MARKETING: MAKING YOUR WORLD BETTER

SOLVING AN ETHICAL CONTROVERSY

CONTEMPORARY MARKETING

FOURTH CANADIAN EDITION

DAVID L. KURTZ
University of Arkansas

H.F. (HERB) MACKENZIE
Brock University

KIM SNOW
York University

NELSON
EDUCATION

Contemporary Marketing, Fourth Canadian Edition

by David L. Kurtz, H.F. (Herb) MacKenzie, and Kim Snow

Vice President, Editorial Higher Education:
Anne Williams

Publisher:
Amie Plourde

Marketing Manager:
Dave Stratton

Developmental Editor:
Lacey McMaster

Photo Researcher and Permissions Coordinator:
Julie Pratt

Production Project Manager:
Jennifer Hare

Production Service:
Vipra Fauzdar, MPS Limited

Copy Editor:
Wendy Thomas

Proofreader:
Nancy Sixsmith

Indexer:
Edwin Durbin

Design Director:
Ken Phipps

Managing Designer:
Franca Amore

Interior Design Revisions:
Peter Papayanakis

Cover Design:
Trinh Truong

Cover Image:
© VLADGRIN/iStockphoto

Compositor:
MPS Limited

Library and Archives Canada Cataloguing in Publication Data

Kurtz, David L., author
    Contemporary marketing / David L. Kurtz, University of Arkansas, H.F. (Herb) MacKenzie, Brock University, Kim Snow, York University. — Fourth Canadian edition.

Revision of: Contemporary marketing : Toronto : Nelson Education, 2012.
Includes bibliographical references and index.
ISBN 978-0-17-653092-1 (bound)

    1. Marketing—Textbooks.
2. Marketing—Management—Textbooks. I. MacKenzie, H. F., author II. Snow, Kim, 1956–, author III. Title.

HF5415.K87 2015
658.8C2014-906606-6

ISBN-13: 978-0-17-653092-1
ISBN-10: 0-17-653092-4

Dedicated to my three dogters: Meghan, her granddogter Emma, and Ceilidh who, together, comfort me while writing and help keep my feet warm.
Herb Mackenzie

To Diane and Bill Weir
Kim Snow

This edition of Contemporary Marketing *is also dedicated to the Cengage Learning and Nelson Education sales representatives.*

The sales representatives have been crucial in helping us not only get the message out regarding the innovations in Contemporary Marketing *but also in acting as our eyes and ears—providing insights that have allowed the authors to continually innovate and improve our product.*

brief contents

Preface xx
Authors xxix

contents

chapter 2

STRATEGIC PLANNING IN CONTEMPORARY MARKETING   32

chapter 3

THE MARKETING ENVIRONMENT, ETHICS, AND SOCIAL RESPONSIBILITY   60

chapter 4

DIGITAL MARKETING AND SOCIAL MEDIA: LIVING IN THE CONNECTED WORLD   94

part 2
UNDERSTANDING BUYERS AND MARKETS

chapter 7
SERVING GLOBAL MARKETS   188

part 3

TARGET MARKET SELECTION

chapter 8

MARKETING RESEARCH, DECISION SUPPORT SYSTEMS, AND SALES FORECASTING 216

chapter 9

MARKET SEGMENTATION, TARGETING, AND POSITIONING 244

part 4

PRODUCT DECISIONS

chapter 10

PRODUCT AND SERVICE STRATEGIES   274

chapter 11
DEVELOPING AND MANAGING BRAND AND PRODUCT STRATEGIES   304

part 5

DISTRIBUTION DECISIONS

chapter 12

MARKETING CHANNELS AND SUPPLY CHAIN MANAGEMENT   330

chapter 13

RETAILERS, WHOLESALERS, AND DIRECT MARKETERS   364

part 6

PROMOTIONAL DECISIONS

chapter 14

INTEGRATED MARKETING COMMUNICATIONS, ADVERTISING, AND DIGITAL COMMUNICATIONS 394

chapter 15
PERSONAL SELLING AND SALES PROMOTION 434

part 7

PRICING DECISIONS

chapter 16
PRICING CONCEPTS AND STRATEGIES 472

Dear Principles of Marketing Student:

Contemporary Marketing, Fourth Canadian Edition, was written for you. Our goal is to provide you with a truly "contemporary" resource containing the most current and relevant marketing information available.

An important theme of this book is connecting with the customer. We've done this by writing with you in mind. Chapter-opening features examine a successful product or organization and conclude with a short **Connecting With Customers** summary that helps you evaluate how this success was achieved. We've even made it easier for you to connect with what you've studied by providing answers to each chapter's **assessment check** questions—a perfect way to verify you've understood all the key concepts. From student focus groups we learned what features work and what needed improvement. New **Marketing: Making Your World Better** boxes have been added to each chapter to illustrate how marketing affects our lives every day. **The Marketing and the SME** boxes have been updated and examine how small and medium-sized companies market their products and services. (This benefits student readers because these are the companies where many of you will find employment.)

Career Readiness tip boxes in each chapter equip you with a winning playbook for business and social settings. Topics include "How to Be a Social Media Marketing Manager," "Making a Good Impression at That First Real Job," "Getting the Best Price on Your Auto Purchase," and many more.

Solving an Ethical Controversy features integrated into each chapter provide you with a thorough treatment of many of the ethical issues affecting marketing. They list the pros and cons of real-world ethics quandaries such as "Celebrities and Oil: Do They Mix?" "Are Your Kids Virtually Unhealthy?" The end-of-chapter Ethics Exercises give you additional hands-on experience with ethical decisions.

Contemporary Marketing, Fourth Canadian Edition, is truly student focused. Why are we so certain that you will find the text easy to understand, lively, and engaging? Because a dedicated group of marketing students worked with us on the text to help achieve this goal. They generously donated their time to provide feedback. We're convinced that this book truly connects with our customers. We hope you agree.

H.F. (Herb) MacKenzie

Kim Snow

preface

Products often begin their lives as something extraordinary, and as they grow, they continue to evolve. The most successful products in the marketplace are those that know their strengths and have branded and marketed those strengths to form a passionate, emotional connection with loyal users and relationships with new users every step of the way. Just like the very best brands in the business world, *Contemporary Marketing* continues to evolve, both as a product and as a brand. This fourth Canadian edition of *Contemporary Marketing* continues to develop and grow with new cases and examples, as well as a new emphasis on social media. As with every good brand, though, the patterns of innovation and excellence established at the beginning remain steadfast. The goals and standards of *Contemporary Marketing* remain intact and focused on excellence, as always. We present to you a text and supplement package that will not only show you why we've been the standard-bearer for so long, but also prove to you why *Contemporary Marketing* remains . . . in a class by itself!

FEATURES OF THE FOURTH CANADIAN EDITION

Here are just a few of the important themes, trends, and practices we've focused on for this edition:

- *Connecting with Customers*: Every opening vignette in the text concludes with a short summary entitled "Connecting with Customers." This enhances the discussion of whatever organization or product was discussed in that opening scenario and asks students to think critically about what they have done and continue to do to remain at the top of their markets. Understanding this connection can be a student's best help in understanding how marketing is conducted every day.

- *Strategic Focus*: The fourth Canadian edition of *Contemporary Marketing* continues to place the marketing planning chapter near the beginning of the text so that it can be assigned much earlier in the term, helping to equip students with a solid foundation of strategic thinking. Appendix A—"Creating an Effective Marketing Plan"—is included at the end of the text. It provides detailed, real-life planning material and includes a planning case that illustrates the strategic marketing planning concepts discussed in Chapter 2. Each chapter closes with a special section assessing strategic implications of chapter concepts on marketing. Finally, Appendix C—"Financial Analysis in Marketing"—provides additional strategic and analytic tools for the reader.

- *Contemporary Topics*: The focus on ethics and social responsibility of the earlier editions is maintained through the new "Marketing: Making Your World Better" boxes, which appear in each chapter. Unique to the Canadian edition, these boxes describe issues in environmentally aware marketing today and illustrate the effect that marketing has on our daily lives. "Marketing and the SME" boxes explore the unique opportunities and challenges small and medium-sized businesses face in today's rapidly changing environment. These boxed features are sure to appeal to students by providing real-life examples related to the theoretical concept they are learning.

- *Updated Content*: In addition to new boxed features, 90 percent of the existing boxes have been revised. All the chapter-opening vignettes are new or revised. References have been thoroughly updated; approximately 90 percent are dated 2012 or later. A number of new, relevant advertisements and photos appear throughout the chapters, providing real-life context for concepts discussed.

- *Case Studies*: In the fourth Canadian edition, there are still two cases in every chapter, one shorter and one longer and more comprehensive. This provides the instructor with flexibility to adjust to time constraints and multiple sections or to use different case assignments for different terms. The end-of-case questions have been fine-tuned to require more critical thinking. Overall, more than 75 percent of the cases are new, while the remaining cases have been updated.

- *Concise Coverage*: A common complaint among both instructors and students is that Principles of Marketing texts are much too long to be covered in a single term. At the same time, they quickly state that they do not want a watered-down version of a text in the form of an "essentials" edition. The authors have worked diligently to streamline the fourth Canadian edition. Wording and examples have been carefully selected with chapter length in mind. The result is a text that provides the rigour and comprehensiveness instructors expect but is still short enough to cover.

- *Marketoids*: Also unique to the Canadian edition are "Marketoids," a trivia element in chapter margins. This feature introduces Canadian content in a fun yet informative way. All Marketoids have been updated in this edition; because this has been such a popular feature with students, those who wish can follow **www.twitter/mktgtoid** to receive a new Marketoid during many working days of the academic year.

KEY CHAPTER CHANGES

Here is an outline of the key changes and new features of the fourth Canadian edition. A list of all boxed feature titles can be found on the inside front cover of this textbook.

PART 1 DESIGNING CUSTOMER-ORIENTED MARKETING STRATEGIES

Chapter 1 Marketing: The Art and Science of Satisfying Customers

The opening vignette describes how NASCAR is connecting with a whole new generation of fans, largely because of Twitter. A new boxed feature—Marketing: Making Your World Better—reviews three *Journal of Marketing* articles written by Richard N. Farmer at 10-year intervals and asks whether marketing is ethical and irrelevant or moral and honourable. The chapter concludes with a case that describes the world's favourite cookie—Oreos—and the role that marketing has played in its success as it has reached its 100th birthday. The chapter has been condensed considerably, but the necessary topics for an introduction to marketing have been retained: how marketing is defined, the history of marketing, nontraditional marketing applications and their application to nonprofit organizations, and how marketing has evolved from transaction-based to relationship marketing.

Chapter 2 Strategic Planning in Contemporary Marketing

Chapter 2 provides an important foundation for analyzing all aspects of marketing by demonstrating the importance of gathering reliable information to create an effective marketing plan. Marketing planning identifies the markets a company can best serve, as well as the most appropriate mix of approaches to satisfy the customers in those markets. The opening vignette describes how even the best companies can make strategic mistakes. Google sold ownership of Motorola after owning it for only a short period, resulting in the loss of billions of dollars. The chapter concludes with a case that describes the changing marketing strategy at BlackBerry and raises the question of the company's future.

Chapter 3 The Marketing Environment, Ethics, and Social Responsibility

This chapter begins by describing five forces in marketing's external environment—competitive, political–legal, economic, technological, and social–cultural. They are the foundation for making decisions that involve the four marketing mix elements and the target market. The second focus of this chapter is marketing ethics and social responsibility. This section describes the nature of marketers' responsibilities both to business and to society at large. The chapter concludes with a case that describes Canada's greenest beer manufacturer: Steam Whistle Brewing.

Chapter 4 Digital Marketing and Social Media: Living in the Connected World

The impact of digital marketing, use of the Web as part of the marketing communication process, designing effective websites, and assessing website effectiveness are covered in this chapter. Social media is covered in this chapter, including social platforms and tools and preparing a social media marketing plan. The chapter opens with a case about Pinterest and ends with cases describing how Procter & Gamble uses social media and other social media promotions.

PART 2 UNDERSTANDING BUYERS AND MARKETS

Chapter 5 Consumer Behaviour

Several significant trends within the Canadian population and how these changes are affecting consumer behaviour are included in this chapter. Some of these trends are the retirement of baby boomers and the ever-increasing diversity of the Canadian population. The chapter begins with a discussion on how shopping habits are changing in Canada and ends with a case describing how Pepsi-Cola has responded to the movement toward healthier eating habits.

Chapter 6 Business-to-Business (B2B) Marketing

Chapter 6 discusses buying behaviour in organizational, or B2B, markets: how businesses, government, and marketing intermediaries purchase products that are used in their daily operations, are combined with other products to create finished goods, or are resold to other businesses or to consumers. Important topics include segmenting B2B markets, characteristics of B2B markets, business market demand, outsourcing and offshoring, the buying process, and roles within the buying centre. The chapter concludes with a case that describes WFS Ltd., one of Canada's leading industrial distributors, and how it manages relationships with the many customers it serves.

Chapter 7 Serving Global Markets

The discussion of strategies, challenges, and opportunities for Canadian companies entering global markets is covered in this chapter. The statistics throughout the chapter have been updated, and new examples such as Hyundai's strategy for international expansion have been added. The chapter closes with a case on how consumers throughout the world are evolving and how Starbucks expanded into India.

PART 3 TARGET MARKET SELECTION

Chapter 8 Marketing Research, Decision Support Systems, and Sales Forecasting

Topics relating to big data and social media research, such as the gamification of market research, have been added to this chapter. In addition, the topic of ethnographic research has been expanded. New examples of how companies perform and use market research have been added throughout the chapter.

Chapter 9 Market Segmentation, Targeting, and Positioning

Recent research relating to the increasing importance of women as consumers and the movement of people from the eastern provinces to the west has been added to this chapter. Updated research on the cultural needs of Chinese, South Asian, and Black Canadian consumers has also been added. The topic of the cohort effect and the video-game generation has been expanded.

PART 4 PRODUCT DECISIONS

Chapter 10 Product and Service Strategies

The chapter begins with an in-depth look at how successful Apple has been with its product development by focusing its high-tech innovations at the young, college- or university-educated male consumer. The section on the globalization of services has been updated and expanded. The chapter concludes with a new case about the development of Frebreze fabric refresher by Procter & Gamble.

Chapter 11 Developing and Managing Brand and Product Strategies

New topics in Chapter 11 include how Under Armour developed its brand of innovative sports attire by sponsoring professional teams in England, Israel, Chile, Mexico, and Greece. Examples of the growth in sales of private label and environmentally friendly product sales have been included in this chapter.

PART 5 DISTRIBUTION DECISIONS

Chapter 12 Marketing Channels and Supply Chain Management

The opening vignette describes how Kiva robots are being used in many companies where distribution is important by creating fast, efficient movement of products and speedier order fulfillment, along with lower labour costs. Chapter 12 discusses the role and types of marketing channels in marketing strategy, the channel decisions that marketers must make, channel conflict and cooperation, and logistics and supply chain management.

Chapter 13 Retailers, Wholesalers, and Direct Marketers

Chapter 13 discusses retailers, wholesalers, and direct marketers, and how they deliver products to their customers in a dynamic environment. The opening vignette describes how Loblaw Companies grew by more than 30 percent through the acquisition of Shoppers Drug Mart, one of the largest business deals in Canadian history. The chapter concludes with a case that describes Tilley Endurables, a major Canadian retailer that "was built by a hat."

PART 6 PROMOTIONAL DECISIONS

Chapter 14 Integrated Marketing Communications, Advertising, and Digital Communications

The chapters on integrated marketing communications, advertising, and digital communications have been streamlined into one chapter. Heavy emphasis has been placed on the growth of social media, particularly mobile communications, throughout this chapter while still covering the traditional communications methods.

Chapter 15 Personal Selling and Sales Promotion

The opening vignette describes how Salesforce.com is using technology to improve both the efficiency and the effectiveness of the sales forces of its customers. The chapter explores personal selling strategies, giving special attention to the relationship-building opportunities that the selling situation presents. Sales promotion, and how it can enhance promotional effectiveness, is also discussed. The chapter concludes with a case that describes a Canadian distributor of food equipment solutions and the selling philosophy of its president, Alex Pettes.

PART 7 PRICING DECISIONS
Chapter 16 Pricing Concepts and Strategies

The opening vignette describes Dollarama, the Canadian retailer that dominates the dollar store industry. Chapter 16 includes many important pricing topics: pricing objectives and the marketing mix, methods for determining prices, pricing policies and strategies, global considerations and pricing, and pricing and the law. The chapter concludes with a case that describes what happens when a major company makes an error with its pricing strategy or fails to honour its pricing promises.

PEDAGOGY

As with the previous editions of *Contemporary Marketing*, the fourth Canadian edition is packed with pedagogical features to keep students interested and bring the text topics to life:

- *Assessment, Assessment, Assessment*: In every university and college marketing department in the country, assessment and assurance of learning among students have become increasingly important. As a result, we've provided students with assessment checks after every main heading in every chapter. Answers at the end of the chapter help students self-review to ensure they've understood the chapter's contents.

- *Critical Thinking*: In response to our reviewers, and reflecting the importance of analysis and independent thought in today's classrooms, Critical Thinking Exercises are included at the end of each chapter.

- *Business Etiquette*: Schools realize that it has become increasingly important to understand proper business etiquette when entering the business world, so more and more schools are adding business etiquette to their curriculums. Every chapter of *Contemporary Marketing* contains a Career Readiness box, addressing all aspects of proper behaviour, including communications etiquette, the importance of body language, and even the most effective way to create customer relationships. Student focus groups revealed that this box is, perhaps surprisingly, one of the most-read and popular features of *Contemporary Marketing*!

- *Ethical Awareness*: Every chapter includes a special experiential feature called "Solving an Ethical Controversy." This feature is designed to facilitate class debates on current ethical issues. Each begins with a brief background and is followed by a series of pro and con points designed to elicit class discussion of the issues. In addition, an Ethics Exercises section appears at the end of each chapter. These are short case scenarios that can be used as homework assignments or as a basis for classroom discussion.

- *Additional Pedagogical Features*: The authors conducted a thorough review of *Contemporary Marketing*'s instructional elements. In addition to the pedagogy described above, the fourth Canadian edition continues to offer these user-friendly features.
  1. *Review of Chapter Objectives*. In addition to a review of each chapter learning objective, a series of review questions is included as part of the chapter review.
  2. *Marketing Terms You Need to Know*. Page numbers are included.
  3. *Project and Teamwork Exercises*. This section includes discussion questions.

THE CONTEMPORARY MARKETING RESOURCE PACKAGE

With its precedent-setting learning materials, *Contemporary Marketing* has continued to improve on its signature package features—equipping students and instructors with the most comprehensive collection of learning tools, teaching materials, and innovative resources available. As expected, the fourth Canadian edition continues to serve as the industry benchmark by delivering the most extensive, technologically advanced, user-friendly package on the market.

FOR THE INSTRUCTOR

The Nelson Education Teaching Advantage (NETA)

The Nelson Education Teaching Advantage (NETA) program delivers research-based instructor resources that promote student engagement and higher-order thinking to enable the success of Canadian students and educators. Be sure to visit Nelson Education's **Inspired Instruction** website at **http://www.nelson.com/inspired/** to find out more about NETA.

All NETA and other key instructor ancillaries are provided in the Instructor's Resources at **www.nelson.com/instructor**, giving instructors the ultimate tool for customizing lectures and presentations.

- **NETA Test Bank:** The NETA Test Bank is available in a new, cloud-based platform. **Nelson Testing Powered by Cognero®** is a secure online testing system that allows you to author, edit, and manage test bank content from any place you have Internet access. No special installations or downloads are needed, and the desktop-inspired interface, with its drop-down menus and familiar, intuitive tools, allows you to create and manage tests with ease. You can create multiple test versions in an instant and import or export content into other systems. Tests can be delivered from your learning management system, your classroom, or wherever you want.

  The **NETA Test Bank** for *Contemporary Marketing* was written by H.F. (Herb) MacKenzie and Kim Snow, the Canadian textbook authors. It includes over 1800 multiple-choice questions written according to NETA guidelines for effective construction and development of higher-order questions. Also included are approximately 1400 true/false, 300 essay, and 300 matching questions. To access the online Cognero Test Bank for *Contemporary Marketing*, Fourth Canadian Edition, select the text resources through **www.nelson.com/instructor**. Printable Word and PDF versions of the Test Bank are available through your sales and editorial representative.

- **NETA PowerPoint:** Microsoft® PowerPoint® lecture slides for every chapter have been adapted for the fourth Canadian edition by H.F. (Herb) MacKenzie and Kim Snow, the Canadian textbook authors, ensuring consistency with the content of the book. We offer two separate collections. The **Basic PowerPoint** collection contains 10 to 20 slides per chapter. This collection is a basic outline of the chapter. The **Expanded PowerPoint** collection includes 25 to 45 slides per chapter and provides a more complete overview of the chapter. Many of the slides feature key figures, tables, and photographs from the fourth Canadian edition of *Contemporary Marketing*. NETA principles of clear design and engaging content have been incorporated throughout, making it simple for instructors to customize the deck for their courses.

- **Image Library:** This resource consists of digital copies of figures, short tables, and photographs used in the book. Instructors may use these jpegs to customize the NETA PowerPoint or create their own PowerPoint presentations.

- **TurningPoint®:** Another valuable resource for instructors is **TurningPoint® classroom response software** customized for *Contemporary Marketing*. Now you can author, deliver, show, access, and grade, all in PowerPoint, with no toggling back and forth between screens. With JoinIn you are no longer tied to your computer. You can walk about your classroom as you lecture, showing slides and collecting and displaying responses with ease. If you can use PowerPoint, you can use JoinIn on TurningPoint.

- **Video Cases:** Enhance your classroom experience with the exciting and relevant videos provided on DVD and directly to students through **MindTap**, prepared to accompany *Contemporary Marketing*. There are three sets of video cases designed to enrich and support chapter concepts:

  End-of-Chapter Video Cases: We have included a video case for each and every chapter, designed to exceed your every expectation. These cases focus on successful real companies' processes, strategies, and procedures. Real employees explain real marketing situations with which they have been faced, bringing key concepts from the chapter to life.

  CBC End-of-Part Video Cases: These videos will add visual impact and current, real-world examples to your lectures.

Scripps Networks Interactive & Food Network Continuing Video Case: You've come to expect only the best from us in choosing our continuing video case concepts, and we do not disappoint with our focus on a fresh, timely topic: how Scripps Networks Interactive and Food Network use a strategic blend of media outlets to connect and market to consumers.

- **NETA Instructor's Guide:** Adapted by H.F. (Herb) MacKenzie and Kim Snow, the Canadian text authors, the Instructor's Guide contains both chapter-related and book-related materials. The chapter materials include features such as brief overviews and lecture outlines (organized by learning objective and correlated to PowerPoint slides). The Instructor's Guide also contains collaborative learning exercises for each chapter, giving students a completely different way to apply chapter concepts to their own lives.

- **Answers to End-of-Chapter Questions:** This resource contains answers to end-of-chapter materials and various critical-thinking exercises.

- **Resource Integration Guide (RIG):** The RIG is written to provide the instructor with a clear and concise guide to all of the ancillaries that accompany the text as well as how best to use these items in teaching a Principles of Marketing course. Not only are all of the book's ancillaries organized clearly for you, but we also provide planning suggestions, lecture ideas, and help in creating assignments. This guide will help instructors prepare for teaching the course, execute teaching plans, and evaluate student performance.

- **Media Guide:** The Media Guide includes teaching materials for end-of-chapter video cases, CBC End-of-Part video cases, and Scripps continuing video case.
  End-of-Chapter Video Cases: A complete set of written cases accompanies these chapter videos. The written segments contain discussion questions, answers to which can be found in the Media Guide, as can a complete video synopsis, a list of text concepts covered in the videos, and even more critical-thinking exercises.
  CBC End-of-Part Video Cases: Teaching notes for these current, dynamic videos are included in this Media Guide.
  Scripps Networks Interactive & Food Network Continuing Video Case: Written case segments and discussion questions accompany these videos, which are divided into seven parts intended to complement the text.

- **DayOne:** Day One—Prof InClass is a PowerPoint presentation that instructors can customize to orient students to the class and their text at the beginning of the course.

MindTap

MindTap for *Contemporary Marketing* is a personalized teaching experience with relevant assignments that guide students to analyze, apply, and elevate thinking, allowing instructors to measure skills and promote better outcomes with ease. A fully online learning solution, MindTap combines all student learning tools—readings, multimedia, activities, and assessments—into a single Learning Path that guides the student through the curriculum. Instructors personalize the experience by customizing the presentation of these learning tools to their students, even seamlessly introducing their own content into the Learning Path.

FOR THE STUDENT

MindTap

Stay organized and efficient with **MindTap**—a single destination with all the course material and study aids you need to succeed. Built-in apps leverage social media and the latest learning technology. For example:

- ReadSpeaker will read the text to you.
- Flashcards are prepopulated to provide you with a jump start for review—or you can create your own.

- You can highlight text and make notes in your MindTap Reader. Your notes will flow into Evernote, the electronic notebook app that you can access anywhere when it's time to study for the exam.
- Self-quizzing allows you to assess your understanding.

Visit **http://www.nelson.com/student** to start using MindTap. Enter the Online Access Code from the card included with your text. If a code card is *not* provided, you can purchase instant access at NELSONbrain.com.

ACKNOWLEDGMENTS TO THE FOURTH CANADIAN EDITION

Your authors have benefited immensely from the comments and suggestions of many reviewers and colleagues. This input has come via focus groups, publisher reviews, contributions to supplementary text materials, emailed suggestions, conference networking, classroom visits, and coffee shop chats. Regardless of the format, all these ideas have helped shape the fourth Canadian edition of *Contemporary Marketing* into a text that serves as the benchmark for other texts.

We'd like to thank the outstanding reviewers whose diligent and thoughtful comments were instrumental in our revisions:

Tom Arhontoudis, George Brown College
Stephen Charko, McMaster University
Brock Cordes, University of Manitoba
Craig Dyer, Red River College
Dwight Heinrichs, University of Regina
Charles Hendriks, York University
Warveni Jap, Thompson Rivers University
Wonkyong (Beth) Lee, Western University
Leighann Neilson, Carleton University
Surjit Rai, Northern Alberta Institute of Technology
Michel Rod, Carleton University
John Russell, Lethbridge College
Michael Shekter, George Brown College
Taiwo Soetan, Red River College
Frances Steciuk, George Brown College
Neil Tracey, Kwantlen Polytechnic University
Padma Vipat, Douglas College

As with the previous edition, we continue to be grateful to the students from York University and Kwantlen Polytechnic University who provided thoughtful feedback and suggestions on how to make the book student friendly. Student involvement resulted in a significant impact on the development of this book—helping the authors and Nelson Education produce the most student-focused introductory marketing book in Canada. Our sincere thanks go to these individuals.

At York University:

Riaz Backer
Josha Chakkalakal
Stephanie Critelli
Elisa Damaso
Tracy Gibbons
Hekmat Kaadan
Varun Kalia
Inna Khvedantsevich
Rachel Lichtman

Nehal Mehra
Jovan Milosevic
Meisham Molou
Khanh Nguyen
Tiago Nunes
Nimesh Shah
Natalie Vacianna
Alexandra Vinichenko

At Kwantlen Polytechnic University:

Alina Monica Dobre	Ivjoat Kyle Rosode
Chris Kozminski	Quyen Tu
Carolyn Molzahn	Jerrica Velo
Penny Purvis	Bria Yelland

Finally, this new edition would never have become a reality without our highly competent editorial, production, and marketing teams at Nelson Education. Sincere thanks go to Anne Williams, Vice President, Editorial, Higher Education; Amie Plourde, Publisher; Lacey McMaster, Developmental Editor; Sarah Fisher, Editorial Assistant; Jennifer Hare, Production Project Manager; Peter Papayanakis, Designer; David Stratton, Marketing Manager; and Joanne McNeil, Manufacturing Manager. Special thanks also go to freelancers for their dedicated and diligent work: Julie Pratt, Photo Researcher and Permissions Editor; and Wendy Thomas, Copy Editor.

We are grateful for the many suggestions and contributions of dozens of people who teach the introductory marketing course on a regular basis and are in the best position to comment on what works best—and what doesn't work at all. Every recommendation made a difference in the creation of the fourth Canadian edition. We welcome any comments, suggestions, or constructive criticisms you wish to provide.

H.F. (Herb) MacKenzie & Kim Snow

authors

Dr. H.F. (Herb) MacKenzie is an associate professor of marketing at the Goodman School of Business, Brock University, St. Catharines, Ontario. He has taught in the undergraduate, graduate, and executive education programs at universities in Canada, Europe, and the Middle East and has been consulting to both private- and public-sector businesses since 1985. He has over 15 years of industrial sales and sales management experience and has published many cases, conference proceedings, and articles in the areas of sales management, buyer–seller relationships, and distribution channel management. He has co-authored Canadian editions of textbooks on selling, sales management, and marketing and has edited five Canadian marketing casebooks. He has received numerous awards from his students, including Professor of the Year, Marketing Professor of the Year, and Faculty of Business Faculty Award of Excellence (twice).

H.F. (Herb) MacKenzie

Dr. KIM SNOW is an associate professor of marketing at York University in Toronto. Dr. Snow received her MBA and PhD from the University of Bradford, U.K., and her Diploma in Business Administration from Wilfrid Laurier University. She has been a member of the faculty at York University since 1992. She has published numerous articles in the area of service marketing, service quality, customer satisfaction, and marketing research. She has been faculty advisor for the American Marketing Association Student Chapter at York University and has been a judge on several student chapter competitions. She has been a member of the Editorial Advisory Board and Internet Editor for the *Managing Service Quality Journal*. Prior to joining York University, Kim spent 17 years working in the financial services industry.

Kim Snow

During **DAVE KURTZ**'s high school days, no one in Salisbury, Maryland, would have mistaken him for a scholar. In fact, he was a mediocre student, so bad that his father steered him toward higher education by finding him a succession of backbreaking summer jobs. Thankfully, most of them have been erased from his memory, but a few linger, including picking peaches, loading watermelons on trucks headed for market, and working as a pipefitter's helper. Unfortunately, these jobs had zero impact on his academic standing. Worse yet for Dave's ego, he was no better than average as a high school athlete in football and track.

But four years at Davis & Elkins College in Elkins, West Virginia, turned him around. Excellent teachers helped get Dave on a sound academic footing. His grade point average soared—enough to get him accepted by the graduate business school at the University of Arkansas, where he met Gene Boone. Gene and Dave became longtime co-authors; together, they produced more than 50 books. Dave and Gene were involved in several entrepreneurial ventures.

Today, Dave is back teaching at the University of Arkansas, after tours of duty in Ypsilanti, Michigan; Seattle, Washington; and Melbourne, Australia. He is the proud grandfather of six "perfect" kids and a sportsman with a golf handicap too high to mention. Dave, his wife, Diane, and four demanding canine companions (Daisy, Lucy, Molly, and Sally) live in Rogers, Arkansas. Dave holds a distinguished professorship at the Sam M. Walton College of Business in nearby Fayetteville, home of the Arkansas Razorbacks.

chapter 1

Marketing: The Art and Science of Satisfying Customers

CHAPTER OBJECTIVES

(1) Define *marketing*, explain how it creates utility, and describe its role in the global marketplace.

(2) Contrast marketing activities during the five eras in the history of marketing.

(3) Explain the importance of avoiding marketing myopia.

(4) Describe the characteristics of not-for-profit marketing.

(5) Identify and briefly explain each of the five types of nontraditional marketing.

(6) Explain the shift from transaction-based marketing to relationship and social marketing.

(7) Identify the universal functions of marketing.

(8) Demonstrate the relationship among ethical business practices, social responsibility, sustainability, and marketplace success.

NASCAR TWEETS ARE HERE TO STAY

Cell phones haven't exactly been standard equipment for NASCAR racing drivers, but after photos of a fiery mid-race crash were tweeted directly from the track by one of the competitors in the Daytona 500, they might well be.

"Fire!" tweeted driver Brad Keselowski, 28, who was in second place when the race was temporarily halted by the accident (another driver struck a jet dryer on the track, starting a massive fire). Keselowski then took a photo of the flames and posted it as "My view"; it was re-tweeted more than 5,000 times that evening, and, within hours, his Twitter followers had tripled to more than 200,000. To their credit, some fans posted to make sure Keselowski was safe and not tweeting while driving—then or later when his own car crashed on Lap 187 of NASCAR's biggest race. He wasn't, and NASCAR, which bans the use of electronic devices while driving, later decided not to fine him, a decision Keselowski also tweeted.

The widely reported incident may provide a welcome boost to NASCAR's popularity. After a few years of suffering declining interest among its primary target market of males 18 to 34, which has pulled TV ratings down, NASCAR is actively looking for ways to re-engage with fans. Using social media is one of several strategies in the organization's innovative five-year plan to broaden audiences and reach them in new ways. NASCAR has hired a director of digital and social strategy and made training for everyone, from race drivers to support staff, in the use of social media a top priority. NASCAR has also regained control of its own Twitter feeds, which used to be run by Turner.com but are now back in the hands of an internal team.

Keselowski's exchanges with fellow Twitter users on the night of the Daytona 500, which had been bumped to a prime-time TV slot due to weather, were picked up and mentioned by a television commentator, alerting thousands more Twitterers to the conversation. Keselowski already had a big Twitter fan base, having recently pasted 5,000 fans' Twitter handles to the bed of his truck for a race. But the night of the crash, he added enough new followers for an observer to call them "a top-10 fan base," suggesting there's at least one NASCAR driver who needs little if any social media training.[1]

connecting with customers

NASCAR has always been popular with some demographics, but it is connecting now with a whole new group of fans largely because of Twitter. Twitter helps make a race personal. Through tweets, fans know what their favourite race drivers are thinking and experiencing. "NASCAR has a distinct niche in Twitter because NASCAR drivers are truly very friendly people," explains one race fan. "When given a popular social network where they can openly interact with their fans and share information about their lives, they think it's great and run with it." Some NASCAR drivers have hundreds of thousands of Twitter followers: Brad Keselowski has more than 295,000, Kevin Harvick has over 250,000, and Jimmie Johnson has more than 215,000. In 2013, NASCAR returned to Canada when the Camping World Truck series appeared for the first time at Canadian Tire Motorsport Park with a spectacular show. The winner, 17-year-old Chase Elliott, moved into the lead in the final lap to win the race.

Chapter Overview

- "I only drink Tim Hortons coffee."
- "Swiss Chalet has my favourite chicken dishes."
- "My next car will be a Ford Focus."
- "I go to all the Winnipeg Jets games at MTS Centre."

These words are music to a marketer's ears. They may echo the click of an online purchase, the *ping* of a cash register, the cheers of fans at a stadium. Customer loyalty is the watchword of 21st-century marketing. Individual consumers and business purchasers have so many goods and services from which to choose—and so many different ways to purchase them—that marketers must continually seek out new and better ways to attract and keep customers. When the world learned that Facebook had assigned two dozen engineers to improve the site's search engine, users and investors were abuzz. A more powerful search engine would mean significantly enhanced capability for Facebook users—and a direct assault on Google, the market leader in search engines and one of Facebook's chief rivals.[2]

The technology revolution continues to change the rules of marketing during this first decade of the 21st century and will continue to do so in years beyond. The combined power of telecommunications and computer technology creates inexpensive global networks that transfer voice messages, text, graphics, and data within seconds. These sophisticated technologies create new types of products and demand new approaches to marketing existing products. Newspapers are learning this lesson the hard way, as circulation continues to decline around the country, due in large part to the rising popularity of blogs and auction and job-posting sites. Electronic reading devices such as Kobo and the Amazon Kindle, on the other hand, have been picking up speed and enthusiastic fans.

Communications technology also contributes to the globalization of today's marketplace, where businesses manufacture, buy, and sell across national borders. You can bid at eBay on a potential bargain or eat a Big Mac or drink Coca-Cola almost anywhere in the world; your MP3 player was probably manufactured in China or South Korea. Both Honda and Toyota manufacture cars in Canada, while some Volkswagens are imported from Mexico. Finished products and components routinely cross international borders, but successful global marketing also requires knowledge to tailor products to regional tastes. Restaurants in Newfoundland and Labrador, for example, often have cod tongues on their menu. This delicacy is seldom found elsewhere in Canada.

Rapidly changing business landscapes create new challenges for companies, whether they are giant multinational firms or small boutiques, profit-oriented or not-for-profit. Organizations must react quickly to shifts in consumer tastes, competitive offerings, and other market dynamics. Fortunately, information technologies give organizations fast new ways to interact and develop long-term relationships with their customers and suppliers. Such links have become a core element of marketing today.

Every company must serve customer needs—create customer satisfaction—to succeed. We call customer satisfaction an art because it requires imagination and creativity, and a science because it requires technical knowledge, skill, and experience. Marketing strategies are the tools that marketers use to identify and analyze customers' needs, then show that their company's goods and services can meet those needs. Tomorrow's market leaders will be companies that can make the most of these strategies to create satisfied customers.

This Canadian edition of *Contemporary Marketing* focuses on the strategies that allow companies to succeed in today's interactive marketplace. This chapter sets the stage for the entire text, examining the importance of creating satisfaction through customer relationships. Initial sections describe the historical development of marketing and its contributions to society. Later sections introduce the universal functions of marketing and the relationship between ethical business practices and marketplace success. Throughout the chapter—and the entire book—we discuss customer loyalty and the lifetime value of a customer. ◆◆◆

---

① Define *marketing*, explain how it creates utility, and describe its role in the global marketplace.

WHAT IS MARKETING?

Production and marketing of goods and services—whether it's a new crop of organically grown vegetables or digital cable service—are the essence of economic life in any society. Like most business disciplines, marketing had its origins in economics. Later, marketing borrowed concepts from areas such as psychology and sociology to explain how people made purchase decisions. Mathematics, anthropology, and other disciplines also contributed to the evolution of marketing. These will be discussed in later chapters.

table 1.1 **Four Types of Utility**

TYPE	DESCRIPTION	EXAMPLES	ORGANIZATIONAL FUNCTION RESPONSIBLE
Form	Conversion of raw materials and components into finished goods and services	Dinner at Swiss Chalet; iPod; shirt from Mark's Work Wearhouse	Production*
Time	Availability of goods and services when consumers want them	Dental appointment; digital photographs; LensCrafters eyeglass guarantee; Canada Post Xpresspost	Marketing
Place	Availability of goods and services at convenient locations	Soft-drink machines outside gas stations; on-site day care; banks in grocery stores	Marketing
Ownership (possession)	Ability to transfer title to goods or services from marketer to buyer	Retail sales (in exchange for currency or credit card payment)	Marketing

*Marketing provides inputs related to consumer preferences, but the actual creation of form utility is the responsibility of the production function.

Economists contributed the concept of **utility**—the want-satisfying power of a good or service. Table 1.1 describes the four basic kinds of utility: form, time, place, and ownership.

Form utility is created when the firm converts raw materials and component inputs into finished goods and services. Because of its appearance, gold can serve as a beautiful piece of jewellery, but because it also conducts electricity well and does not corrode, it has many applications in the manufacture of electronic devices like cell phones and global positioning satellite units. By combining glass, plastic, metals, circuit boards, and other components, Canon makes a digital camera and Sharp produces an LED television. With fabric and leather, Coach manufactures its high-fashion line of handbags. With a ship and the ocean, a captain and staff, and food and entertainment, Royal Caribbean creates a cruise. Although the marketing function focuses on influencing consumer and audience preferences, the organization's production function creates form utility.

Zip.ca and Redbox take advantage of time and place utility. Zip.ca video rental machines can be found mainly at Metro grocery store locations in Ontario. Redbox, on the other hand, has been establishing video rental machine locations at many popular locations where consumers shop, from Newfoundland and Labrador to Vancouver. Marketing creates time, place, and ownership utilities. *Time and place utility* occur when consumers find goods and services available when and where they want to purchase them. Vending machines and convenience stores focus on providing place utility for people buying newspapers, snacks, and soft drinks. The owners of Golf Without Limits created time and place utility when they opened their indoor golf centres in Waterloo and London, Ontario. Customers can play a round of simulated golf at nearly 40 golf courses, many of them world-class, regardless of season, weather, or time of day.[3]

The transfer of title to goods or services at the time of purchase creates *ownership utility.* Purchasing an all-inclusive tropical vacation on Expedia.ca or buying a new Samsung Smart TV

utility Want-satisfying power of a good or service.

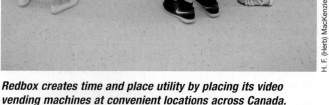
Redbox creates time and place utility by placing its video vending machines at convenient locations across Canada.

H. F. (Herb) MacKenzie

creates ownership utility. All organizations must create utility to survive. Designing and marketing want-satisfying goods, services, and ideas are the foundation for the creation of utility. But where does the process start? In the toy industry, manufacturers try to come up with items that children will want to play with—creating utility. But that's not as simple as it sounds. At the Toy Fair held each February in New York, Canadian and U.S. retailers pore over the products displayed at booths of manufacturers and suppliers, looking for the next Webkinz toys or Lego building blocks—trends that turn into classics and generate millions of dollars in revenues over the years. Marketers also look for ways to revive flagging brands. The classic yo-yo might be making a high-tech comeback, as a line of precision-engineered models have emerged in limited editions, made of titanium and sporting price tags as lofty as $500.[4]

But how does an organization create a customer? Most take a three-step approach: identifying needs in the marketplace, finding out which needs the organization can profitably serve, and developing goods and services to convert potential buyers into customers. Marketing specialists are responsible for most of the activities necessary to create the customers the organization wants. These activities include the following:

- identifying customer needs

- designing products that meet those needs

- communicating information about those goods and services to prospective buyers

- making the items available at times and places that meet customers' needs

- pricing the merchandise and services to reflect costs, competition, and customers' ability to buy

- providing the necessary service and follow-up to ensure customer satisfaction after the purchase[5]

A DEFINITION OF MARKETING

marketing
Organizational function and a set of processes for creating, communicating, and delivering value to customers and for managing customer relationships in ways that benefit the organization and its stakeholders.

The word *marketing* encompasses such a broad scope of activities and ideas that settling on one definition is often difficult. Ask three people to define marketing, and three different definitions are likely to follow. We are exposed to so much advertising and personal selling that most people link marketing only to those activities. But marketing begins long before a product hits the shelf. It involves analyzing customer needs, obtaining the information necessary to design and produce goods or services that match buyer expectations, satisfying customer preferences, and creating and maintaining relationships with customers and suppliers. Marketing activities apply to profit-oriented businesses such as Canadian Tire and Amazon.ca as well as not-for-profit organizations such as Mothers Against Drunk Driving and the Canadian Cancer Society. Even towns, cities, and provinces and territories of Canada engage in marketing activities. Today's definition takes all these factors into account. Marketing is an organizational function and a set of processes for creating, communicating, and delivering value to customers and for managing customer relationships in ways that benefit the organization and its stakeholders.[6]

The expanded concept of marketing activities permeates all organizational functions in businesses and not-for-profit organizations. It assumes that organizations conduct their marketing efforts ethically and that these efforts serve the best interests of both society and the organization. The concept also identifies the marketing variables—product, price, promotion, and distribution—that combine to provide customer satisfaction. In addition, it assumes that the organization begins by identifying and analyzing who its potential customers are and what they need. At all points, the concept emphasizes creating and maintaining long-term relationships with customers and suppliers.

TODAY'S GLOBAL MARKETPLACE

Several factors have forced marketers—and entire nations—to extend their economic views to events outside their own national borders. First, international agreements are being negotiated in attempts to expand trade among nations. Second, the growth of electronic commerce and related computer technologies is bringing previously isolated countries into the marketplace for buyers and sellers around the globe. Third, the interdependence of the world's economies is a reality because no nation produces all the raw materials and finished goods its citizens need or consumes all its output without exporting some to other countries. Evidence of this interdependence is illustrated by the introduction of the euro as a common currency to facilitate trade among the nations of the European Union and the creation of trade agreements such as the North American Free Trade Agreement (NAFTA), the Comprehensive Economic and Trade Agreement (CETA) between Canada and the European Union, and the World Trade Organization (WTO).

Rising oil prices affect the price that Canadian consumers pay for just about everything—not just gasoline at the pump. Dow Chemical raised the prices of its products up to 20 percent to adjust to its rising cost for energy. Dow supplies companies in industries such as agriculture and health care, all of which will be affected by the price hike. Airlines, too, are trying to respond to a near-doubling of the cost of jet fuel. Many have started charging customers for redeeming their reward miles, and Air Canada now charges $25 (per direction) for a checked bag on economy domestic flights, $35 on economy flights to the United States, and $100 for a second checked bag on flights to Europe.[7]

To remain competitive, companies must continually search for the most efficient manufacturing sites and most lucrative markets for their products. Canadian marketers now find tremendous opportunities serving customers not only in traditional industrialized nations but also in Latin America and emerging economies in central Europe, the Middle East, Asia, and Africa, where rising standards of living create increased customer demand for the latest products. Expanding operations beyond the Canadian market gives domestic companies access to more than 6.5 billion international customers. China is now the second-largest market in the world—only the United States is larger. But with regard to new automobile sales, China is the world's largest market. In 1993, there were only 37,000 private cars in China but industry observers estimate that Chinese customers will soon purchase 20 to 25 million cars a year.[8] So automakers worldwide are extending their operations to China. In addition, companies based in these emerging economies are beginning to compete in the global market. In one recent year, China exported nearly $50 billion in merchandise to Canada while it imported $16.3 billion from Canada. China has grown to become Canada's second-largest trading partner behind the United States.[9] Chinese-manufactured cars will, most likely, eventually be available in Canada. Interestingly, however, signs are mounting that China's increasing prosperity may be reducing its attractiveness as a low-cost labour source. Rising costs are already driving some foreign manufacturers out of the country. Mexico has taken the lead as the lowest-cost country for outsourced production, with India and Vietnam second and third, respectively; China stands in sixth place.[10]

Service firms also play a major role in today's global marketplace. Telecommunications firms like South Africa's MTN, Luxembourg's Millicom International, and Egypt's Orascom Telecom Holding have carved out new global markets for their products by following the lead of Finnish firm Nokia, among the first high-tech firms to create durable and affordable cell phones specifically designed for emerging markets. The opportunities for such telecom innovators will continue to grow as long as electricity-reliant personal computers remain out of reach for millions in the developing world. Canada is also an attractive market for foreign competitors because of its size, standard of living, and its proximity to the United States. Companies such as Procter & Gamble, Michelin, Home Depot, Lowe's, and Honda operate production, distribution, service, and retail facilities in Canada. Foreign ownership of Canadian companies has increased also. Recently, Calgary-based Nexen Inc. was sold to China National Offshore Oil Company in a controversial takeover worth $15.1 billion.[11]

Although many global marketing strategies are almost identical to those used in domestic markets, more and more companies are tailoring their marketing efforts to the needs and preferences of consumers in foreign markets. It is often difficult to standardize a brand name on a global basis. The Japanese, for example, like the names of flowers or girls for their automobiles, names such as Bluebird, Blue-bonnet, Violet, and Gloria. Canadians, on the other hand, prefer rugged outdoorsy names such as Wrangler, Challenger, Mustang, and Cherokee.

assessment check 1

1.1 Define *marketing* and explain how it creates utility.

1.2 What three factors have forced marketers to embrace a global marketplace?

② **Contrast marketing activities during the five eras in the history of marketing.**

exchange process
Activity in which two or more parties give something of value to each other to satisfy perceived needs.

production orientation
Business philosophy stressing efficiency in producing a quality product, with the attitude toward marketing that "a good product will sell itself."

FOUR ERAS IN THE HISTORY OF MARKETING

The essence of marketing is the **exchange process**, in which two or more parties give something of value to each other to satisfy perceived needs. Often people exchange money for tangible goods, such as video games, clothes, or groceries. In other situations, they exchange money for intangible services, such as a haircut or an education. Many exchanges involve a combination of goods and services, such as dinner in a restaurant— where dinner represents the good and the wait staff represents the service. People also make exchanges when they donate money or time to a charitable cause, such as Habitat for Humanity. Managing customer relationships such as these are the essence of successful marketing.

Although marketing has always been a part of business, its importance has varied greatly. Figure 1.1 identifies five eras in the history of marketing: (1) the production era, (2) the sales era, (3) the marketing era, (4) the relationship era, and (5) the social era. The "Marketing and the SME" feature describes how Saskatoon Funeral Home has survived through all five marketing eras by constantly embracing change.

THE PRODUCTION ERA

Before 1925, most firms—even those operating in highly developed economies in Western Europe and North America—focused narrowly on production. Manufacturers stressed production of quality products and then looked for people to purchase them. The prevailing attitude of this era held that a high-quality product would sell itself. This **production orientation** dominated business philosophy for decades; business success often was defined solely in terms of production successes.

The production era reached its peak during the early part of the 20th century. Henry Ford's mass-production line exemplifies this orientation. Ford's slogan "They [customers] can have any color they want, as long as it's black" reflected the prevalent attitude toward marketing. Production shortages and intense consumer demand ruled the day. It is easy to understand how production activities took precedence.

However, building a new product is no guarantee of success, and marketing history is cluttered with the bones of miserable product failures despite major innovations—more than 80 percent of new products fail. Inventing an outstanding new product is not enough because it must also fill a perceived marketplace need. Otherwise, even the best-engineered, highest-quality product will fail. Even Henry Ford's horseless carriage took a while to catch on. People were afraid of motor vehicles;

figure 1.1

Five Eras of Marketing History

ERA	Production	Sales	Marketing	Relationship	Social
PREVAILING ATTITUDE	"A good product will sell itself."	"Creative advertising and selling will overcome consumers' resistance and persuade them to buy."	"The consumer rules! Find a need and fill it."	"Long-term relationships with customers and other partners lead to success."	"Connecting to consumers via Internet and social media sites is an effective tool."
APPROXIMATE TIME PERIOD*	Prior to 1920s	Prior to 1950s	Since 1950s	Since 1990s	Since 2000s

*In Canada and other highly industrialized economies.

MARKETING AND THE SME	**Saskatoon Funeral Home: 100 Years Old and Still Alive**

NORTH America's longest continually operated company is Hudson's Bay Company, founded in 1670. It is nearly 200 years older than Canada. But for most businesses—especially family-owned businesses—100 years is a challenge. What does it take to survive 100 years and span all five eras of marketing history, from the production to the social era? Saskatoon Funeral Home is a living enterprise and the last locally owned full-service funeral provider in the city. Its history provides some answers.

William Edwards founded Saskatoon Funeral Home in 1910 and it has been an industry innovator since. William brought the first motorized equipment for funeral and ambulance service to Saskatchewan. When his son Arnold succeeded him in 1960, he soon established Saskatchewan's first crematorium—controversial at the time. Arnold's son Bill, the current president, eventually joined the firm, and his son Morgan (fourth generation) joined in 2006 as the general manager, the same year that a separate crematorium centre for pets was opened: Family Pet Cremation.

What else has the company accomplished that sets it apart in the funeral services industry? In 1995, the family opened the 2,100-square-metre W.A. Edwards Family Centre to provide a public space for funeral receptions after funerals. The centre provides meeting and grief counselling space for more than 80 community groups and also houses an extensive bereavement resource lending library. The centre was recognized that year as the "Best New Idea" at a meeting of independent funeral homes held in Chicago, Illinois. In 2003, the Tribute Planning Centre was opened, a store where visitors can purchase grief literature, books, brochures, videos, and funeral supplies, without interrupting or being interrupted by a funeral service. This centre also received numerous awards for innovation. That same year, the company established the Our Children Live Forever in Our Hearts program and received international recognition. The program recognizes babies lost at or before birth through an annual memorial service now attended by hundreds of people. Today, Saskatoon Funeral Home is the only one in Saskatchewan that provides on-site guardianship 24 hours a day, seven days a week. Bill explains, "What that means is if you bring a loved one into our care, they are never left here alone."

Saskatoon Funeral Home has also received the Saskatoon Achievement in Business Excellence Hall of Fame Award, the Saskatchewan ABEX award for community involvement, and the 2011 Family Enterprise of the Year Award by the Canadian Association of Family Enterprise. The firm has a long history of connecting with its community. Bill explains that to succeed over time, it is necessary to constantly embrace change: "You always want to be moving forward in some fashion and providing new and innovative approaches to what consumers need and want."

Sources: "Saskatoon Funeral Home; For More Than 100 Years and Spanning Four Generations, Saskatoon Funeral Home Has Been a Family Business—and Remains the City's Longest Serving Family-Run Funeral and Cremation Provider," *Star-Phoenix* (Saskatoon), September 30, 2013, E8, available **www.thestarphoenix.com**, accessed January 13, 2014; Jennifer Jacoby-Smith, "Saskatoon Funeral Home Continues Legacy of Innovation," *Star-Phoenix* (Saskatoon), October 5, 2011, p. E14; Rory MacLean, "Good Heaven Edwards Family Inspired to Continue Funeral Business," *Star-Phoenix* (Saskatoon), December 3, 2010, p. C10; Canadian Association of Family Enterprise website, available **www.cafecanada.ca/events/feya2011**, accessed January 13, 2014.

they spat out exhaust, stirred up dust on dirt roads, got stuck in mud, and tied up horse traffic. Besides, at the speed of 11 kilometres per hour, they caused all kinds of accidents and disruption. It took savvy marketing by some early salespeople—and eventually a widespread perceived need—to change people's minds about the product. Today, most of us could not imagine life without a car and have refined that need to preferences for certain types of vehicles, such as SUVs, convertibles, trucks, and hybrids.

THE SALES ERA

As production techniques in North America and Europe became more sophisticated, output grew during the period from the 1920s into the early 1950s. As a result, manufacturers began to increase their emphasis on effective sales forces to find customers for their output. In this era, firms attempted to match their output to the potential number of customers who would want it. Companies with a **sales orientation** assume that customers will resist purchasing nonessential goods and services and that the task of personal selling and advertising is to persuade them to buy.

Although marketing departments began to emerge from the shadows of production and engineering during the sales era, they tended to remain in subordinate positions. Many chief marketing

sales orientation Belief that consumers will resist purchasing nonessential goods and services, with the attitude toward marketing that only creative advertising and personal selling can overcome consumers' resistance and persuade them to buy.

executives held the title of sales manager. But selling is only one component of marketing. As marketing scholar Theodore Levitt once pointed out, "Marketing is as different from selling as chemistry is from alchemy, astronomy from astrology, chess from checkers."

THE MARKETING ERA AND THE EMERGENCE OF THE MARKETING CONCEPT

seller's market Market in which there are more buyers for fewer goods and services.

buyer's market Market in which there are more goods and services than people willing to buy them.

consumer orientation Business philosophy incorporating the marketing concept that emphasizes first determining unmet consumer needs and then designing a system for satisfying them.

marketing concept Company-wide consumer orientation with the objective of achieving long-run success.

Personal incomes and consumer demand for goods and services dropped rapidly during the Great Depression of the 1930s, thrusting marketing into a more important role. Organizational survival dictated that managers pay close attention to the markets for their goods and services. This trend ended with the outbreak of World War II, when rationing and shortages of consumer goods became commonplace. The war years, however, created only a pause in an emerging trend in business: a shift in the focus from products and sales to satisfying customer needs.

The marketing concept, a crucial change in management philosophy, can be linked to the shift from a **seller's market**—one in which there were more buyers for fewer goods and services—to a **buyer's market**—one in which there were more goods and services than people willing to buy them. When World War II ended, factories stopped manufacturing war supplies and started turning out consumer products again, an activity that had, for all practical purposes, stopped during the war.

The advent of a strong buyer's market created the need for **consumer orientation** by businesses. Companies had to market goods and services, not just produce and sell them. This realization has been identified as the emergence of the marketing concept. Marketing would no longer be regarded as a supplemental activity performed after completion of the production process. Instead, the marketer would play a leading role in product planning. *Marketing* and *selling* would no longer be synonymous terms.

Today's fully developed **marketing concept** is a *company-wide consumer orientation* with the objective of achieving long-run success. All facets—and all levels, from top to bottom—of the organization must contribute first to assessing and then to satisfying customer wants and needs. Whether marketing manager, accountant, or product designer, every employee plays a role in reaching potential customers. Even during tough economic times, when companies tend to emphasize cutting costs and boosting revenues, the marketing concept focuses on the objective of achieving long-run success instead of short-term profits. Because the firm's survival and growth are built into the marketing concept, company-wide consumer orientation should lead to greater long-run profits.

Apple exemplifies the marketing concept in every aspect of its business. Its products are consistently stylish and cutting edge but without overwhelming users with every possible feature. "A defining quality of Apple has been design restraint," says one industry consultant. That hallmark restraint is a characteristic of Apple's late founder, Steve Jobs, and is reflected in the work of Apple's designers, managers, and engineers, whose contributions to the company's new products Jobs credited for the company's ability to constantly surprise the marketplace. Apple's recently released iPad Mini and iPad Air represent product enhancements designed to anticipate needs many consumers didn't even realize they had. Within three days of its release, Apple said it had sold 3 million of the new model. "The new iPad is a blockbuster … the strongest iPad launch yet," said Philip Schiller, Apple's senior vice-president of worldwide marketing.[12] A strong market orientation— the extent to which a company adopts the marketing concept—generally improves market success and overall performance. It also has a positive effect on new-product development and the introduction of innovative products. Companies that implement market-driven strategies are better able to understand their customers' experiences, buying habits, and needs. Like Apple, these companies can, therefore, design products with advantages and levels of quality compatible with customer requirements.

H. F. (Herb) MacKenzie

Apple exemplifies the marketing concept, creating consistently stylish and cutting-edge products that have high consumer satisfaction and loyalty.

THE RELATIONSHIP ERA

The fourth era in the history of marketing emerged during the final decade of the 20th century and continues to grow in importance. Organizations now build on the marketing era's customer orientation by focusing on establishing and maintaining relationships with both customers and suppliers. Relationship marketing involves long-term, value-added relationships developed over time with customers and suppliers. Strategic alliances and partnerships among manufacturers, retailers, and suppliers often benefit everyone. The Boeing 787 Dreamliner, which has been under development and construction since 2004, is the result of an international team of companies working on the technology, design, and construction of the planes. Boeing and more than 40 global suppliers, connected virtually at 135 sites around the world, worked together to complete the planes. Despite three years of production delays, the fuel-efficient aircraft was still in demand: at its launch, Boeing had orders for about 800 Dreamliners.[13] The concept of relationship marketing, which is the current state of customer-driven marketing, is discussed in detail later in Appendix B.

relationship marketing Development and maintenance of long-term, cost-effective relationships with individual customers, suppliers, employees, and other partners for mutual benefit.

THE SOCIAL ERA

We are now half-way through the second decade of the 21st century, and the social era of marketing is in full swing, thanks to consumers' accessibility to the Internet and the creation of social media sites such as Facebook, Twitter, YouTube, LinkedIn, Pinterest, and Snapchat. Building on the relationship era, companies now routinely use the Web and social networking sites to connect to consumers as a way to market goods and services. On a personal level, see the "Career Readiness" feature for suggestions on creating and connecting to your own personal network, a key to success in marketing and in business generally.

Marketoid

The Oreo cookie, introduced in 1912, has survived all five marketing eras. Originally, the cookie was sold in bulk, priced at $0.30 per pound.

CONVERTING NEEDS TO WANTS

Every consumer must acquire goods and services on a continuing basis to fill certain needs. Everyone must satisfy the fundamental needs for food, clothing, shelter, and transportation by purchasing things or, in some instances, temporarily using rented property and hired or leased transportation. By focusing on the benefits resulting from these products, effective marketing converts needs to wants. A need for a pair of pants may be converted to a desire for jeans—and further, a desire for jeans from Abercrombie & Fitch or Bootlegger. The need for food may be converted to a desire for a panini at Tim Hortons or groceries from Sobeys or Real Canadian Superstore. But if the need for transportation isn't converted to a desire for a Hyundai Elantra or a Chevrolet Malibu, extra vehicles may sit unsold on a dealer's lot.

CAREER READINESS   **How to Be a Social Media Marketing Manager**

ARE you empathic, enthusiastic about connecting with others, well organized, and tech-savvy? If so, you might have the makings of a social media marketing manager, a dynamic new career that's springing up in companies that want to take creative control of their online communication with customers, suppliers, and potential new markets. Here are some ideas for handling the job successfully:

1. Make the most of any customer-service experience you've acquired; it will serve you well in figuring out how to reach people effectively with tools such as Facebook, Twitter, LinkedIn, Pinterest, and YouTube.
2. Take a course to learn about video production. Online video offers marketers countless opportunities and can be quick and inexpensive to produce. Experience here could be invaluable.

3. Make sure you spend enough time listening to your customers. Listening is the most important communication skill, whether in person or online.
4. Connect with others in your industry. Share what you've learned and learn from the best practices of others in this young and growing field.
5. Keep your company's online presence unique—with a distinctive point of view and consistently creative and original content such as contests, blogs, photos, audio, and, of course, video too.

Sources: "Tips for Social Media Manager Training," Black Box Social Media .com, **http://blackboxsocialmedia.com**, accessed March 17, 2012; Karrian Graf, "Qualities of a Social Media Manager," Karrian Graf.com, **www .karrianngraf.com**; Kent Lewis, "First Look: Social Media (Marketing) Evangelist Job Description," iMediaConnection.com, March 10, 2012, **http://blogs .imediaconnection.com**; Kent Lewis, "Creative Best Practices Social Media," iMediaConnection, July 23, 2011, **http://blogs.imediaconnection.com**.

Consumers need to communicate. But converting that need to the desire for certain types of communication requires skill. It also requires listening to what consumers want. Consumers' demand for more cell phone and wireless services seems nearly unlimited, particularly with the surge in social networking sites—providing tremendous opportunities for companies. New products appear continually to feed that demand, such as increasingly popular broadband wireless services and the veritable flood of applications now available for smartphones, enabling consumers to use their phones in new ways—for example, to research health information, check for symptoms, and even count calories.[14]

③ Explain the importance of avoiding marketing myopia.

marketing myopia Management's failure to recognize the scope of its business.

AVOIDING MARKETING MYOPIA

The emergence of the marketing concept has not been devoid of setbacks. One troublesome problem led marketing scholar Theodore Levitt to coin the term **marketing myopia**. According to Levitt, marketing myopia is management's failure to recognize the scope of its business. Product-oriented rather than customer-oriented management endangers future growth. Levitt cites many service industries—such as dry cleaning and electric utilities—as examples of marketing myopia. But many firms have found innovative ways to reach new markets and develop long-term relationships.

For instance, for a long time, Apple has worked to develop greener and more sustainable manufacturing processes and products. Apple has recently built a 20-megawatt solar farm and a 5-megawatt fuel-cell farm, described by some observers as the largest such company-owned facilities in the United States. In addition, the company recently won a patent for a simple, reliable process for recharging its products from solar energy sources.[15] Table 1.2 illustrates how firms in a number of industries have overcome myopic thinking by developing broader marketing-oriented business ideas that focus on consumer need satisfaction.

EXTENDING THE TRADITIONAL BOUNDARIES OF MARKETING

Today's organizations—both profit-oriented and not-for-profit—recognize universal needs for marketing and its importance to their success. During a television commercial break, viewers might be exposed to an advertisement for a Honda Civic, an appeal to help feed children in foreign countries, a message by a political candidate, and a commercial for Tim Hortons—all in the space of about two minutes. Two of these ads are paid for by firms attempting to achieve profitability and other

table 1.2 *Avoiding Marketing Myopia*

COMPANY	MYOPIC DESCRIPTION	COMPANY MOTTO—AVOIDING MYOPIA
Honda Canada	Automobiles, ATVs, motorcycles, marine engines	The power of dreams
MasterCard	Credit card company	There are some things money can't buy. For everything else, there's MasterCard.
Target Canada	Discount retailer	Expect more. Pay less.
3M	Industrial manufacturer	Innovative technology for a changing world
Xerox	Photocopier manufacturer	The Document Company
La-Z-Boy	Furniture manufacturer	Live life comfortably.

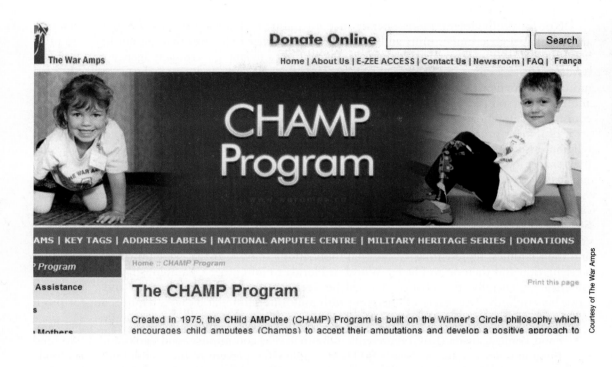

Marketing helps raise money to support social causes. The War Amps is a not-for-profit organization that offers comprehensive services to child amputees and their families. Its CHAMP Program is unique in the world.

objectives. The appeal for funds to feed children and the political ad are examples of communications by not-for-profit organizations and individuals.

MARKETING IN NOT-FOR-PROFIT ORGANIZATIONS

There are an estimated 165,000 not-for-profit and charity organizations in Canada, representing nearly $106 billion—or 7.1 percent—of GDP, making this sector larger than the retail, automotive, or manufacturing sectors. It employs more than 2 million Canadians, and an additional 12 million Canadians are volunteers. That makes not-for-profit organizations big business. Canada has the second-largest not-for-profit and voluntary sector in the world, following the Netherlands. (The United States is the fifth-largest.) Many people assume this sector is mostly government funded, but some not-for-profit organizations do not receive any funding from government. In fact, sales of goods and services generate nearly 50 percent of total income for the core not-for-profit sector. Colleges, universities, and hospitals, though, are an exception. They receive about 75 percent of their funding from government sources, mostly from provincial governments.[16]

Marketing helps bring awareness to important social causes. Food Banks Canada is a not-for-profit organization that represents community food banks across Canada and encourages both individual and corporate involvement.

Not-for-profit organizations operate in both public and private sectors. Federal, provincial, and municipal government units and agencies pursue service objectives that are not keyed to profitability targets. The Canada Border Services Agency is a federal government agency that provides border security services and helps facilitate the flow of people and goods across the Canadian border; individual provincial government departments regulate labour safety, environmental conservation and natural resources, and alcohol control; municipal school boards are responsible for overseeing educational and curriculum standards for their district. The private sector contains an even greater array of not-for-profit organizations, including zoos, hospitals, universities and colleges, ethnic and religious associations, and charities, such as the Make-a-Wish Foundation of Canada. Regardless of their size or location, all these organizations need funds to operate. Adopting the marketing concept can make a great difference in their ability to meet their service objectives.

Some not-for-profits form partnerships with business firms that promote the organization's cause or message. Since it came to Canada in 1994, Walmart Canada has raised more than $80 million to donate to Children's Miracle Network hospitals across the country. In 2013, the company sponsored the Children's Miracle Network Champions program. Twelve special children and their families, representing 12 hospital foundations across Canada, were flown to Toronto for a celebration and then on to Disney World in Florida to join other Champions from across North America.[17] Generally, the alliances formed between not-for-profit organizations and commercial firms benefit both. The reality of operating with multimillion-dollar budgets requires not-for-profit organizations to maintain a focused business approach. Consider some recent examples:

- Food Banks Canada (FBC) represents more than 800 community food banks and 3,000 food programs across Canada. Nearly 900,000 people, 36.4 percent of them children, access food banks monthly in Canada. FBC moves about 7 million kilograms of food industry donations annually to its members, almost exclusively with donated transportation. Some of the many participating companies are McCain Foods; Kraft Canada; Loblaw Companies of Canada; Kellogg Canada; and PepsiCo, whose Quaker Oats brand contributed 3 million servings of oatmeal.[18]

- The Heart & Stroke Foundation is focused on improving the health of Canadians by reducing the severity and occurrence of heart disease and stroke. In one recent year, the foundation provided grants to nearly 1,500 Canadian researchers and, since being founded in 1952, it has invested $1.35 billion in heart and stroke research. In the 2012–13 school year, the foundation engaged 750,000 children in 4,000 Canadian schools through its Jump Rope for Heart program that promotes healthy activity for children.[19]

- Sometimes, not-for-profit organizations are organized quickly for very specific purposes. In August 2013, Alberta Flood Aid organized a benefit concert at McMahon Stadium in Calgary. Musicians, including Nickelback, Jann Arden, Tom Cochrane, Colin James, Loverboy, Corb Lund, and Randy Bachman, entertained about 32,000 people at the venue and raised nearly $2.2 million to aid victims of one of Canada's worst natural disasters.[20]

The diversity of not-for-profit organizations suggests the presence of numerous organizational objectives other than profitability. In addition to their organizational goals, not-for-profit organizations differ from profit-seeking firms in several other ways.

CHARACTERISTICS OF NOT-FOR-PROFIT MARKETING

④ **Describe the characteristics of not-for-profit marketing.**

bottom line Reference to overall company profitability.

The most obvious distinction between not-for-profit organizations and for-profit—commercial—firms is the financial **bottom line**, business jargon that refers to the overall profitability of an organization. For-profit organizations measure profitability, and their goal is to generate revenues above and beyond their costs to make money for all stakeholders involved, including employees, shareholders, and the organization itself. Not-for-profit organizations hope to generate as much revenue as possible to support their causes, whether it is feeding children, preserving wilderness, or helping single mothers find work. Historically, not-for-profits have had less-exact goals and marketing objectives than for-profit firms, but in recent years, many of these groups have recognized that, to succeed, they must develop more cost-effective ways to provide services, and they must compete with other organizations for donors' dollars. Marketing can help them accomplish these tasks. Some groups are finding, for instance, that online social network sites, such as Facebook and Twitter, can bring them increased attention. But they are also using specialized networks devoted to social causes such as YourCause.com and easy payment systems such as Piryx to generate funds.[21]

Other distinctions exist between for-profit and not-for-profit organizations as well, each of which influences marketing activities. Like profit-seeking firms, not-for-profit organizations may market tangible goods and/or intangible services. The Canadian Breast Cancer Foundation (CBCF) benefits from the sale of pink products, goods that signal support for breast cancer education and research. In 2013, the annual CFL Pink game was played between the Toronto Argonauts and the Winnipeg Blue Bombers. The CBCF received proceeds of the night's 50/50 draw, and a portion of ticket sales sold through argonauts.ca/groups, and was on the concourse throughout the game, accepting donations and selling pink goods. As well, the Argonauts wore pink Reebok gear during the game, and this merchandise was sold at the Jays Shop at Gate 5 on game day.[22] But profit-seeking businesses tend to focus their marketing on just one public—their customers. Not-for-profit organizations, however, must often market to multiple publics, which complicates decision making about the correct markets to target. Many deal with at least two major publics— their clients and their sponsors—and often many other publics as well. A college or university targets prospective students as recipients of its marketing program, but it also markets to current students, parents of students, major donors, alumni, faculty, staff, local businesses, and local government agencies.

A service user of a not-for-profit organization may have less control over the organization's destiny than would be true for customers of a profit-seeking firm. Not-for-profit organizations also often possess some degree of monopoly power in a given geographic area. An individual contributor might object to United Way's inclusion of a particular local agency, but that agency will still receive a portion of that donor's contribution.

assessment check 4

4.1 What is the most obvious distinction between a not-for-profit organization and a commercial organization?

4.2 Why do for-profit and not-for-profit organizations sometimes form alliances?

NONTRADITIONAL MARKETING

⑤ **Identify and briefly explain each of the five types of nontraditional marketing.**

As marketing evolved into an organization-wide activity, its application has broadened far beyond its traditional boundaries of for-profit organizations engaged in the creation and distribution of tangible goods and intangible services. In many cases, broader appeals focus on causes, events, individuals, organizations, and places. Table 1.3 lists and describes five major categories of nontraditional marketing: person marketing, place marketing, cause marketing, event marketing, and organization marketing. These categories can overlap—promotion for an organization may also encompass a cause; a promotional campaign may focus on both an event and a place.

PERSON MARKETING

Person marketing involves efforts designed to cultivate the attention, interest, and preferences of a target market toward a celebrity or authority figure. Celebrities can be real people or fictional characters. Political candidates engage in person marketing as they promote their candidacy for office. Authors such as Suze Orman of *The Road to Wealth* use person marketing to promote their books. Rachael Ray uses person marketing to promote her *Every Day with Rachael Ray* magazine, where she appears on every cover.

An extension of person marketing involves *celebrity endorsements*, in which well-known athletes, entertainers, and experts or authority figures promote products for companies or social causes for not-for-profit organizations. When David Beckham retired from soccer in 2013, he was earning $6.5 million for his soccer talent; most of his $44 million income came from endorsement deals with H&M, Breitling, Adidas, and others.[23] And when NBA MVP Derrick Rose signed a 14-year, $250-million contract as a global spokesperson for Adidas, that, combined with his $95-million contract extension, made him the highest-paid athlete in basketball.[24] However, some celebrity endorsements are questionable and difficult to explain. As its business fortunes declined, BlackBerry

person marketing
Marketing efforts designed to cultivate the attention, interest, and preference of a target market toward a person (typically a political candidate or celebrity).

table 1.3 *Categories of Nontraditional Marketing*

TYPE	BRIEF DESCRIPTION	EXAMPLES
Person marketing	Marketing efforts designed to cultivate the attention and preference of a target market toward a person	Milos Raonic, Canada's 2013 male athlete of the year; Drake, Canadian rapper and actor
Place marketing	Marketing efforts designed to attract visitors to a particular area; improve consumer images of a city, province, or country; and/or attract new business	Prince Edward Island: Canada's Green Province Nova Scotia: Canada's Ocean Playground Saskatchewan: Land of Living Skies
Cause marketing	Identification and marketing of a social issue, cause, or idea to selected target markets	"You booze, you cruise, you lose." "Smoke. Stink. Die." "Today a reader. Tomorrow a leader."
Event marketing	Marketing of sporting, cultural, and charitable activities to selected target markets	Grey Cup Rogers Cup Calgary Stampede
Organization marketing	Marketing efforts of mutual-benefit organizations, service organizations, and government organizations that seek to influence others to accept their goals, receive their services, or contribute to them in some way	United Way: "Change starts here." Canadian Red Cross: "You can help when help is most needed." Canadian Professional Sales Association: "Serving the sales community since 1874"

place marketing
Marketing efforts to attract people and organizations to a particular geographic area.

named Alicia Keys, a singer with no tech or real business experience, its global creative director.[25] Many celebrities, however, are becoming better known and better connected with their fans. Katy Perry has more Twitter followers than any other celebrity: 48.5 million. Justin Bieber follows closely with 47.8 million followers, and Taylor Swift has more than 5 million followers on photo-sharing app Instagram.[26]

PLACE MARKETING

Another category of nontraditional marketing is **place marketing**, which attempts to attract customers to particular areas. Cities, provinces, regions, and countries publicize their tourist attractions to lure vacation travellers. They also promote themselves as good locations for businesses. Place marketing has become more important in the world economy—not only for tourism but also to recruit business and workers. A recent report by Deloitte & Touche recommended boosting tourism as a means to increase international trade. Its analysis suggests that a tourist increase of 1 percent would increase Canadian exports by more than $800 million in the following two years. To increase tourism, though, Canada needs to be more creative in reaching the new demographics of world travellers and appealing to their needs.[27]

Although tourism is not the only aspect of place marketing, tourism has a major economic impact and is one of the world's fastest-growing businesses.

Gros Morne National Park has been designated a UNESCO World Heritage Site and is one of many attractions for tourists to Newfoundland and Labrador.

RuthChoi/Shutterstock.com

Unfortunately, the number of tourists travelling to Canada has declined by 20 percent since 2000. In 2012, there were 16 million tourist arrivals, mostly from the United States. But since then, the number of U.S. visitors declined as the value of the Canadian dollar rose and as emerging markets became more popular tourist destinations.[28] China is expected to become the world's largest market for tourism, as well as a source of tourists—tourists from China spent $102 billion in other countries in 2012. While there were more than 83 million Chinese tourists who visited around the world, only 273,300 visited Canada, injecting $486 million into the Canadian economy. Between 2011 and 2012, the number of Chinese tourists worldwide grew by 41 percent, but the number of visits by Chinese tourists to Canada grew by only 18.3 percent. We are falling behind. In fact, Canada was once the second-most popular tourist destination in the world, behind Italy. It now ranks 18th, although the Canadian Tourism Commission is hoping to reverse this trend as it has recently launched an aggressive marketing program in China.[29]

CAUSE MARKETING

A third category of nontraditional marketing, **cause marketing**, refers to the identification and marketing of a social issue, cause, or idea to selected target markets. Cause marketing covers a wide range of issues, including literacy, physical fitness, awareness of childhood obesity, environmental protection, elimination of birth defects, child-abuse prevention, and preventing drunk driving.

As mentioned earlier, an increasingly common marketing practice is for profit-seeking firms to link their products to social causes. Canadian Tire has sponsored the Jumpstart program since 2005 and in 2012 reached an important milestone: more than a half million Canadian children between the ages of 4 and 18 who would otherwise not be able to participate in sports were helped to do so. Jumpstart, through its 332 Jumpstart chapters across Canada, invested more than $12 million in 2012 to help cover the costs of registration, equipment, and transportation for financially disadvantaged children. A range of 73 sports and recreational activities were covered by Jumpstart, including hockey, golf, soccer, and baseball, and less popular activities, such as breakdancing, cheerleading, and gymnastics.[30]

Surveys show strong support for cause-related marketing by both consumers and company employees. In one recent survey, 92 percent of consumers had a more positive image of companies that support important social causes, and four of five respondents said that they would change brands to support a cause if the price and quality of the two brands remained equal.

EVENT MARKETING

Event marketing refers to the marketing of sporting, cultural, and charitable activities to selected target markets. It also includes the sponsorship of such events by firms seeking to increase public awareness and bolster their images by linking themselves and their products to the events. Sports sponsorships have gained effectiveness in increasing brand recognition, enhancing image, boosting purchase volume, and increasing popularity with sports fans in demographic segments corresponding to sponsor business goals.

Some people might say that the premier sporting event is baseball's World Series. Others claim it's the Olympics or the World Cup. Still others might argue that it's the Super Bowl, which many consumers claim they watch only to see the debut of commercials. Those commercials are expensive, costing, on average, US$3.5 million for 30 seconds of airtime. But in Super Bowl LXVI, for example, they reached a record 111.3 million viewers.[31] Companies now also feed their commercials to websites and make them available for downloading to personal computers, tablets, and smartphones. Experienced marketers caution that firms planning such a big expenditure should make it part of a larger marketing plan, not just a single shot at fame.

For those who prefer the international pageantry of the Olympics, marketers have plenty of plans. The promotion of upcoming Olympics—both summer and winter—begins years in advance. Before the end of each Olympics, hosts of the next games unveil their logo and the

cause marketing
Identification and marketing of a social issue, cause, or idea to selected target markets.

event marketing
Marketing of sporting, cultural, and charitable activities to selected target markets.

Marketoid

Shortly before the opening day of the Sochi 2014 Winter Games, its Facebook page registered merely 32,000 likes. Following the Olympics games, the site had 452,000 likes.

Event marketing for the Olympics begins years in advance. A groundbreaking ceremony was held in 2014 for the Sliding Centre for the PyeongChang 2018 Olympic Winter Games.

JUNG YEON-JE/AFP/Getty Images

organization marketing Marketing by mutual-benefit organizations, service organizations, and government organizations intended to influence others to accept their goals, receive their services, or contribute to them in some way.

marketing takes off from there. Corporate sponsors such as Adidas try to target the next Olympic gold-medal winners, draping them in clothing and gear with company logos. The 2014 Winter Olympics in Sochi, Russia, afforded opportunities for hundreds of firms to provide wine and beer for hospitality events, jewellery, team uniforms, electricity generation services, mattresses and mattress toppers, beauty salon services, Internet services, gas, cold and flu remedies, groceries, fitness equipment, logistics services, hand sanitizers, and much more.[32]

ORGANIZATION MARKETING

Organization marketing attempts to influence others to accept the goals of, receive the services of, or contribute in some way to an organization. Organization marketing includes mutual-benefit organizations (conservation groups, labour unions, and political parties), service and cultural organizations (colleges and universities, hospitals, and museums), and government organizations. Many organizations use organizational marketing to help raise funds. The University of Toronto recently launched Boundless, the largest fund-raising campaign in Canadian university history. Chancellor David Peterson stated, "We will look to our global network of friends and alumni—who now number more than 500,000 across 174 countries—to join us in this exciting campaign." The university's previous campaign raised $1 billion by its close in 2003 and remains the most successful in Canadian history. The target for Boundless is $2 billion.[33]

assessment check 5

5.1   Identify the five major categories of nontraditional marketing.

5.2   Give an example of a way in which two or more of these categories might overlap.

MARKETING: MAKING YOUR WORLD BETTER | **Marketing: Unethical and Irrelevant or Moral and Honourable?**

THE most widely read marketing publication by marketing academics is undoubtedly *Journal of Marketing*. Beginning in 1967, at about 10-year intervals, it published three articles that critically evaluated marketing as a profession. Richard N. Farmer authored the "Would You Want…" trilogy, the last of which was published posthumously.

The first article (1967) was "Would You Want Your Daughter to Marry a Marketing Man?" Farmer is very critical of marketing, arguing that it is both unethical—made up of con men and fast-buck artists—and irrelevant: focused on pushing shoddy consumer products while failing to address any of the world's important problems. He concludes his article by asking, "Who wants his daughter to marry a huckster?"

The second article (1977) was "Would You Want Your Son to Marry a Marketing Lady?" Still critical, he begins to see the value of marketing. It still pushes silly consumer products and wastes scarce resources, without addressing increasing ecological concerns. But, he argues, countries that have embraced marketing and free enterprise—even if they peddle soap and promote lousy TV commercials—are economic winners. People in those countries enjoy better medical care, improved education systems, and a higher standard of living compared with countries with planned economies. Some marketers have even begun to explore selling more socially useful products. At the same time, government forced the hiring of women and minorities on the private sector, resulting in more highly capable people entering the marketing profession. He concludes: "Do I want my son to marry a marketing lady? Well, you see, it's this way…."

The third article (1987) was "Would You Want Your Granddaughter to Marry a Taiwanese Marketing Man?" Farmer explores the role that marketing plays in increasing international business. The wealth in newly industrialized countries increases, and with the increase in the standard of living, there is also an increase in longevity. Countries begin to open up, resulting in better educated people, more consumption of goods, increased longevity, and a freer flow of information. Farmer argues that marketing saves lives. But there is another important result from an intimately connected world: people don't fight. Wars become less likely. By saving lives and minimizing wars, marketing, he argues, just might be the most moral field of all. Farmer concludes, as he walks with his granddaughter and she suggests that the bright, young Taiwanese marketing student she is dating might be Mr. Right, "Honey, you see, it's this way…."

How applicable are Richard Farmer's views today?

Sources: Richard N. Farmer, "Would You Want Your Daughter to Marry a Marketing Man?," *Journal of Marketing*, January 1967, pp. 1–3; Richard N. Farmer, "Would You Want Your Son to Marry a Marketing Lady?, *Journal of Marketing*, January 1977, pp. 15–18; Richard N. Farmer, "Would You Want Your Granddaughter to Marry a Taiwanese Marketing Man?" *Journal of Marketing*, October 1987, pp. 111–116.

FROM TRANSACTION-BASED MARKETING TO RELATIONSHIP MARKETING

⑥ **Explain the shift from transaction-based marketing to relationship and social marketing.**

As marketing progresses through the 21st century, a significant change is taking place in the way companies interact with customers. The traditional view of marketing as a simple exchange process, or **transaction-based marketing**, is being replaced by a different, longer-term approach that emphasizes building relationships one customer at a time. Traditional marketing strategies focused on attracting customers and closing deals. Today's marketers realize that, although it's important to attract new customers, it's even more important to establish and maintain a relationship with them so they become loyal repeat customers. These efforts must expand to include suppliers and employees as well. Over the long term, this relationship may be translated to the lifetime value of a customer—the revenues and intangible benefits that a customer brings to an organization over an average lifetime, minus the investment the firm has made to attract and keep the customer.

transaction-based marketing Buyer and seller exchanges characterized by limited communications and little or no ongoing relationships between the parties.

Marketers realize that consumers are getting more and more sophisticated. They quickly recognize marketing messages and may turn away from them if the messages don't contain information that consumers want and need. So marketers need to develop new techniques to establish and build trusting relationships between companies and their customers. As defined earlier in this chapter, relationship marketing refers to the development, growth, and maintenance of long-term, cost-effective exchange relationships with individual customers, suppliers, employees, and other partners for mutual benefit. It broadens the scope of external marketing relationships to include suppliers, customers, and referral sources. In relationship marketing, the term *customer* takes on a new meaning. Employees serve customers within an organization as well as outside it; individual employees and their departments are customers of and suppliers to one another. They must apply the same high standards of customer satisfaction to intradepartmental relationships as they do to external customer relationships. Relationship marketing recognizes the critical importance of internal marketing to the success of external marketing plans. Programs that improve customer service inside a company also raise productivity and staff morale, resulting in better customer relationships outside the firm.

figure 1.2

Converting New Customers to Advocates

Relationship marketing gives a company new opportunities to gain a competitive edge by moving customers up a loyalty ladder—from new customers to regular purchasers, then to loyal supporters of the firm and its goods and services, and finally to advocates who not only buy its products but recommend them to others, as shown in Figure 1.2.

Relationship building begins early in marketing. It starts with determining what customers need and want, then developing high-quality products to meet those needs. It continues with excellent customer service during and after purchase. It also includes programs that encourage repeat purchases and foster customer loyalty. Marketers may try to rebuild damaged relationships or rejuvenate unprofitable customers with these practices as well. Sometimes modifying a product or tailoring customer service to meet the needs of these customers can go a long way toward rebuilding a relationship.

USING SOCIAL MARKETING TO BUILD RELATIONSHIPS

Today's technology allows people to transmit memos, reports, and drawings quickly and inexpensively over phone lines, cables, or wireless devices. People can subscribe to personalized news services that deliver article summaries on specified topics directly to their personal computers, tablets, or smartphones. They can communicate via social media, email, voice mail, text messages, videoconferencing, and computer networks; pay bills using various apps or online banking services; and use online resources to get information about things such as theatre events or a local furniture store's special sale.

CONVERTING NEW CUSTOMERS TO ADVOCATES

As an increasing number of Internet users in Canada use wireless devices such as smartphones or tablets to access the Web and check their email, the stage is set for **mobile marketing**—marketing messages transmitted via wireless technology.

mobile marketing Marketing messages transmitted via wireless technology.

interactive marketing
Buyer–seller
communications in
which the customer
controls the amount
and type of information
received from a marketer
through such channels
as the Internet and
virtual reality kiosks.

social marketing The
use of online
social media as a
communications
channel for marketing
messages.

Interactive media technologies combine computers and telecommunications resources to create software that users can control. Putting power into the hands of customers allows better communication, which can build relationships. **Interactive marketing** refers to buyer–seller communications in which the customer controls the amount and type of information received from a marketer. This technique provides immediate access to key product information when the consumer wants it, and it is increasingly taking place at in-store virtual-reality kiosks and on social media sites such as Facebook, Twitter, LinkedIn, and blogs. **Social marketing** is the use of online social media as a communications channel for marketing messages. Social media is now the top online activity. Facebook has 1.19 billion monthly active users; 874 million (over 73 percent) access it through mobile devices.[34] If Facebook were a country, it would be the third-most populous in the world after India. By contrast, Twitter reports 215 million monthly active users; 163.5 million (76 percent) access it through mobile devices. Users tweet 500 million messages per day.[35] Facebook is accessed daily by 63 percent of its users, Instagram by 57 percent, Twitter by 46 percent, Pinterest by 23 percent, and LinkedIn by 13 percent.[36] Over three-fourths of the Fortune 100 companies have joined Twitter, and more than 60 percent use Facebook.[37] Even small businesses are actively using social media. A Bank of Montreal report found that 46 percent use social media to promote their company's brand and 38 percent use it for sales.[38]

Interactive marketing allows marketers and consumers to customize their communication. Customers may come to companies for information, creating opportunities for one-to-one marketing. They also can tell the company what they like or dislike about a product, and they can just as easily click the exit button and move on to another area. A survey by Insights West found that more than one-third of social media users in British Columbia posted online complaints. Seventy percent were ignored; 23 percent received an online apology.[39] As companies become more social media–savvy, the challenge will be to encourage actionable complaints and turn unhappy customers into loyal supporters or even advocates. Air Canada provides an excellent example. When Shane Gibson, author of *Sociable! How Social Media Is Turning Sales and Marketing Upside-down,* was waiting to catch a flight in Winnipeg, he was told he might get bumped from his confirmed flight because an earlier plane had been cancelled. Gibson tweeted his predicament as he was scheduled to deliver a presentation to 140 Ford dealers in Toronto the next day. Air Canada tweeted back and within a few minutes he was called to his flight. The following day, Air Canada tweeted to wish him good luck with his presentation in Toronto.[40]

By converting indifferent or unhappy customers into loyal ones, companies generate repeat sales. The cost of maintaining existing customers is far below the cost of finding new ones, and these loyal customers are profitable. Some of the best repeat customers are those who are also willing to spread the word—create a buzz—about a product. *Buzz marketing* can be very effective in attracting new customers by bridging the gap between a company and its products. Companies as diverse as Apple and Tim Hortons have tapped customers to create a buzz about their products. Firms that make the most efficient use of buzz marketing warn that it is not a "one-way" approach to building customer relationships. Buzz can be purely visual, too. "Visual buzz" can be thought of as the tangible expression of an issue or position. October is pink ribbon month, and many thousands of people across Canada show their support for breast cancer awareness by wearing pink ribbons. In November, many men support a new 'stache. The month has become known as Movember. In one recent year, 247,441 Canadian males registered their moustache in an effort to raise awareness and money for prostate and testicular cancer and men's mental health issues. In 2013, Dalhousie University in Halifax, Nova Scotia, was the event's leading fund-raising school per capita in Canada; 645 students and faculty raised $93,566. The University of Toronto was its top overall global fund-raiser, where 977 participants raised $148,449.[41]

Effective relationship marketing often relies heavily on information technologies such as computer databases that record customers' tastes, price preferences, and lifestyles. This technology helps companies become one-to-one marketers who gather customer-specific information and provide individually customized goods and services. The firms target their marketing programs to appropriate groups rather than relying on mass-marketing campaigns. Companies that study customer preferences and react accordingly gain distinct competitive advantages.

Courtesy of General Motors of Canada Limited

GM Canada promotes its products in Mandarin on its website to engage this important segment of automobile consumers.

DEVELOPING PARTNERSHIPS AND STRATEGIC ALLIANCES

Relationship marketing does not apply just to individual consumers and employees. It also affects a wide range of other markets, including business-to-business relationships with the firm's suppliers and distributors as well as other types of corporate partnerships. In the past, companies have often viewed their suppliers as adversaries against whom they must fiercely negotiate prices, playing one off against the other. But this attitude has changed radically, as both marketers and their suppliers discover the benefits of collaborative relationships.

The formation of **strategic alliances**—partnerships that create competitive advantages—is also on the rise. Alliances take many forms, including product-development partnerships that involve shared costs for research and development and marketing, and vertical alliances in which one company provides a product or component to another firm, which then distributes or sells it under its own brand. Sears Canada entered into a strategic alliance with Buffalo International to design and manufacture the complete line of Nevada denim-based clothing that will be sold by Sears across Canada.[42]

Not-for-profit organizations often make use of strategic alliances to raise awareness and funds for their causes or to achieve their goals. Second Harvest is Canada's largest food rescue program. It has in one year delivered nearly 3.4 million kilograms of fresh food to needy people in Toronto. Sobeys is one of the larger companies that have partnered with Second Harvest, providing it with 226,000 kilograms of food. The Sobeys group of companies has also supported many local food banks across Canada through collecting food and cash donations.[43]

strategic alliances Partnerships in which two or more companies combine resources and capital to create competitive advantages in a new market.

assessment check 6

6.1 How does relationship marketing give companies a competitive edge?

6.2 Why are interactive and social marketing important tools for marketers?

6.3 What is a strategic alliance?

⑦ **Identify the universal functions of marketing.**

COSTS AND FUNCTIONS OF MARKETING

Firms must spend money to create time, place, and ownership utilities. Numerous attempts have been made to measure marketing costs in relation to overall product costs, and most estimates have ranged between 40 and 60 percent of total costs. On average, one-half of the costs involved in a product, such as a Subway sandwich, a pair of Gap jeans, or a financial planning lecture, can be traced directly to marketing. These costs are not associated with wheat, metal, or other raw materials. Nor are they associated with baking, welding, or any of the other production functions necessary for creating form utility. What functions does marketing perform, and why are they important in creating customer satisfaction?

As Figure 1.3 reveals, marketing is responsible for the performance of eight universal functions: buying, selling, transporting, storing, standardizing and grading, financing, risk taking, and securing marketing information. Some functions are performed by manufacturers; others by marketing intermediaries such as retailers or wholesalers (described in Chapter 13).

exchange functions
Buying and selling.

Buying and selling represent **exchange functions**. Buying is important to marketing on several levels. Marketers must determine how and why consumers buy certain goods and services. To be successful, they must try to understand consumer behaviour. In addition, retailers and other intermediaries must seek out products that will appeal to their customers. Marketers must also anticipate consumer preferences for purchases to be made several months later. Selling is the second half of the exchange process. It involves advertising, personal selling, and sales promotion in an attempt to match the firm's goods and services to consumer needs.

Transporting and storing are physical distribution functions. Transporting involves physically moving goods from the seller to the purchaser. Storing involves warehousing goods until they are needed for sale. Manufacturers, wholesalers, and retailers all typically perform these functions.

The final four marketing functions—standardizing and grading, financing, risk taking, and securing marketing information—are often called facilitating functions because they help the marketer perform the exchange and physical distribution functions. Quality and quantity control standards and grades, frequently established by government, reduce the need for purchasers to inspect each item. For example, if you request a certain size tire for your automobile, you expect to get it.

Financing is another marketing function because buyers often need access to funds to finance inventories prior to sales. Manufacturers often provide financing for their wholesale and retail customers. Some types of wholesalers perform similar functions for their markets. Finally, retailers frequently allow their customers to buy on credit, with either store charge cards or major credit cards.

figure 1.3

Eight Universal Marketing Functions

1. **Buying**
   Ensuring product offerings are available in sufficient quantities to meet customer demands

2. **Selling**
   Using advertising, personal selling, and sales promotion to match products to customer needs

3. **Transporting**
   Moving products from their point of production to locations convenient for purchasers

4. **Storing**
   Warehousing products until needed for sale

5. **Standardizing and Grading**
   Ensuring product offerings meet quality and quantity controls of size, weight, and other variables

6. **Financing**
   Providing credit for channel members (wholesalers and retailers) and consumers

7. **Risk Taking**
   Dealing with uncertainty about future customer purchases

8. **Securing Marketing Information**
   Collecting information about consumers, competitors, and channel members for use in making marketing decisions

The seventh function, risk taking, is part of most ventures. Manufacturers create goods and services based on research and their belief that consumers need them. Wholesalers and retailers acquire inventory based on similar expectations of future consumer demand. Entrepreneurial risk takers accommodate these uncertainties about future consumer behaviour when they market goods and services.

The final marketing function involves securing marketing information. Marketers gather information about potential customers—who they are, what they buy, where they buy, and how they buy. By collecting and analyzing marketing information, marketers can understand why consumers purchase some products while passing others by. This information also helps determine what consumers want and need—and how to offer goods and services to satisfy them. So marketing is the direct connection between a firm and its customers, the link that helps build and maintain lasting relationships.

assessment check 7

7.1 Which two marketing functions represent exchange functions?

7.2 Which two functions represent physical distribution functions?

7.3 Which four functions are facilitating functions?

ETHICS AND SOCIAL RESPONSIBILITY: DOING WELL BY DOING GOOD

8 Demonstrate the relationship among ethical business practices, social responsibility, sustainability, and marketplace success.

Ethics are moral standards of behaviour expected by a society. Most companies do their best to abide by an ethical code of conduct, but sometimes organizations and their leaders fall short. Several years ago, energy giant Enron collapsed, taking with it the retirement savings of its employees and investors. In another scandal, executives from Tyco were convicted of using millions of company dollars for their personal benefit. And chemical manufacturer Monsanto was convicted not only of polluting a rural area's water sources and soil for decades but also of ignoring evidence its own scientists had gathered indicating the extent and severity of the pollution.

Most businesspeople do follow ethical practices. Over half of all major corporations now offer ethics training to employees, and most corporate mission statements include pledges to protect the environment, contribute to communities, and improve workers' lives. This book encourages you to follow the highest ethical standards throughout your business and marketing career.

Social responsibility includes marketing philosophies, policies, procedures, and actions whose primary objective is to enhance society and protect the environment through sustainable products and practices. Walmart and Real Canadian Superstore, for instance, have made great strides in reducing their in-store energy use. Social responsibility often takes the form of philanthropy, making gifts of money or time to humanitarian causes. Many firms, both large and small, include social responsibility programs as part of their overall mission. These programs often produce such benefits as improved customer relationships, increased employee loyalty, marketplace success, and improved financial performance.

Sustainable products, which can be produced, used, and disposed of with minimal impact on the environment, are another goal of socially responsible firms. Many such firms have added annual sustainability reports and a top-level executive position to develop and promote their sustainability efforts. One such executive is DuPont's chief sustainability officer, Linda Fisher, who says about the challenges companies face in operating in environmentally responsible ways, "We believe the global companies that succeed in responding successfully and sustainably to 21st-century challenges will be those that master the art of collaboration. We are building alliances with customers, companies, governments, NGOs (nongovernmental organizations), visionaries, thought leaders, and others around the world in an effort to address needs sustainably at the local level. We've adopted a new model that we call 'inclusive innovation'—solving problems by designing solutions in cooperation with those who will benefit directly from the product."[44]

What is the role of marketing in sustainability efforts? According to Fisher, DuPont's goals "address all stages of product development, from R&D efforts through marketing and sales. They also mark a turning point in our corporate thinking. Establishing goals that relied on our ability to help our customer do better for the environment and their consumers meant sustainability had to be embedded in the way we do business. Now the business of sustainability at DuPont was truly going to be business

ethics Moral standards of behaviour expected by a society.

social responsibility Marketing philosophies, policies, procedures, and actions that have the enhancement of society's welfare as a primary objective.

sustainable products Products that can be produced, used, and disposed of with minimal impact on the environment.

SOLVING AN ETHICAL CONTROVERSY

Celebrities and Oil: Do They Mix?

MARKETERS have long used celebrity endorsers because of their visibility. But sometimes, celebrities decide to market their personal opinions. This often benefits not-for-profit organizations and enhances the awareness of and concern for important social causes. Sometimes those opinions are controversial. In early 2014, Canadian—or at least once Canadian—rocker Neil Young campaigned against the Canadian government's handling of the Alberta oil sands development. Through his Honor (yes, spelled as Americans do) the Treaties concerts in Toronto, Winnipeg, Regina, and Calgary, Young hopes to raise $75,000 to aid the Athabasca Chipewyan First Nation in its legal battle against Shell Canada mine projects in the tar sands region.

Should celebrities promote for or against economic, political, or social causes when they may not have the expertise to do so?

PRO

1. Canadians are free to argue with or ignore any of the comments or people with whom they disagree when it comes to economic, social, or political issues.

2. Because of celebrities' visibility, when they engage in such topics, they foster thought and communication on important and controversial topics that might not otherwise get discussed.

CON

1. Taxes paid by oil companies help reduce the federal deficit and support important infrastructure projects across Canada. Federal equalization payments that are in part a result of Alberta oil have a big impact on the social and economic well-being of people in many parts of Canada.

2. Many of the highest-paying jobs held by Aboriginals are in or near the oil sands region. Arguably, one of the best social programs for young Aboriginals is a good job and a good income that will provide them with labour skills, economic self-sufficiency, and a positive self-image.

Where do you stand: pro or con?

Sources: Brad Wheeler, "Neil Young Renews Push on Treaty Rights, Oil-Sands Development," **www.theglobeandmail.com**, January 13, 2014; CTVNews.ca Staff, "Neil Young Says 'Rock Stars Don't Need Oil' in Response to PM's Spokesperson," **www.ctvnews.ca**, January 14, 2014, both accessed January 14, 2014.

Marketoid

Postsecondary institutions that were recently listed among Canada's greenest employers: Georgian College, Red River College, University of British Columbia, University of Northern British Columbia, University of Alberta, and York University.

as usual."[45] Other sustainability and social responsibility officers agree that sustainability must permeate the firm's corporate strategy from the top down, so all areas in the firm can align their environmental goals in the same direction for the greatest effectiveness. As IBM notes in its A Smarter Planet website, "To be sustainable, organizations must embrace a new objective: optimize operations to minimize environmental impact and improve social outcomes in a manner that also maximizes performance."[46]

Firms stand to gain needed credibility from their efforts to protect the environment by reducing waste and pollution. Not only has the recent economic downturn made it important for them to cut waste and cost as never before, including the costs of damage to the environment, but consumers now are more aware of the real need for such drives—and ready to support them. Recent research by global management consulting firm Accenture suggests that nearly two-thirds of respondents indicated willingness to pay a premium for goods or services that lower greenhouse gas emissions.[47] Nokia recently won praise for its efforts to eliminate dangerous or polluting ingredients in its products. According to the company, 100 percent of the material used to manufacture Nokia cell phones is recyclable. What's more, Nokia offers a recycling program with about 6,000 drop-off centres in 100 countries.[48]

One area where Canadian consumers are growing increasingly informed and where we see behaviour change is in housing, as home owners show more interest in green housing. According to EnerQuality Corporation, a firm that designs and delivers green building programs for residential construction, nearly 30 Ottawa-based firms build to at least Energy Star standards, and more than 20 percent of low-rise residential buildings now built in Ontario meet or exceed Energy Star standards. Roy Nandram, president of Ottawa's RND Construction, sees client education as important to ensuring increased demand for green housing. He says, "People are aware of greening and might have some knowledge of insulation and good windows, but they don't really understand it." Nandram suggests to clients that an extra $20,000 for insulation might cost $100 per month to finance, but it will reduce energy costs by that much, and, he says, that's at today's energy prices.[49]

assessment check 8

8.1 Define *ethics*.

8.2 What is social responsibility?

8.3 What are sustainable products?

Strategic Implications

Unprecedented opportunities have emerged from electronic commerce and computer technologies in business today. These advances and innovations have allowed organizations to reach new markets, reduce selling and marketing costs, and enhance their relationships with customers and suppliers. Thanks to the Internet and social media tools, business has grown into a global market.

Both profit-seeking and not-for-profit organizations must broaden the scope of their activities to prevent myopic results in their enterprises. If they fail to do so, they lose out on promising opportunities.

Marketers must constantly look for ways to create loyal customers and build long-term relationships with those customers, often on a one-to-one basis. They must be able to anticipate customer needs and satisfy them with innovative goods and services. They must be able to do this faster and better than the competition. And they must conduct their business according to the highest ethical and sustainability standards. ◆◆◆

REVIEW OF CHAPTER OBJECTIVES

① **Define *marketing*, explain how it creates utility, and describe its role in the global marketplace.**

Marketing is an organizational function and a set of processes for creating, communicating, and delivering value to customers and for managing customer relationships in ways that benefit the organization and its stakeholders. Utility is the want-satisfying power of a good or service. Four basic kinds of utility exist: form, time, place, and ownership. Marketing creates time, place, and ownership utilities. Three factors have forced marketers to embrace a global marketplace: expanded international trade agreements, new technologies that have brought previously isolated nations to the marketplace, and greater interdependence of the world's economies.

② **Contrast marketing activities during the five eras in the history of marketing.**

During the production era, businesspeople believed that quality products would sell themselves. The sales era emphasized convincing people to buy. The marketing concept emerged during the marketing era, in which there was a company-wide focus on consumer orientation with the objective of achieving long-term success. The relationship era focuses on establishing and maintaining relationships between customers and suppliers. Relationship marketing involves long-term, value-added relationships. The social era encourages companies to use the Web and social media sites to connect to consumers as a way to market goods and services.

③ **Explain the importance of avoiding marketing myopia.**

Marketing myopia is management's failure to recognize a company's scope of business. It focuses marketers too narrowly on products and thus misses potential opportunities to satisfy customers. To avoid it, companies must broadly define their goals so they focus on fulfilling consumer needs.

④ **Describe the characteristics of not-for-profit marketing.**

Not-for-profit organizations operate in both public and private sectors. The biggest distinction between not-for-profits and commercial firms is the bottom line—whether the firm is judged by its profitability levels. Not-for-profit organizations may market to multiple publics. A customer or service user of a not-for-profit organization may have less control over the organization's destiny than do customers of a profit-seeking firm. In addition, resource contributors to not-for-profits may try to exert influence over the organization's activities. Not-for-profits and for-profits may form alliances that effectively promote each other's causes and services.

(5)   **Identify and briefly explain each of the five types of nontraditional marketing.**

Person marketing focuses on efforts to cultivate the attention, interest, and preferences of a target market toward a celebrity or noted figure. Place marketing attempts to attract visitors, potential residents, and businesses to a particular destination. Cause marketing identifies and markets a social issue, cause, or idea. Event marketing promotes sporting, cultural, charitable, or political activities. Organization marketing attempts to influence others to accept the organization's goals or services and contribute to it in some way.

(6)   **Explain the shift from transaction-based marketing to relationship and social marketing.**

Relationship marketing represents a dramatic change in the way companies interact with customers. The focus on relationships gives a firm new opportunities to gain a competitive edge by moving customers up a loyalty ladder from new customers to regular purchasers and then to loyal supporters and advocates. Over the long term, this relationship may be translated to the lifetime value of a customer. Interactive technologies and social marketing (via Facebook, Twitter, and the like) allow marketers direct communication with customers, permit more meaningful exchanges, and put the customer in control. Organizations may form partnerships—called *strategic alliances*—to create a competitive advantage. These alliances may involve product development, raising awareness, and other activities.

(7)   **Identify the universal functions of marketing.**

Marketing is responsible for eight universal functions, divided into three categories: (1) exchange functions (buying and selling); (2) physical distribution (transporting and storing); and (3) facilitating functions (standardization and grading, financing, risk taking, and securing market information).

(8)   **Demonstrate the relationship among ethical business practices, social responsibility, sustainability, and marketplace success.**

Ethics are moral standards of behaviour expected by a society. Companies that promote ethical behaviour and social responsibility usually produce increased employee loyalty and a better public image. This image often pays off in customer growth, since many buyers want to associate themselves with—and be customers of—such firms. Social responsibility involves marketing philosophies, policies, procedures, and actions whose primary objective is the enhancement of society and the protection of the environment through sustainable products and practices. These actions also generally promote a firm's public image.

assessment check answers ✓

1.1 Define *marketing* and explain how it creates utility.
Marketing is an organizational function and a set of processes for creating, communicating, and delivering value to customers and for managing customer relationships in ways that benefit the organization and its stakeholders. It creates time, place, and ownership utilities.

1.2 What three factors have forced marketers to embrace a global marketplace?
International agreements are being negotiated in attempts to expand trade among nations. The growth of technology is bringing previously isolated countries into the marketplace. The interdependence of the world's economies is now a reality.

2.1 What is the major distinction between the production era and the sales era?
During the production era, businesspeople believed that quality products would sell themselves. But during the sales era, emphasis was placed on selling—persuading people to buy.

2.2 What is the marketing concept?
The marketing concept is a company-wide consumer orientation with the objective of achieving long-term success.

2.3 Describe the relationship era of marketing.
The relationship era focuses on building long-term, value-added relationships over time with customers and suppliers.

3.1 What is marketing myopia?

Marketing myopia is management's failure to recognize the scope of a company's business.

3.2 Give an example of how a firm can avoid marketing myopia.

A firm can find innovative ways to reach new markets with existing goods and services.

4.1 What is the most obvious distinction between a not-for-profit organization and a commercial organization?

The biggest distinction between for-profit and not-for-profit organizations is the bottom line—whether an organization is judged by its profitability.

4.2 Why do for-profit and not-for-profit organizations sometimes form alliances?

For-profits and not-for-profits may form alliances to promote each other's causes and offerings. For-profits may do so as part of their social responsibility efforts.

5.1 Identify the five major categories of nontraditional marketing.

The five categories of nontraditional marketing are person, place, cause, event, and organization marketing.

5.2 Give an example of a way in which two or more of these categories might overlap.

Overlap can occur in many ways. An organization might use a person to promote its cause or event. Two organizations might use one marketing effort to promote an event and a place—for example, Subway donating money to the Special Olympics in honour of one of its spokespersons, speed skater Apolo Ohno, who ran the New York Marathon.

6.1 How does relationship marketing give companies a competitive edge?

Relationship marketing can move customers up a loyalty ladder, generating repeat sales and long-term relationships.

6.2 Why are interactive and social marketing important tools for marketers?

Interactive marketing technologies create direct communication with customers, allow larger exchanges, and put the customer in control. Social marketing media (Facebook, Twitter, for example) let companies show customers they are listening and will respond quickly.

6.3 What is a strategic alliance?

A strategic alliance is a partnership formed between two organizations to create a competitive advantage.

7.1 Which two marketing functions represent exchange functions?

Buying and selling are exchange functions.

7.2 Which two functions represent physical distribution functions?

Transporting and storing are physical distribution functions.

7.3 Which four functions are facilitating functions?

The facilitating functions are standardization and grading, financing, risk taking, and securing market information.

8.1 Define *ethics*.

Ethics are moral standards of behaviour expected by a society.

8.2 What is social responsibility?

Social responsibility involves marketing philosophies, policies, procedures, and actions whose primary objective is the enhancement of society.

8.3 What are sustainable products?

Sustainable products are those that can be produced, used, and disposed of with minimal impact on the environment.

MARKETING TERMS YOU NEED TO KNOW

These terms are printed in blue in the text. They are defined in the margins of the chapter and in the Glossary that begins on p. G-1.

utility 5
marketing 6
exchange process 8
production orientation 8
sales orientation 9
seller's market 10
buyer's market 10
consumer orientation 10
marketing concept 10

relationship marketing 11
marketing myopia 12
bottom line 14
person marketing 15
place marketing 16
cause marketing 17
event marketing 17
organization marketing 18
transaction-based marketing 19

mobile marketing 19
interactive marketing 20
social marketing 20
strategic alliances 21
exchange functions 22
ethics 23
social responsibility 23
sustainable products 23

PROJECT AND TEAMWORK EXERCISES

1. Consider each of the following firms and describe how the firm's goods and/or services can create different types of utility. If necessary, go online to the company's website to learn more about it. You can do this alone or in a team.
   a. Visa, MasterCard, or American Express
   b. Swiss Chalet, The Keg, or Red Lobster
   c. Calgary Stampede or Montreal Jazz Festival
   d. Amazon.ca or chapters.indigo.ca
   e. Sobeys, Real Canadian Superstore, Overwaitea, or another grocery store chain

2. With a classmate, choose a Canadian-based company whose products you think will do well in certain markets overseas. The company can be anything from a music group to a clothing retailer—anything that interests you. Suggestions are Panago Pizza, Arcade Fire, Molly Maid, or Lululemon Athletica. Then write a plan for how you would target and communicate with overseas markets.

3. Choose a company that interests you from the following list, or select one of your own. Research the company online, through business magazines, or through other sources to learn what seems to be the scope of its business. Write a brief description of the company's current scope of business. Then describe strategies for avoiding marketing myopia and expanding the company's scope of business over the next 10 years.
   a. General Electric
   b. TD Canada Trust
   c. Delta Hotels and Resorts
   d. Purolator
   e. Canadian Tire

4. With a classmate, choose one of the following not-for-profit organizations. Then come up with a for-profit firm with which you think your organization could form a strategic alliance. Create a presentation—an ad, a poster, or the like—illustrating and promoting the partnership.
   a. Canadian Cancer Society
   b. Make-A-Wish Foundation of Canada
   c. Habitat for Humanity Canada
   d. Save the Children Canada
   e. Humane Society of Canada

5. Research one of the following electronics companies, or another of your choosing, and study its efforts to improve the sustainability of its products, particularly their safe disposal. What does the company do well in this area? What could it do better?
   a. Toshiba
   b. Nintendo
   c. Microsoft
   d. Fujitsu
   e. Samsung

CRITICAL THINKING EXERCISES

1. How does an organization create a customer?
2. How can marketers use interactive and social marketing to convert needs to wants and ultimately build long-term relationships with customers?
3. Why is utility such an important feature of marketing?
4. What benefits—monetary and nonmonetary—do social responsibility programs bring to a business?
5. Why is determining the lifetime value of a customer an important analysis for a company to make?
6. Why is it important for a firm to establish high ethical standards for sustainability? What role do you think marketers play in implementing these standards?

ETHICS EXERCISE

At a local coffee shop you run into a friend who works for a social media firm that competes with yours. After a brief conversation, he remembers an errand he has to run, and he rushes off with a hasty good-bye. As you gather your things to leave a few minutes later, you realize your friend left a file folder on the chair; inside is a report about a client. Your company is very interested in doing some work for this client in the future.

1. Would you take a quick look inside the folder before you return it to your friend? Why or why not?
2. Would you share any information in the report with anyone in your office? Why or why not?
3. When you return the folder to your friend, would you mention the report and offer your own commentary on it? Why or why not?

CASE 1.1

Oreos Turn 100 Years Young

Perhaps it's not entirely marketing expertise that has made Oreo reportedly the most popular cookie in the world. Recent research suggests—at least with lab rats—the Oreo cookie might be more addictive than cocaine. Besides, it also tastes good, and it's fun to eat. But marketing has certainly helped the beloved chocolate wafer sandwich sail past competitors to celebrate its 100th birthday.

Successful early advertising pushed Oreos ahead of Hydrox, its nearest (and now defunct) rival. Wise strategizing led Oreo's producer Kraft Foods to tailor the cream and wafers to different consumer tastes in China, Japan, Indonesia, and Argentina, and later to switch to a trans-fat-free formula. Innovative marketing led to partnerships with Burger King, Carl's Jr., and the Cheesecake Factory, all of which now promote the use of Oreos as ingredients in their dessert offerings. Oreos have gone digital, too. The cookie racked up the most Facebook "likes" ever in a single day and now has 23 million Facebook fans. So it's understandable that 70 million cookies are eaten globally every day, earning $2 billion a year for the Nabisco brand. But perhaps the most elaborate marketing plan of all was the year-long global birthday party.

Kraft—the owner of Nabisco—celebrated with live events, prizes, promotions, and public relations efforts around the world, plus a special ad campaign and online happenings, all tied to the theme "Celebrate the kid inside." Fans could post photos, stories, and videos to a special Facebook gallery and qualify to be a "Birthday of the Day" celebrant on their own special day. "Flash" birthday parties culminated in a multinational celebration

in New York. China hosted a fireworks display, a playground for all ages was opened in Indonesia, and there were party games and cake in Dubai and piñatas in Venezuela. Fans in 200 countries watched these events in real time on Facebook, too. Television ads showcased adults and kids sharing Oreos and milk, print ads commemorated iconic moments of the last 100 years, and the company website featured games and recipes. There was even a special birthday variety of the treat in stores around the world, with rainbow candy sprinkles. (Note: In 2012, Kraft Foods spun off its global snacking and food brands to Mondelez International.)

Questions for Critical Thinking

1. How did Oreo's birthday celebration activities meet the definition of marketing?
2. What accounted for Oreo's popularity on Facebook, and is Mondelez International using this factor to the best marketing advantage?

Sources: Amy Verner, "Oreos More Addictive Than Cocaine, Study Finds," **www .theglobeandmail.com**, October 16, 2013, accessed January 16, 2014; Nadia Arumugam, "Oreo Cookie Celebrates 100th Birthday with Sprinkles and World Domination," *Forbes*, March 8, 2012, **www.forbes.com**; Brian Palmer, "The Unsinkable O," Slate.com, March 6, 2012, **www.slate.com**; Rob Manker, "Oreo at 100," *The Chicago Tribune*, March 6, 2012, **http://articles.chicagotribune.com**; news release, "The World's Favorite Cookie Invites Fans from Around the World to 'Celebrate the Kid Inside' with Every Twist, Lick and Dunk," March 5, 2012, **www .kraftfoodscompany.com**; Kim Peterson, "Oreo Turns 100," Money.com, March 5, 2012, **http://money.msn.com**; Stuart Elliott, "The Oreo Turns 100, with a Nod to the Past," *The New York Times*, February 28, 2012, **www.nytimes.com**.

CASE 1.2

Geoffrey B. Small Is Big on Quality, Customers, Community

Geoffrey B. Small is a leading avant-garde fashion designer who wants you to think about your clothes—but not the style or colour of the outfit you are wearing today, not what a great bargain it was, not the brand name or which celebrities wear the same design. He wants you to dig deeper than that, thinking about the quality and origin of fabrics you wear, their impact on the environment, and your own view of social responsibility as a consumer. Even if you can't afford his clothes (created in one or two of a kind, limited editions), you can take away his messages about quality, value, service to the customer and community, and the importance of activism.

Now based in Italy—with easy access to the Paris fashion shows—Small began his career selling jeans at the Gap. Today, he shrugs off the marketing tactics of the large, name-brand

clothing designers and retail outlets, which he believes do little or nothing to create utility for the consumer, because they hide the true cost of the clothes they are selling. "Corporate advertising has made people unaware of what they're really spending their money on, and what things are really costing them," says Small. Cheap fabrics, poor construction, and lack of attention to detail all add up to low prices and nearly disposable garments—costing consumers more money in the long run. "We have to re-educate a lot of consumers because what they think is cheap is not cheap at all," asserts Small. "It's the most expensive."

Small's clothing designs provide form utility by creating the highest-quality garments. Although customers often have to wait months for these hand-made garments, Small believes this is an asset. "Fifty years ago, machine-made products were perfect, new, and exciting," explains Small. That's no longer the case. "We don't care how long it takes," he insists. "We don't care what it costs. What we care about is that it's the very, very best it can possibly be," which is what his customers want. Consumers may view Small's clothes in motion at runway shows or at a select group of exclusive retail shops, or communicate with him directly. When they take ownership of a suit or coat, they have a highly individualized piece of clothing that some might call a work of art. "Customers are screaming for something personal and special," Small points out, "something that has a bond between one human being and another."

Small views his relationships with customers as critical to his success, referring to them as the "best and only financial backers" a designer should have. Since his clothes are made to last decades—25 to 30 years—he looks toward developing customer relationships that will survive just as long. "We're in a field where you normally do a lot of marketing," he observes. "I think it's more important to focus on great product, great service, value to the customer, and communicating with the customer honestly." That honest communication—about his products and his beliefs—has built Small a devoted following.

It would be easy for Small to hide in his design studio sketching clothes for a few high-end customers who want the novelty of something edgy and different to wear. Doing so could lead him into the quicksand of marketing myopia. But that's not Small's style. He looks for new ways to satisfy customers without compromising his ideals—in fact, he stitches his ideals right into the fabrics of his clothing. Small is a genuine activist for social causes as well as environmental sustainability, which has proved to be an effective tool for connecting with the people who appreciate his designs. Customers see his activism, and when they make a choice about where to spend their money, they choose his brand. "That's where we want to be positioned," says Small. "We want to do more than just supply clothes. We want to play a role in the community."

Looking to the future, Small believes it is his company's responsibility to set an example for other businesses. "The biggest challenge now is not to compromise," he admits, "[but] to focus on one piece at a time and make it the absolute best it can be."

Questions for Critical Thinking

1. Why is the link between relationship marketing and social responsibility so important to Small's business success?
2. Geoffrey B. Small is an avant-garde designer and unconventional businessperson. What examples does he set, and what might marketers for large corporations learn from his views and practices?

Sources: "The Amazing Geoffrey B. Small Story," company website, **www.geoffreybsmall.net/gbsstory.htm**, accessed June 15, 2012; Geoffrey B. Small, "The Environment of Young Designers," Not Just a Label, **www.notjustalabel.com**, accessed June 15, 2012; Claire Ruhlin, "Recycle, Reconstruct, Redesign," Community, April, 24, 2012, **http://communityathens.blogspot.com**; Eugene Rabkin, "Review: Geoffrey B. Small, Fall/Winter 2012," StyleZeitgeist Magazine, January 2012, **www.sz-mag.com**.

chapter 2

Strategic Planning in Contemporary Marketing

CHAPTER OBJECTIVES

1. Distinguish between strategic planning and tactical planning.

2. Explain how marketing plans differ at various levels in an organization.

3. Identify the steps in the marketing planning process.

4. Describe successful planning tools and techniques, including Porter's Five Forces model, first and second mover strategies, SWOT analysis, and the strategic window.

5. Identify the basic elements of a marketing strategy.

6. Describe the environmental characteristics that influence strategic decisions.

7. Describe the methods for marketing planning, including business portfolio analysis, the BCG market share/market growth matrix, and the strategic growth opportunity matrix.

GOOGLE'S STRATEGIC PLAN: RECOVERING FROM A HICCUP

Strategy planning is important to the success of all firms, and especially in the fast-paced world of high technology. Today's winners can be struggling tomorrow. Think BlackBerry. Fortunately, firms, when they develop and implement good strategy, can sometimes rebound. Google has for years consistently been ranked among the most valuable global brands. Interbrand ranked it second behind Apple in 2013, with a brand value of $93.3 billion. In business for less than 20 years, Google has made many good strategic moves. But even Google can have a hiccup.

In 2014, Google sold ownership of Motorola to China's Lenovo for $2.91 billion—less than two years after it paid $12.5 billion to buy the smartphone handset maker. It's not quite as bad as it appears, however. Motorola had $3 billion in cash on its balance sheet when it was bought by Google, and Google gained $2.4 billion by selling off Motorola's set-top box unit. That just leaves about $7 billion remaining to account for after the sale.

Why did Google buy Motorola in the first place? Many analysts thought it an odd acquisition. Motorola was a manufacturer of technology hardware. Google had little, if any, manufacturing experience. The two companies differed radically in their missions, profit margins, and distribution methods. Google appears to have simply wanted ownership of Motorola's patents. Patents ensure exclusive access to protected technologies and are highly desired assets among tech and telecom firms. Licensing rights to them are avidly contested in court. While consumers may love smartphones for their features and convenience, technology companies value smartphone technology for its potential to spur the creation of "the next great thing." When Canada's Nortel Network Corp. went bankrupt, a consortium of firms, including BlackBerry, Microsoft, Apple, and Sony, purchased more than 6,000 wireless-tech patents and applications, easing their access to promising new technologies. Google's stated strategy for buying Motorola was to access its enormous treasury of patents—17,000 mobile tech patents and 7,500 more patents pending—to defend itself and manufacturers of Android handsets, including Samsung and HTC, in patent suits. In effect, it appears to have paid about $7 billion for these patents.

Unfortunately, Google wasn't able to extract the value it expected from the patents. At the same time, ownership of Motorola created tension in the relationships between Google and the other smartphone manufacturers that were using Google's Android operating system. Speculation was even that Samsung would develop its own operating system and would drop Android. In addition, Motorola was "bleeding" money—costing Google hundreds of millions of dollars each quarter. The decision was made to sell, but Google retained the rights to most of the patents—originally valued at $5.5 billion when Google bought Motorola—and has only licensed them to Lenovo. The decision to unload Motorola to Lenovo certainly appears to be a good one. Investors agreed. Google's stock immediately gained $28.08 per share following the announcement.

Google's CEO Larry Page stated, "This move will enable Google to devote our energy to driving innovation across the Android ecosystem, for the benefit of smartphone users everywhere." Google can get back to its mission: to organize the world's information and make it universally accessible and useful. At the same time, Motorola's new owner benefits from gaining a strong brand, a good product portfolio of smartphones, strong and established relationships with more than 50 wireless carriers around the globe, and talented employees, positioning it to become a much stronger global competitor in the smartphone handset business.

Google's purchase of Motorola may have been a mistake, but its sale of Motorola seems to be a hit. Relations between Google and Samsung also improved following the sale. The two companies recently signed a broad patent, cross-licensing deal. Hopefully, for Google, a valuable lesson was learned: a several-billion-dollar lesson.[1]

Marketoid

A google of "Google" on March 31, 2014, produced nearly 3.6 billion results, and took 0.22 seconds.

connecting with customers

Google has always shown an unerring ability to "read" the marketplace and discern what will engage customers. That is how it grew to become the world's second-most-valued brand. The key to building brand value is to have an enormous number of very satisfied customers who interact regularly with the brand, and who trust what the brand stands for and what it is trying to do. Google is admired by many consumers and businesses around the world. In fact, today, people don't simply search for something on the Web, they "google" it. But, Google's success does not come from luck. Like other flourishing enterprises, Google is constantly gathering information about the market; analyzing what it finds; and planning, both for the near and long terms. It can be excused for an occasional hiccup.

Chapter Overview

- "More and more consumers are purchasing smaller, more fuel-efficient vehicles, such as the Ford Focus, Fusion, and Escape. The market for large trucks and SUVs is dwindling. Are fuel-efficient vehicles the wave of the future? Should we commit to building more of them and feature them prominently in our marketing?"

- "We have fewer customers eating at our restaurant on weekends. Should we revamp our menu? Lower our prices? Use special promotions? Update the dining room decor?"

- "Recent marketing research shows we are not reaching our customer target—consumers in their early to mid-20s. Should we consider another advertising agency?"

arketers face strategic questions every day—planning strategy is a critical part of the job. The marketplace changes continually in response to changes in consumer tastes and expectations, technological developments, competitors' actions, economic trends, and political and legal events, as well as product innovations and pressures from suppliers and distributors. Although the causes of these changes often lie outside a marketer's control, effective planning can anticipate many of the changes.

When the price of gas and jet fuel soared recently, travellers opted to stay closer to home—taking "staycations" instead of booking vacations to exotic, faraway places. This represents an opportunity for places such as Vancouver, British Columbia, and Ottawa, Ontario. Local parks, nearby lakes, indoor playgrounds or gyms, museums, art galleries, and restaurants can market themselves as potential alternatives. Any destination that promotes itself to potential vacationers within a short drive could find itself adding up the profits.

This chapter provides an important foundation for analyzing all aspects of marketing by demonstrating the importance of gathering reliable information to create an effective plan. These activities provide a structure for a firm to use its unique strengths. Marketing planning identifies the markets a company can best serve as well as the most appropriate mix of approaches to satisfy the customers in those markets. While this chapter focuses on planning, we will examine in greater detail the task of marketing research and decision making in Chapter 8. ◆◆◆

MARKETING PLANNING: THE BASIS FOR STRATEGY AND TACTICS

planning Process of anticipating future events and conditions and of determining the best way to achieve organizational goals.

Everyone plans. We plan which courses we want to take, which movie we want to see, and which outfit to wear to a party. We plan where we want to live and what career we want to pursue. Marketers plan as well. **Planning** is the process of anticipating future events and conditions and of determining the best way to achieve organizational objectives. Of course, before marketing planning can even begin, an organization must define its objectives. Planning is a continuous process that includes identifying objectives and then determining the actions through which a firm can attain those objectives. The planning process creates a blueprint for marketers, executives, production staff, and everyone else in the organization to follow for achieving organizational objectives. It also defines checkpoints so that people within the organization can compare actual performance with expectations to indicate whether current activities are moving the organization toward its objectives.

Planning is important for both large and small companies. For years, Sir Richard Branson—founder of the airline Virgin Galactic—dreamed of launching a spaceship designed for commercial travel. The dream required complex design and engineering plans, including the launch of prototypes and rigorous rounds of safety testing. After one of the prototypes became the first privately owned, manned craft to reach space, the company's engineers went to work on a similar craft designed for commercial use, called SpaceShipTwo. Meanwhile, the idea of space travel has been marketed to wealthy clients, offering them the opportunity to pay $200,000 or more for a brief suborbital ride. Actor Ashton Kutcher became the 500th person to sign up for the historic trip. If the idea catches on, Branson and Virgin Galactic will have positioned themselves strategically to become the first—and possibly the only—firm to offer commercial space travel for the near future.[2] Here on earth—and at the other end of the size spectrum—Freed & Freed, a fourth-generation, family-owned apparel manufacturer in Winnipeg, Manitoba, refocused and revitalized its core business

Marketoid

Zainab Azim, age 11, and her 10-year-old brother Ali from Milton, Ontario, are hoping to be the youngest space travellers aboard Virgin Galactic. Their tickets, paid for by their father, cost $250,000 each.

and now includes among its customer base the Canadian military; the Royal Canadian Mounted Police; and most recently Hudson's Bay, for whom it manufactured Team Canada clothing for the 2014 Sochi Olympic Games. In less than five years, its 34-year-old president, Marissa Freed, has grown the business from 20 to 100 employees.[3]

Marketing planning—implementing planning activities devoted to achieving marketing objectives— establishes the basis for any marketing strategy. Product lines, pricing decisions, selection of appropriate distribution channels, and decisions relating to promotional campaigns all depend on plans formulated within the marketing organization. In today's boundaryless organizations, many planning activities take place over the Internet with *virtual conferences*—teleconferences with computer interfaces. These conferences represent a new way to build relationships among people who are in different geographic locations. Relationships like these are also important for new employees to help ensure their success.

Richard Branson, shown here in a spacesuit costume to promote a contest, executed complex design and engineering plans to get Virgin Galactic into space.

See the "Career Readiness" feature for some other tips about making a good impression in your first real job.

marketing planning Implementing planning activities devoted to achieving marketing objectives.

An important trend in marketing planning centres on relationship marketing, which is a firm's effort at developing long-term, cost-effective links with individual customers and suppliers for mutual benefit. Good relationships with customers can arm a firm with vital strategic weapons, and that's as true in business-to-business industries as anywhere else.

Many companies now include relationship-building goals and strategies in their plans. Relationship marketers frequently maintain databases to track customer preferences. These marketers may also manipulate product spreadsheets to answer what-if questions related to prices and marketing performance. At Procter & Gamble, the inspiration for new or better products often comes from customers themselves. The company operates in more than 180 countries with 138,000 employees, many of whom serve as the eyes and ears of the firm. Some P&G marketers actually spend time in the homes of consumers, observing how they cook and eat meals, when they play, and where they shop.

CAREER READINESS **Making a Good Impression at That First Real Job**

CONGRATULATIONS—you've won the job! Now how do you ensure you'll stand out at work for all the right reasons? Here are some tips:

- **Pay attention to the basics.** Every organization is different, so be sure to adopt your new employer's particular dress code and work ethic. Always be prompt, ask intelligent questions, avoid overly casual attire, do your Web surfing at home.
- **Remember names.** You'll meet a lot of new people in your first few weeks; make an effort to remember their names. Use mnemonics (memory tricks) if you need to, and if you forget a name, apologize and ask again.
- **Monitor your words and actions.** You never know who is connected or influential, especially when you're new, so be tactful, be circumspect, and avoid gossip.

- **Network with co-workers at all levels.** Meetings and team projects are good opportunities to meet helpful peers, invaluable support staff, and potential mentors. If opportunities like these don't readily come your way, volunteer.
- **Get involved outside work.** Participating in company outings, sports, and social responsibility efforts like community projects shows you're an enthusiastic member of the team.

Good luck!

Sources: Margaret Steen, "Eight Mistakes to Avoid in Your First 'Real' Job," **Monster.com**, accessed March 22, 2012, **http://career-advice.monster .com**; Randall S. Hansen and Katharine Hansen, "Quintessential Careers: Your First Days Working at a New Job: 20 Tips to Help You Make a Great Impression," Quintessential Careers.com, **www.quintcareers.com**, accessed March 22, 2012; "7 Tips for Department Meeting Rookies," Great Leadership, **www .greatleadershipbydan.com**, accessed March 22, 2012.

Other employees are trained simply to have conversations with friends and family about their lifestyles and the goods or services they use. All of this interaction helps build relationships, and the information helps develop products.[4]

(1) **Distinguish between strategic planning and tactical planning.**

STRATEGIC PLANNING VERSUS TACTICAL PLANNING

Planning is often classified on the basis of its scope or breadth. Some extremely broad plans focus on long-range organizational objectives that will significantly affect the firm for five or more years. Other more targeted plans cover the objectives of individual business units over shorter periods.

strategic planning
Process of determining an organization's primary objectives and adopting courses of action that will achieve these objectives.

Strategic planning can be defined as the process of determining an organization's primary objectives and then adopting courses of action that will eventually achieve these objectives. This process includes, of course, allocation of necessary resources. The word *strategy* dates back to a Greek term meaning "the general's art." Strategic planning has a critical impact on a firm's destiny because it provides long-term direction for its decision makers.

tactical planning
Planning that guides the implementation of activities specified in the strategic plan.

Strategic planning is complemented by tactical planning, which guides the implementation of activities specified in the strategic plan. Unlike strategic plans, tactical plans typically address shorter-term actions that focus on current and near-future activities that a firm must complete to implement its larger strategies. The "Marketing: Making Your World Better" feature describes how a "brilliant tactical move" by the executive chairman of Loblaw Companies supports his strategic vision for the organization.

Sometimes tactical planning requires swift decision making and actions. Disturbances onboard commercial flights are rare, but when they occur, there is urgency for action to protect traveller safety. In a recent flight between Warsaw, Poland, and Toronto, a drunken man attempted to

---

MARKETING: MAKING YOUR WORLD BETTER

Loblaw Companies: Ethics and Social Responsibility Help Drive Sales

UNDER the leadership of executive chairman Galen G. Weston, Loblaw Companies has continued to demonstrate its commitment to being a socially responsible and highly ethical organization, from Weston's first television ad in 2007 in which he promised that Loblaw would reduce landfill waste by offering an inexpensive reusable shopping bag as an alternative to the ubiquitous plastic bag, to his speech in May 2013 at the annual shareholders meeting where he made it clear that his company shared very much the responsibility for the disaster that killed 1129 factory workers earlier that year in Bangladesh. Loblaw's continued initiatives include reducing customers' plastic shopping bag use, diverting landfill waste throughout the company's supply chain, improving fuel efficiency in its truck fleet, and reducing energy consumption and greenhouse gas emissions at its many locations. These many initiatives helped Loblaw gain recognition as one of "Canada's Greenest Employers" in 2013, for the fourth consecutive year.

But many people might have missed Weston's commitment to improving the health of Canadians through better product offerings at the company's many stores. Almost everyone is aware of the Loblaw 2013 takeover of Shoppers Drug Mart. Analysts were quick to tout it as a brilliant tactical business move. But it also fit very well with Weston's personal vision: "I've long believed becoming a Canadian health and wellness and

nutrition champion represented the most powerful next chapter for Loblaw." The company's Blue Menu products promote lower fat and sodium and higher fibre, and more than 400 of them have recently been repackaged to make their nutritional information more customer-friendly. Weston has promised that Loblaw products will be free of artificial flavours and colours and that Loblaw will buy 100 percent of the company's seafood from sustainable sources. Loblaw now offers more than 100 Marine Stewardship Council–certified wild-caught seafood items, the most of any Canadian retailer. Loblaw has also committed to fresher choices through more local sourcing, again helping to reduce greenhouse gases as produce is transported over shorter distances.

Beyond its commitment to improving the health and welfare of its customers, Loblaw Companies has also been able to demonstrate its commitment to employees. In 2012, for example, the company was named among Canada's Top 100 Employers, Top Employers for Young People, Best Employers for New Canadians, and Best Diversity Employers.

Sources: Loblaw Companies Limited 2012 Annual Report, available **www .loblaw.ca**, accessed January 20, 2014; James Cowan, "Galen G. Weston," *Canadian Business*, Winter 2013–2014, pp. 20–22, 24–25; Loblaw news release, "Loblaw Named One of Canada's Greenest Employers for Fourth Consecutive Year," April 22, 2013, **www.loblaw.ca**, January 20, 2014.

strangle a flight attendant after being refused alcohol service. Flight attendants approached a physically imposing passenger and asked for help, not knowing that he was the goalie for a recreational men's hockey team composed of 17 Ontario police officers who were returning from a tournament. They quickly subdued the unruly passenger who was held until he was arrested at the Toronto airport. In an industry where safety is paramount, such action helps airlines focus on their strategic goal of providing safe air travel and restores customer trust.[5]

PLANNING AT DIFFERENT ORGANIZATIONAL LEVELS

Planning is a major responsibility for every manager, so managers at all organizational levels devote portions of their workdays to planning. Top management—boards of directors, chief executive officers (CEOs), chief operating officers (COOs), and functional vice presidents, such as chief marketing officers—spend greater proportions of their time engaged in planning than do middle-level and supervisory-level managers. Also, top managers usually focus their planning on long-range strategic issues. In contrast, middle-level managers—such as advertising executives, regional sales managers, and marketing research directors—tend to focus on operational planning, which includes creating and implementing tactical plans for their own units. Supervisors often develop specific programs to meet goals in their areas of responsibility. Table 2.1 summarizes the types of planning undertaken at various organizational levels.

When it is most effective, the planning process includes input from a wide range of sources: employees, suppliers, and customers. Some marketing experts advocate developing a network of "influencers"—people who have influence over other people's opinions through authority, visibility, or expertise—to provide input and spread the word about company plans and products. According to a recent survey of more than 400 private Canadian companies, more than half indicated that mobile computing is a technology priority and that they planned to use social media to support marketing and sales.[6]

assessment check 1

1.1 Define *planning*.

1.2 Give an example of strategic planning and tactical planning.

(2) **Explain how marketing plans differ at various levels in an organization.**

assessment check 2

2.1 How do marketing plans differ at different levels of the organization?

2.2 Why is it important to get input from others when planning?

table 2.1 **Planning at Different Managerial Levels**

MANAGEMENT LEVEL	TYPE OF PLANNING EMPHASIZED AT THIS LEVEL	EXAMPLES
Top Management		
Board of directors	Strategic planning	Organization-wide objectives; fundamental strategies; long-term plans; total budget
Chief executive officer (CEO)		
Chief operating officer (COO)		
Divisional vice presidents		
Middle Management		
General sales manager	Tactical planning	Quarterly and semi-annual plans; business unit budgets; divisional policies and procedures
Business unit manager		
Director of marketing research		
Supervisory Management		
District sales manager	Operational planning	Daily and weekly plans; unit budgets; departmental rules and procedures
Supervisor—telemarketing office		

③ **Identify the steps in the marketing planning process.**

STEPS IN THE MARKETING PLANNING PROCESS

The marketing planning process begins at the corporate level with the definition of a firm's mission. It then determines its objectives, assesses its resources, and evaluates environmental risks and opportunities. Guided by this information, marketers within each business unit then formulate a marketing strategy, implement the strategy through operating plans, and gather feedback to monitor and adapt strategies when necessary. Figure 2.1 shows the basic steps in the process.

DEFINING THE ORGANIZATION'S MISSION AND OBJECTIVES

mission Essential purpose that differentiates one company from others.

The planning process begins with activities to define the firm's **mission**, the essential purpose that differentiates the company from others. The mission statement specifies the organization's overall goals and operational scope and provides general guidelines for future management actions. Adjustments in this statement reflect changing business environments and management philosophies.

Although business writer Peter Drucker cautioned that an effective mission statement should be brief enough "to fit on a T-shirt," organizations typically define themselves with slightly longer statements. But they often condense their mission statement into a catchy slogan such as these:

- Sephora: "The beauty authority."
- Sobeys: "Better food for all."
- Home Hardware: "Homeowners helping homeowners."
- IBM: "Welcome to the decade of smart."
- Tim Hortons: "Always fresh."

An organization lays out its basic objectives, or goals, in its complete mission statement. These objectives in turn guide development of supporting marketing objectives and plans. Soundly conceived objectives should state specific intentions such as the following:

- Generate a 15 percent profit over the next 24 months.
- Reduce waste by 20 percent over the next 36 months.
- Add 25 new outlets within the next year.
- Improve five products within the next six months.
- Enter the Chinese market by 2015.
- Cut manufacturing costs by 10 percent by year-end.

Marketoid

Miles Gilbert "Tim" Horton (1930–1974) was a star defenceman with the Toronto Maple Leafs from 1949 to 1970 but ended his career with the Buffalo Sabres when he died in a car accident in St. Catharines, Ontario. The first Tim Hortons location served two items: coffee and doughnuts, including two original creations, the Apple Fritter and the Dutchie.

figure 2.1

The Marketing Planning Process

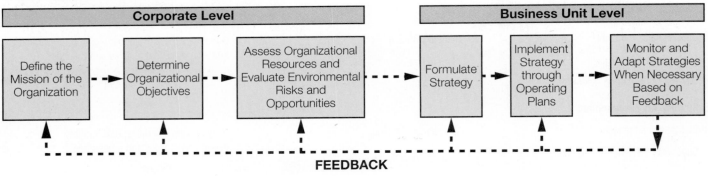

ASSESSING ORGANIZATIONAL RESOURCES AND EVALUATING ENVIRONMENTAL RISKS AND OPPORTUNITIES

The third step of the marketing planning process involves an assessment of an organization's strengths, weaknesses, and available opportunities. Organizational resources include the capabilities of the firm's production, marketing, finance, technology, and employees. An organization's planners pinpoint its strengths and weaknesses. Strengths help them to set objectives, develop plans for meeting those objectives, and take advantage of marketing opportunities.

Chapter 3 will discuss environmental factors that affect marketing opportunities. Environmental effects can emerge both from within the organization and from the external environment. For example, social media have transformed interpersonal communications as well as communications between companies and their customers.

FORMULATING, IMPLEMENTING, AND MONITORING A MARKETING STRATEGY

Once a firm's marketers figure out their company's best opportunities, they can develop a marketing plan designed to meet the overall objectives. A good marketing plan revolves around an efficient, flexible, and adaptable marketing strategy.

A **marketing strategy** is an overall, company-wide program for selecting a particular target market and then satisfying consumers in that market through a careful blending of the elements of the marketing mix—product, distribution, promotion, and price—each of which is a subset of the overall marketing strategy.

In the two final steps of the planning process, marketers put the marketing strategy into action; then they monitor performance to ensure that objectives are being achieved. Sometimes strategies need to be modified if the product's or company's actual performance is not in line with expected results. For years, Toronto-based Sun Life Financial, Canada's third-largest insurer, has sold life insurance and retirement-income plans to individuals and groups in the United States. But when the firm observed that profit margins on individual policies had begun to decline, the company revised its strategy and discontinued those sales, limiting its target market to groups. As Sun Life CEO Dean Connor put it, "We're changing course, and setting a new vision."[7]

One large rent-to-own retailer recently discovered how poor implementation can have severely negative consequences for its business, as described in the "Solving an Ethical Controversy" feature.

> **marketing strategy**
> Overall company-wide program for selecting a particular target market and then satisfying consumers in that market through the marketing mix.

> **Porter's Five Forces**
> Model developed by strategy expert Michael Porter, which identifies five competitive forces that influence planning strategies: the threat of new entrants, the threat of substitute products, rivalry among competitors, the bargaining power of buyers, and the bargaining power of suppliers.

assessment check 3

3.1 Distinguish between an organization's mission and its objectives.

3.2 What is the importance of the final step in the marketing planning process?

SUCCESSFUL STRATEGIES: TOOLS AND TECHNIQUES

(4) Describe successful planning tools and techniques, including Porter's Five Forces model, first and second mover strategies, SWOT analysis, and the strategic window.

We can identify a number of successful marketing planning tools and techniques. This section discusses four of them: Porter's Five Forces model, first and second mover strategies, SWOT analysis, and the strategic window. All planning strategies have the goal of creating a sustainable competitive advantage for a firm, in which other companies simply cannot provide the same value to their customers that the firm does—no matter how hard they try.

PORTER'S FIVE FORCES MODEL

A number of years ago, the renowned business strategist Michael E. Porter identified five competitive forces that influence planning strategies in a model called **Porter's Five Forces**. Porter later updated his model to include the impact of the Internet on the strategies that

SOLVING AN ETHICAL CONTROVERSY   Don't Remove Your Underwear

AFTER the Byrds rented a laptop from a national rent-to-own retailer, they were in for a shock. In an apparent mix-up, at least one of their payments had not been recorded. A retailer employee arrived at their door demanding payment and produced a webcam picture showing Brian Byrd playing online poker. Crystal Byrd later recalled that once when she was sitting at the computer in her underwear while she checked her college grades, she noticed that the computer's webcam light had flashed. Investigation revealed that PC Rental Agent software was installed on the laptop. The program allowed the owner to shut down a laptop when it was stolen or when its user was behind in payments. More troubling, when operated in Detective Mode, the software captured key strokes and screen shots and snapped webcam pictures, all without the user's knowledge, and transmitted them to an external location. The software developer, DesignerWare, sold its program to seven rent-to-own companies that operated about 1,600 stores, and it was subsequently installed on about 420,000 computers, many in Canada.

The Byrds' experience appears to not be an isolated incident. A former sales manager related how her store got access to bank accounts and lots of other personal information, as well as hundreds of photos, some of which she called "shocking." Lawyers have subsequently retrieved hundreds of thousands of screen shots, photos, and key logs extracted from one retail chain's servers. Canada's privacy commissioner is also conducting an investigation.

As the legal computer owner, should a rent-to-own retailer be allowed to monitor computer activity?

PRO

1. Consumers are advised as part of the rental agreement that the owner has the right to install monitoring or tracking software "solely in an attempt to locate and recover the computer."
2. As the legal owner of the computer, the business should be allowed to install whatever software it deems appropriate to protect its investment.

CON

1. When a computer is reported stolen, the computer owner should not be permitted to violate someone's privacy to see if they are lying. People have a right to be presumed innocent unless proven otherwise.
2. Signing a contract, even with a consent clause, is not sufficient. Each time that monitoring or tracking software is activated, the computer user should be warned on the computer screen.

Where do you stand: pro or con?

Sources: David Kravets, "Rent-to-Own Laptops Secretly Photographed Users Having Sex, FTC Says," September 25, 2012, **http://www.wired.com**, accessed January 14, 2014; Richard Warnica, "Keep Your Pants On," *Canadian Business*, December 10, 2012, pp. 13–14; Dan Goodwin, "How Spyware on Rental PCs Captured Users' Most Intimate Moments," December 18, 2012, **http://arstechina .com**, accessed January 14, 2014.

businesses use. As illustrated by Figure 2.2, the five forces are potential new entrants; bargaining power of buyers; bargaining power of suppliers; threat of substitute products; and rivalry among competitors.

Potential new entrants are sometimes blocked by the cost or difficulty of entering a market. It is a lot more costly and complicated to begin building aircraft than it is to start a home-based marketing consulting business. The Internet has reduced the barriers to market entry in many industries. In fact, most businesses now view an Internet presence as a requirement for success. If customers have considerable bargaining power, they can greatly influence a firm's strategy. The Internet can increase a customer's buying power by providing information that might not otherwise be easily accessible, such as supplier alternatives and price comparisons. Firms continue to compete to develop the most effective Internet marketing, because they know that customers are savvy users of technology. Microsoft and Google, for example, operate competing online advertising exchanges—Microsoft's AppNexus and Google's DoubleClick—which allow ad sellers and buyers to negotiate in real time.[8]

The number of available suppliers to a manufacturer or retailer affects their bargaining power. If a seafood restaurant in Alberta has only one supplier of Nova Scotia scallops, that supplier has significant bargaining power. But seafood restaurants located throughout Nova Scotia have many scallop suppliers available, which gives their suppliers less bargaining power.

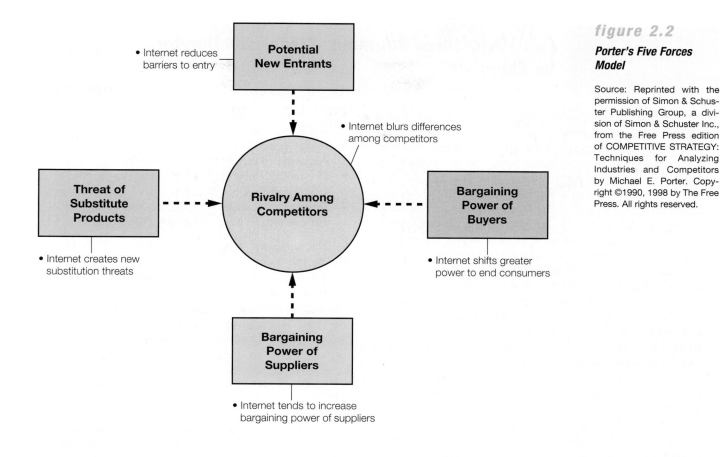

figure 2.2

Porter's Five Forces Model

Source: Reprinted with the permission of Simon & Schuster Publishing Group, a division of Simon & Schuster Inc., from the Free Press edition of COMPETITIVE STRATEGY: Techniques for Analyzing Industries and Competitors by Michael E. Porter. Copyright ©1990, 1998 by The Free Press. All rights reserved.

If customers have the opportunity to replace a company's products with the goods or services from a competing firm or industry, the company's marketers may have to take steps to find a new market, change prices, or compete in other ways to maintain an advantage. McDonald's made what some considered a bold move when the firm announced the launch of its "McCafé," offering upgraded coffee drinks such as lattes, cappuccinos, and mochas—in direct competition with Starbucks and other premium coffee outlets. McCafé's beverage offerings later expanded with fruit smoothies, shakes, frappés, and frozen lemonade. As McDonald's president Don Thompson says, "We want to be a beverage destination. For us, growing markets with great margins is the place to be."9

When Tim Hortons® started offering its Crispy Chicken Sandwich, it entered into direct competition with KFC and McDonald's. The threat of a substitute product can create a need for a company's marketers to find new ways to compete.

The four previous forces influence the rivalry among competitors. In addition, issues such as cost and differentiation or lack of differentiation of products—along with the Internet—influence the strategies that companies use to stand out from their competitors. With increased availability of information, which tends to level the playing field, rivalry heats up among competitors who try to differentiate themselves from the crowd.

FIRST MOVER AND SECOND MOVER STRATEGIES

Some firms like to adopt a first mover strategy—attempting to capture the greatest market share and develop long-term relationships by being the first to enter the market with a product or service, as Virgin Galactic hopes to do by being the first to offer commercial space travel. Being first may also refer to entering new markets with existing products or creating significant innovations that effectively turn an old product into a new one. Naturally, this strategy has its risks—companies

first mover strategy
Theory advocating that the company that is first to offer a product in a marketplace will be the long-term market winner.

MARKETING
AND THE SME

Fairway Divorce Solutions: Kinder and Gentler for Everyone

FRANCHISING—discussed more in Chapter 12—is an increasingly popular "go-to-market" strategy as many small businesses search for growth opportunities. One such company, Fairway Divorce Solutions, is changing the way divorce happens. Karen Stewart, president and CEO of the company, is turning divorce from a confrontational to a cooperative process, and she is franchising her process across North America. Karen has designed a new divorce process because of her own unsatisfactory experience. Hell, in a word, is how she describes her own divorce. The proceedings lasted four years and cost upwards of $500,000. Using her background as a stockbroker, financial planner, and certified divorce financial analyst, Karen created a system that is focused on reducing the time and emotional stress of divorce, while protecting the assets and children of divorcing couples. To promote her business, Karen has invested heavily in marketing and advertising. She uses public relations and a branding company to coordinate the company's entry into new markets. She also is very active with public speaking engagements, uses Twitter and several blogs—including video blogs and a blog on the Fairway website—and other social media to increase the company's visibility.

The company's expressed purpose helps avoid marketing myopia. On the website, "Our Purpose" is clear about its goals:

- To protect children from the needless harm they suffer in traditional divorce
- To give couples a positive, affordable, and time-saving alternative to ending their relationships
- To establish a new standard of civility and common sense for divorce in the 21st century
- To provide a mediation model for conflict resolution that can expand beyond the world of divorce

The company website states, "Divorce is an event in your life, but it does not need to define your life." A person's future is often determined by how they respond to critical life situations, and divorce is certainly one of those. Helping to manage the process by removing emotions from decision making and working to preserve the dignity of the family, Fairway Divorce Solutions' aim is to provide a fairer way to divorce.

Sources: Fairway Divorce Solutions website, **www.fairwaydivorce.com**, accessed January 13, 2014; Jen Gerson, "The Last Stand; Political Correctness May Rule the Land, But Not the Calgary Stampede," *National Post*, July 5, 2012, p. A5; "Fairway Divorce Solutions," *Franchise Canada*, July/August 2012, pp. 33–34, available **www.fairwaydivorce.com/news/media/paving-the-way/**, accessed January 13, 2014; Kim Shiffman, "We're Not Going to Take It," *Profit*, May 2010, pp. 12, 14.

that follow can learn from mistakes by first movers. Some well-known first movers are Ford, IBM, Apple, and MySpace. Each of these firms has stumbled at one time or another, but each is still in business. Ford has been making a remarkable comeback, and IBM has risen from the ashes several times. Fairway Divorce Solutions is a first mover that is changing the divorce process, as described in the "Marketing and the SME" feature.

second mover strategy Theory that advocates observing closely the innovations of first movers and then introducing new products that improve on the original offering to gain advantage in the marketplace.

Other businesses thrive on a **second mover strategy**, observing closely the innovations of first movers and then improving on them to gain advantage in the marketplace. Facebook appeared after MySpace. Target has followed in the footsteps of Walmart. RBC Capital's Derek Spronck suggests second-mover advantage may be why Brazil's Embraer has been able to extend its dominance in regional jet sales over Canada's Bombardier, predicting that it could achieve 63 percent market share by 2015.[10] Sometimes first movers are completely replaced by second movers and disappear from the marketplace altogether such as Books.com, which preceded Amazon.com.

SWOT ANALYSIS

SWOT analysis Analysis that helps planners compare internal organizational strengths and weaknesses with external opportunities and threats.

An important strategic planning tool, **SWOT analysis**, helps planners compare internal organizational strengths and weaknesses with external opportunities and threats. (SWOT is an acronym for *strengths, weaknesses, opportunities,* and *threats.*) This form of analysis provides managers with a critical view of the organization's internal and external environments and helps them evaluate the firm's fulfillment of its basic mission.

A company's strengths reflect its **core competencies**—what it does well. Core competencies are capabilities that customers value and competitors find difficult to duplicate. As Figure 2.3 shows,

figure 2.3
SWOT Analysis

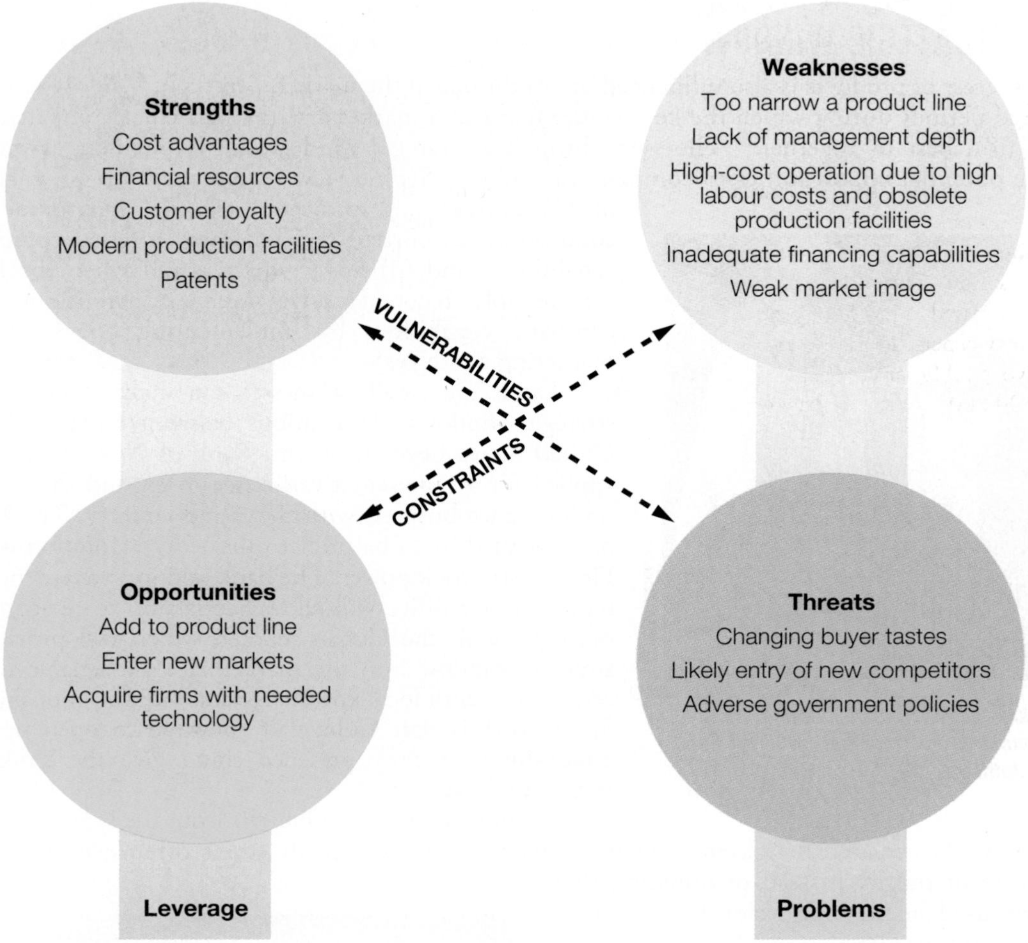

Strengths
Cost advantages
Financial resources
Customer loyalty
Modern production facilities
Patents

Weaknesses
Too narrow a product line
Lack of management depth
High-cost operation due to high labour costs and obsolete production facilities
Inadequate financing capabilities
Weak market image

VULNERABILITIES

CONSTRAINTS

Opportunities
Add to product line
Enter new markets
Acquire firms with needed technology

Threats
Changing buyer tastes
Likely entry of new competitors
Adverse government policies

Leverage

Problems

matching an internal strength with an external opportunity produces a situation known as *leverage*. Marketers face a problem when environmental threats attack their organization's weaknesses. Planners anticipate constraints when internal weaknesses or limitations prevent their organization from taking advantage of opportunities. These internal weaknesses can create vulnerabilities for a company—environmental threats to its organizational strength. While beverage maker Dr Pepper Snapple Group (DPSG) was under the umbrella of Britain's Cadbury, sales of its once popular drinks fizzled as distribution networks were neglected and marketers sometimes waited for weeks or months for decisions from Cadbury headquarters. But once DPSG achieved a spin-off, it could concentrate on what it does best: making, distributing, and selling its more than 50 brands, which include Dr Pepper, Snapple, 7Up, and Canada Dry. Although soft-drink consumption continues to decline in Canada and the United States, Dr Pepper has been able to increase its market share for five consecutive years. In fact, 13 of the company's 14 brands hold the No. 1 or No. 2 position in their flavour category. The strategies that DPSG has implemented since it became a stand-alone company continue to fuel its success as it builds and enhances its leading brands: pursuing profitable channels, packages, and categories; and strengthening its route to market and improving its operating efficiency.[11]

Even if a company focuses on its core competencies, sometimes it needs to broaden its offerings to maintain a competitive edge. When marketing research revealed that parents were adding water to their children's juice drinks in order to reduce calories, DPSG came up with a new version of its Mott's apple juice, containing 40 percent less sugar but a full serving of juice. It's called Mott's for

strategic window
Limited periods during which the key requirements of a market and the particular competencies of a firm best fit together.

Tots. Another success has been Canada Dry Green Tea Ginger Ale, for consumers who are looking for the potential health benefits of green tea.[12]

THE STRATEGIC WINDOW

The success of products is also influenced by conditions in the market. **Strategic windows** are the limited periods during which the key requirements of a market and the particular competencies of a firm best fit together.[13] The view through a strategic window shows planners a way to relate potential opportunities to company capabilities. Such a view requires a thorough analysis of (1) current and projected external environmental conditions, (2) current and projected internal company capabilities, and (3) how, whether, and when the firm can feasibly reconcile environmental conditions and company capabilities by implementing one or more marketing strategies.

Plato's Closet has found a strategic window. It has expanded greatly in recent years as young men and women are increasingly willing to sell and buy gently used brand-name clothing.

Large and small businesses can make the most of strategic windows. As relations between Cuba and the United States begin to warm, Bank of Nova Scotia has applied for a representative licence to expand the bank's trade-finance business with the island country. The bank had operated in Cuba prior to the 1959 revolution when Fidel Castro took power. The bank said in a statement, "A representative office will allow Scotiabank to re-acquaint ourselves with the Cuban market, which will provide a strategic window into the marketplace and enable us to acquire in-depth local knowledge and build relationships." Speculation is that Cuba will continue to open up, so establishing an early presence could give the bank an important head start.[14]

Small businesses can benefit from the same strategic window. As consumers tighten their belts, pawn shops and thrift stores often experience an increase in traffic. Instead of donating their gently used, name-brand clothing to a not-for-profit organization such as Goodwill or the Salvation Army, males and females ages 12 to 24 might take those items to a local consignment shop such as Plato's Closet—and then make a few purchases while there. The franchise operation, with more than 300 stores across Canada and the United States, appeals to consumers who enjoy a bargain.[15]

assessment check 4

4.1 Briefly explain each of Porter's Five Forces.

4.2 What are the benefits and drawbacks of a first mover strategy?

4.3 What are the four components of the SWOT analysis? What is a strategic window?

⑤ **Identify the basic elements of a marketing strategy.**

ELEMENTS OF A MARKETING STRATEGY

Success for a product in the marketplace—whether it is a tangible good, a service, a cause, a person, a place, or an organization—depends on an effective marketing strategy. It's one thing to develop a great product, but if customers don't get the message about it, the product will die. An effective marketing strategy reaches the right buyers at the right time, persuades them to try the product, and develops a strong relationship with them over time. The basic elements of a marketing strategy consist of (1) the target market and (2) the marketing mix variables of product, distribution, promotion, and price that combine to satisfy the needs of the target market. The outer circle in Figure 2.4 lists environmental characteristics that provide the framework within which marketing strategies are planned.

THE TARGET MARKET

A customer-driven organization begins its overall strategy with a detailed description of its **target market**: the group of people toward whom the firm decides to direct its marketing efforts and ultimately its merchandise. Sears Canada stores serve a target market consisting of consumers purchasing for themselves and their families. Other companies, such as Bombardier, market most of their products to business buyers such as Porter Airlines and government purchasers. Still other firms provide goods and services to retail and wholesale buyers. In every instance, however, marketers pinpoint their target markets as accurately as possible. Although the concept of dividing markets into specific segments is discussed in more detail in Chapter 9, it's important to understand the idea of targeting a market from the outset. Although it may be hard to imagine the classic Oreo cookie as anything other than two discs of chocolate with a white cream filling, it had to be reformulated for the Chinese market. Consumers there favoured wafer cookies and found the original Oreo cookie too sweet. So the manufacturer introduced the Oreo wafer stick, a rectangular chocolate-covered wafer that immediately became a hit. In 2011, the company introduced Oreo double fruits with combinations of fruit-flavoured creams, such as orange-mango, between the familiar biscuits. Packaging sizes and advertising were also changed to appeal to the Chinese market, and Oreo's market share grew exponentially to become the top-selling cookie in China. Lessons learned there helped Mondelez International, a 2012 spin-off from Kraft Foods, improve its product development and marketing around the world. Kitchener, Ontario, native Shawn Warren, the company's vice president of snacks for Asia-Pacific, says, "We do it in different ways around the world, but it's still the ritual of twist, lick, and dunk."[16]

Diversity plays an ever-increasing role in targeting markets. By 2017, Canada is expected to have 1.8 million Chinese and another 1.8 million South Asian people—combined, they will make up approximately half of all visible minorities. Canada's banks are certainly paying attention. The Royal Bank of Canada already advertises in Punjabi, Hindi, Mandarin, and Cantonese. Scotiabank advertises during festivals such as Eid, Diwali, and Chinese New Year. TD Canada Trust employs ethnic, bi- or multi-lingual staff and makes sure there is promotional material at its branches in languages that ethnic Canadians prefer. Targeting consumers in specific global markets also represents a challenge—and an opportunity. India is an enormous market that is culturally diverse within itself, containing 27 geographical states, numerous languages and religious practices, and a variety of lifestyles. Traditional Indian culture is infused with Western influences. And while nearly half of all Indian citizens earn less than $1 per day, a growing middle class boasts more than 50 million active users of social media. A recent Nielsen survey predicts that, soon, Indians will be more likely to access the internet by their smartphone than their personal computer. Also, according to the survey, respondents want marketers to engage them with contests, sales and promotions, and tips on how to use their good or service.[17]

figure 2.4

Elements of a Marketing Strategy and Its Environmental Framework

target market Group of people to whom a firm decides to direct its marketing efforts and ultimately its goods and services.

Marketoid

The 1901 Canadian Census recorded about 25 different ethnic groups; the 2011 National Household Survey reported more than 200 ethnic origins. There were 13 different ethnic groups that reported more than 1 million members.

MARKETING MIX VARIABLES

Once marketers select a target market, they direct their company's activities toward profitably serving that segment. Although they must manipulate thousands of variables to reach this goal, marketing decision making can be divided into four strategies: product, distribution, promotion, and pricing strategies. The total package forms the **marketing mix**—the blending of the four basic elements to fit the needs and preferences of a specific target market. While the fourfold classification is useful to study and analyze, remember that the marketing mix can—and should—be an ever-changing combination of variables to achieve success.

marketing mix Blending of the four strategy elements—product, distribution, promotion, and pricing—to fit the needs and preferences of a specific target market.

Your music
**never sounded
so good.**

QuietComfort® 15
Acoustic Noise Cancelling® headphones

Welcome to a better sounding world, where your music comes alive as never before. The QC®15 headphones are our best, with Bose® technologies that deliver sound more naturally than conventional headphones. And a significant improvement in the noise reduction helps you focus on each nuance of your music, as distractions fade into the background. "These are fabulous," says Murray Hill of Canada.com. Simply put, the sound is beautiful." It's a difference you need to hear to believe. We're so sure you'll be delighted, we'll even pay to ship them to your door.

To learn more: 1-XXX-XXX-XXXX, ext. XXXXX
Bose.com/headphones

BOSE
Better sound through research

TRAVELERS'
CHOICE
2012

©2013 Bose Corporation. The distinctive design of the headphone oval ring is a trademark of Bose Corporation. Quote reprinted with permission. Award as voted by TripAdvisor travelers.

Image of Bose Headphones used with permission of Bose Corporation

Bose has always been focused on continually improving its products to produce better sound. Now it's also focused on creating better quiet.

Figure 2.4 illustrates the focus of the marketing mix variables on the central choice of the target market. In addition, decisions about product, distribution, promotion, and price are affected by the environmental factors in the outer circle of the figure. The environmental variables may play a major role in the success of a marketing program, and marketers must consider their probable effects.

Product Strategy

In marketing, the word *product* means more than a good, service, or idea. Product is a broad concept that also encompasses the satisfaction of all consumer needs in relation to a good, service, or idea. So **product strategy** involves more than just deciding what goods or services the firm should offer to a group of consumers. It also includes decisions about customer service, package design, brand names, trademarks, patents, warranties, the life cycle of a product, positioning the product in the marketplace, and new product development. Sometimes, new products are simply modifications of existing products, such as Lay's chocolate-covered potato chips. Lay's has identified millennial women as a target segment that is increasingly seeking such snacks.[18]

Distribution Strategy

Marketers develop **distribution strategies** to ensure that consumers find their products in the proper quantities at the right times and places. Distribution decisions involve modes of transportation, warehousing, inventory control, order processing, and selection of marketing channels. Marketing channels are made up of institutions such as retailers and wholesalers—intermediaries that may be involved in a product's movement from producer to final consumer.

Technology is opening new channels of distribution in many industries. The Internet has caused the biggest revolution in distribution since the mail-order catalogue. Computer software and digital music files are obvious candidates, but a wide variety that includes DVDs, contact lenses, and even motorcycles can be found on the Web. E-readers such as the Kobo tablet or Amazon's Kindle allow consumers to download and read books and periodicals that were once the domain of the printed page. Some publications, such as *Canadian Business* (**www.canadianbusiness.com**) and the *Globe and Mail* (**www.theglobeandmail.com**), offer both online and print content; the online content is free with a print subscription or can be purchased separately. Online visitors can usually access a small number of articles each month for free before a subscription is required. Other publications have abandoned print altogether or were established entirely online in the first place.

Promotion Strategy

Promotion strategy involves the communications links between sellers and buyers. Organizations use varied ways to send messages about their goods, services, and ideas. They may communicate messages directly through salespeople or indirectly through advertisements and promotions. Increasingly, Canadian businesses are turning to social media and the Internet to get their message out. In December 2013, WestJet organized an elaborate Christmas surprise for 250 passengers on flights from Toronto and Hamilton, Ontario, to Calgary, Alberta. Before boarding their planes, passengers who approached a video kiosk where they viewed a blue-suited Santa were asked what they wanted for Christmas. While they were in-flight, WestJet staff in Calgary hurried to purchase the gifts they wanted and the passengers found them on the baggage carousel when they arrived. The

product strategy
Decisions about what goods or services a firm will offer its customers; also includes decisions about customer service, packaging, brand names, and the like.

distribution strategy
Planning that ensures that consumers find their products in the proper quantities at the right times and places.

promotion strategy
Communications links between buyers and sellers. Function of informing, persuading, and influencing a buyer's purchase decision.

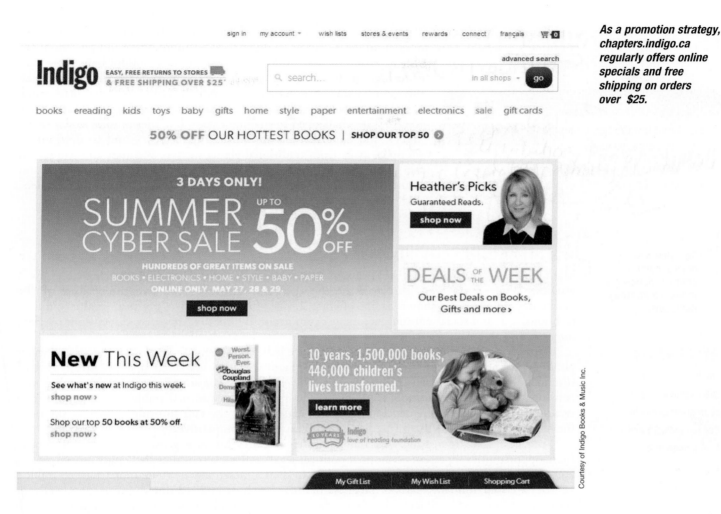

As a promotion strategy, chapters.indigo.ca regularly offers online specials and free shipping on orders over $25.

company's YouTube video went viral, viewed more than 15 million times during its first four days, and approximately 35 million times by the New Year. Mitch Joel, president of digital marketing agency Twist Image, says, "The whole win of this is people are willingly spending five to six minutes with WestJet."[19]

In developing a promotional strategy, marketers blend the various elements of promotion to communicate most effectively with their target market. Many companies use an approach called integrated marketing communications (IMC) to coordinate all promotional activities so that the consumer receives a unified and consistent message. Consumers might receive newsletters, email updates, discount coupons, catalogues, invitations to company-sponsored events, and any number of other types of marketing communications about a product. Honda dealers mail maintenance and service reminders to their customers. A political candidate may send volunteer workers through a neighbourhood to invite voters to a local reception.

Pricing Strategy

Pricing strategy deals with the methods of setting profitable and justifiable prices. It is closely regulated and subject to considerable public scrutiny. One of the many factors that influence a marketer's pricing strategy is competition. The computer industry has become all too familiar with price cuts by both current competitors and new market entrants. After years of steady growth, the market has become saturated with low-cost computers, driving down profit margins even farther. A good pricing strategy should create value for customers, building and strengthening their relationship with a firm and its products. But sometimes conditions in the external marketing environment cause difficulties in pricing strategies. Political unrest overseas, the soaring price of fuel, or a freeze

pricing strategy
Methods of setting profitable and justifiable prices.

that destroys crops could all affect the price of goods and services. If the economy is booming, consumers generally have more confidence and are willing to shop more often and pay more for discretionary goods. But when the economy takes a downturn, consumers look for bargains—they want high quality at low prices. It is a challenge for marketers to strike the right balance in order to make enough profits to survive and grow. Currently, luxury retailers such as Hudson's Bay Company and Holt Renfrew are challenged to maintain sales, but sales at local dollar stores and cheaper supermarkets are continuing to grow—and are even luring shoppers away from traditional giants such as Walmart and Target. In fact, more than half of dollar-store shoppers think that the products and brands sold at these stores are comparable to those sold at other retailers, and more than half of high-income consumers shop at dollar stores.[20]

> ## assessment check 5 ✓
>
> **5.1** What are the two components of every marketing strategy?
>
> **5.2** Identify the four strategic elements of the marketing mix.

⑥ **Describe the environmental characteristics that influence strategic decisions.**

Marketoid

The RCMP seized $38 million worth of counterfeit goods in Canada in 2012, up from $7.6 million in 2005.

THE MARKETING ENVIRONMENT

Marketers do not make decisions about target markets and marketing mix variables in a vacuum. They must take into account the dynamic nature of the five dimensions of the marketing environment shown back in Figure 2.4 (p. 45): competitive, political-legal, economic, technological, and social-cultural factors. It's important to note that these five dimensions overlap, interact, and fluctuate.

Concerns about the natural environment have led to new regulations concerning air and water pollution, which affect the political-legal environment in which marketers operate. Efforts toward sustainability are now social-cultural factors as well because consumer awareness is turning into consumer preference. Automobile engineers, for instance, have turned public concerns and legal issues into opportunities by developing hybrid cars. In fact, the race to bring to market the most fuel-efficient vehicles for the future has become extremely competitive.

Businesses are increasingly looking to foreign shores for new growth markets. Of course, these opportunities represent economic, political-legal, and social-cultural challenges as well. Many automobile manufacturers are now entrenched in the Chinese market where more than 20 million vehicles are sold annually. Sales of Japanese brands were hurt in 2012 due to protests and calls for boycotts of Japanese products following a flare-up of tensions between China and Japan over two uninhabited islands in the East China Sea. Toyota, Honda, and Nissan all achieved major gains in sales in 2013, but the big winner was Ford Motor Company. With a lineup of new vehicles, including the Ford Focus, and revamped vehicles, including the Mondeo—sold in North America as the Fusion—Ford sales in China increased by almost 50 percent, approaching nearly 1 million units. Ford still trails General Motors and Volkswagen, which each sell about 3 millions units annually in China.[21]

Technology continually changes the marketing environment. Marketers are now increasing efforts to get their messages to consumers via smartphone with free mobile apps. For example, Tim Hortons provides an app that lets customers pay for their coffee with their smartphone. Using the Canadian Tire app, you can get sale alerts and preview the weekly flyer early; scan product bar codes for pricing, information, and inventory; watch product videos; compare ratings and reviews; and locate your nearest store or gas bar. Toronto developers recently created the Think Dirty app. Consumers can scan the bar codes of their favourite personal care products in-store to find a list of product ingredients and see on the "Dirty Meter" how the product is rated on a 10-point scale. For products that score high on the scale, the app will suggest "cleaner" alternatives. The app's database has over 11,000 products from 1,000 brands. For products not in the database, the Think Dirty team encourages consumers to scan the bar code and submit the product for review.[22] In the competitive environment, some experts have coined the phrase *rule of three*, meaning that in any industry, the three strongest, most efficient companies dominate between 70 and 90 percent of the market. Here are a few examples—all of which are household names:

- *Supermarkets:* Loblaws, Sobeys, Walmart

- *Cereal manufacturers:* General Mills, Kellogg's, Post

- *Running shoes:* Nike, Adidas, Reebok
- *Airlines:* Air Canada, WestJet, Porter Airlines
- *Wireless providers:* Bell, Rogers, Telus
- *Pharmaceuticals:* Merck, Pfizer, Bristol-Myers Squibb

While it may seem like an uphill battle for the remaining hundreds of companies in any given industry, each of these firms can find a strategy for gaining competitive ground.

The social-cultural environment includes a variety of factors, including prevailing cultural norms. As the novelty of bidding for auction items on eBay has worn off for consumers who don't necessarily have the time or desire to wait several days or a week for auction results, eBay has begun to reshape itself. Fixed-price merchandise has become the new norm. The "Buy It Now" option—designed with smartphones in mind—now accounts for more than 60 percent of eBay purchases. The company expects mobile purchases to add revenues of nearly $5 billion per year.[23] This new trend also reflects economic factors,

assessment check 6

6.1 What are the five dimensions of the marketing environment?

6.2 How is concern over the natural environment affecting the other dimensions?

Domino's Pizza® has an Android app that lets customers place orders for pizza. The company reports that online and phone orders represent one-third of its business.

Domino's® is a registered trademark of Domino's IP Holder and used with permission.

including how much consumers are willing and able to spend. The entire marketing environment provides a framework for all marketing activity. Marketers consider environmental dimensions when they develop strategies for segmenting and targeting markets and when they study consumer and organizational buying behaviour.

⑦ **Describe the methods for marketing planning, including business portfolio analysis, the BCG market share/market growth matrix, and the strategic growth opportunity matrix.**

METHODS FOR MARKETING PLANNING

As growing numbers of companies have discovered the benefits of effective marketing planning, they have developed planning methods to assist in this important function. This section discusses business portfolio analysis and the strategic business unit concept, the market share/market growth matrix, and the strategic growth opportunity matrix.

BUSINESS PORTFOLIO ANALYSIS

Although a small company may offer only a few items to its customers, a larger organization frequently offers and markets many products to widely diverse markets. CIBC and BMO offer a wide range of financial products to businesses and consumers; Kraft Foods stocks supermarket shelves with a wide variety of products that include macaroni and cheese, cheese, and mayonnaise, and offers nonfood products such as cookware and cutlery online. Top managers at these larger firms need a method for spotting product lines that deserve more investment as well as lines that aren't living up to expectations. So they conduct a portfolio analysis, in which they evaluate their company's products and divisions to determine which are strongest and which are weakest. Similar to how securities analysts review their portfolios of stocks and bonds, deciding which to retain and which to discard, marketing planners must assess their products, the regions in which they operate, and other marketing mix variables. This is where the concept of an SBU comes in.

strategic business units (SBUs) Key business units within diversified firms.

Strategic business units (SBUs) are key business units within diversified firms. Each SBU has its own managers, resources, objectives, and competitors. A division, product line, or single product may define the boundaries of an SBU. Each SBU pursues its own distinct mission, and each develops its own plans independently of other units in the organization. A manufacturer that sells many different brands of laundry detergent may consider each a separate strategic business unit. PartSource, a chain of automotive specialty stores, is a strategic business unit of Canadian Tire.

Strategic business units focus the attention of company managers so that they can respond effectively to changing consumer demand within limited markets. Companies may have to redefine their SBUs as market conditions dictate. IBM was once known as a manufacturer of high-quality clocks. Today, the firm markets everything related to computers—computer servers and systems, software, Internet security, and printing paper and toner. Its slogan, "Welcome to the Decade of Smart," conveys the firm's forward-thinking philosophy. The old IBM clocks have become valuable collectibles.[24]

THE BCG MARKET SHARE/MARKET GROWTH MATRIX

To evaluate each of their organization's strategic business units, marketers need some type of portfolio performance framework. A widely used framework was developed by the Boston Consulting Group (BCG). This market share/market growth matrix places SBUs in a four-quadrant chart that plots market share—the percentage of a market that a firm controls (or company sales divided by total market sales)—against market growth potential. The position of an SBU along the horizontal axis indicates its market share relative to those of competitors in the industry. Its position along the vertical axis indicates the annual growth rate of the market. After plotting all of a firm's business units, planners divide them according to the matrix's four quadrants. Figure 2.5 illustrates this matrix by labelling the four quadrants stars, cash cows, question marks, and dogs. Firms in each quadrant require a unique marketing strategy.

Stars represent units with high market shares in high-growth markets. These products or businesses are high-growth market leaders. Although they generate considerable income, they need considerable inflows of cash to finance further growth. BlackBerry was the number one selling smartphone in North America as recently as 2010—and third in the world—but it has been losing market share ever since. By the end of 2013, Apple iPhone had maintained its lead in smartphone sales, but Google Android led as the number one smartphone platform with more than 50 percent market share.[25] Apple will come under increasingly intense competition and must continue to offer new models to demanding and tech-savvy consumers. *Cash cows* command high market shares in low-growth markets. Marketers for such an SBU want to maintain this status for as long as possible. The business produces strong cash flows, but instead of investing heavily in the unit's own promotions and production capacity, the firm can use this cash to finance the growth of other SBUs with higher growth potentials. For instance, Microsoft might use the profits from sales of its Windows operating system to finance research and development for new Internet-based technologies.[26]

Question marks achieve low market shares in high-growth markets. Marketers must decide whether to continue supporting these products or businesses since question marks typically require considerably more cash than they generate. If a question mark cannot become a star, the firm should pull out of the market and target other markets with greater potential. Ford Motor Company sold off its luxury brands Jaguar and Aston-Martin in order to concentrate on its more economical, fuel-efficient vehicles. *Dogs* manage only low market shares in low-growth markets. SBUs in this category promise poor future prospects, and marketers should seriously consider withdrawing from these businesses or product lines. In some cases, these products can be sold to other firms, where they are a better fit. IBM sold its PC business to Chinese manufacturer Lenovo so that it could concentrate on its business services.

figure 2.5

BCG Market Share/Market Growth Matrix

	Relative Market Share	
	High	Low
High (Industry Growth Rate)	**Stars** Generate considerable income **Strategy:** Invest more funds for future growth	**Question Marks** Have potential to become stars or cash cows **Strategy:** Either invest more funds for growth or consider disinvesting
Low (Industry Growth Rate)	**Cash Cows** Generate strong cash flow **Strategy:** Milk profits to finance growth of stars and question marks	**Dogs** Generate little profits **Strategy:** Consider withdrawing

Laundry detergent has long been a cash cow for Procter & Gamble.

H. F. (Herb) MacKenzie

STRATEGIC GROWTH OPPORTUNITY MATRIX

As part of its strategy planning, a company needs to consider potential growth opportunities. Once it has performed a portfolio analysis, a logical step for a company is to consider which among its strategic business units it will focus its attention upon for growth. Ansoff's strategic growth opportunity matrix is illustrated in Figure 2.6, showing the four growth options.

Market penetration is a strategy that a company uses when it attempts to build market share by selling existing products to existing customers. It is the least risky of growth strategies as the company is familiar with both its customers and its products. However, it is often difficult to increase market share in mature markets as any increase must come at the expense of competitors. It is sometimes easier in fast-growing markets. Even if a number of competitors are aiming at growth, they are not all aware of how well others are doing. A company that is happy with its 20 percent growth may not

figure 2.6

Ansoff's Strategic Growth Opportunity Matrix

	Present Product	New Product
Present Market	**Market Penetration** When Tim Hortons promotes its Roll up the Rim to Win contest, it is following a market penetration strategy.	**Product Development** When KFC Canada introduced the Double Down, it was following a product development strategy.
New Market	**Market Development** When McCain Foods entered the African market to sell its frozen french fries, it was following a market development strategy.	**Diversification** When Zippo Manufacturing introduced a new cologne, it was following a diversification strategy.

Source: From LAMB/HAIR/MCDANIEL/FARIA/WELLINGTON. Marketing, 4E. © 2008 Nelson Education Ltd. Reproduced by permission. **www.cengage.com/permissions**

---

assessment check 7 ✓

7.1 What are SBUs?

7.2 Identify the four quadrants in the BCG matrix.

7.3 Identify the four strategic growth opportunities.

---

realize that a competitor is growing at 40 percent. When Tim Hortons implements its Roll up the Rim to Win® promotion each year, its intention is to further penetrate its market—that is, increase market share.

Market development occurs when a company tries to attract new customers for its existing products, sometimes by geographic expansion, but often by simply targeting new segments of customers. Lululemon Athletica operates 226 stores in Canada, the United States, Australia, and New Zealand. It plans to open stores in the United Kingdom and has a test boutique in Hong Kong's trendy Soho district. Industry experts see its greatest medium-term opportunities in the United States but suggest it needs to look outside North America for longer-term growth. Lululemon is also promoting its new Ivivva banner, targeted at young girls, and it is expanding its focus to include men.[27]

Product development occurs when a company develops new products that it hopes to sell to existing customers. New Brunswick–based McCain Foods recently launched a low-fat French fry that it will sell exclusively through Burger King. Several previous manufacturers launched low-fat fries, but all were ultimately unsuccessful. McCain's fries, though, appear to have lower fat content, fewer calories, and the same great taste as regular fries, and they will sell to consumers at a small price premium.[28]

A product development strategy could also include introducing modified products, such as the introduction of iPad Air.

Diversification is the most risky of growth strategies as companies that follow this strategy attempt to sell new products to new markets—that is, they have little experience with either. Zippo Manufacturing Company, maker of the famous Zippo lighter, is being forced to consider diversification options as the worldwide tobacco industry becomes an increasingly "dying" industry—sorry for the pun. Zippo recently launched a new cologne in Italy, and it is now available on Amazon.ca.

Strategic Implications

Never before has planning been as important to marketers as the 21st century speeds ahead with technological advances. Marketers need to plan carefully, accurately, and quickly if their companies are to gain a competitive advantage in today's global marketplace. They need to define their organization's mission and understand the different methods for formulating a successful marketing strategy. They must consider a changing, diverse population and the boundaryless business environment created by the Internet. They must be able to evaluate when it's best to be first to get into a market and when it's best to wait. They need to recognize when they've got a star and when they've got a dog—when to hang on and when to let go. As daunting as this seems, planning can reduce the risk and worry of bringing new goods and services to the marketplace. ◆◆◆

REVIEW OF CHAPTER OBJECTIVES

① Distinguish between strategic planning and tactical planning.

Strategic planning is the process of identifying an organization's primary objectives and adopting courses of action toward these objectives. In other words, strategic planning focuses on the big picture of which industries are central to a firm's business. Tactical planning guides the implementation of the activities specified in the strategic plan. Once a strategy is set, operational managers devise methods (tactics) to achieve the larger goals.

② Explain how marketing plans differ at various levels in an organization.

Top management spends more time engaged in strategic planning than do middle- and supervisory-level managers, who tend to focus on narrower, tactical plans for their units. Supervisory managers are more likely to engage in developing specific plans designed to meet the goals assigned to them—for example, streamlining production processes so that they operate more efficiently.

③ Identify the steps in the marketing planning process.

The basic steps in the marketing planning process are defining the organization's mission and objectives; assessing organizational resources and evaluating environmental risk and opportunities; and formulating, implementing, and monitoring the marketing strategy.

④ Describe successful planning tools and techniques, including Porter's Five Forces model, first and second mover strategies, SWOT analysis, and the strategic window.

Porter's Five Forces are identified as the five competitive factors that influence planning strategies: potential new entrants, bargaining power of buyers, bargaining power of suppliers, threat of substitute products, and rivalry among competitors. With a first mover strategy, a firm attempts to capture the greatest market share by being first to enter the market; with a second mover strategy, a firm observes the innovations of first movers and then improves on them to gain advantage. SWOT analysis (strengths, weaknesses, opportunities, and threats) helps planners compare internal organizational strengths and weaknesses with external opportunities and threats. The strategic window identifies the limited periods during which the key requirements of a market and the competencies of a firm best fit together.

⑤ Identify the basic elements of a marketing strategy.

Development of a marketing strategy is a two-step process: (1) selecting a target market and (2) designing an effective marketing mix to satisfy the chosen target. The target market is the group of people toward whom a company decides to direct its marketing efforts. The marketing mix blends four strategy elements to fit the needs and preferences of a specific target market: product strategy, distribution strategy, promotional strategy, and pricing strategy.

⑥ Describe the environmental characteristics that influence strategic decisions.

The five dimensions of the marketing environment are competitive, political-legal, economic, technological, and social-cultural. Marketers must also address growing concern about the natural environment—including new regulations—and increasing cultural diversity in the global marketplace.

⑦ Describe the methods for marketing planning, including business portfolio analysis, the BCG market share/market growth matrix, and the strategic growth opportunity matrix.

The business portfolio analysis evaluates a company's products and divisions, including strategic business units (SBUs). The SBU focuses the attention of company managers so they can respond effectively to changing consumer demand within certain markets. The BCG matrix places SBUs in a four-quadrant chart that plots market share against market growth potential. The four quadrants are stars, cash cows, question marks, and dogs. The strategic growth opportunity matrix identifies four growth alternatives: penetration (same products, same markets), market development (same products, new markets), product development (new products, same markets), and diversification (new products, new markets).

assessment check answers ✓

1.1 Define *planning*.

Planning is the process of anticipating future events and conditions and of determining the best way to achieve organizational objectives.

1.2 Give an example of strategic planning and tactical planning.

To survive in a challenging environment that includes soaring fuel costs, several airlines have decided to partner with their competitors as part of their strategic planning. Tactical plans include cutting the number of flights and charging passengers extra for checked baggage.

2.1 How do marketing plans differ at different levels of the organization?

Top managers usually focus their planning activities on long-range strategic issues. In contrast, middle-level managers focus on operational planning, which includes creating and implementing tactical plans for their own units. Supervisors develop specific programs to meet the goals in their areas of responsibility.

2.2 Why is it important to get input from others when planning?

Input from a variety of sources—other employees, suppliers, or customers—helps ensure that many ideas are considered. Involving those people in planning can also turn them into advocates for the plan.

3.1 Distinguish between an organization's mission and its objectives.

The firm's mission is the essential purpose that differentiates the company from others. Its objectives guide development of supporting marketing objectives and plans. Avon's mission is to be "the company for women." One of its objectives might be to convert all its packaging to recycled materials.

3.2 What is the importance of the final step in the marketing planning process?

In the final step of the marketing planning process, managers monitor performance to ensure that objectives are being achieved.

4.1 Briefly explain each of Porter's Five Forces.

Porter's Five Forces are the threats of potential new entrants, which increases competition in a market; bargaining power of buyers, which can depress prices; bargaining power of suppliers, which can increase cost or reduce selection; threat of substitute products, which can lure customers to other products; and rivalry among competitors, which can bring about price wars or divert companies from their main goals.

4.2 What are the benefits and drawbacks of a first mover strategy?

The benefits of a first mover strategy include being able to capture the greatest market share and develop long-term relationships with customers. Disadvantages include the possibility that companies that follow can learn from mistakes by first movers. Procter & Gamble has been a first mover with its line of Swiffer products.

4.3 What are the four components of the SWOT analysis? What is a strategic window?

SWOT analysis helps planners compare internal organizational strengths and weaknesses with external opportunities and threats. SWOT is an acronym for *strengths*, *weaknesses*, *opportunities*, and *threats*. A strategic window defines the limited periods during which the key requirements of a market and the particular competencies of a firm best fit together.

5.1 What are the two components of every marketing strategy?

The basic elements of a marketing strategy are (1) the target market and (2) the marketing mix variables.

5.2 Identify the four strategic elements of the marketing mix.

The marketing mix consists of product, distribution, promotion, and pricing strategies.

6.1 What are the five dimensions of the marketing environment?

The five dimensions of the marketing environment are competitive, political-legal, economic, technological, and social-cultural factors.

6.2 How is concern over the natural environment affecting the other dimensions?

Concerns over the natural environment have led to new and tighter regulations on pollution, which affect the political-legal environment in which marketers operate. Efforts toward sustainability are now social-cultural factors as well because consumer awareness is turning into consumer preference.

7.1 What are SBUs?

Strategic business units (SBUs) are key business units within diversified firms. Each SBU has its own managers, resources, objectives, and competitors.

7.2 Identify the four quadrants in the BCG matrix.

The BCG matrix labels SBUs stars, cash cows, question marks, and dogs. Stars are the SBUs with high market shares in high-growth markets; cash cows command high market shares in low-growth markets; question marks achieve low market shares in high-growth markets; and dogs manage only low market shares in low-growth markets.

7.3 Identify the four strategic growth opportunities.
The four strategic growth opportunities are penetration (same products, same markets), market development (same products, new markets), product development (new products, same markets), and diversification (new products, new markets).

MARKETING TERMS YOU NEED TO KNOW

These terms are printed in blue in the text. They are defined in the margins of the chapter and in the Glossary that begins on p. G-1.

planning 34	Porter's Five Forces 39	marketing mix 45
marketing planning 35	first mover strategy 41	product strategy 46
strategic planning 36	second mover strategy 42	distribution strategy 46
tactical planning 36	SWOT analysis 42	promotion strategy 46
mission 38	strategic window 44	pricing strategy 47
marketing strategy 39	target market 45	strategic business units (SBUs) 50

PROJECT AND TEAMWORK EXERCISES

1. Choose one of the following companies, or select another one whose goods and services are familiar to you. On your own or with a classmate, formulate a mission statement for that company. Then create a list of objectives that reflect your company's mission.
    a. Sobeys
    b. Petro-Canada
    c. Tim Hortons
    d. Telus
2. Using a first mover strategy, Apple's iPod and iPhone have clearly established the lead in their markets. Research the products of another firm that produces either a digital music player or a smartphone to learn about its strategy. How has a second mover strategy benefited the firm? Has the second mover firm been able to catch Apple in sales?
3. When rivals Samsung and Sony each unveiled its new 3D TVs at a major electronics store, some consumers couldn't tell the difference between the two. But the firm's strategies were very different. Sony opted to use outside manufacturing firms to build its TVs, stating that the move would help cut costs and keep the company strong. But Samsung manufactures its own TVs, including its own computer chips. Since then, the two firms have experienced quite different outcomes.[29] With a classmate, research the two companies and their 3D TVs, evaluating their marketing strategy. Who is the target market for both of these TVs? How do product, distribution, promotion, and pricing fit into each firm's overall marketing strategy? In your opinion, how did the firms' strategies affect their respective outcomes?
4. Select one of the following industries and research which firms might fall into the top three in the industry, creating a rule of three:
    a. online securities trading
    b. upscale hotels
    c. electronics retailing
    d. automotive manufacturing
5. On your own or with a classmate, research one of the following large corporations. Select several product lines and classify each in the BCG matrix.
    a. 3M
    b. Johnson & Johnson
    c. Condé Nast Publications
    d. General Electric (GE)

CRITICAL THINKING EXERCISES

1. Suppose you are a marketer for a Canadian manufacturer of pet supplies. Two top executives have proposed expanding the company by opening retail stores and marketing pets on-site—puppies, kittens, rabbits, birds, fish, and the like. What are the potential benefits and drawbacks of making a move like this? How would you advise your company to proceed?
2. Netflix has made thousands of streaming videos available to its subscribers. How does this strategy demonstrate a strategic window for the company?
3. Choose one of the following products and describe how it may (or already has) become vulnerable to substitution. Then describe an overall strategy—with two or three tactics—for reducing this vulnerability.

a. printed copies of periodicals or books
b. television
c. telephone landlines
d. travel agencies
4. Research the website of one of the following retail firms to identify its target market. Then outline a strategy for expanding that target market.
   a. Tim Hortons
   b. Aritzia

c. Roots Canada
d. Dollarama
e. Target Canada
5. Research a company such as Molson Breweries or Loblaw Companies Limited that has a number of different successful SBUs. What factors do you think make these units—and this company—successful from a marketing standpoint?

ETHICS EXERCISE

A recent news story reported research from a major centre for disease control and prevention: bread is the number one source of sodium in the average North American diet. In fact, most people get twice as much sodium from bread and rolls as they do from a bag of salty snacks such as chips or pretzels.[30] Imagine that you are a marketer for a baking company whose main product lines are bread and rolls. For years, your company has focused on "heart-healthy" as a key claim.

1. You have been assigned to create a new strategy and tactics for your firm's Facebook page. Would you continue to emphasize the heart-healthy message? Would you refer to the research study or simply ignore it?

2. As you review the Facebook site, you note that packaging for your company's bread uses the words "heart-healthy." Would you bring this to the attention of the marketing group responsible for product packaging? Or would you look for a way to obscure the package design online? Defend your answer.

CASE 2.1

Hotels Market New Comforts Just for Millennials

Poised to become the largest consumer group in Canadian history, the 8.9 million Millennials (also called Generation Y; born between 1981 and 2000) wield tremendous spending power, earning about $225 billion a year. They differ from baby boomers (born between 1946 and 1964) in many ways, including their preferences when staying at a hotel. Millennials feel "interesting is more important than comfort." They also lack brand loyalty for hotels, making competition for their business fierce.

Hotel chains are therefore hurrying to upgrade their facilities to attract these young guests in sneakers and baseball caps, who aren't completely at home in quiet lobbies that reek of Olde England. Chains like Hilton, Starwood, Marriott, and InterContinental have installed sleek and comfortable new lounges with stylish bars, plush furniture, areas for socializing, out-in-the-open power consoles for recharging electronics, and electronic concierge services. They've added state-of-the-art gyms, happy hours, free wine and tea tastings, yoga classes, designer shower heads, check-in kiosks to replace registration desks, and of course Wi-Fi access and high-speed Internet, which one observer described as "almost like air to Millennials." Nearly 60 percent of Millennials own a smartphone, and 14 percent own a tablet, twice the percentage of non-Millennials.

While baby boomers enjoy the solitude of their rooms after a long day of business or sightseeing, Millennials like to visit several restaurants and bars during their travels, so some hotels are introducing multiple eateries and lounges, all designed with different themes to create variety and keep guests from spending their entertainment budgets elsewhere. New York's Plaza Hotel puts an iPad in every room that lets guests control light and temperature, skim the morning news, and place room-service orders. Starwood Hotels and Resorts Worldwide set up a 20-member team to monitor and respond to guests' complaints and suggestions—but not at a desk in the lobby. This team works solely online, constantly monitoring Twitter posts by their outspoken guests.

And, of course, hotels are increasing their own online presence, including on Facebook, Twitter, Google+, and YouTube, since the vast majority of travel arrangements are now made online. It's all part of the hotel industry's effort to woo a group of Canadians whose travel increased by 89 percent between 2011 and 2012. The business has come a long way from placing chocolates on the pillow at night.

Questions for Critical Thinking

1. Hotel chains see Millennials as "critical" to their financial growth. What are some reasons for this?
2. How should the hotel industry use social media to connect with younger travellers?

Sources: Megan Haynes, "Millennials by the Numbers," **strategyonline.ca**, August 21, 2013; "Generation Y: More Emotional, Less Loyal," Market Metrix.com, accessed March 22, 2012, **www.marketmetrix.com**; Janet Morrissey, "The Millennials Check In," *The New York Times*, March 13, 2012, **www.nytimes.com**; Corey Eridon, "Why User-Generated Content Is More Important than You Think," Hubspot .com, February 7, 2012, **http://blog.hubspot.com**; Nancy Trejos, "Aloft Hotels Test Out iPad Concierge," *USA Today*, December 30, 2011, **http://travel.usatoday.com**.

CASE 2.2

BlackBerry: On the Ropes, but Going Down or Bouncing Back?

BlackBerry—formerly Research in Motion—could be "on the ropes." The question is whether it will drop to the canvas or bounce back with a knockout punch. Many of Canada's former technology stars have gone to the canvas: Nortel Networks, Corel, and Biovail, to name a few. Some have exited the ring (Nortel), some continue to fight (Corel), and some have tried to re-invent themselves (Biovail). The best choice is not always clear.

In 1999, BlackBerry revolutionized the mobile communications industry. It grew rapidly, selling smartphones and technology to governments and businesses where data security was a major concern. The company's BlackBerry Messenger (BBM) remains today the most secure communications platform on the market. To protect its advantage and to promote the sale of BlackBerry devices, the company adamantly refused to allow alternative devices to operate on its BBM system.

In 2007, Apple shook up the mobile communications industry with its wildly popular iPhone, which quickly caught consumer interest. Response was so great that BlackBerry responded by developing its own consumer-focused devices. BlackBerry executives could see tremendous opportunity in the fast-growing consumer market, and they felt their enterprise business—the real strength of the company—was secure from competition. Apple ramped things up again in 2010: the iPad came to market along with a fourth-generation iPhone. The iPad became a popular workplace tool quickly supported by many businesses. At the same time, the new iPhone was improved so that it could operate smoothly on many company servers. The iPhone was not as secure as the BlackBerry, but the gap was closing. Companies began to allow employees to BYOD—bring your own device—to work and were soon asking BlackBerry to adapt its BlackBerry enterprise server (BES) to also manage Apple and iPhone devices. At the time, BlackBerry was struggling to develop new smartphones to compete with the iPhone and newer entrants, while also trying to develop the PlayBook to compete with the iPad in the emerging tablet market. The company remained strongly focused on the consumer market, and this let competitors focus on developing multi-device platforms to compete in the enterprise market. Several companies, many, and possibly all, of which might never have been able to launch had

BlackBerry defended its position in the enterprise market, have appeared. An updated BlackBerry enterprise system, BES 10, was introduced in 2013, providing a single, unified management console that manages not only BlackBerry but also iOS and Android smartphones. BES 10 was quickly adopted by many notable BlackBerry customers, including Air Canada, MetLife, Citigroup, and PwC Canada. BlackBerry has had particular success in India with its BES 10 enterprise system: more than a thousand enterprise adoptions during 2013.

In late 2013, with BlackBerry's revenues in freefall, there were rumours of an impending sale of the company. But, the sale never materialized. Near the end of 2013, John Chen took over as chief executive officer and was quick to announce, "Our 'for sale' sign has been taken down and we are here to stay." He publicly announced a new strategy for BlackBerry: a refocus on enterprise customers, a sales force that will target regulated industries, and an outsourcing deal with Taiwan-based electronics giant Foxconn Technology Group. BlackBerry will return to its roots: selling smartphones and the technology to secure and manage mobile communications to enterprise customers. The main focus will be enterprise customers in regulated industries, where communications security is critical. This is why BlackBerry remains so popular with governments around the world. BlackBerry plans to open a "security technology centre" in Washington, D.C., to work with a number of U.S. government agencies, including the Department of Defence. Finally, the five-year outsourcing contract will allow BlackBerry to continue its focus on designing and producing high-end smartphones while Foxconn will focus on lower-priced devices for emerging markets.

Mr. Chen announced he would try to avoid future job cuts beyond the 4,500 that were cut in late 2013. That, however, did not apply to the executive ranks. He quickly dismissed the company's chief marketing officer and its chief operating officer, an indication that BlackBerry will be moving away from the consumer market. He also announced that all touch-screen devices will be discontinued; they will all have a keyboard. A further indication came in January 2014 when BlackBerry announced it would be discontinuing its sponsorship of Alicia Keys, who had been hired as "global creative director" for the launch of the BlackBerry 10 smartphone. Hopes were that Ms. Keys would be able to win back some of the millions of consumers who replaced their BlackBerry devices with Apple or Android smartphones. The questionable decision to sponsor her in the first place cost the company reportedly in excess of $1 million. BlackBerry consumer sales have remained strong in some emerging markets, though. In South Africa, BlackBerry market share has grown from 18 to 23 percent in 2013 but is even higher among college and university students where it has a 57 percent market share. It seems to have the possibility of further growth as a survey of South Africans found that 29 percent plan to buy a BlackBerry. A threat, however, is that sales may quickly disappear if BlackBerry doesn't promote a cheaper range of phones in emerging markets. Much less expensive phones are already appearing in many of these markets.

Where is BlackBerry heading next? BlackBerry continues to add new features to BBM, such as voice-over IP calling, while it is also trying to transition its BlackBerry Messaging service from a simple instant messaging system into a promising social network. It is testing BBM Channels, a new service that will allow users to set up channels—similar to Facebook pages—so that BBM users can interact with brands, companies, and other BBM users. To pave the way, of course, BlackBerry made the BBM service—once kept exclusive to BlackBerry devices to encourage their sales—available to its competitors. This move increased the number of BBM users almost instantly from 60 to 80 million. BlackBerry says that dozens of brands have been experimenting with BBM Channels, including Tim Hortons and

Maple Leaf Sports & Entertainment (owners of the Toronto Maple Leafs, Toronto Raptors, and Toronto FC). Plans are to introduce BBM Channels for iPhone and Android by early 2014, a long-overdue move.

Ultimately, Chen's goal is to make BlackBerry revenue neutral by the end of 2014 and profitable by 2016.

Questions for Critical Thinking

1. Is BlackBerry following a first mover or a second mover strategy? Explain.
2. Using Ansoff's Strategic Growth Opportunity Matrix, explain which growth opportunities BlackBerry appears to be following. Which growth option do you feel is the best one for BlackBerry at this time?

Sources: Company press release, "Enterprises in India Move To BlackBerry 10," http://press.blackberry.com, January 15, 2014; Gemma Karstens-Smith, "Tech Companies Aim to Wow: Trade Show Gets Underway to the Delight of Those Eager to Launch Their Cutting-Edge Innovations," *Toronto Star*, January 8, 2014, p. B1; Sean Silcoff and Susan Krashinsky, "BlackBerry and Alicia Keys: The Duet That Didn't Sell," *Globe and Mail*, January 3, 2014, p. B1; Matt Hartley, "Chen Comes Out Swinging; CEO Vows the Days of Making Fun of BlackBerry Are Over," National Post, December 21, 2013, p. FP1; Matt Hartley, "BlackBerry Goes on the Offensive to Retain Clients; Interim CEO Chen Issues Open Letter," *National Post*, December 3, 2013, p. FP5; Geoffrey York, "In Africa, BlackBerry Finds a Land of Growth," *Globe and Mail*, November 27, 2013, p. B1; Matt Hartley, "Don't Shoot the Messenger; Can BBM Become a Successful Social Network?" *National Post*, November 26, 2013, p. FP1; Sean Silcoff, Iain Marlow, and Tim Kiladze, "'This Game Is Not Over'," *Globe and Mail*, October 19, 2013, p. B6.

chapter 3

The Marketing Environment, Ethics, and Social Responsibility

CHAPTER OBJECTIVES

1. Identify the five components of the marketing environment.

2. Explain the types of competition marketers face and the steps necessary for developing a competitive strategy.

3. Describe how marketing activities are regulated and how marketers can influence the political-legal environment.

4. Outline the economic factors that affect marketing decisions and consumer buying power.

5. Discuss the impact of the technological environment on a firm's marketing activities.

6. Explain how the social-cultural environment influences marketing.

7. Describe the ethical issues in marketing.

8. Identify the four levels of the social responsibility pyramid.

CHIPOTLE KEEPS IT SUSTAINABLE

Micro-breweries were the trend in the 1990s, but farm-to-table restaurants are the trend today, from Raincity Grill in Vancouver, British Columbia—with its 100-mile menu—to Terre Rouge Bistro Marche in Charlottetown, Prince Edward Island—with its daily changing menu. But "farm fresh" sustainable food is also making itself known in the fast-food industry. Chipotle Mexican Grill has long relied on its use of fresh, natural, and sustainably grown meats and other ingredients as a marketing advantage and a positive way of "changing the way people think about and eat fast food." The chain's more than 1,500 fast-food outlets served approximately 15 million pounds (nearly 7 million kilograms) of locally grown farm produce— lettuce, tomatoes, onions, peppers— in 2013. Chipotle has grown from a single restaurant opened in 1993 in the United States, to include locations in Canada, the United Kingdom, and France.

Chipotle is looking for even more ways to do business responsibly. Among its new initiatives are the Chipotle Cultivate Foundation, which was formed to support individuals and organizations dedicated to creating a more sustainable future, such as family farms and ranches and their communities. Breaking with its long practice of relying on radio, billboards, and digital advertising, Chipotle also recently produced an entertaining two-minute animated film called *Back to the Start*, about a family farm that learns the benefits of sustainable farming. Originally shown online and in movie theatres, the film features a soundtrack with Willie Nelson covering a Coldplay song and proved a fitting broadcast ad for the Grammy Awards, where its message and novelty made it a surprise hit. It even became one of the top 10 advertisements of the year in Internet buzz and had racked up more than 8 million views on YouTube by 2014. A second animated movie, *The Scarecrow*, has been viewed nearly 12 million times. It is a companion film to Chipotle's new app-based game. (The free app can be downloaded at **www.scarecrowgame.com**.)

Cultivate is also the name of Chipotle's annual food and music festival, featuring well-known chefs, exhibits about how food is grown, and, of course, music. Chipotle has already donated millions of dollars to like-minded groups such as Jamie Oliver's Food Revolution and the Nature Conservancy, emphasizing its commitment to sustainable farming and natural ingredients. The chain's customers can earn loyalty points, redeemable online, not for making extra purchases but for demonstrating their knowledge about how food is produced. And a recent effort to shift its marketing focus led the company to devise one-of-a-kind lunch bags made from its own recycled billboards, which would otherwise go to landfills. The bags were available for sale on Earth Day, accompanied by a free meal.[1]

connecting with customers

Chipotle Mexican Grill differentiates itself by articulating its mission as selling fresh, natural, and sustainably grown food. Achieving that mission requires Chipotle to integrate eco-friendly practices throughout its operations—a task that can be costly and challenging. For example, large-scale industrialized farming—often regarded as cost-saving for the consumer—has replaced many independent family farms. However, many of the savings claimed by large commercial farms come at the expense of farm communities and the environment. By supporting the responsible use of resources, Chipotle continues in its quest to change how people think about fast food while also demonstrating corporate social responsibility.

Chapter Overview

Change is a fact of life for all people, including marketers. Adapting to change in an environment as complex and unpredictable as the world's energy usage is perhaps the supreme challenge. Montreal-based Bombardier has invested $3.9 billion in the development of its C Series jets. With the rising cost of fuel, Bombardier is betting that many customers will be swayed by its assurance that the new jets will burn 20 percent less fuel.[2]

Although some change may be the result of crises, more often it is the result of a gradual trend in lifestyle, income, population, and other factors. Consumers are increasingly interested in buying "green" products—goods that minimize their impact on the environment. Technology can trigger a sudden change in the marketplace: in one fell swoop, it appeared that Internet music downloads had replaced traditional CDs. And within mere months of offering its iPhone, Apple introduced the iPod touch MP3 player, which borrowed touchscreen technology from the iPhone.

Marketers must anticipate and plan for change. They must set goals to meet the concerns of customers, employees, shareholders, and members of the general public. Industry competition, legal constraints, the impact of technology on product designs, and social concerns are some of the many important factors that shape the business environment. All potentially have an impact on a firm's goods and services. Although external forces frequently are outside the marketer's control, decision makers must still consider those influences together with the variables of the marketing mix in developing—and occasionally modifying—marketing plans and strategies that take these environmental factors into consideration.

This chapter begins by describing five forces in marketing's external environment—competitive, political-legal, economic, technological, and social-cultural. Figure 3.1 identifies them as the foundation for making decisions that involve the four marketing mix elements and the target market. These forces provide the frame of reference within which all marketing decisions are made. The second focus of this chapter is marketing ethics and social responsibility. This section describes the nature of marketers' responsibilities both to business and to society at large. ◆◆◆

① **Identify the five components of the marketing environment.**

figure 3.1

Elements of the Marketing Mix within an Environmental Framework

ENVIRONMENTAL SCANNING AND ENVIRONMENTAL MANAGEMENT

Marketers constantly monitor crucial trends and developments in the business environment. **Environmental scanning** is the process of collecting information about the external marketing environment to identify and interpret potential trends. The goal of this process is to analyze the information and decide whether these trends represent significant opportunities or pose major threats to the company. The firm can then determine the best response to a particular environmental change.

We are currently seeing unprecedented rising fuel and energy costs in Canada and an increasing concern about greenhouse gas emissions. RenewABILITY Energy Inc., based in Waterloo, Ontario, recently launched its Power-Pipe drain-water heat-recovery system, which reclaims and recycles hot water that would otherwise go down the drain. Cost savings due to reduced energy demand can be as high as 40 percent and, along with reduced energy needs, there is a decrease in greenhouse gas emissions. This new product has applications in university residences, health clubs, apartment buildings, food processing plants, pulp and paper mills, and even in private homes. Ontario has recently become the first jurisdiction in North America—following the United Kingdom, France, and the Netherlands—to provide energy credits for drain-water heat-recovery technology within its building code.[3]

Environmental scanning is a vital component of effective **environmental management**. Environmental management involves marketers' efforts to achieve organizational objectives by predicting and influencing the competitive, political-legal, economic, technological, and social-cultural environments. In the political-legal environment, managers who are seeking modifications of regulations, laws, or tariff restrictions may lobby legislators or contribute to the campaigns of sympathetic politicians. Business and consumer groups continuously lobby government. The Canadian Federation of Small Business, for example, has been lobbying the federal government for a tax reduction from 11 to 9 percent for small businesses. It has also been lobbying against increased Employment Insurance premiums, previously projected for 2014 and 2015. The Canadian government has promised to reduce taxes once the budget is balanced and has promised a three-year Employment Insurance premium freeze through 2016.[4]

For many domestic and international firms, competing with established industry leaders frequently involves **strategic alliances**—partnerships with other firms in which the partners combine resources and capital to create competitive advantages in a new market. Strategic alliances are especially common in international marketing, where partnerships with local firms provide regional expertise for a company expanding its operations abroad. Members of such alliances share risks and profits. Alliances are considered essential in a country such as China, where laws require foreign firms doing business there to work with local companies. Through successful research and development efforts, firms may influence changes in their own technological environments. A research breakthrough may lead to reduced production costs or a technologically superior new product. While changes in the marketing environment may be beyond the control of individual marketers, managers continually seek to predict their impact on marketing decisions and to modify operations to meet changing market needs. Even modest environmental shifts can alter the results of those decisions.

> ## assessment check 1 ✓
>
> **1.1** Define *environmental scanning*.
>
> **1.2** How does environmental scanning contribute to environmental management?

THE COMPETITIVE ENVIRONMENT

As organizations vie to satisfy customers, the interactive exchange creates the **competitive environment**. Marketing decisions by individual firms influence consumer responses in the marketplace. They also affect the marketing strategies of competitors. As a consequence, decision makers must continually monitor competitors' marketing activities—their products, distribution channels, prices, and promotional efforts. The "Marketing and the SME" feature describes how one small Canadian company entered a very competitive marketplace.

Few organizations have **monopoly** positions as the sole supplier of a good or service in the marketplace. Utilities, such as natural gas, electricity, water, and cable TV service, have traditionally accepted considerable regulation from local authorities who controlled such marketing-related factors as rates, service levels, and geographic coverage. In exchange, the utilities gained exclusive rights to serve a particular group of consumers. But the deregulation movement of the past three decades has ended total monopoly protection for most utilities. Many shoppers can choose from alternative cable TV and Internet providers, cell phone and traditional telephone carriers, and even gas and electric utilities. Some firms, such as pharmaceutical giants Merck and Pfizer, have *temporary* monopolies from patents on new drugs. When Health Canada approves a new drug for lowering cholesterol or improving sleep, its manufacturer is typically granted exclusive rights to produce and market the product during the life of the patent. This gives the manufacturer a chance to recoup the millions spent on developing and launching the drug. Once the patent expires, all bets are off—and competitors can flood the market with generic versions of the drug.

But what about professional sports teams who are part of a league? Is it lawful for their league to operate as a monopoly without violating anticompetitive laws? Consider the experience of apparel manufacturer American Needle. For 20 years, the company had a contract to make team caps for the National Football League (NFL), but it lost the business after the league engaged Reebok as its exclusive provider. American Needle sued the NFL, saying its 32 teams had operated as a monopoly with regard to licensed providers. In a 9–0 ruling, the decision was that the NFL had violated antitrust laws.[5]

environmental scanning Process of collecting information about the external marketing environment to identify and interpret potential trends.

Marketoid

In one recent two-year period, Canada's direct investment in Russia quadrupled to $4.2 billion; the political crisis following Russia's 2014 involvement in Ukraine, and Canada's imposition of economic sanctions against Russia, threatened existing and future business opportunities.

environmental management Attainment of organizational objectives by predicting and influencing the competitive, political-legal, economic, technological, and social-cultural environments.

strategic alliance Partnership in which two or more companies combine resources and capital to create competitive advantages in a new market.

competitive environment Interactive process that occurs in the marketplace among marketers of directly competitive products, marketers of products that can be substituted for one another, and marketers competing for the consumer's purchasing power.

monopoly Market structure in which a single seller dominates trade in a good or service for which buyers can find no close substitutes.

Kik Kicks Butt

HAVE you ever heard of Kik Interactive? When the Waterloo, Ontario–based company was launched in the fall of 2010, it had registered a million users within about two weeks. By mid-2012, that number rose to 30 million, and before the end of 2013, there were 100 million users: 50 percent from the United States and about 3 percent from Canada. Kik Interactive was originally launched as a free instant messaging app by a group of University of Waterloo students, hoping to compete with BlackBerry. The founder and CEO, Ted Livingston, had been a co-op student at BlackBerry, and when Kik was launched, BlackBerry sued for patent infringement. An out-of-court settlement was reached in fall 2013.

Kik is adding 250,000 new users every day, across 220 countries. Each week, Kik users send about 4.5 billion messages via this free alternative to text messaging, currently sent through wireless carriers such as Bell Canada, Rogers, Telus, and Fido. British research firm Informa Telecoms & Media predicts that text-messaging revenues will decline 20 percent by 2018 as a result of chat apps.

While all of this is impressive, Kik does have some major competition. WhatsApp, for example, has about 350 million users. Livingston says that if the future is simply instant messaging, WhatsApp might be positioned to win. But he has moved Kik in a new direction: content delivery through the mobile Web. Kik has been bringing out millions of Cards, which are actually apps. Unlike competitors' apps, though, these are not native apps but are "little" websites running inside a mobile browser. When Kik launched its Costume Party game app, it had 1 million users in less than 22 hours. Another advantage that Kik users have is that they don't need to tie their accounts to a phone number. Users simply choose a username and the app behaves like email. As a mobile Web-based content provider, Kik delivers seamlessly and its HTML5-powered Cards seem to give it an advantage that its larger rivals will have difficulty matching.

Sources: Devindra Hardawar, "Kik Messenger Hits 100M Users, with 145M HTML5-Powered Kik Cards Added," Venture Beat, December 12, 2103, available **http://venturebeat.com**; "Sean Silcoff, "Upstart Kik Hits Milestone, Outpaces BBM," *Globe and Mail*, December 13, 2013, p. B3; Canadian Press, "Report: BlackBerry and Kik Settle over Instant-Messaging App," October 8, 2013; Armina Ligaya, "Kik Surpasses BlackBerry's BBM; 80 Million Users Tops Bitter Rival's 60 Million, *National Post*, August 21, 2013, p. FP1.

oligopoly Market structure in which relatively few sellers compete and where high start-up costs form barriers to keep out new competitors.

Rather than seeking sole dominance of a market, corporations increasingly prefer to share the pie with just a few rivals. Referred to by economists as an **oligopoly**, this structure of a limited number of sellers in an industry where high start-up costs form barriers to keep out new competitors deters newcomers from breaking into markets, while ensuring that corporations remain innovative. Commercial airplane manufacturers operate within an oligopolostic industry, currently dominated by Europe-based Airbus Industrie and U.S.-based Boeing. After earlier failures at building and marketing commercial airplanes, the Chinese government once again is attempting to enter this exclusive club. With the increasing numbers of Chinese air travellers, the government founded the Commercial Aircraft Corporation of China (COMAC) to build fuel-efficient jets domestically, in the hope that China can "buy local" and reduce its dependence on aircraft made in the West. COMAC has recently signed a cooperation agreement with its competitor, Canada's Bombardier, to explore opportunities for common systems and procedures between the two companies' aircraft.[6]

(2) **Explain the types of competition marketers face and the steps necessary for developing a competitive strategy.**

TYPES OF COMPETITION

Marketers face three types of competition. The most *direct* form occurs among marketers of similar products, such as when a Petro-Canada station opens across the street from an Esso retail outlet. The cell phone market provides consumers with such alternative suppliers as Bell, Rogers, Fido, and Telus.

Costco—which sells a wide variety of goods, such as home generators and birthday cakes—also takes direct aim at luxury retailers. Costco offers diamond jewellery, cashmere sweaters, Fendi handbags, and even Suzuki grand pianos.[7]

A second type of competition is *indirect* and involves products that are easily substituted. In the fast food industry, pizza competes with chicken, hamburgers, and tacos. In entertainment, a movie could be substituted for a concert or a night at the bowling alley. Canada's Wonderland, Six Flags La Ronde, and Vancouver's Playland—traditional hot spots for family vacations—now compete with outdoor adventure trips. Approximately one-half of Canadian adults will decide not to make this year's vacation a tranquil week at the beach or a trip to an amusement park. Instead, they'll choose to do something more adventurous— thrill-filled experiences such as skydiving, whitewater rafting, participating in an archaeological dig, or rock climbing. So marketers have to find ways to attract consumers to their specific brand as well as to their type of product.

A change such as a price increase or an improvement in a product's attributes can also affect demand for substitute products. As the prices for one type of energy soar, consumers look for cheaper, and more environmentally friendly, alternatives. Growing consumer interest in energy efficiency has led shoppers to look for products that have earned the Energy Star. In Canada, Energy Star is a program created through a voluntary arrangement between Natural Resources Canada and manufacturers and resellers of appliances, building materials, computers, new homes, tools, and other products that Energy Star assesses for levels of energy performance.[8] Advances in technology can give rise to other substitute products.

These products are all indirect competitors of each other. The consumer who has a need for a midday treat can fulfill that need with any one of them.

Wireless fidelity, or Wi-Fi, makes the Internet available via radio waves and can be accessed at any number of public "hot spots" in a variety of locations, including airports, coffee shops, hotels, and libraries. The number of registered hot spots continues to grow worldwide and is expected to reach 5.8 million by 2015.[9] While some hosts charge a fee, Wi-Fi increasingly is offered at no charge. And as technology continues to advance, industry observers expect Wi-Fi eventually will be replaced as the wireless standard. The likely "next generation" successor, LTE (an acronym for long-term evolution), offers enhanced capabilities for numerous applications and boasts a stronger, more secure signal and significantly greater range than does Wi-Fi. All of Canada's major Internet providers currently provide an LTE network.

The final type of competition occurs among all organizations that compete for consumers' purchases. Traditional economic analysis views competition as a battle among companies in the same industry (direct competition) or among substitutable goods and services (indirect competition). But marketers know that *all* firms compete for a limited number of dollars that consumers can or will spend. In this broader sense, competition means that purchase of a Honda Accord might compete with a Norwegian Cruise Line vacation.

Because the competitive environment often determines the success or failure of a product, marketers must continually assess competitors' marketing strategies. New products, updated features or technology, increased service, and lower prices are all variations that marketers look for. When changes occur in the competition, marketers must decide how to respond.

DEVELOPING A COMPETITIVE STRATEGY

Marketers at every successful firm must develop an effective strategy for dealing with the competitive environment. One company may compete in a broad range of markets in many areas of the world. Another may specialize in particular market segments, such as those determined by customers' geographic location, age, or income characteristics. Determining a **competitive strategy** involves answering the following three questions:

1. Should we compete?

2. If so, in what markets should we compete?

3. How should we compete?

The answer to the first question depends on the firm's resources, objectives, and expected profit potential.   A firm may decide not to pursue or continue operating a potentially successful venture that does not mesh with its resources, objectives, or profit expectations. The board of directors of Foster's Group voted to "demerge" the company's two divisions—a well-known Australian

Marketoid

Loblaw Companies operate more than 2,300 corporate, franchised, and associate-owned locations that together employ about 192,000 full- and part-time workers across Canada. Loblaw stores see more than 14 million shoppers each week.

competitive strategy Methods through which a firm deals with its competitive environment.

brewery and an international wine business—because of their different industry dynamics and business requirements. As independent businesses, Foster's and Treasure Wine Estates would be able to identify and implement cost savings.[10] Answering the second question requires marketers to acknowledge their firm's limited resources—sales personnel, advertising budgets, product development capability, and the like. They must allocate these resources to the areas of greatest opportunity. Some companies gain access to new technologies or markets through acquisitions and mergers. SAP, a leading provider of business management software, recently bought SuccessFactors, a leader in cloud-based human capital management solutions. The purchase enabled SAP to build its position in the cloud, strengthen its presence in the growing human capital management market, and gain a greater foothold in social media—an area where SuccessFactors excels.[11]

Answering the third question requires marketers to make product, distribution, promotion, and pricing decisions that give the firm a competitive advantage in the marketplace. Firms can compete on a variety of bases, including product quality, price, and customer service. Stoneyfield Farm invites visitors on its website to follow it on Twitter and Pinterest, and, on its home page, visitors can "Like" the statement "I believe that eating organic is good for me and my family." The company competes on an environmental basis by using organic ingredients. Its commitment to organic products has resulted in Stonyfield Farm becoming the world's largest producer of organic yogurt and the third-largest overall yogurt producer behind Yoplait and Dannon, even though it is higher priced.[12]

time-based competition Strategy of developing and distributing goods and services more quickly than competitors.

© AP Images/Russel A. Daniels

Time-based competition allowed for the creation of the electronic boarding pass to reduce the incidence of phony boarding passes.

TIME-BASED COMPETITION

With increased international competition and rapid changes in technology, a steadily growing number of firms are using time as a strategic competitive weapon. **Time-based competition** is the strategy of developing and distributing goods and services more quickly than competitors. Although a video option on cell phones came late to the Canadian market, the new feature was a big hit, attracting new customers to cell phone providers. The flexibility and responsiveness of time-based competitors enable them to improve product quality, reduce costs, and expand product offerings to satisfy new market segments and enhance customer satisfaction.

In rapidly changing markets—particularly those that involve technology—time-based competition is critical to a firm's success. Technology firms love to debut their latest inventions and ideas each year at the International Consumer Electronics Show. In 2014, Sony announced its plans to launch a video-game streaming service that would work with its smartphones, tablets, and consoles. Intel introduced several new wearable devices: smart earbuds, a smart watch, a smart earphone headset, and a charging "bowl" where all the gadgets can be placed for recharging.[13]

assessment check 2 ✓

2.1 Distinguish between direct and indirect competition and give an example of each.

2.2 What is time-based competition?

③ **Describe how marketing activities are regulated and how marketers can influence the political-legal environment.**

THE POLITICAL-LEGAL ENVIRONMENT

Before you play the game, learn the rules! It is a bad idea to start playing a new game without first understanding the rules, yet some businesspeople exhibit a lack of knowledge about marketing's political-legal environment—the laws and their interpretations that require firms to operate under certain competitive conditions and to protect consumer rights. Ignorance of laws, ordinances, and regulations, or noncompliance with them, can result in fines, negative publicity, and expensive civil damage suits.

The existing Canadian legal framework was constructed on a piecemeal basis, often in response to issues that were important at the time individual laws were enacted. Businesspeople need considerable diligence to understand its relationship to their marketing decisions. Numerous laws and regulations affect those decisions, many of them vaguely stated and inconsistently enforced by a multitude of different authorities.

Regulations enacted at the federal, provincial, and municipal levels affect marketing practices, as do the actions of independent regulatory agencies. These requirements and prohibitions touch on all aspects of marketing decision making: designing, labelling, packaging, distributing, advertising, and promoting goods and services. To cope with the vast, complex, and changing political-legal environment, many large firms maintain in-house legal departments; small firms often seek professional advice from outside lawyers. All marketers, however, should be aware of the major regulations that affect their activities.

political-legal environment Component of the marketing environment consisting of laws and interpretations of laws that require firms to operate under competitive conditions and to protect consumer rights.

GOVERNMENT REGULATION

Marketing decisions are influenced by many laws and regulations—federal, provincial and territorial, and municipal. Table 3.1 lists many of the most important federal laws that affect marketing decisions in Canada. These laws have been enacted to ensure fair and competitive trade practices and to protect Canadian consumers.

The **Competition Act** is the most comprehensive legislation in Canada, and you will continue to see references to it in several later chapters. It replaced earlier pro-competition legislation, the 1923 Combines Investigation Act, which proved to be largely ineffective, partly because all violations under the Act had to be treated as criminal acts and guilt was almost impossible to prove, and partly because competition had to be virtually eliminated before legal action would be taken. Dissatisfaction with this Act eventually led to the passing of the Competition Act in 1975, later amended in 1986 when additional changes dealing primarily with mergers and acquisitions were made. The Competition Act is administered by Industry Canada, whose mission is to "foster a growing competitive, knowledge-based Canadian economy." Among the areas Industry Canada is responsible for is "setting rules and services that support the effective operation of the marketplace." The Competition Act assists in this effort by fostering competition and by protecting consumers, both of which are necessary to have a healthy marketplace. Many of the laws and regulations within the Competition Act can be roughly categorized within three specific marketing areas: pricing, promotion, or distribution.

Among the pricing practices that are covered by the Competition Act are price fixing, bid rigging, price discrimination, predatory pricing, double ticketing, and resale price maintenance. Promotion issues include misleading advertising (or even verbal product misrepresentation), referral selling, and bait-and-switch selling. Distribution issues include refusal to deal, exclusive dealing, and pyramid selling. Table 3.2 summarizes these practices. Many of these topics are discussed in greater detail in later chapters that deal with these specific marketing areas.

Many of these practices, such as price fixing, bid rigging, price discrimination, predatory pricing, and misleading advertising, are criminal offences. Others such as tied selling, refusal to deal, and exclusive dealing are noncriminal offences where actions are taken based on how each particular situation reduces or interferes with competition or otherwise affects consumers in the marketplace.

Provincial and territorial consumer protection legislation in Canada is generally focused on the rights of buyers and sellers with respect to direct sales contracts. These sales include direct mail or

Competition Act The most comprehensive legislation in Canada, designed to help both consumers and businesses by promoting a healthy competitive environment.

table 3.1 **Selected Federal Legislation of Interest to Canadian Marketers**

Agreement on Internal Trade Implementation Act

Bills of Exchange Act

Boards of Trade Act

Broadcasting Act

Canadian Tourism Commission Act

Competition Act

Competition Tribunal Act

Consumer Packaging and Labelling Act

Copyright Act

Food and Drugs Act

Hazardous Products Act

Industrial Design Act

Interest Act

Official Languages Act

Patent Act

Personal Information Protection and Electronic Documents Act

Precious Metals Marking Act

Radiocommunication Act

Standards Council of Canada Act

Telecommunications Act

Textile Labelling Act

Timber Marking Act

Trade-marks Act

Weights and Measures Act

table 3.2 **Some Marketing Practices Covered by the Competition Act**

Price Issues

Price fixing	Sellers collude to set prices higher than they would be in a free market
Bid rigging	Sellers collude to set prices with respect to one or more bids or quotations
Price discrimination	A seller charges different prices for the same quantity and quality of products to two customers who are in competition with each other
Predatory pricing	Sellers set prices so low they deter competition from entering a market, or with the intention to drive competition from the market
Double ticketing	An item has been ticketed with two prices (the lowest price must prevail although there are now limits to protect sellers)
Resale price maintenance	Manufacturers or other channel members try to influence the price at which products are sold to subsequent buyers

Promotion Issues

Misleading advertising	Representations, in print or made orally, concerning a product are false or misleading
Referral selling	Price reductions or other inducements are offered to a customer for the names of other potential customers
Bait-and-switch selling	Sellers attract customers with low prices but then offer another product at a higher price because they are unable to provide the originally promoted item
Tied selling	A seller requires a buyer to purchase another product or to refrain from purchasing a product from a specific manufacturer as a condition to getting the product they want

Distribution Issues

Refusal to deal	Sellers refuse to sell to legitimate buyers
Exclusive dealing	A seller refuses to sell to another channel member unless that customer agrees to buy only from that seller
Pyramid selling	Salespeople are paid to recruit additional salespeople, and each new salesperson pays to "invest" in the scheme, with some of that investment going to earlier participants in the scheme—not to be confused with genuine multi-level marketing plans

telemarketing sales, door-to-door sales, and seminar sales where customers are enticed to a hotel, convention centre, or some other venue where the intention is to sell a product or service to them. This legislation is commonly referred to as the Consumer Protection Act or the Direct Seller's Act in most provinces or territories. These laws are also called "cooling-off" laws because an important aspect they have in common is the right of the buyer to reconsider a buying decision that was made under the persuasive influence of a salesperson. The cooling-off period may vary depending on the provincial or territorial legislation. A notice that informs the customer of the cooling-off period must be part of the contract. If a buyer demands that a contract be cancelled, the seller must return the purchase price and any trade-in that was taken (or a sum of money equal to the value of the trade-in) within a specified period of time. Companies should know the legislation that covers each territory where they sell.

As you can see with federal legislation and with varied provincial and territorial legislation, there is a need to harmonize laws, regulations, and practices in order to raise awareness and to improve the marketplace for Canadian consumers. The Consumer Measures Committee, created under the Agreement on Internal Trade, is a joint federal, provincial, and territorial committee that focuses attention on common issues. In the areas of direct selling, cost of credit disclosure, the manufacture and selling of upholstered and stuffed articles, Internet sales contracts, and prohibited debt collection practices, harmonization is now complete.[14]

GOVERNMENT REGULATORY AGENCIES

Governments at all levels have established regulatory agencies that influence marketing decisions and practices, including those related to product development and commercialization, packaging, pricing, advertising, personal selling, and distribution. Federal agencies may provide advice and assistance to Canadian businesses or may have responsibility to regulate specific industries. Those that regulate industries usually have well-defined responsibilities. The National Energy Board, for example, regulates the construction and operation of interprovincial and international pipelines and power lines; pipeline traffic, tolls, and tariffs; the export and import of natural gas; and the export of oil and electricity, among other things. It also conducts studies into specific energy matters, holds public inquiries, monitors Canada's energy supplies, and provides energy advice to the Minister of Natural Resources in areas where it has expertise derived from its regulatory functions.[15]

One agency that is particularly important to marketers is the Canadian Radio-television and Telecommunications Commission (CRTC), which has the authority to regulate and supervise all aspects of the Canadian broadcasting system. The CRTC works closely with the broadcasting and telecommunications industry to establish standards relating to television violence, gender portrayal, ethnic and minority representation, advertising to children, quality and accessibility of service, and customer billing practices. The CRTC also regulates the companies that supply industry-related technology, including cable television, mobile telephones, satellite television and radio, and direct-to-home television. The CRTC also has the primary enforcement responsibility for Canada's new anti-spam law when anti-spam rules come into effect in 2014, safeguards on software installations come into effect in 2015, and a private right of action that will facilitate lawsuits comes into effect in 2017.[16] Some examples of other Canadian federal regulatory agencies and their major areas of responsibility are provided in Table 3.3.

OTHER REGULATORY FORCES

Public and private consumer interest groups and self-regulatory organizations are also part of the legal environment. Consumer interest organizations have mushroomed since the late 1970s, and today, hundreds of groups operate at national, provincial and territorial, and municipal levels. These organizations seek to protect consumers in as many areas as possible. People for the Ethical Treatment of Animals (PETA), which operates in Canada, the United States, India, Germany, and many other countries, opposes the use of animals for product testing. The Humane Society

table 3.3   **Some Examples of Canadian Federal Regulatory Agencies**

FEDERAL AGENCY	MAJOR AREAS OF RESPONSIBILITY
Canada Border Services Agency	To ensure the security and prosperity of Canada by managing the access of people and goods to and from Canada
Canadian Environmental Assessment Agency	To provide Canadians with high-quality environmental assessments that contribute to informed decision making in support of sustainable development
Canadian Intellectual Property Office	To accelerate Canada's economic development by fostering the use of intellectual property systems and the exploitation of intellectual property information; encouraging invention, innovation, and creativity in Canada; administering the intellectual property systems in Canada (patents, trademarks, copyrights, industrial designs, and integrated circuit topographies); promoting Canada's international intellectual property interests
Canadian Space Agency	To promote the peaceful use and development of space, to advance the knowledge of space through science, and to ensure that space science and technology provide social and economic benefits for Canadians
Communications Research Centre Canada	To be the federal government's centre of excellence for communications R&D, ensuring an independent source of advice for public policy purposes; to help identify and close the innovation gaps in Canada's communications sector by engaging in industry partnerships, building technical intelligence, and supporting small and medium-sized high-technology enterprises
Measurement Canada	To ensure equity and accuracy where goods and services are bought and sold on the basis of measurement, in order to contribute to a fair and competitive marketplace for Canadians
Technology Partnerships Canada	To provide funding support for strategic research and development and demonstration projects that will produce economic, social, and environmental benefits to Canadians

of Canada tries to "protect animals and the earth." Other groups attempt to advance the rights of minorities, Canadian seniors, the homeless, and other special-interest causes. The power of these groups has also grown. Pressure from anti-alcohol groups such as Mothers Against Drunk Driving has had an impact on criminal laws and offender sentencing in Canada.

Self-regulatory groups represent industries' attempts to set guidelines for responsible business conduct. Advertising Standards Canada (ASC) is the advertising industry's self-regulatory body. Its mission is to ensure the integrity and viability of advertising in Canada. ASC administers the Canadian Code of Advertising Standards, the principal instrument of self-regulation. ASC tries to promote truth and accuracy in advertising and to ensure that advertising is not offensive to viewers, listeners, or readers. It provides consumers with a mechanism to complain about any particular advertisement. It reviews and advocates voluntary resolution of advertising-related complaints between consumers and businesses. ASC also provides industry with a mechanism to resolve competitive disputes about advertising, and with a clearance service that is a fee-based review of advertising copy to help ensure that advertising complies with current laws and regulations.[17] In addition to ASC, many individual trade associations set business guidelines and codes of conduct and encourage members' voluntary compliance.

The Canadian Marketing Association (CMA) has over 800 corporate members who include the country's largest financial institutions, insurance companies, retailers, publishers, charitable organizations, and relationship marketers. It is the Canadian marketing industry's leading advocate on legislative matters and has participated in a variety of government-led initiatives on such issues as privacy, electronic commerce, consumer protection, and the prevention of telemarketing fraud. The CMA has a number of internal task forces that develop self-regulatory standards and policies on ethics, privacy, and marketing to children and teenagers and has developed the Code of Ethics and Standards of Practice to which its members must adhere. In an effort to protect consumer privacy and curb unwanted mail or phone solicitation, the CMA provides a Do Not Contact service, which its members honour.

CONTROLLING THE POLITICAL-LEGAL ENVIRONMENT

Most marketers comply with laws and regulations. Doing so not only serves their customers but also avoids legal problems that could ultimately damage a firm's image and hurt profits. But smart marketers get ahead of the curve by providing products that will meet customers' future needs while also addressing government goals. Showing remarkable forward thinking, Toyota was one of the first automakers to commit to building hybrid cars. Its efforts were supported by a government tax break for purchasers of the first hybrids. Consumer groups and political action committees within industries may try to influence the outcome of proposed legislation or change existing laws by engaging in political lobbying or boycotts. Lobbying groups frequently enlist the support of customers, employees, and suppliers to assist their efforts.

④ Outline the economic factors that affect marketing decisions and consumer buying power.

THE ECONOMIC ENVIRONMENT

The overall health of the economy influences how much consumers spend and what they buy. This relationship also works the other way. Consumer buying plays an important role in the economy's health; in fact, consumer spending accounts for nearly 60 percent of the nation's total **gross domestic product (GDP)**, the sum of all goods and services produced by a nation in a year.[18] Because marketing activities are directed toward satisfying consumer wants and needs, marketers must first understand how economic conditions influence the purchasing decisions consumers make.

Marketing's **economic environment** consists of forces that influence consumer buying power and marketing strategies. They include the stage of the business cycle, inflation and deflation, unemployment, income, and resource availability.

gross domestic product (GDP) Sum of all goods and services produced by a nation in a year.

STAGES IN THE BUSINESS CYCLE

Historically, the economy has tended to follow a cyclical pattern consisting of four stages: prosperity, recession, depression, and recovery. Consumer buying differs in each stage of the **business cycle**, and marketers must adjust their strategies accordingly. In times of prosperity, consumer spending maintains a brisk pace, and buyers are willing to spend more for premium versions of well-known brands. Growth in services such as banking and restaurants usually indicates a strong economy. When economists predict such conditions as low inflation and low unemployment, marketers respond by offering new products, increasing their promotional efforts, and expanding distribution. They might even raise prices to widen profit margins. But high prices for some items—such as energy—can affect businesses and consumers alike. Skyrocketing gasoline prices have led many consumers to seek other forms of transportation, including the e-bicycle; sales are expected to grow from 31 million units in 2013 to 38 million units by 2020. While China accounts for 90 percent of unit sales, Europe accounts for more than 20 percent of global e-bicycle revenue.[19] E-bicycles enable many consumers— especially those in China, India, and Europe—to postpone the more costly purchase of a car.

During economic slowdowns, consumers focus on more basic, functional products that carry lower price tags. They limit travel, restaurant meals, and entertainment. They skip expensive vacations and cook their own meals. During a recession, marketers consider lowering prices and increasing promotions that include special offers to stimulate demand. They may also launch value-priced products likely to appeal to cost-conscious buyers.

Consumer spending sinks to its lowest level during a depression. The last true depression in Canada occurred during the 1930s. Although a severe depression could occur again, most experts see it as a slim possibility. Through its monetary and fiscal policies, the federal government attempts to control extreme fluctuations in the business cycle that lead to depression.

In the recovery stage, the economy emerges from recession and consumer purchasing power increases. But while consumers have money to spend, caution often restrains their willingness to buy. A family might buy a new car if no-interest financing is available. A couple might decide to book a trip through a discount travel firm such as Expedia.ca or Travelocity.ca. Companies like these can make the most of an opportunity and develop loyal customers by offering superior service at lower prices. Recovery still remains a difficult stage for businesses just climbing out of a recession

economic environment Factors that influence consumer buying power and marketing strategies, including stage of the business cycle, inflation, unemployment, income, and resource availability.

business cycle Pattern of stages in the level of economic activity: prosperity, recession, depression, and recovery.

Skyrocketing gas prices have led consumers to seek other forms of transportation. In just a few years, the electric bicycle has grown to an $11-billion industry.

H. F. (Herb) MacKenzie

because they must earn profits while trying to gauge uncertain consumer demand. Many cope by holding down costs. Some trim payrolls and close branch offices. Others cut back on business travel budgets, substituting teleconferencing and videoconferencing.

Business cycles, like other aspects of the economy, are complex phenomena that, despite the efforts of government, businesspeople, and others to control them, sometimes have a life of their own. Unforeseen natural disasters such as the 2013 floods throughout Alberta and in Toronto—described by the Insurance Bureau of Canada as respectively the largest and third-largest natural insured catastrophes in Canadian history—have negatively affected the Canadian economy, as have power outages that affected hundreds of thousands of Canadians across much of eastern Canada during the 2013 Christmas season. Many residences and businesses were without power for extended periods of time, some more than a week. The most effective marketers know how to recognize ways to serve their customers during the best of times—and the worst of times.

THE GLOBAL ECONOMIC CRISIS

Sometimes business cycles take a severe turn and affect consumers and businesses across the globe. That is the case with the 2008 global recession, called the worst economic downturn since the Great Depression of the 1930s. Typically, nations' GDP rates grow—some modestly at 2 to 4 percentage points a year and some, such as rapidly expanding India and China, at or near double digits. With the crisis, economists predicted that the world economy might shrink for the first time in 60 years.

A struggling economy generates its own downward spiral: fearing worse days ahead, consumers and businesses become cautious about spending money, and as they spend less, demand for many products also drops. Lessened demand forces employers to take extraordinary steps just to stay in business: institute a shortened workweek with reduced salaries or even slash the workforce. Canada was certainly not immune to the effects of the global recession, but it weathered the recession better than most nations.

Especially during a recession, marketers look to emphasize value in their offerings. Some slash prices or offer sales to help customers stretch their budget dollars. Automakers Ford and Hyundai recently assured new-car buyers that they would assist them with payments for a period of time if they lost their jobs or would take the cars back to avoid damaging consumers' credit. Retailers that emphasized affordable products, such as Walmart and McDonald's, saw their sales increase. With the severity of the recession, all marketers needed to reevaluate their strategies and concentrate on their most promising products. But it remains to be seen whether or how much consumers, now used to price reductions and special offers, will change their habits once they regain their economic footing in a recovery.

INFLATION AND DEFLATION

inflation Rising prices caused by some combination of excess consumer demand and increases in the costs of one or more factors of production.

A major constraint on consumer spending, which can occur during any stage of the business cycle, is **inflation**—rising prices caused by some combination of excess demand and increases in the costs of raw materials, component parts, human resources, or other factors of production. Inflation devalues money by reducing the products it can buy through persistent price increases. These rising prices increase marketers' costs, such as expenditures for wages and raw materials, and the resulting higher prices may therefore negatively affect sales. The Bank of Canada has a target inflation rate of 1 to 3 percent, and in recent years, inflation has been at the lower end of the range: 1 to 1.5 percent.[20]

If inflation is so bad, is its opposite, *deflation*, better? At first, it might seem so. Falling prices mean that products are more affordable. But deflation can be a long and damaging downward spiral, causing a freefall in business profits, lower returns on most investments, and widespread job layoffs. The last time that Canada experienced significant deflation was in the Great Depression of the 1930s.

UNEMPLOYMENT

unemployment Proportion of people in the economy that do not have jobs but are actively seeking work.

Unemployment is defined as the proportion of people in the economy who are actively seeking work but do not have jobs. Unemployment rises during recessions and declines in the recovery and prosperity stages of the business cycle. Like inflation, unemployment affects the ways consumers

MARKETING: MAKING YOUR WORLD BETTER   You Don't Need a Green Thumb to Get a Green Job

TRADITIONALLY, the colour green was described as dark, light, or bright. Today, we are more likely to describe green as army, asparagus, emerald, forest, hunter, jade, jungle, lime, moss, olive, pine, or sea green. Traditionally, "green" jobs were largely science-based positions: contaminant and waste management, environmental engineering, water conservation and quality management, soil testing, forest conservation, agronomy, etc. Today, green jobs are more likely to be cross-functional or cross-disciplinary, and many require only a marginal understanding of science. That's great news for many people, including want-to-be marketers. The green job market is hot; there are many opportunities for people who are simply passionate about the environment. This could include accountants, builders, economists, journalists, lawyers, and marketers. Green jobs are growing much faster than jobs in the overall economy. In Canada, environmental employment has grown from about 250,000 workers ten years ago to about 700,000 today. Approximately 2.2 million Canadians—about 12 percent of the workforce—spend at least a portion of their time on environment-related activities.

There are increasing opportunities for green entrepreneurs, people who want to start green businesses. As green products become more popular, opportunities for green manufacturers will open up, and they will employ green salespeople and green marketers. One new green service firm, Carbonzero, is a Toronto-based firm that uses recognized international carbon accounting standards to measure greenhouse gas emissions for clients and then helps them reduce or neutralize their impact on the environment.

Many green jobs will continue to require technical or scientific backgrounds, and entry standards for some jobs are high—either a master's degree or a Ph.D. However, a major task for many organizations within the environmental industry will be their ability to "sell" green science and gain popular acceptance. There will be key positions for those who can work with teams of people from various stakeholder groups—company technical people and senior-level management, government agencies, public interest groups—and communicate effectively with them. According to ECO Canada—the largest online resource for environmental jobs, training, and certification in Canada—more businesses are demanding professionals who can link business skills with environment-related expertise, and the two competencies they most often seek are these:

- Corporate Environmental Program Planning and Implementation
- Environmental Business, Technology, and Product Development.

Each is listed in approximately one-third of green job postings. If you are passionate about the environment, find a job you can be passionate about.

Sources: Carbonzero website, **www.carbonzero.ca**, accessed January 15, 2014; ECO Canada website, **www.eco.ca**, accessed January 15, 2014; Wallace Immen, "Wanted: Jobs with Meaning," *Globe and Mail*, April 22, 2013, p. B11.

---

behave. Unless personal savings and employment insurance or union benefits effectively offset lost earnings, unemployed people have relatively little income to spend—they buy food, pay the rent or mortgage, and try to keep up with utility bills. Canada's unemployment rate has been hovering near 7 percent in recent years. Of course, this varies by region of the country and by demographics; the unemployment rate for young people, for example, was nearly double the national rate.[21] Not surprisingly, when jobs are created, consumer confidence rises, and consumer spending increases. The "Marketing: Making Your World Better" feature describes green jobs, an opportunity for those who are passionate about the environment to also help reduce unemployment in Canada.

INCOME

Income is another important determinant of marketing's economic environment because it influences consumer buying power. By studying income statistics and trends, marketers can estimate market potential and develop plans for targeting specific market segments. A rise in income represents a potential for increasing overall sales. Many marketers are particularly interested in **discretionary income**, the amount of money people have to spend after buying necessities such as food, clothing, and housing. Those whose industry involves the necessities seek to turn those needs into preferences for their goods and services. When the Canadian economy slows down, consumers frequently experience a drop in their net worth because their homes and stock investments lose value. At the same time, Canadians spend less on nonessential items, and a greater proportion of

Marketoid

More than 120,000 jobs were created in Toronto in 2013, but the city's unemployment rate increased to 8.4 percent, higher than any of Canada's major metropolitan areas.

discretionary income Money available to spend after buying necessities such as food, clothing, and housing.

their income goes toward food and other necessities. When the economy is reasonably stable as it currently is in Canada, consumer spending tends to increase. A long period of low interest rates is partly responsible for increasing consumer debt, which, at the end of 2013, was at a record high.[22]

Changes in average earnings powerfully affect discretionary income. Historically, periods of major innovation have been accompanied by dramatic increases in living standards and rising incomes. Automobiles, televisions, telephones, and computers are just a few of the innovations that have changed consumers' lives—and standards of living. Statistics Canada tracks personal income and discretionary income; then determines how much of that income is spent on personal consumption. Marketers can use these figures to plan their approaches to everything from product development to the promotion of their goods and services.

Not only does income affect how much money individuals donate to not-for-profit organizations, but it can also affect the amount of time they're willing to spend on charitable efforts. And some firms have also demonstrated their commitment not only to charities but also to conducting business in a responsible manner. Such activities often fall under the theme of corporate social responsibility (CSR). But charitable giving is not all there is to CSR, as the "Career Readiness" feature shows.

RESOURCE AVAILABILITY

Resources are not unlimited. Shortages—temporary or permanent—can result from several causes, including lack of raw materials, component parts, energy, or labour. The global financial crisis, coupled with extreme weather conditions such as drought and typhoons, signals the possibility of worldwide food shortages.[23]

demarketing Process of reducing consumer demand for a good or service to a level that the firm can supply.

One reaction to a shortage is **demarketing**, the process of reducing consumer demand for a product to a level that the firm can reasonably supply. Oil companies publicize tips on how to cut gasoline consumption, and utility companies encourage homeowners to install more insulation to reduce heating costs. Volvo IT's mobile app, Commute Greener, encourages environmentally friendly commuting. Users can calculate the environmental impact of their trips to and from work or school and can even form groups on Facebook to create friendly competition in green commuting.[24] A shortage presents marketers with a unique set of challenges. They may have to allocate limited supplies, a sharply different activity from marketing's traditional objective of expanding sales

---

CAREER READINESS   **Landing a Job in CSR**

ARE you eager to turn your passion for environmental causes or "green" technology into a career in corporate social responsibility? You can, if you keep some important ideas in mind.

- Make sure you know what CSR really is. While charitable giving still plays a big role in many companies' CSR efforts, and rightly so, it's not the whole story, as this chapter shows. Many CSR experts today feel "it's all about the environment," including problems such as climate change and waste reduction.
- Be ready to promote your CSR experience. Don't have any? Volunteer or work a related internship to show your commitment to your field and gain a track record of real accomplishment. It's not enough to say you recycle at home.

- Practise your persuasive skills. Convincing other people within and outside your organization to change their behaviour will be a big part of your daily responsibility.
- Hone your leadership and communication skills. These are critical in any field, but particularly in small departments like CSR that interact with other areas in a company such as marketing, operations, legal, and human resources.
- Cover the basics. Perfect your résumé, network effectively, study the companies you're interested in, and prepare thoroughly for interviews.

Sources: "Landing a CSR Job," WetFeet.com, accessed March 26, 2012, **www.wetfeet.com**; C.B. Bhattacharya, "Corporate Social Responsibility: It's All About Marketing," *Forbes*, accessed March 26, 2012, **www.forbes.com**; James Epstein-Reeves, "How to Find a CSR Job in a Big Company," *Forbes*, March 13, 2012, **www.forbes.com**.

volume. Shortages may require marketers to decide whether to spread limited supplies over all customers or limit purchases by some customers so that the firm can completely satisfy others.

Marketers today have also devised ways to deal with increased demand for fixed amounts of resources. In its annual *Green Book,* the American Council for an Energy Efficient Economy (ACEEE) gives cars a "green score," rating vehicles on their manufacturers' use of scarce resources and attention to the environment in the production process. The recent winner? The ACEEE rated the electric battery-powered Mitsubishi i-MIEV at the top.[25]

THE INTERNATIONAL ECONOMIC ENVIRONMENT

In today's global economy, marketers must also monitor the economic environment of other nations. Just as in Canada, a recession in the United States, Europe, or Japan changes buying habits. Changes in foreign currency rates compared with the Canadian dollar also affect marketing decisions. The high value of the Canadian dollar in recent years has made it more expensive to ship Canadian goods to the United States and has made it less attractive for U.S. companies to operate manufacturing plants here. In early 2014, the Canadian dollar was weakening and there were indications that it might continue to do so for the foreseeable future. Such a weakening would be welcomed by Canadian manufacturers whose exports will rise, but not welcomed by importers who would have to pay more for their purchases. The tourism sector would be a big winner: international tourists would have greater purchasing power when visiting Canada, and Canadian tourists would be encouraged to visit other parts of Canada as international travel would become more expensive for them.

As China exports more and more goods to the world, including Canada, some people voice concern over the widening trade gap. Only recently have broad economic reforms allowed China to play in the global marketplace. Some wonder if China's entry into world markets might help the West economically. However, with China's gross domestic product still relatively small, economists say the country cannot rescue the world economy—yet. But they point to China's rapidly expanding economy, fuelled in part by a growing middle class with vast, untapped marketing potential.[26]

Politics in other countries affect the international economic environment as well. For example, even though Egypt is not an oil exporter, political unrest in that country had an effect on global oil prices in 2013. Much of the oil from North Africa and the Middle East flows through the Suez Canal, controlled by Egypt.[27]

The 2008 global recession has pushed some members of the European Union to the brink of bankruptcy, and the EU and the International Monetary Fund have provided financial bailouts for Greece, Ireland, and Portugal, with Greece receiving a second bailout in two years. The economies of two other EU members, Spain and Italy, are also faltering.[28]

> **assessment check 4** ✓
>
> **4.1** Identify and describe briefly the four stages of the business cycle.
>
> **4.2** Explain how inflation and income affect consumer buying decisions.

THE TECHNOLOGICAL ENVIRONMENT

(5) **Discuss the impact of the technological environment on a firm's marketing activities.**

The **technological environment** represents the application to marketing of knowledge based on discoveries in science, inventions, and innovations. Technology leads to new goods and services for consumers; it also improves existing products, offers better customer service, and often reduces prices through new, cost-efficient production and distribution methods. Technology can quickly make products obsolete—email, for example, quickly eroded both letter writing and the market for fax machines—but it can just as quickly open new marketing opportunities, in entirely new industries.

Pets have been wearing RFID—radio-frequency identification—transmitters for years, in case they got lost. Now RFID tags are used in many industries to locate items as varied as library books and laundry detergent. An RFID tag contains a computer chip with an antenna. A reader scans the tag and transmits the data from the tag to a computer. This innovation means that retailers, manufacturers, and others can locate and track inventory without opening packages. Guests on Disney Cruise Line ships wear wristbands with embedded RFID tags. The wristbands provide access

technological environment Applications to marketing of knowledge based on discoveries in science, inventions, and innovations.

to the ship's amenities and replace the need for a key card. To open their room, guests simply tap the door with the hand wearing the wristband. But the use of RFID to track the movement of humans is controversial because of the privacy implications.[29] Technology can sometimes address social concerns. In response to societal pressure for fuel savings and environmental improvements, automakers used technology to develop more fuel-efficient vehicles and reduce dangerous emissions. Increased use of ethanol made from corn was another solution, but researchers have stepped up efforts to develop biofuels to replace gasoline. One such fuel, cellulosic ethanol, comes from cellulose—grass clippings, wood chips, yard waste—anything organic, even old tires. The biofuel emits significantly fewer greenhouse gases than gasoline and, if spilled, is less damaging to the environment. Scientists believe advances in technology eventually will make the fuel cost-effective to produce. Meanwhile, several start-up companies are working to create fuel from another organic source: algae. Low-cost, fast-growing, and carbon neutral, algae shows promise as a source of alternative energy.[30]

Industry and government—as well as educational and other not-for-profit institutions—all play roles in the development of new technology. The Canadian Environmental Technology Advancement Corporation-WEST (CETAC-WEST) was established in 1994 by Environment Canada and is a not-for-profit corporation dedicated to helping small to medium-sized enterprises (SMEs) across western Canada develop and commercialize new environmental technologies. More than 150 innovators, entrepreneurs, and small businesses now make up its alumni, and its graduates have an impressive record. Among those that have been in business more than 10 years, there is a 94 percent survival rate, compared to a normal Canadian SME 10-year survival rate of about 20 percent. An example alumnus is Ground Effects, a private company that now has 35 employees and annual revenue of $10 million. One of its activities is cleaning up water used to fracture wells so that it can be reused in the process.[31] Many of Canada's universities now have offices focused on transferring and commercializing technology that results from their research.

Another major source of technology is the government, including the military. Air bags originated from airplane ejection seats, digital computers were first designed to calculate artillery trajectories, and the microwave oven is a derivative of military radar systems. Even the Internet was first developed by the U.S. Department of Defense as a secure military communications system. Although the United States has long been the world leader in research, competition from rivals in Europe, Japan, and other Asian countries is intense.

VoIP—Voice over Internet Protocol A phone connection through a personal computer with any type of broadband Internet connection.

APPLYING TECHNOLOGY

Marketers monitor the technological environment for a number of reasons. Creative applications of new technologies not only give a firm a definite competitive edge but can also benefit society. Marketers who monitor new technology and successfully apply it may also enhance customer service.

VoIP—Voice over Internet Protocol—is an alternative to traditional telecommunications services provided by companies such as Rogers Communications. The telephone is not connected to a traditional phone jack but instead is connected to a personal computer with any type of broadband Internet connection. Special software transmits phone conversations over the Internet, rather than through telephone lines. A VoIP user dials the phone as usual. Recipients can receive calls made using VoIP through regular telephone connections—land or wireless. Moreover, you can call another person who has VoIP using a regular landline or cell phone. Globally, VoIP continues to attract growing numbers of users—both consumers and businesses—mainly because of the cost savings. The VoIP business is also growing worldwide, with hundreds of service providers in the United States alone. One of the largest, Skype, has more than 663 million customers.[32]

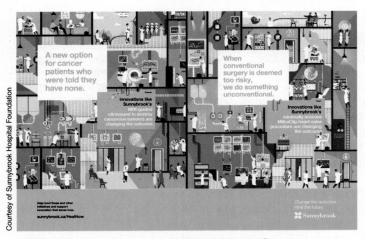

Continual improvements in technology help save time, save money, and, sometimes, save lives.

As convenient as the Internet, cell phones, and Wi-Fi are for businesspeople and consumers, the networks that facilitate these connections aren't yet compatible with each other. So engineers are working on a new standard that would enable these networks to connect with each other—paving the way for melded services such as video exchanges between a cell phone and a computer. Called the Internet Protocol Multimedia Subsystem (IPMS), the new standard will attempt to create a common interface so that data can be carried across networks between different devices. The implications for various communications providers are enormous—not only will they find new ways to cooperate but they will also find new ways to compete. Subsequent chapters discuss in more detail how companies apply technologies—such as databases, blogs, and interactive promotional techniques—to create a competitive advantage.

> **assessment check 5**
>
> **5.1 What are some of the consumer benefits of technology?**
>
> **5.2 Why must marketers monitor the technological environment?**

THE SOCIAL-CULTURAL ENVIRONMENT

⑥ **Explain how the social-cultural environment influences marketing.**

As a nation, Canada is becoming older, more affluent, and more culturally diverse. The birthrate is falling, and *microculture* populations are rising. People express concerns about the environment, buying ecologically friendly products that reduce pollution. They value the time at home with family and friends, cooking meals at home and exchanging vacation photos over the Internet. Marketers need to track these trends to be sure they are in tune with consumers' needs and desires. These aspects of consumer lifestyles help shape marketing's **social-cultural environment**—the relationship among marketing, society, and culture.

social-cultural environment Component of the marketing environment consisting of the relationship among the marketer and society and its culture.

To remain competitive, marketers must be sensitive to society's demographic shifts and changing values. These variables affect consumers' reactions to different products and marketing practices. As the baby boom generation—those born between 1946 and 1965—reaches middle age and retirement, marketers are scrambling to identify this generation's needs and wants. Fuelled by hopes of a long life with plenty of time and money to spend, the baby boom generation views retirement much differently than their predecessors did. Marketers already know that boomers feel young at heart and enjoy their leisure time, but they aren't playing canasta and shuffleboard—they're becoming "social media mavens" who spend a significant portion of their free time surfing the Web and connecting with friends and family and accessing sites such as Facebook and LinkedIn on their smartphones.[33] Some even launch a second career, starting their own small business. And boomers have a whole new take on the concept of grandparenting. More than past generations, boomer grandparents get actively involved in their grandchildren's daily lives and are more inclined to spend money on them. An estimated 20 percent of all travel involves grandchildren with grandparents, with or without their parents along. As they age, boomers will need health care goods and services and, should they live longer, they may need such things as physical therapy for a repaired knee or a motorized scooter to get around. Another social-cultural consideration is the increasing importance of cultural diversity. Canada is a mixed society composed of various micromarkets, each with its unique values, cultural characteristics, consumer preferences, and purchasing behaviours. Rogers Communications has been actively targeting these important micromarkets and offers 24/7 programming in many languages including Cantonese, Mandarin, Italian, Spanish, Portuguese, Greek, Hindi, Punjabi, and Bengali.[34] Marketers also need to learn about cultural and societal differences among countries abroad, particularly as business becomes more and more global. Marketing strategies that work in Canada often fail when directly applied in other countries and vice versa. In many cases, marketers must redesign packages and modify products and advertising messages to suit the tastes and preferences of different cultures. Chapter 7 explores the social-cultural aspects of international marketing.

CONSUMERISM

Changing societal values have led to **consumerism**, defined as a social force within the environment that aids and protects the buyer by exerting legal, moral, and economic pressures on business. Today,

consumerism Social force within the environment designed to aid and protect the consumer by exerting legal, moral, and economic pressures on business and government.

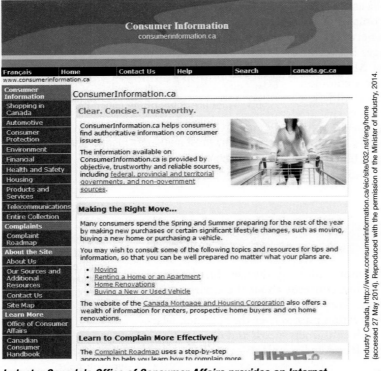

Industry Canada's Office of Consumer Affairs provides an Internet gateway to help keep Canadian consumers informed.

everyone—marketers, industry, government, and the public—is acutely aware of the impact of consumerism on the nation's economy and general well-being.

Marketers see a rise in consumer activism. Imports of Canadian seal products have been banned from the United States, the European Union, and many other countries, and groups such as Boycott Canada and Harpseals.org argue for a tourism boycott of Canada to bring attention to the annual seal hunt. Many Canadian consumers have opposed and still oppose the use of plastic shopping bags, most of which end up as solid waste in landfills, clog sewers, or litter waterways. Increasingly, however, retailers are helping to curb the use of plastic bags. Loblaw Companies instituted a small fee in 2007 for customers who use these bags and has been able to reduce their consumption by more than 5 billion bags in just over five years. Whole Foods discontinued the use of plastic shopping bags throughout its stores in Canada, the United States, and the United Kingdom. Both retailers—and others, including Canadian Tire and Target Canada—sell reasonably priced, reusable cloth alternatives. Whole Foods also offers a discount to shoppers for not using plastic bags.[35]

But firms cannot always adjust to meet the demands of consumer groups. The choice between pleasing all consumers and remaining profitable—thus surviving—defines one of the most difficult dilemmas facing business. Given these constraints, what do consumers have the right to expect from the companies from which they buy goods and services? The most frequently quoted answer came from a speech made by former U.S. president John F. Kennedy more than four decades ago. Although this list does not amount to a definitive statement, it offers good rules of thumb that explain basic **consumer rights**:

consumer rights In their most basic form, these rights are a person's right to choose goods and services freely, to be informed about these products and services, to be heard, and to be safe.

1. *The right to choose freely.* Consumers should be able to choose from among a range of goods and services.

2. *The right to be informed.* Consumers should be provided with enough education and product information to enable them to be responsible buyers.

3. *The right to be heard.* Consumers should be able to express their legitimate displeasure to appropriate parties—that is, sellers, consumer assistance groups, and consumer affairs offices.

4. *The right to be safe.* Consumers should be assured that the goods and services they purchase are not injurious with normal use. Goods and services should be designed in such a way that the average consumer can use them safely.*

These rights have formed the conceptual framework of much of the legislation enacted in Canada and the United States during the first five decades of the consumer rights movement. However, the question of how best to guarantee them remains unanswered. In Canada, different classes of consumer products fall under the jurisdiction of different government agencies. Regulations concerning food are administered by the Canadian Food Inspection Agency. Food labelling regulations force disclosure of such details as expiration date, ingredients, and nutritional values on packaged foods. Vehicles fall under the jurisdiction of Transport Canada. Provincial governments may regulate the marketing of farm products, such as eggs and milk, and of service providers, such as homeopathic and chiropractic practitioners and insurance agents and brokers. They, and sometimes municipal governments, may regulate pesticide use.

Consumers' right to safety encompasses a vast range of products, such as automobiles and children's toys. Sometimes it seems as though safety recalls are reported in the media too regularly.

---

*Papers of John F. Kennedy. Presidential Papers. President's Office Files. Speech Files. Special message to Congress on protecting consumer interest, 15 March 1962. (http://www.jfklibrary.org/Asset-Viewer/Archives/JFKPOF-037-028.aspx)

You might even receive a letter in the mail from a manufacturer informing you of a recall for a part on your refrigerator or car. Health Canada makes it convenient for consumers to learn about product recalls. Its website, **www.hc-sc.gc.ca**, consolidates information on safety-related issues and includes a link on consumer product safety. There, consumers can find another link that provides advisories, warnings, and recall information. The user-friendly site organizes information into broad categories: children's products, personal care products, household products, recreational products, pesticides, and more.

Consumerism, along with the rest of the social-cultural environment for marketing decisions at home and abroad, is expanding in scope and importance. Today, no marketer can initiate a strategic decision without considering the society's norms, values, culture, and demographics. Understanding how these variables affect decisions is so important that some firms have created a new position—typically, manager of public policy research—to study the future impact on their organizations of a changing societal environment.

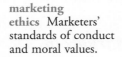

assessment check 6

6.1 Define *consumerism*.

6.2 Identify the four consumer rights.

ETHICAL ISSUES IN MARKETING

⑦ **Describe the ethical issues in marketing.**

The five environments described so far in this chapter do not completely capture the role that marketing plays in society and the consequent effects and responsibilities of marketing activities. Because marketing is closely connected with various public issues, it invites constant scrutiny. Moreover, since marketing acts as an interface between an organization and the society in which it operates, marketers often carry much of the responsibility for dealing with social issues that affect their firms.

Marketing operates outside the firm. It responds to that outside environment and in turn is acted on by environmental influences. Relationships with employees, suppliers, the government, consumers, and society as a whole frame the social issues that marketers must address. The way that marketers deal with these social issues has a significant effect on their firm's eventual success. The diverse social issues that marketers face can be divided into two major categories: marketing ethics and social responsibility. While these two categories certainly overlap, this simple classification system provides a method for studying these issues.

Environmental influences have directed increased attention toward marketing ethics, defined as the marketer's standards of conduct and moral values. Ethics concern matters of right and wrong: the responsibility of individuals and firms to do what is morally right. As Figure 3.2 shows, each element of the marketing mix raises its own set of ethical questions. Before any improvements to a firm's marketing program can be made, each of them must be evaluated.

marketing ethics Marketers' standards of conduct and moral values.

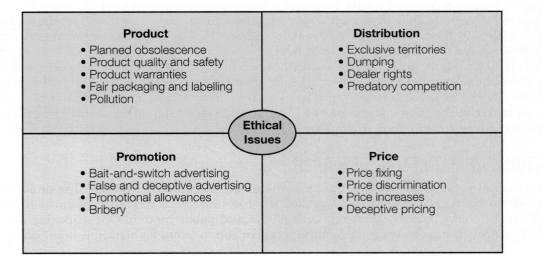

figure 3.2

Ethical Questions in Marketing

Marketoid

Vancouver telemarketer Dillon Sherif (a.k.a. Nuraldin Shareef Karim) was sentenced to more than 14 years in prison and ordered to pay restitution of nearly $1 million after he was convicted of scamming mainly U.S. senior citizens.

Creating an ethics program may be complicated and time consuming, but it is worthwhile. A code of ethics may mitigate some responsibility and help reduce some fines and sentences, but responsibility for its implementation ultimately rests with senior executives. If management doesn't openly support it, communicate its value internally, reward ethical behaviour, and punish unethical behaviour, its value becomes questionable. A step-by-step framework for building an effective program is shown in Figure 3.3. Because ethical behaviour is so important to business conduct, some firms and universities have taken an unusual step. They invite convicted corporate criminals to speak to employees and students about their mistakes and the consequences of their actions.[36]

Ensuring ethical practices means promising customers and business partners not to sacrifice quality and fairness for profit. In exchange, organizations hope for increased customer loyalty toward their brands. Yet issues involving marketing ethics are not always clear-cut. The issue of cigarette advertising, for example, has divided the ranks of advertising executives. Is it right for advertisers to promote a product that, while legal, has known health hazards?

For years, charges of unethical conduct have plagued the tobacco industry. In the largest civil settlement in history, tobacco manufacturers agreed to pay $206 billion (U.S.) to 46 U.S. states. Four other states—Florida, Minnesota, Mississippi, and Texas—had separate settlements totalling another $40 billion (U.S.). The settlement frees tobacco companies from claims for the cost of treating sick smokers. In Canada, British Columbia was the first province to launch a lawsuit against tobacco manufacturers, and by 2012, every province of Canada had launched a similar suit. The payoff in Canada will likely be much higher in Canada than in the United States because of Canada's public health care system, where health care costs are borne entirely by government. Canada's two most populous provinces—Ontario and Quebec—are seeking $50 billion and $60 billion respectively. In addition, Quebec has also certified a $27 billion class-action lawsuit on behalf of 1.8 million Quebec smokers. There are a reported 800 lawsuits against tobacco companies worldwide.[37]

People develop standards of ethical behaviour based on their own systems of values, which help them deal with ethical questions in their personal lives. However, the workplace may generate serious conflicts when individuals discover that their ethical beliefs are not necessarily in line with those of their employer. For example, employees may think that shopping online during a lunch break using a work computer is fine, but the company may decide otherwise. The quiz in Figure 3.4 highlights other everyday ethical dilemmas. (See pages 91–92 for the answers.)

How can these conflicts be resolved? In addition to individual and organizational ethics, individuals may be influenced by a third basis of ethical authority—a professional code of ethics that transcends both organizational and individual value systems. A professional peer association can exercise collective oversight to limit a marketer's individual behaviour. Any code of ethics must anticipate the variety of problems that marketers are likely to encounter. Promotional matters tend to receive the greatest attention, but ethical considerations also influence marketing research, product strategy, distribution strategy, and pricing.

ETHICS IN MARKETING RESEARCH

Invasion of personal privacy has become a critical issue in marketing research. The proliferation of databases, the selling of address lists, and the ease with which consumer information can be gathered through Internet technology have all increased public concern. One marketing research tool particularly problematic is the promise of cash or gifts in return for marketing information that

figure 3.4

Test Your Workplace Ethics

Workplace Ethics Quiz

The spread of technology into the workplace has raised a variety of new ethical questions, and many old ones still linger. Compare your answers with those of others surveyed on pages 91–92.

Office Technology

1. Is it wrong to use company email for personal reasons?
   ❑ Yes   ❑ No

2. Is it wrong to use office equipment to help your children or spouse do schoolwork?
   ❑ Yes   ❑ No

3. Is it wrong to play computer games on office equipment during the workday?
   ❑ Yes   ❑ No

4. Is it wrong to use office equipment to do Internet shopping?
   ❑ Yes   ❑ No

5. Is it unethical to blame an error you made on a technological glitch?
   ❑ Yes   ❑ No

6. Is it unethical to visit pornographic websites using office equipment?
   ❑ Yes   ❑ No

Gifts and Entertainment

7. What's the value at which a gift from a supplier or client becomes troubling?
   ❑ $25   ❑ $50   ❑ $100

8. Is a $50 gift to a boss unacceptable?
   ❑ Yes   ❑ No

9. Is a $50 gift from the boss unacceptable?
   ❑ Yes   ❑ No

10. Of gifts from suppliers: Is it okay to take a $200 pair of football tickets?
    ❑ Yes   ❑ No

11. Is it okay to take a $120 pair of theatre tickets?
    ❑ Yes   ❑ No

12. Is it okay to take a $100 holiday food basket?
    ❑ Yes   ❑ No

13. Is it okay to take a $25 gift certificate?
    ❑ Yes   ❑ No

14. Can you accept a $75 prize won at a raffle at a supplier's conference?
    ❑ Yes   ❑ No

Truth and Lies

15. Due to on-the-job pressure, have you ever abused or lied about sick days?
    ❑ Yes   ❑ No

16. Due to on-the-job pressure, have you ever taken credit for someone else's work or idea?
    ❑ Yes   ❑ No

Source: Ethics and Compliance Officer Association (ECOA), Waltham, Massachusetts, USA, and Ethical Leadership Group, a NAVEX Global company, Lake Oswego, Oregon, USA. Surveys sampled a cross-section of workers at large companies across the United States. Used with permission from the ECOA.

can then be sold to direct marketers. Consumers commonly disclose their demographic information in return for an email newsletter or a favourite magazine.

Privacy issues have mushroomed with the growth of the Internet, with huge consequences for both consumers and marketers. During the busy 2013 Christmas season, a data security breach at Target resulted in the theft of personal information of more than 70 million customers. CEO Gregg Steinhafel promised that customers would have "zero liability for the cost of any fraudulent charges arising from the breach." Further, customers involved would have free credit monitoring and identity theft protection for one year.[38] Not all privacy issues arise because of criminal activity. Americans—and many affected people and governments around the world—were upset when they learned that the U.S. National Security Agency was spying on them. While Google, Facebook, and other Internet giants pressure the U.S. government to change the way they gather intelligence, data centres in Canada are positioning themselves for added business. The Canadian Cloud Council CEO Robert Hart says, "I think right now Canadian and international organizations have a monumental opportunity to capture a lot of business from organizations that no longer want to deal with the States." The cloud computing market is expected to be worth $200 billion by 2016, and the United States could lose as much as $35 billion due to declining international confidence in U.S. data security.[39] Canadians concerned about Internet privacy can get a lot of information from the Electronic Commerce Branch of Industry Canada at **www.ic.gc .ca/eic/site/ecic-ceac.nsf/eng/home** and by exploring its various programs and services. The Canadian Marketing Association also provides valuable services for Canadian consumers at **www .the-cma.org**. The site gives tips for protecting your privacy, dealing with spam, identifying fraudulent offers, and resolving complaints. You may also register online for its Do Not Contact service. This will reduce the number of contacts you receive because members of the Canadian

Marketoid

Canada has enacted anti-spam legislation that came into effect in 2014. Fines for noncompliance can be very costly: up to $1 million for individuals and up to $10 million for corporations.

BusinessEthics.ca is a Canadian resource for business ethics. Concern with business ethics has led to the growth of ethics institutes across Canada.

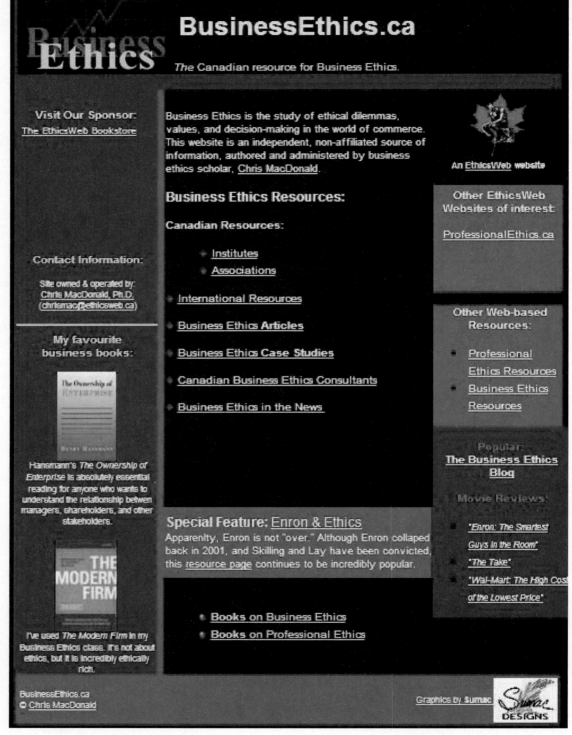

Dr. Chris MacDonald, Ryerson University

Marketing Association agree to not contact registered users. Canadians can also visit the Canadian Radio-television and Telecommunications Commission website at **www.lnnte-dncl.gc.ca/ index-eng** and register on Canada's National Do-Not-Call List, hoping to reduce the number of unwanted calls they receive.

ETHICS IN PRODUCT STRATEGY

Product quality, planned obsolescence, brand similarity, and packaging questions all raise ethical issues. Feeling the competition, some marketers have tried packaging practices that might be considered misleading, deceptive, or unethical. Larger packages take up more shelf space, and consumers notice them. An odd-sized package makes price comparisons difficult. Bottles with concave bottoms give the impression that they contain more liquid than they actually do. Are these packaging practices justified in the name of competition, or are they deceptive? Growing regulatory mandates appear to be narrowing the range of discretion in this area.

How do you evaluate the quality of a product like a beverage? By flavour or by ingredients? Citing several studies, some consumer advocates say that the ingredients in soft drinks—mainly the high sugar content—can be linked to obesity in consumers, particularly children. Not surprisingly, the beverage industry disagrees, arguing that lack of exercise and a poor diet in general are greater contributors to weight gain than regular consumption of soft drinks.

K-cups (54-pack, 80-pack, and 100-pack) all come in over-size cartons. The cartons in this photo, all from different manufacturers, are "full."

ETHICS IN DISTRIBUTION

Two ethical issues influence a firm's decisions regarding distribution strategy:

1. What is the appropriate degree of control over the distribution channel?

2. Should a company distribute its products in marginally profitable outlets that have no alternative source of supply?

The question of channel control typically arises in relationships between manufacturers and franchise dealers. For example, should an automobile dealership, a gas station, or a fast food outlet be forced to purchase parts, materials, and supplementary services from the parent organization?

The second question concerns marketers' responsibility to serve unsatisfied market segments even if the profit potential is slight. Should marketers serve retail stores in low-income areas, serve users of limited amounts of the firm's product, or serve a declining rural market? These problems are difficult to resolve because they often involve individuals rather than broad segments of the general public. An important first step is to ensure that the firm consistently enforces its channel policies.

ETHICS IN PROMOTION

Promotion raises many ethical questions, because it is the most direct link between a firm and its customers. Personal selling has always been a target of criticism—and jokes about untrustworthiness. Used-car dealers, horse traders, and purveyors of quick remedies have been the targets of such barbs. But promotion covers many areas, ranging from advertising to direct marketing—and it is vital for marketers to monitor their ethics in all marketing communications. Truth in advertising— representing accurately a product's benefits and drawbacks, warranties, price, and availability—is the bedrock of ethics in promotion.

Marketing to children has been under close scrutiny for many years because children have not yet developed the skills to receive marketing messages critically. They simply believe everything they see and hear. With childhood obesity a serious concern in Canada, Kellogg Company announced it would change how it advertises its breakfast cereals to children worldwide, focusing solely on products that meet nutrition guidelines. Other organizations such as General Mills, Kraft Foods, and Quaker Oats pledged to also emphasize healthy choices. However, the Internet has become a new landscape of advertising to children, and this raises potential concerns as discussed in the "Solving an Ethical Controversy" feature.

SOLVING AN ETHICAL CONTROVERSY   Are Your Kids Virtually Unhealthy?

JUST when we seem to have the issue of advertising to children somewhat under control, along comes advergaming: a free online game that promotes a particular product, service, or company by integrating it into the game. These games increasingly target children and often promote unhealthy foods loaded with fat, sugar, and sodium. Among the prominent products are Pop Tarts, Honey Nut Cheerios, Apple Jacks, Dr Pepper, and Oreo cookies. A KFC advergame, Snack in the Face, allows players to win KFC snacks. Recent research demonstrated that children who play games featuring unhealthy foods ate 56 percent more unhealthy snacks than those who played games featuring healthy foods and 16 percent more than children in a control group who played games without any featured foods.

Advergames engage children for periods of time considerably longer than traditional television advertising that characteristically lasts for 30 seconds and actually require active engagement and interaction rather than simply passive viewing. While advertising clearly separates program content—the show—from the advertisement, advergames blur the line since advertising is the entertainment.

Should advergaming be left to industry self-regulation by the companies that sponsor them, even when they clearly target children?

PRO

1. It should be parents' responsibility to educate children to make healthy food choices.
2. Providing engaging experiences for consumers, young and older, is a logical extension of advertising in today's connected world.

CON

1. Winning at the game—for example, filling up a bottle of Dr Pepper by matching an array of sweets on the screen—encourages children to want unhealthy products in the real world.
2. Many manufacturers have promised to responsibly advertise their products to children, but some seem to be failing in this new landscape of advertising.

Where do you stand: pro or con?

Sources: Sandra Jones and Jeffrey Thom, "Advergames Play with Nutrition by Making Fast Food Rewarding," **http://theconversation.com**, December 6, 2013; Susan Krashinsky, "Advertising Food to Children Moves from TV to Online Games," **www.theglobeandmail.com**, October 17, 2013; Anna Almendraia, "'Advergames' That Market Food to Children Push Mostly Junk, Study Says," **www.huffingtonpost.com**, October 9, 2013; Alice Park, "Can Online Games Influence What Kids Eat?" **http://heartland.time.com**, January 10, 2012, all accessed January 14, 2014.

Promoting certain products to postsecondary students can raise ethical questions as well. These students are a prime market for firms that sell such products as electronics and beer. And although laws prohibit the sale of alcohol to students who are under the legal drinking age, companies often advertise beer through popular items such as hats, shirts, bar signs, and other collectible items.

ETHICS IN PRICING

Pricing is probably the most regulated aspect of a firm's marketing strategy. As a result, most unethical price behaviour is also illegal. Some aspects of pricing, however, are still open to ethics abuses. For example, should some customers pay more for merchandise if distribution costs are higher in their areas? Do marketers have an obligation to warn vendors and customers of impending price, discount, or return policy changes?

Some credit card companies target consumers with poor credit ratings and offer them what industry observers call "subprime" or "fee-harvesting" credit cards. Under such an arrangement, the company lures consumers to sign up for the card, promising to improve their credit rating. The cardholder is then charged exorbitant annual fees, leaving them in worse financial shape than before.[40] Some retailers have a reputation for approving applicants who have a poor credit rating. Unfortunately, the cards can be used only at that retailer's, they have low credit limits, and customers are charged high interest payments. While consumers are almost always informed of credit card terms on their agreements, the print is usually tiny and the language hard to understand. For instance, a credit card issuer might advertise the benefits of its premium card. But the fine print explains that the firm is allowed to substitute a different plan—with a higher interest rate—if the applicant doesn't qualify for the premium card.

All these concerns must be dealt with in developing a professional ethic for pricing products. The ethical issues involved in pricing for today's highly competitive and increasingly computerized markets are discussed in greater detail in Chapter 16.

SOCIAL RESPONSIBILITY IN MARKETING

⑧ **Identify the four levels of the social responsibility pyramid.**

Companies can do business in such a way that everyone benefits—customers, the companies themselves, and society as a whole. While ethical business practices are vital to a firm's long-term survival and growth, **social responsibility** raises the bar even higher. In marketing, social responsibility involves accepting an obligation to give equal weight to profits, consumer satisfaction, and social well-being in evaluating a firm's performance. In addition to measuring sales, revenues, and profits, a firm must also consider ways in which it has contributed to the overall well-being of its customers and society.

social responsibility Marketing philosophies, policies, procedures, and actions that have the enhancement of society's welfare as a primary objective.

Social responsibility allows a wide range of opportunities for companies to shine. If they are reluctant at first, government legislation can mandate socially responsible actions. Government may require firms to take socially responsible actions in matters of environmental policy, deceptive product claims, and other areas. Also, consumers, through their power to repeat or withhold purchases, may force marketers to provide honest and relevant information and fair prices. The four dimensions of social responsibility—economic, legal, ethical, and philanthropic—are shown in Figure 3.5. The first two dimensions have long been recognized, but ethical obligations and the need for marketers to be good corporate citizens have increased in importance in recent years.

figure 3.5

The Four-Step Pyramid of Corporate Social Responsibility

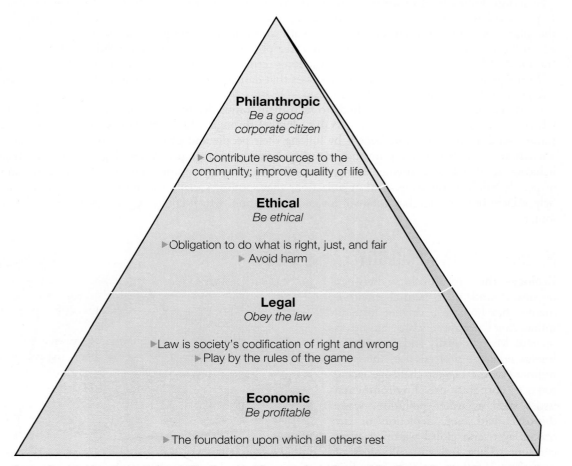

Philanthropic
Be a good corporate citizen

▶Contribute resources to the community; improve quality of life

Ethical
Be ethical

▶Obligation to do what is right, just, and fair
▶ Avoid harm

Legal
Obey the law

▶Law is society's codification of right and wrong
▶ Play by the rules of the game

Economic
Be profitable

▶The foundation upon which all others rest

Source: Reprinted from Archie B. Carroll, "The Pyramid of Corporate Social Responsibility: Toward the Moral Management of Organizational Stakeholder," Business Horizons 34, July-August, 1991, with permission from Elsevier.

The locus for socially responsible decisions in organizations has always been an important issue. But who should accept specific accountability for the social effects of marketing decisions? Responses include the district sales manager, the marketing vice president, the firm's CEO, and even the board of directors. Probably the most valid assessment holds that all marketers, regardless of their stations in the organization, remain accountable for the social aspects of their decisions.

MARKETING'S RESPONSIBILITIES

The concept of business' social responsibility traditionally has concerned managers' relationships with customers, employees, and shareholders. In general, managers traditionally have felt responsible for providing quality products at reasonable prices for customers, adequate wages and decent working environments for employees, and acceptable profits for shareholders. Only occasionally did the concept extend to relations with the government and rarely with the general public.

Today, corporate responsibility has expanded to cover the entire societal framework. A decision to temporarily delay the installation of a pollution-control device may satisfy the traditional sense of responsibility. Customers would continue to receive an uninterrupted supply of the plant's products, employees would not face layoffs, and shareholders would still receive reasonable returns on their investments. Contemporary business ethics, however, would not accept this choice as socially responsible.

Contemporary marketing decisions must consider their global effect. Some clothing manufacturers and retailers have come under fire for buying from foreign suppliers who force employees to work in dangerous conditions or pay less than a living wage. The illegally constructed Rana Plaza collapsed in 2013, killing 1,129 workers in Bangladesh, the worst garment industry disaster in history. Approximately 30 brands of clothing were manufactured at the complex, including Loblaw Companies' Joe Fresh. To its credit, Loblaw Companies was among the first to take action. Following its own inspections, the company immediately pulled out of seven factories. It promised to compensate directly the employees of New Wave Style who were employed at the plaza—victims or their dependants—with three months wages. Loblaw has also donated $1 million to help victims with medical care, physical therapy, mobility aids, and vocational training.[41] Marketers must also consider the long-term effects of their decisions and the well-being of future generations. Manufacturing processes that damage the environment or that use up natural energy resources are easy targets for criticism.

Marketers can use several methods to help their companies behave in socially responsible ways. Chapter 1 discussed cause marketing as one channel through which companies can promote social causes—and at the same time benefit by linking their people and products to worthy undertakings. Socially responsible marketing involves campaigns that encourage people to adopt socially beneficial behaviours, such as safe driving, eating more nutritious food, or improving the working conditions of people half a world away. And organizations that sponsor socially responsible programs not only help society but also develop goodwill for an organization, which could help the bottom line in the long run.

MARKETING AND ECOLOGY

Ecology—the relationship between organisms and their natural environments—has become a driving force in influencing the ways in which businesses operate. Many industry and government leaders rank the protection of the environment as the biggest challenge facing today's corporations. Environmental issues such as water pollution, waste disposal, acid rain, depletion of the ozone layer, and global warming affect everyone. They influence all areas of marketing decision making, including product planning and public relations,

Several manufacturers of printer cartridges provide postage-paid envelopes so consumers can mail back the empty cartridges for recycling.

© Maurice Savage/Alamy

spanning such topics as planned obsolescence, pollution control, recycling waste materials, and resource conservation.

In creating new-product offerings that respond to consumer demands for convenience by offering extremely short-lived products, such as disposable diapers, ballpoint pens, razors, and cameras, marketers occasionally find themselves accused of intentionally offering products with limited durability—in other words, of practising planned obsolescence. In addition to convenience-oriented items, other products become obsolete when rapid changes in technology create superior alternatives. In the computer industry, changes take place so quickly that every province now has environmental handling fees that are charged when consumers purchase electronic products. For example, the fee charged when a desktop computer is purchased ranges from $3.00 in Ontario to $15.00 in Manitoba and Saskatchewan.[42]

Public concern about pollution of such natural resources as water and air affects some industries, such as pharmaceuticals or heavy-goods manufacturing, more than others. Still, the marketing system annually generates billions of tons of packaging materials such as glass, metal, paper, and plastics that add to the world's growing piles of trash and waste. Recycling such materials, as many manufacturers do, is another important aspect of ecology. Recycling can benefit society by saving natural resources and energy as well as by alleviating a major factor in environmental pollution—waste disposal.

Unwanted and outdated electronic waste is the latest trash to overrun landfills as technology advances motivate Canadians to ditch their old electronics for newer models. Increasingly, consumers wonder how to dispose of their old computers, monitors, printers, TVs, phones, cameras, and other gadgets, especially since many of the older models contain lead and other hazardous materials requiring special handling. Best Buy and Future Shop sponsor a recycling program under which customers can drop off a wide variety of unwanted electronics products—even if they weren't bought at their store.[43] There are some restrictions at specific store locations.

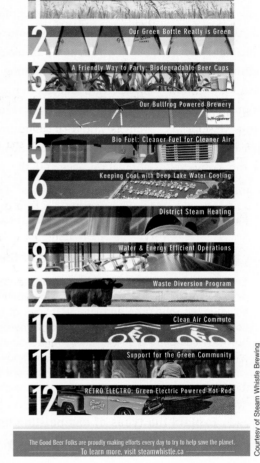

STEAM WHISTLE BREWING'S
GREEN initiatives

Steam Whistle Brewing strives to be a model green manufacturer, crafting our all-natural Pilsner while minimizing our environmental footprint.

1 All Natural Ingredients
2 Our Green Bottle Really is Green
3 A Friendly Way to Party: Biodegradable Beer Cups
4 Our Bullfrog Powered Brewery
5 Bio Fuel: Cleaner Fuel for Cleaner Air
6 Keeping Cool with Deep Lake Water Cooling
7 District Steam Heating
8 Water & Energy Efficient Operations
9 Waste Diversion Program
10 Clean Air Commute
11 Support for the Green Community
12 RETRO ELECTRO: Green Electric Powered Hot Rod

The Good Beer Folks are proudly making efforts every day to try to help save the planet. To learn more, visit steamwhistle.ca

Courtesy of Steam Whistle Brewing

The good beer folks at Steam Whistle Brewing proudly strive to minimize their environmental footprint.

Many companies respond to consumers' growing concern about ecological issues through **green marketing**—the production, promotion, and reclamation of environmentally sensitive products. In the green marketing revolution of the early 1990s, marketers were quick to tie their companies and products to ecological themes. Consumers have responded by purchasing more and more of these goods, providing profits and opportunities for growth to the companies that make and sell them. The Sustainability Consortium, an independent organization dedicated to driving sustainability in consumer goods, is working with companies such as Dell, HP, Toshiba, and Walmart to create standards to help consumers make green choices in electronics.[44] The Motel 6 chain and Sofitel and Studio 6 brands—all part of the Accor North America portfolio—committed to a green rating program after Accor piloted it recently. Three of Marriott's brands—Courtyard, Residence Inn, and TownPlace Suites—have earned certification by the U.S. Green Building Council. And Fairmont Hotels & Resorts was recently named one of the top five eco-friendly hotel chains by a leading environmental organization, and one of Canada's 2013 greenest employers.[45]

green marketing Production, promotion, and reclamation of environmentally sensitive products.

assessment check 8

8.1 Identify the four levels of the social responsibility pyramid.

8.2 What are the benefits of green marketing?

Strategic Implications

Marketing decisions that businesses make are influenced by changes in the competitive, political-legal, economic, technological, and social-cultural environments. Marketing ethics and social responsibility will continue to play important roles in business transactions in your hometown and around the globe.

As the Internet and the rapid changes in technology that it represents are fully absorbed into the competitive environment, competition is even more intense than before. Much of the competition will result from innovations in technology and scientific discoveries. Business in the 21st century is propelled by information technologies, but sustained by creative thinking and the willingness of marketers to meet challenges. Marketers will face new regulations as the political and legal environment responds to changes in Canada and abroad. As the population ages and the social-cultural environment evolves, marketers will seek to meet the demands for new goods and services for consumers, such as increased health-related merchandise. As always, they will try to anticipate and make the most of every opportunity afforded by the business cycle.

Ethics and social responsibility must underlie everything that marketers do in the 21st century—those who find ways to "do well by doing good" will succeed. ◆◆◆

REVIEW OF CHAPTER OBJECTIVES

① **Identify the five components of the marketing environment.**

The five components of the marketing environment are (1) *the competitive environment*—the interactive process that occurs in the marketplace as competing organizations seek to satisfy markets; (2) *the political-legal environment*—the laws and interpretations of laws that require firms to operate under competitive conditions and to protect consumer rights; (3) *the economic environment*—environmental factors resulting from business fluctuations and resulting variations in inflation rates and employment levels; (4) *the technological environment*—applications to marketing of knowledge based on discoveries in science, inventions, and innovations; and (5) *the social-cultural environment*—the component of the marketing environment consisting of the relationship among the marketer and society and its culture.

② **Explain the types of competition marketers face and the steps necessary for developing a competitive strategy.**

Three types of competition exist: (1) direct competition among marketers of similar products; (2) competition among goods or services that can be substituted for one another; and (3) competition among all organizations that vie for the consumer's purchasing power. To develop a competitive strategy, marketers must answer the following questions: (1) Should we compete? The answer depends on the firm's available resources and objectives as well as its expected profit potential. (2) If so, in what markets should we compete? This question requires marketers to make product, pricing, distribution, and promotional decisions that give their firm a competitive advantage. (3) How should we compete? This question requires marketers to make the technical decisions involved in setting a comprehensive marketing strategy.

③ **Describe how marketing activities are regulated and how marketers can influence the political-legal environment.**

Marketing activities are influenced by federal, provincial and territorial, and municipal laws that require firms to operate under competitive conditions and to protect consumer rights. The Competition Act, administered by Industry Canada, is the most comprehensive legislation in Canada. Government regulatory agencies can provide advice and assistance to Canadian businesses or, like the National Energy Board, can have responsibility to regulate specific industries. Public and private consumer interest groups and industry self-regulatory groups also affect marketing activities. Marketers can seek to influence public opinion and legislative actions through advertising, political action committees, and political lobbying.

④ **Outline the economic factors that affect marketing decisions and consumer buying power.**

The primary economic factors are (1) the stage in the business cycle, (2) inflation and deflation, (3) unemployment, (4) income, and (5) resource availability. All are vitally important to marketers because of their effects on consumers' willingness to buy and consumers' perceptions regarding changes in the marketing mix variables.

⑤ **Discuss the impact of the technological environment on a firm's marketing activities.**

The technological environment consists of applications to marketing of knowledge based on discoveries in science, inventions, and innovations. This knowledge can provide marketing opportunities. It results in new products and improves existing ones, and it is a frequent source of price reductions through new production methods or materials. Technological applications also pose a threat because they can make existing products obsolete overnight. The technological environment demands that marketers continually adapt to change, since its scope of influence reaches into consumers' lifestyles, competitors' products, and industrial users' demands.

⑥ **Explain how the social-cultural environment influences marketing.**

The social-cultural environment is the relationship among marketing, society, and culture. To remain competitive, marketers must be sensitive to society's demographic shifts and changing values, which affect consumers' reactions to different products and marketing practices. Marketers must consider the increasing importance of cultural diversity, both in Canada and abroad. Changing societal values have led to consumerism. Consumerism is the social force within the environment designed to aid and protect the consumer by exerting legal, moral, and economic pressures on business. Consumer rights include the following: (1) the right to choose freely, (2) the right to be informed, (3) the right to be heard, and (4) the right to be safe.

⑦ **Describe the ethical issues in marketing.**

Marketing ethics encompass the marketer's standards of conduct and moral values. Each element of the marketing mix raises its own set of ethical questions. Ethics in product strategy may involve quality and safety, packaging and labelling, and pollution. Ethics in distribution may involve territorial decisions. In promotion, ethical issues include honesty in advertising and promotion to children. Pricing may raise questions about price fixing and discrimination, price increases, and deceptive pricing.

⑧ **Identify the four levels of the social responsibility pyramid.**

The four dimensions of social responsibility are (1) *economic*—to be profitable, the foundation upon which the other three levels of the pyramid rest; (2) *legal*—to obey the law, society's codification of right and wrong; (3) *ethical*—to do what is right, just, and fair and to avoid wrong doing; (4) *philanthropic*—to be a good corporate citizen, contributing to the community and improving quality of life.

assessment check answers ✓

1.1 Define *environmental scanning*.
Environmental scanning is the process of collecting information about the external marketing environment to identify and interpret potential trends.

1.2 How does environmental scanning contribute to environmental management?
Environmental scanning contributes to environmental management by providing current information about the five different environments so marketers can predict and influence changes.

2.1 Distinguish between direct and indirect competition and give an example of each.
Direct competition occurs among marketers of similar products, such as supermarkets or gas stations. Indirect competition involves products that are easily substituted. Pizza could compete with chicken wings or tacos. A trip to Canada's Wonderland could compete with a trip to a Toronto Blue Jays game.

2.2 What is time-based competition?
Time-based competition is the strategy of developing and distributing goods and services more quickly than competitors.

3.1 What are the purposes of the Competition Act?
The purposes of the Competition Act are to foster competition and protect consumers, both of which are necessary to have a healthy marketplace.

3.2 Name a self-regulatory group and describe its mission.
Advertising Standards Canada is the advertising industry's self-regulatory body. Its mission is to ensure the integrity and viability of advertising in Canada.

4.1 Identify and describe briefly the four stages of the business cycle.

The four stages of the business cycle are prosperity, recession, depression, and recovery. During prosperity, companies introduce new products, spend on promotion, and expand distribution. Consumer spending is at its highest. In a recession, consumer spending drops. Companies use special offers to increase demand and may introduce value-priced products. In a depression, consumer spending is at its lowest. During recovery, consumer spending increases, but businesses face uncertainty as they must earn a profit while trying to manage uncertain consumer demand.

4.2 Explain how inflation and income affect consumer buying decisions.

Inflation devalues money and therefore may restrict some purchasing, particularly goods and services that are not considered necessary. Income also influences consumer buying power—the more discretionary income a household has, the more goods and services can be purchased.

5.1 What are some of the consumer benefits of technology?

Technology can lead to new or improved goods and services, offer better customer service, and reduce prices. It can also address social concerns.

5.2 Why must marketers monitor the technological environment?

Marketers need to monitor the technological environment in order to stay current with—and possibly ahead of—competitors. If they don't, they may wind up with obsolete offerings.

6.1 Define *consumerism*.

Consumerism is a social force within the environment that aids and protects the buyer by exerting legal, moral, and economic pressures on business.

6.2 Identify the four consumer rights.

The four consumer rights are as follows: the right to choose freely, the right to be informed, the right to be heard, and the right to be safe.

7.1 Define *marketing ethics*.

Marketing ethics refers to the marketer's standards of conduct and moral values.

7.2 Identify the five areas in which ethics can be a problem.

The five areas of ethical concern for marketers are marketing research, product strategy, distribution, promotion, and pricing.

8.1 Identify the four levels of the social responsibility pyramid.

The four levels of social responsibility are economic, legal, ethical, and philanthropic.

8.2 What are the benefits of green marketing?

Green marketing, which responds to consumers' growing concerns about ecological issues, offers consumers high-quality products without health risks or damage to the environment. Many industries, including appliances, consumer electronics, construction, and hospitality, are finding that incorporating green practices rejuvenates their business.

MARKETING TERMS YOU NEED TO KNOW

These terms are printed in blue in the text. They are defined in the margins of the chapter and in the Glossary that begins on p. G-1.

environmental scanning 62	Competition Act 67	VoIP—Voice over Internet Protocol 76
environmental management 63	gross domestic product (GDP) 70	social-cultural environment 77
strategic alliance 63	economic environment 70	consumerism 77
competitive environment 63	business cycle 71	consumer rights 78
monopoly 63	inflation 72	marketing ethics 79
oligopoly 64	unemployment 72	social responsibility 85
competitive strategy 65	discretionary income 73	green marketing 87
time-based competition 66	demarketing 74	
political-legal environment 66	technological environment 75	

PROJECT AND TEAMWORK EXERCISES

1. With a classmate, choose two firms that compete directly with each other. Select two of the following or choose your own. Then develop a competitive strategy for your firm while your partner develops a strategy for his or hers. Present the two strategies to the class. How are they similar? How are they different?
   a. Home Depot and Rona or Lowe's
   b. Apple and Samsung or BlackBerry
   c. Paramount Canada's Wonderland and Six Flags La

   Ronde or Vancouver's Playland
   d. Visa and MasterCard or American Express
   e. Bell Canada and Rogers Communications or Telus
   f. Tim Hortons and Starbucks or Second Cup

2. Track your own consumer purchasing decisions as they relate to your income. Compare your decisions during the academic year and the summer. Do you have a summer job that increases your income? How does that affect your decisions?

3. Canada Post essentially enjoys a monopoly on the delivery of most mail. With a classmate, develop a strategy for a business that would compete with Canada Post in areas that firms such as Purolator, UPS, FedEx, and DHL do not already address.

4. Choose one of the following products. Working in pairs or small groups, present arguments for and against having Canada impose certain regulations on the advertising of your product. (Note that some products already do have regulations—you can argue for or against them.)
   a. alcoholic beverages
   b. smokeless tobacco
   c. casinos or provincial lotteries
   d. prescription medications

5. With a classmate, research one of the recent large cases involving unethical and illegal activities by executives for companies such as Enron, MCI, Nortel Networks, Martha Stewart Living Omnimedia, and Hollinger International. Describe the charges made against these executives and the outcome. Do you think they were fairly charged and punished? Why or why not?

CRITICAL THINKING EXERCISES

1. Environmental scanning is important for any business wanting to identify important trends that may affect its future marketing actions. Identify five current trends that are predicted to have a major influence on Canadian businesses in the next decade. Explain how or whether each of these trends will affect you personally as a consumer.

2. Suppose you and a friend want to start a company that markets frozen fish dinners. What are some of the questions about the competitive environment that you would like to have answered before you begin production? How will you determine who your customers are likely to be? How will you reach them?

3. The social-cultural environment can have a strong influence on the decisions marketers must make. In recent years, animal rights groups have targeted the manufacture and sale of foie gras, a European food delicacy made from goose and duck liver. Activists cite the cruel treatment of these birds, while chefs and restaurant owners claim otherwise. Animal rights groups are pressuring restaurants to stop serving foie gras. Others argue that consumers should be allowed a choice. What aspects of the social-cultural environment are affecting the marketing of foie gras? Which of the other components of the marketing environment may come into play, and how?

4. Approximately 400 million rebates—worth about $6 billion—are offered to Canadian and U.S. consumers by marketers every year. But do consumers like them? Often rebates require more effort than a consumer is willing to make to receive the cash back. Critics of the promotional effort say that marketers know this—and are banking on consumers' not redeeming them, resulting in extra income for retailers and manufacturers. Do you think rebate programs are ethical? Why or why not?

5. The disposal of nuclear waste has been an ongoing public safety issue, one with which marketers who work for nuclear power companies must deal. Most of Canada's nuclear waste is stored in Ontario, but smaller amounts exist in Quebec and New Brunswick. The Ontario government has been trying to negotiate nuclear storage at several Ontario towns but has met considerable resistance. Supporters argue that this is important to building Ontario's nuclear power capacity, while critics are skeptical of its safety and usefulness. As a marketer, how would you approach this issue?

ETHICS EXERCISE

Some retail firms protect their inventory against theft by locking their premises after hours even though maintenance and other workers are inside the stores working all night. Employees have charged that they are forbidden to leave the premises during work hours and that during an emergency, such as illness or injury, precious time is lost waiting for a manager to arrive who is authorized to unlock the doors. Although workers could open an emergency exit, in some cases they claim that they will be fired for doing so.

Employers assert that managers with keys are on the premises (or minutes away) and that locking employees in ensures their own safety as well as cutting down on costly "shrinkage."

1. Under what circumstances, if any, do you think locking employees in at night is appropriate?

2. If you feel this practice is appropriate, what safeguards do you think should be put into effect? What responsibilities do employers and employees have in such circumstances?

ETHICS QUIZ ANSWERS

Here is how others have responded to the quiz on page 81.
1. 34 percent said personal email on company computers is wrong.
2. 37 percent said using office equipment for schoolwork is wrong.
3. 49 percent said playing computer games at work is wrong.
4. 54 percent said Internet shopping at work is wrong.
5. 61 percent said it is unethical to blame your error on technology.
6. 87 percent said it's unethical to visit pornographic sites at work.

7. 33 percent said $25 is the amount at which a gift from a supplier or client becomes troubling, while 33 percent said $50, and 33 percent said $100.
8. 35 percent said a $50 gift to the boss is unacceptable.
9. 12 percent said a $50 gift from the boss is unacceptable.
10. 70 percent said it's unacceptable to take the $200 football tickets.
11. 70 percent said it's unacceptable to take the $120 theatre tickets.
12. 35 percent said it's unacceptable to take the $100 food basket.
13. 45 percent said it's unacceptable to take the $25 gift certificate.
14. 40 percent said it's unacceptable to take the $75 raffle prize.
15. 11 percent reported they lied about sick days.
16. 4 percent reported they have taken credit for the work or ideas of others.

CASE 3.1

PWYW: Doing Well by Doing Good

Have you ever had an occasion where you could simply PWYW (pay what you want)? Some venues refer to this as PWYC (pay what you can). Of course you have. Think about tips. You may refuse to leave a tip, and there is no limit to how much you may tip: 100 percent, or even more. The PWYW model has been used often in theatre, for example. Canada's National Arts Centre in Ottawa; the Neptune Theatre in Halifax, Nova Scotia; Theatre Calgary, in Calgary, Alberta; and the Citadel Theatre in Edmonton, Alberta, all have performances where patrons are free to choose what they pay. The Bata Shoe Museum in Toronto has a PWYW admission every Thursday evening, with a suggested donation of $5. The band Radiohead made headlines in 2007 when it launched its album *In Rainbows*. Few outside of the band really know whether the band made more money than it would have had it used the more traditional distribution model.

Panera Bread Co. operates 1,761 locations across 45 U.S. states and in Ontario in Canada. It has been experimenting with PWYW pricing for several years. After seeing how demoralizing it can be for a person waiting for a handout, Panera's president Ron Shaich—since named chairman of the board and CEO—converted three locations into a separate not-for-profit operation. It has since expanded to five locations, and there are now 48 locations that sell the company's turkey chili as a PWYW item. The menu at the not-for-profit locations is the same as elsewhere in the popular salad and sandwich chain, but a donation box and the honour system replace the cash register in what Shaich calls "community cafés of shared responsibility." These Panera locations do not charge for meals. Instead, customers get receipts with their orders that explain what the meal would have cost in a conventional Panera store.

About 60 percent of customers leave the suggested amount; 20 percent leave more; and the remainder pay less or nothing. The PWYW model generates 70 to 80 percent of the revenue produced in the company's for-profit stores, an amount Shaich calls enough to make a profit while doing good. Customers are requested to come no more than once a day for the PWYW opportunity. Those who come in a few times a week to have a meal are asked to volunteer in the store, in keeping with posted signs reading, "We are not about a handout. We are about a hand up for those who really need it."

University of California professor Leif Nelson has some interesting results from one research study where the PWYW option was combined with a charitable cause. His study included people who were offered an opportunity to purchase a funfair keepsake at a specified price, and the rest were told they could pay whatever price they chose. At the specified price, sales were increased only a small amount when people were informed of the charitable affiliation. However, in the PWYW option, when customers were told that 50 percent of the price they paid would go to charity, significantly higher profit was generated. Clearly, doing good can be profitable.

Questions for Critical Thinking

1. When the PWYW model is used by a for-profit business, is it simply "a marketing ploy." Explain your reasoning.
2. Panera donates millions in cash and food each year but feels the cafés allow a direct connection to those in need. Why would that matter?

Sources: Company websites, **www.panerabread.com**; **www.batashoemuseum .ca**; **www.neptunetheatre.com**; **http://nac-cna.ca**; **http://theatrecalgary.com**; **www.citadeltheatre.com**, January 16, 2014; Colette Symanowitz, "Pay What You Want: Does It Work?" *Finweek*, May 9, 2013, pp. 42–44.

CASE 3.2

Steam Whistle Brewing: Doing the Right Thing, Really, Really Well

Why would a company wish to be "green"? For the very cynical, the answer is simply that it would not; that is, unless it is forced due to government regulation—enforced to protect the environment. Those who are less cynical might suggest that it would do so to get a competitive advantage, leading to future rewards. Maybe it would like to be first among competitors to promote its "greenness." This, of course, assumes that stakeholders value green companies, and there is increasing evidence that investors, customers, and employees all value companies that are socially responsible. There is a third reason: altruism. It might be difficult to prove altruism as the motive for greening a company, but surely there are companies owned or managed by people who simply want to "do the right thing."

One company that has been doing the right thing since its inception is Toronto-based Steam Whistle Brewing, not only leading its industry in green initiatives but arguably North America's greenest brewery. What makes Steam Whistle Brewing so green?

The company prides itself on "doing one thing, really, really well." Since its first beer came off the production line in 2000, Steam Whistle Brewing has made a single product: a Pilsner of exceptional quality. While beers can have upwards of 100 or more ingredients, Steam Whistle's Pilsner has only four: pure spring water, malted barley, hops, and yeast, all GMO-free—that is, free of genetically modified organisms. Although listing beer ingredients is not required in Canada, Steam Whistle Brewing proudly lists its ingredients on every bottle. And, every day, 110,000 green bottles go through the production line. These unique bottles contain 30 percent more glass than regular beer bottles, so they can be recycled up to 45 times, about three times more than other bottles. The company's logo is painted on each bottle, replacing the need for paper labels. This saves trees but also reduces the contaminants from glue and ink that would result from washing paper labels from used bottles. Steam Whistle Brewing proudly recycles every element it can from its packaging line, including broken glass, old bottle caps, cardboard cartons, and even shrink wrap, resulting in 94 percent of waste from operations being diverted from landfill. It was the first Canadian brewery to use 100-percent biodegradable cups for outdoor events. Made from cornstarch resin, these cups are completely compostable within 50 days. Leftover edibles at the company's several hundred events held each year are donated to a local street mission or a women's shelter. Organic waste unfit for consumption is composted. Even the "spent grain" from the brewing process is recycled. It is shipped to farmers to use for animal feed.

Since 2006, Canada Clean Fuels has been supplying biodiesel B20 fuel so that the Steam Whistle truck fleet has an environmentally friendly fuel alternative. This B20 biofuel is a mixture of soya and recycled cooking oils from restaurants. In 2011, the company added a new truck to its vintage fleet: a 1958 Chevy Apache, which it dubbed "Retro Electro." The custom-built truck was rescued from a metal scrap heap and was retrofitted with a high-efficiency electric motor. Steam Whistle Brewing gets its electricity from Bullfrog Power, a provider of green power, sourced from wind and hydro facilities that have been certified by Environment Canada as low impact and currently available in six of Canada's provinces.

To provide a comfortable working environment, Steam Whistle Brewing uses a unique green alternative to air conditioning, provided through Enwave Energy Corporation. Enwave draws cold water from Lake Ontario and passes it through pipes at Steam Whistle Brewing, where it chills the surrounding environment. The water then continues along to become part of Toronto's potable water supply. Using this system to chill the brewery work environment reduces the amount of carbon dioxide that would have been generated by conventional air conditioning by about 71 tonnes—or the equivalent of 16 fewer cars on the highway

per annum. It also reduces electricity consumption by about what would be consumed by seven homes. Steam Whistle Brewing uses steam exclusively to heat water for brewing, for bottle washing, and for climate control, again supplied by Enwave Energy. This allows the company to use steam only as needed, rather than having to operate its own on-site gas-burning boiler that would need to be continually operating. To further conserve energy, Steam Whistle Brewing installed a state-of-the-art brew house that reduces the energy needed for brewing by recirculating the steam-heated water back into the system. It also reduces water consumption by nearly 70 percent compared to the older brew house it had been using. The company has been leaving lights off whenever possible, taking advantage of the natural light that is abundant throughout their heritage building. Motion sensors also help reduce electricity use, and energy-efficient bulbs and fixtures are installed as older ones need to be replaced. By keeping the older fixtures and bulbs in place as long as possible, the company helps reduce what it would otherwise have to send to landfill.

Steam Whistle Brewing has an active management plan to be as environmentally responsible as possible. But it goes beyond its manufacturing and administrative operations. The company encourages employees to use bike paths and mass transit where possible. It provides showers, a towel service, and a covered bike rack for employees. The employees have a strong sense of social responsibility and of being part of a culture where sustainability is important. Steam Whistle Brewing sponsors hundreds of charitable, cultural, and community events each year. Consumers can connect with Steam Whistle through its website or its mobile site, Twitter, Facebook, and Instagram. Visitors to Toronto can even tour the company's operations. In 2014, touring Steam Whistle Brewing was ranked 13 of 139 activities to do in Toronto.

Creating a strong identity for a brand is always important, but particularly for those that are considered "badge" products, such as beer. Badge products through association say something about the user's personality or character and speak to others about the user; for example, "By having invested in this premium, socially conscious product, it demonstrates my beliefs." Sybil Taylor, the company's communications director, says, "That's why we think it's important that we share our environmental story. It's just one part of our personality, but it's an important part."

Questions for Critical Thinking

1. What is meant by Steam Whistle's "personality"? Describe it and explain why it is important.
2. Explain how each of the five forces in marketing's external environment—competitive, political-legal, economic, technological, and social-cultural—can affect Steam Whistle's green strategy.
3. How does Steam Whistle Brewing rate on the four-step pyramid of corporate social responsibility? Does it meet all the criteria for a socially responsible company? Explain.

Sources: Company website, **www.steamwhistle.ca**, January 16, 2014; Company website, **www.bullfrogpower.com**, January 16, 2014; Company website, **www .enwave.com**, January 16, 2014; Company website, **www.tripadvisor.ca**, January 16, 2014; Wallace Immen, "Two 'Fired Guys' Poured Ambition into Steam Whistle," *Globe and Mail*, October 3, 2013, p. B15; Personal correspondence, Sybil Taylor, communications director, Steam Whistle Brewing, August 18, 2011.

chapter 4

Digital Marketing and Social Media: Living in the Connected World

CHAPTER OBJECTIVES

1. Describe the impact of digital marketing.

2. Discuss how marketers use the communication function of the Web as part of their online marketing function.

3. Outline the steps involved in developing successful marketing websites and identify methods for assessing website effectiveness.

4. Define social media, social media platforms, and social media tools and describe how consumers use social media.

5. Outline the elements of a written social media marketing plan and describe the different means of monitoring, measuring, and managing the social media marketing campaign.

6. Discuss ethical and legal issues encountered by marketers in social media marketing and identify the different types of positions in social media marketing.

PINTEREST SURGES AHEAD

Proving that a picture is worth a thousand words, about 70 percent of all Facebook activity revolves around uploading and sharing photos, and 10 percent of all the photos ever taken in the history of the world were snapped within the last 12 months. As cameras spread into more smart devices, and social media provide more opportunities to share the results, the online world is becoming increasingly visual.

So it's no surprise that Pinterest, the website where a community of users create bulletin board–like pages to "pin" and link photos of interest, is one of the fastest-growing online phenomena. Founded in late 2009 to little fanfare, the site took off like a rocket one year later. It now boasts over 11 million unique visitors a month, many of whom spend more time on the site than the typical LinkedIn or Twitter user, and it recently attracted $27 million in venture capital.

Unlike the youth-oriented Facebook and Twitter, however, Pinterest found its audience mostly among women aged 30 to 40, who use it to share photos and links to recipes and knitting patterns, blogs, child-care tips, and favourite fashion items. Given that this demographic group controls purchasing decisions for many households, marketers for food, clothing, and electronics companies are looking for ways to capitalize. One food company discovered that consumer topics, rather than brand-related promotions, attract Pinterest users, so the site has become a great way to drive people to the company's recipe database. Happily for retailers, Pinterest has added a red "Pin It" button so members can link their boards to merchandisers' online catalogues with a single click. The new button is rapidly spreading to shopping sites, showing up next to similar buttons from Twitter and Facebook.

Given its link-sharing nature, Pinterest is a natural referral tool, and, in one recent month, it drove more referral traffic to third-party websites than even Twitter. To increase its utility and ease of use, the site added user profiles with prominent photos of the people each user most often "re-pins," so boards offer a visual snapshot of social influence for each member of the Pinterest community.

To make it even more effective for their goods and services, marketers will need to thoroughly master Pinterest's visual basis and community nature.[1]

connecting with customers

Pinterest tells its subscriber audience, "We want you to discover inspiration for just about anything." True to this declaration, Pinterest is a forum where subscribers can share photos of all the things that inspire them, such as recipes and consumer goods. The site's simple grid structure has proved popular with its millions of users. Ben Silbermann, the site's founder, says, "We want to be this snapshot of what you're about and we wanted to represent that visually."

In a recent month, Pinterest sent more referral traffic—traffic that arrives at a company's website from another source, such as a social media site—than Twitter. Companies recognize the tremendous potential of Pinterest to drive sales via marketing and to connect with their customers.

Chapter Overview

During the past decade, marketing has become the cutting-edge tool for success on the Internet. Profit-seeking organizations are not the only benefactors of the Internet; organizations of all kinds are emphasizing marketing's role in achieving set goals. Contemporary marketing continues to perform its function of bringing buyers and sellers together; it just does it faster and more efficiently than ever before. With just a few ticks of the clock and a few clicks of a mouse, the Internet revolutionizes every aspect of life. New terms and new tools have emerged, such as *shopping blog, RSS, VoIP,* and *XML,* and old words have new meanings never imagined a few years ago: *Web, Net, surfer* and *server, banner* and *browser, tweet* and *twitter, online* and *offline.*

Electronic business, or **e-business**, refers to conducting business via the Internet and has turned virtual reality into reality. With a computer and Internet access, a virtual marketplace is open 24/7 to provide almost anything anywhere to anyone, including clothes, food, entertainment, medicine, and information. You can pay your cell phone bill, make travel reservations, do research for a term paper, post a résumé at an employment bulletin board, or buy a used car—perhaps at a lower price than you could in person.

Today the Internet has moved beyond the computer to include mobile phones and tablets and has introduced new tools. Facebook. Twitter. Foursquare. Tumblr. You know what all these names represent: social media. You may have accounts on most of them—or one, at the very least. You might follow NASCAR drivers like Brad Keselowski and Kevin Harvick. Maybe you prefer tracking country music star Carrie Underwood or want to keep up with the latest on the stars of the *Hunger Games* trilogy. You can find all these on various social media. They know it, and so do their sponsors and promoters.

This chapter examines the current status and potential of e-business and digital marketing. We explore the scope of e-business and outline how marketers use the Internet to succeed. We explore the profile of online buyers and sellers and describe some of the challenges associated with marketing on the Web. We discuss how marketers use the communication function of the Internet and examine how to build an effective Web presence.

This chapter also explores the ways that organizations use social media to market their goods and services. This chapter presents an overview of the different types of social media, such as blogs and social networking sites, and examines how they work. We look at how consumers use social media—and why. Then we turn to the marketer's point of view: social media marketing. We outline the elements of a formal social media marketing plan. Next, the chapter addresses the legal and ethical issues surrounding the use of social media, and we take a look at marketing careers in social media. ◆◆◆

---

① **Describe the impact of digital marketing.**

e-business Conducting online transactions with customers by collecting and analyzing business information, carrying out the exchanges, and maintaining online relationships with customers.

Marketoid

In Canada, 45 percent of companies have a website.

digital marketing Strategic process of creating, distributing, promoting, and pricing goods and services to a target market over the Internet or through digital tools.

DIGITAL MARKETING

In the past decade, the number of Internet users in North America and worldwide has grown dramatically. Today, over 270 million people—more than 78 percent of the North American population—have access to the Internet at home, school, work, or public access sites. The number of Internet users worldwide totals over 2.4 billion.[2] The map in Figure 4.1 shows the number of Internet users and Internet penetration rates for each of the world's continents and regions. *Internet penetration* is the percentage of a region's population who use the Internet.

Today, *e-business* describes the wide range of business activities taking place via Internet applications such as email and virtual shopping carts. E-business can be divided into the following five broad categories: (1) *e-tailing,* or virtual storefronts on websites; (2) business-to-business transactions; (3) electronic data interchanges (EDI), the business-to-business exchange of data; (4) email, instant messaging, blogs, podcasts, vlogs (video blogs), and other Web-enabled communication tools and their use as media for reaching prospective and existing customers; and (5) the gathering and use of demographic, product, and other information through Web contacts.

The component of e-business of particular interest to marketers is *electronic marketing,* or **digital marketing**, the strategic process of creating, distributing, promoting, and pricing goods and services to a target market over the Internet or through such digital tools as smartphones. Digital marketing is the means by which e-business is achieved.

The application of these electronic tools to contemporary marketing has the potential to greatly reduce costs and increase customer satisfaction by increasing the speed and efficiency of marketing interactions. Just as e-business is a major function of the Internet, digital marketing is an integral component of e-business.

figure 4.1

Number of Internet Users and Internet Penetration Rate (by Region)

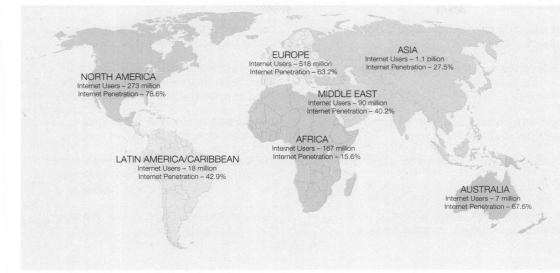

NORTH AMERICA
Internet Users – 273 million
Internet Penetration – 78.6%

EUROPE
Internet Users – 518 million
Internet Penetration – 63.2%

ASIA
Internet Users – 1.1 billion
Internet Penetration – 27.5%

MIDDLE EAST
Internet Users – 90 million
Internet Penetration – 40.2%

AFRICA
Internet Users – 167 million
Internet Penetration – 15.6%

LATIN AMERICA/CARIBBEAN
Internet Users – 18 million
Internet Penetration – 42.9%

AUSTRALIA
Internet Users – 7 million
Internet Penetration – 67.6%

Source: Data from Internet World Stats, **www.internetworldstats.com**, accessed Sept 29, 2013

OPPORTUNITIES OF DIGITAL MARKETING

Digital marketing offers countless opportunities to reach consumers. This radical departure from traditional brick-and-mortar operations provides contemporary marketers the benefits summarized in Table 4.1.

In addition to the benefits listed here, an effective online presence can improve the performance of traditional marketing operations. Recent surveys of consumers found that, whether they purchase online or in person, well over half of shoppers do online product research before buying. In one recent survey, 70 percent of online shoppers said research would continue to be a critical factor in purchasing decisions over the next year, and a third use their mobile phones to scan QR or bar codes to search for information on a product or to compare prices.[3] The Internet is thus a powerful force in shaping consumer behaviour, even if it is seldom the only avenue most consumers pursue in their search for product information. Meanwhile, with online sales growing by well over 10 percent each year while retail stores sales remain flat, brick-and-mortar stores are fighting back with options that online sellers can't deliver. The cookware and kitchen appliance dealer Williams-Sonoma offers in-store cooking classes and demonstrations; participants can get a 10 percent discount on in-store purchases on the day of the class.[4]

Courtesy of Pizza Pizza Limited

A website is usually included as part of a company's digital marketing strategy. Many of these websites allow the customer to place orders, as in the Pizza Pizza example.

B2C DIGITAL MARKETING

One area of e-business that consistently grabs news headlines is Internet shopping. Known as **business-to-consumer (B2C) digital marketing**, it is selling directly to consumers over the Internet. Driven by convenience and improved security for transmitting credit card numbers and other financial information, online retail sales—sometimes called *e-tailing*—have grown rapidly in recent years. Canadians consumers are shopping online but not as many as in other countries. One recent study of consumers in 11 countries showed that Canadian and Italian consumers had the lowest online shopping rate, with only 78 percent of Canadian consumers shopping online.[5]

business-to-consumer (B2C) digital marketing Selling directly to consumers over the Internet.

table 4.1   *Digital Marketing Capabilities*

CAPABILITY	DESCRIPTION	EXAMPLE
Global reach	The ability to reach anyone connected to the Internet anywhere in the world	Independent filmmakers use the Internet to generate audiences and sales for their films.
Personalization	Creating products to meet customer specifications	Lululemon Athletica has a website feature that allows buyers to mix and match items to create complete outfits to suit their individual tastes.
Interactive marketing	Buyer–seller communications through such channels as the Internet and interactive kiosks	Dell maintains the IdeaStorm site where users trade ideas, information, and product feedback.
Right-time marketing	The ability to provide a product at the exact time needed	The WestJet website lets customers make advance reservations, check in online, check flight status, and sign up for the carrier's rewards program.
Integrated marketing	Coordination of all promotional activities to produce a unified, customer-focused promotional message	Sony uses the slogan "Make. Believe" in both online and offline promotions.

interactive marketing Buyer–seller communications in which the customer controls the amount and type of information received from a marketer through such channels as the Internet and virtual reality kiosks.

electronic storefronts Company websites that sell products to customers.

electronic shopping cart File that holds items the online shopper has chosen to buy.

Virtually all major retailers have staked their claims in cyberspace by setting up **electronic storefronts**, websites where they offer items for sale to consumers. Clothing retailer American Eagle sees e-retailing as a "significant growth opportunity" for all its brands and has been enjoying double-digit increases in electronic sales from year to year. The company's attractive website offers a store locator and wish list feature, gift card purchasing, a feedback link, and the opportunity to sign up for sales and other promotions. Clothing is organized by category—tops, bottoms, accessories, footwear, and so on—and the site has separate sections for sales and clearance items as well as for new arrivals and Web exclusives.[6]

Generally, online retailers—such as Gap.com and BestBuy.com—provide an online catalogue where visitors click on items they want to buy. These items are placed in a file called an **electronic shopping cart** or *shopping bag*. When the shopper indicates that he or she wants to complete

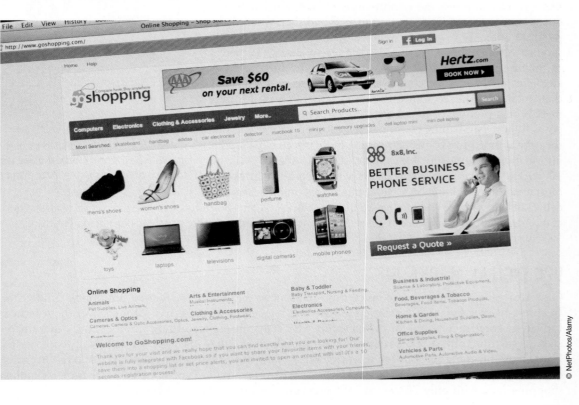

An effective online presence can improve the performance of traditional marketing operations.

the transaction, the items in the electronic shopping cart are listed on the screen, along with the total amount due, so the customer can review the whole order and make changes before paying.

BENEFITS OF DIGITAL MARKETING

Many consumers prefer shopping online to the time needed to drive to a store and select purchases. Why do consumers shop online? Three main reasons are most often cited in consumer surveys: competitive pricing, access and convenience, and personalized service.

Adrian Brown/Bloomberg/Getty Images

Google Product Search offers convenience to online shoppers. The website offers a wide range of products.

Many of the best deals on products, such as airfares and hotels, can be found on the Internet. Expedia.com is just one of several sites that offer packages with combinations of flight, hotel, and car rental, plus special sales and last-minute flight specials at attractive prices organized by city and date of travel.[7] The Web is an ideal method for savvy shoppers to compare prices from dozens—even hundreds—of sellers. Online shoppers can compare features and prices at their leisure. **Bots** aid consumers in comparison shopping. Bots—short for *robots*—are search programs that check hundreds of sites, gather and assemble information, and bring it back to the sender.

bot (shopbot) Software program that allows online shoppers to compare the price of a particular product offered by several online retailers.

A second important factor in prompting online purchases is shopper convenience. Cybershoppers can order goods and services from around the world at any hour of the day or night. Most digital marketers allow customers to register their credit card and shipping information for quick use in making future purchases. Customers are required to select a username and password for security. Later, when they place another order, registered customers are asked to type in their password. Digital marketers typically send an email message confirming an order and the amount charged to the buyer's credit card. Another email is sent once the product is shipped, along with a tracking number, which the customer can use to follow the order through the delivery process. After acquiring Like.com, Google is currently routing users from its Boutiques.com page to Google Product Search, which showcases items as varied as washing machines, clothing, and watches. Shoppers can download Google Catalogs, an app for tablets that brings their favourite online catalogues together. Google Shopper, a smartphone app, allows subscribers to scan the cover art of books and electronic products such as DVDs or games to find those products—or simply say the name of a product to find it. This app also allows subscribers to see nearby offers, find local stores, scan bar codes of products for more information, and check out online prices. Google Offers lists participating restaurants in the subscriber's local area.[8]

Although online shopping transactions often operate with little or no human interaction, successful B2C digital marketing companies know how important personalization is to the quality of the shopping experience. Customer satisfaction is greatly influenced by the marketer's ability to offer service tailored to many customers. But each person expects a certain level of customer service. Consequently, most leading online retailers offer customized features on their websites. How does personalized marketing work online? Say you buy a book at Chapters.Indigo.ca and register with the site. The site welcomes you back for your next purchase by name. Using special software that analyzes your previous purchases, it also suggests several other books you might like. You even have the option of receiving periodic emails informing you of new products. Some websites offer customized products to match individual consumer requirements. For instance, Nike offers online shoppers the opportunity to customize a running shoe, personalizing such features as the outsole, the amount of cushioning, and the width. Other sites provide online chat options. Visitors to the site can communicate with a company representative who can answer their questions in real time.

ONLINE BUYERS AND SELLERS

Recent research paints a picture of the characteristics of online users and buyers (see Figure 4.2). In Canada there are over 25 million possible Internet shoppers because that is the number of Internet users over the

figure 4.2

Characteristics of Canadian Internet Users

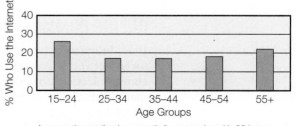

Average time online in a month (home and work): 30 hours
Average number of Web pages viewed per person in a month (home and work): 2,773

Source: "UPS Pulse of the Online Shopper: A Customer Experience Study," Canada Study, September 2013

Oleksiy Mark/Shutterstock.com

New mobile payment systems allow shoppers to make secure credit card purchases.

Marketoid

More than 10 percent of Canadian companies sell goods or services online.

② **Discuss how marketers use the communication function of the Web as part of their online marketing function.**

spam Popular name for junk email.

age of 15. Seventy-eight percent of Canadians say they have shopped online but only 71 percent of those living in Quebec shop online. A higher number of men shop online than women. Canadian online shoppers are aware of the length of time it will take for their purchases to arrive at their door but are happy to wait as long as 10 days. Canadian online shoppers are also price conscious but 15 percent of them have never shopped for special offers or bargains.[9]

Realizing that customers would have little or no opportunity to rely on many of the sense modes—smelling the freshness of direct-from-the-oven bread, touching the soft fabric of a new cashmere sweater, or squeezing fruit to assess its ripeness—early online sellers focused on offering products consumers were familiar with and tended to buy frequently, such as books and music. Other popular early online offerings were computer hardware and software and airline tickets.

Event tickets, computers, and peripherals top the list of products sold online. Sales of clothing and accessories have increased, with books showing a decline.[10]

CHALLENGES IN DIGITAL MARKETING

For all the advantages, digital marketing faces some problems and challenges. Some of the most significant are developing safe online payment systems, protecting consumer privacy, preventing fraud and scams, improving site design and customer service, and reducing potential channel conflicts and copyright disputes. Table 4.2 outlines some of these issues.

assessment check 1 ✓
1.1 Define *digital marketing*.
1.2 What are the major benefits of digital marketing?
1.3 What are the major challenges in digital marketing?

MARKETING AND WEB COMMUNICATION

There are four main functions of the Internet: digital business, entertainment, information, and communication. Even though digital business is growing rapidly, communication still remains the most popular Web function. One survey estimates that about 90 *trillion* emails are sent per year. The volume of email today exceeds regular mail (sometimes called *snail mail*) by something like 81 to one.[11] The WWF uses a website to inform people about their National Sweater Day event as described in the "Marketing: Making Your World Better" feature.

Firms also use email to inform customers about events such as new products and special promotions. While using email in this manner can be quite cost effective, companies have to be careful. A growing number of customers consider such emails to be **spam**, the popular name for junk email. A recent study found as much as 95 percent of all email is spam, up from 70 percent three years before the study.[12] It is no wonder many Internet users employ *spam filters* that automatically eliminate junk email from their in-boxes.

ONLINE COMMUNITIES AND SOCIAL NETWORKS

In addition to email, many firms use Internet forums, newsgroups, electronic bulletin boards, and social networks that appeal to people with common interests. All these sites take advantage of the communication power of the Internet. Members congregate online and exchange views and information on topics of interest. These communities may be organized for commercial or noncommercial purposes.

To get the most from social networking communities, marketers may want to implement a mix of strategies, such as preparing their websites for social networking, carrying out email campaigns, and advertising on social networking sites.[13] Online communities and social networks are discussed in greater detail later in the chapter.

table 4.2   *Challenges in Digital Marketing*

CHALLENGE	DESCRIPTION	SOLUTION
Safety of Online Payment	Consumers are concerned about the safety of sending credit card numbers over the Internet.	Internet browsers contain encrypttion systems. Encryption—the process of encoding data for security Secure Sockets Layer (SSL)—technology that secures a website by encrypting information and providing authentication (example VeriSign). Payment services—examples PayPal, Google Checkout
Privacy Issues	Collection and use of personal information through the use of cookies or spyware. Cookies and spyware are software programs that collect data. Hackers take information without the company's permission.	Internet privacy organizations assure consumers their information won't be used without their permission. Firewalls or electronic barriers between a company's internal network and the Internet limit access into and out of a network. Firewalls won't stop all hackers.
Frauds and Scams	Phishing is a high-tech scam that uses authentic-looking email or pop-up messages to get unsuspecting victims to reveal personal information. Vishing is a scam that collects information through voice response systems.	Most phishing and vishing scams ask the user to update or validate personal information usually for a bank account, Internet service provider, etc. The best solution to this problem is the users themselves. No organization like a bank would ask for personal information through the Internet.
Site Design and Customer Service	Well-designed websites draw more customers. Customers want quick deliveries and easy ways to return products.	Design sites so that products are easy to find and customer questions can be answered quickly. Use three-dimensional photos and videos. Allow customers to track a delivery or have products picked up from a retail store.
Channel Conflicts and Copyright Disputes	If manufacturers sell through their sites, they compete with the stores selling their products. This situation is called channel conflict. If material written or produced by a third party is placed on a site, copyright permission from the owner may be required.	Many manufacturers do not sell from their sites to avoid channel conflict. Obtaining permission from the owner of material to be placed on the site avoids any copyright issues.

Sources: Company website, **www.symantec.com**, accessed April 29, 2012; U.S. Small Business Administration, "Online Payment Services," **www.sba.gov**, accessed April 29, 2012; Katy Bachman, "Big Week in Washington for Online Privacy Issues," Adweek, **www.adweek.com**, accessed April 29, 2012; Antone Gonsalves, "10 Biggest Security Breaches of 2011," CRN, **www.crn.com**, accessed April 30, 2012; Government website, **www.ic3.gov**, accessed April 30, 2012; "2011 CyberSecurity Watch Survey: Organizations Need More Skilled Cyber Professionals to Stay Secure," Marketwire, **www.marketwire.com**, accessed April 30, 2012; David Jacoby, "Facebook Security Phishing Attack in the Wild," Securelist, **www.securelist.com**, accessed April 30, 2012; Amanda Ciccatelli, "Pindrop Security Helps Victims Address Mounting Vishing Attacks," TMCnet, **www.tmcnet.com**, accessed April 30, 2012; Mark Brohan, "Big Design Changes Drive Growth Online at Under Armour," Internet Retailer, **www.internetretailer.com**, accessed April 30, 2012; "Top 500 List," Internet Retailer, **www.internetretailer.com**, accessed April 30, 2012; Zak Stambor, "Daily Deals Spur Repeat Business," Internet Retailer, **www.internetretailer.com**, accessed April 30, 2012; Timothy B. Lee, "Google Tries to Kick Authors Guild Out of Court in Book Case," Ars Technica, **http://arstechnica.com**, accessed April 30, 2012

BLOGS AND PODCASTS

Another popular online communication method is the **blog**. Short for *Web log*, the term *blog* describes a Web page that is a publicly accessible journal for an individual or organization. Typically updated daily or even more frequently, these hybrid diary-guide sites are read regularly. Using *RSS (Really Simple Syndication)* software, readers continually are kept up to date on new material posted on their favourite blogs whenever they are online. Unlike email and instant messaging, blogs let readers post comments and ask questions aimed at the author, called a *blogger.* Some blogs also

blog Short for *Web log*—an online journal for an individual or organization.

MARKETING: MAKING YOUR WORLD BETTER — National Sweater Day

SINCE February 2010 the WWF (World Wildlife Fund) with support from the Loblaw Companies have been promoting energy conservation and building relationships with the organization by staging National Sweater Day. The event, aimed at university and college students, asked people to turn down their thermostats by a couple of degrees and wear a sweater for the day. The hope was that if people could get used to the lower temperatures for a day they might continue to keep their thermostats lower.

A website was designed to promote the event, SweaterDay.ca, featuring grandmothers. The idea to use grandmothers came from grandmothers knitting or purchasing ugly sweaters that were never worn. The website contained lots of information about the initiative, including packages explaining how businesses and schools could get involved and videos of grandmothers knitting sweaters. Visitors to the website could even request a call from a grandmother on the day reminding them to reduce their heat. One year website visitors could even request the type of granny to deliver the message ranging from sweet to cranky. In another year

the campaign included a granny recruitment effort. The material provided to participating schools included ideas for supporting events such as organizing a collection to donate sweaters to a charity or taking pictures of sweaters for photo displays. Schools were also encouraged to offer rewards (heart-shaped chocolates or hot cocoa) to participants and to invite local media to cover their activities.

The campaign has increased in popularity each year by using a combination of social media, radio, and television. In addition to the dedicated website, the WWF promoted the event on its Twitter and FaceBook accounts. Other organizations contributed to the event by sponsoring sweater fashion shows, sweater design contests, and sweater parties.

Sources: WWF website, "National Sweater Day," **www.wwf.ca**, accessed December 29, 2013; Public website, "How Do You Motivate Canadians to Turn Down Their Thermostats," **www.publicinc.com**, accessed December 29, 2013; Chris Powell, "WWF Brings Back Grannies for Sweater Day," *Marketing*, **www.marketingmag.ca**, January 18, 2013; Matt Semansky, "WWF Puts Grannies on the Phone for National Sweater Day," *Marketing*, **www.marketingmag.ca**, February 2, 2012.

---

wiki Web page that anyone can edit.

podcast Online audio or video file that can be downloaded to other digital devices.

Many companies have their own Facebook page to interact with customers and build up a fan base.

incorporate **wikis**. A wiki is a Web page anyone can edit so a reader can, in addition to asking questions or posting comments, actually make changes to the Web page. **Podcasts** are another emerging technology. Anyone from bloggers to traditional media sources can prepare an audio or video recording and then post it to a website from which it can be downloaded to any digital device that can play the file.

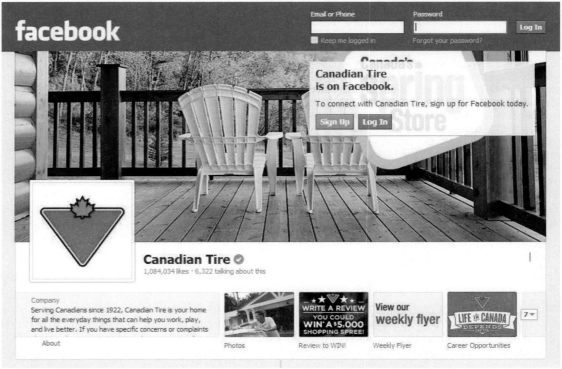

Given the growing interest in blogs and podcasts, it hasn't taken long for marketers to incorporate them into their e-business strategies. Blogs and podcasts are discussed in more detail in the social media section of the chapter.

PROMOTIONS ON THE WEB

Rather than rely completely on their websites to attract buyers, companies frequently expand their reach in the marketplace by placing ads on sites their prospective customers are likely to visit. Banner ads, the most common form of Internet advertising, are typically small, strip messages placed in high-visibility areas of frequently visited websites. Pop-up ads are separate windows that pop up with an advertising message. The effectiveness of pop-up ads, however, is questionable. First, scam artists use pop-ups. Second, many Internet users simply hate pop-up ads—even those from legitimate companies. Consequently, most ISPs now offer software that blocks pop-up ads. Google and Microsoft also offer free pop-up ad-blocking software.

Preroll video ads, marketing messages that play before an online video, are becoming more popular, although users have shown some resistance. YouTube is one of the few sites to let viewers opt out of watching them. One company that sells preroll video advertising recently launched a new service that, for a small fee, allows viewers to opt out of viewing the ads.[14] Widgets are tiny applications Internet users can copy and add to their social networking pages or their personal websites to play music, video, or slide shows. Marketers are adopting the use of widgets at a rapid rate.[15]

Another type of online advertising is search marketing. This is considered one of the most effective forms of Web-based advertising. Companies pay search engines fees to have their websites or ads pop up after a user enters certain words into the search engine, or to make sure their firm's listing appears toward the top of the search results. Google and other search engines feature "Sponsored Links" on the right side of the search results page. A user who clicks on one of the sites listed under Sponsored Links is taken to that site, and the company pays the search engine a small fee. Google and Microsoft, among others, have made major investments in improving their search marketing services and capabilities.

Another way companies use the Web to promote their products is through online coupons. For instance, customers can visit a company's website—for example, Aeropostale (**www.aeropostale.com**)—to learn about items on sale then print a discount coupon redeemable at participating retailers.

banner ad Strip message placed in high-visibility areas of frequently visited websites.

pop-up ad Separate window that pops up with an advertising message.

preroll video ad Brief marketing message that appears before expected video content.

widgets Tiny applications that Internet users can copy and add to their own pages to play music, video, or slide shows.

search marketing Paying search engines, such as Google, a fee to make sure the company's listing appears toward the top of the search results.

Marketoid

In a three-year period, 51 percent of Canadian companies purchased information and communication technologies.

> ### assessment check 2
>
> **2.1** What are online communities and social networks? Explain how online communities can help companies market their products and improve customer service.
>
> **2.2** What are blogs, wikis, and podcasts?
>
> **2.3** Explain the differences between a banner ad, pop-up ad, preroll video ad, widget, and search marketing.

BUILDING AN EFFECTIVE WEB PRESENCE

(3) Outline the steps involved in developing successful marketing websites and identify methods for assessing website effectiveness.

An e-business website can serve many purposes. It can broaden customer bases, provide immediate access to current catalogues, accept and process orders, and offer personalized customer service. As technology becomes increasingly easy to use, anyone with Internet access can open an account and place a simple website on the Internet. How people or organizations use their sites to achieve their goals determines whether their sites will succeed. Figure 4.3 lists some key questions to consider in developing a website.

SUCCESSFUL SITE DEVELOPMENT

Most Web experts agree: "It is easier to build a bad website than a good one." When judging websites, success means different things to different businesses. One firm might be satisfied by maintaining a popular site that conveys company information or reinforces name recognition—just

figure 4.3

Questions to Consider in Developing a Website

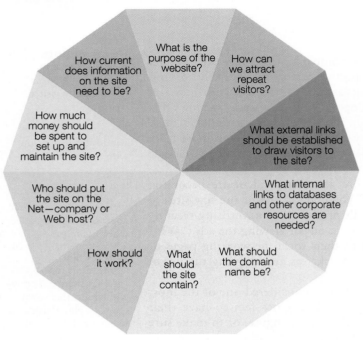

as a billboard or magazine ad does—without requiring any immediate sales activity. Websites like those of your local newspaper draw many visitors who want the latest news, and Yahoo! and Google are successful because they attract heavy traffic. Besides enhancing their brands, popular websites such as these add to their success by selling advertising space to other businesses.

Internet merchants need to attract customers who conduct business on the spot. Entrepreneurs are wise to clearly define their business goals, perhaps by creating a community of enthusiasts to build up sales in advance and to pay due attention to tried-and-true marketing tools, including television advertising, that can complement Internet efforts. Listening to consumers is as important as talking to them via a company website or blog.

ESTABLISHING GOALS

What is the company's goal for its website? Answering this question is the first and most important step in the website development process. For the broadband telephone service provider Vonage, the primary objective is to sign up new customers. So the website designers put a link called "Sign Up" prominently in the upper portion of the home page.

Objectives for the website also determine the scope of the project. If the company's goal is to sell merchandise online, the site must incorporate a way for customers to place orders and ask questions about products, as well as provide links to the company's databases to track inventory and deliveries. The plan should include not only the appearance of the website but also the company's behind-the-scenes resources for making the website deliver on its promises.

Websites like the one for Amazon are successful because they attract heavy traffic and offer shoppers a variety of products and deals as well as opportunities to join in discussions on a variety of topics via community forums.

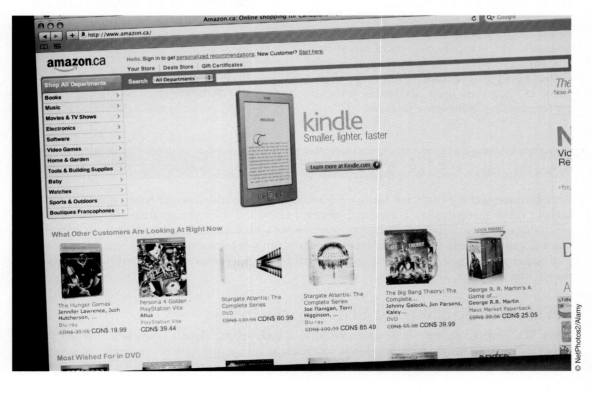

Other key decisions are whether to create and maintain a site in-house or to contract with outside designers. Some companies prefer to retain control over content and design by producing their own sites. However, because acquiring the expertise to develop websites can be very time-consuming, hiring specialists may be more cost effective. Naming the website is another important early step in the planning process. A domain name should reflect the company and its products and be easy to remember. However, with millions of domain names already registered, the search for a unique, memorable, and easily spelled name can be difficult.

IMPLEMENTATION AND INTEREST

Implementing the goals of the site is the next stage, and content is one of the most important factors in determining whether visitors return to a site. People obviously are more inclined to visit a site that provides material that interests them. Many e-business websites try to distinguish themselves by offering additional features. For example, Amazon's website lures traffic to the site with daily and hourly deals (called Lightning deals); a separate clothing store; garden supplies; music, movie, and book downloads; and online community forums on a variety of topics. Many sites offer links to other sites that may interest visitors.

Standards for good content vary for every site, but available resources should be relevant to viewers; easy to access and understand; updated regularly; and written or displayed in a compelling, entertaining way. When the World Wide Web was a novelty, a page with a picture and a couple of paragraphs of text seemed entertaining. But such "brochureware" falls far short of meeting today's standards for interactivity, including the ability to accept customer data and orders, keep up-to-the-minute inventory records, and respond quickly to customer questions and complaints. Also, today's Internet users are less patient about figuring out how to make a site do what it promises. They won't wait 10 minutes for a video clip to download or click through five different pages to complete a purchase. Revamping a site can help maintain interest and keep users on the site longer. Facebook recently rolled out a new design for its home page that is more than just cosmetic. The changes are meant to improve site navigation and gather useful links and information in one part of the site.[16]

After making content decisions and designing the site, the next step is connecting to the Internet by placing the required computer files on a server. Companies can have their own dedicated Web servers or contract to place their websites on servers at Internet Service Providers (ISPs) or other host companies. Most small businesses lack the necessary expertise to set up and run their own servers; they are better off outsourcing to meet their hosting and maintenance needs. They also need to draw business to their site. This usually requires a listing with the major search engines, such as Google, Ask.com, and Bing.

PRICING AND MAINTENANCE

As with any technological investment, website costs are an important consideration. The highly variable cost of a website includes not only development expenses but also the cost of placing the site on a Web server, maintaining and updating it, and promoting it. A reasonably tech-savvy employee with off-the-shelf software can create a simple piece of brochureware for a few hundred dollars. A website that can handle e-business will cost several thousand dollars. Creating the website requires an understanding of how to link the website to the other company information systems.

Although developing a commercial website with interactive features can cost tens of thousands of dollars, putting it online can cost as little as $30 a month for a spot on the server of a Web host such as Yahoo!

It's also important for a website to stay current. Visitors don't return to a site if they know that the information never changes or that claims about inventory or product selection are not relevant or current; consequently, updating design and content is another major expense. In addition, site maintenance should include running occasional searches to test that links to the company's website are still active.[17]

ASSESSING SITE EFFECTIVENESS

How does a company gauge the return from investing in a website? Measuring the effectiveness of a website is tricky, and the appropriate process often depends on the purpose of the website. Figure 4.4 lists some measures of effectiveness. Profitability is relatively easy to measure in companies that

figure 4.4

Measures of Website Effectiveness

Web-to-store shoppers
Consumers who use the
Internet as a tool when
shopping at brick-and-
mortar retailers.

click-through rate
Percentage of people
presented with a banner
ad who click on it.

conversion rate
Percentage of visitors to
a website who make a
purchase.

engagement Amount
of time users spend on
sites.

generate revenues directly from online product orders, advertising, or subscription sales. The airlines, for example, generate a portion of their bookings online through their websites. However, what's not clear is how many of those tickets would have sold through other channels if the airlines did not have a website. Also, evidence exists that so-called **Web-to-store shoppers**—a group that favours the Internet primarily as a research tool and time-saving device for retail purchases made in stores—are a significant consumer niche.

For many companies, revenue is not a major website objective. Most company websites are classified as corporate websites, not shopping sites, meaning that firms use their sites to showcase their products and to offer information about their organizations. For such companies, online success is measured by increased brand awareness and brand loyalty, which presumably translates into greater profitability through offline transactions.

Some standards guide efforts to collect and analyze traditional consumer purchase data, such as how many residents in a certain area purchased a new Jeep in the previous year, watched a certain television program, or tried Starbucks Blond Roast coffee. Still, the Internet presents several challenges for marketers. Although information sources are getting better, it is difficult to be sure how many people use the Internet, how often, and what they actually do online. Some Web pages display counters that measure the number of visits. However, the counters can't tell whether someone has spent time on the page or skipped over it on the way to another site, or whether that person is a first-time or repeat viewer.

Advertisers typically measure the success of their ads by **click-through rates**, meaning the percentage of people presented with a banner ad who click on it, thereby linking to a website or a pop-up page of information related to the ad. Recently, the average click-through rate has been declining to about 0.10 percent of those viewing an ad. This rate is much lower than the 1.38 to 3.42 percent response rate for direct-mail advertisements. Low click-through rates have made Web advertising less attractive than when it was new and people were clicking on just about anything online. Selling advertising has therefore become a less reliable source of e-business revenue.

As e-business gains popularity, new models for measuring its effectiveness are being developed. A basic measurement is the **conversion rate**, the percentage of visitors to a website who make purchases. A conversion rate of 3 to 5 percent is average by today's standards. A company can use its advertising cost, site traffic, and conversion rate data to find out the cost to win each customer. E-business companies are trying to boost their conversion rates by ensuring their sites download quickly, are easy to use, and deliver on their promises. Many are turning to one of several firms that help companies improve the performance of their websites. Nielsen/Net Ratings developed a new way to rate websites that measures **engagement**, or how much time users spend on sites, rather than counting how many pages of a site they view. Google Analytics is a tool for tracking the number of visitors to a site, which pages they visit, where they come from, and whether they buy, among other statistics.[18]

Many new analytical programs offer similar measurements of consumer wireless activity. These programs aim to integrate analytics from mobile, social, and Web channels. They can analyze marketing data from Facebook pages, iTunes Connect, and other media platforms. The programs aim to provide a more holistic view of customer engagement and brand performance.[19]

assessment check 3 ✓

3.1 What are the basic questions a company should ask itself when planning a website?

3.2 How does the type of website affect measures of effectiveness?

3.3 Explain the difference between click-through rate, conversion rate, and engagement.

④ Define social media, social media platforms, and social media tools and describe how consumers use social media.

WHAT IS SOCIAL MEDIA?

You post a video on YouTube. You tag a friend on Facebook. You create a pinboard of your favourite foods on Pinterest. You start a blog about your motorcycle adventures. These are just a few of the ways you might use social media in your daily life. **Social media** is defined collectively as the different forms of electronic communication (such as networking websites or blogs) through which users can create online communities to exchange information, ideas, messages, and other content, such as videos or music.[20]

Although innovators constantly find new ways to branch out the tree of social media, to date there are several basic forms. These may be divided into two main categories: social media platforms and social media tools. A social media platform is a type of software or technology that allows users to build, integrate, or facilitate a community, interaction among users, and user-generated content. The popular blogging site Wordpress is a social media platform, as are social networking sites Facebook and Foursquare. A social media tool enables users to communicate with each other online. Examples are apps, blog postings and comments, and video shares.

The different types of social media often overlap with each other. For example, you can create a forum on LinkedIn to discuss job training, or post a video to your Facebook page. In addition, the media sites themselves cross boundaries; for example, StumbleUpon, which is a Web search engine that directs users to Web pages based on their interests, has its own Facebook page, Twitter account, and blog.

SOCIAL MEDIA PLATFORMS

Social media platforms act as a home base for an online community. To access the conversations held there, users must become members. Usually, this is a matter of typing in a valid email address and creating a password, followed by providing some kind of profile. But some social media platforms require an invitation or sponsor who is already a member. When you join, be sure to learn the site's rules. For example, Facebook strictly regulates where you can run a contest promotion on your timeline as well as how you may choose and contact the winner. If you violate these rules, your firm could be banned from the site.[21] Table 4.3 outlines some social media platforms.

social media Different forms of electronic communication through which users can create online communities to exchange information, ideas, messages, and other content, such as videos or music.

social media platform A type of software or technology that allows users to build, integrate, or facilitate a community, interaction among users, and user-generated content.

social media tool Software (such as an app or blog) that enables users to communicate with each other online.

table 4.3 **Social Media Platforms**

PLATFORM	DESCRIPTION	EXAMPLES	MARKETING USES
Social Networking Sites	A website that provides virtual communities through which people can share information, post opinions, and increase their circle of online friends	Facebook, Twitter, LinkedIn	Companies like Walmart and Target use Facebook to build relationships with customers. Not-for-profit organizations use Facebook to promote their events. Keywords are important for marketing campaigns that include Facebook so that network users can land in the right place.
Bookmarking Sites	A platform that gives users a place to save, organize, and manage links to websites and other Internet resources	StumbleUpon; Pinterest combines bookmarking with social networking	Pinterest allows the user to create a virtual scrapbook or bulletin board that can be shared with others. The virtual scrapbook created on Pinterest can be linked to other websites such as Facebook, a retail store, or a magazine.
Social News Sites	A platform where users can post news items to links to outside articles; then vote on which postings get the most prominent display	Digg, Reddit	Because viewers vote using whatever criteria they want, it is difficult for marketers to determine if their messages get through to the desired audience.
Blogging Sites and Forums	Blogging sites are platforms where a host or writer posts information or opinions on various topics and followers may respond. Online forums are platforms where users post messages and hold conversations on specific topics.	Blogging sites— Wordpress, Tumblr	Fashion brands use Tumblr to place pictures of their fashions.
Microblog	A blog posting that contains only a few words	Twitter	Tweets are short—140 characters. Companies pay celebrities huge sums to tweet about their goods and services to followers.

Sources: PC Magazine Encyclopedia, **www.pcmag.com**, accessed August 19, 2013; "10 Successful Social Media Campaign Tips," Nimble, April 9, 2012, **www.nimble.com**; Kristin Laird, "What You Need to Know About Pinterest," Marketing Magazine, March 23, 2013, **www.marketingmag.ca**; Tim Grahl, "The 6 Types of Social Media," Out:think, **www.outthinkgroup.com**, accessed May 8, 2012; Lauren Indvik, "Why Fashion's Top Brands Are Flocking to Tumblr," Mashable, **http://mashable.com**, accessed May 11, 2012; Alicia Androich, "YouTube Pulse event shows how brands can make most of the platform," Marketing Magazine, June 18, 2013, **www.marketingmag.ca**; Rebecca Harris, "Skip the hard sell and be more useful: Jay Baer Q & A," Marketing Magazine, May 29, 2013, **www.marketingmag.ca**.

Mark Zuckerberg, the founder of Facebook, presents his online profile from Facebook.

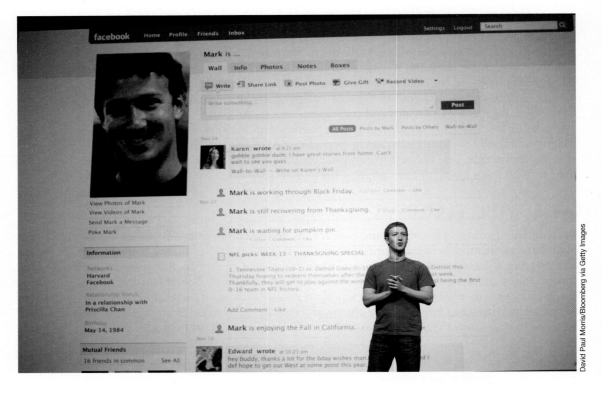

Marketoid

Almost 90 percent of Canadian companies use the Internet.

Marketoid

Roughly 35 percent of Canadian companies use traditional advertising methods, such as print ads, to direct customers to their websites.

app Short for *application*, a free or purchased software download that links users to a wide range of goods and services, media and text content, social media platforms, search engines, and the like.

SOCIAL MEDIA TOOLS

Social media tools make the conversation happen. Blog comments, tags, photo and video shares, apps, and other technology items make up the social media toolkit. Social media tools include media sharing, blog and microblog postings, apps, and QR codes.

Media sharing services like YouTube and Flickr allow you to upload and share media, such as photos and video. Most also let you create a profile or comment on a posting. Some videos have gone viral and shot their makers to fame, as in the case of pop singer Justin Bieber. Marketers realize that a viral video can translate to a jump in demand—and sales—for their products.

Blogging allows people to communicate in greater detail than microblogging does. Individuals blog about topics such as their favourite foods, their pet peeves, or the best vacation spots within driving distance. Marketers use blog postings to educate consumers and business customers about new products, to ask for feedback about particular goods and services, to notify the public about social responsibility initiatives, and to manage public relations crises. Many companies designate certain staff members as bloggers, while others hire professional bloggers either in-house or on a consulting basis, because they believe in the power of skilled blogging to influence readers' opinions about their goods and services. When Turkish Airlines wanted to deflate the negative publicity about antigovernment riots in Istanbul they arranged for bloggers from six Canadian magazines and websites to have a free visit. The bloggers shared highlights of their trip with their readers with descriptions and photos.[22]

Microblogging, on the other hand, offers short bursts of news. Recently, PepsiCo unveiled a partnership with Twitter through which it will offer free downloadable songs to consumers who include a Pepsi hashtag in their tweets and streaming video of live concerts. PepsiCo's Twitter followers may tweet the names of songs they want played—thus influencing concert playlists.[23]

App—short for *application*— is a purchased or free software download that links users to a wide range of goods and services, media and text content, social media platforms, search engines, individual businesses or organizations—just about anything you can think of. It's difficult to determine exactly how many apps exist because new ones are being created at such a rapid rate.

There are apps available for Android-powered mobile phones, for Apple devices, and for Nokia, BlackBerry, and Palm. And there are apps for computer tablets, as well as for the iPad. Apps allow you to download music, play games, or make dinner reservations. Marketers know that potential and existing customers use all kinds of apps, and they want to tap into the opportunities created by this phenomenon.

QR codes, short for "quick response," are two-dimensional bar codes that can be read by some mobile phones with cameras (often, a dedicated QR code reader is necessary as well). The codes look like small black-and-white squares with patterns and appear in various ads. Once a mobile phone snaps a picture and "reads" the code, the information contained in the code is shared with the user—it might lead to a video, give details about a product, or offer a coupon.

QR code Short for "quick response," a two-dimensional bar code that can be read by some mobile phones with cameras.

WHY SHOULD MARKETERS TURN TO SOCIAL MEDIA?

Despite its relatively brief existence, social media has quickly grown to be an important tool for marketers to build relationships with customers, strengthen brands, launch new products, enter new markets, and boost sales. Once considered the domain of teens and young adults, sites like YouTube and Facebook report that their user base is now much broader. More than 60 percent of adults are connected to one or more social media sites; 46 percent of Facebook users are age 45 or older.[24]

Denys Prykhodov/Shutterstock.com

QR codes help companies connect with their customers.

Not every effort at social media is successful. When Ford got ready to launch its new Ford Fiesta, the carmaker recruited 100 influential bloggers and gave them each a Fiesta to drive for a specified period of time. For the most part, the bloggers liked the car and generated buzz about the "Fiesta Movement" campaign. "Fiesta Movement was a groundbreaking campaign that put Ford on the social-media map," says Ford's manager of digital and multimedia communications. But the bloggers (and Ford) didn't take into account the fact that the company's more popular subcompact—the Focus—was undergoing a major design overhaul and wasn't yet available. Thus, while Ford sold more than 69,000 Fiestas that year, sales dropped off dramatically the following year, because car buyers preferred the revamped Focus.[25]

MARKETING AND THE SME
New Types of Consulting Firms Emerge

SOCIAL media and digital marketing have not only changed how companies market their products and services but it also takes different skills to create the websites and the content and videos that go on them. Many new companies are springing up to perform these tasks. Notch Video and the Performance Content Group are two new companies that create digital content. Both companies started business in 2013 but the people who started them and work with them are marketing veterans.

Notch Video was created by Justin Creally and Mia Pearson. The two realized that all the websites, YouTube, and Facebook marketing required video but traditional ad agencies were charging too much to produce the video. Their model was to have people with all the skills needed to produce a video—writers, editors, producers, and directors—mount their profiles on the Notch Video website. A company looking for people to produce their videos could connect directly through the website with people in a certain geographic area or with the skills sets they were looking for. Notch Video does not charge for its matching service but its also offers traditional consulting services for those who want them.

The Performance Content Group was started by Deb Hall and Michael Girgis. Their company looks at data from several sources and then helps its clients understand what content needs to go on which social media platform and when to put it there. They analyze data to determine what trends are emerging and who the customers are. This information then allows others to develop the proper content to get the right message out to those customers.

Companies like Notch Video and the Performance Content Group may be new but others are sure follow as the social media trend continues.

Sources: "Girgis and Hall: Putting the Performance in Content," *Marketing*, **www.marketing mag.ca**, December 18, 2013; The Performance Content Group website, **www.pcglab.com**, accessed December 30, 2013; Notch Video website, **www.notchvideo.com**, accessed December 31, 2013; Tom Gierasimczuk, "Creative Newsroom: Newsy Content Marketing," *Marketing*, **www.marketingmag.ca**, March 22, 2013; Rebecca Harris, "North Strategic Gets into the Video Business," *Marketing*, **www.marketingmag.ca**, November 5, 2013.

social media marketing (SMM) The use of social media portals to create a positive influence on consumers or business customers toward an organization's brand, products, public image, or website.

Effective **social media marketing (SMM)** uses social media portals to create a positive influence on consumers or business customers toward an organization's brand, goods and services, public image, or website. Of course, this can also apply to an individual like a sports celebrity or entertainment star. Marketers generally view the goal of social media marketing as developing a conversation with potential customers—resulting in a purchase, subscription to an email newsletter, registration in an online community, participation in an event, and so forth. If the online conversation is successful, it will go viral—sparking others to join in. Helping companies produce effective social media marketing are some new types of consulting firms as described in the "Marketing and the SME" feature.

Not-for-profit organizations also create social media marketing campaigns to expand their reach. Although the organization is 100 years old, Big Brothers Big Sisters recently launched its "Start Something Web Series" to highlight individual success stories. Videos were posted on its YouTube channel, which then spread via website shares and Facebook postings.[26]

Social media marketing contains three essential features:

1. *It creates a buzz.* Buzz is the engine that drives social media marketing. Buzz carries the marketing message from one user to the next until it becomes viral, spreading as far and as rapidly as possible. The message doesn't have to be related directly to a firm's goods or services, but it must be compelling and memorable.

2. *It creates ways for customers or fans to engage in conversations with each other and the organization.* Social networking sites, blogs, and forums promote these conversations.

3. *It allows customers to promote the firm's messages themselves.* Social networking sites like Facebook and Twitter enable customers to easily become a firm's promoter.

HOW CONSUMERS USE SOCIAL MEDIA

For businesses to be successful at using social media to reach their customers, they need to understand how consumers use social media to decide whether to buy certain goods and services. Figure 4.5 shows the top 10 social-networking sites by the estimated number of visitors per month with Facebook, Twitter, and Linkedin leading the pack.

Studies show an overall link between social media and trends in consumer behaviour. For example, 43 percent of all consumers online follow or are fans of a brand. Fifteen percent of consumers between the ages of 16 and 24 would rather receive customer service through social media than any other channel. Smartphone users are twice as active on social media as non-smartphone users. And social media users are more apt to dine out on a regular basis than nonusers.[27]

According to one recent report, in a survey conducted by comScore and Group M Search, roughly half of online consumers use a combination of search engines and social media to make purchase decisions. Fifty-eight percent of consumers start with search engines like Google or Bing, while 24 percent go straight to social media. Here's the twist: 46 percent of consumers who start with social media then turn to search engines.

Shoppers who start with search engines do so because these provide the greatest amount of information about products and companies. Search engines also help with comparison shopping, particularly when it comes to price. More than 86 percent surveyed say that search engines are extremely important to their buying decisions. "Consumers at a ratio of 2 to 1 cite quality and depth of information as reasons for using search versus social media," says the report.[28] Marketers can use this kind of insight to develop social media marketing campaigns that incorporate—or start consumers at—search engines.

Marketoid

Canadian firms with 100 or more full-time employees account for 59 percent of online sales.

figure 4.5

Most Popular Social Networking Sites

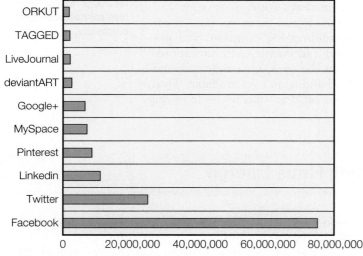

Source: "Top 15 Most Popular Social Networking Sites: August 2013," eBizMBA website, **www.ebizmba.com**, accessed August 25, 2013.

Marketoid

Only 4 percent of the total goods and services sold in Canada are e-sales.

Consumers rely on the communities created by social media for their buying decisions in the following ways:

- To learn about new goods and services.

- To conduct research and share information.

- To make final purchase decisions.

Some experts contend that social media can shift the way consumers behave within entire industries. For example, consumers are visiting retail stores but when they find an item they are interested in they go online with their smartphones to get more information. This process is called "showrooming." The customer may actually purchase the item online if they find it for a lower price. Some industry experts are blaming the practice of showrooming for significantly affecting the retail industry in Canada. Showrooming started in 2011 when Amazon introduced its smartphone app Price Check. Online comparison shopping evolved from the Price Check program that compared prices of products that only Amazon carried to allowing the shopper to compare prices at any online retailer.[29]

Courtesy of Kruger Products L.P. Reprinted with permission of Facebook.

Many organizations share photos on Facebook, allowing them to share information about themselves.

assessment check 4

4.1 What are social networking sites?

4.2 Define *social media marketing*.

4.3 Why do online shoppers often begin with search engines?

CREATING A SOCIAL MEDIA MARKETING PLAN

⑤ **Outline the elements of a written social media marketing plan and describe the different means of monitoring, measuring, and managing the social media marketing campaign.**

Like every other type of marketing, effective social media marketing (SSM) requires setting goals and developing strategies to reach a target audience. The **social media marketing plan** identifies and describes all three of these variables, the tactics required to implement the plan, and the budget and expected returns, along with methods for monitoring and measuring the campaign's effectiveness.

A social media marketing plan contains many of the same elements found in a traditional marketing plan or business plan. The formal plan is important because it documents in writing the firm's goals and strategies for the SMM initiative, its budget and expected returns, and the company's chosen methods for monitoring, measuring, and managing the effort. A well-written plan contains clear, concise prose that covers the salient points and answers anticipated questions. Although the format and length of SMM plans may vary from firm to firm (or even from project to project), most contain the following information:

- *An executive summary.* This is a paragraph or two explaining the *who, what, when, where, how,* and *why* of the plan. An effective summary gives compelling reasons why the plan should be adopted—for example, to remain competitive in a particular market. Most marketers write the executive summary last, even though it appears first in the plan.

- *A brief overview.* The overview briefly describes the overall market conditions, the firm's current position in social media, and any other factors that the social media marketing effort will address.

- *Analysis of the competition.* The plan examines competitors' presence in social media, including which platforms and tools they select and an evaluation of their overall effectiveness.

social media marketing plan A formal document that identifies and describes goals and strategies, targeted audience, budget, and implementation methods, as well as tactics for monitoring, measuring, and managing the SMM effort.

figure 4.6

Cycle of Social Media Marketing

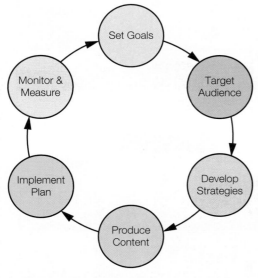

Source: Based on Ron Jones, "6 Steps in Developing a Social Media Strategy," Clickz, January 9, 2012, **www.clickz.com**.

influencers Individuals with the capability of affecting the opinions or actions of others.

Marketoid

Business-to-business online sales reached $136 billion in 2013; they are expected to reach $34 billion by 2018.

- *The body of the plan.* The remaining sections of the SMM plan cover the following: statement of goals and strategies, target audience, budget (including human resource needs), and expected returns, as well as methods for implementing, monitoring, measuring, and managing the SMM campaign.

The following sections describe in detail the steps in creating the plan for a social media marketing campaign. As marketers develop goals and strategies, decide on methods of implementation, and consider how to monitor, measure, and manage a social media marketing initiative, they keep in mind the elements of the formal document they will produce.

STRATEGIES OF A SOCIAL MEDIA MARKETING PLAN

Before embarking on a social media marketing campaign, it's important for social media marketers to understand two major distinctions between traditional marketing and SMM. First, traditional marketing seeks to control the content and message received by an audience. But SMM actively solicits the audience's participation in the message, and more often than not the audience creates its own message—that's the nature of interactivity. Second, successful social media marketing efforts require the audience's trust. It may take a while for this trust to solidify—and, in fact, some parts of the SMM effort may be directed toward trust building—but without credibility, the two-way conversation between company and consumer can't occur. The audience will cease to participate, and the effort will fail.

We can break the process of developing a social media marketing campaign into six basic phases, keeping in mind that they actually represent a cycle: set goals, target the audience, develop strategies, produce content, implement the plan, monitor, and measure.[30] Figure 4.6 illustrates the cycle of social media marketing.

Marketers must also keep in mind the importance of listening throughout all phases of the campaign. Since the basis for social media is conversation, smart marketers use social media to listen to what is being said about their own company and its products and their competitors. Social media is also helpful for connecting with **influencers**—individuals with the capability of affecting the opinions and actions of others. If you want to stay current on upcoming fashion trends, follow stylist Rachel Zoe's Facebook page. Oprah Winfrey and Justin Bieber were on a recent list of the top 10 most powerful celebrities.[31] You can find all of them on various forms of social media.

SETTING GOALS

A successful social media marketing campaign starts with clear goals. Marketers should ask themselves: "What do we want to accomplish through this campaign?" Examples of social media marketing goals are building brand awareness and reaching new customers.

Tourism Calgary launched a social media campaign after the region was devastated by floods.

Once goals are established, marketers are better able to develop strategies and choose the right platforms or outlets for their messages. Clear goals also help everyone involved in the campaign to aim their efforts in the right direction. "In the aftermath of the Alberta floods Tourism Calgary wanted to let everyone know the destination was open for business. A video featuring the city's tourist attractions, restaurants, and hotels was produced and uploaded to YouTube."[32]

Goals should also be flexible. Conditions in the marketing environment may change, and marketers should be able to adapt their goals without scrapping an entire plan. Upon measuring the results of a campaign, marketers may determine that a change is necessary. A social media effort might be so successful that a firm wants to expand its goals. Unexpected customers may appear, in which case marketers could tweak the message or add another type of social media to the mix in order to serve them. A new social networking site could pop up and attract visitors at a high rate—leading marketers to reevaluate not only their choice of platforms but also their immediate goals. Or a company might decide to return to its roots to reconnect with customers.

TARGETING THE AUDIENCE

"Who are we trying to reach?" This is the first question marketers ask when they begin to develop strategies for any marketing effort—including one involving social media. Social media efforts customize marketers' approach to targeted audiences more than many types of traditional marketing, because they are interactive. A television commercial for the latest Ford Escape could reach school-age children, parents of large families, teenagers with limited money for a new car, young professionals who prefer a sport model, and many others not in the market for a sport utility vehicle. But visitors who follow the model on Pinterest can view or pin pictures of road trips. Those who click on the Ford Canada Web page might visit the Ford YouTube page where they can view videos and pictures about the company and the vehicle.[33] The social media effort targets interested consumers much more specifically than a television commercial.

How do social media marketers arrive at a target audience? It depends on the goal of the marketing effort. If it's to create brand awareness, the audience will be broader than for strengthening relationships with existing customers. Marketers narrow this target further by determining which social media will be best suited to certain types of consumers. People who want to learn more about a product and its features are more apt to search out this information on Facebook or Google+, while those interested in a promotional event more likely will follow Twitter. Although Chapter 9 discusses the concept of market segmentation and targeting in detail, here we examine ways for marketers to target their audience for social media campaigns.

In order to pinpoint the audience for social media marketing, firms gather information on the following:

- *Demographics.* This refers to features of the group (or groups) within the larger population that the firm wants to reach. Characteristics include age, gender, geographic location, income, ethnicity, and marital status.

- *What the group (or organization) needs or wants.* Marketers identify what their potential customers need or want—say, gluten-free foods or sports apparel—and determine if and how the firm's products could satisfy this.

- *Which of the firm's products and social media will meet the needs and wants of particular groups of people.* Marketers not only identify a target group, they also pinpoint which of their goods and services will best serve that group, and begin to determine through which social media they should deliver the messages that will spark interest and interaction.

Developing the best strategies for social media marketing requires thoroughly understanding the target audience in order to influence its behaviour as a result of interaction—whether it's to make an immediate purchase, spread the word, sign an online petition, participate in a survey, or visit a brick-and-mortar store.[34]

DEVELOPING STRATEGIES AND CHOOSING TACTICS

Every strategy in an effective social media marketing campaign traces back to the campaign's goals—and ultimately links to a firm's overall strategic goals. Once marketers answer the question of who they are trying to reach by targeting their audience, they ask a second vital question in social media marketing: "How do we engage the audience in a conversation?" Then they develop strategies for developing and delivering the content that will drive the interaction. They decide:

- *Which social media platforms to use, and how to combine them to reach and engage with the audience.* McDonald's used a combination of platforms in its McDonald's goes to the movies campaign. The company asked its customers to submit a product story using only 140 characters. The story could be submitted through Twitter or online.[35]

- *Which social media tools should deliver the campaign's content, and how best to link them with the selected social media platforms.* There's an app for just about everything, and tools like QR codes are gaining rapidly in popularity as well. Consumers who scan QR codes generally expect a coupon or deal on products.

- *Who will participate in the conversation on behalf of the company (staff members, professional bloggers, celebrities, and other influencers).* Marketers looking for a list of top influencers in a particular industry can browse those compiled online by SocMetrics for fields as varied as advertising and design, politics, and public relations.[36]

- *How to make it easy for potential customers to locate and participate in the conversation.* One way to do this is to create a specific landing page for a marketing campaign instead of directing consumers to the company's home page first. This works especially well for larger companies that are marketing many products. Another way to make it easy for potential customers is to have an eye-catching ad on the company's website with a link to a specific landing page. This is the technique used by LG Canada when it launched its new G2 phone. Information about the company's "One Finger Challenge" contest was on its home page with a link to the Facebook page where customers could upload photos.[37]

Once strategic decisions are made, marketers zoom in on specific tactics like recruiting specific influencers, setting up a photo or naming contest, offering coupons or discounts, highlighting loyal customers or fans, sending out regular updates, and the like.

CREATING CONTENT

Marketers create content with the firm's goals and strategies in mind. The idea is to reach the targeted audience and engage them with the company's brand. For companies that manage to build followers on social media, this is a huge branding opportunity.[38]

SMM content differs from traditional marketing in that it is, by definition, a two-way street. In order for SMM to succeed, the content of its messages must engage the target audience in the conversation. According to the Content Marketing Institute (CMI), nine out of ten organizations already use some type of content marketing (usually in a combination of traditional and social media marketing), and 60 percent report that they plan to increase their content marketing budgets over the next year.[39] **Content marketing** involves creating and distributing relevant and targeted material to attract and engage an audience, with the goal of driving them to a desired action.[40]

Content for an effective SMM campaign has the following qualities:

- A strong brand focus.

- A focus on the audience rather than the organization.

- Targeted keywords.

- Relevant information.

- Shareworthy text and images.

- Invitations to generate content via posts, shares, discussions, reviews, or other forms of dialogue with the organization as well as with fellow customers.

- Promotions that offer discounts, gifts, or other special deals in exchange for participation.

Marketers who use social media to reach their targeted audience are entering into conversations with customers—and must respect the conventions of personal interaction if they want to build successful relationships. Social networking sites often have strict rules about advertising, and some have rules governing membership. Marketers shouldn't try to sidestep these in an effort to get marketing messages to users—it will backfire and may result in a ban from any kind of presence on the site.

Each social media channel has an intended use by its community. Marketers should be aware of these functions and stay within those parameters. For example, LinkedIn members can join discussion groups or send each other direct messages. The same thing goes for Facebook, Twitter, and other sites. Smart marketers understand the distinction and tailor their postings accordingly. Businesses also

---

Marketoid

Over 50 percent of Canadian retailers have a website.

---

content marketing
Creating and distributing relevant and targeted material to attract and engage an audience, with the goal of driving them to a desired action.

should avoid creating social media profiles for the sole purpose of marketing. Most people do not care to see unwanted product messages on the personal blogs or forums in which they participate. Failure to follow these conventions may result in posts being hidden or unfollowed—or outright public criticism.

Before hitting that "publish" button, marketers must be absolutely certain that the content they are making public is exactly what they want to say—and that it will be received in the intended manner. It's always a good idea to ask, "What could go wrong with this message?" This is particularly true if the organization is multinational and messages are being received by potential customers around the world. In addition, marketers should avoid sending spam. A person who follows a page or group doesn't necessarily want regular promotional messages and may ultimately decide to stop following the page or group if too many messages are sent by the company.

Social media strategists advise organizations *not* to delete comments, no matter how painful or unflattering they may be (unless they are profane, obscene, or illegal). Instead, they recommend that marketers weather legitimate criticism and deal directly with an online crisis instead of trying to avoid it. When Volkswagen deleted negative Facebook comments related to Greenpeace's accusations that the carmaker used "its huge political muscle to lobby against environmental laws," a firestorm ensued. Social media experts observed that the crisis could have died down much sooner if Volkswagen had responded to the comments and offered to continue any discussions at its own website.[41]

IMPLEMENTING THE PLAN

Like traditional marketing plans, the social media marketing plan requires a timeline for implementation. Marketers may decide to create separate schedules for the rollout onto each social media platform. In addition, the SMM plan builds in a specified time period for engaging with the public, offering special promotions, and the like. Finally, the timeline includes managing, monitoring, and measuring the success of the effort.

As the marketing effort is launched, someone representing the firm must stand watch to respond to customers who comment on blog posts, review products, ask questions, post videos and photos, or enter contests. The good thing about social media is that it operates around the clock; the bad thing about social media is that marketers never have down time. But they can use software products such as Hootsuite, a social media management system (or dashboard) to manage multiple social profiles, schedule messages and tweets, track brand mentions, and analyze social traffic.[42]

There are specialty apps available to marketers that can assist them to manage various aspects of their marketing plan. One type of app enables marketers to post with pictures or video and has a version that allows companies to customize the app name and send visitors who click on it to the company's website instead of to an application. Various apps allow firms to add newsletter signups to their pages. Other types of apps help companies manage the customer feedback function. These apps can direct the Facebook or website visitor to a specific department or can allow fans to ask questions directly from a Facebook page.[43]

Experts recommend that marketers refrain from scheduling content more than a week away because information can change, consumer responses may shift, and events might occur that would change the content. Since marketers must continually update content, there's no point in doing it so far ahead that the content will be almost guaranteed to require revisions before posting. But as long as marketers are prepared to account for some bumps that will require changes, scheduling the rollout of content should be a relatively smooth process.

MONITORING, MEASURING, AND MANAGING THE SMM CAMPAIGN

It's one thing to launch a social media marketing campaign, but without tracking its course, the campaign may sink or run aground. The role of **social media monitoring** is to track, measure, and evaluate a firm's social media marketing initiatives. Marketers must also manage their company's SMM efforts by making changes when necessary.

One of the greatest challenges faced by social media marketers is monitoring the progress of an SMM effort, partly because its reach can stretch far beyond the capabilities of the company. But various **social media analytics** tools help marketers track (find and follow social content), measure, and interpret data related to SMM initiatives.

social media monitoring The process of tracking, measuring, and evaluating a firm's social media marketing initiatives.

social media analytics Tools that help marketers trace, measure, and interpret data related to social media marketing initiatives.

figure 4.7

Social Media Measuring

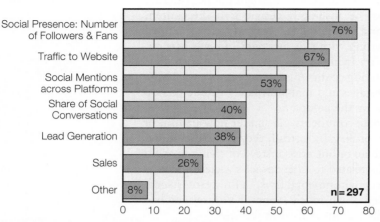

Source: AwarenessHub, LLC, **www.awarenesshub.com**

return on investment (ROI) The rate of revenues received for every dollar spent on an expense.

Monitoring and measuring help marketers understand what their customers need and want, ultimately making adjustments to SMM or product offerings to satisfy those customers. Marketers select monitoring tools based on the needs of their own firms. Social media analytics software are all designed to assist companies in monitoring their social media engagement.

Firms also calculate the **return on investment (ROI)** of their social media marketing initiatives, using reach (the percentage of people in a target market who are exposed to the marketing effort at least once) and frequency (the number of times an individual is exposed to the marketing material during the campaign) as variables. Expenses (such as employee time spent answering customer tweets or Facebook questions) are weighed against savings (employees not having to make in-person calls to customers). Although not all marketers agree on the validity of measuring SMM campaigns this way, companies do concede that they look for quantitative ways like this to evaluate the efficiency of the marketing effort.

Measuring the success of a social media marketing plan includes such factors as share of voice (number of conversations about the company versus competitors and overall market), awareness of the company or brand, level of engagement by the targeted audience, influence created, and popularity among target audience members.[44] Figure 4.7 identifies several metrics that companies typically measure; for example, more than 75 percent of firms measure their social media presence (based on number of followers and fans).

Managing a social media marketing campaign—or a company's overall social media efforts—requires skill, expertise, and understanding of the company's brand, its competitors, and the social media environment. This means maintaining a grasp on the success or failure of previous strategies, knowledge of the benefits and drawbacks of the different social media platforms and tools, and an ability to interpret data without losing sight of the overall goal. It also means being flexible enough to change tactics when necessary to avert or minimize a crisis.

assessment check 5

5.1   What is content marketing?

5.2   What is one major drawback to social media as it pertains to scheduling?

5.3   What is the function of social media monitoring?

⑥ **Discuss ethical and legal issues encountered by marketers in social media marketing and identify the different types of positions in social media marketing.**

ETHICAL AND LEGAL ISSUES AND CAREERS IN SOCIAL MEDIA MARKETING

Social media marketers face ethical and legal issues, such as privacy and accountability, as part of their job. As rapidly as the various social media evolve and expand, so too new ethical situations will appear. Firms will have to stay apprised of new threats as well as the solutions to problems. Marketers who maintain an educated and cautious approach to these issues—laced with common sense—will be best prepared to meet challenges head on.

As more and more businesses engage in social media marketing, many people are now seeking careers in the field—either with companies looking to boost their social media presence or with firms that specialize in assisting these companies with their marketing efforts. People are also developing successful careers in social media itself, with firms like Facebook, Twitter, Pinterest, and others.

WORKPLACE ETHICS

Recent studies have begun to examine correlations between social media use (particularly during the workday) and ethical behaviour. This has led companies to begin instituting formal policies about social networking in the workplace.[45]

Many companies are now drafting written policies for the use of social media by individuals in the workplace as well as by groups such as the marketing department for company purposes. Well-written social media policies have the following qualities:

- Are consistent with a firm's organizational culture and values;

- Explain why employees should take certain steps or actions (or avoid them);

- Are broad enough to cover the major points, but brief enough to fit onto two pages; and

- Are linked to other relevant company policies and guidelines.[46]

Many organizations also maintain a presence with their own YouTube channel.

BE HONEST

Social media messages travel at lightning speed around the world; potentially millions of people may view a message in a matter of seconds or minutes. This means that postings, ads, comments, and even images come under intense scrutiny—and must be checked for accuracy, fair and realistic claims or promises, balance and objectivity, and potential for misinterpretation. Honesty is the best policy when marketing via social media; transparent communications help develop trust among followers and may ultimately contribute to strengthening a firm's brand.

RESPECT PRIVACY

Although marketers try to gather as much information as possible about a targeted audience, they must not distribute any personal information without consent. Because social media is interactive by its nature, marketers must be vigilant about confidentiality and not letting personal information or other data accidentally slip into unauthorized hands. Violation of these practices and other privacy laws and guidelines could destroy a company's reputation and cost millions of dollars.

After Sony revealed a breach of its PlayStation Network customers' personal data, people complained that the firm took too long to notify them. Although Sony temporarily turned off its PlayStation Network and Music Unlimited service and hired an outside security firm to investigate the unauthorized intrusion, the company's reputation was damaged.[47]

In the quickly changing social media world, organizations need to be nimble when dealing with security measures that affect them and their customers. The "Solving an Ethical Controversy" feature discusses a password breach that posed challenges for LinkedIn and its members.

BE ACCOUNTABLE

Mistakes happen. When they do, smart social media marketers take action to solve the problem or resolve the issue. First, they acknowledge the problem and take responsibility for it. Second, they communicate with the right people, via the most relevant channel(s), and promise to take steps necessary to correct the situation. Third, they implement the agreed-upon changes or make other concessions and evaluate ways to avoid similar problems in the future. While it's important for businesses to be accountable for their actions, they must do so in a realistic manner, making changes that are relevant to the situation.

LinkedIn Security Breach: Who's at Fault?

LINKEDIN is one of the social media sites that professionals use to connect to business colleagues, existing clients, and potential customers. Recently, the company announced that it suffered a security breach related to subscribers' passwords. The passwords of more than 6 million subscribers (about 4 percent of its members worldwide) were posted to a hacker site. Two security firms were able to confirm the breach by searching for known passwords of colleagues within the massive password file that spread around the Internet.

Should LinkedIn be responsible for keeping members' passwords secure?

PRO

1. The company should take precautions to ensure the level of encryption used in its security process is impenetrable.

2. Because of their professional nature, LinkedIn profiles may contain business-related information that should not be shared with anyone outside of the user's authorized network.

CON

1. Most Internet users have become complacent when it comes to selecting usernames and passwords.
2. Let users beware: Passwords should be made more random and difficult to crack—and not easy to "guess" based on user information provided on social media sites.

Where do you stand: pro or con?

Sources: Matthew J. Schwartz, "LinkedIn Defends Security Practices, Leadership," *Information Week*, June 13, 2012, **www.informationweek.com**; Benny Evangelista, "LinkedIn Password Breach Erodes Confidence," *San Francisco Chronicle*, June 8, 2012, **www.sfgate.com**; Vicente Silveira, "Taking Steps to Protect Our Members," *LinkedIn Blog*, June 7, 2012, **http://blog.linkedin.com**; Michael Hickins, "LinkedIn Password Breach Illustrates Endemic Security Issue," *The Wall Street Journal*, June 6, 2012, **http://blogs.wsj.com**.

figure 4.8

Job Titles in Social Media Marketing

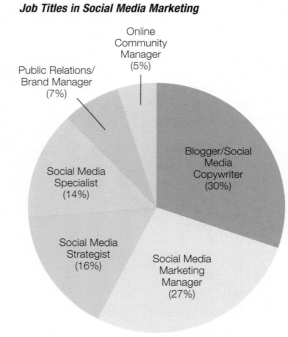

Source: "Social Media Jobs Salary Guide," *Onward Search*, May 23, 2012, **www.onwardsearch.com**.

CAREERS IN SOCIAL MEDIA MARKETING

Figure 4.8 shows a breakdown of overall social media job titles in North America. Even if you aren't looking for a position specifically in social media marketing, it's likely that you will undertake at least some portion of your job hunt through social media. See the "Career Readiness" feature for some suggestions on using social media to find a job.

Job titles vary from company to company, but here is a sampling of the different types of positions in social media marketing:

- *Social media marketing manager (or digital marketing manager).* The person who oversees all the company's social media functions, ranging from blogging copywriter to social media strategist.

- *Social media strategist.* The primary decision maker who runs the firm's social media program.

- *Brand manager.* The person who is responsible for online public relations and management of the brand over social media sites.

- *Online community manager.* The person who manages external engagement with customers in social media channels (such as Facebook, Twitter, blogs, or community forums).

- *Influencer relations.* The liaison between a company and those considered to be influencers within the social media community.

Using Social Media to Find a Job

NINETY percent of companies now use social media for recruitment. How can you use social media to look like a rock star in the job market? Here are some tips.

- Know what each social media site does best.
- Facebook is mostly social, but recruiters routinely check applicants' walls. Post responsibly, segregate your friend groups appropriately, and monitor friends' posts and tags about you.
- Reserve LinkedIn for actively building your professional network. Instead of adding purely social friends and family to your LinkedIn network, friend them on Facebook instead.
- Protect your network's integrity by refusing LinkedIn requests from anyone you don't know or whose work isn't related to your career.

- Be proactive on LinkedIn. Find people who work for companies of interest and identify links in your network who can introduce you to them.
- If you connect your LinkedIn account to your blog or Twitter feed, remember that you've just given potential employers access to all those additional posts.
- Use Twitter tools to search biographies of followers and those you follow, for networking purposes.
- Always be professional when you post. The rule about social media remains: Don't post anything you wouldn't want to read in tomorrow's news.

Sources: Rachel Levy, "How to Use Social Media in Your Job Search," About .com, accessed April 3, 2012, **http://jobsearch.about.com**; Dan Taylor, "How to Use Social Media and Look Like a Rock Star on a Recruiter's Radar," Social Media blog at The NextWeb.com, March 25, 2012, **http://thenextweb.com**; Terri Lee Ryan, "Tips for Using Social Media in Your Job Search," Chicago Now.com, February 14, 2012, **www.chicagonow.com**.

- *Social media specialist.* Job descriptions vary depending on company size and needs, but this employee may do anything from overseeing blog copy to implementing a company's entire social media program.

- *Social media analytics.* This candidate usually has a background in marketing research or Web analytics and is responsible for measuring the results of a social media marketing effort.

- *Social media design.* The individual who oversees the look and feel of an online community, Facebook page, or other branded content. This person often has a background in graphic design.

- *Social media developer.* Responsibilities generally include the programming necessary to build and assemble the features for social tools, such as blogs and communities.[48]

- *Content programmer.* The employee who creates content and generates discussions about topics related to the company's social media presence, such as product releases and lifestyle conversations.

- *Blogger or copywriter.* The person who writes blogs as well as other social media copy.

Social media marketing jobs offer a wide range in salaries (depending on level, company size, geographic location, and so forth). Corporations are allocating a portion of their online ad spending to social media marketing, and that number is likely to increase—potentially creating more jobs.[49]

Marketoid

Approximately one in four Canadian companies has used paid search methods to increase awareness of their websites.

assessment check 6

6.1 How does the interactivity of social media cause potential privacy issues?

6.2 Why is it likely that more jobs in social media marketing will be created in the near future?

Strategic Implications

The future is bright for marketers who continue to take advantage of the tremendous potential of e-business and digital marketing. Online channels, such as podcasts, that seem cutting edge today will be eclipsed within the next decade by newer technologies, some of which haven't even been invented yet. First and foremost, e-business empowers consumers. For instance, already a significant percentage of car buyers show up at a dealership armed with information on dealer costs and option packages—information they obtained online. And the percentage of informed buyers is only going to increase. This trend isn't about being market led or customer focused; it is about consumer control. Some argue that the Internet represents the ultimate triumph of consumerism.

When a new medium of communication emerges, marketers must pay attention. In a short span of time, social media has rooted itself in our global culture. Thus companies are figuring out how to use this new mode of communication—which creates a two-way conversation—with potential and existing customers.

Despite false starts and various pitfalls, marketers are quickly learning the benefits of using social media to reach their targeted audiences. According to one survey, 85 percent of marketers say that the number-one benefit of social media marketing is generating more exposure for their business; 69 percent report that the greatest benefit is increasing traffic; and 65 percent say it's providing insight into the marketplace.[50]

Despite these numbers, the various social media platforms, tools, and services continue to expand at a rapid rate, opening up opportunities for firms to adopt social media for their competitive advantage and for people looking to build careers in social media marketing. Industry experts anticipate significant growth for social media sites. Thus marketers will be on constant watch for new developments and ways they can harness the power of social media to reach and engage their customers. ◆◆◆

REVIEW OF CHAPTER OBJECTIVES

① Describe the impact of digital marketing.

In the past decade, the number of Internet users in North America and worldwide has grown dramatically. The component of e-business of particular interest to marketers is *electronic marketing*, or digital marketing. Digital marketing is the means by which e-business is achieved. The application of these electronic tools to contemporary marketing has the potential to greatly reduce costs and increase customer satisfaction by increasing the speed and efficiency of marketing interactions. Just as e-business is a major function of the Internet, digital marketing is an integral component of e-business.

② Discuss how marketers use the communication function of the Web as part of their online marketing function.

Communication remains the most popular function of the Internet. Companies have long used email to communicate with customers, suppliers, and other partners. Online communities are groups of people who share common interests. Companies use online communities, such as forums and electronic bulletin boards, and social networking sites to communicate with and obtain feedback from customers and other partners. Blogs are online journals that have gained popularity in recent years. Wikis are Web pages anyone can edit, and podcasts are audio and video files that can be downloaded from the Web to any digital device. Web-based promotions include advertising on other websites using banner ads and pop-up ads, preroll video ads, widgets, and search marketing. Banner ads are strip messages placed in high-visibility areas of frequently visited websites. A pop-up ad is a separate window that pops up with an advertising message. Preroll video ads appear before a selected video, and widgets are interactive applications users can add to their pages to play music, video, and slide shows. Search marketing is an arrangement by which a firm pays a search engine such as Google a fee to make sure the firm's listing appears toward the top of the search results.

③ **Outline the steps involved in developing successful marketing websites, and identify methods for assessing website effectiveness.**

Businesses establish websites to expand their customer bases, increase buyer awareness of their products, improve consumer communications, and provide better service. Before designing a website, a company's decision makers must first determine what they want to achieve with the site.

Other important decisions are who should create, host, and manage the site; how to promote it; and how much funding to allocate. Successful websites contain informative, up-to-date, and visually appealing content. Sites should also download quickly and be easy to use. Finally, management must develop ways of assessing how well a site accomplishes its objectives. Common methods of measuring the effectiveness of websites are profitability, click-through rates, conversion rates, and engagement.

④ **Define social media, social media platforms, and social media tools and describe the how consumers use social media.**

Social media is defined collectively as the different forms of electronic communication through which users can create online communities to exchange information, ideas, messages, and other content such as videos and music. A social media platform is a type of software or technology that allows users to build, integrate, or facilitate a community, provide interaction among users, and generate user-authored content. Social networking sites and bookmarking sites are social media platforms. Social media tools enable users to communicate with each other online. Examples are apps and QR codes. Consumers use social media to learn about new goods and services, conduct research and share information, and make final purchase decisions.

⑤ **Outline the elements of a written social media marketing plan and describe the different means of monitoring, measuring, and managing the social media marketing plan.**

The formal social media marketing plan contains an executive summary explaining the "who, what, when, where, how, and why" of the plan; a brief overview of market conditions and other factors; a competition analysis; and a body including goals and strategies, target audience, budget with expected returns, and methods for implementing and managing the effort.

Clear and flexible goals help marketers set the SMM campaign in the right direction and enable firms to adapt to changing circumstances. Social media marketing efforts customize their approach to targeted audiences more than any other type of marketing because they are interactive, so it is important for marketers to link the targeted audience with the goals.

Effective content has the following qualities: a strong brand focus; emphasis on the audience instead of the organization; targeted keywords; relevant information; shareworthy text and images; invitations to the audience to generate its own content; and offers for discounts or deals.

Marketers often use social media analytics tools to help them track, measure, and interpret data related to the SMM effort. They calculate the return on investment (ROI) of the marketing campaign, typically measuring success by share of voice, awareness of company or brand, level of audience engagement, influence created, and popularity.

⑥ **Discuss ethical and legal issues encountered by marketers in social media marketing and identify the different types of positions in social media marketing.**

Social media marketers face ethical and legal issues in their marketing efforts, as well as workplace ethics by employees. Social media marketing efforts should be honest, respect privacy (for example, when collecting data from users), and accountable. When mistakes happen, marketers must acknowledge the problems and take responsibility for fixing them.

SMM jobs include social media marketing manager, social media strategist, brand manager, online community manager, influencer relations, social media analytics, social media design, content programmer, and blogger or copywriter.

assessment check answers ✓

1.1 Define *digital marketing*.

Digital marketing is the strategic process of creating, distributing, promoting, and pricing goods and services to a target market over the Internet.

1.2 What are the major benefits of digital marketing?

The major benefits of digital marketing are the elimination of geographical boundaries, personalized marketing, interactive marketing, right-time marketing, and integrated marketing.

1.3 What are the major challenges in digital marketing?

The major challenges include developing safe online payment, privacy concerns, and fraud and scams. In addition, poor site design and customer service, unreliability of delivery and returns, and lack of retail expertise have limited e-business success.

2.1 What are online communities and social networks? Explain how online communities can help companies market their products and improve customer service.

Online communities and social networks can take several forms and include Internet discussion groups and electronic bulletin boards, as well as networking sites such as Facebook and Twitter. Users log in and participate by sending comments and questions or receiving information from other forum members. Companies use online communities to ask questions and exchange information with customers.

2.2 What are blogs, wikis, and podcasts?

A blog, short for *Web log*, is a web page that serves as a publicly accessible journal for an individual or organization. A wiki is a web page anyone can edit. A podcast is an audio or video file that can be downloaded from a website to a digital device. Companies use blogs, wikis, and podcasts as tools to build and maintain customer relationships.

2.3 Explain the differences between a banner ad, pop-up ad, preroll video ad, widget, and search marketing.

Banner ads are strip messages placed in high-visibility areas of frequently visited websites. A pop-up ad is a separate window that pops up with an advertising message. Preroll video ads are brief marketing messages that appear before expected video content. Widgets are tiny applications Internet users can copy and add to their own pages to play music, video, or slide shows. Search marketing is an arrangement by which a firm pays a search engine—such as Google—a fee to make sure the firm's listing appears toward the top of the search results.

3.1 What are the basic questions a company should ask itself when planning a website?

The first question deals with the purpose of the website. The second deals with whether the firm should develop the site itself or outsource it to a specialized firm. The third question is determining the name of the site.

3.2 How does the type of website affect measures of effectiveness?

For a shopping site, profitability is an important measure of effectiveness, though profitability can be difficult to measure given the tendencies of Web-to-store shoppers. For other websites, online success is measured by increased brand awareness and loyalty, which presumably translate into greater profitability through offline transactions.

3.3 Explain the difference between click-through rate, conversion rate, and engagement.

The click-through rate is the percentage of viewers who, when presented with a banner ad, click on it. The conversion rate is the percentage of visitors to a website who actually make purchases. Engagement measures how long a user spends on a site instead of how many pages they view.

4.1 What are social networking sites?

Social networking sites are the websites that provide virtual communities for people to share daily activities, post opinions on various topics, and increase their circle of friends.

4.2 Define *social media marketing*.

SMM uses the social media portals to create a positive influence on consumers or business customers toward an organization's brand, products, public image, or website.

4.3 Why do online shoppers often begin with search engines?

Search engines provide the greatest amount of information about products and companies.

5.1 What is content marketing?

Content marketing involves creating and distributing relevant and targeted material to attract and engage an audience, with the goal of driving viewers to a desired action.

5.2 What is the one major drawback to social media as it pertains to scheduling?

Because social media operates around the clock, marketers rarely have down time.

5.3 What is the function of social media monitoring?

The role of social media monitoring is to track, measure, and evaluate a firm's social media marketing initiatives.

6.1 How does the interactivity of social media cause potential privacy issues?

Marketers are collecting personal data about users that could possibly slip into unauthorized hands.

6.2 Why is it likely that more jobs on social media marketing will be created in the near future?

Businesses are increasingly engaging in social media marketing, potentially creating more jobs in this field in the coming years.

MARKETING TERMS YOU NEED TO KNOW

These terms are printed in blue in the text. They are defined in the margins of the chapter and in the Glossary that begins on p. G-1.

e-business 96
digital marketing 96
business-to-consumer (B2C) digital marketing 97
interactive marketing 98
electronic storefronts 98
electronic shopping cart 98
bot (shopbot) 99
spam 100
blog 101
wiki 102

podcast 102
banner ad 103
pop-up ad 103
preroll video ad 103
widgets 103
search marketing 103
Web-to-store shoppers 106
click-through rate 106
conversion rate 106
engagement 106
social media 107

social media platform 107
social media tool 107
app 108
QR code 109
social media marketing (SMM) 110
social media marketing plan 111
influencers 112
content marketing 114
social media monitoring 115
social media analytics 115
return on investment (ROI) 116

PROJECT AND TEAMWORK EXERCISES

1. In small teams, research the benefits of purchasing the following products online:
   a. tablet computers
   b. hotel rooms in Vancouver
   c. movie tickets
   d. auto insurance

2. Assume your team is assigned to develop the website for a large online clothing retailer that also has traditional retail stores. Research the characteristics of Web users and online shoppers. What features would you want to incorporate into your website?

3. Working with a partner, identify and visit 10 different websites. Which of these sites, in your opinion, have the highest and lowest conversion rates? Explain your choices and suggest some ways in which the conversion rates of all 10 sites could be improved.

4. For a week, keep a log on your social media use as a consumer. Which sites and tools do you frequent? Why? How much time do you spend on each daily? Weekly? Do you interact with social media marketing efforts? Create a profile of yourself as a consumer, describing preferences, influencers, and any other factors that are relevant to your online interaction with SMM.

5. With a classmate, select a television commercial or print ad for a product, such as an upcoming concert or theatre production, a hybrid vehicle, a clothing retailer, a new smartphone model, or a line of low-fat snacks. Create a poster or brief PowerPoint presentation showing how you would transform this from a traditional marketing effort into social media marketing. Customize your plan for the targeted audience.

CRITICAL THINKING EXERCISES

1. Who are typical online buyers and sellers? What are some of the strategic implications of these facts to online marketers?

2. Some marketers argue that search marketing is a more effective means of using the Web to advertise than traditional pop-up or banner ads. Research the concept of search marketing. What are some of the benefits of using search marketing?

3. Log on to the Facebook, Tumblr, or Pinterest page of a company that you like or follow. What are people saying about the company, its goods and services, problems they'd like solved, or new products they'd like to see? How do they describe their experiences and their general views as consumers?

4. When designing a social media marketing plan, marketers must be sure to select and use channels as they were intended—or risk difficulties. For each of the following, state your choice of channel type (social networking site, microblog, bookmarking site, and so forth) and explain why.
   a. discussion of product attributes
   b. opinion survey
   c. exchange of ideas for saving energy
   d. personal stories
   e. video contest featuring pets

5. How do you view the future of social media—and social media marketing? Write a description citing three or four trends or developments you think may evolve over the next decade.

ETHICS EXERCISE

One of the lingering obstacles to digital marketing revolves around privacy concerns. Virtually all websites collect user data. Internet service providers, for example, can track where users go on the Web and store that information. Search engines keep detailed data on Internet searches by users. Those who argue that additional privacy laws and regulations are needed claim that users never know exactly what information is collected, nor when it is collected. Moreover, there is no means for determining whether websites follow their own privacy policies.

On the other hand, some say current laws and regulations are adequate because they make it illegal for firms to misrepresent their privacy policies or fail to disclose the type of information collected. Furthermore, there is no evidence that Internet companies are quietly passing on specific customer information to outside parties. Aside from the strictly legal issues, Web privacy raises a number of ethical issues as well.

Assume your company collects and stores personal information about its online customers. The company's privacy policy allows the company to give limited amounts of that information to "selected" third parties.

1. Is this policy, in your opinion, appropriate and adequate? What ethical issues does your company's policy raise?
2. How would you change the privacy policy to reflect your ethical concerns?
3. From strictly an economic perspective, is the company's existing policy adequate and appropriate?

CASE 4.1

Procter & Gamble Goes Digital

Undertaking marketing research to find out what background colour works best in online ads is just one way Procter & Gamble (P&G) is ramping up its digital marketing campaign. These efforts aren't breaking the company's advertising budget either. P&G wants to gradually *reduce* its advertising expenditures, saving as much as $1 billion, partly by emphasizing cost-efficient digital over pricey television ads and increasing digital's share of the company's overall marketing budget. The idea is to use social media, in particular, to build relationships with customers, so when they're making product choices in the store, they'll select P&G as the brand they're most comfortable with, even if it isn't always the cheapest one.

As technology and its marketing strategy both evolve, the company is making what it sees as a natural transition from search ads to banner ads and on to social media. For example, P&G recently noticed online chatter about Pepto Bismol on weekend mornings, most likely from people who had overeaten the night before. After it launched a Facebook campaign touting the indigestion reliever whose sales had been relatively flat for several years, market share grew 11 percent.

Another motivator for P&G's move to digital is that members of its primary target audience, women 25 to 45, spend 14 percent more time on Facebook than other users—that usage added up to almost 500 minutes per person in one recent month. P&G also works through Twitter and YouTube, creates product blogs, and has Facebook pages for all its major products, plus online advocacy campaigns on topics inspired by customer focus groups. The company's Facebook presence for its Secret deodorant, for example, addresses bullying among teen girls and helped launch the online "Mean Stinks" anti-bullying campaign, featuring Amber Riley of the TV hit *Glee*. Marketing for Secret has gone entirely digital, in fact. "These days, social media is an integral part of brand building," says the company's head of e-business.

And what colour works best on Facebook? P&G discovered that orange "can have a dramatic impact on purchase intent," says its marketing director.

Questions for Critical Thinking

1. Do you agree with P&G that online marketing will save money without hurting its brands in the marketplace? Why or why not?
2. What nonfinancial advantages of online marketing can P&G try to achieve? How will these benefits help it increase market share?

Sources: Lauren Coleman-Lochner, "Social Networking Takes Center Stage at P&G," *Bloomberg Businessweek*, March 29, 2012, **www.businessweek.com**; Emily Glazer, "P&G's Marketing Chief Looks to Go Digital," *The Wall Street Journal*, March 13, 2012, **http://online.wsj.com**; Jack Neff, "P&G Finds Orange Ads Work Better on Facebook," *Advertising Age*, February 27, 2012, **www.adage.com**; Jack Neff, "Marketers: Digital Offers Us More for Less," *Advertising Age*, February 27, 2012, **www.adage.com**.

CASE 4.2

Social Media Promotions

Social media has significantly expanded the opportunities available to organizations on how they market their products. As countries around the world see their economies improving, the amount being spent on marketing is increasing and most predictions see this trend continuing for some time to come. A significant amount of the increases are being directed toward social media. Some industry experts even predict that organizations will spend more on social media than some more traditional advertising like radio and magazines. The increase in social media ad spending is due in part to the increasing number of people who have smartphones and tablets. This trend is also predicted to continue.

As with most new technologies, the rapid development of social media as an advertising medium has not always been successful. Many organizations have experimented with social media while others are sitting back to see what works for other companies. A recent survey of Canadian retailers shows that many are taking a cautious approach to social media. During the Christmas season, most retailers spend heavily on advertising and yet less than 40 percent of those included in the survey stated that they would be using social media. These retailers are using a very focused approach to social media with 99 percent on Facebook but just over 50 percent using Twitter. The customer demographics and product type seem to be the main drivers of what social media is being used. For young women, Pinterest works for products in the fashion industry while for products that need to be demonstrated YouTube or Vine videos are the medium of choice. Most Canadian retailers say that some form of social media will be included in their overall marketing strategy throughout the coming year.

Some companies have used social media successfully. WestJet is one company that has used social media for several years, particularly during its holiday advertising. In a recent year, it used a real-time marketing promotion called "The WestJet Christmas Miracle" that was documented and uploaded to social media. The company set up an interactive video booth in the airport with a Santa clad in WestJet blue asking travellers of a particular flight what they wanted for Christmas. The travellers, young and old, asked Santa for everything from a big-screen television to socks and underwear. WestJet employees went to work as Santa's elves shopping for all the items the passengers asked for. The gifts were then wrapped, and when the flight landed instead of luggage coming down the turnstile, brightly coloured presents arrived to shocked passengers. The company did not stop giving with the passengers of that flight. When the number of viewers of the video on YouTube grew to a certain point, the company donated flights to their partner charity, Ronald McDonald House. This type of promotion may be expensive for companies but the benefits include the large number of viewers who watch the videos, the word of mouth generated from them, and the internal goodwill for those employees who got to be part of the experience.

Not all social media promotions are geared to holidays. Ford Motor Company teamed up with the YouTube channel Just For Laughs Gags to produce a short video called "Valet Thief–Police Pursuit Prank." In the video, a bag full of money is thrown from a Ford Focus and several people in the area are caught up in the drama of the police trying to determine where the money came from. A representative from Ford said the spot was "aimed at 25 to 40 years living in a urban market." This stunt was also aired in cinemas toward the same market.

Companies like WestJet and Ford are using social media to promote their products and services in unique ways. It is likely we will see more of this as more companies feel comfortable with social media.

Questions for Critical Thinking

1. In your view, do WestJet and Ford use social media effectively? Why or why not?
2. What do you think the benefits of these social media promotions are? What are the drawbacks?

Sources: Alicia Androich, "WestJet Gives Shocked Travellers Gifts in Real-Time," *Marketing*, **www.marketingmag.ca**, December 9, 2013; Sarah Mahoney, "Retailers Backing Away From Mobile," *Marketing Daily*, **www.mediapost.com**, December 5, 2013: Chris Powell, "Digital, Mobile and Big-Event Sports Boost Ad World in 2014," *Marketing*, **www.marketingmag.ca**, December 9, 2013; Michelle DiPardo, "Ford Teams up with Just For Laughs Gags for Focus Stunt," *Marketing*, **www .marketingmag.ca**, November 14, 2013; "WestJet and Santa Surprise Travellers with a Holiday Miracle," WestJet website, **http://westjet2.mediaroom .com**, December 9, 2013; "Valet Thief–Police Pursuit Prank (JFL Gags X Ford)," YouTube, November 11, 2013.

chapter 5

Consumer Behaviour

CHAPTER OBJECTIVES

1. Define *consumer behaviour* and describe the role it plays in marketing decisions.

2. Describe the interpersonal determinants of consumer behaviour: cultural, social, and family influences.

3. Explain each of the personal determinants of consumer behaviour: needs and motives, perceptions, attitudes, learning, and self-concept theory.

4. Distinguish between high-involvement and low-involvement purchase decisions.

5. Outline the steps in the consumer decision process.

6. Differentiate among routinized response behaviour, limited problem solving, and extended problem solving by consumers.

IS SOCIAL MEDIA CHANGING HOW WE SHOP?

Social media has affected how companies market their products but it has also changed how customers shop for products. In order to be successful, marketers need to understand the customers who shop online and how these customers interface with the various online sites. The growing importance of this area of marketing has prompted many studies to be conducted in order to better understand who these customers are.

Shopping online requires Internet access, and no one can question that Canada is a connected nation since 83 percent of Canadians have Internet access. There is very little difference in the numbers across the country, with Newfoundland and New Brunswick at the low end at only a 77 percent connection rate, and British Columbia with the highest rate of Internet users at 87 percent. These statistics indicate that the majority of Canadians have access to the technology that allows them to shop online.

Canadians are using this Internet access to shop online. According to Statistics Canada, in the two-year period from 2010 to 2012, the value of purchases Canadian consumers made online increased by 24 percent, and 5 percent more Internet users made online purchases. Some of the most popular online purchases were travel arrangements, tickets for entertainment events, and clothing.

The age of the shopper is related to who shops online. The highest number of online shoppers is aged 25 to 34: 69 percent of those in this age group make online purchases. Age is not the only factor that helps marketers understand the online consumer. One study researching the online shopping habits of women found that another determining factor was the amount of time they were spending online. Women who spent more time online generally were also likely to be shopping online. The study found that 18 percent of female online users worldwide fit into the heavy-user category, making them the most likely online shoppers. This study found that most Canadian women were not considered to be heavy users of the Internet for shopping— only 14 percent were classified as heavy Internet users. The only other area of the world with such low numbers for heavy Internet usage and online shopping was South Africa. The study also identified other characteristics of frequent online shoppers. Women classified as heavy users and online shoppers tended to be younger, with almost 40 percent of them under the age of 40 and with average household incomes above $60,000. This group of shoppers is not looking for coupons or deals but brands that add value to their lives.

Not all online shoppers are purchasing products when they visit a website—some are looking for information. One study found that 51 percent of Canadians who were shopping online were just looking for information. These shoppers wanted to find store locations or were determining if point-of-sale promotions were available.

Online shoppers are also accessing the Internet from a variety of locations and devices. Another study found that 75 percent of smartphone owners used their phones while shopping in retail stores. These shoppers were accessing the retailer's website to obtain information about products they discovered in the stores. Canadians also use different devices to connect to the Internet when shopping.

The majority of online shoppers, however, are looking to save money. They want prices to be comparable to or lower than what they would find in the stores, and many won't purchase online unless the shipping is free.

If retailers observe and understand these trends, they can tailor their marketing strategies to influence shoppers to make purchases. For example, if a retailer understands which customers use social media as part of their shopping experience, they can develop social media campaigns as part of their marketing programs. However, Canadian retailers are cautious about developing mobile-related technologies, particularly the location-based apps. There are several reasons for their cautious approach. The technology is expensive to implement, retailers fear that it will have to be updated frequently, and not enough customers are requesting it. Most experts agree that because so many customers now have smartphones, these devices will become a more important part of the shopping experience.[1]

connecting with customers

Customers' shopping habits vary depending on their characteristics and on influences like social media. Companies selling products are better at connecting with their customers when they understand why their customers' shopping behaviour has changed. More and more customers are shopping online but not all customers want the same things from their online shopping experience.

Chapter Overview

Why does your best friend drive five kilometres out of the way for Tim Hortons coffee when the local coffee shop is much closer? Why do people prefer one brand of pop over another? The answers to these questions aren't obvious but they directly affect every aspect of the marketing strategy, from product development to pricing, distribution, and promotion. Developing a marketing strategy requires an understanding of the process by which consumers buy goods and services for their personal use and organizational buyers purchase business products.

A variety of influences affects both individuals buying items for themselves and personnel purchasing products for their firms. This chapter focuses on individual purchasing behaviour, which applies to all of us. Consumer behaviour is the process through which the ultimate buyer makes purchase decisions for small items such as toothbrushes as well as big-ticket items such as autos and vacations. Chapter 6 will shift the focus to business buying decisions.

The study of consumer behaviour builds on an understanding of human behaviour in general. In their efforts to understand why and how consumers make buying decisions, marketers borrow extensively from the sciences of psychology and sociology. The work of psychologist Kurt Lewin, for example, provides a useful classification scheme for influences on buying behaviour.

Lewin's work determined that behaviour is a function of the interactions of personal influences and pressures exerted by outside environmental forces.

Consumer behaviour is influenced by the interactions of interpersonal influences—such as culture, friends, classmates, co-workers, and relatives—and personal factors—such as attitudes, learning, and perception. In other words, inputs from others and an individual's psychological makeup affect his or her purchasing behaviour. Before looking at how consumers make purchase decisions, we first consider how both interpersonal and personal factors affect consumers. ◆◆◆

---

① **Define *consumer behaviour* and describe the role it plays in marketing decisions.**

consumer behaviour Process through which buyers make purchase decisions.

Marketoid

Canadians purchase almost $19 billion worth of merchandise online annually.

culture Values, beliefs, preferences, and tastes handed down from one generation to the next.

INTERPERSONAL DETERMINANTS OF CONSUMER BEHAVIOUR

You don't make purchase decisions in a vacuum. You might not be aware of it, but every buying decision you make is influenced by a variety of external and internal factors. Consumers often decide to buy goods and services based on what they believe others expect of them. They may want to project positive images to peers or to satisfy the unspoken desires of family members. They may buy a certain book because someone they respect recommended it. Or they may make reservations at a particular restaurant based on a good review in the newspaper. They may buy a home in a certain neighbourhood they think will impress their family and friends. Students may even choose which college or university to attend based on where their parents went, how the school ranked for certain features, or on their friends' impression of the school. Marketers recognize three broad categories of interpersonal influences on consumer behaviour: cultural, social, and family influences. Figure 5.1 shows how these interpersonal determinants as well as personal determinants influence the consumer decision-making process. Personal determinants and the decision-making process are discussed later in the chapter.

CULTURAL INFLUENCES

Culture can be defined as the values, beliefs, preferences, and tastes handed down from one generation to the next. Culture is the broadest environmental determinant of consumer behaviour. Marketers need to understand its role in consumer decision making, both in Canada and abroad. They must also monitor trends in cultural values as well as recognize changes in these values.

Marketing strategies and business practices that work in one country may be offensive or ineffective in another. Strategies may even have to be varied from one area of a country to another. Nowhere is that more true than in Canada, where the population continues to diversify at a rapid pace. When you insert your bank card into an ATM, the first option on the screen often is what language you prefer for the transaction. Companies like Kraft Canada are tailoring their marketing strategies to different cultural groups, including developing products aimed at Chinese and South Asian consumers. Kraft launched its new products with advertising aimed at these markets and through designated websites featuring culturally inspired recipes.[2] The Canadian population is also moving rapidly away from the two original cultural groups; today, fewer Canadians identify themselves as of British or French ethnic origin.

figure 5.1

Integrated Model of the Consumer Decision Process

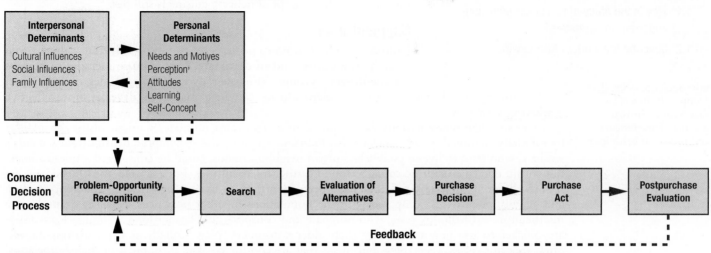

Source: Roger Blackwell, Paul W. Minard, and James F. Engel, *Consumer Behavior*, 10th Edition (Mason, OH: South-Western, 2004).

Core Values in Canadian Culture

Some cultural values change over time, but basic core values do not. Core values are underlying motivations that move society forward and are shaped by the people one grows up with. The Canadian Marketing Association has identified four core Canadian values, which are these: a unique balance between individualism and collectivism, an attitude of tolerance and acceptance, a heightened appreciation for a quality of life, and an essentially peaceful predisposition.[3] Michael Adams, president of the research company Environics, has studied the social values of the Canadian population for over 20 years. His extensive work in studying changing social values has covered not only the Canadian population but how we compare to our U.S. neighbours.[4]

Values that change over time also have their effects. As technology rapidly changes the way people exchange information, consumers adopt values that include communicating with anyone, anytime, anywhere in the world. The generation that includes older teens and young twenty-somethings is adept at learning and using rapidly changing communications technology, including smartphones. They regularly communicate through social media. Marketers are recognizing this, and in anticipation of more consumers adopting new communications technology, they are increasing their allocation of resources to reach consumers in this way. Starbucks customers can use a Starbucks app on their smartphone to pay for their purchases, reload their card, and even send a gift card to one of their phone or Facebook contacts.[5]

International Perspective on Cultural Influences

Cultural differences are particularly important for international marketers. Marketing strategies that prove successful in one country often cannot extend to other international markets because of cultural variations. Europe is a good example, with many different languages and a wide range of lifestyles and product preferences. Even though the continent is becoming a single economic unit as a result of the expansion of the European Union and the widespread use of the euro as currency, cultural divisions continue to define multiple markets.

For years, Domino's has been a known quantity in North America, and now its business has gone global. Nearly half of its stores are outside North America and soon, management predicts, overseas stores will outstrip domestic ones. "We move very fast in international markets," says Domino's executive Peter Doyle. "When we see opportunities, we act on them."

What's behind this global success? In part, management says, it's fitting the product to local tastes. The Taiwanese like shrimp and peapods on their pizza; in England, tuna and sweet corn are favourites. And sometimes, a new ingredient just takes off. When Domino's arrived in Japan, the Japanese had no word for "pepperoni." Today, pepperoni is one of the most popular toppings in Japan.

(2) **Describe the interpersonal determinants of consumer behaviour: cultural, social, and family influences.**

microcultures Smaller groups within a society that have their own distinct characteristics and modes of behaviour.

While Domino's believes pizza is universal, in some countries, it's still an acquired taste. In China, for example, dairy hasn't always been part of the diet, and the concept of delivery cuisine is still new.[6]

Microcultures

Cultures are not homogeneous groups with universal values, even though core values tend to dominate. Each culture includes numerous **microcultures**—groups with their own distinct modes of behaviour. Understanding the differences among microcultures can help marketers develop more effective marketing strategies.

Canada, like many nations, is composed of a significant number of microcultures that differ by ethnicity, nationality, age, social class, location, religion, and geographic distribution. Canada's wealthy, who tend to live in established urban neighbourhoods, could be considered a microculture, but within that microculture could be found further microcultures. For example, the Quebec market has 15 different lifestyle types that have been identified as having significantly different product and activity preferences compared with the populations in other provinces. Another example of a microculture is Orthodox Jews, who purchase and consume only kosher foods. Younger consumers are quicker to use new technology than older consumers. New Canadians from various nations often seek out spices, vegetables, and meats that are considered tasty or popular in their homelands. Understanding these and other differences among microcultures contributes to successful marketing of goods and services.

Canada's racial mix continues to change. According to Statistics Canada, by 2031, between 25 and 28 percent of Canadians will be foreign-born, and 29 to 32 percent will belong to a group that classifies itself as a visible minority. This would be the highest proportion of the population ever and represents a 3 percent increase from the previous census when just over 16 percent of the population classified themselves in this group.[7]

Other changes predicted for these microculture segments of the population will affect what products companies market and how they market them. For example, the composition of microculture segments is likely to change. By 2031, it is expected that the group identifying themselves as South Asian is likely to be larger than the Chinese group, making these the two largest ethnic groups in Canada. Blacks and Filipinos are predicted to remain as the third- and

The importance of family is a core value in Canadian culture. Boston Pizza has special offers to promote families dining together.

Courtesy of Boston Pizza International Inc.

fourth-largest groups but the fastest-growing groups will be made up of those who are of West Asian and Arab heritage. These cultural groups tend to be younger than the rest of the population and are predicted to remain so. Toronto, Vancouver, and Montreal will be home to most of these cultural groups—71 percent—as is the case today, but they will represent an increasing percentage of the populations in these cities.[8]

Marketers need to be sensitive to these changes and to the differences in shopping patterns and buying habits among ethnic segments of the population. Businesses must develop marketing messages that consider the needs of these different types of consumers. For example, members of one microculture might be attracted to bargain offers while those of another might be offended by them. Marketing concepts may not always cross cultural boundaries without changes. For example, new immigrants may not be familiar with cents-off coupons and contests. Marketers may need to provide specific instructions when targeting such promotions to these groups. Although no cultural or ethnic microculture is entirely homogeneous, researchers have found that each of these ethnic segments has identifiable consumer behaviour profiles.

Canada has one of the highest proportions of population born outside the country. Figure 5.2 shows the percentage of the population that was foreign born for several countries. The only country with a higher percentage than Canada is Australia.

Quebecois

One group, the Quebecois or French Canadians, is more often viewed as one of Canada's two main cultural groups. From a marketing point of view, it doesn't make a difference whether you treat the Quebecois as a microculture or one of Canada's two main cultural groups. What does matter is that this group is very large and significantly different from the rest of Canada in many ways. However, like other cultural groups, the French-speaking inhabitants of Quebec and the pockets of French-speaking communities across the rest of Canada are not a homogeneous group. Quebec is the largest French-speaking area in North America but there are also a large number of English-speaking residents in the province and as many other nationalities in the province as there are in the rest of Canada. Almost a quarter of the population of Quebec lives in Montreal, and 63 percent of those are French speaking. Quebecois are more likely to live in cities than in rural areas.[9]

The population of Quebec, like many areas of Canada, is getting older. Currently, Quebec ranks as one of the oldest populations, with a median age of 41.4 as opposed to the median age for Canada at 39.9. There are currently over 1.3 million Quebecers over the age of 65 and for the first time ever there are more seniors living in Quebec than children.[10]

Consumer behaviour depends on psychological and social factors. Jacques Bouchard, founder of a Quebec advertising agency and the father of made-in-Quebec advertising, studied the psychological and social factors that were important to Quebecois. The results of his work indicate that while the Quebecois are looking more and more like the rest of Canada, strong differences still exist in many areas, and there are lasting influences from the days when the differences were much greater. More recent research still supports the findings of Bouchard. For example, the Quebecois are very brand loyal and prefer brands they consider as local. For marketers, this means it is difficult entering this market with brands that are established elsewhere in the country or the world. Companies that understand these differences have been successful in this market. Home Depot, for example, was having difficulty in the market until it changed its

figure 5.2

Percentage of the Total Population That Was Foreign-Born

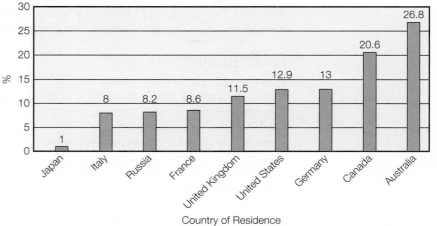

Country of Residence

Source: "Immigration and Ethnocultural Diversity in Canada," National Household Survey, 2011, Statistics Canada, Catalogue no. 99-010-X2011001, page 7.

MARKETING AND THE SME

Headspace: The Knowledge to Build Brands in Quebec

"SUCCESSFUL brand building in Quebec is knowing when to adopt, adapt, or create for Quebec" is the statement that Eric Blais and his team at Headspace marketing use to describe marketing in Quebec. He advises his clients, "There are an awful lot of similarities between Quebec and ROC [rest of Canada], and they certainly often don't require a different approach. But sometimes, the differences can be a competitive advantage that you can leverage." Eric was born in Quebec and grew up there, but offices of Headspace are situated in both Toronto and Montreal.

Recently the company decided to do some research to determine if the "36 keys" identified by Jacques Bouchard were still relevant to the Quebec market. The study involved 3,000 participants across the country. This new research identified what Blais calls "Five Heartstrings" or attitudes that are stronger in Quebec than in the rest of Canada. These include the following:

1. Living in the moment—Today is more important than tomorrow
2. Chez nous—Their sense of local pride is strong
3. Joyful living—They are pleasure seekers
4. All about me—Looking out for themselves is important
5. Life, uncomplicated—They prefer all aspects of their life to be simple

In addition to the "five heartstrings," this study determined that the Quebecois have a higher brand loyalty than the rest of Canada. French participants of the study scored roughly 10 percent higher on questions relating to brand loyalty.

Headspace Consulting uses this research to help companies like Weston Foods Canada develop promotional campaigns for the Quebec market. One such campaign for the Country Harvest Brand bread featured Quebec-born actress Pascale Bussières. One of the reasons Bussières agreed to act as spokesperson for the brand was the partnership with the organization Food Banks of Quebec.

Sources: Matt Semansky, "Plus ça Change…," *Marketing*, **www.marketingmag.ca**, October 27, 2008; Headspace website, **http://headspacemarketing.com**, accessed January 4, 2014; Caroline Fortin, "Weston Makes Bussieres Spokesperson for Quebec," *Marketing*, **www.marketingmag.ca**, February 28, 2013; Caroline Fortin, "Headspace Says It Knows What Quebec Consumers Want," *Marketing*, **www.marketingmag.ca**, May 16, 2013; Susan Krashinsky, "Target Take Note: Quebec Market Tricky for Outsiders," *The Globe and Mail*, **www.theglobeandmail.com**, March 4, 2013.

advertising strategy. Target stores also experienced some problems launching into the Quebec market. Brand awareness for Target stores was 92 percent in the rest of Canada but roughly 20 percent lower in Quebec.[11] Some marketing consulting firms specialize in the Quebec market, as discussed in the "Marketing and the SME" feature.

Marketing to the Quebec population has moved through several distinct phases. Up to the 1970s, marketers used the same marketing strategies for Quebec as they used for the rest of Canada and merely translated advertising copy into French. Then along came Jacques Bouchard. He put forward the "twin beds" theory: where advertising was concerned, Quebec and the rest of Canada shared the same bedroom but slept in different beds. He demonstrated that marketing campaigns would be more successful if they were designed specifically for the Quebec market. Today, with the distinctions that have made Quebec unique disappearing and the move toward global markets, the "twin beds" theory is being challenged. Some feel that the Quebec identity has become so strong and established that the Quebecois are feeling less threatened by marketing that is more Canadian or global rather than specific to their market.[12]

Chinese Canadians

Chinese immigrants have been coming to Canada since 1788, when they first landed on Vancouver Island. This group didn't represent a significant number until the 1980s, a decade that saw a large insurgence of Hong Kong Chinese before the colony was repatriated by China in 1997. Along with the Hong Kong group came their wealth, talents, education, and an entrepreneurial spirit to invest in Canada. They established themselves in four major centres across the country: Vancouver, Toronto, Calgary, and Edmonton. These relatively large clusters mean that their cultural influence will be maintained for some time. The influx of people from Asian countries is expected to slow in the coming years but this group will maintain a large influence on Canadian society.[13]

The impact of this cultural group on marketing strategies is significant. Chinese-Canadian consumers spend $34.6 billion annually. The average Chinese household saves 24 percent of their annual income. This group is generally young, is made up of early adopters, and likes high-end brands, particularly if they perceive they are getting the products at a good price. They relate best to advertising and packaging in their own language, feeling that it shows respect. They like to shop in Chinese malls and supermarkets such as T&T Supermarkets that carry imported products. This group also responds more favourably to advertising than the average Canadian.[14]

South Asian Canadians

Like the Chinese Canadians, the South Asian Canadian group comes from several cultures, including Punjabi, Urdu, and Tamil. This is the second-largest cultural group in Canada but is expected to surpass the Chinese by 2031. A large number of this group was born in Canada. The largest number lives in Toronto and surrounding communities, but significant numbers can be found in all the larger centres across the country. A smaller number of this group is elderly, suggesting that parents and grandparents did not accompany the family when they moved to Canada. South Asians tend to associate more with their own sub-ethnic group rather than the South Asian community as a whole, a feature that fragments the segment into even smaller groups who maintain strong links with the communities they left.[15]

Some companies, Home Depot being a notable example, have started to develop marketing campaigns aimed at the South Asian market. Their marketing program included in-store workshops demonstrating home repair projects, as well as in-store signage and bag stuffers, in Punjabi and Hindi. Home Depot also placed ads in Hindi and Punjabi newspapers. One marketing trend for this group is to take advantage of the South Asians' love for pop culture by sponsoring music festivals and getting the stars of Bollywood movies to promote products and brands.[16]

Other Cultural Groups

More than 80 ethnic groups live in Canada. Many of these groups live in clusters or pockets across the country. For example, Winnipeg has a large Filipino population. Communities where these population clusters live have developed cultural infrastructures that include newspapers, social clubs, and even radio stations. In order to effectively market to specific cultural groups, both an understanding of these infrastructures and access to them are helpful. In Canada, as in most multicultural nations, marketing too is becoming more multicultural so it is important to understand which aspects of a marketing strategy will be affected by cultural influences and which won't.[17]

SOCIAL INFLUENCES

Every consumer belongs to a number of social groups. A child's earliest group experience comes from membership in a family. As children grow older, they join other groups such as friendship groups, neighbourhood groups, school groups, organizations, and sports teams. Adults are also members of various groups at work and in the community.

Group membership influences an individual's purchase decisions and behaviour in both overt and subtle ways. Every group establishes certain norms of behaviour. Norms are the values, attitudes, and behaviours that a group deems appropriate for its members. Group members are expected to comply with these norms. Members of such diverse groups as the Harley Owners Group (H.O.G.), the Canadian Medical Association, and any local social or cultural club tend to adopt their organization's norms of behaviour. Norms can even affect nonmembers. Individuals who aspire to membership in a group may adopt its standards of behaviour and values.

Differences in group status and roles can also affect buying behaviour. Status is the relative position of any individual member in a group; roles define behaviour that members of a group expect of individuals who hold specific positions within that group. Some groups (such as Rotary

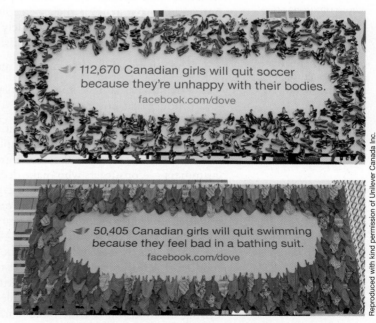

Some companies like Unilever use creative promotions, like attaching bathing suits or soccer cleats to their billboards, in order to change social influences.

Club or Lions Club) define formal roles, and others (such as a book club among friends) impose informal expectations. Both types of groups supply each member with both status and roles; in doing so, they influence that person's activities—including his or her purchase behaviour.

Social media provides an opportunity for individuals to form and be influenced by new types of groups. Mailing lists and chat rooms allow groups to form around common interests. Some of these online virtual communities can develop norms and membership roles similar to those found in real-world groups. For example, to avoid criticism, members must observe rules for proper protocol in posting messages and participating in chats.

People often make purchases designed to reflect their status within a particular group, particularly when the purchase is considered expensive by society. In the past few years, affluent consumers have spent money on home renovations and exotic trips. Loyal customers of Apple products are willing to pay top dollar for the latest gadgets, apps, and upgrades, not only because of their high quality, but because of the status they reflect.

As the economy fluctuates, affluent shoppers actually achieve status by shopping at discount stores and consignment shops. Searching for the best value becomes the new norm—and status symbol.[18] But these consumers are willing to spend more on fresh or organic produce, often found at upscale grocery markets. And they like to tout the health and environmental benefits of these foods. Over the past several years, as the economy has dipped and adjusted itself, a new norm has emerged for most consumers, regardless of their economic standing—restrained spending and an emphasis on value. In fact, a certain amount of frugality has become chic.

Groups influence an individual's purchase decisions more than is realized. Most people tend to adhere in varying degrees to the general expectations of any group that they consider important, often without conscious awareness of this motivation. The surprising impact of groups and group norms on individual behaviour has been called the Asch phenomenon, named after social psychologist S.E. Asch, who through his research first documented characteristics of individual behaviour. Asch found that individuals would conform to majority rule, even if that majority rule went against their beliefs. The Asch phenomenon can be a big factor in many purchase decisions, from major choices such as buying a house or car to more minor purchases, such as deciding whether to buy a pair of shoes on sale.

Reference Groups

reference groups
People or institutions whose opinions are valued and to whom a person looks for guidance in his or her own behaviour, values, and conduct, such as family, friends, or celebrities.

Discussion of the Asch phenomenon raises the subject of reference groups—groups whose value structures and standards influence a person's behaviour. Consumers usually try to coordinate their purchase behaviour with their perceptions of the values of their reference groups. The extent of reference-group influence varies widely among individuals. Strong influence by a group on a member's purchase requires two conditions:

1. The purchased product must be one that others can see and identify.

2. The purchased item must be conspicuous; it must stand out as something unusual, a brand or product that not everyone owns.

Reference-group influence would significantly affect the decision to buy a luxury home in an upscale neighbourhood, for example, but it would have little or no impact on the decision to purchase a loaf of bread. Reference group influence can create what some marketers call "elastic customers"—consumers who make decisions to save or splurge in the same economy. During a slow economy, a customer might purchase generic brands at the supermarket but, because of reference group influence, spend those savings on designer jeans or a flat-screen TV. Banking on the fact that grandparents like to show off their grandchildren to friends—and are willing to spend money to do so, even if they skimp on themselves—some retailers offer premium-priced apparel for babies and small children. Roots and the Gap both have lines of premium-priced clothing for children and toddlers.[19] A reference group that tries to change consumer consumption patterns is described in the "Marketing: Making Your World Better" feature.

Children are especially vulnerable to the influence of reference groups. They often base their buying decisions on outside forces such as what they see on television and the Internet (including social network sites) or the opinions of friends. Understanding this phenomenon, marketers sometimes take a step back so that older children, preteens, and teens can shop—even if they don't have

One Earth—One Chance...

that is the motto of the Sierra Club of Canada. The organization started in 1963 as a Canadian chapter of the U.S. organization and now has chapters across the country, including youth groups. The Sierra Club's mission is to "empower people to protect, restore and enjoy a healthy and safe planet."

The organization encourages its members to be as environmentally aware in their day-to-day lives as their educational and advocacy campaigns promote. Not only does the organization influence the consumer behaviour of its members but also the people of the many partner foundations, corporations, other organizations, and the general public. The organization's partners are as diverse as the projects the Sierra Club takes on, including the RBC Foundation and Frito Lay Canada.

Internal programs in place to reduce the Sierra Club's environmental footprint include encouraging its staff to use public transit, reducing the amount of paper used by the organization, and using only recycled paper. The group encourages the use of fair-trade organic coffee, tea, and chocolate. Even the organization's office equipment is second-hand and when no longer needed is recycled.

The external causes the Sierra Club is involved in include promoting a nuclear-free Canada, saving the Churchill River from power development projects, and slowing globalization by speaking out against free trade. Another project, ActionH2O, involves water conservation whereby the club is working with cities and towns to find ways to better manage the country's water supply. Club members support projects in areas where wild life is threatened through bad management, or where a species is threatened by logging or oil production.

The Sierra Club has been successful at getting its environmental message out and is an important part of the environmental movement in Canada. Members are often asked to give their advice on any new environmental issue affecting any region of the country.

Sources: Sierra Club Canada website, **www.sierraclub.ca**, January 5, 2014; "The Real Truth about Wind Energy: A Literature Review on Wind Turbines in Ontario," **www.sierraclub.ca**, June 10, 2011; Joe Castaldo, "Environment: Nuclear Options," **www.canadianbusiness.com**, April 11, 2011; Matthew McClearn, "Food: Something's Fishy," **www.canadianbusiness.com**, April 8, 2011.

---

their own money to spend. More retailers now welcome teens who browse but don't buy. These retailers know they are still developing loyal customers—the teens will return when they have their own or their parents' money.

In addition, marketers are recognizing the power of the Internet, including smartphones and social networking sites, as a tool for reaching children and teens—not just to market new or existing products, but to learn more about reference groups and upcoming trends. Ninety-five percent of consumers ages 12 to 17 are online, visiting social networking sites, getting information, and forming opinions from these interactions. They download music, play games, and participate in interactive marketing online, but still prefer to shop at brick-and-mortar stores; less than 50 percent are making online purchases.[20]

Marketoid

Sixty-nine percent of Internet users between the ages of 25 and 34 make online purchases.

Social Classes

Research has identified six classes within the social structures of both small and large North American cities: the upper-upper, lower-upper, upper-middle, and lower-middle classes, followed by the working class and lower class. Class rankings are determined by occupation, income, education, family background, and residence location. Note that income is not always a primary determinant; pipe fitters paid at union scale earn more than many university professors, but their purchase behaviour may be quite different. Still, the ability to make certain purchases such as a private jet or an ocean-view home is an important factor in determining class.

Family characteristics, such as the occupations and incomes of one or both parents, have been the primary influences on social class. People in one social class may aspire to a higher class and therefore exhibit buying behaviour common to that class rather than to their own. For example, middle-class consumers often buy items they associate with the upper classes. Marketers of certain luxury goods appeal to these consumers. Tiffany—traditionally associated with high-end luxury goods—now offers its items in price ranges and locations attractive to middle-class consumers. Saks Fifth Avenue, the luxury retailer recently purchased by the Hudson Bay Company, launched a private label collection of men's suits priced lower than some of its premier brands. The new collection features Italian-made wool suits and dress shirts.[21]

Marketers use language in their marketing messages designed to appeal to certain social classes or to those who aspire to them. Two examples are the Ocean Club, Bahamas—"50 years....oh the tales we could tell. Live the moment"—and American Express Travel—"Extraordinary is being able to afford a trip that you just can't afford to miss."[22]

Opinion Leaders

In nearly every reference group, a few members act as **opinion leaders**. These trendsetters are likely to purchase new products before others in the group and then share their experiences and opinions via word of mouth. As others in the group decide whether to try the same products, they are influenced by the reports of opinion leaders. Generalized opinion leaders are rare; instead, individuals tend to act as opinion leaders for specific goods or services based on their knowledge of and interest in those products. Their interest motivates them to seek out information from mass media, manufacturers, and other sources and, in turn, transmit this information to associates through interpersonal communications. Opinion leaders are found within all segments of the population.

Information about goods and services may flow from the Internet, television, or other mass media to opinion leaders and then from opinion leaders to others. In other instances, information flows directly from media sources to all consumers. In still other instances, a multi-step flow carries information from mass media to opinion leaders and then on to other opinion leaders before dissemination to the general public.

A product for those aspiring to a higher social class.

opinion leaders
Trendsetters who purchase new products before others in a group and then influence others in their purchases.

Some opinion leaders influence purchases by others merely through their own actions. Oprah Winfrey is one such individual. Through her on-air book clubs, she encouraged millions of viewers to read. And through many on-air wellness programs, she motivated viewers to commit to a more healthful lifestyle through diet and exercise. Winfrey launched her "No Phone Zone" campaign, urging viewers to sign an online pledge to refrain from texting or talking on their phones while driving. Winfrey continues to influence viewers' behaviour with her latest TV program, "Oprah's Next Chapter."[23]

FAMILY INFLUENCES

Most people are members of at least two families during their lifetimes—the ones they are born into and those they eventually form later in life. The family group is perhaps the most important determinant of consumer behaviour because of the close, continuing interactions among family members. Like other groups, each family typically has norms of expected behaviour, different roles, and status relationships for its members.

The traditional family structure consists of a husband, wife, and children. However, according to Statistics Canada, this structure has been steadily changing over the last century. Today, only about 67 percent of all households are headed by married couples. Many couples are separated or divorced, so single heads of households are more common. In addition, there has been an increase in households headed by same-sex couples. Women are having fewer children, giving birth later in life, and spacing their children farther apart. More women are choosing to live alone, with or without children. And more senior citizens are living alone or without younger generations present in their homes.[24] Still, to target a market for their goods

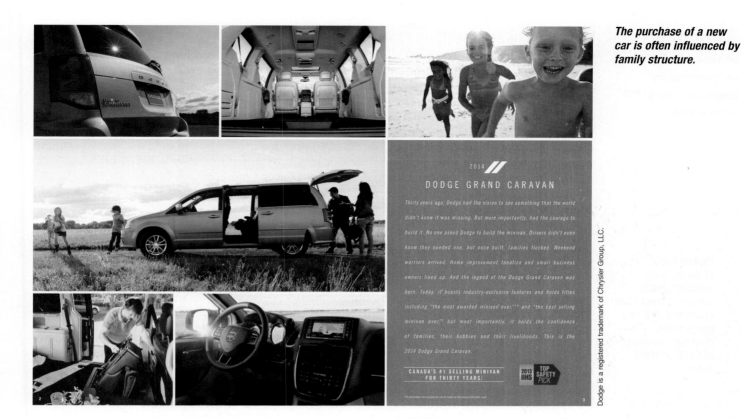

The purchase of a new car is often influenced by family structure.

and services, marketers find it useful to describe the role of each spouse in a household in terms of the following four categories:

1. *Autonomic role* is seen when the partners independently make equal numbers of decisions. Personal-care items would fall into the category of purchase decisions each would make for him- or herself.

2. *Husband-dominant role* occurs when the husband usually makes certain purchase decisions. Buying a wood stove or generator is a typical example.

3. *Wife-dominant role* has the wife making most of the buying decisions. Children's clothing is a typical wife-dominant purchase.

4. *Syncratic role* refers to joint decisions. The purchase of a house follows a syncratic pattern.

Numbers 2 and 3 on this list have changed dramatically over the years. The increasing occurrence of the two-income family means that women have a greater role in making large family purchases, such as homes, vacations, and automobiles. And studies show that women take the lead in choosing entertainment, such as movies and restaurants. Women now outspend men in the purchase of electronics. Conversely, as more highly educated women begin to out-earn their spouses, men are appearing more frequently at the grocery store because their wives are still at the office.[25] In addition, men are taking a more active role in child care. Both of these shifts in family life mean that marketers must consider both genders as potential customers when creating their marketing messages.

Studies of family decision making have also shown that households with two wage earners are more likely than others to make joint purchasing decisions. Members of two-income households often do their shopping in the evening and on weekends because of the number of hours spent at the workplace. Shifting family roles have created new markets for a variety of products. Goods and services that save time, promote family togetherness, emphasize safety, or encourage health and fitness appeal to the family values and influences of today.

assessment check 2

2.1 List the interpersonal determinants of consumer behaviour.

2.2 What is a microculture?

2.3 Describe the Asch phenomenon.

Children and Teenagers in Family Purchases

Children and teenagers represent a huge market, and they influence what their parents buy, from cereal to cars. These consumers are bombarded with messages from a variety of media. They are presented with a wide array of choices. Preteens and teens now have their own spending money but they are careful shoppers. A recent study showed that 59 percent of teen shoppers did research on products before they bought them. Some of the research was conducted over social media. This group of shoppers is also less concerned about brands, with 65 percent of them stating people place too much emphasis on branded products, and only 48 percent of them stated they would buy a branded product if it stood for something they believed in.[26]

Children and teens are wired but they are moving away from Facebook to other social media like Twitter, Instagram, and Tumblr. They feel there are too many adults on Facebook. These teens have not deleted their Facebook accounts—they just don't use them as much.[27]

③ Explain each of the personal determinants of consumer behaviour: needs and motives, perceptions, attitudes, learning, and self-concept theory.

PERSONAL DETERMINANTS OF CONSUMER BEHAVIOUR

Consumer behaviour is affected by a number of internal, personal factors in addition to interpersonal ones. Each individual brings unique needs, motives, perceptions, attitudes, learned responses, and self-concepts to buying decisions. This section looks at how these factors influence consumer behaviour.

NEEDS AND MOTIVES

need Imbalance between a consumer's actual and desired states.

Individual purchase behaviour is driven by the motivation to fill a perceived need. A **need** is an imbalance between the consumer's actual and desired states. A person who recognizes or feels a significant or urgent need will then seek to correct the imbalance. Marketers attempt to arouse this sense of urgency by making a need "felt" and then influencing consumers' motivation to satisfy their needs by purchasing specific products.

motive Inner state that directs a person toward the goal of satisfying a need.

Motives are inner states that direct a person toward the goal of satisfying a need. The individual takes action to reduce the state of tension and return to a condition of equilibrium.

Maslow's Hierarchy of Needs

Psychologist Abraham H. Maslow developed a theory that characterized needs and arranged them into a hierarchy. Maslow identified five levels of needs, beginning with physiological needs and progressing to the need for self-actualization. A person must at least partially satisfy lower-level needs, according to Maslow, before higher needs can affect behaviour. In developed countries, where relatively large per capita incomes allow most people to satisfy the basic needs on the hierarchy, higher-order needs may be more important to consumer behaviour. Table 5.1 illustrates products and marketing themes designed to satisfy needs at each level.

Physiological Needs

Needs at the most basic level concern essential requirements for survival, such as food, water, shelter, and clothing. Pur promotes its water filtration system with the slogan "Your water should be Pur." Its ads emphasize the need for clean water: "When you realize how often water touches your family's life, you discover just how important healthy, great-tasting water is."

Safety Needs

Second-level needs include financial or lifestyle security, protection from physical harm, and avoidance of the unexpected. To gratify these needs, consumers may buy insurance, retirement plans, or security devices. In one of its ads Fidelity asks, "Will you be ready for the retirement you have in mind?" The answer to the question is "Let Fidelity be your guide."

Courtesy of Agropur Dairy Cooperative/Natrel Division

Children often influence what their parents buy.

table 5.1   ***Marketing Strategies Based on Maslow's Hierarchy of Needs***

Physiological Needs	Products	Food, water, medicines, vitamins, exercise equipment and gym memberships, health care and cleaning products, sleep aids and mattresses, food for pets
	Marketing Themes	Colgate Total: "No. 1 recommended by dentists and hygienists." Purina pet food: "A difference you can see."
Safety Needs	Products	Health and life insurance, computer antivirus software, smoke and carbon monoxide detectors, antibacterial cleaners, auto safety features
	Marketing Themes	Allstate Insurance: "Protect what's important to you for less." Lysol Household Cleaner: "Disinfect to protect."
Belongingness Needs	Products	Cosmetics, food, entertainment, fashion, appliances and home furnishings, clubs and organizations, cars
	Marketing Themes	Payless Shoes: "Save now. Feel good." Ford: "Drive one."
Esteem Needs	Products	Fashion, jewellery, gourmet foods, electronics, cosmetics, luxury cars, credit cards, investments, sports and hobbies, travel
	Marketing Themes	Rolex watches: "A crown for every achievement." L'Oréal Paris: "Because you're worth it."
Self-Actualization Needs	Products	Education, cultural events, sports, hobbies, motivational seminars, technology, travel, investments
	Marketing Themes	Gatorade: "Is it in you?" Tony Robbins: "Unleash the power within."

Social/Belongingness Needs

Satisfaction of physiological and safety needs leads a person to attend to third-level needs—the desire to be accepted by people and groups important to that individual. To satisfy this need, people may join organizations and buy goods or services that make them feel part of a group. Air Canada's Altitude program is an example. Members have lounge access at the airport along with other benefits.

Esteem Needs

People have a universal desire for a sense of accomplishment and achievement. They also wish to gain the respect of others and even to exceed others' performance once lower-order needs are satisfied. Pandora's jewellery ads encourage consumers to buy its pieces because "Life has its moments—make them unforgettable."

Self-Actualization Needs

At the top rung of Maslow's ladder of human needs is people's desire to realize their full potential and to find fulfillment by expressing their unique talents and capabilities. Companies that run exotic adventure trips aim to satisfy consumers' needs for self-actualization. Not-for-profit organizations that invite paying volunteers to assist in such projects as archaeological digs or building homes for the needy appeal to these needs as well. Four Seasons resorts advertises one of its African locations by showing two of its guests riding elephants through the mist. "It's said they never forget," reads the tag line. "Neither will you."

Maslow believed that a satisfied need no longer has to be met. Once the physiological needs are met, the individual moves on to pursue satisfaction of higher-order needs. Consumers are periodically motivated by the need to relieve thirst and hunger, but their interests soon return to focus on satisfaction of safety, social, and other needs in the hierarchy. People may not always progress through the hierarchy; they may fixate on a certain level. For example, consumers who lived through

THE WORLD'S MOST AWARDED SINGLE MALT

The Glenfiddich range has won more medals for taste in international competitions than any other single malt Scotch whisky. The passion to create 'the best dram in the valley' began with our founder, William Grant, and has carried on through generations of care from our family. With complex notes of honey and raisins, our 15 year old is created using an innovative technique called the Solera Process, and produces a subtle marriage of influences.

Discover more at Glenfiddich.com

FAMILY RUN SINCE 1887

Glenfiddich SINGLE MALT SCOTCH WHISKY

Courtesy of William Grant & Sons Distillers Ltd.

Glenfiddich: Appealing to self-actualization needs

an economic downturn may always be motivated to save money in order to avoid financial insecurity—a second-level need. Marketers who understand this can create opportunities for their firms by offering money-saving goods and services.

Critics have pointed out a variety of flaws in Maslow's reasoning. For example, some needs can be related to on more than one level, and not every individual progresses through the needs hierarchy in the same order; some bypass social and esteem needs and are motivated by self-actualization needs. However, the hierarchy of needs can offer an effective guideline for marketers who want to study consumer behaviour.

PERCEPTIONS

Perception is the meaning that a person attributes to incoming stimuli gathered through the five senses—sight, hearing, touch, taste, and smell. Certainly, a buyer's behaviour is influenced by his or her perceptions of a good or service. Researchers now recognize that people's perceptions depend as much on what they want to perceive as on the actual stimuli. It is for this reason that Holt Renfrew and Godiva chocolates are perceived differently from Walmart and Hershey, respectively.

A person's perception of an object or event results from the interaction of two types of factors:

1. Stimulus factors—characteristics of the physical object such as size, colour, weight, and shape

2. Individual factors—unique characteristics of the individual, including not only sensory processes but also experiences with similar inputs and basic motivations and expectations

perception Meaning that a person attributes to incoming stimuli gathered through the five senses.

Perceptual Screens

The average North American consumer is constantly bombarded by marketing messages. A typical supermarket now carries 30,000 different packages, each serving as a miniature billboard vying to attract consumers' attention. Over 6,000 commercials a week are aired on network TV. As marketers compete for attention—and dollars—they get more creative about where they place their messages. Consumers might find a carton of eggs stamped with the name of a television show or takeout cartons emblazoned with the name of a major airline. Old-fashioned billboards—once thought to be obsolete—have made a comeback with 3D elements and large digital advertising screens.

The problem with all these messages is they create clutter in the minds of the consumer, causing them to ignore many promotional messages. People respond selectively to messages that break through their **perceptual screens**—the mental filtering processes through which all inputs must pass. Doubling the size of an ad, using certain colours or graphics, or developing unique packaging are some techniques that marketers use to get a positive response from consumers. For example, colour is so suggestive that its use on product packaging and logos often is the result of a long and careful selection process. Red grabs the attention, and orange has been shown to stimulate appetite. Blue is associated with water—you'll find blue on cleaning products. Green connotes low-fat or healthful food products. The psychological concept of closure also helps marketers create messages that stand out. Closure is the human tendency to perceive a complete picture from an incomplete stimulus. Advertisements that allow consumers to do this often succeed in breaking through perceptual screens.

Word of mouth is probably the oldest marketing technique in existence. It is also one of the most effective. If one satisfied customer tells a friend, relative, neighbour, or co-worker about a positive experience with a product, that message quite often breaks through the listener's perceptual screen because trust between the two already exists.

On the other end of the scale lie newer, technology-based marketing tools. These include virtual reality (in which a consumer can test-drive a car or tour a resort) and social media such

perceptual screens Mental filter or block through which all inputs must pass to be noticed.

attitudes A person's enduring favourable or unfavourable evaluations, emotions, or action tendencies toward some object or idea.

as Facebook, Twitter, and LinkedIn. While investment in these new tools is increasing rapidly, it is interesting to note that the old methods remain strong.

With selective perception at work screening competing messages, it is easy to see the importance of marketers' efforts in developing brand loyalty. Satisfied customers are less likely to seek information about competing products. Even when competitive advertising is forced on them, they are less apt than others to look beyond their perceptual filters at those appeals. Loyal customers simply tune out information that does not agree with their existing beliefs and expectations.

Another method marketers are using to break through a customer's perceptual screen is by targeting them with ads specifically for them as described in the "Solving an Ethical Controversy" feature.

ATTITUDES

Perception of incoming stimuli is greatly affected by our attitudes. In fact, a consumer's decision to purchase an item is strongly based on his or her attitudes about the product, store, or salesperson. **Attitudes** are a person's enduring favourable or unfavourable evaluations, emotions, or action tendencies toward some object or idea. As attitudes form over time through individual experiences and group contacts, they become highly resistant to change. New fees, a reduction in service hours, or a change in location can be difficult for customers to accept. Because favourable attitudes likely affect brand preferences, marketers are interested in determining consumer attitudes toward their offerings. Numerous attitude-scaling devices have been developed for this purpose.

Can our work today build a better tomorrow?

Our answer is Yes.

We're all part of something bigger and we all have a stake in shaping the future. So are there better ways to sustain our quality of life not just this year or next, but for generations to come?

We're Canada's largest energy company. Come and see how we're creating opportunities for employment and economic prosperity as we take on the essential questions around energy in the world we share.

Come and see whatyescando.com

SUNCOR

Courtesy of Suncor Energy

Consumers' perceptions about energy companies can influence the purchases they make.

SOLVING AN ETHICAL CONTROVERSY

Should Facial Recognition Technology Go Incognito?

IT'S already a commonplace marketing strategy to put cookies on users' computers that allow companies to identify their likes and dislikes in order to target online ads to these preferences. Now a parallel strategy is about to roll out that uses facial recognition technology to identify people as males or females in specific age brackets. The first users are expected to be bars, clubs, and restaurants that want to monitor the mix of customers, but other marketers see many opportunities. Facial recognition mechanisms at store entrances can help ensure customers see only digital and mobile ads that matter to them, for instance, but privacy advocates are concerned about potential misuse of the technology, such as lack of an opt-in or opt-out feature.

Is it acceptable for companies to use facial recognition technology without telling customers?

PRO

1. Identifying customers lets markets pinpoint their ads, so people won't see advertising that doesn't relate to or interest them.

2. People who see messages about the right product at the right time are more likely to buy, benefiting everyone.

CON

1. Facial recognition technology is yet another way for companies to amass personal data about people without their consent.

2. Unless there are industry standards, including an opt-out feature like Facebook had to add when its facial-recognition photo-tagging function angered users, companies will make up their own rules.

Where do you stand: pro or con?

Sources: Wendy Davis, "Consumers Union Urges Opt-In Consent for Facial Recognition Tech," MediaPost.com, **www.mediapost.com**, accessed April 20, 2012; Kashmir Hill, "Kraft to Use Facial Recognition Technology to Give You Macaroni Recipes," *Forbes*, **www.forbes.com**, accessed April 20, 2012; Shan Li and David Sarno, "Advertisers Start Using Facial Recognition to Tailor Pitches," *The Los Angeles Times*, **http://articles.latimes.com**, accessed April 20, 2012.

Courtesy of Earth Day Canada/DDB Canada Toronto

Consumer attitudes about the environment can be affected by advertising.

Attitude Components

An attitude has cognitive, affective, and behavioural components. The *cognitive* component refers to the individual's information and knowledge about an object or concept. The *affective* component deals with feelings or emotional reactions. The *behavioural* component involves tendencies to act in a certain manner. For example, in deciding whether to shop at a specific retailer for a tablet computer, a consumer might obtain information about what the store offers from advertising, visits to the store, and input from family, friends, and co-workers—the cognitive component. The consumer might also receive affective input by listening to others about their shopping experiences at this store. Affective input might lead the person to make a judgment about the people who shop there and whether those people represent a group with which he or she would like to be associated. The consumer might decide to buy his or her new tablet at that store—the behavioural component. All three components maintain a relatively stable and balanced relationship to one another. Together, they form an overall attitude about an object or idea.

Changing Consumer Attitudes

A favourable consumer attitude is vital to the success of a marketing effort. Marketers can approach this in one of two ways:

1. by attempting to produce consumer attitudes that will lead to a purchase of an existing product, or

2. by evaluating existing consumer attitudes and creating or modifying products to appeal to these attitudes.

It's always easier to create and maintain a positive attitude toward a product than it is to change an unfavourable to a favourable. But if consumers view a product unfavourably, all is not lost. The seller may redesign it, offer new or desired options, or enhance service. Sometimes an attitude isn't unfavourable but consumers just don't feel a need for the product—they aren't motivated to make the purchase. So marketers must find a way to change shoppers' attitude to include the desire to buy. For example, although most consumers don't necessarily have a negative attitude toward sweet potatoes, they might not have a strong enough positive attitude to cause them to add sweet potatoes to their grocery list. In order to boost sales, marketers recently began to provide more information about sweet potatoes, including their high content of vitamins, antioxidants, and dietary fibre. This information addressed the cognitive component of consumers' attitude toward sweet potatoes, pushing it enough toward the positive that shoppers began to buy them more often.[28]

Courtesy of The Sun Products Corporation

Companies often introduce new products in response to changing attitudes, as with Snuggle Free Clear Fabric Softener, a product that has no dyes or perfumes added.

Modifying the Components of Attitude

Attitudes frequently change in response to inconsistencies among the three components. The most common inconsistencies result when new information changes the cognitive or affective components of an attitude. Marketers can modify attitudes by providing evidence of product benefits and by correcting misconceptions. Marketers may also change attitudes by engaging buyers in new behaviour. Free samples, for instance, can change attitudes by getting consumers to try a product.

Sometimes new technologies can encourage consumers to modify their attitudes. Consumers who sign up to receive Internet coupons for goods and services might be more likely to try these products without knowing a lot about them. Personalized shopping alerts from firms such as Amazon.ca might encourage consumers to purchase a new book or video by making shoppers feel as though the retailer cares about their individual reading or viewing preferences.

LEARNING

Marketers are concerned with the process by which consumer decisions change over time and with the current status of those decisions. **Learning**, in a marketing context, refers to immediate or expected changes in consumer behaviour as a result of experience. The learning process includes the component of drive, which is any strong stimulus that impels action. Fear, pride, greed, thirst, pain avoidance, and rivalry are examples of drives. Learning also relies on a cue—any object or signal in the environment that determines the nature of the consumer's response to a drive. Examples of cues are a newspaper advertisement for a new Thai restaurant—a cue for a hungry person—and a Shell sign near a highway—a cue for a motorist who needs gasoline. A response is an individual's reaction to a set of cues and drives. The hungry person might go to the restaurant or the driver stop at the Shell station for gas.

> **learning** Knowledge or skill that is acquired as a result of experience, which changes consumer behaviour.

Reinforcement is the reduction in drive that results from a proper response. As a response becomes more rewarding, it creates a stronger bond between the drive and the purchase of the product, likely increasing future purchases by the consumer. Reinforcement is the rationale that underlies frequent-buyer programs, which reward repeat purchasers for their loyalty. These programs may offer points for premiums, frequent-flyer miles, and the like. However, so many companies now offer these programs that marketers must find ways to differentiate them. And firms that don't offer the programs quickly learn that consumers will bypass their products and move on to those of competitors.

Applying Learning Theory to Marketing Decisions

Learning theory has some important implications for marketing strategists, particularly those involved with consumer packaged goods. Marketers must find a way to develop a desired outcome such as repeat purchase behaviour gradually over time. **Shaping** is the process of applying a series of rewards and reinforcements to permit more complex behaviour to evolve.

> *Marketoid*
>
> **Tickets to concerts or movies are purchased by 52 percent of online shoppers.**

Both promotional strategy and the product itself play a role in the shaping process. Marketers want to motivate consumers to become regular buyers of certain merchandise. Their first step in getting consumers to try the product might be to offer a free sample package that includes a substantial discount coupon for the next purchase. This example uses a cue as a shaping procedure. If the item performs well, the purchase response is reinforced and followed by another inducement—the coupon. The reason a sample works so well is that it allows the consumer to try the product at no risk. Supermarket shoppers have the opportunity to sample products on a regular basis. Generally a display is set up near the aisle where the item is sold, staffed by a person who dispenses the sample along with a coupon for a future purchase.

> **shaping** Process of applying a series of rewards and reinforcements to permit more complex behaviour to evolve over time.

The second step is to entice the consumer to buy the item with little financial risk. The discount coupon enclosed with the free sample prompts this action. Suppose the package that the consumer purchases has another, smaller discount coupon enclosed. Again, satisfactory product performance and the second coupon provide reinforcement.

The third step is to motivate the person to buy the item again at a moderate cost. A discount coupon accomplishes this objective, but this time the purchased package includes no additional coupon. The only reinforcement comes from satisfactory product performance.

The final test comes when the consumer decides whether to buy the item at its true price without a discount coupon. Satisfaction with product performance provides the only continuing reinforcement. Repeat purchase behaviour is shaped by effective application of learning theory within a marketing strategy context.

Air Canada: Providing reinforcement for customer loyalty.

How to Avoid Major Distractions at Work

PHONE calls, email, and visitors are all part of every workday, but they can distract you from work. Here are some tips for getting your focus back.

1. Set a realistic schedule that prioritizes the week's tasks—including responding to emails—by deadline and importance. Now you have specific goals to focus on in orderly fashion. Update this schedule at the beginning or end of each week.
2. Check email just three times a day—morning, lunch, and close of business—and turn your email application off in between. If you can train yourself to check only twice a day, even better.
3. Don't hesitate to tell people you're busy or have a deadline. If you are polite, they'll understand. If they insist,

invite them to walk with you while you grab lunch or head back to your office.

4. Let family members use the office number to reach you in an emergency, leaving you free to shut your personal phone off at work so personal calls don't interrupt you.
5. Leave Facebook, Twitter, LinkedIn, and the rest for off-hours. If your company doesn't already block these sites from employees' computers, you'll be grateful you can turn your smartphone off at work.

Sources: "How to Avoid the 5 Major Distractions at Work," CareerBright.com, **http://careerbright.com**, accessed April 11, 2012; Caroline Potter, "Work, Interrupted: Six Ways to Avoid Distractions," Monster.com, **http://career-advice.monster.com**, accessed April 11, 2012; Michael Pollick, "How Can I Avoid Distractions at Work?" *Wise Geek*, **www.wisegeek.com**, accessed April 11, 2012.

SELF-CONCEPT THEORY

self-concept A person's multifaceted picture of himself or herself.

Our **self-concept**—our multifaceted picture of ourselves—plays an important role in our consumer behaviour. Perhaps you see yourself as a creative person, someone who thinks outside the box. You pride yourself on keeping up with the latest trends—in fact, you like to think of yourself as a trendsetter, ahead of the wave. You might express this self-concept by wearing certain clothes, such as those offered by the Ed Hardy brand. Ed Hardy was created by designer Christian Audigier and tattoo artist Don Ed Hardy. The cooperation of these two creative people brought to market jeans, jackets, sweatshirts, sunglasses, hats, and other items bearing tattoo art. Fashion industry experts acknowledge that the Ed Hardy line established a new trend in "street fashion."[29] Perhaps your self-concept lets you see yourself as a genius multi-tasker, but if you find that you're often distracted at work, see the "Career Readiness" feature for some tips on regaining your focus.

The concept of self emerges from an interaction of many of the influences—both personal and interpersonal—that affect buying behaviour. The individual's needs, motives, perceptions, attitudes, and learning lie at the core of his or her conception of self. In addition, family, social, and cultural influences affect self-concept.

A person's self-concept has four components: real self, self-image, looking-glass self, and ideal self. The *real self* is an objective view of the total person. The *self-image*—the way an individual views himself or herself—may distort the objective view. The *looking-glass self*—the way an individual thinks others see him or her—may also differ substantially from self-image because people often choose to project different images to others than their perceptions of their real selves. The *ideal self* serves as a personal set of objectives, since it is the image to which the individual aspires.

assessment check 3

3.1 Identify the personal determinants of consumer behaviour.

3.2 What are the human needs categorized by Abraham Maslow?

3.3 How do perception and learning differ?

In purchasing goods and services, people are likely to choose products that move them closer to their ideal self-images. For example, suppose your ideal self-image is one of a trendsetter, but you generally have a hard time wearing anything other than conventional clothes. You might buy a designer purse or jacket in an effort to break out of the box and bring you closer to your ideal self-image. Social network media such as Facebook appeal to people's ideal self-image—users are often likely to post pictures and entries that paint themselves in a flattering light.

THE CONSUMER DECISION PROCESS

④ Distinguish between high-involvement and low-involvement purchase decisions.

Although we might not be aware of it, as consumers we complete a step-by-step process in making purchasing decisions. The time and effort devoted to a particular purchasing decision depend on how important it is.

Purchases with high levels of potential social or economic consequences are said to be **high-involvement purchase decisions**. Buying a car or deciding where to go to university or college are examples of high-involvement decisions. Routine purchases that pose little risk to the consumer are **low-involvement purchase decisions**. Purchasing a candy bar from a vending machine is a good example.

Consumers generally invest more time and effort in buying decisions for high-involvement products than in those for low-involvement products. A home buyer will visit a number of listings, compare asking prices, apply for a mortgage, have the selected house inspected, and even have friends or family members visit the home before signing the final papers. Few buyers invest that much effort in choosing between two different brands of chocolate bars. Believe it or not, though, they will still go through the steps of the consumer decision process—but on a more compressed scale.

Figure 5.1, on page 129, shows the six steps in the consumer decision process. First, the consumer recognizes a problem or unmet need, searches for goods or services, and evaluates the alternatives before making a purchase decision. The next step is the actual purchase act. After buying the item, the consumer evaluates whether he or she made the right choice. Much of marketing involves steering consumers through the decision process in the direction of a specific product.

Consumers apply the decision process in solving problems and taking advantage of opportunities. Such decisions permit them to correct differences between their actual and desired states. Feedback from each decision serves as additional experience in helping guide subsequent decisions.

high-involvement purchase decision Buying decision that evokes high levels of potential social or economic consequences.

low-involvement purchase decision Routine purchase that poses little risk to the consumer, either socially or economically.

assessment check 4 ✓

4.1 Differentiate between high-involvement decisions and low-involvement decisions.

4.2 Categorize each of the following as a high- or low-involvement product: shampoo, computer, popcorn, apartment, cell phone service.

PROBLEM OR OPPORTUNITY RECOGNITION

⑤ Outline the steps in the consumer decision process.

During the first stage in the decision process, the consumer becomes aware of a gap between the existing situation and a desired situation. You have experienced this yourself. Perhaps you realize there is little food in the refrigerator. You are really hungry for a sandwich. By identifying the problem—an empty refrigerator—you can resolve it with a trip to the grocery store. Sometimes the problem is more specific. You might have a full refrigerator but no mustard or mayonnaise for sandwiches. This problem requires a solution as well.

Suppose you are unhappy with a particular purchase—say, a brand of cereal. Or maybe you just want a change from the same old cereal every morning. This is the recognition of another type of problem or opportunity—the desire for change.

What if you just got a raise at work? You might want to try some of the prepared gourmet take-home dinners offered by the local supermarket. These dinners are more expensive than the groceries you have purchased in the past, but now they are within financial reach. The marketer's main task during this phase of the decision-making process is to help prospective buyers identify and recognize potential problems or needs. This task may take the form of advertising, promotions, or personal sales assistance. A supermarket employee might suggest appetizers or desserts to accompany your gourmet take-home dinner.

SEARCH

During the second step in the decision process, the consumer gathers information about the attainment of a desired state. This search identifies different ways to solve the problem. A high-involvement purchase might mean conducting an extensive information search, whereas low-involvement purchases require much less research.

The search may cover internal or external sources of information. An internal search is simply a mental review: Is there past experience with the product? Was it good or bad? An external search involves gathering information from all kinds of outside sources—for instance, family, friends, co-workers or classmates, advertisements or salespeople, online reviews, and consumer magazines.

Get a Scotiabank® Second Opinion.

Have your investment questions answered. Even the ones you haven't asked yet. Come in for a free, no-obligation review today.

Let's get started.

www.scotiabank.com/secondopinion

You're richer than you think® · Scotiabank®

Courtesy of Scotiabank

Purchasing an investment would be a high-involvement decision.

evoked set Number of alternatives that a consumer actually considers in making a purchase decision.

evaluative criteria Features that a consumer considers in choosing among alternatives.

Because conducting an external search requires time and effort, it is usually done for high-involvement purchases.

The search identifies alternative brands or models for consideration and possible purchase. The number of alternatives that a consumer actually considers in making a purchase decision is known in marketing as the **evoked set**. In some searches, consumers already know of the brands that merit further consideration; in others, their external searches develop such information. The number of brands included in the evoked set vary depending on both the situation and the person. An immediate need, such as filling a nearly empty gas tank, might limit the evoked set. But a driver with half a tank of gas, with more time to make a decision, might expand the evoked set to choose from a broader range of options that include lower prices or certain brands.

Consumers can now choose among more alternative products than ever before. This variety can confuse and complicate the analysis necessary to narrow the range of choices. Instead of comparing one or two brands, a consumer often faces a dizzying array of brands and sub-brands. Products that once included only one or two categories—regular coffee versus decaffeinated—are now available in many different forms—cappuccino, latte, tall skinny latte, flavoured coffee, espresso, and iced coffee, just to name a few possibilities. Researchers have conducted studies showing that too many choices—and resulting decisions—can cause anxiety and stress.[30] Recognizing this, and wanting to help consumers find their way through the maze of choices, some firms have set up online sites where shoppers can compare products.

Marketers try to influence buying decisions during the search process by providing persuasive information about their offerings in a format useful to consumers. The marketer must find creative ways to penetrate a consumer's evoked set of alternatives.

EVALUATION OF ALTERNATIVES

The third step in the consumer decision process is to evaluate the evoked set of options. Actually, it is difficult to completely separate the second and third steps because some evaluation takes place as the search progresses; consumers accept, discount, distort, or reject information as they receive it. For example, knowing that you are looking for a new pair of boots, your roommate might tell you about this great online site for shoes she visited recently. But you don't particularly like her taste in shoes or boots, so you reject the information, even though the site might have a pair of boots that you would have bought.

The outcome of the evaluation stage is the choice of a brand or product in the evoked set or possibly a decision to keep looking for alternatives. To complete this analysis, the consumer must develop a set of evaluative criteria to guide the selection. **Evaluative criteria** are the features that a consumer considers in choosing among alternatives. These criteria can either be objective facts (government tests of an automobile's mileage) or subjective impressions (a favourable view of a brand of clothing). Common criteria include price, brand name, and country of origin. Evaluative criteria can vary with the consumer's age, income level, social class, and culture; what's important to a senior citizen might not matter at all to a student. When it comes to dining out, an affluent senior might look for a restaurant with an upscale atmosphere and high-quality food; a budget-conscious student might choose a place that's inexpensive and fast to accommodate study hours or classes.

Marketers attempt to influence the outcome of this stage in three ways. First, they try to educate consumers about attributes that they view as important in evaluating a particular class of goods. They also identify which evaluative criteria are important to an individual and attempt to show why a specific brand fulfills those criteria. Finally, they try to induce a customer to expand the evoked set to include the product being marketed.

PURCHASE DECISION AND PURCHASE ACT

The search and alternative evaluation stages of the decision process result in the purchase decision and the actual purchase. At this stage, the consumer has evaluated each alternative in the evoked set based on his or her personal set of evaluative criteria and narrowed the alternatives down to one.

The consumer then decides where—or from whom—to make the purchase. Sometimes this decision is part of the evaluation; perhaps one seller is offering a better price or better warranty than another. The purchase may be made online or in person at a retail store. The delivery options might also influence the decision of where to purchase an item. For example, a local electronics store might deliver your HDTV for free, whereas an online retailer might charge $50 for delivery.

POST-PURCHASE EVALUATION

The purchase act produces one of two results. The buyer feels either satisfaction at the removal of the discrepancy between the existing and desired states or dissatisfaction with the purchase. Consumers are generally satisfied if purchases meet their expectations.

Sometimes, however, consumers experience some post-purchase anxiety called **cognitive dissonance**. This anxiety results from an imbalance among a person's knowledge, beliefs, and attitudes. A consumer may experience dissonance after choosing a particular automobile over several other models when some of the rejected models have desired features that the chosen one does not provide.

Dissonance is likely to increase (1) as the dollar values of purchases increase, (2) when the rejected alternatives have desirable features that the chosen alternatives do not provide, and (3) when the purchase decision has a major effect on the buyer. In other words, dissonance is more likely with high-involvement purchases than with those that require low involvement. If you buy a soft drink and you don't like the flavour, you can toss it and buy a different one. But if you have spent more than $1,000 on a TV and you aren't satisfied with it, you will most likely experience dissonance. You might try to reduce the dissonance by focusing on good reviews about your choice. Or you might show a friend all the neat features on your TV—without pointing out anything you find dissatisfactory.

Marketers can help buyers reduce cognitive dissonance by providing information that supports the chosen alternative. Automobile dealers recognize the possibility of buyer's remorse and often follow up purchases with letters or telephone calls from dealership personnel offering personal attention to any customer problems. Advertisements that stress customer satisfaction also help reduce cognitive dissonance.

A final method of dealing with cognitive dissonance is to change products. The consumer may ultimately decide that one of the rejected alternatives would have been the best choice and vows to purchase that item in the future. Marketers may capitalize on this with advertising campaigns that focus on the benefits of their products or with tag lines that say something like "If you're unhappy with them, try us." But making a different choice isn't always an option, particularly if the item requires a large investment in time and money. If you decide you aren't happy with your TV, you could try selling it, perhaps on a website like eBay or Craigslist, before purchasing another one.

CLASSIFYING CONSUMER PROBLEM-SOLVING PROCESSES

As mentioned earlier, the consumer decision processes for different products require varying amounts of problem-solving efforts. Marketers recognize three categories of problem-solving behaviour: routinized response, limited problem solving, and extended problem solving. Some

Marketoid

Over 50 percent of online shoppers purchase travel arrangements such as airline tickets and hotel reservations.

cognitive dissonance Imbalance among knowledge, beliefs, and attitudes that occurs after an action or decision is taken, such as a purchase.

assessment check 5

5.1 List the steps in the consumer decision process.

5.2 What is meant by the term *evoked set*?

5.3 What are evaluative criteria?

⑥ Differentiate among routinized response behaviour, limited problem solving, and extended problem solving by consumers.

table 5.2   *Consumer Problem Solving*

	ROUTINIZED RESPONSE BEHAVIOUR	LIMITED PROBLEM SOLVING	EXTENSIVE PROBLEM SOLVING
Price	Low	Moderate	High
Level of involvement of the purchaser	Low	Moderate	High
The number of brands considered	Few	Moderate	Several
Frequency of purchases	High	Moderate	Low
Customer's perceived risk	Low	Moderate	High
Sometimes called	Habitual Buying Behaviour	Variety-Seeking or Dissonance-Reducing Buying Behaviour	Complex Buying Behaviour

marketers base this problem-solving behaviour on the following: price, the level of involvement of the purchaser, the number of brands to choose from, frequency of purchases, and the customer's perceived risk.[31] Table 5.2 provides a summary. The classification of a particular purchase within this framework clearly influences the consumer decision process.

Routinized Response Behaviour

routinized response behaviour Rapid consumer problem solving in which no new information is considered; the consumer has already set evaluative criteria and identified available options.

Consumers make many purchases routinely by choosing a preferred brand or one of a limited group of acceptable brands. This type of rapid consumer problem solving is referred to as **routinized response behaviour**. A routine purchase of a regular brand of canned soup or the renewal of a magazine subscription are examples. The consumer has already set evaluative criteria and identified available options. External search is limited in such cases, which characterize extremely low-involvement products.

Limited Problem Solving

limited problem solving Situation in which the consumer invests some small amount of time and energy in searching for and evaluating alternatives.

Consider the situation in which the consumer has previously set evaluative criteria for a particular kind of purchase but then encounters a new, unknown brand. The introduction of a new shampoo is an example of a **limited problem solving** situation. The consumer knows the evaluative criteria for the product but has not applied these criteria to assess the new brand. Such situations demand moderate amounts of time and effort for external searches. Limited problem solving is affected by the number of evaluative criteria and brands, the extent of external search, and the process for determining preferences. Consumers making purchase decisions in this product category are likely to feel involvement in the middle of the range.

Extended Problem Solving

extended problem solving Situation that involves lengthy external searches and long deliberation; results when brands are difficult to categorize or evaluate.

Extended problem solving results when brands are difficult to categorize or evaluate. The first step is to compare one item with similar ones. The consumer needs to understand the product features before evaluating alternatives. Most extended problem-solving efforts involve lengthy external searches. High-involvement purchase decisions—cars, homes, and educational programs—usually require extended problem solving.

assessment check 6

6.1 What is routinized response behaviour?

6.2 What does limited problem solving require?

6.3 Give an example of an extended problem-solving situation.

Strategic Implications

Marketers who plan to succeed with today's consumers will understand how their potential market behaves. Cultural influences will play a big role in marketers' relationships with consumers, particularly as firms conduct business on a global scale but also as they try to reach diverse populations in Canada. In addition, family characteristics are changing—more seniors are living alone—which forecasts a change in the way families make purchasing decisions. One of the biggest shifts in family spending is the amount of power children and teenagers now wield in the marketplace. These young consumers are more and more involved and in some cases know more about certain products, such as electronics, than their parents do and very often influence purchase decisions. This holds true even with high-involvement purchases like the family car.

Marketers constantly work toward changing or modifying components of consumers' attitudes about their products to gain a favourable attitude and purchase decision. Finally, they will refine their understanding of the consumer decision process and use their knowledge to design effective marketing strategies. ◆◆◆

REVIEW OF CHAPTER OBJECTIVES

① **Define *consumer behaviour* and describe the role it plays in marketing decisions.**

Consumer behaviour refers to the buyer behaviour of individual consumers. Consumer behaviour plays a huge role in marketing decisions, including what goods and services to offer, to whom, and where. If marketers can understand the factors that influence consumers, they can develop and offer the right products to those consumers.

② **Describe the interpersonal determinants of consumer behaviour: cultural, social, and family influences.**

Cultural influences, such as the general work ethic or the desire to accumulate wealth, come from society. Core values may vary from culture to culture. Social or group influences include social class, opinion leaders, and reference groups with which consumers may want to be affiliated. Family influences may come from spouses, parents, grandparents, or children.

③ **Explain each of the personal determinants of consumer behaviour: needs and motives, perceptions, attitudes, learning, and self-concept theory.**

A need is an imbalance between a consumer's actual and desired states. A motive is the inner state that directs a person toward the goal of satisfying a need. Perception is the meaning that a person attributes to incoming stimuli gathered through the five senses. Attitudes are a person's enduring favourable or unfavourable evaluations, emotions, or action tendencies toward something. Learning refers to the immediate or expected changes in consumer behaviour as a result of experience. In self-concept theory, a person's view of himself or herself plays a role in purchasing behaviour. In purchasing goods and services, people are likely to choose products that move them closer to their ideal self-images.

④ **Distinguish between high-involvement and low-involvement purchase decisions.**

Purchases with high levels of potential social or economic consequences are called high-involvement purchase decisions. Examples are buying a new car or home. Routine purchases that pose little risk to the consumer are called low-involvement purchase decisions. Choosing a chocolate bar or a newspaper are examples.

⑤ **Outline the steps in the consumer decision process.**

The consumer decision process consists of six steps: problem or opportunity recognition, search, alternative evaluation, purchase decision, purchase act, and post-purchase evaluation. The time involved in each stage of the decision process is determined by the nature of the individual purchases.

⑥ **Differentiate among routinized response behaviour, limited problem solving, and extended problem solving by consumers.**

Routinized response behaviour refers to repeat purchases made of the same brand or limited group of items. Limited problem solving occurs when a consumer has previously set criteria for a purchase but then encounters a new brand or model. Extended problem solving results when brands are difficult to categorize or evaluate. High-involvement purchase decisions usually require extended problem solving.

assessment check answers ✓

1.1 Why is the study of consumer behaviour important to marketers?

If marketers can understand the behaviour of consumers, they can offer the right products to consumers who want them.

1.2 Describe the work of Kurt Lewin.

Kurt Lewin proposed that behaviour is the function of the interactions of personal influences and pressures exerted by outside environmental forces. This research sheds light on how consumers make decisions.

2.1 List the interpersonal determinants of consumer behaviour.

The interpersonal determinants of consumer behaviour are cultural, social, and family influences.

2.2 What is a microculture?

A microculture is a group within a culture that has its own distinct mode of behaviour.

2.3 Describe the Asch phenomenon.

The Asch phenomenon is the impact of groups and group norms on individual behaviour.

3.1 Identify the personal determinants of consumer behaviour.

The personal determinants of consumer behaviour are needs and motives, perceptions, attitudes, learning, and self-concept theory.

3.2 What are the human needs categorized by Abraham Maslow?

The human needs categorized by Abraham Maslow are physiological, safety, social/belongingness, esteem, and self-actualization.

3.3 How do perception and learning differ?

Perception is the meaning that a person attributes to incoming stimuli. Learning refers to immediate or expected changes in behaviour as a result of experience.

4.1 Differentiate between high-involvement decisions and low-involvement decisions.

High-involvement decisions have high levels of potential social or economic consequences, such as selecting a college or university to attend. Low-involvement decisions pose little financial, social, or emotional risk to the buyer, such as a magazine or litre of milk.

4.2 Categorize each of the following as a high- or low-involvement product: shampoo, computer, popcorn, apartment, cell phone service.

High-involvement products are the computer, apartment, and cell phone service. Low-involvement products are the shampoo and popcorn.

5.1 List the steps in the consumer decision process.

The steps in the consumer decision process are problem or opportunity recognition, search, alternative evaluation, purchase decision, purchase act, and post-purchase evaluation.

5.2 What is meant by the term *evoked set*?

The evoked set is the number of alternatives that a consumer actually considers in making a purchase decision.

5.3 What are evaluative criteria?

Evaluative criteria are the features that a consumer considers in choosing among alternatives.

6.1 What is routinized response behaviour?

Routinized response behaviour is the repeated purchase of the same brand or limited group of products.

6.2 What does limited problem solving require?

Limited problem solving requires a moderate amount of a consumer's time and effort.

6.3 Give an example of an extended problem-solving situation.

An extended problem-solving situation might involve the purchase of a car or a postsecondary education.

MARKETING TERMS YOU NEED TO KNOW

These terms are printed in blue in the text. They are defined in the margins of the chapter and in the Glossary that begins on p. G-1.

consumer behaviour 128
culture 128
microcultures 130
reference groups 134
opinion leaders 136
need 138
motive 138

perception 140
perceptual screens 140
attitudes 141
learning 143
shaping 143
self-concept 144
high-involvement purchase decision 145

low-involvement purchase decision 145
evoked set 146
evaluative criteria 146
cognitive dissonance 147
routinized response behaviour 148
limited problem solving 148
extended problem solving 148

PROJECT AND TEAMWORK EXERCISES

1. Choose a person whom you believe to be a true opinion leader. It might be a media celebrity, a political leader, a sports figure, or someone in another category entirely. Research ways in which the person has possibly shaped consumer attitudes toward various goods and services. Present your findings in class.

2. Consider your own participation in family purchases. How much influence did you have on your family's decisions as a child? As a teenager? Over what types of products did you have an influence—or not? Has this influence changed over time? Why or why not? Compare your answers with those of classmates.

3. One major trend in consumer spending that is likely to last for the next several years is a focus on value. Discount stores have been profitable during the economic downturn, and their popularity shows no sign of abating.[32] While consumers search for bargains, manufacturers and retailers of luxury goods are struggling to change consumer attitudes toward their products. On your own or with a classmate, choose one of the following

luxury brands (or select one of your own) and create an advertisement for the product that seeks to change consumer attitudes about your product:
   a. Mercedes-Benz car
   b. Louis Vuitton leather goods
   c. Tiffany jewellery
   d. Four Seasons Hotels and Resorts

4. Consider a purchase decision involving one of the following types of products: a tablet computer, a smartphone, or a vacation. Develop an evoked set of three alternatives for your purchase decision. Then create a list of evaluative criteria that you would use to choose among the alternatives. Research your alternatives in more detail—online, at a store, at a friend's apartment, and the like. Finally, make your purchase decision. Describe to the class how you made your decision—and why.

5. Choose a partner and select a low-involvement, routinized consumer product such as toothpaste or detergent. Create an ad that you think could stimulate consumers to change their preferred brand to yours.

CRITICAL THINKING EXERCISES

1. Describe a group to which you belong—it might be a team or a club. Outline the norms of the group, the major roles that different members play, and your own status within the group. Have you ever sought to change your status? Why or why not?

2. What are the two conditions that must exist for a consumer to be influenced by a reference group? Have you ever made a purchase based on reference group influence? If so, what was the purchase and how did you come to the decision to make it? If not, why not?

3. Marketers point out that the five levels in Maslow's hierarchy of needs are sometimes combined or even bypassed by consumers making purchase decisions. Explain how each of the following could fulfill more than one need:

   a. a download of "We Are the World"
   b. a retirement investment account
   c. body wash
   d. dinner at a restaurant

4. What are some ways marketers can break through consumers' perceptual screens? If you were a marketer for a line of pet food for cats and dogs, what method might you use?

5. Suppose you are employed by a large electronics retailer, and a customer comes to you with cognitive dissonance over the purchase of an expensive computer system from your store the previous week. How would you work with the customer to help dispel that dissonance?

ETHICS EXERCISE

Marketers of online news content are struggling to change consumer attitudes about whether it is fair to charge for this content. While consumers are already willing to pay for movies, music, and games, they don't want to pay for news—whether it is from online versions of newspapers and magazines or online feeds of radio and talk shows. Yet these news formats are created by paid professionals and can be expensive to produce. Increasingly, some newspapers and magazines have created "pay walls" that require readers, after a while, to pay for a digital subscription.[33]

1. Express your own view. Is it ethical for marketers of online news content to begin charging consumers for

their services? If so, under what circumstances? If not, why not?

2. Go online to research different news sources—those that are free (such as the headlines offered on Yahoo!) and those for which there is a charge (such as online magazine or newspaper subscriptions). Is there a difference in features or the extent of services offered?

3. Based on your research and your knowledge of consumer behaviour, what steps do you think news marketers might take to change consumer attitudes about whether news should be offered for free?

CASE 5.1

How Colour Is Used in Marketing

Everyone has a favourite colour. When someone asks us what it is, we usually answer without hesitation. As consumers, we gravitate toward that colour in just about everything—clothing, room decor, cars, and the like. (Do you have a friend who always wears black? Or a roommate who insists on decorating entirely in purple?) We're also drawn to our favourite colour when we see it in packaging. Marketers know this. They do a great deal of research to determine greater complexities in the perception of colour, as well as cultural determinants of colour preferences. To break through consumers' perceptual screens so they are attracted to the products being offered, marketers need to understand how colour is perceived in order to use it effectively.

Scientists know that colour literally affects the body and mind. Colours stimulate the nervous system and create emotional states. For example, red increases the heart and breathing rate. It also represents danger and caution. Advertisements that display words or product details—such as tooth decay prevention—against a red background may cause consumers to respond with a purchase in order to avoid getting cavities. McDonald's use of red in its colour scheme subliminally encourages consumers to order and eat their food quickly—the whole idea of fast food.

On the other hand, blue has a calming influence on the nervous system and evokes peace, freedom, optimism, trustworthiness, and creativity. If marketers want to emphasize the teeth-whitening properties of the toothpaste described earlier, using advertisements or packaging with a blue background would likely be most effective. The colour blue also suggests intelligence. IBM has always been known as "Big Blue." For a firm that develops and promotes high-tech products, the link to trustworthiness, creativity, and intelligence helps create a positive attitude among consumers. Green is another positive marketing colour, commonly

representing nature, freshness, health, abundance, and money. General Mills has a green "G" as part of its logo. Freshness, health, nature, and abundance are all qualities that consumers would like to find in the food they buy.

Colour has certain meanings in different cultures—in Canada white signifies cleanliness and purity, but in China, white is associated with funerals and mourning. So a Canadian manufacturer of bedding or tablecloths would not want to try to market its crisp white linens to Chinese consumers. And whereas yellow signifies happiness in Canada, the colour symbolizes sadness in Greece and jealousy in France. This presents a difficulty for global marketers such as McDonald's, whose signature brand colours are red and yellow. Although the golden arches remain their true colour at the restaurants themselves, visitors to the McDonald's France site will find that pale blue and pale yellow are the predominant colours that appear on the site.

Understanding the psychology of colour—the way it can be used to affect perception and shape consumer attitudes toward goods and services—is an important tool for marketers. The next time you find yourself reaching for the green bottle of vitamins or asking to test-drive the blue car, at least you'll know why.

Questions for Critical Thinking

1. Choose one of the following companies. What colour does it use predominantly in its logo or packaging? How do these colours affect the perception of its product?
   a. Boston Pizza
   b. Microsoft
   c. Mountain Equipment Co-op
   d. Starbucks
   e. Harvey's Hamburgers

2. Should a global firm like McDonald's or General Mills change the colours of its logo or packaging depending on the country in which it is marketing? Why or why not? How might this affect consumer attitudes toward the company and its products?

Sources: "Strategic Use of Color in Marketing Materials," Keysteps Internet Marketing, **www.keysteps.com**, February 23, 2010; Darrell Zahorsky, "What Color Is Your Business?" Small Business Information, About.com, **http://sbinformation .about.com**, February 23, 2010; Elaine Love, "Psychology of Colors Marketing," *Golden Nuggets for Entrepreneurs*, **http://leloveforlife.blogspot.com**, February 4, 2010; "Internet Marketing and the Psychology of Color," *Money Easy Tips*, **http:// moneyeasytips.com**, January 30, 2010; "Marketing and the Psychology of Color," ArticlesBase.com, **www.articlesbase.com**, November 20, 2009; Nancy Pekala, "Color Me Creative: New Study Analyzes the Psychology of Color," Marketing-Power.com, **www.marketingpower.com**, February 27, 2009.

CASE 5.2

Pepsi-Cola Gets a Boost from Healthier Beverages

Pepsi was experiencing a drop in market share, declining sales, and a flat share price. It was time for PepsiCo to engineer a change in its corporate fortunes in the North American beverage market.

In addition to trimming costs, the firm added $500 to $600 million to its beverage advertising and marketing budget. It hired new Pepsi spokespeople, including actress Eva Longoria and rapper Nicki Minaj, and it introduced a mid-calorie Pepsi. But for several years North American consumers have been turning away from carbonated soft drinks and choosing healthier beverages such as juices, teas, flavoured water, and sports drinks. So PepsiCo wanted to leverage that behavioural change by pumping up its Gatorade brand.

Gatorade was associated for years with male-dominated team sports at the youth level. Now PepsiCo will link it to a wider range of consumers, including women, and a broader spectrum of other athletic activities, such as skateboarding, surfing, tennis, and dance, each represented by a professional athlete. The company recently introduced the G Series, a product extension that offers three types of Gatorade, one for each of three phases of athletic activity: Prime, Perform, and Recover. Relying on marketing research revealing that high school and college athletes spend more on clothing and equipment than they do on nutrition products, PepsiCo is also unveiling a new Gatorade marketing campaign featuring prominent athletes like Usain Bolt and Abby Wambach that stresses the importance of what you put *in* your body, as opposed to what you put *on* it.

Some Gatorade ads carried a hashtag, to help PepsiCo monitor social media buzz in its new Gatorade Mission Control centres in the United States, the United Kingdom, and Latin America. The company also sent out a special sales and marketing team called G-Force, which included any former college athletes, to foster marketing relationships with local retailers. "It's an aggressive, grass-roots effort," says Gatorade's president.

All these changes and improvements did have some effect on the company's performance. Pepsi still trailed Coke in market share with Coke's market share at 42 percent and Pepsi's at 31 percent. On the positive side, the company's share price increased by over 15 percent while Coke experienced a share price increase of just over 12 percent.

Questions for Critical Thinking

1. How can PepsiCo capitalize on what it has learned about the buying behaviour of young athletes?
2. Gatorade's president says, "We probably know more about who on Twitter is the most influential influencer of end user athletes than Twitter does, because we've made it our business to know that." What can social media tell PepsiCo about the market for Gatorade?

Sources: "PepsiCo Bubbles to $71 by Pumping up Pepsi Next," *Forbes*, April 9, 2012, **www.forbes.com**; "Q&A with Sarah Robb O'Hagan, Global CMO and North American President, Gatorade," *Marketing*, March 19, 2012, **www.marketingmag .com**; "Pepsi Can Bubble up to $71 But Needs Next Nooyi Thing," Forbes, February 21, 2012, **www.forbes.com**; Jennifer Rooney, "Sarah Robb O'Hagan Shares Gatorade's Strategy to Be Sports Nutrition Leader," *Forbes*, January 3, 2012, **www.forbes.com**; Natalie Zmuda, "Gatorade's New Selling Point: We're Necessary Performance Gear," *Advertising Age*, January 2, 2012, **www.adage.com**; David Brown, "Infographic: Does This Mean Kanye Will Drink Pepsi?" *Marketing*, **www .marketingmag.ca**, February 25, 2013; "Pepsi Feels Shareholder Pressure to Buy Mondelez," *Marketing*, **www.marketingmag.ca**, July 17, 2013.

chapter 6

Business-to-Business (B2B) Marketing

CHAPTER OBJECTIVES

①　Explain each of the components of the business-to-business (B2B) market.

②　Describe the major approaches to segmenting business-to-business (B2B) markets.

③　Identify the major characteristics of the business market and its demand.

④　Discuss the decision to make, buy, or lease.

⑤　Describe the major influences on business buying behaviour.

⑥　Outline the steps in the organizational buying process.

⑦　Classify organizational buying situations.

⑧　Explain the buying centre concept.

⑨　Discuss the challenges of and strategies for marketing to government, institutional, and international buyers.

GE AND B2B

GE knows that about 90 percent of B2B buyers report using social media in their decision processes. In fact, the company has developed an enviable reputation in its industry for its forward thinking and successful use of social media and a growing list of mobile apps to find and generate new corporate business. GE's B2B marketing arm uses popular sites such as LinkedIn, where it hosts several targeted groups; Facebook, where its page has garnered more than a quarter-million "likes"; and Twitter. The company has been featured in a video on Apple's website as a prime example of how mobile apps for the iPad and iPhone can transform businesses, and it now has its own GE Mobile App store. With these digital and social media efforts, GE is building on the high standards it sets for the B2B customer experience in the industries in which it operates, which are as diverse as aviation, energy, media, health care technology, and financial services.

GE wants to deliver content it considers "micro-relevant," which means it reaches just the right customers rather than the biggest audience, and with content that's specific to their needs. Its mobile apps allow restaurants to estimate the energy savings they can reap with more energy-efficient lighting, for instance, or let railroads monitor their tracks and gather diagnostics on their locomotives. Another app helps manage gas turbines and electric transformers, while still more offer business intelligence and presentations.

The company is so enthusiastic about using social media to reach its business-to-business (B2B) customers that it has even embraced the possibilities offered by Pinterest, the rapidly growing scrapbook-like website that's especially popular with women 20 through 40. Some B2B marketers feel Pinterest has little to offer them, but GE is finding that its sample posts—selected inspirational words from Thomas Edison (the company's founder)—have drawn considerable Pinterest traffic. "We're experimenting," says the firm's executive director of global digital marketing, "and we're learning."

Despite the social media initiatives the company has already undertaken, GE believes it has only scratched the surface of mobile and social media marketing, especially for its B2B customers. Look for more to come.[1]

connecting with customers

GE recognizes the potential for B2B outreach, given how many buyers rely on social media when making purchasing decisions. The company has wholeheartedly committed itself to social media, availing itself of social networking sites such as Facebook, LinkedIn, and Pinterest. Its Mobile App Store lists B2B applications, such as order tracking, order status, price, and availability. Its Ecomagination website features ideas that combine inventiveness and environmental consciousness. The company connects with customers in the many industries it serves by focusing on specific ones and providing them with specific content.

Chapter Overview

We are all aware of the consumer marketplace. As consumers, we're involved in purchasing needed items almost every day. In addition, we can't help noticing the barrage of marketing messages aimed at us through a variety of media. But the business-to-business marketplace is, in fact, significantly larger. Just to compare Internet sales, online retail sales in Canada are expected to reach only $34 billion by 2018; however, in 2013, total online sales of goods and services exceeded $136 billion.[2] Whether through face-to-face transactions, via telephone, or over the Internet, business marketers each day deal with complex purchasing decisions involving multiple decision makers. They often involve the steady building of relationships between companies and customers as well as the ability to respond to changing circumstances in existing markets. Customer satisfaction and customer loyalty are major factors in the development of these long-term relationships and are often determined by factors other than price.

This chapter discusses buying behaviour in the business or organizational market. **Business-to-business (B2B) marketing** deals with organizational purchases of goods and services to support production of other products, to facilitate daily company operations, or for resale. But you ask, "How do I go about distinguishing between consumer purchases and B2B transactions?" Actually, it's pretty simple. Just ask yourself two questions:

1. Who is buying the good or service?

2. Why is the purchase being made?

Consumer buying involves purchases made by people like you and me. We purchase items for our own use and enjoyment—and not for resale. By contrast, B2B purchases are made by businesses, government, and marketing intermediaries to be resold, combined with other items to create a finished product for resale, or used up in the day-to-day operations of the organization. So answer the two questions— "Who is buying?" and "Why?"—and you have the answer. ◆◆◆

business-to-business (B2B) marketing
Organizational sales and purchases of goods and services to support production of other products, for daily company operations, or for resale.

NATURE OF THE BUSINESS MARKET

Firms usually sell fewer standardized products to organizational buyers than to ultimate consumers. Whereas you might purchase a cell phone for your personal use, a company generally has to purchase an entire communications system from a supplier such as Bell Canada, whose Unified Communications service provides processes and tools to seamlessly enable real-time collaboration for a business customer's suppliers, customers, and employees.[3] Purchases such as these require greater customization, more decision making, and usually more decision makers. So the buying and selling process becomes more complex, often involving teams of decision makers and taking an average of 6 to 36 months to make decisions. Because of the complexity of the purchases, customer service is extremely important to B2B buyers. Advertising plays a much smaller role in the business market than in the consumer market, although advertisements placed in business magazines or trade publications are common. Business marketers advertise primarily to announce new products, to enhance their company image and presence, and to attract potential customers who would then deal directly with a salesperson. Personal selling plays a much bigger role in business markets than in consumer markets, distribution channels are shorter, customer relationships tend to last longer, and purchase decisions can involve many decision makers. Table 6.1 compares the marketing practices commonly used in both B2B and consumer marketing.

Like final consumers, an organization purchases products to fill needs. However, its primary need—meeting the demands of its own customers—is similar from firm to firm. A manufacturer buys raw materials such as wood pulp, fabric, or grain to create the company's product. A wholesaler or retailer buys the manufactured products—paper, clothing, or cereal—to resell. Mattel buys products such as plastic and paints to produce its toys, Canadian Tire buys finished toys to sell to the public, and passenger airlines buy and lease aircraft from manufacturers such as Bombardier and Boeing. Institutional purchasers such as government agencies and nonprofit organizations also buy products to meet the needs of their constituents, whether it is global positioning system (GPS) mapping devices or meals ready to eat for troops in the field.

table 6.1   *Comparing Business-to-Business Marketing and Consumer Marketing*

	BUSINESS-TO-BUSINESS MARKETING	CONSUMER MARKETING
Product	Relatively technical in nature, exact form often variable, accompanying services very important	Standardized form, service important but less than for business products
Promotion	Emphasis on personal selling	Emphasis on advertising
Distribution	Relatively short, direct channels to market	Product passes through a number of intermediate links en route to consumer
Customer relations	Relatively enduring and complex	Comparatively infrequent contact, relationship of relatively short duration
Decision-making process	Diverse group of organization members makes decision	Individual or household unit makes decision
Price	Competitive bidding for unique items, list prices for standard items	List prices

Companies also buy services from other businesses. A firm may purchase legal and accounting services, an office cleaning service, a call centre service, or a recruiting service. Jan-Pro is a commercial cleaning service company in business since 1991. The chain has approximately 120 master franchise offices throughout Canada, the United States, and nine other countries, and more than 12,000 individual franchise operations.[4]

Environmental, organizational, and interpersonal factors are among the many influences in B2B markets. Budget, cost, and profit considerations all play parts in business buying decisions. In addition, the business buying process typically involves complex interactions among many people. An organization's goals must also be considered in the B2B buying process. Later sections of the chapter will explore these topics in greater detail.

Some firms focus entirely on business markets. For instance, DuPont sells materials such as polymers, coatings, and colour technologies to manufacturers that use them in a variety of products. Caterpillar makes construction and mining equipment, diesel and natural gas engines, and industrial gas turbines. SAP provides collaborative business software that lets companies work with customers and business partners using databases and other applications from every major software vendor. Other firms sell to both consumer and business markets. Intel's digital and wireless computer technology is found in business computing systems and personal computers. Bell Canada, Rogers

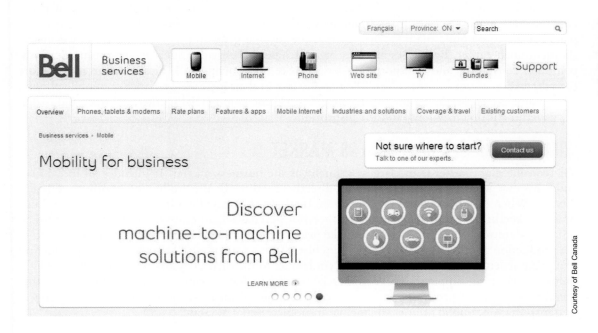

Many companies that are well-known consumer marketers also provide specialized goods and services for business customers.

Courtesy of Bell Canada

SOLVING AN ETHICAL CONTROVERSY

Making It Harder to Commit Mobile Crime

PHONE spoofing is a strategy that allows callers to subvert caller ID by hiding behind someone else's number. Although the Canadian Radio-television and Telecommunications Commission (CRTC) requires that telemarketers display the telephone number that they are calling from, scammers are increasingly using phone spoofing services for illegal purposes. Criminals can perpetrate identify theft under cover of a legitimate business's phone number and gain access to mobile voice mailboxes, obtaining just enough personal information about the owner to enter the victim's online bank and credit card accounts and raid them for sensitive information. They can then call the bank to transfer cash or trigger the issuance of duplicate credit cards. Most major mobile carriers offer customers password protection for voice mail, making it more difficult for fraudsters to get in.

Should mobile phone carriers be required to make it harder for crooks to use phone spoofing?

PRO

1. Privacy advocates find it "alarming that virtually anyone can get access to your payment and purchase information." Phone carriers can easily make this crime more difficult.

2. Businesses are especially at risk because banks often don't reimburse them for financial losses from online accounts. Losses in North America and Europe can total $1 billion a year.

CON

1. Business and individual mobile users want ready access to their information. Mandating an extra step such as password verification reduces the convenience of the voice-mail service for them.

2. Business owners should be savvy enough to use all available tools, such as the password option, to protect themselves from possible fraud.

Where do you stand: pro or con?

Sources: Federal Communications Commission, "Caller ID and Spoofing," **www.fcc.gov**, accessed April 21, 2012; Bryon Acohido, "Caller ID Spoofing Scams Aim for Bank Accounts," *USA Today*, March 15, 2012, **www.usatoday.com**; Matt Richtel, "Who's on the Line? Increasingly, Caller ID Is Duped," *The New York Times*, November 22, 2011, **www.nytimes.com**; Ron Lieber, "Your Voice Mail May Be Even Less Secure Than You Thought," *The New York Times*, August 19, 2011, **www.nytimes.com**.

Communications, and Telus sell Internet and phone service to both consumers and businesses. Note also that marketing strategies developed in consumer marketing are often appropriate for the business sector, too. Final consumers are often the end users of products sold into the business market and, as explained later in the chapter, can influence the buying decision.

The B2B market is diverse. Transactions can range from orders as small as a box of paper clips or copy-machine toner for a home-based business to transactions as large as thousands of parts for an automobile manufacturer or massive turbine generators for an electric power plant. As mentioned earlier, businesses are also big purchasers of services, such as telecommunications, computer consulting, and transportation services. See the "Solving an Ethical Controversy" feature for a discussion of one of the problems companies face in their increasing reliance on mobile phones. Four major categories define the business market: (1) the commercial market, (2) trade industries, (3) government organizations, and (4) institutions.

COMPONENTS OF THE BUSINESS MARKET

① **Explain each of the components of the business-to-business (B2B) market.**

commercial market Individuals and firms that acquire products to support, directly or indirectly, production of other goods and services.

The **commercial market** is the largest segment of the business market. It includes all individuals and firms that acquire products to support, directly or indirectly, the production of other goods and services. When Dell buys computer chips from Intel, when Sobeys buys flour for an ingredient in its on-site baked breads, and when an office supervisor purchases light bulbs or cleaning services for an office in Manitoba, these transactions all take place in the commercial market. Some products aid in the production of other items (the computer chips). Others are physically used up in the production of a good or service (the flour). Still others contribute to the firm's day-to-day operations (the light bulbs and cleaning supplies). The commercial market includes manufacturers, farmers, and other members of resource-producing industries; construction contractors; and providers of such services as transportation, public utilities, financing, insurance, and real estate.

The second segment of the organizational market, trade industries, includes retailers and wholesalers, known as resellers, who operate in this sector. Most resale products, such as clothing, appliances, sports equipment, and automobile parts, are finished goods that the buyers sell to final consumers. ACCO Brands supplies paper clips, ring binders, vinyl envelopes, sheet protectors, and fasteners to Office Depot.[5] In other cases, the buyers may complete some processing or repackaging before reselling the products. A retail meat market may purchase a side of beef and then cut individual pieces for its customers. Lumber dealers and carpet retailers may purchase in bulk and then provide quantities and sizes to meet customers' specifications. In addition to resale products, trade industries buy computers, display shelves, and other products needed to operate their businesses. All these goods—as well as maintenance items and specialized services, such as scanner installation, newspaper inserts, and radio advertising—represent organizational purchases.

The government category of the business market includes domestic units of government—federal, provincial or territorial, and municipal—as well as foreign governments. This important market segment makes a wide variety of purchases, such as highways, military uniforms, and Internet services. The primary motivation of government purchasing is to provide some form of public benefit, such as national defence or pollution control. But government agencies have also become creative when it comes to selling—local police departments and federal and provincial agencies sell unclaimed shipments, seized assets, and surplus goods through public sales, public tenders, and auctions. Lucky bidders might buy a custom yacht for their business, a sausage grinder for their restaurant, or an auto transmission for their delivery truck through an Internet auction.[6] GC Surplus, through eight sales centres across Canada, is the federal government organization responsible for selling surplus goods for more than 100 federal departments and agencies. During any week, it might dispose of vehicles, boats, household appliances, office furniture, jewellery, tools and agricultural equipment, and many other items.

Institutions, both public and private, are the fourth component of the business market. This category includes a wide range of organizations, such as hospitals, churches, skilled care and rehabilitation centres, colleges and universities, museums, and not-for-profit agencies. Some institutions—such as in higher education—must rigidly follow standardized purchasing procedures, but others have less formal buying practices. Business-to-business marketers often benefit by setting up separate divisions to sell to institutional buyers.

B2B E-MARKETING: THE INTERNET CONNECTION

UPS's website is not designed to be flashy. Although it contains some graphics and a link to sign up for Webinars, its main purpose is not entertainment. Instead, it provides lots of practical information to help the firm's customers. The site enables customers to check rates, compare services, schedule package pickups and deliveries, track shipments, and order shipping supplies. This information is vital to UPS's customers, most of whom are businesses. Customers access the site thousands of times a day.

Business-to-business (B2B) e-marketing is the use of the Internet for business transactions between organizations. Although most people are familiar with such online firms as eBay and Amazon.com, the number of consumer transactions is dwarfed by their B2B counterparts. About 91 percent of all Internet sales are B2B transactions.[7] Many business-to-business marketers have set up private portals that allow their customers to buy needed items. Service and customized pages are accessed through passwords provided by B2B marketers. Online auctions and virtual marketplaces offer other ways for buyers and vendors to connect with each other over the Internet.

During the early Internet boom, start-up companies rushed to connect buyers and sellers without considering basic marketing principles such as targeting their customers and making sure to fulfill their needs. As a result, many of these companies failed. But the companies that survived—and new firms that have learned lessons from others' mistakes—have established a much stronger marketing presence. For instance, they recognize that their business customers have a lot at stake and expect greater value and utility from the goods and services they purchase as well as streamlined marketing communications such as email, blogs, and podcasts.[8] In addition to generating sales revenue, B2B e-marketing also provides detailed product descriptions whenever needed. Payments and other information are exchanged on the Web, and B2B e-marketing can slash order-processing expenses. Business-to-business transactions, which typically involve more steps than consumer purchases, can be much more efficient on the Internet. Orders placed over the Internet usually contain fewer

trade industries Retailers or wholesalers that purchase products for resale to others.

resellers Marketing intermediaries that operate in the trade sector.

Marketoid

GC Surplus sells seized goods as well as surplus government items. In one recent year, it sold more than $3.2 million of seized goods.

business-to-business (B2B) e-marketing Use of the Internet for business transactions between organizations.

© The Seam, LLC

The Seam survived the Internet boom and bust and now brings together global buyers of commodities like cotton, peanuts, and grain.

errors than handwritten ones, and when mistakes occur, the technology can locate them quickly. So the Internet is an attractive option for business buying and selling.

B2B e-marketing activity has become more varied in recent years. In addition to using the Web to conduct individual sales transactions and provide product information, companies use such tools as EDI, Web services, extranets, private exchanges, electronic exchanges, and e-procurement. The Internet also opens up foreign markets to sellers. One such firm, a cotton exchange called The Seam, survived the Internet boom and bust and is now bringing together global buyers of commodities like cotton, peanuts, and grain.[9]

Proprietary B2B Transactions

One of the oldest applications of technology to business transactions is *electronic data interchange (EDI)*, computer-to-computer exchanges of price quotations, purchase orders, invoices, and other sales information between buyers and sellers. EDI requires compatible hardware and software systems to exchange data

---

MARKETING: MAKING YOUR WORLD BETTER	**Environmental Rebels Wanted: Must Be High-Energy and Creative**

INCREASINGLY, Canadian offices are going paperless and this is getting easier to do as technology continues to advance. For example, office workers are able to share files without printing them, and even work on them simultaneously, by using software such as Google Docs and Microsoft Office 365. Software such as Dropbox, Google Drive, and YouSendIt allows people to share and store files, particularly large ones. Many companies still scan and fax documents, and this is even easier today. There are a number of portable and desktop scanner options. TurboScan is an app that allows people to use their camera as a scanner and will even convert the file to PDF format for easy storage and emailing. Companies are also emailing invoices and collecting payments electronically. And the good news: you don't have to be a large company to go paperless.

Idea Rebel, a digital marketing agency with offices in Vancouver and Toronto, was founded with a view to sustainability. All "rebels" who work for the company must keep a reusable mug for their daily java. They commute to work by public transit, by bicycle, or by walking. Power use in the office is kept to a minimum and so is paper. The office does not have a printer nor does it provide notepads. Nearly all of the approximately 30 employees have two computer screens and an iPad on their desk. Designers get larger screens, and other employees get 21-inch screens. Employees take notes on their iPads and make heavy use of whiteboards. Idea Rebel has had to face one major problem that all paperless offices face: employees frequently must communicate with external constituents as well as internally. Customers and suppliers frequently insist

on printed communications. Idea Rebel has found an obvious solution: it simply turns down business from clients who insist on paper. There appears to be a sufficient number of clients who are happy to deal with a paperless supplier, though. Among the company's clients are such iconic names as Lululemon Athletica, CTV, Virgin, WestJet, Mountain Equipment Co-op, RE/MAX, and BMW.

For companies that want to go paperless, or nearly paperless, there are some considerations and advice. Do not try to go from paper to paperless overnight. Have a plan and look for continuous improvement. Be sure that files are backed up. Communicate with employees and get their buy-in as the process proceeds. Idea Rebel had an advantage here. It started as a paperless office, and owner Jamie Garratt recognized the importance of office culture to make his vision succeed. The company website encourages applications and states, "Our offices are high-energy, socially responsible, and active and we look for people who fit that description." Most companies have to change an existing culture. But the value to companies that succeed continues as the process unfolds. In addition to the savings from printing, mailing, and storing paper, there are savings from being able to find documents more easily and quickly, and the advantage that employees can access documents while away from the office by using cloud-based products such as Microsoft's Remote Desktop Services.

Sources: Idea Rebel website, **www.idearebel.com**, March 7, 2014; Bryan Borzykowski, "How One Company Went Completely Paperless," *The Globe and Mail*, June 14, 2103, p. B10; Kate Harrison, "5 Steps to a (Nearly) Paperless Office," **www.forbes.com**, April 19, 2013, accessed March 9, 2014.

over a network. Use of EDI cuts paper flow, speeds the order cycle, and reduces errors. In addition, by receiving daily inventory status reports from vendors, companies can set production schedules to match demand. The "Marketing: Making Your World Better" feature describes how one Canadian company is completely cutting paper flow, even refusing business from customers who insist on paper documents.

Early EDI systems were limited due to the requirement that all parties had to use the same computer operating system. That changed with the introduction of *Web services*—Internet-based systems that allow parties to communicate electronically with one another regardless of the computer operating system they use. Web services rely on open-source XML (Extensible Markup Language, a formatting language) standards.

The Internet also offers an efficient way for businesses to collaborate with vendors, partners, and customers through *extranets,* secure networks used for e-marketing and accessible through the firm's website by external customers, suppliers, or other authorized users. Extranets go beyond ordering and fulfillment processes by giving selected outsiders access to internal information. Like other forms of e-marketing, extranets provide additional benefits such as enhanced relationships with business partners. *Intranets* are secure internal networks that help companies share information among employees, no matter how many or how widespread they are. The office-supply firm Staples has thousands of employees in 26 countries. In-store devices connect them to the company's intranet, The Hub, where they can exchange information and find job-related software. The Hub also carries customer-success stories and best practices from various Staples stores, as well as video updates on company news. Andrea Quinn, Staples's retail communications manager, says, "The Hub is one of our primary vehicles to talk to all store associates." The Hub recently has twice been named one of the ten best-designed intranets by the Nielsen Norman Group, a usability consulting agency.[10]

Security and access authorization remain critical issues, and most companies create virtual private networks that protect information travelling over public communications media. These networks control who uses a company's resources and what users can access. Also, they cost considerably less than leasing dedicated lines.

The next generation of extranets is the *private exchange*, a secure website where a company and its suppliers share all types of data related to e-marketing, from product design through order delivery. A private exchange is more collaborative than a typical extranet, so this type of arrangement is sometimes called *c-business.* The participants can use it to collaborate on product ideas, production scheduling, distribution, order tracking, and any other functions a business wants to include. For example, Walmart has a private exchange it calls RetailLink. The system permits Walmart employees to access detailed sales and inventory information. Suppliers such as Procter & Gamble and Nestlé, in turn, can look up Walmart sales data and forecasts to manage their own inventory and logistics, helping them better meet the needs of the world's largest retailer and its millions of customers worldwide.

E-Procurement on Open Exchanges

In the early stages of B2B transactions, marketers believed all types of products would be traded online. Entrepreneurs created electronic exchanges to bring buyers and sellers together in one electronic marketplace and cater to a specific industry's needs, but the performance of these sites was disappointing. Many suppliers weren't happy with the pressure to come in with the lowest bid each time, and buyers preferred to cultivate long-term relationships with their suppliers, even if those suppliers sometimes charged slightly more. Purchasing agents simply didn't see enough benefits from electronic exchanges to abandon suppliers they knew.

Evolving from electronic exchanges is **e-procurement**, Web-based systems that enable all types of organizations to improve the efficiency of their bidding and purchasing processes. Royal Dutch/ Shell Group, a group of energy companies with operations in 140 countries, purchases millions of dollars of parts, components, supplies, and services every day. Recently the firm decided to replace its network of more than 100 different purchasing systems with a streamlined new system to unify procurement and reduce costs. "E-procurement enables us to make radical changes to the way we buy, the speed at which we buy, the way we and our suppliers work together, and the way we can use information to manage our business in the connected economy," said the company's strategic sourcing advisor.[11] E-procurement provides considerable benefits in public sector purchasing, and this will be discussed later in this chapter.

e-procurement Use of the Internet by organizations to solicit bids and purchase goods and services from suppliers.

DIFFERENCES IN FOREIGN BUSINESS MARKETS

When The Seam first moved into other countries, its marketers had to consider the fact that foreign business markets may differ due to variations in government regulations and cultural practices. Some business products need modifications to succeed in foreign markets. In Australia, Japan, and Great Britain, for instance, motorists drive on the left side of the road. Automobiles must be modified to accommodate such differences.

Business marketers must be willing to adapt to local customs and business practices when operating abroad. They should also research cultural preferences. Factors as deceptively simple as the time of a meeting and methods of address for associates can make a difference. A company even needs to consider what ink colours to use for documents because colours can have different meanings in different countries.

assessment check 1 ✓

1.1 Define *B2B marketing*.

1.2 What is the commercial market?

1.3 Define *EDI* and *Web services*.

1.4 Briefly explain how e-procurement works.

② **Describe the major approaches to segmenting business-to-business (B2B) markets.**

SEGMENTING B2B MARKETS

Business-to-business markets include wide varieties of customers, so marketers must identify the different market segments they serve. By applying market segmentation concepts to groups of business customers, a firm's marketers can develop a strategy that best suits a particular segment's needs. The overall process of segmenting business markets divides markets based on different criteria, usually organizational characteristics and product applications. Among the major ways to segment business markets are demographics (size), customer type, end-use application, and purchasing situation.

SEGMENTATION BY DEMOGRAPHIC CHARACTERISTICS

As with consumer markets, demographic characteristics define useful segmentation criteria for business markets. For example, firms can be grouped by size or based on sales revenues or number of employees. Marketers may develop one strategy to reach Fortune 500 corporations with complex purchasing procedures and another strategy for small firms where decisions are made by one or two people. According to one study, many firms are actually increasing their outreach to small and midsize businesses. Microsoft, for instance, targets small-business customers online but also recently partnered with a user-contributed website called Kirtsy.com that focuses on female small-business owners.

Together Microsoft and Kirtsy offered free, informal hands-on instruction to groups around Canada and the United States in using social media as marketing tools. Said a senior marketing manager for Microsoft Office Live, "Today, there are lots of options for small business owners looking to leverage the Web to bring down marketing costs and connect with customers.... By holding these sessions, we hope to help entrepreneurs gain some valuable insights they can take back and immediately use to grow their businesses."[12]

SEGMENTATION BY CUSTOMER TYPE

Another useful segmentation approach groups prospects according to type of customer. Marketers can apply this concept in several ways. They can group customers by broad categories—manufacturer, service provider, government agency, not-for-profit organization, wholesaler, or retailer—and also by industry. These groups may be further divided using other segmentation approaches discussed in this section.

customer-based segmentation Dividing a business-to-business market into homogeneous groups based on buyers' product specifications.

Customer-based segmentation is a related approach often used in the business-to-business marketplace. Organizational buyers tend to have much more precise—and complex—requirements for goods and services than ultimate consumers do. As a result, business products often fit narrower market segments than consumer products, which leads some firms to design business goods and services to meet detailed buyer specifications. The "Marketing and the SME" feature describes how one Canadian company refocused from government to private industry, where purchasing

MARKETING AND THE SME	**You Need a Salesperson to Succeed When Working with Private Dirt**

KELSEY Ramsden has an amazing story to tell. When she was 14, she worked for her father as a flag girl in the Yukon while construction of the Alaska Highway was in progress. She eventually went on to successfully complete her MBA at the Richard Ivey School of Business in London, Ontario, and today she is president of Belvedere Place Developments of Kelowna, British Columbia. While her career progressed, Kelsey battled cervical cancer, gave birth to four children, was ranked No. 1 on the Chatelaine/Profit W100 list of Canada's top female entrepreneurs, and was one of two Canadian women recognized among the 12 winners of the Ernst & Young 2013 Entrepreneurial Winning Women. Impressive? Absolutely. And Kelsey Ramsden is still under 40 years old.

What has led to Kelsey's success? She grew her small construction company—sales less than $5 million approximately five years ago—to be a major player in the Canadian construction industry. Because Belvedere is a privately held company, 2013 sales are not available, but estimates are somewhere between $40 and $50 million. It began with a very strategic decision Kelsey made a few years ago. Her company was focused on government contracts, but with the 2009 recession, competitors nearly doubled. Companies that had not previously been interested in small government

contracts were targeting them to simply stay solvent. Kelsey decided to re-invent Belvedere Place Developments to focus on private industry customers: subdivision developers, mines, and companies in the gas and oil sector.

Private industry customers, unlike the government, are not simply focused on lowest cost. But to succeed, you need a professional salesperson: someone to prospect for and qualify potential customers, someone who can build quality relationships with them, and someone who can handle customer concerns and close sales. Kelsey hired a business development manager—one of many titles given to today's salespeople—to knock on doors and seek business. It helped that Belvedere Place Developments had managed many successful contracts in the public sector and had a history of meeting specifications, on time and on budget. And not only has her company become a success in Canada, it has been expanding internationally. Kelsey expects that half of her company's revenues will come from outside Canada by the end of 2014.

Sources: "Relationship Building Fuels Growth," *National Post*, February 10, 2014, p. FP8; Canada NewsWire (Ottawa), "Two Canadians Win Spots in EY's Prestigious 2013 Entrepreneurial Winning Women™ Program," November 15, 2013; Eleanor Beaton, "Different Dirt," *Profit*, November 2012, pp. 52–53; Laura Bickle, "Breaking Ground," *Chatelaine*, November 2012, pp. 192–194.

was less concerned with price but more concerned with relationships. Another firm, Tetra Tech provides a variety of environmental services, such as technology development, design, engineering, and remediation for organizations around the world. Because the company's customers include government agencies as well as private firms—and because customers' needs are different—Tetra Tech FW has more than 60 offices in Canada and 350 offices worldwide that offer a range of programs to suit each type of customer. For instance, the firm provides consulting services for utilities, helps communities clean up polluted water sources, and even conducts missions to clear public and private sites of unexploded military supplies.[13]

North American Industry Classification System (NAICS)

For many decades, the Canadian and U.S. governments used a system for subdividing the business marketplace into detailed segments. The Standard Industrial Classification (SIC) system standardized efforts to collect and report information on industrial activity, but the systems varied between the two countries.

SIC codes divided firms into broad industry categories: agriculture, forestry, and fishing; mining and construction; manufacturing; transportation; communication; electric, gas, and sanitary services; wholesale trade; retail trade; finance, insurance, and real-estate services; public administration; and nonclassifiable establishments. The system assigned each major category within these classifications its own two-digit number. Three-digit and four-digit numbers further subdivided each industry into smaller segments.

For roughly 70 years, B2B marketers used SIC codes as a tool for segmenting markets and identifying new customers. The system, however, became outdated with implementation of the North American Free Trade Agreement. Each NAFTA member—the United States, Canada, and Mexico—had its own system for measuring business activity. NAFTA required a joint classification

table 6.2 *NAICS Classifications for Wine Manufacturers*

31	Manufacturing
312	Beverage and Tobacco Product Manufacturing
3121	Beverage Manufacturing
31213	Wineries
312130	Canadian Wineries

Source: NAICS, U.S. Census Bureau, **http://www.census.gov/epcd/www/naics.html**.

North American Industry Classification System (NAICS)
Classification used by NAFTA countries to categorize the business marketplace into detailed market segments.

system that would allow marketers to compare business sectors among the member nations. In effect, marketers required a segmentation tool they could use across borders. The **North American Industry Classification System (NAICS)** replaced the SIC and provides more detail than previously available. The NAICS created new service sectors to better reflect the economy of the 21st century. They include information on health care and social assistance and professional, scientific, and technical services.

Table 6.2 demonstrates the NAICS system for wine manufacturers. The NAICS uses six digits, compared with the four digits used in the SIC. The first five digits are fixed among the members of NAFTA. The sixth digit can vary among U.S., Canadian, and Mexican data. In short, the sixth digit accounts for specific data needs of each nation.[14] Knowing that Canadian wine manufacturers are classified under NAICS code 312130 allows suppliers to the wine industry to quickly identify and get valuable information on potential customers.

SEGMENTATION BY END-USE APPLICATION

Marketoid

NAICS Canada 2012 consists of 20 sectors, 102 subsectors, 323 industry groups, 711 industries, and 922 national industries.

A third basis for segmentation, **end-use application segmentation**, focuses on the precise way in which a business purchaser will use a product. For example, a printing equipment manufacturer may serve markets as varied as a local utility, a bicycle manufacturer, and the Department of National Defence. Each end use of the equipment may dictate unique specifications for performance, design, and price. Praxair, a supplier of industrial gases, for example, might segment its markets according to user. Steel and glass manufacturers might buy hydrogen and oxygen, while food and beverage manufacturers need carbon dioxide. Praxair also sells krypton, a rare gas, to companies that produce lasers, lighting, and thermal windows. Many small- and medium-sized companies also segment markets according to end-use application. Instead of competing in markets dominated by large firms, they concentrate on specific end-use market segments. The approximately two dozen companies that manufacture wooden baseball bats for Major League Baseball focus on specific end users who are very different from the youth and high school players using aluminum bats. In 2012, Miguel Cabrera of the Detroit Tigers was the first Triple Crown winner in 45 years: .330 batting average, 44 home runs, and 108 runs batted in. He is one of many leading batters in Major League Baseball who use bats manufactured by The Original Maple Bat Corporation of Ottawa, Ontario.[15]

end-use application segmentation
Segmenting a business-to-business market based on how industrial purchasers will use the product.

SEGMENTATION BY PURCHASE CATEGORIES

Firms have different structures for their purchasing functions, and B2B marketers must adapt their strategies according to those organizational buyer characteristics. Some companies designate centralized purchasing departments to serve the entire firm, and others allow each unit to handle its own buying. A supplier may deal with one purchasing agent or several decision makers at various levels. Each of these structures results in different buying behaviour.

When the buying situation is important to marketers, they typically consider whether the customer has made previous purchases or if this is the customer's first order, offering special rates or programs for valued clients. Most hotel chains and car rental companies across Canada provide discounts to government employees; special discounts for air crew from commercial airlines are also common.

customer relationship management (CRM)
Combination of strategies and tools that drives relationship programs, reorienting the entire organization to a concentrated focus on satisfying customers.

Increasingly, businesses that have developed **customer relationship management (CRM)** systems—strategies and tools that reorient an entire organization to focus on satisfying customers— can segment customers by the stage of the relationship between the business and the customer.

A B2B company, for example, might develop different strategies for newly acquired customers than it would for existing customers to which it hopes to cross-sell new products. Similarly, building loyalty among satisfied customers requires a different approach than developing programs to "save" at-risk customer relationships. An example of a very popular CRM software program is discussed in the opening vignette for Chapter 15.

assessment check 2 ✓

2.1 What are the four major ways marketers segment business markets?

2.2 What is the NAICS?

CHARACTERISTICS OF THE B2B MARKET

③ **Identify the major characteristics of the business market and its demand.**

Businesses that serve both B2B and consumer markets must understand the needs of their customers. However, several characteristics distinguish the business market from the consumer market: (1) geographic market concentration, (2) the sizes and numbers of buyers, (3) the purchase decision process, and (4) buyer–seller relationships. The next sections consider how these traits influence business-to-business marketing.

GEOGRAPHIC MARKET CONCENTRATION

The Canadian business market is more geographically concentrated than the consumer market. Manufacturers converge in certain regions of the country, making these areas prime targets for business marketers. For example, the Canadian chemical industry is largely concentrated in Alberta, Ontario, and Quebec. The oil and gas industry is largely concentrated in Newfoundland and Labrador and Alberta.

Certain industries locate in particular areas to be close to customers. Firms may choose to locate sales offices and distribution centres in these areas to provide more attentive service. It makes sense that the Ottawa and Washington areas are favoured by companies that sell to the Canadian and U.S. governments, respectively. BlackBerry, once known for its strong association with governments worldwide due to the security of its communications platform, recently announced it will open a new security centre in Washington, D.C., as it gets back to its roots and refocuses on the B2B market.[16]

The Canadian automobile assembly industry is concentrated in southwestern Ontario. There is no surprise that so many automobile parts manufacturers are located in this area as well. As the suppliers to the industry concentrate near their customers, they then make the area more attractive for industry expansion. As Internet-based technology continues to improve, allowing companies to transact business even with distant suppliers, business markets may become less geographically concentrated. Much of government spending, for example, is now directed through the Internet.

SIZES AND NUMBERS OF BUYERS

In addition to geographic concentration, the business market features a limited number of buyers. Marketers can draw on a wealth of statistical information to estimate the sizes and characteristics of business markets. The federal government is the largest single source of such statistics. Information can be accessed from several important sources: Statistics Canada (**www.statcan.gc.ca**), Industry Canada (**www.ic.gc.ca**), and Strategis (**www.strategis.ic.gc.ca**). Many government units and trade organizations also operate websites that contain helpful information.

Many buyers in limited-buyer markets are large organizations. A few large buyers, such as Tim Hortons, McDonald's, Wendy's, and Burger King, dominate the fast-food industry. These chains have the power to name the price they will pay for eggs and meats and can dictate living conditions and standards of labour on ranches.

In a limited-buyer market such as fast food, a few large buyers—McDonald's, Wendy's, Tim Hortons, and Burger King—are the major customers.

H. F. (Herb) MacKenzie

Trade associations and business publications provide additional information on the business market. Private firms such as Dun & Bradstreet publish detailed reports on individual companies. These data serve as a useful starting point for analyzing a business market. Finding data in such a source requires an understanding of the NAICS, which identifies much of the available statistical information.

Having an enormous number of business customers with varying needs can pose quite a logistical challenge for a firm.

THE PURCHASE DECISION PROCESS

To market effectively to other organizations, businesses must understand the dynamics of the organizational purchase process. Suppliers who serve business-to-business markets must work with many buyers, especially when selling to larger customers. Decision makers at several levels may influence final orders, and the overall process is more formal and professional than the consumer purchasing process. Purchasers typically require a longer time frame because B2B involves more complex decisions. Suppliers must evaluate customer needs and develop proposals that meet technical requirements and specifications. Also, buyers need time to analyze competing proposals. Often, decisions require more than one round of bidding and negotiation, especially for complicated purchases.

BUYER–SELLER RELATIONSHIPS

An especially important characteristic of B2B marketing is the relationship between buyers and sellers. These relationships are often more complex than consumer relationships, and they require superior communications among the organizations' personnel. Satisfying one major customer may mean the difference of millions of dollars to a firm.

Relationship marketing involves developing long-term, value-added customer relationships. A primary goal of business-to-business relationships is to provide advantages that no other vendor can provide—for instance, lower price, quicker delivery, better quality and reliability, customized product features, or more favourable financing terms. For the business marketer, providing these advantages means expanding the company's external relationships to include suppliers, distributors, and other organizational partners. CDW, for instance, relies on a variety of vendors to meet its own business, government, and education customers' technology needs with hardware, software, networking, and data storage. It has developed the CDW Supplier Diversity Program to increase and improve relationships with small-business suppliers owned by minorities, women, and veterans and thus must manage its supplier as well as its customer relationships successfully.[17]

Close cooperation, whether through informal contacts or under terms specified in contractual partnerships and strategic alliances, enables companies to meet buyers' needs for quality products and customer service. This holds true both during and after the purchase process. Tetra Tech EC is a wholly owned subsidiary of Tetra Tech, mentioned earlier. Tetra Tech EC has instituted formal Client Service Quality and Shared Vision programs, designed to engage customers in continuous communication leading to customer satisfaction.

Relationships between for-profit and not-for-profit organizations are just as important as those between two commercial organizations. Walmart is a long-time corporate sponsor of Children's Miracle Network, an international organization that helps improve children's health and welfare by raising funds for state-of-the-art care, cutting-edge research, and education. Since 1994, when Walmart came to Canada, it has raised and donated more than $80 million to Children's Miracle Network member hospitals across the country.[18]

EVALUATING INTERNATIONAL BUSINESS MARKETS

Business purchasing patterns differ from one country to the next. Researching these markets poses a particular problem for B2B marketers. Of course, as explained earlier, NAICS is correcting this problem in the NAFTA countries.

In addition to quantitative data such as the size of the potential market, companies must also carefully weigh its qualitative features. This process involves considering cultural values, work styles, and the best ways to enter overseas markets in general. The Coca-Cola Company has a presence in 90 markets worldwide. The company manages the sometimes volatile variations in culture and politics in Eurasia and Africa with a structure of six locally based business units in South Africa, Kenya, Turkey, Russia, India, and Dubai. A functional team in Istanbul manages finance, marketing, and strategy, working with each business unit to devise a strategic plan for that unit's market. For example, the business unit in Turkey developed a special marketing campaign for the Muslim holy month of Ramadan. The campaign proved so successful that the company expanded it to other Muslim countries where Coca-Cola has a presence. The president of Coca-Cola's Eurasia and Africa Group says, "This is not a bureaucratic approval-based system. Of course, there are approvals, but once the strategy and business plan are approved, local teams can execute."[19]

In today's international marketplace, companies often practise global sourcing, which involves contracting to purchase goods and services from suppliers worldwide. This practice can result in substantial cost savings, although product quality must be carefully monitored. India, China, and Malaysia are the world's top destinations for global IT sourcing. Some other countries in the top 30 outsourcing destinations are the Philippines, Indonesia, Malaysia, Sri Lanka, Thailand, and Vietnam in Asia; and Colombia, Costa Rica, Mexico, Argentina, Brazil, Peru, Chile, and Panama in Central and South America.[20]

Global sourcing requires companies to adopt a new mind-set; some must even reorganize their operations. Among other considerations, businesses sourcing from several multinational locations should streamline the purchase process and minimize price differences due to labour costs, tariffs, taxes, and currency fluctuations.

global sourcing
Purchasing goods and services from suppliers worldwide.

derived demand
Demand for a resource that results from demand for the goods and services that are produced by that resource.

---

assessment check 3a

3.1 Why is geographic segmentation important in the B2B market?

3.2 In what ways is the buyer–seller relationship important in B2B marketing?

3.3 What is global sourcing?

BUSINESS MARKET DEMAND

The previous section's discussion of business market characteristics demonstrated considerable differences between marketing techniques for consumer and business products. Demand characteristics also differ in these markets. In business markets, the major categories of demand are derived demand, joint demand, inelastic demand, volatile demand, and inventory adjustments. Figure 6.1 summarizes these different categories of business market demand.

DERIVED DEMAND

The term **derived demand** refers to the linkage between demand for a company's output and its purchases of resources such as machinery, components, supplies, and raw materials. The demand for computer microprocessor chips is *derived* from the demand for personal computers. If more businesses and individuals buy new computers, the demand for chips increases; if fewer computers are sold, the demand for chips decreases. Lear Corporation, for instance, supplied auto seats and other interior parts to companies like Ford and General Motors. In the wake of the car makers' plant closings and reduced production plans, demand for Lear products declined.[21]

Organizational buyers purchase two general categories of business products: capital items and expense items. Derived demand ultimately affects both. Capital items are long-lived business assets that must be depreciated over time. *Depreciation* is an accounting term that refers to charging a portion of a capital item's cost as a deduction against the company's annual revenue for purposes of determining its net income. Examples of capital items are major installations such as new manufacturing plants, office buildings, and computer systems.

Expense items, in contrast, are items consumed within short time periods. Accountants charge the cost of such products against income in the year of purchase. Examples of expense items are the supplies necessary to operate the business, such as paper clips or machine lubricants.

Marketoid

Chinese demand for red wine is driving global demand. In 2013, China passed France in total red wine consumption: 155 million 9-litre cases (1.87 billion bottles) versus France's 150 million cases. However, France's per capita consumption at 51.9 litres by far exceeds China's 1.5 litres.

figure 6.1

Categories of Business Market Demand

joint demand Demand for a product that depends on the demand for another product used in combination with it.

inelastic demand Demand that, throughout an industry, will not change significantly due to a price change.

just-in-time (JIT)/ JIT II Inventory practices that seek to boost efficiency by cutting inventories to absolute minimum levels. With JIT II, suppliers' representatives work at the customer's facility.

sole sourcing Purchasing a firm's entire stock of an item from just one vendor.

VOLATILE DEMAND

Derived demand creates volatility in business market demand. Assume that the sales volume for a gasoline retailer is increasing at an annual rate of 5 percent. Now suppose that the demand for this gasoline brand slows to a 3 percent annual increase. This slowdown might convince the firm to keep its current gasoline pumps and replace them only when market conditions improve. In this way, even modest shifts in consumer demand for a gasoline brand would greatly affect the pump manufacturer.

JOINT DEMAND

Another important influence on business market demand is **joint demand**, which results when the demand for one business product is related to the demand for another business product used in combination with the first item. Both lumber and concrete are required to build most homes. If the lumber supply falls, the drop in housing construction will most likely affect the demand for concrete. Another example is the joint demand for electrical power and large turbine engines. If consumers decide to conserve power, demand for new power plants drops, as does the demand for components and replacement parts for turbines.

INELASTIC DEMAND

Inelastic demand means that demand throughout an industry will not change significantly due to a price change. If the price of lumber drops, a construction firm will not necessarily buy more lumber from its suppliers unless another factor—such as lowered mortgage interest rates—causes more consumers to purchase new homes.

INVENTORY ADJUSTMENTS

Adjustments in inventory and inventory policies can also affect business demand. Assume that manufacturers in a particular industry consider a 60-day supply of raw materials the optimal inventory level. Now suppose that economic conditions or other factors induce these firms to increase their inventories to a 90-day supply. The change will bombard the raw-materials supplier with new orders.

Further, **just-in-time (JIT)** inventory policies seek to boost efficiency by cutting inventories to absolute minimum levels and by requiring vendors to deliver inputs as the production process needs them. JIT allows companies to better predict which supplies they will require and the timing for when they will need them, markedly reducing their costs for production and storage. Widespread implementation of JIT has had a substantial impact on organizations' purchasing behaviour. Firms that practise JIT tend to order from relatively few suppliers. In some cases, JIT may lead to **sole sourcing** for some items—in other words, buying a firm's entire stock of a product from just one supplier. Electronic data interchange (EDI) and quick-response inventory policies have produced similar results in the trade industries. The latest inventory trend, **JIT II**, leads suppliers to place representatives at the customer's facility to work as part of an integrated, on-site customer–supplier team. Suppliers plan and order in consultation with the customer. This streamlining of the inventory process improves control of the flow of goods.

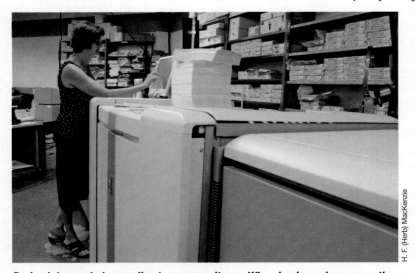

H. F. (Herb) MacKenzie

Derived demand also applies to expense items. When business increases, the need for printing services increases, and demand for paper, printing ink, and other supplies increases.

Although inventory adjustments are critical in manufacturing processes, they are equally vital to wholesalers and retailers. Limited Brands, which owns Victoria's Secret and Bath & Body Works, recently upgraded its technology infrastructure and distribution centres. With a large variety of products, Victoria's Secret and Bath & Body Works benefited from improved inventory management, which sped up the process of keeping popular items in stock and removing those that didn't sell.[22]

THE MAKE, BUY, OR LEASE DECISION

(4)   **Discuss the decision to make, buy, or lease.**

Before a company can decide what to buy, it should decide whether to buy at all. Organizational buyers must figure out the best way to acquire needed products. In fact, a firm considering the acquisition of a finished good, component part, or service has three basic options:

1. Make the good or provide the service in-house.

2. Purchase it from another organization.

3. Lease it from another organization.

Manufacturing the product itself, if the company has the capability to do so, may be the best route. It may save a great deal of money if its own manufacturing division does not incur costs for overhead that an outside vendor would otherwise charge.

On the other hand, most firms cannot make all the business goods they need. Often, it would be too costly to maintain the necessary equipment, staff, and supplies. Therefore, purchasing from an outside vendor is the most common choice. Xerox manufactures more than 50 different types of colour printers to meet nearly any business need—from affordable colour laser printers to high-performance ink-jet printers. Its wide array of products, coupled with its track record of a century of supplying businesses, has made it a leader in the B2B printer market.[23] Companies can also look outside their own plants for goods and services that they formerly produced in-house, a practice called *outsourcing* that the next section will describe in more detail.

In some cases, however, a company may choose to lease inputs. This option spreads out costs compared with lump-sum costs for upfront purchases. The company pays for the use of equipment for a certain period. A small business may lease a copier for a few years and make monthly payments. At the end of the lease term, the firm can buy the machine at a prearranged price or replace it with a different model under a new lease. This option can provide useful flexibility for a growing business, allowing it to easily upgrade as its needs change.

Companies can also lease sophisticated computer systems and heavy equipment. For example, some airlines prefer to lease airplanes rather than buy them outright because short-term leases allow them to adapt quickly to changes in passenger demand.

THE RISE OF OUTSOURCING AND OFFSHORING

Chances are, if you dial a call centre for a firm such as Dell, GE, or Nestlé, your call will be answered by someone in India. In recent years, there has been a growing concern related to the movement of jobs to lower-cost overseas locations, a business practice referred to as **offshoring**. This relocation of business processes to a lower-cost location can involve production offshoring or services offshoring. China has emerged as the preferred destination for production offshoring, while India has emerged as the dominant player in services offshoring.

Some firms want to remain closer to home but take advantage of the benefits of locating some of their operations outside their home country, a practice known as **nearshoring**. In today's highly competitive marketplace, firms look to improve efficiency and cut costs on just about everything, including customer service, human resources, accounting, information technology, manufacturing, and distribution. **Outsourcing**—using outside vendors to produce goods and services formerly produced in-house—is a trend that continues to rise. Businesses outsource for several reasons: (1) they

offshoring Movement of high-wage jobs from Canada to lower-cost overseas locations.

nearshoring Moving jobs to vendors in countries close to the business's home country.

outsourcing Using outside vendors to produce goods and services formerly produced in-house.

need to reduce costs to remain competitive, (2) they need to improve the quality and speed of software maintenance and development, and (3) outsourcing has begun to offer greater value than ever before.

Outsourcing allows firms to concentrate their resources on their core business. It also allows access to specialized talent or expertise that does not exist within the firm. The most frequently outsourced business functions are information technology (IT) and human resources, with other white-collar service jobs such as accounting, drug research, technical R&D, and film animation. Although most outsourcing is done by North American–based companies, the practice is rapidly becoming commonplace in Asia, Europe, and Central America.

China still leads the way in offshore manufacturing, making two-thirds of the world's copiers, microwaves, DVD players, and shoes, and virtually all of the world's toys. In recent years, however, China's very success and the resulting rise of an increasingly wealthy middle class have pushed up its labour and management costs and may have helped shift many companies to suppliers in Vietnam and India, where such costs are still low.[24]

Outsourcing can be a smart strategy if a company chooses a vendor that can provide high-quality products and perhaps at a lower cost than could be achieved by the company itself. This priority allows the outsourcer to focus on its core competencies. Successful outsourcing requires companies to carefully oversee contracts and manage relationships. Some vendors now provide performance guarantees to assure their customers that they will receive high-quality services that meet their needs.

PROBLEMS WITH OUTSOURCING AND OFFSHORING

Outsourcing and offshoring are not without their downsides. Many companies discover that their cost savings are less than vendors sometimes promise. Also, companies that sign multiyear contracts may find that their savings drop after a year or two. When proprietary technology is an issue, outsourcing raises security concerns. Similarly, companies that are protective of customer data and relationships may think twice about entrusting functions like customer service to outside sources.

In some cases, outsourcing and offshoring can reduce a company's ability to respond quickly to the marketplace, or they can slow efforts in bringing new products to market. Suppliers who fail to deliver goods promptly or provide required services can adversely affect a company's reputation with its customers.

Outsourcing and offshoring are controversial topics with unions, especially in the auto industry, as the percentage of component parts made in-house has steadily dropped. These practices can create conflicts between nonunion outside workers and in-house union employees, who fear job loss. Management initiatives to outsource jobs can lead to strikes and plant shutdowns. Even if they do not lead to disruption in the workplace, outsourcing and offshoring can have a negative impact on employee morale and loyalty.

assessment check 4

4.1 Identify two potential benefits of outsourcing.

4.2 Identify two potential problems with outsourcing.

(5) **Describe the major influences on business buying behaviour.**

THE BUSINESS BUYING PROCESS

Suppose that CanMap, Inc., a hypothetical manufacturer of GPS devices for automakers, decides to upgrade its manufacturing facility with $5 million in new automated assembly equipment. Before approaching equipment suppliers, the company must analyze its needs, determine goals that the project should accomplish, develop technical specifications for the equipment, and set a budget. Once it receives vendors' proposals, it must evaluate them and select the best one. But what does *best* mean in this context? The lowest price or the best warranty and service contract? Who in the company is responsible for such decisions?

The business buying process is more complex than the consumer decision process. Business buying takes place within a formal organization's budget, cost, and profit considerations. Furthermore, B2B and institutional buying decisions usually involve many people with complex interactions among individuals and organizational goals. To understand organizational buying behaviour, business marketers require knowledge of influences on the purchase decision process, the stages in the organizational buying model, types of business buying situations, and techniques for purchase decision analysis.

INFLUENCES ON PURCHASE DECISIONS

B2B buying decisions react to various influences, some external to the firm and others related to internal structure and personnel. In addition to product-specific factors such as purchase price, installation, operating and maintenance costs, and vendor service, companies must consider broader environmental, organizational, and interpersonal influences.

Environmental Factors

Environmental conditions such as economic, political, regulatory, competitive, and technological considerations influence business buying decisions. CanMap may wish to defer purchases of the new equipment in times of slowing economic activity. During a recession, sales to automakers might drop because households hesitate to spend money on a new car. The company would look at the derived demand for its products, possible changes in its sources of materials, employment trends, and similar factors before committing to such a large capital expenditure.

Environmental factors include natural disasters, such as the earthquake that struck Japan, temporarily shutting down many industries, such as car manufacturing. During plant shutdowns, the purchasing of parts and equipment declines.

Environmental factors can also include natural disasters, such as the devastating earthquake and tsunami that struck Japan. Among the many industries affected was car manufacturing. The Toyota Prius is made only in Japan and was out of stock for several months, along with other models like the Camry. More recently, however, almost all the Japanese auto plants are back on line, some even ahead of schedule.[25]

Political, regulatory, and competitive factors also come into play in influencing purchase decisions. Passage of a privacy law that restricted GPS tracking would affect demand, as would competition from smartphones and other devices containing map features. Finally, technology plays a role in purchase decisions. When GPS systems were first introduced, many customers bought separate units to install in their cars. But as more new cars come factory-equipped with the units, the market for stand-alone boxes naturally decreases.

Organizational Factors

Successful business-to-business marketers understand their customers' organizational structures, policies, and purchasing systems. A company with a centralized procurement function operates differently from one that delegates purchasing decisions to divisional or geographic units. Trying to sell to the local store when head office merchandisers make all the decisions would clearly waste salespeople's time. Buying behaviour also differs among firms. For example, centralized buying tends to emphasize long-term relationships, whereas decentralized buying focuses more on short-term results. Personal selling skills and user preferences carry more weight in decentralized purchasing situations than in centralized buying.

How many suppliers should a company patronize? Because purchasing operations spend over half of each dollar their companies earn, consolidating vendor relationships can lead to large cost savings. However, a fine line separates maximizing buying power from relying too heavily on a few suppliers. Many companies engage in **multiple sourcing**—purchasing from several vendors. Spreading orders ensures against shortages if one vendor cannot deliver on schedule. However, dealing with many sellers can be counterproductive and take too much time. Each company must set its own criteria for this decision.

multiple sourcing
Purchasing from several vendors.

Interpersonal Influences

Many people may influence B2B purchases, and considerable time may be spent obtaining the input and approval of various organization members. Both group and individual forces are at work here. When committees handle buying, they must spend time to gain majority or unanimous approval. Also, each individual buyer brings to the decision process individual preferences, experiences, and biases. See the "Career Readiness" feature for some tips on negotiating with these individual buyers.

CAREER READINESS **How to Negotiate with Customers**

IN a business situation, there will be occasions when you'll need to rely on your negotiating skills to interact with customers. Here are some tried-and-true tips.

1. Do your homework first. Before you begin a negotiation, you should already have a good general idea what the customer's needs and wants are, and what other options they have for meeting these.
2. Listen. Now it pays to be a bit of a detective and simply listen while the other party tells you what you need to know in order to close the deal.
3. Read body language. Don't overlook the importance of what people are telling you with their gestures, position, and eye contact.
4. Agree in advance about what you are negotiating. Don't assume that it is price. Customers may want to

negotiate a better deal on service, an earlier delivery date, more add-on features, replacement parts, and the like.

5. Believe in the value of what you're selling.
6. Avoid the word "between." If you propose a range, you give the other party the ability to choose the lower price or later delivery date, giving up ground when you don't need to.
7. Don't commit anything to writing until the negotiation is over.

Sources: Ed Brodow, "Ten Tips for Negotiating in 2012," Brodow.com, **www.brodow.com,** accessed April 16, 2012; Mark Hunter, "6 Sales Negotiation Tips You MUST Know," The Sales Hunter.com, **http://thesaleshunter.com,** accessed April 16, 2012; Mike Hoffman, "5 Things You Should Never Say While Negotiating," Inc., **www.inc.com,** accessed April 16, 2012.

Business marketers should know who will influence buying decisions in an organization for their products and should know each of their priorities. To choose a supplier for an industrial press, for example, a purchasing manager and representatives of the company's production, engineering, and quality control departments may jointly decide on a supplier. Each of these principals may have a different point of view that the vendor's marketers must understand.

To effectively address the concerns of all people involved in the buying decision, sales personnel must be well versed in the technical features of their products. They must also interact well with employees of the various departments involved in the purchase decision. Sales representatives for medical products—traditionally called detailers—frequently visit hospitals and doctors' offices to discuss the advantages of their new products and leave samples with clinical staff.

The Role of Merchandisers and Category Advisors

merchandisers Trade sector buyers who secure needed products at the best possible prices.

Many large organizations attempt to make their purchases through systematic procedures employing professional buyers. In the trade industries, these buyers, often referred to as **merchandisers**, are responsible for securing needed products at the best possible prices. Canadian Tire has buyers for hardware items and sporting goods that will ultimately be sold to consumers. Ford has buyers for components that will be incorporated into its cars and trucks. A firm's purchasing or merchandising unit devotes all its time and effort in determining needs, locating and evaluating alternative suppliers, and making purchase decisions.

Purchase decisions for capital items vary significantly from those for expense items. Firms often buy expense items routinely with little delay. Capital items, however, involve major fund commitments and usually undergo considerable review.

systems integration Centralization of the procurement function within an internal division or as a service of an external supplier.

One way in which a firm may attempt to streamline the buying process is through **systems integration**, or centralization of the procurement function. One company may designate a lead division to handle all purchasing. Another firm may choose to designate a major supplier as the systems integrator. This vendor then assumes responsibility for dealing with all the suppliers for a project and for presenting the entire package to the buyer. In trade industries, this vendor is sometimes called a **category advisor** or **category captain**.

category advisor (category captain) Trade industry vendor who develops a comprehensive procurement plan for a retail buyer.

A business marketer may set up a sales organization to serve national accounts

assessment check 5

5.1 Identify the three major factors that influence purchase decisions.

5.2 What are the advantages and disadvantages of multiple sourcing?

that deals solely with buyers at geographically concentrated corporate headquarters. A separate field sales organization may serve buyers at regional production facilities.

Corporate buyers often use the Internet to identify sources of supply. They view online catalogues and websites to compare vendors' offerings and to obtain product information. Some use Internet exchanges to extend their supplier networks.

MODEL OF THE ORGANIZATIONAL BUYING PROCESS

⑥ **Outline the steps in the organizational buying process.**

An organizational buying situation takes place through a sequence of activities. Figure 6.2 illustrates an eight-stage model of an organizational buying process. Although not every buying situation will require all these steps, this figure provides a good overview of the whole process.

Stage 1: Anticipate or Recognize a Problem, Need, or Opportunity and a General Solution

Both consumer and business purchase decisions begin when the recognition of problems, needs, or opportunities triggers the buying process. Perhaps a firm's computer system has become outdated or an account representative demonstrates a new service that could improve the company's performance. Companies may decide to hire an outside marketing specialist when their sales stagnate.

The problem may be as simple as needing to provide a good cup of coffee to a firm's employees. The founders of Keurig Incorporated, which supplies about 2.5 million individually brewed cups of coffee to homes and offices each day, started by asking themselves, "Why do we brew coffee a pot at a time when we drink it a cup at a time?"[26]

figure 6.2

Stages in the B2B Buying Process

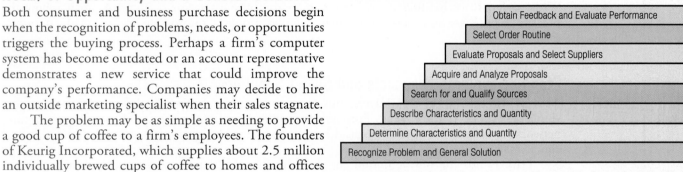

Obtain Feedback and Evaluate Performance	8
Select Order Routine	7
Evaluate Proposals and Select Suppliers	6
Acquire and Analyze Proposals	5
Search for and Qualify Sources	4
Describe Characteristics and Quantity	3
Determine Characteristics and Quantity	2
Recognize Problem and General Solution	1

Source: Based on Michael D. Hutt and Thomas W. Speh, *Business Marketing Management: A Strategic View of Industrial and Organizational Markets*, 8th edition (Mason, OH: South-Western, 2004).

Stage 2: Determine the Characteristics and Quantity of a Needed Good or Service

The coffee problem described in stage 1 translated into a service opportunity for Keurig. The small firm was able to offer a coffee system that would brew one perfect cup of coffee at a time, according to the preferences of each employee. After finding success in the offices of many accounting, law, and medical practices, the company developed a single-cup brewer for home use and has most recently introduced a unique full-colour touch screen that allows coffee lovers to readily customize each cup's temperature and strength. Recently, Keurig unveiled its Vue V1200 commercial brewer, intended for office use. Along with a touch screen and strength selection, the Vue V1200 also has radio frequency identification technology (RFID), which further ensures the quality of the final brew.[27]

Stage 3: Describe Characteristics and the Quantity of a Needed Good or Service

After determining the characteristics and quantity of needed products, B2B buyers must translate these ideas into detailed specifications. Customers told Keurig they wanted a foolproof, individual coffee maker. The Keurig system supplies a plastic K-Cup portion pack, containing ground coffee that the individual simply places in the coffee maker—no measuring of water or coffee is required. Out comes the perfect cup of coffee. Firms can easily base the quantity requirements of the Keurig system on the number of coffee-drinking employees they have or the amount of space they occupy.

The founders of Keurig Incorporated asked themselves, "Why do we brew coffee a pot at a time when we drink it a cup at a time?"

Stage 4: Search for and Qualify Potential Sources

Both consumers and businesses search for good suppliers of desired products. The choice of a supplier may be relatively straightforward—for instance, because there was no other machine like it, its early adopters had no trouble selecting the Keurig coffee system. Other searches may involve more complex decision making. A company that wants to buy a group life or health insurance policy, for example, must weigh the varying provisions and programs of many different vendors.

Stage 5: Acquire and Analyze Proposals

The next step is to acquire and analyze suppliers' proposals, which are often submitted in writing. If the buyer is a government or public agency, this stage of the purchase process may involve competitive bidding. During this process, each marketer must develop its bid, including a price that will satisfy the criteria determined by the customer's problem, need, or opportunity. While competitive bidding is less common in the business sector, a company may follow the practice to purchase nonstandard materials, complex products, or products that are made to its own specifications.

Stage 6: Evaluate Proposals and Select Suppliers

Next in the buying process, buyers must compare vendors' proposals and choose the one that seems best suited to their needs. Proposals for sophisticated equipment, such as a large computer networking system, can include considerable differences among product offerings, and the final choice may involve trade-offs.

Price is not the only criterion for the selection of a vendor. Relationship factors such as communications and trust may also be important to the buyer. Other issues are reliability, delivery record, time from order to delivery, quality, and order accuracy. These are particularly important in the package delivery business. UPS recently announced that it is equipping its drivers worldwide with a new hand-held computer intended to speed uploading of package-tracking information and hence delivery to customers. This mobile device, called the Delivery Information Acquisition Device or DIAD V, is half the size and weight of the previous generation of package trackers. It also has a colour camera for proof of delivery, is sturdier, and can store more information. The DIAD V is the first to use Qualcomm's Gobi Radio Technology, which allows the device to switch instantly to another cellular carrier if the signal is lost. Dave Barnes, the chief information officer at UPS, says, "This computer accelerates the transfer of customer tracking data and makes it possible for UPS customers to track almost 16 million deliveries worldwide each day."[28]

H. F. (Herb) MacKenzie

In business-to-business markets, price is often much less important than quality. Product failure for an inexpensive item can have tremendous financial consequences for a company.

Stage 7: Select an Order Routine

Once a supplier has been chosen, buyer and vendor must work out the best way to process future purchases. Ordering routines can vary considerably. Most orders will, however, include product descriptions, quantities, prices, delivery terms, and payment terms. Today, companies have a variety of options for submitting orders: written documents, phone calls, faxes, or electronic data interchange (EDI).

Stage 8: Obtain Feedback and Evaluate Performance

At the final stage, buyers measure vendors' performances. Sometimes this judgment will involve a formal evaluation of each supplier's product quality, delivery performance, prices, technical knowledge, and overall responsiveness to customer needs. At other times, vendors are measured according to whether they have lowered the customer's costs or reduced its employees' workloads. In general, bigger firms are more likely to use formal evaluation procedures, while smaller companies lean toward informal evaluations. Regardless of the method used, buyers should tell vendors how they will be evaluated.

Sometimes firms rely on independent organizations to gather quality feedback and summarize results. J.D. Power and Associates conducts research and provides information to a variety of firms so that they can improve the quality of their goods and services.

> **assessment check 6**
>
> 6.1 Why does the organizational buying process contain more steps than the consumer buying process?
>
> 6.2 List the steps in the organizational buying process.

CLASSIFYING BUSINESS BUYING SITUATIONS

⑦ **Classify organizational buying situations.**

As discussed earlier, business buying behaviour responds to many purchasing influences, such as environmental, organizational, and interpersonal factors. This buying behaviour also involves the degree of effort that the purchase decision demands and the levels within the organization where it is made. Like consumer behaviour, marketers can classify B2B buying situations into three general categories, ranging from least to most complex: (1) straight rebuying, (2) modified rebuying, and (3) new-task buying. Business buying situations may also involve reciprocity. The following sections look at each type of purchase.

Straight Rebuying

The simplest buying situation is a **straight rebuy**, a recurring purchase decision in which a customer reorders a product that has satisfied needs in the past. The buyer already likes the product and terms of sale, so the purchase requires no new information. The buyer sees little reason to assess competing options and so follows a routine repurchase format. A straight rebuy is the business market equivalent of routinized response behaviour in the consumer market. Purchases of low-cost items such as paper clips and pencils for an office are typical examples of straight rebuys. Marketers who maintain good relationships with customers by providing high-quality products, superior service, and prompt delivery can go a long way toward ensuring straight rebuys.

straight rebuy Recurring purchase decision in which a customer repurchases a good or service that has performed satisfactorily in the past.

modified rebuy Situation in which a purchaser is willing to reevaluate available options for repurchasing a good or service.

Modified Rebuying

In a **modified rebuy**, a purchaser is willing to reevaluate available options. Buyers may see some advantage in looking at alternative offerings within their established purchasing guidelines. They might take this step if their current supplier has let a rebuy situation deteriorate because of poor service or delivery performance. Price, quality, and innovation differences can also provoke modified rebuys. Modified rebuys resemble limited problem solving in consumer markets.

B2B marketers want to induce current customers to make straight rebuys by responding to all their needs. Competitors, on the other hand, try to lure those buyers away by raising issues that will convince them to reconsider their decisions.

New-Task Buying

The most complex category of business buying is the **new-task buy**—a first-time or unique purchase situation that requires considerable effort by the decision makers. The consumer market equivalent of new-task buying is extended problem solving.

A new-task buy often requires a purchaser to carefully consider alternative offerings and vendors. A company entering a new field must seek suppliers of component parts that it has never before purchased. This new-task buying would require several stages, each yielding a decision of some sort. These decisions would include developing product requirements, searching out potential suppliers, and evaluating proposals. Information requirements and decision makers can complete the entire buying process, or they may change from stage to stage.

Marketoid

The Supply Chain Management Association— formed in 2013 through the amalgamation of the Purchasing Management Association of Canada and Supply Chain and Logistics Association of Canada—has 8,000 members who control more than $130 billion in annual purchasing.

new-task buy First-time or unique purchase situation that requires considerable effort by decision makers.

Reciprocity

reciprocity Buying from suppliers who are also customers.

Reciprocity—a practice of buying from suppliers that are also customers—is a controversial practice in a number of procurement situations. An office equipment manufacturer may favour a particular supplier of component parts if the supplier has recently made a major purchase of the manufacturer's products. Reciprocal arrangements traditionally have been common in industries featuring homogeneous products with similar prices, such as the chemical, paint, petroleum, rubber, and steel industries.

Reciprocity suggests close links among participants in the organizational marketplace. It can add to the complexity of B2B buying behaviour for new suppliers who are trying to compete with preferred vendors. Business-to-business buyers in Canada see it as a positive, widespread practice. In Japan, close ties between suppliers and customers are common. In the United States, reciprocal agreements are viewed as attempts to reduce competition.

value analysis Systematic study of the components of a purchase to determine the most cost-effective approach.

ANALYSIS TOOLS

Two tools that help professional buyers improve purchase decisions are value analysis and vendor analysis. **Value analysis** examines each component of a purchase in an attempt to either delete the item or replace it with a more cost-effective substitute. Airplane designers have long recognized the need to make planes as light as possible. Value analysis supports using DuPont's synthetic material Kevlar in airplane construction because it weighs less than the metals it replaces. The resulting fuel savings are significant for the buyers in this marketplace.

vendor analysis Assessment of supplier performance in areas such as price, back orders, timely delivery, and attention to special requests.

Vendor analysis carries out an ongoing evaluation of a supplier's performance in categories such as price, EDI capability, back orders, delivery times, liability insurance, and attention to special requests. In some cases, vendor analysis is a formal process. Some buyers use a checklist to assess a vendor's performance. A checklist quickly highlights vendors and potential vendors that do not satisfy the purchaser's buying requirements.

assessment check 7 ✓

7.1 What are the four classifications of business buying situations?

7.2 Differentiate between value analysis and vendor analysis.

⑧ **Explain the buying centre concept.**

THE BUYING CENTRE CONCEPT

buying centre Participants in an organizational buying decision.

The buying centre concept provides a vital model for understanding B2B buying behaviour. A company's **buying centre** encompasses everyone who is involved in any aspect of its buying activity. A buying centre may include the architect who designs a new research laboratory, the scientist who works in the facility, the purchasing manager who screens contractor proposals, the chief executive officer who makes the final decision, and the vice president for research who signs the formal contracts for the project. Buying centre participants in any purchase seek to satisfy

This buying centre includes the buyer, who is also the gatekeeper; the decider, who is the company's financial manager; and two influencers: a technician, who will be the user, and an engineer, who will decide the specifications. One role can be filled by more than one person; one person can fill more than one role.

H. F. (Herb) MacKenzie

personal needs, such as participation or status, as well as organizational needs. A buying centre is not part of a firm's formal organizational structure. It is an informal group whose composition and size vary among purchase situations and firms.

BUYING CENTRE ROLES

Buying centre participants play different roles in the purchasing decision process. **Users** are the people who will actually use the good or service. Their influence on the purchase decision may range from negligible to extremely important. Users sometimes initiate purchase actions by requesting products, and they may also help develop product specifications. Users often influence the purchase of office equipment.

Gatekeepers control the information that all buying centre members will review. They may exert this control by distributing printed product data or advertisements or by deciding which salespeople will speak to which individuals in the buying centre. A purchasing agent might allow some salespeople to see the engineers responsible for developing specifications but deny others the same privilege. The office manager for a medical group may decide whether to accept and pass along sales literature from a pharmaceutical detailer or sales representative.

Influencers affect the buying decision by supplying information to guide evaluation of alternatives or by setting buying specifications. Influencers are typically technical staff such as engineers or quality control specialists. Sometimes a buying organization hires outside consultants, such as architects, who influence its buying decisions.

The **decider** chooses a good or service, although another person may have the formal authority to do so. The identity of the decider is the most difficult role for salespeople to pinpoint. A firm's buyer may have the formal authority to buy, but the firm's chief executive officer may actually make the buying decision. Alternatively, a decider might be a design engineer who develops specifications that only one vendor can meet.

The **buyer** has the formal authority to select a supplier and to implement the procedures for securing the good or service. The buyer often surrenders this power to more influential members of the organization, though. The purchasing manager often fills the buyer's role and executes the details associated with a purchase order.

B2B marketers face the task of determining the specific role and the relative decision-making influence of each buying centre participant. Salespeople can then tailor their presentations and information to the precise role that an individual plays at each step of the purchase process. Business marketers have found that their initial—and in many cases, most extensive—contacts with a firm's purchasing department often fail to reach the buying centre participants who have the greatest influence, since these people may not work in that department at all.

Consider the selection of meeting and convention sites for trade or professional associations. The primary decision maker could be an association board or an executive committee, usually with input from the executive director or a meeting planner; the meeting planner or association executive might choose meeting locations, sometimes with input from members; finally, the association's annual-meeting committee or program committee might make the meeting location selection. Because officers change periodically, centres of control may change frequently. As a result, destination marketers and hotel operators must constantly assess how an association makes its decisions on conference locations.

INTERNATIONAL BUYING CENTRES

Two distinct characteristics differentiate international buying centres from domestic ones. First, marketers may have trouble identifying members of foreign buying centres because of cultural differences in decision-making methods. Second, a buying centre in a foreign company often includes more participants than Canadian companies involve. International buying centres employ from 1 to 50 people, with 15 to 20 participants being commonplace. Global B2Bmarketers must recognize and accommodate this greater diversity of decision makers.

user Individual or group that actually uses a business good or service.

gatekeeper Person who controls the information that all buying centre members will review.

influencers Typically, technical staff such as engineers who affect the buying decision by supplying information to guide evaluation of alternatives or by setting buying specifications.

decider Person who chooses a good or service, although another person may have the formal authority to complete the sale.

buyer Person who has the formal authority to select a supplier and to implement the procedures for securing a good or service.

assessment check 8 ✓

8.1   Identify the five roles of people in a buying centre decision.

8.2   What are some of the problems that Canadian marketers face in dealing with international buying centres?

International buying centres can change in response to political and economic trends. Many European firms once maintained separate facilities in each European nation to avoid tariffs and customs delays. When the European Union lowered trade barriers between member nations, however, many companies closed distant branches and consolidated their buying centres. The Netherlands has been one of the beneficiaries of this trend.

⑨ **Discuss the challenges of and strategies for marketing to government, institutional, and international buyers.**

DEVELOPING EFFECTIVE BUSINESS-TO-BUSINESS MARKETING STRATEGIES

A business marketer must develop a marketing strategy based on a particular organization's buying behaviour and on the buying situation. Clearly, many variables affect organizational purchasing decisions. This section examines three market segments whose decisions present unique challenges to B2B marketers: units of government, institutions, and international markets. Finally, it summarizes key differences between consumer and business marketing strategies.

CHALLENGES OF GOVERNMENT MARKETS

Marketoid

Public Works and Government Services Canada was established in 1841 and has been instrumental in the construction of Canada's canals, roads and bridges, Houses of Parliament, post offices, and federal buildings. Today, the department employs approximately 12,100 people.

Government markets include the federal government, provincial and territorial governments, and municipal governments. These markets are large and are extremely important to many business marketers in Canada. Purchasing authorities for the various levels and units involved in these markets purchase a wide variety of products, including computers and office supplies; aircraft and component parts; vehicles and automotive supplies; safety clothing and equipment; and concrete and lumber. To compete effectively, business marketers must understand the unique challenges of selling to government units. One challenge results because government purchases typically involve dozens of interested parties who specify, evaluate, or use the purchased goods and services. These parties may or may not work within the government agency that officially handles a purchase. For example, much of the purchasing for the federal government is done through Public Works and Government Services Canada (PWGSC). More than $14 billion is injected into the Canadian economy each year through PWGSC purchasing activity.[29]

Contractual guidelines create another important influence in selling to government markets. The government buys products under two basic types of contracts: fixed-price contracts, in which seller and buyer agree to a set price before finalizing the contract; and cost-reimbursement contracts, in which the government pays the vendor for allowable costs, including profits, incurred during performance of the contract. Each type of contract has advantages and disadvantages for B2B marketers. Although the fixed-price contract offers more profit potential than the alternative, it also carries greater risks from unforeseen expenses, price hikes, and changing political and economic conditions.

While there is some variability between departments, purchasing procedures are largely determined by the size of the individual purchase. For purchases below $5,000, most departments use acquisition cards (credit cards), local purchase orders, or releases against standing offers. A standing offer is not a formal contract. PWGSC issues standing offers for a variety of regularly purchased goods and services that are often needed by several government units. Business marketers agree to provide these goods and services at specific prices for a particular period of time and under a predetermined set of terms and conditions. Once a standing offer has been issued by PWGSC, government units must generally use the standing offer for any purchases of items that are included in the standing offer and that meet the buying unit's requirements. The government saves money by increasing the volume it purchases from holders of standing offers, and the business marketers who hold the standing offers benefit from increased sales.

For purchases over $5,000, most federal government units use the services of PWGSC, which then asks for proposals from qualified suppliers. Business marketers may register online with Buyandsell.gc.ca so that they can freely access Canadian government tender notices for products

Buyandsell.gc.ca is a procurement website and is the main location for suppliers to find information about doing business with the Government of Canada.

and services that they might wish to provide. Many business marketers also access MERX to keep informed about tenders in the public and private sectors. MERX is a privately owned e-tendering service used by more than 2,500 organizations, including the federal government; many provincial, territorial, and municipal governments; and other public sector purchasing authorities. Since public sector purchasing authorities have different thresholds at which purchasing procedures come into effect, business marketers need to know the particular policies used by each of the units to which they wish to sell.

While provincial and territorial governments individually purchase much less than the federal government, collectively they are more important. Purchasing procedures for provincial and territorial government purchasing units are generally similar to those used by the federal government; however, there is even more variability between them. Alberta, for example, uses the Alberta Purchasing Connection for its e-tendering requirements. The province of Nova Scotia has been hosting the annual Supplier Development Reverse Trade Show for many years. Businesses wishing to sell to the Nova Scotia government are encouraged to attend. Public sector units manage display booths, and representatives from private sector businesses visit them to access information on government purchasing needs and to explore whether these units might benefit from the products and services that these private businesses sell. Business marketers need to be aware of any unique conditions that exist in each province or territory where they sell.

CHALLENGES OF INSTITUTIONAL MARKETS

Institutions constitute another important market. Institutional buyers include a wide variety of organizations, such as schools, colleges, universities, hospitals, libraries, churches, and not-for-profit agencies.

Institutional markets are characterized by widely diverse buying practices. Some institutional purchasers behave like government purchasers because laws and political considerations determine

H. F. (Herb) MacKenzie

Buying practices can differ among institutions of the same type. In a small business, the administrative assistant might purchase office supplies; in a large business, supplies are often purchased by a professional purchasing person.

their buying procedures. Many of these institutions, such as hospitals and prisons, may even be managed by government units.

Buying practices can differ between institutions of the same type. In a small hospital, the chief dietitian may approve all food purchases, while in a larger medical facility, food purchases may go through a committee consisting of the dietitian and a business manager, purchasing agent, and cook. Other hospitals may belong to buying groups, perhaps health maintenance organizations or local hospital cooperatives. Still others may contract with outside firms to prepare and serve all meals.

Within a single institution, a variety of buying influences may affect decisions. Many institutions staffed by professionals, such as physicians, nurses, researchers, and instructors, may also employ purchasing managers or even entire purchasing departments. Conflicts may arise among these decision makers. Professional employees may prefer to make their own purchase decisions and resent giving up control to the purchasing staff. This conflict can force a business marketer to cultivate both professionals and purchasers. A salesperson for a pharmaceutical firm must convince physicians of the value to patients of a certain drug while simultaneously convincing the hospital's purchasing department that the firm offers competitive prices, good delivery schedules, and prompt service. Group purchasing is an important factor in institutional markets because many organizations join cooperative associations to pool purchases for quantity discounts. For example, the Niagara Public Purchasing Committee purchases for 52 participating agencies—including health care and educational institutions and government agencies—in the regional municipality of Niagara. Each purchasing authority can decide when and if it would like to participate in the tendering for any particular product or service. Responsibility for calling tenders and negotiating prices is shared among them, but control of ordering, scheduling, receiving, and payment remains with individual purchasing authorities.[30]

Diverse practices in institutional markets pose special challenges for B2B marketers. They must maintain flexibility in developing strategies for dealing with a range of customers, from large cooperative associations and chains to midsized purchasing departments and institutions to individuals. Buying centres can work with varying members, priorities, and levels of expertise. Discounts and effective distribution functions play important roles in obtaining—and keeping—institutions as customers.

CHALLENGES OF INTERNATIONAL MARKETS

To sell successfully in international markets, business marketers must consider buyers' attitudes and cultural patterns within areas where they operate. In Asian markets, a firm must maintain a local presence to sell products. Personal relationships are also important to business deals in Asia. Companies that want to expand globally often need to establish joint ventures with local partners. International marketers must also be poised to respond to shifts in cultural values.

Local industries, economic conditions, geographic characteristics, and legal restrictions must also be considered in international marketing. Many local industries in Spain specialize in food and wine; therefore, a maker of forklift trucks might market smaller vehicles to Spanish companies than to German firms, which require bigger, heavier trucks to serve the needs of that nation's large automobile industry.

remanufacturing
Efforts to restore older products to like-new condition.

Remanufacturing—production to restore worn-out products to like-new condition—can be an important marketing strategy in a nation that cannot afford to buy new products. Developing countries often purchase remanufactured factory machinery, which costs 35 to 60 percent less than new equipment.

Foreign governments represent another important business market. In many countries, the government or state-owned companies dominate certain industries, such as construction and other infrastructure sales. Additional examples are airport and highway construction, telephone system equipment, and computer networking equipment. Sales to a foreign government can involve an array of regulations. Many governments, like that of Canada, limit foreign participation in their defence programs. Joint ventures and countertrade are common, as are local content laws, which mandate domestic production of a certain percentage of a business product's components.

> **assessment check 9** ✓
>
> 9.1 What are some influences on government purchases?
>
> 9.2 Why is group purchasing important in institutional purchases?
>
> 9.3 What special factors influence international buying decisions?

Strategic Implications

To develop marketing strategies for the B2B sector, marketers must first understand the buying practices that govern the segment they are targeting, whether it is the commercial market, trade industries, government, or institutions. Similarly, when selling to a specific organization, strategies must take into account the many factors that influence purchasing. B2B marketers must identify people who play the various roles in the buying decision. They must also understand how these members interact with one another, other members of their own organizations, and outside vendors. Marketers must be careful to direct their marketing efforts to their organization, to broader environmental influences, and to individuals who operate within the constraints of the firm's buying centre. ◆◆◆

REVIEW OF CHAPTER OBJECTIVES

① **Explain each of the components of the business-to-business (B2B) market.**

The B2B market is divided into four segments: the commercial market, trade industries, governments, and institutions. The commercial market consists of individuals and firms that acquire products to be used, directly or indirectly, to produce other goods and services. Trade industries are organizations, such as retailers and wholesalers, that purchase for resale to others. The primary purpose of government purchasing, at all levels, is to provide some form of public benefit. The fourth segment, institutions, includes a diverse array of organizations, such as hospitals, schools, museums, and not-for-profit agencies.

② **Describe the major approaches to segmenting business-to-business (B2B) markets.**

Business markets can be segmented by (1) demographics, (2) customer type, (3) end-use application, and (4) purchasing situation. The North American Industry Classification System (NAICS), instituted after the passage of NAFTA, helps further classify types of customers by the use of six digits.

③ **Identify the major characteristics of the business market and its demand.**

The major characteristics of the business market are geographic concentration, size and number of buyers, purchase decision procedures, and buyer–seller relationships. The major categories of demand are derived demand, volatile demand, joint demand, inelastic demand, and inventory adjustments.

④ **Discuss the decision to make, buy, or lease.**

Before a company can decide what to buy, it must decide whether to buy at all. A firm has three options: (1) make the good or service in-house, (2) purchase it from another organization, or (3) lease it from another organization. Companies may outsource goods or services formerly produced in-house to other companies either within their own home country or to firms in other countries. The shift of high-wage jobs from the home country to lower-wage locations is known as *offshoring*. If a company moves production to a country close to its own borders, it uses a *nearshoring* strategy. Each option has its benefits and drawbacks, including cost and quality control.

⑤ **Describe the major influences on business buying behaviour.**

B2B buying behaviour tends to be more complex than individual consumer behaviour. More people and time are involved, and buyers often seek several alternative supply sources. The systematic nature of organizational buying is reflected in the use of purchasing managers to direct such efforts. Major organizational purchases may require elaborate and lengthy decision-making processes involving many people. Purchase decisions typically depend on combinations of such factors as price, service, certainty of supply, and product efficiency.

⑥ **Outline the steps in the organizational buying process.**

The organizational buying process consists of eight general stages: (1) anticipate or recognize a problem, need, or opportunity and a general solution; (2) determine characteristics and quantity of needed good or service; (3) describe characteristics and quantity of needed good or service; (4) search for and qualify potential sources; (5) acquire and analyze proposals; (6) evaluate proposals and select supplier(s); (7) select an order routine; and (8) obtain feedback and evaluate performance.

⑦ **Classify organizational buying situations.**

Organizational buying situations differ. A straight rebuy is a recurring purchase decision in which a customer stays with an item that has performed satisfactorily. In a modified rebuy, a purchaser is willing to reevaluate available options. New-task buying refers to first-time or unique purchase situations that require considerable effort on the part of the decision makers. Reciprocity involves buying from suppliers that are also customers.

⑧ **Explain the buying centre concept.**

The buying centre includes everyone who is involved in some fashion in an organizational buying action. There are five buying centre roles: users, gatekeepers, influencers, deciders, and buyers.

⑨ **Discuss the challenges of and strategies for marketing to government, institutional, and international buyers.**

A government purchase typically involves dozens of interested parties. Social goals and programs influence government purchases. Many Canadian government purchases involve complex contractual guidelines and often require detailed specifications and a bidding process. Institutional markets are challenging because of their diverse buying influences and practices. Group purchasing is an important factor, since many institutions join cooperative associations to get quantity discounts. An institutional marketer must be flexible enough to develop strategies for dealing with a range of customers. Discounts and effective distribution play an important role. An effective international business marketer must be aware of foreign attitudes and cultural patterns. Other important factors are economic conditions, geographic characteristics, legal restrictions, and local industries.

assessment check answers ✓

1.1 Define *B2B marketing*.
Business-to-business, or B2B, marketing deals with organizational purchases of goods and services to support production of other products, to facilitate daily company operations, or for resale.

1.2 What is the commercial market?
The commercial market consists of individuals and firms that acquire products to be used, directly or indirectly, to produce other goods and services.

1.3 Define *EDI* and *Web services*.
An EDI is a computer-to-computer exchange of invoices, purchase orders, price quotations, and other sales information between buyers and sellers. All parties must use the same computer operating system. Web services consist of Internet-based systems that allow parties to communicate and exchange data regardless of the computer operating system they use.

1.4 Briefly explain how e-procurement works.
E-procurement systems are Web-based systems that enable all types of organizations to improve the efficiency of their bidding and purchasing processes.

2.1 What are the four major ways marketers segment business markets?
Business markets can be segmented by (1) demographics, (2) customer type, (3) end-use application, and (4) purchasing situation.

2.2 What is the NAICS?

The North American Industry Classification System (NAICS) is a unified system for Canada, Mexico, and the United States to classify B2B market segments.

3.1 Why is geographic segmentation important in the B2B market?

Certain industries locate in particular areas to be close to customers. Firms may choose to locate sales offices and distribution centres in these areas to provide more attentive service. For example, the Ottawa area is favoured by companies that sell to the federal government.

3.2 In what ways is the buyer–seller relationship important in B2B marketing?

Buyer–seller relationships are often more complex than consumer relationships, and they require superior communication among the organizations' personnel. Satisfying one major customer may mean the difference of millions of dollars to a firm.

3.3 What is global sourcing?

Global sourcing involves contracting to purchase goods and services from suppliers worldwide.

3.4 How does derived demand create volatile demand?

Business demand often is derived from consumer demand. Even modest shifts in consumer demand can produce disproportionate—and volatile—shifts in business demand.

3.5 Give an example of joint demand.

Both lumber and concrete are required to build most homes. If the lumber supply falls, the drop in housing construction will most likely affect the demand for concrete.

3.6 How might JIT II strengthen marketing relationships?

JIT II leads suppliers to place representatives at the customer's facility to work as part of an integrated, on-site customer–supplier team. Suppliers plan and order in consultation with the customer. This streamlining of the inventory process improves control of the flow of goods.

4.1 Identify two potential benefits of outsourcing.

Outsourcing allows firms to concentrate their resources on their core business. It also allows access to specialized talent or expertise that does not exist within the firm.

4.2 Identify two potential problems with outsourcing.

Many companies discover that their cost savings are less than vendors sometimes promise. Also, companies that sign multi-year contracts may find that their savings drop after a year or two.

5.1 Identify the three major factors that influence purchase decisions.

In addition to product-specific factors such as purchase price, installation, operating and maintenance costs, and vendor service, companies must consider broader environmental, organizational, and interpersonal influences.

5.2 What are the advantages and disadvantages of multiple sourcing?

Spreading orders ensures against shortages if one vendor cannot deliver on schedule. However, dealing with many sellers can be counterproductive and take too much time.

6.1 Why does the organizational buying process contain more steps than the consumer buying process?

The additional steps arise because business purchasing introduces new complexities that do not affect consumers.

6.2 List the steps in the organizational buying process.

The steps in organizational buying are (1) anticipate or recognize a problem, need, or opportunity and a general solution; (2) determine characteristics and quantity of needed good or service; (3) describe characteristics and quantity of needed good or service; (4) search for and qualify potential sources; (5) acquire and analyze proposals; (6) evaluate proposals and select supplier(s); (7) select an order routine; and (8) obtain feedback and evaluate performance.

7.1 What are the four classifications of business buying situations?

The four classifications of business buying are (1) straight rebuying, (2) modified rebuying, (3) new-task buying, and (4) reciprocity.

7.2 Differentiate between value analysis and vendor analysis.

Value analysis examines each component of a purchase in an attempt to either delete the item or replace it with a more cost-effective substitute. Vendor analysis carries out an ongoing evaluation of a supplier's performance in categories such as price, EDI capability, back orders, delivery times, liability insurance, and attention to special requests.

8.1 Identify the five roles of people in a buying centre decision.

There are five buying centre roles: users (those who use the product), gatekeepers (those who control the flow of information), influencers (those who provide technical information or specifications), deciders (those who actually choose the product), and buyers (those who have the formal authority to purchase).

8.2 What are some of the problems that Canadian marketers face in dealing with international buying centres?

International buying centres pose several problems. First, there may be cultural differences in decision-making methods. Second, a buying centre in a foreign company typically includes more participants than is common in Canada. Third, international buying centres can change in response to political and economic trends.

9.1 What are some influences on government purchases?

Social goals and programs often influence government purchases.

9.2 Why is group purchasing important in institutional purchases?

Group purchasing is an important factor because many institutions join cooperative associations to get quantity discounts.

9.3 What special factors influence international buying decisions?

An effective international business marketer must be aware of foreign attitudes and cultural patterns. Other important factors are economic conditions, geographic characteristics, legal restrictions, and local industries.

MARKETING TERMS YOU NEED TO KNOW

These terms are printed in blue in the text. They are defined in the margins of the chapter and in the Glossary that begins on p. G-1.

business-to-business (B2B) marketing 156
commercial market 158
trade industries 159
resellers 159
business-to-business (B2B) e-marketing 159
e-procurement 161
customer-based segmentation 162
North American Industry Classification System (NAICS) 164
end-use application segmentation 164
customer relationship management (CRM) 164
global sourcing 167

derived demand 167
joint demand 168
inelastic demand 168
just-in-time (JIT) / just-in-time II 168
sole sourcing 168
offshoring 169
nearshoring 169
outsourcing 169
multiple sourcing 171
merchandisers 172
systems integration 172
category advisor (category captain) 172
straight rebuy 175

modified rebuy 175
new-task buy 175
reciprocity 176
value analysis 176
vendor analysis 176
buying centre 176
user 177
gatekeeper 177
influencers 177
decider 177
buyer 177
remanufacturing 180

PROJECT AND TEAMWORK EXERCISES

1. In small teams, research the buying process through which your school purchases the following products:
   a. computers for your school's computer lab
   b. computers for your campus bookstore
   c. garbage bags used by your campus custodial staff
   d. vehicles for your campus security and maintenance staff
   Be prepared to discuss how the buying process differs for these products.

2. In pairs or individually, select a firm in your area and ask to interview the person who is in charge of purchasing. In particular, ask the person about the importance of buyer–seller relationships in his or her industry. Report your findings to the class.

3. In pairs, select a business product in one of two categories—capital or expense—and determine how derived demand will affect the sales of the product. Create a chart showing your findings.

4. As a team, research a firm such as BlackBerry, Bombardier, or General Motors to learn how it is using outsourcing and/or offshoring. Then report on what you think the benefits and drawbacks to the firm might be.

5. Imagine that you and your teammates are buyers for a firm such as Tim Hortons, Canadian Tire, Delta Hotels & Resorts, or another firm you like. Map out a logical buying process for a new-task purchase for your organization.

CRITICAL THINKING EXERCISES

1. Imagine that you are a wholesaler for dairy products such as yogurt and cheese, which are produced by a cooperative of small farmers. Describe what steps you would take to build relationships with both the producers—farmers—and retailers, such as supermarkets.

2. Describe an industry that might be segmented by geographic concentration. Then identify some of the types of firms that might be involved in that industry. Keep in mind that these companies could be involved in other industries as well.

3. Imagine that you are in charge of making the decision to lease or buy a fleet of automobiles for the limousine service for which you work. What factors would influence your decision and why?

4. Do you think online selling to the federal government benefits marketers? What might be some of the drawbacks to this type of selling?

Suppose you work for a well-known local restaurant, and a friend of yours is an account representative for a supplier of restaurant equipment. You know that the restaurant owner is considering upgrading some of the kitchen equipment. Although you have no purchasing authority, your friend has asked you to arrange a meeting with the restaurant owner. You have heard unflattering rumours about this supplier's customer service.

1. Would you arrange the meeting between your friend and your boss?
2. Would you mention the customer-service rumours either to your friend or your boss?
3. Would you try to influence the purchase decision in either direction?

CASE 6.1

Zappos Offers Insights to Other Businesses

How many firms throw open their doors to the business community, essentially offering access to trade secrets so other companies can learn and grow? Zappos does this—in fact, the online shoe retailer has created an entire division devoted to the effort, called Zappos Insights. Based on the company's core value of open and honest communication, Zappos conducts business-to-business marketing in an unusual way: giving away information for free. Zappos is well known among other businesses for two things it does extremely well: providing top-notch customer service and building a culture that spreads happiness.

Zappos's focus on customer service was born of necessity. When it started in the late 1990s, the company didn't have any money to market the novel idea of online shoe selling. So its founders sank everything they had into customer service, including the idea of free shipping both ways. As the company built its business and its reputation, it also created a culture in which people liked to work. "It's an environment where people are in service to each other," explains Robert Richman, product manager for Zappos Insights. Zappos's expertise in customer service has become a product itself, as Zappos Insights offers training to other firms in how to do what it does so well.

Access to the Zappos culture starts for free, with a tour of the company and information available to everyone online. From there, businesses can join Zappos Insights and pay for various levels of training, such as a two-day on-site boot camp at Zappos or a customized program conducted at an individual company's location. Membership benefits include training modules on leadership development, techniques for keeping team members engaged and empowered, and strategies for delivering Zappos's signature "WOW" service to customers. At a one-day seminar, a business owner or executive learns applications for such tenets as "culture drives success," "getting the culture right," "getting the right people on board," "creating a fun physical environment creates energy," and "communication is everything, and everything is communication." These aren't just taglines. They are organizational values that Zappos has proved to be successful.

Zappos segments its B2B customers by sifting through the data it has collected on companies that request the free portion of its program and determining what kind of business they do (customer type) as well as how they might use Zappos training to further their business (end-use application). In essence, explains Robert Richman, it's about "offering a lot of free value and then seeing who wants to go deeper." In fact, Zappos Insights doesn't advertise or send direct email—for the most part, companies come to them. They may be as varied as Google, Eli Lilly, and Intuit—but they all want one thing: a culture driven by customer service. Why isn't Zappos worried about sharing its methods? "Culture can't be duplicated because it's based on people," says Richman. "So because of that, it's completely different when transferred from company to company."

The decision for an organization to pay for an in-depth membership to Zappos Insights requires consideration of certain factors, such as price (there are several levels) and availability (businesses can attend workshops and seminars at Zappos, or have Zappos come to them). The buying situation itself varies as well. As a client enters into a new relationship with Zappos Insights, it's a new-task purchase. Managers are involved not only in the purchase but probably in the experience itself. If a company continues its membership, adding services, upgrading, or renewing, it becomes a modified rebuy. Reciprocity also occurs, as some of Zappos' vendors are enrolled in the Zappos Insights program.

When you think about strategies for businesses marketing to each other, you might not necessarily consider the strategy of delivering happiness. But Zappos Insights places the concept of happiness in the business environment at the top of its list. The training programs offered by Zappos Insights "play into the larger vision of delivering happiness, because we are essentially training the people who are responsible for hundreds of thousands of other people," says Robert Richman. "We've seen the trickle effect." As Zappos trains companies to build places where employees like to work, all those employees deliver better experiences to their customers. "It's a rising tide that raises all boats," Richman muses. "If we create stronger cultures, everybody in business will have better relationships."

Questions for Critical Thinking

1. Describe the buyer–seller relationship between Zappos Insights and its business clients.
2. How would you classify the business market demand for Zappos Insights training? Explain your answer.

Sources: Company website, **www.zapposinsights.com**, accessed July 5, 2012; Michael Kerr, "Zapped by Zappos: Lessons in How to Build a Workplace Culture That WOWS!" Humor at Work, **www.mikekerr.com**, accessed July 5, 2012; "Zendesk Joins Forces with Zappos Insights and Groupon to Launch Its First Ever Customer Service Hero Tour," PR Newswire, February 27, 2012, **www.prnewswire.com**.

CASE 6.2

WFS Ltd.

WFS Ltd.—formerly Windsor Factory Supply—is a 100-percent employee-owned, full-line industrial distributor and, as such, all of its sales are B2B sales. It represents more than 3,500 suppliers and sells to more than 4,500 customers—mainly manufacturers, but also many government and institutional accounts. (It does for many business customers what Walmart and Canadian Tire do for consumers.) The company started in Windsor, Ontario, in 1955 as a two-person operation and had grown to 247 employees at the start of 2014. Sales the first year were approximately $50,000, but have been approaching $100 million in recent years.

The company was fortunate in many ways. First, it was strategically located close to the centre of automotive manufacturing in Canada, and the three large North American automobile manufacturers all became important customers. Second, it was close to the Canada–United States border. Many U.S. manufacturers who sold through Canadian distributors selected ones located in or near Toronto. That meant customers in Windsor who wanted to buy these products would have to place orders with a distributor located some distance away, wait for the distributor to order the material from the United States, and then wait for delivery of the material from the U.S. manufacturer—sometimes physically routed through their Canadian distributor. Deliveries could take days or even weeks. WFS would send two trucks across the border into Detroit each morning, one to each end of the city. When Canadian customers wanted important material from the United States, WFS would find a Detroit-area distributor, negotiate a discount as it would act as a sub-distributor, and bring the material into Canada, often the same day that the customer requested it.

Such willingness to provide outstanding service for its major customers helped WFS quickly grow. By the 1990s, the company had five additional locations: Leamington, Sarnia, Wallaceburg, London, and Mississauga. In early 2008, WFS acquired another industrial distributor, adding three more locations. Today, WFS has ten sales branches and warehouses in Ontario; a warehouse in Detroit, Michigan; and a sales branch and warehouse in South Carolina, which it built to serve one of its major customers there. WFS has always been willing to negotiate supply contracts with important customers. It operates what is referred to as commodity management programs, whereby it will carry inventory and manage the supply of a large number of specific items, guaranteeing their availability when and where the customer needs them. Sometimes, these programs result in on-site inventory agreements.

WFS has a strong internal culture and a healthy business philosophy. The company's foundation is built on quality, satisfaction, and dependability. President Rick Thurston describes the company philosophy: "Our business is built on relationships. Of course, we are always looking for opportunities, but we know that sometimes it is important to curb growth so that quality service to existing accounts is not compromised."

Questions for Critical Thinking

1. Describe how environmental factors, organizational factors, and interpersonal influences will affect sales for WFS.
2. How important is the buying centre concept to WFS? Explain.
3. How can commodity management programs and other special inventory management programs be used to add value for WFS's customers? How can such programs contribute to the company's long-term success?

Sources: WFS website, **www.wfsltd.com**, February 13, 2014; Rick Thurston, personal interview and correspondence, January 27, 2014.

chapter 7

Serving Global Markets

CHAPTER OBJECTIVES

① Describe the importance of global marketing from the perspectives of the individual firm and the nation.

② Identify the major components of the environment for global marketing.

③ Outline the basic functions of GATT, WTO, NAFTA, FTAA, and the European Union.

④ Identify the alternative strategies for entering international markets.

⑤ Differentiate between a global marketing strategy and a multi-domestic marketing strategy.

⑥ Describe the alternative marketing mix strategies used in global marketing and explain the attractiveness of Canada as a target market for international marketers.

Zoran Karapancev/Shutterstock.com

HYUNDAI THINKS BIG

Hyundai ranks in the top five among global automakers, but it wants more. The Korean company, which began operations in Canada in 1983, has seen an enormous growth in North American sales. But the company is hoping to do better than merely ride out what some observers predict could be a shrinking auto market worldwide in the next few years. In fact, Hyundai not only wants to move up in the rankings of automakers, it also wants to begin appealing to car buyers' aspirations to drive a "modern premium," the company's new definition of luxury. The CEO of the firm's ad agency draws an analogy between Hyundai and the world leader in digital technology, comparing Hyundai to Apple, where style and function justify a price premium.

Having already established a solid record of value and fuel economy, Hyundai is often a car buyer's "left-brain choice," says its vice president of marketing. So now the firm has planned a vigorous new marketing campaign designed to strengthen its appeal to buyers' emotions. Its Elantra sedan, recently voted the North American Car of the Year, features both best-in-class standard fuel economy and an appealingly sleek, sculpted design with plenty of interior room. With models like this, along with its Sonata, Genesis, and Santa Fe

SUV, the company wants to grow worldwide and also keep ahead of Chinese and Indian automakers that are quickly gaining ground in their own potentially huge markets. Hyundai is not the only car maker "that wants to succeed up-market," says the ad agency's CEO. "That's where the margins are."

Hyundai's chief financial officer expects price competition in Europe to heat up in the near future, perhaps shaking up the market for European automakers and providing an opportunity for the company to grow its market share there, in the same way it is doing in Canada and the United States. Some of Hyundai's success came at the expense of Japanese automakers, whose production capacity was hurt by the disastrous earthquake and tsunami, which interrupted their parts supply lines for months. Hyundai builds most of its cars in South Korea but also has manufacturing plants in the United States, and it will soon open a diesel engine factory in India.

Hyundai's success in the North American market has also caused the company some problems, mainly keeping up with the demand. Manufacturing plants in the United States and Korea are producing the maximum number of cars. Other companies may have decided to build more manufacturing plants but not Hyundai. It has decided to take a

couple of years to focus on designing new vehicles and improving customer satisfaction before increasing its manufacturing capacity.

Hyundai has shown itself to be an up-and-coming name in a competitive world market, thanks in no small part to aggressive advertising and the creation of products that combine value with fuel economy. Industry observers say the company has been successful because it understands what consumers want and applies that knowledge to developing products that appeal, particularly to North American consumers. For decades, industry observers say, North American automakers relied on their gut instinct rather than customer data to develop and market cars. Now Hyundai offers consumers a "left-brained" choice—that is, a decision supported by logic and rationality and not merely feelings. Which is not to say that look and feel don't enter into the decision to buy a Hyundai. The company boasts a design network that takes its inspiration from consumers around the globe. The team studies the lifestyles and interests of drivers in all their markets in order to come up with the sleek, imagination-capturing designs that typify a Hyundai.[1]

connecting with customers

Hyundai connects with its customers by concentrating on design and customer satisfaction. For North American consumers, the notion of "modern premium"—how Hyundai defines a luxury car—is something new.

Chapter Overview

Canadian and foreign companies are crossing national boundaries in unprecedented numbers in search of new markets and profits.

Global trade can be divided into two categories: **exporting**, marketing domestically produced goods and services abroad; and **importing**, purchasing foreign goods and services. Figure 7.1 shows the nations with which Canada trades. The United States accounts for 62 percent of our imported products and 73 percent of our exported products. Japan, the United Kingdom, and the European Union countries account for another 11 percent of exports.[2] Global trade is vital to a nation and its marketers for several reasons. It expands markets, makes production and distribution economies of scale possible, allows companies to explore growth opportunities in other nations, and makes them less dependent on economic conditions in their home nations. Many also find that global marketing and trade can help them meet customer demand, reduce costs, and provide valuable information on potential markets around the world.

For North American marketers, global trade is especially important because the Canadian and U.S. economies represent a mature market for many products. Outside North America, however, it is a different story. Economies in many parts of sub-Saharan Africa, Asia, Latin America, central Europe, and the Middle East are growing rapidly. This opens up new markets for Canadian products as consumers in these areas have more money to spend and as the need for goods and services by foreign companies expands.

Global trade also builds employment. The United Nations estimates that 82,000 transnational corporations are operating today, employing more than 77 million workers directly and through subsidiaries.[3]

Global marketers carefully evaluate the marketing concepts described in other chapters. However, transactions that cross national borders involve additional considerations. For example, different laws, varying levels of technological capability, economic conditions, cultural and business norms, and consumer preferences often require new strategies. Companies that want to market their products worldwide must reconsider each of the marketing variables (product, distribution, promotion, and price) in terms of the global marketplace. To succeed in global marketing, today's marketers answer questions such as these:

- How do our products fit into a foreign market?

- How can we turn potential threats into opportunities?

- Which strategic alternatives will work in global markets?

Many of the answers to these questions can be found by studying techniques used by successful global marketers. This chapter first considers the importance and characteristics of foreign markets. It then examines the international marketing environment, the trend toward multinational economic integration, and the steps that most firms take to enter the global marketplace. Next, the importance of developing a global marketing mix is discussed. The chapter closes with a look at Canada as a target market for foreign marketers. ◆◆◆

---

① **Describe the importance of global marketing from the perspectives of the individual firm and the nation.**

THE IMPORTANCE OF GLOBAL MARKETING

As the list of Canada's and the world's largest companies shown in Table 7.1 reveals, most if not all are in global markets. For most companies—large and small—global marketing is rapidly becoming a necessity. The demand for foreign products in the fast-growing economies of Pacific Rim and other Asian nations offers one example of the benefits of thinking globally. Canada is often viewed as an exporter of natural resources such as lumber, wheat, and energy products, but other products such as machinery and industrial products are equally important to our economy. In a recent year, Canada exported over $100 billion of energy products, over $47 billion in consumer goods, and over $62 billion in automotive products.[4]

The United States is by far our largest trading partner, as shown in Figure 7.1. However, the amount of trade with the United States as a percentage of Canada's total trade has been declining. The amount of trade with Europe and Asia, particularly China, has been steadily increasing. Our next largest trading partner is the European Union, which has purchased over $21 billion worth of goods from us in one year. Japan and the United Kingdom also play an important role in our international trade, purchasing over $10 and $19 billion a year respectively.[5]

exporting Marketing domestically produced goods and services in foreign countries.

importing Purchasing foreign goods and services.

Walmart currently ranks as the world's largest private employer, with 2.2 million employees, and its largest retailer. If Walmart were a country, industry observers estimate, its gross domestic product would be the 25th-largest in the world. Walmart's goods represent 15 percent of all U.S. imports from China. The retail giant imports more from China than do Taiwan and Russia combined. Walmart allocates billions of dollars in expansion efforts in Africa, China, Central America, India, Japan, and South America.[6]

The rapid globalization of business and the boundless nature of the Internet have made it possible for every marketer to become an international marketer. However, becoming an Internet global marketer is not necessarily easy. While larger firms have the advantage of more resources and wider distribution systems, smaller companies can build websites for as little as a few hundred dollars and can bring products to market quickly. The Internet allows companies like HootSuite, the Vancouver-based social media firm to expand globally. The company has over 7 million customers around the world and has opened offices in London, Sydney, Hong Kong, New York, and San Francisco. HootSuite executives plan to expand their customer base in Europe, Asia, and Latin America over the next few years.[7]

Just as some firms depend on foreign and Internet sales, others rely on purchasing raw materials abroad as input for their domestic manufacturing operations. A furniture manufacturer may depend on purchases of South American mahogany, while furniture retailers are taking advantage of Chinese-made styling and quality and that country's traditionally low prices.

figure 7.1

Top Canadian Trading Partners

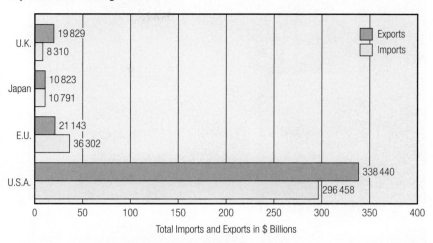

Source: Adapted from Statistics Canada's Summary Table, Imports, exports and trade balance of goods on a balance-of-payments basis, by country or country grouping; **http://www40.statcan.gc.ca/l01/cst01/gblec02a-eng.htm?sdi=imports%20exports%20trade%20balance%20goods** (accessed January 27, 2014).

Marketoid

On January 1, 2014, the North American Free Trade Agreement had been in existence for 20 years.

table 7.1 **Largest Companies in the World and in Canada**

	WORLD'S LARGEST COMPANIES		CANADA'S LARGEST COMPANIES
RANK	COMPANY	COUNTRY OF ORIGIN	BY PROFIT
1	ICBC	China	Royal Bank of Canada
2	China Construction Bank	China	Bank of Nova Scotia
3	JPMorgan Chase	United States	Toronto-Dominion Bank
4	General Electric	United States	Bank of Montreal
5	Exxon Mobil	United States	Imperial Oil
6	HSBC Holdings	United Kingdom	Canadian Imperial Bank of Commerce
7	Royal Dutch Shell	Netherlands	Suncor Energy
8	Agricultural Bank of China	China	BCE Inc.
9	Berkshire Hathaway	United States	Canadian National Railway Corp.
10	PetroChina	China	Potash Corporation of Saskatchewan

Sources: Data from "The World's Biggest Public Companies - Forbes," **forbes.com**, January 27, 2014; "Top 1000: Exclusive Rankings of Canada's Most Profitable Companies," *The Globe and Mail*, **theglobeandmail.com**, January 27, 2014.

JTB PHOTO/Glow Images

The global coverage and international reputation of the Hilton name combine to generate additional sales revenues around the world as both business and vacation travellers select accommodations for their stays.

SERVICE EXPORTS

Manufacturing no longer accounts for the lion's share of annual production output in Canada. Today, a large portion of the nation's gross domestic product (GDP) comes from services—banking, entertainment, business and technical services, retailing, and communications. Services also account for more than 75 percent of all employment in Canada. This profound shift from a largely manufacturing to a largely service economy is also reflected in the nation's exports.[8]

The importance of service exports to all nations and the difficulty in measuring service transactions has prompted the International Monetary Fund (IMF) to classify and define service categories and transactions, assisting government statistical agencies to collect and compare data. Service categories include travel, transportation, government services, and other (such as business services). A service transaction is included in a country's export numbers when a client, the service, or the supplier crosses a border or a commerce presence is set up abroad.[9]

Canada measures imports and exports of services under three major categories: travel, transportation, and commercial services. One important area of service exports is tourism. International visitors to Canada represent $17.4 billion to the Canadian economy. There are over 600,000 Canadians working in more than 150,000 businesses that cater to tourism across the country. Throughout the world more than 1 billion international travellers spent over $1 trillion. These numbers are forecasted to increase over the next couple of decades.[10]

BENEFITS OF GOING GLOBAL

Besides generating additional revenue, firms expand their operations outside their home country to gain other benefits, including new insights into consumer behaviour, alternative distribution strategies, and advance notice of new products. By setting up foreign offices and production facilities, marketers may encounter new products, new approaches to distribution, or clever new promotions that they may be able to apply successfully in their domestic market or in other international markets. Often, these ventures require firms to send employees abroad on special assignments; see the "Career Readiness" feature for some tips for successful international business travel.

Global marketers are typically well positioned to compete effectively with foreign competitors. A major key to achieving success in foreign markets is a firm's ability to adapt its products to local preferences and culture. Restaurants like McDonald's succeeded in other countries by paying attention to local tastes and modifying its menus. Similarly, Yum! Brands, parent of KFC, Pizza Hut, and Taco Bell successfully launched KFC in China by catering to Chinese tastes. China's first fast-food chain, KFC, augmented its familiar chicken-based menu with such Chinese staples as fish, porridge, fried dough, beef rice, bean curd, and egg tarts. Today, the company is repeating its global success in India, where Taco Bell, KFC, and Pizza Hut are leading brands.[11]

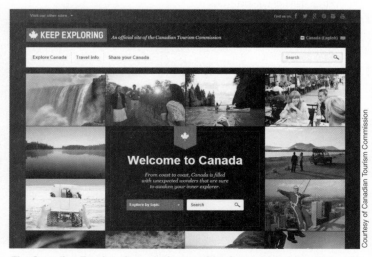

Courtesy of Canadian Tourism Commission

The Canadian Tourism Commission provides international travellers with easy access to information about Canadian companies and events.

CAREER READINESS   Tips for International Travel

SAVVY international business travellers learn as much as possible in advance about local customs and etiquette in their destination, including key phrases in the local language. Another best practice is to stow important documents, including passport, travel tickets, and driver's licence, on your person, since you'll need them to board a plane or rent a car. Here are tips for getting the most from your digital devices while travelling abroad.

1. Make sure you have the right voltage converters for the countries you'll visit (check **www.voltageconverters .com**). Don't count on borrowing or buying these when you arrive; bring your own.
2. Pack chargers and adaptors for all your electronics in carry-on luggage.
3. Keep your laptop with you at all times while in transit, and back up work regularly to protect against computer crashes or theft.

4. Make sure your mobile phone will operate overseas. You may need a special SIM card, even if your phone uses GSM technology (a radio frequency accepted across the globe).
5. Put key customer service phone numbers on speed dial before you go: your airline or travel website in case of flight problems, your credit card company, your bank, and your hotel.

Bon voyage!

Sources: "4 Excellent International Business Travel Tips," *Business Trip*, **www .cpechrd.org**, accessed April 20, 2012; Carolyn M. Brown, "7 Tips for Foreign Business Travel," *Inc.*, **www.inc.com**, accessed April 20, 2012; Kathleen Ameche, "Business Travel Tips: Top 5 Business Traveler Nightmares and How To Prevent Them," Best Traveling Guide.net, January 11, 2012, **www .besttravelingguide.net**; Trisha Garbrick, "International Business Travel Tips," Best Traveling Guide.net, **www.besttravelingguide.net**, January 11, 2012.

Subway has more than 41,000 stores in 105 countries. After opening its first overseas Subway (in 1984 in Bahrain), the company targeted 10 markets for further expansion, primarily Australia, New Zealand, Japan, and countries in Europe. When other regions showed strong growth—like Russia—the company added them to the list. Subway now plans to have 1,000 stores in Russia over the next several years. But tastes differ around the globe. While all Subways feature the same basic menu, cultural and religious preferences often help shape the fare. For example, a sandwich prepared with beef or pork in North America is likely to use lamb, chicken, or turkey instead in Muslim

Marketoid

Since NAFTA was signed in 1994, Canada's GDP has risen by over $1 trillion.

KFC is a leading brand in India. Yum! Brands repeats its success from China by continuing to cater to local tastes.

© Stuart Kelly/Alamy

or Hindu countries. In India, lamb, pepperoni, and salami are popular meat choices. And while the type of bread may vary, there's one thing Subway customers can count on: it's baked on-site, daily.[12]

Since companies must perform the marketing functions of buying, selling, transporting, storing, standardizing and grading, financing, risk taking, and obtaining market information in both domestic and global markets, some may question the wisdom of treating global marketing as a distinct subject. But as this chapter will explain, there are similarities and differences that influence strategies for both domestic and global marketing.

② Identify the major components of the environment for global marketing.

THE INTERNATIONAL MARKETING ENVIRONMENT

As in domestic markets, the environmental factors discussed in Chapter 3 have a powerful influence on the development of a firm's global marketing strategies. Marketers must pay close attention to changing demand patterns as well as competitive, economic, social-cultural, political-legal, and technological influences when they venture abroad.

INTERNATIONAL ECONOMIC ENVIRONMENT

A nation's size, per capita income, and stage of economic development determine its prospects as a host for international business expansion. Nations with low per capita incomes may be poor markets for expensive industrial machinery but good ones for agricultural hand tools. These nations cannot afford the technical equipment that powers an industrialized society. Wealthier countries may offer prime markets for many industries, particularly those producing consumer goods and services and advanced industrial products.

But some less-industrialized countries are growing fast. India and China, for example, may rival the United States in world economic importance in a generation or two. Although the per capita GDP of Canada or the United States at $42,300 and $51,700, respectively, ranks far above China's $9,100 and India's $3,800, these nations have much larger populations and thus more potential human capital to develop in the future.[13] Their ability to import technology and foreign capital, as well as to train scientists and engineers and invest in research and development, ensures that their growth will be rapid and their income gaps with the developed countries will close quickly. Most recently, India's GDP rose 3.2 percent and China's rose 7.7 percent, but Canada's and the United States' GDP grew only 1.7 and 2.8 percent repectively.[14]

Infrastructure, the underlying foundation for modern life and efficient marketing that includes transportation, communications, banking, utilities, and public services, is another important economic factor to consider when planning to enter a foreign market. An inadequate infrastructure may constrain marketers' plans to manufacture, promote, and distribute goods and services in a particular country. People living in countries blessed with navigable waters often rely on them as inexpensive, relatively efficient alternatives to highways, rail lines, and air transportation. Thai farmers use their nation's rivers to transport their crops. Their boats even become retail outlets in so-called floating markets such as the one located outside the capital city of Bangkok. Often the population in rural areas begins to shift to where the infrastructure is more developed. This change is happening in both China and India, with suburbs springing up around some of India's largest cities. And although both countries' populations continue to grow, India is expected to outstrip China by the year 2050, with a projected population of 2 billion (compared to 1.3 billion expected in China).[15] Marketers expect developing economies to have substandard utility and communications networks. China encountered numerous problems in establishing a modern communications industry infrastructure. The Chinese government's answer was to bypass the need for landline telephone connections by leapfrogging technologies and moving directly to cell phones.

exchange rate Price of one nation's currency in terms of another country's currency.

Changes in exchange rates can also complicate international marketing. An **exchange rate** is the price of one nation's currency in terms of another country's currency. Fluctuations in exchange rates can make a nation's currency more valuable or less valuable compared with those of other nations. In today's global economy, imbalances in trade, dependence on fossil fuels, and other conditions affect the currencies of many countries, not just one or two. The rising cost of energy and raw materials, stricter business standards, higher labour costs, and a faltering U.S. dollar contributed to price increases for most goods produced in China.[16]

At the beginning of the 21st century, most members of the European Union switched to the euro as the replacement to their traditional francs and liras. The long-range idea behind this common currency is that switching to a single currency would strengthen Europe's competitiveness in the global marketplace. Russian and many Eastern European currencies are considered *soft currencies* that cannot be readily converted into such hard currencies as the dollar, euro, or Japanese yen.

INTERNATIONAL SOCIAL-CULTURAL ENVIRONMENT

Before entering a foreign market, marketers should study all aspects of that nation's culture, including language, education, religious attitudes, and social values. The French love to debate and are comfortable with frequent eye contact. In China, humility is a prized virtue, colours have special significance, and it is insulting to be late. Swedes value consensus and do not use humour in negotiations. Navigating these rules that are commonly understood among the citizens of a country takes time, patience, and a willingness to learn about other cultures.

Language plays an important role in global marketing. Table 7.2 lists the world's 10 most frequently spoken languages. Marketers must make sure not only to use the appropriate language or languages for a country but also ensure that the message is correctly translated and conveys the intended meaning.

Firms that rely on call centres located in India and staffed by Indian nationals have discovered an occasional language gap. But these employees do speak English, the worldwide language of commerce. Despite some glitches, the call centres, along with other outsourced operations, are booming, creating jobs and a new middle class in India. The country's economy has benefited hugely from the influx of foreign direct investment that came after the country loosened restrictions of foreign ownership. India now boasts the fastest-growing market for wireless services: mobile phone sales tripled in a two-year period. In one recent year, IBM opened seven offices in India. Big Blue has more workers in India than in any other country.[17]

INTERNATIONAL TECHNOLOGICAL ENVIRONMENT

More than any innovation since the telephone, Internet technology has made it possible for both large and small firms to be connected to the entire world. The Internet transcends political, economic, and

Marketoid

Since NAFTA was signed in 1994, there are 4.7 million more jobs in Canada.

table 7.2   *The World's Most Frequently Spoken Languages*

RANK	LANGUAGE	NUMBER OF SPEAKERS
1	Mandarin (Chinese)	1.2 billion
2	Spanish	414 million
3	English	335 million
4	Hindi	260 million
5	Arabic	237 million
6	Portuguese	203 million
7	Bengali	193 million
8	Russian	167 million
9	Japanese	122 million
10	Javanese	84 million

Source: Lewis, M. Paul, Gary F. Simons, and Charles D. Fennig (eds.). 2014. Ethnologue: Languages of the World, Seventeenth edition. Dallas, Texas: SIL International. Online version: **http://www.ethnologue.com**.

In Europe, demonstrators made a banner to look like a farm as part of the effort to ban the cultivation of GMO crops.

cultural barriers, reaching to every corner of the globe. It has made it possible for marketers to add new business channels. It also helps developing nations in becoming competitive with industrialized nations. However, a huge gap still exists between the regions with the greatest Internet usage and those with the least. Asia, Europe, and North America together account for over 75 percent of the world's total Internet usage; Latin America and the Caribbean follow with just over 10 percent; while Africa accounts for 7 percent; Oceania/Australia just over 1 percent; and the Middle East just over 3 percent. Despite those numbers, Africa and the Middle East have seen the greatest growth in Internet users.[18]

Technology presents challenges for global marketers that extend beyond the Internet and other telecommunications innovations. A major issue involving food marketers is genetic re-engineering. Although Canadian grocery shelves are filled with foods grown with genetically modified organisms (GMOs), most Canadians are unaware they are eating GMO foods because no labelling disclosures are required. In Europe, a number of countries—including Austria, Bulgaria, France, Germany, and Hungary—have banned the cultivation of GMO crops, but the European Court of Justice has yet to issue a ruling that would ban GMOs throughout the European Union. With soaring food costs and global grain shortages, governments the world over are rethinking their position on foods made from crops that are engineered to resist pests and drought.[19] This complex issue affects almost every marketer in the global food industry.

INTERNATIONAL POLITICAL-LEGAL ENVIRONMENT

Global marketers must continually stay abreast of laws and trade regulations in each country in which they compete. Political conditions often influence international marketing as well. Political unrest in places such as the Middle East, Afghanistan, Africa, Eastern Europe, Spain, and South America sometimes results in acts of violence, such as destruction of a firm's property or even deaths from bombings or other violent acts. As a result, many Western firms have set up internal **political risk assessment (PRA)** units or turned to outside consulting services to evaluate the political risks of the marketplaces in which they operate.

The political environment also involves labour conditions in different countries. For decades, Chinese labourers have suffered workplace abuses such as forced labour and withholding of pay.

political risk assessment (PRA)
Units within a firm that evaluate the political risks of the marketplaces in which they operate as well as proposed new marketplaces.

SOLVING AN ETHICAL CONTROVERSY Taking Responsibility for Working Conditions Abroad

MAGAZINES and newspapers have recently published stories about abusive, unsafe working and living conditions endured by poorly paid employees building iPads and iPhones in Chinese factories operated by Foxconn. Foxconn employs 1.2 million people and manufactures about 40 percent of consumer electronics worldwide for Amazon, IBM, Dell, Hewlett-Packard, Lenovo, Nintendo, Nokia, Sony, Toshiba, and Samsung, as well as Apple. Apple says it conducts rigorous audits of all its suppliers and requires them to correct abuses when found. Critics say consumers would be horrified if they knew what really lay behind their sleek electronic devices.

Should foreign companies be responsible for unsafe working conditions in China?

PRO

1. If customers of Foxconn and other manufacturers threatened to take their profitable business elsewhere, conditions would quickly improve.

2. Apple and other firms must act responsibly wherever they do business.

CON

1. What consumers may frown on is often necessary or accepted business practice in other countries.
2. Foreign customers of companies like Foxconn have no right to dictate how its factories should be run.

Where do you stand: pro or con?

Sources: "Activists Take Apple Workers' Rights Campaign to Facebook," Technology News.com, March 7, 2012, **http://news.mindprocessors.com**; Kristin Samuelson, "China and Worker Rights," *The Chicago Tribune*, February 19, 2012, p. B5; Marc Gunther, "The Bigger Picture Behind Apple's China Problem," GreenBiz.com, February 7, 2012, **www.greenbiz.com**; Charles Duhigg and David Barboza, "In China, Human Costs Are Built into an iPad," *The New York Times*, January 25, 2012, **www.nytimes.com**.

While recently enacted labour laws give workers more rights, violations still exist.[20] See the "Solving an Ethical Controversy" feature for a further discussion.

The legal environment for firms operating abroad results from three forces: (1) international law, (2) Canadian law, and (3) legal requirements of host nations. International law emerges from the treaties, conventions, and agreements that exist among nations. Canada has several agreements or treaties with other governments. These agreements set terms for various aspects of commercial relations with other countries, such as the right to conduct business in the treaty partner's domestic market. Other international business agreements concern worldwide standards for various products, patents, trademarks, reciprocal tax treaties, export control, international air travel, and international communications. Since the 1990s, Europe has pushed for mandatory **International Organization for Standardization (ISO) certification**—internationally recognized standards that ensure a company's goods, services, and operations meet established quality levels. The organization has two sets of standards: the ISO 9000 series of standards sets requirements for quality in goods and services; the ISO 14000 series sets standards for operations that minimize harm to the environment. Today, many companies follow these certification standards as well. Currently, 164 countries participate in both series.[21] The "Marketing: Making Your World Better" feature discusses further ISO standards and guidelines. The International Monetary Fund (IMF), another major player in the international legal environment, lends foreign exchange to nations that require it to conduct international trade. These agreements facilitate the entire process of world marketing.

The second dimension of the international legal environment, Canadian law, includes various trade regulations, tax laws, and import/export requirements that affect international marketing. The laws regarding international trade are administered by several different government agencies. For example, Agriculture and Agri-Food Canada working with other government agencies has the responsibility for the agri-food (agriculture and food) trade policy. Other regulations such as the Export and Import Permit Act (EIPA) fall under Foreign Affairs, Trade and Development Canada. The EIPA controls the flow of certain types of goods, including textiles, clothing, steel, and military items. Several government agencies, including the Canada Business Network, a federal government website, are set up to assist companies to work through the various legal requirements. The Canada Business Network is a comprehensive site that presents information to companies about all aspects of importing and exporting. The federal government provides individual assistance to large and

International Organization for Standardization (ISO) certification Internationally recognized standards that ensure a company's goods and services meet established quality levels and that ensure its operations minimize harm to the environment.

| MARKETING: MAKING YOUR WORLD BETTER | **ISO and the Environment** |

ISO stands for International Organization for Standardization, a nongovernmental body that establishes management systems standards and certification processes used throughout the world. In fact, hundreds of thousands of organizations, both private and public, in 164 countries have implemented ISO best practices.

The ISO has several families of standards and guidelines:

- 9000 series: Quality Management
- 14000 series: Environmental Management
- 26000 series: Social Responsibility
- 50001 series: Energy Management
- 31000 series: Risk Management
- 22000 series: Food Safety Management
- 27001 series: Information Security Management
- 20121 series: Sustainable Events

For the groups that are standards, like quality management and environmental management, companies can be recognized through a certification process.

The 14000 series of standards provides guidance to organizations that want to be certified on environmental issues. These standards enable organizations to be proactive in controlling their impact on the environment with regard to the quality of air, water, and soil, as well as noise and the transport of dangerous goods.

The 20121 series, event sustainability management, includes relatively new guidelines aimed at providing organizations with information to allow large and small events to have the least impact on the environment. These guidelines support policies of minimum material waste, minimum energy consumption, and maximum social benefit.

The London 2012 Olympics and Paralympic Games were one of the first events to use these guidelines. The Olympic organizers were able to achieve outstanding results. They began planning the environmental aspects of the games when they were preparing the bid to host the games even before the ISO had finalized the guidelines. Event organizers were able to divert 99 percent of construction waste and 63 percent of the materials delivered to the site arrived by boat or rail, and the permanent buildings on the site emit 50 percent less carbon dioxide than other comparable buildings.

Sources: ISO website, **www.iso.org**, accessed February 6, 2014; "Sustainability of the Olympic Park," The Institution of Engineering and Technology website, **www.theiet.org**, accessed February 6, 2014; "Why This Could Be the Greenest Super Bowl Yet," GreenBiz.com website, January 14, 2014, **www.greenbiz.com**.

small companies wanting to enter foreign markets through its Trade Commissioner Service. The Canadian Trade Commissioner Service can also connect you to business contacts in more than 150 cities throughout the world with its LinkedIn network.[22]

Finally, legal requirements of host nations affect foreign marketers. Despite China's many advances in recent years—and even as it attempts to build a modern economy—the Chinese government continues to censor the Internet. More than 420 million Chinese currently use the Internet, and an active cadre of Chinese "hacktivists" works to outwit the government's firewall and help fellow citizens gain unfettered access.[23]

TRADE BARRIERS

tariff Tax levied against imported goods.

Assorted trade barriers also affect global marketing. These barriers fall into two major categories: **tariffs**—taxes levied on imported products—and administrative, or non-tariff, barriers. Some tariffs impose set taxes per kilogram, litre, or unit; others are calculated according to the value of the imported item. Administrative barriers are more subtle than tariffs and take a variety of forms such as customs barriers, quotas on imports, unnecessarily restrictive standards for imports, and export subsidies. Because the GATT and WTO agreements (discussed later in the chapter) eliminated tariffs on many products, countries frequently use non-tariff barriers to boost exports and control the flows of imported products.

Canada and other nations are constantly negotiating tariffs and other trade agreements. Two significant agreements are the North American Free Trade Agreement (NAFTA) and the Free Trade Area of the Americas (FTAA). NAFTA involves Canada, the United States, and Mexico. The FTAA involves Canada and 34 other countries within North, South, and Central America, including large countries like the United States, Argentina, and Brazil, and smaller ones like Bahamas and Haiti.[24] A list of other trade barriers is outlined in Table 7.3.

table 7.3   *Trade Barriers*

Revenue tariffs	Taxes designed to raise funds for the importing government
Protective tariffs	Taxes designed to raise the retail price of an imported product to match or exceed that of a similar domestic product
Import quotas	Trade restrictions limiting the number of units of certain goods that can enter a country for resale
Embargo	Complete ban on the import of specified products
Subsidies	Government financial support of a private industry
Exchange control	Method used to regulate international trade among importing organizations by controlling access to foreign currencies
Dumping	Controversial practice of selling a product in a foreign market at a price lower than what it receives in the producer's domestic market

Tariffs

Tariffs can be classified as either revenue or protective tariffs. Most early government revenue came from revenue tariffs. Protective tariffs are usually higher than revenue tariffs. Some countries use tariffs in a selective manner to encourage or discourage certain consumption practices and thereby reduce access to their local markets. For example, Canada has a policy called General Preferential Tariff (GPT) in which we give preferential treatment to imports from developing countries. As of January 1, 2015, the number of countries covered under the GPT was reduced to 103 countries from 175. The countries benefiting from the GPT is reviewed every two years to ensure they still qualify for the reduced tariff status.[25]

Other Trade Barriers

In addition to direct taxes on imported products, governments may erect a number of other barriers ranging from special permits and detailed inspection requirements to quotas on foreign-made items in an effort to stem the flow of imported goods—or halt them altogether. In one of the longest-running trade disputes, European shoppers paid about twice as much for bananas as did North Americans. Through a series of import licence controls, Europe had limited the importation of bananas from Latin American countries in an effort to protect producers from former European colonies in Africa and the Caribbean, who pay no tariff. The World Trade Organization ruled that the European tariffs on imported bananas unfairly discriminated against Latin American banana growers. After 16 years of wrangling, the European Union reached an agreement with Latin American growers, which will make them subject to lower tariffs—and likely lower-cost bananas in Europe.[26] Other forms of trade restrictions are import quotas and embargoes.

The ultimate quota is the embargo. Since 1960, the United States has maintained an embargo against Cuba in protest against Fidel Castro's dictatorship and policies such as expropriation of property and disregard for human rights. Not only do the sanctions prohibit Cuban exports—cigars and sugar are the island's best-known products—from entering the country, but they also apply to companies that profit from property that Cuba's communist government expropriated from Americans following the Cuban revolution.

Thanks to a WTO ruling on banana importation, European shoppers are likely to see more bananas from Latin America in their supermarkets—along with a more affordable price.

Benis Arapovic/Shutterstock.com

Courtesy of Emirates

Some industries, such as airlines, need special approvals from government agencies in order to do business in Canada.

assessment check 2 ✓

2.1 What are the three criteria that determine a nation's prospects as a host for international business expansion?

2.2 What are the two major categories of trade barriers?

Another trade barrier is subsidies. China has long subsidized the cost of many products to boost consumption. When Chinese wireless carriers recently subsidized the cost of 3G (third-generation) handsets, they saw a four-fold increase in sales.[27] Some nations also limit foreign ownership in the business sector. And still another way to block international trade is to create so many regulatory barriers that it is almost impossible to reach target markets. China presents a maze of regulations controlling trade, and while the government continues to lift barriers, experienced businesspeople agree that it's important to have personal connections, or *guanxi*, to help navigate the bureaucratic challenges.[28]

Foreign trade can also be regulated by exchange control through a central bank or government agency. The exchange control authority can allocate, expand, or restrict foreign exchange according to existing national policy.

DUMPING

The practice of selling a product in a foreign market at a price lower than it commands in the producer's domestic market is called dumping. Critics of free trade often argue that foreign governments give substantial support to their own exporting companies. Government support may permit these firms to extend their export markets by offering lower prices abroad. In retaliation for this kind of interference with free trade, some governments add import tariffs to products that foreign firms are dumping on their markets to bring prices in line with their domestically produced goods. In Canada, the Special Import Measures Act covers anti-dumping regulations.[29]

China recently fined the United States for dumping chicken feet into the Chinese market. Poultry processors in the United States see China as an attractive destination for the item, considered worthless in North America but regarded as a delicacy in southern China.[30]

③ **Outline the basic functions of GATT, WTO, NAFTA, FTAA, and the European Union.**

free trade area Region in which participating nations agree to the free trade of goods among themselves, abolishing tariffs and trade restrictions.

customs union Establishment of a free trade area plus a uniform tariff for trade with nonmember unions.

common market Extension of a customs union by seeking to reconcile all government regulations affecting trade.

MULTINATIONAL ECONOMIC INTEGRATION

A noticeable trend toward multinational economic integration has developed since the end of World War II. Multinational economic integration can be set up in several ways. The simplest approach is to establish a **free trade area** in which participating nations agree to the free trade of goods among themselves, abolishing all tariffs and trade restrictions. A **customs union** establishes a free trade area plus a uniform tariff for trade with nonmember nations. A **common market** extends a customs union by seeking to reconcile all government regulations affecting trade. Despite the many factors in its favour, not everyone is enthusiastic about free trade. Canadians and Americans have lost jobs when employers outsourced their work to countries like Mexico where wages are lower. Now, workers in Mexico face the same outsourcing threat as their employers begin out-sourcing work to China, where wages are even lower. Although productivity and innovation are said to grow quickly with free trade, workers often find themselves working longer and for reduced pay as operations move overseas. But many firms view the change as a way to offer superior service.

GATT AND THE WORLD TRADE ORGANIZATION

The **General Agreement on Tariffs and Trade (GATT)**, a trade accord that has sponsored several rounds of major tariff negotiations, substantially reducing worldwide tariff levels, has existed for six decades. In 1994, a seven-year series of GATT conferences, called the Uruguay Round, culminated in one of the biggest victories for free trade in decades.

The Uruguay Round reduced average tariffs by one-third, or more than $700 billion. Among its major victories were these:

- Reduced farm subsidies, which opened vast new markets for exports

- Increased protection for patents, copyrights, and trademarks

- Included services under international trading rules, creating opportunities for financial, legal, and accounting firms

- Phased out import quotas on textiles and clothing from developing nations, a move that cost textile workers thousands of jobs when their employers moved many of these domestic jobs to lower-wage countries, but benefited retailers and consumers

A key outcome of the GATT talks was establishment of the **World Trade Organization (WTO)**, a 153-member organization that succeeds GATT. The WTO oversees GATT agreements, serves as a forum for trade, negotiations, and mediates disputes. It also monitors national trade policy and works to reduce trade barriers throughout the world. Unlike GATT, WTO decisions are binding. Countries that seek to become members of the WTO must participate in rigorous rounds of negotiations that can last several years. Russia holds the record: having applied for membership in 1993, its application was approved in 2011.[31]

To date, the WTO has made only slow progress toward its major policy initiatives—liberalizing world financial services, telecommunications, and maritime markets. Trade officials have not agreed on the direction for the WTO. Big differences between developed and developing nations create a major roadblock to WTO progress, and its activities so far have focused more on dispute resolution through its Dispute Settlement Body than on reducing trade barriers. But the WTO also provides important technical assistance and training for the governments of developing countries.[32]

NAFTA

More than two decades after the passage of the **North American Free Trade Agreement (NAFTA)**, an agreement between Canada, the United States, and Mexico that removes trade restrictions among the three nations, negotiations among the nations continue. The three nations insist that they will not create a trade bloc similar to the European Union—that is, they will not focus on political integration but instead on economic cooperation. NAFTA is particularly important to Canadian marketers because the United States is this country's largest trading partner.

But NAFTA is a complex issue, and from time to time groups in one or more of the three countries chafe under the agreement. In Mexico, farm workers have charged that NAFTA puts their industry at a disadvantage. In the United States, critics argue that U.S. workers lose jobs to cheap labour south of the border. In Canada, some observers claim NAFTA has compromised the country's oil reserves. Yet since NAFTA's passage, these three countries daily conduct more than $2 billion in trade with each other and have experienced GDP growth as a result.[33]

THE FREE TRADE AREA OF THE AMERICAS

NAFTA was the first step toward creating the **Free Trade Area of the Americas (FTAA)**, stretching the length of the entire Western Hemisphere, from Alaska's Bering Strait to Cape Horn at South America's southern tip, encompassing 34 countries, a population of 800 million, and a combined gross domestic product of more than $11 trillion. The FTAA would be the largest free trade zone on earth and would offer low or nonexistent tariffs; streamlined customs; and no quotas, subsidies, or other barriers to trade. In addition to Canada, the United States, and Mexico, 31 other countries have joined with the proposed FTAA, including Argentina, Brazil, Chile, Colombia, Ecuador, Guatemala, Jamaica, Peru, Trinidad and Tobago, Uruguay, and Venezuela. The FTAA still has many hurdles to overcome as countries wrangle for conditions that are most favourable to them.[34]

THE EUROPEAN UNION

The best-known example of a multinational economic and monetary union or community is the **European Union (EU)**. As Figure 7.2 shows, 28 countries make up the EU: Finland, Sweden, Denmark,

General Agreement on Tariffs and Trade (GATT) International trade accord that has helped reduce world tariffs.

Marketoid

In the years since NAFTA has been in place, trilateral trade has increased almost fourfold.

World Trade Organization (WTO) Organization that replaces GATT, overseeing GATT agreements, making binding decisions in mediating disputes, and reducing trade barriers.

North American Free Trade Agreement (NAFTA) Accord removing trade barriers among Canada, Mexico, and the United States.

Free Trade Area of the Americas (FTAA) Proposed free trade area stretching the length of the entire Western Hemisphere and designed to extend free trade benefits to additional nations in North, Central, and South America.

European Union (EU) Customs union that is moving in the direction of an economic and monetary union by adopting a common currency, removing trade restrictions, and permitting free flow of goods and workers throughout the member nations.

figure 7.2

The 28 Members of the European Union

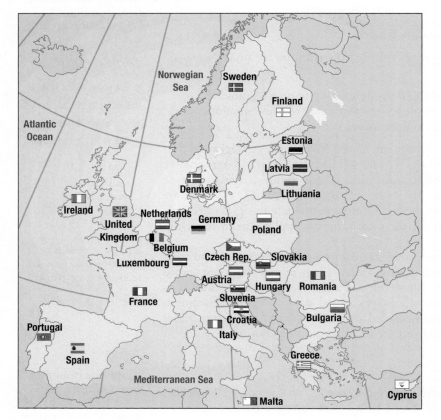

the United Kingdom, Ireland, the Netherlands, Belgium, Germany, Luxembourg, France, Austria, Italy, Greece, Spain, Portugal, Hungary, Poland, the Czech Republic, Slovakia, Slovenia, Estonia, Latvia, Lithuania, Malta, Bulgaria, Romania, Croatia, and Cyprus. Five countries—Iceland, Montenegro, Serbia, Macedonia, and Turkey—are candidates for membership. With a total population of more than 505 million people, the EU forms a huge market.[35]

The goal of the EU is to eventually remove all barriers to free trade among its members, making it as simple and painless to ship products between England and Spain as it is between Newfoundland and British Columbia. Also involved is the standardization of currencies and regulations that businesses must meet. Introduced in 1999, the EU's euro is the common currency in 18 member countries, with other EU countries planning to phase it in over time. Only Denmark, Sweden, and the United Kingdom have declined to use the euro.[36]

In addition to simplifying transactions among members, the EU looks to strengthen its position in the world as a political and economic power. Its recently ratified Treaty of Lisbon is designed to further streamline operations and enables the EU to enter into international agreements as a political entity. Mexico negotiated a trade agreement with the EU that makes it easier for European companies to set up operations in Mexico. The agreement gives EU companies the same privileges enjoyed by Canada and the United States and brings new investors to Mexico.

In some ways, the EU is making definite progress toward its economic goals. It is drafting standardized eco-labels to certify that products are manufactured according to certain environmental standards as well as creating guidelines governing marketers' uses of customer information. Marketers can also protect some trademarks throughout the entire EU with a single application and registration process through the Community Trade Mark (CTM), which simplifies doing business and eliminates having to register with each member country. Yet marketers still face challenges when selling their products in the EU. Customs taxes differ, and no uniform postal system exists. Using one toll-free number for several countries will not work, either, because each country has its own telephone system for codes and numbers.

assessment check 3 ✓

3.1 What is the World Trade Organization (WTO)?

3.2 What countries are parties to NAFTA?

3.3 What is the goal of the European Union (EU)?

④ **Identify the alternative strategies for entering international markets.**

GOING GLOBAL

Globalization affects almost every industry and every individual throughout the world. Traditional marketers who decide to take their firms global may do so because they already have strong domestic market shares or their target market is too saturated to offer any substantial growth. Sometimes, by evaluating key indicators of the marketing environment, marketers can move toward globalization at an optimal time.

The German footwear firm Adidas made a big jump into the global market after its successful "Impossible Is Nothing" ad campaign, announcing it would purchase rival Reebok in an effort to overtake number one competitor Nike. Using the benefits of the EU while also making a play for the Asian market, Adidas marketers believe they have a good chance at winning the global game. Making deals with athletes, such as British soccer legend David Beckham and heptathlete Jessica Ennis, and licensing agreements for major sports leagues have helped Adidas strengthen its brand in major markets around the world. The firm scored one of its biggest coups by signing National Basketball League superstar Derrick Rose to a 14-year contract.[37]

Most large firms—and many smaller businesses—already participate in global commerce, and virtually every domestic marketer, large or small, recognizes the need to investigate whether to market its products overseas. It is not an easy step to take, requiring careful evaluation and preparation of a strategy. Common reasons that marketers cite for going global are globalization of customers, new customers in emerging markets, globalization of competitors, reduced trade barriers, advances in technology, and enhanced customer responsiveness.

STRATEGIES FOR ENTERING INTERNATIONAL MARKETS

Successful global marketing starts at the top. Without the enthusiasm and support of senior managers, an initiative is likely to fail. When making the decisions to enter a global market and how to enter these markets, managers face a danger of evaluating the success of entering global markets based on cultural values, experiences, or knowledge of their domestic markets. This often unconscious evaluation of global markets based on domestic experiences is referred to as the **self-reference criterion**.[38] Managers making decisions to enter into a global market often consult with companies who specialize in cultural differences as described in the "Marketing and the SME" feature.

self-reference criteria
The unconscious reference to one's own cultural values, experiences, and knowledge as a basis for decisions.

MARKETING AND THE SME | Itim International and the Hofstede Centre

ITIM International and the Hofstede Centre are both owned by the human resource consulting firm FeedbackDialog, which has its main office in Finland. Both organizations are based on the work of Professor Geert Hofstede but each has its own focus. Itim International, which began operations in 1985, aims to assist companies to use culture as a strategic asset. The goal of the Hofstede Centre, which opened in 2012, is to provide educational programs to those who want to better understand the work of Professor Hofstede.

Professor Hofstede is a social psychologist who began his career with the multinational firm IBM. It was there that he started his research on how to explain the cultures of different countries. Based on attitude surveys of employees from 40 different countries, Professor Hofstede developed a four-dimensional scale that identified different aspects of culture within these countries. Professor Hofstede's original dimensions were these:

- Power distance—how people within a culture that have less power accept that power is distributed unequally
- Uncertainty avoidance—the society's tolerance for uncertainty
- Individualism—the degree of individualism versus collectivism within a society

- Masculinity—emotional roles between genders

Further research by Michael Bond and Michael Minkov added two more dimensions to Professor Hofstede's model:

- Long-term orientation versus short-term orientation
- Indulgence versus restraint

Using these dimensions, countries around the world are assigned scores that can assist management in making decisions. This research has helped companies make decisions about what countries to expand into, the best approach to expanding into different cultures, and how to communicate effectively in different cultures.

This research also shows that even with the global explosion of social media and the advancement of technology, the differences in culture between nations is growing wider.

Sources: Geert Hofstede, "Dimensions of National Cultures," Geert Hofstede website, **http://geerthofstede.com**, accessed February 8, 2014; Feedback-Dialog website, **www.feedbackdialog.com**, accessed February 9, 2014; The Hofstede Centre website, **http://geert-hofstede.com**, accessed February 8, 2014; Marieke de Mooij website, **http://mariekedemooij.com**, accessed February 9, 2014.

figure 7.3

*Levels of Involvement in
International Marketing*

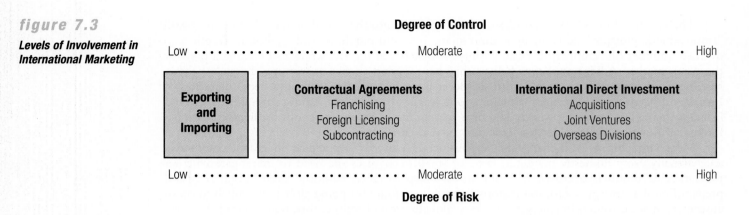

Once marketers have researched and identified markets for expansion, they may choose from among three basic strategies for entering international markets: importing and exporting; contractual agreements such as franchising, licensing, and subcontracting; and international direct investment. As Figure 7.3 shows, the level of risk and the firm's degree of control over global marketing increase with greater involvement. Firms often use more than one of these entry strategies.

IMPORTING AND EXPORTING

An importer is a firm that brings in goods produced abroad to sell domestically or to be used as components in its products. In making import decisions, the marketer must assess local demand for the product, taking into consideration factors such as the following:

- Ability of the supplier to maintain agreed-to quality levels

- Flexibility in filling orders that might vary considerably from one order to the next

- Response time in filling orders

- Total costs—including import fees, packaging, and transportation—in comparison with costs of domestic suppliers

Exporting, another basic form of global marketing, involves a continuous effort in marketing a firm's merchandise to customers in other countries. Many firms export their products as the first step in reaching international markets. Furniture manufacturer and retailer IKEA has built an entire exporting strategy around its modular furniture. Because IKEA's furniture is lightweight, packs flat, and comes in components that customers can assemble, the firm can ship its goods almost anywhere in the world at a low cost, unlike manufacturers of traditional furniture.[39]

First-time exporters can reach foreign customers through one or more of three alternatives: export-trading companies, export-management companies, or offset agreements. An export-trading company (ETC) buys products from domestic producers and resells them abroad. While manufacturers lose control over marketing and distribution to the ETC, it helps them export through a relatively simple and inexpensive channel, in the process providing feedback about the overseas market potential of their products.

The second option, an export-management company (EMC), provides the first-time exporter with expertise in locating international buyers, handling necessary paperwork, and ensuring that its goods meet local labelling and testing laws. However, the manufacturer retains more control over the export process when it deals with an EMC than if it were to sell the goods outright to an export-trading company. Smaller firms can get assistance with administrative needs such as financing and preparation of proposals and contracts from large EMC contractors.

The final option, entering a foreign market under an offset agreement, teams a small firm with a major international company. The smaller firm essentially serves as a subcontractor on a large foreign project. This entry strategy provides new exporters with international experience, supported by the assistance of the primary contractor in such areas as international transaction documentation and financing.

CONTRACTUAL AGREEMENTS

As a firm gains sophistication in global marketing, it may enter contractual agreements that provide several flexible alternatives to exporting. Both large and small firms can benefit from these methods. Franchising and foreign licensing, for example, are good ways to take services abroad. Subcontracting agreements may involve either production facilities or services.

Franchising

A **franchise** is a contractual arrangement in which a wholesaler or retailer (the franchisee) agrees to meet the operating requirements of a manufacturer or other franchiser. The franchisee receives the right to sell the products and use the franchiser's name as well as a variety of marketing, management, and other services. Fast-food companies such as McDonald's have been active franchisers around the world.

franchise Contractual arrangement in which a wholesaler or retailer agrees to meet the operating requirements of a manufacturer or other franchiser.

One advantage of franchising is risk reduction by offering a proven concept. Standardized operations typically reduce costs, increase operating efficiencies, and provide greater international recognition. However, the success of an international franchise depends on its willingness to balance standard practices with local customer preferences. McDonald's and Pizza Hut are expanding into India with special menus that feature lamb, chicken, and vegetarian items, in deference to Hindu and Muslim customers who do not eat beef or pork.

Foreign Licensing

A second method of going global through the use of contractual agreements is **foreign licensing**. Such an agreement grants foreign marketers the right to distribute a firm's merchandise or use its trademark, patent, or process in a specified geographic area. These arrangements usually set certain time limits, after which agreements are revised or renewed.

foreign licensing Agreement that grants foreign marketers the right to distribute a firm's merchandise or to use its trademark, patent, or process in a specified geographic area.

Licensing offers several advantages over exporting, including access to local partners' marketing information and distribution channels and protection from various legal barriers. Because licensing does not require capital outlays, many firms, both small and large, regard it as an attractive entry strategy. Like franchising, licensing allows a firm to quickly enter a foreign market with a known product. The arrangement also may provide entry into a market that government restrictions close to imports or international direct investment. Entertainment software producer Electronic Arts entered into a licensing agreement with the European soccer league to provide *UEFA EURO 2012,* a video game that re-creates the 2012 European Football Championship. Posing as the team of their choice, gamers can relive exciting real-life sports moments as they compete for the European championship.[40]

Subcontracting

A third strategy for going global through contractual agreements is **subcontracting**, in which the production of goods or services is assigned to local companies. Using local subcontractors can prevent mistakes involving local culture and regulations. Manufacturers might subcontract with a local company to produce their goods or use a foreign distributor to handle their products abroad or provide customer service. Manufacturing within the country can provide protection from import duties and may be a lower-cost alternative that makes it possible for the product to compete with local offerings. But it can also have a downside if local suppliers don't make the grade or if a manufacturer imposes an unrealistically tight timeframe on a supplier to deliver the product, leading to long hours or sweatshop conditions in the factory.

subcontracting Contractual agreements that assign the production of goods or services to local or smaller firms.

INTERNATIONAL DIRECT INVESTMENT

Another strategy for entering global markets is international direct investment in foreign firms, production, and marketing facilities. With so many Canadians coming from different parts of the world, it is not surprising that foreign direct investment inflows and outflows—the total of Canadian investments abroad and foreign investments in Canada—are important to our economic growth. Canadian firms invested over $700 billion in other countries in 2012. Total foreign investment into Canada for the same period amounted to $633 billion.[41]

Furniture manufacturer IKEA has built its entire exporting strategy around modular furniture, which is lightweight, packs flat, and is easy to ship.

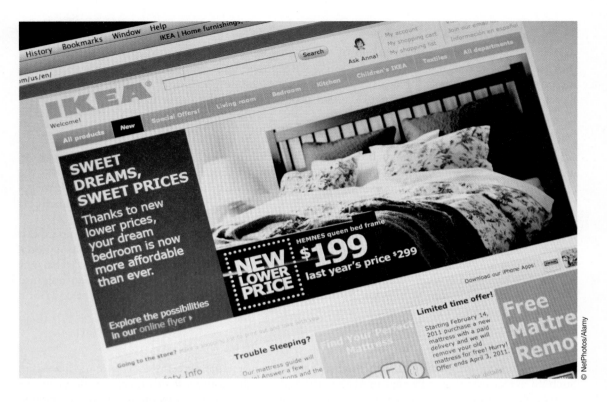

Although high levels of involvement and high-risk potential are characteristics of investments in foreign countries, firms choosing this method often have a competitive advantage. Direct investment can take several forms. A company can acquire an existing firm in a country where it wants to do business, or it can set up an independent division outside its own borders with responsibility for production and marketing in a country or geographic region. Chinese firms have been seeking to purchase businesses in other countries, mostly in industries involving natural resources such as oil, natural gas, metals, and coal. However, they have been making inroads in industrial, technology, and finance companies as well.[42]

multinational corporation Firm with significant operations and marketing activities outside its home country.

Companies may also engage in international marketing by forming joint ventures, in which they share the risks, costs, and management of the foreign operation with one or more partners. These partnerships join the investing companies with nationals of the host countries. While some companies choose to open their own facilities overseas, others share with their partners. Because India puts limits on foreign direct investment, Walmart formed a partnership with Indian conglomerate Bharti Enterprises to open wholesale cash-and-carry stores in India. The stores do business under the name BestPrice Modern Wholesale. In October 2013, the two companies announced that the partnership would be discontinued and that Walmart would continue doing business in India using the BestPrice Modern name.[43]

Although joint ventures offer many advantages, foreign investors have encountered problems in several areas throughout the world, especially in developing economies. Lower trade barriers, new technologies, lower transport costs, and vastly improved access to information mean that many more partnerships will be involved in international trade.

assessment check 4 ✓

4.1 What are the three basic strategies for entering global markets?

4.2 What is a franchise?

4.3 What is international direct investment?

⑤ **Differentiate between a global marketing strategy and a multi-domestic marketing strategy.**

FROM MULTINATIONAL CORPORATION TO GLOBAL MARKETER

A **multinational corporation** is a firm with significant operations and marketing activities outside its home country. Examples of multinationals are General Electric, Siemens, and Mitsubishi in heavy electrical equipment, and Timex, Seiko, and Citizen in watches. Since they first became a force in international business in the 1960s, multinationals have evolved in some important ways.

First, these companies are no longer exclusively North American–based. Today, it is as likely for a multinational to be based in Japan, Germany, or Great Britain as in North America. Second, multinationals no longer think of their foreign operations as mere outsourcing appendages that carry out the design, production, and engineering ideas conceived at home. Instead, they encourage constant exchanges of ideas, capital, and technologies among all the multinational operations.

Multinationals often employ huge foreign workforces relative to their North American staffs. A large percentage of all Ford and IBM personnel are located outside North America. These workforces are no longer seen merely as sources of cheap labour. On the contrary, many multinationals centre technically complex activities in locations throughout the world. Texas Instruments does much of its research, development, design, and manufacturing in East Asia. In fact, it is increasingly common for multinationals to bring product innovations from their foreign facilities back to North America.

Multinationals have become global corporations that reflect the interdependence of world economies, the growth of international competition, and the globalization of world markets. For example, 60 percent of households in Hong Kong get their television services through ultra-high-speed broadband connections that turn their TVs into computers, a concept that has been slower to catch on in North America. European and Asian consumers were the first to use smart cards with embedded memory chips for retail purchases. Chile has emerged as a highly attractive destination for multinational firms seeking to expand their "global footprint" by outsourcing some functions, particularly if the firms serve both English- and Spanish-speaking customers. Swiss engineering and technology giant ABB chose Chile as the site of its first remote service centre. The centre provides real-time monitoring, diagnostic, and technical assistance for a number of ABB's businesses.[44]

DEVELOPING AN INTERNATIONAL MARKETING STRATEGY

In developing a marketing mix, international marketers may choose between two alternative approaches: a global marketing strategy or a multi-domestic marketing strategy. A **global marketing strategy** defines a standard marketing mix and implements it with minimal modifications in all foreign markets. This approach brings the advantage of economies of scale to production and marketing activities. Procter & Gamble (P&G) marketers follow a global marketing strategy for Pringles potato chips, its leading export brand. P&G sells one product with a consistent formulation in every country and meets 80 percent of worldwide demand with only six flavours of Pringles and one package design. This standardized approach saves money since it allows large-scale production runs and reinforces the brand's image. In addition, a global strategy can foster collaborative innovation, as with the development of Pringles Stixx, an extension of the popular product line. Pringles's strong global performance played heavily in Kellogg's recent decision to acquire the brand from P&G.[45]

A global marketing perspective can effectively market some goods and services to segments in many nations that share cultures and languages. This approach works especially well for products with strong, universal appeal such as Nike, luxury items like Rolex watches, and high-tech brands like Microsoft. Global advertising outlets, such as international editions of popular consumer and business magazines and international transmissions of TV channels such as CNN, MTV, and the CNBC financial network, help marketers deliver a single message to millions of global viewers.

A global marketing strategy can be highly effective for luxury products that target upscale consumers everywhere. Marketers of diamonds and luxury watches, for instance, typically use advertising with little or no copy—just a picture of a beautiful diamond or watch with the name discreetly displayed on the page.

But a global strategy doesn't always work, as Domino's Pizza discovered after it opened stores in Asia. With its "30 minutes or it's free" policy, the company has been known for the fastest pizzas rather than the best-tasting ones. Apparently for Asians, the 30-minute guarantee wasn't attractive enough to offset how the food tasted, and Domino's ended up closing more than 50 stores in Hong Kong, Indonesia, Singapore, and Thailand. Domino's learned from its mistakes. It developed a new recipe for its pizzas and re-entered the Singapore market.[46]

A major benefit of a global marketing strategy is its low cost to implement. Most firms, however, find it necessary to practise market segmentation outside their home markets and tailor their marketing mixes to fit the unique needs of customers in specific countries. This **multi-domestic marketing strategy** assumes that differences between market characteristics and

global marketing strategy Standardized marketing mix with minimal modifications that a firm uses in all of its domestic and foreign markets.

multi-domestic marketing strategy Application of market segmentation to foreign markets by tailoring the firm's marketing mix to match specific target markets in each nation.

Domino's® new global strategy involved a pizza makeover to meet local preferences in Asia. Domino's has re-entered the Singapore market with 13 new stores.

assessment check 5

5.1 What is a multinational corporation?

5.2 What is the difference between a global marketing strategy and a multi-domestic marketing strategy?

competitive situations in certain nations require firms to customize their marketing decisions to effectively reach individual marketplaces. Many marketing experts believe that most products demand multi-domestic marketing strategies to give them realistic global marketing appeal. Cultural, geographic, language, and other differences simply make it difficult to send one message to many countries. Specific situations may allow marketers to standardise some parts of the marketing process but customize others.

⑥ **Describe the alternative marketing mix strategies used in global marketing and explain the attractiveness of Canada as a target for international marketers.**

INTERNATIONAL PRODUCT AND PROMOTIONAL STRATEGIES

Global marketers can choose from among five strategies for selecting the most appropriate product and promotion strategy for a specific foreign market: straight extension, promotion adaptation, product adaptation, dual adaptation, and product invention. As Figure 7.4 indicates, the strategies centre on whether to extend a domestic product and promotional strategy into international markets or adapt one or both to meet the target market's unique requirements.

A firm may follow a one-product, one-message straight extension strategy as part of a global marketing strategy. This strategy permits economies of scale in production and marketing. Also, successful implementation creates universal recognition of a product for consumers from country to country. Levi's global advertising campaign, "Go Forth," uses a poem called "The Laughing Heart," written by the late Charles Bukowski, that reads, in part, "Your life is your life. Know it while you have it." Levi's kicked off the campaign on its Facebook page, then moved to TV with a commercial running in 19 languages, including French, German, Japanese, and Spanish.

The Levi's message will also run in movie theatres worldwide.[47]

Other strategies call for product adaptation, promotion adaptation, or both. Marketers in the greeting card industry adapt their product and messaging to cultural differences. For example, Russians are unlikely to send a card to a man on his 40th birthday. Reason: a common superstition in Russia that says big parties for a man celebrating that milestone attract "the Death." In Japan, where the parent–child relationship is formal, cards intended for a parent are also formal and express less sentimentality. And most cultures outside North America don't respond to images of Santa Claus and the Easter Bunny.[48]

figure 7.4

Alternative International Product and Promotional Strategies

		Product Strategy		
Promotion Strategy		Same Product	Product Adaptation	New Product
	Same Promotion	**Straight Extension** General Mills Cheerios Coca-Cola Mars Snickers candy bar	**Product Adaptation** Campbell's soup	**Product Invention** Nonelectric sewing machines Manually operated washing machines
	Different Promotion	**Promotion Adaptation** Bicycles/motorcycles Outboard motors	**Dual Adaptation** Coffee Some clothing	

Finally, a firm may select product invention to take advantage of unique foreign market opportunities. To match user needs in developing nations, an appliance manufacturer might introduce a hand-powered washing machine even though such products became obsolete in industrialized countries years ago. Although Chapter 11 discusses the idea of branding in greater detail, it is important to note here the importance of a company's recognizable name, image, product, or even slogan around the world.

Marketoid

One in seven Canadian jobs depends on trade with the United States.

INTERNATIONAL DISTRIBUTION STRATEGY

Distribution is a vital aspect of overseas marketing. Marketers must set up proper channels and anticipate extensive physical distribution problems. Foreign markets may offer poor transportation systems and warehousing facilities—or none at all. Global marketers must adapt promptly and efficiently to these situations to profit from overseas sales.

A distribution decision involves two steps. First, the firm must decide on a method of entering the foreign market. Second, it must determine how to distribute the product within the foreign market through that entry channel. After Chrysler Group introduced the Fiat 500 in North America, sales were flat—a phenomenon that management attributed to an insufficient distribution network. The following year, the automaker launched its Fiat 500 Abarth with an edgy campaign featuring a supermodel. Fiat marketing head Matt Davis believes the Abarth can fill a niche: "It's like the Italian sports car for the everyday driver."[49]

PRICING STRATEGY

Pricing can critically affect the success of an overall marketing strategy for foreign markets. Considerable competitive, economic, political, and legal constraints often limit pricing decisions. Global marketers can succeed if they thoroughly understand these requirements.

Companies must adapt their pricing strategies to local markets and change them when conditions change. In India, Unilever's partner Hindustan Lever offers "penny packets" of shampoo to lower-income consumers, who typically cannot afford to buy an entire bottle of shampoo. Although local firms follow the same practice, Hindustan Lever wants to develop loyalty among these consumers so that if they move up the income scale, they will be more apt to buy the firm's higher-priced products as well.

An important development in pricing strategy for international marketing has been the emergence of commodity marketing organizations that seek to control prices through collective action. The Organization of Petroleum Exporting Countries (OPEC) is a good example of this kind of collective export organization.

COUNTERTRADE

In a growing number of nations, the only way a marketer can gain access to foreign markets is through **countertrade**—a form of exporting in which a firm barters products rather than selling

countertrade Form of exporting whereby goods and services are bartered rather than sold for cash.

them for cash. Less-developed nations sometimes impose countertrade requirements when they lack sufficient foreign currency to attain goods and services they want or need from exporting countries. These countries allow sellers to exchange their products only for domestic products as a way to control their balance-of-trade problems.

Countertrade became popular two decades ago, when companies wanted to conduct business in eastern European countries and the former Soviet Union. Those governments did not allow exchanges of hard currency, so this form of barter facilitated trade. PepsiCo made one of the largest countertrades ever when it exchanged $3 billion worth of Pepsi-Cola for Russian Stolichnaya vodka, a cargo ship, and tankers from the former Soviet Union.

CANADA AS A TARGET FOR INTERNATIONAL MARKETERS

Foreign marketers regard Canada as an inviting target. It offers access to North American markets, high levels of discretionary income, political stability, a generally favourable attitude toward foreign investment, and a relatively well-controlled economy.

Among the best-known industries in which foreign manufacturers have established Canadian production facilities is automobiles. Most of the world's leading auto companies have built assembly plants here. America's big three automakers (Ford, General Motors, and Chrysler) and Japan's (Honda and Toyota) all have manufacturing plants in Canada.

Canada is a country rich in natural resources that are in demand worldwide as manufacturing increases in many areas of the world. This makes companies in the natural resource sector attractive for foreign investment. It is also one area of foreign investment that is meeting with some resistance and calls for caution from Canadian business leaders. Business leaders have been warning for years that foreign ownership of resources, telecommunications, and infrastructure-related companies could cause problems for Canada in the future. The Canadian government has recently put more restrictions on foreign companies purchasing natural resource interests in Canada.[50]

assessment check 6

6.1 What are the five strategies for selecting the most appropriate product and promotion strategy for a specific international market?

6.2 What is countertrade?

6.3 What characteristics of Canada make it an inviting target for international marketers?

Foreign car manufacturers have taken advantage of Canadian consumers' desire for foreign cars by locating many assembly plants in Canada. This assembly-line worker is employed in Toyota's plant in Cambridge, Ontario.

Norm Betts/Bloomberg/Getty Images

All the concern over foreign ownership and foreign companies investing in Canada may be academic, however. Foreign investors continue to purchase Canadian companies, invest in Canadian stocks, and purchase Canadian bonds. Increasingly, foreign multinationals will invest in Canadian assets as they seek to produce goods locally and control distribution channels.

Strategic Implications

The last decade has marked a new era of truly global marketing, in which the world's marketplaces are accessible to nearly every firm. Marketers in both small, localized firms and giant businesses need to reevaluate the strengths and weaknesses of their current marketing practices and realign their plans to meet the new demands of this era.

Marketers are the pioneers in bringing new technologies to developing nations. Their successes and failures will determine the direction global marketing will take and the speed with which it will be embraced. Actions of international marketers will influence every component of the marketing environments: competitive, economic, social-cultural, political-legal, and technological.

The greatest competitive advantages will belong to those marketers who capitalize on the similarities of their target markets and adapt to the differences. In some instances, the actions of marketers today help determine the rules and regulations of tomorrow. Marketers need flexible and broad views of an increasingly complex customer. Goods and services will likely become more customized as they are introduced in foreign markets—yet some recognizable brands seem to remain universally popular just as they are. New and better products in developing markets will create and maintain relationships for the future. ◆◆◆

REVIEW OF CHAPTER OBJECTIVES

① **Describe the importance of global marketing from the perspectives of the individual firm and the nation.**

Global marketing expands a company's market, allows firms to grow, and makes them less dependent on their own country's economy for success. For the nation, global trade provides a source of needed raw materials and other products not available domestically in sufficient amounts, opens up new markets to serve with domestic output, and converts countries and their citizens into partners in the search for high-quality products at the lowest possible prices. Companies find that global marketing and international trade can help them meet customer demand, reduce certain costs, provide information on markets around the world, and increase employment.

② **Identify the major components of the environment for global marketing.**

The major components of the international environment are competitive, economic, social-cultural, political-legal, and technological. A country's infrastructure also plays an important role in determining how effective marketers will be in manufacturing, promoting, and distributing their goods and services.

③ **Outline the basic functions of GATT, WTO, NAFTA, FTAA, and the European Union.**

The General Agreement on Tariffs and Trade is an accord that has substantially reduced tariffs. The World Trade Organization oversees GATT agreements, mediates disputes, and tries to reduce trade barriers throughout the world. The North American Free Trade Agreement removes trade restrictions among Canada, Mexico, and the United States. The proposed Free Trade Area of the Americas seeks to create a free trade area covering the entire Western Hemisphere. The European Union is an economic and monetary union whose goal is to remove all barriers to free trade among its members.

④ **Identify the alternative strategies for entering international markets.**

Several strategies are available to marketers, including exporting, importing, franchising, foreign licensing, subcontracting, and direct investment. This progression moves from the least to the most involvement by a firm.

⑤ **Differentiate between a global marketing strategy and a multi-domestic marketing strategy.**

A global marketing strategy defines a standard marketing mix and implements it with minimal modifications in all foreign markets. A multi-domestic marketing strategy requires firms to customize their marketing decisions to reach individual marketplaces.

⑥ **Describe the alternative marketing mix strategies used in global marketing and explain the attractiveness of Canada as a target market for international marketers.**

Product and promotional strategies include the following: straight extension, promotion adaptation, product adaptation, dual adaptation, and product invention. Marketers may also choose among distribution, pricing, and countertrade strategies.

Canada is attractive as a target market for marketers because it is close to the United States and has high levels of discretionary income, political stability, a relatively favourable attitude toward foreign investment, and a relatively well-controlled economy.

assessment check answers ✓

1.1 Define *importing* and *exporting*.
Importing involves purchasing foreign goods and services. Exporting refers to marketing domestically produced goods and services abroad.

1.2 What must global marketers be able to do effectively to reach international markets?
Global marketers must be able to adapt their goods and services to local preferences.

2.1 What are the three criteria that determine a nation's prospects as a host for international business expansion?
A nation's size, per capita income, and stage of economic development determine its prospects as a host for international business expansion.

2.2 What are the two major categories of trade barriers?
The two categories of trade barriers are tariffs and nontariffs.

3.1 What is the World Trade Organization (WTO)?
The World Trade Organization (WTO) oversees GATT agreements and mediates disputes. It also continues efforts to reduce trade barriers around the world.

3.2 What countries are parties to NAFTA?
The United States, Canada, and Mexico are parties to NAFTA.

3.3 What is the goal of the European Union (EU)?
The European Union seeks to remove all barriers to free trade among its members and strengthen its position in the world as an economic and political power.

4.1 What are the three basic strategies for entering global markets?
The three basic strategies are importing and exporting, contractual agreements, and international direct investment.

4.2 What is a franchise?
A franchise is a contractual agreement in which a wholesaler or retailer (the franchisee) agrees to meet the operating requirements of a manufacturer or other franchiser.

4.3 What is international direct investment?
International direct investment is direct investment in foreign firms, production, and marketing facilities.

5.1 What is a multinational corporation?
A multinational corporation is a firm with significant operations and marketing activities outside the home country.

5.2 What is the difference between a global marketing strategy and a multi-domestic marketing strategy?
A global marketing strategy defines a marketing mix and implements it with minimal modifications in all foreign markets. A multi-domestic marketing strategy requires that firms customize their marketing decisions to reach individual marketplaces.

6.1 What are the five strategies for selecting the most appropriate product and promotion strategy for a specific international market?
The five strategies are the following: straight extension, promotion adaptation, product adaptation, dual adaptation, and product invention.

6.2 What is countertrade?
Countertrade is a form of exporting in which a firm barters products rather than selling them for cash.

6.3 What characteristics of Canada make it an inviting target for international marketers?
Canada is an inviting target because it offers access to North American markets, has high levels of discretionary income, has political stability, has a generally favourable attitude toward foreign investment, and has a relatively well-controlled economy.

MARKETING TERMS YOU NEED TO KNOW

These terms are printed in blue in the text. They are defined in the margins of the chapter and in the Glossary that begins on p. G-1.

exporting 190
importing 190
exchange rate 194
political risk assessment (PRA) 196
International Organization for
    Standardization (ISO) certification 197
tariff 198
free trade area 200
customs union 200
common market 200

General Agreement on Tariffs and Trade
    (GATT) 200
World Trade Organization (WTO) 201
North American Free Trade Agreement
    (NAFTA) 201
Free Trade Area of the Americas
    (FTAA) 201
European Union (EU) 201
self-reference criteria 203
franchise 205

foreign licensing 205
subcontracting 205
multinational corporation 206
global marketing strategy 207
multi-domestic marketing strategy 207
countertrade 209

PROJECT AND TEAMWORK EXERCISES

1. Imagine that you and a classmate are marketers for one of the following companies: Apple Inc., Burger King, General Mills, or Mattel Toys. Choose one of the following markets into which your company could expand: Mexico, India, or China. Research the country's infrastructure, social-cultural environment, technological environment, and any trade barriers your firm might encounter. Then present your findings to the class, with a conclusion on whether you think the expansion would be beneficial.

2. Assume you are a marketer for Weight Watchers International, a global company that holds meetings in more than 25 countries. With a classmate, identify a country that Weight Watchers has not yet reached and write a brief plan for entering that country's market. Then create a print ad for that market (you can write the ad copy in English). It may be helpful to visit the Weight Watchers website or Facebook page for some ideas.

3. Rio de Janeiro, Brazil, is hosting the 2016 Summer Olympics. By yourself or with a classmate, identify a company that might benefit from promoting its goods or services at the Rio de Janeiro Olympics. In a presentation, describe which strategy you would use: straight extension, product or promotion adaptation, dual adaptation, or product invention.

4. Suppose you work for a firm that is getting ready to introduce a tablet computer to the Chinese marketplace. With a classmate, decide which strategies your firm could use most effectively for entering this market. Present your ideas either in writing or to the class.

5. Chinese automaker Geely (pronounced *jeely*) announced plans to enter the North American market. With a classmate, research Geely to find out more about the cars, then create an ad for the firm, targeting Canadian consumers.

CRITICAL THINKING EXERCISES

1. Few elements in the global marketing environment are more difficult to overcome than the unexpected, such as natural disasters or outbreaks of disease such as the avian flu. Travel may be curtailed or halted by law, by a breakdown in infrastructure, or simply by fear on the part of consumers. Suppose you work for a firm that has resorts on several continents. As a marketer, what kinds of contingency plans might you recommend for your firm in the event of an unexpected disaster?

2. Zippo lighters have been around for decades. But as the number of smokers in Canada continues to decline, Zippo has spent the last half century scouting the world for new markets. Today, Zippo is a status symbol among Chinese consumers, who prefer North American products. Recently, Zippo also broadened its product line to include watches,

writing instruments, and items for outdoor enthusiasts. Can you think of other product lines that would be logical extensions for Zippo? And if Zippo decided to introduce additional product lines, which would work better: a global marketing strategy or a multi-domestic strategy? Explain the reasons for your choice.

3. Do you agree with the goals and ideas of the proposed FTAA? Why or why not?

4. Do you agree with countertrade as a legitimate form of conducting business? Why or why not? Describe a countertrade agreement that Microsoft might make in another country.

5. Foreign investment continues to grow in Canada. Do you think this is a positive trend for Canadian businesses and consumers? Why or why not?

ETHICS EXERCISE

Cheap—and illegal—copies of pirated popular movies, video games, and music are often available for sale in Asia within days of their worldwide release. The entertainment industry has so far had little success in stopping the flow of these copies into consumers' hands. Do you think multinational economic communities should be more effective at combating piracy? Why or why not? What actions could they take?

CASE 7.1

The Changing Global Consumer

The demographics of the global consumer are changing. These changes are the results of economic shifts throughout the world. For the first time in over 100 years, the combined output of China, India, and Brazil equalled that of Canada, Germany, the United States, Italy, France, and the United Kingdom combined. This represents a major movement of economic power from North America and Europe to Asia, South America, and Africa and has implications for marketers throughout the world.

One major change for marketers is the growing middle class in areas of the world like China, India, Africa, and parts of Central and South America. The growth in Asian and African economies means that there is a significant movement of poor into middle class. Middle-class consumers have more discretionary income to spend on goods and services.

The increase in the number of middle-class consumers in areas like China, India, and Africa presents both an opportunity and a challenge to marketers. The growth of this segment of the population has not followed a uniform pattern; some areas have seen a rapid growth of middle-class consumers, while other areas have seen a growing period followed by a slump. There are some general trends, however, such as the movement of the population into urban areas.

Experts predict that the middle class in China will continue to grow at a fast pace for the next decade, making up over 50 percent of the population or 400 million people by 2020. Today 85 percent of the Chinese middle class live in the wealthiest 100 cities but the growth of the middle class is expected to include three times as many urban locations during this growth period. These consumers are expected to increase their spending on personal items, education, transportation, and communications. The number of seniors in the middle class is also expected to increase. The older consumers will be more cautious with their spending, save more, and be less likely to travel or purchase expensive clothing.

The middle class in India will face a slightly different pattern of growth in the next decade than the Chinese. India's economy will experience more peaks and troughs rather than seeing a steady upward climb, according to recent studies. The middle class in India fits into the upper-middle-class segment with fewer in the lower end of the middle-class range. The top 20 percent of Indian households account for the majority of spending with some predictions being as high as over half. The majority of the Indian population does not earn a regular wage; only 40 percent of those living in cities and 10 percent of the rural population are employed in jobs with regular paycheques. The remainder are classified as self-employed. The self-employed will see greater fluctuations in their earnings.

One of the least-researched groups of consumers is the growing middle class in areas of Africa. Africa still has a large number of people living in poverty and high unemployment in many areas, but there are pockets of Africa where economic growth is equal to that of the Middle East. Middle-class African consumers are very positive about their future and expect to be better off in the future. More than half of Africans have access to the Internet. Contrary to popular belief, this segment is very brand conscious and values quality. They want the latest styles and features and a shopping experience that is up to date.

Whether the predictions of experts about the growing middle class in China, India, and Africa come true or not, it is a safe bet that the shift in economic power from North America to these regions will continue.

Questions for Critical Thinking

1. If you are the marketing manager for a consumer product company, how would you take advantage of these untapped markets?
2. If you were going to introduce a new product into India, China, or Africa, would you use the same strategy for each region? Why or why not?

Sources: Damian Hattingh, Bill Russo, Ade Sun-Basorun, and Arend Van Wamelen, "The Rise of the African Consumer: A Report from McKinsey's Africa Consumer Insights Center," October 2012, McKinsey & Company website, **www.mckinsey .com**; Rama Bijapurkar, "The Future of Indian Consumer Markets," Livemint & *The Wall Street Journal*, December 25, 2013, **www.livemint.com**; Yuval Atsmon and Max Magni, "Meet the Chinese Consumer of 2020," March 2012, McKinsey & Company website, **www.mckinsey.com**; Richard Warnica, "Reversal of Fortune," *Canadian Business*, July 13, 2013, pp. 32–36.

CASE 7.2

Starbucks Takes Coffee to India

Although India has long been a tea-drinking culture, the country's southern area is home to huge coffee farms. And thanks to a growing youth market and an increasingly comfortable middle class, more of India's 1.2 billion people are discovering the joys of coffee every year.

Enter Starbucks.

The coffee giant is making a later debut in the Indian market than it planned, after outlasting the government's reluctance to upset local firms by allowing foreign business ownership. To comply with regulations, Starbucks has signed a 50-50 partnership with Tata Global Beverages, the country's largest coffee producer and owner of a hotel chain and in-flight food service, which opens two more business avenues for its partner.

Starbucks is focusing initially on retail stores and hopes to open 50 cafés in Mumbai and New Delhi in its first year. In its favour are huge momentum from its U.S. success, its status as an "aspirational brand" that represents affordable luxury to many Indians, and the desire among India's youth for an inexpensive place to socialize away from home and parents. Tata's local expertise will help Starbucks overcome some deficiencies of the country's infrastructure, such as still-developing road and rail systems.

Challenges Starbucks faces in India include the success of a home-grown competitor: Café Coffee Day recently expanded to 1,200 stores in 175 cities. Other opportunistic competitors include Lavarazza from Italy and Coffee Bean & Tea Leaf from California. Starbucks will also have to overcome price resistance; Café Coffee Day sells its small cappuccino for about $1. Finally, as one industry analyst observed, "There are certain things that different cultures never accept." Starbucks will need to correctly adapt its business and customer strategies, and its product offerings, to India's unique and vibrant culture.

Starbucks is pinning its hopes on the 25 percent growth recently observed in India's coffee-drinking market. The head of one Indian consulting firm sees no reason why the chain could not successfully expand to 5,000 stores over the long term. If Starbucks targets only the top 20 percent of India's population, he says, that market is the size of the United States.

Questions for Critical Thinking

1. How can Starbucks best adapt its model for its cafés and menus to a young and middle-class Indian market?
2. What can Starbucks do to compensate for competitors taking advantage of its late entry to the Indian market?

Sources: Elliot Hannon, "Will Global Coffee Giant Starbucks Conquer India?" *Time*, January 31, 2012, **http://globalspin.blogs.time.com**; Vikas Baja, "After a Year of Delays, the First Starbucks Is to Open in Tea-Loving India This Fall," *The New York Times*, January 30, 2012, **www.nytimes.com**; Melissa Allison, "Finally Starbucks Announces Plans for India Debut," *The Seattle Times*, January 30, 2012, **http://seattletimes.nwsource.com**.

chapter 8

Marketing Research, Decision Support Systems, and Sales Forecasting

CHAPTER OBJECTIVES

(1) Describe the development of the marketing research function and its major activities.

(2) Explain the steps in the marketing research process.

(3) Distinguish between primary and secondary data and identify the sources of each type.

(4) Explain the different sampling techniques used by marketing researchers and identify the methods by which marketing researchers collect primary data.

(5) Explain the challenges of conducting marketing research in global markets and outline the most important uses of computer technology in marketing research.

(6) Identify the major types of forecasting methods.

THE FUTURE OF MARKETING RESEARCH: BIG DATA

"Big Data" is a term that has become almost synonymous with market research. It refers to data that are collected from many interactions customers have with an organization. The data from all these interactions are collected into a database that analysts can integrate into the organization's decision making. The ideal situation is for all this integration and analysis to be accomplished in real time. Companies are making steady progress to that point, but most aren't there yet.

A recent study found that 29 percent of organizations felt they had too little data and a further 39 percent said their data were not collected frequently enough or quickly enough to make real-time, market-driven decisions. This study also showed that most organizations felt that such data-driven marketing would be necessary in the future if firms wanted to be successful.

One company that uses the data they collect to better understand their customers' behaviour is Target Stores. The large U.S. retailer, which recently expanded into Canada, is acknowledged as one of the world's most savvy marketers around, thanks to its long practice of collecting information about its customers. Target assigns loyal buyers a unique identifier called a Guest ID number, which records demographic information like customers' age, income, marital status, credit cards carried, neighbourhood, and even the distance they live from the store. The Guest ID program tracks information supplied when customers pay with credit cards, use coupons, fill out surveys or rebate slips, call customer service, or visit Target's website. And, like most other major retailers, Target can buy additional market research information that delves even deeper into customers' personal history and buying habits. As one marketing research consultant said, "We're living through a golden age of behavioural research."

Target's marketing analysts devise ways of sifting all its market and customer data in order to predict purchases and develop more effective marketing programs. For instance, the company uses customer data to send customized coupon booklets featuring all the grocery items a customer purchased the preceding week. A former scientist for Amazon.com agrees that such data-crunching has risen to the top of many marketers' agendas: "Mathematicians are suddenly sexy," he says.

Shopping routines are particularly hard to break, which is one reason it is so important to a company like Target to find out which cues and rewards will encourage retail habits that lead to its doors. Target would like to pinpoint customers who are shopping for very special nonroutine occasions, such as the birth of a child, when it seems the one thing most people can count on is that all their habits will be disrupted and new ones will be formed.

With all the information it collects, says Target, it may someday be sending you coupons for products before you know you want them.

The collection of large amounts of data about individuals is not without some controversy. Many people feel the collection of so much information about our day-to-day habits is an invasion of privacy. Others feel that unless companies really know what they are doing with the analysis of the data they will produce information that is incorrect.[1]

connecting with customers

While the principle "Know your audience" applies to all companies, it is particularly important in competitive industries like retail, where businesses engage daily in an all-out battle to attract—and keep—customers. Understanding the customer mind-set is a critical and ongoing task.

Chapter Overview

Collecting and managing information about what customers need and want is a challenging task for any marketer. Marketing research is the process of collecting and using information for marketing decision making. Data come from a variety of sources. Some results come from well-planned studies designed to elicit specific information. Other valuable information comes from sales force reports, accounting records, and published reports. Still other data emerge from controlled experiments and computer simulations. Thanks to new database technologies, some data that companies collect are compiled for them by research specialists, and some are collected and compiled by in-house staff. Marketing research, by presenting pertinent information in a useful format, aids decision makers in analyzing data and in suggesting possible actions.

This chapter discusses the marketing research function. Marketers use research to understand their customers, target customer segments, and develop long-term customer relationships—all keys to profitability. Information collected through marketing research underlies much of the material on market segmentation discussed in the following chapter. Clearly, the marketing research function is the primary source of the information needed to make effective marketing decisions. The use of technology to mine data and gather business and competitive intelligence is also discussed, as is technology's vast impact on marketing research decision making and planning. This chapter also explains how marketing research techniques are used to make accurate sales forecasts, a critical component of marketing planning. ◆◆◆

---

① **Describe the development of the marketing research function and its major activities.**

marketing research
Process of collecting and using information for marketing decision making.

Marketoid

Canadian households spend more than $55,000 annually on goods and services.

THE MARKETING RESEARCH FUNCTION

Before looking at how marketing research is conducted, we must first examine its historical development, the people and organizations it involves, and the activities it entails. Because an underlying purpose of research is to find out more about consumers, research is clearly central to effective customer satisfaction and customer relationship programs. Media technologies such as the Internet and virtual reality are opening up new channels through which researchers can tap into consumer information.

DEVELOPMENT OF THE MARKETING RESEARCH FUNCTION

More than 130 years have passed since the first organized marketing research project was undertaken in 1879. A second important milestone in the development of marketing research occurred 32 years later, when the first commercial research department was organized at Curtis Publishing, publishers of *The Saturday Evening Post.*

Most early research gathered little more than written testimonials from purchasers of firms' products. Research methods became more sophisticated during the 1930s as the development of statistical techniques led to refinements in sampling procedures and greater accuracy in research findings.

In recent years, advances in computer technology have significantly changed the complexion of marketing research. Besides accelerating the pace and broadening the base of data collection, computers have aided marketers in making informed decisions about problems and opportunities. Simulations, for example, allow marketers to evaluate alternatives by posing "what-if" questions. Marketing researchers at many consumer goods firms simulate product introductions through computer programs to determine whether to risk real-world product launches or even to subject products to test marketing.

WHO CONDUCTS MARKETING RESEARCH?

The size and organizational form of the marketing research function are usually tied to the structure of the company. Some firms organize research units to support different product lines, brands, or geographic areas. Others organize their research functions according to the types of research they need performed, such as sales analysis, new-product development, advertising evaluation, or sales forecasting.

Many firms outsource their research needs and thus depend on independent marketing research firms. These independent organizations might specialize in handling just part of a larger study, such as conducting consumer interviews. Firms can also contract out entire research studies.

Marketers usually decide whether to conduct a study internally or through an outside organization based on cost. Another major consideration is the reliability and accuracy of the information collected by an outside organization. Because collecting marketing data is what these outside organizations do full time, the information they gather is often more thorough and accurate than that collected by less experienced in-house staff. Often, an outside marketing research firm can provide technical assistance and expertise not available within the company's marketing unit. Interaction with outside suppliers also helps to ensure that a researcher does not conduct a study only to validate a favourite viewpoint or preferred option.

The Marketing Research and Intelligence Association is a not-for-profit association with chapters across Canada representing all aspects of the research industry.

Marketing Research and Intelligence Association

Some companies combine their market research with environmental issues as described in the "Marketing: Making Your World Better" feature.

Marketing research companies range in size from sole proprietorships to national and international firms such as Nielsen Company. They can be classified as syndicated services,

---

MARKETING: MAKING YOUR WORLD BETTER — Loyalty Cards Go Green

COMPANY reward programs were originally designed to accomplish two things: reward loyal customers and collect information about those customers. One of the best known of these programs is LoyalOne. The company began operations in 1991 as the Air Miles Reward Program with a unique concept. Before the Air Miles Reward Program, loyalty programs were company specific so information collected was limited to one company. The Air Miles concept was simple—one company in an industry sector could offer common rewards and receive customer information gathered from all participating companies. The company has grown from the simple Air Miles Program to assisting its clients with analysis of the results of its research and even assisting with the communication associated with its loyalty programs.

With regard to market research, the company can track sales by segment, number of shoppers in a segment that are shopping at a particular retail store, and whether that segment is likely to increase or decrease their sales. In one case, LoyaltyOne analysis discovered that a retailer who was relying on sales trends to measure success was not attracting the customer segments it was aiming for.

The company also is interested in good environmental practices. Its Air Miles for Social Change Program works with organizations and governments to increase the use of public transit, encourages people to more active, and promotes energy conservation.

This interest does not stop with its rewards program. The company itself has several programs to encourage its employees to be environmentally friendly and promote a positive work environment. Internal programs are in place to reduce waste, conserve energy, and minimize the company's impact on climate. These programs are working. The company has received a number of awards, including Best Employer in Canada, Canada's Top 100 Employers, and Canada's Greenest Employer.

Sources: Brian Ross, "Tale of Two Segments: Using Data to Reach High-Potential Customers," *Marketing*, November 12, 2012, **www.marketingmag.ca**; Jeffrey Berry, "Column: The Secret to Apps That 'Stick,'" *Marketing*, October 30, 2013, **www.marketingmag.ca**; Rebecca Harris, "Direct Antidote Rebrands as Squareknot," *Marketing*, May 8, 2013, **www.marketingmag.ca**; LoyaltyOne company website, **www.loyalty.com**, accessed January 11, 2014.

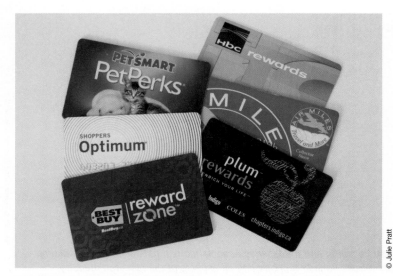

© Julie Pratt

Loyalty programs reward loyal customers and collect valuable information about consumer behaviour.

syndicated service
Organization that provides standardized data to all customers.

Marketoid

The average Canadian household increases its household spending by more than 2 percent annually.

full-service research supplier Marketing research organization that contracts with clients to conduct complete marketing research projects.

limited-service research supplier Marketing research firm that specializes in a limited number of research activities, such as conducting field interviews or performing data processing.

full-service suppliers, or limited-service suppliers, depending on the types of services they offer to clients. Some full-service organizations are also willing to take on limited-service activities.

Syndicated Services

An organization that regularly provides a standardised set of data to all customers is called a **syndicated service**. Companies providing syndicated product research may base their reports on personal interviews, exposure to advertising, or point-of-sale scanner data captured from a retail store. Clients include advertisers, advertising agencies, magazines, newspapers, broadcasters, and cable TV networks.

One syndicated service provider is J.D. Power and Associates, a global marketing information firm that specializes in surveying customer satisfaction, product quality, and buyer behaviour. Among its customers are companies in the telecommunications, travel and hotel, marine, utilities, health care, building, consumer electronics, automotive, and financial services industries.[2]

Full-Service Research Suppliers

An organization that contracts with clients to conduct complete marketing research projects is called a **full-service research supplier**. Environics Research Group, which has offices across Canada and the United States, is an example of a full-service company.[3] A full-service supplier becomes the client's marketing research arm, performing all the steps in the marketing research process (discussed later in this chapter).

Limited-Service Research Suppliers

A marketing research firm that specializes in a limited number of activities, such as conducting field interviews or performing data processing, is called a **limited-service research supplier**. Syndicated services can also be considered a type of limited-service research supplier.

Customer Satisfaction Measurement Programs

In their marketing research, firms often focus on tracking the satisfaction levels of current customers. For example, one research firm charges a monthly fee and provides services such as designing and managing a firm's customer feedback area on its website to moderating online discussion groups and analyzing comments.[4] Some marketers have gained valuable insights by tracking the dissatisfaction that led customers to abandon certain products for those of competitors. Some customer defections are only partial; customers may remain somewhat satisfied with a business but not completely satisfied. Such attitudes could lead them to take their business elsewhere. Studying the underlying causes of customer defections, even partial defections, can be useful for identifying problem areas that need attention.

Some organizations conduct their own measurement programs through online polls and surveys. Some fast-food restaurants and retailers have their employees point out special codes printed on their receipts. Entering the code on the company website brings up a customer satisfaction survey that offers respondents a chance to win prizes.[5]

---

assessment check 1 ✓

1.1 Identify the different classifications of marketing research suppliers and explain how they differ from one another.

1.2 What research methods can be used to measure customer satisfaction?

THE MARKETING RESEARCH PROCESS

② Explain the steps
in the marketing
research process.

As discussed earlier, business executives rely on marketing research to provide the information they need to make effective decisions regarding their firm's current and future activities. The chances of making good decisions improve when the right information is provided at the right time during decision making. To achieve this goal, marketing researchers often follow the six-step process shown in Figure 8.1. In the initial stages, researchers define the problem, conduct exploratory research, and formulate a hypothesis to be tested. Next, they create a design for the research study and collect needed data. Finally, researchers interpret and present the research information. The following sections take a closer look at each step of the marketing research process.

DEFINE THE PROBLEM

A popular anecdote advises that well-defined problems or research questions are half-solved. A well-defined problem permits the researcher to focus on securing the exact information needed for the solution. Defining a question that is concise increases the speed and accuracy of the research process.

Researchers must carefully avoid confusing symptoms of a problem with the problem itself. A symptom merely alerts marketers that a problem exists. For example, suppose that a maker of frozen pizzas sees its market share drop from 8 to 5 percent in six months. The loss of market share is a symptom of a problem the company must solve. To define the problem, the firm must look for the underlying causes of its market share loss.

A logical starting point in identifying the problem might be to evaluate the firm's target market and marketing mix elements. Suppose, for example, a firm has recently changed its promotional strategies. Research might then seek to answer the question "What must we do to improve the effectiveness of our marketing mix?" The firm's marketers might also look at possible environmental changes. Perhaps a new competitor entered the firm's market. Decision makers will need information to help answer the question "What must we do to distinguish our company from the new competitor?"

When marketers at Target came up with what they called the "PFresh" concept—adding grocery departments in Target stores—the company first tested the concept for two years in two locations. After the company implemented PFresh in over 100 stores and saw sales rise over $4.5 million, it expanded more broadly. Target used the same concept when it opened its stores in Canada by partnering with Sobeys.[6]

CONDUCT EXPLORATORY RESEARCH

Once a firm has defined the question it wants to answer, researchers can begin exploratory research. **Exploratory research** seeks to discover the cause of a specific problem by discussing the problem with informed sources both within and outside the firm and by examining data from other information sources. Marketers might talk with their wholesalers, retailers, and customers. They might also ask for input from the sales force or look for overall market clues. The term *informal investigation* is often used for exploratory interviews with informed individuals outside the researchers' firms.

In addition, exploratory research can include evaluation of company records, such as sales and profit analyses, and available competitive data. Marketing researchers often refer to internal data collection as a situation analysis. Typical sources of internal

Marketoid

**Households in Alberta
spend the most with
an average household
spending more than
$64,000 on goods and
services annually.**

exploratory research
Process of discussing
a marketing problem
with informed sources
both within and outside
the firm and examining
information from
secondary sources.

figure 8.1

The Marketing Research Process

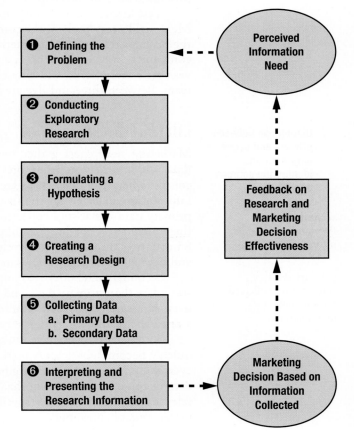

sales analysis In-depth evaluation of a firm's sales.

hypothesis Tentative explanation for some specific event.

data are sales records, financial statements, and marketing cost analyses. For example, marketers analyze sales performance records. Easily prepared from company invoices or a computer database system, this sales analysis typically compares actual and expected sales based on a detailed sales forecast by territory, product, customer, and salesperson. One company that performs this type of analysis is Randa Luggage, the global designer and licensed distributor of upscale luggage brands like Anne Klein, Perry Ellis, and Nautica. The firm recently installed a centralized software system to track the comings and goings of the millions of items it distributes annually. Reports trigger restocking and inventory decisions and provide information for financial statements and reporting.[7] Other types of internal data are identified in Table 8.1 on page 225.

FORMULATE A HYPOTHESIS

After defining the problem and conducting an exploratory investigation, the marketer needs to formulate a hypothesis—a tentative explanation for some specific event. A hypothesis is a statement about the relationship among variables that carries clear implications for testing this relationship. It sets the stage for more in-depth research by further clarifying what researchers need to test. For example, a restaurant might want to see whether good customer service is related to its increased sales, so its marketers would conduct a survey of customers to test this hypothesis.

Not all studies test specific hypotheses; however, a carefully designed study can benefit from the rigour introduced by developing a hypothesis before beginning data collection and analysis.

CREATE A RESEARCH DESIGN

To test hypotheses and find solutions to marketing problems, a marketer creates a research design, a master plan or model for conducting marketing research. In planning a research project, marketers must be sure that the study will measure what they intend to measure. A second important research design consideration is the selection of respondents. Marketing researchers use sampling techniques (discussed later in the chapter) to determine which consumers to include in their studies.

Test kitchens and willing research participants are indispensable in the fast-food business. At McDonald's test kitchen, the company reviews 1,800 new menu ideas each year. After input from the business research and marketing teams about where the firm is looking to pick up business, the company's and suppliers' chefs and suppliers get together for brainstorming. About 30 ideas each year get a closer look, and about half of those are presented to the fast-food chain's management team. Between three and five are actually launched in a given year.[8]

(3) **Distinguish between primary and secondary data and identify the sources of each type.**

secondary data Previously published information.

primary data Information collected for a specific investigation.

COLLECT DATA

Marketing researchers gather two kinds of data: secondary data and primary data. Secondary data are information from previously published or compiled sources. Data Statistics Canada collects when it does a census are secondary data when used by companies. Primary data refer to information collected for the first time specifically for a marketing research study. An example of primary data is statistics collected by a company from a survey that asks current customers about their preferences for product improvements. Global research firm Ipsos collects primary data in 85 countries throughout the world. The company conducts thousands of projects and focus groups and over 70 million interviews in a year and employs over 16,000 people.[9]

Secondary data offer two important advantages: (1) it is almost always less expensive to gather secondary than primary data, and (2) researchers usually spend less time to locate and use secondary data. A research study that requires primary data may take three to four months to complete, while a researcher can often gather secondary data in a matter of days.

Secondary data do have limitations that primary data do not. First, published information can quickly become obsolete. A marketer analyzing the population of various areas may discover that even the most recent census figures are already out of date because of rapid growth and changing demographics. Second, published data collected for an unrelated purpose may not be completely relevant to the marketer's specific needs. For example, census data do not reveal the brand preferences of consumers.

Although research to gather primary data can cost more and take longer, the results can provide richer, more detailed information than secondary data offer. The choice between secondary and primary data is tied to cost, applicability, and effectiveness. Many marketing research projects combine secondary and primary data to fully answer marketing questions. This chapter examines specific methods for collecting both secondary and primary data in later sections.

> **assessment check 2** ✓
>
> 2.1 What are the six steps in the marketing research process?
>
> 2.2 What is the goal of exploratory research?

INTERPRET AND PRESENT RESEARCH INFORMATION

The final step in the marketing research process is to interpret the findings and present them to decision makers in a format that allows managers to make effective judgments. Possible differences in interpretations of research results may occur between marketing researchers and their audiences due to differing backgrounds, levels of knowledge, and experience. Both oral and written reports should be presented in a manner designed to minimize such misinterpretations.

Marketoid

The average Canadian household spends more than $11,000 on transportation annually.

Marketing researchers and research users must cooperate at every stage in the research process. Too many studies go unused because management considers the results are of little use, once they hear lengthy discussions of research limitations or unfamiliar terminology. Marketing researchers must remember to direct their reports toward management and not to other researchers. They should spell out their conclusions in clear and concise terms that can be put into action. Reports should confine technical details of the research methods to an appendix, if they are included at all. By presenting research results to all key executives at a single sitting, researchers can ensure that everyone will understand the findings. Decision makers can then quickly reach consensus on what the results mean and what actions are to be taken.

MARKETING RESEARCH METHODS

Clearly, data collection is an integral part of the marketing research process. One of the most time-consuming parts of collecting data is determining what method the marketer should use to obtain the data. This section discusses the most commonly used methods by which marketing researchers find both secondary and primary data.

SECONDARY DATA COLLECTION

Secondary data come from many sources. The overwhelming quantity of secondary data available at little or no cost challenges researchers to select only data that are relevant to the problem or issue being studied.

Secondary data consist of two types: internal and external data. Internal data, as discussed earlier, include sales records, product performance reviews, sales force activity reports, and marketing cost reports. External data come from a variety of sources, including government records, syndicated research services, and industry publications. Computerized databases provide access to vast amounts of data from both inside and outside an organization. The following sections on government data, private data, and online sources focus on databases and other external data sources available to marketing researchers.

Government Data

All levels of government—federal, provincial, and municipal—provide information, much of it free. The two largest sources of information are two federal government agencies, Statistics Canada (**www.statcan.gc.ca**) and Industry Canada (**www.ic.gc.ca**).

In early May every five years, Statistics Canada mails surveys to every home in Canada. In 2011, the census consisted of eight questions that had been used on the previous survey and two added questions on language. Another change that occurred in 2011 was the elimination of the longer version of the survey. For the first time, the questions that were in included in the second version of the questionnaire became part of the National Household Survey. The National Household Survey is conducted within a month of the census and covers approximately 4.5 million households.[10]

Industry Canada's website contains a wealth of data, including company directories, guides on business and the environment, and Industry Canada services. Marketers can use such secondary data to learn about markets and their customers.

Industry Canada's mission is to "foster a growing, competitive, knowledge-based Canadian economy." In order to achieve this mission, Industry Canada provides business and consumer information on its website, including information about consumer trends, laws, exporting, investing, and financing, as well as economic statistics.[11]

Provincial and municipal governments also provide information about their areas. Some of the information on their websites comes from Statistics Canada, but other information is collected locally. The aim of these government-sponsored websites is to provide relevant information quickly.

Private Data

Many private organizations provide information for marketing decision makers. A trade association may be an excellent source of data on activities in a particular industry. The advertising industry continuously collects data on audiences reached by various media. Business and trade magazines also publish a wide range of valuable data. General business magazines such as *Marketing, Strategy,* and *Canadian Business* can also be good sources. Because few libraries carry specialized trade journals, the best way to gather data from them is either directly from the publishers or through online periodical databases like ProQuest Direct's *ABI/Inform,* available at many libraries.

Several firms offer information to businesses by subscription. These companies provide global database services with continuing data on consumer attitudes, lifestyles, and buying behaviour in many countries.

Electronic systems that scan Universal Product Code (UPC) bar codes speed purchase transactions, and they also provide data used for inventory control, ordering, and delivery. Techniques that rely on radio-frequency identification (RFID) technology (tags that use a tiny chip with identification information that can be read by a scanner using radio waves) are in growing use. American Apparel, a rapidly growing chain of clothing stores, tested RFID tags for stocking and inventory replenishment in some of its locations. The company found the tags reduced internal shrinkage by as much as 75 percent in some stores and enabled customers to find more items in the right size and colour on the selling floor, increasing sales and freeing salespeople from restocking chores so they could spend more time helping shoppers. In addition, inventory counts that once occupied several salespeople for an entire day were more accurately handled by two people in a couple of hours. Based on its experience, American Apparel installed the RFID technology in all its stores.[12]

Online Sources of Secondary Data

The tools of cyberspace sometimes simplify the hunt for secondary data. Hundreds of databases and other sources of information are available online. A well-designed, Internet-based marketing research project can cost less yet yield faster results than offline research.

The Internet has spurred the growth of research aggregators—companies that acquire, catalogue, reformat, segment, and then resell premium research reports that have already been published. Aggregators put valuable data within reach of marketers who lack the time or the budget to commission custom research. Because Web technology makes their databases easy to search, aggregators are able to compile detailed, specialized reports quickly and cost-effectively.[13] Social networking sites also yield valuable marketing information. Social networks may also provide secondary private data. Google Analytics is a business tool for measuring online sales, tracking email, social media, and ad campaigns, and benchmarking key measures against competitors. Marketers use Google Analytics to collect information from sites mentioned on Twitter and other social media sites. Facebook has partnered with Nielsen Company to study the relationship between paid and unpaid advertising

Marketoid

Canadian households spend more than $7,500 annually on food.

table 8.1   *Sources of Secondary Data*

INTERNAL SOURCES OF SECONDARY DATA

Sales analysis	In-depth evaluation of a firm's sales by territory, product, customer, and salesperson
Accounting data	Using the firm's financial statements companies can compare their performance over a number of years.
Marketing cost analysis	The evaluation of expenses for tasks such as selling, warehousing, advertising, and delivery to determine the profitability of particular customers, territories, or product lines

EXTERNAL SOURCES OF SECONDARY DATA

Government data	All levels of government—federal, provincial, and municipal—provide information. The two sources from the federal government are Statistics Canada (**www.statcan.gc.ca**) and Industry Canada (**www.ic.gc.ca**).
Private data	Trade organizations, magazines, trade journals, periodic databases, research companies, data from UPC scanners, and RFID technology
Online sources	Aggregator companies and social networking sites

on brand awareness and engagement.[14] YouTube's Insight service gives its video-uploading account holders an array of statistics, graphs, and maps about the audiences they attract, far more specific than just the number of views it used to collect.[15]

However, marketers must carefully evaluate the validity of any information they find on the Internet. People without in-depth knowledge of a subject may post information. Similarly, Web pages might contain information gathered using questionable research methods. The phrase *caveat emptor* ("let the buyer beware") should guide evaluation of secondary data on the Internet. Table 8.1 provides a summary of sources of secondary data.

assessment check 3 ✓

3.1 Distinguish between primary and secondary data.

3.2 What are the major methods of collecting secondary data?

SAMPLING TECHNIQUES

Before undertaking a study to gather primary data, researchers must first identify which participants to include in the study. **Sampling** is the process of selecting survey respondents or research participants. This step is important because if a study fails to involve consumers who accurately reflect the target market, the research is likely to yield misleading conclusions.

The total group of people that the researcher wants to study is called the **population** or universe. For a political campaign study, the population would be all eligible voters. For research about a new lipstick line, it might be all women in a certain age bracket. The sample is a representative group chosen from this population. Researchers rarely gather information from a study's total population, resulting in a census. Unless the total population is small, the costs of a census are simply too high. Sometimes limitations can reduce the size of the sample. Online surveys often draw large self-selected, rather than random, groups of respondents who don't usually represent the total population. Vague questions and surveys that are too long further reduce the number of respondents and can skew the results even further.[16]

Samples can be classified as either probability samples or nonprobability samples. A **probability sample** is one that gives every member of the population a chance of being selected. Types of probability samples include simple random samples, stratified samples, and cluster samples.

In a simple random sample, every member of the relevant universe has an equal opportunity of selection. The weekly lotteries sponsored by provincial lottery organizations, such as British Columbia Lottery Corporation, where every numbered ball has an equal chance of dropping out of the machine, are an example of a simple random sample. In a stratified sample, randomly selected subsamples of different groups are represented in the total sample. Stratified samples provide efficient,

④ **Explain the different sampling techniques used by marketing researchers and identify the methods by which marketing researchers collect primary data.**

sampling Process of selecting survey respondents or research participants.

population Total group that researchers want to study.

probability sample Sample that gives every member of the population a chance of being selected.

representative groups that are relatively homogeneous for a certain characteristic for such studies as opinion polls, in which groups of individuals share various divergent viewpoints. In a cluster sample, researchers select a sample of subgroups (or clusters) from which they draw respondents. Each cluster reflects the diversity of the whole population being sampled. This cost-efficient type of probability sample is widely used when the entire population cannot be listed or enumerated.

nonprobability sample
Sample that involves personal judgment somewhere in the selection process.

In contrast, a **nonprobability sample** relies on personal judgment somewhere in the selection process. In other words, researchers decide which particular groups to study. Types of nonprobability samples are convenience samples and quota samples. A convenience sample is a nonprobability sample selected from among readily available respondents; this sample is often called an *accidental sample* because those included just happen to be in the place where the study is being conducted. Mall intercept surveys and TV call-in opinion polls are good examples. Marketing researchers sometimes use convenience samples in exploratory research but not in definitive studies. A quota sample is a nonprobability sample that is divided to maintain the proportion of certain characteristics among different segments or groups as is seen in the population as a whole. In other words, each field worker is assigned a quota that specifies the number and characteristics of the people to contact. It differs from a stratified sample, in which researchers select subsamples by some random process; in a quota sample, they hand-pick participants.

PRIMARY RESEARCH METHODS

Marketers use a variety of methods for conducting primary research, as Figure 8.2 shows. The principal methods for collecting primary data are observation, surveys and interviews, and controlled experiments. The choice among these methods depends on the issues under study and the decisions that marketers need to make. In some cases, researchers may decide to combine techniques during the research process.

Observation Method

In observational studies, researchers view the overt actions of subjects being studied. Marketers trying to understand how consumers behave in certain situations find observation to be a useful technique. Observation tactics may be as simple as counting the number of cars passing by a potential site for a fast-food restaurant or checking the licence plates at a shopping centre near a provincial border or near the Canada–U.S. border to determine where shoppers live.

Technological advances provide increasingly sophisticated ways for observing consumer behaviour. The television industry relies on data from people meters, which are electronic remote-control

figure 8.2

Types of Primary Research

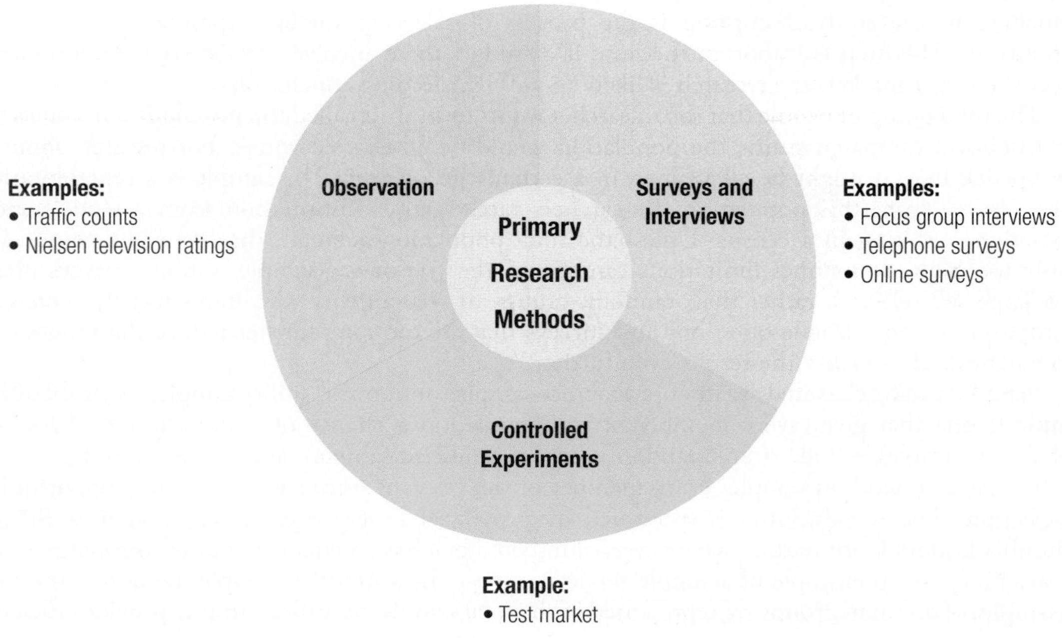

Examples:
- Traffic counts
- Nielsen television ratings

Observation

Surveys and Interviews

Examples:
- Focus group interviews
- Telephone surveys
- Online surveys

Primary Research Methods

Controlled Experiments

Example:
- Test market

devices that record the TV-viewing habits of individual household members to measure the popularity of TV shows. Traditional people meters require each viewer to press a button each time he or she turns on the TV, changes channels, or leaves the room.

Some observers expect that communications technology will also change the way consumers respond to advertising. Internet users are more willing than ever to use real money for purchases that arise during social gaming and social networking sessions. For instance, in *Diablo III*, a video game, players can sell items they discover while playing the game—or buy the loot they can't find while they play.[17]

Videotaping consumers in action is also gaining acceptance as a research technique. Cookware manufacturers may videotape consumers cooking in their own kitchens to evaluate how they use their pots and pans. A toothbrush manufacturer asked a marketing research firm to videotape consumers brushing their teeth and using mouthwash in its quest to develop products that would leave behind the sensation of cleanliness and freshness.

In an effort to understand what makes younger consumers tick, a trend-forecasting firm gathers the reflections of more than 30,000 teens in 40 markets across five continents. These primary data are used to create the firm's annual study report, a "living, breathing" document of teen insights.[18]

Interpretative Research—Ethnographic Studies

Another type of primary research is **interpretative research**, a method in which a researcher observes a customer or group of customers in their natural setting and interprets their behaviour based on an understanding of the social and cultural characteristics of that setting.

Interpretative research has attracted considerable interest in recent years. Developed by social anthropologists as a method for explaining behaviour that operates below the level of conscious thought, interpretative research can provide insights into consumer behaviour and ways in which consumers interact with brands.

In interpretative research, the researcher first spends an extensive amount of time studying the culture, and for that reason, the studies often are called *ethnographic* studies. The word *ethnographic* means that a researcher takes a cultural perspective of the population being studied. For that reason, interpretative research often is used to interpret consumer behaviour within a culture where language, ideals, values, and expectations are subject to different cultural influences. After experiencing a number of product failures in low-income markets in Latin America, Procter & Gamble (P&G) began an "immersion research" program called "Living It," in which P&G managers and executives spent time with low-income families around the world, living in their homes to develop a better understanding of their needs and desires. P&G's subsequent sales suggest that the effort was worthwhile. Among the mistakes the firm corrected was a low-sudsing detergent it introduced in Mexico, unaware that most of its customers there were manual labourers who associated suds with cleaning power.[19]

Interpretative research focuses on understanding the meaning of a product or the consumption experience in a consumer's life. Its methods capture consumers interacting with products in their environment—in other words, capturing what they actually do, not what they say they do. Typically, subjects are filmed in specific situations, such as socializing with friends in a bar for research into beverage consumption, or for extended periods of time for paid participants. Paid participants may be followed by a videographer who records their day-to-day movements and interactions, or they may film themselves. Some companies even pay consumers to wear mini-video cameras attached to visors and linked to a sound recorder. These systems record consumer behaviour while participants are shopping or doing chores.

An iPhone application developed by a British research agency allows ethnographic researchers to take photos, notes, and audio and video clips of subjects while conducting their studies. Users can organize the material by theme and send it to their email account to review it later.[20]

interpretative research Observational research method developed by social anthropologists in which customers are observed in their natural setting and their behaviour is interpreted based on an understanding of social and cultural characteristics; also known as *ethnography*, or going native.

Survey and Interview Methods

Observation alone cannot supply all the desired information. Researchers must ask questions to get information on attitudes, motives, and opinions. It is also difficult to get exact demographic information—such as income levels—from observation. To discover this information, researchers can use either interviews or questionnaires.

Marketoid

Canadian households spend more than $1,500 annually on communications.

Telephone Interviews

Many respondents are hesitant to give personal information about themselves over the telephone. Results may be biased by the omission of typical households where adults are off working during the day. Other households, particularly market segments such as single women and physicians, are likely to have unlisted numbers. While computerized random dialling can give access to unlisted numbers, it may be restricted in some areas. The Telecommunications Act excludes marketing research from the national Do Not Call Registry.[21]

The popularity of caller-ID systems to screen unwanted calls is another obstacle for telephone researchers.

Other obstacles restrict the usefulness of telephone surveys abroad. In areas where telephone ownership is rare, survey results will be highly biased. Telephone interviewing is also difficult in countries that lack directories or charge landline telephone customers on a per-minute basis, or where call volumes congest limited phone line capacity.

Personal Interviews

mall intercepts
Interviews conducted inside retail shopping centres.

The best means for obtaining detailed information about consumers is usually the personal interview because the interviewer can establish rapport with respondents and explain confusing or vague questions. In addition to contacting respondents at their homes or workplaces, marketing research firms can conduct interviews in rented space in shopping centres, where they gain wide access to potential buyers of the merchandise they are studying. These locations sometimes feature private interviewing space, videotape equipment, and food-preparation facilities for taste tests. As mentioned earlier, interviews conducted in shopping centres are typically called **mall intercepts**. Downtown retail districts and airports provide other valuable locations for marketing researchers.

Focus Groups

focus group
Simultaneous personal interview of a small group of individuals, which relies on group discussion about a certain topic.

Marketers also gather research information through the popular technique of focus group interviews. A **focus group** brings together 8 to 12 individuals in one location to discuss a subject of interest. Unlike other interview techniques that elicit information through a question-and-answer format, focus groups usually encourage a general discussion of a predetermined topic.

In a focus group, the leader, or moderator, typically begins by explaining the purpose of the meeting and suggesting an opening topic. The moderator's main purpose, however, is to stimulate interaction among group members to encourage their discussion of numerous points. The moderator may occasionally interject questions as catalysts to direct the group's discussion. The moderator's job is difficult, requiring preparation and group facilitation skills.

Focus group sessions often last one or two hours. Researchers usually record the discussion on tape, and observers frequently watch through a one-way mirror. Some research firms also allow clients to view focus groups in action through videoconferencing systems.

Focus groups are a particularly valuable tool for exploratory research, developing new-product ideas and preliminary testing of alternative marketing strategies. They can also aid in the development of well-structured questionnaires for larger-scale research.[22]

Researchers are finding ways to re-create the focus group environment over the Internet. With experienced moderators who have the technical skills to function fluently online, it is possible to gain valuable qualitative

Test kitchens inform marketers by allowing companies to introduce new products to a test market and avoid risking a real-world product launch that consumers might not like.

© AP Images/Larry Crowe

information at a fraction of the cost it takes to run a traditional focus group session. Online focus groups can be both cost and time efficient, with immediate results in the form of chat transcripts. The convenience of online conversations tends to improve attendance as well, particularly among those who are otherwise difficult to include, such as professionals and people who travel frequently, and the problem of peer pressure is virtually eliminated. Some drawbacks include the lack of ability to see body language and nonverbal cues, the difficulty of testing any products in which taste or smell are relevant, and the potential for samples to be nonrepresentative because they are limited to those who have Internet access and a certain comfort level with technology.

Electronic systems that scan UPC bar codes speed purchase decisions and allow customers to check a price before committing to the purchase.

Mail Surveys

Although personal interviews can provide very detailed information, cost considerations usually prevent an organization from using personal interviews in a large-scale study. Mail surveys can help marketers track consumer attitudes through ongoing research.

Mail questionnaires do, however, have several limitations: the response rate can be low, mail surveys usually take a considerably longer time to conduct, and unanticipated questions may occur. Researchers try to minimize these limitations by carefully developing and pretesting questionnaires. Researchers can boost response rates by keeping questionnaires short and by offering incentives—typically discount coupons or money.

Online Surveys and Other Internet-Based Methods

The growing population of Internet users has spurred researchers to conduct online surveys. For some tips on creating surveys for mobile devices, see the "Career Readiness" feature.

Businesses and other organizations are increasingly including questionnaires on their Web pages to solicit information about consumer demographics, attitudes, and comments and suggestions for improving goods and services or improving marketing messages. Online polling is also increasingly popular. Worldwide, nearly one minute of every five that consumers spend online is spent on social networking sites, and this trend shows no sign of slowing down. Facebook has the largest number of unique users—more than 800 million users worldwide.[23] While companies have struggled for ways to measure the impact of social media, more tools than ever exist for tracking which ones drive traffic to any particular site or sites and thus would be the best sites on which to post polls and questionnaires.

CAREER READINESS   Designing Surveys for Mobile Devices

MARKETING surveys are increasingly migrating to mobile devices. But to earn a high response rate, such mobile questionnaires need to specifically reflect the electronic environment. Here are some tips for designing mobile surveys that get responses.

1. Design the survey with the mobile environment in mind. Consider the smartphone's smaller screen, for instance, and choose larger type and colours with good contrast.
2. Limit your use of images. Some email clients block them, and they slow down loading time on mobile devices.
3. Keep your survey short and simple. Try to reduce the amount of scrolling up and down respondents have to do for each question, and limit yourself to no more than 12 questions.

4. Offer an incentive. It doesn't have to be big, but incentives have been shown to draw five times as many responses.
5. Make sure you don't require the respondent to navigate away to a separate browser or interrupt the task he or she is doing.
6. Where possible, try to offer the choice to complete the survey on a computer. Completing a survey on a mobile device can take as much as 50 percent longer.

Sources: Andrew Grenville, "When Is Long and Slow More Satisfying? When It's Mobile Research," Vision Critical.com, April 10, 2012, **http://vcu .visioncritical.com**; Sherrie Mersdorf, "5 Best Practices for Designing Mobile Surveys," Survey Event.com, **http://survey.event.com**, accessed April 10, 2012; Jennifer Okula, "A KISS Is Not Enough: How to Launch Mobile Intercept Surveys," iMediaConnection.com, **http://blogs.imediaconnection.com**, accessed April 10, 2012.

MARKETING AND THE SME

MARKETING AND THE SME | Hootsuite—The Little Company That Grew

HOOTSUITE is a Vancouver-based company that has developed a social media management system. The company has gone from a start-up to employing over 300 people in less than five years. It can boast that over 75 percent of the Fortune 1000 companies use its product, including Sony, Pepsi, and Virgin. The company has won numerous awards, including a Mashable Award for the best social management tool and the Digi for being Canada's top digital company.

The programs the company has developed allow firms to manage multiple social networks with ease, schedule messages and tweets, track brand mentions over various social media platforms, and analyze social media traffic.

For each social media platform, Hootsuite has different measurement tools. For Facebook, its program allows companies to monitor and measure activity such as the number of likes or page activity. On Twitter you track the number of followers or mentions. Its programs even provide Ow.ly Click Stats, where a company can view statistics by date or geographic location. There are over 40 analytical models to choose from or Hootsuite will design one specifically for your situation.

In order to keep all its customers up to date with what is happening on social media, the company offers training programs through its Hootsuite University. The university courses are free for Hootsuite customers but others can enroll for a small monthly fee. A student can listen to lectures or take online tests to become a certified graduate.

All this success has been driven by a college drop-out, Ryan Holmes. After two career false starts—a paintball company and a pizza restaurant—Holmes founded the media company that developed Hootsuite in 2009. Today Holmes is identified as the authority on how businesses that can use social media most effectively.

Sources: Chris Powell, "Expansion on the Horizon with HootSuite's $165 Million in New Funding," *Marketing*, August 12, 2013, **www.marketingmag.ca**; "HootSuite Closes 2013 with Strong Fourth Quarter," January 16, 2014, **www.marketwatch.com**; Russ Martin, "2012 Media Players of the Year Shortlist: HootSuite," *Marketing*, November 15, 2012, **www.marketingmag.ca**; Company website, **http://hootsuite.com**, accessed January 18, 2014.

At present, no industry-wide standards define techniques for measuring Web use. Some sites ask users to register before accessing the pages; others merely keep track of the number of "hits," or number of times a visitor accesses a page. Marketers have tried to place a value on a site's "stickiness"—longer-lasting site visits—as a means of measuring effectiveness. Others use "cookies," which are electronic identifiers deposited on viewers' computers, to track click-through behaviour—the paths users take as they move through the site. However, because some consumers change their Internet service providers frequently and special software is available to detect and remove them, cookies have lost some of their effectiveness. One company that helps businesses track their social media campaigns is Hootsuite as described in the "Marketing and the SME" feature.

Research suggests that most marketing executives are unsure of the return they are getting for their online marketing efforts—and even how to measure it. Meanwhile, some observers believe the traditional measure of ROI, or return on investment, must evolve into one or more other results that are easier for online marketers to actually measure, such as the sales success rate, the ability to build self-moderating customer service programs within social networks, or the creation of brand advocates, perhaps tracked with click-through sales or promotional codes. Others look to turn the often intangible effects of social media into new measures like user time spent interacting with others, degree of user involvement, and level of user attention.[24]

Certainly, observing consumers online, where users spend more time than with any other medium including TV, offers marketers the opportunity to monitor the buying decision process, understand what turns a browser into

Courtesy of SurveyMonkey.com

SurveyMonkey.com provides assistance with all aspects of online surveys.

table 8.2   *Survey Methods*

TECHNIQUE	BENEFITS	DRAWBACKS
Telephone interviews	Quick, inexpensive, good method for obtaining small amounts of impersonal information, high response rate	Many people refuse to take part, negative association with telemarketing
Personal interviews	Best for obtaining detailed personal information, can be location based	Expensive, time-consuming
Focus groups	Quick, relatively inexpensive, provide insights	Success depends on participants
Mail surveys	Cost effective, provide anonymity, can provide demographic data	Low response rate, time-consuming, impersonal
Online surveys	Fast, increased sample sizes, can be done anywhere, lower costs, less intrusive	Sample may be biased

a buyer, see how shoppers compare product features, and grasp the relative impacts on purchase decisions of marketing and price. Details like these help advertisers grow increasingly accurate about where they place their messages.

Experimental Method

The third—and least-used—method for collecting primary data is the **controlled experiment**. A marketing research experiment is a scientific investigation in which a researcher controls or manipulates a test group (or groups) and compares the results with those of a control group that did not receive the experimental controls or manipulations.

The most common use of this method by marketers is **test-marketing**, or introducing a new product in a specific area and then observing its degree of success. Up to this point, a product development team may have gathered feedback from focus groups. Other information may have come from shoppers' evaluations of competing products. Test-marketing is the first stage at which the product performs in a real-life environment.

Procter & Gamble have used streaming ads on Facebook and MySpace to invite users to try free samples of new products or incentives.[25] Some firms omit test-marketing and move directly from product development to full-scale production. These companies cite three problems with test-marketing:

1. *Test-marketing is expensive.* A firm can spend more than $1 million depending on the size of the test-market city and the cost of buying media to advertise the product.

2. *Competitors quickly learn about the new product.* By studying the test market, competitors can develop alternative strategies.

3. *Some products are not well suited to test-marketing.* Few firms test-market long-lived, durable goods such as cars because of the major financial investments required for their development, the need to establish networks of dealers to distribute the products, and requirements for parts and servicing.

Companies that decide to skip the test-marketing process can choose several other options. A firm may simulate a test-marketing campaign through computer-modelling software. By plugging in data on similar products, it can develop a sales projection for a new product. Another firm may offer an item in just one region or in another country, adjusting promotions and advertising based on local results before going to other geographic regions. Another option may be to limit a product's introduction to only one retail chain to carefully control and evaluate promotions and results.

controlled experiment
Scientific investigation in which a researcher manipulates a test group (or groups) and compares the results with those of a control group that did not receive the experimental controls or manipulations.

test-marketing
Marketing research technique that involves introducing a new product in a specific area and then measuring its degree of success.

assessment check 4

4.1 What is sampling?

4.2 What are the different types of probability and nonprobability samples?

4.3 What are the major methods of collecting primary data?

4.4 Identify the different types of survey methods.

4.5 How is interpretative research typically conducted and when should ethnographic research be used?

⑤ **Explain the challenges of conducting marketing research in global markets and outline the most important uses of computer technology in marketing research.**

CONDUCTING INTERNATIONAL MARKETING RESEARCH

As corporations expand globally, they need to gather correspondingly more knowledge about consumers in other countries. Although marketing researchers follow the same basic steps for international studies as for domestic ones, they often face some very different challenges.

Organizations can tap into many secondary sources as they research global markets. One major information source is the government, particularly Industry Canada. Another useful source for Canadian companies is the U.S. government. Both Industry Canada and the U.S. Department of Commerce publish reports that discuss marketing activities in many other countries. Commercial guides for almost every country in the world are compiled by local embassies. Industry Canada provides information on competition, international agreements, and directories of local contacts through its online database or its international trade offices located across the country.[26]

When conducting international research, companies must be prepared to deal with both language issues—communicating their message in the most effective way—and cultural issues, or capturing local citizens' interests while avoiding missteps that could unintentionally offend them. Companies also need to take a good look at a country's business environment, including political and economic conditions, trade regulations affecting research studies and data collection, and the potential for short- and long-term growth. Many marketers recommend using local researchers to investigate foreign markets.

Businesses may need to adjust their data collection methods for primary research in other countries because some methods do not easily transfer across national frontiers. Face-to-face interviewing, for instance, remains the most common method for conducting primary research outside North America.

Due to the buying power of the teen market, it is important to capture the attitudes and opinions of this age group.

© Richard G. Bingham II/Alamy

While mail surveys are a common data collection method in developed countries, they are useless in many other nations because of low literacy rates, unreliable mail service, and a lack of address lists. Telephone interviews may also not be suitable in other countries, especially those where many people do not have phones. Focus groups can be difficult to arrange because of cultural and social factors. In Latin American countries, for example, highly educated consumers make up a sought-after and opinionated minority, but they have little time to devote to lengthy focus group discussions. Middle- to lower-income Latin Americans may not be accustomed to articulating their opinions about products and grow reticent in the presence of others, whereas in some countries where violence and kidnapping are common, affluent consumers are reluctant to attend meetings with strangers. To help with such difficulties, a growing number of international research firms offer experience in conducting global studies.

COMPUTER TECHNOLOGY IN MARKETING RESEARCH

The ability to quickly gather and analyze business intelligence can create a substantial strategic advantage. Computer databases provide a wealth of data for marketing research, whether they are maintained outside the company or designed specifically to gather important facts about its customers. This section addresses important uses of computer technology related to marketing research: marketing information systems (MISs), marketing decision support systems (MDSSs), data mining, business intelligence, and competitive intelligence.

MARKETING INFORMATION SYSTEMS (MIS)

In the past, many marketing managers complained that their information problems resulted from too much rather than too little information. Reams of data were difficult to use and not always relevant. At times, information was almost impossible to find. Modern technological advances have made constraints like these obsolete.

A **marketing information system (MIS)** is a planned, computer-based system designed to provide decision makers with a continuous flow of information relevant to their areas of responsibility. A component of the organization's overall management information system, a marketing information system deals specifically with marketing data and issues.

A well-constructed MIS serves as a company's nerve centre, continually monitoring the market environment—both inside and outside the organization—and providing instantaneous information. Marketers can store data for later use, classify and analyze that data, and retrieve it easily when needed.

> **marketing information system (MIS)** Planned, computer-based system designed to provide managers with a continuous flow of information relevant to their specific decisions and areas of responsibility.

MARKETING DECISION SUPPORT SYSTEMS (MDSS)

A **marketing decision support system (MDSS)** consists of software that helps users quickly obtain and apply information in a way that supports marketing decisions. Taking MIS one step further, it allows managers to explore and connect such varying information as the state of the market, consumer behaviour, sales forecasts, competitors' actions, and environmental changes. MDSSs consist of four main characteristics: they are interactive, investigative, flexible, and accessible. An MDSS can create simulations or models to illustrate the likely results of changes in marketing strategies or market conditions.

> **marketing decision support system (MDSS)** Marketing information system component that links a decision maker with relevant databases and analysis tools.

While an MIS provides raw data, an MDSS develops this data into information useful for decision making. For example, an MIS might provide a list of product sales from the previous day. A manager could use an MDSS to transform this raw data into graphs illustrating sales trends or reports estimating the impacts of specific decisions, such as raising prices or expanding into new regions.

DATA MINING

Data mining is the process of searching through computerized data files to detect patterns. It focuses on identifying relationships that are not obvious to marketers—in a sense, answering questions that marketing researchers may not even have thought to ask. The data are stored in a huge database called a *data warehouse*. Software for the marketing decision support system is often associated with the data warehouse and is used to mine data. Once marketers identify patterns and connections, they use this intelligence to check the effectiveness of different strategy options.

> **data mining** Process of searching through customer databases to detect patterns that guide marketing decision making.

Data mining is an efficient way to sort through huge amounts of data and to make sense of that data. It helps marketers create customer profiles, pinpoint reasons for customer loyalty or the lack thereof, analyze the potential returns on changes in pricing or promotion, and forecast sales. Data mining also offers considerable advantages in retailing, the hotel industry, banking, utilities, and many other areas and holds the promise of providing answers to many specific strategic questions. Some are concerned, however, about the rapidly growing amount of personal data being gathered by companies like Facebook and Google, and the uses to which it may be put in the absence of any regulations governing such use. See the "Solving an Ethical Controversy" feature for a discussion.

> ### *Marketoid*
> The average Canadian household spends over $2,200 on restaurant meals annually.

Companies are using data mining to find small but important segments that had not been discovered through research methods. Other companies are using data mining to determine how their brands are being perceived by their customers.[27]

BUSINESS INTELLIGENCE

Business intelligence is the process of gathering information and analyzing it to improve business strategy, tactics, and daily operations. Using advanced software tools, marketers gather information from both within and outside the organization. Business intelligence can thus tell the firm how its own sales operation is doing or what its top competitors are up to.

The key is not only gathering the information but also getting it into a form that employees can make sense of and use for decision making and strategizing. Software can help users collect, aggregate, and create reports with outside information available on the Web from such databases as Dun & Bradstreet. As with other types of research, some research companies specialize in collecting business intelligence information.

SOLVING AN ETHICAL CONTROVERSY

Who Should Profit from Your Data?

FACEBOOK makes over $3 billion in advertising a year by targeting ads based on information its users voluntarily post about them. Google makes more than 10 times as much with ads based on the contents of users' Gmail and Web searches. Other organizations use personal information gleaned online to turn people down for jobs, insurance coverage, or loans and credit, sometimes based on information about others with similar profiles, rather than on accurate data about the individuals themselves.

Should online companies be allowed to profit from using your personal data?

PRO

1. Privacy is a subjective concept; not everyone objects to the use of data they voluntarily provide, and those who do can leave it offline.

2. Knowing consumers' likes and dislikes lets companies efficiently target their marketing to present only the messages those users will welcome.

CON

1. No laws limit what online companies and data aggregators can do with the information they collect, so they do as they please without regard to individuals' privacy.
2. The possibilities for abuse and theft of the collected data are too great.

Where do you stand: pro or con?

Sources: "Protect Yourself Online," *Consumer Reports,* June 2012, pp. 12–13; Doug Walp, "Facebook Users Should Be Wary of Company's Data Mining," *The Daily Athenaeum,* April 24, 2012, **www.thedaonline.com**; Lori Andrews, "Facebook Is Using You," *The New York Times*, **www.nytimes.com**, accessed April 24, 2012; "The Pros and Cons of Data Mining with Facebook Applications," Connected Internet, **www.connectedinternet.co.uk**, accessed April 24, 2012.

assessment check 5

5.1 What are some organizations that can serve as sources of international secondary marketing data?

5.2 Distinguish between an MIS and an MDSS.

5.3 What is data mining?

5.4 Describe the process of collecting business and competitive intelligence.

COMPETITIVE INTELLIGENCE

Competitive intelligence is a form of business intelligence that focuses on finding information about competitors using published sources, interviews, observations by salespeople and suppliers in the industry, government agencies, public filings such as patent applications, and other secondary sources, including the Internet. Its aim is to uncover the specific advantages a competitor has, such as new-product launches, new features in existing goods or services, or new marketing or promotional strategies. Even a competitor's advertising can provide clues. Marketers use competitive intelligence to make better decisions that strengthen their own competitive strategy in turn.

(6) **Identify the major types of forecasting methods.**

sales forecast An estimate of a firm's sales for a specified future period.

qualitative forecasting Use of subjective techniques to forecast sales, such as the jury of executive opinion, Delphi technique, sales force composite, and surveys of buyer intentions.

SALES FORECASTING

A basic building block of any marketing plan is a **sales forecast**, an estimate of a firm's revenue for a specified future period. Sales forecasts play major roles in new-product decisions, production scheduling, financial planning, inventory planning and procurement, distribution, and human-resource planning. An inaccurate forecast may lead to incorrect decisions in each of these areas. A number of software programs offer companies sales forecasting applications to help automate the forecasting process.

Marketing research techniques are used to deliver effective sales forecasts. A sales forecast is also an important tool for marketing control because it sets standards against which to measure actual performance. Without such standards, no comparisons can be made.

Planners rely on short-run, intermediate, and long-run sales forecasts. A short-run forecast usually covers a period of up to one year, an intermediate forecast covers one to five years, and a long-run forecast extends beyond five years. Although sales forecasters use an array of techniques to predict the future—ranging from computer simulations to studying trends identified by futurists—their methods fall into two broad categories: qualitative and quantitative forecasting.

Qualitative forecasting techniques rely on subjective data that report opinions rather than exact historical data. **Quantitative forecasting** methods, by contrast, use statistical computations

table 8.3   *Benefits and Limitations of Various Forecasting Techniques*

TECHNIQUES	BENEFITS	LIMITATIONS
Qualitative Methods		
Jury of executive opinion	Opinions come from executives in many different departments; quick; inexpensive	Managers may lack background knowledge and experience to make meaningful predictions
Delphi technique	Group of experts may predict long-term events such as technological breakthroughs	Time-consuming; expensive
Sales force composite	Salespeople have expert customer, product, and competitor knowledge; quick; inexpensive	Inaccurate forecasts may result from low estimates of salespeople concerned about their influence on quotas
Survey of buyer intentions	Useful in predicting short-term and intermediate sales for firms that serve only selected customers	Intentions to buy may not result in actual purchases; time-consuming; expensive
Quantitative Methods		
Market test	Provides realistic information on actual purchases rather than on intent to buy	Alerts competition to new-product plans; time-consuming; expensive
Trend analysis	Quick; inexpensive; effective with stable customer demand and environment	Assumes the future will continue the past; ignores environmental changes
Exponential smoothing	Same benefits as trend analysis, but emphasizes more recent data	Same limitations as trend analysis, but not as severe due to emphasis on recent data

such as trend extensions based on past data, computer simulations, and econometric models. As Table 8.3 shows, each method has benefits and limitations. Consequently, most organizations use a combination of both techniques.

QUALITATIVE FORECASTING TECHNIQUES

Planners apply qualitative forecasting methods when they want judgmental or subjective indicators. Qualitative forecasting techniques include the jury of executive opinion, Delphi technique, sales force composite, and survey of buyer intentions.

Jury of Executive Opinion

The technique called the **jury of executive opinion** combines and averages the outlooks of top executives from such areas as marketing, finance, and production. Top managers bring the following capabilities to the process: experience and knowledge about situations that influence sales, open-minded attitudes toward the future, and awareness of the bases for their judgments. This quick and inexpensive method generates good forecasts for sales and new-product development. It works best for short-run forecasting.

Delphi Technique

Like the jury of executive opinion, the **Delphi technique** solicits opinions from several people, but it also gathers input from experts outside the firm, such as academic researchers, rather than relying completely on company executives. It is most appropriately used to predict long-run issues, such as technological breakthroughs, that could affect future sales and the market potential for new products.

The Delphi technique works as follows: a firm selects a panel of experts and sends each a questionnaire relating to a future event. After combining and averaging the answers, the firm

quantitative forecasting Use of statistical forecasting techniques such as trend analysis and exponential smoothing.

Marketoid

Households headed by seniors spent the highest percentage of their income on food at 12.5 percent.

jury of executive opinion Qualitative sales forecasting method that assesses the sales expectations of various executives.

Delphi technique Qualitative sales forecasting method that gathers and redistributes several rounds of anonymous forecasts until the participants reach a consensus.

develops another questionnaire based on these results and sends it back to the same people. The process continues until it identifies a consensus. Although firms have successfully used Delphi to predict future technological breakthroughs, the method is both expensive and time-consuming.

Sales Force Composite

sales force composite
Qualitative sales forecasting method based on the combined sales estimates of the firm's salespeople.

The **sales force composite** technique develops forecasts based on the belief that organization members closest to the marketplace—those with specialized product, customer, and competitive knowledge—offer the best insights concerning short-term future sales. It typically works from the bottom up. Management consolidates salespeople's estimates first at the district level, then at the regional level, and finally countrywide to obtain an aggregate forecast of sales that reflects all three levels.

The sales force composite approach has some weaknesses, however. Because salespeople recognize the role of their sales forecasts in determining sales quotas for their territories, they are likely to make conservative estimates. Moreover, their narrow perspectives from within their limited geographic territories may prevent them from considering the impact on sales of trends developing in other territories, forthcoming technological innovations, or the major changes in marketing strategies. Consequently, the sales force composite gives the best forecasts in combination with other techniques.

Survey of Buyer Intentions

survey of buyer intentions Qualitative sales forecasting method that samples opinions among groups of present and potential customers concerning their purchase intentions.

A **survey of buyer intentions** gathers input through mail-in questionnaires, online feedback, telephone polls, and personal interviews to determine the purchasing intentions of a representative group of present and potential customers. This method suits firms that serve limited numbers of customers but often proves impractical for those with millions of customers. Also, buyer surveys gather useful information only when customers willingly reveal their buying intentions. Moreover, customer intentions do not necessarily translate into actual purchases. These surveys may help a firm to predict short-run or intermediate sales, but they employ time-consuming and expensive methods.

QUANTITATIVE FORECASTING TECHNIQUES

Quantitative techniques attempt to eliminate the subjectiveness of the qualitative methods. They include such methods as market tests, trend analysis, and exponential smoothing.

Test Markets

One quantitative technique, the test market, frequently helps planners in assessing consumer responses to new-product offerings. The procedure typically begins by establishing one or more test markets to gauge consumer responses to a new product under actual marketplace conditions. Market tests also permit experimenters to evaluate the effects of different prices, alternative promotional strategies, and other marketing mix variations by comparing results among different test markets.

The primary advantage of market tests is the realism that they provide for the marketer. However, these expensive and time-consuming experiments may also communicate marketing plans to competitors before a firm introduces a product to the total market.

Trend Analysis

trend analysis
Quantitative sales forecasting method that estimates future sales through statistical analyses of historical sales patterns.

Trend analysis develops forecasts for future sales by analyzing the historical relationship between sales and time. It implicitly assumes that the collective causes of past sales will continue to exert similar influences in the future. When historical data are available, planners can quickly and inexpensively complete trend analysis. Software programs can calculate the average annual increment of change for the available sales data. This average increment of change is then projected into the future to come up with the sales forecast. So, if the sales of a firm have been growing $15.3 million on average per year, this amount of sales could be added to last year's sales total to arrive at next year's forecast.

Of course, trend analysis cannot be used if historical data are not available, as in new-product forecasting. Also, trend analysis makes the dangerous assumption that future events will continue in the same manner as the past. Any variations in the determinants of future sales will cause deviations from the forecast. In other words, this method gives reliable forecasts during periods of steady growth and stable demand. If conditions change, predictions based on trend analysis may become worthless. For this reason, forecasters have applied more sophisticated techniques and complex, new forecasting models to anticipate the effects of various possible changes in the future.

exponential smoothing Quantitative forecasting technique that assigns weights to historical sales data, giving the greatest weight to the most recent data.

Exponential Smoothing

A more sophisticated method of trend analysis, the **exponential smoothing** technique, weighs each year's sales data, giving greater weight to results from the most recent years. Otherwise, the statistical approach used in trend analysis is applied here. For example, last year's sales might receive a 1.5 weight, while sales data from two years ago could get a 1.4 weighting. Exponential smoothing is considered the most commonly used quantitative forecasting technique.

assessment check 6

6.1 Describe the jury of executive opinion.

6.2 What is the Delphi technique?

6.3 How does the exponential smoothing technique forecast sales?

Strategic Implications

Marketing research can help an organization develop effective marketing strategies. Most new products eventually fail to attract enough buyers to remain viable. Why? A major reason is the seller's failure to understand market needs.

Consider, for example, the hundreds of dot-com companies that went under. A characteristic shared by all those failing businesses is that virtually none of them was founded on sound marketing research. Very few used marketing research techniques to evaluate sales potential, and even fewer studied consumer responses after the ventures were initiated. While research might not have prevented every dot-com meltdown, it might have helped a few of those businesses survive.

Marketing research ideally matches new products to potential customers. Marketers also conduct research to analyze sales of their own and competitors' products, to gauge the performance of existing products, to guide the development of promotional campaigns, and to develop and refine products. All these activities enable marketers to fine-tune their marketing strategies and reach customers more effectively and efficiently.

Marketing researchers have at their disposal a broad range of techniques with which to collect both quantitative and qualitative data on customers, their lifestyles, behaviours, attitudes, and perceptions. Vast amounts of data can be rapidly collected, accessed, interpreted, and applied to improve all aspects of business operations. Because of customer relationship management technology, that information is no longer generalized to profile groups of customers—it can be analyzed to help marketers understand every customer. ◆◆◆

REVIEW OF CHAPTER OBJECTIVES

① **Describe the development of the marketing research function and its major activities.**

Marketing research, or the collection and use of information in marketing decision making, is changing faster than ever before. Today, the most common marketing research activities are (1) determining market potential, market share, and market characteristics and (2) conducting sales analyses and competitive product studies. Some large companies have internal marketing research departments. However, outside suppliers still remain vital to the research function. Some perform the complete research task, while others specialize in a limited area or provide specific data services.

(2) **Explain the steps in the marketing research process.**

The marketing research process can be divided into six specific steps: (1) defining the problem, (2) conducting exploratory research, (3) formulating hypotheses, (4) creating a research design, (5) collecting data, and (6) interpreting and presenting the research information. A clearly defined problem focuses on the researcher's search for relevant decision-oriented information. Exploratory research refers to information gained both within and outside the firm. Hypotheses, tentative explanations of specific events, allow researchers to set out specific research designs—that is, the series of decisions that, taken together, make up master plans or models in order to conduct the investigations. The data collection phase of the marketing research process can involve either or both primary (original) and secondary (previously published) data. After the data are collected, researchers must interpret and present the results in a way that will be meaningful to management.

(3) **Distinguish between primary and secondary data and identify the sources of each type.**

Primary data can be collected by the firm's own researchers or by independent marketing research companies. Three principal methods of primary data collection are observation, survey and interview, or experiment. Secondary data can be classified as either internal or external. Sources of internal data include sales records, product evaluation, sales force reports, and records of marketing costs. Sources of external data include the government and private sources, such as business magazines. Both external and internal data can also be obtained from computer databases.

(4) **Explain the different sampling techniques used by marketing researchers and identify the methods by which marketing researchers collect primary data.**

Samples can be categorized as either probability samples or nonprobability samples. A probability sample is one in which every member of the population has a known chance of being selected. Probability samples include simple random samples, in which every item in the relevant universe has an equal opportunity to be selected; stratified samples, which are constructed such that randomly selected subsamples of different groups are represented in the total sample; and cluster samples, in which geographic areas are selected from which respondents are drawn. A nonprobability sample is arbitrary and does not allow application of standard statistical tests. Nonprobability sampling techniques include convenience samples, in which readily available respondents are picked, and quota samples, which are divided so that different segments or groups are represented in the total sample.

The methods marketing researchers use to collect primary data include observation, survey and interviews, and experiments. Observation data are gathered by observing consumers via devices such as people meters or videotape. Survey and interview data can be collected through telephone interviews, mail surveys, personal interviews, focus groups, or a variety of online methods. Telephone interviews give the researcher a fast and inexpensive way to get small amounts of information but generally not detailed or personal information. Personal interviews are costly but allow researchers to get detailed information from respondents. Mail surveys are a means of conducting national studies at a reasonable cost; their main disadvantage is potentially inadequate response rates. Focus groups elicit detailed, qualitative information that provides insight not only into behaviour but also into consumer attitudes and perceptions. Online surveys can yield fast responses but face obstacles such as the adequacy of the probability sample. The experimental method creates verifiable statistical data through the use of test and control groups to reveal actual benefits from perceived benefits.

(5) **Explain the challenges of conducting marketing research in global markets and outline the most important uses of computer technology in marketing research.**

The major challenge of conducting marketing research in global markets is finding information. Many resources are available to help organizations research global markets. Government resources include Statistics Canada, Industry Canada, small-business development centres, and foreign embassies. Private companies, such as marketing research firms and companies that distribute research from other sources, are another resource. Electronic networks offer online international trade forums, in which marketers can establish global contacts.

Important uses of computer technology in marketing research include (1) a marketing information system (MIS)—a planned, computer-based system designed to provide managers with a continuous flow of information relevant to their specific decision-making needs and areas of responsibility; (2) a marketing decision support system (MDSS)—a marketing information system component that links a decision maker with relevant databases and analysis tools; (3) data mining—the process of searching through consumer information files or data warehouses to detect patterns that guide marketing decision making; (4) business intelligence—the process of gathering information and analyzing it to improve business strategy, tactics, and daily operations; and (5) competitive intelligence—the form of business intelligence that focuses on finding information about competitors using published sources, interviews, observations by salespeople and suppliers in the industry, government agencies, public filings such as patent applications, and other secondary methods, including the Internet.

⑥ Identify the major types of forecasting methods.

There are two categories of forecasting methods. Qualitative methods are more subjective since they are based on opinions rather than exact historical data. They include the jury of executive opinion, the Delphi technique, the sales force composite, and the survey of buyer intentions. Quantitative methods are more factual and numerical measures such as test markets, trend analysis, and exponential smoothing.

assessment check answers ✓

1.1 Identify the different classifications of marketing research suppliers and explain how they differ from one another.

Marketing research suppliers can be classified as syndicated services, which regularly send standardized data sets to all customers; full-service suppliers, which contract to conduct complete marketing research projects; or limited-service suppliers, which specialize in selected activities.

1.2 What research methods can be used to measure customer satisfaction?

Some companies look at feedback from existing customers—for instance, hiring marketing research firms to collect and analyze customer feedback at their websites. Other firms collect feedback about customer defections—why a customer no longer uses a product. Other organizations conduct research through online polls and surveys.

2.1 What are the six steps in the marketing research process?

The marketing research process can be divided into six specific steps: (1) defining the problem, (2) conducting exploratory research, (3) formulating hypotheses, (4) creating a research design, (5) collecting data, and (6) interpreting and presenting the research information.

2.2 What is the goal of exploratory research?

Exploratory research seeks to discover the cause of a specific problem by discussing the problem with informed sources within and outside the firm and examining data from other information sources.

3.1 Distinguish between primary and secondary data.

Primary data are original; secondary data have been previously published.

3.2 What are the major methods of collecting secondary data?

Secondary data consist of two types: internal and external data. Internal data include sales records, product performance reviews, sales force activity reports, and marketing cost reports. External data come from a variety of sources, including government records, syndicated research services, and industry publications. Computerized databases provide access to vast amounts of data from both inside and outside an organization.

4.1 What is sampling?

Sampling is the process of selecting representative survey respondents or research participants from the total universe of possible participants.

4.2 What are the different types of probability and nonprobability samples?

Types of probability samples are simple random samples, stratified samples, and cluster samples. Nonprobability samples are convenience samples and quota samples.

4.3 What are the major methods of collecting primary data?

Three principal methods of primary data collection are observation, survey and interview, and experiment.

4.4 Identify the different types of survey methods.

Different survey methods may include telephone interviews, personal interviews, focus groups, mail surveys, and online or other Internet-based methods.

4.5 How is interpretative research typically conducted and when should ethnographic research be used?

Interpretative research observes a customer or group of customers in their natural setting and interprets their behaviour based on social and cultural characteristics of that setting. Ethnographic research is used to look at the consumer behaviour of different groups of people.

5.1 What are some organizations that can serve as sources of international secondary marketing data?

Industry Canada and the U.S. Department of Commerce offer reports and guides for many countries.

5.2 Distinguish between an MIS and an MDSS.

A marketing information system (MIS) is a planned, computer-based system designed to provide managers with a continuous flow of information relevant to their specific decision-making needs and areas of responsibility. A marketing decision support system (MDSS) is a marketing information system component that links a decision maker with relevant databases and analysis tools to help answer "what-if" questions.

5.3 What is data mining?

Data mining is the process of searching through huge consumer information files or data warehouses to detect patterns that can help marketers ask the right questions and guide marketing decision making.

5.4 Describe the process of collecting business and competitive intelligence.

Business intelligence is the process of gathering information and analyzing it to improve business strategy, tactics, and daily operations. Competitive intelligence focuses on finding information about competitors using published sources, interviews, observations by salespeople and suppliers in the industry, government agencies, public filings such as patent applications, and other secondary methods including the Internet.

6.1 Describe the jury of executive opinion.

The jury of executive opinion combines and averages the outlooks of top executives from areas such as marketing, finance, and production.

6.2 What is the Delphi technique?

The Delphi technique solicits opinions from several people within the firm but also includes input from experts outside the firm such as academic researchers.

6.3 How does the exponential smoothing technique forecast sales?

Exponential smoothing weighs each year's sales data, giving greater weight to results from the most recent years.

MARKETING TERMS YOU NEED TO KNOW

These terms are printed in blue in the text. They are defined in the margins of the chapter and in the Glossary that begins on p. G-1.

marketing research 218
syndicated service 220
full-service research supplier 220
limited-service research supplier 220
exploratory research 221
sales analysis 222
hypothesis 222
secondary data 222
primary data 222
sampling 225
population 225

probability sample 225
nonprobability sample 226
interpretative research 227
mall intercepts 228
focus group 228
controlled experiment 231
test-marketing 231
marketing information system (MIS) 233
marketing decision support system (MDSS) 233
data mining 233

sales forecast 234
qualitative forecasting 234
quantitative forecasting 235
jury of executive opinion 235
Delphi technique 235
sales force composite 236
survey of buyer intentions 236
trend analysis 236
exponential smoothing 237

PROJECT AND TEAMWORK EXERCISES

1. Nielsen Company offers data collected by optical scanners from the United Kingdom, France, Germany, Belgium, the Netherlands, Austria, Italy, and Finland. These scanner data track sales of UPC-coded products in those nations. In small teams, imagine that you are one of Nielsen's clients. One team might be a retail chain, another team might be an Internet company, and still another team a toy manufacturer. Discuss the types of marketing questions these data might help you answer. Share your list with other teams.

2. Sandwich maker Subway opened its first overseas store in 1984, in the Middle East. Today, it has over 36,000 stores in 100 countries. Discuss some of the challenges Subway might face in conducting marketing research in potential new international markets. What types of research would you recommend the company use in choosing new countries for expansion?

3. Working alone or with a partner, choose a new product idea, or a variation on an existing product, that you think would appeal to your classmates, such as yogurt or an energy drink in a new flavour, and devise a test-marketing plan for it. Determine where you will test your product and which variables you will assess, such as price and promotional

activities. Be prepared to present your plan to the class and include a description of the information you hope your test market will provide.

4. Interpretative research offers marketing researchers many possibilities, including the opportunity to improve product features such as packaging for food or over-the-counter medication that is difficult for seniors or people with disabilities to open. List some other ways in which you think this observation method can help make existing product offerings more appealing or more useful to specific kinds of users. What kind of products would you choose, and how would you test them?

5. McDonald's conducts extensive marketing research for all its new products, including new menu items for its overseas stores. Due to cultural and other differences and preferences, the company cannot always extrapolate its results from one country to another. For instance, Croque McDo fried ham-and-cheese sandwiches are unlikely to be as popular in North America as they are in France, which invented the *croque monsieur* sandwich on which McDonald's product is based. Can you think of any other kinds of firms that share this limitation on global applications of their research? In contrast, what sorts of questions *could* multinational firms answer on a global basis? Why?

CRITICAL THINKING EXERCISES

1. Some companies are broadening their markets by updating classic products to appeal to younger people's tastes and preferences. What primary and secondary market information would you want to have if you were planning to reinvigorate an established brand in each of the following categories? Where and how would you obtain the information?
   a. household cleaner
   b. moist packaged cat food
   c. spray starch
   d. electrical appliances

2. Marketers sometimes collect primary information by using so-called *mystery shoppers* who visit stores anonymously (as if they were customers) and note such critical factors as store appearance and ambiance, items in stock, and quality of service, including waiting time and courtesy of employees. (The CEO of Staples has gone on mystery shopper trips and sometimes asked his mother to make similar trips.) Prepare a list of data that you would want to obtain from a mystery shopper surveying a chain of gas stations in your area. Devise a format for gathering the information that combines your

need to compile the data electronically and the researcher's need to remain undetected while visiting the stores.

3. Select a sales forecasting method (or combination of methods) for each of the following information needs and explain why you chose it.
   a. prediction of next year's sales based on last year's figures
   b. prediction of next year's sales based on weighted data from the last five years
   c. expected sales categorized by district and by region
   d. estimated product usage for the next year by typical consumers
   e. probable consumer response to a new product

4. The Internet provides ready access to secondary information but is also a portal to an almost limitless store of primary information via social networking sites, message boards, chat rooms, e-mail questionnaires, newsgroups, and website registration forms. What are some specific drawbacks of each of these methods for obtaining primary information from customers?

ETHICS EXERCISE

Consumer groups sometimes raise objections to marketers' methods of collecting primary data from customers. They object to such means as product registration forms; certain types of games, contests, or product offers; and "cookies" and demographic questionnaires on company websites. Marketers believe that such tools offer them an easy way to collect data. Most strictly control the use of such data and never link identifying information with consumers' financial or demographic profiles. However, the possibility of abuse or error always exists.

Research the code of ethics of the Canadian Marketing Association (CMA), American Marketing Association (AMA), and the Marketing Research and Intelligence Association (MRIA). Note especially the guidelines for use of the Internet in marketing research.

1. Check the websites of a few large consumer-products companies. How effective do you think these sites are at informing visitors about the use of "cookies" on the sites? Do you think marketers could or should improve their protection of site visitors' privacy? If so, how?

2. Do you think the code of ethics of these organizations would be violated if marketers compile a mailing list based on information provided on warranty and product registration cards and then use the list to send customers new-product information? Why or why not? Does your opinion change if the company also sends list members special discount offers and private sale notices?

CASE 8.1

The Gamification of Marketing Research

Reward programs were originally designed to accomplish two things: reward loyal customers and collect information about those customers who like reward programs. In 2012 the average Canadian participated in more than six different reward programs. In 2013 that number increased to over seven, a more than 7 percent increase in one year, and over 90 percent of Canadians belonged to at least one loyalty program. The challenge for companies now is how to make their loyalty programs stand out from all others. In order to differentiate their loyalty programs, some companies are turning to games.

There's no stopping a good idea. As millions of avid fans enjoy online games like Farmville, businesses are responding with similar games on corporate websites, but their purpose isn't to amass virtual goods or defeat alien armies. Rather, these games are designed to build customer relationships, reward loyalty, and, not incidentally, gather market research data.

Samsung Nation rewards users who post comments on the company's website, answer other users' questions, and link to Samsung.com from their Twitter accounts. Although a television set was offered as the top prize, players reaching higher levels in Samsung Nation enjoy only virtual rewards like coloured badges and titles like "Connoisseur." They also spend more time on the company's site, share more product information, and let Samsung track their online behaviour. The CEO of a company that designs corporate games like Samsung's says his client companies "use gamification to measure and influence user behaviour to meet their business goals." Increased site activity impresses potential customers; positive user comments can increase sales with lower marketing costs; and peer reviews are seen as highly trustworthy. For marketers, who also get to swell their customer databases, gamification is a win–win strategy.

Gaming has moved beyond the Internet to mobile devices. In a joint program between the Scotiabank and Cineplex, gaming has come to the movie theatres in real time. Movie goers can "check in" when they arrive at the theatre and answer movie trivia questions, playing with other movie goers in the same theatre. The one with the highest number of correct answers wins. The prizes are not big—extra points on their Scene Scotiacard or a free drink. The Scotiabank and Cineplex Scene loyalty program was successful even before the introduction of the TimePlay app, with 14 percent of Canadians participating in the program. Scotiabank customers could link their Scene program to their debit or card cards and collect points toward free movies at Cineplex theatres.

Corporate games attract some unexpected demographic groups, like women in their late 30s, who don't fit the typical gamer profile, or the under-35 crowd, who collect their reward points through Facebook or Twitter. That boosts companies' confidence that the data they're gathering accurately reflect their target segments. Sears, Groupon, Warner Brothers, and Verizon Wireless have adopted gaming techniques to draw more users to their websites, extend the time they spend there, or increase their loyalty to a brand. Some companies track hundreds of actions by millions of people.

Whether companies use traditional loyalty programs or attach a gaming element to them, these programs do cause some concern for participants. The biggest concern for most participants is privacy. The majority of people who participate in loyalty programs, about 90 percent, want these programs to provide them with information about the program through direct communication but they have concerns about how the information they provide is being used. This is a tricky balancing act for program administrators because they need personal information in order to provide the communications directed at each participant. Given the popularity of these programs and how important the data are that companies get from them, it is likely marketers will find the balance between privacy and personal communications records.

Questions for Critical Thinking

1. Critics say marketing games manipulate customers into giving away an increasing amount of personal information without the real thrill of game playing. Do you agree? Why or why not?

2. Some companies say they are cautious about adopting gamification techniques because of concerns about keeping the collected data secure. Are they right? Why or why not?

Sources: Kristin Laird, "Loyalty Program: Don't Be Creepy," *Marketing*, February 26, 2013, **www.marketingmag.ca**; Rebecca Harris, "Social Media Contests: A Winning Tactic?" *Marketing*, January 7, 2014, **www.marketingmag.ca**; Sarah Barmak, "Game-Changing in Loyalty," *Marketing*, January 13, 2014, **www .marketingmag.ca**; "The 2013 Maritz Loyalty Report™, Canadian Edition," March 2013, Maritz Canada company website, **www.maritzcanada.com**, accessed January 19, 2014; Erica Swallow, "How Three Businesses Scored Big with Gamification," *Entrepreneur*, March 6, 2012, **www.entrepreneur.com**; David Rosenbaum, "The Games Businesses Play," *CFO*, February 14, 2012, **www3.cfo .com**; Natasha Singer, "You've Won a Badge (and Now We Know All About You)," *The New York Times*, February 4, 2012, **www.nytimes.com**; Erica Swallow, "How Badgeville Is Gamifying the Internet," *Entrepreneur*, January 20, 2012, **www .entrepreneur.com;** Becky Yerak, "How To Score the Loyal Customer," *Chicago Tribune*, January 17, 2012, pp. B1, B6.

CASE 8.2

High-Performance Analytics

Companies that sell products and services to the ultimate consumer are not the only ones trying to figure out how to deal with the mountains of data being collected today. The market research companies are struggling with the problem as well. One company that has made some progress in the area of big data is SAS—which stands for statistical analysis system. The company was created in 1976 after its founder developed a statistical software product. Today its products are found in 140 countries around the world.

One of the company's latest challenges has been to develop statistical processes that enable companies to analyze large amounts of data quickly. The company identified three trends in market research: there was an ever-increasing amount of data available to companies, more companies were depending on data analysis in their decision making, and new technologies were constantly being developed. The solution is called High-Performance Analytics (HPA). This technique allows for in-memory processing that significantly reduces data processing time. For example, one company reduced its data-processing time from 176 hours to less than 90 seconds.

Companies are using this high-powered analytical tool for several different applications. A sporting goods store used it to better understand its customers' purchasing behaviour in order to improve its direct marketing. By analyzing the locations of its best customers, it was able to improve its direct marketing program and experienced a 60 percent increase in responses to a direct marketing campaign.

Staples performed an analysis to determine the differences between its online and in-store customer behaviour. As a result of this analysis, Staples can now determine when one of its regular customers reduces its spending. The company can now send a personalized promotion to these customers in order to increase their spending at Staples.

Big data is not just the latest buzz in marketing, but as more companies realize the benefits this method of analyzing large amounts of data will become the norm for all companies.

Questions for Critical Thinking

1. What are some ways marketers could use High-Performance Analytics? What are the advantages and disadvantages of these uses?
2. How can High-Performance Analytical techniques be used in connection with a company's social media?

Sources: Tapan Patel, "Three Reasons Marketers Should Care About High-Performance Analytics," *Marketing*, November 12, 2012, **www.marketingmag.ca**; "Boosting Profits, Loyalty Through Better Marketing," SAS company website, **www.sas.com**, accessed January 19, 2014; "Scotiabank Mines Data to Generate Leads," SAS company website, **www.sas.com**, accessed January 19, 2014; Company Information, SAS company website, **www.sas.com**, accessed January 19, 2014.

chapter 9

Market Segmentation, Targeting, and Positioning

CHAPTER OBJECTIVES

① Identify the essential components of a market, outline the role of market segmentation in developing a marketing strategy, and describe the criteria necessary for effective segmentation.

② Explain the geographic, demographic, and psychographic approaches to segmenting consumer markets.

③ Describe product-related segmentation.

④ Identify the steps in the market segmentation process and discuss four basic strategies for reaching target markets.

⑤ Summarize the types of positioning strategies, and explain the reasons for positioning and repositioning products.

MOOOO-RE MILK PLEASE

Recent studies have found that Canadians are not drinking enough milk or dairy products to remain healthy. Preschool children have the best record of dairy consumption, but once they start school and the beverage choice increases, the consumption of milk declines. The amount of milk consumed continues to decline throughout their lives. One study found that for those in the 10- to 16-year-age bracket, 61 percent of boys did not drink enough milk to remain healthy. Age is not the only factor influencing the amount of milk consumed. Milk consumption is also dependent on culture. Of the two largest cultural groups coming to Canada, South Asian and Chinese, only the South Asians are large consumers of milk.

These statistics were startling enough to the health care community but they were a call to action for the various organizations that promote dairy products across the country. The challenge was to decide what types of promotional material would get the message out to the different regions of the country and across so many different customer groups.

The Dairy Farmers of Canada have used a calendar featuring recipes that use dairy products. The calendar is distributed across the country by including it in regional newspapers. The organization hopes that families will display the calendar in their kitchens to remind them every day to consume dairy products. But while a kitchen calendar might get the message out to families, it did not seem to be as effective for other customer groups.

The Dairy Farmers of Canada targeted other groups of customers with their "Get Enough" campaign. Aimed at educating consumers about the benefits of drinking milk, the "Get Enough" campaign included television commercials in both French and English; ads in the popular magazines *Chatelaine* and *Canadian Living*; and billboard ads in Halifax, Montreal, Toronto, and Calgary.

Another ad campaign, "Milk Every Moment," was based on research showing that teenagers and young adults responded to nostalgia-style promotions. This campaign included commercials of very young children acting silly. The commercials were accompanied by a photo contest and were shown in theatres and on social media.

A campaign that is aimed specifically at physically active young men is the "Recharge with Milk" promotion. This promotion positions chocolate milk as an alternative to sports drinks by showing the benefits of chocolate milk as a recovery beverage after a strenuous workout. The campaign was one of four sponsors of the series of programs that followed two National Hockey League teams as they prepared for the Winter Classic Game played on New Year's Day. These programs were a good match because the audience was primarily 18- to 49-year-old males.

Another innovative promotional campaign aimed at a broader market was developed by the Quebec Milk Bureau and its ad agencies. This campaign was based on relationships with food and emotional relationships. Three television ads were made with the theme of relationships. The first was a holiday-themed spot featuring Santa with milk and cookies, and the second was a family eating cake and drinking milk. The third in the series was a grittier story of two brothers. The commercial starts off in a park where the older brother protects the younger one from bullies. When the boys get to their apartment, which has peeling paint and leaky taps and is clearly in a less affluent section of the city, they share a glass of milk and a peanut butter sandwich.

Calendars in kitchens across the country aimed at families, billboards in major cities, gritty commercials in the Quebec market, and hockey programs may seem diverse ways to get Canadians consuming more dairy products, but these promotions and others like them across the country seem to be working.[1]

connecting with customers

Milk marketing associations across the country are using innovative techniques to make different customer groups aware of the health benefits of drinking milk. By using social media to reach teens, providing recipes for the cook in the family, and catching attention with gritty commercials to reach a broader market, these organizations are connecting with their customers.

Chapter Overview

Each of us is unique. We come from different backgrounds, live in different households, and have different interests and goals. You and your best friend may shop at different stores, listen to different music, play different sports, and take different courses in college or university. Suppose you like country music, but your best friend prefers oldies hits. Marketers for all kinds of music-related products, whether they're digital songs or live concerts, want to capture your interest as well as that of your friends. Do you play an instrument or sing, or are you a fan who goes to clubs and downloads music? Marketers look at current customers and potential customers to figure out what their characteristics are, whether they can identify certain subgroups, and how they can best offer products to meet their needs. Your interests and needs, your lifestyle and income, the city where you live, and your age all contribute to the likelihood that you will

listen to and buy certain types of music. All these factors make up a market. A **market** is composed of people with sufficient purchasing power, authority, and willingness to buy. And marketers must use their expertise to understand the market for a good or service, whether it's a download by your favourite artist, a new radio station, or a 12-string guitar.

Many markets include consumers with different lifestyles, backgrounds, and income levels. Nearly everyone buys toothpaste, but that does not mean every consumer has the same lifestyle, background, or income. So it is unusual for a single marketing mix strategy to attract all sectors of a market. By identifying, evaluating, and selecting a target market to pursue, such as consumers who prefer toothpaste made with all-natural ingredients or those who want an extra-whitening formula, marketers are able to develop more efficient and effective marketing strategies. On the other hand, some products—such

as luxury sports cars or fly fishing supplies—are intended for a more specific market. In either case, the **target market** for a product is the specific segment of consumers most likely to purchase a particular product.

Marketing now takes place on a global basis more than ever, incorporating many target markets. To identify those markets, marketers must determine useful ways for segmenting different populations and communicating with them successfully. This chapter discusses useful ways to accomplish this objective, explaining the steps of the market segmentation process and strategies for reaching target markets. Finally, it looks at the role of positioning in developing a marketing strategy. ◆◆◆

Marketoid

The per capita consumption of skim milk is almost eight litres per year.

---

① **Identify the essential components of a market, outline the role of market segmentation in developing a marketing strategy, and describe the criteria necessary for effective segmentation.**

market Group of people with sufficient purchasing power, authority, and willingness to buy.

target market Specific group of people a firm believes is most likely to buy its goods and services.

TYPES OF MARKETS

Products are usually classified as either consumer products or business products. **Consumer products** are bought by ultimate consumers for personal use, such as cell phones or fashion magazines. **Business products** are goods and services purchased for use either directly or indirectly in the production of other goods and services for resale. Most goods and services purchased by individual consumers, such as downloaded music or restaurant meals, are considered consumer products. Rubber and raw cotton are examples of items generally purchased by manufacturers and are, therefore, classified as business products. B.F. Goodyear buys rubber to manufacture tires; textile manufacturers convert raw cotton into cloth.

However, in many cases, a single product can serve different uses. Tires purchased for the family car constitute consumer products, but tires purchased by the Ford Motor Company to be mounted on its Ford Focus are business products because they become part of another product destined for resale. Or a product that was once a business product might be modified for consumer use, and vice versa. A line of professional cookware sold to restaurants—a business product—could be adapted by its manufacturer to become a line of cookware for home use—a consumer product. If you want to determine the classification of an item, just think about who is going to buy the product, who will use it, and how or why the product will be used. The bottle of mouthwash you buy at the supermarket is a consumer product, but if a large hotel chain purchases large quantities of the same mouthwash from a wholesaler, it becomes a business product.

THE ROLE OF MARKET SEGMENTATION

There are more than 7 billion people in the world today, more than 35 million of whom live in Canada.[2] In today's business world, there are too many variables in consumer needs, preferences, and purchasing power to attract all consumers with a single marketing mix. That's not to say that firms must actually change products to meet the needs of different market segments—although they often do—but they must attempt to identify the factors that affect purchase decisions and then group consumers according to the presence or absence of these factors. Finally, they adjust marketing strategies to meet the needs of each group.

Consider motor vehicles. Unlike a century ago, when Henry Ford pronounced that customers could order any colour of car they liked—as long as it was black—today there is a make, model, and colour for every taste and budget. But auto manufacturers need to adjust their messages for different markets. And savvy marketers are looking toward markets that show growth, such as the South Asian population, which is the fastest-growing ethnic group in the country, and the aging baby boomers, whose needs for goods and services are changing.[3]

The division of the total market into smaller, relatively homogeneous groups is called **market segmentation**. Both profit-oriented and not-for-profit organizations practise market segmentation.

CRITERIA FOR EFFECTIVE SEGMENTATION

Segmentation doesn't automatically guarantee success in the marketing arena; instead, it is a tool for marketers to use. Its effectiveness depends on four basic requirements.

1. The market segment must present measurable purchasing power and size.

With jobs, incomes, and decision-making power, female consumers represent a hefty amount of purchasing power. Women control or influence the purchase of 85 percent of all consumer goods, including such items as stocks for investment, personal computers, and family vehicles.[4] With this information in mind, car manufacturers and dealers now market directly to women. Not all car manufacturing companies have successfully made the switch from male-dominated ads, however. Both Honda and Ford have recently launched ads that alienated the very audiences they were trying to attract.[5]

2. Marketers must find a way to promote effectively and to serve the market segment.

Because women now wield such purchasing power in the technology market, marketers need to find different ways to appeal to them. Some companies have taken this advice to heart by creating ads featuring working moms.

3. Marketers must then identify segments that are sufficiently large to give them good profit potential.

Women in the baby boomer age group, those who were born after the World War II, are particularly attractive to marketers. These women are now transitioning into new phases of their lives. Whether they are retiring, their children are leaving home, or they are becoming grandmothers, they will be purchasing products at each stage. This group represents about 16 percent of the Canadian population and they are part of the wealthiest, healthiest, and best-educated group in Cananda.[6]

4. The firm must aim for segments that match its marketing capabilities.

consumer products
Products bought by ultimate consumers for personal use.

business products
Goods and services purchased for use either directly or indirectly in the production of other goods and services for resale.

market segmentation
Division of the total market into smaller, relatively homogeneous groups.

Winter feels better on America's Best Beaches. Including Clearwater Beach, voted "Best Place to Watch a Sunset" by USA TODAY. And St. Pete Beach, TripAdvisor's #1 beach in the U.S. Plan your sun-soaked getaway today.

ST. PETERSBURG CLEARWATER
VisitStPeteClearwater.com

Courtesy of VisitStPeteClearwater.com

The Official Florida Tourism Marketing Corporation uses geographic segmentation with its ad directed at Canadians.

Targeting a large number of small markets can be an expensive, complex, and inefficient strategy, so smaller firms may decide to stick with a particular niche, or target market. But Harley-Davidson, once thought to be the exclusive domain of men, has experienced a surge in purchases by women, who represent the fastest-growing segment of the motorcycle business and currently account for nearly one in four motorcyclists. So Harley-Davidson runs targeted ads in women's magazines and hosts events geared specifically for women, featuring demonstrations and social gatherings where women riders can meet and network.[7]

SEGMENTING CONSUMER MARKETS

Market segmentation attempts to isolate the traits that distinguish a certain group of consumers from the overall market. An understanding of the group's characteristics—such as age, gender, geographic location, income, and buying patterns—plays a vital role in developing a successful marketing strategy. In most cases, marketers seek to pinpoint a number of factors affecting buying behaviour in the target segment. Marketers in the travel industry consider employment trends, changes in income levels and buying patterns, age, lifestyle, and other factors when promoting their goods and services. To boost flagging attendance at its theme parks, Disney World advertises to adults who are empty nesters and groups of friends instead of focusing entirely on families with young children. Marketers rarely identify totally homogeneous segments, in which all potential customers are alike; they always encounter some differences among members of a target group, but they must be careful to ensure that their segments accurately reflect consumers.

In the next sections, we discuss the four common bases for segmenting consumer markets: geographic segmentation, demographic segmentation, psychographic segmentation, and product-related segmentation. These segmentation approaches can give important guidance for marketing strategies, provided they identify significant differences in buying behaviour.

assessment check 1

1.1 Define *target market*.

1.2 Distinguish between a consumer product and a business product.

1.3 Define *market segmentation* and describe the role of market segmentation.

1.4 Identify the four criteria for effective segmentation.

② Explain the geographic, demographic, and psychographic approaches to segmenting consumer markets.

geographic segmentation Division of an overall market into homogeneous groups based on their locations.

GEOGRAPHIC SEGMENTATION

Marketers have long practised **geographic segmentation**—dividing an overall market into homogeneous groups on the basis of their locations. Geographic location does not ensure that all consumers in a location will make the same buying decisions, but this segmentation approach does help identify some general patterns.

The over 35 million people living in Canada are not scattered evenly across the country. Instead, they are concentrated in major metropolitan areas. Toronto is the largest city, with a population of 5.9 million. Montreal is the second-largest with 3.9 million, and third place goes to Vancouver at 2.4 million.[8] Figure 9.1 shows populations of the 10 largest cities in Canada.

The provinces with the most residents are Ontario (13.5 million), Quebec (8.1 million), British Columbia (4.5 million), Alberta (4.0 million), and Manitoba (1.2 million). In contrast, Prince Edward Island has a population of only 145,200, 35,000 of whom live in Charlottetown.[9]

A look at the worldwide population distribution illustrates why so many firms are pursuing customers around the globe. China has the most citizens, with 1.3 billion people, and India is second with 1.2 billion. The United States is third with about 316 million, and Indonesia is fourth with 251 million. Japan is a distant tenth with 127 million.[10] As in Canada, much of the world's population lives in urban environments. The two largest cities in the world are Shanghai, China, with 21.3 million, and Mumbai, India, with 14.3 million. The two largest metropolitan areas are Tokyo, Japan, with more than 38.1 million and Mexico City, with 27.7 million.[11]

Population size alone, however, may not be reason enough for a business to expand into a specific country. Businesses also need to look at a wide variety of economic variables. Some businesses may decide to combine their marketing efforts for countries that share similar population and product-use

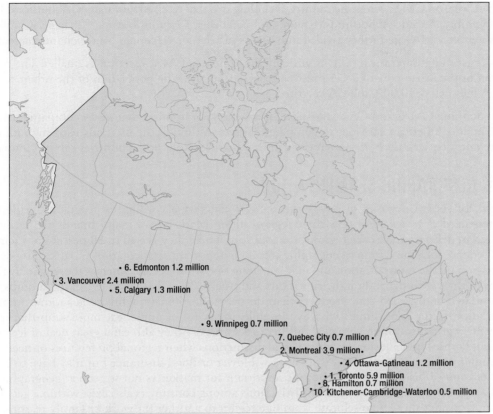

figure 9.1

Canada's 10 Largest Cities

• 6. Edmonton 1.2 million
• 3. Vancouver 2.4 million
• 5. Calgary 1.3 million
• 9. Winnipeg 0.7 million
7. Quebec City 0.7 million •
2. Montreal 3.9 million •
• 4. Ottawa-Gatineau 1.2 million
• 1. Toronto 5.9 million
• 8. Hamilton 0.7 million
• 10. Kitchener-Cambridge-Waterloo 0.5 million

Source: Adapted from Statistics Canada, "Population of Census Metropolitan Areas" available at **http://www40.statcan .gc.ca/l01/cst01/demo05a.htm**, accessed February 20, 2014.

census metropolitan area (CMA)
Geographic area surrounding an urban core with a population of at least 100,000.

patterns instead of treating each country as an independent segment. This grouping is taking place with greater frequency throughout the European Union as the currency and trade laws of the member nations are becoming more unified.

While population numbers indicate the overall size of a market, other geographic indicators such as job growth give useful guidance to marketers, depending on the type of products they sell. Automobile manufacturers might segment geographic regions by household income because it is an important factor in the purchase of a new car.

Geographic areas also vary in population migration patterns. The most recent Canadian census data show a movement of people to the western provinces. For the first time ever, slightly more people live in the western provinces—30.7 percent of the population as opposed to 30.6 percent from Ontario east. The fastest-growing metropolitan areas are all in the west, seven of them in Alberta. The fastest-growing metropolitan area was a suburb of Calgary, which experienced a 42.9 percent growth rate.[12]

The move from urban to suburban areas after World War II created a need to redefine the urban marketplace. This trend radically changed cities' traditional patterns of retailing and led to the decline in many downtown shopping areas—although recent trends have been toward the revitalization of downtown areas. Subsequently, traditional city boundaries became almost meaningless for marketing purposes.

In an effort to respond to these changes, the government has classified urban data into the following categories:

1. A **census metropolitan area (CMA)** is the largest classification. A CMA is a geographic area surrounding an urban core with a population of at least 100,000. Once Statistics Canada classifies an area as a CMA, it will always count as a CMA, even if the population drops below 100,000. As of the 2011 census,

Harley-Davidson hosts "garage parties" around the country, targeted specifically to women.

there were 33 CMAs across the country, including two that received new names: Abbotsford, British Columbia, became Abbotsford-Mission, and Kitchener, Ontario, became Kitchener-Cambridge-Waterloo. CMAs are further divided into census subdivisions if certain conditions are present.

census agglomeration (CA) Geographic area with a population over 10,000.

2. A **census agglomeration (CA)** is virtually the same as a CMA, except it is smaller. The population of the urban core of a CA must be at least 10,000. If the population of the urban core of a CA falls below 10,000, the CA is retired.

In defining CMAs and CAs, Statistics Canada has kept in mind that many companies use both Canadian and American statistics to compare markets. Although the methods used by both countries are not identical, they are similar enough that markets from both countries can be compared.[13]

USING GEOGRAPHIC SEGMENTATION

Demand for some categories of goods and services can vary according to geographic region, and marketers need to be aware of how these regions differ. Marketers of major brands are particularly interested in defining their **core regions**, the locations where they get 40 to 80 percent of their sales.

core region Region from which most major brands get 40 to 80 percent of their sales.

Residence location within a geographic area is an important segmentation variable. City dwellers often rely on public transportation and may get along fine without cars, whereas those who live in the suburbs or rural areas depend on their own cars and trucks. Also, those who live in the suburbs spend more on lawn and garden-care products than do people in the city. Climate is another important segmentation factor. Consumers who live in chilly areas, for example, eat more soup than people who live in warmer southern climates. But here's a surprise—they also eat a great deal of ice cream!

demographic segmentation Division of an overall market into homogeneous groups based on variables such as gender, age, income, occupation, education, sexual orientation, household size, and stage in the family life cycle; also called *socioeconomic segmentation*.

Geographic segmentation provides useful distinctions when regional preferences or needs exist. A consumer might not want to invest in a snow blower or flood insurance but may have to because of the location of his or her home. But it's important for marketers not to stop at geographic location as a segmentation method because distinctions among consumers also exist within a geographic location. Consider those who relocate from one region to another for work or family reasons. They may bring with them their preferences from other parts of the country. Using several segmentation variables is probably a much better strategy for targeting a specific market.

GEOGRAPHIC INFORMATION SYSTEMS (GISs)

Once used mainly by the military, geographic information systems (GISs) are computer systems that assemble, store, manipulate, and display data by their location. GISs simplify the job of analyzing marketing information by relating data to their locations. The result is a geographic map overlaid with digital data about consumers in a particular area. A growing number of companies benefit from using a GIS to locate new outlets, assign sales territories, plan distribution centres—and map out the most efficient delivery routes. Google Earth is a recent application of GIS technology that allows computer users to view different parts of the world close up. Users simply type in an address and zoom into it, whether it's a house, a theme park, a school, or a store.

Geographic information systems are becoming more mobile and more social as people increasingly turn to applications like Foursquare and Facebook Places to locate restaurants, movies, and stores. Retail stores can send ads to mobile phones, shoppers can find the location of a product within the store, or information about items on the shoppers' lists can be sent using geographic information systems. While this technology is slower to develop in Canada, countries like the United States and China are already experimenting with it.[14]

Geographic segmentation is illustrated by the buying habits of suburban homeowners.

Courtesy of Canadian Stone Industries

DEMOGRAPHIC SEGMENTATION

The most common method of market segmentation—**demographic segmentation**—defines consumer groups according to demographic variables such as gender, age, income, occupation, education, sexual orientation, household size, and stage in the family life cycle. This approach is also called *socioeconomic segmentation*. Marketers review vast quantities of available data to complete a plan for demographic segmentation. One of the primary sources for demographic data in Canada is Statistics Canada. Marketers can obtain many of the census statistics online at **www.statcan.gc.ca**.

The following discussion considers the most commonly used demographic variables. Keep in mind, however, that while demographic segmentation is helpful, it can also lead to stereotyping—a preconception about a group of people—which can alienate a potential market or cause marketers to miss a potential market altogether. The idea is to use segmentation as a starting point, not as an end point.

SEGMENTING BY GENDER

Gender is an obvious variable that helps define the markets for certain products, but segmenting by gender can be tricky. In some cases, the segmenting is obvious—lipstick for women, facial shaving products for men. But in recent years, the lines have become increasingly blurred. Men wear earrings and use skin-care products, once both the province of women. Women purchase power tools and pickup trucks, once considered traditionally male purchases. So marketers of cars and trucks, power tools, jewellery, and skin-care products have had to change the way they segment their markets. Nivea, well known for its skin-care products for women and babies, created an entire line of men's skin-care products called Nivea for Men. Some companies successfully market the same—or similar—products to both men and women. Visa markets its small-business credit card services to firms owned by both men and women.

As purchasing power in many households has shifted toward women, marketers have learned that female consumers who regularly use the Internet make most of the decisions about retail items. Based on this information, Yahoo! recently launched Shine, a site specifically for women. The site offers content in a variety of areas such as entertainment and finance and provides opportunities for advertisers to reach a targeted female audience. Puffs and Oral-B are among the brands that advertise on the site.[15]

SEGMENTING BY AGE

Age is another variable that marketers use to segment their markets. As with gender, age seems to be an easy distinction to make—baby food for babies, retirement communities for seniors. But the distinctions become blurred as consumers' roles and needs change, as age distribution shifts, and as changes in each group take place. Baby aspirin is no longer marketed just to parents for their infants; now it is also marketed to adults to help prevent heart disease.

School-Age Children

School-age children—and those who are even younger—exert considerable influence over family purchases, as marketers are keenly aware, particularly in the area of food. Children as young as 2 make choices about what they want to eat, play with, and wear. Advertisements for such products as breakfast cereals, snack foods, and beverages are designed to attract the attention of children under the age of 12—who in turn persuade their families to purchase them. With childhood obesity on the rise, nutritionists and pediatricians are concerned about the nutritional value of foods marketed to children. In fact, a recent study revealed that the advertising of junk food plays a key role in childhood obesity.[16] See the "Solving an Ethical Controversy" feature for a discussion of the role of high-fructose corn syrup, a high-calorie ingredient whose use in a wide variety of foods concerns many.

Some food and broadcast companies have formed organizations like Companies Committed to Kids (formerly Concerned Children's Advertisers) in order to promote responsible advertising toward children but very little regulation in this area exists.[17]

Segmenting by age.

SOLVING AN ETHICAL CONTROVERSY

Free to Choose High-Fructose Corn Syrup

HIGH-FRUCTOSE corn syrup is a common ingredient in many processed foods and drinks consumers buy and eat every day, such as soft drinks, baked goods, and even yogurt. Made from corn kernels blended into thick syrup, the ingredient is cheaper than sugar but high in calories with either little nutritional value or none (depending on whom you ask). It is blamed for a wide variety of health problems (including childhood obesity) and environmental impacts.

Should high-fructose corn syrup be banned from foods and soft drinks?

PRO

1. Long-term consumption leads to high levels of body fat and cholesterol, which can contribute to obesity, diabetes, and heart disease.

2. High-fructose corn syrup requires the cultivation of corn as a monoculture, depleting the soil of nutrients while flooding soil and groundwater with pesticides.

CON

1. High-fructose corn syrup helps baked, canned, and frozen goods look better and stay fresh and moist longer.
2. Even calories, in moderation, have their place in a balanced diet. Consumers should be able to make their own choices about what they eat.

Where do you stand: pro or con?

Sources: Jennifer K. Nelson, "Nutrition and Healthy Eating," Mayo Clinic.com, **www.mayoclinic.com**, accessed April 22, 2012; Marin Gazzaniga, "Sickeningly Sweet: The Effects of High-Fructose Corn Syrup," MSN.com, **http://health .ms.com**, accessed April 22, 2012; Amanda Hermes, "The Pros & Cons of High Fructose Corn Syrup," Live Strong.com, **www.livestrong.com**, accessed April 22, 2012; Nanci Heilmich, "Study: Kids Get More Added Sugar from Foods than Drinks," USA Today, February 20, 2012, **http://yourlife.usatoday.com**.

Tweens and Teens

Tweens—also called *preteens*—and teens are a rapidly growing market. This group packs a wallop when it comes to spending, and it influences purchases made by their families. Although members of this group don't fall into a single category—they reflect the diversity of the population in general—the most popular purchases are candy and snacks, soft drinks, clothing, music, and electronics. If marketers could characterize this group with one word, it would likely be *interactive*. They grew up with the Internet, and they expect to be actively involved in their own entertainment. They might rather determine the outcome of a video game than watch to see who won a hockey game on TV. Even the TV shows they watch—like *American Idol*—provide opportunities for input. They are completely comfortable in a digital world, and many cannot imagine life without their smartphones and iPods. When they want to communicate with friends—or parents—they send text messages. They expect a vast array of choices in programming, media alternatives, and interactive experiences. The big challenge for marketers is keeping up with them—let alone staying a step ahead. Phone companies and car companies have increased their spending on advertising to older teens, while snacks, clothing, and video games claim the attention of the younger set.[18]

Some companies have expanded their product lines to include specific offerings to tweens and teens. Lululemon Athletica, which specializes in athletic wear for women, recently launched a website featuring Ivivva, a new line of athletic and dance clothing for girls.[19]

Generation X

Generation X The group born between 1966 and 1981—who are in their 30s to early 40s.

The group born between 1966 and 1981, now generally in their early 30s to late 40s, are often referred to as **Generation X**. Members of this group faced some economic and career challenges as they began their adult lives and started families: Housing costs were high and debt associated with postsecondary education loans and credit cards was soaring. But their financial squeeze should ease as they enter their prime earning years. This group is very family oriented—not defining themselves by their careers as much as previous generations—well educated, and optimistic. Like their younger counterparts, Gen Xers are comfortable with the Internet. Even if they make a purchase at a retail store, they are likely to have researched their choices online. But like their elders, they were raised on television—so the TV is still an important marketing tool.[20]

As this generation matures, they are growing more concerned about social issues and protecting the natural environment, both of which they view as affecting the well-being of their children. As a result, they are turning to goods and services that support certain causes. Singer-songwriter Jack Johnson, in his mid-30s, recorded an album using solar energy. He requires his concert promoters to recycle and launched an online social networking site, All At Once, where fans can support environmental not-for-profit organizations. Johnson, a member of Generation X, appeals both to his own age group and older teens.[21]

Baby Boomers

Baby boomers—people born between 1947 and 1965—are a popular segment to target because of their numbers and income levels. Almost one in every three Canadians was born in this period. This group has been described as rebellious and spoiled, when in fact only about 25 percent of the boomers fit that description. They came of age with early television and with TV commercials serving as a backdrop to most of their lives. They tried new breakfast cereals, ate TV dinners, and can recall when cigarettes were advertised on television.[22]

baby boomers People born between the years of 1947 and 1965.

Not surprisingly, baby boomers are a lucrative segment for many marketers. By the year 2020, this group will be spending $1 trillion annually.[23] Different subgroups within this generation complicate segmentation and targeting strategies. Some boomers put off having children until their 40s, while others their age have already become grandparents. Boomers tend to value health and quality of life—a fact not lost on marketers for products like organic food, financial investments, travel, and fitness. But boomers are also quick to embrace new technology, even as they age. According to a recent study, baby boomers make up about 36 percent of Internet users. In addition, about 65 percent of all boomers maintain a Facebook page.[24]

The motorcycle industry has boomers clearly in its sights. As a group, baby boomers are significantly more physically active than their counterparts in previous generations. However, boomers are beginning to experience the wide range of health problems that typically come with age—back pain and muscle aches—making it difficult for them to continue to ride their two-wheel motorcycles. With baby boomers making up more than 40 percent of the motorcycling population, several manufacturers have introduced trikes—that is, three-wheeled motorcycles. The trikes even include luxury features like GPS navigation, cruise control, and stereo speakers.[25]

Seniors

Marketers also recognize a trend dubbed the greying of the population. By 2031, 23 percent of the Canadian population will be over 65. As Canadians have continued to live longer, the median age of the Canadian population has dramatically increased.

The current median age is now 39.9 years, up from 25.4 years in 1996. The average life expectancy in Canada has increased for both genders to age 79 for men and to age 83 for women. Explanations for these increases in life spans include better medicines and healthier lifestyles.[26] With discretionary income and rates of home ownership higher than those of other age groups, they also account for a high proportion of new car sales and travel dollars spent. Many marketers have found that seniors are a group worth targeting. Although many seniors live on modest, fixed incomes, those who are well off have both time and money to spend on leisure activities and luxury goods.

Other important characteristics of the group are the following:

- Families experienced economic hardship during this group's childhood.

- They built the suburbs.

- They value hard work.

- They like to associate with people who have similar views and backgrounds.

A New Perspective on Retirement Living

If you think you know Waterside Retirement Lodge, maybe it's time to think again! Visitors are astonished at the lively, independent lifestyle available at Waterside. Spacious apartments, a choice of meal options, a great fitness and recreation program – and as much independence and privacy as you want. **Granny wouldn't recognize this kind of retirement living!**

Call Lorree or Tanya today to book a tour and discover a refreshing new perspective.

705-429-8626
239 Zoo Park Rd, Wasaga Beach
www.jarlette.com

WATERSIDE Retirement Lodge Inc.

Making Waves in Retirement Living!

Courtesy of Jarlette Health Services. Photo © Masterfile Corporation

This ad is aimed at those who are retired or thinking of retiring.

- They are concerned with personal safety.

- They spend money conservatively, but have reached a level of financial comfort where they like to indulge in some luxury.

- They are not likely to be the first to try new products.[27]

Understanding just a few of these characteristics helps marketers develop goods and services and create marketing messages that will reach this group. Road Scholar, a branch of Elderhostel, is a nonprofit organization that has been offering educational travel for seniors since 1975. Its "Adventures in Lifelong Learning" currently offers 6,500 educational tours in every area of Canada and 150 countries. Instead of guides, the tours are run by instructors who are experts in their fields and by local educators. Lectures and field trips are part of the package, and the Road Scholar Travel Assistance Plan, included in the cost of the programs, ensures that anyone with a medical emergency will be cared for. Participants pay tuition rather than fees, and the program is supported by donations.[28]

The Cohort Effect: The Video-Game Generation

cohort effect Tendency of members of a generation to be influenced and bound together by events occurring during their key formative years— roughly 17 to 22 years of age.

Marketers can learn from a sociological concept called the **cohort effect**, the tendency of members of a generation with common characteristics—like an interest in sustainability—to be influenced and bound together by significant events occurring during their key formative years, roughly ages 17 to 22. These events help define the core values of the age group that eventually shapes consumer preferences and behaviour. For elderly seniors, the events would be the Great Depression and World War II because many were in this age bracket at that time. For older baby boomers, it would be the Vietnam War and the women's rights movement.

The current cohort—generally consisting of those born during the late 1970s to the early 1990s—may be the most cohesive to date. Marketers have called this group by several names: Generation Y, the Millennial Generation, Generation Next, and the Echo Boomers (an echo of baby boomers). Others called it the 9/11 Generation because its members were in their formative years during the terrorist attacks of September 11, 2001.

But something else happened during this group's formative years to shape its preferences and behaviours: while they were coming of age, so too were video games. For this reason, we call this cohort the **Video-Game Generation**.

Video-Game Generation A group called by several names: Generation Y, the Millennial Generation, Generation Next, the 9/11 generation, and the Echo Boomers (an echo of baby boomers), whose preferences were shaped at the same time as video games.

The early versions of video games were developed during the 1950s and 1960s and were displayed on oscilloscopes, mainframe computers, and television screens. Atari and Magnavox were the first commercial entrants on the scene, with Atari introducing its Pong game, and Magnavox launching the Odyssey home video-game system. During the late 1970s and 1980s, other competitors entered the market: Activision, Commodore, Nintendo, Sega, and more. As the technology improved, the games and systems became more sophisticated, with 3-D, realistic graphics, laser disks, and hand-held consoles. The industry has continued to evolve, with the introduction of PlayStation, the Nintendo DS, Microsoft's Xbox, and the Wii. Today, more consumers regularly play video games—at home, on their mobile phone, on the beach, anywhere—than go to the movies.

Members of the Video-Game Generation are highly visual and are generally comfortable with all forms of technology. They gravitate to activities that provide constant entertainment and immediate gratification. They get their information from social media like Facebook as opposed to traditional media, and they prefer instant messaging and texting to email.

The significance of the cohort effect for marketers lies in understanding the general characteristics of the Video-Game Generation as it responds to its life-defining events. The social and economic influences it experiences help form members' long-term beliefs and goals in life—and can have a lasting effect on their buying habits and the product choices they make.[29]

SEGMENTING BY ETHNIC GROUP

According to Statistics Canada, the ethnic makeup of our population is changing. Other than the two largest ethnic groups, English and French, between 29 and 32 percent of the people in Canada will be from different ethnic backgrounds by 2031. Since 2006, 66 percent of Canada's population growth has been the result of immigration.[30]

Figure 9.2 show the makeup of Canada's ethnic population. The three largest groups, Chinese, South Asians, and Blacks, account for 75 percent of those indicating an ethnic category on the Statistics Canada census; however, the South Asian group may catch up to the Chinese in numbers by 2017. From a marketer's perspective, it is important to understand the spending patterns of these groups.[31]

French and English

Many companies today realize there are major differences between the French- and English-speaking markets in Canada besides language, but these markets have not always been treated differently. Marketers from various organizations have attempted to reach the Quebecois market, but for many years, companies ran their English ads in Quebec in direct translations.[32]

The father of made-in-Quebec marketing, Jacques Bouchard, spent 30 years studying the Quebecois consumer. He explains the differences between the French and English consumers using a six-element model based on roots.

- Root number one, Rural Root, refers to Quebecois who feel the need to be closer to nature. There is a high number of fishermen and hunters, and they crave a simple life but describe their lives as hectic. They like to keep their traditions alive.

- The Minority Root describes Quebecois in relation to other parts of the world. They live for the moment, generally are tolerant and understanding, and have a matriarchal family structure.

- The North American Root explains how they enjoy an American lifestyle—they love to shop and describe their homes as "lived in."

- The Catholic Root looks at the influence of religion.

- The Latin Root is reflected in the importance of enjoying life.

- The French Root is evident in their feeling of connection with a region.[33]

One tradition that has not changed is the love for hockey in Quebec. Boston Pizza uses that relationship to get hockey fans into their restaurants when the Montreal team is playing by offering free chicken wings during the game.[34]

Chinese Canadians

One of the largest ethnic groups in Canada, the Chinese, is not a homogeneous segment. While it is true that most Chinese Canadians live in Toronto and Vancouver, they did not all come from the same areas of the world, nor are their shopping habits similar.

When Hong Kong was repatriated, a large number of fairly wealthy immigrants arrived in Canada; since then, arrivals from Hong Kong have slowed while those arriving from mainland China, Taiwan, and Southeast Asia are on the increase. People from each of these environments bring different values with them based on their home country and, in some cases, a different language. Hong Kong, for example, is heavily influenced by its past connection to Britain, and people from Hong Kong place higher importance on recognition and status. Physical comforts and luxuries are important to consumers from mainland China. The only democratic Chinese country is Taiwan, where national identity plays an important role. The values that all Chinese cultures share include a trust in family, hard work, thrift, and a tendency to save and invest in both tangible and liquid assets.[35]

figure 9.2

Canadian Visible Minority Populations

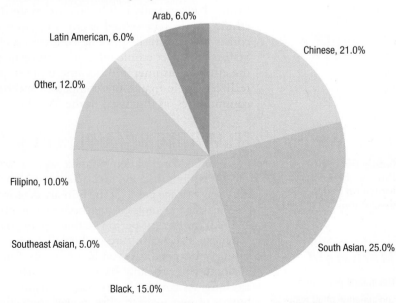

Source: Adapted from the Statistics Canada website article "NHS Profile, Canada 2011," available at **statcan.gc.ca**, accessed February 22, 2014.

Chinese consumers tend to be superstitious—colours and numbers are important. They like red and gold, but not white because it is the colour of mourning. When pricing products and services, the numbers 2, 3, 8, and 9 are good, but 4 is considered unlucky. It is important for the Chinese to look respected or important to their friends and family. Status is important to this market, so they are purchasers of luxury products. Advertising in their language is important to older Chinese consumers, with 55 percent of them watching culturally specific programs every day. There is more than one language, depending on where they came from. Younger Chinese customers generally speak English. Chinese consumers read their ethnic newspapers and spend more time on the Internet than other Canadians. Marketers who understand these characteristics will be more successful when marketing to this group.[36]

South Asian Canadians

South Asians are another large group in Canada, but they are the largest ethnic group in Ontario. Their countries of origin include India, Pakistan, and Bangladesh. This group is value and brand conscious. They have a greater tendency to be conspicuous consumers as a way of demonstrating success. The female head of the household is often the major decision maker for most items, such as food, appliances, cars, and homes. Purchase decisions in this group are often influenced by the attitudes of family and friends. This group watches cricket, Bollywood movies, and television programming from their country of origin. This is not a homogeneous group. While many are well educated, just as many come from small villages and have blue-collar jobs. Family is important to this group. It is not unusual for more than one generation to be living together.[37]

Black Canadians

The Black Canadian group represents an $11-billion market annually. This group has not received the same amount of attention from marketers as the Chinese or South Asian Canadians. Members of this community originate in Africa or the Caribbean. Canadian marketers are often criticized about the type of marketing that is directed at Black Canadians. Within this community there are many micro-cultures, and a strategy that works for one may not work for another. This group is also compared to the Black community in the United States, and while some within this group are not offended by this, others are. Members of this group are heavy purchasers of skin- and hair-care products, but often have difficulty finding products that will work with their skin and hair colours and textures.[38]

Other Ethnic Groups

Ethnic backgrounds in Canada are more diverse than just those mentioned, and the number of ethnic groups represented is growing. So is their spending. The Hispanic/Latino group in Canada comes from Spanish-speaking countries such as Mexico and is not nearly as large as in the United States. Whatever ethnic influences motivate the shopping habits of Canadians, one thing is for sure: the ethnic consumer will become more important in the future if projected immigration rates are realized. Some marketing companies specialize in meeting the needs of Canada's different ethnic communities, as discussed in the "Marketing and the SME" feature.

SEGMENTING BY FAMILY LIFE CYCLE STAGES

family life cycle
Process of family formation and dissolution.

Still another form of demographic segmentation employs the stages of the family life cycle—the process of family formation and dissolution. The underlying theme of this segmentation approach is that life stage, not age per se, is the primary determinant of many consumer purchases. As people move from one life stage to another, they become potential consumers for different types of goods and services.

An unmarried person setting up an apartment for the first time is likely to be a good prospect for inexpensive furniture and small home appliances. This consumer probably budgets carefully, ruling out expenditures on luxury items. On the other hand, a young single person who is still living at home will probably have more money to spend on products such as a car, entertainment, and clothing. As couples marry, their consumer profiles change. Couples without children are frequent buyers of personalized gifts, power tools, furniture, and homes. Eating out and travel may also be part of their lifestyles.

Marketoid

The annual per capita consumption of all milk products is over 75 litres.

Multicultural Communications

CANADA'S diverse cultural population often requires unique promotional strategies designed specifically for different cultural groups. Two companies that specialize in developing promotional strategies and material for these different groups are AV Communications and Monsoon Communications.

AV Communications is a full-service advertising agency that assists clients with their multicultural communications in print and online. They developed promotional material for the Chinese, South Asian, Filipino, Latin American, Caribbean, and African customers of companies such as Western Union and Rogers. One of their campaigns for Western Union, its "5 for 50" holiday promotion, won a CASSIES award. (The CASSIES awards are presented for business effectiveness through advertising.) The "5 for 50" campaign involved posters that included QR codes and were displayed in shopping malls and on public transit targeting different cultural groups. Scanning the QR codes with a smartphone would take the customer to a special Western Union website where they would receive a price discount on a money transfer. Another of AV Communication's award-winning campaigns was a BMW Chinese New Year campaign. Using a red background— red signifying good luck in the Chinese community—and the tagline "BMW wishes you a smooth ride for the new year," the artwork for this campaign showed only the front of the car.

Monsoon Communications works with several of the Loblaw group of companies as well as Kraft and the Heart & Stroke Foundation. For the Heart & Stroke foundation, it modified the campaign "Make Health Last" to reach the South Asian community. Targeting South Asians aged 40 to 55, this promotion aimed to educate its audience about lifestyle and attitude changes that could reduce the likelihood of health problems. The South Asian community was the target audience because this group has a higher risk of heart disease than the general population. The campaign included television and radio ads as well as print. The promotion for Loblaw included a video of the well-known chef Vikram Vij promoting the freshness of the produce at the grocery store.

Both AV Communications and Monsoon Communications understand the importance of reaching a diverse market.

Sources: Rebecca Harris, "Monsoon Aims to 'Make Health Last' for South Asian Community," *Marketing*, May 13, 2013, **www.marketingmag.ca**; AV Communications website, **http://avcommunications.ca**, accessed February 26, 2014; Chris Daniels, "Facebook? Big Deal, Are You on Weibo?" *Marketing*, April 17, 2014, **www.marketingmag.ca**; Kristin Laird, "Marketer Shortlist 2013: Heart & Stroke Foundation," *Marketing*, December 10, 2013, **www.marketingmag.ca**; Monsoon Communications website, **http://monsooncommunications.ca**, accessed February 26, 2014.

The birth of a first child changes any couple's consumer profile considerably; parents must buy cribs, changing tables, baby clothes, baby food, car seats, and similar products. Parents usually spend less on the children who follow the first because they have already bought many essential items for

the first child. Today, the average woman gives birth to fewer children than she did a century ago and usually waits until she is older to have them. The most recent statistics show that the fertility rate in Canada is 1.6, and that 51 percent of women have their first child after the age of 30.[39] This means that if they work outside the home, older women are likely to be more established financially, with more money to spend. However, if a woman chooses to stay at home after the birth of a child, income can drop dramatically.

Families typically spend the most during the years their children are growing—on basics such as housing, food, and clothing and more specialized items such as braces and college. Thus they often look to obtain value wherever they can. Marketers can create satisfied and loyal customers among this group by giving them the best value possible.

Once the children are grown and on their own—or at least off to university or college—married couples enter the empty-nest stage. Empty nesters may have the disposable incomes necessary to purchase premium

Many firms have websites designed specifically for the Quebec market.

Book your FREE design consultation today

Custom designed storage solutions for everyday life.
Make the most of your space. Call 416 385 8855.
simplyclosets.ca

simply closets

Courtesy of Simply Closets

This ad is an example of segmenting by family life cycle stage.

products once university or college tuitions and mortgages are paid off. They may travel more, eat out more often, redecorate the house, or go back to school themselves. They may treat themselves to a new and more luxurious car or buy a vacation home. In later years, empty nesters may decide to sell their homes and become customers for retirement or assisted living communities. They may require home-care services or more health care products. However, many older adults will continue to work a couple of days a week. A recent study found that about a third of Canadians expect to be working past the age 65, the traditional retirement age. The majority of them stated that they could not afford to retire at age 65, but felt they could do so by age 67.[40]

One trend noted by researchers in the past decade is an increase in the number of grown children who have returned home to live with their parents. Called boomerangs, some of these grown children bring along families of their own. The latest census data revealed that 42 percent of adults in the 20- to 29-year-old age range lived with their parents.[41] Another trend is the growing number of grandparents who care for grandchildren on a regular basis—making them customers all over again for baby and child products such as toys, food, and safety devices. Cangrands, the national group that supports grandparents who are raising their grandchildren, estimates there are over 60,000 children in Canada in this situation.[42]

SEGMENTING BY HOUSEHOLD TYPE

According to Statistics Canada, from 1981 to 2011, the average size of households in Canada declined from 2.9 to 2.5 people.[43] There are several reasons for the trend toward smaller households: lower fertility rates (including the decision to have fewer children or no children at all), young people's tendency to postpone marriage, the frequency of divorce, and the ability and desire of many people to live alone.

Today's households represent a wide range of diversity. They include households with a married couple and their children; households that are blended through divorce or loss of a spouse and remarriage; those headed by a single parent, same-sex parents, or grandparents; couples without children; groups of friends; and single-person households.

Couples without children may be young or old. If they are seniors, their children may have already grown and are living on their own. The percentage of couples with no children under the age of 25 living at home has increased steadily for the last 10 years. Couples living common-law (living together but not married) have also seen a significant increase, reaching 16.7 percent by 2011. This trend is strongest in Quebec and the Territories, where common-law relationships represent 25 to 32 percent of all families.[44] Couples who are younger and do not have children are considered attractive to marketers because they often have high levels of income, allowing them to spend more freely. These couples typically eat out often, take expensive vacations, and buy luxury cars.

The 2001 census was the first time data on same-sex partnerships were collected. In the 2011 census, same-sex couples represented only 0.8 percent of all couples, with 54 percent of these being male.[45] Since same-sex marriage was legalized in Canada in 2005, same-sex couples in Canada have the same legal, social, and financial benefits as opposite-sex couples.

People live alone for a variety of reasons—sometimes by choice and sometimes by necessity such as divorce or widowhood. In response, marketers have modified their messages and their products to meet the needs of single-person households. Food manufacturers are downsizing products and offering more single-serving foods such as soup and macaroni and cheese.

Regardless of the type of household, households are often used to collect information about trends in society, as can be seen by the ongoing study of households and the environment discussed in the "Marketing: Making Your World Better" feature.

| MARKETING: MAKING YOUR WORLD BETTER | **Households and the Environment** |

ENVIRONMENTAL trends are so important in today's society that Statistics Canada, Environment Canada, Health Canada, Natural Resources Canada, and several provincial organizations have joined forces to collect information about how Canadian households are adapting to environmentally friendly products and practices. The results of the studies are available on the Statistics Canada website under EnviroStats.

As part of this initiative, Statistics Canada performed the Households and the Environment Survey (HES). Over 20,000 households across Canada were asked questions relating to household activities that would have both positive and negative impacts on the environment. Topics covered included water and energy use, indoor environments, household hazardous waste, disposal of electronic waste, and purchasing decisions. The results were compared to similar studies conducted since the 1990s.

With regard to water, the survey found almost 68 percent of households drank tap water. Canadian households that primarily drank bottled water continued to drop in the two-year period from the previous survey. The survey also found that 63 percent of Canadian households had water-saving showerheads, up from 42 percent in 1994, and 47 percent had a water-saving toilet, up from 15 percent in 1994.

The energy-use part of the survey found that Canadians are purchasing more environmentally friendly devices. The number of households using at least one compact fluorescent light increased from 19 percent in 1994 to 76 percent. Households with programmable thermostats increased from 16 percent in 1994 to 54 percent, and about 83 percent of households with programmable thermostats had actually programmed them to control the temperature. The latest survey found that 13 percent of homes in Canada had had an energy audit performed within a two-year period, and 89 percent had had an energy audit performed within the last 10 years.

The study also highlighted how Canadians were dealing with household hazardous waste. Just over 60 percent of households with leftover or unwanted medications disposed of them correctly. Roughly the same percentage of households with unwanted paint or solvents dropped them off at disposal centres.

Source: "Households and the Environment: 2011," Statistics Canada, Catalogue no. 11-526-X

SEGMENTING BY INCOME AND EXPENDITURE PATTERNS

Part of the earlier definition of *market* described people with purchasing power. Not surprisingly, then, a common basis for segmenting the consumer market is income. Marketers often target geographic areas known for the high incomes of their residents. Or they might consider age or household type when determining potential buying power.

Engel's Laws

How do expenditure patterns vary with income? Over a century ago, Ernst Engel, a German statistician, published what became known as Engel's laws—three general statements based on his studies of the impact of household income changes on consumer spending behaviour. According to Engel, as household income increases, the following will take place:

1. A smaller percentage of expenditures goes for food.

2. The percentage spent on housing, household operations, and clothing remains constant.

3. The percentage spent on other items (such as recreation and education) increases.

Are Engel's laws still valid? Recent studies say yes, with a few exceptions. Researchers note a steady decline in the percentage of total income spent on food and beverages as income increases. Although high-income families spend greater absolute amounts on food items, their purchases represent declining percentages of their total expenditures compared with low-income families.[46] In addition, the overall percentage of income spent on food has declined over the last century.[47] But as food prices become inflated, consumers change how they shop—they may spend the same to buy fewer items, spend more to buy the same items, or try to spend less and buy as many items as possible within the new budget. Marketers note that consumers are more selective, on the alert for bargains at the supermarket.

An ad targeting people with significant disposable income.

The second law remains partly accurate. However, the percentage of fixed expenditures for housing and household operations has increased over the past 30 years, and the percentage spent on clothing rises with increased income. The third law remains true, with the exception of personal-care costs, which appear to decline as a percentage of increased income.

Engel's laws can help marketers target markets at all income levels. Regardless of the economic environment, consumers still buy luxury goods and services. One reason is that some companies now offer their luxury products at different price levels. Mercedes-Benz has its lower-priced C-class models, while the jewellery store Birks sells a $100 sterling silver heart pendant with chain. Both these firms continue to offer their higher-priced items as well, but have chosen to broaden their market by serving other consumers.

DEMOGRAPHIC SEGMENTATION ABROAD

Marketers often face a difficult task in obtaining the data necessary for demographic segmentation abroad. Many countries do not have scheduled census programs. Germany skipped counting from 1970 to 1987, and France conducts a census about every seven years. In contrast, Japan conducts a census every five years; however, the mid-decade assessments are not as complete as the end-of-decade counts.

Also, some foreign data include demographic divisions not found in the Canadian census. Not all countries collect information on religious affiliation, for instance. On the other hand, some of the standard segmentation data for Canadian markets are not available abroad. Many nations do not collect income data. Great Britain, Japan, Spain, France, and Italy are examples. Similarly, family life-cycle data are difficult to apply in global demographic segmentation efforts. Ireland acknowledges only three marital statuses—single, married, and widowed—while Latin American nations and Sweden count their unmarried cohabitants.

psychographic segmentation Division of a population into groups that have similar attitudes, values, and lifestyles.

One source of global demographic information is the Industry Canada website. Industry Canada provides a searchable online database of population statistics for many countries. Another source is the United Nations, which sponsors national statistical offices that collect demographic data on a variety of countries.

Some companies have expanded their product lines to include specific offerings to tweens and teens, such as lululemon's ivivva.

PSYCHOGRAPHIC SEGMENTATION

Marketers have traditionally referred to geographic and demographic characteristics as the primary bases for dividing consumers into homogeneous market segments. Still, they have long recognized the need for fuller, more lifelike portraits of consumers in developing their marketing programs. As a result, psychographic segmentation can be a useful tool for gaining sharper insight into consumer purchasing behaviour.

WHAT IS PSYCHOGRAPHIC SEGMENTATION?

Psychographic segmentation divides a population into groups that have similar values and lifestyles. Lifestyle refers to a person's mode of living; it describes how an individual operates on a daily basis. Consumers' lifestyles are composites of their individual psychological profiles, including their needs, motives, perceptions, and attitudes. A lifestyle also bears the mark of many other influences, such as family, job, social activities, and culture.

The most common method for developing psychographic profiles of a population is to conduct a large-scale survey that asks consumers to agree or disagree with a collection of several hundred AIO statements. These **AIO statements** describe various activities, interests, and opinions. The resulting data allow researchers to develop lifestyle profiles. Marketers can then develop a separate marketing strategy that closely fits the psychographic makeup for each lifestyle segment.

Marketing researchers have conducted psychographic studies on hundreds of goods and services such as beer and air travel. Many businesses turn to psychographic research in an effort to learn what consumers in various demographic and geographic segments want and need.

VALS™

The **VALS™** segmentation system divides consumers into eight psychographic categories: innovators, thinkers, believers, achievers, strivers, experiencers, makers, and survivors.

A quarter century ago, the research and consulting firm SRI International developed a psychographic segmentation system called VALS, an acronym for *VALues and Lifestyles*. Initially VALS categorized consumers by their social values—how they felt about issues such as legalization of marijuana or abortion. Today VALS is owned and managed by SRI Consulting Business Intelligence (SRIC-BI), an SRI spin-off that has revised the system to link it more closely with consumer buying behaviour. The revised VALS system categorizes consumers by characteristics that correlate with purchase behaviour. It is based on two key concepts: resources and innovation. VALS divides consumers into eight psychographic categories: innovators, thinkers, achievers, experiencers, believers, strivers, makers, and survivors. Figure 9.3 details the profiles for these categories and their relationships.

The VALS framework in the figure displays differences in resources as vertical distances, and primary innovation is represented horizontally. The resource dimension measures income, education, self-confidence, health, eagerness to buy, and energy level. The innovation dimension divide consumers into three groups: principle-motivated consumers, who have a set of ideas and morals—principles—that they live by; achievement-motivated consumers, who are influenced by symbols of success; and action-motivated consumers, who seek physical activity, variety, and adventure.

SRIC-BI has created several specialized segmentation systems based on this approach. Japan-VALS segments the Japanese marketplace with an emphasis on early adopters of new ideas and products. GeoVALS estimates the percentage of each VALS type by U.S. zip code.[48]

Other tools available are Canada's Social Value Tribes, developed by Michael Adams and Environics Research Group Ltd. Environics crunches the numbers on hundreds of personal variables that include political views, religious affiliations, and social attitudes and comes up with 12 psychographic categories within three tribes that reflect Canadian social values.

figure 9.3

The VALS™ Framework

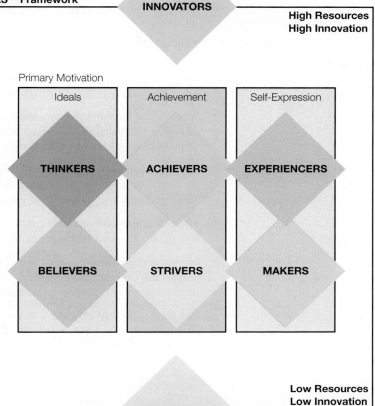

Source: SRI Consulting Business Intelligence, **www.sric-bi.com/VALS/**

AIO statements Items on lifestyle surveys that describe various activities, interests, and opinions of respondents.

VALS™ Segmentation system that divides consumers into eight psychographic categories: innovators, thinkers, achievers, experiencers, believers, strivers, makers, and survivors.

Depending on your own variables, you might be a "thrill-seeking materialist" or an "aimless dependent," both fitting into the Gen X Tribe.[49]

PSYCHOGRAPHIC SEGMENTATION OF GLOBAL MARKETS

As JapanVALS suggests, psychographic profiles can cross national boundaries. An international marketing research firm surveyed 7,000 people in 35 countries. From the resulting data, the company identified six psychographic consumer segments that exist in all 35 nations, although to varying degrees:

- *Strivers*, the largest segment, value professional and material goals more than the other groups. One-third of the Asian population and one-fourth of Russians are strivers. They are slightly more likely to be men than women.

- *Devouts* value duty and tradition. While this segment is made up of 22 percent of all adults, they are most common in Africa, the Middle East, and developing Asia. They are least common in Western Europe and developed Asian countries. Worldwide, they are more likely to be female.

- *Altruists* emphasize social issues and societal well-being. Making up 18 percent of all adults, this group shows a median age of 44 and a slightly higher percentage of women.

- *Intimates* value family and personal relationships. They are divided almost equally between males and females. One North American or European in four would be categorized as intimates, but only 7 percent of consumers in developing Asia fall into this category.

- *Fun seekers*, as you might guess from their name, focus on personal enjoyment and pleasurable experiences. They make up 12 percent of the world's population, with a male–female ratio of 54 to 46. Many live in developed Asia.

- *Creatives*, the smallest segment, account for just 10 percent of the global population. This group seeks education, technology, and knowledge; and their male–female ratio is roughly equal.

Researchers note that some principles and core beliefs—such as protecting the family—apply to more than one psychographic segment.

Baby boomers are a lucrative segment for many marketers.

forestpath/Shutterstock.com

USING PSYCHOGRAPHIC SEGMENTATION

No one suggests that psychographic segmentation is an exact science, but it does help marketers quantify aspects of consumers' personalities and lifestyles to create goods and services for a target market. Psychographic profile systems like VALS can paint useful pictures of the overall psychological motivations of consumers. These profiles produce much richer descriptions of potential target markets than other techniques can achieve. The enhanced detail aids in matching a company's image and product offerings with the types of consumers who use its products.

Identifying which psychographic segments are most prevalent in certain markets helps marketers plan and promote more effectively. Often, segments overlap. In a recent study of mobile phone users, researchers discovered five distinct segments, which they named basic planners, mobile professionals, pragmatic adopters, social connectors, and mobitati. The mobitati segment represents those mobile phone users whose phones are such an important part of their lives they cannot live without them. Mobile phones have become so prevalent that the user population is large enough to be studied and segmented.[50]

Psychographic segmentation is a good supplement to segmentation by demographic or geographic variables. For example, marketers may have access to each consumer type's media preferences in network television, cable television, Internet use, radio format, magazines, and newspapers. Psychographic studies may then refine the picture of segment characteristics to give a more elaborate lifestyle profile of the consumers in the firm's target market. A psychographic study could help marketers of goods and services across the country predict what kinds of products consumers in particular cities would be drawn to and eliminate those that are not attractive.

PRODUCT-RELATED SEGMENTATION

Product-related segmentation involves dividing a consumer population into homogeneous groups based on their relationships to the product. This segmentation approach can take several forms:

1. Segmenting based on the benefits that people seek when they buy a product

2. Segmenting based on usage rates for a product

3. Segmenting according to consumers' brand loyalty toward a product

SEGMENTING BY BENEFITS SOUGHT

This approach focuses on the attributes that people seek and the benefits they expect to receive from a good or service. It groups consumers into segments based on what they want a product to do for them. Consumers who drink Starbucks premium coffees are not just looking for a dose of caffeine. They are willing to pay extra to savour a pleasant experience, one that makes them feel pampered and appreciated. Women who work out at Curves want to look their best and feel healthy. Pet owners who feed their cats and dogs Science Diet believe that they are giving their animals a great-tasting, healthy pet food.

Even if a business offers only one product line, however, marketers must remember to consider product benefits. Two people may buy the same product for very different reasons. A box of baking soda could end up serving as a refrigerator freshener, a toothpaste substitute, an antacid, or a deodorizer for a cat's litter box.

SEGMENTING BY USAGE RATES

Marketers may also segment a total market by grouping people according to the amounts of a product that they buy and use. Markets can be divided into heavy-user, moderate-user, and light-user segments. The **80/20 principle** holds that a big percentage of a product's revenues—maybe 80 percent—comes from a relatively small, loyal percentage of total customers—perhaps 20 percent. The 80/20 principle is sometimes referred to as Pareto's Principle. Although the percentages need not exactly equal these figures, the general principle often holds true: relatively few heavy users of a product can account for much of its consumption.

Depending on their goals, marketers may target heavy, moderate, or light users as well as nonusers. A company may attempt to lure heavy users of another product away from their regular brands to try a new brand. Nonusers and light users may be attractive prospects because other companies are ignoring them. Usage rates can also be linked to other segmentation methods such as demographic and psychographic segmentation.

SEGMENTING BY BRAND LOYALTY

A third product-related segmentation method groups consumers according to the strength of the brand loyalty they feel toward a product. A classic example of brand loyalty segmentation is a frequent purchase program—it might be frequent flyer, frequent stay, or frequent purchase of shoes or gasoline. Other companies attempt to segment their market by developing brand loyalty over a period of time, through consumers' stages of life. Children whose parents dress them in Baby Gap clothes may grow up to wear Gap Kids and Gap clothing.

③ **Describe product-related segmentation.**

product-related segmentation Division of a population into homogeneous groups based on their relationships to the product.

80/20 principle Generally accepted rule that 80 percent of a product's revenues come from 20 percent of its total customers.

Companies fight for loyalty on just about every front. After McDonald's rolled out its McCafé line of coffee drinks, Burger King announced it would begin serving Seattle's Best Coffee in its restaurants. After McDonald's launched its free coffee loyalty program, Tim Hortons followed with its loyalty program in which customers can earn "Tim Cash" if they pay for their coffee with a credit card.[51]

USING MULTIPLE SEGMENTATION BASES

Segmenting a market can help marketers increase their accuracy in reaching the right consumers. Like other marketing tools, segmentation is probably best used in a flexible manner—for instance, combining geographic and demographic segmentation techniques or dovetailing product-related segmentation with segmentation by income and expenditure patterns. The important point to keep in mind is that segmentation is a tool to help marketers get to know their potential customers better and ultimately satisfy their needs with the appropriate goods and services.

assessment check 3 ✓

3.1 List the three approaches to product-related segmentation.

3.2 What is the 80/20 principle?

④ **Identify the steps in the market segmentation process and discuss four basic strategies for reaching target markets.**

THE MARKET SEGMENTATION PROCESS

To this point, the chapter has discussed various bases on which companies segment markets. But how do marketers decide which segmentation base—or bases—to use? Firms may use a management-driven method, in which segments are predefined by managers based on their observation of the behavioural and demographic characteristics of likely users. Or they may use a market-driven method, in which segments are defined by asking customers which attributes are important. Then marketers follow a four-stage process.

1. DEVELOP A RELEVANT PROFILE FOR EACH SEGMENT

After identifying promising segments, marketers should understand the customers in each one. This in-depth analysis of customers helps managers accurately match buyers' needs with the firm's marketing offers. The process must identify characteristics that both explain the similarities among customers within each segment and account for differences among segments.

The task at this stage is to develop a profile of the typical customer in each segment. Such a profile might include information about lifestyle patterns, attitudes toward product attributes and brands, product-use habits, geographic locations, and demographic characteristics.

2. FORECAST MARKET POTENTIAL

In the second stage, market segmentation and market opportunity analysis combine to produce a forecast of market potential within each segment. Market potential sets the upper limit on the demand that competing firms can expect from a segment. Multiplying by market share determines a single firm's maximum sales potential. This step should define a preliminary go or no-go decision from management because the total sales potential in each segment must justify resources devoted to further analysis. For example, in deciding whether to market a new product to teens, electronics firms need to determine the demand for it and the disposable income of that group.

3. FORECAST PROBABLE MARKET SHARE

Once market potential has been estimated, a firm must forecast its probable market share. Competitors' positions in targeted segments must be analyzed, and a specific marketing strategy must be designed to reach these segments. These two activities may be performed simultaneously. Moreover, by settling on a marketing strategy and tactics, a firm determines the expected level of resources it must commit—that is, the costs it will incur to tap the potential demand in each segment.

Apple's iPod took the marketplace by storm, followed by the iPhone, and analysts believe these two products helped boost sales of the iMac computers as well. Most recently, Apple's latest version of the iPad was met with a flood of orders: 3 million were sold over the first weekend alone, about three times as many as during the launch of the original iPad.[52]

4. SELECT SPECIFIC MARKET SEGMENTS

The information, analysis, and forecasts accumulated throughout the entire market segmentation decision process allow management to assess the potential for achieving company goals and to justify committing resources in developing one or more segments. Demand forecasts, together with cost projections, determine the profits and the return on investment (ROI) that the company can expect from each segment. Marketing strategy and tactics must be designed to reinforce the firm's image, yet keep within its unique organizational capabilities.

At this point in the analysis, marketers weigh more than monetary costs and benefits; they also consider many difficult-to-measure but critical organizational and environmental factors. The firm may lack experienced personnel to launch a successful attack on an attractive market segment. Similarly, a firm with a dominant market position may face possible legal problems with the Competition Bureau if it increases its market concentration or is seen to be engaging in anticompetitive acts.[53] This assessment of both financial and nonfinancial factors is a difficult but vital step in the decision process.

STRATEGIES FOR REACHING TARGET MARKETS

Marketers spend a lot of time and effort developing strategies that will best match their firm's product offerings to the needs of particular target markets. An appropriate match is vital to the firm's marketing success. Marketers have identified four basic strategies for achieving consumer satisfaction: undifferentiated marketing, differentiated marketing, concentrated marketing, and micromarketing. Social media is rapidly becoming a profitable means of reaching

---

CAREER READINESS   **Reaching Target Markets with Social Media**

SOCIAL media allows for more precise targeting of consumer and other markets than ever before. How can *you* make the most of it? Here are some tips.

1. Know your target market and its most important segments. How does your audience use your product, and what unsolved problems do they face?
2. Join the online communities where your target audience gathers, including Facebook, LinkedIn, Twitter, Google+, and Pinterest, and influential blogs.
3. Understand how these sites and their users differ from each other. All social media sites are not alike.
4. Start by spending some time listening, so you can learn about users' concerns, problems, and preferences. Learn and follow the social conventions of each community as well.

5. Start chiming in with helpful tips and advice that revolve around your market, not your product. Help users solve problems rather than pitching your product or service.
6. Find additional content that matters to your audience, and share it with them.
7. If you add more tools, like widgets, make sure they're easy to use and require minimal effort.
8. Consider using audio and video. A large number of people watch a video online every day.

Sources: Elizabeth Wilson, "Know Your Target Market," *Entrepreneur*, **www.entrepreneur.com**, accessed April 21, 2012; Phil Mershon, "5 Social Media Tips for Finding and Engaging Your Target Audience: New Research," Social Media Examiner.com, March 28, 2012, **www.socialmediaexaminer.com**; Jen Williams, "Reaching Your Target Market Through Social Media," Pronet Advertising.com, February 29, 2012, **www.pronetadvertising.com**.

audiences in all these strategies; see the "Career Readiness" feature for some ways to do so successfully.

UNDIFFERENTIATED MARKETING

undifferentiated marketing Strategy that focuses on producing a single product and marketing it to all customers; also called *mass marketing*.

A firm may produce only one product or product line and promote it to all customers with a single marketing mix; such a firm is said to practise **undifferentiated marketing**, sometimes called *mass marketing*. Undifferentiated marketing was much more common in the past than it is today.

While undifferentiated marketing is efficient from a production viewpoint, the strategy also brings inherent dangers. A firm that attempts to satisfy everyone in the market with one standard product may suffer if competitors offer specialized alternatives to smaller segments of the total market and better satisfy individual segments. In fact, firms that implement strategies of differentiated marketing, concentrated marketing, or micromarketing may capture enough small segments of the market to defeat another competitor's strategy of undifferentiated marketing. The golden arches of McDonald's have always stood for quick, inexpensive meals. Consumers could count on the same food and same dining experience at every McDonald's they visited. But McDonald's marketers are changing the firm's strategy somewhat in response to a trend that says consumers want a little luxury with their burger and fries and a more varied dining experience from restaurant to restaurant. Some stores feature wall-mounted televisions and a colour scheme featuring earth tones. The company also introduced new products such as Fruit & Nut Oatmeal.[54]

DIFFERENTIATED MARKETING

differentiated marketing Strategy that focuses on producing several products and pricing, promoting, and distributing them with different marketing mixes designed to satisfy smaller segments.

concentrated marketing Focusing marketing efforts on satisfying a single market segment; also called *niche marketing*.

Firms that promote numerous products with differing marketing mixes designed to satisfy smaller segments are said to practise **differentiated marketing**. By providing increased satisfaction for each of many target markets, a company can produce more sales by following a differentiated marketing strategy than undifferentiated marketing would generate. A marketer of a variety of meat products might practise a differentiated strategy. In order to increase sales, it might introduce a new snack food for children to take to school for lunch. In general, however, differentiated marketing also raises costs. Production costs usually rise because additional products and variations require shorter production runs and increased setup times. Inventory costs rise because more products require added storage space and increased efforts for record keeping. Promotional costs also rise because each segment demands a unique promotional mix.

Despite higher marketing costs, however, an organization may be forced to practise differentiated marketing to diversify and reach new customers. The travel industry now recognises the need to target smaller groups of travellers with specialized interests. One company, for instance, may target seniors with trips that focus on history, hiking, golfing, cooking, or other special interests. The Sierra Club and other environmental organizations, in addition to commercial operators, offer guided nature walks where participants could learn about the history of an area, environmental management practices, and ecological services.[55]

CONCENTRATED MARKETING

Marketoid

The per capita consumption of cheese in Canada is over 10 kilograms per year.

Rather than trying to market its products separately to several segments, a firm may opt for a concentrated marketing strategy. With **concentrated marketing** (also known as *niche marketing*), a firm focuses its efforts on profitably satisfying only one market segment. This approach can appeal to a small firm that lacks the financial resources of its competitors and to a company that offers highly specialised goods and services. American Express, a large firm with many financial products, introduced two new credit cards designed for very specific markets: The Knot for engaged couples, and The Nest for newlyweds.

The Prairie Milk Marketing Partnership is using a concentrated strategy to reach the 9- to 17-year-old market. The Prairie Milk Marketing Partnership realizes that every age group drinks milk, but forming healthy eating at this age is a tough sell. The promotion features a television ad where a teenage girl does not succeed at activities like skateboarding and soccer but performs well at gymnastics. The message that teens needs to persevere until they find what they love or are good at was reinforced with photo contests at the Milk Every Moment website.[56]

MICROMARKETING

The fourth targeting strategy, still more narrowly focused than concentrated marketing, is **micromarketing**, which involves targeting potential customers at a very basic level, such as by postal code, specific occupation, or lifestyle. Ultimately, micromarketing can target even individuals themselves. The salesperson at your favourite clothing boutique may contact you when certain merchandise that she thinks you will like arrives at the store. The Internet allows marketers to make micromarketing even more effective. By tracking specific demographic and personal information, marketers can send email directly to individual consumers who are most likely to buy their products. If you purchase a book via Chapters.Indigo.ca, the company will offer to send you email notices about other books that may be of interest.

But micromarketing, like niche marketing, can become too much of a good thing if companies spend too much time, effort, and marketing dollars to unearth a market that is too small and specialised to be profitable. In addition, micromarketing may cause a company to lose sight of other larger markets. So it's important for marketers to assess the situation and pursue the most profitable markets.

SELECTING AND EXECUTING A STRATEGY

Although most organizations adopt some form of differentiated marketing, no single best choice suits all firms. Any of the alternatives may prove most effective in a particular situation. The basic determinants of a market-specific strategy are (1) company resources, (2) product homogeneity, (3) stage in the product life cycle, and (4) competitors' strategies.

A firm with limited resources may have to choose a concentrated marketing strategy. Small firms may be forced to select small target markets because of limitations in their sales force and advertising budgets. On the other hand, an undifferentiated marketing strategy suits a firm selling items perceived by consumers as relatively homogeneous. Marketers of grain, for example, sell standardized grades of generic products rather than individual brand names. Some petroleum companies implement undifferentiated marketing to distribute their gasoline to the mass market.

The firm's strategy may also change as its product progresses through the stages of the life cycle. During the early stages, undifferentiated marketing might effectively support the firm's effort to build initial demand for the item. In the later stages, however, competitive pressures may force modifications in products and in the development of marketing strategies aimed at segments of the total market.

The strategies of competitors also affect the choice of a segmentation approach. A firm may encounter obstacles to undifferentiated marketing if its competitors actively cultivate smaller segments. In such instances, competition usually forces each firm to adopt a differentiated marketing strategy.

Having chosen a strategy for reaching their firm's target market, marketers must then decide how best to position the product. The concept of **positioning** seeks to put a product in a certain position, or place, in the minds of prospective buyers. Marketers use a positioning strategy to distinguish their firm's offerings from those of competitors and to create promotions that communicate the desired position.

To achieve this goal of positioning, marketers follow a number of positioning strategies. Possible approaches include positioning a product according to the following categories:

1. *Attributes*—Kashi, "7 whole grains on a mission"

2. *Price/quality*—Omega watches, "We measure the 100th of a second that separates winning from taking part"

---

assessment check 4

4.1 Identify the four stages of the process of market segmentation.

4.2 Why is forecasting important to market segmentation?

4.3 Explain the difference between undifferentiated and differentiated marketing strategies and the benefits of concentrated marketing.

---

micromarketing Targeting potential customers at very narrow, basic levels, such as by postal code, specific occupation, or lifestyle—possibly even individuals themselves.

⑤ **Summarize the types of positioning strategies, and explain the reasons for positioning and repositioning products.**

positioning Placing a product at a certain point or location within a market in the minds of prospective buyers.

Sobeys Inc. positions its Compliments private label products against the competition by promoting quality and value.

figure 9.4

Hypothetical Positioning Map for Selected Retailers

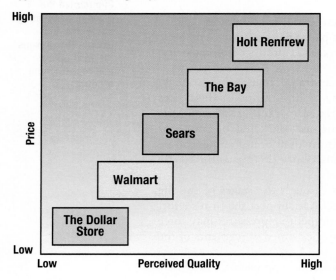

positioning map A tool that helps marketers place products in a market by graphically illustrating consumers' perceptions of competing products within an industry.

repositioning Changing the position of a product within the minds of prospective buyers relative to the positions of competing products.

3. *Competitors*—Walmart, "Save Money, Live Better"

4. *Application*—Blue Cross, "Enjoy the Benefits of Good Health"

5. *Product user*—Fisher-Price, "Play, Laugh, Grow"

6. *Product class*—BMW, the "ultimate driving experience"

Whatever strategy they choose, marketers want to emphasize a product's unique advantages and to differentiate it from competitors' options. A **positioning map** provides a valuable tool in helping managers position products by graphically illustrating consumers' perceptions of competing products within an industry. Marketers can create a competitive positioning map from information solicited from consumers or from their accumulated knowledge about a market. A positioning map might present two different characteristics— price and perceived quality—and show how consumers view a product and its major competitors based on these traits. The hypothetical positioning map in Figure 9.4 compares selected retailers based on possible perceptions of the prices and quality of their offerings.

Sometimes changes in the competitive environment force marketers to **reposition** a product—changing the position it holds in the minds of prospective buyers relative to the positions of competing products. Repositioning may even be necessary for already successful products or firms in order to gain greater market share. *Encyclopaedia Britannica*, published in multivolume print editions for 224 years, recently announced that it would be available only online. The company updates the online edition, which is far bigger than any print version, every 20 minutes.[57]

Strategic Implications

To remain competitive, today's marketers must accurately identify potential customers. They can use a variety of methods to accomplish this, including segmenting markets by gender and geographic location. The trick is to figure out the best combination of methods for segmentation to identify the most lucrative, long-lasting potential markets. Marketers must also remain flexible, responding to markets as they change—for instance, following a generation as it ages or reaching out to new generations by revamping or repositioning products.

The greatest competitive advantage will belong to firms that can pinpoint and serve markets without segmenting them to the point where they are too small or specialized to garner profits. Marketers who can reach and communicate with the right customers have a greater chance of attracting and keeping those customers than marketers who are searching for the wrong customers in the wrong place. ◆◆◆

REVIEW OF CHAPTER OBJECTIVES

① **Identify the essential components of a market, outline the role of market segmentation in developing a marketing strategy, and describe the criteria necessary for effective segmentation.**

A market consists of people and organizations with the necessary purchasing power, willingness, and authority to buy. Consumer products are purchased by the ultimate consumer for personal use. Business products are purchased for use directly or indirectly in the production of other goods and services. Certain products may fall into both categories.

Market segmentation is the process of dividing a total market into several homogeneous groups. It is used in identifying a target market for a good or service. Segmentation is the key to deciding a marketing strategy.

Effective segmentation depends on these four basic requirements: (1) The segment must have measurable purchasing power and size; (2) marketers can find a way to promote to and serve the market; (3) marketers must identify segments large enough for profit potential; and (4) the firm can target a number of segments that match its marketing capabilities.

② **Explain the geographic, demographic, and psychographic approaches to segmenting consumer markets.**

Geographic segmentation divides the overall market into homogeneous groups according to population locations. Demographic segmentation classifies the market into groups based on characteristics such as age, gender, and income level. Psychographic segmentation uses behavioural profiles developed from analyses of consumers' activities, opinions, interests, and lifestyles to identify market segments.

③ **Describe product-related segmentation.**

Product-related segmentation can take three basic forms: segmenting based on the benefits that people seek when they buy a product; segmenting based on usage rates for a product; and segmenting according to consumers' brand loyalty toward a product.

④ **Identify the steps in the market segmentation process and discuss four basic strategies for reaching target markets.**

Market segmentation is the division of markets into relatively homogeneous groups. Segmentation follows a four-step sequence: (1) developing user profiles; (2) forecasting the overall market potential; (3) estimating market share; and (4) selecting specific market segments.

Four strategies are (1) undifferentiated marketing, which uses a single marketing mix; (2) differentiated marketing, which produces numerous products, each with its own mix; (3) concentrated marketing, which directs all the firm's marketing resources toward a small segment; and (4) micromarketing, which targets potential customers at basic levels, such as postal code or occupation.

⑤ **Summarize the types of positioning strategies, and explain the reasons for positioning and repositioning products.**

Positioning strategies include positioning a good or service according to attributes, price and/or quality, competitors, application, product user, and product class. Positioning helps distinguish a firm's products from those of competitors and provides a basis for marketing communications. Repositioning a product—changing the position it holds in consumers' minds—may be necessary to gain greater market share.

assessment check answers ✓

1.1 Define *target market*.
A target market is the specific segment of consumers most likely to purchase a particular product.

1.2 Distinguish between a consumer product and a business product.
A consumer product is purchased by the ultimate buyer for personal use. A business product is purchased for use directly or indirectly in the production of other goods and services.

1.3 Define *market segmentation* and describe the role of market segmentation.
Market segmentation is the process of dividing a total market into several homogeneous groups.

The role of market segmentation is to identify the factors that affect purchase decisions and then group consumers according to the presence or absence of these factors.

1.4 Identify the four criteria for effective segmentation.
The four criteria for effective segmentation are these: (1) the market segment must present measurable purchasing power and size, (2) marketers must find a way to promote effectively and to serve the market segment, (3) marketers must identify segments that are sufficiently large to give them good profit potential, and (4) the firm must aim for segments that match its marketing capabilities.

2.1 Under what circumstances are marketers most likely to use geographic segmentation?
Marketers usually use geographic segmentation when regional preferences exist and when demand for categories of goods and services varies according to geographic region.

2.2 What is demographic segmentation and what are the major categories of demographic segmentation?
Demographic segmentation defines consumer groups according to demographic variables. The major categories of demographic segmentation are gender, age, ethnic group, family life cycle, household type, income, and expenditure patterns.

2.3 What is psychographic segmentation?
Psychographic segmentation divides a population into groups that have similar values and lifestyles.

2.4 Name the eight categories of VALS.
The eight categories are innovators, thinkers, achievers, experiencers, believers, strivers, makers, and survivors.

3.1 List the three approaches to product-related segmentation.
The three approaches are segmenting by benefits sought, segmenting by usage rates, and segmenting by brand loyalty.

3.2 What is the 80/20 principle?
The 80/20 principle states that a big percentage (80 percent) of a product's revenues comes from a relatively small number (20 percent) of loyal customers.

4.1 Identify the four stages of the process of market segmentation.
The four stages are developing user profiles, forecasting the overall market potential, estimating market share, and selecting specific market segments.

4.2 Why is forecasting important to market segmentation?
Forecasting is important because it can define a preliminary go or no-go decision based on sales potential. It can help a firm avoid a disastrous move or point out opportunities.

4.3 Explain the difference between undifferentiated and differentiated marketing strategies and the benefits of concentrated marketing.
Undifferentiated marketing promotes a single product line to all customers with a single marketing mix. Differentiated marketing promotes numerous products with different marketing mixes designed to satisfy smaller segments. Concentrated marketing can allow a firm to focus on a single market segment, which is especially appealing to smaller firms and those that offer highly specialized goods and services.

5.1 What are the four determinants of a market-specific strategy?
The four determinants are company resources, product homogeneity, stage in the product life cycle, and competitors' strategies.

5.2 What is the role of positioning in a marketing strategy?
Positioning places a product in a certain position in the minds of prospective buyers so that marketers can create messages that distinguish their offerings from those of competitors.

MARKETING TERMS YOU NEED TO KNOW

These terms are printed in blue in the text. They are defined in the margins of the chapter and in the Glossary that begins on p. G-1.

market 246	demographic segmentation 250	product-related segmentation 263
target market 246	Generation X 252	80/20 principle 263
consumer products 246	baby boomers 253	undifferentiated marketing 266
business products 246	cohort effect 254	differentiated marketing 266
market segmentation 247	Video Game Generation 254	concentrated marketing 266
geographic segmentation 248	family life cycle 256	micromarketing 267
census metropolitan area (CMA) 249	psychographic segmentation 260	positioning 267
census agglomeration (CA) 250	AIO statements 261	positioning map 268
core region 250	VALS™ 261	repositioning 268

PROJECT AND TEAMWORK EXERCISES

1. On your own or with a partner, choose one of the following consumer products and think about how it could be used as a business product. Then create a business advertisement for your product.
   a. lawn care products
   b. microwave oven
   c. tennis balls
   d. bottled water
   e. electric car
   f. vacuum cleaner

2. With a classmate, choose one of the following products you believe is generally targeted for either men or women and create an advertisement for the product aimed at the opposite gender.
   a. barbecue grill and accessories
   b. hunting or fishing supplies
   c. nail salon
   d. minivan
   e. online video game

3. Create a chart showing how your family's income and expenditure patterns have changed over the years as the family life cycle changes. You don't need exact figures, just the general picture. If possible, interview other family members for additional information.

4. With a classmate, choose a product and come up with a slogan representing each of the six positioning approaches for the product.

5. On your own or with a classmate, select one of the following products. Visit the firm's website to see how the product is positioned, then create an advertisement showing how you think marketers could reposition the product to gain greater market share.
   a. Gatorade
   b. Dove soap
   c. Barilla pasta
   d. Fiskars scissors
   e. Hallmark cards

CRITICAL THINKING EXERCISES

1. Create a profile of yourself as part of a market segment. Include the following:
   a. geographic location
   b. gender and age
   c. household type
   d. income and spending habits.

2. Select one of the following products and explain how you would use segmentation by income and expenditure patterns to determine your targeted market.
   a. Disney theme parks
   b. Sony Cyber-shot camera
   c. Stouffer's Lean Cuisine
   d. Kia Soul car

3. How do you think the Internet has affected differentiated marketing techniques?

4. Choose one of the following products and describe a marketing approach that segments the target market by benefits sought:
   a. Kryptonite bicycle lock
   b. college or university
   c. Pella windows and doors
   d. Coke Zero
   e. Dairy Queen ice cream

5. Visit the website for a large company such as Kraft Foods, Sony, or Campbell Soups. Look for ways the firm practises differentiated marketing. How do you think this approach benefits the firm?

ETHICS EXERCISE

Marketers are making a new pitch to men—at the risk of political incorrectness. Marketers for firms such as Unilever and Wendy's have been frustrated at not being able to reach young male consumers with their messages. After searching for clues about what this crowd likes, these firms have created marketing campaigns designed to grab their attention—perhaps at the expense of other consumers. Some advertising is designed to appeal to "bad boy" attitudes, low-brow humour, and sex.

1. What are some of the pitfalls of this kind of segmentation?
2. Do you think these ads will be successful in the long run? Why or why not?
3. Should marketers be concerned about offending one market segment when trying to reach another? Why or why not?

CASE 9.1

Segmenting the Alcohol Market in Canada

The Canadian market for alcoholic beverages is roughly $21 billion a year. Statistics Canada keeps track of sales in this market with three categories: beer, wine, and spirits. The spirits category includes drinks like vodka, rum, and brandy.

Canadians are beer drinkers. Beer sales represented 44 percent of the total alcoholic beverage market for the year ending March 2012. However, beer sales have been declining in relation to the other categories, down from 50 percent 10 years earlier. The per capita consumption of beer is over 80 litres per person. Ontario, Quebec, and British Columbia saw the highest beer sales. The highest per capita beer sales were in the Yukon, where beer consumption was at 385 bottles per year.

In contrast to the beer market, wine sales have been increasing. Wine sales accounted for 31 percent of the total market. Red wine accounted for 57 percent of all wines sales. Imported products, both red and white wines, remained fairly constant with 76 percent of red wines and 63 percent of white wines sold in Canada coming from other countries. The highest total wine sales were in Quebec, Ontario, and British Columbia. On a per capita basis, Quebec had the highest wine sales and Yukon came in second.

Sales of spirits have been declining. Sales of whisky-type products were the highest in market share, accounting for 27 percent of spirit sales. Vodka sales have been increasing, amounting to 24 percent of the category. The provinces with the highest sales of spirits are Ontario, British Columbia, and Quebec. On a per capita basis, the highest consumers of spirits could be found in the Yukon, Nunavut, and Northwest Territories.

Marketers of beer, wine, and spirits would be interested in finding out why the drinking habits of Canadians are changing. One reason drinking habits are changing could be the shift in demographics of the population. As the largest group of Canadians—the baby boomers—age, they tend to drink fewer alcoholic beverages, but the good news for the makers of beer, wine, and spirits is that the next largest group in Canada, the video-game generation, is now in its prime drinking years.

The video-game generation represents 26 percent of the population or just over 8.5 million people. This group could be attending college or university, still living with their parents, just buying their first house, or just starting out on their careers.

A recent study of the video-game generation's drinking habits showed that 32 percent were casual drinkers, 28 percent were regular drinkers, 23 percent did not drink at all, and 17 percent drank alcohol only on special occasions. Men were more likely to be regular drinkers, with 35 percent falling into that category.

This study segmented the video-game generation into six segments they called simple lifers, fireflies, sparks, stampeders, achievers, and pacers. The heaviest drinkers were in the stampede segment. Stampeder was the only segment that was entirely male and made up 14 percent of the group. Stampeders like to party, play video games, and watch sports, and just over 18 percent of them are French Canadian.

Over half of the men were beer drinkers and over a quarter of them preferred craft beers. Over half of this group also drank spirits, and the amount of spirits increased with age.

The results of the study into the drinking habits of the video-game generation help to explain the changes in sale patterns of alcohol reported by Statistics Canada. The results can also assist marketers of alcoholic beverages better understand their customers in order to develop effective marketing strategies.

Questions for Critical Thinking

1. If a winery wanted to expand its target markets further, what segment or segments of the market might the firm include? Can you think of value profiles for those segments?
2. What promotions—social media, mobile, etc.—could a beer company like Molson Coors use to reach its target markets?

Sources: Jonathan Nadeau and David Coletto, "Canadian Millennials and Beverage Alcohol," January 30, 2013, Abacus Data Inc. website, **http://abacusinsider.com**, accessed February 28, 2014; Bill Kaufmann, "Statistic Canada's Report of Boosted Beer Sales in Alberta No Bitter Pil for Brewers," *Calgary Sun*, April 11, 2013, **www .calgarysun.com**; "Control and Sale of Alcoholic Beverages, for the Year Ending March 31, 2013," Statistics Canada, April 11, 2013, **www.statcan.gc.ca**.

CASE 9.2

Cruise Companies Learn How to Cater to Distinct Market Segments

The typical cruise ship passenger may not actually exist. While the core target market for cruise vacations is 25 or older, with a passport and a household income of at least $40,000, who is likely to have cruised at least once before, that description now covers a large proportion of the population. That's why cruise marketers no longer think in terms of an "average" customer. So many different specialty cruises are springing up to appeal to different market segments that almost anyone can find themselves in a target group.

What's your passion? Whether you like to cook, quilt, tango, snorkel, listen to jazz, play baseball, garden, watch movies, gaze at Impressionist art, explore investment strategies, hold a family reunion, or engage in a host of other pursuits, there's a themed cruise for you, with specific on-board and on-shore activities, workshops, and seminars hosted by skilled instructors. Even if you're attending a business meeting or conference rather than enjoying a vacation, you may well find yourself cruising for the occasion. Business managers find that meetings on cruise ships can save as much as a third of the cost of land-based gatherings, once all cost factors like meals, lodging, travel, and audio-visual equipment are taken into account. Besides, says the co-founder of a company that plans such events, cruising "excites people."

Passengers do fall into a number of traditional demographic categories that cruise marketers find useful. Analyzing factors like country of origin, language, economic status, and psychographics, marketers have devised distinct market segments. "Explorers" are well-to-do repeat customers, a small group that's profitable but challenging to please. "Admirals" are older and loyal; they appreciate a traditional experience. "Marines" are young professionals on the lookout for a better experience each time; they're eager to parasail, surf, and rock climb. "Little Mermaids" are upper-middle-class families in search of a memorable vacation, while "Escapers" just want to get away from the daily grind without worries or complications. Finally, "Souvenirs" are in search of the best deal; price is their priority.

Marketers even have a term for those whose interest and income make them unlikely to become cruise customers. They are "Adrift."

Questions for Critical Thinking

1. Is segmenting customers as "Explorers," "Admirals," and the like a useful marketing tool? Why or why not?
2. Which segments of the cruise market are most likely to be influenced by social media? Why?

Sources: Organization website, *Cruise Market Watch*, **www.cruisemarketwatch.com**, accessed April 21, 2012; "CLIA's 2011 Cruise Market Profile Study Reports Positive Customer Attitudes," Cruising.org, **www.cruising.org**, accessed April 21, 2012; "Specialty Cruises Ride Wave of Popularity with Landry & Kling," Market Watch.com, April 2, 2012, **www.marketwatch.com**; Anne Campbell, "Pursue Your Passions at Sea: Specialty Cruises," *USA Today*, January 23, 2012, **http://travel.usatoday.com**; Kayleigh Kulp, "Businesses Cruise More to Meetings—Literally," CNN Travel.com, November 28, 2011, **www.cnn.com**.

chapter 10

Product and Service Strategies

© Pixellover RM 8/Alamy

CHAPTER OBJECTIVES

1. Define product, distinguish between goods and services and how they relate to the goods–services continuum, and explain the importance of the service sector in today's marketplace.

2. Describe the classifications of consumer and business goods and services.

3. Explain how quality is used by marketers as a product strategy and why firms develop lines of related products.

4. Describe the way marketers typically measure product mixes and make product mix decisions.

5. Explain the concept of the product life cycle and identify the different stages.

6. Describe how a firm can extend a product's life cycle, and explain why certain products may be deleted.

APPLE'S PRODUCTS SHINE

Apple has become one of the most successful and innovative companies in the world. It is no accident that the maker of the Mac, the iPhone, the iPod, and the iPad draws more than 1 million people to its 407 stores every day; or that it generates more than $20 billion in sales each year, more per square foot of retail space than even the fabled Tiffany & Company. What is the strategy behind Apple's success? It relies on both product and service.

First, of course, Apple leads the industry in the design of sleek and highly functional products that are dependable and intuitively easy to use. Nearly all of its products have revolutionized or created and then dominated a market. The quality, features, and hi-tech appeal of Apple products ensures that millions of homes have at least one; in fact, the average number owned is three, and one in four households plan to buy another Apple product in the next year. Though the most typical customers are young, college- or university-educated males, the popularity of Apple devices cuts across all age groups and geographic areas. The vice president of one marketing research firm says, "It's a fantastic business model—the more [Apple] products you own, the more likely you are to buy more."

Apple also introduces new devices, and new versions of existing products, at a dizzying rate. Innovation truly drives the firm, and it is not afraid to let new products take sales away from older ones. Its new CEO, Tim Cook, says the company would rather let the iPad cannibalize sales of the Mac than lose those sales to a competing company.

Another big factor in Apple's continued success is the care with which it treats customers in its stores. Steve Jobs, the company's late founder, helped select "Enriching lives" as Apple's retail vision, rather than focusing on selling per se. Staff in the stores don't earn commissions and are trained to create memorable customer experiences, even for visitors who don't buy anything. Building relationships, offering help and training, troubleshooting, and solving problems are stressed as part of the effort to touch customers at an emotional level and motivate them to become loyal to the Apple brand. That's why they recommend it to others.

With all this to offer, Apple can feel confident that its merchandise and customer service can command a premium price.[1]

connecting with customers

From the Macintosh computer to the iPhone, iPod, and iPad, the Apple brand is an indisputable success story. But success didn't come without a plan and a vision. Steve Jobs's vision for Apple centred on products that were well made, functional, and easy to use—products that would become part of the fabric of life for consumers worldwide.

Chapter Overview

We've discussed how marketers conduct research to determine unfilled needs in their markets, how customers behave during the purchasing process, and how firms expand their horizons overseas. Now our attention shifts to a company's marketing mix, the blend of four elements of a marketing strategy—product, distribution, promotion, and price—to satisfy the target market. This chapter focuses on how firms select and develop the goods and services they offer, starting with planning which products to offer. The other variables of the marketing mix—distribution channels, promotional plans, and pricing decisions—must accommodate the product strategy selected.

Marketers develop strategies to promote both tangible goods and intangible services. Any such strategy begins with investigation, analysis, and selection of a particular target market, and it continues with the creation of a marketing mix designed to satisfy that segment. Both tangible goods and intangible services intend to satisfy consumer wants and needs, but the marketing efforts supporting them may be vastly different. Many firms sell both types of products, offering innovative goods and ongoing service to attract and retain customers for the long term. Doing so can be profitable, as you'll see in this chapter.

This chapter examines both the similarities and the differences in marketing goods and services. It then presents basic concepts—product classifications, development of product lines, and the product life cycle—that marketers apply in developing successful products. Finally, the chapter discusses product deletion and product mix decisions. ◆◆◆

---

① **Define product, distinguish between goods and services and how they relate to the goods–services continuum, and explain the importance of the service sector in today's marketplace.**

WHAT IS A PRODUCT?

At first, you might think of a product as an object you hold in your hand, such as a baseball or a toothbrush. You might also think of the car you drive as a product. But this doesn't take into account the idea of a service as a product. Nor does it consider the idea of what the product is used for. So a television is more than a box with a screen and a remote control. It's really a means of providing entertainment—your favourite movies, news programs, or reality shows. Marketers acknowledge this broader conception of product; they realize that people buy *want satisfaction* rather than objects.

You might feel a need for a television to satisfy a want for entertainment. You might not know a lot about how the device itself works, but you understand the results. If you are entertained by watching TV, then your wants are satisfied. If, however, the television is working just fine but you don't like the programming offered, you may need to satisfy your desire for entertainment by changing your service package to include premium channels. The service and its offerings is a product.

Marketers think of a product as a compilation of package design and labelling, brand name, availability, warranty, reputation, image, and customer-service activities that add value for the customer. Consequently, a **product** is a bundle of physical, service, and symbolic attributes designed to satisfy a customer's wants and needs.

product Bundle of physical, service, and symbolic attributes designed to satisfy a customer's wants and needs.

service Intangible task that satisfies the needs of consumer and business users.

good Tangible products that customers can see, hear, smell, taste, or touch.

goods–services continuum Spectrum along which goods and services fall according to their attributes, from pure good to pure service.

WHAT ARE GOODS AND SERVICES?

Services are intangible products. A general definition identifies **services** as intangible tasks that satisfy the needs of consumer and business users. But you can't hold a service in your hand the way you can **goods**, which are tangible products that customers can see, hear, smell, taste, or touch. Most service providers cannot transport or store their products; customers simultaneously buy and consume these products, like haircuts, car repairs, and visits to the dentist. One way to distinguish services from goods is the **goods–services continuum**, as shown in Figure 10.1.

This spectrum helps marketers visualize the differences and similarities between goods and services. A car is a pure good, but the dealer may also offer repair and maintenance services or include the services in the price of a lease. The car falls at the pure good extreme of the continuum because the repair and maintenance services are an adjunct to the purchase. A dinner at an exclusive restaurant is a mix of goods and services. It combines the physical goods of gourmet food with the intangible

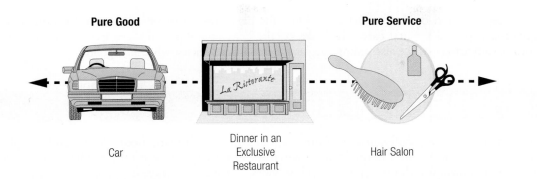

Pure Good   **Pure Service**

Car   Dinner in an   Hair Salon
                       Exclusive
                       Restaurant

figure 10.1

The Goods–Services Continuum

services of attentive wait staff, elegant surroundings, and perhaps a visit to your table by the chef or restaurant owner to make sure your meal is perfect. At the other extreme, a dentist provides pure service—cleaning teeth, filling cavities, taking X-rays. The dentist's office may also sell items such as electric toothbrushes or night guards, but it's the service that is primary in patients' minds.

You can begin to see the diversity of services. Services can be distinguished from goods in several ways:

1. *Services are intangible.* Services do not have physical features that buyers can see, hear, smell, taste, or touch prior to purchase. Service firms essentially ask their customers to buy a promise—that the haircut be stylish, that the insurance will cover injuries, that the lawn will be mowed.

2. *Services are inseparable from the service providers.* Consumer perceptions of a service provider become their perceptions of the service itself. The name of a doctor, lawyer, or hair stylist is synonymous with the service they provide. A bad haircut can deter customers, while a good one will attract more to the salon. A house-cleaning service depends on its workers to leave each house spotless, because its reputation is built on this service.

3. *Services are perishable.* Providers cannot maintain inventories of their services. A day spa can't stockpile facials or pedicures. A travel agent can't keep quantities of vacations on a shelf. For this reason, some service providers, such as airlines and hotels, may raise their prices during times of peak demand—such as school vacation times—and reduce them when demand declines.

4. *Companies cannot easily standardize services.* However, many firms are trying to change this. Most fast-food chains promise that you'll get your meal within a certain number of minutes and that it will taste the way you expect it to. A hotel chain may have the same amenities at each location—a pool, fitness room, free breakfast, or movies.

5. *Buyers often play important roles in the creation and distribution of services.* Service transactions frequently require interaction between buyer and seller at the production and distribution stages. When a traveller arrives at the airport to pick up a rental car, he or she may have a choice of vehicle and additional amenities, such as a GPS unit or car seat for a child. If the car is ready to go immediately, the customer will likely be satisfied. If the desired car is not available, is not clean, or doesn't have a full tank of gas, the customer may not book with this company again.

6. *Service standards show wide variations.* An upscale steakhouse and your school cafeteria are both restaurants. Their customers, however, experience considerably different cuisine, physical surroundings, service standards, and prices.

hxdbzxy/Shutterstock.com

It isn't easy for companies to standardize services, but they do try. For example, a hotel chain might have the same amenities at each location, including a beautiful indoor pool.

Keep in mind that a product often blurs the distinction between services and goods. Avis is a service that provides rental cars, which are goods. Lenscrafters provides eye examinations—services from optometrists—while also selling eyeglasses and contact lenses, which are goods.

IMPORTANCE OF THE SERVICE SECTOR

You would live a very different life without service firms to fill many needs. You could not place a phone call, log on to the Internet, flip a switch for electricity, or even take a college or university course if organizations did not provide such services. During an average day, you probably use many services without much thought, but these products play an integral role in your life.

The service sector makes a crucial contribution to the Canadian economy by providing both products and jobs. Several of Canada's largest companies are pure services, such as the Royal Bank of Canada and the Bank of Nova Scotia. Other large companies, BCE Bell Enterprises, for example, provide communication services to businesses and consumers.[2]

The Canadian service sector now makes up about three-quarters of the economy and is growing faster than the goods-producing sector. The service sector employs about 75 percent of Canadians and continues to increase. Many service-sector jobs are knowledge intensive and therefore employ a high number of university- and college-educated employees. Some of Canada's highest-paying jobs are also in services.[3]

Services also play a crucial role in the international competitiveness of Canadian firms. The value of Canadian service exports is almost $75 billion per year. The United States is Canada's largest trading partner in services, as it is in manufactured goods. The European Union is Canada's second-largest trading partner for service exports. International trade of services is less dependent on the U.S. market for service exports than companies in the goods-producing sector.[4]

Services also play a crucial role in the international competitiveness of firms. Some economists believe a more precise measurement of service exports is required to provide an accurate picture of the movement of services. Several trends are affecting service exports statistics. One of these trends is offshoring service jobs, such as customer call centres, to nations like India. The telecommunications industry has been offshoring jobs since the 1990s with the result that there are 10 percent fewer jobs in this industry today.[5]

While some firms have found success with offshoring their call centres, others have recently returned their call centres to North America after determining they would save money and improve customer service efficiency be doing so.[6] Termed *backshoring,* this trend is growing and actually becoming a marketing tool for firms. "Foreign call centres feed into the perception that companies aren't interested in their customers," notes one marketing researcher. And some companies bringing their call centres back to North America are taking another approach using home-based hourly workers, often managed by a private company.

An emerging trend, homeshoring, sometimes called *insourcing,* enables firms to save on office space, furnishings, and supplies. Firms that practise homeshoring are experiencing several benefits, including a reduction in the use of energy and other natural resources, which decreases these firms' impact on the environment. Because employees are not commuting to work every day, and because an office does not have to be heated, cooled, and supplied with electricity and water every day, firms experience not only reduced costs but also a drop in emissions. These companies can highlight their green practices in marketing messages to customers.

wavebreakmedia ltd/Shutterstock.com

Homeshoring allows companies to save on office space, furnishings, and supplies as well as reducing their impact on the environment.

Observers cite several reasons for the growing importance of services, including consumers' desire for speed and convenience and the technological advances that allow firms to fulfill this demand. Services that involve wireless communications, data backup and storage, and even meal preparation for busy families are on the rise. Consumers are also looking to advisors to help plan for a financially secure future and for insurance to protect their homes and families.

Most service firms emphasize marketing as a significant activity for two reasons. First, the growth potential of service transactions represents a vast marketing opportunity. Second, the environment for services is changing. For instance, increased competition is forcing traditional service industries to differentiate themselves from their competitors. Providing superior service is one way to develop long-term customer relationships and compete more effectively. Relationship marketing is just one of the ways service firms can develop and solidify their customer relationships.

> **assessment check 1** ✓
>
> **1.1** Define the term *product*.
>
> **1.2** Why is the understanding of want satisfaction so important to marketers?
>
> **1.3** Describe the goods–services continuum and list the six characteristics that distinguish services from goods.
>
> **1.4** Identify two reasons why services are important to the Canadian economy and business environment.
>
> **1.5** Why do service firms emphasize marketing?

CLASSIFYING GOODS AND SERVICES FOR CONSUMER AND BUSINESS MARKETS

> ② **Describe the classifications of consumer and business goods and services.**

A firm's choices for marketing a good or service depend largely on the offering itself and on the nature of the target market. Product strategies differ for consumer and business markets. Consumer products (sometimes called B2C products) are those destined for use by ultimate consumers. Business products or **business-to-business (B2B) products** (also called *industrial* or *organizational products*), as discussed in Chapter 6, contribute directly or indirectly to the output of other products for resale. Marketers further subdivide these two major categories into more specific categories, as discussed in this section.

Some products fall into both categories. A case in point is prescription drugs. Traditionally, pharmaceutical companies marketed prescription drugs to doctors, who then made the purchase decision for their patients by writing the prescription. Thus the medications could be classified as a business product. However, many drug companies now advertise their products in consumer-oriented media, including magazines, the Internet, and television. Even though it is not legal to show these ads on Canadian television, Canadian cable and satellite television services provide access to American channels so Canadian consumers see these ads.

business-to-business (B2B) product Product that contributes directly or indirectly to the output of other products for resale; also called industrial or organizational product.

TYPES OF CONSUMER PRODUCTS

The most widely used product classification system focuses on the buyer's perception of a need for the product and his or her buying behaviour. However, **unsought products** are marketed to consumers who may not yet recognize any need for them. Examples of unsought products are long-term-care insurance and funeral services.

However, relatively few products fall into the unsought category. Most consumers recognize their own needs for various types of consumer purchases and actively seek them, so customer buying behaviour variations are the key to distinguishing the various categories. The most common classification scheme for sought products divides consumer goods and services into three groups based on customers' buying behaviour: convenience, shopping, and specialty. Figure 10.2 illustrates samples of these three categories, together with the unsought classification.

unsought products Products marketed to consumers who may not yet recognize a need for them.

Convenience Products

Convenience products refer to goods and services that consumers want to purchase frequently, immediately, and with minimal effort. Milk, bread, and toothpaste are convenience products. Convenience services include 24-hour convenience stores, walk-in hair salons, copy shops, and dry cleaners.

Marketers further subdivide the convenience category into impulse items, staples, or emergency items. **Impulse goods and services** are purchased on the spur of the moment, such as a visit to a

convenience products Goods and services that consumers want to purchase frequently, immediately, and with minimal effort.

impulse goods and services Products purchased on the spur of the moment.

figure 10.2

Classification of Consumer Products

Specialty Products

Lexus and Infiniti luxury cars, tax lawyer, Versace designer clothes, Botox injections

Unsought Products

Pre-need funeral plans, long-term health care (nursing home) insurance, remedial math programs

Consumer Products

Convenience Products

Impulse Items: Magazines, snack foods
Staples: Gasoline, dry cleaning, milk
Emergency Items: Emergency vet visit, plumbing repair kit, asthma inhalers

Shopping Products

Homogeneous: Airplane flights, computers
Heterogeneous: Child care, furniture, Pilates or yoga instructors, Caribbean cruise

staples Convenience goods and services that consumers constantly replenish to maintain a ready inventory.

emergency goods and services Products bought in response to unexpected and urgent needs.

car wash or a pack of gum tossed in the shopping cart at the register. Some marketers have even come up with ways to make impulse shopping on the Internet attractive. Canada Flowers, a site that provides flowers, gift baskets, and plants, promotes same-day delivery on its website. Consumers can order such items as roses for a birthday or a "get well soon" arrangement, and it will be delivered the same day anywhere in Canada.[7]

Staples are convenience goods and services that consumers constantly replenish to maintain a ready inventory; gasoline, toothpaste, and dry cleaning are good examples. Marketers spend many hours and dollars creating messages for consumers about these products, partly because there are so many competitors.

Emergency goods and services are bought in response to unexpected and urgent needs. A snow shovel purchased during a snowstorm and an emergency visit to a vet with a sick pet are examples. Depending on your viewpoint, the products offered by Canada Flowers as last-minute gifts could also fall into this category!

Since consumers devote little effort to purchase decisions about convenience products, marketers must strive to make these exchanges as simple as possible. Store location can boost a convenience product's visibility. Marketers compete vigorously for prime locations, which can make all the difference between a consumer choosing one gas station, vending machine, or dry cleaner over another.

In addition, location *within* a store can make the difference between success and failure of a product, which is why manufacturers fight so hard for the right spot on supermarket shelves. Typically, the larger and more powerful grocery manufacturers such as Kraft, Kellogg, and General Mills get the most visible spots. But visibility to consumers sometimes comes at a price, often through a practice called slotting allowances, or slotting fees, money paid by producers to retailers to guarantee display of their merchandise. According to retailers, the purpose of slotting allowances is to cover their losses if a product doesn't sell. The practice of slotting fees has been investigated and it was discovered that these fees are far from uniform; they vary greatly across product categories, in both whether fees are charged and, if they are, how large the fees will be.

Shopping Products

In contrast to the purchase of convenience items, consumers buy **shopping products** only after comparing competing offerings on such characteristics as price, quality, style, and colour. Shopping products typically cost more than convenience purchases. This category includes tangible items such as clothing, furniture, and appliances as well as services such as child care, home renovations, auto repairs, and insurance. The purchaser of a shopping product lacks complete information prior to the buying trip and gathers information during the buying process.

Several important features distinguish shopping products: physical attributes, service attributes such as warranties and after-sale service terms, prices, styling, and

An unsought product.

Courtesy of Western Financial Insurance Company

Suzanne Tucker/Shutterstock.com

Emergency goods and services are bought in response to urgent needs.

places of purchase. A store's name and reputation have considerable influence on people's buying behaviour. The personal selling efforts of salespeople also provide important promotional support.

Buyers and marketers treat some shopping products, such as refrigerators and washing machines, as relatively *homogeneous* products. To the consumer, one brand seems largely the same as another. Marketers may try to differentiate homogeneous products from competing products in several ways. They may emphasize price and value, or they may attempt to educate buyers about less obvious features that contribute to a product's quality, appeal, and uniqueness.

Other shopping products seem *heterogeneous* because of basic differences among them. Examples are furniture, physical-fitness training, vacations, and clothing. Differences in features often separate competing heterogeneous shopping products in the minds of consumers. Perceptions of style, colour, and fit can all affect consumer choices.

shopping products
Products that consumers purchase after comparing competing offerings.

Specialty Products

Specialty products offer unique characteristics that cause buyers to prize those particular brands. They typically carry high prices, and many represent well-known brands. Examples of specialty goods are Hermès scarves, Kate Spade handbags, Ritz-Carlton resorts, Tiffany jewellery, and Lexus automobiles. Specialty services include professional services such as financial, legal, and medical services.

Purchasers of specialty goods and services know exactly what they want—and they are willing to pay accordingly. These buyers begin shopping with complete information, and they refuse to accept substitutes. Because consumers are willing to exert considerable effort to obtain specialty products, producers can distribute them through relatively few retail locations. In fact, some firms intentionally limit the range of retailers that carry their products to add to their cachet. Both highly personalized service by sales associates and image advertising help marketers promote specialty items. Because these products are available in so few retail outlets, advertisements frequently list their locations or give toll-free telephone numbers that provide customers with this information.

In recent years, some makers of specialty products have broadened their market by selling some of their goods through company-owned discount outlets. But these stores nearly always carry items from previous years' inventory. The stores attract consumers who want to own specialty items but who cannot or do not wish to pay their high prices. One company making shopping and specialty products is described in the "Marketing and the SME" feature.

specialty products
Products that offer unique characteristics that cause buyers to prize those particular brands.

Canadian-Made Snowshoes

A small town just outside Quebec City is home to two companies both manufacturing and selling a similar product—snowshoes. The two companies are GV Snowshoes and Faber & Co. The town is Huron-Wendake, which is part of the Huron nation reserve.

The story of the two companies is pretty similar; both are family run, and both have a wide variety of snowshoes and related products, such as bindings and poles. Faber has been in business longer, over 140 years, while GV started making snowshoes 50 years ago.

No one knows when the first snowshoes were used, but one of the first references to them was in 1608 by Samuel de Champlain when he was describing how native Canadians could travel in the winter without sinking in the snow. Today you can still get a traditional wood and rawhide version, as well as aluminum and hybrid types.

Stephen Vincent, one of the owners of GV Snowshoes, explains that the market for snowshoes is not dependent on economic conditions or styles but rather the amount of snow that falls during the winter: the more snow, the more snowshoes are sold. The market has changed from using them to get around in rural Canada, although some models are still designed for wilderness travels, to using them in more urban settings, which has led to smaller snowshoes. Today the snowshoe user is slightly more likely to be female (54 percent of users) and living in a city. Vincent explains they sell all the snowshoes they can manufacture, with 60 percent of sales to residents of Quebec, 20 percent to customers throughout the rest of Canada, 10 percent to the United States, and the remainder to customers in Europe and South America. The company has also supplied the Canadian, Russian, and Finnish militaries with snowshoes. Sales increased when the company switched to aluminum frames, but according to Vincent the company waited too long to make the switch and it has been working to regain its lost market share.

Whether you enjoy winter sports in the country or your local park, if you are snowshoeing, chances are pretty good that the shoes came from a little town near Quebec City.

Sources: Mark Cardwell, "Tiny Huron Village of Wendake Is a Giant in the Snowshoe Industry," *Montreal Gazette*, February 25, 2014, **www.montrealgazette.com**; Faber Snowshoes company website, **www.fabersnowshoes.com**, accessed March 3, 2014; GV Snowshoes company website, **www.gvsnowshoes.com**, accessed March 3, 2014; Timothy Giilck, "Gear Review: GV Wide Trail Snowshoes," *Snowshoe Magazine*, March 2, 2014, **www.snowshoemag.com**; Patrick White, "Let It Snow Shoes," *Globe and Mail Report on Business*, March 2014, page 12.

CLASSIFYING CONSUMER SERVICES

Like tangible goods, services are also classified based on the convenience, shopping, and specialty products categories. But added insights can be gained by examining several factors that are unique to classifying services. Service firms may serve consumer markets, business markets, or both. A firm offering architectural services may design either residential or commercial buildings or both. A cleaning service may clean houses, offices, or both. In addition, services can be classified as equipment-based or people-based. A car wash is an equipment-based service, whereas a law office is people-based. Marketers may ask themselves any of these five questions to help classify certain services:

1. What is the nature of the service?

2. What type of relationship does the service organization have with its customers?

3. How much flexibility is there for customization and judgment on the part of the service provider?

4. Do demand and supply for the service fluctuate?

5. How is the service delivered?[8]

A marketer attempting to classify the activities of a boarding kennel would answer these questions in one way; a marketer evaluating a lawn care service would come up with different answers. For example, customers would bring their pets to the kennel to receive service, while the lawn care staff would travel to customers' homes to provide service. Workers at the kennel are likely to have closer interpersonal relationships with pet owners—and their pets—than lawn care workers, who might not meet their customers at all. A marketer assessing demand for the services of a ski resort or a food concession at the beach is likely to find fluctuations by season. And a dentist has flexibility in making decisions about a patient's care, whereas a delivery service must arrive with a package at the correct destination, on time.

table 10.1   **Marketing Impact of the Consumer Products Classification System**

	CONVENIENCE PRODUCTS	SHOPPING PRODUCTS	SPECIALTY PRODUCTS
Consumer Factors			
Planning time involved in purchase	Very little	Considerable	Extensive
Purchase frequency	Frequent	Less frequent	Infrequent
Importance of convenient location	Critical	Important	Unimportant
Comparison of price and quality	Very little	Considerable	Very little
Marketing Mix Factors			
Price	Low	Relatively high	High
Importance of seller's image	Unimportant	Very important	Important
Distribution channel length	Long	Relatively short	Short
Number of sales outlets	Many	Few	Very few
Promotion	Advertising and promotion by producer	Personal selling and advertising by both producer and retailer	Personal selling and advertising by both producer and retailer

APPLYING THE CONSUMER PRODUCTS CLASSIFICATION SYSTEM

The three-way classification system of convenience, shopping, and specialty goods and services helps to guide marketers in developing a successful marketing strategy. Buyer behaviour patterns differ for the three types of purchases. For example, classifying a new food item as a convenience product leads to insights about marketing needs in branding, promotion, pricing, and distribution decisions. Table 10.1 summarizes the impact of this classification system on the development of an effective marketing mix.

The classification system, however, also poses a few problems. The major obstacle in implementing this system results from the suggestion that all goods and services must fit within one of the three categories. Some fit neatly into one category, but others share characteristics of more than one category. For example, how would you classify the purchase of a new car? Before classifying the expensive good, which is handled by a few dealers in the area as a specialty product, consider other characteristics. New car buyers often shop extensively among competing models and dealers before deciding on the best deal. And there is a wide range of models, features, and prices to consider. At one end of the spectrum is a basic Ford that could be purchased for less than $20,000. At the other end is what people are calling European super cars such as the Lamborghini Murcielago, at $470,000, or the Aston Martin One-77, priced at more than $1.4 million. These cars are fast, powerful, and hard to find—which boosts their value.[9]

So it's a good idea to think of the categorization process as a continuum representing degrees of effort expended by consumers. At one end of the continuum, they casually pick up convenience items; at the other end, they search extensively for specialty products. Shopping products fall between these extremes. In addition, car dealers may offer services, both during and after the sale, that play a big role in the purchase decision. On this continuum, the new car purchase might appear between the categories of shopping and specialty products but closer to specialty products.

A second problem with the classification system emerges because consumers differ in their buying patterns. One person may walk into a hair salon and request a haircut without an appointment, while another may check references and compare prices before selecting a stylist.

Jewellery: A specialty product.

Ingvald Kaldhussater/Shutterstock.com

figure 10.3

Classification of Business Products

Installations
Airplane
Office tower
Oil drilling rig
Regional shopping centre

Components
Fabric
Computer chips
Diesel engines for trucks
Motors for lawn mowers

Business Services
Oil rig services
Trucking
Security services
Railroad

Business Products

Accessory Equipment
Electric grinders
Smartphone
Computer

MRO
Staples
Scotch tape
Copy paper
Duct tape

Raw Materials
Sugar
Crude oil
Milk
Iron ore

But the first consumer's impulse purchase of a haircut does not make hair styling services a convenience item. Marketers classify goods and services by considering the purchase patterns of the majority of buyers.

TYPES OF BUSINESS PRODUCTS

Business buyers are professional customers. Their job duties require rational, cost-effective purchase decisions. For instance, General Mills applies much of the same purchase decision process to buying flour that Kellogg's does.

The classification system for business products emphasizes product uses rather than customer buying behaviour. B2B products generally fall into one of six categories for product uses: installations, accessory equipment, component parts and materials, raw materials, supplies, and business services. Figure 10.3 illustrates the six types of business products.

Installations

The specialty products of the business market are called **installations**. This classification includes major capital investments for new factories and heavy machinery and for telecommunications systems. Purchases of new airplanes by Air Canada or Air Inuit are considered installations.

Since installations last for long periods of time and their purchases involve large sums of money, they represent major decisions for organizations. Negotiations often extend over several months and involve numerous decision makers. Vendors often provide technical expertise along with tangible goods. Representatives who sell custom-made equipment work closely with buying firms' engineers and production personnel to design the most satisfactory products possible.

Price typically does not dominate purchase decisions for installations, although a recent order for 230 Boeing 737s by the Indonesia-based carrier Lion Air totalled a record $22.4 billion.[10] A purchasing firm buys such a product for its efficiency and performance over its useful life. The firm also wants to minimize breakdowns. Downtime is expensive because the firm must pay employees while they wait for repairs on the machine. In addition, customers may be lost during downtime; in the case of an airline, travellers may choose to fly with another company. Installations are major investments often designed specifically for the purchasers. Training of the buyer's workforce to operate the equipment correctly, along with significant after-sale service, is usually involved. As a result, marketers of these systems typically focus their promotional efforts on employing highly trained sales representatives, often with technical backgrounds. Advertising, if the firm uses it at all, emphasizes company reputation and directs potential buyers to contact local sales representatives.

Most installations are marketed directly from manufacturers to users. Even a one-time sale may require continuing contacts for regular product servicing. Some manufacturers prefer to lease extremely expensive installations to customers rather than sell the items outright, and they assign personnel directly to the lessees' sites to operate or maintain the equipment.

Accessory Equipment

Only a few decision makers may participate in a purchase of accessory equipment—capital items that typically cost less and last for shorter periods than installations. Although quality and service exert important influences on purchases of accessory equipment, price may significantly affect these decisions. Accessory equipment includes products such as power tools, computers, and smartphones. Although these products are considered capital investments and buyers depreciate their costs over several years, their useful lives generally are much shorter than those of installations.

installations Business products like factories, assembly lines, and huge machinery that are major capital investments.

accessory equipment Capital items like desktop computers and printers that typically cost less and last for shorter periods of time than installations.

Marketing these products requires continuous representation and dealing with the widespread geographic dispersion of purchasers. To cope with these market characteristics, a wholesaler—often called an industrial distributor—might be used to contact potential customers in its own geographic area. Customers usually do not require technical assistance, and a manufacturer of accessory equipment often can distribute its products effectively through wholesalers. Advertising is an important component in the marketing mix for accessory equipment.

Component Parts and Materials

Whereas business buyers use installations and accessory equipment in the process of producing their own final products, **component parts and materials** represent finished business products of one producer that become part of the final products of another producer. Some materials, such as flour, undergo further processing before becoming part of the finished product. Textiles, paper pulp, and chemicals are also examples of component parts and materials. Bose supplies its luxury sound systems to auto manufacturers such as Audi, Infiniti, Porsche, and Cadillac. Marketers for the auto manufacturers believe that Bose systems are a good match between premium sound and their luxury vehicles, comparing the high performance of the Bose sound systems to the high performance of their cars.[11]

Purchasers of component parts and materials need regular, continuous supplies of uniform-quality products. They generally contract to purchase these items for set periods of time. Marketers commonly emphasize direct sales, and satisfied customers often become regular buyers. Wholesalers sometimes supply fill-in purchases and handle sales to smaller purchasers.

> **component parts and materials** Finished business products of one producer that become part of the final products of another producer.

Raw Materials

Farm products, such as beef, cotton, eggs, milk, poultry, and soybeans; and natural resources, such as coal, copper, iron ore, and lumber, constitute **raw materials**. These products resemble component parts and materials in that they become part of the buyers' final products. Cargill supplies many of the raw materials for finished food products—dry corn ingredients, flour, food starch, oils and shortenings, soy protein and sweeteners, and beef and pork. Food manufacturers then take these materials and turn them into finished products, such as cake and barbecued ribs.[12]

See the "Solving an Ethical Controversy" feature to find out what happened when one cereal company discovered that consumers don't distinguish between "natural" and "organic" ingredients.

> **raw materials** Natural resources such as farm products, coal, copper, or lumber, which become part of a final product.

SOLVING AN ETHICAL CONTROVERSY   Natural vs. Organic: Who Is Responsible for Knowing the Difference?

BUYERS of Kashi brand cereal were recently shocked to realize that the product, billed as "natural" by its maker, Kellogg Co., contained nonorganic soybeans, genetically modified as protection against a popular weed-killer. An organic grocer took the cereal off the shelves, and the news quickly went viral, resulting in an online uproar, to which Kashi responded with a Facebook video. Kashi said it did not violate consumers' trust by labelling its product "natural," which it defines as minimally processed without artificial ingredients. The use of the term *organic*, on the other hand, is regulated. Kashi did not call its cereal organic.

Are companies responsible for noting the difference between natural and organic in their products?

PRO

1. Consumers want wholesome products, and companies that want their business should be upfront about what is in their products.

2. Companies are taking advantage of consumers' confusion about the difference between "natural" and "organic."

CON

1. Consumers should educate themselves about what "organic" means under the law.
2. As long as labels comply with the laws, companies can use whatever terms they want.

Where do you stand: pro or con?

Sources: Stephanie Armour, "Kellogg's Kashi Targeted as Web Food Fighting Escalates," *Bloomberg Businessweek*, May 7, 2012, **www.businessweek.com**; Barry Silverstein, "Kashi GMO Flap Stirs Debate on 'Natural' and 'Organic,'" *Brand Channel*, May 2, 2012, **www.brandchannel.com**; Elizabeth Weise, "Kashi Cereal's 'Natural' Claims Stir Anger," *USA Today*, April 29, 2012, **www.usatoday.com**; Emily Leaman, "Kashi Cereal Lovers Red-Faced over Company's 'Natural' Claims," *Philadelphia Magazine's Be Well Philly*, April 26, 2012, **http://blogs.phillymag.com**.

Anson Hung/GetStock.com

Installation product.

supplies Regular expenses that a firm incurs in its daily operations.

MRO items Business supplies made up of maintenance items, repair items, and operating supplies.

Most raw materials carry grades determined according to set criteria, assuring purchasers of the receipt of standardized products of uniform quality. As with component parts and materials, vendors commonly market raw materials directly to buying organizations. Wholesalers are increasingly involved in purchasing raw materials from foreign suppliers.

Price is seldom a deciding factor in a raw materials purchase since the costs are often set at central markets, determining virtually identical transactions among competing sellers. Purchasers buy raw materials from the firms they consider best able to deliver the required quantities and qualities.

Courtesy of International Business Machines Corporation, © 2013 International Business Machines Corporation.

Business services.

Supplies

If installations represent the specialty products of the business market, operating supplies are its convenience products. **Supplies** constitute the regular expenses that a firm incurs in its daily operations. These expenses do not become part of the buyer's final products.

Supplies are also called **MRO items** because they fall into three categories: (1) maintenance items, such as brooms, filters, and light bulbs; (2) repair items, such as nuts and bolts used in repairing equipment; and (3) operating supplies, such as printer ink cartridges, mouse batteries, and pens. Staples sells all kinds of supplies to small, medium, and large businesses. Companies can purchase everything in the way of office necessities: paper, labels, and file folders. The firm also offers services such as printing and binding.[13]

A purchasing manager regularly buys operating supplies as a routine job duty. Wholesalers often facilitate sales of supplies due to the low unit prices, the small order size, and the large number of potential buyers. Since supplies are relatively standardized, heavy price competition frequently keeps costs under control. However, a business buyer spends little time making decisions about these products. Exchanges of products frequently demand simple telephone, Web, or EDI (electronic data interchange) orders or regular purchases from a sales representative of a local wholesaler.

table 10.2   *Marketing Impact of the Business Products Classification System*

FACTOR	INSTALLATIONS	ACCESSORY EQUIPMENT	COMPONENT PARTS AND MATERIALS	RAW MATERIALS	SUPPLIES	BUSINESS SERVICES
Organizational Factors						
Planning time	Extensive	Less extensive	Less extensive	Varies	Very little	Varies
Purchase frequency	Infrequent	More frequent	Frequent	Infrequent	Frequent	Varies
Comparison of price and quality	Quality very important	Quality and price important	Quality important	Quality important	Price important	Varies
Marketing Mix Factors						
Price	High	Relatively high	Low to high	Low to high	Low	Varies
Distribution channel length	Very short	Relatively short	Short	Short	Long	Varies
Promotion method	Personal selling by producer	Advertising	Personal selling	Personal selling	Advertising by producer	Varies

Business Services

The **business services** category covers the intangible products that firms buy to facilitate their production and operating processes. Examples of business services are financial services, leasing and rental services that supply equipment and vehicles, insurance, security, legal advice, and consulting. As mentioned earlier, many service providers sell the same services to both consumers and organizational buyers—telephone, gas, and electric, for example—although service firms may maintain separate marketing groups for the two customer segments.

Organizations also purchase many adjunct services that assist their operations but are not essentially a part of the final product. Cisco Systems offers its TelePresence meeting service to businesses seeking to link people in a single interactive conference. The service combines voice, data, and video on the same network, providing an interactive and collaborative experience for participants.[14]

Price may strongly influence purchase decisions for business services. The buying firm must decide whether to purchase a service or provide that service internally. This decision may depend on how frequently the firm needs the service and the specialized knowledge required to provide it. In the case of TelePresence, firms may decide the cost of the service is offset by savings in travel expenses for meeting participants. In addition, the service offers convenience.

Purchase decision processes vary considerably for different types of business services. A firm may purchase window-cleaning services through a routine and straightforward process similar to that for buying operating supplies. In contrast, a purchase decision for highly specialized environmental engineering advice requires complex analysis and perhaps lengthy negotiations similar to those for purchases of installations. This variability of the marketing mix for business services and other business products is outlined in Table 10.2.

The purchase of the right business services can make a difference in a firm's competitiveness. The Regus Group provides businesses with facilities for meetings and conferences in 600 cities in more than 100 countries. These facilities are fully furnished and equipped with every electronic medium and amenity a business could possibly need. They are staffed with trained support personnel. Regus serves large and small companies, including those relying on mobile and home-based workers. The firm's services allow businesses to customize their office and meeting needs while saving money during periods when office space is not necessary on a full-time basis.[15]

business services
Intangible products that firms buy to facilitate their production and operating processes.

QUALITY AS A PRODUCT STRATEGY

No matter how a product is classified, nothing is more frustrating to a customer than having a new item break after just a few uses or having it not live up to expectations. The smartphone that hisses static at you unless you stand still or the seam that rips out of your new jacket aren't life-altering

(3) **Explain how quality is used by marketers as a product strategy and why firms develop lines of related products.**

Cisco Systems offers its TelePresence meeting service to businesses to link people from around the world in a single interactive conference.

experiences, but they do leave an impression of poor quality that likely will lead you to make different purchases in the future. Then there's the issue of service quality—the store that seems to have no salespeople or the computer help line that leaves you on hold for 20 minutes.

Quality is a key component to a firm's success in a competitive marketplace. The efforts to create and market high-quality goods and services have been referred to as **total quality management (TQM)**. TQM expects all of a firm's employees to continually improve products and work processes with the goal of achieving customer satisfaction and world-class performance. This means that engineers design products that work, marketers develop products that people want, and salespeople deliver on their promises. Managers are responsible for communicating the goals of total quality management to all staff members and for encouraging workers to improve themselves and take pride in their work. Of course, achieving maximum quality is easier said than done, and the process is never complete. Many companies solicit reviews or feedback from customers to improve goods and services.

total quality management (TQM) Continuous effort to improve products and work processes with the goal of achieving customer satisfaction and world-class performance.

WORLDWIDE QUALITY PROGRAMS

Although the movement began in the 1920s as an attempt to increase product quality by improving the manufacturing process, it was during the 1980s that the quality revolution picked up speed in corporations. The campaign to improve quality found leadership in large manufacturing firms such as Ford, Xerox, and Motorola that had lost market share to Japanese competitors. Smaller companies that supplied parts to large firms then began to recognize quality as a requirement for success. Some companies today are using a process called Sigma Six, in which cross-functional teams work at improving the quality of their products and services by eliminating virtually all defects. Today, commitment to quality has spread to service industries, not-for-profit organizations, government agencies, and educational institutions.

In order to assist Canadian companies improve quality and to advance the quality movement in Canada, an independent, not-for-profit organization was developed to work in partnership with the Canadian government. Excellence Canada, formerly the National Quality Institute (NQI), provides advice on change management, facilitates organizational assessments, organizes events to promote quality, offers educational certification programs, and presents the annual Canada Awards for Excellence.[16] In the United States, the Malcolm Baldrige National Quality Award was established in 1987 to recognize excellence in management.

The quality movement is also strong in European countries. The European Union's ISO 9001:2008 standards define international, generic criteria for quality management and quality assurance. These standards were originally developed by the International Organization for Standardization in Switzerland to ensure consistent quality among products manufactured and sold throughout the nations of the European Union (EU). The standards now include criteria for systems of management as well. Although most other ISO standards are specific to particular products or processes, ISO 9001 applies to any organization, regardless of the goods or services it produces. Many European companies require suppliers to achieve ISO certification, which is a rigorous process that takes several months to complete, as a condition of doing business with them. The Canadian member body of ISO is the Standards Council of Canada.[17]

BENCHMARKING

Firms often rely on an important tool called **benchmarking** to set performance standards. The purpose of benchmarking is to achieve superior performance that results in a competitive advantage in the marketplace. A typical benchmarking process involves three main activities: identifying manufacturing or business processes that need improvement, comparing internal processes to those of industry leaders, and implementing changes for quality improvement.

Benchmarking requires two types of analyses: internal and external. Before a company can compare itself with another, it must first analyze its own activities to determine strengths and weaknesses. This assessment establishes a baseline for comparison. External analysis involves gathering information about the benchmark partner to find out why the partner is perceived as the industry's best. A comparison of the results of the analysis provides an objective basis for making improvements. From time to time, firms of all sizes, but particularly large firms, benchmark their operations and practices against their competitors and other players in their industry. Often, organizations follow a formal, complex program, but benchmarking can also take a simpler, more informal approach as well. Sometimes companies use benchmarking to determine how they are doing to reduce waste, as described in the "Marketing: Making Your World Better" feature.

assessment check 2

2.1. What are the three major classifications of consumer products?

2.2 Identify five factors marketers should consider in classifying consumer services.

2.3 What are the six main classifications of business products?

2.4 What are the three categories of supplies?

ISO 9001:2008 Standards that define international, generic criteria for quality management and quality assurance.

benchmarking Method of measuring quality by comparing performance against industry leaders.

MARKETING: MAKING YOUR WORLD BETTER — Fast Food Goes Green

COMPANIES like McDonald's and Tim Hortons have often been criticized for the amount of trash they produce. Much of it can be found littering the roadsides and city streets. Even small differences in the amount of garbage these companies produce or other sustainability programs they put in place can make a big impact on the environment. Both companies and others in the fast-food industry are trying to make an environmental difference through internal programs and by sponsoring environmental events.

The challenge for companies in this industry is not only the fact that they use large amounts of different types of packaging in order that food reaches the customers while it is still hot but that they deal with a large number of suppliers for the food they serve as well as the containers it's served in.

Tim Hortons makes public the results of its environmental efforts annually in its "Sustainability and Responsibility Report." The report contains such information as how many farmers take part in the Tim Hortons Coffee Partnership Program; for example, it currently has just over 1,400 and is aiming for 2,800 farmers to participate. Not only does the report identify the

corporate environment goals but it also provides a summary of the company's performance for each goal and what the next steps are for the company.

McDonald's approach to the problem does not provide the same level of detailed information as Tim Hortons. The McDonald's website does describe its efforts to reduce, reuse, and recycle, and in some cases provides examples. McDonald's also has a program in place to support the farmers that grow the coffee beans. McDonald's has joined forces with two organizations: TechnoServe and SCAN (Sustainable Commodities Assistance Network) to provide training programs for farmers in Central America and Guatemala. Their goal is to train 13,000 farmers in environmentally friendly growing practices.

These companies are so large and produce so many meals even small moves to reduce waste or programs to support the environment make big differences.

Sources: McDonald's Canada company website, **www.mcdonalds.ca**, March 5, 2014; Tim Hortons company website, **www.timhortons.com**, March 5, 2014; Larry West, "Progress Is Slow on Reducing, Reusing and Recycling Fast Food Waste," About.com website, **http://environment.about.com**, accessed March 5, 2014.

Courtesy of Telefonaktiebolaget L M Ericsson

Professional services: An important part of the service sector.

service encounter
Point at which the customer and service provider interact.

service quality
Expected and perceived quality of a service offering.

QUALITY OF SERVICES

Everyone has a story about bad and good service, the waiter who forgot a dinner order, a car mechanic who offered a ride to and from the repair shop. As a consumer, your perception of the quality of the service you have purchased is usually determined during the **service encounter**—the point at which the customer and service provider interact. Employees such as cashiers and customer service representatives have a powerful impact on their customers' decision to return or not. You might pass the word to your friends about the friendly staff at a local breakfast eatery, the slow cashiers at a local grocery store, or the huge scoops of ice cream you got at the nearby ice cream stand. Those words form powerful marketing messages about the services you received.

Service quality refers to the expected and perceived quality of a service offering, and it has a huge effect on the competitiveness of a company. It may be getting harder for companies to maintain their level of service quality. According to a recent study conducted by the research company Colloquy, customer expectations have increased by 30 percent and are at a 20-year high.[18]

Service quality is determined by five variables:

1. *Tangibles*, or physical evidence. A tidy office and clean uniform are examples.

2. *Reliability*, or consistency of performance and dependability.

3. *Responsiveness*, or the willingness and readiness of employees to provide service. A salesperson who asks, "How may I help you?" is an example.

4. *Assurances*, or the confidence communicated by the service provider.

5. *Empathy*, or the service provider's efforts to understand the customer's needs and then individualize the service.

If a gap exists between the level of service that customers expect and the level they think they have received, it can be favourable or unfavourable. If you get a larger steak than you expected or your plane arrives ahead of schedule, the gap is favourable, and you are likely to try that service again. But if your steak is tiny, cold, and overcooked or your plane is two hours late, the gap is unfavourable, and you will probably find another restaurant or decide to drive next time. Emails are another way that customers judge a company's service. See the "Career Readiness" feature for some tips about sending effective emails, both within and outside the company.

CAREER READINESS   Email: Think Before You Send

TEXTING, tweeting, and social networking are popular, but they haven't replaced email in business communication. It is true, however, that many people still make basic email errors that can backfire. Here's how to avoid some of them.

- Always use grammatically correct and concise language, avoid abbreviations and jargon, and watch your tone. Sarcasm and humour are easily misunderstood.
- Proofread everything.
- Never send an email whose presence on tomorrow's front page would embarrass you. If you're angry, wait an hour before writing anything, and think before sending. You never know who is storing your message.
- Make one point per email; many readers don't notice the second or third.
- Include an accurate subject line so your recipient can prioritize incoming messages.

- Be cautious about forwarding other people's emails, about blind copying others on your emails, and about hitting the infamous "Reply all" button.
- Never forward chain emails.
- Ask yourself whether your message is important enough to spend a stamp on it. If not, don't send it.
- Answer incoming email promptly and completely.
- Finally, remember the human touch. A phone call or quick visit to someone's office can be more effective than a long, complicated email.

Sources: Seth Godin, "Email Checklist," Typepad.com, **http://sethfodin .typepad.com**, accessed May 8, 2012; "Email Etiquette," **Emailreplies.com**, **http://emailreplies.com**, accessed May 8, 2012; Alina Tugeno, "What to Think About before You Hit 'Send,'" *The New York Times*, April 20, 2012, **www.nytimes.com**; Emily Suess, "12 Tips for Writing More Effective Business Emails," *Small Business Bonfire*, February 20, 2012, **http:// smallbusinessbonfire.com**.

DEVELOPMENT OF PRODUCT LINES

Few firms today market only one product. A typical firm offers its customers a **product line**—that is, a series of related products. The motivations for marketing complete product lines rather than concentrating on a single product include the desire to grow, enhancing the company's position in the market, optimal use of company resources, and exploiting the product life cycle. The following subsections examine each of the first three reasons. The final reason, exploiting the stages of the product life cycle, is discussed in the section that focuses on strategic implications of the product life cycle concept.

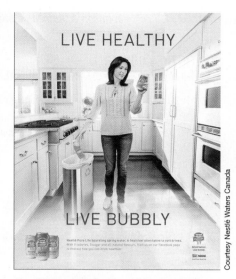

LIVE HEALTHY

LIVE BUBBLY

Courtesy Nestlé Waters Canada

Nestlé expands its line of bottled water with a product aimed at consumers who are health conscious.

DESIRE TO GROW

A company limits its growth potential when it concentrates on a single product, even though the company may have started that way, as retailer Roots did with its single negative-heel shoe. Now the company sells a complete line of casual wear for men and women, not to mention clothing for children and babies along with bags and home furnishings. The company has grown to 120 stores in Canada and the United States, with 100 more in Asia, in addition to its online retailing. The company customizes its products for films, television shows, musical groups, and sports teams.[19]

product line Series of related products offered by one company.

ENHANCING THE COMPANY'S POSITION IN THE MARKET

A company with a line of products often makes itself more important to both consumers and marketing intermediaries than a firm with only one product. A shopper who purchases a hat for outdoor activities often buys related clothes. For instance, Tilley Endurables offers a wide range of products, allowing consumers to completely outfit themselves for outdoor activities or travel. They can purchase hats, pants, shorts, dresses, and the bags to pack them in. The company sells its products in company stores in Ontario, Quebec, and British Columbia; through its mail-order catalogue; and on the Internet. In addition, many other stores throughout Canada and around the world carry Tilley clothes. The company started making hats, advertising them in sailing magazines, and selling them at boating shows. Few would know about Tilley products if the company had not expanded beyond its original hat.[20]

OPTIMAL USE OF COMPANY RESOURCES

By spreading the costs of its operations over a series of products, a firm may reduce the average production and marketing costs of each product. The Calgary Stampede is a good example. Once the site of a single 10-day event, today the Stampede Development Park is the location of year-round events promoting tourism, economic development, education, and entertainment.[21]

> **assessment check 3** ✓
>
> 3.1 What is TQM?
>
> 3.2 What are the five variables of service quality?
>
> 3.3 List the four reasons for developing a product line.

④ Describe the way marketers typically measure product mixes and make product mix decisions.

THE PRODUCT MIX

A company's **product mix** is the assortment of product lines and individual product offerings that the company sells. The right blend of product lines and individual products allows a firm to maximize sales opportunities within the limitations of its resources. Marketers typically measure product mixes according to width, length, and depth.

product mix Assortment of product lines and individual product offerings that a company sells.

table 10.3 *Johnson & Johnson's Mix of Health Care Products*

OVER-THE-COUNTER MEDICINES	NUTRITIONALS	SKIN AND HAIR CARE	ORAL CARE	MEDICAL DEVICES AND DIAGNOSTICS
Motrin pain reliever	Lactaid digestive aid	Aveeno lotions	REACH dental floss	Ethicon surgical instruments and systems
Tylenol pain reliever	Splenda sweetener	Clean & Clear facial cleansers and toners	Rembrandt Deeply White	OneTouch diabetes management products
Reactine Allergy		Johnson's baby shampoo	Listerine mouth wash	Orthopaedic joint replacement products
		Neutrogena soaps and shampoos	Listerine Pocketpaks	ACCLARENT ear, nose, and throat products

Sources: Information from Johnson & Johnson websites, **www.jnjcanada.com**, accessed March 6, 2014, and **www.jjmc.ca**, accessed March 6, 2014.

PRODUCT MIX WIDTH

The *width* of a product mix refers to the number of product lines the firm offers. As Table 10.3 shows, Johnson & Johnson offers a broad line of retail consumer products in the Canadian market, as well as business-to-business products to the medical community. Consumers can purchase over-the-counter medications, nutritional products, dental care products, and first-aid products, among others. Health care professionals can obtain prescription drugs, medical and diagnostic devices, and wound treatments. LifeScan, one of Johnson & Johnson's subsidiaries, offers a range of products under the OneTouch brand designed to help diabetes patients manage their condition. DePuy, another subsidiary, manufactures orthopaedic implants and joint replacement products. At the drugstore, consumers can pick up some of J&J's classic products, such as Motrin and Visine.[22]

PRODUCT MIX LENGTH

The *length* of a product mix refers to the number of different products a firm sells. Table 10.3 identifies some of the hundreds of health care products offered by Johnson & Johnson. Some of J&J's most recognizable brands are Band-Aid, Motrin, Tylenol, and Neutrogena.

PRODUCT MIX DEPTH

Depth refers to variations in each product that the firm markets in its mix. Johnson & Johnson's Band-Aid brand bandages come in a variety of shapes and sizes, including Perfect Fit, Flexible Fabric for Knuckle and Fingertip, and Advance Healing Blister Cushions.

PRODUCT MIX DECISIONS

Establishing and managing the product mix have become increasingly important marketing tasks. Adding depth, length, and width to the product mix requires careful thinking and planning—otherwise a firm can end up with too many products, including some that don't sell well. To evaluate a firm's product mix, marketers look at the effectiveness of its depth, length, and width. Has the firm ignored a viable consumer segment? It may improve performance by increasing product line depth to offer a product variation that will attract the new segment. Can the firm achieve economies in its sales and distribution efforts by adding complementary product lines to the mix? If so, a wider product mix may seem appropriate. Does the firm gain equal contributions from all products in its portfolio? If not, it may decide to lengthen or shorten the product mix to increase revenues. Geox is an Italian shoe manufacturer known for its patented breathable fabric that keeps feet cool and comfortable. With sales of more than $1.1 billion, Geox is expanding both ways: in width and length. The firm offers trendy shoe styles, including strappy sandals and retro-inspired

Geox is expanding its product mix to include shoes and apparel for women, men, and children.

Alessia Pierdomenico/Bloomberg via Getty Images

bowling shoes. In addition, Geox has launched apparel and shoe lines for men and children, made of similar breathable fabrics that help keep consumers cool and dry.[23]

Another way to add to the mix is to purchase product lines from other companies. Or a firm can acquire entire companies through mergers or acquisitions. Canadian Tire expanded its sporting goods and sporting apparel lines by purchasing the Forzani Group of stores, which includes Sport Chek and Nevada Bob's Golf retailers. The company has continued to expand its product mix by purchasing the Pro Hockey Life stores.[24]

A firm should assess its current product mix for another important reason: to determine the feasibility of a line extension. A **line extension** adds individual offerings that appeal to different market segments while remaining closely related to the existing product line. To reinforce its "do it yourself" theme, Home Depot broadened its existing Martha Stewart Living product line to include carpets, storage units, and lighting. Home Depot marketers say the additions will especially appeal to female shoppers, who make up half their customers.[25]

The marketing environment also plays a role in a marketer's evaluation of a firm's product mix. In the case of Home Depot, the growing proportion of women who like to do their own redecorating and the increased interest in Martha Stewart–branded merchandise all helped influence the retailer's decision to extend the product line.

Careful evaluation of a firm's current product mix can also help marketers in making decisions about brand management and new-product introductions. Chapter 11 examines the importance of branding, brand management, and the development and introduction of new products.

line extension
Development of individual offerings that appeal to different market segments while remaining closely related to the existing product line.

assessment check 4

4.1 Define *product mix*.

4.2 How do marketers typically measure product mixes?

⑤ **Explain the concept of the product life cycle and identify the different stages.**

THE PRODUCT LIFE CYCLE

Products, like people, pass through stages as they age. Successful products progress through four basic stages: introduction, growth, maturity, and decline. This progression, known as the **product life cycle**, is shown in Figure 10.4.

product life cycle
Progression of a product through introduction, growth, maturity, and decline stages.

figure 10.4

Stages in the Product Life Cycle

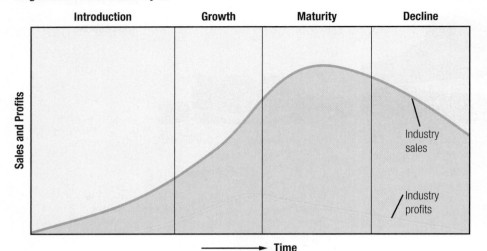

The product life cycle concept applies to products or product categories within an industry, not to individual brands. For instance, smartphones and tablet computers moved rapidly from the introduction stage into the growth stage. Digital cameras are now in the maturity stage, while traditional film cameras are in decline. There is no set schedule or time frame for a particular stage of the life cycle. Some products pass through certain stages rapidly, while others move more slowly. CDs have been around for more than a quarter of a century but are declining, due in part to the increase in digital music downloads.[26]

introductory stage First stage of the product life cycle, in which a firm works to stimulate demand for the new market entry.

growth stage Second stage of the product life cycle, which begins when a firm starts to realize substantial profits from its investment in the product.

Marketoid

Over 75 percent of the labour force works in service industries.

INTRODUCTORY STAGE

During the **introductory stage** of the product life cycle, a firm works to stimulate demand for the new market entry. Products in this stage might bring new technology to a product category. Since the product is unknown to the public, promotional campaigns stress information about its features. Additional promotions try to induce distribution channel members to carry the product. In this phase, the public becomes acquainted with the item's merits and begins to accept it.

A product whose introductory stage has been successful is the GPS mapping device. Although global positioning systems have been around for a number of years, their introduction to the consumer market was more recent. By promoting its practical application and making the devices easy to use, marketers have seen GPS sales increase rapidly, moving the products quickly toward the growth stage.[27]

Technical problems and financial losses are common during the introductory stage as companies fine-tune product design and spend money on advertising. Many users remember early problems with the Internet—jammed portals, order-fulfilling glitches, dot-coms that went bust. Users of GPS devices reported some glitches but also conceded that some problems stem from learning how to operate the devices correctly.

GPS mapping devices have had a successful introductory stage.

GROWTH STAGE

Sales volume rises rapidly during the **growth stage** as new customers make initial purchases and early buyers repurchase the product, such as smartphones and GPS devices. The growth stage usually begins when a firm starts to realize substantial profits from its investment. Word-of-mouth reports, mass advertising, and lowered prices all encourage hesitant buyers to make trial purchases of new products. In the case of big-screen TVs, low prices generally have not been a factor—many cost several thousand dollars. "Big-screen" now refers to a TV that is about 60 inches. As sales volume rises, competitors enter the marketplace, creating new challenges for marketers. As plasma technology was gradually replaced by LCD and LED-LCD models, companies with competing technologies vied for dominance, the TVs themselves grew larger, and prices continued to vary considerably.[28]

MATURITY STAGE

Sales of a product category continue to grow during the early part of the maturity stage, but eventually they reach a plateau as the backlog of potential customers dwindles. By this time, many competitors have entered the market, and the firm's profits begin to decline as competition intensifies.

At this stage in the product life cycle, differences between competing products diminish as competitors discover the product and promotional characteristics most desired by customers. Available supplies exceed industry demand for the first time. Companies can increase their sales and market shares only at the expense of competitors, so the competitive environment becomes increasingly important. In the maturity stage, heavy promotional outlays emphasize any differences that still separate competing products, and brand competition intensifies. Some firms try to differentiate their products by focusing on attributes such as quality, reliability, and service. Others focus on redesign or other ways of extending the product life cycle. Nike athletic shoes could be said to be in the maturity stage. With hundreds of athletic shoes on the market, it is difficult to differentiate competing products. But a Nike innovation has enabled the manufacture of shoes that weigh considerably less yet are able to take the pounding of a professional athlete. The innovation is Flywire, a lightweight thread made of Vectran fibres. Flywire shoes are so simple and inexpensive to manufacture that Nike could be looking at a whole new life cycle for its time-honoured shoes. Not only is the Flywire technology used for footwear, but it can be incorporated into athletic clothing as well. The 2014 Canadian Olympic hockey teams had the Flywire technology in their sweaters. The sweater design was based on classic jerseys of the past, but the new technology made them 15 percent lighter than the uniforms worn at the Vancouver games.[29]

DECLINE STAGE

In the decline stage of a product's life, innovations or shifts in consumer preferences bring about an absolute decline in industry sales. Dial telephones became touch-tone phones, which evolved to portable phones, which were replaced by conventional cell phones, which in turn were replaced by camera phones, and now smartphones are on the market.

Some manufacturers refuse to give up in the decline stage. Young consumers, accustomed to CDs and digital downloads, are beginning to turn their attention to vinyl records. They have discovered their parents' and grandparents' collection of LPs and have hauled old record turntables out of the attic. If curiosity led them to the discovery, the sound and graphics of a record seem to be holding their interest. Marketers in the music industry have taken notice, and some bands have begun to issue limited numbers of records along with CDs and MP3 formats. They don't expect vinyl to become the primary medium for music, but are happy to resurrect a classic product for a new generation of listeners.[30]

The traditional product life cycle differs from fad cycles. Fashions and fads profoundly influence marketing strategies. Fashions are currently popular products that tend to follow recurring life cycles. For example, bell-bottom pants that were popular in the 1960s and 1970s have returned as flares or boot-cut pants. In contrast, fads are products with abbreviated life cycles. Most fads experience short-lived popularity and then quickly fade, although some maintain residual markets among certain segments. Webkinz (the stuffed animals that have their own online Webkinz World) are an example of a fad.

Marketoid

The average weekly earnings in the service sector is about $185 less than in the goods-producing sector.

maturity stage Third stage of the product life cycle, in which industry sales level out.

decline stage Final stage of the product life cycle, in which a decline in total industry sales occurs.

assessment check 5

5.1 Identify the four stages of the product life cycle.

5.2 During which stage or stages are products likely to attract the most new customers?

EXTENDING THE PRODUCT LIFE CYCLE

⑥ Describe how a firm can extend a product's life cycle, and explain why certain products may be deleted.

Marketers usually try to extend each stage of the life cycles for their products as long as possible. Product life cycles can stretch indefinitely as a result of decisions designed to increase the frequency of use by current customers; increase the number of users for the product; find new uses; or change package sizes, labels, or product quality.

Nivea increases the number of users by changing the package size.

INCREASING FREQUENCY OF USE

During the maturity stage, the sales curve for a product category reaches a maximum point if the competitors exhaust the supply of potential customers who previously had not made purchases. However, if current customers buy more frequently than they formerly did, the total number of sales will rise even though no new buyers enter the market.

For instance, consumers buy some products during certain seasons of the year. Marketers can boost purchase frequency by persuading these people to try the product year-round. For decades, most people used sunscreen only during warm and sunny seasons of the year. With greater warnings about the risks of sun damage and skin cancer, however, companies now advertise the benefits of using sunscreen year-round.

INCREASING THE NUMBER OF USERS

A second strategy for extending the product life cycle seeks to increase the overall market size by attracting new customers who previously have not used the product. Marketers may find their products in different stages of the life cycle in different countries. This difference can help firms extend product growth. Items that have reached the maturity stage in Canada may still be in the introductory stage somewhere else.

After years of operating exclusively in the United States and Canada, retail chain J. Crew recently announced it would open stores in Europe and Asia, with London and Hong Kong as its first new locations. Although J. Crew's CEO had earlier remarked that expanding overseas would distract the company from its North American operations, J. Crew now sees stores in Europe and Asia as an attractive way to grow sales.[31]

FINDING NEW USES

Finding new uses for a product is an excellent strategy for extending a product's life cycle. Examples of new applications for mature products are oatmeal as a cholesterol reducer, antacids as a calcium supplement, and aspirin for promoting heart health.

Marketers sometimes conduct contests or surveys to identify new uses for their products. They may post the results or their own new ideas on their websites. Arm & Hammer's website lists a variety of alternative uses throughout the house for its baking soda. Consumers can use baking soda to clean crayon off walls, as an antacid to settle an upset stomach, and as an agent to balance the pH in swimming pool water. The firm has even developed packaging with special vents to control odours in freezers and refrigerators.[32]

CHANGING PACKAGE SIZES, LABELS, OR PRODUCT QUALITY

Many firms try to extend their product life cycles by introducing physical changes in their offerings. Alternatively, new packaging and labels with updated images and slogans can help revitalize a product. General Mills found a way to remodel the packaging for its iconic Cheerios brand and create a more sustainable design. Previously, Cheerios that sold at club stores like Costco came in an oversized box with two bags of cereal inside; for many homes, the box was cumbersome and didn't fit on a pantry shelf. In addition, the bags contained a considerable amount of head space because the cereal would settle during transit. However, a new technology developed at General Mills permits the Cheerios to settle while still on the production line, allowing more dense packing and a smaller box. For club shoppers, the new package actually consists of two smaller, detachable boxes—easier to store and serve. The new design also saves paperboard and even reduces the company's carbon footprint because more boxes can fit on a truck.[33]

Changes in packaging can lengthen a product's life cycle. Food marketers have brought out small packages designed to appeal to one-person households and extra-large containers for customers who want to buy in bulk. Other firms offer their products in convenient packages for use away from home or at the office. The popularity of the single-cup brewing machine has skyrocketed, leading numerous coffee sellers, including Tim Hortons, to introduce single-cup versions of their brand.[34]

assessment check 6 ✔

6.1 Describe the four strategies for extending a product's life cycle.

6.2 Under what circumstances do firms decide to delete a product from their line?

PRODUCT DELETION DECISIONS

To avoid wasting resources promoting unpromising products, marketers must sometimes prune product lines and eliminate marginal products. Marketers typically face this decision during the late maturity and early decline stages of the product life cycle. Periodic reviews of weak products should justify either eliminating or retaining them. After battling it out with Sony in the DVD player arena, Toshiba conceded defeat and announced it would stop making its HD DVD player. That left Sony the winner in the marketplace with its Blu-ray format.

A firm may continue to carry an unprofitable item to provide a complete line for its customers. For example, while most grocery stores lose money on bulky, low-unit-value items such as salt, they continue to carry these items to meet shopper demand.

Shortages of raw materials sometimes prompt companies to discontinue production and marketing of previously profitable items. A firm may even drop a profitable item that fails to fit into its existing product line or fails to fit the direction in which the firm wants to grow. Some of these products return to the market carrying the names of other firms that purchase these "orphan brands" from the original manufacturers. In the largest relaunch in hotel history, InterContinental Hotels Group undertook a $1-billion relaunch of its Holiday Inn chain. Over several years, 3,300 Holiday Inns re-emerged with a redesigned logo; updated lobbies and guest bathrooms; and new signage, landscaping, lighting, and bedding. What's more, all employees will be retrained under the chain's new "Stay Real" program.[35]

Strategic Implications

Marketers who want their businesses to succeed will continue to develop new goods and services to attract and satisfy customers. They will engage in continuous improvement activities, focusing on quality and customer service. And they will continually evaluate their company's mix of products.

Marketers everywhere are constantly developing new and better products that fit their firm's overall strategy. Technological innovations are one area in which new products quickly replace old ones. Marketers are sometimes faced with the dilemma of lagging sales for formerly popular products. They must come up with ways to extend the lives of certain products to increase their firm's profitability and sometimes must recognize and delete those that no longer meet expectations. ◆◆◆

REVIEW OF CHAPTER OBJECTIVES

① **Define product, distinguish between goods and services and how they relate to the goods–services continuum, and explain the importance of the service sector in today's marketplace.**

Marketers define a product as the bundle of physical, service, and symbolic attributes designed to satisfy customers' wants and needs. Goods are tangible products that customers can see, hear, smell, taste, or touch. Services are intangible tasks that satisfy the needs of customers. Goods represent one end of a continuum, and services represent the other. The service sector makes a crucial contribution to the Canadian economy by means of products and jobs. The service sector now makes up more than 75 percent of the economy. Services have grown because of consumers' desire for speed, convenience, and technological advances.

② **Describe the classifications of consumer and business goods and services.**

Consumer products—both goods and services—are classified as convenience products (frequently purchased items), shopping products (products purchased after comparison), and specialty products (those that offer unique characteristics that consumers prize).

Business products are classified as installations (major capital investments), accessory equipment (capital items that cost less and last for shorter periods than installations), component parts and materials (finished business products of one producer that become part of the final products of another producer), raw materials (natural resources such as lumber, beef, or cotton), supplies (the regular expenses that a firm incurs in daily operations), and business services (the intangible products that firms buy to facilitate their production and operating processes).

③ **Explain how quality is used by marketers as a product strategy and why firms develop lines of related products.**

Many companies use total quality management (TQM) in an effort to encourage all employees to participate in producing the best goods and services possible. Companies may also participate in ISO 9001:2008 certification or benchmarking to evaluate and improve quality. Consumers often evaluate service quality on the basis of tangibles, reliability, responsiveness, assurance, and empathy, so marketers of service firms strive to excel in all these areas.

Companies usually produce several related products rather than individual ones to achieve the objectives of growth, optimal use of company resources, and increased company importance in the market, and to make optimal use of the product life cycle.

④ **Describe the way marketers typically measure product mixes and make product mix decisions.**

Marketers must decide the right width, length, and depth of product lines. Width is the number of product lines. Length is the number of products a company sells. Depth refers to the number of variations of a product available in a product line. Marketers evaluate the effectiveness of all three elements of the product mix. They may purchase product lines from other companies or extend the product line if necessary. Firms may also acquire entire companies and their product lines through mergers and acquisitions.

⑤ **Explain the concept of the product life cycle and identify the different stages.**

The product life cycle outlines the stages that a product goes through, including introduction, growth, maturity, and decline. During the introductory stage, marketers work to stimulate demand for the new product. New customers make initial purchases and repurchases of the product in the growth stage. Sales continue to grow during the maturity stage but eventually level off. In the decline stage, sales are reduced due to innovations or a shift in consumer preferences.

⑥ **Describe how a firm can extend a product's life cycle, and explain why certain products may be deleted.**

Marketers can extend the product life cycle by increasing frequency of use or number of users; finding new uses for the product; or changing package size, label, or quality. If none of these is successful, or if the product no longer fits a firm's line, the firm may decide to delete a product from its line.

assessment check answers ✓

1.1 Define the term *product*.

A product is a bundle of physical, service, and symbolic attributes designed to satisfy a customer's wants and needs.

1.2 Why is the understanding of want satisfaction so important to marketers?

The understanding of want satisfaction is important to marketers because it helps them understand why people purchase certain goods and services.

1.3 Describe the goods–services continuum and list the six characteristics that distinguish services from goods.

The goods–services continuum is a spectrum that helps marketers visualize the differences and similarities between goods and services.

The six characteristics distinguishing services from goods are the following: (1) services are intangible, (2) services are inseparable from the service providers, (3) services are perishable, (4) companies cannot easily standardize services, (5) buyers often play important roles in the creation and distribution of services, and (6) service standards show wide variations.

1.4 Identify two reasons why services are important to the Canadian economy and business environment.

The service sector makes an important contribution to the economy with products and jobs. Services also play a vital role in the international competitiveness of Canadian firms.

1.5 Why do service firms emphasize marketing?

The growth of potential service transactions represents a vast marketing opportunity, and the environment for services is changing—so marketers need to find new ways to reach customers.

2.1 What are the three major classifications of consumer products?

The three major classifications are convenience products, shopping products, and specialty products.

2.2 Identify five factors marketers should consider in classifying consumer services.

The five factors are the following: (1) the nature of the service, (2) the relationship between the service organization and its customers, (3) flexibility for customization, (4) fluctuation of supply and demand, and (5) the way the service is delivered.

2.3 What are the six main classifications of business products?

The six main classifications of business products are the following: (1) installations, (2) accessory equipment, (3) component parts and materials, (4) raw materials, (5) supplies, and (6) business services.

2.4 What are the three categories of supplies?

The three categories of supplies are maintenance items, repair items, and operating supplies.

3.1 What is TQM?

TQM stands for total quality management, a process that expects all of a firm's employees to continually improve its products and work processes.

3.2 What are the five variables of service quality?

The five variables of service quality are tangibles, reliability, responsiveness, assurances, and empathy.

3.3 List the four reasons for developing a product line.

The four reasons firms want to develop product lines are the following: (1) a desire to grow, (2) enhancing the company's position in the market, (3) optimal use of company resources, and (4) exploiting the stages of the product life cycle.

4.1 Define *product mix*.

The product mix is a company's assortment of product lines and individual product offerings.

4.2 How do marketers typically measure product mixes?

The product mix is measured by width, length, and depth.

5.1 Identify the four stages of the product life cycle.

The four stages of the product life cycle are introduction, growth, maturity, and decline.

5.2 During which stage or stages are products likely to attract the most new customers?

Products usually attract the most new customers during the introductory and growth stages.

6.1 Describe the four strategies for extending a product's life cycle.

The four strategies are increasing frequency of use, increasing the number of users, finding new users, and changing packaging or quality.

6.2 Under what circumstances do firms decide to delete a product from their line?

Firms may decide to delete a product if none of the strategies for extending a product's life works, if raw materials become unavailable, or if the product no longer fits the existing or future product line.

MARKETING TERMS YOU NEED TO KNOW

These terms are printed in blue in the text. They are defined in the margins of the chapter and in the Glossary that begins on p. G-1.

product 276	goods–services continuum 276	convenience products 279
service 276	business-to-business (B2B) product 279	impulse goods and services 279
good 276	unsought products 279	staples 280

PROJECT AND TEAMWORK EXERCISES

1. On your own or with a classmate, choose one of the following goods (or choose one of your own). Visit the company's website to learn as much as you can about your product and the way it is marketed. Then create a marketing strategy for developing the services to support your product and make it stand out from others.
   a. LG smartphone
   b. Mini Cooper car
   c. IKEA furniture
   d. Apple iPad

2. On your own or with a classmate, create an advertisement for an unsought product such as a remedial reading or math course, a warranty for a big-screen TV, a first-aid kit, or the like. How can your ad turn an unsought product into one actually desired by consumers?

3. Consider a customer service experience you have had in the last month or so. Was it positive or negative? Describe your experience to the class and then discuss how the firm might improve the quality of its customer service—even if it is already positive.

4. With a classmate, choose one of the following firms or another that interests you. Visit the firm's website and measure its product mix. Then create a chart like the one for Johnson & Johnson in Table 10.3, identifying the company's major product lines, along with a few specific examples.
   a. Champion athletic clothing
   b. Condé Nast magazines
   c. Wyndham Hotels
   d. Panasonic
   e. Audi

5. With the same classmate, create a plan for further extending one of the firm's product lines. Describe the strategy you would recommend for extending the line as well as new products that might be included.

CRITICAL THINKING EXERCISES

1. Draw a line representing the goods–services continuum. Then place each of the following along the continuum. Briefly explain your decision.
   a. Skype
   b. Teleflora.com
   c. Walmart
   d. Kia dealership
   e. Netflix

2. Make a list of all the convenience products you buy in a week. Does the list change from week to week based on need or your budget? What would it take to make you switch from one product to another?

3. Imagine your favourite restaurant. List as many installations, raw materials, and supplies as you think the restaurant owner or manager must be responsible for purchasing.

4. Why is it important for even a small company to develop a line of products?

5. Choose one of the following goods and services and describe your strategy for taking it to the next stage in its product life cycle. For products in the maturity or decline stage, describe a strategy for extending their life cycle.
   a. iPad (growth)
   b. MP3 players (maturity)
   c. text messaging (growth)
   d. landline phones (decline)
   e. duct tape (maturity)

6. Describe a fad that has come and gone during your lifetime, such as Beanie Babies. Did you take part in the fad? Why or why not? How long did it last? Why do you think it faded?

ETHICS EXERCISE

The airline industry has suffered recent setbacks, such as the high cost of fuel, that have forced the major carriers to cut back on many of their services. Some airlines have started charging passengers for checked luggage and others have announced they are going to even charge for carry-on bags. Most airlines charge for in-flight snacks or don't serve any at all. Airlines have reduced the number of flights they operate to certain destinations, packing planes full to overflowing; some restrict the use of frequent flyer miles, making it difficult to cash them in. Then there are the record-setting delays and lost luggage claims. All these factors add up to less than enjoyable flying experiences for many travellers, many of whom are going to find other modes of transportation or just stay home.[36] Suppose you are a marketer for one of the major airlines. Your company is facing difficulty providing acceptable service to the passengers on its flights, but you need to find a way to emphasize the positive features of your airline's service.

1. Using the five variables of service quality as your guideline, what steps would you take—within your realm of control—to close the gap between the level of service passengers expect and the level they have been receiving?
2. How might you attract business customers? Would you give them a level of service that is different from families and other consumers who are flying for pleasure?

CASE 10.1

The Canadian Word for Coffee—Tims

What could be more Canadian than hockey? How about a coffee and doughnut? Even more Canadian would be a coffee and doughnut shop started by and named after a hockey player. Tim Hortons is so Canadian that terms like "double double" (coffee with double cream and double sugar) and "Tims" (coffee) are part of everyday language across the country. If that weren't enough of a sign that Tim Hortons is doing it right, it has even received awards for its marketing activities. The reasons it is so successful are easy—quality products and an efficient operation.

In 1964, an NHL player, Tim Horton, opened a coffee shop in Hamilton, Ontario. The original store sold only beverages and doughnuts, but it was a place for the average person to meet friends. In 1965, Ron Joyce left the Hamilton police department to run the store, and in 1967, he became a full partner in the company. Tragedy struck in 1974, when Tim Horton, then playing for the Buffalo Sabres, was killed in a car accident returning home after a game in Toronto. Shortly after the accident, Joyce bought Horton's share of the business to become sole owner of the 40-store chain. It was at this time that the company decided to focus all its efforts on providing an always-fresh product and outstanding service. Another important milestone in the company's history occurred in 1995, when it merged with Wendy's International Inc., a company based in the United States. Since 2006, Tim Hortons has been operating as a stand-alone public company with its stocks trading on both the Toronto and New York exchanges. There are more than 3,400 stores in Canada, more than 800 in the United States, almost 250 in the United Kingdom and Ireland, and more than 20 in the United Arab Emirates and Oman.

The number of menu items has expanded significantly since the first restaurant was opened. While product development was important to the success of the company, two things were kept in mind: the ever-changing tastes of its customers and the stores' ability to deliver a quality product and service.

When the first Tim Hortons opened, only two items were on the menu—coffee and doughnuts. There was a large number of varieties of doughnuts. It took 14 years before the menu saw any significant changes. It was at this time that the Timbit was introduced. While some could argue that a Timbit is still a doughnut, its introduction was the start of many new menu items. The 1980s were a decade of expansion for the menu with new items appearing almost annually. First to appear on the menu was the muffin, followed closely by cakes, pies, croissants, and cookies. The first lunch menu item appeared in 1985 when soup and chili were added. The lunch menu continued to expand into the 1990s with sandwiches. Around this time the company also started to move away from its traditional menu aimed at the average Canadian by adding flavoured and iced cappuccinos and café mochas to the menu.

In 2005, the company made its first move into the breakfast market by introducing yogurt and fruit to its lineup. A year later the company was ready to take on McDonald's for the breakfast market. Research conducted at the time showed that Tim Hortons was the most popular place for Canadians to stop for their morning coffee, but McDonald's Egg McMuffin was the most popular breakfast sandwich. Tim Hortons was in the right position in the market to take advantage of the fast-growing segment. It introduced its egg breakfast sandwich, which is available on a fresh baked biscuit, English muffin, or bagel with sausage or bacon and cheese. The product introduction was accompanied by a promotional campaign to get the word out.

What's next for Tim Hortons? If the company stays true to its past strategic plans, it will continue expanding its menus and its global locations.

Questions for Critical Thinking

1. At what stage of the product life cycle is Tim Hortons? What steps can be taken to manage the product portfolio?

2. How important do you think product and service quality are as a product strategy for Tim Hortons?

Sources: Kristin Laird, "Tim Hortons Dumps Ice Cream, Launches Loyalty Program," *Marketing*, February 20, 2014, **www.marketingmag.ca**; "Tim Hortons Moving to Persian Gulf," *Marketing*, **www.marketingmag.ca**, February 7, 2011; "Tim Hortons Makes Smoothie Move," *Marketing*, March 3, 2011; "Tim Hortons Charts Course for Global Expansion," *Marketing*, **www.marketingmag.ca**, May 14, 2010; "Tim Hortons Closing Poorly Performing U.S. Stores, Kiosks," *Marketing*, **www.marketingmag.ca**, November 11, 2010; Kristin Laird, "Tim Hortons Serves up New Challenge to McDonald's in the Morning," *Marketing*, **www.marketingmag.ca**, January 29, 2010; Rebecca Harris, "Down-Home Smarts," *Marketing*, February 7, 2005, pp. 15–19; Tim Hortons website, **www.timhortons.com**, accessed March 8, 2014; "Tim Hortons Is Marketing's Marketer of the Year," *Marketing Daily*, February 4, 2005; Rebecca Harris, "A Cup of Canadiana: Tim Hortons, Oakville, Ont.," *Marketing*, December 13, 2004.

CASE 10.2

Procter & Gamble and the Febreze Product Line

Procter & Gamble, the large multinational that produces and sells several household brands such as Tide and Pampers, has a history of innovation. The company introduces new versions of products every year, but rarely does it introduce an entirely new type of product. In 1998 the company introduced a product that did not fit into any of its other product lines. That product was Febreze Fabric Refresher.

Febreze was the first product to eliminate unwanted odours in fabric. Up to this point, there were lots of air freshener products on the market, but they did not eliminate odours—they just tried to cover them up. At first consumers had to be convinced that the product actually did what the company claimed and to be shown that it added value to the household cache of cleaning products. Procter & Gamble was able to overcome these initial challenges and experienced an unprecedented new product launch. Within the first year, Febreze attained a 38 percent household penetration rate.

The new product launch was so successful the company quickly began expanding the product line. The next new product was a spray mist that could be used to eliminate odours in fabric and in a room. Today there is a fabric spray designed specifically for bedding, one to eliminate pet odours, and another to reduce allergens. In addition to the spray and mist products, there are products that you plug into the wall, ones that have wax inserts that melt, and others that have oils and candles. You can even get products that can clip onto the vents in car. All these products come in a variety of scents—sweet, fruity, or exotic—or without any fragrance at all. One line of products is designed to help you fall asleep.

It is likely that the product line is going to continue to grow given that Procter & Gamble sells more than $1 billion a year of Febreze products. The products are available globally, with strong sales in North America, Japan, and Europe.

Questions for Critical Thinking

1. Do you think it is a good idea for Procter & Gamble to expand the Febreze product line further? If so, how?

2. What stage of the product life cycle is Febreze currently in? How can Procter & Gamble extend the product life cycle for Febreze?

Sources: The Partnering Group website, **www.thepartneringgroup.com**, accessed March 11, 2014; Elle Byron, "Febreze Joins P&G's $1 Billion Club," *Wall Street Journal*, March 9, 2011, **http://online.wsj.com**; Febreze website, **http://febreze.com**, accessed March 11, 2014.

chapter 11

Developing and Managing Brand and Product Strategies

CAREY PRICE

CHAPTER OBJECTIVES

1. Define a brand and identify the different types of brands.

2. Explain the strategic value of brand equity and the benefits of category and brand management.

3. Discuss how companies develop a strong identity for their products and brands.

4. Identify and briefly describe each of the new-product development strategies.

5. Describe the consumer adoption process.

6. List the stages in the new-product development process and explain the relationship between product safety and product liability.

UNDER ARMOUR SCORES

It might seem unlikely that a college athlete's efforts to overcome being "short and slow" could grow into a billion-dollar sports apparel company, but that's the story behind Under Armour. Founder Kevin Plank was a football player who believed the sweat-collecting properties of cotton gear slowed him down on the field. Soon he was spending most of his spare time and meagre savings on testing fabrics from tailors' shops to find a material that would carry moisture away from the body.

If he had been working in the apparel industry, Plank says, "I would have been too scared to do anything." But by being dogged and depending on his former teammates and their friends to test his sample shirts, Plank not only refined his product ideas, he also managed to start a successful word-of-mouth campaign that soon had him scrambling to fill orders from college teams.

Now the company is pulling in over $1 billion in annual sales and is expanding internationally, opening offices and expanding its retail distribution around the world. Under Armour still makes its iconic moisture-wicking shirts, but it has added other athletic gear, including mouth guards, sports bras, basketball shoes, running shoes, and football cleats. It is the official uniform sponsor of a number of overseas teams, including the Tottenham Hotspurs in England; the Welsh Rugby Union; and soccer teams in Israel, Mexico, Chile, and Greece. Under Armour also launched its first major media marketing campaign in Europe, where its vice president of global marketing says, "It's time to tell our story . . . because we've built authenticity with our presence on the field." International sales make up about 10 percent of the company's business.

Under Armour provides the clothing for some Olympic teams and has positioned itself as the go-to supplier for young athletes who can grow up with the company, unlike long-established brands like Nike that represent an older generation.

The company's plans include even more growth and expansion. Its first-ever football cleat sold out online in two hours before moving into stores, and next up are innovative "coldblack" shirts, with a special fabric designed to reflect sunlight to keep wearers cool and dry. The company sees products aimed at women and youths as areas for growth. Company research shows that women are wearing athletic clothing in places other than the gym, making the company's focus on style increasingly important. The youth market or, as Under Armour calls them, the Next segment has double the growth rate of its other segments. Plank sees many opportunities for the brand, and Under Armour is poised to take them.

Under Armour has moved into the digital world with its acquisition of MapMyFitness, an application designed to help athletes plan and monitor their workouts. The application works with Android, iPhone, or BlackBerry mobile devices, allowing users to keep track of the routes they take; find a new route to run, walk, or bike; or record their workout activities. The application also allows users to record their food intake to determine an overall picture of their health.

Under Armour recently announced that it would expand its business to Europe, launching a new TV and social media campaign in several European countries. Its most recent annual report stated, "We believe the future success of our brand depends on developing our business outside of North America." The company also has a presence in China.

Unlike other firms, Under Armour does all its own campaigns and creative designs. Its employees' average age is 30, and many are ex-athletes. In one recent year, 26,000 prospective employees sent in their résumés, but just 215 landed spots in the firm.[1]

connecting with customers

Under Armour has successfully connected with customers from different segments of the market—men, women, and the youth market—by providing athletic wear to meet their needs. Expanding internationally and into the digital market provides the company with new opportunities to connect with customers.

Chapter Overview

Brands play a huge role in our lives. We try certain brands for all kinds of reasons: on recommendations from friends, because we want to associate ourselves with the images certain brands possess, or because we remember colourful advertisements. We develop loyalty to certain brands and product lines for varying reasons as well—the quality of a product, price, and habit are a few examples. This chapter examines the way companies make decisions about developing and managing the products and product lines that they hope will become consumer necessities. Developing and marketing a product and product line and building a desired brand image are costly propositions. To protect its investment and maximize the return on it, a specialized marketer called a *category manager* must carefully nurture both existing and new products. The category manager is responsible for an entire product line.

This chapter focuses on two critical elements of product planning and strategy. First, it looks at how firms build and maintain identity and competitive advantage for their products through branding. Second, it focuses on the new-product planning and development process. Effective new-product planning and meeting the profit responsibility that a category manager has for a product line require careful preparation. The wants and desires of consumers change constantly, and successful marketers manage to keep up with—or stay just ahead of—those changes. ◆◆◆

① **Define a brand and identify the different types of brands.**

Marketoid

Over 60 percent of adults over the age of 25 have a postsecondary education.

brand Name, term, sign, symbol, design, or some combination that identifies the products of one firm while differentiating them from the competition's.

MANAGING BRANDS FOR COMPETITIVE ADVANTAGE

Think of the last time you went shopping for groceries. As you moved through the store, chances are your recognition of various brand names influenced many of your purchasing decisions. Perhaps you chose Colgate toothpaste over competitive offerings or loaded Heinz ketchup into your cart instead of the store brand. Walking through the snack food aisle, you might have reached for Doritos or Lay's potato chips without much thought.

Marketers recognize the powerful influence that products and product lines have on customer behaviour, and they work to create strong identities for their products and protect them. Branding is the process of creating that identity. A **brand** is a name, term, sign, symbol, design, or some combination that identifies the products of one firm while differentiating these products from competitors' offerings. Canada's best managed brands as determined by Interbrand are illustrated in Table 11.1.

As you read this chapter, consider how many brands you are aware of—both those you are loyal to and those you have never tried or have tried and abandoned. Table 11.2 shows some selected

table 11.1 *Canada's Most Valuable Brands*

CANADA	$ VALUE (US MILLIONS)
1 Royal Bank of Canada	11,060
2 TD Bank	10,855
3 Scotiabank	7,717
4 Bank of Montreal	7,114
5 Bell	7,081
6 Canadian Imperial Bank of Commerce	5,028
7 Rogers	4,787
8 Telus	4,290
9 Enbridge	4,093
10 Bombardier	4,090

Source: "Top 100 Brands," The Globe and Mail: Report on Business, March 2014, page 57.

table 11.2 *Selected Brands, Brand Names, and Brand Marks*

BRAND TYPE	
Private brand	Sam's Choice (Walmart) or President's Choice (Loblaw)
Family brand	RAID insect sprays or Campbell soups
Individual brand	Purex or Clorox
Brand name	Kleenex or Cheetos
Brand mark	Colonel Sanders for KFC or Mr. Peanut for Planters

brands, brand names, and brand marks. Satisfied buyers respond to branding by making repeat purchases of the same product because they identify the item with the name of its producer. One buyer might derive satisfaction from an ice cream cone with the brand name Chapman; another might derive the same satisfaction from one with the name Breyers or Neilson.

BRAND LOYALTY

Brands achieve widely varying consumer familiarity and acceptance. A snowboarder might insist on a Burton snowboard, but the same consumer might show little loyalty to particular brands in another product category such as soap. Marketers measure brand loyalty in three stages: brand recognition, brand preference, and brand insistence.

Brand recognition is a company's first objective for newly introduced products. Marketers begin the promotion of new items by trying to make them familiar to the public. Advertising offers one effective way for increasing consumer awareness of a brand. Coca-Cola is a familiar brand worldwide, and it drew on customers' recognition of its Dasani bottled water brand when it introduced the PlantBottle, made from 30 percent plant fibre. Other tactics for creating brand recognition include offering free samples or discount coupons for purchases. Once consumers have used a product, seen it advertised, or noticed it in stores, it moves from the unknown to the known category, which increases the probability that some of those consumers will purchase it. Sometimes customers can misinterpret a marketing message, however, as happened to Nutella. See the "Solving an Ethical Controversy" feature to find out the result.

At the second level of brand loyalty, **brand preference**, buyers rely on previous experiences with the product when choosing it, if available, over competitors' products. You may prefer Nike shoes or Roots clothes to other brands and buy their new lines as soon as they are offered. If so, those products have established brand preference.

Brand insistence, the ultimate stage in brand loyalty, leads consumers to refuse alternatives and to search extensively for the desired merchandise. A product at this stage has achieved a monopoly position with its consumers. Although many firms try to establish brand insistence with all consumers, few achieve this ambitious goal. Companies that offer specialty or luxury goods and services, such as Rolex watches or Lexus automobiles, are more apt to achieve this status than those that offer mass-marketed goods and services.

TYPES OF BRANDS

Brands are classified in many ways: private, manufacturer's or national, family, and individual brands. In making branding decisions, firms weigh the benefits and disadvantages of each type of brand. Some firms, however, sell their goods without any efforts at branding. These items are called **generic products**. They are characterized by plain labels, little or no advertising, and no brand names. Common categories of generic products include food and household staples. These no-name products were first sold in Europe at prices as much as 30 percent below those of branded products. This product strategy was introduced in North America three decades ago. The market shares for generic products increase during economic downturns but subside when the economy improves. However, many consumers request generic substitutions for certain brand-name prescriptions at the pharmacy whenever they are available.

brand recognition
Consumer awareness and identification of a brand.

brand preference
Consumer reliance on previous experiences with a product to choose that product again.

brand insistence
Consumer refusal of alternatives and extensive search for desired merchandise.

generic products
Products characterized by plain labels, no advertising, and the absence of brand names.

SOLVING AN ETHICAL CONTROVERSY
Who Is Responsible for the Truth of Advertising Claims?

SOME customers were shocked to find that Nutella, the chocolate-hazelnut spread from Europe that's becoming increasingly popular in North America, was not an especially nutritious food, despite promotional material showing a mother and children eating it in their kitchen, which these customers believe suggested Nutella was part of a healthy breakfast for kids. When competitor Kraft launched its chocolate peanut spread, the promotional material included the line "50% less sugar than the leading hazelnut spread." Nutella countered with the claim that their product has "91% less sodium than the leading smooth peanut butter."

Should consumers be responsible for correctly interpreting advertising claims?

PRO

1. Anyone reading the product label would know it contains 11 grams of sugar and 6 grams of fat per serving.
2. When has chocolate been a healthy breakfast food?

CON

1. Promotional material for Nutella deliberately put the product in a wholesome setting, suggesting it has nutritional value.
2. The ads market Nutella as particularly suitable for kids' breakfasts, despite its high calorie content.

Where do you stand: pro or con?

Sources: Nutella website, **www.nutella.ca**, accessed March 14, 2014; Vanessa Milne, "Kraft Gets Competitive with New Chocolatey Peanut Butter," *Marketing*, February 21, 2014, **www.marketingmag.ca**; "Nutella Health Claims Net $3.05 Million Settlement in Class-Action Lawsuit," CBS News.com, **www.cbsnews.com**, accessed May 14, 2012; Caroline Scott-Thomas, "Ferrero Backs away from Nutella Health Claims in $3M Class Action Settlement," Food Navigator USA, April 30, 2012, **www.foodnavigator-usa.com**; Laurent Belsie, "Nutella Settles Lawsuit. You Can Get $20," *The Christian Science Monitor*, April 27, 2012, **www.csmonitor.com**; Carly Rothman, "In Nutella Lawsuit over False Health Claims, a Two-Fold Lesson," NJ.com, April 27, 2012, **www.nj.com**.

---

manufacturer's brand Brand name owned by a manufacturer or other producer.

private brand Brand offered by a wholesaler or retailer.

captive brand National brands that are sold exclusively by a retail chain.

Manufacturers' Brands versus Private Brands

Manufacturers' brands, also called *national brands*, define the image that most people form when they think of a brand. A **manufacturer's brand** refers to a brand name owned by a manufacturer or other producer. Well-known manufacturers' brands include Hewlett-Packard, Sony, Pepsi-Cola, Dell, and Heinz. In contrast, many large wholesalers and retailers place their own brands on the merchandise they market. The brands offered by wholesalers and retailers are usually called **private brands** (or private labels). Although some manufacturers refuse to produce private label goods, most regard such production as a way to reach additional market segments. Walmart offers many private label products at its stores, including its Old Roy dog food.

The growth of private brands has paralleled that of chain stores. Manufacturers not only sell their well-known brands to stores but also put the store's own label on similar products. Such leading manufacturers as Westinghouse and Heinz generate ever-increasing percentages of their total incomes by producing goods for sale under retailers' private labels. Private brands are popular in the grocery business. Canadians spend $6.4 billion annually on private label packaged food, representing more than 12 percent market share in that category. From 2008 to 2012 more than 4,900 new private label packaged food products were introduced in Canada. The majority of these new products were introduced by Walmart, Loblaw, and Sobeys.[2]

Consistent with its corporate goal to buy and sell environmentally friendly products, office supply retailer Staples launched Sustainable Earth by Staples, a private label line of environmentally friendly products. The line

Coca-Cola is a familiar brand worldwide, and it drew on customers' recognition of its Dasani bottled water brand when it introduced the PlantBottle, made from 30 percent plant fibre.

Scott Olson/Getty Images

includes recycled paper and paper products, paper towels, compostable cups for hot beverages, and other items that create minimal impact on the environment.[3]

Captive Brands

The nation's major retailers—for example, Canadian Tire—have come up with a spin-off of the private label idea. So-called **captive brands** are national brands that are sold exclusively by a retail chain. Captive brands typically provide better profit margins than private labels. One of Canadian Tire's captive brands is the Debbie Travis line of home decor products. Canadian Tire is hoping to not only increase its decor business but also attract younger shoppers into its stores.[4]

Family and Individual Brands

A **family brand** is a single brand name that identifies several related products. For example, KitchenAid markets a complete line of appliances under the KitchenAid name; and Johnson & Johnson offers a line of baby powder, lotions, plastic pants, and baby shampoo under its name. All Heinz products, such as the company's tomato ketchup and its vegetable soup, carry the Heinz brand.

Alternatively, a manufacturer may choose to market a product as an **individual brand**, which uniquely identifies the item itself, rather than promoting it under the name of the company or under an umbrella name covering similar items. Unilever, for example, markets Knorr, Bertolli, Lipton, and Slim-Fast food products; Pond's and Sunsilk beauty products; and Lifebuoy and Dove soaps. PepsiCo's Quaker Oats unit markets Aunt Jemima breakfast products and Gatorade beverages. Individual brands cost more than family brands to market because the firm must develop a new promotional campaign to introduce each new product to its target market. Distinctive brands are extremely effective aids in implementing market segmentation strategies.

On the other hand, a promotional outlay for a family brand can benefit all items in the line. Family brands also help marketers introduce new products to both customers and retailers. Since supermarkets stock thousands of items, they hesitate to add new products unless they are confident they will be in demand.

Family brands should identify products of similar quality, or the firm risks harming its overall product image. If Rolls-Royce marketers were to place the Rolls name on a low-end car or a line of discounted clothing, they would severely tarnish the image of the luxury car line. Conversely, Lexus, Infiniti, and Porsche put their names on luxury sport utility vehicles to capitalize on their reputations and to enhance the acceptance of the new models in a competitive market.

Individual brand names should, however, distinguish dissimilar products. Kimberly-Clark markets two different types of diapers for infants under its Huggies and Pull-Ups names. Procter & Gamble offers shaving products under its Gillette name; laundry detergent under Cheer, Tide, and other brands; and dishwasher detergent under Cascade.

Companies like Catelli use a family branding strategy for all their pasta products.

Now 100% Canadian whole grain wheat and nothing more.

CATELLI
*Healthy Harvest
Moisson Santé*

CATELLI
Goodness that brings us together.

Used with permission of Catelli Foods Corporation

Marketoid

In the 25 to 34 age group, almost 60 percent of the women have university degrees.

family brand Single brand name that identifies several related products.

individual brand Single brand that uniquely identifies a product itself.

assessment check 1

1.1 What is a brand?

1.2 Differentiate among brand recognition, brand preference, and brand insistence.

1.3 Identify the different types of brands.

1.4 How are generic products different from branded products?

BRAND EQUITY

As individuals, we often like to say that our strongest asset is our reputation. The same is true of organizations. A brand can go a long way toward making or breaking a company's reputation. A strong brand identity backed by superior quality offers important strategic advantages for a firm. First, it increases the likelihood that consumers will recognize the firm's product or product line when they make purchase decisions. Second, a strong brand identity can contribute to buyers'

(2) **Explain the strategic value of brand equity and the benefits of category and brand management.**

MARKETING: MAKING YOUR WORLD BETTER   Finding "Genuine Goodness" in Canada

SHREDDIES, the 100 percent whole wheat cereal produced by Post Foods in Niagara Falls, Ontario, has used different promotions since the company started making the product in 1939. The idea behind its "Genuine Goodness" campaign came from the link between the genuine goodness of having a bowl of Shreddies for breakfast and how it makes people feel good inside. When people feel good inside, they often perform good acts in their communities, so the campaign was launched in order to find those people who were doing good deeds.

The first part of the campaign involved the company asking the public to submit stories of people in their communities who were doing nice things for others. These stories were judged by a panel selected by the company. When the panel had chosen five finalists from the stories submitted, Canadians across the country were asked to vote on the person they felt demonstrated genuine goodness by performing acts that benefited their communities.

The first contest winner was Greg Epp from Saskatoon, Saskatchewan. Greg's contribution to his community was maintaining the local outdoor skating rink. Every morning, regardless how cold or stormy, Greg gets up early and goes to the rink.

He clears the snow and floods the ice surface so those in his neighbourhood can enjoy some outdoor skating. The second annual winners were two sisters from Oakville, Ontario. The two started a charity they called "Books with No Bounds." They have collected more than 27,000 books for children in isolated communities in Northern Ontario.

After the contest was over, the company continued to promote "Genuine Goodness." For each winner, the company produced a television commercial featuring the winner's story. For every finalist the company donated a supply of Shreddies to their local food bank and for each "share" of the stories on the dedicated Facebook site the company donates an additional box of cereal.

Sources: "Shreddies Finds Genuine Goodness in Saskatoon Resident," Market Wired website, March 4, 2013, **www.marketwired.com**; "Shreddies Finds Canadian Goodness for New Campaign," *Marketing*, February 8, 2013, **www.marketingmag.ca**; "Top Five Finalists Announced in Shreddies 'Search for Goodness,'" Market Wired website, December 12, 2013, **www.marketwired.com**; Kristin Laird, "Watch This: Building on 'Genuine Goodness' (Shreddies)," *Marketing*, March 20, 2014, **www.marketingmag.ca**; Company website, **www.postfoods.ca**, accessed March 26, 2014.

---

brand equity Added value that a respected, well-known brand name gives to a product in the marketplace.

Marketoid

The most common college and university degrees are business, management, and marketing.

perceptions of product quality. Branding can also reinforce customer loyalty and repeat purchases. A consumer who tries a brand and likes it will probably look for that brand on future store visits. All these benefits contribute to a valuable form of competitive advantage called *brand equity*.

Brand equity refers to the added value that a certain brand name gives to a product in the marketplace. Brands with high equity confer financial advantages on a firm because they often command comparatively large market shares, and consumers may pay little attention to differences in prices. Studies have also linked brand equity to high profits and stock returns. Service companies are also aware of the value of brand equity. Sometimes companies increase their brand equity using promotional contests that connect with customers, as discussed in the "Marketing: Making Your World Better" feature.

In global operations, high brand equity often facilitates expansion into new markets. Currently, Apple, Google, and Coca-Cola are the most valuable—and most recognized—brands in the world.[5] Similarly, Disney's brand equity allows it to market its goods and services in Europe and Japan—and now China. What makes a global brand powerful? According to Interbrand Corp., which measures brand equity in dollar values, a strong brand is one that has the power to increase a company's sales and earnings. A global brand is generally defined as one where at least 20 percent of total sales are generated outside its home country.

The global advertising agency Young & Rubicam (Y&R) developed another brand equity system called the Brand Asset Valuator. Y&R's database of consumers' brand perceptions contains more than 700,000 consumer interviews and information on 44,000 brands across 49 countries. According to Y&R, a firm builds brand equity sequentially on four dimensions of brand personality.[6] These four dimensions are differentiation, relevance, esteem, and knowledge:

- *Differentiation* refers to a brand's ability to stand apart from competitors. Brands such as Porsche and Victoria's Secret stand out in consumers' minds as a symbol of unique product characteristics.

- *Relevance* refers to the real and perceived appropriateness of the brand to a big consumer segment. A large number of consumers must feel a need for the benefits offered by the brand. Brands with high relevance are Hallmark and Microsoft.

- *Esteem* is a combination of perceived quality and consumer perceptions about the growing or declining popularity of a brand. A rise in perceived quality or in public opinion about a brand enhances a brand's esteem. But negative impressions reduce esteem. Brands with high esteem are General Mills and Honda.

- *Knowledge* refers to the extent of customers' awareness of the brand and understanding of what a good or service stands for. Knowledge implies that customers feel an intimate relationship with a brand. Examples are Jell-O and Band-Aid.[7]

THE ROLE OF CATEGORY AND BRAND MANAGEMENT

Because of the tangible and intangible value associated with strong brand equity, marketing organizations invest considerable resources and effort in developing and maintaining these dimensions of brand personality. Traditionally, companies assigned the task of managing a brand's marketing strategies to a **brand manager**. Today, because they sell about 80 percent of their products to national retail chains, major consumer goods companies have adopted a strategy called **category management**. In this strategy a manufacturer's category manager maximizes sales for the retailer by overseeing an entire product line, often tracking sales history with data from the retail checkout point and aggregating it with sales data for the entire category (obtained from third-party vendors) and qualitative data such as customer surveys.[8]

Unlike traditional product managers, category managers have profit responsibility for their product group and also help the retailer's category buyer maximize sales for the whole category, not just the particular manufacturer's product. These managers are assisted by associates usually called *analysts*. Part of the shift to category management was initiated by large retailers, which realized they could benefit from the marketing muscle of large grocery and household goods producers such as Kraft and Procter & Gamble. As a result, producers began to focus their attention on in-store merchandising instead of mass-market advertising. Some manufacturers that are too small to dedicate a category manager to each retail chain assign a category manager to each major channel, such as grocery, convenience, drugstore, and so on.[9]

Some of the steps companies follow in the category management process are defining the category based on the target market's needs, scoping out a consumer's decision process when shopping in the category, identifying consumer groups and the store clusters with the greatest sales potential, creating a marketing strategy and performance goal for each cluster and using a scorecard to measure progress, defining and executing the tactics, and tracking progress.[10] Hershey's vending division offers category management services to its institutional customers, providing reduced inventory costs, improved warehouse efficiency, and increased sales.[11]

brand manager
Marketer within an organization who is responsible for a single brand.

category management
Product management system in which a category manager— with profit and loss responsibility—oversees a product line.

assessment check 2

2.1 What is brand equity?

2.2 What are the four dimensions of brand personality?

2.3 Define *brand manager*.

2.4 How does category management help retailers?

PRODUCT IDENTIFICATION

(3) Discuss how companies develop a strong identity for their products and brands.

Organizations identify their products in the marketplace with brand names, symbols, and distinctive packaging. Almost every product that is distinguishable from another gives buyers some means of identifying it. Sunkist Growers, for instance, stamps its oranges with the name Sunkist. Iams stamps a pawprint on all of its pet food packages. For well over 100 years, Prudential Insurance Co. has used the Rock of Gibraltar as its symbol. Choosing how to identify the firm's output represents a major strategic decision for marketers. Produce growers have another option besides gummed paper stickers for identifying fruits and vegetables: dissolvable fruit stickers. This technology marks fruits and vegetables with a label that includes the PLU (price look up) code and eliminates the sticky labels. Washing the fruit or vegetable dissolves the label, which turns into an organic produce wash that eliminates wax, pesticides, dirt, and bacteria.[12]

BRAND NAMES AND BRAND MARKS

brand name Part of a brand consisting of words, numbers, or letters that can be spoken and that identifies and distinguishes a firm's offerings from those of its competitors.

brand mark Symbol or pictorial design that distinguishes a product.

A name plays a central role in establishing brand and product identity. The American Marketing Association defines a **brand name** as the part of the brand that can be spoken. It can consist of words, numbers, or letters that form a name that identifies and distinguishes the firm's offerings from those of its competitors. Firms can also identify their brands by brand marks. A **brand mark** is a symbol or pictorial design that distinguishes a product such as Mr. Peanut for Planters nuts.

Effective brand names are easy to pronounce, recognize, and remember. Short names, such as Nike, Ford, and Bounty, meet these requirements. Marketers try to overcome problems with easily mispronounced brand names by teaching consumers the correct pronunciations. For example, early advertisements for the Korean carmaker Hyundai explained that the name rhymes with *Sunday*. Sensitivity to clear communication doesn't end with the choice of brand name; marketers should also be aware of how well they get their point across in interpersonal communications.

A brand name should also give buyers the correct connotation of the product's image. Nissan's X-Terra connotes youth and extreme sports to promote the off-road SUV. ConAgra's Healthy Choice food line presents an alternative to fast foods that may be high in sodium or fat, and the iPod Nano uses a name that aptly suggests its tiny size. A brand name must also qualify for legal protection. The Trade-marks Act states that registered trademarks should not contain names or surnames unless the name is viewed in the mind of the consumer as that product, such as McDonald's. Clearly descriptive words such as *sweet* for baked goods cannot become registered trademarks.[13]

Marketers feel increasingly hard pressed to coin effective brand names, as multitudes of competitors rush to stake out brand names for their own products. Some companies register names before they have products to fit the names to prevent competitors from using them. Some marketers use humour to connect with potential customers. Harley-Davidson's Fat Boy series of motorcycles has become very successful because buyers liked the name.[14]

When a class of products becomes generally known by the original brand name of a specific offering, the brand name may become a descriptive generic name. If this occurs, the original owner may lose exclusive claim to the brand name. The generic names *nylon, aspirin, escalator, kerosene,* and *zipper* started as brand names. Other generic names that were once brand names are *cola, yo-yo, linoleum,* and *shredded wheat.*

trademark Brand for which the owner claims exclusive legal protection.

Marketers must distinguish between brand names that have become legally generic terms and those that seem generic only in many consumers' eyes. Consumers often adopt legal brand names as descriptive names. Jell-O, for instance, is a brand name owned exclusively by Kraft Foods, but many consumers casually apply it as a descriptive name for gelatine desserts. Similarly, many people use the term Kleenex to refer to facial tissues. English and Australian consumers use the brand name Hoover as a verb for vacuuming. One popular way to look something up on the Internet is now to "Google it." Xerox is such a well-known brand name that people frequently—though incorrectly—use it as a verb to mean photocopying. To protect its valuable trademark, Xerox Corporation has created advertisements explaining that Xerox is a brand name and registered trademark and should not be used as a verb.

TRADEMARKS

Businesses invest considerable resources in developing and promoting brands and brand identities. The high value of brand equity encourages firms to take steps in protecting the expenditures they invest in their brands.

A **trademark** is a brand for which the owner claims exclusive legal protection. A trademark should not be confused with a trade name, which identifies a company. The Coca-Cola Company is a trade name, but Coke is a trademark of the company's product. Some trade names duplicate companies' brand names.

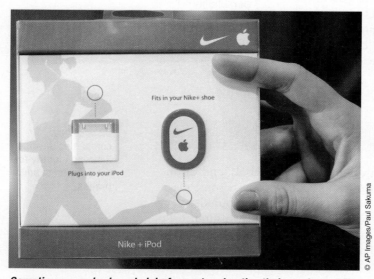

Fits in your Nike+ shoe

Plugs into your iPod

Nike + iPod

© AP Images/Paul Sakuma

Sometimes popular brands join forces to advertise their products. Nike and Apple combined their marketing efforts in an ad campaign for Nike + iPod Sport Kit.

Protecting Trademarks

Trademark protection confers the exclusive legal right to use a brand name, brand mark, and any slogan or product name abbreviation. It designates the origin or source of a good or service. Frequently, trademark protection is applied to words or phrases, such as *Bud* for Budweiser.

Firms can also receive trademark protection for packaging elements and product features such as shape, design, and typeface. In Canada, the Trade-marks Act allows companies to register "distinguishing guises," which identify the shape of the product, packaging, or wrapping. The act gives companies the right to take legal action for trademark infringement even if other products using its brand are not particularly similar or easily confused in the minds of consumers. The Trade-marks Office, the government agency responsible for registering trademarks, will not police or monitor a trademark to ensure no one else is infringing on it.[15]

The Internet may be the next battlefield for trademark infringement cases. Some companies are attempting to protect their trademarks by filing infringement cases against companies using similar Internet addresses or using unauthorized versions of the same name.

Balderson is the trademark for cheese produced by Parmalat Canada.

Trade Dress

Visual cues used in branding create an overall look sometimes referred to as **trade dress**. These visual components may be related to colour selections, sizes, package and label shapes, and similar factors. For example, McDonald's golden arches, Merrill Lynch's bull, and the yellow of Shell's seashell are all part of these products' trade dress. A combination of visual cues may also constitute trade dress. Consider a Mexican food product that uses the colours of the Mexican flag: green, white, and red. Trade dress disputes have led to numerous courtroom battles.

DEVELOPING GLOBAL BRAND NAMES AND TRADEMARKS

Cultural and language variations make brand-name selection a difficult undertaking for international marketers; an excellent brand name or symbol in one country may prove disastrous in another. An advertising campaign for E-Z washing machines failed in the United Kingdom because the British, like Canadians, pronounce *z* as "zed," unlike Americans. A firm marketing a product in several countries must also decide whether to use a single brand name for universal promotions or tailor names to individual countries. Most languages contain *o* and *k* sounds, so *okay* has become an international word. Most languages also have a short *a,* so Coca-Cola works as an effective brand abroad.

PACKAGING

A firm's product strategy must also address questions about packaging. Like its brand name, a product's package can powerfully influence buyers' purchase decisions.

Marketers are applying increasingly scientific methods to their packaging decisions. Rather than experimenting with physical models or drawings, more and more package designers work with special computer graphics programs that create three-dimensional images of packages in thousands of colours, shapes, and typefaces. Another software program helps marketers design effective packaging by simulating the displays shoppers see when they walk down supermarket aisles.

Companies conduct marketing research to evaluate current packages and to test alternative package designs. When Nestlé Prepared Foods recently wanted to update the packaging of its Lean Cuisine line of frozen entrees and dinners, the company conducted extensive market research. Lean Cuisine was introduced more than 30 years ago as a line of healthful meals, but as the company's design manager put it, the brand is about bringing out the best by helping people to eat healthier

Marketoid

Students taking science, technology, engineering, and engineering technology courses represent over 18 percent of all postsecondary students in Canada.

trade dress Visual components that contribute to the overall look of a brand.

every day. The company believed the old package design didn't reflect this attitude. Nestlé worked with a design firm to develop packaging that would reflect Lean Cuisine's "vibrant and optimistic personality." Another innovation was the packaging of some items in steam-in bags, which are increasingly popular in today's time-pressed world.[16]

A package serves three major objectives: (1) protection against damage, spoilage, and pilferage; (2) assistance in marketing the product; and (3) cost effectiveness. Let's briefly consider each of these objectives.

Protection against Damage, Spoilage, and Pilferage

The original objective of packaging was to offer physical protection for the merchandise. Products typically pass through several stages of handling between manufacturing and customer purchases, and a package must protect its contents from damage. Furthermore, packages of perishable products must protect the contents against spoilage in transit and in storage until purchased by the consumer. Fears of product tampering have forced many firms to improve package designs. Over-the-counter medicines are sold in tamper-resistant packages covered with warnings informing consumers not to purchase merchandise without protective seals intact. Many grocery items and light-sensitive products are packaged in tamper-resistant containers as well. Products such as spaghetti sauce and jams, packaged in glass jars, often come with vacuum-depressed buttons in the lids that pop up the first time the lids are opened.

Many packages offer important safeguards for retailers against pilferage. Shoplifting and employee theft cost retailers millions of dollars each year. To limit this activity, many packages feature oversized cardboard backings too large to fit into a shoplifter's pocket or purse. Efficient packaging that protects against damage, spoilage, and theft is especially important for international marketers, who must contend with varying climatic conditions and the added time and stress involved in overseas shipping.

Assistance in Marketing the Product

The proliferation of new products, changes in consumer lifestyles and buying habits, and marketers' emphasis on targeting smaller market segments have increased the importance of packaging as a promotional tool. Many firms are addressing consumers' concerns about protecting the environment by designing packages made of biodegradable and recyclable materials. To demonstrate serious concern regarding environmental protection, Procter & Gamble, Coors, McDonald's, and other firms have created ads that describe their efforts in developing environmentally sound packaging.

In a grocery store where thousands of different items compete for notice, a product must capture the shopper's attention. Marketers combine colours, sizes, shapes, graphics, and typefaces to establish distinctive trade dress that sets their products apart from the products of competitors. Packaging can help establish a common identity for a group of items sold under the same brand name. Like the brand name, a package should evoke the product's image and communicate its value.

Packages can also enhance convenience for the buyers. Pump dispensers, for example, facilitate the use of products as varied as mustard and insect repellent. Squeezable bottles of honey and ketchup make the products easier to use and store. Packaging provides key benefits for convenience foods such as meals and snacks packaged in microwavable containers, juice drinks in aseptic packages, and frozen entrees and vegetables packaged in single-serving portions.

Some firms increase consumer utility with packages designed for reuse. Empty peanut butter and jelly jars have long doubled as drinking glasses. Parents can buy bubble bath in animal-shaped plastic bottles suitable for bathtub play. Packaging is a major component in Avon's overall marketing strategy. The firm's decorative, reusable bottles have even become collectibles.

Cost-Effective Packaging

Although packaging must perform a number of functions for the producer, marketers, and consumers, it must do so at a reasonable cost. Sometimes changes in the packaging can make packages both cheaper and better for the environment. Kimberly-Clark is best known to consumers for its Kleenex, Scott, and Huggies brands, but its Kimberly-Clark Health Care and Kimberly-Clark Professional divisions make products for the medical field. Recently, those two divisions introduced new packaging for disposable medical gloves. Someone trying to take one glove out of a package often pulls out several that have to be discarded. The new SmartPULL packaging has a dual-opening tab for its paper cartons that greatly reduces wasted gloves.[17]

Labelling

Labels were once a separate element that was applied to a package; today, they are an integral part of a typical package. Labels perform both promotional and informational functions. A **label** carries an item's brand name or symbol, the name and address of the manufacturer or distributor, information about the product's composition and size, and recommended uses. The right label can play an important role in attracting consumer attention and encouraging purchases.

A number of regulations control package labelling in Canada, some at the federal level and others at the provincial level. The federal government has enacted the Competition Act, the Hazardous Products Act, the Food and Drugs Act, the Consumer Packaging and Labelling Act, and the Textile Labelling Act. The Competition Act, which is administered by the Competition Bureau, regulates false or misleading information. The Hazardous Products Act protects consumers by regulating the sale, advertising, or importing of potentially dangerous materials. The Food and Drugs Act regulates the information required on the labels of food, drugs, cosmetics, and medical devices. Consumer textile articles are dealt with under the Textile Labelling Act. The Consumer Packaging and Labelling Act specifically relates to labels for food products, ensuring that accurate information describes ingredients and quantities in both French and English.[18]

The **Universal Product Code (UPC)** designation is another important aspect of a label or package. Introduced in 1974 as a method for cutting expenses in the supermarket industry, UPCs are numerical bar codes printed on packages. Optical scanner systems read these codes, and computer systems recognize items and print their prices on cash register receipts. Although UPC scanners are costly, they permit both considerable labour savings over manual pricing and improved inventory control. The Universal Product Code is also a major asset for marketing research. However, many consumers feel frustrated when only a UPC is placed on a package without an additional price tag because they do not always know how much an item costs if the price labels are missing from the shelf.

Radio-frequency identification (RFID) tags—electronic chips that carry encoded product identification—may replace some of the functions of UPC codes, such as price identification and inventory tracking. But consumer privacy concerns about the amount of information RFID tracking can accumulate may limit their use to aggregate packaging such as pallets, rather than units sized for individual sale.

BRAND EXTENSIONS

Some brands become so popular that marketers may decide to use them on unrelated products in pursuit of instant recognition for the new offerings. The strategy of attaching a popular brand name to a new product in an unrelated product category is known as **brand extension**. This practice should not be confused with line extensions, which refers to new sizes, styles, or related products. A brand extension, in contrast, carries over from one product nothing but the brand name. In establishing brand extensions, marketers hope to gain access to new customers and markets by building on the equity already established in their existing brands. This is the strategy behind Nautica's brand extension from fashion to furniture and bedding. Nintendo extended its participative Wii video-game line with Wii Fit Plus, an extension on its popular Wii Fit fitness software.[19]

Targeting young girls, Mattel extended its Barbie fashion doll brand in an effort to sustain the interest of older children. It launched the "Barbie My Dreams," an online interactive platform.

Nestlé introduces a new Aero chocolate bar but keeps the packaging close to the original.

label Branding component that carries an item's brand name or symbol, the name and address of the manufacturer or distributor, information about the product, and recommended uses.

Universal Product Code (UPC) Numerical bar code system used to record product and price information.

brand extension Strategy of attaching a popular brand name to a new product in an unrelated product category.

Reproduced with kind permission of Unilever Canada Inc.

Unilever introduces a new product.

brand licensing Firm's authorization of other companies to use its brand names.

assessment check 3 ✓

3.1 Distinguish between a brand name and a trademark.

3.2 What are the three purposes of packaging?

3.3 Describe brand extension and brand licensing.

"Barbie My Dreams" allows mothers and daughters to interact in an environment that is similar to Pinterest, only coloured pink. Members of the site can follow what Barbie loves or create their own Dreamboard. There are games for members to play. New content is added to the site on a weekly basis in order to keep the young Barbie fans interested.[20]

BRAND LICENSING

A growing number of firms have authorized other companies to use their brand names. Even colleges and police services have licensed their logos and trademarks. This practice, known as **brand licensing**, expands a firm's exposure in the marketplace, much as a brand extension does. The brand name's owner also receives an extra source of income in the form of royalties from licensees, typically 8 to 12 percent of wholesale revenues.[21]

Brand experts note several potential problems with licensing, however. Brand names do not transfer well to all products. The PetSmart PetsHotel was a winner, as was *American Idol* camp, but losers were Precious Moments coffins, Donald Trump steaks, and Girls Gone Wild apparel. If a licensee produces a poor-quality product or an item ethically is incompatible with the original brand, the arrangement could damage the reputation of the brand. Consider the failure of two odd brand extensions: Burger King perfume and Colgate Kitchen Entrees.[22]

Harley-Davidson has been selling motorcycles for over 100 years, basing its marketing campaigns on the association of its bikes with masculinity and the open road. Although some fans have gone so far as to get tattooed with the Harley-Davidson name and logo, most are content with buying branded T-shirts, ornaments, and socks. Thinking that introducing more branded products would bring more sales, the company launched Harley-Davidson aftershave, perfume, and even wine coolers. But those brand extensions were too much for even the most devoted fans.[23]

NEW-PRODUCT PLANNING

(4) **Identify and briefly describe each of the new-product development strategies.**

As its offerings enter the maturity and decline stages of the product life cycle, a firm must add new items to continue to prosper. Regular additions of new products to the firm's line help protect it from product obsolescence.

New products are the lifeblood of any business, and survival depends on a steady flow of new entries. Some new products may implement major technological breakthroughs. Other new products simply extend existing product lines. In other words, a new product is one that either the company or the customer has not handled before.

market penetration strategy Strategy that seeks to increase sales of existing products in existing markets.

product positioning Consumers' perceptions of a product's attributes, uses, quality, and advantages and disadvantages relative to competing brands.

market development strategy Strategy that concentrates on finding new markets for existing products.

PRODUCT DEVELOPMENT STRATEGIES

A firm's strategy for new-product development varies according to its existing product mix and the match between current offerings and the firm's overall marketing objectives. The current market positions of products also affect product development strategy. Figure 11.1 identifies four alternative development strategies as market penetration, market development, product development, and product diversification.

A **market penetration strategy** seeks to increase sales of existing products in existing markets. Firms can attempt to extend their penetration of markets in several ways. They may modify products, improve product quality, or promote new and different ways to use products. Packaged goods marketers often pursue this strategy to boost market share for mature products in mature markets. Product positioning often plays a major role in such a strategy.

Product positioning refers to consumers' perceptions of a product's attributes, uses, quality, and advantages and disadvantages relative to competing brands. Marketers often conduct marketing research studies to analyze consumer preferences and to construct product positioning maps that plot their products' positions in relation to those of competitors' offerings.

Hyundai Motors has repositioned its Hyundai brand in North America. Although Hyundai entered the North American market as an inexpensive alternative to other cars, the company has ratcheted up the look and feel of its sedans to emphasize quality and safety as well as eco-friendliness. Some models have been recognised in the industry as award winners for both style and safety.[24]

A **market development strategy** concentrates on finding new markets for existing products. Market segmentation, discussed in Chapter 9, provides useful support for such an effort. Many companies in Canada pursue this strategy particularly when trying to reach large ethnic markets. Bell Mobility promoted a model of a red Samsung phone around the Chinese New Year celebration with ads featuring horses for the year of the horse.[25]

The strategy of **product development** refers to the introduction of new products into identifiable or established markets. Responding to moviegoers' recently revived interest in 3-D, Panasonic introduced a 3-D home entertainment system. The system includes a pair of special 3-D eyewear as well as a Blu-ray disk player for playing movies at home in 3-D format. Other manufacturers soon followed suit. However, the 3-D glasses are expensive and dedicated—for example, Panasonic glasses won't work with a Samsung system. Currently, the major 3-D television manufacturers are working to make the glasses compatible across systems.[26]

Firms may also choose to introduce new products into markets in which they have already established positions to try to increase overall market share. These new offerings are called *flanker brands*. The fragrance industry uses this strategy extensively when it develops scents that are related to their most popular products. The flanker scents are related in both their smell and their names. Calvin Klein has built a family of flanker brands around its original Calvin fragrance for men. The flanker brands include Eternity, Obsession, CK One, and Euphoria, all in men's and women's scents; and Beauty for women and CK Free for men. Recently, the company introduced "summer" versions of CK One and Eternity.[27]

Finally, a **product diversification strategy** focuses on developing entirely new products for new markets. Some firms look for new target markets that complement their existing markets; others look in completely new directions. PepsiCo's CEO regards obesity as one of the world's most significant health issues and wants her company to be part of the solution, not the problem. PepsiCo began diversifying its product line beyond items that are "fun for you" to items that are "good for you," including juices, nuts, and oatmeal several years ago. However, the company recently announced that, while it will continue to promote "good for you" items, it will also spend an additional $500 million on advertising and marketing of Pepsi's traditionally more profitable soft drinks and snacks, with a renewed emphasis on new product development.[28]

In selecting a new-product strategy, marketers should keep in mind an additional potential problem: **cannibalization**. Any firm wants to avoid investing resources in a new-product introduction that will adversely affect sales of existing products. A product that takes sales from another offering in the same product line is said to cannibalize that line. A company can accept some loss of sales from existing products if the new offering will generate sufficient additional sales to warrant its investment in its development and market introduction.

figure 11.1

Alternative Product Development Strategies

	Old Product	New Product
Old Market	Market Penetration	Product Development
New Market	Market Development	Product Diversification

product development Introduction of new products into identifiable or established markets.

product diversification strategy Developing entirely new products for new markets.

cannibalization Loss of sales of an existing product due to competition from a new product in the same line.

Established companies introduce new products.

assessment check 4

4.1 Distinguish between market penetration and market development strategies.

4.2 What is product development?

4.3 What is product diversification?

(5) **Describe the consumer adoption process.**

THE CONSUMER ADOPTION PROCESS

In the **adoption process**, consumers go through a series of stages from first learning about the new product to trying it and deciding whether to purchase it regularly or to reject it. These stages in the consumer adoption process can be classified as follows:

adoption process
Stages that consumers go through in learning about a new product, trying it, and deciding whether to purchase it again.

1. *Awareness.* Individuals first learn of the new product, but they lack full information about it.
2. *Interest.* Potential buyers begin to seek information about it.
3. *Evaluation.* They consider the likely benefits of the product.
4. *Trial.* They make trial purchases to determine its usefulness.
5. *Adoption/Rejection.* If the trial purchase produces satisfactory results, they decide to use the product regularly.

Marketers must understand the adoption process to move potential consumers to the adoption stage. Once marketers recognize a large number of consumers at the interest stage, they can take steps to stimulate sales by moving these buyers through the evaluation and trial stages. When Colgate launched its new Speed Stick Gear line of deodorants aimed at adventurous millennial males, the company created awareness and interest using an ice wall and sampling. A 60-foot-high wall of ice was created in downtown Toronto and, with the help of professional climbers, people were encouraged to climb it. A team of brand ambassadors handed out samples of the product to those who visited the tower.[29]

ADOPTER CATEGORIES

consumer innovators
People who purchase new products almost as soon as the products reach the market.

First buyers of new products, the so-called **consumer innovators**, are people who purchase new products almost as soon as these products reach the market. Later adopters wait for additional information and rely on the experiences of initial buyers before making trial purchases. Consumer innovators welcome innovations in each product area. Some computer users, for instance, rush to install new software immediately after each update becomes available.

A number of studies about the adoption of new products have identified five categories of purchasers based on relative times of adoption. These categories, shown in Figure 11.2, are consumer innovators, early adopters, early majority, late majority, and laggards.

diffusion process
Process by which new goods or services are accepted in the marketplace.

While the adoption process focuses on individuals and the steps they go through in making the ultimate decision about whether to become repeat purchasers of the new product or to reject it as a failure to satisfy their needs, the **diffusion process** focuses on all members of a community or social system. The focus here is on the speed at which an innovative product is accepted or rejected by all members of the community.

Figure 11.2 shows the diffusion process as following a normal distribution from a small group of early purchasers (called *innovators*) to the final group of consumers (called *laggards*) to make trial purchases of the new product. A few people adopt at first, and then the number of adopters increases rapidly as the value of the product becomes apparent. The adoption rate finally diminishes as the number of potential consumers who have not adopted, or purchased, the product diminishes. Typically, innovators make up the first 2.5 percent of buyers who adopt the new product; laggards are the last 16 percent to do so. Figure 11.2 excludes those who never adopt the product.

figure 11.2

Categories of Adopters Based on Relative Times of Adoption

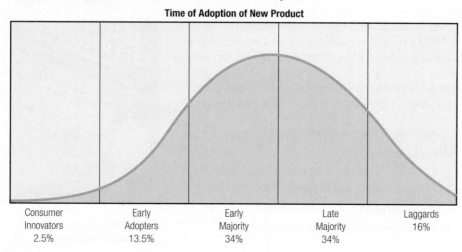

Time of Adoption of New Product

| Consumer Innovators 2.5% | Early Adopters 13.5% | Early Majority 34% | Late Majority 34% | Laggards 16% |

IDENTIFYING EARLY ADOPTERS

It's no surprise that identifying consumers or organizations that are most likely to try a new product can be vital to a product's success. By reaching these buyers early in the product's development or introduction, marketers can treat these adopters as a test market, evaluating the product and discovering suggestions for modifications. Since early purchasers often act as opinion leaders from whom others seek advice, their attitudes toward new products quickly spread to others. Acceptance or rejection of the innovation by these purchasers can help forecast its expected success. New-car models are multiplying, for instance, and many are sporting a dizzying variety of options such as ports to accommodate—and integrate—the driver's iPod, wireless phone, and laptop. Improved stability controls, collision warnings, and "smart engines" that save fuel are also available.

A large number of studies have established the general characteristics of first adopters. These pioneers tend to be younger, are better educated, and enjoy higher incomes than other consumers. They are more mobile than later adopters and change both their jobs and addresses more often. They also rely more heavily than later adopters on impersonal information sources; more hesitant buyers depend primarily on company-generated promotional information and word-of-mouth communications.

Rate of Adoption Determinants

Frisbees progressed from the product introduction stage to the market maturity stage in a period of six months. In contrast, it took 13 years to convince corn farmers to use hybrid seed corn, an innovation capable of doubling crop yields. Five characteristics of a product innovation influence its adoption rate:

1. *Relative advantage.* An innovation that appears far superior to previous ideas offers a greater relative advantage—reflected in lower price, physical improvements, or ease of use—and increases the product's adoption rate.

2. *Compatibility.* An innovation consistent with the values and experiences of potential adopters attracts new buyers at a relatively rapid rate. Consumers already comfortable with the miniaturization of communications technology may be attracted to smartphones, for instance, and the iPhone's small screen.

3. *Complexity.* The relative difficulty of understanding the innovation influences the speed of acceptance. In most cases, consumers move slowly in adopting new products that they find difficult to understand or use. Farmers' cautious acceptance of hybrid seed corn illustrates how long an adoption can take.

4. *Possibility of trial use.* An initial free or discounted trial of a good or service means that adopters can reduce their risk of financial loss when they try the product. A coupon for a free item or a free night's stay at a hotel can accelerate the rate of adoption.

5. *Observability.* If potential buyers can observe an innovation's superiority in a tangible form, the adoption rate increases. In-store demonstrations or even advertisements that focus on the superiority of a product can encourage buyers to adopt a product.

Marketers who want to accelerate the rate of adoption can manipulate these five characteristics, at least to some extent. An informative promotional message about a new allergy drug could help consumers overcome their hesitation in adopting this complex product. Effective product design can emphasize an item's advantages over the competition. Everyone likes to receive something for free, so giving away small samples of a new product lets consumers try it at little or no risk. In-home demonstrations or trial home placements of items such as furniture or carpeting can achieve similar results. Marketers must also make positive attempts to ensure the innovation's compatibility with adopters' value systems.

ORGANIZING FOR NEW-PRODUCT DEVELOPMENT

A firm needs to be organized in such a way that its personnel can stimulate and coordinate new-product development. Some companies contract with independent design firms to develop new products. Many assign product-innovation functions to one or more of the following entities: new-product committees, new-product departments, product managers, and venture teams.

New-Product Committees

The most common organizational arrangement for activities in developing a new product is to centre these functions in a new-product committee. This group typically brings together experts in such areas as marketing, finance, manufacturing, engineering, research, and accounting. Committee members spend less time conceiving and developing their own new-product ideas than reviewing and approving new-product plans that arise elsewhere in the organization. The committee might review ideas from the engineering and design staff or perhaps from marketers and salespeople who are in constant contact with customers.

Since members of a new-product committee hold important jobs in the firm's functional areas, their support for any new-product plan likely foreshadows approval for further development. However, new-product committees in large companies tend to reach decisions slowly and maintain conservative views. Sometimes members compromise so they can return to their regular responsibilities.

New-Product Departments

Many companies establish separate, formally organized departments to generate and refine new-product ideas. The departmental structure overcomes the limitations of the new-product committee system and encourages innovation as a permanent full-time activity. The new-product department is responsible for all phases of a development project within the firm, including screening decisions, developing product specifications, and coordinating product testing. The head of the department wields substantial authority and typically reports to the chief executive officer, chief operating officer, or a top marketing executive.

Product Managers

product manager
Marketer within an organization who is responsible for an individual product or product line; also called a brand manager.

A **product manager** is another term for a brand manager, a function mentioned earlier in the chapter. This marketer supports the marketing strategies of an individual product or product line. Procter & Gamble, for instance, assigned its first product manager in 1927, when it made one person responsible for Camay soap.

Product managers set prices, develop advertising and sales promotion programs, and work with sales representatives in the field. In a company that markets many products, product managers fulfill key functions in the marketing department. They provide individual attention for each product; and support and coordinate efforts of the firm's sales force, marketing research department, and advertising department. Product managers often lead new-product development programs, including creation of new-product ideas and recommendations for improving existing products.

However, most consumer goods companies such as Procter & Gamble and General Mills have either modified the product manager structure or done away with it altogether in favour of a category management structure. Category managers have profit and loss responsibility, which is not characteristic of the product management system. This change has largely come about because of customer preference, but it can also benefit a manufacturer by avoiding duplication of some jobs and competition among the company's own brands and its managers.

Venture Teams

venture team Associates from different areas of an organization who work together in developing new products.

A **venture team** gathers a group of specialists from different areas of an organization to work together in developing new products. The venture team must meet criteria for return on investment, uniqueness of product, serving a well-defined need, compatibility of the product with existing technology, and strength of patent protection. Although the organization sets up the venture team as a temporary entity, its flexible life span may extend over a number of years. When purchases confirm the commercial potential of a new product, an existing division may take responsibility for that product, or it may serve as the nucleus of a new business unit or of an entirely new company. Some marketing organizations differentiate between venture teams and task forces. A new-product task force assembles an interdisciplinary group working on temporary assignment through their functional departments. Its basic activities centre on coordinating and

CAREER READINESS | How to Be a Team Player

WORK groups and teams are more popular than ever. How can you turn your team assignment into a success for you and for your teammates?

- Cover the basics. That means being on time and prepared for meetings (virtual or face-to-face), completing your assigned tasks, communicating, and contributing actively to discussions.
- Help others in the group. Volunteer your assistance; perhaps you can help a team member catch up on his or her assignment or lend an extra effort to achieving a group goal.
- Be respectful of others. Listen to others' opinions with an open mind, accommodate their differences, and avoid criticizing.
- Play an active social role as appropriate for your organization. Go to lunch with team members or join company

extracurricular activities. You'll get to know team members in a different setting and might even make new connections across the organization that can help you and the team.

- Promote a positive team atmosphere. Some conflict is unavoidable, but don't be the source or the cause of it. Keep a positive attitude and avoid complainers and troublemakers.
- Be the person who gets things done. Your efforts won't go unnoticed.

Sources: "Tips to Succeeding as a Team Player," Bayt.com, **www.bayt.com**, accessed May 14, 2012; "How to Be a Successful Team Player at Work," eHow, **www.ehow.com**, accessed May 14, 2012; "How to Be a Team Player," *Doostang News*, **http://blog.doostang.com**, accessed May 14, 2012; Marty Brounstein, "Ten Qualities of an Effective Team Player," Dummies.com, **www.dummies.com**, accessed May 14, 2012.

integrating the work of the firm's functional departments on a specific project. Check out the "Career Readiness" feature for some tips about working successfully in a group or team.

Unlike a new-product committee, a venture team does not disband after every project. Team members accept project assignments as major responsibilities, and the team exercises the authority it needs to both plan and implement a course of action. To stimulate product innovation, the venture team typically communicates directly with top management, but it functions as an entity separate from the basic organization.

assessment check 5 ✓

5.1 Who are consumer innovators?

5.2 What characteristics of a product innovation can influence its adoption rate?

THE NEW-PRODUCT DEVELOPMENT PROCESS

⑥ List the stages in the new-product development process and explain the relationship between product safety and product liability.

Once a firm is organized for new-product development, it can establish procedures for moving new-product ideas to the marketplace. Developing a new product is often time-consuming, risky, and expensive. Usually, firms must generate dozens of new-product ideas to produce even one successful product. In fact, the failure rate of new products averages 80 percent. Products fail for a number of reasons, including inadequate market assessments, lack of market orientation, poor screening and project evaluation, product defects, and inadequate launch efforts. And these blunders cost a bundle: firms invest nearly half of the total resources devoted to product innovation on products that become commercial failures. Sometimes new products are the beginning of entirely new companies, as discussed in the "Marketing and the SME" feature.

A new product is more likely to become successful if the firm follows a six-step development process shown in Figure 11.3: (1) idea generation, (2) screening, (3) business analysis, (4) development, (5) test marketing, and (6) commercialization. Of course, each step requires decisions about whether to proceed further or abandon the project. And each step involves a greater financial investment.

Traditionally, most companies have developed new products through phased development, which follows the six-step process in an orderly sequence. Responsibility for each phase passes first from product planners to designers and engineers, to manufacturers, and finally to marketers. The phased-development method can work well for firms that dominate mature markets and can develop variations on existing products. But with rapid changes in technology and markets, many companies feel pressured to speed up the development process.

| MARKETING AND THE SME | **From Idea to Dragons' Den—Flavor Fork** |

WHEN Troy Biever, the owner of a pizza restaurant, could not find a utensil to infuse sauce into the meat he barbecued he decided to invent one. His first step was to purchase a domain name so he could sell his invention online. He took his idea to a concept designer, who incorporated his ideas into a computer program to come up with the original design. An industrial designer took the concept and prepared it into a form that could be used to produce a prototype. Another firm took the work of the industrial designer and produced the first version of the product on a 3-D printer. When the invention was ready to be produced, Troy looked to China to find a company to manufacture the product.

Troy was now ready to start selling the product he named the Flavor Fork. Troy believed the unique design of the product would make it stand out. The handle of the fork held a syringe, which could be loaded with sauce to be injected from the fork into the meat. The fork end was interchangeable with a brush or a spatula. Troy had no marketing team or a distribution system in place so he decided to load up his car and visit stores himself. His plan worked. Specialty cooking stores, Canadian Tire, and Home Hardware all agreed to put his product on the shelf.

In order to get more exposure for his product and to make a pitch for additional funds to help him expand, Troy appeared on the television program *Dragon's Den*. The appearance netted him a partner, Arlene Dickinson, who agreed to help with distributing Flavor Fork, particularly into the United States. Troy overcame a large number of challenges in taking his idea from concept to market, but his challenges are still not over. He will need additional capital in order to maintain inventory, and large retailers are hesitant to work with companies that have only one product.

Sources: Nary Teresa Bitti, "Can Flavor Fork Make a U.S. Splash with Dragons' Den's Arlene Dickinson?" *Financial Post*, March 17, 2014, **www.financialpost.com**; Viola Pruss, "Flavor Fork Gets Deal on Dragons' Den," *St. Albert Gazette*, March 19, 2014, **www.stalbertgazette.com**; Company website, **http://flavorfork.com**, accessed March 20, 2014.

This time pressure has encouraged many firms to implement accelerated product development programs. These programs generally consist of teams with design, manufacturing, marketing, and sales personnel who carry out development projects from idea generation to commercialization. This method can reduce the time needed to develop products because team members work on the six steps concurrently rather than in sequence.

Whether a firm pursues phased development or parallel product development, all phases can benefit from planning tools and scheduling methods such as the program evaluation and review technique (PERT) and the critical path method (CPM). These techniques, originally developed by the U.S. Navy, map out the sequence of each step in a process and show the time allotments for each activity. Detailed PERT and CPM flowcharts help marketers to coordinate all activities entailed in the development and introduction of new products.

IDEA GENERATION

New-product development begins with ideas from many sources: suggestions from customers, the sales force, research and development specialists, competing products, suppliers, retailers, and independent inventors. Bose Corporation has built its brand by staying at the forefront of technology.

figure 11.3

Steps in the New-Product Development Process

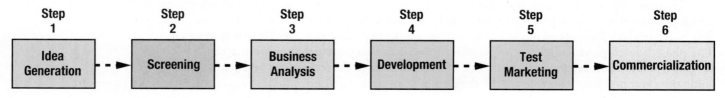

Step 1	Step 2	Step 3	Step 4	Step 5	Step 6
Idea Generation	Screening	Business Analysis	Development	Test Marketing	Commercialization

Spending an estimated $100 million a year on research, the company leads the market for products using advanced technology; sound systems for businesses, cars, and consumer home use; and the award-winning Wave radio and Acoustic Wave music systems.[30] With the goal of winning 1 billion new customers over the next decade, the cosmetics and beauty company L'Oréal opened a global research centre in Paris for the sole purpose of developing new hair colouring, hair care, and hair styling products.[31] Similarly, ongoing research by scientists at lawn-care industry leader Scotts Miracle-Gro helps the company fine-tune its understanding of consumer needs as it develops products and incorporates environmentally responsible behaviour throughout its operations.[32]

SCREENING

Screening separates ideas with commercial potential from those that cannot meet company objectives. Some organizations maintain checklists of development standards in determining whether a project should be abandoned or considered further. These checklists typically include factors such as product uniqueness; availability of raw materials; and the proposed product's compatibility with current product offerings, existing facilities, and present capabilities. The screening stage may also allow for open discussions of new-product ideas among different parts of the organization.

BUSINESS ANALYSIS

A product idea that survives the initial screening must then pass a thorough business analysis. This stage consists of assessing the new product's potential market, growth rate, and likely competitive strengths. Marketers must evaluate the compatibility of the proposed product with organizational resources.

Concept testing subjects the product idea to additional study prior to its actual development. This important aspect of a new product's business analysis represents a marketing research project that attempts to measure consumer attitudes and perceptions about the new-product idea. Focus groups and in-store polling can contribute effectively to concept testing. The screening and business analysis stages generate extremely important information for new-product development because they (1) define the proposed product's target market and customers' needs and wants and (2) determine the product's financial and technical requirements. Firms that are willing to invest money and time during these stages tend to be more successful at generating viable ideas and creating successful products.

concept testing
Method for subjecting a product idea to additional study before actual development by involving consumers through focus groups, surveys, in-store polling, and the like.

DEVELOPMENT

Financial outlays increase substantially as a firm converts an idea into a visible product. The conversion process is the joint responsibility of the firm's development engineers, who turn the original concept into a product; and of its marketers, who provide feedback on consumer reactions to the product design, package, colour, and other physical features. Many firms implement computer-aided design and manufacturing systems to streamline the development stage, and prototypes may go through numerous changes before the original mock-up becomes a final product.

Marketoid

More than 40 percent of Canadians with doctorate degrees studied outside Canada.

TEST-MARKETING

As discussed in Chapter 8, many firms test-market their new-product offerings to gauge consumer reaction. After a company has developed a prototype, it may decide to test-market it to measure consumer reactions under normal competitive conditions. Test-marketing's purpose is to verify that the product will perform well in a real-life environment. If the product does well, the

Companies like Unilever are constantly developing new products.

company can proceed to commercialization. If it flops, the company has two options. It can fine-tune certain features and reintroduce it or pull the plug on the project altogether. Industries that rely heavily on test-marketing are snack foods and movies. Of course, even if a product tests well and reaches the commercialization stage, it may still take a while to catch on with the general public.

COMMERCIALIZATION

When a new-product idea reaches the commercialization stage, it is ready for full-scale marketing. Commercialization of a major new product can expose the firm to substantial expenses. It must establish marketing strategies; fund outlays for production facilities; and acquaint the sales force, marketing intermediaries, and potential customers with the new product.

THE STAGE-GATE PROCESS

Some companies have moved away from the traditional product development process to a stage-gate process. This development process also has stages starting with Idea Generation and moving through Scoping, Building a Business Case, Development, Testing and Validation to Product Launch. The major difference in the stage-gate development process is that in between each of the development stages is a gate. When the development team reaches a gate, they need to evaluate the project based on predetermined criteria and make a decision on whether to end the development process, put the process on hold, or proceed with further development.[33]

PRODUCT SAFETY AND LIABILITY

product liability
Responsibility of manufacturers and marketers for injuries and damages caused by their products.

A product can fulfill its mission of satisfying consumer needs only if it ensures safe operation. Manufacturers must design their products to protect users from harm. Products that lead to injuries, either directly or indirectly, can have disastrous consequences for their makers. **Product liability** refers to the responsibility of manufacturers and marketers for injuries and damages caused by their products. Chapter 3 discussed some of the major consumer protection laws that affect product safety. Product safety is controlled by laws that are administered by different government agencies as well as voluntary standards. The laws covering product safety include the Hazardous Products Act, the Motor Vehicle Safety Act, and many acts and regulations under the Canadian Food Inspection Agency. These laws cover many areas of product safety, such as regulating and even banning certain products, requiring packaging that is not injurious to children, and ensuring food safety. In addition to the laws relating to product safety, there are standards. Standards are technical specifications or other criteria that companies adhere to either voluntarily or because they are required to by law. Canada has the National Standards System that outlines the development of standards for the country. The National Standards System is overseen by the Standards Council of Canada, a federal Crown corporation.[34]

Regulatory activities and the increased number of liability claims have prompted companies to sponsor voluntary improvements in safety standards. Safety planning is now a vital element of product strategy, and many companies now publicize the safety planning and testing that go into the development of their products. Volvo, for example, is well known for the safety features it designs into its automobiles, and consumers recognize that fact when they decide to purchase a Volvo.

assessment check 6

6.1 Where do ideas for new products come from?

6.2 What is concept testing and what happens in the commercialization stage?

6.3 What role do the various product safety acts play in protecting consumers?

6.4 What role do standards play in protecting the safety of consumers?

Strategic Implications

Marketers who want to see their products reach the marketplace successfully have a number of options for developing them, branding them, and developing a strong brand identity among consumers and business customers. The key is to integrate all the options so that they are compatible with a firm's overall business and marketing strategy and ultimately the firm's mission. As marketers consider ideas for new products, they need to be careful not to send their companies in so many different directions as to dilute the identities of their brands, making it nearly impossible to keep track of what their companies do well. Category management can help companies develop a consistent product mix with strong branding while at the same time meeting the needs of customers. Looking for ways to extend a brand without diluting it or compromising brand equity is also an important marketing strategy. Finally, marketers must continue to work to produce high-quality products that are also safe for all users. ◆◆◆

REVIEW OF CHAPTER OBJECTIVES

① **Define a brand and identify the different types of brands.**

Marketers recognize the powerful influence products and product lines have on customer behaviour, and they work to create strong identities for their products and protect them. Branding is the process of creating that identity. A brand is a name, term, sign, symbol, design, or some combination that identifies the products of one firm while differentiating these products from competitors' offerings.

A generic product is an item characterized by a plain label, no advertising, and no brand name. A manufacturer's brand is a brand name owned by a manufacturer or other producer. Private brands are brand names placed on products marketed by a wholesaler or retailer. A family brand is a brand name that identifies several related products. An individual brand is a unique brand name that identifies a specific offering within a firm's product line to avoid grouping it under a family brand.

② **Explain the strategic value of brand equity and the benefits of category and brand management.**

Brand equity provides a competitive advantage for a firm because consumers are more likely to buy a product that carries a respected, well-known brand name. Brand equity also eases the path for global expansion.

Category management is beneficial to a business because it gives direct responsibility for creating profitable product lines to category managers and their product group. Consumers respond to branding by making repeat purchases of favoured goods and services. Therefore, good management of brands and categories of brands or product lines can result in a direct response from consumers, increased profits and revenues for companies, and greater consumer satisfaction. Brand and category managers can also enhance relationships with business customers such as retailers.

③ **Discuss how companies develop a strong identity for their products and brands.**

Effective brands communicate to a buyer an idea of the product's image. Trademarks, brand names, slogans, and brand icons create an association that satisfies the customer's expectation of the benefits that using or having the product will yield.

④ **Identify and briefly describe each of the new-product development strategies.**

The success of a new product can result from four product development strategies: (1) market penetration, in which a company seeks to increase sales of an existing product in an existing market; (2) market development, which concentrates on finding new markets for existing products; (3) product development, which is the introduction of new products into identifiable or established markets; and (4) product diversification, which focuses on developing entirely new products for new markets.

⑤ **Describe the consumer adoption process.**

In the adoption process, consumers go through a series of stages from learning about the new product to trying it and deciding whether to purchase it again. The stages are called awareness, interest, evaluation, trial, and adoption/rejection.

⑥ **List the stages in the new-product development process and explain the relationship between product safety and product liability.**

The stages in the six-step new-product development process are (1) idea generation, (2) screening, (3) business analysis, (4) development, (5) test-marketing, and (6) commercialization. These steps may be performed sequentially or, in some cases, concurrently.

Product safety refers to the goal of manufacturers to create products that can be operated safely and will protect consumers from harm. Product liability is the responsibility of marketers and manufacturers for injuries and damages caused by their products. There are major consumer protection laws in place to protect consumers from faulty products.

assessment check answers

1.1 What is a brand?
A brand is a name, term, sign, symbol, design, or some combination that identifies the products of one firm while differentiating these products from competitors' offerings.

1.2 Differentiate among brand recognition, brand preference, and brand insistence.
Brand recognition is a company's first objective for newly introduced products and aims to make these items familiar to the public. Brand preference means buyers rely on previous experiences with the product when choosing it over competitors' products. Brand insistence leads consumers to refuse alternatives and to search extensively for the desired merchandise.

1.3 Identify the different types of brands.
The different types of brands are manufacturer's (or national) brands, private brands, captive brands, family brands, and individual brands.

1.4 How are generic products different from branded products?
Generic products are characterized by plain labels, little or no advertising, and no brand names.

2.1 What is brand equity?
Brand equity refers to the added value that a certain brand name gives to a product in the marketplace.

2.2 What are the four dimensions of brand personality?
The four dimensions of brand personality are differentiation, relevance, esteem, and knowledge.

2.3 Define *brand manager*.
A brand manager is the person at a company with the task of managing a brand's marketing strategies.

2.4 How does category management help retailers?
Category management helps retailers by providing a person—a category manager—to oversee an entire product line and maximize sales for that retailer. It teams the consumer-goods producer's marketing expertise with the retailer's in-store merchandising efforts to track and identify new opportunities for growth.

3.1 Distinguish between a brand name and a trademark.
A brand name is the part of the brand consisting of letters or words that can be spoken and that forms a name distinguishing a firm's offerings from competitors. A trademark is a brand for which the owner claims exclusive legal protection.

3.2 What are the three purposes of packaging?
A package serves three major objectives: (1) protection against damage, spoilage, and pilferage; (2) assistance in marketing the product; and (3) cost effectiveness.

3.3 Describe brand extension and brand licensing.
Brand extension is the strategy of attaching a popular brand name to a new product in an unrelated product category. Brand licensing is the strategy of authorizing other companies to use a brand name.

4.1 Distinguish between market penetration and market development strategies.
In a market penetration strategy, a company seeks to increase sales of an existing product in an existing market. In a market development strategy, the company concentrates on finding new markets for existing products.

4.2 What is product development?
Product development refers to the introduction of new products into identifiable or established markets.

4.3 What is product diversification?

A product diversification strategy focuses on developing entirely new products for new markets.

5.1 Who are consumer innovators?

Consumer innovators are the first buyers of new products—people who purchase new products almost as soon as these products reach the market.

5.2 What characteristics of a product innovation can influence its adoption rate?

Five characteristics of a product innovation influence its adoption rate: relative advantage, compatibility, complexity, possibility of trial use, and observability.

6.1 Where do ideas for new products come from?

New-product development begins with ideas from many sources: suggestions from customers, the sales force, research and development specialists, assessments of competing products, suppliers, retailers, and independent inventors.

6.2 What is concept testing and what happens in the commercialization stage?

Concept testing subjects the product idea to additional study prior to its actual development. When a new-product idea reaches the commercialization stage, it is ready for full-scale marketing.

6.3 What role do the various product safety acts play in protecting consumers?

The various safety acts regulate the safety of consumer products such as food and automobiles.

6.4 What role do standards play in protecting the safety of consumers?

Standards are technical specifications or other criteria that companies adhere to either voluntarily or because they are required to by law.

MARKETING TERMS YOU NEED TO KNOW

These terms are printed in blue in the text. They are defined in the margins of the chapter and in the Glossary that begins on p. G-1.

brand 306	category management 311	product development 317
brand recognition 307	brand name 312	product diversification strategy 317
brand preference 307	brand mark 312	cannibalization 317
brand insistence 307	trademark 312	adoption process 318
generic products 307	trade dress 313	consumer innovators 318
manufacturer's brand 308	label 315	diffusion process 318
private brand 308	Universal Product Code (UPC) 315	product manager 320
captive brand 309	brand extension 315	venture team 320
family brand 309	brand licensing 316	concept testing 323
individual brand 309	market penetration strategy 316	product liability 324
brand equity 310	product positioning 317	
brand manager 311	market development strategy 317	

PROJECT AND TEAMWORK EXERCISES

1. Locate an advertisement for a product that illustrates an especially effective brand name, brand mark, packaging, and overall trade dress. Explain to the class why you think this product has a strong brand identity.

2. With a classmate, search a grocery store for a product that you think could benefit from updated or new package design. Then sketch out a new package design for the product, identifying and explaining your changes as well as your reasons for the changes. Bring the old package and your new package design to class to share with your classmates.

3. What category of consumer adopter best describes you? Do you follow the same adoption pattern for all products, or are you an early adopter for some and a laggard for others? Create a graph or chart showing your own consumer adoption patterns for different products.

4. Which product labels do you read? Over the next several days, keep a brief record of the labels you check while shopping. Do you read nutritional information when buying food products? Do you check care labels on clothes before you buy them? Do you read the directions or warnings on a product you haven't used before? Make notes about what influenced your decision to read or not read the product labels. Did you feel they provided enough information, too little, or too much?

5. Some brands achieve customer loyalty by retaining an air of exclusivity and privilege, even though that often comes along with high price tags. Louis Vuitton, the maker of luxury leather goods, is one such firm. What kind of brand loyalty is this, and how does Vuitton achieve it?

CRITICAL THINKING EXERCISES

1. In this chapter, you learned that Mattel has launched "Barbie My Dreams," an online interactive platform, in an attempt to sustain the interest of older girls in the Barbie brand. Do you think this strategy will work for Mattel? Why or why not? Identify another well-known product that appeals to a specific age group. Do you think a similar strategy would be successful? Why or why not?

2. General Mills and several other major food makers have begun producing organic foods. But they have deliberately kept their brand names off the packaging of these new products, thinking that the kind of customer who goes out of his or her way to buy organic products is unlikely to trust multinational brands. Other companies, however, such as Heinz and PepsiCo, are betting that their brand names will prove to be persuasive in the $25-billion organic foods market. Which strategy do you think is more likely to be successful? Why?

3. Recently some consumer groups have called for a ban on super-sized sugary drinks at fast-food restaurants and sports arenas. Those involved believe that obesity is an epidemic and want governments to take the lead in doing something about the problem. While some government officials are behind the ban, some industry groups and companies are unhappy about it. Do you think a ban on super-sized drinks will help in the fight against obesity? If you were a marketing manager for a fast-food restaurant chain, how would you handle the situation if a ban got approved?

4. Brand names contribute enormously to consumers' perception of a brand. One writer has argued that alphanumeric brand names, such as the Toyota RAV4, Jaguar's X-Type sedan, the Xbox game console, and the GTI from Volkswagen, can translate more easily overseas than "real" names like Golf, Jetta, Escalade, and Eclipse. What other advantages and disadvantages can you think of for each type of brand name? Do you think one type is preferable to the other? Why?

ETHICS EXERCISE

As mentioned in the chapter, some analysts predict that bar codes may soon be replaced by a wireless technology called *radio frequency identification (RFID)*. RFID is a system of installing tags containing tiny computer chips on, say, supermarket items. These chips automatically radio the location of the item to a computer network where inventory data are stored, letting store managers know not only where the item is at all times but also when and where it was made and its colour and size. Proponents of the idea believe RFID will cut costs and simplify inventory tracking and reordering. It may also allow marketers to respond quickly to shifts in demand, avoid under- and overstocking, and reduce spoilage by automatically removing outdated perishables from the shelves. Privacy advocates, however, think the chips provide too much product-preference information that might be identified with individual consumers. In the meantime, Walmart is requiring its major suppliers to begin using the new technology on products stocked by the giant retailer.

1. Do you think RFID poses a threat to consumer privacy? Why or why not?

2. Do you think the technology's possible benefits to marketers outweigh the potential privacy concerns? Are there also potential benefits to consumers, and if so, what are they?

3. How can marketers reassure consumers about privacy concerns if RFID comes into widespread use?

CASE 11.1

Branding Canada—Canada. Keep Exploring.

Tourism is big business. Tourism represents almost 2 percent of Canada's gross domestic product, amounting to just below $82 billion annually. International visitors to Canada who stayed at least one night spent just over $12 billion with an additional $7 billion coming from visitors from the United States. In one year, about 16 million international visitors came into the country—some for business reasons, some to visit family, and others for a holiday. In order to look after all these visitors to the country, approximately 608,000 Canadians work in jobs related to the tourism sector.

The Canadian Tourism Commission (CTC), the federal government body responsible for tourism, groups visitors into three market segments according to the number of visitors. Most visitors to Canada come from the United States. The second group is considered to be Canada's core tourism market. Visitors from the United Kingdom, France, Germany, and Australia are part of this group. The third group of countries is considered to be Canada's emerging or transitional markets. Visitors from Japan, South Korea, Mexico, Brazil, China, and India are in this group.

Canada collects a large amount of data about visitors in order to assist companies in the tourism sector to satisfy their needs. Two major sources of information about Canadian visitors are Statistics Canada and the Canada Border Services Agency. For example, we know that most visitors, roughly 40 percent, visit during the months of July, August, and September. The data also indicate that visitors to Canada are getting younger, with 20 percent of all international visitors falling into the age group of under 24 years old.

Because tourism is so important to the Canadian economy, several organizations are responsible for promoting Canada. At the federal level the CTC has this responsibility. Every province and many regions also have groups that develop promotional material. The CTC is a Crown corporation responsible to the Minister of Industry. The CTC focuses its marketing activities toward international markets. The organization has developed several tools to assist companies direct their marketing toward international markets, including the Brand Standards Guide, an Experience toolkit, and a market segmentation tool called Explorer Quotient.

Several marketing programs have also been developed by the CTC, including Signature Experiences, 35 Million Directors, and a social media initiative. The "Signature Experiences Collection" is a set of 163 exotic tourism experiences ranging from whale watching in British Columbia to lobster fishing in Prince Edward Island. In the 35 Million Directors programs, Canadians across the country were asked to share the photos and videos of their most memorable experience or locations. From over 8,000 photos and videos, the CTC produced a two-minute YouTube program. The CTC also started an Instagram site asking for user-generated content.

Not all marketing organizations across the country aim their promotions at foreign visitors. Banff Lake Louise Tourism aimed its promotion at other Canadian destinations with a social media contest. Searching through social media posts to find people who were about to leave on a skiing or snowboarding vacation, Banff Lake Louise Tourism would ask them to change their travel plans with an all-expenses-paid trip to Banff. The aim of this promotion was to encourage winners, who were already using social media, to talk about their free trip.

Companies within the tourism industry also promote Canada. One popular trip is a journey on a Rocky Mountaineer train through the mountains. Rocky Mountaineer is a privately owned passenger rail service offering trips of one to two days or a couple of weeks. The company's latest promotional material included a television commercial in which people on a rail trip through the mountains were asked to describe their experience. The travellers were speechless but the smiles on their faces portrayed the enjoyment they were feeling.

Questions for Critical Thinking

1. What are the main elements the different marketing organizations are using to build a brand identity for Canada? Discuss the effectiveness of each strategy.
2. Are there any other branding strategies these marketing organizations could use to brand the country? What are they? Why do you think these strategies would be more effective?

Sources: Eve Lazarus, "Rocky Mountaineer Takes Speechless Travelers to New Markets," *Marketing,* November 13, 2013, **www.marketingmag.ca**; Rocky Mountaineer website, **www.rockymountaineer.com**, accessed March 23, 2014; "Delivering Value for Canada's Tourism Businesses Through Innovation and Efficiency," Canadian Tourism Commission, 2012 Annual Report; Eve Lazarus, "Banff Stalks Social Media, Lures Skiers from Other Resorts," *Marketing,* January 27, 2014, **www.marketingmag .ca**; "Tourism Snapshot: 2012 Year-in-Review," Canadian Tourism Commission.

CASE 11.2

Yogurt Wars

Yogurt is one of the fastest-growing food categories in the grocery store. This is surprising to some since the origins of yogurt can be traced back to the herdsmen of Central Asia around 6000 B.C. Yogurt became a grocery staple in North America during the 1950s and '60s, and today there are varieties of yogurt for every meal, for snacks, and to drink. One food expert has even named yogurt the food of the decade.

Canadians are eating more yogurt—91 percent of Canadians purchase yogurt regularly and sales have grown 10 percent per year—but Canadians still lag in per person consumption. In Canada, individuals consume an average of 11 kilograms of yogurt a year as opposed to Europe, where the consumption per person is 35 kilograms annually.

The importance of this food category to companies in the dairy business is not surprising given the growth rates. One company in particular, Ultima Foods, the Quebec-based dairy cooperative, had a long-term licence agreement with General Mills to produce the Yoplait brand of yogurt. When it was time to renew the licence, negotiations did not progress to Ultima's liking, so the company decided to launch its own brand of yogurt products—after all, it had the manufacturing and distributing facilities already in place. The company invested $60 million in research and development. The research included interviews with 4,000 Canadians throughout the development process, including product, packaging, and name development. The result was a new brand of yogurt that included 40 products in seven product lines.

Ultima Foods is not the only company developing new yogurt products. In one year, 83 new yogurt products were launched into the Canadian market. One area of the market that is particularly popular is Greek yogurt. Greek yogurt products represent one-quarter of all yogurt sales, the largest segment of the market.

Questions for Critical Thinking

1. What factors account for the rising popularity of yogurt?
2. Do you think the sales trend will continue upward? Why or why not?

Sources: "The History of Yogurt," The Dairy Goodness website, **www.dairygoodness .ca**, accessed March 26, 2014; Rebecca Harris, "logo Emerges from Cross-Border Marketing Shuffle," *Marketing,* September 14, 2012, **www.marketingmag.ca**; Rebecca Harris, "Danone Goes Greek with New Campaign," *Marketing,* February 18, 2014, **www.marketingmag.ca**; Grainne Burns, "Yogurt: The Most Versatile Grocery Aisle Product," *Marketing,* March 7, 2014, **www.marketingmag.ca**.

chapter 12

Marketing Channels and Supply Chain Management

CHAPTER OBJECTIVES

① Describe the types of marketing channels and the roles they play in marketing strategy.

② Outline the major channel strategy decisions.

③ Describe the concepts of channel management, conflict, and cooperation.

④ Identify and describe the different vertical marketing systems.

⑤ Explain the roles of logistics and supply-chain management in an overall distribution strategy.

⑥ Identify the major components of a physical distribution system.

⑦ Compare the major modes of transportation.

⑧ Discuss the role of transportation intermediaries, combined transportation modes, and warehousing in improving physical distribution.

KIVA ROBOTS ADD TO DISTRIBUTION OPTIONS

If you happen to be in an Amazon.com warehouse in the near future and spy some squat, square orange objects scurrying around the stacks, you're seeing the online retailer's new Kiva robots at work. You might also see them at warehouses belonging to Staples, Crate and Barrel, Gap, Toys "R" Us, and Diapers.com, as well as at other prominent retailers' fulfillment centres. Think Logistics, a third-party logistics (3PL) provider, also uses them in its large distribution warehouse in Vaughan, Ontario.

Kiva Systems, founded in 2003, was recently purchased by Amazon, which will not only continue utilizing the battery-operated robots in its own warehouses but also blend them into the fulfillment services it offers other companies. "Kiva's technology is another way to improve productivity by bringing the products directly to employees to pick and stow," says Amazon's vice president of fulfillment.

Kiva has grown tremendously since its founding, hiring more employees every quarter and recording a 130 percent increase in sales in one recent year, for total revenues of more than $100 million. The company charges its clients $1 to $2 million for a robot "start-up kit"; outfitting a customer's entire warehouse with robots can cost 10 times as much and require six months of planning, testing, and training for human logistics managers. The payoff? Big savings at the warehouse, in both time and cost.

By locating the items in an order, moving around the warehouse to retrieve them, and stacking them on its surface to ferry them to employees, a Kiva robot can help fill three to four times as many orders as a worker acting alone who must walk the warehouse to retrieve items. Speedier order fulfillment makes customers happy, of course, because orders are shipped sooner than before, but employees are happy, too. At Crate and Barrel, for instance, 50 people and 50 robots now pack up 2,000 orders a day, but the humans do much less physical labour, without noisy conveyor belts. Amazon says it will not eliminate any jobs at its own facilities as a result of its $775-million purchase of the company.

The robots rely on sophisticated software that Kiva can customize for each of its clients, while a Wi-Fi network and floor grid of two-dimensional barcodes helps them navigate the space. They can even determine when they need to go recharge themselves.[1]

connecting with customers

Early in his career, Mick Mountz worked for an online grocery retailer that subsequently went bankrupt, the consequence of an inefficient fulfillment system. Mountz began to question whether it was possible to have a warehouse run by robots. Instead of having employees wandering around looking for inventory, could robots find inventory and bring it to human workers? He founded Kiva Systems and eventually convinced Staples to try a pilot program. Today, Staples has 1,000 Kiva robots in two of its distribution centres, and many other companies where distribution is critical are also buying Kiva robots. These customers see the value that Kiva Systems creates: fast, efficient movement of products and speedier order fulfillment, along with lower labour costs.

Chapter Overview

Distribution—moving goods and services from producers to customers—is the second marketing mix variable and an important marketing concern. Firms depend on waterways like the Panama Canal to be able to move their goods from one destination to another. A distribution strategy has two critical components: (1) marketing channels and (2) logistics and supply chain management.

A **marketing channel**—also called a **distribution channel**—is an organized system of marketing institutions and their interrelationships that enhances the physical flow and ownership of goods and services from producer to consumer or business user. The choice of marketing channels should support the firm's overall marketing strategy. In contrast, **logistics** refers to the process of coordinating the flow of information, goods, and services among members of the marketing channel. **Supply-chain management** is the control of activities of purchasing, processing, and delivery through which raw materials are transformed into products and made available to final consumers. Efficient logistical systems support customer service, enhancing customer relationships—an important goal of any marketing strategy.

A key aspect of logistics is physical distribution, which covers a broad range of activities aimed at efficient movement of finished goods from the end of the production line to the consumer. Although some marketers use the terms *transportation* and *physical distribution* interchangeably, these terms do not carry the same meaning. **Physical distribution** extends beyond transportation to include such important decision areas as customer service, inventory control, materials handling, protective packaging, order processing, and warehousing.

Well-planned marketing channels and effective logistics and supply-chain management provide ultimate users with convenient ways for obtaining the goods and services they desire. This chapter discusses the activities, decisions, and marketing intermediaries involved in managing marketing channels and logistics. Chapter 13 looks at other players in the marketing channel: retailers, direct marketers, and wholesalers. ◆◆◆

---

① **Describe the types of marketing channels and the roles they play in marketing strategy.**

distribution Movement of goods and services from producers to customers.

marketing (distribution) channel System of marketing institutions that enhances the physical flow of goods and services, along with ownership title, from producer to consumer or business user.

logistics Process of coordinating the flow of information, goods, and services among members of the distribution channel.

THE ROLE OF MARKETING CHANNELS IN MARKETING STRATEGY

A firm's distribution channels play a key role in its overall marketing strategy because these channels provide the means by which the firm makes the goods and services available to ultimate users. Channels perform four important functions. First, they facilitate the exchange process by reducing the number of marketplace contacts necessary to make a sale. Suppose you've had a Nintendo Wii hand-held game player in the past and been satisfied with it, so when you see an ad for the Nintendo Wii U, you are interested. You visit the Nintendo website, where you learn more about the Wii U and its unique features. You are particularly drawn to the games *Marvel Avengers: Battle for Earth* and *NBA 2K13*. But you want to see the game console in person, so you locate a dealer near enough for you to visit.[2] The dealer forms part of the channel that brings you—a potential buyer—and Nintendo—the seller—together to complete the exchange process. It's important to keep in mind that all channel members benefit when they work together; when they begin to disagree or—worse yet—compete directly with each other, everyone loses.

Distributors adjust for discrepancies in the market's assortment of goods and services via a process known as *sorting*, the second channel function. A single producer tends to maximize the quantity it makes of a limited line of goods, while a single buyer needs a limited quantity of a wide selection of merchandise. Sorting alleviates such discrepancies by channelling products to suit both the buyer's and the producer's needs.

The third function of marketing channels involves standardizing exchange transactions by setting expectations for products, and it involves the transfer process itself. Channel members tend to standardize payment terms, delivery schedules, prices, and purchase lots among other conditions.

Standardization helps make the transactions efficient and fair. The final marketing channel function is to facilitate searches by both buyers and sellers. Buyers search for specific goods and services to fill their needs, while sellers attempt to learn what buyers want. Channels bring buyers and sellers together to complete the exchange process. Hundreds of distribution channels exist today, and no single channel best serves the needs of every company. Instead of searching for the best channel for all products, a marketing manager must analyze alternative channels in light of consumer needs to determine the most appropriate channel or channels for the firm's goods and services.

Marketers must remain flexible because channels may change over time. Today's ideal channel may prove inappropriate in a few years. Or the way a company uses that channel may change. Like many other companies, Procter & Gamble has used digital advertising for many years, taking advantage of digital's ability to home in on customers' needs. But finding the right combination of tactics—apps, tablets, mobile, social, and many others—is never easy. The world's largest advertiser, the company recently announced that it would shift its marketing focus even further to digital. Alex Tosolini, P&G's vice president of global e-business, says that the evolving nature of digital media prompted a change "from static marketing campaigns that we launch and adjust infrequently to real-time always-on brand building."[3]

The following sections examine the diverse types of channels available to marketers and the decisions marketers must make to develop an effective distribution strategy that supports their firm's marketing objectives.

If you are interested in learning more about the xBox One, you may want to try it at a local dealer.

supply-chain management Control of the activities of purchasing, processing, and delivery through which raw materials are transformed into products and made available to final consumers.

physical distribution Broad range of activities aimed at efficient movement of finished goods from the end of the production line to the consumer.

marketing intermediary (middleman) Wholesaler or retailer that operates between producers and consumers or business users.

TYPES OF MARKETING CHANNELS

The first step in selecting a marketing channel is determining which type of channel will best meet both the seller's objectives and the distribution needs of customers. Figure 12.1 depicts the major channels available to marketers of consumer and business goods and services.

Most channel options involve at least one **marketing intermediary**. The "Marketing and the SME" feature explains how pets purchased through marketing intermediaries frequently come from questionable sources; however, even if you purchase your pet directly from a breeder, you need to take care that you are dealing with a reputable one. A marketing intermediary (or *middleman*) is an organization that operates between producers and consumers or business users. Retailers and wholesalers are both marketing intermediaries. A retail store owned and operated by someone other than the manufacturer of the products it sells is one type of marketing inter-

mediary. A **wholesaler** is an intermediary that takes title to the goods it handles and then distributes these goods to retailers, other distributors, or B2B customers. Wholesalers are able to stockpile nonperishable goods, but perishables are another story. The specialty coffee market, once only 1 percent of the total, has increased to roughly 20 percent in only the last 25 years. The recent rise in the price of coffee and a worldwide increase in demand have made it more difficult for both wholesalers and independent specialty retailers to keep coffee affordable.[4]

Canadian companies are increasingly communicating with their target customers through Twitter and other social media. Many Canadians are now following Molson Coors on Twitter.

figure 12.1

Alternative Marketing Channels

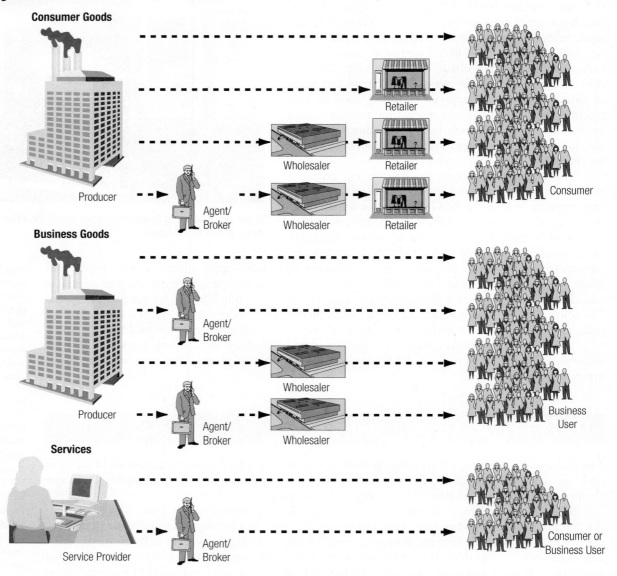

wholesaler Channel intermediary that takes title to the goods it handles and then distributes these goods to retailers, other distributors, or B2B customers.

A short marketing channel involves few intermediaries. In contrast, a long marketing channel involves many intermediaries working in succession to move goods from producers to consumers. Business products usually move through short channels due to geographic concentrations and comparatively fewer business purchasers. Service firms market primarily through short channels because they sell intangible products and need to maintain personal relationships within their channels. Haircuts, manicures, and dental cleanings are all provided through short channels. Not-for-profit organizations also tend to work with short, simple, and direct channels. Any marketing intermediaries in such channels usually act as agents, such as independent ticket agencies or fund-raising specialists.

direct channel Marketing channel that moves goods directly from a producer to the business purchaser or ultimate user.

DIRECT SELLING

The simplest and shortest marketing channel is a direct channel. A **direct channel** carries goods directly from a producer to the business purchaser or ultimate user. This channel forms part of

MARKETING AND THE SME	Direct Selling: It's Good for the Dogs; Not Always So Good for You

IF you ask most people what a puppy mill is, they will tell you it is a disreputable breeding operation that sells its dogs to retailers, either directly or through brokers who wholesale dogs to pet stores. Some people are even aware of the cruelty that is endemic in the industry. Dogs are kept in crowded, substandard housing, often with poor sanitation; fed the cheapest of food; and denied exercise, human contact, and veterinary care. Breeding dogs often die young—sometimes after only four to six years—and puppies are frequently sold before they are ready. It is no wonder that many of these puppies have behavioural problems or develop medical conditions early in their lives.

Increasingly, cities and towns in Canada are banning the sale of puppies from pet stores. Unfortunately, puppy mills are increasingly selling directly to would-be owners at flea markets, or through newspaper ads, or online. Craigslist and BuySellTrade.ca have stopped allowing ads for family pets, but Kijiji Canada has no plans to do so. Kijiji prefers to "filter out" bad users. However, its ability to do so is questionable. Gail Benoit, a Nova Scotia woman convicted of animal cruelty and who is believed to have sold as many as 30,000 dogs over a 13-year period, had been banned from Kijiji. However, she has continued to try to find ways around the ban by using fake identities, different computers, and getting others to post ads for her.

How do you find a good breeder? The best way is to visit the breeder's operation. How many dogs does the breeder have? How often do they breed? Look at the bitch and at the littermates. See if the dogs react to you and to other people. Investigate the dogs' living conditions. Ask what health tests have been done on the dogs, both parents and pups. Does the breeder show dogs, and what breed clubs does the breeder belong to? Be very suspicious of any breeder that is not cooperative. Remember that when you buy directly from a breeder, there is no guarantee that you are not buying from a puppy mill. Canadians love their dogs, all 6.4 million of them, but puppy mills are a multimillion-dollar industry in Canada. Your dog should be a lifelong commitment. Consider carefully; choose wisely; love sincerely.

Cindy Berube is just one of thousands of reputable and responsible dog breeders in Canada. She maintains a small group of breeding Portuguese water dogs and has only a few litters each year. All her dogs live with her family and interact with them. They participate in conformation events (dog shows), obedience trials, agility trials, and water-work trials. New puppies are handled daily and get desensitized to sights and sounds through planned activities that begin only a few days after they are born. Prospective pet owners are interviewed and must complete a questionnaire before they are allowed to buy one of her puppies. Through her website, **www.charbr.com**, Cindy provides prospective owners with information on raising puppies, and she provides pictures and information on all her dogs and previous litters. She is firmly committed to her breed and wants to ensure that all her puppies go to great homes.

Sources: Cindy Berube, personal interview, March 7, 2014; Benjamin Shingler, "Popular Classified Website Kijiji Pressed to End Sale of Household Pets," Canadian Press (Toronto), September 8, 2013; Selena Ross, "Benoit Charged with Fraud in Stolen Dog Case," **www.thechronicleherald.ca**, March 5, 2013, accessed March 8, 2014; Humane Society International website, "Puppy Mills in Canada," **www.hsi.org**, accessed March 7, 2014.

direct selling, a marketing strategy in which a producer establishes direct sales contact with its product's final users. Direct selling is an important option for goods that require extensive demonstrations in convincing customers to buy. The "Career Readiness" feature contains suggestions for closing a successful sale.

Direct selling plays a significant role in business-to-business marketing. Most major installations, accessory equipment, and even component parts and raw materials are sold through direct contacts between producing firms and final buyers. Many people in business enjoy successful sales careers. Think about the textbook you are now reading. Probably it was originally purchased by your campus bookstore. But it would be the publisher's salesperson who sold the book to the bookstore, most likely after the Nelson Education salesperson helped convince your instructor to choose this text for his or her course. Direct selling is also important in consumer-goods markets. Direct sellers such as Avon Canada, Pampered Chef, and Tupperware Canada sidestep competition in store aisles by developing networks of independent representatives who sell their products directly to consumers. Many of these companies practise a direct selling strategy called the *party plan*, originally popularized by Tupperware. Jewellery boutique

direct selling Strategy designed to establish direct sales contact between producer and final user.

| CAREER READINESS | **How to Successfully Close a Sale** |

CLOSING a sale is often a challenge, but several steps can improve your success rate. Here are some basic strategies, and a few you might not have thought of.

- There's no substitute for preparation. Research your customer so you know what the company's needs are and what they've purchased before.
- Know the value of your product. It's not the same thing as the price.
- During the sales call, listen more than you speak. Some experienced salespeople say you should be talking only 20 percent of the time and listening the rest.
- Use your speaking time to ask about the challenges your customer faces, who all the decision makers are that you need to influence, and how you can help solve their problems.

- Assume that any buyer concerns raised are legitimate and address them as such. Your response to buyer concerns tells the prospect a lot about how you will treat him or her as a customer.
- Remain seated. Standing up, even if the prospect has done so, signals a change in the situation and can end negotiations before you're ready.
- Always carry a pen. More than one sale has been lost for want of a pen to sign with.
- Don't forget to say thank you.

Sources: Paul Chenier, "7 Tips for Closing a Sale in One Call," AskMen.com, **www.askmen.com**, accessed May 18, 2012; Barry Farber, "8 Steps to a Successful Sales Call," *Entrepreneur*, **www.entrepreneur.com**, accessed May 18, 2012; "12 Expert Tips for Closing That Sale," SoldLab.com, **www.soldlab.com**, accessed May 18, 2012; Grant Cardone, "12 Commandments for Closing a Sale," *Entrepreneur*, January 11, 2012, **www.entrepreneur.com**.

Marketoid

A Stella & Dot salesperson in Hamilton, Ontario, earned more than $250,000 in one recent year, taking home $63,000 in her best month.

company Stella & Dot—recently new to Canada—is one such business. Launched by entrepreneur Jessica Herrin, Stella & Dot jewellery is sold at home-based parties, or "trunk shows," by independent sales representatives. The jewellery, which appeals to women of all ages, is accessible and affordable—and is often worn by TV celebrities. Stella & Dot recently topped $200 million in sales.[5] The Internet provides another direct selling channel for both B2B and B2C purchases. Canadian women who wish to wear designer dresses—but don't want to pay full price for them—can rent them from **rentfrockrepeat.com** and receive them a day or two before their planned event. After their event, they simply return their rental dress in a prepaid return envelope via Canada Post.

Direct mail can be an important part of direct selling—or it can encourage a potential customer to contact an intermediary such as a retailer. Either way, it is a vital communication piece for many marketers.

CHANNELS USING MARKETING INTERMEDIARIES

Although direct channels allow simple and straightforward marketing, they are not practical in every case. Some products serve markets in different areas of the country or world, or have large numbers of potential end users. Other categories of goods rely heavily on repeat purchases. The producers of these goods may find more efficient, less expensive, and less time-consuming alternatives to direct channels by using marketing intermediaries. This section considers five channels that involve marketing intermediaries.

Producer to Wholesaler to Retailer to Consumer

The traditional channel for consumer goods proceeds from producer to wholesaler to retailer to user. This method carries goods between literally thousands of small producers with limited lines and local retailers. A firm with limited financial resources will rely on the services of a wholesaler that serves as an immediate source of funds and then markets to hundreds of retailers. On the other hand, a small retailer can draw on a wholesaler's specialized distribution skills. In addition, many manufacturers hire their own field sales representatives to service retail accounts with marketing information. Wholesalers may then handle the actual sales transactions.

Producer to Wholesaler to Business User

Similar characteristics in the organizational market often attract marketing intermediaries to operate between producers and business purchasers. The term *industrial distributor* commonly refers to intermediaries in the business market that take title to the goods.

Producer to Agent to Wholesaler to Retailer to Consumer

In markets served by many small companies, a unique intermediary—the agent—performs the basic function of bringing buyer and seller together. An agent may or may not take possession of the goods, but never takes title. The agent merely represents a producer by seeking a market for its products or a wholesaler (which does take title to the goods) by locating a supply source.

Producer to Agent to Wholesaler to Business User

Like agents, brokers are independent intermediaries who may or may not take possession of goods, but never take title to these goods. Agents and brokers also serve the business market when small producers attempt to market their offerings through large wholesalers. Such an intermediary, often called a **manufacturers' representative**, provides an independent sales force to contact wholesale buyers. A kitchen equipment manufacturer may have its own manufacturers' representatives to market its goods, for example.

Producer to Agent to Business User

For products sold in small units, only merchant wholesalers can economically cover the markets. A merchant wholesaler is an independently owned wholesaler that takes title to the goods. By maintaining regional inventories, this wholesaler achieves transportation economies, stockpiling goods and making small shipments over short distances. For a product with large unit sales, however, and for which transportation accounts for a small percentage of the total cost, the producer-agent-business user channel is usually employed. The agent in effect becomes the producer's sales force, but bulk shipments of the product reduce the intermediary's inventory management function.

DUAL DISTRIBUTION

Dual distribution refers to movement of products through more than one channel to reach the firm's target market. Sears Canada, for instance, has a three-pronged distribution system, selling through stores, catalogues, and the Internet. Marketers usually adopt a dual distribution strategy either to maximize their firm's coverage in the marketplace or to increase the cost effectiveness of the firm's marketing effort. Nintendo and Netflix recently partnered to offer entertainment through more than one channel. Traditionally, customers order their favourite movies online and have the DVDs delivered to their mailboxes. Under the new agreement, Netflix subscribers with a monthly subscription can stream movies and TV programs and view them on their Wii console at no extra cost.[6]

REVERSE CHANNELS

While the traditional concept of marketing channels involves the movement of goods and services from producer to consumer or business user, marketers should not ignore **reverse channels**— channels designed to return goods to their producers. Reverse channels have gained increased importance with rising prices for

manufacturers' representative Agent wholesaling intermediary that represents manufacturers of related but noncompeting products and receives a commission on each sale.

dual distribution Network that moves products to a firm's target market through more than one marketing channel.

reverse channel Channel designed to return goods to their producer.

As more retailers sell online, reverse channels become increasingly important. Canada Post offers a convenient solution.

Marketoid

Canadians generate about 418 kilograms of waste per person annually, and only 27 percent of that is recycled. Almost all Canadian households (95 percent) have access to recycling programs; 98 percent of those households recycle. More than half of them report that they do so to reduce demand for raw materials.

raw materials, increasing availability of recycling facilities, and passage of additional antipollution and conservation laws. Purchase a new set of tires, and you'll probably pay a recycling charge for disposing of the old tires. The intent is to halt the growing litter problem of illegal tire dumps. Automotive and marine batteries contain potentially toxic materials, including 11 kilograms of lead, plastic, and sulphuric acid. Despite this, 99 percent of the elements in a spent battery can be reclaimed, recycled, and reused in new batteries. Environmentally friendly consumers can turn in their old batteries at the time they purchase new ones. To help in this effort, the Canadian Automobile Association (CAA) holds an annual CAA Great Battery Roundup during which consumers can drop off their dead batteries.[7]

Some reverse channels move through the facilities of traditional marketing intermediaries. In provinces that require bottle deposits, retailers and local bottlers may perform these functions in the consumer beverage industry. For other products, manufacturers—or governments—establish redemption centres, develop systems for rechannelling products for recycling, and create specialized organizations to handle disposal and recycling. Nike's Reuse-A-Shoe program collects people's cast-off athletic shoes and recycles virtually the entire shoe. These recycling efforts are likely to help build customer loyalty and enhance the brands' reputations.[8]

Reverse channels also handle product recalls and repairs. An appliance manufacturer might send recall notices to the buyers of a washing machine. An auto manufacturer might send notices to car owners advising them of a potential problem and offering to repair it at no cost through local dealerships.

> ### assessment check 1
>
> 1.1 Distinguish between a marketing channel and logistics.
>
> 1.2 What are the different types of marketing channels?
>
> 1.3 What four functions do marketing channels perform?

(2) **Outline the major channel strategy decisions.**

CHANNEL STRATEGY DECISIONS

Marketers face several strategic decisions in choosing channels and marketing intermediaries for their products. Selecting a specific channel is the most basic of these decisions. Marketers must also resolve questions about the level of distribution intensity, assess the desirability of vertical marketing systems, and evaluate the performance of current intermediaries.

SELECTION OF A MARKETING CHANNEL

Consider the following questions: What characteristics of a franchised dealer network make it the best channel option for a company? Why do operating supplies often go through both agents and merchant wholesalers before reaching their actual users? Why would a firm market a single product through several channels? Marketers must answer many such questions in choosing marketing channels.

A variety of factors affect the selection of a marketing channel. Some channel decisions are dictated by the marketplace in which the company operates. In other cases, the product itself may be a key variable in picking a marketing channel. Finally, the marketing organization may base its selection of channels on its size and competitive factors. Individual firms in a single industry may choose different channels as part of their overall strategy to gain a competitive edge. Book publishers, for instance, may sell through bookstores, directly to consumers on their own websites, or through nontraditional outlets, including specialty retailers such as craft stores or home improvement stores.

Market Factors

Channel structure reflects a product's intended markets, either for consumers or business users. Business purchasers usually prefer to deal directly with manufacturers (except for routine supplies or small accessory items), but most consumers make their purchases from retailers. Marketers often sell products that serve both business users and consumers through more than one channel. Sometimes marketers must adapt to customers' preferences for ethical supply chain behaviour. See the "Solving an Ethical Controversy" feature to learn how consumers brought about change in the cocoa industry.

SOLVING AN ETHICAL CONTROVERSY	Hershey's Takes Responsibility for Its Supply Chain

A DECADE ago, when consumers learned of abusive conditions under which thousands of children were forced to work in Africa's cocoa industry, most major chocolate manufacturers bowed to public pressure. They promised to end human trafficking and child labour in Ivory Coast, which produces 40 percent of the world's cocoa, and to buy sustainably produced ingredients. Hershey's, however, lagged behind other chocolate producers who made a commitment to ensure their products are made without child labour. Several human rights organizations recently banded together and besieged the Hershey's Facebook page, asking the company to "raise the bar" when it came to using suppliers who use child labour and inspiring more than 50,000 people to sign a petition on Change.org to get Hershey's to stop using suppliers who abused their young workers.

Should companies be responsible for the actions of their suppliers?

PRO

1. Consumers want to know the products they're buying are not associated with abusive labour practices.

2. Multinational companies with small, unregulated suppliers that depend on their business have an opportunity to do good by insisting on fair labour practices.

CON

1. Companies should not try to control what their suppliers in other cultures do or impose their own (or their customers') value systems on them.
2. Companies are responsible to their shareholders for finding the lowest-cost and most efficient production methods.

Where do you stand: pro or con?

Sources: "Why Hershey?" organization website, Raise the Bar.org, **www.raisethebarhershey.org**, accessed May 18, 2012; Mindy Lubber, "U.S. Companies Must Raise the Bar on Supply Chain Conditions," *Forbes*, May 17, 2012, **www.forbes.com**; Julie Bort, "Group Used Facebook to Make Hershey Act on Child Slavery," BusinessInsider.com, February 1, 2012, **http://articles.businessinsider.com**; Alyce Lomax, "Hershey's Gets a Bit Safer for Africa's Exploited Kids," Daily Finance.com, February 2, 2012, **www.dailyfinance.com**; Nick Malawskey, "Hershey Co. Invests $10 Million to Education Programs, CocoaLink in West Africa," PennLive.com, January 30, 2012, **www.pennlive.com**.

Other market factors also affect channel choice, including the market's needs, its geographic location, and its average order size. To serve a concentrated market with a small number of buyers, a direct channel offers a feasible alternative. But in serving a geographically dispersed potential trade area in which customers purchase small amounts in individual transactions—the conditions that characterize the consumer-goods market—distribution through marketing intermediaries makes sense.

Product Factors

Product characteristics also guide the choice of an optimal marketing channel strategy. Perishable goods, such as fresh fruit and vegetables, milk, and fruit juice, move through short channels. Trendy or seasonal fashions, such as swimsuits and ski wear, are also examples.

Vending machines represent another short channel. Typically, you can buy a bag of Skittles, Lay's potato chips, or a bottle of Dasani water from a vending machine. But how about underwear, fresh flowers, gold bars, dried squid, or nail polish? All of these things can be found today in vending machines. In Paris, France, five Nailmatic vending machines dispense 63 different shades of nail polish so you can be sure to get just the right shade for you.[9] Complex products, such as custom-made installations and computer equipment, are often sold directly to ultimate buyers. In general, relatively standardized items that are also nonperishable pass through comparatively long channels. Products with low unit costs, such as cans of dog food, bars of soap, and packages of gum, typically travel through long channels. Perishable items such as fresh flowers, meat, and produce require much shorter channels.

Perishable goods must move through short channels, sometimes directly from the grower to the consumer.

Organizational and Competitive Factors

Companies with strong financial, management, and marketing resources feel less need for help from intermediaries. A large, financially strong manufacturer can hire its own sales force, warehouse its own goods, and extend credit to retailers or consumers. But a small firm with fewer resources may do better with the aid of intermediaries. Suzie Chemel and Jennifer Ger started Foxy Originals when they were still in university and began selling their fashion jewellery at flea markets, eventually expanding their sales through fashion boutiques across Canada and the United States. They recently launched a new line—Foxy by Foxy Originals—to be sold through Target Canada. Ms Chemel says, "This was an extremely exciting opportunity for us and for our company and we saw it as the next step for Foxy to expand in Canada."[10]

A firm with a broad product line can usually market its products directly to retailers or business users because its own sales force can offer a variety of products. High sales volume spreads selling costs over a large number of items, generating adequate returns from direct sales. Single-product firms often view direct selling as unaffordable.

The manufacturer's desire for control over marketing its products also influences channel selection. Some manufacturers choose to sell their products only at their own stores. Manufacturers of specialty or luxury goods, such as scarves from Hermès and watches from Rolex, limit the number of retailers that can carry their products.

Businesses that explore new marketing channels must be careful to avoid upsetting their channel intermediaries. Conflicts frequently arose as companies began to establish an Internet presence in addition to traditional outlets. Today, firms look for new ways to handle both without damaging relationships. In an aggressive social media campaign, the athletic apparel and equipment manufacturer Under Armour recently unveiled a revamped website to showcase its new products, such as shoes, athletic bags, and hats. The site also has live chat and customer review apps. However, retail sales—most notably through two major sporting goods chains—still account for 26 percent of Under Armour sales. The new website also features a much more conspicuous brick-and-mortar store locater. John Rogers, Under Armour's vice president of global e-commerce, says, "The new store finder ensures consumers can find all stores near them to touch, feel, and try on Under Armour gear, but online we focus on telling the innovation and leadership product stories that create strong desire for our products across all distribution channels."[11] Table 12.1 summarizes the factors that affect the selection of a marketing channel. The table also examines the effect of each factor on the channel's overall length.

table 12.1   *Factors Influencing Marketing Channel Strategies*

	CHARACTERISTICS OF SHORT CHANNELS	CHARACTERISTICS OF LONG CHANNELS
Market factors	Business users	Consumers
	Geographically concentrated	Geographically dispersed
	Extensive technical knowledge and regular servicing required	Little technical knowledge and regular servicing not required
	Large orders	Small orders
Product factors	Perishable	Durable
	Complex	Standardized
	Expensive	Inexpensive
Organizational factors	Manufacturer has adequate resources to perform channel functions	Manufacturer lacks adequate resources to perform channel functions
	Broad product line	Limited product line
	Channel control important	Channel control not important
Competitive factors	Manufacturer feels satisfied with marketing intermediaries' performance in promoting products	Manufacturer feels dissatisfied with marketing intermediaries' performance in promoting products

DETERMINING DISTRIBUTION INTENSITY

Another key channel strategy decision is the intensity of distribution. *Distribution intensity* refers to the number of intermediaries through which a manufacturer distributes its goods in a particular market. Optimal distribution intensity should ensure adequate market coverage for a product. Adequate market coverage varies depending on the goals of the individual firm, the type of product, and the consumer segments in its target market. In general, however, distribution intensity varies along a continuum with three general categories: intensive distribution, selective distribution, and exclusive distribution.

Lay's potato chips is a convenience good so consumers expect to find it just about everywhere: the supermarket, the convenience store, or even at their local drugstore. Lay's must use an intensive distribution strategy.

Intensive Distribution

An **intensive distribution** strategy seeks to distribute a product through all available channels in a trade area. Because Lay's practises intensive distribution for its snack products, you can pick up a bag of Lay's potato chips just about anywhere—the supermarket, the convenience store, and even the drugstore. Usually, an intensive distribution strategy suits items with wide appeal across broad groups of consumers.

> **intensive distribution**
> Distribution of a product through all available channels.

Selective Distribution

In another market coverage strategy, **selective distribution**, a firm chooses only a limited number of retailers in a market area to handle its line. Italian design firm Gucci sells its merchandise only through a limited number of select boutiques worldwide. By limiting the number of retailers, marketers can reduce total marketing costs while establishing strong working relationships within the channel. Moreover, selected retailers often agree to comply with the company's strict rules for advertising, pricing, and displaying its products. *Cooperative advertising*—in which the manufacturer pays a percentage of the retailer's advertising expenditures and the retailer prominently displays the firm's products—can be used for mutual benefit, and marginal retailers can be avoided. Where service is important, the manufacturer usually provides training and assistance to the dealers it chooses.

> **selective distribution**
> Distribution of a product through a limited number of channels.

Exclusive Distribution

When a producer grants exclusive rights to a wholesaler or retailer to sell its products in a specific geographic region, it practises **exclusive distribution**. The automobile industry provides a good example of exclusive distribution. A city with a population of 460,000 may have a single Honda dealer. Exclusive distribution agreements also govern marketing for some major appliance and apparel brands.

Marketers may sacrifice some market coverage by implementing a policy of exclusive distribution. However, they often develop and maintain an image of quality and prestige for the product. If it's harder to find a Free People silk dress, the item seems more valuable. In addition, exclusive distribution limits marketing costs since the firm deals with a smaller number of accounts. In exclusive distribution, producers and retailers cooperate closely in decisions concerning advertising and promotion, inventory carried by the retailers, and prices.

> **exclusive distribution**
> Distribution of a product through a single wholesaler or retailer in a specific geographic region.

Legal Problems of Exclusive Distribution

Exclusive distribution presents potential legal problems in three main areas: exclusive dealing, market restriction, and tied selling. Although none of these practices is illegal *per se*, all may break the law if they reduce competition or tend to create monopolies.

As part of an exclusive distribution strategy, marketers may try to enforce an exclusive dealing agreement, which prohibits a marketing intermediary (a wholesaler or, more typically, a retailer) from handling competing products. Producers of high-priced shopping goods, specialty goods, and accessory equipment often require such agreements to ensure total concentration on their own product lines. Such contracts violate the Competition Act only if the producer's or dealer's sales volumes represent a substantial percentage of total sales in the market area. While exclusive distribution is legal for companies first entering a market, such agreements violate the Competition Act if used by firms with a sizable market share seeking to bar competitors from the market.

closed sales territory Exclusive geographic selling region of a distributor.

Producers may also try to set up **closed sales territories** to restrict their distributors to certain geographic regions. This protects distributors from rival dealers in their exclusive territories. Some beverage distributors have closed territories, as do distributors of plumbing fixtures.[12] But the downside of this practice is that the distributors sacrifice opportunities to open new facilities or market the manufacturers' products outside their assigned territories. The legality of a system of closed sales territories depends on whether the restriction decreases competition. If so, it will violate the Competition Act.

The legality of closed sales territories also depends on whether the system imposes horizontal or vertical restrictions. Horizontal territorial restrictions result from agreements between retailers or wholesalers to avoid competition among sellers of products from the same producer. Such agreements consistently have been declared illegal. Vertical territorial restrictions—those between producers and wholesalers or retailers—are more likely to meet legal criteria. Such agreements likely satisfy the law in cases where manufacturers occupy relatively small market shares. In such instances, the restrictions may actually increase competition among competing brands; the wholesaler or retailer faces no competition from other dealers carrying the manufacturer's brand, so it can concentrate on effectively competing with other brands.

tying agreement An arrangement that requires a marketing intermediary to carry items other than those they want to sell.

The third legal question of exclusive distribution involves **tying agreements**, which allow channel members to become exclusive dealers only if they also carry products other than those that they want to sell. In the apparel industry, for example, an agreement might require a dealer to carry a comparatively unpopular line of clothing to get desirable, fast-moving items. Tying agreements are reviewable under the Competition Act and not an offence. These practices are, therefore, not prohibited unless an order has been obtained after a review by the Competition Tribunal. Prohibiting such practices is more likely to happen when they reduce competition or create monopolies that keep competitors out of major markets.

WHO SHOULD PERFORM CHANNEL FUNCTIONS?

A fundamental marketing principle governs channel decisions. A member of the channel must perform certain central marketing functions. Responsibilities of the different members may vary, however. Although independent wholesalers perform many functions for manufacturers, retailers, and other wholesaler clients, other channel members could fulfill these roles instead. A manufacturer might bypass its wholesalers by establishing regional warehouses, maintaining field sales forces, serving as sources of information for retail customers, or arranging details of financing. For years, auto manufacturers have operated credit units that offer new-car financing.

An independent intermediary earns a profit in exchange for providing services to manufacturers and retailers. This profit margin is low, however, ranging from 1 percent for food wholesalers to 5 percent for durable goods wholesalers. Manufacturers and retailers could retain these costs, or they could market directly and reduce retail prices—but only if they could perform the channel functions and match the efficiency of the independent intermediaries.

To grow profitably in a competitive environment, an intermediary must provide better service at lower costs than manufacturers or retailers can provide for themselves. In this case, consolidation of channel functions can represent a strategic opportunity for a company.

assessment check 2 ✓

2.1 Identify four major factors in selecting a marketing channel.

2.2 Describe the three general categories of distribution intensity.

③ **Describe the concepts of channel management, conflict, and cooperation.**

CHANNEL MANAGEMENT AND LEADERSHIP

Distribution strategy does not end with the choice of a channel. Manufacturers must also focus on channel management by developing and maintaining relationships with the intermediaries in their marketing channels. Positive channel relationships encourage channel members to remember their partners' goods and market them. Manufacturers also must carefully manage the incentives offered to induce channel members to promote their products. This effort includes weighing decisions about pricing, promotion, and other support efforts that the manufacturer performs.

Increasingly, marketers are managing channels in partnership with other channel members. Effective cooperation allows all channel members to achieve goals that they could not achieve on their own. Keys to successful management of channel relationships include the development of high levels of coordination, commitment, and trust between channel members.

Not all channel members wield equal power in the distribution chain, however. The dominant member of a marketing channel is called the **channel captain**. This firm's power to control a channel may result from its control over some type of reward or punishment to other channel members, such as granting an exclusive sales territory or taking away a dealership. Power might also result from contractual arrangements, specialized expert knowledge, or agreement among channel members about their mutual best interests.

In the grocery industry, consumer goods manufacturers, such as Procter & Gamble and Kraft Foods, once were considered channel captains. Today, retail giants such as Loblaw, Sobeys, Provigo, Safeway, and Costco face competition from discounters such as Giant Tiger and Dollarama. To survive in the competitive grocery industry, supermarket owners are diversifying their retail formats from traditional stores to include natural and organic and upscale items in their stores to satisfy a wider variety of customers, and to compete with chains such as Whole Foods Market and smaller specialty stores. But the pressure on traditional chains is coming from stores that have not traditionally been involved in the grocery market: Walmart, Target, and Shoppers Drug Mart. Walmart is continuing its expansion in the grocery market; in fact, its grocery receipts now account for 55 percent of its U.S. sales and it is continuing to expand its distribution within Canada. It recently opened a 400,000-square-foot fresh food distribution centre near Balzac, Alberta, and in 2014 announced plans for a new 500,000-square-foot distribution centre to be opened nearby.[13]

channel captain
Dominant and controlling member of a marketing channel.

CHANNEL CONFLICT

Marketing channels work smoothly only when members cooperate in well-organized efforts to achieve maximum operating efficiencies. Yet channel members often perform as separate, independent, and even competing forces. Two types of conflict—horizontal and vertical—may hinder the normal functioning of a marketing channel.

Horizontal Conflict

Horizontal conflict sometimes results from disagreements among channel members at the same level, such as two or more wholesalers or two or more retailers; or among marketing intermediaries of the same type, such as two competing discount stores or several retail florists. More often, horizontal conflict causes sparks between different types of marketing intermediaries that handle similar products. For example, Netflix, Streampix, Hulu, and Amazon all offer streaming video service, allowing subscribers to view movies and, especially, TV shows on their televisions, computers, or mobile devices. The networking equipment maker Cisco predicts that by 2018, there will be 1.4 mobile-connected devices for every person on earth: more than 10 billion such devices, including sensors, tablets, and smartphones. The company also estimates that about three-quarters of Internet traffic will be

The vertical conflict that arose when consumers made their own travel arrangements online has been mostly resolved as consumers rely increasingly on travel advisors to help them plan the right vacation.

H. F. (Herb) MacKenzie

streamed video. Although carriers are trying to slow down the rush of video use on mobile devices by charging higher prices for heavy data consumption, more and more people are buying and using smartphones that can carry videos, especially with some models of smartphones now available for less than $100.[14]

Vertical Conflict

Vertical relationships may result in frequent and severe conflict. Channel members at different levels find many reasons for disputes, such as when retailers develop private brands to compete with producers' brands, or when producers establish their own retail stores or create mail-order operations that compete with retailers. Producers may annoy wholesalers and retailers when they attempt to bypass these intermediaries and sell directly to consumers. When booking plane flights and other travel arrangements online first became feasible, travellers dispensed with the services of travel agents and made their own arrangements. But it can sometimes take several hours to search airline websites to find the best combination of price and travel dates. In the wake of the recession, travellers have become much more cautious about spending money. And they have gotten much choosier about exactly what kind of vacation they want. Thus travel agencies are experiencing a revival. Their job is also changing as they develop long-term, more advisory relationships with their clients.[15]

THE GREY MARKET

grey goods Goods produced for sale in one market and then diverted to another market.

Another type of channel conflict results from activities in the grey market. As Canadian manufacturers license their technology and brands abroad, they sometimes find themselves in competition in the Canadian market against versions of their own brands produced by overseas affiliates. These **grey goods**, goods produced for sale in one market and then diverted to another market, enter Canadian channels through the actions of unauthorized foreign distributors. While licensing agreements usually prohibit foreign licensees from selling in Canada, and exclusive distribution agreements prohibit manufacturers from selling to non-authorized Canadian resellers, no such rules inhibit their distributors. Other countries also have grey markets. For example, while Amazon is not licensed to sell its Kindle in China, the product is available on China's grey market.

Similarly, even before the iPad's official global release, enterprising individuals had bought them up for resale at an inflated price in Hong Kong. A recent study indicated that half of iPad sales in China have been from the grey market.[16]

assessment check 3 ✓

3.1 What is a channel captain? What is its role in channel cooperation?

3.2 Identify and describe the three types of channel conflict.

ACHIEVING CHANNEL COOPERATION

vertical marketing system (VMS) Planned channel system designed to improve distribution efficiency and cost effectiveness by integrating various functions throughout the distribution chain.

The basic antidote to channel conflict is effective cooperation among channel members. Cooperation is best achieved when all channel members regard themselves as equal components of the same organization. The channel captain is primarily responsible for providing the leadership necessary to achieve this kind of cooperation.

Imax, Sony, and Discovery Communications formed a joint venture to create a 3-D television channel. The new channel, to be distributed by Discovery, will present a programming mix that includes sports, entertainment, and some natural-history shows.[17]

④ Identify and describe the different vertical marketing systems.

VERTICAL MARKETING SYSTEMS

Efforts to reduce channel conflict and improve the effectiveness of distribution have led to the development of vertical marketing systems. A **vertical marketing system (VMS)** is a planned channel system designed to improve distribution efficiency and cost effectiveness by integrating various functions throughout the distribution chain.

A vertical marketing system can achieve this goal through either forward or backward integration. In **forward integration**, a firm attempts to control downstream distribution. For example, a manufacturer might set up a retail chain to sell its products. **Backward integration** occurs when a firm attempts to gain greater control over inputs in its production process. A manufacturer might acquire the supplier of a raw material the manufacturer uses in the production of its products. Backward integration can also extend the control of retailers and wholesalers over producers that supply them.

A VMS offers several benefits. First, it improves chances for controlling and coordinating the steps in the distribution or production process. It may lead to the development of economies of scale that ultimately saves money. A VMS may also let a manufacturer expand into profitable new businesses. However, a VMS also involves some costs. A manufacturer assumes increased risk when it takes control of an entire distribution chain. Manufacturers may also discover that they lose some flexibility in responding to market changes.

Marketers have developed three categories of VMSs: corporate systems, administered systems, and contractual systems. These categories are outlined in the sections that follow.

CORPORATE AND ADMINISTERED SYSTEMS

When a single owner runs organizations at each stage of the marketing channel, it operates a **corporate marketing system**. Roots, for example, sells its branded products through more than 120 retail locations in Canada and the United States, and close to 100 stores in Asia.[18] An **administered marketing system** achieves channel coordination when a dominant channel member exercises its power. Even though Goodyear sells its tires through independently owned and operated dealerships, it controls the stock that these dealerships carry. Another example of a channel captain leading an administered channel is McKesson Canada, a health care technology company and pharmaceutical distributor.

CONTRACTUAL SYSTEMS

Instead of common ownership of intermediaries within a corporate VMS or the exercising of power within an administered system, a **contractual marketing system** coordinates distribution through formal agreements among channel members. In practice, three types of agreements set up these systems: wholesaler-sponsored voluntary chains, retail cooperatives, and franchises.

Wholesaler-Sponsored Voluntary Chain

Sometimes an independent wholesaler will try to preserve a market by strengthening its retail customers through a wholesaler-sponsored voluntary chain. The wholesaler adopts a formal agreement with its retailers to use a common name and standardized facilities and to purchase the wholesaler's goods. The wholesaler may even develop a line of private brands to be stocked by the retailers. This practice often helps smaller retailers compete with rival chains—and strengthens the wholesaler's position as well.

True Value Company has approximately $2 billion in sales through its more than 4,000 retail locations that serve 54 countries.[19] Because a single advertisement will promote all the retailers in the trading area, a common store name and similar inventories allow it to save on advertising costs.

Retail Cooperative

In a second type of contractual VMS, a group of retailers establishes a shared wholesaling operation to help them compete with chains. This is known as a **retail cooperative**. The retailers purchase ownership shares in the wholesaling operation and agree to buy a minimum percentage of their inventories from this operation.

forward integration
Process through which a firm attempts to control downstream distribution.

backward integration Process through which a firm attempts to gain greater control over inputs in its production process, such as raw materials.

corporate marketing system VMS in which a single owner operates the entire marketing channel.

administered marketing system VMS that achieves channel coordination when a dominant channel member exercises its power.

contractual marketing system VMS that coordinates channel activities through formal agreements among participants.

Wee Piggies & Paws was started by mompreneur Debbie Cornelius as a home-based business and now has franchise locations in Canada, the United States, Mexico, and the United Kingdom.

retail cooperative
Group of retailers that establish a shared wholesaling operation to help them compete with chains.

franchise Contractual arrangement in which a wholesaler or retailer agrees to meet the operating requirements of a manufacturer or other franchiser.

The members typically adopt a common store name and develop common private brands. Home Hardware is a Canadian retail cooperative.

Franchise

A third type of contractual vertical marketing system is the **franchise**, in which a wholesaler or dealer (the franchisee) agrees to meet the operating requirements of a manufacturer or other franchiser. Franchising is a huge and growing industry. There are more than 78,000 franchise units (franchisees) in Canada, controlled by more than 1,000 franchisors. Thirty-five percent of all sales in the restaurant sector in Canada come from franchise operations, while 45 percent of all retail sales do.[20] Among the most popular franchise operations in Canada are Canadian Tire, Rona, Subway, 7-Eleven, RE/MAX, Tim Hortons, and M&M Meat Shops.

Franchise owners pay anywhere from several thousand to more than a million dollars to purchase and set up a franchise. Typically, they also pay a royalty on sales to the franchising company. In exchange for these initial and ongoing fees, the franchise owner receives the right to use the company's brand name as well as services such as training, marketing, advertising, and volume discounts. Major franchise chains justify the steep price of entry since it allows new businesses to sell winning brands. But if the brand enters a slump or the corporation behind the franchise makes poor strategic decisions, franchisees are often hurt.

assessment check 4

4.1 What are vertical marketing systems (VMSs)? Identify the major types.

4.2 Identify the three types of contractual marketing systems.

⑤ **Explain the roles of logistics and supply-chain management in an overall distribution strategy.**

LOGISTICS AND SUPPLY-CHAIN MANAGEMENT

Pier 1 imports its eclectic mix of items from vendors in more than 50 countries, most representing small companies. If high-demand items or seasonal products are late into its six North American distribution centres or are shipped in insufficient quantities, the company may miss opportunities to deliver popular shopping choices to its more than 1,000 retail stores and could lose ground to such competitors as Pottery Barn and Crate and Barrel. The situation facing Pier 1 illustrates the importance of logistics. Careful coordination of Pier 1's supplier network, shipping processes, and inventory control is the key to its continuing success. In addition, the store's buyers develop relationships with suppliers in all participating countries.[21]

supply chain Complete sequence of suppliers and activities that contribute to the creation and delivery of merchandise.

upstream management Controlling part of the supply chain that involves raw materials, inbound logistics, and warehouse and storage facilities.

downstream management Controlling part of the supply chain that involves finished product storage, outbound logistics, marketing and sales, and customer service.

Effective logistics requires proper supply-chain management, the control of activities of purchasing, processing, and delivery through which raw materials are transformed into products and made available to final consumers. The **supply chain**, also known as the *value chain,* is the complete sequence of suppliers and activities that contribute to the creation and delivery of goods and services. The supply chain begins with the raw-material inputs for the manufacturing process of a product and then proceeds to the actual production activities. The final link in the supply chain is the movement of finished products through the marketing channel to customers. Each link of the chain benefits the consumers as raw materials move through manufacturing to distribution. The chain encompasses all activities that enhance the value of the finished goods, including design, quality manufacturing, customer service, and delivery. Customer satisfaction results directly from the perceived value of a purchase to its buyer.

To manage the supply chain, businesses must look for ways to maximize customer value in each activity they perform. Supply-chain management takes place in two directions: upstream and downstream, as illustrated in Figure 12.2. **Upstream management** involves managing raw materials, inbound logistics, and warehouse and storage facilities. **Downstream management** involves managing finished product storage, outbound logistics, marketing and sales, and customer service.

Companies choose a variety of methods for managing the supply chain. They can include high-tech systems such as radio-frequency identification (discussed in the next section) and regular person-to-person meetings. JDA Software Group helps other businesses track and manage their global supply chains. Using its proprietary software, JDA helps its clients enhance customer service and improve inventory management.[22] Logistics plays a major role in giving customers what they

figure 12.2

The Supply Chain of a Manufacturing Company

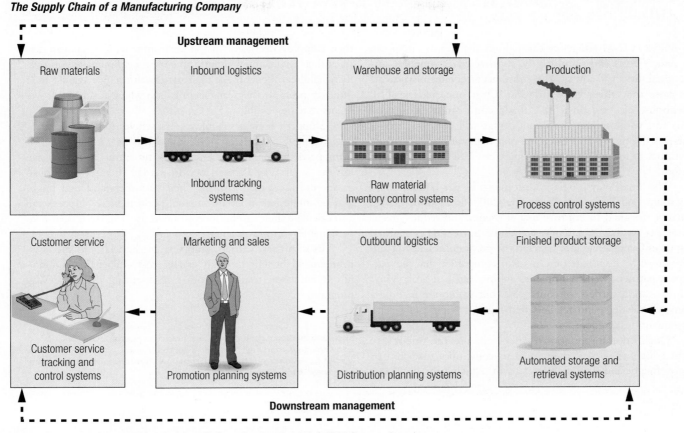

Source: From STAIR/REYNOLDS, *Principles of Information Systems*, 7E. © 2006 Cengage Learning.

need when they need it and thus is central in the supply chain. Another important component of this chain, *value-added service*, adds some improved or supplemental service that customers do not normally receive or expect. The following sections examine methods for streamlining and managing logistics and the supply chain as part of an overall distribution strategy. The "Marketing: Making Your World Better" feature explains how the SmartWay program is helping many Canadian companies improve their environmental performance.

RADIO FREQUENCY IDENTIFICATION (RFID)

One tool that marketers are using to help manage logistics is **radio frequency identification (RFID)** technology. With RFID, a tiny chip with identification information that can be read from a distance by a radio-frequency scanner is placed on an item. These chips are already widely used in tollway pass transmitters, allowing drivers to zip through toll booths without stopping or rolling down their windows to toss change into baskets.

They are also embedded in employee ID cards that workers use to open office doors without keys. But businesses such as retail giant Walmart, manufacturer Procter & Gamble, credit card firms MasterCard and Visa, and German retailer Metro AG are eagerly putting the technology to wider use; they say it will speed deliveries, make consumer bar codes obsolete, and provide marketers with valuable information about consumer preferences. Walmart requires its biggest suppliers to attach RFID tags to pallets and cases of products such as Coca-Cola and Dove soap, saying that the technology will vastly improve its ability to track inventory and keep the right amount of products in stock.

radio frequency identification (RFID) Technology that uses a tiny chip with identification information that can be read from a distance by a scanner using radio waves.

MARKETING: MAKING YOUR WORLD BETTER — SmartWay: A Win-Win-Win-Win Program

IMPROVING efficiency throughout the supply chain can reduce costs and significantly improve environmental sustainability. Of course, the most necessary improvements are those that affect transportation. Over one-quarter of all greenhouse gas emissions in Canada come from transportation, and without improvements things will continue to get worse as the number of tractor-trailer registrations in Canada continues to increase, up nearly one-third in a recent five-year period.

The SmartWay program, introduced by the United States Environmental Protection Agency in 2004, is a public-private initiative designed to improve fuel efficiency and reduce greenhouse gas emissions and air pollution. Since 2012, Natural Resources Canada has administered the program in Canada and there are now hundreds of Canadian companies that are participant partners. What companies are interested in SmartWay? Transportation carriers, of course, are, but so too are manufacturers, wholesalers, and retailers that regularly ship and receive large quantities of goods.

Qualified transportation carriers can use the SmartWay Partner logo to market themselves to companies that ship or receive freight and that are interested in reducing the impact of

their shipping decisions on the environment. Carriers can also track their environmental performance to help manage improvement, and can benchmark their own performance against their industry peers so they can begin to see where future improvements may be possible.

Shippers, such as manufacturers, wholesalers, and retailers, that regularly make transportation decisions can also benefit from participating in the SmartWay program. They too can use the SmartWay Partner logo to market themselves to businesses and consumers that are their customers and that might also be interested in environmental performance. Shippers can also calculate their carbon footprint and use it to track their own sustainability improvements.

In summary, carriers, shippers, consumers, and the environment all benefit through greater cost efficiencies and pollution reduction resulting from implementing the SmartWay program.

Sources: Supply Chain Management Association, "SmartWay Comes to Canada," http://scmanational.ca; Environmental Protection Agency, "About SmartWay," www.epa.gov/smartway; Natural Resources Canada, "SmartWay," www.nrcan.gc.ca/energy/efficiency/transportation/commercial-vehicles/smartway/7615, all accessed May 1, 2014.

Several manufacturers have released an iPhone case with a built-in RFID reader, active RFID tags, and software that allows a user to alert friends, find people or things, or create a "virtual leash."[23]

ENTERPRISE RESOURCE PLANNING

enterprise resource planning (ERP) system Software system that consolidates data from among a firm's various business units.

Software is an important aspect of logistics management and the supply chain. An **enterprise resource planning (ERP) system** is an integrated software system that consolidates data from among the firm's units. Roughly two-thirds of ERP system users are manufacturers concerned with production issues such as sequencing and scheduling. German software giant SAP offers systems that allow businesses to manage their customer relations. Recently, ERP suppliers have begun offering cloud-based technology, with its emphasis on subscription-based solutions.[24]

As valuable as it is, ERP and its related software aren't always perfect. For example, ERP failures were blamed for Hershey's inability to fulfill all its candy orders during one Halloween period, when a fall-off in sales was blamed on a combination of shipping delays, inability to fill orders, and partial shipments while candy stockpiled in warehouses. Several major retailers were forced to shift their purchases to other candy vendors.

LOGISTICAL COST CONTROL

In addition to enhancing their products by providing value-added services to customers, many firms are focusing on logistics for another important reason: to cut costs. Distribution functions currently represent almost half of a typical firm's total marketing costs. To reduce logistical costs, businesses are re-examining each link of their supply chains to identify activities that do not add value for customers. By eliminating, reducing, or redesigning these activities, they can often cut costs and boost efficiency. As just described, new technologies such as RFID can save businesses millions—or even billions—of dollars.

Because of increased security requirements in recent years, businesses involved in importing and exporting have faced a major rise in logistical costs. U.S. Customs and Border Protection has initiated a voluntary program for transportation carriers that requires them to ensure the integrity of their own security practices. Canadian carriers that participate in the Customs-Trade Partnership Against Terrorism (C-TPAT) program are much less likely to have their shipments undergo a security exam at the border and are eligible to receive expedited service at major border crossings.[25]

Third-Party Logistics

Some companies try to cut costs and offer value-added services by outsourcing some or all of their logistics functions to specialist firms. **Third-party (contract) logistics firms** (3PL firms) specialize in handling logistical activities for their clients. Third-party logistics is a huge industry, estimated to exceed $250 billion among the global Fortune 500 companies. Walmart, Procter & Gamble, and General Motors each use 50 or more 3PLs.[26]

Through outsourcing alliances, producers and logistical service suppliers cooperate in developing innovative, customized systems that speed goods through carefully constructed manufacturing and distribution pipelines. Although many companies have long outsourced transportation and warehousing functions, today's alliance partners use similar methods to combine their operations.

third-party (contract) logistics firm Company that specializes in handling logistics activities for other firms.

assessment check 5

5.1 What is upstream management? What is downstream management?

5.2 Identify three methods for managing logistics.

PHYSICAL DISTRIBUTION

(6) Identify the major components of a physical distribution system.

A firm's physical distribution system is an organized group of components linked according to a plan for achieving specific distribution objectives. It contains the following elements:

1. *Customer service.* What level of customer service the distribution activities should support.

2. *Transportation.* How the firm should ship its products.

3. *Inventory control.* How much inventory the firm should maintain at each location.

4. *Protective packaging and materials handling.* How the firm can package and efficiently handle goods in the factory, warehouse, and transport terminals.

5. *Order processing.* How the firm should handle orders.

6. *Warehousing.* Where the distribution system will locate stocks of goods and the number of warehouses the firm should maintain.

All these components function in interrelated ways. Decisions made in one area affect efficiency in others. The physical distribution manager must balance each component so that the system avoids stressing any single aspect to the detriment of overall functioning. A firm might decide to reduce transportation costs by shipping its products by less costly—but slow—water transportation. But slow deliveries would likely force the firm to maintain higher inventory levels, raising those costs. This mismatch between system elements often leads to increased production costs. So balancing the components is crucial.

The general shift from a manufacturing economy to a service economy in Canada has affected physical distribution in two key ways. First, customers require more flexible—yet reliable—transportation service. Second, the number of smaller shipments is growing much faster than the number of large shipments. Although traditional, high-volume shipments will continue to grow, they will represent a lower percentage of the transportation industry's revenues and volume.

THE PROBLEM OF SUBOPTIMIZATION

Logistics managers seek to establish a specified level of customer service while minimizing the costs of physically moving and storing goods. Marketers must first decide on their priorities for customer service and then figure out how to fulfill those goals by moving goods at the best cost. Meshing together all the physical distribution elements is a huge challenge that firms don't always meet.

suboptimization
Condition that results when individual operations achieve their objectives but interfere with progress toward broader organizational goals.

Suboptimization results when the managers of individual physical distribution functions attempt to minimize costs, but the impact of one task on the others leads to less than optimal results. Imagine a hockey team composed of record-holding players. Unfortunately, despite the individual talents of the players, the team fails to win a game. This is an example of suboptimization. The same thing can happen at a company when each logistics activity is judged by its own accomplishments instead of the way it contributes to the overall goals of the firm. Suboptimization often happens when a firm introduces a new product that may not fit easily into its current physical distribution system.

Effective management of the physical distribution function requires some cost trade-offs. By accepting relatively high costs in some functional areas to cut costs in others, managers can minimize their firm's total physical distribution costs. Of course, any reduction in logistical costs should support progress toward the goal of maintaining customer-service standards.

CUSTOMER-SERVICE STANDARDS

Customer-service standards state the goals and define acceptable performance for the quality of service that a firm expects to deliver to its customers. Internet retailers such as CanadaFlowers.ca thrive because of their ability to ship within hours of receiving an order. This company accepts orders 360-plus days per year and, through an established network of local florists, can deliver the same day to most towns and cities across Canada.[27] An auto repair shop might set a standard to complete oil changes within 30 minutes. A business might set a standard to answer incoming phone calls within three rings. All are examples of customer service standards.

Designers of a physical distribution system begin by establishing acceptable levels of customer service. These designers then assemble physical distribution components in a way that will achieve this standard at the lowest possible total cost. This overall cost breaks down into five components: (1) transportation, (2) warehousing, (3) customer service/order processing, (4) administrative costs, and (5) inventory control.

TRANSPORTATION

The transportation industry employs approximately 900,000 Canadians, making it extremely important to the Canadian economy aside from the movement of goods across Canada or between Canada and its many trade partners. It was largely deregulated a number of years ago.[28] Deregulation has been particularly important for motor carriers, railroads, and air carriers. Many transporters are now free to develop unique solutions to shippers' needs. The trucking industry now operates far more efficiently than it did under government regulation; many carriers have reduced empty mileage by two-thirds. Approximately 11 million trucks cross the Canada–U.S. border each year.[29] Railroads are enjoying a new boom: once hauling mostly commodities like corn and grain, they now transport cross-country the huge loads of goods coming from China through coastal ports. Railroads can move a greater amount of freight for less fuel than trucks. Canadian National Railway (CN) and Canadian Pacific Railway (CP) are the two dominant freight rail operators. Together, they carry about 75 percent of overall tonnage, but account for more than 95 percent of annual rail tonne-kilometres. CN crosses Canada from coast to coast and follows the Mississippi River to the Gulf of Mexico as the result of a number of U.S. acquisitions. CP operates 22,500 route-kilometres through six Canadian provinces and 13 U.S. states.[30]

Typically adding 10 percent to the cost of a product, transportation and delivery expenses represent the largest

H. F. (Herb) MacKenzie

Trucks are very important for moving products across Canada and between Canada and the United States. Approximately 11 million trucks cross the Canada–U.S. border every year.

category of logistics-related costs for most firms. Also, for many items—particularly perishable ones such as fresh fish or produce—transportation makes a central contribution to satisfactory customer service.

Many logistics managers have found that the key to controlling their shipping costs is careful management of relationships with shipping firms. Freight carriers use two basic rates: class and commodity rates. A class rate is a standard rate for a specific commodity moving between any pair of destinations. A carrier may charge a lower commodity rate, sometimes called a *special rate,* to a favoured shipper as a reward for either regular business or a large-quantity shipment. Railroads and inland water carriers frequently reward customers in this way. In addition, the railroad and motor carrier industries sometimes supplement this rate structure with negotiated, or contract, rates. In other words, the two parties finalize terms of rates, services, and other variables in a contract.

Classes of Carriers

Freight carriers are classified as common, contract, and private carriers. **Common carriers**, often considered the backbone of the transportation industry, provide transportation services as for-hire carriers to the general public. The government still regulates their rates and services, and they cannot conduct their operations without permission from the appropriate regulatory authority. Common carriers move freight via all modes of transport. FedEx is a major common carrier serving businesses and consumers. One way the firm remains competitive is by developing new methods for enhancing customer service. FedEx has a service called InSight, a free online service that essentially reverses the package-tracking process—instead of following a package from shipment to delivery, customers can go online to find out what is going to be delivered to them that day. One FedEx customer that has benefited greatly from this new service is a greenhouse, which ships perishable goods—begonias, miniature poinsettias, and other plants—to florists and nursery departments of such big-box stores as Home Depot, Lowe's, and Walmart. With InSight, the company can easily track the status of its shipments.[31]

Contract carriers are for-hire transporters that do not offer their services to the general public. Instead, they establish contracts with individual customers and operate exclusively for particular industries, such as the motor freight industry. These carriers operate under much looser regulations than common carriers.

Private carriers do not offer services for hire. These carriers provide transportation services solely for internally generated freight. As a result, they observe no rate or service regulations. Many large retailers operate their own private fleets in Canada.

common carriers Businesses that provide transportation services as for-hire carriers to the general public.

contract carriers For-hire transporters that do not offer their services to the general public.

private carriers Transporters that provide service solely for internally generated freight.

> ## assessment check 6 ✓
>
> **6.1 What are the six major elements of physical distribution?**
>
> **6.2 What is suboptimization?**

Major Transportation Modes

Logistics managers choose among five major transportation alternatives: railroads, motor carriers, water carriers, pipelines, and air freight. Each mode has its own unique characteristics. Logistics managers select the best options by matching these features to their specific transportation needs.

⑦ **Compare the major modes of transportation.**

Railroads

Railroads continue to control the largest share of the freight business as measured by tonne-kilometres. The term *tonne-kilometre* indicates shipping activity required to move one tonne of freight one kilometre. Rail shipments quickly rack up tonne-kilometres because this mode provides the most efficient way to move bulky commodities over long distances. Rail carriers generally transport huge quantities of coal, chemicals, grain, nonmetallic minerals, lumber and wood products, and automobiles. The railroads have improved their service standards through a number of innovative concepts, such as unit trains, run-through trains, **intermodal operations**, and double-stack container trains. Unit trains carry much of the coal, grain, and other high-volume commodities shipped, running back and forth between single loading points (such as a mine) and single destinations (such as a power plant) to deliver a commodity. Run-through trains bypass intermediate terminals to speed up schedules. They work similarly to unit trains, but a run-through train may carry a variety of commodities.

intermodal operations Combination of transport modes such as rail and highway carriers (piggyback), air and highway carriers (birdyback), and water and highway carriers (fishyback) to improve customer service and achieve cost advantages.

Marketoid

Canadian railways carry more than 310 million tonnes of freight annually and consume about 1.9 billion litres of fuel. There are more than 46,000 kilometres of railway tracks in Canada. Share of transportation and warehousing GDP by transportation mode: truck (28.4 percent), air (9.2 percent), rail (8.6 percent), pipeline (8.2 percent), and water (1.8 percent).

In piggyback operations, one of the intermodal operations, highway trailers and containers ride on railroad flatcars, thus combining the long-haul capacity of the train with the door-to-door flexibility of the truck. A double-stack container train pulls special rail cars equipped with bathtub-shaped wells so they can carry two containers stacked on top of one another. By nearly doubling train capacity and slashing costs, this system offers enormous advantages to rail customers. Both Canadian Pacific Railway and Canadian National Railway are focused on lowering fuel consumption and smog-causing emissions. With modern aerodynamically designed double-stacked intermodal freight trains, it is possible to replace as many as 300 trucks on the highway, greatly reducing emissions and stress on roads and bridges.[32]

Motor Carriers

Canadian for-hire truckers haul more than 224 billion tonne-kilometres of freight annually: 61 percent of it domestically and 39 percent of it internationally. Approximately $1.5 billion in trade crosses the Canada–U.S. border daily, and 57 percent of that, by value, is by truck.[33] Trucking offers some important advantages over the other transportation modes, including relatively fast shipments and consistent service for both large and small shipments. Motor carriers concentrate on shipping manufactured products, while railroads typically haul bulk shipments of raw materials.

Technology is also improving the efficiency of trucking. Walmart Canada and Innovative Trailer Design recently unveiled the Supercube trailer. It is 14 percent longer than a conventional trailer and has a lower floor and a "dromedary" box behind the cab. These trailers carry 28 percent more freight and are only 3 percent heavier than conventional trailers. In a recent pilot study using these trailers, Walmart Canada was able to reduce transportation costs by 24 percent and cut greenhouse gas emissions by 14 percent.[34] Many trucking firms now track their fleets via satellite communications systems, and in-truck computer systems allow drivers and dispatchers to make last-minute changes in scheduling and delivery. The Internet is also adding new features to motor carrier services.

Even so, the trucking industry must adjust to changes in the marketing environment. Trucking firms report a shortage of long-haul drivers, causing delays in some deliveries and higher costs, along with the rising cost of fuel, to customers. Some firms offer drivers regional runs and dedicated routes for more predictable work hours, as well as better pay. They also recruit husband-and-wife teams for the long-haul routes, which is becoming a popular practice.

Water Carriers

Two basic types of transport methods move products over water: inland or barge lines and ocean-going, deepwater ships. Barge lines efficiently transport bulky, low-unit-value commodities such as grain, gravel, lumber, sand, and steel. Montreal-based Canada Steamship Lines operates a fleet of 20 self-unloaders and bulk carriers on the Great Lakes–St. Lawrence Waterway system.[35]

Ocean-going ships carry a growing stream of containerized freight between ports around the world. Vancouver, Canada's largest port, handled 135 million tonnes of cargo in 2013.[36] Supertankers from global companies such as Maersk Sealand are the size of three football fields, almost double the capacity of other vessels. At full capacity, the ships can cut the cost of shipping a container across the Pacific by one-fifth. Shippers that transport goods via water carriers incur very low costs compared to the rates for other transportation modes. Standardized modular shipping containers maximize savings by limiting loading, unloading, and other handling. Canada's four major container ports have all experienced growth in recent years, measured in 20-foot equivalent units (TEUs). In 2012, Vancouver handled 2.7 million TEUs, Montreal handled 1.4 million, Prince Rupert handled 565,000, and Halifax handled 417,000.[37]

Ships often carry large refrigerated containers, called reefers, for transporting such varied items as fresh produce and medical supplies. These containers, along with their non-refrigerated counterparts, improve shipping efficiency because they can easily be removed from a ship and attached to trucks or trains. Although shipping by water has traditionally been less expensive than other modes of transportation, costs for this mode have increased dramatically because of tightened security measures. Freight rates are based on the size of the vessel, the cost of fuel, and security requirements.

DHL XML Services offers a fully integrated Web service that advises clients of DHL's availability, shipping times, and rates; provides for shipment and courier booking; and has a shipment tracking capability from over 140 countries. It also features in-house label printing and tracking. The company's totally customizable EDI Solutions provides for large-volume shipping and multi-site logistical operations.[38]

The expansion of the Panama Canal should be completed within the next few years. Once it is widened and deepened, the Panama Canal will allow larger-sized ships to pass through the all-water route from Asia to Canada's Atlantic coast. The expansion will double the amount of freight that can go through the canal and will have a significant impact on distribution.

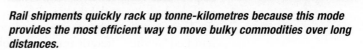

Rail shipments quickly rack up tonne-kilometres because this mode provides the most efficient way to move bulky commodities over long distances.

Pipelines

Although the pipeline industry ranks third after railroads and motor carriers in tonne-kilometres transported, many people scarcely recognize its existence. Oil pipelines carry two types of commodities: crude (unprocessed) oil and refined products, such as gasoline, jet fuel, and kerosene. In addition, one so-called *slurry pipeline* carries coal in suspension after it has been ground up into a powder and mixed with water. TransCanada Pipelines owns about 68,500 kilometres of pipeline and transports most of Western Canada's natural gas to markets in Canada and the United States.[39] Enbridge is Canada's largest transporter of crude oil and delivers more than 2.2 million barrels per day of crude oil and liquids through its 24,738-kilometre system, the world's longest system.[40]

Although pipelines offer low maintenance and dependable methods of transportation, a number of characteristics limit their applications. They have fewer locations than water carriers, and they can accommodate shipments of only a small number of products. Finally, pipelines represent a relatively slow method of transportation; liquids travel through this method at an average speed of only five to six kilometres per hour.

Air Freight

Although the air freight industry grew steadily for many years, recently that growth has levelled off—at least in certain market sectors, such as overnight delivery service. But firms are adapting. UPS recently revamped its services, now offering an expanded international express service called UPS Express Freight. The service provides guaranteed time-definite, overnight to three-day door-to-door delivery, including customs clearance, to large global metropolitan areas. UPS is also offering two less expensive, nonguaranteed services: UPS Air Freight Direct and UPS Air Freight Consolidated. Both are available worldwide and provide package pickup, delivery, and customs clearance.[41] Purolator Courier remains Canada's largest domestic air shipper, handling more than 1.4 million pieces for pick-up and delivery each day. Purolator handles more than 196,000 kilograms of air freight each night.[42]

Comparing the Five Modes of Transport

Table 12.2 compares the five transportation modes on several operating characteristics. Although all shippers judge reliability, speed, and cost in choosing the most appropriate transportation methods, they assign varying

> **Marketoid**
>
> In one recent year, Air Canada earned $131 million on revenues of $12.1 billion; WestJet earned $242.2 million on revenues of $3.4 billion.

TransCanada Pipelines transports most of Western Canada's natural gas to markets in Canada and the United States.

table 12.2 **Comparison of Transport Modes**

MODE	SPEED	DEPENDABILITY IN MEETING SCHEDULES	FREQUENCY OF SHIPMENTS	AVAILABILITY IN DIFFERENT LOCATIONS	FLEXIBILITY IN HANDLING	COST
Rail	Average	Average	Low	Low	High	Average
Water	Very slow	Average	Very low	Limited	Very high	Very low
Truck	Fast	High	High	Very extensive	Average	High
Pipeline	Slow	High	High	Very limited	Very low	Low
Air	Very fast	High	Average	Average	Low	Very high

importance to specific criteria when shipping different goods. For example, while motor carriers rank highest in availability in different locations, shippers of petroleum products frequently choose the lowest-ranked alternative, pipelines, for their low cost. Examples of types of goods most often handled by the different transports follow:

- *Railroads:* lumber, iron, steel, coal, automobiles, grain, chemicals;
- *Motor carriers:* clothing, furniture, fixtures, lumber, plastic, food, leather, machinery;
- *Water carriers:* fuel, oil, coal, chemicals, minerals, and petroleum products; automobiles, electronics, and many low-value products from foreign manufacturers;
- *Pipelines:* oil, diesel fuel, jet fuel, kerosene, natural gas; and
- *Air freight:* flowers, medical testing kits, and gourmet food products directly to consumers.

assessment check 7 ✓

7.1 Identify the five major modes of transport.

7.2 Which mode of transport is currently experiencing resurgence, and why?

⑧ **Discuss the role of transportation intermediaries, combined transportation modes, and warehousing in improving physical distribution.**

Freight Forwarders and Supplemental Carriers

Freight forwarders act as transportation intermediaries, consolidating shipments to gain lower rates for their customers. The transport rates on less-than-truckload (LTL) and less-than-carload (LCL) shipments often double the per-unit rates on truckload (TL) and carload (CL) shipments. Freight forwarders charge less than the highest rates but more than the lowest rates. They profit by consolidating shipments from many customers until they can ship at TL and CL rates. The customers gain two advantages from these services: lower costs on small shipments and faster delivery service than they could achieve with their own LTL and LCL shipments.

In addition to the transportation options reviewed so far, a logistics manager can ship products via a number of auxiliary, or supplemental, carriers that specialize in small shipments. These carriers include Purolator, Canpar, UPS, FedEx, and Canada Post.

Intermodal Coordination

Transportation companies emphasize specific modes and serve certain kinds of customers, but they sometimes combine their services to give shippers the service and cost advantages of each. *Piggyback* service, mentioned in the section on rail transport, is the most widely used form of intermodal coordination. *Birdyback* service, another form of intermodal coordination, sends motor carriers to pick up a shipment locally and deliver that shipment to local destinations; an air carrier takes it between airports near

H. F. (Herb) MacKenzie

Distribution warehouses assemble and redistribute goods, keeping them moving as much as possible.

those locations. *Fishyback* service sets up a similar intermodal coordination system between motor carriers and water carriers.

Intermodal transportation generally gives shippers faster service and lower rates than either mode could match individually because each method carries freight in its most efficient way. However, intermodal arrangements require close coordination between all transportation providers.

Recognizing this need, multimodal transportation companies have formed to offer combined activities within single operations. Piggyback service generally joins two separate companies—a railroad and a trucking company. A multimodal firm provides intermodal service through its own internal transportation resources. Shippers benefit because the single service assumes responsibility from origin to destination. This unification prevents disputes over which carrier delayed or damaged a shipment.

WAREHOUSING

Products flow through two types of warehouses: storage and distribution warehouses. A storage warehouse holds goods for moderate to long periods in an attempt to balance supply and demand for producers and purchasers. For example, Conestoga Cold Storage operates five fully automated controlled-atmosphere—also called *cold storage*—warehouses in Canada. It has a total storage volume of 27 million cubic feet where it stores and consolidates shipments to serve all points in Canada and the United States.[43] In contrast, a *distribution warehouse* assembles and redistributes goods, keeping them moving as much as possible. Many distribution warehouses or centres physically store goods for less than 24 hours before shipping them to customers.

Logistics managers have attempted to save on transportation costs by developing central distribution centres. A manufacturer might send a single, large, consolidated shipment to a break-bulk centre—a central distribution centre that breaks down large shipments into several smaller ones and delivers them to individual customers in the area. Many Internet retailers use break-bulk distribution centres.

Cornwall, Ontario, a small town of 46,000 people, is becoming one of the most important distribution hubs for eastern Canada. A general merchandise distribution centre was built there more than a decade ago to serve Walmart locations in eastern Ontario, Quebec, and the Atlantic provinces. Today, the facility employs more than 1,000 associates and covers 1.42 million square feet. Shoppers Drug Mart, The Benson Group, and Target Canada also have large distribution centres there. Cornwall offers the advantage of being close to Montreal, a city with a metropolitan-area population of nearly 4 million people, but the town is in Ontario, a friendlier business environment: lower land prices, business taxes, property taxes, and fuel costs; a larger nonunionized labour force; and less political bureaucracy. In addition, Ontario-based companies do not have to contend with Quebec's strict language and labour policies.[44] As long as these political conditions exist, Cornwall will likely continue to see increased jobs and business opportunities at the expense of Quebec.

Automated Warehouse Technology

Logistics managers can cut distribution costs and improve customer service dramatically by automating their warehouse systems. Although automation technology represents an expensive investment, it can provide major labour savings for high-volume distributors such as grocery chains. A computerized system might store orders, choose the correct number of cases, and move those cases in the desired sequence to loading docks. This kind of warehouse system reduces labour costs, worker injuries, pilferage, fires, and breakage.

Warehouse Locations

Every company must make a major logistics decision when it determines the number and locations of its storage facilities. Two categories of costs influence this choice: (1) warehousing and materials handling costs and (2) delivery costs from warehouses to customers. Large facilities offer economies of scale in facilities and materials handling systems; per-unit costs for these systems decrease as volume increases. Delivery costs, on the other hand, rise as the distance from warehouse to customer increases.

Warehouse location also affects customer service. Businesses must place their storage and distribution facilities in locations from which they can meet customer demands for product availability and delivery times. They must also consider population and employment trends. For example, because of Moncton's central location in the Atlantic region, many firms have established distribution centres in the area. Pratt & Whitney Canada, a designer and manufacturer of aircraft engines, has eight distribution centres and can deliver parts anywhere in the world within 12 hours. Locations include Sydney, Australia; Singapore; Amsterdam, Holland; and Memphis, Tennessee.[45]

INVENTORY CONTROL SYSTEMS

Inventory control captures a large share of a logistics manager's attention because companies need to maintain enough inventory to meet customer demand without incurring unneeded costs for carrying excess inventory. Some firms attempt to keep inventory levels under control by implementing just-in-time (JIT) production. Others are beginning to use RFID technology, discussed earlier in this chapter.

Retailers often shift the responsibility—and costs—for inventory from themselves back to individual manufacturers. **Vendor-managed inventory (VMI)** systems like this are based on the assumption that suppliers are in the best position to spot understocks or surpluses, cutting costs along the supply chain that can be translated into lower prices at the checkout. Datalliance provides VMI platform services in consumer and industrial applications. In the retail sector, it helps manufacturers that want to replenish supplies by sending them directly to retail stores rather than to distribution centres. Among its clients are Elizabeth Arden, Honeywell, Johnson & Johnson, and Siemens.[46]

ORDER PROCESSING

Like inventory control, order processing directly affects the firm's ability to meet its customer service standards. A company may have to compensate for inefficiencies in its order processing system by shipping products via costly transportation modes or by maintaining large inventories at many expensive field warehouses.

Order processing typically consists of four major activities: (1) conducting a credit check; (2) keeping a record of the sale, which involves tasks such as crediting a sales representative's commission account; (3) making appropriate accounting entries; and (4) locating orders, shipping them, and adjusting inventory records. A stockout occurs when an order for an item is not available for shipment. A firm's order-processing system must advise affected customers of a stockout and offer a choice of alternative actions.

As in other areas of physical distribution, technological innovations improve efficiency in order processing. Many firms are streamlining their order processing procedures by using email and the Internet. The outdoor-gear retailer REI, for example, pushes customers toward Web ordering—its least costly fulfillment channel—in its catalogues, store receipts, signs, mailers, and membership letters.

PROTECTIVE PACKAGING AND MATERIALS HANDLING

Logistics managers arrange and control activities for moving products within plants, warehouses, and transportation terminals, which together make up the **materials handling system**. Two important concepts influence many materials handling choices: unitizing and containerization.

Unitizing combines as many packages as possible into each load that moves within or outside a facility. Logistics managers prefer to handle materials on pallets (platforms, generally made of wood, on which goods are transported). Unitizing systems often lash materials in place with steel bands or shrink packaging. A shrink package surrounds a batch of materials with a sheet of plastic that shrinks after heating, securely holding individual pieces together. Unitizing promotes efficient materials handling because each package requires minimal labour to move. Securing the materials together also minimizes damage and pilferage. American-Canadian Ridley Inc. manufactures animal feeds, which it sells to breeders and growers. The company uses an efficient process in distributing its products as unitized pallets—that is, a pallet holding merchandise ready for storage and shipping

vendor-managed inventory (VMI) Inventory management system in which the seller—based on an existing agreement with a buyer—determines how much of a product is needed.

materials handling system Set of activities that moves production inputs and other goods within plants, warehouses, and transportation terminals.

Marketoid

By comparison, in one recent year, container traffic at Chinese ports included 155 million TEUs (20-foot equivalent units), while Canadian ports handled 5.3 million TEUs.

to customers. To create these pallets, the company invested in a palletizing line that can handle 24 bags of feed per minute. The machine sprays a food-grade, water-soluble material called Lock n' Pop onto each bag, preventing spillage. The bags then enter a robotic palletizer. Instead of stretch wrap, the palletizer can be programmed with two types of adhesive spray for stacking the pallets. Dustin Varvil, Ridley's director of manufacturing, says, "We replaced 55 cents per pallet of stretch wrap with 5 cents of Lock n' Pop while eliminating a sizeable invest-ment in new stretch equipment."[47] Logistics managers extend the same concept through **containerization**—combining several unitized loads. A container of oil rig parts, for example, can be loaded in Alberta, trucked or shipped by rail to Vancouver, and then loaded on a ship headed to Saudi Arabia.

In addition to the benefits outlined for unitizing, containerization also markedly reduces the time required to load and unload ships. Con-tainers limit in-transit damage to freight because individual packages pass through few handling systems en route to purchasers.

containerization
Process of combining several unitized loads into a single, well-protected load for shipment.

assessment check 8

8.1 What are the benefits of intermodal transportation?

8.2 Identify the two types of warehouses and explain their function.

Strategic Implications

Several factors, including the burgeoning e-commerce envi-ronment, are driving changes in channel development, logistics, and supply-chain management. As the Internet continues to revolutionize the ways manufacturers deliver goods to ultimate consumers, marketers must find ways to promote cooperation among existing dealer, retailer, and distributor networks while harnessing the power of the Web as an alterna-tive channel. This system demands not only delivery of goods and services faster and more efficiently than ever before but also superior service to Web-based customers.

In addition, increased product proliferation—grocery stores typi-cally stock almost 50,000 different items—demands logistics systems that can manage many brands deliv-ered through many channels world-wide. Those channels must be finely tuned to identify and rapidly rectify problems such as retail shortfalls or costly overstocks. The trend toward leaner retailing, in which the burden of merchandise tracking and inventory control is switching from retailers to manufacturers, means that to be effec-tive, logistics and supply chain systems must result in cost savings. ◆◆◆

REVIEW OF CHAPTER OBJECTIVES

① **Describe the types of marketing channels and the roles they play in marketing strategy.**

Marketing (distribution) channels are the systems of marketing institutions that enhance the physical flow of goods and services, along with ownership title, from producer to consumer or business user. In other words, they help bridge the gap between producer or manufacturer and business customer or consumer. Types of channels are direct selling, selling through intermediaries, dual distribution, and reverse channels. Channels perform four functions: facilitating the exchange process, sorting, standardizing exchange processes, and facilitating searches by buyers and sellers.

② **Outline the major channel strategy decisions.**

Decisions include selecting a marketing channel and determining distribution intensity. Selection of a mar-keting channel may be based on market factors, product factors, organizational factors, or competitive fac-tors. Distribution may be intensive, selective, or exclusive.

③ Describe the concepts of channel management, conflict, and cooperation.

Manufacturers must practise channel management by developing and maintaining relationships with the intermediaries in their marketing channels. The channel captain is the dominant member of the channel. Horizontal and vertical conflict can arise when there is disagreement among channel members. Cooperation is best achieved when all channel members regard themselves as equal components of the same organization.

④ Identify and describe the different vertical marketing systems.

A vertical marketing system (VMS) is a planned channel system designed to improve distribution efficiency and cost effectiveness by integrating various functions throughout the distribution chain. This coordination may be achieved by forward integration or backward integration. Options include a corporate marketing system, operated by a single owner; an administered marketing system, run by a dominant channel member; and a contractual marketing system, based on formal agreements among channel members.

⑤ Explain the roles of logistics and supply-chain management in an overall distribution strategy.

Effective logistics requires proper supply-chain management. The supply chain begins with raw materials, proceeds through actual production, and then continues with the movement of finished products through the marketing channel to customers. Supply-chain management takes place in two directions: upstream and downstream. Tools that marketers use to streamline and manage logistics include radio frequency identification (RFID), enterprise resource planning (ERP), and logistical cost control.

⑥ Identify the major components of a physical distribution system.

Physical distribution involves a broad range of activities concerned with efficient movement of finished goods from the end of the production line to the consumer. As a system, physical distribution consists of six elements: (1) customer service, (2) transportation, (3) inventory control, (4) materials handling and protective packaging, (5) order processing, and (6) warehousing. These elements are interrelated and must be balanced to create a smoothly functioning distribution system and to avoid suboptimization.

⑦ Compare the major modes of transportation.

The five major modes of transport are railroads, motor carriers, water freight, pipelines, and air freight. Railroads rank high on flexibility in handling products; average on speed, dependability in meeting schedules, and cost; and low on frequency of shipments. Motor carriers are relatively high in cost but rank high on speed, dependability, shipment frequency, and availability in different locations. Water carriers balance their slow speed, low shipment frequency, and limited availability with lower costs. The special nature of pipelines makes them rank relatively low on availability, flexibility, and speed, but they are also low in cost. Air transportation is high in cost but offers very fast and dependable delivery schedules.

⑧ Discuss the role of transportation intermediaries, combined transportation modes, and warehousing in improving physical distribution.

Transportation intermediaries facilitate movement of goods in a variety of ways, including piggyback, birdyback, and fishyback services—all forms of intermodal coordination. Methods such as unitization and containerization facilitate intermodal transfers.

assessment check answers ✓

1.1 Distinguish between a marketing channel and logistics. A marketing channel is an organized system of marketing institutions and their interrelationships designed to enhance the flow and ownership of goods and services from producer to user. Logistics is the actual process of coordinating the flow of information, goods, and services among members of the marketing channel.

1.2 What are the different types of marketing channels?

The different types of marketing channels are direct selling, selling through intermediaries, dual distribution, and reverse channels.

1.3 What four functions do marketing channels perform?

The four functions of marketing channels are (1) facilitating the exchange process by reducing the number of marketplace contacts necessary for a sale, (2) sorting, (3) standardizing exchange transactions, and (4) facilitating searches by buyers and sellers.

2.1 Identify four major factors in selecting a marketing channel.

The four major factors in selecting a marketing channel are market, product, organizational, and competitive.

2.2 Describe the three general categories of distribution intensity.

Intensive distribution seeks to distribute a product through all available channels in a trade area. Selective distribution chooses a limited number of retailers in a market area. Exclusive distribution grants exclusive rights to a wholesaler or retailer to sell a manufacturer's products.

3.1 What is a channel captain? What is its role in channel cooperation?

A channel captain is the dominant member of the marketing channel. Its role in channel cooperation is to provide the necessary leadership.

3.2 Identify and describe the three types of channel conflict.

Horizontal conflict results from disagreements among channel members at the same level. Vertical conflict occurs when channel members at different levels disagree. The grey market causes conflict because it involves competition in the Canadian market of brands produced by overseas affiliates.

4.1 What are vertical marketing systems (VMSs)? Identify the major types.

Vertical marketing systems are planned channel systems designed to improve the effectiveness of distribution, including efficiency and cost. The three major types are corporate, administered, and contractual.

4.2 Identify the three types of contractual marketing systems.

The three types of contractual systems are wholesale-sponsored voluntary chains, retail cooperatives, and franchises.

5.1 What is upstream management? What is downstream management?

Upstream management involves managing raw materials, inbound logistics, and warehouse and storage facilities. Downstream management involves managing finished product storage, outbound logistics, marketing and sales, and customer service.

5.2 Identify three methods for managing logistics.

Methods for managing logistics include RFID technology, enterprise resource planning (ERP) systems, and logistical cost control.

6.1 What are the six major elements of physical distribution?

The major elements of physical distribution are customer service, transportation, inventory control, materials handling and protective packaging, order processing, and warehousing.

6.2 What is suboptimization?

Suboptimization occurs when managers of individual functions try to reduce costs but create less than optimal results.

7.1 Identify the five major modes of transport.

The five major modes of transport are railroads, motor carriers, water carriers, pipelines, and air freight.

7.2 Which mode of transport is currently experiencing a resurgence, and why?

Railroad transport is currently experiencing a resurgence because of the cost of fuel and its efficiency in transporting large amounts of freight for less fuel.

8.1 What are the benefits of intermodal transportation?

Intermodal transportation usually provides shippers faster service and lower rates than a single mode could offer.

8.2 Identify the two types of warehouses and explain their function.

The two types of warehouses are storage and distribution. Storage warehouses hold goods for moderate to long periods of time in order to balance supply and demand. Distribution warehouses assemble and redistribute goods as quickly as possible.

MARKETING TERMS YOU NEED TO KNOW

These terms are printed in blue in the text. They are defined in the margins of the chapter and in the Glossary that begins on p. G-1.

distribution 332	dual distribution 337	forward integration 345
marketing (distribution) channel 332	reverse channel 337	backward integration 345
logistics 332	intensive distribution 341	corporate marketing system 345
supply-chain management 332	selective distribution 341	administered marketing system 345
physical distribution 332	exclusive distribution 341	contractual marketing system 345
marketing intermediary (middleman) 333	closed sales territory 342	retail cooperative 345
wholesaler 333	tying agreement 342	franchise 346
direct channel 334	channel captain 343	supply chain 346
direct selling 335	grey goods 344	upstream management 346
manufacturers' representative 337	vertical marketing system (VMS) 344	downstream management 346

PROJECT AND TEAMWORK EXERCISES

1. The traditional channel for consumer goods runs from producer to wholesaler to retailer to user. With a classmate, select a product from the following list (or choose one of your own) and create a chart that traces its distribution system. You may go online to the firm's website for additional information.
   a. a kayak from the Mountain Equipment Co-op website or catalogue
   b. a ticket to a Toronto Blue Jays baseball game or a ticket to an Edmonton Oilers hockey game
   c. HD TV from Costco
2. On your own or with a classmate, identify, draw, and explain a reverse channel with which you are familiar. What purpose does this reverse channel serve to businesses? To the community? To consumers?
3. With a classmate, choose a product you think would sell best through a direct channel. Then create a brief sales presentation for your product and present it to the class. Ask for feedback.
4. With a classmate, choose a franchise that interests you. Visit the website of the company to learn more about how its goods and services are distributed. Create a chart outlining the firm's physical distribution system.
5. It takes a lot to move an elaborate stage performance like Cirque du Soleil, Big Apple Circus, or a rock band from one location to another while it is on tour. With a classmate, choose a touring performance that interests you—a music group, a circus, a theatre performance, or the like—and imagine you are in charge of logistics. Create a chart showing what modes of transportation you would select to move the performance, how you would warehouse certain items during downtime, and what methods you would use to control costs.

CRITICAL THINKING EXERCISES

1. Imagine a vending machine that would charge more for hot drinks—coffee, tea, and cocoa—during cold weather. What is your opinion of a temperature-sensitive vending machine? Consumers who live in colder climates might pay more over a longer time period each year than consumers who live in warmer climates. Would your opinion change if alternatives were nearby, say, a convenience store or a vending machine that is not temperature sensitive? Do you think such a machine would be successful? Why or why not?
2. Auto dealerships often have exclusive distribution rights in their local markets. How might this affect the purchase choices consumers make? What problems might a dealership encounter with this type of distribution?
3. Choose one of the following firms and identify which marketing channel or channels you think would be best for its goods or services. Then explain the market factors, product factors, and organizational and competitive factors contributing to your selection.
   a. Chapters
   b. The Keg restaurant or Swiss Chalet
   c. *Canadian Business* magazine
   d. Canada's Wonderland in Toronto, or Playland in Vancouver
   e. Lululemon
4. In their most basic form, RFID tags track the progress of products from warehouse to retail shelf to checkout counter. But they have great potential to provide marketers with more information about consumers' purchase patterns. In what ways might RFID technology be used to serve customers better? What problems might arise?
5. After a trip to India, where you were inspired by the craftsmanship of artisans who make jewellery and artifacts, you decide to establish an import business focusing on their work. How would you determine distribution intensity for your business? What mode (or modes) of transportation would you use to get the goods to Canada? How and where would you warehouse the goods? Explain your answers.

> ### *ETHICS EXERCISE*

As more and more firms do business globally, transporting goods from one part of the world to another, there has been a surge in piracy—criminals making off with cargo shipments filled with everything from component parts to finished goods. A tractor-trailer loaded with electronics might be stolen from a truck; or from a warehouse stacked with pallets of new clothing, TVs, or just about anything else that might be susceptible to theft. Large, sophisticated cargo-theft gangs have been identified by law enforcement authorities in Halifax, Montreal, Toronto, and Vancouver. However, members of the supply chain can work together to close the net around would-be thieves, developing stronger relationships with each other and law enforcement.[48]

1. What steps might manufacturers take to achieve the kind of channel cooperation that could reduce or prevent cargo theft?

2. How might transportation firms use security measures to build trust with customers and strengthen their position in the marketplace?

CASE 12.1

Natural Disasters Disrupt the Global Supply Chain

Aside from tragic human losses and incalculable damage to property, manufacturers around the world were affected by two unprecedented disasters in 2011. First came the magnitude 9.0 earthquake and tsunami that hit Japan, followed by deadly flooding in Thailand. While damage to Japan's automotive parts makers and Thailand's disk drive industry immediately affected customers such as Honda and Apple, manufacturers as far away as Canada, the United States, and Denmark, making products such as aircraft tires, shoes, automobiles, and computer equipment, also were hampered by supply chain disruptions.

Danish shoe manufacturer ECCO used scuba divers to retrieve specialized shoe moulds from a flooded Thai factory to continue producing at other locations. Honda employees in the United States grappled with temporarily reduced hours while awaiting parts from Thailand. Honda Canada's car production was reduced to the point where its dealers could get only 30 to 50 percent of their normal inventory volume. Toyota's manufacturing plants in Canada and China experienced several months of drastically reduced production. Nissan, meanwhile, sent car parts normally intended for U.S. plants to Asia in order to continue production. Apple and Hewlett-Packard predicted reduced future earnings, based on supply disruptions after hard-drive manufacturer Seagate suffered damage to its two Thai factories. And without hard drives, computer manufacturers had less need of computer chips, so Intel also predicted lower revenues.

In Japan alone, the economic costs of the earthquake and tsunami were running at $210 billion before the year was over, and losses in Thailand reached an estimated $30 billion only weeks after the floods receded.

The two disasters' lingering (and sometimes cascading) effects led some companies to reconsider their reliance on lean, decentralized manufacturing methods, including just-in-time, all of which increase efficiency and reduces costs but may leave companies vulnerable to supply chain disruptions. Natural disasters are unavoidable, and even early warning offers limited advantages.

With the likelihood of more extreme weather to come, some companies have pulled back from lean methods and invested once again in redundancy—multiple suppliers, backup facilities, and stockpiles of critical parts. After all, in an insurance company's survey completed before the earthquake in Japan, 600 CFOs were asked what threat to their revenue drivers they most feared. The most common answer: supply chain disruptions.

Questions for Critical Thinking

1. Do you think companies are wise to favour backup systems over lean manufacturing? Why or why not?

2. In what other ways could companies safeguard their supply chains, including transportation methods, against natural disasters?

Sources: Regina Cline, "One Year Later, Natural Disasters Still Rattling Supply Chains," Bloomberg BNA, **www.bna.com**, accessed May 18, 2012; Bill Powell, "The Global Supply Chain: So Very Fragile," CNNMoney.com, **http://tech.fortune .cnn.com**, accessed May 18, 2012; Thomas Farole and Julia Oliver, "Shoe Molds and Scuba Divers: How Natural Disasters Affect Our Supply Chains," World Bank Growth and Crisis Blog, **http://blogs.worldbank.org**, accessed May 18, 2012; "Supply Chain News: Did Major Supply Chain Disruptions from Natural Disasters in 2011 Really Change Approach to Supply Chain Risk Management?" *Supply Chain Digest*, January 19, 2012, **www.scdigest.com**; "Update on How Japanese Earthquake and Tsunami Are Impacting Honda Canada," May 9, 2012, available **http:// hondawest.wordpress.com/2011/05/09/update-on-how-japanese-earthquake -and-tsunami-are-impacting-honda-canada/**, accessed March 3, 2014.

CASE 12.2

Geoffrey B. Small Wants to Remain "Small"

Designer Geoffrey B. Small doesn't want you to buy his clothes. In fact, he might be disappointed if you were able to find them in a store at all. Small is a fashion designer who cut his teeth in the clothing industry by selling jeans at the Gap. Today, Small's overall marketing channel strategy is the opposite of the Gap's: the fewer pieces he sells, the more successful he becomes.

Small is blunt about the importance of exclusive distribution to the image of his goods and his relationships with retail partners as well as consumers. "We have one of the tightest distributions in the world-designer industry," says Small. "It's very difficult to find our collection. So it's very exclusive, and that's by choice, that's important for our customer. We're not for everybody, and we're not interested in being available to everybody." Small explains that the benefits of exclusive distribution outweigh the drawbacks. While it's true that his firm doesn't sell as many clothes as other clothing manufacturers (sometimes Small makes only four pieces of one design), he believes that reverse psychology works. "People want what they can't have," he observes. "Exclusivity is a fundamental part of our field," he comments. "If you're too available, nobody makes money." Small makes his profit by selling less—not more.

The flip side to the exclusivity coin is the mandate that a product represent the very best quality of its type in the world. Small is confident that his clothes meet the highest standards for fabric, tailoring, and workmanship. To achieve this goal, he headquarters his business in Italy right near his suppliers. "If you're trying to make the very best clothes in the world today in terms of materials, components, and accessories in collaborative work-partnerships, there's only one place in the world—and that's Italy." The designer deliberately keeps his supply chain very short. "We're in a region in Italy where we're very close to the best suppliers in the world, and we work with them," Small says.

Small partners with two fabric makers: one is the oldest woollen maker in the world, and the other is a multigenerational family company. Small is working with the second firm to develop what he hopes will be the world's best organic fibre, with the ultimate goal of making the world's best sustainable fabrics to be used in luxury fashion design. He is proud of the way these textile manufacturers complement the expertise his team brings to the design table. They bring "a level of artisanal excellence that is unique in the world," says Small. He also notes that the components of his garments reflect the highest concentration of handwork available that he's aware of.

Small also maintains a close relationship with his other channel partners, the retailers who carry his finished garments. Despite the extremely limited production runs of his clothing, Small's designs can be found in 10 countries. In addition to producing a handful of items to be sold across retailers (sometimes one jacket or pair of pants per country), Small works with his retail partners to come up with designs exclusively for the customers of a particular store. Because so few items are produced in any given year, Small says that visiting every store is difficult—but he does it. "The store is where the action is," he explains. He likes to meet with retail staff who, he believes, are the most connected to customers—yet are often underappreciated. Small believes that the retail staff holds key information about consumer needs and preferences. Small also likes to speak directly with customers on his retail visits, engaging in one-on-one communication with the people who buy his clothes.

You won't see a Geoffrey B. Small line at Walmart, Target, or even at the Gap any time soon. Small doesn't want to sell you his clothes unless you share his outlook on fashion, appreciate his designs and fabrics, will happily pay top dollar for them, and know the right retailers. Although he wants to grow his business, he insists on doing it his own way: with the marketing channels as precise and tight as one of his hand-sewn stitches.

Questions for Critical Thinking

1. Over the next 10 years, do you think Small's insistence on exclusivity will continue to benefit his business or begin to be detrimental? Why?
2. In your opinion, why does Small have such successful partnerships throughout his marketing channels?

Sources: "The Amazing Geoffrey B. Small Story," Company website, **www.geoffreybsmall.net/gbstory.htm**, accessed June 15, 2012; Geoffrey B. Small, "The Environment of Young Designers," Not Just a Label, **www.notjustalabel.com**, accessed June 15, 2012; Claire Ruhlin, "Recycle, Reconstruct, Redesign," Community, April 24, 2012, **http://communityathens.blogspot.com**; Eugene Rabkin, "Review: Geoffrey B. Small, Fall/Winter 2012," *StyleZeitgeist Magazine*, January 2012, **www.sz-magazine.com**.

Retailers, Wholesalers, and Direct Marketers

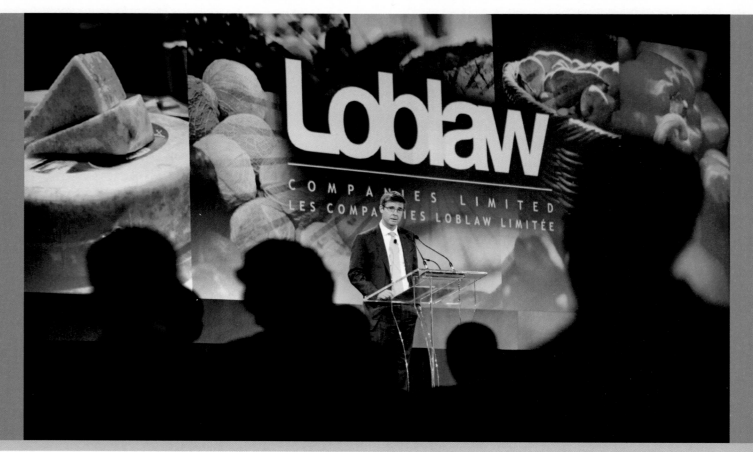

CHAPTER OBJECTIVES

① Explain the wheel of retailing.

② Discuss how retailers select target markets.

③ Show how the elements of the marketing mix apply to retailing strategy.

④ Explain the concepts of retail convergence and scrambled merchandising.

⑤ Identify the functions performed by wholesaling intermediaries.

⑥ Outline the major types of independent wholesaling intermediaries and the appropriate situations for using each.

⑦ Compare the basic types of direct marketing and nonstore retailing.

⑧ Describe how the Internet has altered the wholesaling, retailing, and direct marketing environments.

LOBLAW COMPANIES AND SHOPPERS DRUG MART: 1 + 1 = 3

What do you get when Canada's largest grocery retailer combines with Canada's largest drugstore chain? You get a giant retail behemoth that will be the country's largest purchaser of many of the products that overlap in the two companies' product mix. In one of the largest deals ever in Canadian business history, Loblaw Companies acquired Shoppers Drug Mart in a $12.4-billion deal that was officially completed on March 28, 2014. The combined company will operate more than 2,700 grocery stores and more than 1,800 pharmacies across Canada.

Why the deal, and why now? Loblaw Companies has been operating primarily in Canada's slow-growing grocery sector, where sales growth has been restricted largely to the rate of price inflation and population growth, neither of which provide much promise for future growth. At the same time, there has been tremendous square-footage growth in food retail across Canada as retailers have been entering the grocery market or expanding their operations to include an increasing number of grocery items. With one acquisition, Loblaw Companies has added approximately $11 billion in top-line revenue to its already impressive sales of more than $30 billion—not just growth, but very fast growth. And business synergies as the result of managing the combined operations promise to increase profits through cost reductions.

But there are other reasons why this acquisition makes sense. By acquiring Shoppers, Loblaw Companies thwarted a rumoured potential takeover by U.S.-based Walgreens. At the same time, Loblaw Companies got access to an increasingly important urban customer base. Zoning restrictions make it very difficult to open large-format stores in urban settings but, by acquiring Shoppers locations, Loblaw Companies gets immediate access to retail locations where it can begin to sell its most important retail products. Loblaw Companies manages one of Canada's best private-label brands: President's Choice (PC). Consumers will get their favourite PC products at Shoppers stores. They will also be able to find some Life brand products—Shoppers' popular private-label brand—at Loblaw locations. These urban locations may be even more important to Loblaw Companies in the future. As more retailers are considering online grocery sales—even Amazon.ca has added 15,000 nonperishable grocery items to its product mix recently—Loblaw Companies will be able to accept online grocery orders and deliver them to urban consumers at Shoppers locations. Other grocery retailers will not be capable of providing this same level of service.

Although the deal closed in 2014, Loblaw Companies made its first offer for Shoppers Drug Mart in 2011 and followed it with several additional offers until a deal was finally agreed upon in 2013, subject to the approval of the Competition Bureau of Canada. When the deal finally received approval, the Competition Bureau did put some limits on the acquisition. Loblaw Companies was required to sell 18 stores and nine pharmacy operations where it was determined that Loblaw Companies would have too much market power; i.e., where there would not be sufficient competition. As well, the Competition Bureau required some behavioural changes in how Loblaw Companies managed its relationships with key vendors, such as demanding price freezes and even retroactive price discounts. Although other retailers have been making similar demands recently, there is real concern about the ability of Loblaw Companies to leverage its increased size and buying power to engage in increased anticompetitive behaviour.

The acquisition deal topped off a number of important initiatives managed by executive chairman Galen Weston, Jr., who took over from his father in 2006. It was certainly a factor that helped him earn the title Canadian Press Business Newsmaker of the Year for 2013. Weston received 22 percent of the votes, well ahead of BCE's chief executive George Cope and Thorstein Heins, CEO of BlackBerry, who were tied for second with 17 percent of the votes.[1]

connecting with customers

How does Loblaw Companies connect with its customers? Obviously, as Canada's largest grocery retailer, it must do many things right. President's Choice is just a start, but the retailer manages a number of popular retail banners—Loblaw, Zehrs, No Frills, Real Canadian Superstore, and more—that allows it to meet the needs of almost all Canadians. And it doesn't hurt that its executive chairman, Galen Weston, Jr.—the face of the company—is approachable, friendly, and charismatic. He has been positioning Loblaw Companies with a health and wellness strategy and seems genuinely concerned with the health of Canadians. He also won kudos following his recent humanitarian initiative on behalf of Loblaw Companies to help workers and their dependants following a recent tragedy in Bangladesh. His youth, his values, and his fresh approach resonate well with Canadian consumers.[2]

Chapter Overview

In exploring how today's retailing sector operates, this chapter introduces many examples that explain the combination of activities involved in selling goods to ultimate consumers. Then the chapter discusses the role of wholesalers and other intermediaries who deliver goods from the manufacturers into the hands of retailers or other intermediaries. Finally, the chapter looks at nonstore retailing. Direct marketing, a channel consisting of direct communication to consumers or business users, is a major form of nonstore retailing. It includes not just direct mail and telemarketing but also direct-response advertising, infomercials, and Internet marketing. The chapter concludes by looking at a less pervasive but growing aspect of nonstore retailing—automatic merchandising. ◆◆◆

① **Explain the wheel of retailing.**

retailing Activities involved in selling merchandise to ultimate consumers.

Marketoid

In its first full year in Canada, 2013, Target had sales of $1.3 billion— just over $10 million per store—but suffered a loss of $941 million.

RETAILING

Retailers are the marketing intermediaries that are in direct contact with ultimate consumers. Retailing describes the activities involved in selling merchandise to these consumers. Retail outlets serve as contact points between channel members and ultimate consumers. In a very real sense, retailers represent the distribution channel to most consumers since a typical shopper has little contact with manufacturers and virtually no contact with wholesaling intermediaries. Retailers determine locations, store hours, number of sales personnel, store layouts, merchandise selections, and return policies—factors that often influence the consumers' images of the offerings more strongly than consumers' images of the products themselves. Both large and small retailers perform the major channel activities: creating time, place, and ownership utilities.

Retailers act as both customers and marketers in their channels. They sell products to ultimate consumers, and at the same time, they buy from wholesalers and manufacturers. Because of their critical location in the marketing channel, retailers often perform a vital feedback role. They obtain information from customers and transmit that information to manufacturers and other channel members.

EVOLUTION OF RETAILING

The development of retailing illustrates the marketing concept in operation. Early retailing in North America can be traced to the establishment of trading posts, such as the Hudson's Bay Company, and to pack peddlers who carried their wares to outlying settlements. The first type of retail institution, the general store, stocked a wide range of merchandise that met the needs of an isolated community or rural area. Supermarkets appeared in the early 1930s in response to consumers' desire for lower prices. In the 1950s, discount stores delivered lower prices in exchange for reduced services. The emergence of convenience food stores in the 1960s satisfied consumer demand for fast service, convenient locations, and expanded hours of operation. The development of off-price retailers in the 1980s and 1990s reflected consumer demand for brand-name merchandise at prices considerably lower than those of traditional retailers. In recent years, Internet-enabled retailing has increased in influence and importance.

wheel of retailing Hypothesis that each new type of retailer gains a competitive foothold by offering lower prices than current outlets charge; the result of reducing or eliminating services.

A key concept, known as the wheel of retailing, attempts to explain the patterns of change in retailing. According to the wheel of retailing, a new type of retailer gains a competitive foothold by offering customers lower prices than current outlets charge and maintains profits by reducing or eliminating services. Once established, however, the innovator begins to add more services, and its prices gradually rise. It then becomes vulnerable to new low-price retailers that enter with minimum services—and so the wheel turns, as illustrated in Figure 13.1. The Canadian retail graveyard is littered with former giants such as Eaton's, Woolco, Kmart, Zellers, and catalogue retailer Consumers Distributing.

Many major developments in the history of retailing appear to fit the wheel's pattern. Early department stores, chain stores, supermarkets, discount stores, hypermarkets, and catalogue retailers all emphasized limited service and low prices. Most of these retailers gradually increased prices as they added services.

Some exceptions disrupt this pattern, however. Suburban shopping centres, convenience food stores, and vending machines never built their appeals around low prices. Still, the wheel pattern has been a good indicator enough times in the past to make it an accurate indicator of future retailing developments.

The wheel of retailing suggests that retailing is always changing. Retailers must continually change to meet the changing needs of Canadian consumers. As more fast-food and casual family-dining options are increasingly available across Canada, Swiss Chalet has been changing its menu to attract families that wish to dine out. Although Swiss Chalet has been known primarily for its rotisserie chicken, diners can now have hamburgers, fish and chips, ribs, wraps and flatbreads, and several rice and pasta dishes.

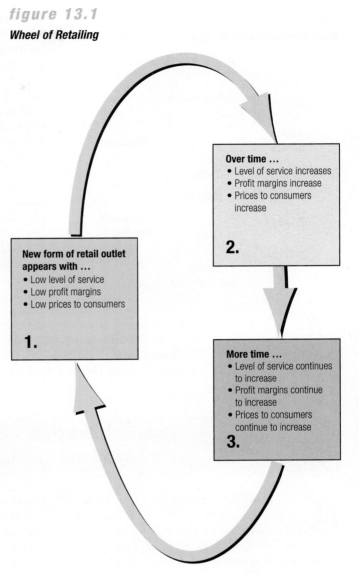

figure 13.1

Wheel of Retailing

assessment check 1 ✓

1.1 What is retailing?

1.2 Explain the wheel of retailing concept.

RETAILING STRATEGY

Like manufacturers and wholesalers, a retailer develops a marketing strategy based on the firm's goals and strategic plans. The organization monitors environmental influences and assesses its own strengths and weaknesses in identifying marketing opportunities and constraints. A retailer bases its key decisions on two fundamental steps in the marketing strategy process: (1) selecting a target market and (2) developing a retailing mix to satisfy the chosen market. The retailing mix specifies merchandise strategy, customer-service standards, pricing guidelines, target market analysis, promotion goals, location/distribution decisions, and store atmosphere choices. The combination of these elements projects a desired retail image. Retail image communicates the store's identity to consumers. As Figure 13.2 points out, components of retailing strategy must work together to create a consistent image that appeals to the store's target market.

As more fast-food chains such as Chipotle, Applebee's, and Chili's open stores with modern, fresher visuals, the big burger chains are remodelling to catch up. These remodels are expensive: $375,000 to $750,000 or more, per location. Denny Lynch, senior vice president of communications at Wendy's, explains that the more modern approach will include new colours and textures and more glass on the building exteriors. To encourage franchisees to renovate, Wendy's has been offering cash incentives up to $100,000 to its franchisees.[3]

(2) **Discuss how retailers select target markets.**

SELECTING A TARGET MARKET

A retailer starts to define its strategy by selecting a target market. Factors that influence the retailer's selection are the size and profit potential of the market and the level of competition for its business. Retailers pore over demographic, geographic, and psychographic profiles to segment markets. In the

Marketoid

Dollarama Group dominates the dollar store business in Canada, with 800 locations and sales exceeding $2 billion annually.

figure 13.2

Components of Retail Strategy

end, most retailers identify their target markets by certain demographics. The "Marketing: Making Your World Better" feature describes two online retailers that have targeted the parents and caregivers of Canada's youngest consumers.

The importance of identifying and targeting the right market is dramatically illustrated by the erosion of department store retailing. While mall anchor stores struggle to attract customers, stand-alone store Target makes a memorable splash with edgy advertising that incorporates its signature red doughnut-shaped logo in imaginative ways. And although Target can be categorized as a discount retailer, it has differentiated itself from competitors such as Walmart by offering trendy, quality merchandise at low prices. Target entered the Canadian marketplace with 124 locations across all 10 provinces and has since announced additional planned store openings for Quebec, Ontario, Manitoba, Alberta, and British Columbia.[4]

Deep-discount retailers, such as Dollarama and Buck-or-Two, with their less glamorous locations and low-priced merchandise displayed in narrow aisles, target lower-income bargain hunters. Attracted by cents-off basics, such as shampoo, cereal, and laundry detergent, customers typically pick up higher-margin goods—toys or chocolates—on their way to the checkout.

By creating stores with wide aisles and clean presentation and offering friendly service and high-end product lines such as Laura Ashley paints, home improvement chain Lowe's competes with arch rivals Home Depot and Rona. Lowe's ambiance helps make the store more appealing to

---

MARKETING: MAKING YOUR WORLD BETTER

Babies Have Had a Bum Wrap for Years: It's Time for a Change

CANADIAN retailers are increasingly adding sustainable, or green, products to their shelves, but they frequently face two major problems: price, and convincing Canadian consumers that these products perform at least as well as conventional alternatives.

Some of the latest green products are manufactured wholly or in part from bamboo, and while they may not always solve the first problem, price, they frequently outperform existing products. Bamboo is the fastest-growing plant in the world—some species grow as much as 1.5 metres per day. Bamboo forests release 35 percent more oxygen into the atmosphere than equivalent forests. The "woody" plant combines strength with versatility, making it possible to manufacture flooring, tile, countertops, kitchen cabinets, bathroom vanities, and, once it is pulped and spun, one of the world's softest yarns. From this yarn, manufacturers are making goods as varied as diapers, panties, and boxer briefs; sweaters and T-shirts; and even suits, bath towels, and bedroom linens. You can find a variety of bamboo products at Canadian retailers, large and small.

For the smallest Canadians, nothing is better than bamboo diapers. They can be purchased online from Lil Helper, a company started by two young men who met at Ryerson University and who each now hold a master's degree in aerospace. Their company got its name because its owners, Mohammed Gandhi and Nader Abu El Samid, built their business on a simple philosophy: to provide a *lil help* to babies, who are the end users; to parents and caregivers, who are the purchasers; and to the environment, which benefits when Canadians use products manufactured from sustainable materials. Canadian handmade bamboo baby products are also available online from Babibu, a business started by mompreneur Sarah Lopez. All Babibu products—including diapers, beanies, bibs, booties, scratch mittens, rompers, shorts, dresses, and many other items—are handmade in Canada and come in 11 different colours. Both Lil Helper and Babibu also sell through a number of retailers across Canada. Babies—who have had a bum wrap for years—now have better bum wraps. Bamboo is especially suited for diapers: it is 60 percent more absorbent than cotton and dries 20 percent more quickly. It is hypoallergenic and naturally antibacterial, and its tiny micro-holes promote ventilation, helping it prevent bad odour longer. Bamboo diapers thus provide many advantages for babies, and one major advantage for parents.

Sources: Babibu website, **www.babibu.ca**, accessed March 8, 2014; Lil Helper website, **www.lilhelper.ca**, accessed March 8, 2014.

female shoppers, who do almost 44 percent of all do-it-yourself projects and account for half of all home improvement purchases.[5]

After identifying a target market, a retailer must then develop marketing strategies to attract these chosen customers to its stores or website. The following sections discuss tactics for implementing different strategies.

assessment check 2 ✓

2.1 How does a retailer develop a marketing strategy?

2.2 How do retailers select target markets?

MERCHANDISING STRATEGY

(3) **Show how the elements of the marketing mix apply to retailing strategy.**

A retailer's merchandising strategy guides decisions regarding the items it will offer. A retailer must decide on general merchandise categories, product lines, specific items within lines, and the depth and width of its assortments. Joe Fresh, a Loblaw clothing brand, was originally sold through Loblaw stores, but has since opened many stand-alone locations in Canada and the United States where it can show off its stylish, well-priced clothing and accessories. The big-box electronics retailer Best Buy recently expanded its product offerings to include a full line of musical instruments.

To develop a successful merchandise mix, a retailer must weigh several priorities. First, it must consider the preferences and needs of its previously defined target market, keeping in mind that the competitive environment influences these choices. The retailer must also consider the overall profitability of each product line and product category.

Retail outlets are contact points between manufacturers and consumers.

Category Management

As mentioned in Chapter 11, a popular merchandising strategy is *category management,* in which a category manager oversees an entire product line for both vendors and retailers and is responsible for the profitability of the product group. Category management seeks to improve the retailer's product category performance through more coordinated buying, merchandising, and pricing. Rather than focusing on the performance of individual brands, such as Flex shampoo or Kleenex tissue, category management evaluates performance according to each product category. Laundry detergent, skin-care products, and paper goods, for example, are each viewed as individual profit centres, and different category managers supervise each group. Those that underperform are at risk of being dropped from inventory, regardless of the strength of individual brands. To improve their profitability, for example, some department stores have narrowed their traditionally broad product categories to eliminate high-overhead, low-profit lines such as toys, appliances, and furniture.

stockkeeping unit (SKU) Offering within a product line such as a specific size of liquid detergent.

The Battle for Shelf Space

As discussed in Chapter 12, large-scale retailers are increasingly taking on the role of channel captain within many distribution networks. Some have assumed traditional wholesaling functions, while others dictate product design and specifications to manufacturers. The result is a shift in power from the manufacturers of top-selling brands to the retailer that makes them available to customers.

Adding to the pressure is the increase in the number of new products and variations on existing products. To identify the varying items within a product line, retailers refer to a specific product offering as a **stockkeeping unit (SKU)**. Within the skin-care category, for example, each facial cream, body moisturizer, and sunscreen in each of a variety of sizes and formulations is a separate SKU. The proliferation of new SKUs has resulted in a fierce battle for space on store shelves.

Shelf space is important if you want to be noticed: If you're not on the shelf, you can't be chosen when the consumer makes his or her choice.

Courtesy of Home Hardware. Reprinted by permission of Facebook.

Home Hardware celebrates 50 years of providing expert advice to its customers.

Increasingly, major retailers, such as Target and Loblaw, make demands in return for providing shelf space. They may, for example, seek pricing and promotional concessions from manufacturers as conditions for selling their products. Retailers such as Walmart also require that manufacturers participate in their electronic data interchange (EDI) and quick-response systems. Manufacturers unable to comply may find themselves unable to penetrate the marketplace.

Slotting allowances are just one of the range of nonrefundable fees grocery retailers receive from manufacturers to secure shelf space for new products. Manufacturers may pay a national retailer thousands of dollars to get their new product displayed on store shelves.[6] Other fees include failure fees (imposed if a new product does not meet sales projections), annual renewal fees (a "pay to stay" inducement for retailers to continue carrying brands), trade allowances, discounts on high-volume purchases, survey fees for research done by the retailers, and even fees to allow salespeople to present new items.

CUSTOMER-SERVICE STRATEGY

Some stores build their retailing strategy on heightened customer services for shoppers. Gift wrapping, alterations, return privileges, product demonstrations, bridal registries, consultants, interior design services, delivery and installation, and perhaps even electronic shopping via store websites are all examples of services that add value to the shopping experience. A retailer's customer-service strategy must specify which services the firm will offer and whether it will charge customers for these services. Those decisions depend on several conditions: store size, type, and location; merchandise assortment; services offered by competitors; customer expectations; and financial resources.

The basic objective of all customer services focuses on attracting and retaining target customers, thus increasing sales and profits. Some services—such as convenient restrooms, lounges, and complimentary coffee—enhance shoppers' comfort. Other services are intended to attract customers by making shopping easier and faster than it would be without the services. Some retailers, for example, offer child-care services for customers.

Consumers can also get "virtual assistance" from companies like Virtuosity and CallWave, which manage phone calls by allowing users to switch among voice mail, email, and real-time cell and landline calls using voice commands. Virtuosity's Virtual Assistant software can answer, screen, and route calls much like a living, breathing administrative assistant. Similarly, CallWave's Voicemail-to-Text service screens mobile calls, converts voice mail to text, and helps users manage their time.[7]

A customer-service strategy can also support efforts in building demand for a line of merchandise. Despite the trend toward renovation, redecorating, and do-it-yourself home projects, Home Depot was experiencing slowing sales until its recent decision to revamp its own stores, improve customer service, and upgrade its marketing efforts. Home Depot experienced solid growth with the strategy, assuring its customers with its familiar slogan, "More saving. More doing."

PRICING STRATEGY

Prices reflect a retailer's marketing objectives and policies. They also play a major role in consumer perceptions of a retailer. Consumers realize, for example, that when they enter a Hermès boutique, they will find such expensive merchandise as leather handbags priced at $3,275 and up, along with men's belts at $650 and up. In contrast, customers of Big Lots or Winners expect totally different merchandise and prices, and to see new items each time they visit.

Markups and Markdowns

markup Amount that a retailer adds to the cost of a product to determine its selling price.

The amount that a retailer adds to a product's cost to set the final selling price is the **markup**. The amount of the markup typically results from two marketing decisions:

1. *Services performed by the retailer.* Other things being equal, stores that offer more services charge larger markups to cover their costs.

2. *Inventory turnover rate.* Other things being equal, stores with a higher turnover rate can cover their costs and earn a profit while charging a smaller markup.

A retailer's markup exerts an important influence on its image among present and potential customers. In addition, the markup affects the retailer's ability to attract shoppers. An excessive markup may drive away customers; an inadequate markup may not generate sufficient income to cover costs and return a profit. Retailers typically state markups as percentages of either the selling prices or the costs of the products.

Marketers determine markups based partly on their judgments of the amounts that consumers will pay for a given product. When buyers refuse to pay a product's stated price, however, or when improvements in other items or fashion changes reduce the appeal of current merchandise, a retailer must take a **markdown**. The amount by which a retailer reduces the original selling price—the discount typically advertised for a sale item—is the markdown. Markdowns are sometimes used to evaluate merchandisers. For example, a department store might base its evaluations of buyers partly on the average markdown percentages for the product lines for which they are responsible.

markdown Amount by which a retailer reduces the original selling price of a product.

The formulas for calculating markups and markdowns are provided in the "Financial Analysis in Marketing" appendix at the end of the text.

LOCATION/DISTRIBUTION STRATEGY

Retail experts often cite location as a potential determining factor in the success or failure of a retail business. A retailer may choose to locate at an isolated site, in a central business district, or in a planned shopping centre. The location decision depends on many factors, including the type of merchandise, the retailer's financial resources, characteristics of the target market, and site availability.

In recent years, many localities have become saturated with stores. As a result, some retailers have re-evaluated their location strategies. A chain may close individual stores that do not meet sales and profit goals. Other retailers have experimented with nontraditional location strategies. GoodLife Fitness, Canada's largest fitness company with 877,000 members, has approximately 50 of its more than 300 clubs in Real Canadian Superstore locations. These stores offer high traffic and ample parking, and attract women aged 35 to 50 with high household incomes. Real Canadian Superstore strengthened its position as a one-stop shop for customers; and GoodLife Fitness benefited from increased visibility, credibility, and access to Canada's fastest-growing fitness segment.[8]

Locations in Planned Shopping Centres

Over the past several decades, retail trade has shifted away from traditional downtown retailing districts and toward suburban shopping centres. A **planned shopping centre** is a group of retail stores designed, coordinated, and marketed to shoppers in a geographic trade area. Together, the stores provide a single convenient location for shoppers as well as free parking. They facilitate shopping by maintaining uniform hours of operation, including evening and weekend hours.

planned shopping centre Group of retail stores planned, coordinated, and marketed as a unit.

There are five main types of planned shopping centres. The smallest, the *neighbourhood shopping centre*, is likely to consist of a group of smaller stores, such as a drugstore, a dry cleaner, a card and gift shop, and perhaps a hair-styling salon. This kind of centre provides convenient shopping for 5,000 to 50,000 shoppers who live within a few minutes' commute. It contains 5 to 15 stores, and the product mix is usually confined to convenience items and some limited shopping goods.

A *community shopping centre* serves 20,000 to 100,000 people in a trade area extending a few kilometres from its location. It contains anywhere from 10 to 30 retail stores, with a branch of a local department store or some other large store as the primary tenant. In addition to the stores found in a neighbourhood centre, a community centre probably encompasses more stores featuring shopping goods, some professional offices, a bank branch, and perhaps a movie theatre or supermarket. Community shopping centres typically offer ample parking, and tenants often share some promotion costs. With the advent of stand-alone big-box retailers, some community shopping centres have declined in popularity. Some department stores are also moving away from the strategy of locating in shopping centres and opting for freestanding stores. A *regional shopping centre* is a large facility with at least 300,000 square feet of shopping space. Its marketing appeal usually emphasizes major department stores with the power to draw customers, supplemented by as many as 200 smaller stores. A successful regional centre needs a location within 30 minutes' driving time of at least 250,000 people. A regional centre—or a super-regional centre such as the West Edmonton Mall—provides a wide assortment of convenience, shopping, and specialty goods, plus many professional and personal service facilities. Some shopping centres are going green, working to reduce their carbon footprint with mandatory recycling programs, maximizing the use of natural light, and installing heat-reflecting roofing that reduces the need for air conditioning.[9]

A *power centre*, usually located near a regional or super-regional mall, brings together several huge specialty stores, such as Rona, Designer Depot, Costco, Canadian Tire, Michaels, or Pier 1 Imports, as stand-alone stores in a single trading area. Rising in popularity during the 1990s, power centres offered value because they underpriced department stores and provided a huge selection of specialty merchandise. Heated competition from cost-cutter Walmart and inroads from more upscale discounters such as Target are currently hurting the drawing power of these centres. A fifth type of planned centre has emerged, known as a *lifestyle centre*. This retailing format seeks to offer a combination of shopping, movie theatres, stages for concerts and live entertainment, decorative fountains and park benches in greenways, and restaurants and bistros in an attractive outdoor environment. At around 300,000 to 1 million square feet, the centres are large, but they seek to offer the intimacy and easy access of neighbourhood village retailing with a fashionable cachet. Convenience, safety, and pleasant ambiance are also part of the appeal. Canada's first lifestyle centre, The Village at Park Royal located in West Vancouver, has old-fashioned gas lamps and a lighthouse. Each store differs in design and colour, and the main street has many sculptures and plantings, along with a pond and stepping stones where children can play. There are no big anchor stores but rather a mix of just the right upscale tenants—Aritzia, J. Crew, Sephora, Maison Birks, Whole Foods Market, and Lululemon Athletica, for instance. Restaurants are also much more prominent in lifestyle centres than in enclosed malls.[10]

To fill the empty spaces in malls and attract shoppers, malls are increasingly adding businesses that offer entertainment and experiences. Today, many shopping centres include movie theatre complexes, indoor playgrounds, arcade games, bowling alleys, and more. The West Edmonton Mall boasts more than 800 stores and services. It covers 5.3 million square feet, the equivalent of 48 city blocks. The mall boasts the world's largest indoor amusement park, which includes the world's largest indoor triple-loop roller coaster, the world's largest indoor wave pool, and the world's largest indoor lake.[11]

PROMOTIONAL STRATEGY

To establish store images that entice more shoppers, retailers use a variety of promotional techniques. Through its promotional strategy, a retailer seeks to communicate to consumers information about its stores—locations, merchandise selections, hours of operation, and prices. If merchandise selection changes frequently to follow fashion trends, advertising is typically used to promote current styles effectively. In addition, promotions help retailers attract shoppers and build customer loyalty.

Innovative promotions can pay off in unexpected ways. General Electric recently put one of its latest-model refrigerators on a flatbed truck, hooked it up to a generator, and sent it across the country with a chef and a refrigerator engineer. A film crew recorded the trip in reality-show style, following the two men on a 3,200-kilometre journey to Texas to reach a wildlife biologist in the field and cook a meal for him. During the trip, which took a week, the chef picked up supplies along the way from local farmers and fishermen, carefully storing them in the refrigerator. The film was turned into a Web series, "Freshpedition," and was promoted through a TV commercial as well as the company's Facebook and Twitter accounts.[12]

National retail chains often purchase advertising space in newspapers, on radio, and on television. Other retailers promote their goods over the Internet or use wireless technology to send marketing messages to customers' cell phones. Consumers are increasingly using their smartphones and tablet devices to surf the Web. Analytics firm Flurry provides clients with details on how mobile phone and tablet users engage with apps and recently launched Ad Analytics, which measures data on how smartphone and tablet users interact with advertisements within apps.[13]

Retailers also try to combine advertising with in-store merchandising techniques that influence buyer behaviour at the point of purchase. As part of Whole Foods Market's goal of "satisfying and delighting our customers," stores reach out to engage their communities by offering in-store education on food, free samples, and lively social media content.[14]

A friendly, well-trained, and knowledgeable salesperson plays a vital role in conveying the store's image to consumers and in persuading shoppers to buy. To serve as a source of information,

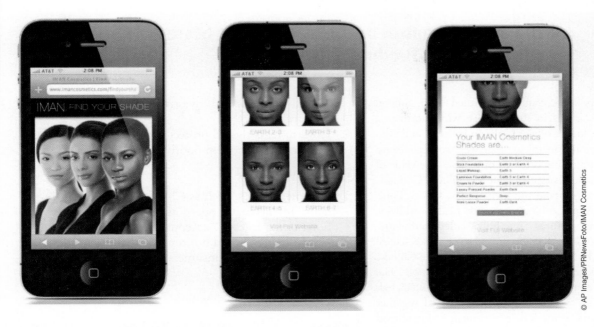

From anywhere in the world, a shopper can launch the IMAN Cosmetics "Find Your Shade" app to find just the right makeup for her skin tone.

a salesperson must possess extensive knowledge regarding credit policies, discounts, special sales, delivery terms, layaways, and returns. To increase store sales, the salesperson must persuade customers that the store sells what those customers need. To this end, salespeople should receive training in selling up and suggestion selling.

By *selling up*, salespeople try to persuade customers to buy higher-priced items than originally intended. For example, an automobile salesperson might convince a customer to buy a more expensive model than the car that the buyer had initially considered. Of course, the practice of selling up must always respect the constraints of a customer's real needs. If a salesperson sells customers something that they really do not need, the potential for repeat sales dramatically diminishes.

Another technique, *suggestion selling*, seeks to broaden a customer's original purchase by adding related items, special promotional products, or holiday or seasonal merchandise. Here, too, the salesperson tries to help a customer recognize true needs rather than unwanted merchandise. Beauty advisors in upscale department stores are masters of suggestion selling. Smartphones can become beauty advisors, too. Recently, IMAN Cosmetics, which specializes in cosmetics for women of colour, introduced an application called "Find Your Shade." IMAN has added QR codes to all of its products, online advertising, promotional materials, and some in-store items, including signs. When a customer scans the code, it directs her to her skin colour, along with advice on selecting the right products for her colouring.[15]

Just as knowledgeable and helpful sales personnel can both boost sales and set retailers apart from competitors, poor service influences customers' attitudes toward a retailer. Increasing customer complaints about unfriendly, inattentive, and uninformed salespeople have prompted many retailers to intensify their attention to training and motivating salespeople. Older training methods are giving way to online learning in many firms.

STORE ATMOSPHERICS

While store location, merchandise selection, customer service, pricing, and promotional activities all contribute to a store's consumer awareness, stores also project their personalities through **atmospherics**—physical characteristics and amenities that attract customers and satisfy their shopping needs. Atmospherics include both a store's exterior and interior decor.

A store's exterior appearance, including architectural design, window displays, signs, and entryways, helps to identify the retailer and attract its target market shoppers. The Canadian Tire red triangle and green maple leaf is an exterior element that readily identifies this retailer. Other retailers design eye-catching exterior elements aimed at getting customers' attention. Consumers readily recognize Tim Hortons, Chapters, and Future Shop locations by their building designs. Many of the more than 100 Canadian locations of East Side Mario's attract

atmospherics
Combination of physical characteristics and amenities that contribute to a store's image.

SOLVING AN ETHICAL CONTROVERSY

Who Should Control the Spread of Fake Stores and Counterfeit Products?

TORONTO police recently confiscated $6.5 million worth of fake goods in the city: ice wine, cosmetics, contact lenses, knock-offs of Cialis and Viagra, and even Toronto Transit Commission tokens that were smuggled into Canada in shower curtains imported from China. The value of the Canadian black market is estimated at $30 billion. Counterfeiters often copy prestige-brand products: Rolex, Gucci, Louis Vuitton, Coach, and Apple. A blogger recently made worldwide headlines after posting pictures of a fully staffed, authentic-looking Apple store in China that also proved to be a fake, like all the products inside. The store was so authentic that the Chinese staff members really believed they were working for Apple. The global proliferation of counterfeit electronics continues unabated, especially in Asia, with counterfeit products cobbled together from fake or stolen parts. Wide-scale government action abroad seems unlikely, especially in Asia, where sophisticated fakes—like replaceable-battery iPhones—are often preferred by consumers, because the products are less expensive than the real thing.

Should governments step in and do more to stop the flood of fakes?

PRO

1. All governments should respect intellectual property rights so multinational companies can safely bring jobs and investment dollars to their countries.
2. Governments should protect their citizens from fake products that perform poorly, if at all.

CON

1. In some cultures, such as China's, innovation is difficult, intellectual property is not protected, and functioning fakes are accepted.
2. Governments should not restrict what companies manufacture, and consumers should look out for themselves.

Where do you stand: pro or con?

Sources: CBC News, "Fake Goods Valued at $6.5M Seized in Toronto," **www.cbc.ca**, November 29, 2013, accessed March 7, 2014; Alex Boutilier, "Ottawa Targets $30B in Counterfeit Goods: Commission to Gauge the Magnitude of Market for Pirated Goods," *Toronto Star*, November 2, 2013, p. A14; "Fake Apple Store: Update with Video," WordPress.com, **http://birdabroad .wordpress.com**, accessed June 2, 2012; Nick Bilton, "Fake Apple Stores Get Fake News Video," *The New York Times*, **http://bits.blogs.nytimes .com**, accessed June 2, 2012; "Are You Listening, Steve Jobs?" WordPress .com, **http://birdabroad.wordpress.com**, accessed June 2, 2012; Michael Wilson, "An iPhone That's Cheaper, But Fake," *The New York Times*, February 24, 2012, **www.nytimes.com**; Louis Bedigian, "Apple's Worst Nightmare Comes from an Unlikely Source," *Forbes*, January 6, 2012, **www.forbes.com**.

Atmospherics—such as layout, colour, lighting, sounds, scents, and cleanliness—affect a customer's restaurant value perception, as does its wine list.

customers with their signature giant tomatoes on their buildings. Sometimes the design can be too good to be true; as fake electronics continue to flood global markets, counterfeiters have even managed to open fake Apple stores in China. See the "Solving an Ethical Controversy" feature to learn more.

The interior decor of a store should also complement the retailer's image, respond to customers' interests, and, most important, induce shoppers to buy. Interior atmospheric elements include store layout, merchandise presentation, lighting, colour, sounds, scents, and cleanliness. At one time, Tim Hortons locations could be described as dark, smoky, and male-dominated, attractive only to a small group of customers. The company improved its product offering, but more important, it consciously decided to improve its atmospherics to appeal particularly to women and families. Tim Hortons was among the first Canadian food outlets to isolate smoking and then to ban it outright. Much of the interior visual appearance was improved, and the bar stool counters, a common store feature, were replaced with family-friendly tables. As a result, Tim Hortons customers now cross all income groups and ages. You are as likely to see a Lexus in the parking lot as you are to see a pickup truck.

When designing the interior and exterior of a store, marketers must remember that many people shop for reasons other than just purchasing needed products. Other common reasons for shopping are escaping the routine of

assessment check 3

3.1 What is an SKU?

3.2 What are the two components of a markup?

3.3 What are store atmospherics?

daily life, avoiding weather extremes, fulfilling fantasies, and socializing with family and friends. When it comes to fast-food restaurants, consumers judge the perceived price value of what they receive not just by their food experience but also by the behaviour of the wait staff, the store's location, and the store appearance.[16]

TYPES OF RETAILERS

Because new types of retailers continue to evolve in response to changes in consumer demand, a universal classification system for retailers has yet to be devised. Certain differences do, however, define several categories of retailers: (1) forms of ownership, (2) shopping effort expended by customers, (3) services provided to customers, (4) product lines, and (5) location of retail transactions.

As Figure 13.3 points out, most retailing operations fit in different categories. A 7-Eleven outlet may be classified as a convenience store (category 2) with self-service (category 3) and a relatively broad product line (category 4). It is both a store-type retailer (category 5) and a member of a chain (category 1).

CLASSIFICATION OF RETAILERS BY FORM OF OWNERSHIP

Perhaps the easiest method for categorizing retailers is by ownership structure, distinguishing between chain stores and independent retailers. In addition, independent retailers may join wholesaler-sponsored voluntary chains, band together to form retail cooperatives, or enter into franchise agreements with manufacturers, wholesalers, or service-provider organizations. Each type of ownership has its own unique advantages and strategies.

Chain Stores

Chain stores are groups of retail outlets that operate under central ownership and management and handle the same product lines. Chains have a major advantage over independent retailers in economies of scale. Volume purchases allow chains to pay lower prices than their independent rivals must pay. Since a chain may encompass hundreds of retail stores, it can afford extensive advertising; sales training; and sophisticated computerized systems for merchandise ordering, inventory management, forecasting, and accounting. Also, the large sales volume and wide geographic reach of a chain may enable it to advertise in a variety of media.

Independent Retailers

The Canadian retailing structure supports a large number of small stores, many medium-size stores, and a small number of large stores. The retail industry represents Canada's largest segment of small businesses: 146,000 firms that employ 795,000 people, an average of just under 5.5 people per firm.[17] Most of these retail locations are independent retailers.

Independent retailers compete with chains in a number of ways. The traditional advantage of independent stores is friendly, personalized service. Cooperatives offer another strategy for independents. For instance, cooperatives such as Best Western Hotels and Pharmasave help independents compete with chains by providing volume buying power as well as advertising and marketing programs.

CLASSIFICATION BY SHOPPING EFFORT

Another classification system is based on the reasons consumers shop at particular retail outlets. This approach categorizes stores as convenience, shopping, or specialty retailers.

Convenience retailers focus their marketing appeals on accessible locations, long store hours, rapid checkout service, and adequate parking facilities. Local food stores, gasoline stations, and dry

Marketoid

Founded in 1909, UFA Co-operative—a retailer cooperative with about 110,000 members—now operates 35 retail stores, four fertilizer plants, and more than 110 petroleum outlets.

convenience retailer Store that appeals to customers with accessible location, long hours, rapid checkout, and adequate parking.

figure 13.3

Bases for Categorizing Retailers

Shopping Effort Expended by Customers
Convenience Retailers
Shopping Stores
Specialty Outlets

Services Provided for Customers
Self-Service
Self-Selection
Limited-Service
Full-Service

Form of Ownership
Corporate Chain
Independent Retailer

Product Lines
Specialty Retailer
Limited-Line Retailer
General Merchandise Retailer

Location of Retail Transactions
Retail Stores
Nonstore and Internet Retailing

Alimentation Couche-Tard is Canada's convenience store leader. It operates more than 6,600 locations under the Couche-Tard and Mac's banners.

H. F. (Herb) MacKenzie

Marketoid

In 2014, Nestlé opened its very first Kit Kat store in Japan, with such limited-edition varieties as Sublime Bitter, Special Sakura Green Tea, and Special Chilli.

specialty retailer Store that combines carefully defined product lines, services, and reputation to persuade shoppers to spend considerable shopping effort there.

cleaners fit this category. Alimentation Couche-Tard is Canada's convenience store leader. It employs more than 60,000 people and has more than 6,600 locations that operate under the Couche-Tard and Mac's banners across all 10 Canadian provinces and 38 states of the United States. It also has more than 2,200 locations in Europe and more than 4,200 locations that are operated under the Circle K banner in Asia, Mexico, and the United Arab Emirates through licensing agreements.[18]

Shopping stores typically include furniture stores, appliance retailers, clothing outlets, and sporting goods stores. Consumers usually compare prices, assortments, and quality levels at competing outlets before making purchase decisions. Consequently, managers of shopping stores attempt to differentiate their outlets through advertising, in-store displays, well-trained and knowledgeable salespeople, and appropriate merchandise assortments.

Specialty retailers combine carefully defined product lines, services, and reputations in attempts to convince consumers to expend considerable effort to shop at their stores. Examples include Edie Hats (Vancouver), The Camera Store (Calgary), Woodlands Gallery (Winnipeg), and Aerobics First (Halifax). Many specialty retailers, such as Gap, La Senza, and Running Room, have locations across Canada.

CLASSIFICATION BY SERVICES PROVIDED

Another category differentiates retailers by the services they provide to customers. This classification system consists of three retail types: self-service, self-selection, or full-service retailers.

The 7-Eleven convenience stores are classified as self-service stores, while Safeway and Sobeys grocery stores are examples of self-selection stores. Both categories sell convenience products people can purchase frequently with little assistance. Full-service retailers such as Holt Renfrew focus on fashion-oriented merchandise, backed by a complete array of customer services.

CLASSIFICATION BY PRODUCT LINES

Product lines also define a set of retail categories and the marketing strategies appropriate for firms within those categories. Grouping retailers by product lines produces three major categories: specialty stores, limited-line retailers, and general merchandise retailers.

Specialty Stores

A *specialty store* typically handles only part of a single product line. However, it stocks this portion in considerable depth or variety. Specialty stores include a wide range of retail outlets: examples are fish markets, grocery stores, men's and women's shoe stores, and bakeries. Although some specialty stores are chain outlets, most are independent small-scale operations. They represent perhaps the greatest concentration of independent retailers who develop expertise in one product area and provide narrow lines of products for their local markets. The "Marketing and the SME" feature describes how a small number of specialty pizza shops in Nova Scotia has been able to expand well beyond their local geographic area by selling a product that is still demanded by loyal customers long after they leave home.

Specialty stores should not be confused with specialty products. Specialty stores typically carry convenience and shopping goods. The label *specialty* reflects the practice of handling a specific, narrow line of merchandise. For example, Denman Bike Shop, with two locations in Vancouver, sells bicycles to meet everyone's needs; and also offers a huge selection of seats, bells, lights, grips, baskets, handlebars, and more. And, if your bicycle needs service, it can do that too.[19]

MARKETING AND THE SME | Getting Your Fix from Home

WHEN students visit home from college or university, they often return with many of their favourite foods, compliments of mom and dad. Sometimes care packages arrive at school via Canada Post or courier. But what happens when you move a long distance away, maybe to seek employment in another province, or even outside Canada, and you get homesick for some of your favourite food items from your former community? Many small restaurants and food producers create unique products that you just can't get anywhere else on earth. Some Canadians are turning to UPS or other couriers to get their "hometown fix."

Pictou County, Nova Scotia, is famous for pizzas that are unlike any others. Just ask a Pictonian. What makes pizzas from there so special? Many small pizza makers use Halifax-based Brothers famous pepperoni. Instead of the regular pizza sauce, they make a special, spicy brown sauce. Pictou County pizzas are available in several restaurants in Halifax that are trying to attract former residents from Pictou County. Yes, the pepperoni is shipped 160 kilometres to Pictou Country, gets baked in a pizza, and the pizza gets returned 160 kilometres to Halifax. But that's not the farthest these pizzas have travelled. Pictou County pizzas are regularly shipped to Ontario, Alberta, and even British Columbia. For about $80, UPS will deliver six frozen Pictou County pizzas to Fort McMurray, Alberta—more expensive because it is not the easiest place to reach in Canada. Pictou County pizzas have even been

delivered to Afghanistan. One Pictou Country pizzeria claims it ships as many as 15 pizza orders by courier each month.

If you ever get to Pictou County, be sure to visit one of the small pizzerias that are known for their famous pizza: Sam's (New Glasgow, Stellarton, Trenton), Alice's (New Glasgow), or Acropole (New Glasgow, Pictou, Westville). In 2014, the Pictou County Rotary Club International sponsored the inaugural Pictou County Pizza Competition. Following blind taste tests, the "celebrity" judges awarded Acropole first place, a title it will defend as the planned annual event promises to grow in future years.

Once you try a Pictou County pizza, you'll understand why the Pizza Hut that once opened there didn't last very long. Oh, while you're in Pictou County, you might want to try Cameron's oatmeal pudding, similar but not the same as white pudding, and unavailable anywhere else in Canada. You can buy it in many local supermarkets, such as Sobeys. Or, if you want, you can have it shipped overnight by UPS to almost anywhere in Canada. (A shipment left Pictou County the day this was written and arrived in St. Catharines the following day. Unfortunately, it was a six-day supply.)

Sources: H.F. (Herb) MacKenzie, many personal experiences; Heather Brimicombe, "Acropole New Glasgow Named Best Pizza in Pictou County," **www.ngnews.ca**, April 27, 2014; Amy MacKenzie, "UPS Store Shipping Pictou County Pizza across Canada," **www.ngnews.ca**, April 9, 2013; "Pictou County Pizza," available **http://thelocaltravelerns.com/2012/05/24/pictou-county-pizza**, accessed March 10, 2014.

Limited-Line Retailers

Customers find a large assortment of products within one product line or a few related lines in a **limited-line store**. This type of retail operation typically develops in areas with a large enough population to sufficiently support it. Examples of limited-line stores are Golf Town (golf clothing and equipment) and The Brick (furniture). These retailers cater to the needs of people who want to select from complete lines in purchasing particular products.

A unique type of limited-line retailer is known as a **category killer**. These stores offer huge selections and low prices in single product lines. Stores within this category—for example, Best Buy, Toys "R" Us, and Home Depot—are among the most successful retailers in the nation. Category killers at first took business away from general merchandise discounters, which were not able to compete in selection or price. Recently, however, expanded merchandise and aggressive cost cutting by warehouse clubs and by Walmart have turned the tables. Competition from Internet companies that are able to offer unlimited selection and speedy delivery have also taken customers away. While they still remain a powerful force in retailing, category killers are not invulnerable.

limited-line store Retailer that offers a large assortment within a single product line or within a few related product lines.

category killer Store offering huge selections and low prices in single product lines.

General Merchandise Retailers

General merchandise retailers, which carry a wide variety of product lines that are all stocked in some depth, distinguish themselves from limited-line and specialty retailers by the large number of product lines they carry. Walmart and Target are examples of general merchandise retailers. The general store described earlier in this chapter is a primitive form of a general merchandise retailer.

general merchandise retailer Store that carries a wide variety of product lines, stocking all of them in some depth.

This category includes variety stores, department stores, and mass merchandisers such as discount stores, off-price retailers, and hypermarkets.

Variety Stores

A retail outlet that offers an extensive range and assortment of low-price merchandise is called a *variety store*. Less popular today than they once were, many of these stores have evolved into or given way to other types of retailers such as discount stores. Giant Tiger is an example of today's variety store. The country's variety stores now account for less than 1 percent of all retail sales. However, variety stores remain popular in other parts of the world. Many retail outlets in Spain and Mexico are family-owned variety stores.

Department Stores

department store Large store that handles a variety of merchandise, including clothing, household goods, appliances, and furniture.

In essence, a **department store** is a series of limited-line and specialty stores under one roof. By definition, this large retailer handles a variety of merchandise, including men's, women's, and children's clothing and accessories; household linens and dry goods; home furnishings; and furniture. It serves as a one-stop shopping destination for almost all personal and household products. The Bay and Sears Canada are classic examples.

Department stores built their reputations by offering wide varieties of services, such as charge accounts, delivery, gift wrapping, and liberal return privileges. As a result, they incur relatively high operating costs, averaging about 45 to 60 percent of sales.

Department stores have faced intense competition over the past several years. Relatively high operating costs have left them vulnerable to competition from specialty stores, discount stores, and Internet retailers. In addition, department stores' traditional locations in downtown business districts have suffered from problems associated with limited parking, traffic congestion, and population migration to the suburbs.

Department stores have fought back in a variety of ways. Some have closed certain sections, such as electronics, in which high costs kept them from competing with discount houses and category killers. They have added bargain outlets, expanded parking facilities, and opened major branches in regional shopping centres. Marketers have attempted to revitalize downtown retailing in many cities by modernizing their stores, expanding store hours, making special efforts to attract the tourist and convention trade, and serving the needs of urban residents.

Mass Merchandisers

mass merchandiser Store that stocks a wider line of goods than a department store, usually without the same depth of assortment within each line.

Mass merchandising has made major inroads into department store sales by emphasizing lower prices for well-known brand-name products, high product turnover, and limited services. A **mass merchandiser** often stocks a wider line of items than a department store but usually without the same depth of assortment within each line. Discount houses, off-price retailers, hypermarkets, and catalogue retailers are all examples of mass merchandisers.

Discount Houses

discount house Store that charges low prices but may not offer services such as credit.

A **discount house** charges low prices and offers fewer services. Early discount stores sold mostly appliances. Today, they offer soft goods, drugs, food, gasoline, and furniture.

By eliminating many of the "free" services provided by traditional retailers, these operations can keep their markups 10 to 25 percent below those of their competitors. Some of the early discounters have since added services, stocked well-known name brands, and boosted their prices. In fact, many now resemble department stores.

A discount format that is gaining strength is the *warehouse club*. These no-frills, cash-and-carry outlets offer consumers access to name-brand products at deeply discounted prices. Selection at warehouse clubs includes such varied items as gourmet popcorn, books, peanut butter, luggage, bakery products, and electronics sold in vast warehouse-like settings. Attracting business away from almost every retailing segment, warehouse clubs now even offer fresh food and oil changes. Customers must be members to shop at warehouse clubs. Costco is Canada's predominant warehouse club since Sam's Club has closed its Canadian operations.

Off-Price Retailers

Another version of a discount house is an *off-price retailer*. This kind of store stocks only designer labels or well-known brand-name clothing at prices equal to or below regular wholesale prices and then passes the cost savings along to buyers. While many off-price retailers are located in outlets in downtown areas or in freestanding buildings, a growing number are concentrating in *outlet malls*—shopping centres that house only off-price retailers.

Inventory at off-price stores changes frequently as buyers take advantage of special price offers from manufacturers selling excess merchandise. Off-price retailers such as Winners, HomeSense, and Home Outfitters also keep their prices below those of traditional retailers by offering fewer services. Off-price retailing has been well received by today's shoppers. France-based retailer Vente-privée.com sells high-fashion overstock merchandise through invitation-only clearance sales conducted solely on the Web.[20]

Hypermarkets and Supercentres

Another innovation in discount retailing is the creation of **hypermarkets**—giant one-stop shopping facilities that offer wide selections of grocery and general merchandise products at discount prices. Store size determines the major difference between hypermarkets and supercentres. Hypermarkets typically fill up 200,000 or more square feet of selling space, about a third larger than most **supercentres**. With regard to merchandise strategy, hypermarkets generally carry a larger proportion of food items than supercentres, including fresh meat, fish, and produce. Despite great success in Europe, hypermarkets have had limited success in North America. Meijer is a regional hypermarket chain that operates more than 190 locations in five U.S. states.[21]

hypermarket Giant one-stop shopping facility offering wide selections of grocery items and general merchandise at discount prices, typically filling up 200,000 or more square feet of selling space.

supercentre Large store, usually smaller than a hypermarket, that combines groceries with discount store merchandise.

CLASSIFICATION OF RETAIL TRANSACTIONS BY LOCATION

Although most retail transactions occur in stores, nonstore retailing serves as an important marketing channel for many products. In addition, both consumer and business-to-business marketers rely on nonstore retailing to generate orders or requests for more information that may result in future orders.

Direct marketing is a broad concept that includes direct mail, direct selling, direct response retailing, telemarketing, Internet retailing, and automatic merchandising. The last sections of this chapter will consider each type of nonstore retailing.

④ **Explain the concepts of retail convergence and scrambled merchandising.**

RETAIL CONVERGENCE AND SCRAMBLED MERCHANDISING

Many traditional differences no longer distinguish familiar types of retailers, rendering any set of classifications less useful. **Retail convergence**, whereby similar merchandise is available from many retail outlets distinguished by price more than any other factor, is blurring distinctions between types of retailers and the merchandise mix they offer. A few years ago, a customer looking for a fashionable coffeepot might have headed straight for Williams-Sonoma or Starbucks. Today, she's just as likely to pick one up at Canadian Tire or Walmart, where she can check out new spring fashions or stock up on paper goods. The Gap is no longer pitted only against American Eagle Outfitters or L.L. Bean but against designer-label brands at department stores and Joe Fresh at Real Canadian Superstore, too. Grocery stores compete with Walmart Supercenter and Costco. Walmart has beefed up its already robust product mix to include VUDU broadband streaming services for the consumer electronics products it sells alongside the apparel, housewares, fine jewellery, and more.[22] All these examples highlight how important it is to know your competition. See the "Career Readiness" feature for some tips on how to stay ahead of your competitors.

Scrambled merchandising—in which a retailer combines dissimilar product lines in an attempt to boost sales volume—has also muddied the waters. Drugstores, such as the newly renovated Shoppers Drug Mart stores, not only fill prescriptions but offer cameras,

retail convergence A situation in which similar merchandise is available from many retail outlets, resulting in the blurring of distinctions between type of retailer and merchandise offered.

scrambled merchandising Retailing practice of combining dissimilar product lines to boost sales volume.

assessment check 4 ✓

4.1 How do we classify retailers by form of ownership?

4.2 Categorize retailers by shopping effort and by services provided.

4.3 List several ways to classify retailers by product line.

A classic article in the *Harvard Business Review* claimed that railroads would have continued to grow if they had correctly identified their competition as everyone in the transportation business. How can you thoroughly analyze your competitors to avoid making a similar mistake?

- Define "competition" to include anything and everything that might take your customers away. Anticipate market entries from existing and new directions. Movie theatres compete with all forms of live and recorded entertainment, for instance, not just other theatre chains.
- Become your competitors' customer. Buy and try the product; visit the store and the website; talk to other customers in person or online. What are your competitors doing well? Where are they weak?

- Go to trade shows and conferences, and let competitors' reps tell you all about their new products, goals, and selling strategies.
- Investigate competitors' company websites, Facebook and Twitter pages, and blogs. Sign up for their marketing messages, including newsletters and mobile ads. How effectively are they reaching their customers—and yours?
- On a search engine, type in "Link:" followed by the full URL of your competitors' website, to see which sites are sending Web traffic to your rivals. Will they do the same for you?

Sources: "Analyze the Competition to Keep Your Edge," All Business.com, **www .allbusiness.com**, accessed May 24, 2012; "Tips to Analyzing Your Competition Online," Best Contractor Leads.com, **http://bestcontractorleads.com**, accessed May 24, 2012; "7 Tips for Analyzing the Business Competition," *USA Today*, **www.usatoday.com**, accessed May 24, 2012.

cards, magazines, small appliances, home decor accessories, and even fresh and prepared foods. Pharmacists not only dispense prescription drugs, they also dispense medical advice for a number of illnesses and, more recently, offer free flu shots.

(5) **Identify the functions performed by wholesaling intermediaries.**

wholesaler Channel intermediary that takes title to goods it handles and then distributes these goods to retailers, other distributors, or B2B customers.

wholesaling intermediary Comprehensive term that describes wholesalers as well as agents and brokers.

WHOLESALING INTERMEDIARIES

Recall from Chapter 12 that several distribution channels involve marketing intermediaries called **wholesalers**. These firms take title to the goods they handle and sell those products primarily to retailers or to other wholesalers or business users. They sell to ultimate consumers only in insignificant quantities if at all. **Wholesaling intermediaries**, a broader category, include not only wholesalers but also agents and brokers, who perform important wholesaling activities without taking title to the goods.

FUNCTIONS OF WHOLESALING INTERMEDIARIES

As specialists in certain marketing functions, as opposed to production or manufacturing functions, wholesaling intermediaries can perform these functions more efficiently than producers or consumers. The importance of these activities results from the utility they create, the services they provide, and the cost reductions they allow.

Creating Utility

Wholesaling intermediaries create three types of utility for consumers. They enhance time utility by making products available for sale when consumers want to purchase them. They create place utility by helping to deliver goods and services for purchase at convenient locations. They create ownership (or possession) utility when a smooth exchange of title to the products from producers or intermediaries to final purchasers is complete. Possession utility can also result from transactions in which actual title does not pass to purchasers, as in rental-car services.

Providing Services

Table 13.1 lists a number of services provided by wholesaling intermediaries. The list clearly indicates the marketing utilities—time, place, and possession utility—that wholesaling intermediaries create or

table 13.1   *Wholesaling Services for Customers and Producer-Suppliers*

SERVICE	BENEFICIARIES OF SERVICE	
	Customers	Producer-Suppliers
Buying Anticipates customer demands and applies knowledge of alternative sources of supply; acts as purchasing agent for customers.	Yes	No
Selling Provides a sales force to call on customers, creating a low-cost method for servicing smaller retailers and business users.	No	Yes
Storing Maintains warehouse facilities at lower costs than most individual producers or retailers could achieve. Reduces risk and cost of maintaining inventory for producers.	Yes	Yes
Transporting Customers receive prompt delivery in response to their demands, reducing their inventory investments. Wholesalers also break bulk by purchasing in economical carload or truckload lots, then reselling in smaller quantities, thereby reducing overall transportation costs.	Yes	Yes
Providing Marketing Information Offers important marketing research input for producers through regular contacts with retail and business buyers. Provides customers with information about new products; technical information about product lines; reports on competitors' activities and industry trends; and advisory information concerning pricing changes, legal changes, and so forth.	Yes	Yes
Financing Grants credit that might be unavailable for purchases directly from manufacturers. Provides financing assistance to producers by purchasing products in advance of sale and by promptly paying bills.	Yes	Yes
Risk Taking Evaluates credit risks of numerous, distant retail customers, and small-business users. Extends credit to customers that qualify. By transporting and stocking products in inventory, the wholesaler assumes risk of spoilage, theft, or obsolescence.	Yes	Yes

enhance. These services also reflect the basic marketing functions of buying, selling, storing, transporting, providing market information, financing, and risk taking.

Of course, many types of wholesaling intermediaries provide varying services, and not all of them perform every service listed in the table. Producer-suppliers rely on wholesaling intermediaries for distribution and selection of firms that offer the desired combinations of services. In general, however, the critical marketing functions listed in the table form the basis for any evaluation of a marketing intermediary's efficiency. The risk-taking function affects each service of the intermediary.

Dominion Citrus Limited, based in Etobicoke, Ontario, supplies fresh produce and various packaging and sorting services to retailers, food service companies, and other food distribution businesses. It procures, processes, packs, sorts, grades, warehouses, and distributes to over 400 customers, mainly in Ontario and Quebec, but also in the United States and Europe.[23]

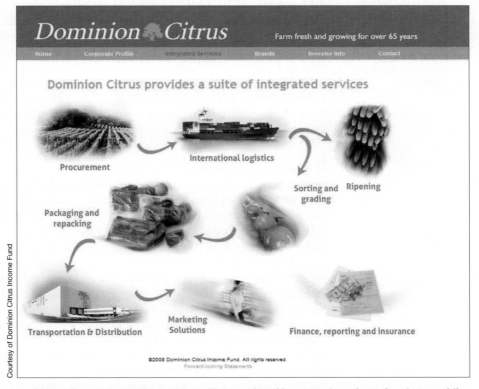

Courtesy of Dominion Citrus Income Fund

Dominion Citrus is a wholesaler that offers a suite of integrated services aimed at providing value-added solutions to its customers.

figure 13.4

Transaction Economies through Wholesaling Intermediaries

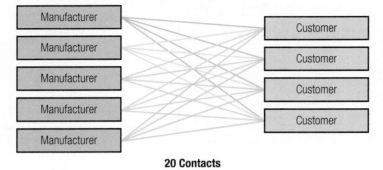

20 Contacts

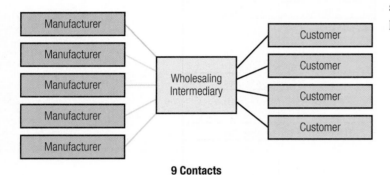

9 Contacts

Lowering Costs by Limiting Contacts

When an intermediary represents numerous producers, it often cuts the costs of buying and selling. The transaction economies are illustrated in Figure 13.4, which shows five manufacturers marketing their outputs to four different customers. Without an intermediary, these exchanges create a total of 20 transactions. Adding a wholesaling intermediary reduces the number of transactions to nine.

WFS Ltd.—formerly Windsor Factory Supply—represents more than 3,500 suppliers and sells to more than 4,500 customers. The company now has 10 Canadian branches, a branch in South Carolina, and a warehouse near Detroit, Michigan. With sales approaching $100 million, WFS sells such things as maintenance, repair, and operating supplies; plumbing supplies; and health and safety equipment.[24]

assessment check 5

5.1 What is a wholesaler? How does it differ from a wholesaling intermediary?

5.2 How do wholesaling intermediaries help sellers lower costs?

TYPES OF WHOLESALING INTERMEDIARIES

⑥ Outline the major types of independent wholesaling intermediaries and the appropriate situations for using each.

Various types of wholesaling intermediaries operate in different distribution channels. Some provide wide ranges of services or handle broad lines of goods; while others specialize in individual services, goods, or industries. Figure 13.5 classifies wholesaling intermediaries by two characteristics: ownership and title flows (whether title passes from manufacturer to wholesaling intermediary). There are three basic ownership structures: (1) manufacturer-owned facilities, (2) independent wholesaling intermediaries, and (3) retailer-owned cooperatives and buying offices. The two types of independent wholesaling intermediaries are merchant wholesalers, which take title of the goods, and agents and brokers, which do not.

Manufacturer-Owned Facilities

Several factors lead manufacturers to distribute their goods directly through company-owned facilities. Some perishable goods need rigid control of distribution to avoid spoilage; other goods require complex installation or servicing. Some goods need aggressive promotion. Goods with high-unit values allow profitable sales by manufacturers directly to ultimate purchasers. Manufacturer-owned facilities include sales branches, sales offices, trade fairs, and merchandise marts.

A *sales branch* carries inventory and processes orders for customers from available stock. Branches provide a storage function like independent wholesalers and serve as offices for sales representatives in their territories. They are prevalent in marketing channels for chemicals, commercial machinery and equipment, motor vehicles, and petroleum products.

A *sales office*, in contrast, does not carry inventory, but it does serve as a regional office for a manufacturer's sales personnel. Locations close to the firm's customers help limit selling costs and support active customer service. For example, many Ontario manufacturers have established sales offices in eastern and western Canada.

A *trade fair* (or trade exhibition) is a periodic show at which manufacturers in a particular industry display their wares for visiting retail and wholesale buyers. For example, the Canadian Gift Association (CanGift) holds a trade fair biannually in Toronto where exhibitors display their

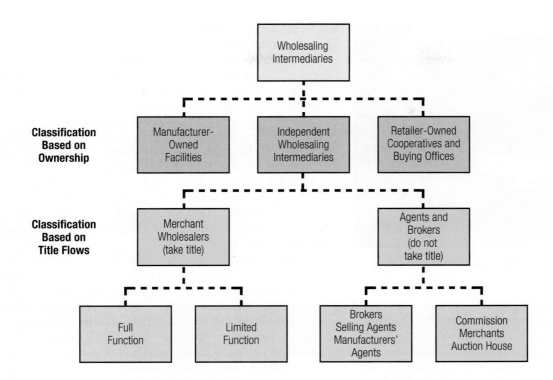

figure 13.5

**Major Types
of Wholesaling
Intermediaries**

products to more than 25,000 retail buyers. Smaller gift fairs are held regularly in Halifax, Calgary, Vancouver, and many other Canadian cities.

A *merchandise mart* provides space for permanent showrooms and exhibits, which manufacturers rent to market their goods. One of the world's largest merchandise marts is Chicago's Merchandise Mart Center, a 7-million-square-foot complex that hosts more than 30 seasonal buying markets each year. Many large merchandise marts are located in the United States, but they attract exhibitors from Canada and around the world.

Independent Wholesaling Intermediaries

Many wholesaling intermediaries are independently owned. These firms fall into two major categories: merchant wholesalers and agents and brokers.

Merchant Wholesalers

A **merchant wholesaler** takes title to the goods it handles. Merchant wholesalers account for roughly 60 percent of all sales at the wholesale level. Further classifications divide these wholesalers into full-function or limited-function wholesalers, as indicated in Figure 13.5. WFS Ltd., mentioned in the previous section, is a merchant wholesaler.

A full-function merchant wholesaler provides a complete assortment of services for retailers and business purchasers. Such a wholesaler stores merchandise in a convenient location, allowing customers to make purchases on short notice and minimizing inventory requirements. The firm typically maintains a sales force that calls on retailers, makes deliveries, and extends credit to qualified buyers. Full-function wholesalers are common in the drug, grocery, and hardware industries. In the business-goods market, full-function merchant wholesalers (often called *industrial distributors*) sell machinery, inexpensive accessory equipment, and supplies.

A **rack jobber** is a full-function merchant wholesaler that markets specialized lines of merchandise to retailers. A rack jobber supplies the racks, stocks the merchandise, prices the goods, and makes regular visits to refill shelves. Sometimes rack jobbers are the exclusive supplier of a retailer—as in the case of Anderson Merchandisers, a rack jobber in the entertainment sector, which grew by being the supplier to Walmart stores' consumer electronics departments.[25]

Limited-function merchant wholesalers fit into four categories: cash-and-carry wholesalers, truck wholesalers, drop shippers, and mail-order wholesalers. Limited-function wholesalers serve the

merchant wholesaler Independently owned wholesaling intermediary that takes title to the goods it handles; also known as an industrial distributor in the business goods market.

rack jobber Full-function merchant wholesaler that markets specialized lines of merchandise to retail stores.

Auction house eBay offers a wide variety of products in all price ranges.

H. F. (Herb) MacKenzie

truck wholesaler (truck jobber) Limited-function merchant wholesaler that markets perishable food items.

drop shipper Limited-function merchant wholesaler that accepts orders from customers and forwards these orders to producers, which then ship directly to the customers who placed the orders.

mail-order wholesaler Limited-function merchant wholesaler that distributes catalogues instead of sending sales personnel to contact customers.

food, coal, lumber, cosmetics, jewellery, sporting goods, and general merchandise industries.

A *cash-and-carry wholesaler* performs most wholesaling functions except for financing and delivery. Although feasible for small stores, this kind of wholesaling generally is unworkable for large-scale grocery stores. Today, cash-and-carry operations typically function as departments within regular full-service wholesale operations. Cash-and-carry wholesalers are becoming less popular in Canada but are still commonplace in some European countries.

A **truck wholesaler**, or **truck jobber**, markets perishable food items such as bread, tobacco, potato chips, candy, and dairy products. Truck wholesalers make regular deliveries to retailers, perform sales and collection functions, and promote product lines.

A **drop shipper** accepts orders from customers and forwards these orders to producers, which then ship the desired products directly to customers. Although drop shippers take title to goods, they never physically handle or even see the merchandise. These intermediaries often operate in industries selling bulky goods—such as coal and lumber—that customers buy in large lots.

A **mail-order wholesaler** is a limited-function merchant wholesaler that distributes physical or online catalogues as opposed to sending sales representatives to contact retail, business, and institutional customers. Customers then make purchases by mail, phone, or online. Such a wholesaler often serves relatively small customers in outlying areas. Mail-order operations mainly exist in the hardware, cosmetics, jewellery, sporting goods, and specialty food lines as well as in general merchandise. Some popular mail-order products are pharmaceuticals, roasted bean coffee, Christmas trees and wreaths, and popcorn.

Table 13.2 compares the various types of merchant wholesalers and the services they provide. Full-function merchant wholesalers and truck wholesalers rank as relatively high-cost intermediaries due to the number of services they perform; while cash-and-carry wholesalers, drop shippers, and mail-order wholesalers provide fewer services and set lower prices since they incur lower operating costs.

Agents and Brokers

A second group of independent wholesaling intermediaries, agents and brokers, may or may not take possession of the goods they handle, but they never take title. They normally perform fewer services than merchant wholesalers, working mainly to bring together buyers and sellers. Agents and brokers fall into five categories: commission merchants, auction houses, brokers, selling agents, and manufacturers' representatives (reps).

table 13.2   **Comparison of the Types of Merchant Wholesalers and Their Services**

		LIMITED-FUNCTION WHOLESALER			
SERVICE	**Full-Function**	**Cash-and-Carry**	**Truck**	**Drop Shipper**	**Mail-Order**
Anticipates customer needs	Yes	Yes	Yes	No	Yes
Carries inventory	Yes	Yes	Yes	No	Yes
Delivers	Yes	No	Yes	No	No
Provides market information	Yes	Rarely	Yes	Yes	No
Provides credit	Yes	No	No	Yes	Sometimes
Assumes ownership risk by taking title	Yes	Yes	Yes	Yes	Yes

Commission merchants, who predominate in the markets for agricultural products, take possession when producers ship goods such as grain, produce, and livestock to central markets for sale. Commission merchants act as producers' agents and receive agreed-upon fees when they make sales. Since customers inspect the products and prices fluctuate, commission merchants receive considerable latitude in marketing decisions. The owners of the goods may specify minimum prices, but the commission merchants sell these goods at the best possible prices. The commission merchants then deduct their fees from the sales proceeds.

An *auction house* gathers buyers and sellers in one location and allows potential buyers to inspect merchandise before submitting competing purchase offers. Auction house commissions typically reflect specified percentages of the sales prices of the auctioned items. Auctions are common in the distribution of tobacco, used cars, artwork, livestock, furs, and fruit. The Internet has led to a new type of auction house that connects customers and sellers in the online world. A well-known example is eBay, which auctions a wide variety of products in all price ranges.

Brokers work mainly to bring together buyers and sellers. A broker represents either the buyer or the seller, but not both, in a given transaction, and the broker receives a fee from the client when the transaction is completed. Intermediaries that specialize in arranging buying and selling transactions between domestic producers and foreign buyers are called *export brokers*. Brokers operate in industries characterized by large numbers of small suppliers and purchasers, such as real estate, frozen foods, and used machinery. Since they provide one-time services for sellers or buyers, they cannot serve as effective channels for manufacturers seeking regular, continuing service. A firm that seeks to develop a more permanent channel might choose instead to use a selling agent or manufacturers' agent.

A **selling agent** typically exerts full authority over pricing decisions and promotional outlays, and it often provides financial assistance for the manufacturer. Selling agents act as independent marketing departments because they can assume responsibility for the total marketing programs of client firms' product lines. Selling agents mainly operate in the coal, lumber, and textiles industries. For a small, poorly financed, production-oriented firm, such an intermediary might prove the ideal marketing channel.

While a manufacturer may deal with only one selling agent, a firm that hires **manufacturers' representatives** often delegates marketing tasks to many of these agents. Such an independent salesperson may work for a number of firms that produce related, noncompeting products. Manufacturers' reps are paid on a commission basis, such as 6 percent of sales. Unlike selling agents, who may contract for exclusive rights to market a product, manufacturers' agents operate in specific territories. They may develop new sales territories or represent relatively small firms and those firms with unrelated lines. Jeff Walker of Puslinch, Ontario, is a manufacturers' agent that serves the truck market in Ontario. He represents a number of manufacturers and sells truck accessories, such as grill guards, running boards, bed rails, hydraulic systems, electrical components, heavy duty aluminum racks, stainless steel moose guards, remote-operated trailer testers, and more.[26]

The importance of selling agents in many markets has declined because manufacturers want better control of their marketing programs than these intermediaries allow. In contrast, the volume of sales by manufacturers' agents has more than doubled and now accounts for 37 percent of all sales by agents and brokers. Table 13.3 compares the major types of agents and brokers on the basis of the services they perform.

commission merchant Agent wholesaling intermediary who takes possession of goods shipped to a central market for sale, acts as the producer's agent, and collects an agreed-upon fee at the time of the sale.

broker Agent wholesaling intermediary who does not take title to or possession of goods in the course of its primary function, which is to bring together buyers and sellers.

selling agent Agent wholesaling intermediary for the entire marketing program of a firm's product line.

manufacturers' representative Agent wholesaling intermediary who represents manufacturers of related but noncompeting products and who receives a commission on each sale.

Marketoid

Acklands-Grainger, Canada's largest merchant wholesaler with 175 branches and six distribution centres from coast to coast, has a 3,168-page catalogue that features more than 300,000 items.

table 13.3 **Services Provided by Agents and Brokers**

SERVICE	Commission Merchant	Auction House	Broker	Manufacturers' Agent	Selling Agent
Anticipates customer needs	Yes	Sometimes	Sometimes	Yes	Yes
Carries inventory	Yes	Yes	No	No	No
Delivers	Yes	No	No	Sometimes	No
Provides market information	Yes	Yes	Yes	Yes	Yes
Provides credit	Sometimes	No	No	No	Sometimes
Assumes ownership risk by taking title	No	No	No	No	No

RETAILER-OWNED COOPERATIVES AND BUYING OFFICES

Retailers may assume numerous wholesaling functions in an attempt to reduce costs or provide special services. Independent retailers sometimes band together to form buying groups that can achieve cost savings through quantity purchases. Other groups of retailers establish retailer-owned wholesale facilities by forming cooperative chains. Large chain retailers often establish centralized buying offices to negotiate large-scale purchases directly with manufacturers.

⑦ **Compare the basic types of direct marketing and nonstore retailing.**

DIRECT MARKETING AND OTHER NONSTORE RETAILING

Although most retail transactions occur in stores, nonstore retailing is an important marketing channel for many products. Both consumer and business-to-business marketers rely on nonstore retailing to generate leads or requests for more information that may result in future orders.

direct marketing Direct communications, other than personal sales contacts, between buyer and seller, designed to generate sales, information requests, or store or website visits.

Direct marketing is a broad concept that includes direct mail, direct selling, direct-response retailing, telemarketing, Internet retailing, and automatic merchandising. Direct and interactive marketing expenditures amount to hundreds of billions of dollars in yearly purchases across North America. The last sections of this chapter consider each type of nonstore retailing.

DIRECT MAIL

Direct mail is a major component of direct marketing. It comes in many forms, such as sales letters, postcards, brochures, booklets, catalogues, house organs (periodicals published by organizations to cover internal issues), and DVDs. Both not-for-profit and profit-seeking organizations make extensive use of this distribution channel.

Direct mail offers several advantages such as the ability to select a narrow target market, achieve intensive coverage, send messages quickly, choose from various formats, provide complete information, and personalize each mailing piece. Response rates are measurable and higher than other types of advertising. In addition, direct mailings stand alone and do not compete for attention with magazine articles and television programs. On the other hand, the per-reader cost of direct mail is high; effectiveness depends on the quality of the mailing list; and some consumers object strongly to direct mail, considering it "junk mail."

Direct-mail marketing relies heavily on database technology in managing lists of names and in segmenting these lists according to the objectives of the campaign. Recipients get targeted materials, often personalized with their names within the ad's content.

Catalogues are a popular form of direct mail, with more than 10,000 different consumer specialty mail-order catalogues—and thousands more for business-to-business sales—finding their way to almost every home and business in Canada and the United States. In a typical year, mail-order catalogues generate billions of dollars in consumer and business markets. Catalogue marketing continues to grow at a faster rate than brick-and-mortar retailers. Catalogues can be a company's only or primary sales method. L.L. Bean and Spiegel are well-known examples. Brick-and-mortar retailers such as Canadian Tire, Tilley Endurables, Cabela's, and IKEA Canada also distribute catalogues. Cabela's sells outdoor and adventure clothing and equipment and operates several retail locations in western Canada. The company states that its foundation is its world-famous catalogue business and that it creates more than 100 different catalogues each year.[27]

Environmental concerns and new technologies are changing catalogue marketing. Today's online catalogues can be updated quickly, providing consumers with the latest information and prices. They allow marketers to display products in three-dimensional views and can include video sequences of product demonstrations.

DIRECT SELLING

Through direct selling, manufacturers completely bypass retailers and wholesalers. Instead, they set up their own channels to sell their products directly to consumers. Avon, Amway, Pampered Chef, and Tupperware are all direct sellers. This channel was discussed in detail in Chapter 12.

DIRECT-RESPONSE RETAILING

Customers of a direct-response retailer can order merchandise by mail or telephone, by visiting a mail-order desk in a retail store, or by computer or fax machine. The retailer then ships the merchandise to the customer's home or to a local retail store for pickup.

Many direct-response retailers rely on direct mail, such as catalogues, to create telephone and mail-order sales and to promote in-store purchases of products featured in the catalogues. Some firms, such as Lillian Vernon, make almost all their sales through catalogue orders. Mail-order sales have grown at about twice the rate of retail store sales in recent years.

Direct-response retailers are increasingly reaching buyers through the Internet and through unique catalogues that serve special market niches. Many catalogues sell specialty products, such as kitchenware for the professional cook, art supplies, or supplies for the home renovator.

Direct-response retailing also includes home shopping, which runs promotions on cable television networks to sell merchandise through telephone orders. One form of home shopping, the *infomercial,* has existed for years. Infomercials can be short—one to two minutes—or run up to 30 minutes. Both have demonstrated success at generating revenues. Collette Liantonia is known as the "Queen of Infomercials," having produced more than 2,000 of them over 30 years. Among them are pitches for the George Foreman Grill, the Perfect Pasta Pot, and Pajama Jeans.[28]

> **assessment check 7** ✓
>
> **7.1** What is direct marketing?
>
> **7.2** What is direct mail?

TELEMARKETING

Telemarketing refers to direct marketing conducted entirely by telephone. It is the most frequently used form of direct marketing. It provides marketers with a high return on their expenditures, an immediate response, and the opportunity for personalized two-way conversations. Telemarketing is discussed in further detail in Chapter 15.

INTERNET RETAILING

⑧ **Describe how the Internet has altered the wholesaling, retailing, and direct marketing environments.**

Internet-based retailers sell directly to customers via virtual storefronts on the Web. They usually maintain little or no inventory, ordering directly from vendors to fill customer orders received via their websites. In recent years, conventional retailers have anxiously watched the rise—and then the demise—of many poorly planned, financed, and marketed Internet-based retailers. During the dot-com bust, 130 e-tailers failed. Even early successes like Ezshop, an online home furnishings retailer, eventually ran aground. Traditional retailers, using the Web to support brick-and-mortar stores— the so-called *brick-and-click retailers*—have had much better staying power. Sears Canada, Future Shop, and Canadian Tire, for example, have succeeded in extending their expertise to the Web. Costco offers thousands of products on its website, many of which are not available at store locations. Customers can also request email alerts or go online to read the *Costco Connection* magazine.

AUTOMATIC MERCHANDISING

The world's first vending machines dispensed holy water for five-drachma coins in Egyptian temples around 215 B.C. This retailing method has grown rapidly ever since; today, approximately 5,000 North American vending machine operators sell more than $6 billion in convenience goods annually.[29]

Although vending machines have traditionally been limited to snacks and soft drinks, some Canadians were probably excited to hear that marijuana vending machines would be coming to Canada in a partnership between California-based Medbox and an unnamed Canadian firm.

assessment check 8 ✓

8.1 Describe Internet-based retailers.

8.2 Explain how the Internet has enhanced retailers' functions.

In less than a week, Health Canada clarified that this would not happen.[30] However, Canadian marketers have begun to realize the potential of this underused marketing tool. The three major soft-drink companies recently agreed to remove sweetened drinks such as pop and iced tea from vending machines in elementary and high schools nationwide. The calorie-laden drinks will be replaced by bottled water, low-fat milk, and 100 percent fruit juice or sports drinks. The ability to accept credit cards has enabled vending machines to sell high-end items like iPods, headphones, and Sony PlayStation games. Technological advances such as touch screens, animation, and digital imagery make the buying experience fun—and even allow customers to read the back of the package before they buy.[31]

Strategic Implications

As the Internet revolution steadily becomes a way of life—both for consumers and for the businesses marketing goods and services to them—technology will continue to transform the ways in which retailers, wholesalers, and direct marketers connect with customers.

In the retail sector, the unstoppable march toward lower and lower prices has forced retailers from Sears Canada to dollar stores to reevaluate everything, including their logistics, supply networks, and profit margins. Many have used the power of the Internet to strengthen such factors as store image, the merchandising mix, customer service, and the development of long-term relationships with customers.

Though manufacturers first anticipated that Internet technology would enable them to bypass such intermediaries as wholesalers and agents, bringing them closer to the customer, the reality is quite different. Successful wholesalers have been able to establish themselves as essential links in the supply, distribution, and customer-service network. By leveraging technology, they have been able to carve out new roles, providing such expert services as warehousing or fulfillment to many retail clients.

The Internet has empowered direct marketers by facilitating ever more sophisticated database segmentation. Traditional catalogue and direct mail marketers have integrated Internet sites, Web advertising, and emailing programs into a cohesive targeting, distribution, and repeat-buying strategy. ◆◆◆

REVIEW OF CHAPTER OBJECTIVES

① Explain the wheel of retailing.

The wheel of retailing is the hypothesis that each new type of retailer gains a competitive foothold by offering lower prices than current suppliers and maintains profits by reducing or eliminating services. Once established, the innovator begins to add more services, and its prices gradually rise, making it vulnerable to new low-price retailers. This turns the wheel again.

② Discuss how retailers select target markets.

A retailer starts to define its strategy by selecting a target market. The target market dictates, among other things, the product mix, pricing strategy, and location strategy. Retailers deal with consumer behaviour at the most complicated level, and a clear understanding of the target market is critical. Strategies for selecting target markets include merchandising, customer services, pricing, location/distribution, and promotional strategies.

③ Show how the elements of the marketing mix apply to retailing strategy.

A retailer must first identify a target market and then develop a product strategy. Next, it must establish a customer-service strategy. Retail pricing strategy involves decisions on markups and markdowns. Location is often the determining factor in a retailer's success or failure. A retailer's promotional strategy and store atmosphere play important roles in establishing a store's image.

④ **Explain the concepts of retail convergence and scrambled merchandising.**

Retail convergence is the coming together of shoppers, goods, and prices, resulting in the blurring of distinctions between types of retailers and the merchandise mix they offer. Similar selections are available from many sources and are differentiated mainly by price. Scrambled merchandising refers to retailers' practice of carrying dissimilar product lines in an attempt to generate additional sales volume. Retail convergence and scrambled merchandising have made it increasingly difficult to classify retailers.

⑤ **Identify the functions performed by wholesaling intermediaries.**

The functions of wholesaling intermediaries include creating utility, providing services, and lowering costs by limiting contacts.

⑥ **Outline the major types of independent wholesaling intermediaries and the appropriate situations for using each.**

Independent wholesaling intermediaries can be divided into two categories: merchant wholesalers and agents and brokers. The two major types of merchant wholesalers are full-function merchant wholesalers, such as rack jobbers; and limited-function merchant wholesalers, including cash-and-carry wholesalers, truck wholesalers, drop shippers, and mail-order wholesalers. Full-function wholesalers are common in the drug, grocery, and hardware industries.

Limited-function wholesalers are sometimes used in the food, coal, lumber, cosmetics, jewellery, sporting goods, and general merchandise industries. Agents and brokers do not take title to the products they sell; this category includes commission merchants, auction houses, brokers, selling agents, and manufacturers' reps. Companies seeking to develop new sales territories, firms with unrelated lines, and smaller firms use manufacturers' reps. Commission merchants are common in the marketing of agricultural products. Auction houses are used to sell tobacco, used cars, livestock, furs, and fruit. Brokers are prevalent in the real estate, frozen foods, and used machinery industries.

⑦ **Compare the basic types of direct marketing and nonstore retailing.**

Direct marketing is a distribution channel consisting of direct communication to a consumer or business recipient. It generates orders and sales leads that may result in future orders. Because direct marketing responds to fragmented media markets and audiences, growth of customized products, and shrinking network broadcast audiences, marketers consider it an important part of their planning efforts. While most Canadian retail sales take place in stores, such nonstore retailing activities as direct mail, direct selling, direct-response retailing, telemarketing, Internet retailing, and automatic merchandising are important in marketing many types of goods and services.

⑧ **Describe how the Internet has altered the wholesaling, retailing, and direct marketing environments.**

The Internet has affected everything from how supply networks operate to how relationships are formed with customers. Successful wholesalers have carved out a niche as a source of expertise offering faster, more efficient, Web-enabled distribution and fulfillment. The Internet has allowed retailers to enhance their merchandising mix and their customer service by, among other things, giving them access to much broader selections of goods. Direct marketers have merged their traditional catalogue or direct mail programs with an Internet interface that allows for faster, more efficient, and more frequent contact with customers and prospects.

assessment check answers ✓

1.1 What is retailing?
Retailing describes the activities involved in selling merchandise to ultimate consumers.

1.2 Explain the wheel-of-retailing concept.
The wheel of retailing is the hypothesis that each new type of retailer gains a competitive foothold by offering lower prices than current suppliers and maintains profits by reducing or eliminating services.

2.1 How does a retailer develop a marketing strategy?

A retailer develops a marketing strategy based on its goals and strategic plans.

2.2 How do retailers select target markets?

Strategies for selecting target markets include merchandising, customer service, pricing, location/distribution, and promotional strategies.

3.1 What is an SKU?

An SKU, or stockkeeping unit, is a specific product offering within a product line.

3.2 What are the two components of a markup?

A markup consists of the product's cost and an amount added by the retailer to determine its selling price.

3.3 What are store atmospherics?

Store atmospherics are physical characteristics and amenities that attract customers and satisfy their shopping needs.

4.1 How do we classify retailers by form of ownership?

There are two types of retailers by form of ownership: chain stores and independent retailers.

4.2 Categorize retailers by shopping effort and by services provided.

Convenience retailers and specialty retailers are classified by shopping effort; self-service, self-selection, and full-service describe retailers in terms of services provided.

4.3 List several ways to classify retailers by product line.

Retailers classified by product line include specialty stores, limited-line retailers, and general-merchandise retailers. General-merchandise retailers include variety stores, department stores, and mass merchandisers.

5.1 What is a wholesaler? How does it differ from a wholesaling intermediary?

A wholesaler is a channel intermediary that takes title to goods it handles and then distributes these goods to retailers, other distributors, or B2B customers. A wholesaling intermediary can be a wholesaler, an agent, or a broker and performs wholesaling activities without taking title to the goods.

5.2 How do wholesaling intermediaries help sellers lower costs?

Wholesaling intermediaries lower the number of transactions between manufacturers and retail outlets, thus lowering distribution costs.

6.1 What is the difference between a merchant wholesaler and a rack jobber?

A merchant wholesaler takes title to the goods it handles. A rack jobber is a full-function merchant wholesaler that markets specialized lines of merchandise to retailers.

6.2 Differentiate between agents and brokers.

Agents and brokers may or may not take possession of the goods they handle but they never take title. Brokers work mainly to bring together buyers and sellers. A selling agent typically exerts full authority over pricing decisions and promotional outlays and often provides financial assistance for the manufacturer.

7.1 What is direct marketing?

Direct marketing is a distribution channel consisting of direct communication to a consumer or business recipient. It generates orders and sales leads that may result in future orders.

7.2 What is direct mail?

Direct mail is a form of direct marketing that includes sales letters, postcards, brochures, booklets, catalogues, house organs, and DVDs.

8.1 Describe Internet-based retailers.

Internet-based retailers sell directly to customers via virtual storefronts on the Web. They usually maintain little or no inventory, ordering directly from vendors to fill customers' orders.

8.2 Explain how the Internet has enhanced retailers' functions.

The Internet has allowed retailers to enhance their merchandising mix and their customer service by, among other things, giving them access to much broader selections of goods. Direct marketers have merged their traditional catalogue or direct-mail programs with an Internet interface that allows for faster, more efficient, and more frequent contact with customers and prospects.

MARKETING TERMS YOU NEED TO KNOW

These terms are printed in blue in the text. They are defined in the margins of the chapter and in the Glossary that begins on p. G-1.

retailing 366
wheel of retailing 366
stockkeeping unit (SKU) 369
markup 370
markdown 371
planned shopping centre 371
atmospherics 373
convenience retailer 375
specialty retailer 376
limited-line store 377
category killer 377

general merchandise retailer 377
department store 378
mass merchandiser 378
discount house 378
hypermarket 379
supercentre 379
retail convergence 379
scrambled merchandising 379
wholesaler 380
wholesaling intermediary 380
merchant wholesaler 383

rack jobber 383
truck wholesaler (truck jobber) 384
drop shipper 384
mail-order wholesaler 384
commission merchant 385
broker 385
selling agent 385
manufacturers' representative 385
direct marketing 386

PROJECT AND TEAMWORK EXERCISES

1. Research and then classify each of the following retailers:
   a. Canadian Tire
   b. Bonnie Togs
   c. Danier Leather
   d. Stoney Creek Furniture
   e. Golf Town

2. Visit a local Walmart store and observe such aspects as product placement, shelf placement, inventory levels on shelves, traffic patterns, customer service, and checkout efficiency. Discuss what makes Walmart the world's most successful retailer.

3. Winners has become known for trendy clothes and stylish housewares, all readily available in spacious stores at reasonable prices. Visit a local Winners store or the company's website and compare its product selection to a hardware store and/or a department store. Make a list of each store's advantages and disadvantages, including convenience, location, selection, service, and general prices. Do any of its product lines overlap? How are they different from each other?

4. Match each industry with the most appropriate type of wholesaling intermediary.

_____ hardware	a. drop shipper
_____ perishable foods	b. truck wholesaler
_____ lumber	c. auction house
_____ wheat	d. full-function merchant wholesaler
_____ used cars	e. commission merchant

5. In teams, develop a retailing strategy for an Internet retailer. Identify a target market and then suggest a mix of merchandise, promotion, service, and pricing strategies that would help a retailer to reach that market via the Internet. What issues must Internet retailers address that do not affect traditional store retailers?

6. With a classmate, visit two or three retail stores that compete with one another in your area and compare their customer-service strategies. (You might wish to visit each store more than once to avoid making a snap judgment.) Select at least five criteria and use them to assess each store. How do you think each store sees its customer-service strategy as fitting into its overall retailing strategy? Present your findings in detail to the class.

7. Visit a department store and compare at least two departments' pricing strategies based on the number of markdowns you find and the size of the discount. What, if anything, can you conclude about the success of each department's retailing strategy?

8. Think of a large purchase you make on a nonroutine basis, such as a new winter coat or expensive clothing for a special occasion. Where will you shop for such items? Will you travel out of your way? Will you go to the nearest shopping centre? Will you look on the Internet? Once you have made your decision, describe any strategies used by the retailer that led you to this decision. What would make you change your mind about where to shop for this item?

9. Outlet malls are a growing segment of the retail market. Visit a local outlet mall or research one on the Internet. What types of stores are located there? How do the product selection and price compare with typical stores?

10. Addition Elle is a national chain of stores that feature clothing for plus-size women. Recommend an appropriate retailing strategy for this type of retailer.

CRITICAL THINKING EXERCISES

1. Retail chain Anthropologie sells a unique mix of women's clothing and home furnishings. Since its founding in 1992, Anthropologie has opened stores across the United States, in Canada, and in Great Britain. The retailer aims to create a shopping "experience" where its customers—independent-minded, college-educated female professionals between ages 30 and 45—can find their own look. No two Anthropologie stores are exactly alike, and the chain does not use advertising. Visit the website at **www.anthropologie.com**. How does it differentiate itself from its competitors?

2. Several major retailers have begun to test the extreme markdown strategy that lies behind popular "dollar" stores such as Great Canadian Dollar Store or Dollar Giant. Walmart and A&P, for example, are opening sections in selected stores that feature items such as snacks and beauty supplies priced at $1. Is this experiment simply a test of pricing strategy? What else might motivate these retailers to offer such deep discounts?

3. When A and B Sound, a company with 21 music stores that controlled 20 percent of recorded music sales in Western Canada, went bankrupt it was only one symptom of the general decline of the retail music store. Industry analysts blame such things as music downloading programs and changes in consumers' tastes. Most, however, feel that music stores will somehow remain viable. What are some changes that these retailers could make in their merchandising, customer service, pricing, location, and other strategies to try to reinvent their business?

4. McDonald's has traditionally relied on a cookie-cutter approach to its restaurant design. One store looked essentially like every other—until recently. The chain has decided to loosen its corporate design mandate to fit within special

markets and to update its image with customers. Research McDonald's makeover efforts. What types of changes has the company made and where? How have changes in

atmospherics helped the chain with customers? Have the changes you researched modified your perception of McDonald's at all? If so, how?

ETHICS EXERCISE

As the largest company in the world, with 2.2 million employees worldwide and $466 billion (U.S.) in sales in a recent year, many people would argue that Walmart has become too big and powerful. It has twice as many stores in Mexico as it does in Canada, and it is the largest private sector employer in that country. It imports so much from China that, if it were a country, Walmart would be China's eighth-largest trading partner, ahead of Britain and Russia. Some observers believe Walmart is also responsible for the low inflation rates and high productivity gains of recent years in Canada and the United States, accounting for as much as 12 percent of total productivity gains since the late 1990s. However, its unbeatable buying power and efficiency have forced

many local stores to close when Walmart opens a new store in their area.

1. Some economists fear what might happen to the economy if Walmart has a bad year (so far, it has had more than four decades of nonstop growth). Should retailers have that much influence on the economy? Why or why not?

2. Walmart is selective about what it sells, refusing, for instance, to carry music or computer games with mature ratings, magazines with content that it considers too adult, or a popular morning-after pill. Because of its sheer size, these decisions can become influential in the culture. Do you think this is a positive or negative effect of the growth of this retailer? Why?

CASE 13.1

Costco Plays Catch-Up in Online Sales

Costco, the $105-billion warehouse-style chain, is the third-largest retailer in North America. With low prices, low employee turnover, and steady growth, the company would seem to be an all-around success. It even boasts above-average survey scores on the quality of the shopping experience and customer service in its 648 stores worldwide.

But Costco is playing catch-up online, a sector that's growing faster than in-store retailing and where nimble competitors like Walmart hope to gain most of their future expansion. A rarity in store retailing because it has been profitable since day one, Costco has big plans for boosting its e-commerce business, but it has also missed some opportunities.

Costco.com and Costco.ca take in more than $2 billion a year with a broad assortment of products that are not always found in the stores. These are as varied as electronics and lawn furniture, caskets, and pricey diamond jewellery (delivered by Brink's). The convenience of free shipping and assembly are usually included. Most of Costco's online customers are a bit more affluent than customers of the warehouse stores, and their average purchases tend to be bigger too.

But despite being a brick-and-mortar presence in Mexico, Australia, Japan, Korea, Taiwan, and the United Kingdom, Costco currently limits its online operations to Canada and the United States. Critics have also found flaws in the company's online marketing efforts. Customers are not always aware of the product variety online, nor do they realize that the special offers outlined in

the company's emails, which go to about 12 million registered customers, promote products unique to the website. Another problem is that products on the website don't readily turn up in shoppers' search engine results because of the way the website's pages are named, a condition Costco hopes to improve via the technical process of search engine optimization. The website also isn't as user-friendly as it could be, say critics, with "rookie mistakes" like visual clutter and poorly labelled photographs. One search engine consultant said the company's online division is "undoubtedly leaving some sales on the table."

Questions for Critical Thinking

1. How can Costco better inform its online customers of the product variety available there and the real value of its special offers?

2. What priority do you think Costco should put on expanding its online business abroad? Is this more or less important than improving sales from the existing e-commerce operations in Canada and the United States? Explain your reasoning.

Sources: "Costco, Company Profile, available **http://phx.corporate-ir.net/ phoenix.zhtml?c=83830&p=irol-homeprofile**, March 4, 2014; Melissa Allison, "Costco Makes Plans for Boosting Its Online Sales," *The Seattle Times*, May 5, 2012, **http://seattletimes.nwsource.com**; Brad Tuttle, "Survey: Costco Given Retail Crown for Best Shopping Experience," *Time*, February 10, 2012, **http:// moneyland.time.com**; David W. Fuller, Tim Talevich, and Brenda Shecter, "The Empire Built on Values," *The Costco Connection*, January 2012, pp. 24–27.

CASE 13.2

Tilley Endurables: The Company a Hat Built

What is water-repellent, mildew-proof, machine-washable, guaranteed for life, insured against loss or theft (50 percent deductible), comes with an owner's manual printed in seven languages, floats in water, blocks UV rays, and is made from preshrunk 10-ounce cotton duck? That's easy: it's the original Tilley hat, a simple product that helped launch a major Canadian retailer.

It all started in 1980 after Alex Tilley, an avid sailor, became frustrated with sailing hats that blew off his head when sailing and then either sank before they could be retrieved or shrank after getting wet. He decided to oversee the building of a better hat. He soon had some prototypes he was comfortable attaching his name to and began selling them from his home in suburban Toronto. To build sales, Alex tried advertising. His first ads appeared in *Gam,* a Canadian sailing magazine, and he paid for them with some Tilley hats. He sent a Tilley hat to the editor of *Yachting* and was fortunate to get a one-third-page editorial. Within a year, he was selling Tilley hats at boat shows across North America, sometimes in the hundreds.

Next Alex decided to add a second product: Tilley shorts. Again, the focus was on quality. Lockstitches were used, and all the stress points were bar-tacked. The seat was double-layered so that any friction would be between the two layers and not between the cloth and a boat deck. These too were guaranteed for life, but they were priced at a 50 percent premium over competitors' products. Sales were disappointing and Alex eventually decided that it was "time to drop [his] shorts." Fortunately, Canada had a team in the 1983 America's Cup races, and Alex decided to present the team with complimentary hats and shorts. Word spread quickly, and at the Annapolis Sailboat Show that fall people began to ask for the shorts. They also asked for pants, not for sailing but for travelling, again requesting the same quality.

What does Tilley Endurables sell today? The company's product line expansion has been phenomenal. From the original Tilley hat, Tilley Endurables now offers more than 50 models of hats—for summer and winter, in various colours and materials. There is a full range of travel and adventure clothing, including shorts, pants, shirts, jackets, dresses, and all types of travel accessories—all of superior quality. Nearly everything Tilley Endurables sells is made in Canada where, Alex says, "we can keep an eye on it." Exceptions include a water bottle made in Washington, and "the world's best socks," made to Alex's "unholey" specifications.

From its humble beginning through home sales and its expansion into a mail-order business in 1984, the company now has six retail locations: two in Toronto—including the company's flagship store—and one each in Montreal, Brossard (Montreal), Mississauga, and Vancouver. There is also a website, **www.tilley .com**, where visitors can see its online catalogue—or request a printed version. The website also provides considerable value-added information and services for travellers and adventurers: how to protect against pickpockets, how to pack "smart," tips for travelling by plane, how and where to research information on destinations, and much more.

Tilley products can be purchased through one of several hundred retailers across Canada. Outside Canada, Tilley products are available from more than 2,600 retailers. And the good news: It doesn't matter where you buy your Tilley products, the price you pay will be identical. You won't be able to find Tilley products on sale, regardless of where you look. No matter where you go, a $75 Tilley hat is a $75 Tilley hat.

What has been responsible for Tilley's success? Referring to everything Tilley Endurables sells, Alex says, "We make the best in the world. Then we make it better!" Alex Tilley has travelled to more than 1,000 cities in more than 50 countries, wear-testing and researching potential products, always questioning how these products can be improved for Tilley Endurables. His favourite country: Guatemala. His favourite people to visit: the Balinese, the Bhutanese, and the people of Newfoundland and Labrador. How does Alex want to be remembered? He says, "I would like my epitaph to be 'A good man who built a better hat.'"

Questions for Critical Thinking

1. Describe the retailing strategy of Tilley Endurables (target market and retailing mix).
2. How does Tilley Endurables manage its channel relationships to help prevent horizontal conflict? Explain how horizontal conflict can lead to vertical conflict.

Sources: Tilley Endurables website, **www.tilley.com**, accessed March 24, 2014; Judy Steed, "It Takes Hard Work to Be Endurable: A Childhood Fall Means Alex Tilley Must Rely on Those Around Him to Help When Memory Fails," *Toronto Star,* August 29, 2009; Andy Holloway, "Alex Tilley," *Canadian Business,* January 16–January 29, 2006, p. 66.

chapter 14

Integrated Marketing Communications, Advertising, and Digital Communications

CHAPTER OBJECTIVES

1. Explain how integrated marketing communications relates to the development of an optimal promotional mix and describe the communication process.

2. Identify the elements of the promotional mix.

3. Name the major advertising objectives, categories, and strategies of advertising and describe the process of creating an advertisement.

4. Compare the major types of advertising appeals and the major advertising media.

5. Explain the role of public relations, publicity, cross-promotion, and ethics in an organization's promotional strategy.

6. Discuss the factors that influence the effectiveness of a promotional mix and how marketers measure effectiveness.

MOBILE DEVICES— THE ADVERTISING GAME CHANGER

Did you read a newspaper today? Did you read a paper copy or an online version? Did you listen to the radio or watch television? Did you use your smartphone or tablet to access the programs you wanted? Consumers have never had available the variety of options to get information or be entertained as they have today. This variety of options presents opportunities and challenges for marketers wanting to get their messages out. Marketers have the opportunity to place their ads where more viewers can see them, such as sites that can be accessed with mobile devices. The challenge for marketers is to know what sites consumers view with their mobile devices and how to measure how many people are actually seeing the ads.

There is no question that advances in technology, both hardware and software, have changed the way we interact with companies. The number of smartphones and tablets owned by Canadians has been steadily increasing. Currently just under half of all Canadians have a smartphone, and just over 20 percent of Canadians have a tablet. Canadians are using their mobile devices to search for store or restaurant locations, to search for specific products or brands, and to take advantage of discounts when purchasing products. Canadians are also using their mobile devices to watch their favourite television programs or videos. Some experts even predict that in the near future, the mobile screen will be viewed more often than television.

Companies are responding to these changes in consumer behaviour by changing their communications strategies. They are changing how many funds they allocate to each medium and where they place ads, and some companies are even using special techniques for their mobile communications strategies. Today the highest amount of dollars spent on advertising goes to television ads. Television ads are expensive to produce, and it is expensive to purchase the air time to broadcast the ads. Experts say this will change, though. Over the next several years, the amount of money spent on television advertising is expected to remain at a constant level while the amount spent on Internet and mobile advertising is expected to increase significantly. Some experts predict the amount spent on Internet advertising will increase by over 50 percent, and the amount spent on mobile advertising will increase by nearly 100 percent over the next couple of years. Some of these increases predicted for Internet and mobile advertising are because social media platforms like Facebook are now charging companies to place ads that could be placed in the past for free.

The type of advertising companies are doing on the Internet is also changing. Today over 40 percent of Internet advertising dollars are being spent on search ads—those ads that pop up when you do a search on Google—and roughly 30 percent on display ads. Classified ads make up another roughly 20 percent and the smallest amount is spent on video advertising. Within the next couple of years, it is predicted that video ads will account for the largest amount of Internet ad spending.

At the same time that companies are changing how they advertise on the Internet and mobile devices, they are also changing how they buy advertising space. In the past, advertising agencies purchased the advertising space whether it was on television, in a magazine, or in a newspaper. Today more and more companies are turning to programmatic buying and real-time bidding. Programmatic buying is similar to automated stock purchases, where companies purchase their own ad space based on past data. This process can be totally automatic or the process can be started by a person. Real-time bidding allows companies to purchase ad space instantaneously.[1]

connecting with customers

As more and more Canadians use smartphones and tablets to connect with the companies and the brands they like, companies are taking advantage of the opportunity to connect with customers. Companies are able to provide information about products or services and even offer discounts when the customer is purchasing a product with mobile technology.

Chapter Overview

Two of the four components of the marketing mix—product and distribution strategies—were discussed in previous chapters. The two chapters in Part 6 analyze the third marketing mix variable—promotion. **Promotion** is the function of informing, persuading, and influencing the consumer's purchase decision.

This chapter introduces the concept of integrated marketing communications. It describes the elements of a firm's promotional mix and discusses the factors that influence its effectiveness. Chapter 15 completes this part of the book by focusing on two other elements of the promotional mix: personal selling and sales promotion.

Throughout *Contemporary Marketing*, special emphasis has been given to showing how technology is changing the way marketers approach *communication*, the transmission of a message from a sender to a receiver. Consumers receive **marketing communications**—messages that deal with buyer–seller relationships—from a variety of media, including television, radio, magazines, direct mail, the Internet, and smartphones. Marketers can broadcast an ad on the Web to mass markets or design a customized appeal targeted to a small market segment. Each message the customer receives from any source represents the brand, company, or organization. A company needs to coordinate all these messages for maximum total impact and to reduce the likelihood the consumer will completely tune them out.

To prevent this loss of attention, marketers are turning to **integrated marketing communications (IMC)**, which coordinates all promotional activities—media advertising, direct mail, personal selling, sales promotion, public relations, and sponsorships—to produce a unified, customer-focused promotional message as shown in Figure 14.1. IMC is a broader concept than marketing communications and promotional strategy. It uses database technology to refine the marketer's understanding of the target audience, segment this audience, and select the best type of media for each segment.

IMC involves not only the marketer but all other organizational units that interact with the consumer. Marketing managers set the goals and objectives of the firm's promotional strategy in accordance with overall organizational objectives and marketing goals. Based on these objectives, elements of the promotional strategy are formulated into an integrated communications plan that becomes a central part of the firm's total marketing strategy. The feedback mechanism, including marketing research and field reports, identifies any deviations from the plan and suggests improvements. ◆◆◆

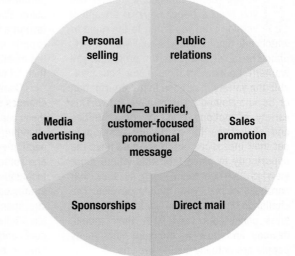

figure 14.1

Integrated Marketing Communications (IMC)

Personal selling

Public relations

Media advertising

IMC—a unified, customer-focused promotional message

Sales promotion

Sponsorships

Direct mail

① Explain how integrated marketing communications relates to the development of an optimal promotional mix and describe the communication process.

INTEGRATED MARKETING COMMUNICATIONS

Stop and think for a moment about all the marketing messages you receive in a day. You click on the television for the news, and you see commercials. Listen to the car radio on the way to work or school, and you can sing along with the jingles. You get catalogues, coupons, and fliers in the mail. People even leave promotional fliers under your car's windshield wiper while it sits in the parking lot. When you go online, you see banner and pop-up ads and marketing-related emails. Marketers know that you are receiving many types of communication. They compete for your attention, so they look for ways to reach you in a coordinated manner through integrated marketing communications.

Successful marketers use the marketing concept and relationship marketing to develop customer-oriented marketing programs. The customer is at the heart of integrated marketing communications. An IMC strategy begins not with the organization's goods and services but with consumer wants or needs, and then works in reverse to the product, brand, or organization. It sends receiver-focused rather than product-focused messages.

Rather than separating the parts of the promotional mix and viewing them as isolated components, IMC looks at these elements from the consumer's viewpoint: as information about the brand, company, or organization. Even though the messages come from different sources—sales presentations, word of mouth, TV, radio, newspapers, and social media—consumers may perceive them as "advertising" or a "sales pitch." IMC broadens promotion to include all the ways a customer has contact with an organization, adding to traditional media and direct mail such sources as package design, store displays, sales literature, and online and interactive media. Unless the organization takes an integrated approach to present a unified, consistent message, it may send conflicting information that confuses consumers.

Today's business environment is characterized by many diverse markets and media, creating both opportunities and challenges. The success of any IMC program depends on identifying the members of an audience and understanding what they want. Without accurate, current information about existing and potential customers, their purchase histories, needs, and wants, marketers may send the wrong message. But they cannot succeed simply by improving the quality of the messages or by sending more of them. IMC must not only deliver messages to intended audiences but also gather responses from them. Databases and interactive marketing are important IMC tools that help marketers collect information from customers and segment markets according to demographics and preferences. Marketers can then design specialized communications programs to meet the needs of each segment.

The increase in media options provides more ways to give consumers product information; however, it can also create information overload. Marketers have to spread available dollars across fragmented media markets and a wider range of promotional activities to achieve their communication goals. Mass media such as TV ads, while still useful, are no longer the mainstays of marketing campaigns. In fact, companies are spending almost as much on digital advertising as they do on television ads, and digital ad spend is expected to increase. Digital ads are likely to be directed at a more focused target market.[2] Audiences are also more fragmented. So to reach desired groups, organizations are turning to niche marketing by advertising in special-interest magazines, by purchasing time on cable TV channels, by reaching out through telecommunications media such as smartphones or the Internet, and by sponsoring events and activities. Without an IMC program, marketers frequently encounter problems within their own organizations because separate departments have authority and responsibility for planning and implementing specific promotional mix elements.

The coordination of an IMC program often produces a competitive advantage based on synergy and interdependence among the various elements of the promotional mix. With an IMC strategy, marketers can create a unified personality for the product or brand by choosing the right elements from the promotional mix to send the message. At the same time, they can develop more narrowly focused plans to reach specific market segments and choose the best form of communication to send a particular message to a specific target audience. IMC provides a more effective way to reach and serve target markets than less coordinated strategies. Sometimes an IMC strategy involves coordinating with other companies as described in the "Marketing: Making Your World Better" feature.

promotion
Communications link between buyers and sellers. Function of informing, persuading, and influencing a consumer's purchase decision.

marketing communications
Messages that deal with buyer–seller relationships.

integrated marketing communications (IMC) Coordination of all promotional activities to produce a unified, customer-focused promotional message.

Marketoid

Canadian companies spend over $3,500 million on television advertising annually.

The Quaker® brand used a coupon to encourage consumers to try their new products.

MARKETING: MAKING YOUR WORLD BETTER — Doing Good as Part of Your Communications Strategy

MANY companies support good causes, community events, and charities, and some even align themselves with these causes on an ongoing basis. Marketing experts advise this trend will continue to grow for several reasons, including how important it is to women, particularly those with families and the millennial, or video-game, segment.

A recent study showed companies like Unilever and Tim Hortons rated highly as brands Canadian women most valued. Tim Hortons made the list because its Timbits minor sports program was important to women with small children. Unilever made the list because of its Dove "Real Beauty" program. The Dove "Real Beauty" commercials are among the most watched videos, and women admire the global self-esteem campaign aimed at young women.

The millennials, who make up 30 percent of the Canadian population, are now entering the workforce. Unlike the generations before them, this group is demanding more from the companies they work for. This group enters the workforce with high levels of personal debt stemming from their student loans and has lower expectations regarding their economic standing in life. They do expect more from their employers than previous generations.

Not all companies have reached the status of Tim Hortons or Unilever in their ongoing cause marketing programs but many are starting to understand the importance of such campaigns. Bell, for example, has taken on the mental health cause. Bell chose Olympic star Clara Hughes as the spokesperson for a campaign called "Let's Talk." On one day per year, Bell contributes five cents for every long-distance call, text message, or tweet to a mental health initiative across the country. One year the campaign resulted in just under a $5-million contribution by Bell.

Sources: "Millennials Are Slowly Proving to Be More Engaged at Work," Betakit website, **www.betakit.com**, accessed April 20, 2014; David Brown, "Why Women Love Tim Hortons and Walmart: Study," *Marketing*, April 14, 2014, **www.marketingmag.ca**; Vanessa Milne, "Millennials Show Little Optimism for Their Financial Futures," *Marketing*, March 27, 2014, **www.marketingmag.ca**; "Latest Data about Millennials," Strum Consulting Company website, April 9, 2014, **www.strumconsulting.com**; Phillip Haid, "It's Time to Make 'Purpose' the Fifth P in Marketing," *Marketing*, January 30, 2014, **www.marketingmag.ca**; Rebecca Harris, "Bell's Let's Talk Day": Money Raiser and Reputation Builder," *Marketing*, January 7, 2014, **www.marketingmag.ca.**

IMPORTANCE OF TEAMWORK

IMC requires a big-picture view of promotion planning, a total strategy that includes all marketing activities, not just promotion. Successful implementation of IMC requires that everyone involved in every aspect of promotion function as a team, presenting a consistent, coordinated effort at every point of customer contact. This saves time and money, avoids duplication of effort, and increases effectiveness. In other words, the result is greater than the sum of its parts.

Teamwork involves both in-house resources and outside vendors. A firm gains nothing from a terrific advertisement featuring a great product, an informational website, and a toll-free number if unhelpful salespeople frustrate customers when they answer the phones. The company must train its representatives to send a single positive message to consumers and also to solicit information for the firm's customer database.

IMC also challenges the traditional role of the advertising agency. A single agency may no longer fulfill all a client's communications requirements, including traditional advertising and sales promotions, interactive marketing, database development, direct marketing, and public relations. To best serve client needs, agencies must often partner with other firms to get the job done.

Networking, another form of teamwork, is an important skill for building a career. The "Career Readiness" feature provides networking tips.

ROLE OF DATABASES IN EFFECTIVE IMC PROGRAMS

The Internet empowers marketers to gather more information faster and to organize it more easily than ever before. By sharing this detailed knowledge appropriately among all relevant parties, a company can lay the foundation for a successful IMC program.

The move from mass marketing to a customer-specific marketing strategy—a characteristic of online marketing—requires not only a means of identifying and communicating with the firm's target market but also information regarding important characteristics of each prospective customer. Organizations can compile different kinds of data into complete databases with customer information, including names and addresses, demographic data, lifestyle considerations, brand preferences, and buying behaviour. This information provides critical guidance in designing an effective IMC strategy that achieves organizational goals and finds new opportunities for increased sales and profits. This increased ability to acquire huge amounts of data poses a new challenge: how to sift through it efficiently so that it becomes useful information. Newer technology allows researchers to do exactly that—working with millions of sets of data to make very specific analyses.

Direct sampling is another method frequently used to quickly obtain customer opinions regarding a particular firm's goods and services. If you've ever received a free sample of laundry detergent, air freshener or even a newspaper in your mailbox, you've been the recipient of direct sampling.

Marketoid

Canadian companies spend over $2,200 million advertising in daily and weekly newspapers on an annual basis.

THE COMMUNICATION PROCESS

When you have a conversation with someone, do you wonder whether the person understood your message? Do you worry that you might not have heard the person correctly? Marketers have the same concerns—when they send a message to an intended audience or market, they want to make sure it gets through clearly and persuasively. That is why the communication process is so important to marketing. The top portion of Table 14.1 shows a general model of the communication process and its application to promotional strategy.

The **sender** acts as the source in the communication system as he or she seeks to convey a **message** (a communication of information, advice, or a request) to a receiver. An effective message accomplishes three tasks:

1. It gains the receiver's attention.

2. It achieves understanding by both receiver and sender.

3. It stimulates the receiver's needs and suggests an appropriate method of satisfying them.

Table 14.1 also provides several examples of promotional messages. Although the types of promotion may vary from a highly personalized sales presentation to such nonpersonal promotions

sender Source of the message communicated to the receiver.

message Communication of information, advice, or a request by the sender to the receiver.

table 14.1 *Relating Promotion to the Communication Process*

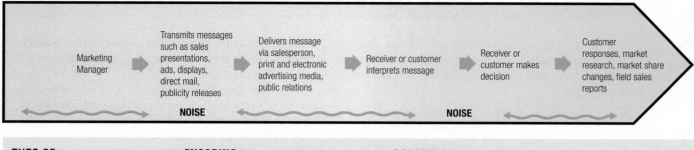

TYPE OF PROMOTION	SENDER	ENCODING BY SENDER	CHANNEL	DECODING BY RECEIVER	RESPONSE	FEEDBACK
Personal selling	IBM software	Sales presentation on new applications of software	IBM sales representative	Office manager and employees discuss sales presentation and those of competing suppliers	Customer places order for new software	Customer asks about a second system for subsidiary company
Dollar-off coupon (sales promotion)	Kellogg's Special K cereal	Coupon for Kellogg's Special K cereal	Coupon insert in weekend newspaper	Newspaper reader sees coupon for Special K cereal	Special K is purchased by consumers using coupon	Kellogg researchers see increase in market share
Television advertising	Paramount Canada's Wonderland	Advertisement developed by Wonderland's advertising agency featuring the new park rides	Network television ads air during program with high percentages of viewers under 20 years old	Teens and young adults see ad and decide to try out the park	Wonderland tickets are purchased	Customers purchase season ticket packages for Wonderland

AIDA concept Steps through which an individual reaches a purchase decision: attention, interest, desire, and action.

as television advertising and dollar-off coupons, each goes through every stage in the communications process.

The three tasks just listed are related to the **AIDA concept** (attention-interest-desire-action), the steps consumers take in reaching a purchase decision. First, the promotional message must gain the potential consumer's attention. It then seeks to arouse interest in the good or service. At the next stage, it stimulates desire by convincing the would-be buyer of the product's ability to satisfy his or her needs. Finally, the sales presentation, advertisement, or sales promotion technique attempts to produce action in the form of a purchase or a more favourable attitude that may lead to future purchases.

The message must be encoded, or translated into understandable terms and transmitted through a communications channel. Decoding is the receiver's interpretation of the message. The receiver's response, known as feedback, completes the system. Throughout the process, noise (in such forms as ineffective promotional appeals, inappropriate advertising media, or poor radio or television reception) can interfere with the transmission of the message and reduce its effectiveness.

The marketer is the message sender in Table 14.1. He or she encodes the message in the form of sales presentations, advertising, displays, or publicity releases. The channel for delivering the message may be a salesperson, a public relations announcement, or an advertising medium. Decoding is often the most troublesome step in marketing communications because consumers do not always interpret promotional messages in the same way that senders do. Since receivers usually decode messages according to their own frames of reference or experiences, a sender must carefully encode a message in a way that matches the frame of reference of the target audience. Consumers today are bombarded daily by hundreds of sales messages through many media channels.

This communications traffic can create confusion as noise in the channel increases. Since the typical person will choose to process only a few messages, ignored messages waste communications budgets.

The AIDA concept is also vital to online marketers. It is not enough to say a website has effective content or high response rates. Marketers must know just how many "eyeballs" are looking at the site, how often they come to view a message, and what they are examining. Most important, they must find out what consumers do besides just look. The bottom line is that if nobody is responding to a website, it might as well not exist. Experts advise attracting users' attention by including people in advertisements and other communications in addition to new content and formats. For the Winter Olympic Games in Sochi, television networks offered programming on several different platforms, including network channels, cable channels, online, on-demand, and on-the-go. The networks saw the Olympics Games as a great opportunity to provide full coverage of the games in whatever medium people wanted. This provided marketers more options to get their messages out to consumers.[3]

Feedback lets marketers evaluate the effectiveness of the message and tailor their responses accordingly. Feedback may take the form of attitude changes, purchases, or nonpurchases. In some instances, organizations use promotion to create favourable attitudes toward their goods or services in the hope of future purchases. Other promotional communications have the objective of directly stimulating consumer purchases. Marketers using infomercials that urge the viewer to call a toll-free number to place orders for their products can easily measure their success by counting the number of calls they receive that result in orders.

Even a nonpurchase is feedback. Failure to purchase may result from ineffective communication in which the receivers do not believe it, don't remember it, or even associate it with another firm's products. Alternatively, receivers may remember it correctly, but the message may have failed to persuade them to buy. So marketers need to be aware of why messages fail.

Noise represents interference at some stage in the communication process. It may result from disruptions such as transmissions of competing promotional messages over the same communications channel, misinterpretation of a sales presentation or advertising message, receipt of the promotional message by the wrong person, or random events such as people conversing or leaving the room during a television commercial. Noise can also result from distractions within an advertising message itself. Buzzwords and jargon can create a linguistic jungle for consumers who are just trying to find out more about a product. In a recent survey of 1,200 adults by a financial services organization it was found that more than half were confused by the language of the investment industry. This confusion often resulted in people making costly investment mistakes.[4]

Noise can be especially problematic in international communications. One problem is that there may be too many competing messages. Italian television channels, for instance, broadcast all advertisements during a single half-hour slot each night. Or technology may be poor, and language translations inaccurate. Nonverbal cues, such as body language and tone of voice, are important parts of the communication process, and cultural differences may lead to noise and misunderstandings. For example, in North America,

individualEYES!
exact eyelights mascara • liner • shadow in 4 customized collections
You've got one-of-a-kind eyes. Make them shine with a shade collection designed to brighten your eyes. **Tell us what makes you a COVERGIRL** @ facebook.com/covergirl

easy breezy beautiful COVERGIRL
Queen Latifah's eyes shine with the Exact Eyelights Collection for brown eyes.

Courtesy of Procter & Gamble

Queen Latifah promoting CoverGirl.

assessment check 1 ✓

1.1 Define *promotion*.

1.2 What is the difference between marketing communications and integrated marketing communications (IMC)?

1.3 Identify the four steps of the AIDA concept.

1.4 What is noise?

the round o sign made with the thumb and first finger means "okay." However, in Mediterranean countries, it means "zero" or "the worst." A Tunisian interprets this same sign as "I'll kill you," and to a Japanese consumer it means "money." It's easy to see how misunderstanding could arise from this single gesture.

② Identify the elements of the promotional mix.

promotional mix
Subset of the marketing mix in which marketers attempt to achieve the optimal blending of the elements of personal and nonpersonal selling to achieve promotional objectives.

ELEMENTS OF THE PROMOTIONAL MIX

Like the marketing mix, the promotional mix requires a carefully designed blend of variables to satisfy the needs of a company's customers and achieve organizational objectives. The **promotional mix** works like a subset of the marketing mix. With the promotional mix, the marketers attempt to create an optimal blend of various elements to achieve promotional objectives. The components of the promotional mix are personal selling and nonpersonal selling, including advertising, sales promotion, direct marketing, public relations, and guerrilla marketing.

Personal selling, advertising, and sales promotion usually account for the bulk of a firm's promotional expenditures. However, direct marketing, guerrilla marketing, sponsorships, and public relations also contribute to integrated marketing communications.

PERSONAL SELLING

personal selling
Interpersonal influence process involving a seller's promotional presentation conducted on a person-to-person basis with the buyer.

Personal selling is the oldest form of promotion, dating back as far as the beginning of trading and commerce. Traders vastly expanded both market sizes and product varieties as they led horses and camels along the Silk Road from China to Europe roughly between 300 B.C. and A.D. 1600, conducting personal selling at both ends. Personal selling may be defined as a seller's promotional presentation conducted on a person-to-person basis with the buyer. It may be conducted face to face, over the telephone, through videoconferencing, or through interactive computer links between the buyer and seller.

Careers in personal sales may include real estate; insurance; financial investment; or sales of tractors, cars, or vacuum cleaners; individuals may work in retail or wholesaling; they may be regional managers or in the field. In other words, the range of jobs, as well as the products they represent, is huge.

NONPERSONAL SELLING

nonpersonal selling
Promotion that includes advertising, product placement, sales promotion, direct marketing, guerrilla marketing, and public relations—all conducted without being face to face with the buyer.

Nonpersonal selling includes advertising, product placement, sales promotion, direct marketing, guerrilla marketing, and public relations. Advertising and sales promotion are usually regarded as the most important forms of nonpersonal selling. About one-third of marketing dollars spent on nonpersonal selling activities are allocated for media advertising; the other two-thirds fund trade and consumer sales promotions.

ADVERTISING

advertising Paid, nonpersonal communication through various media about a business, not-for-profit organization, product, or idea by a sponsor identified in a message that is intended to inform, persuade, or remind members of a particular audience.

Advertising is any paid, nonpersonal communication through various media about a business, not-for-profit organization, product, or idea by a sponsor identified in a message that is intended to inform, persuade, or remind members of a particular audience. It is a major promotional mix component for thousands of organizations. Mass consumption and geographically dispersed markets make advertising particularly appropriate for marketing goods and services aimed at large audiences likely to respond to the same promotional messages.

Advertising primarily involves mass media, such as newspapers, television, radio, magazines, movie screens, and billboards, but also includes electronic and computerized forms of promotion such as Web commercials, streaming videos, and television monitors in supermarkets. The rich potential of the Internet as an advertising channel to reach millions of people one at a time has attracted the attention of companies large and small, local and international. As consumers become increasingly savvy—and tune out messages that don't interest them—marketers are finding new ways to grab their attention.

PRODUCT PLACEMENT

Product placement is a form of nonpersonal selling in which the marketer pays a fee to display his or her product prominently in the film or television show. The practice gained attention in the movie *E.T.: The Extra-Terrestrial* when Elliott, the boy who befriends E.T., lays out a trail of Reese's Pieces candy for the extraterrestrial to follow, to draw the alien from his hiding place. Product sales for Reese's Pieces candies went through the roof. (Interestingly, this was not the moviemaker's first choice of candy; Mars turned down the opportunity to have its M&Ms appear in the film.) Today, hundreds of products appear in movies and on television shows, and the fees charged to marketers for these placements have soared. Samsung was featured prominently in an Oscar event when Ellen DeGeneres hosted the program. She used a Samsung phone to take pictures during the event which were retweeted so often that it caused Twitter to crash.[5] Brands even pay celebrities to post about them on Twitter.

product placement Form of promotion in which a marketer pays a motion picture or television program owner a fee to display a product prominently in the film or show.

SALES PROMOTION

Sales promotion consists of marketing activities other than personal selling, advertising, guerrilla marketing, and public relations that stimulate consumer purchasing and dealer effectiveness. This broad category includes displays, trade shows, coupons, contests, samples, premiums, product demonstrations, and various one-time selling efforts. Sales promotion provides a short-term incentive, usually in combination with other forms of promotion, to emphasize, assist, supplement, or otherwise support the objectives of the promotional program. Restaurants, including those that serve fast food, often place certain items on the menu at a lower price "for a limited time only." Advertisements may contain coupons for free or discounted items for a specified period of time. Or companies may conduct sweepstakes for prizes such as new cars or vacations, which may even be completely unrelated to the products the company is selling.

sales promotion Marketing activities other than personal selling, advertising, guerrilla marketing, and public relations that stimulate consumer purchasing and dealer effectiveness.

Sales promotion geared to marketing intermediaries is called **trade promotion**. Companies spend about as much on trade promotion as on advertising and consumer-oriented sales promotion combined. Trade promotion strategies include offering free merchandise, buyback allowances, and merchandise allowances along with sponsorship of sales contests to encourage wholesalers and retailers to sell more of certain products or product lines.

trade promotion Sales promotion that appeals to marketing intermediaries rather than to consumers.

DIRECT MARKETING

Another element in a firm's integrated promotional mix is direct marketing, the use of direct communication to a consumer or business recipient designed to generate a response in the form of an order, a request for further information (lead generation), or a visit to a place of business to purchase specific goods or services (traffic generation). While many people equate direct marketing with direct mail, this promotional category also includes telemarketing, direct-response advertising and infomercials, direct-response print advertising, and electronic media.

PUBLIC RELATIONS

Public relations refer to a firm's communications and relationships with its various publics. These publics include customers, suppliers, shareholders, employees, the government, and the general public. Public relations programs can conduct either formal or informal contacts. The critical point is that every organization, whether or not it has a formally organized program, must be concerned about its public relations.

public relations Firm's communications and relationships with its various publics.

Publicity is the marketing-oriented aspect of public relations. It can be defined as the nonpersonal stimulation of demand for a good, service, person, cause, or organization through unpaid placement of significant news about it in a published medium or through a favourable presentation of it on the radio or television. Compared with personal selling, advertising, and sales promotion, expenditures for public relations are usually low in most firms. Since companies do not pay for publicity, they have less control over the publication by the press or electronic media of good or bad company news. But this often means that consumers find this type of news source more believable than company disseminated information. Of course, bad publicity can damage a company's reputation and diminish brand equity. Organizations that enjoy good publicity generally try to make the most of it. Those who have suffered from bad publicity try to turn the situation around.

GUERRILLA MARKETING

guerrilla marketing
Unconventional, innovative, and low-cost marketing techniques designed to get consumers' attention in unusual ways.

Guerrilla marketing uses unconventional, innovative, and low-cost techniques to attract consumers' attention. It is a relatively new approach typically used by marketers whose firms are underfunded for a full marketing program. Firms that can't afford the huge costs of print and broadcasting often look for an innovative, low-cost way to reach their market. But some large companies, such as PepsiCo and Toyota, engage in guerrilla marketing as well.

Buzz marketing can be part of guerrilla marketing. This type of marketing works well to reach students and other young adults. Marketing firms may hire students to mingle among their own classmates and friends, creating buzz about a product. Often called *campus ambassadors,* they may wear logo-bearing T-shirts or caps, leave Post-it notes with marketing messages around campus, and chat about the good or service with friends during class breaks or over meals.

Viral marketing is another form of guerrilla marketing that has rapidly caught on with large and small firms. Evian used the paid placement on YouTube of the "roller babies" ad as the central part of its overall campaign. When Chris Hadfield commanded the International Space Station, he sent out Tweets, maintained a blog, and videoed live experiments that were viewed by millions around the world. He not only wanted to bring attention to what was happening on the Space Station but he wanted to get more young people interested in science.[6]

The results of guerrilla marketing can be funny and outrageous—even offensive to some people. But they almost always get consumers' attention. Some guerrilla marketers stencil their company and product names anywhere graffiti might appear. Street artists are hired to plaster company and product logos on blank walls or billboards.

ADVANTAGES AND DISADVANTAGES OF TYPES OF PROMOTION

Marketoid

Canadian companies spend over $1,200 million advertising in community newspapers each year.

As Table 14.2 indicates, each type of promotion has both advantages and shortcomings. Although personal selling entails a relatively high per-contact cost, it involves less wasted effort than do nonpersonal forms of promotion such as advertising. Personal selling often provides more flexible promotion than the other forms because the salesperson can tailor the sales message to meet the unique needs—or objections—of each potential customer.

The major advantages of advertising come from its ability to create instant awareness of a good, service, or idea; build brand equity; and deliver the marketer's message to mass audiences for a relatively low cost per contact. Major disadvantages include the difficulty in measuring advertising effectiveness and high media costs. Sales promotions, in contrast, can be more accurately monitored and measured than advertising, produce immediate consumer responses, and provide short-term sales increases. Direct marketing gives potential customers an action-oriented choice, permits segmentation and customization of communications, and produces measurable results. Public relations efforts such as publicity frequently offer higher credibility than other promotional techniques. For marketers with limited funds, guerrilla marketing can be innovative and effective at a low cost, as long as the tactics are not too outrageous, but it is more difficult to reach people. The marketer must determine the appropriate blend of these promotional mix elements to effectively market the firm's goods and services.

SPONSORSHIPS

sponsorship
Relationship in which an organization provides funds or in-kind resources to an event or activity in exchange for a direct association with that event or activity.

Commercial sponsorships of an event or activity involve personal selling, advertising, sales promotion, and public relations in achieving specific promotional goals. Sponsorships have become a multibillion-dollar business.

Sponsorship occurs when an organization provides money or in-kind resources to an event or activity in exchange for a direct association with that event or activity. The sponsor purchases access to the activity's audience and the image associated with the activity. Sponsorships typically involve advertising, direct mail and sales promotion, publicity in the form of media coverage of the event, and personal selling at the event itself. They also involve relationship marketing, bringing together the event,

table 14.2   *Comparison of the Six Promotional Mix Elements*

	PERSONAL SELLING	ADVERTISING	SALES PROMOTION	DIRECT MARKETING	PUBLIC RELATIONS	GUERRILLA MARKETING
Advantages	Permits measurement of effectiveness Elicits an immediate response Tailors the message to fit the customer	Reaches a large group of potential consumers for a relatively low price per exposure Allows strict control over the final message Can be adapted to either mass audiences or specific audience segments	Produces an immediate consumer response Attracts attention and creates product awareness Allows easy measurement of results Provides short-term sales increases	Generates an immediate response Covers a wide audience with targeted advertising Allows complete, customized, personal message Produces measurable results	Creates a positive attitude toward a product or company Enhances credibility of a product or company	Is low cost Attracts attention because it is innovative Is less cluttered with competitors trying the same thing
Disadvantages	Relies almost exclusively upon the ability of the salesperson Involves high cost per contact	Does not permit totally accurate measurement of results Usually cannot close sales	Is nonpersonal in nature Is difficult to differentiate from competitors' efforts	Suffers from image problem Involves a high cost per reader Depends on quality and accuracy of mailing lists May annoy consumers	May not permit accurate measurement of effect on sales Involves much effort directed toward non-marketing-oriented goals	May not reach as many people If the tactics are too outrageous, they may offend some people

its participants, the sponsoring firms, and their channel members and major customers. Marketers underwrite varying levels of sponsorships, depending on the amount their companies wish to spend and the types of events.

Commercial sponsorship is not a new concept. Aristocrats in ancient Rome sponsored gladiator competitions and chariot races featuring teams that were often supported financially by competing businesses.

Today's sponsorships are most prevalent in sports—golf, soccer, Nascar races, the Olympics, and the World Cup, and thousands of smaller events as well. Companies may also sponsor concerts or art exhibits, reading and child-care programs, programs that support small businesses and create new jobs, and humanitarian or cause-related programs.

The escalating costs of traditional advertising make commercial sponsorships a cost-effective alternative. Except for the really large events, which often have several sponsors, most sponsorships are less expensive than an advertising campaign that relies on television, print, and other media. In addition, sponsors often gain the benefit of media coverage anyway, because associated events are covered by the news. And in the case of naming rights of such venues as sports arenas, the name serves as a perpetual advertisement. Examples are the Rogers Centre in Toronto, the Scotiabank Place in Ottawa, and the Bell Centre in Montreal.

Marketers have considerable control over the quantity and quality of market coverage when they advertise. Sponsors have little control of sponsored events beyond matching the audiences to profiles of their own target markets. Instead, event organizers control the coverage, which typically focuses on the event, not the sponsor. In contrast, a traditional advertisement allows the marketer to create an individual message containing an introduction, a theme, and a conclusion.

assessment check 2

2.1 Differentiate between personal and nonpersonal selling.

2.2 What are the six major categories of nonpersonal selling?

2.3 How is sponsorship different from advertising?

(3) **Name the major advertising objectives, categories, and strategies of advertising and describe the process of creating an advertisement.**

ADVERTISING

Twenty-first-century advertising is closely related to integrated marketing communications (IMC) in many respects. While IMC involves a message dealing with buyer–seller relationships, advertising seeks to inform or persuade members of a particular audience. Marketers use advertising to reach target markets with messages designed to appeal to business firms, not-for-profit organizations, or ultimate consumers.

Companies around the world spend more than $500 billion (U.S.) a year on advertising.[7] The amount spent on advertising varies among countries and industries as well as companies. Companies in the United States spend the most on advertising, contributing just under 30 percent of the overall amount.[8] Procter & Gamble, Unilever, and L'Oréal are the companies spending the most.[9] Procter & Gamble spends just under $3 billion on advertising in a year.[10]

product advertising Nonpersonal selling of a particular good or service.

institutional advertising Promotion of a concept, idea, philosophy, or goodwill of an industry, company, organization, person, geographic location, or government agency.

TYPES OF ADVERTISING

Advertisements fall into two broad categories: product advertising and institutional advertising. **Product advertising** is nonpersonal selling of a particular good or service. This is the type of advertising the average person usually thinks of when talking about most promotional activities.

Institutional advertising, in contrast, promotes a concept, an idea, a philosophy, or the goodwill of an industry, company, organization, person, geographic location, or government agency. This term has a broader meaning than *corporate advertising*, which is typically limited to advertising sponsored by a specific profit-seeking firm. Institutional advertising is often closely related to the public relations function.

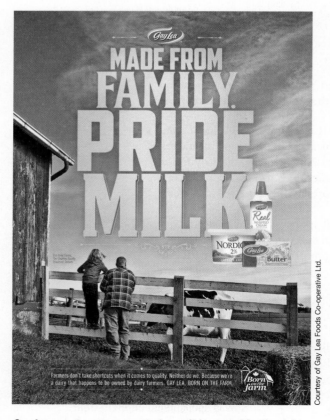

Courtesy of Gay Lea Foods Co-operative Ltd.

Gay Lea wants consumers to know it is owned by the dairy farmers that produce its milk.

OBJECTIVES OF ADVERTISING

Marketers use advertising messages to accomplish three primary objectives: to inform, to persuade, and to remind. These objectives may be used individually or, more typically, in conjunction with each other. For example, an ad for a not-for-profit agency may inform the public of the existence of the organization and at the same time persuade the audience to make a donation, join the organization, or attend a function.

Informative advertising seeks to develop initial demand for a good, service, organization, person, place, idea, or cause. The promotion of any new market entry tends to pursue this objective because marketing success at this stage often depends simply on announcing availability. Informative advertising can also be used to explain the benefits of a product as in the case of Activia, the yogurt whose television ads feature Shakira.[11] Informative advertising is common in the introductory stage of the product life cycle.

Persuasive advertising attempts to increase demand for an existing good, service, organization, person, place, idea, or cause. Persuasive advertising is typically used during the growth stage and the early part of the maturity stage of the product life cycle.

Reminder advertising strives to reinforce a previous promotional activity by keeping the name of a good, service, organization, person, place, idea, or cause before the public. It is common in the latter part of the maturity stage and throughout the decline stage of the product life cycle. Procter & Gamble, for instance, seeks to remind consumers about their products in the "Thank You Mom" series of ads they run during the Olympic Games.[12]

Figure 14.2 illustrates the relationship between advertising objectives and the stages of the product life cycle. Informative advertising tends to work best during the early stages, while reminder advertising is effective later on. Persuasive advertising, if done well, can be effective through the entire life cycle.

Traditionally, marketers stated their advertising objectives as direct sales goals. A more current and realistic standard, however, views advertising as a way to achieve communications objectives, including informing, persuading, and reminding potential customers of the product. Advertising attempts to condition consumers to adopt favourable views regarding a promotional message. The goal of an ad is to improve the likelihood that a customer will buy a particular good or service. In this sense, advertising illustrates the close relationship between marketing communications and promotional strategy.

To get the best value for a firm's advertising investment, marketers must first determine what that firm's advertising objectives are. Effective advertising can enhance consumer perceptions of quality in a good or service, leading to increased customer loyalty, repeat purchases, and protection against price wars. In addition, perceptions of superiority pay off in the firm's ability to raise prices without losing market share.

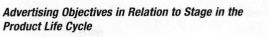

figure 14.2

Advertising Objectives in Relation to Stage in the Product Life Cycle

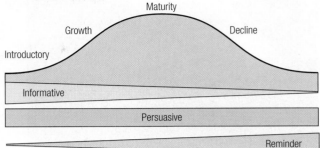

informative advertising Promotion that seeks to develop initial demand for a good, service, organization, person, place, idea, or cause.

persuasive advertising Promotion that attempts to increase demand for an existing good, service, organization, person, place, idea, or cause.

reminder advertising Advertising that reinforces a previous promotional activity by keeping the name of a good, service, organization, person, place, idea, or cause before the public.

ADVERTISING STRATEGIES

If the primary function of marketing is to bring buyers and sellers together, then advertising is the means to an end. Effective advertising strategies accomplish at least one of three tasks: informing, persuading, or reminding consumers. The secret to choosing the best strategy is developing a message that best positions a firm's product in the audience's mind. Among the advertising strategies available for use by marketers are comparative advertising and celebrity advertising as well as plans about global and interactive ads. Channel-oriented decisions such as retail and cooperative advertising can also be devised.

Marketers often combine several of these advertising strategies to ensure that the advertisement accomplishes set objectives. As markets become more segmented, the need for personalized advertising increases.

COMPARATIVE ADVERTISING

Firms whose products are not the leaders in their markets often favour **comparative advertising**, a promotional strategy that emphasizes advertising messages with direct or indirect comparisons to dominant brands in the industry. In contrast, advertising by market leaders seldom acknowledges competing products even exist, and when they do, they usually do not point out any benefits of the competing brand.

Wireless telecommunications carriers have been battling it out in media advertising, promoting their calling plans and inviting comparison to competitors. Some offer "in" calling, free text messaging, no roaming charges, or extended hours at reduced rates.

Generally speaking, when there is competition through advertising, prices tend to go down because people can shop around. This benefit has proved increasingly true for online consumers, who now use shopping bots to help find the best prices on goods and services.

comparative advertising Advertising strategy that emphasizes messages with direct or indirect promotional comparisons between competing brands.

CELEBRITY TESTIMONIALS

A popular technique for increasing advertising readership and improving effectiveness involves the use of celebrity spokespeople. This type of advertising is also popular in foreign countries. In Japan, a majority of ads use celebrities, both local and international stars. Ads using Olympic athletes are also popular.

Both the number of celebrity ads and the dollars spent on those ads have increased in recent years. Professional athletes such as NBA star LeBron James are among the highest-paid product endorsers. In a recent year, James reportedly earned over $40 million in endorsement deals with such firms as the Coca-Cola Company and Nike.[13] In comparison, Sidney Crosby, the NHL's highest-paid player, took in $4.5 million a year in endorsements from companies like Tim Hortons and Bell.[14]

One advantage of associations with big-name personalities is improved product recognition in a promotional environment filled with hundreds of competing 15- and 30-second commercials. Advertisers use the term *clutter* to describe this situation. As e-marketing continues to soar, one inevitable result has been the increase in advertising clutter as companies rush to market their goods and services online.

A celebrity testimonial generally succeeds when the celebrity is a credible source of information for the product being promoted. The most effective ads of this type establish links between the celebrities and the advertised goods or services. Studies of consumer responses show that celebrities improve the product's believability, recall of the product, and brand recognition. However, celebrity endorsements can also go awry. A personality who endorses too many products may create confusion in the marketplace. Customers may remember the celebrity but not the product or brand; or worse they might connect the celebrity to a competing brand. Another problem arises if a celebrity is not credible. When Chrysler engaged Jennifer Lopez to promote its Fiat 500, the campaign fell flat. Viewers were unconvinced that someone with a reputation for luxurious tastes would drive such a modest car.[15]

Victorian Values
Bed, Bath & Decor

128 MILL STREET, CREEMORE, ONTARIO   705-466-6327

Courtesy of Victorian Values

An example of retail advertising.

Some advertisers try to avoid problems with celebrities by using cartoon characters as endorsers. The Geico gecko, the cocky reptile with a Cockney accent, has appeared in Geico ads for years.[16] Some advertisers may actually prefer cartoon characters because the characters can never say anything negative about the product, they do exactly what the marketers want them to do, and they cannot get involved in scandals. The only drawback is high licensing fees; popular animated characters often cost more than live celebrities. Companies may create their own cartoon characters or "talking" animals, which eventually become celebrities in their own right as a result of many appearances in advertisements, as is the case with the Energizer bunny and the Geico gecko.

RETAIL ADVERTISING

retail advertising
Advertising by stores that sell goods or services directly to the consuming public.

Most consumers are confronted daily with **retail advertising**, which includes all advertising by retail stores that sell goods or services directly to the consuming public. While this activity accounts for a sizable portion of total annual advertising expenditures, retail advertising varies widely in its effectiveness. One study showed that consumers often respond with suspicion to retail price advertisements.

An advertiser once quipped that the two most powerful words to use in an ad are "New" and "Free"—and these terms are often capitalized on in retail ads. Although "Free" may be featured only in discussions of customer services, the next best term—"Sale"—is often the centrepiece of retail promotions. And "New" typically describes new lines of products being offered. However, many retail stores continue to view advertising as a secondary activity, although that is changing. Local independent retailers rarely use advertising agencies, perhaps because of the expense. Instead, store managers may accept responsibility for advertising in addition to their other duties. Management can begin to correct this problem by assigning one individual the sole responsibility and authority for developing an effective retail advertising program.

cooperative advertising
Strategy in which a retailer shares advertising costs with a manufacturer or wholesaler.

A retailer often shares advertising costs with a manufacturer or wholesaler in a technique called **cooperative advertising**. For example, an apparel marketer may pay a percentage of the cost of a retail store's newspaper advertisement featuring its product lines. Cooperative advertising campaigns originated to take advantage of the media's practice of offering lower rates to local advertisers than to national ones. Later, cooperative advertising became part of programs to improve dealer relations. The retailer likes the chance to secure advertising that it might not be able to afford otherwise. Cooperative advertising can strengthen vertical links in the marketing channel, as when a manufacturer and retailer coordinate their resources. It can also involve firms at the same level of the supply chain. In a horizontal arrangement, a group of retailers—for example, all the Ford dealers in Edmonton—might pool their resources.

INTERACTIVE ADVERTISING

Since marketers realize that two-way communications provide more effective methods for achieving promotional objectives, they are interested in interactive media. **Interactive advertising** involves two-way promotional messages transmitted through communication channels that induce message recipients to participate actively in the promotional effort. Achieving this involvement is the difficult task facing contemporary marketers. Although interactive advertising has become nearly synonymous with e-commerce and the Web, it also includes other formats such as kiosks in shopping malls or text messages on smartphones. Multimedia technology, the Internet, and commercial digital services are changing the nature of advertising from a one-way, passive communication technique to more effective, two-way marketing communications. Interactive advertising creates dialogue between marketers and individual shoppers, providing more materials at the user's request. The advertiser's challenge is to gain and hold consumer interest in an environment where these individuals control what they want to see.

Successful interactive advertising adds value by offering the viewer more than just product-related information. A website can do more than display an ad to promote a brand; it can create a company store, provide customer service, and offer additional content. Many marketers at companies both large and small are hoping that such ads will soon be so finely targeted that they can cut through increasing "advertising clutter" and reach only consumers who are ready to hear their message. And, despite an economic downturn resulting in only modest gains in ad spending overall, online advertising continues to climb and has the highest growth of all mediums.[17]

interactive advertising Two-way promotional messages transmitted through communication channels that induce message recipients to participate actively in the promotional effort.

Marketoid

Canadian companies spend over $1,500 million on radio advertising annually.

CREATING AN ADVERTISEMENT

With millions of dollars at stake, marketers must create effective, memorable ads that increase sales and enhance their organizations' images. Research helps marketers create better ads by pinpointing goals that an ad needs to accomplish, such as educating consumers about product features, enhancing brand loyalty, or improving consumer perception of the brand. These objectives should guide the design of the ad. Marketers can also discover what appeals to consumers and can test ads with potential buyers before committing funds for a campaign.

Marketers sometimes face specific challenges as they develop advertising objectives for services. They must find a creative way to fill out the intangible images of most services and successfully convey the benefits that consumers receive. The "Always Fresh" message of Tim Hortons, along with a picture of a steaming cup of coffee, is an example of how creative advertising can make the intangible nature of services tangible.

TRANSLATING ADVERTISING OBJECTIVES INTO ADVERTISING PLANS

Once a company defines its objectives for an advertising campaign, it can develop its advertising plan. Marketing research assists managers in making strategic decisions that guide choices in technical areas such as budgeting, copywriting, scheduling, and media selection. Post-tests, which are discussed in greater detail later in the chapter, measure the effectiveness of advertising and form the basis for feedback concerning possible adjustments. The elements of advertising planning are shown in Figure 14.3. Experienced marketers know the importance of following even the most basic steps in the process, such as market analysis.

figure 14.3

Elements of the Advertising Planning Process

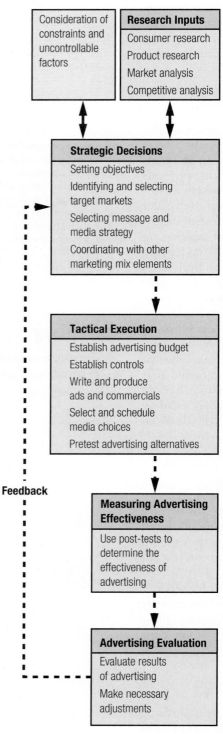

Consideration of constraints and uncontrollable factors	**Research Inputs**
	Consumer research
	Product research
	Market analysis
	Competitive analysis

Strategic Decisions

Setting objectives

Identifying and selecting target markets

Selecting message and media strategy

Coordinating with other marketing mix elements

Tactical Execution

Establish advertising budget

Establish controls

Write and produce ads and commercials

Select and schedule media choices

Pretest advertising alternatives

Feedback

Measuring Advertising Effectiveness

Use post-tests to determine the effectiveness of advertising

Advertising Evaluation

Evaluate results of advertising

Make necessary adjustments

As Chapter 9 explained, positioning involves developing a marketing strategy that aims to achieve a desired position in a prospective buyer's mind. Marketers use a positioning strategy that distinguishes their good or service from those of competitors. Effective advertising then communicates the desired position by emphasizing certain product characteristics, such as performance attributes, price/quality, competitors' shortcomings, applications, user needs, and product classes.

ADVERTISING MESSAGES

The strategy for creating a message starts with the benefits a product offers to potential customers and moves to the creative concept phase, in which marketers strive to bring an appropriate message to consumers by using both visual and verbal components. Marketers work to create an ad with meaningful, believable, and distinctive appeals—one that stands out from the clutter and is more likely to escape zapping by the television remote control or clicking by a mouse.

Usually, ads are created not individually but as part of specific campaigns. An **advertising campaign** is a series of different but related ads that use a single theme and appear in different media within a specified time period. When Weston Bakeries wanted to inject some new interest in its Wonder Bread brand, it worked with its ad agency on a new ad campaign. The campaign, named "The greatest thing since," featured five different televisions ads each telling a different humorous story while preparing a snack using Wonder Bread. The campaign also included social media with promotional material on Facebook.[18]

ADVERTISING APPEALS

Should the tone of the advertisement focus on a practical appeal such as price or gas mileage, or should it evoke an emotional response by appealing to, say, fear, humour, sex? This is another critical decision in the creation of memorable ads that possess the strengths needed to accomplish promotional objectives.

FEAR APPEALS

In recent years, marketers have relied increasingly on fear appeals. Ads for insurance, autos, and even batteries imply that incorrect buying decisions could lead to property loss, injury, or other bad consequences. Companies like Allstate Canada have used fear appeals in their advertising and public relations campaigns.[19]

Fear appeals can backfire, however. Viewers are likely to practise selective perception and tune out statements they perceive as too strong or not credible. Some consumer researchers believe that viewer or reader backlash will eventually occur due to the amount of advertising based on fear appeals.

④ **Compare the major types of advertising appeals and the major advertising media.**

HUMOUR IN ADVERTISING MESSAGES

A humorous ad seeks to create a positive mood related to a product or service, but advertising professionals differ in their opinions of the ads' effectiveness. Some believe that humour distracts attention from brand and product features; consumers remember the humour but not the product. Humorous ads, because they are so memorable, may lose their effectiveness sooner than ads with other kinds of appeals. In addition, humour can be tricky because what one group of consumers finds funny may not be funny at all to another group. Men and women sometimes have a different sense of humour, as do people of different ages. This distinction may become even greater across cultures.

ADS BASED ON SEX

Ads with sex-based appeals immediately attract the consumer's attention. Advertisements for Victoria's Secret lingerie and clothing are designed this way. While many people accept these and other ads, they do not appeal to everyone. And marketers using sex-based appeals know they walk a fine line between what is acceptable to the consumers they want to reach and what is not.

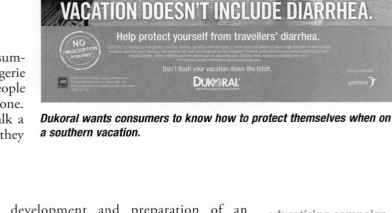

Dukoral wants consumers to know how to protect themselves when on a southern vacation.

DEVELOPING AND PREPARING ADS

The final step in the advertising process—the development and preparation of an advertisement—should flow logically from the promotional theme selected. This process should create an ad that becomes a complementary part of the marketing mix with a carefully determined role in the total marketing strategy. Preparation of an advertisement should emphasize features like its creativity, its continuity with past advertisements, and possibly its association with other company products.

advertising campaign Series of different but related ads that use a single theme and appear in different media within a specified time period.

What immediate tasks should an advertisement accomplish? Regardless of the chosen target, an advertisement should (1) gain attention and interest, (2) inform or persuade, and (3) eventually lead to a purchase or other desired action. It should gain attention in a productive way; that is, it should instill some recall of the good or service. Otherwise, it will not lead to buying action.

Gaining attention and generating interest—cutting through the clutter—can be formidable tasks. Stimulating buying action is often difficult because an advertisement cannot actually close a sale. Nevertheless, if an ad gains attention and informs or persuades, it probably represents a worthwhile investment of marketing resources. Too many advertisers fail to suggest how consumers can purchase the product. Creative design should eliminate this shortcoming.

Figure 14.4 shows the four major elements of a print advertisement: headline, illustration, body copy, and signature. *Headlines* and *illustrations* (photographs, drawings, or other artwork) should work together to generate interest and attention. *Body copy* informs, persuades, and stimulates buying action. The *signature*, which may include the company name, address, phone number, Web address, slogan, trademark, or simply a product photo, names the sponsoring organization. An ad may also have one or more subheadings that either link the main headline to the body copy or subdivide sections of the body copy.

After advertisers conceive an idea for an ad that gains attention, informs and persuades, and stimulates purchases, their next step involves refining the thought sketch into a rough layout.

Figure 14.4

Elements of a Typical Ad

Continued refinements of the rough layout eventually produce the final version of the advertisement design that is ready to be executed, printed, or recorded.

The creation of each advertisement in a campaign requires an evolutionary process that begins with an idea and ultimately results in a finished ad that is ready for distribution through print or electronic media. The idea itself must first be converted into a thought sketch, which is a tangible summary of the intended message. Advances in technology allow advertisers to create novel, eye-catching advertisements. Innovative computer software packages now allow artists to merge several images to create a single image with a natural, seamless appearance.

CREATING INTERACTIVE ADS

Web surfers want engaging, lively content that takes advantage of the medium's capabilities and goes beyond what they find elsewhere. The Web's major advantages make it possible for advertisers to provide that, offering speed, information, two-way communications, self-directed entertainment, and personal choice. Web ads are also vibrant in their visual appeal and some believe they will not experience the swings in spending that traditional ad media do.

Web ads have grown from information-based home pages to innovative, interactive channels for transmitting messages to cyber audiences, including advergames, banners, keyword ads, advertorials, interstitials, pop-ups, and adware. *Advergames* are either online games created by marketers to promote their products to targeted audiences in an interactive way or product placements inserted into online video games. Car manufacturers use these product placements to reach younger audiences who may not watch their television commercials. When the new model of the Louisville Slugger baseball bat was introduced into Canada, Lanctôt Ltée, the Canadian distributor, launched it with an online game called "The Priceless Bat Competition." Players would use their smartphones as a bat and their desktop computers as the playing field. The objective of the game was to determine the price of the new bat—the farther the ball was hit, the lower the price.[20]

Banners, advertisements on a Web page that link to an advertiser's site, are the most common type of advertising on the Internet. They can be free of charge or cost thousands of dollars per month depending on the amount of hits the site receives. Online advertisers often describe their Internet ads in terms of richness, referring to the degree to which new technologies such as streaming video, 3-D animation, JavaScript, video layers, and interactive capabilities are implemented in the banners.

Banners have evolved into a more target-specific technique for Internet advertising with the advent of *missiles:* messages that appear on the screen at exactly the right moment. When a customer visits the site of Company A's competitor, a missile can be programmed to appear on the customer's monitor that allows the customer to click a direct link to Company A's site. However, many people feel the use of such missiles is a questionable practice.

Courtesy of Lanctôt Ltée

When the Canadian distributor of Louisville Slugger sports equipment, Lanctôt Ltée, started promoting its new Z-3000 model of bat, it did it with an interactive website.

Keyword ads are an outcropping of banner ads. Used in search engines, keyword ads appear on the results page of a search and are specific to the term being searched. Advertisers pay search engines to target their ads and display only the banners when users search for relevant keywords, allowing marketers to target specific audiences. For example, if a user searched the term *digital camera*, keyword ads might appear for electronic boutiques or camera shops that sell digital cameras.

Then there are pop-ups, which are little advertising windows that appear in front of the top window of a user's computer screen, and pop-unders, which appear under the top window. Many users complain that interstitials, like pop-ups and missiles, are intrusive and unwanted. Interstitials are more likely to contain large graphics and streaming presentations than banner ads and therefore are more difficult to ignore than typical banner ads. But despite complaints, some studies show that users are more likely to click interstitials than banners.

Perhaps the most intrusive form of online advertising is *adware*, which allows ads to be shown on users' screens through the use of software downloaded to their computers without their consent or through trickery. Such software can be difficult to remove, and some industry experts believe that marketers should avoid dealing with Internet marketing firms that promote the use of adware.

Revenues for *social network advertising* on sites such as Facebook are skyrocketing. In a recent year, Facebook alone had revenues of over $7 billion, and firms are expected to increase the amount they spend on this type of advertising. However, the very nature of the advertising makes it difficult to evaluate and measure its effectiveness. For example, if a virtual bottle of Coca-Cola appears on Facebook or in an online game, how likely is it that consumers will actually purchase Coke the next time they want something to drink?[21]

MEDIA SELECTION AND SCHEDULING

One of the most important decisions in developing an advertising strategy is the selection of appropriate media to carry a firm's message to its audience. The media selected must be capable of accomplishing the communications objectives of informing, persuading, and reminding potential customers of the good, service, person, or idea being advertised.

Research identifies the ad's target market to determine its size and characteristics. Advertisers then match the target characteristics with the media best able to reach that particular audience. The objective of media selection is to achieve adequate media coverage without advertising beyond the identifiable limits of the potential market. Finally, cost comparisons between alternatives should determine the best possible media purchase.

TELEVISION

Television, network and cable combined, still accounts for more than 40 percent of all advertising dollars spent in the world.[22] The attractiveness of television advertising is that marketers can reach local and national markets. Whereas most newspaper advertising revenues come from local advertisers, the greatest share of television advertising revenues comes from organizations that advertise nationally. The newer trend in television advertising is virtual ads—banner-type logos and brief messages that are superimposed onto television coverage of sporting events so that they seem to be a part of the arena's signage but cannot be seen by anyone attending the game. Then there are streaming headlines run by some news stations, which are paid for by corporate sponsors whose names and logos appear within the news stream.

Other trends in television advertising include the abbreviated spot—a 15- or 30-second ad—that costs less to make and is too quick for most viewers to zap with their remote control—and single-advertiser shows. These advertisements work well when viewers are watching live, but as more consumers record programs, many fast-forward past even the briefest commercials. New technology installed in some DVRs enables viewer to skip over commercial content altogether.[23]

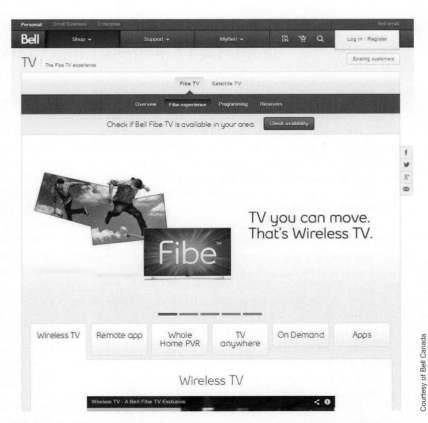

Wireless TV, Whole Home PVRs, or television on your smartphone or tablet—there are more television viewing options than ever before.

Courtesy of Bell Canada

Websites that aggregate TV programming have become top video destinations on the Internet. There viewers can watch complete, high-resolution episodes of current TV programs on their computers, smartphones, or other wireless devices. The sites are free and do not require any additional wires or boxes for access. Instead, viewers see brief ads in order to watch their favourite shows.

In the past decade, ad spending for television has changed significantly mainly due to changes in the industry. The number of specialty channels has increased and the number of homes subscribing to cable, satellite, or the new digital services has also increased. Even though television ad spending still accounts for a large proportion of advertising, other media are closing in. In the last couple of years, online television has started to attract some of the advertising dollars companies were spending on traditional television and other online advertising.[24]

Television advertising offers the advantages of mass coverage, powerful impact on viewers, repetition of messages, flexibility, and prestige. Its disadvantages include loss of control of the promotional message to the telecaster, which can influence its impact; high costs; and some public distrust. Compared with other media, television can suffer from lack of selectivity because specific TV programs may not reach consumers in a precisely defined target market without a significant degree of wasted coverage. However, the growing specialization of cable TV channels can help to resolve the problem. Finally, some types of products are actually banned from television advertising. Tobacco goods, such as cigarettes, cigars, and smokeless tobacco, fall into this category.

With the high cost of television advertising, some companies seek cheaper alternatives, such as print ads, online blogs, and Facebook, particularly for new product launches. Television commercials can promote more than a firm's products; they can highlight an organization's efforts to address a crisis, repair corporate reputations, and attempt to solidify customer loyalty. Often more than one advertising agency will work together to produce a promotional campaign as described in the "Marketing and the SME" feature.

MARKETING AND THE SME — Smaller Ad Agencies Often Work Together

THE first job for many marketing students after they graduate is with a marketing firm or agency. Many of these companies are large multinational organizations located in the major cities, but even more are small firms located across the country. Some of these companies specialize in video, interactive, experiential, traditional advertising; and some take a more general approach. Two such companies are North Strategic and the TraffikGroup.

North Strategic is an awarding-winning communications company, having been awarded the Small Business of the Year award by Air Miles and Top Marketer of the Year by *Marketing* magazine. Some of the companies North Strategic has worked with are Canadian Tire on its "Science of Winter Drinking" campaign and the Royal Bank of Canada on its "Building Olympic Spirit" campaign. North Strategic has offices in Calgary, Montreal, and Toronto.

The TrafffikGroup is based in Toronto. The company has worked on the digital component, packaging, and experiential marketing for Kellogg's Vector "Power Challenge" campaign and the broadcast and digital components of the Sunny D campaign.

More often, companies like TraffikGroup and North Strategic work together on marketing campaigns as the two companies did with the Guinness beer "Anti-Green-Beer" promotion. The campaign ran in March to celebrate St. Patrick's Day. Brand ambassadors were flown in from Ireland to educate Canadians on Irish culture and promote Guinness beer. A website was created to inform those wanting to celebrate St. Patrick's Day where events would be held.

TraffikGroup also teamed with several different marketing companies—SMG, Mosaic, and Wunderman—for the launch of Microsoft's Xbox One. For the national campaign, TraffikGroup was responsible for the digital material, and Wunderman provided the creative aspects of the campaign. The experiential marketing component was developed by Mosaic, and the media part of the campaign was contributed by SMG.

Sources: Jordan Twiss, "Spotted! Microsoft Brings Xbox One to Toronto," Media in Canada website, November 19, 2013, **http://mediaincanada.com**; Rebecca Harris, "Guinness Brings Back Irish Ambassadors for St. Patrick's Day," *Marketing*, March 17, 2014, **www.marketingmag.ca**; Rebecca Harris, "North Strategic Gets into the Video Business," *Marketing*, November 5, 2013, **www.marketingmag.ca**; North Strategic company website, **http://northstrategic.com**, accessed April 16, 2014; TraffikGroup company website, **http://traffikgroup.com**, accessed April 18, 2014; Jennifer Horn, "Creative Report Card: Agencies Full List," *Strategy*, January 29, 2013, **http://strategyonline.ca**.

RADIO

Radio advertising has always been a popular media choice for up-to-the-minute newscasts and for targeting advertising messages to local audiences. But in recent years, radio has become one of the fastest-growing media alternatives. As more and more people find they have less and less time, radio provides immediate information and entertainment at work, at play, and in the car. In addition, as e-commerce continues to grow globally, more people are travelling abroad to seek out new markets. For these travellers, radio stations, including those airing over the Internet, are a means of staying in touch with home—wherever that may be. Marketers frequently use radio advertising to reach local audiences. But in recent years, it has been playing an increasingly important role as a national—and even global—listening favourite. Thousands of online listeners use the Internet to tune in on radio stations from almost every city—an easy-listening station in London, a top-40 Hong Kong broadcaster, or a chat show from Toronto. Other listeners equip their vehicles with satellite radio to maintain contact with their hometown or destination stations during long trips.

Satellite radio providers offer much higher-quality digital signals than regular radio stations, with many more available channels that are mostly free of government regulations and are generally commercial-free. XM Radio, the first such service to be licensed, began airing commercials on a few of its nearly 200 music, sports, and talk channels. XM and its competitor, Sirius Satellite Radio, both charge an annual subscription fee. In May 2011, the Canadian arm of XM and Sirius merged.

Advertisers like radio for its ability to reach people while they drive because they are a captive audience. Other benefits include low cost, flexibility, and mobility. Stations can adapt to local preferences by changing formats, such as going from country and western to an all-news or sports station. The variety of stations allows advertisers to easily target audiences and tailor their messages to those listeners. Disadvantages to radio advertising include highly segmented audiences (reaching most people in a market may require ads placed on several stations), the temporary nature of messages (unlike print ads, radio and TV ads are instantaneous and must be rebroadcast to reach consumers a second time), and a minimum of research information compared with television.

While most radio listening is done in cars or with headset-equipped portables, technology has given birth to Internet radio. Webcast radio allows customers to widen their listening times and choices through their computers. With over 600 radio stations across the country and thousands more around the world streaming live on the Internet, online radio listening continues to grow.[25]

Marketoid

Canadian companies spend over $3,000 million advertising on the Internet annually.

NEWSPAPERS

Newspaper advertising continues to dominate local markets, accounting for more than 25 percent of annual advertising expenditures in Canada.[26] In addition to retail advertisements, classified advertising is an important part of newspaper revenues. Although some predict the decline of newspaper audiences, when online readers are included in circulation figures, newspapers are as popular as ever.[27] Most newspapers have their own websites, which attract a growing number of visitors. Although the amount spent on newspaper advertising in some areas of the world is declining, Canadian newspaper are doing better than most. Two areas where advertising dollars are declining is for classified ads and inserted flyers.[28]

Newspapers' primary advantages start with flexibility because advertising can vary from one locality to the next. Newspapers also allow intensive coverage for ads. Readers sometimes keep the printed advertising message, unlike television or radio advertising messages, and can refer to newspaper ads. Newspaper advertising does have some disadvantages: hasty reading and relatively poor reproduction quality, although that is changing as technology improves.

Newspapers have also begun to struggle to "get through the noise" of other advertisers. To retain big advertisers, some companies have launched annual, semiannual, or monthly magazines featuring a single topic such as fashion or business.

MAGAZINES

Advertisers divide magazines into two broad categories: consumer magazines and business magazines. These categories are also subdivided into monthly and weekly publications. Canadians like to read magazines: there are over 1,200 different Canadian magazines, and Canadian companies spent

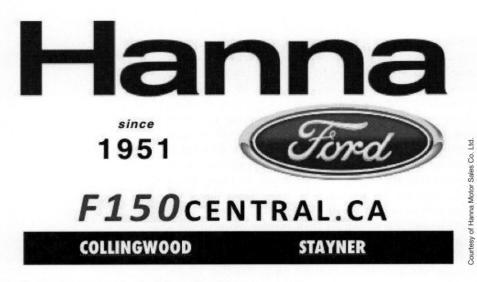

Signage is an example of outdoor advertising.

around $570 million annually to advertise in them.[29] The primary advantages of magazine advertising include the following: the ability to reach precise target markets, quality reproduction, long life, the prestige associated with some magazines. The primary disadvantage is that magazines lack the flexibility of newspapers, radio, and television.

Media buyers study circulation numbers and demographic information for various publications before choosing optimal placement opportunities and in negotiating rates. The same advertising categories have claimed the title for big spenders for several years running. Automotive, retail, and movies and media advertising have held their first, second, and third places, respectively, each year and have continued to show strong growth percentages. Advertisers seeking to promote their products to target markets can reach them by advertising in the appropriate magazines.

DIRECT MAIL

Direct mail advertising consists of sales letters, postcards, leaflets, folders, booklets, catalogues, and house organs (periodicals published by organizations to cover internal issues). Its advantages come from direct mail's ability to segment large numbers of prospective customers into narrow market niches, speed, flexibility, detailed information, and personalization. Disadvantages of direct mail include high cost per reader, dependence on the quality of mailing lists, and some consumers' resistance to it.

The advantages of direct mail explain its widespread use. Data are available on previous purchase patterns and preferred payment methods, as well as household characteristics such as number of children or seniors. Direct mail accounts for an estimated $1243 million of advertising spending each year in Canada.[30] The downside to direct mail is clutter, otherwise known as *junk mail*. So much advertising material is stuffed into people's mailboxes every day that the task of grabbing consumers' attention and evoking some interest is daunting to direct mail advertisers.

OUTDOOR ADVERTISING

Outdoor advertising, sometimes called out-of-home, is perhaps the oldest and simplest media business around. It attracts $486 million in advertising spending, representing about 4 percent of the Canadian total.[31] Traditional outdoor advertising takes the form of billboards, painted displays such as those that appear on the walls of buildings, and electronic displays. Transit advertising includes ads placed both inside and outside buses, subway trains and stations, and commuter trains. Some firms place ads on the roofs of taxicabs, on bus stop shelters and benches, on entertainment and sporting event turnstiles, in public restrooms, and even on parking meters. A section of highway might be cleaned up by a local real estate company or restaurant, with a nearby sign indicating the firm's contributions. All these are forms of outdoor advertising.

Outdoor advertising quickly communicates simple ideas. It also offers repeated exposure to a message and strong promotion for locally available products. Outdoor advertising is particularly effective along metropolitan streets and in other high-traffic areas. But outdoor advertising, just like every other type, is subject to clutter. It also suffers from the brevity of exposure to its messages by passing motorists. Driver concerns about rush-hour safety and limited time also combine to limit the length of exposure to outdoor messages. As a result, most of these ads use striking, simple illustrations, short selling points, and humour to attract people interested in products such as vacations, local entertainment, and lodging.

Another problem involves public concern over aesthetics. Many areas of the country, for example, regulate the placement of outdoor advertising near major highways. Critics have even labelled billboard advertising as "pollution on a stick."

New technologies are helping to revive outdoor advertising. Technology livens up the billboards themselves with animation, large sculptures, and laser images. Three organizations assist companies with outdoor advertising: the Canadian Out-of-Home Measurement Bureau, the Out-of-Home Marketing Association of Canada, and the Canadian Out-of-Home Digital Association.[32]

INTERACTIVE MEDIA

Interactive media—especially the Internet and social media sites—are growing up. Keyword ads dominate online advertising. In a recent year, Google's revenues were over $57 billion, the majority of their revenue coming from ad sales. A growing number of firms are increasing their interactive advertising budgets.[33]

As video and broadcast capabilities expand, advertising comes to cell phones in interesting ways. Mobile advertising revenues in Canada recently hit an estimated $240 million and are expected to continue their explosive growth. Through an emerging technology known as *augmented reality,* virtual imaging can be incorporated into real-time video on a mobile phone, creating an exciting new experience for cell phone users.[34]

OTHER ADVERTISING MEDIA

As consumers filter out appeals from traditional and Internet ads, marketers need new ways to catch their attention. One such device is a special kiosk with Web cameras and software that can recognize, track, and render images on the screen. At the kiosk, customers can see themselves on a screen through the webcam while holding up a two-dimensional brochure of the advertiser's product. The system transforms the picture into a three-dimensional image of the consumer with the product. Marketers believe this type of system increases an advertiser's engagement with the consumer in a new way.[35]

Ads also appear on T-shirts, inlaid in-store flooring, in printed programs of live theatre productions, and as previews on movie DVDs. Directory advertising includes the familiar Yellow Pages and numerous business directories. Some firms pay to have their advertising messages placed on hot-air balloons, blimps, banners behind airplanes, and scoreboards at sporting events. Individuals sometimes agree to paint their own vehicles with advertising messages. The drivers are chosen based on their driving habits, routes, occupations, and living and working locations and are paid a monthly fee for the use of the outside of their vehicles as advertising space.[36]

MEDIA SCHEDULING

Once advertisers have selected the media that best match their advertising objectives and promotional budget, attention shifts to **media scheduling**—setting the timing and sequence for a series of advertisements. A variety of factors influences this decision as well. Sales patterns, repurchase cycles, and competitors' activities are the most important variables.

Seasonal sales patterns are common in many industries. An airline might reduce advertising during peak travel periods and boost its media schedule during low travel months. *Repurchase cycles* may also play a role in media scheduling—products with shorter repurchase cycles will more likely require consistent media schedules throughout the year. Competitors' activities are another influence on media scheduling. A small firm may avoid advertising during periods of heavy advertising by competitors.

Advertisers use the concept of reach, frequency, and gross rating points to measure the effectiveness of media scheduling plans. *Reach* refers to the number of different people or households exposed to an advertisement at least once during a certain period, typically four weeks. *Frequency* refers to the number of times an individual is exposed to an advertisement during a certain period. By multiplying reach times frequency, advertisers quantitatively describe the total weight of a media effort, which is called *gross rating point (GRP = frequency × reach).*

media scheduling
Setting the timing and sequence for a series of advertisements.

4.1 What are some common emotional appeals used in advertising?

4.2 What are the main types of interactive ads?

4.3 What are some advantages radio offers to advertisers? What about newspapers?

4.4 Define *media scheduling* and identify the most important factors influencing the scheduling decision.

Recently, marketers have questioned the effectiveness of reach and frequency to measure the ad success of digital media. The theory behind frequency is that the average advertising viewer needs a minimum of three exposures to a message to understand it and connect it to a specific brand. Web surfers tend to perceptually screen out ads much more quickly—hence, the greater importance of building customer relationships through advertisements.

A media schedule is typically created in the following way. Say an auto manufacturer wants to advertise a new model designed primarily to appeal to professional consumers in their 40s. The model would be introduced in November with a direct mail piece offering test drives. Outdoor, newspaper, and magazine advertising would support the direct mail campaign but also follow through the winter and into the spring and summer. Early television commercials might air during a holiday television special in mid-December, and then one or more expensively produced, highly creative spots would be first aired during the Super Bowl in late January. Another television commercial—along with new print ads—might be scheduled for fall clearance sales as the manufacturer gets ready to introduce next year's models. This example illustrates how marketers might plan their advertising year for just one product.

⑤ **Explain the role of public relations, publicity, cross-promotion, and ethics in an organization's promotional strategy.**

PUBLIC RELATIONS

Earlier, we defined public relations as the firm's communications and relationships with its various publics, including customers, employees, shareholders, suppliers, government agencies, and the society in which it operates. Organizational public relations efforts date back to 1889, when George Westinghouse hired two people to publicize the advantages of alternating current electricity and refute arguments originally championed by Thomas Edison for direct current systems.

Public relations is an efficient, indirect communications channel through which a firm can promote products, although it serves broader objectives than those of other components of promotional strategy. It is concerned with the prestige and image of all parts of the organization. Today, public relations plays a larger role than ever within the promotional mix, and it may emphasize more marketing-oriented information. In addition to its traditional activities, such as surveying public attitudes and creating a good corporate image, PR also supports advertising in promoting the organization's goods and services.

Public relations is in a period of major growth as a result of increased public pressure on industries regarding corporate ethical conduct and environmental and international issues. International expenditures on public relations are growing more rapidly than those for advertising and sales promotion. Many top executives are becoming more involved in public relations as well. The public expects top managers to take greater responsibility for company actions than they have accepted in the past. Those who refuse are widely criticized and censured.

The PR department is the link between the firm and the media. It provides press releases and holds news conferences to announce new products, the formation of strategic alliances, management changes, financial results, or similar developments. The PR department may issue its own publications as well, including newsletters, brochures, and reports.

MARKETING AND NONMARKETING PUBLIC RELATIONS

nonmarketing public relations
Organizational messages about general management issues.

Nonmarketing public relations refers to a company's messages about general management issues. When a company makes a decision that affects any of its publics, input from public relations specialists can help smooth its dealings with those publics. A company that decides to close a plant would need advice on how to deal with the local community, while a firm during a long strike might try to achieve a favourable attitude from the public. Either of these situations might be considered a crisis, as would a massive product recall. Companies that have a plan of action and can effectively handle a crisis by generating positive public relations generally can survive these types of crisis.

In contrast, **marketing public relations (MPR)** refers to focused public relations activities that directly support marketing goals. MPR involves an organization's relationships with consumers or other groups about marketing concerns and can be either proactive or reactive.

With proactive MPR, the marketer takes the initiative and seeks out opportunities for promoting the firm's products, often including distribution of press releases and feature articles. For example, companies send press releases about new products to newspapers, television stations, and relevant consumer, business, and trade publications. It is a powerful marketing tool since it adds news coverage that reinforces direct promotion activities.

Reactive MPR responds to an external situation that has potential negative consequences for the organization. When Honda discovered a problem in the assembly of the driveshaft in certain recent Civic sedans and coupes, it issued a voluntary recall. Although the company had received no reports of accidents related to the matter, it took steps to notify owners and made arrangements for free inspections and replacements.[37]

PUBLICITY

The aspect of public relations that is most directly related to promoting a firm's products is publicity, the nonpersonal stimulation of demand for a good, service, idea, person, or organization by unpaid placement of significant news regarding the product in a print or broadcast medium. It

Courtesy of Kruger Products L.P. ® used under licence

10 years of Scotties. 10 years of support.
For 10 years, Scotties has been a proud supporter of the Canadian Breast Cancer Foundation and their vision of creating a future without breast cancer. So when you choose Scotties, you're not just giving your home a touch of softness. You're giving hope to those who need it most.
facebook.com/ScottiesTissue

HOPE
Scotties
Canada's #1 tissue

Scotties not only promotes its product but also promotes its association with the Canadian Breast Cancer Foundation.

has been said that if advertising is the hammer, publicity is the nail. It creates credibility for the advertising to follow. Firms generate publicity by creating special events, holding press conferences, and preparing news releases and media kits. Many businesses build their brands with virtually no advertising.

While publicity generates minimal costs compared with other forms of promotion, it does not deliver its message entirely for free. Publicity-related expenses include the costs of employing marketing personnel assigned to create and submit publicity releases, printing and mailing costs, and related expenses.

Firms often pursue publicity to promote their images or viewpoints. Other publicity efforts involve organizational activities such as plant expansions, mergers and acquisitions, management changes, and research breakthroughs. A significant amount of publicity, however, provides information about goods and services, particularly new products.

Because many consumers consider news stories to be more credible than advertisements as sources of information, publicity releases are often sent to media editors for possible inclusion in news stories. The media audiences perceive the news as coming from the communications media, not the sponsors. The information in a publicity release about a new good or service can provide valuable assistance for a television, newspaper, or magazine writer, leading to eventual broadcast or publication.

However, not all publicity is positive for a firm. Since companies cannot control the news that surrounds their decisions and actions, negative publicity can create a poor image in consumers' minds. Air travel, once regarded as an exciting adventure, has now become more of a chore. As the

marketing public relations (MPR) Narrowly focused public relations activities that directly support marketing goals.

airline industry struggles to survive increased costs, many carriers have cut flights, raised fares, and added many fees. The result has been bad publicity.

CROSS-PROMOTION

cross-promotion
Promotional technique in which marketing partners share the cost of a promotional campaign that meets their mutual needs.

In recent years, marketers have begun to combine their promotional efforts for related products using a technique called **cross-promotion**, in which marketing partners share the cost of a promotional campaign that meets their mutual needs—an important benefit in an environment of rising media costs. Relationship marketing strategies like co-marketing—a cooperative arrangement in which two businesses jointly market each other's products—and co-branding—a cooperative arrangement in which two or more businesses team up to closely link their names on a single product—are forms of cross-promotion. Marketers realize that these joint efforts between established brands provide greater benefits for both organizations; investments of time and money on such promotions will become increasingly important to many partners' growth prospects.

ETHICS AND PROMOTIONAL STRATEGIES

Chapter 3 introduced the topic of marketing ethics and noted that promotion is the element in the marketing mix that raises the most ethical questions. People actively debate the question of whether marketing communications contribute to better lives.

Even though advertising promoting alcohol or targeting children are technically legal in most areas of Canada, these types of promotions raise ethical issues. In the case of advertising aimed at children, when it comes to influencing parents' purchase decisions, nothing beats influencing kids. By promoting goods and services directly to children, firms can sell not only to them but to the rest of the household, too. However, as the feature "Solving an Ethical Controversy" points out, many question the ethics of promoting directly to children. Their argument: at a time when kids need to learn how to consume healthy food, they are being inundated with promotional messages teaching the opposite.

SOLVING AN ETHICAL CONTROVERSY   **Fast-Food Advertising to Children**

HEADLINES like "Canada's Obesity Rates Triple in Less Than 30 Years" and facts like more than 30 percent of Canadian children are overweight or obese have caused the members of the medical profession to call for some action to be taken. The medical profession believes that a major contributing factor to the weight problem is fast-food advertising directed at children.

Should fast-food advertising to children be banned?

PRO

1. Research shows children familiar with many fast-food ads are twice as likely to be obese as their peers.
2. One study reported that banning fast-food ads could decrease obesity, which invites serious health problems in adulthood, by 17 percent.

CON

1. Parents buy fast food for their children; banning ads on kids' programs won't affect their purchases.

2. Banning advertising comes too close to censorship.

   Where do you stand: pro or con?

Sources: "Curb Junk Food Ads Aimed at Children, Group Says," CBC News, May 9, 2013, **www.cbc.ca**; "Canada's Obesity Rates Triple in Less Than 30 Years," CBC News, March 3, 2014, **www.cbc.ca**; Banaz Al-khalidi, "Backgrounder: Obesity Trends in Canada," EvidenceNetwork.ca, University of Manitoba, August 9, 2013, **http://umanitoba.ca**; Brooks Barnes, "Promoting Nutrition, Disney to Restrict Junk-Food Ads," *The New York Times*, June 5, 2012, **www.nytimes.com**; Doug Tynan, "Whose Responsibility Is Childhood Obesity?" KevinMD.com, accessed May 31, 2012, **www.kevinmd.com**; Anthony Gucciardi, "McDonald's Rejects Anti-Obesity Campaign, 'Proud' of 'Responsible' Menu," InfoWars.com, May 27, 2012, **www.infowars.com**; Mark Brandau, "McDonald's CEO Skinner Takes on Critics at Final Shareholder Meeting," *Nation's Restaurant News*, May 24, 2012, **http://nrn.com**; Emily Bryson York, "McDonald's to Kids: Eat Fruit, Drink Milk, Visit Arches," *Chicago Tribune*, March 5, 2012, **http://articles.chicagotribune.com**; "Familiarity with Television Fast-Food Ads Linked to Obesity," American Academy of Pediatrics, April 29, 2012, **www.aap.org**; Emma Gray, "Do Fast Food Ads Make Kids Fat?" That's Fit.com, **www.thatsfit.com**, accessed April 29, 2012.

Another issue is the insertion of product messages in media programs without full disclosure of the marketing relationship to audiences. To woo younger consumers, especially teens and those in their 20s, advertisers attempt to make these messages appear as different from advertisements as possible; they design ads that seem more like entertainment.

In online ads, it is often difficult to separate advertising from editorial content since many sites resemble magazine and newspaper ads or television infomercials. Another ethical issue surrounding advertising online is the use of cookies, small text files that are automatically downloaded to a user's computer whenever a site is visited. Each time the user returns to that site, the site's server accesses the cookie and gathers information: What site was visited last? How long did the user stay? What was the next site visited? Marketers claim that this device helps them determine consumer preferences and argue that cookies are stored in the user's PC, not the company's website. The problem is that cookies can and do collect personal information without the user's knowledge.

DECEPTIVE ADVERTISING

Deceptive advertising refers to exaggerated claims of a product's superiority or the use of subjective or vague statements that may not be literally true. Although there are a few laws in Canada dealing with deceptive advertising, the Competition Act does regulate deceptive ads relating to pricing.

Exaggeration in ads is not new. Consumers seem to accept advertisers' tendencies to stretch the truth in their efforts to distinguish their products and get consumers to buy. This inclination may provide one reason that advertising does not encourage purchase behaviour as successfully as sales promotions do. A tendency toward exaggeration does raise some ethical questions, though: Where is the line between claims that attract attention and those that provide implied guarantees? To what degree do advertisers deliberately make misleading statements?

Advertising Standards Canada (ASC) is the self-regulatory body for the advertising industry. The members of this organization promote the integrity and viability of advertising, hoping that effective self-control will reduce the number of laws enacted to control abuse. To date they have been effective in doing so. They administer the Canadian Code of Advertising Standards, which includes those aspects covered in the Competition Act, as well as other issues such as those relating to advertising to children. This group also investigates any complaints relating to the industry but they have no authority to enforce their decisions.[38]

ETHICS IN PUBLIC RELATIONS

Several public relations issues open organizations to criticism. Various PR firms perform services for the tobacco industry; publicity campaigns defend unsafe products. Also, marketers must weigh ethics before they respond to negative publicity. For example, do firms admit to problems or product deficiencies, or do they try to cover them up?

assessment check 5

5.1 Distinguish between marketing public relations and nonmarketing public relations.

5.2 What is publicity?

5.3 What are the advantages of cross-promotion?

PROMOTIONAL MIX EFFECTIVENESS

(6) **Discuss the factors that influence the effectiveness of a promotional mix and how marketers measure effectiveness.**

Since quantitative measures are not available to determine the effectiveness of each component of a promotional mix in a given segment, developing an effective promotional mix is one of the marketer's most difficult tasks. Several factors influence the effectiveness of a promotional mix.

NATURE OF THE MARKET

The marketer's target audience has a major impact on the choice of a promotion method. When a market includes a limited number of buyers, personal selling may prove a highly effective technique. However, markets characterized by large numbers of potential customers scattered over sizable geographic areas may make the cost of contact by salespeople prohibitive. In such instances, extensive use of advertising often makes sense. The type of customer also affects the promotional mix. Personal selling works better in high-priced, high-involvement purchases—for instance, a target market made up of business purchasers or wholesale buyers—than in a target market consisting of ultimate consumers. Similarly, pharmaceutical firms use large sales forces to sell prescription drugs directly to physicians and hospitals, but they also advertise to promote over-the-counter medications for the consumer market. So the drug firm must switch its promotional strategy from personal selling to consumer advertising based on the market it is targeting.

NATURE OF THE PRODUCT

The product itself is an important factor in determining promotional mix effectiveness. Highly standardized products with minimal servicing requirements usually depend less on personal selling than do custom products with technically complex features or requirements for frequent maintenance. Marketers of consumer products are more likely to rely heavily on advertising than are business products. For example, soft drinks lend themselves more readily to advertising than do large pieces of business machinery.

Promotional mixes vary within each product category. In the B2B market, for example, installations typically rely more heavily on personal selling than does marketing of operating supplies. In contrast, the promotional mix for a convenience product is likely to involve more emphasis on manufacturer advertising and less on personal selling.

STAGE IN THE PRODUCT LIFE CYCLE

The promotional mix must also be tailored to the product's stage in the product life cycle. In the introductory stage, both nonpersonal and personal selling are used to acquaint marketing intermediaries and final consumers with the merits of the new product. Heavy emphasis on personal selling helps inform the marketplace of the merits of the new good or service. Salespeople contact marketing intermediaries to secure interest in and commitment to handling the newly introduced item. Trade shows are frequently used to inform and educate prospective dealers and ultimate consumers about its merits over current competitive offerings. Advertising and sales promotion are also used during this stage to create awareness, answer questions, and stimulate initial purchases.

As the product moves into the growth and maturity stages, advertising gains relative importance in persuading consumers to make purchases. Marketers continue to direct personal-selling efforts at marketing intermediaries in an attempt to expand distribution. As more competitors enter the marketplace, advertising begins to stress product differences to persuade consumers to purchase the firm's brand. In the maturity and early decline stages, firms frequently reduce advertising and sales promotion expenditures as market saturation is reached and newer products with their own competitive strengths begin to enter the market.

PRICE

The price of an item is the fourth factor that affects the choice of a promotional mix. Advertising dominates the promotional mixes for low-unit-value products due to the high per-contact costs in personal selling. Advertising permits a low promotional expenditure per sales unit because it reaches mass audiences. For low-value consumer goods, such as chewing gum, soft drinks, and snack foods, advertising is the most feasible means of promotion. On the other hand, consumers of high-priced items such as luxury cars expect lots of well-presented information from qualified salespeople. High-tech direct marketing promotions such as video presentations on a notebook computer or via smartphone; fancy brochures; and personal selling by informed, professional salespeople appeal to these potential customers.

FUNDS AVAILABLE FOR PROMOTION

Budget size can present a stumbling block to implementing promotional strategy. A single 30-second television commercial during the Super Bowl telecast costs an advertiser around $4 million.[39] While millions of viewers may see the commercial, making the cost per contact relatively low, such an expenditure exceeds the entire promotional budgets of thousands of firms, a dilemma that at least partially explains how guerrilla marketing got its start. And if a company wants to hire a celebrity to advertise its goods and services, the fee can run into the millions of dollars a year.

Traditional methods used for creating a promotional budget include the percentage-of-sales and fixed-sum-per-unit methods, along with techniques for meeting the competition and achieving task objectives.

The *percentage-of-sales method* is perhaps the most common way of establishing promotional budgets. The percentage can be based on sales either from some past period (such as the previous year) or forecasted for a future period (the current year). While this plan is appealingly simple, it does not effectively support the achievement of basic promotional objectives. Arbitrary percentage allocations can't provide needed flexibility. In addition, sales should depend on promotional allocation rather than vice versa.

The *fixed-sum-per-unit method* allocates a predetermined amount to each sales or production unit. This amount can also reflect either historical or forecasted figures. Producers of high-value consumer durable goods, such as automobiles, often use this budgeting method.

The *meeting competition method* simply matches competitors' outlays, either in absolute amounts or relative to the firms' market shares. But this method doesn't help a company gain a competitive edge. A budget that is appropriate for one company may not be appropriate for another.

The *task-objective method* develops a promotional budget based on a sound evaluation of the firm's promotional objectives. The method has two steps:

1. Define realistic and quantifiable communication goals for the promotional mix (for example, to achieve a 25 percent increase in brand awareness). These objectives become an integral part of the promotional plan.

2. Determine the amount and type of promotional activity required for each objective. Combined, these units become the firm's promotional budget.

A crucial assumption underlies the task-objective approach: marketers can measure the productivity of each promotional dollar. That assumption explains why the objectives must be carefully chosen, quantified, and accomplished through promotional efforts. Generally, budgeters should avoid marketing objectives such as "Achieve a 5 percent increase in sales." A sale is a culmination of the effects of all elements of the marketing mix. A more appropriate promotional objective might be "Achieve an 8 percent response rate from a targeted direct mail advertisement."

Promotional budgeting always requires difficult decisions. Still, recent research studies and the spread of computer-based models have made it a more manageable problem than it used to be.

EVALUATING PROMOTIONAL EFFECTIVENESS

Evaluating the effectiveness of a promotion today is a far different exercise in marketing research than it was even a few decades ago. For years, marketers depended on store audits conducted by large organizations like Nielsen. Other research groups conducted warehouse withdrawal surveys of shipments to retail customers. These studies were designed to determine whether sales had risen as a direct result of a particular promotional campaign. During the 1980s, scanners and automated checkout lanes completely changed marketing research. For the first time, retailers and manufacturers had a tool to obtain sales data quickly and efficiently. The problem was that the collected data were used for little else other than determining how much of which product was bought at what price and at what time.

With the advent of the Internet and the proliferation of social media sites, marketing research has entered another evolutionary period. Now marketers can delve into each customer's purchase behaviour, lifestyle, preferences, opinions, and buying habits. All this information can also be obtained in a matter of seconds.

Most marketers would prefer to use a *direct sales results test* to measure the effectiveness of promotion. Such an approach would reveal the specific impact on sales revenues for each dollar of promotional spending. This type of technique has always eluded marketers, however, due to their inability to control other variables operating in the marketplace. A firm may receive $20 million in additional sales orders following a new $1.5-million advertising campaign, but the market success may really have resulted from the products benefiting from more intensive distribution as

Marketoid

Canadian companies spend over $450 million on billboards and other outdoor advertising in a year.

more stores decide to carry them or price increases for competing products rather than from the advertising outlays.

Marketers often encounter difficulty isolating the effects of promotion from those of other market elements and outside environmental variables. *Indirect evaluation* helps researchers concentrate on quantifiable indicators of effectiveness, such as recall (how much members of the target market remember about specific products or advertisements) and readership (size and composition of a message's audience). The basic problem with indirect measurement is the difficulty in relating these variables to sales.

Marketers need to ask the right questions and understand what they are measuring. Promotion to build sales volume produces measurable results in the form of short-term returns, but brand-building efforts to generate or enhance consumers' perceptions of value in a product, brand, or organization cannot be measured over the short term.

MEASURING ADVERTISING EFFECTIVENESS

Although promotional prices vary widely, advertisers typically pay a fee based on the cost to deliver the message to viewers, listeners, or readers—the so-called *cost per thousand impressions (CPM)*. Billboards are the cheapest way to spend advertising dollars, with television and some newspapers the most expensive. But while price is an important factor in media selection, it is by no means the only one—or all ads would appear on billboards.

Since promotion represents such a major expenditure for many firms, they need to determine whether their campaigns accomplish appropriate promotional objectives. Companies want their advertising agencies and in-house marketers to demonstrate how promotional programs contribute to increased sales and profits. Marketers are well aware of the number of advertising messages and sales promotions consumers encounter daily, and they know these people practise selective perception and simply screen out many messages.

By measuring promotional effectiveness, organizations can evaluate different strategies, prevent mistakes before spending money on specific programs, and improve their promotional programs. As the earlier discussion of promotional planning explained, any evaluation program starts with objectives and goals; otherwise, marketers have no yardstick against which to measure effectiveness. However, determining whether an advertising message has achieved its intended objective is one of the most difficult undertakings in marketing. Sales promotions and direct marketing are somewhat easier to evaluate, because they evoke measurable consumer responses. Like advertising, public relations is also difficult to assess on purely objective terms.

MEDIA AND MESSAGE RESEARCH

media research
Advertising research that assesses how well a particular medium delivers an advertiser's message, where and when to place the advertisement, and the size of the audience.

message research
Advertising research that tests consumer reactions to an advertisement's creative message.

Measures to evaluate the effectiveness of advertising, while difficult and costly, are essential parts of any marketing plan. Without an assessment strategy, marketers will not know whether their advertising achieves the objectives of the marketing plan or whether the dollars in the advertising budget are well spent. To answer these questions, marketers can conduct two types of research. **Media research** assesses how well a particular medium delivers the advertiser's message, where and when to place the advertisement, and the size of the audience. Buyers of broadcast time base their purchases on estimated Nielsen rating points, and the networks have to make good if ratings do not reach promised levels. Buyers of print advertising space pay fees based on circulation. Circulation figures are independently certified by specialized research firms.

The other major category, **message research**, tests consumer reactions to an advertisement's creative message. Pretesting and post-testing, the two methods for performing message research, are discussed in the following sections.

As the role of marketing expands in many organizations, marketers are employing increasingly sophisticated techniques to measure marketing effectiveness not only throughout the company but through the entire marketing channel. As more firms also conduct multichannel promotional efforts, keeping track of the data is a challenge. However, when they do so, they can better track which channels are most effective.

Pretesting

To assess an advertisement's likely effectiveness before it actually appears in the chosen medium, marketers often conduct **pretesting**. The obvious advantage of this technique is the opportunity to evaluate ads when they are being developed. Marketers can conduct a number of different pretests, beginning during the concept phase in the campaign's earliest stages, when they have only rough copy of the ad, and continuing until the ad layout and design are almost completed.

Pretesting uses several evaluation methods. For example, focus groups can discuss their reactions to mock-ups of ads using different themes, headlines, or illustrations. To screen potential radio and television advertisements, marketers often recruit consumers to sit in a studio and indicate their preferences by pressing two buttons, one for a positive reaction to the commercial and the other for a negative reaction. Sometimes proposed ad copy is printed on a postcard that also offers a free product; the number of cards returned represents an indication of the copy's effectiveness. In *blind product tests,* people are asked to select unidentified products on the basis of available advertising copy.

Mechanical and electronic devices offer yet another method of assessing how people read advertising copy. One mechanical test uses a hidden camera to photograph eye movements of readers. The results help advertisers determine headline placement and copy length. Another mechanical approach measures the galvanic skin response—changes in the electrical resistance of the skin produced by emotional reactions.

pretesting Research that evaluates an ad during its development stage.

Post-testing

Post-testing assesses advertising copy after it has appeared in the appropriate medium. Pretesting generally is a more desirable measurement method than post-testing because it can save the cost of placing ineffective ads. However, post-testing can help in planning future advertisements and in adjusting current advertising programs.

One of the most popular post-test methods is a readership test, interviews with people who have read selected magazines to determine whether they observed various ads in them. A copy of the magazine is used as an interview aid, and each interviewer starts at a different point in the magazine. For larger ads, respondents are asked about specifics, such as headlines and copy. All such readership tests, also called recognition tests, assume that future sales are related to advertising readership.

Unaided recall tests are another method of post-testing the effectiveness of advertisements. Respondents do not see copies of the magazine after their initial reading but are asked to recall the ads from memory. Podcasts are a popular medium for advertisers because post-tests reveal that unaided recall among respondents is high. *Inquiry tests* are another popular form of post-test. Advertisements sometimes offer gifts—generally product samples—to people who respond to them. The number of inquiries relative to the advertisement's cost forms a measure of its effectiveness.

Split runs allow advertisers to test two or more ads at the same time. Although advertisers traditionally place different versions in newspapers and magazines, split runs on cable television systems frequently test the effectiveness of TV ads. With this method, advertisers divide the cable TV audience or a publication's subscribers in two: half view advertisement A and the other half view advertisement B. The relative effectiveness of the alternatives is then determined through inquiries or recall and recognition tests.

Regardless of the exact method marketers choose, pretesting and post-testing are expensive efforts that must be used as effectively as possible.

post-testing Research that assesses advertising effectiveness after it has appeared in a print or broadcast medium.

split runs Methods of testing alternative ads by dividing a cable TV audience or a publication's subscribers in two, using two different ads, and then evaluating the relative effectiveness of each.

MEASURING PUBLIC RELATIONS EFFECTIVENESS

Organizations must measure PR results based on their objectives both for the PR program as a whole and for specific activities. In the next step, marketers must decide what they want to measure. This choice includes determining whether the message was heard by the target audience and whether it had the desired influence on public opinion.

The simplest and least costly level of assessment measures outputs of the PR program: whether the target audience received, paid attention to, understood, and retained the messages directed to them. To make this judgment, the staff could count the number of media placements and gauge the extent of media coverage. They could count attendees at any press conference, evaluate the quality of brochures and other materials, and pursue similar activities. Formal techniques include tracking publicity placements, analyzing how favourably their contents portrayed the company, and conducting public opinion polls.

To analyze PR effectiveness more deeply, firms conduct focus groups, interviews with opinion leaders, and more detailed and extensive opinion polls. The highest level of effectiveness measurement looks at outcomes: Did the program change people's opinions, attitudes, and behaviour? PR professionals measure these outcomes through before-and-after polls (similar to pretesting and post-testing) and more advanced techniques like psychographic analysis (discussed in Chapter 9).

EVALUATING INTERACTIVE MEDIA

Marketers have used various methods to measure the effectiveness of Web communications: *hits* (user requests for a file), *impressions* (the number of times a viewer sees an ad), and *click-throughs* (when the user clicks the ad to get more information). *View-through* rates measure responses over time. However, some of these measures can be misleading: it takes more than "eyeballs" to measure the effectiveness of online media. What matters is not how many times a website is visited but how well the communication elicits the desired behaviour.

Traditional numbers that work for other media forms are not necessarily relevant indicators of effectiveness for a website. For one thing, the Web combines both advertising and direct marketing. Web pages effectively integrate advertising and other content, such as demonstrations, coupons, product information, and interactive features, which may often prove to be the page's main—and most effective—feature. For another consideration, consumers generally choose the advertisements they want to see on the Internet, whereas traditional broadcast or print media automatically expose consumers to ads.

Two major techniques for setting Internet advertising rates are cost per impression and cost per response. *Cost per impression* is a measurement technique that relates the cost of an ad to every thousand people who view it. In other words, anyone who sees the page containing the banner or other form of ad creates one impression. This measure assumes the site's primary purpose is to display the advertising message. *Cost per response* (or *click-throughs)* is a direct marketing technique that relates the cost of an ad to the number of people who click it. However, not everyone who clicks on an ad makes a purchase. So marketers measure the *conversion rate*—the percentage of website visitors who actually make a purchase. All three rating techniques have merit. Site publishers point out that click-through rates are influenced by the creativity of the ad's message. Advertisers, on the other hand, point out that the Web ad has value to those who click it for additional information.

Internet marketers price ad banners based on cost per thousand (CPM). Websites that sell advertising typically guarantee a certain number of impressions—the number of times an ad banner is downloaded and presumably seen by visitors. Marketers then set a rate based on that guarantee times the CPM rate.

Marketers can measure performance by incorporating some form of direct response into their promotions. This technique also helps them compare different promotions for effectiveness and rely on facts rather than opinions.

assessment check 6

6.1 What five factors affect the choice of a promotional mix?

6.2 Why is the choice of a mix a difficult task for marketers?

6.3 What is the most common way of establishing a promotional budget?

6.4 What is the direct sales results test? Why is it difficult to administer?

Strategic Implications

With the incredible proliferation of promotional messages in the media, today's marketers—consumers themselves—must find new ways to reach customers without overloading them with unnecessary or unwanted communications. Integrating marketing communications into an overall consumer-focused strategy that meets a company's promotional and business objectives has become more and more critical in a busy global marketplace.

It is difficult to overstate the impact of the Internet and social media on the promotional mix of 21st-century marketers. As greater portions of corporate ad budgets continue to migrate to the Web, marketers must be increasingly aware of the benefits and pitfalls of Internet advertising. But they should not forget the benefits of other types of advertising as well. Promotion industry experts agree that e-business and social media broaden marketers' job tasks, though many promotional objectives still remain the same. ◆◆◆

REVIEW OF CHAPTER OBJECTIVES

(1) **Explain how integrated marketing communications relates to the development of an optimal promotional mix and describe the communication process.**

Integrated marketing communications (IMC) refers to the coordination of all promotional activities to produce a unified, customer-focused promotional message. Developing an optimal promotional mix involves selecting the personal and nonpersonal selling strategies that will work best to deliver the overall marketing message as defined by IMC.

In the communication process, a message is encoded and transmitted through a communications channel; then it is decoded, or interpreted by the receiver; finally, the receiver provides feedback, which completes the system. The AIDA concept (attention, interest, desire, action) explains the steps through which a person reaches a purchase decision after being exposed to a promotional message. The marketer sends the promotional message, and the consumer receives and responds to it via the communication process.

(2) **Identify the elements of the promotional mix.**

The elements of the promotional mix are personal selling and nonpersonal selling (advertising, product placement, sales promotion, direct marketing, and public relations). Guerrilla marketing is frequently used by marketers with limited funds and firms attempting to attract attention for new-product offerings with innovative promotional approaches. Sponsorship occurs when an organization pays money or in-kind resources to an event or activity in exchange for a direct association with that event or activity.

(3) **Name the major advertising objectives, categories, and strategies of advertising and describe the process of creating an advertisement.**

The three major objectives of advertising are to inform, persuade, and remind. The two major categories of advertising are product advertising and institutional advertising. Product advertising involves the nonpersonal selling of a good or service. Institutional advertising is the nonpersonal promotion of a concept, idea, or philosophy of a company or organization.

The major strategies are comparative advertising, which makes extensive use of messages with direct comparisons between competing brands; celebrity, which uses famous spokespeople to boost an advertising message; retail, which includes all advertising by retail stores selling products directly to consumers; and interactive, which encourages two-way communication via the Internet, social media sites, or kiosks.

An advertisement evolves from pinpointing goals, such as educating consumers, enhancing brand loyalty, or improving a product's image. From those goals, marketers move to the next stages: creating a plan, developing a message, developing and preparing the ad, and selecting the appropriate medium (or media).

(4) **Compare the major types of advertising appeals and the major advertising media.**

Advertisements often appeal to consumers' emotions, and these appeals to fear, humour, or sex can be effective. However, marketers need to recognize that fear appeals can backfire; people's sense of humour can differ according to gender, age, and other factors; and use of sexual imagery must not overstep the bounds of taste.

The major media include broadcast (TV and radio), newspapers and magazines, direct mail, outdoor, and interactive. Each medium has benefits and drawbacks. Newspapers are flexible and dominate local markets. Magazines can target niche markets. Interactive media foster two-way communication. Outdoor advertising in a high-traffic location reaches many people every day; television and radio reach even more. Direct mail allows effective segmentation. Once advertisers select the media that best matches their advertising objectives and promotional budgets, their attention shifts to setting the time and sequence for a series of ads.

⑤ **Explain the roles of public relations, publicity, cross-promotion, and ethics in an organization's promotional strategy.**

Public relations consists of the firm's communications and relationships with its various publics, including customers, employees, shareholders, suppliers, government, and the society in which it operates. Publicity is the dissemination of newsworthy information about a product or organization. This information activity is frequently used in new-product introductions. Although publicity is welcomed by firms, negative publicity is easily created when a company enters a grey ethical area with the use of its promotional efforts. Cross-promotion, illustrated by tie-ins between popular movies and fast-food restaurants, permits marketing partners to share the cost of a promotional campaign that meets their mutual needs. Marketers should be careful to construct ethically sound promotional campaigns, avoiding such practices as deception. In addition, negative publicity may occur as a result of some action a firm takes—or fails to take—such as a product recall.

⑥ **Discuss the factors that influence the effectiveness of a promotional mix and how marketers measure effectiveness.**

Marketers face the challenge of determining the best mix of components for an overall promotional strategy. Several factors influence the effectiveness of the promotional mix: (1) the nature of the market, (2) the nature of the product, (3) the stage in the product's life cycle, (4) price, and (5) the funds available for promotion.

Marketers may choose among several methods for determining promotional budgets, including percentage-of-sales, fixed-sum-per-unit, meeting competition, or task-objective, which is considered the most flexible and most effective. Today, marketers use either direct sales results tests or indirect evaluation to measure effectiveness. Both methods have their benefits and drawbacks because of the difficulty of controlling variables.

The effectiveness of advertising can be measured by pretesting and post-testing. Pretesting assesses an ad's effectiveness before it is actually used. Post-testing assesses an ad's effectiveness after it has been used. Commonly used post-tests are readership tests, unaided recall tests, inquiry tests, and split runs.

assessment check answers ✓

1.1 Define *promotion*.
Promotion is the function of informing, persuading, and influencing the consumer's purchase decision.

1.2 What is the difference between marketing communications and integrated marketing communications (IMC)?
Marketing communications are messages that deal with buyer–seller relationships, from a variety of media. IMC coordinates all promotional activities to produce a unified, customer-focused promotional message.

1.3 Identify the four steps of the AIDA concept.
The four steps of the AIDA concept are attention, interest, desire, and action.

1.4 What is noise?
Noise represents interference at some stage in the communication process.

2.1 Differentiate between personal and nonpersonal selling.
Personal selling is promotion conducted person to person between a seller and a buyer. It may take place face to face, over the telephone, through videoconferencing, or by computer links between buyer and seller. Nonpersonal selling is promotion conducted without being face to face with the buyer.

2.2 What are the six major categories of nonpersonal selling?
The six categories of nonpersonal selling are advertising, product placement, sales promotion, direct marketing, public relations, and guerrilla marketing.

2.3 How is sponsorship different from advertising?
Although sponsorship generates brand awareness, the sponsor has little control over the message or even the coverage, unlike advertising.

3.1 What is comparative advertising?
Comparative advertising makes extensive use of messages with direct comparisons between competing brands.

3.2 What makes a successful celebrity testimonial?
Successful celebrity ads feature figures who are credible sources of information for the promoted product.

3.3 What is an advertising campaign?
An advertising campaign is a series of different but related ads that use a single theme and appear in different media within a specified time period.

3.4 What are an advertisement's three main goals?
Advertising's three main goals are to educate consumers about product features, enhance brand loyalty, and improve consumer perception of the brand.

4.1 What are some common emotional appeals used in advertising?
Advertisers often focus on making emotional appeals to fear, humour, or sex.

4.2 What are the main types of interactive ads?
Interactive ads include Internet banners, pop-ups, keyword ads, advertorials, advergames, and interstitials.

4.3 What are some advantages radio offers to advertisers? What about newspapers?
Radio ads allow marketers to target a captive audience and offer low cost, flexibility, and mobility. Newspaper ads are flexible and provide nearly complete coverage of the market. Readers can also refer back to newspaper ads.

4.4 Define *media scheduling* and identify the most important factors influencing the scheduling decision.
Media scheduling sets the timing and sequence for a series of advertisements. Sales patterns, repurchase cycles, and competitors' activities are the most important variables in the scheduling decision.

5.1 Distinguish between marketing public relations and nonmarketing public relations.
Marketing public relations refers to focused public relations activities that directly support marketing goals. Nonmarketing public relations refers to a company's messages about general issues.

5.2 What is publicity?
Publicity is nonpersonal stimulation of demand for a good, service, place, idea, person, or organization by unpaid placement of significant news regarding the subject in a print or broadcast medium.

5.3 What are the advantages of cross-promotion?
Cross-promotion divides the cost of a promotional campaign that meets the mutual needs of marketing partners and provides greater benefits for both in return.

6.1 What five factors affect the choice of a promotional mix?
The five factors are (1) nature of the market, (2) nature of the product, (3) stage in the product life cycle, (4) price, and (5) funds available for promotion.

6.2 Why is the choice of a mix a difficult task for marketers?
Developing an effective promotional mix is difficult, because marketers lack quantitative measures to determine the effectiveness of each component of a promotional mix in a given market segment.

6.3 What is the most common way of establishing a promotional budget?
The most common method of establishing a promotional budget is the percentage-of-sales method.

6.4 What is the direct sales results test? Why is it difficult to administer?
The direct sales results test reveals the specific impact on sales revenues for each dollar of promotional spending. Administering this test is difficult because marketers cannot control other variables operating in the marketplace.

MARKETING TERMS YOU NEED TO KNOW

These terms are printed in blue in the text. They are defined in the margins of the chapter and in the Glossary that begins on p. G-1.

cross-promotion 420   message research 424   post-testing 425
media research 424   pretesting 425   split runs 425

PROJECTS AND TEAMWORK EXERCISES

1. On your own or with a classmate, select a print advertisement that catches your attention and analyze it according to the AIDA concept (attention, interest, desire, action). Identify features of the ad that catch your attention, pique your interest, make you desire the product, and spur you toward a purchase. Present your findings to the class.

2. Watch a television show and see how many products you can find placed within the show. Present your findings to the class.

3. With a classmate, choose a good or service you think could benefit from guerrilla marketing. Imagine you have a limited promotional budget, and come up with a plan for a guerrilla approach. Outline several ideas, and explain how you plan to carry them out. Present your plan to the class.

4. Cut out a print ad and place it on a poster board. With a marker, identify all the elements of the ad. Then identify what you believe is the ad's objective. Next, identify the strategy used. If the ad has an interactive component, note that as well.

CRITICAL THINKING EXERCISES

1. What are some benefits and drawbacks of using celebrity testimonials in advertising? Identify an ad that uses a celebrity's endorsement effectively, and explain why.

2. Identify a corporate sponsorship for a cause or program in your area, or find a local company that sponsors a local charity or other organization. What does the sponsor gain from its actions? Be specific. What does the sponsored organization receive? Is this sponsorship good for your community? Explain.

3. Select two different advertisers' TV or print ads for the same product category (cars or soft drinks, for instance) and decide what emotion each appeals to. Which ad is more effective, and why?

4. Think back to publicity you have heard recently about a company or its products. If it was good publicity, how was it generated, and what media were used? If it was bad publicity, where did you learn about it, and how did the firm try to control or neutralize it?

ETHICS EXERCISE

Pop-up ads, those unsolicited messages that sometimes pop onto your computer screen and block the site or information you're looking for until you close or respond to them, are inexpensive to produce and cost nearly nothing to send. But they are so annoying to some computer users that dozens of special programs have been written to block them from appearing on the screen during Internet use.

1. Do you think that, because they are unsolicited, pop-up ads are also disruptive? Are they an invasion of privacy? Explain your reasoning.

2. Do you consider the use of pop-up ads to be unethical? Why or why not?

CASE 14.1

Not-for-Profit and IMC

Many advertising and marketing companies work with charities and not-for-profit organizations; often these companies donate their time, resources, and creativity in order to help the not-for-profit get a message out. Two such campaigns are the "Surrender Your Say—Twitter Campaign for Tourette Syndrome" and the "Milk Carton 2.0" campaign for the Missing Children's Society of Canada. These two campaigns were aimed at a national audience but some messages are aimed at a local audience or even an international audience.

The "Surrender Your Say—Twitter Campaign for Tourette Syndrome" was produced for the Tourette Syndrome Foundation of Canada by Saatchi & Saatchi Canada, an international advertising agency with offices in more than 70 countries. The Tourette Syndrome Foundation of Canada (TSFC) was founded in 1976 by two men whose children had Tourette syndrome. The two fathers wanted to provide information about the neurological disorder, in which sufferers experience involuntary movements or vocalizations such as facial grimaces or tongue clicking.

In creating the campaign, Saatchi & Saatchi wanted to give people an opportunity to experience what it was like to live with the condition. In order to provide an understanding of the lack of control and anxiety that many with the disorder experience, thousands of Twitter users signed up to lose control over their Twitter accounts. For an entire day the foundation sent out tic-like Tweets generating millions of impressions. The campaign was described by one industry expert as "daring in its simplicity and brilliant in the way that it leveraged true channel understanding to perfectly deliver the marketing objective 140 characters at a time." The promotion won gold in the Media Innovation Awards.

Another gold winner in the Media Innovation Awards was the Milk Carton 2.0 campaign developed by Grey Canada for the Missing Children Society of Canada. Grey, an agency with expertise in all areas of marketing, started in New York City in 1917, with the Canadian office opening in 1958. Established in 1986, the Missing Children Society of Canada has a mission to reunite missing children with their families. The society provides support to families in a number of ways, including a team of investigators that assist police, an emergency response program that sends out information when a child goes missing, and family support programs. The Milk Carton 2.0 campaign provides an opportunity for individuals to donate their Twitter, Foursquare, or Facebook social media feeds to help find missing children and promote awareness for the society. If a child goes missing in the area where a participant in the program lives, the society will send them the information through their social media account.

In addition to the social media part of the program, people were encouraged to sign up at events that included family friendly activities, refreshments, and live entertainment.

When studentsNS, the alliance of postsecondary students' associations in Nova Scotia, wanted to get the message out about sexual assault, they went to the Extreme Group. The Extreme Group is a marketing company located in Halifax. The campaign, called "More than yes," consisted of posters to be displayed on campuses, stickers for condom packages, and a website—**http://morethanyes.ca**. The website included additional resources such as provincial and school support contact information.

The winter Olympic Games in Sochi, Russia, gives another example of a not-for-profit group working with an advertising agency to highlight an issue. Russia's anti-gay laws had prompted a flood of messages around the world. The Canadian Institute of Diversity and Inclusion went to the agency Rethink to produce a 30-second video to be shared through social media channels. Many companies that were official sponsors of the games took it upon themselves to change the ads they were showing during the games in support of the gay community.

Marketing companies, not-for-profit organizations, and even for-profit companies often use marketing communication techniques to get messages out about issues that concern society as a whole.

Questions for Critical Thinking

1. How do marketing companies or advertising agencies benefit from working with not-for-profit companies to produce marketing communications that can benefit society as a whole?
2. Discuss the effectiveness of each type of marketing communication used in the case.

Sources: Jeromy Lloyd, "Sochi Sponsors Flying the Pride Flag," *Marketing*, February 14, 2014, **www.marketingmag.ca**; Jeromy Lloyd, "Watch This: Keep the Olympics Gay (CIDI)," *Marketing*, February 4, 2014, **www.marketingmag.ca**; studentNS website, **http://studentsns.ca**, accessed April 19, 2014; Vanessa Milne, "Student Campaign Moves from 'No Means No' to 'More Than Yes'," *Marketing*, February 13, 2014, **www.marketingmag.ca**; More Than Yes website, **http://morethanyes.ca**, accessed April 19, 2014; Extreme Group website, **www.extremegroup.com**, accessed April 19, 2014; Alicia Androich, "Missing Children Society of Canada Holding Milk Carton 2.0 Sign-up Event," *Marketing*, March 12, 2014; Missing Children of Canada website, **http://mcsc.ca**, accessed April 18, 2014; Tourette Syndrome Foundation of Canada website, **http://Tourette.ca**, accessed April 18, 2014; Grey Advertising Agency website, **http://grey.com/canada,** accessed April 18, 2014; "Saatchi & Saatchi and Tourette Syndrome Foundation Win Best of Show at 2013 MIAs," *Marketing*, November 7, 2013, **www.marketingmag.ca**; Saatchi & Saatchi Canada website, **http://saatchi.ca**, accessed April 18, 2014.

CASE 14.2

Newspapers Are Not Dead Yet

Dailies, weeklies, community, or digital are some of the options readers have to receive news coverage from a newspaper. For several years, experts predicted that newspapers would become obsolete but the opposite is happening. The newspapers are changing with the times and it is working for them.

Canada has over 100 daily newspapers that are available in over 1,000 communities. In fact, over 20 percent more print newspapers are available today than 40 years ago, but Canadians are getting their news on multiple devices. Over 85 percent of Canadians read a newspaper at least once a week, but some get their news from a website and others from an e-reader, smartphone, or tablet. Most Canadians use more than one device to get their news.

Newspaper readership varies depending on whether the paper is a daily or community publication and on demographics. Just over 40 percent of Canadian households receive a daily newspaper but more than 75 percent of Canadians over the age of 18 read a community newspaper on a regular basis. Readership is fairly consistent between men and women, but more of those in the 35- to 50-year-old age group read a daily paper. As income and education increase, so does the percentage of readership for both daily papers and community papers.

The newspapers have made changes to the way they do business in order to survive in recent years. Most newspapers now charge for their online editions. One exception to this is Gesca, publisher of seven newspapers in Quebec. The company aims to target the 18- to 49-year-old market. A spokesperson for the company says, "Younger consumers have figured out how to access consumer content for free, and we chose to create a business model that works with that." And the business model is working for them. The company is hiring additional journalists and videographers at a time when other papers are reducing staff.

Newspapers are making other changes as technology becomes available. One national newspaper is experimenting with integrating custom content into their advertising. The paper will integrate stories, video, and graphics into their editorial content. This new technique may help the papers' online advertising revenues, which have seen increases over the last couple of years, but revenues for their print versions have remained constant or experienced some declines. Newspaper advertising still is a good investment for companies because Canadians not only accept ads in newspapers but trust the information provided in them.

Questions for Critical Thinking

1. Discuss the advantages and disadvantages of paper and online versions of newspapers.
2. Discuss the advantages and disadvantages for companies advertising in newspapers.

Sources: Gesca website, **http://publicite.gesca.ca**, accessed April 19, 2014; Sarah Barmak, "The Globe Soft-Launches Native Ad Program with Ge," *Marketing*, April 147, 2014, **www.marketingmag.ca**; *Canadian Media Director's Council Media Digest* 2012/2013, pp. 53–69; Chris Powell, "Outside the Wall: Why One Media Company Broke Ranks," *Marketing*, January/February 2014, pp. 40–44.

chapter 15

Personal Selling and Sales Promotion

CHAPTER OBJECTIVES

① Describe the role of today's salesperson.

② Describe the four sales channels.

③ Describe the major trends in personal selling.

④ Identify and briefly describe the three basic sales tasks.

⑤ Outline the seven steps in the sales process.

⑥ Identify the seven basic functions of a sales manager.

⑦ Explain the role of ethical behaviour in personal selling.

⑧ Describe the role of sales promotion in the promotional mix and identify the different types of sales promotion.

SALESFORCE.COM EXPANDS ITS CLOUD MARKETING BUSINESS

One of the most influential recent trends in marketing is the use of social media such as Facebook, Twitter, LinkedIn, and Google+ to reach customers, develop relationships with them, and shape their brand preferences and buying habits. Having a presence on these sites is such a given that "Facebook has become the new corporate home page," says one high-tech CEO. Many companies need help today integrating all those social and mobile platforms with their own customer relationship management (CRM) systems, so they know, for instance, what Facebook users are saying about their goods and services and can quickly react. That's where Salesforce.com comes in. About 100,000 companies already rely on this cloud-computing pioneer to help them tap into social media in an effective and efficient way that yields useful information.

Salesforce, a young company with more than 6,000 employees worldwide, initially focused on providing cloud-computing services for sales operations and information management. In 2014, for the sixth consecutive year, it was named one of *Fortune's* "100 Best Companies to Work For," being ranked No. 7. Now it is ramping up its investment in what it calls the Salesforce Marketing Cloud so it can extend its services to chief marketing officers (CMOs), leading a trend that's expected to make corporate marketing departments the biggest information technology spenders in many organizations.

With its recent acquisitions of Buddy Media and Radian6, Salesforce has invested almost $1 billion in two leading companies in the analysis and management of social media information. These acquisitions put Salesforce in a strong position to offer CMOs new integrated marketing services that allow them to track and act on the "crucial insights about themselves" that social media users volunteer online. According to Radian6's CEO, Salesforce's strategy confirms that social media has evolved to become "the central core" of most corporate marketing operations.

Salesforce operates a social network of its own, called Chatter, which serves its own clients exclusively but will now (thanks to the Radian6 acquisition) also allow them to see customers' posts on Facebook, Twitter, blogs, and more data in real time. Salesforce believes it's on track to develop a billion-dollar business with the new suite of services available on its Marketing Cloud. It is so confident it can help its clients excel at multichannel CRM, in fact, that "CRM" is the symbol the company uses for its NYSE stock listing.[1]

connecting with customers

Salesforce.com continues to find ways to connect with customers and to help its customers connect with customers. Salesforce's acquisitions of Radian6 and Buddy Media reflect the firm's plans to strengthen its social marketing presence across various media. As its customers learn how to use the various kinds of social media to market their goods and services, Salesforce's newly unified platform can make that process easier.

Chapter Overview

The Salesforce.com story illustrates how important it is for marketers to not simply sell products but to understand their customers and connect with them through product innovations that make life easier. In exploring personal selling strategies, this chapter gives special attention to the relationship-building opportunities that the selling situation presents.

Personal selling is the process of a seller's person-to-person promotional presentation to a buyer. The sales process is essentially interpersonal, and it is basic to any enterprise. Accounting, engineering, human resource management, production, and other organizational activities produce no benefits unless a salesperson matches his or her company's products to the needs of a customer, and then closes a sale. The fact that almost 10 percent of the Canadian labour force is employed in sales positions testifies to the importance of selling. While the average firm's advertising expenses may represent from 1 to 3 percent of sales revenue, personal selling expenses are likely to equal 10 to 15 percent. This makes personal selling the single largest marketing expense in many firms.

Personal selling is a primary component of a firm's promotional mix when one or more of several well-defined factors are present:

1. Customers are geographically concentrated.

2. Individual orders account for large amounts of revenue.

3. The firm markets goods and services that are expensive, are technically complex, or require special handling.

4. Trade-ins are involved.

5. Products move through short channels.

6. The firm markets to relatively few potential customers.

For example, personal selling is an important component of the promotional mix for a car dealer, although both dealers and manufacturers also rely heavily on advertising. Because cars and trucks are expensive, customers usually like to go to a dealership to compare models, discuss a purchase, or obtain service; and trade-ins often are involved. So a dealer's salespeople provide valuable assistance to the customer.

Table 15.1 summarizes the factors that influence the importance of personal selling in the overall promotional mix based on four variables: consumer, product, price, and marketing channels. This chapter also explores *sales promotion*, which includes all marketing activities other than personal selling, advertising, and publicity that enhance promotional effectiveness. ◆◆◆

---

① Describe the role of today's salesperson.

personal selling
Interpersonal influence process involving a seller's promotional presentation conducted on a person-to-person basis with the buyer.

Marketoid

The world's longest yard sale stretches for 1,110 kilometres and spans six U.S. states from Michigan to Alabama. The annual four-day event has been held for nearly 30 years and starts on the first Thursday in August.

THE EVOLUTION OF PERSONAL SELLING

Selling has been a standard business activity for thousands of years. As long ago as 2000 B.C., the Code of Hammurabi protected the rights of the Babylonian salesman, who was referred to as a *peddler*. Throughout Canadian history, selling has been a major factor in economic growth. Early peddlers travelled with their goods from town to town and farm to farm, helping expand trade among early settlers. Today, professional salespeople are problem solvers who focus on satisfying the needs of customers before, during, and after sales are made. Armed with knowledge about their firm's goods or services, those of competitors, and their customers' business needs, salespeople pursue a common goal of creating mutually beneficial long-term relationships with customers.

Personal selling is a vital, vibrant, dynamic process. As domestic and foreign competition increases emphasis on productivity, personal selling is taking on a more prominent role in the marketing mix. Salespeople must communicate the advantages of their firms' goods and services over those of competitors. They must be able to do the following:

• Focus on a customer's situation and needs and create solutions that meet those needs.

• Follow through and stay in touch before, during, and after the sale.

• Know their own industry and their customers' industry, and have a firm grasp not only of their own firm's capabilities but also of their competitors' abilities.

• Work hard to exceed their customers' expectations.

table 15.1   *Factors Affecting the Importance of Personal Selling in the Promotional Mix*

VARIABLE	CONDITIONS THAT FAVOUR PERSONAL SELLING	CONDITIONS THAT FAVOUR ADVERTISING
Customer	Geographically concentrated	Geographically dispersed
	Relatively low numbers	Relatively high numbers
Product	Expensive	Inexpensive
	Technically complex	Simple to understand
	Custom-made	Standardized
	Special handling requirements	No special handling requirements
	Transactions frequently involve trade-ins	Transactions seldom involve trade-ins
Price	Relatively high	Relatively low
Channels	Relatively short	Relatively long

Relationship marketing affects all aspects of an organization's marketing function, including personal selling. This means marketers in both internal and external relationships must develop different sales skills. Instead of working alone, many salespeople now unite their efforts in sales teams. The customer-focused firm wants its salespeople to form long-lasting relationships with buyers by providing high levels of customer service rather than going for quick sales. Even the way salespeople perform their jobs is constantly changing. Growing numbers of companies have integrated communications and computer technologies into the sales routine. These trends are covered in more detail later in the chapter.

Personal selling is an attractive career choice today. Good salespeople are always in demand as the number of sales positions continues to increase in most industrialized countries. Approximately 10 percent of the Canadian workforce is employed in sales positions.[2] Company executives usually recognize a good salesperson as a performance-oriented person who can solve problems, communicate clearly, and manage relationships. In fact, many corporations are headed by executives who began their careers in sales.

assessment check 1

1.1 What is personal selling?

1.2 What is the main focus of today's salespeople?

THE FOUR SALES CHANNELS

② **Describe the four sales channels.**

Personal selling occurs through several types of communication channels: over-the-counter selling (including online selling), field selling, telemarketing, and inside selling. Each of these channels includes both business-to-business and direct-to-customer selling. Although telemarketing and online selling are lower-cost alternatives, their lack of personal interaction with existing or prospective customers often makes them less effective than personalized, one-to-one field selling and over-the-counter channels. In fact, many organizations use a number of different channels.

OVER-THE-COUNTER SELLING

The most frequently used sales channel, **over-the-counter selling**, typically describes selling in retail and some wholesale locations. Most over-the-counter sales are direct to customer, although business customers are frequently served by wholesalers with over-the-counter sales reps. Customers typically visit the seller's location on their own initiative to purchase desired items. Some visit their favourite stores because they enjoy shopping. Others respond to

over-the-counter selling Personal selling conducted in retail and some wholesale locations in which customers come to the seller's place of business.

Superior companies understand that courteous and knowledgeable counter salespeople can be an important factor in closing sales.

many kinds of appeals, including direct mail; personal letters of invitation from store personnel; and advertisements for sales, special events, and new-product introductions.

Electronics giant Best Buy—the world's largest multi-channel consumer electronics retailer—continues to outsell its competitors; with more than 1,400 stores and 140,000 employees in Canada and the United States, the company gets more than 1.6 billion visitors to its stores and websites annually.[3] Perhaps Best Buy's success is because of the training its salespeople receive. The training focuses on the firm's mantra: CARE Plus. *C* stands for contact with the customer. *A* means asking questions to learn what the customer needs. *R* represents making recommendations to the customer. *E* stands for encouragement, praising the customer for a wise purchase.

Local retailers often know their customers by name. They also know their customers' likes and dislikes. The owner of a bookstore in your hometown might call you when a new book by your favourite author arrives. Taking a page from this type of selling, Amazon.ca creates personalized messages for its customers as well—even though its salespeople have never met their customers in person. Amazon's software can send you reminders for gift purchases, recommend related purchases, or even stop you from making the same purchase twice. The site also welcomes you by name when you log on.

Regardless of a retailer's innovation, a few things remain the same in selling. For example, customers never like hearing salespeople say the following:

- "That's not my department."
- "If it's not on the rack [or shelf], we don't have it."
- "I don't know" or "I'm new here."
- "I'm closing" or "I'm on a break."
- "The computer is down."

While these quotes may seem humorous, they also ring true. You've probably heard them, and you may have said them yourself if you've worked in a retail environment. But each statement conveys the message that the salesperson is not willing or able to serve the customer—exactly the opposite of what every marketer wants to convey.

FIELD SELLING

field selling Sales presentations made at prospective customers' locations on a face-to-face basis.

network marketing Personal selling that relies on lists of family members and friends of the salesperson, who organizes a gathering of potential customers for a demonstration of products.

Field selling involves making sales calls on prospective and existing customers at their businesses or homes. Some situations involve considerable creative effort, such as the sales of major computer installations. Often, the salesperson must convince customers first that they need the good or service and then that they need the particular brand the salesperson is selling. Field sales of large industrial installations such as Bombardier's CSeries or CRJ NextGen commercial jets also often require considerable technical expertise.

Largely because it involves travel, field selling is considerably more expensive than other selling options. Rising prices of fuel, air fares, car rentals, and hotel rates have forced up the cost of business trips. Needing to find ways to trim costs while increasing productivity, some firms have replaced certain travel with conference calls, while others require salespeople to stay in less expensive hotels and spend less on meals. Some firms have simply shortened the time allowed for trips.

In fairly routine field selling situations, such as calling on established customers in industries such as food, textiles, or wholesaling, the salesperson basically acts as an order taker who processes regular customers' orders. But more complex situations may involve weeks of preparation, formal presentations, and many hours of post-sales work. Field selling is a lifestyle that many people enjoy; they also cite some of the negatives, such as travel delays and impact on family life.

Some firms view field selling as a market in itself and have developed goods and services designed to help salespeople do their jobs. Panasonic manufactures the Toughbook series—a line of tablet computers loaded with Microsoft Office software and designed with field sales reps in mind. Each Toughbook has a magnesium alloy case—significantly stronger than the plastic cases of standard computers—and is built for rugged handling. The toughest Toughbook can withstand a six-foot drop and is rain-, dust-, and vibration-resistant.[4]

Taking their cue from the successes of businesses such as Avon, Mary Kay Cosmetics, and Tupperware, thousands of smaller businesses now rely on field selling in customers' homes. Often called network marketing, this type of personal selling relies on lists of family members and friends of the salesperson or "party host" who organizes a gathering of potential customers for an in-home demonstration of products. There are over 75 network marketing companies in Canada, about two-thirds of them members of the Direct Sellers Association of Canada. Combined, they employ more than 900,000 independent sales contractors, sometimes called distributors, and they generate more than $2.2 billion sales.[5]

Panasonic manufactures a family of Toughpad tablet devices and Toughbook laptop computers with field sales reps in mind.

YOSHIKAZU TSUNO/AFP/Getty Images

TELEMARKETING

Telemarketing, a channel in which the selling process is conducted by phone, serves two general purposes—sales and service—and two general markets—business to business and direct to customer. Both inbound and outbound telemarketing are forms of direct marketing.

Outbound telemarketing involves a sales force that relies on the telephone to contact customers, reducing the substantial costs of personal visits to customers' homes or businesses. Technologies such as predictive diallers, autodialling, and random-digit dialling increase chances that telemarketers will reach customers at home. *Predictive diallers* weed out busy signals and answering machines, nearly doubling the number of calls made per hour. *Autodialling* allows telemarketers to dial numbers continually; when a customer answers the phone, the call is automatically routed to a sales representative. *Random-digit dialling* allows telemarketers to reach unlisted numbers and block caller-ID.

A major drawback of telemarketing is that most consumers dislike the practice. The Canadian Radio-television and Telecommunications Commission implemented the Canadian Do Not Call List (DNCL) in late 2008, and, by the end of 2013, there were more than 12 million listed numbers.[6] If an unauthorized telemarketer calls any of these numbers, the CRTC can levy penalties up to $1,500 for individuals or $15,000 for corporations, for each infraction.[7] As one of many recent examples, Nature Carpet Cleaning of Calgary, Alberta, was fined $9,000 total: $1,000 for each of nine violations. The company admitted using numbers from a phone directory without checking to see if they were registered on the DNCL.[8] Imperial Data Supply of Port Moody, British Columbia, was fined $18,000 total, $3,000 for each of six unsolicited fax telemarketing communications it initiated.[9] Organizations exempt from fines are political parties, registered charities, marketing researchers and pollsters, newspapers, and businesses that have had business dealings with the phone call recipient within the previous 18 months. Why do some firms still use telemarketing? The average call cost is low, and companies point to a significant rate of success.

Inbound telemarketing typically involves a toll-free number that customers can call to obtain information, make reservations, and purchase goods and services. When a customer calls a toll-free number, the caller can be identified and routed to the person with whom he or she has done business previously, creating a human touch not possible before. This form of selling provides maximum convenience for customers who initiate the sales process. Many large

Marketoid

The Canadian Professional Sales Association (CPSA) was established in 1874 and now supports approximately 27,000 members, including senior executives, sales managers, sales representatives, sales agents, and entrepreneurs.

telemarketing
Promotional presentation involving the use of the telephone on an outbound basis by salespeople or on an inbound basis by customers who initiate calls to obtain information and place orders.

outbound telemarketing
Sales method in which sales personnel place phone calls to prospects and try to conclude the sale over the phone.

inbound telemarketing
Sales method in which prospects call a seller to obtain information, make reservations, and purchase goods and services.

© iStockphoto.com/kristian sekulic

Some firms use telemarketing because the average call cost is low and companies point to a significant rate of success.

catalogue merchants such as Pottery Barn, L.L. Bean, and Lands' End keep their inbound telemarketing lines open 24 hours a day, 7 days a week.

Many Canadians who seek technical or customer support now reach call centre employees in India. Within Canada, New Brunswick continues to focus on the call centre industry. At the start of 2014, there were 17,000 call centre jobs in the province, down from a peak of 22,000. However, the average annual wage has improved to $33,000. TD Insurance recently hired 275 additional call centre positions in Saint John, New Brunswick.[10] One attractive feature of inbound customer service jobs is that many of them allow employees from across Canada to work from home.

INSIDE SELLING

inside selling Selling by phone, mail, and electronic commerce.

The role of many of today's telemarketers is a combination of field selling techniques applied through inbound and outbound telemarketing channels with a strong customer orientation, called **inside selling**. Inside sales reps perform two primary jobs: they turn opportunities into actual sales, and they support technicians and purchasers with current solutions. Inside sales reps do far more than read a canned script to unwilling prospects. Their role goes beyond taking orders to solving problems, providing customer service, and selling. For this reason, some inside sales positions are paying salaries that approach those of field salespeople, and incentive plans can increase their compensation considerably. A successful inside sales force relies on close working relationships with field sales representatives to solidify customer relationships.

The six-member inside sales force—the Client Experience Team—of the NBA's Detroit Pistons supports the team's marketing efforts, such as special events for season ticket holders, including backstage tours, tipoff parties, and privileges like getting into games 30 minutes early. Season-ticket holders are also issued the official Pistons On-Court Jacket, which comes with an embedded microchip, to get 20 percent off at concessions and 30 percent off merchandise. Pistons sales reps use online chat, telephone, and email to stay connected.[11]

INTEGRATING THE VARIOUS SELLING CHANNELS

Figure 15.1 illustrates how firms are likely to blend alternative sales channels—over-the-counter selling, field selling, telemarketing, and inside selling—to create a successful cost-effective sales organization. Existing customers whose business problems require complex solutions are likely to be best served by the traditional field sales force. Other current customers who need answers but not the same attention as the first group can be served by inside sales reps who call on them as needed. Over-the-counter sales reps serve existing customers by supplying information and advice and completing sales transactions. Telemarketers may be used to strengthen communication with customers or to re-establish relationships with customers that may have lapsed over a few months.

Marketoid

Turf Operations Group, which owns Weed Man franchises across Canada, was recently fined $200,000 after it was found to be making telemarketing calls to Canadians registered on the National Do Not Call List.

assessment check 2 ✓

2.1 What is over-the-counter selling?

2.2 What is field selling?

2.3 Distinguish between inbound and outbound telemarketing.

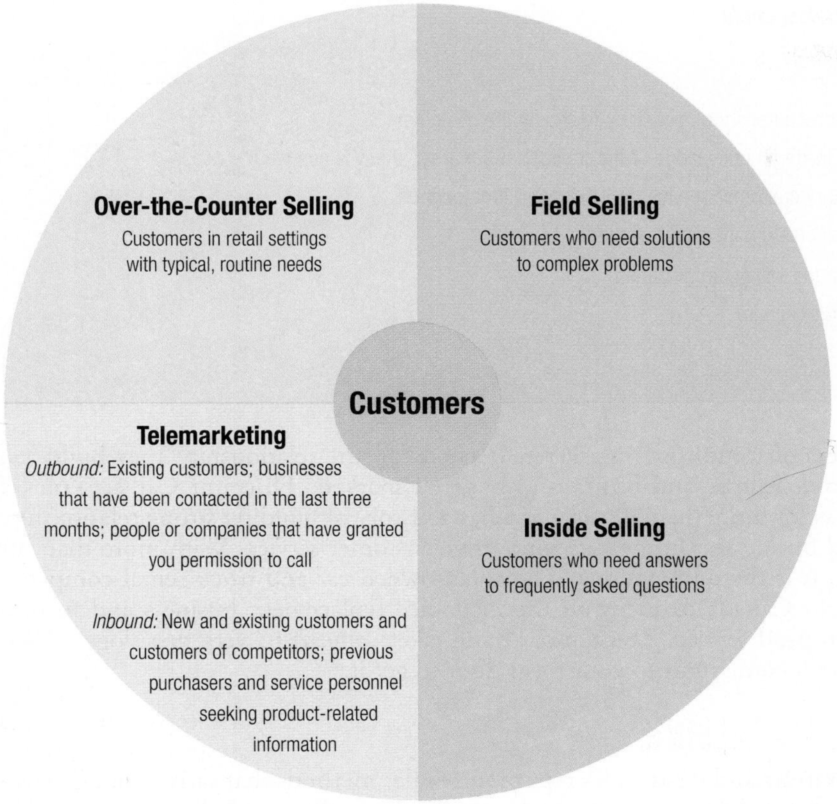

figure 15.1

**Alternative Sales
Channels for Serving
Customers**

Over-the-Counter Selling
Customers in retail settings
with typical, routine needs

Field Selling
Customers who need solutions
to complex problems

Customers

Telemarketing
Outbound: Existing customers; businesses
that have been contacted in the last three
months; people or companies that have granted
you permission to call

Inbound: New and existing customers and
customers of competitors; previous
purchasers and service personnel
seeking product-related
information

Inside Selling
Customers who need answers
to frequently asked questions

TRENDS IN PERSONAL SELLING

③ **Describe the major
trends in personal
selling.**

In today's complex marketing environment, effective personal selling requires different strategies from those used by salespeople in the past. As pointed out in the discussion of *buying centres* in Chapter 6, rather than selling one on one, in B2B settings it is now customary to sell to teams of corporate representatives who participate in the client firm's decision-making process. In business-to-business sales situations involving technical products, customers expect salespeople to answer technical questions—or bring along someone who can. They also want representatives who understand technical jargon and can communicate using sophisticated technological tools. Patience is also a requirement because the B2B sales cycle, from initial contact to closing, may take months or even years. To address all these concerns, companies rely on three major personal selling approaches: relationship selling, consultative selling, and team selling. Regardless of the approach, however, experts agree on a few basic guidelines for conducting successful personal selling.

RELATIONSHIP SELLING

Most firms now emphasize **relationship selling**, a technique for building a mutually beneficial partnership with a customer through regular contacts over an extended period. Such buyer–seller bonds become increasingly important as companies cut back on the number of suppliers and look for companies that provide high levels of customer service and satisfaction. Salespeople must also find ways to distinguish themselves and their products from competitors. To create strong, long-lasting relationships with customers, salespeople must meet buyers' expectations. Table 15.2 summarizes the results of several surveys that indicate what buyers expect of professional salespeople.

relationship selling
Regular contacts
between sales
representatives and
customers over an
extended period to
establish a sustained
seller–buyer relationship.

table 15.2   *What Buyers Expect from Salespeople*

Buyers prefer to do business with salespeople who

- Orchestrate events and bring to bear whatever resources are necessary to satisfy the customer
- Provide counselling to the customer based on in-depth knowledge of the product, the market, and the customer's needs
- Solve problems proficiently to ensure satisfactory customer service over extended time periods
- Demonstrate high ethical standards and communicate honestly at all times
- Willingly advocate the customer's cause within the selling organization
- Create imaginative arrangements to meet buyers' needs
- Arrive well prepared for sales calls

The success of tomorrow's marketers depends on the relationships they build today in both the business-to-consumer and business-to-business markets. Discount Car & Truck Rentals has been in business for more than 30 years and has a history of building strong relationships with both consumers and businesses through its innovative customer service. With more than 300 locations across Canada, it is the only national, Canadian-owned car and truck rental company. It was the first company in Canada to focus on the insurance replacement business and to offer customer pick-up and drop-off service. The company still takes to heart its very first slogan: "We want your business and we'll come right to your front door to get it."[12]

CONSULTATIVE SELLING

consultative selling
Meeting customer needs by listening to customers, understanding their problems, paying attention to details, and following through after the sale.

Field representatives and inside sales reps require sales methods that satisfy today's cost-conscious, knowledgeable buyers. One such method, consultative selling, involves meeting customer needs by listening to customers, understanding—and caring about—their problems, paying attention to details, and following through after the sale. It works hand in hand with relationship selling in building customer loyalty. Inspiration Furniture has a 40,000-square-foot showroom in Vancouver, British Columbia, and carries a huge selection of furniture products with a broad range of price points. Owner Steen Skaaning is a firm believer in the consultative sales process used by his team of sales professionals. He says, "We carry furniture from many different vendors, so it is critical that our sales team stays informed about the features and benefits of our products; in fact, understanding these qualities is more important than just famous 'brand names.'"[13]

Online companies have instituted consultative selling models to create long-term customers. Particularly for complicated, high-priced products that require installation or specialized service, Web sellers must be able to quickly communicate the benefits and features of their products. They accomplish this through consultative selling.

cross-selling Selling several, often unrelated, goods and services to the same customer based on knowledge of that customer's needs.

Cross-selling—offering many goods or services to the same customer—is another technique that capitalizes on a firm's strengths. It costs a bank five times more to acquire a new customer than to cross-sell to an existing one. Moreover, research shows that the more a customer buys from an institution, the less likely that person is to leave. So a customer who opens a chequing account at a local bank may follow with a safety deposit box, retirement savings account, mortgage loan, and guaranteed line of credit.

TEAM SELLING

team selling Selling situation in which several sales associates or other members of the organization are recruited to assist the lead sales representative in reaching all those who influence the purchase decision.

Another development in the evolution of personal selling is team selling, in which the salesperson joins with specialists from other functional areas of the firm to complete the selling process. Teams can be formal and ongoing or created for a specific short-term selling situation. Although some salespeople have hesitated to embrace the idea of team selling, preferring to work alone, a growing number believe that team selling brings better results. Customers often prefer the team approach, which makes them feel well served. Consider a restaurant meal. If the host, servers, wine steward, chef, and kitchen crew are all working well together as a team, your experience at the restaurant is likely to be positive. But if the service stops and starts, your order is recorded wrong, the food is cold, the silverware is dirty, and the staff seems grouchy, you probably won't eat at that restaurant again. In fact, you may not even finish the meal.

Another advantage of team selling is the formation of relationships between companies rather than between individuals. In sales situations that call for detailed knowledge of new, complex, and ever-changing technologies, team selling offers a distinct competitive edge in meeting customers' needs. In most computer software B2B departments, a third of the sales force is made up of technically trained, nonmarketing experts such as engineers or programmers. A salesperson continues to play the lead role in most sales situations, but technical experts bring added value to the sales process. Some companies establish permanent sales-and-tech teams that conduct all sales presentations together; others have a pool of engineers or other professionals who are on call for different client visits.

virtual sales team Network of strategic partners, suppliers, and others who recommend a firm's goods or services.

Some resourceful entrepreneurs have begun building a **virtual sales team**—a network of strategic partners, trade associations, suppliers, and others who are qualified and willing to recommend a firm's goods or services. Michelle Marciniak and Susan Walvius, both former college basketball coaches, came up with a new use for the moisture-wicking fabric that workout clothes are made of—bedsheets. Together they founded Sheex, which makes bedsheets that are cool to the touch and transfer body heat away from the sleeper. Rather than a traditional sales force, a virtual sales force of "sleep ambassadors" promotes Sheex bedsheets. Athletes, such as NFL wide receiver Steve Smith, golfer Diana D'Alessio, and snowboarder Steve Fisher post discount codes via Twitter or other social media. They receive commissions based on sales of Sheex. "It's kind of a virtual sales team of athletes," Susan Walvius says.[14]

assessment check 3 ✓

3.1 Identify the three major personal selling approaches.

3.2 Distinguish between relationship selling and consultative selling.

SALES TASKS

④ **Identify and briefly describe the three basic sales tasks.**

Today's salesperson is more concerned with establishing long-term buyer–seller relationships and helping customers select the correct products for meeting their needs than with simply selling whatever is available. Where repeat purchases are common, the salesperson must be certain that the buyer's purchases are in his or her best interest; otherwise, no future relationship will be possible. The seller's interests are tied to the buyer's in a mutually beneficial relationship.

While all sales activities assist the customer in some manner, they are not all alike. Three basic sales tasks can be identified: (1) order processing, (2) creative selling, and (3) missionary sales. Most of today's salespeople are not limited to performing tasks in a single category. Instead, they often perform all three tasks to some extent. A sales engineer for a computer firm may be doing 50 percent missionary sales, 45 percent creative selling, and 5 percent order processing. Most sales positions are classified on the basis of the primary selling task performed.

Then there's the philosophy that *everyone* in the organization, regardless of what his or her job description is, should be engaged in selling. Calgary-based WestJet believes delivering great customer service is paramount for every employee, from the reservations agent to the baggage handler to the flight attendant. The company website claims, "Sure, it's our aircraft that fly you places, but it's really our people who get you there. In fact, our entire corporate culture has been built around caring for you, our guests, by providing a great guest experience." WestJet was inducted into the Waterstone Hall of Fame after several years of inclusion in the company's study of Canada's 10 Most Admired Corporate Cultures.[15]

ORDER PROCESSING

order processing Selling, mostly at the wholesale and retail levels, that involves identifying customer needs, pointing them out to customers, and completing orders.

Order processing, which can involve both field selling and telemarketing, is most often typified by selling at the wholesale and retail levels. For instance, a Snapple route salesperson who performs this task must take the following steps:

1. *Identify customer needs.* The route salesperson determines that a store has only seven cases of Snapple left in stock when it normally carries an inventory of 40.

2. *Point out the need to the customer.* The route salesperson informs the store manager of the inventory situation.

3. *Complete (write up) the order.* The store manager acknowledges the need for more of the product. The driver unloads 33 cases of Snapple, and the manager signs the delivery slip.

Order processing is part of most selling positions. It becomes the primary task in situations where needs can be readily identified and are acknowledged by the customer. Even in such instances, however, salespeople whose primary responsibility involves order processing will devote some time persuading their wholesale or retail customers to carry more complete inventories of their firms' merchandise or to handle additional product lines. They also are likely to try to motivate purchasers to feature some of their firms' products, increase the amount of shelf space devoted to these items, and improve product location in the stores.

Technology now streamlines order-processing tasks. Some retailers, such as Canadian Tire, now use interactive store kiosks, a recent innovation that provides a touch screen that lets customers browse a store's catalogue, compare brands and product features, check inventory and store location, and even place their order—all from a single user-friendly device, putting an end to endlessly cruising store aisles in search of sales staff.

CREATIVE SELLING

creative selling Personal selling that involves situations in which a considerable degree of analytical decision making on the buyer's part results in the need for skillful proposals of solutions for the customer's needs.

When a considerable amount of decision making is involved in purchasing a good or service, an effective salesperson uses **creative selling** techniques to solicit an order. In contrast to the order-processing task, which deals mainly with maintaining existing business, creative selling generally is used to develop new business either by adding new customers or by introducing new goods and services. New products or upgrades to more expensive items often require creative selling. The salesperson must first identify the customer's problems and needs and then propose a solution in the form of the good or service being offered. When a company is attempting to expand an existing business relationship, creative selling techniques are used in over-the-counter selling, field selling, inside selling, and telemarketing.

Creative selling can generate "buzz" for a product. Digital marketing agency Rockfish developed a creative campaign for BUNN, which manufactures high-quality commercial coffee- and tea-making equipment and sells it from sales offices across North America. BUNN recently launched a line of commercial-quality machines for the home. Rockfish merged BUNN's two at-home websites, initiated a social-media campaign with online interactive videos, search-engine marketing, social media placement, and holiday-themed advertising, all of which resulted in a dramatic increase in website visits and sales.[16]

MISSIONARY SELLING

missionary selling Indirect type of selling in which specialized salespeople promote the firm's goodwill among indirect customers, often by assisting customers in product use.

sales incentives Programs that reward salespeople for superior performance.

Missionary selling is an indirect approach to sales. Salespeople sell the firm's goodwill and provide their customers with information and technical or operational assistance. A cosmetics company salesperson may call on retailers to check on special promotions and overall product movement, even though a wholesaler takes orders and delivers merchandise. For years, large pharmaceutical companies operated the most aggressive missionary selling, courting doctors (the indirect customer) by providing lavish restaurant meals, educational seminars, and other incentives in the hope of persuading them to prescribe a particular brand to patients. While the doctor is clearly the decision maker, the transaction is not complete until the patient hands the prescription over to a pharmacist. But recent changes to the code of ethical practices established by Canada's Research-Based Pharmaceutical Companies (Rx&D) prohibit missionary salespeople from offering incentives of value to their customers. Salespeople must now focus on educating health care professionals. Some pharmaceutical companies are now asking their sales forces to change their focus to becoming resources for doctors in treating patients and providing practical support.[17]

Some missionary salespeople, however, do offer **sales incentives** such as trips, gas cards, free product upgrades, and other inducements to their customers. Missionary sales may involve both field selling and telemarketing. Many aspects of team selling can also be seen as missionary sales, as when technical support salespeople help design, install, and maintain equipment; when they train customers' employees; and when they provide information or operational assistance.

assessment check 4

4.1 What are the three basic sales tasks performed by salespeople?

4.2 What are the three steps of order processing?

THE SALES PROCESS

⑤ **Outline the seven steps in the sales process.**

If you have worked in a retail store, or if you've sold magazine subscriptions or candy to raise money for your school or sports team, you will recognize many of the activities involved in the following list of steps in the sales process. Personal selling encompasses the following sequence of activities: (1) prospecting and qualifying, (2) approach, (3) presentation, (4) demonstration, (5) handling buyer concerns, (6) closing, and (7) follow-up.

As Figure 15.2 indicates, these steps follow the AIDA concept (attention-interest-desire-action). Once a sales prospect has been qualified, an attempt is made to secure his or her attention. The presentation and demonstration steps are designed to generate interest and desire. Successful handling of buyer resistance should arouse further desire. Action occurs at the close of the sale.

Salespeople modify the steps in this process to match their customers' buying processes. A neighbour who eagerly looks forward to the local symphony orchestra's new concert season each year needs no presentation except for details about scheduled performances and perhaps whether any famous musicians will be on the bill. But the same neighbour would expect a demonstration from an auto dealer when looking for a new car or might appreciate a presentation of dinner specials by the waiter prior to ordering a meal at a restaurant.

prospecting Personal selling function of identifying potential customers.

PROSPECTING AND QUALIFYING

Prospecting, the process of identifying potential customers, may involve hours, days, or weeks of effort, but it is a necessary step. Leads about prospects come from many sources: the Internet, computerized databases, trade show exhibits, previous customers, friends and neighbours, other vendors, non-sales employees in the firm, suppliers, and social and professional contacts. Although a firm may emphasize personal selling as the primary component of its overall promotional strategy, direct mail and advertising campaigns are also effective in identifying prospective customers.

Before salespeople begin their prospecting effort, they must be clear about what their firm is selling and create a "brand story," that is, define their product in terms of what it can do for a customer. Because customers are generally looking for solutions to problems or ways to make their lives better or businesses more successful, this focus on the customer is critical. Once they develop a brand story, the sales team must be consistent about telling it at every possible point of contact, whether in a face-to-face conversation with a prospect, in advertising, or in promoting the product to the media.[18]

In addition, salespeople must be well informed about the goods and services of the industry in general. They need to find out how other goods are marketed and packaged. They can try out a service themselves to understand how the industry operates. In these ways, they will understand what prospective customers need and want—and how they can serve them. **Qualifying**—determining that the prospect really is a potential customer—is another important sales task. Not all prospects are qualified to make purchase decisions. Even though an employee in a firm might like your products, he or she might not be authorized to make the purchase. A consumer who test-drives a Porsche might fall in love with it—but not be able to afford the purchase price. Qualifying can be a two-way street. As a sales representative, you might determine that a certain prospect is qualified to make a purchase. But the prospect must agree in order for the process to go forward. If either you or the prospect determine at the outset that there's no chance for a purchase, then it's best to move on.

Marketoid

Stanley Tucker bought the first 1964 Ford Mustang in St. John's, Newfoundland and Labrador, serial number 00001. The car is now in the Henry Ford Museum after Ford Motor Company eventually convinced Tucker to trade it for a new model, the one-millionth Mustang off the assembly line.

qualifying Determining a prospect's needs, income, and purchase authority as a potential customer.

figure 15.2

The AIDA Concept and the Personal Selling Process

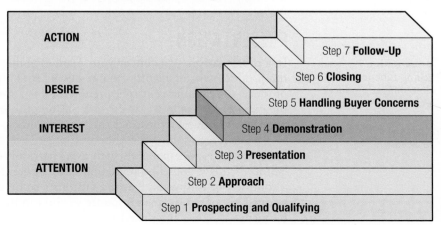

Courtesy of InfoCanada

Salespeople who use Salesgenie have access to 12 million Canadian consumers and 1.5 million Canadian businesses for prospecting.

approach Salesperson's initial contact with a prospective customer.

precall planning Use of information collected during the prospecting and qualifying stages of the sales process and during previous contacts with the prospect to tailor the approach and presentation to match the customer's needs.

APPROACH

Once you have identified a qualified prospect, you need to collect all available, relevant information and plan an **approach**—your initial contact with the prospective customer. If your firm already has a relationship with the customer or has permission to contact the person, you may use telemarketing. But before you do so, gather as much information as you can.

Information gathering makes **precall planning** possible. As mentioned earlier, educate yourself about the industry in general, as well as goods and services offered by competitors. Read any marketing research that is available. Go to trade shows—you can learn a lot about many companies and their products at one location, usually in one day. Also learn as much as you can about the firm you are planning to approach—browse the company's website, find online news articles and press releases about the company, talk with other people in the industry. Know its product offerings well. If possible, buy at least one of the firm's products and use it yourself. Identify ways you can help the firm do whatever it does better. Without invading an individual customer's privacy, see if there is anything you have in common—perhaps you grew up in the same town or you both like to play tennis. All this planning will help you make an effective approach.

As you plan your approach, try to answer the following questions:

- Whom am I approaching and what are their jobs within the company?

- What is their level of knowledge? Are they already informed about the idea I am going to present?

- What do they want or need? Should I speak in technical terms or provide general information?

- What do they need to hear? Do they need to know more about specific products or how those products can serve them? Do they need to know how the product works? Do they need to know about cost and availability?

If you are a retail salesperson, you can ask a shopper questions to learn more about his or her needs and preferences. Say you work at a large sporting-goods store. You might ask a young male shopper whether he works out at home, what equipment he already has, or what his fitness goals are. The answers to these questions should lead you in the direction of a sale.

PRESENTATION

presentation Personal selling function of describing a product's major features and relating them to a customer's problems or needs.

In a **presentation**, you convey your marketing message to the potential customer. You will describe the product's major features, point out its strengths, and cite other customers' successes with the product. One popular form of presentation is a *features-benefits* framework wherein you talk about the good or service in terms that are meaningful to the buyer. If you work for a car dealership, you might point out safety features such as side airbags and built-in car seats to a young couple.

Your presentation should be well organized, clear, and concise. If appropriate, you might use visual sales support materials such as a chart, a brochure, a DVD, or a video streamed from your laptop. If this is your first presentation to a potential customer, it will likely be more detailed than a routine call to give an existing customer some updates. Regardless of the situation, though, be attuned to your audience's response so you can modify your presentation—even on the spur of the moment—to meet their needs.

Many presentations now use computer-based multimedia, which can offer everything from interactivity to current pricing information. Companies such as SlideShare and cloud-based Brainshark, which enable users to share their presentations online, are now offering video capabilities. Users can embed video into their presentations along with traditional PowerPoint slides and other images. Brainsharks' app SlideShark has multi-user functionality.[19] However, technology must be used efficiently to be effective. For example, a company's website can be an excellent selling tool if it is easy for salespeople to present and buyers to use. A salesperson can actually use the site during a presentation by showing a potential customer how to use it to learn about and purchase products.

In a **cold calling** situation, the approach and presentation often take place at the same time. Cold calling means phoning or visiting the customer without a prior appointment and making a sales pitch on the spot. Cold calling requires nerve, skill, and creativity—but salespeople who are successful at it still point to the importance of preparation. See the "Career Readiness" feature for some tips on making cold calling work for you. During economic downturns, the ability to make cold calls becomes even more essential, as Tom Wood discovered recently. Wood is the president and CEO of Floor Coverings International (FCI), a franchisor with locations from Ontario to British Columbia and across most of the United States. FCI struggled financially during the recent recession, with some of its franchisees going out of business altogether. Although FCI had continued its Web ads and local direct mail, Wood decided that the company had to do more to help the remaining franchisees find new potential customers. The company's Fast Start program turned its corporate employees loose to teach franchise owners the tried-and-true methods: knocking on doors, cold calling, and networking. Fast Start also showed the franchisees how to develop relationships with other companies, such as real estate agents, restoration and remodelling companies, and home inspectors, which could be sources of future leads. Wood says, "We were going out and finding customers before they even needed

Making effective presentations is an important skill when selling products, services, or ideas.

cold calling Contacting a prospect without a prior appointment.

flooring. It was a culture shift … but that's just what it took to survive." FCI's franchisees have increased, and sales went up 17 percent in one recent year and 31 percent in the next.[20]

DEMONSTRATION

demonstration Stage in the personal selling process in which the customer has the opportunity to try out or otherwise see how a good or service works before purchase.

One of the most important advantages of personal selling is the opportunity to demonstrate a product. During a **demonstration**, the buyer gets a chance to try the product or at least see how it works. A demonstration might involve a test drive of the latest hybrid car or an in-store cooking class using pots and pans that are for sale. Salespeople at car dealerships have long used the test drive to demonstrate vehicles to prospective customers. It is part of the relationship-building process that makes dealerships critical to the success of automobile manufacturers as explained in the "Marketing and the SME" feature.

Many firms use new technologies to make their demonstrations more outstanding than those of their competitors. Multimedia interactive demonstrations are now common. Visitors to the Black & Decker website can click on a video demonstration of the company's new 20-volt MAX interchangeable lithium ion battery system and can also learn how to reduce their environmental impact by using the latest Black & Decker products.[21] The key to an outstanding demonstration—one that gains the customer's attention, keeps his or her interest, is convincing, and stays in the customer's memory—is planning. But planning should also include time and space for free exchanges of information. During your demonstration, you should be prepared to stop and answer questions, demonstrate a certain feature again, or let the customer try the product firsthand.

Dealers and Dealer Salespeople = Sales Success

WHAT does it take to be successful in the automotive industry? It takes a large manufacturer to produce automobiles that consumers want as few consumers will make such an important purchase without comparing the features and benefits offered by several manufacturers. Few people will buy an automobile they don't like. Ford Motor Company understands this. It introduced the 1958 Edsel, one of the world's greatest automotive marketing failures, but followed it with the 1964 Mustang, a car that sold 22,000 units during its first day on the market. Ford could hardly give the Edsel away, but lineups of people were waiting to purchase the Mustang.

But real success is often determined by the much smaller dealerships that support automotive manufacturers, and many of these succeed based on the performance of key salespeople that they employ. Imagine the Chevrolet dealership that first hired Joe Girard. He sold his first car during his first day on the job and went on to sell 18 vehicles during his second month. Then he was fired. Why? Some of the other salespeople at the dealership complained about Joe, and the manager decided Joe was too aggressive. Joe quickly found employment at another Chevrolet dealership and went on to sell 13,001 vehicles during his 15-year selling career. Joe Girard is now in the *Guinness Book of World Records* as the world's greatest car salesperson: best day, 18 sales; best month, 174 sales; best year, 1,425 sales. He achieved the top vehicle sales in the world 12 times. Why was he so successful? Joe Girard understood the importance of connecting with his customers: before, during, and after the sale.

Today's dealer salespeople—at least the tech-savvy ones—can better connect with customers than ever before, thanks to social media. Chris Van Wiechen, a sales consultant at Collins Nissan in St. Catharines, Ontario, understands this and uses social media to keep in contact with prospective customers. After he has met with a prospect, Chris prepares a video walk-around, where he carefully describes all the features and benefits he wants the prospect to remember. He then uploads the video to YouTube and emails a link to the prospect. Some prospects, during their showroom visit, explain that they must discuss the vehicle purchase with their spouse before making a decision. The video lets them show all the important parts of the sales presentation to their spouse at their convenience. The video also serves as a reminder for the prospect as Chris can carefully describe everything he wishes the prospect to remember when making his or her decision. Chris knows that most prospects will visit several dealerships, talk to several salespeople, and test-drive several cars before making a decision. The video is an opportunity to help the prospect differentiate among salespeople, dealerships, and vehicles, and reinforces the interest Chris has in making a sale.

Sources: Personal interview, Chris Van Wiechen, Collins Nissan, March 7, 2014; Sharon Lagina, "The Joe Girard Story—Lessons from a Top Salesman," **www.dearbornfreepress.com**, April 23, 2012, accessed May 3, 2014; Ford Motor Company, "A Drive through History," available **http://corporate.ford.com/vehicles/ford-mustang-story**, accessed May 3, 2014.

table 15.3   **Common Buyer Concerns**

CONCERN RELATED TO:	QUESTION	STATEMENT
Product	What makes this product unique?	I don't see why this product is better than the one I have.
Price	Is this the best price you can offer?	Your price is certainly not within my budget.
Source	Will you be with this company next year if I have a problem?	I am very satisfied with my current supplier.
Time	Why would I want to buy more hockey equipment in May?	May is a poor month to buy hockey equipment.
Need	Why do I need a new cell phone?	I already have a cell phone that meets my needs.

HANDLING BUYER CONCERNS

Potential customers often have questions and concerns about a good or service they are considering. **Buyer concerns**—sometimes called *objections*—are expressions of sales resistance, so it is reasonable for a salesperson to expect them. There are five types of concerns: product, price, source, time, and need. They may be expressed as questions or statements, as illustrated in Table 15.3. Concerns might appear in the form of stalling or indecisiveness. "Let me call you back," your customer might say, or "I need to talk to Ed about this."

buyer concerns Expressions of sales resistance by the prospect.

You can answer concerns without being aggressive or rude. Use a buyer concern as an opportunity to reassure your buyer about price, features, durability, availability, and the like. If the objection involves price, you might be able to suggest a less expensive model or a payment plan. If the concern involves a comparison to competitive products, point out the obvious—and not so obvious—benefits of your own. If the concern involves a question about availability, a few clicks on your laptop might show how many items are in stock and when they can be shipped.

CLOSING

The moment of truth in selling is the **closing**—the point at which the salesperson asks the prospect for an order. If your presentation has been effective and you have handled all buyer concerns, a closing would be the natural conclusion to the meeting. But you may still find it difficult to close the sale. Closing does not have to be thought of as a hard sell. Instead, a salesperson can ask low-pressure questions such as "Would you like to give this a try?" "Can I answer any more questions for you?" or "May I have your approval to proceed?"

closing Stage of the personal selling process in which the salesperson asks the customer to make a purchase decision.

Other methods of closing include the following:

1. Addressing the prospect's major concern about a purchase and then offering a convincing argument. ("If I can show you how the new heating system will reduce your energy costs by 25 percent, would you be willing to let us install it?")

2. Posing choices for the prospect in which either alternative represents a sale. (Would you prefer the pink sweater or the green one?)

3. Advising the prospect that a product is about to be discontinued or will go up in price soon. (But be completely honest about this—you don't want a customer to learn later that this was not true.)

4. Remaining silent so the prospect can make a decision on his or her own.

5. Offering an extra inducement designed to motivate a favourable buyer response, such as a quantity discount, an extended service contract, or a low-interest payment plan.

Even if the meeting or phone call ends without a sale, the effort is not over. You can use a written note or an email to keep communication open, letting the buyer know that you are ready and waiting to be of service.

assessment check 5

5.1 Identify the seven steps of the sales process.

5.2 Why is follow-up important to the sales effort?

FOLLOW-UP

The word *close* can be misleading because the point at which the prospect accepts the seller's offer is where much of the real work of selling begins. In today's competitive environment, the most successful salespeople make sure that today's customers will also be tomorrow's.

It is not enough to close the sale and move on. Relationship selling involves reinforcing the purchase decision and making sure the company delivers the highest-quality merchandise. As a salesperson, you must also ensure that customer service needs are met and that satisfaction results from all of a customer's dealings with your company. Otherwise, some other company may get the next order.

follow-up Post-sale activities that often determine whether an individual who has made a recent purchase will become a repeat customer.

These post-sale activities, which often determine whether a person will become a repeat customer, constitute the sales **follow-up**. Sales experts believe in a wide array of follow-up techniques, ranging from expensive information folders to less expensive holiday cards and online greetings. Some suggest phone calls at regular intervals. Others prefer automatic email reminders when it is time to renew or reorder. At the very least, however, you should try to contact customers to find out whether they are satisfied with their purchases. This step allows you to psychologically reinforce the customer's original decision to buy. It also gives you an opportunity to correct any problems and ensure the next sale. Follow-up helps strengthen the bond you are trying to build with customers in relationship selling. You have probably experienced follow-up as a customer—if your auto dealership called to see if you were satisfied with recent service, or if your veterinarian phoned to find out if your pet was feeling better.

6 Identify the seven basic functions of a sales manager.

MANAGING THE SALES EFFORT

The overall direction and control of the personal selling effort are in the hands of sales managers. In a typical geographic sales structure, a district or divisional sales manager might report to a regional or zone manager. This manager in turn reports to a national sales manager or vice president of sales.

The sales manager's job requires a unique blend of administrative and sales skills depending on the specific level in the sales hierarchy. Sales skills are particularly important for first-level sales managers because they are involved daily in the continuing process of training and directly leading the sales force. But as people rise in the sales management hierarchy, they require more managerial skills and fewer sales skills to perform well. Candace Plourd recently became the inside sales manager for Jupiter Systems, an international supplier of digital display walls and networked PCs. Her earlier career was in sales, working for Digital Equipment and Compaq. At both companies, she worked in channel sales as well as with end users, managing major accounts such as CVS, American Express, and John Deere. At both companies, she gained experience in delivering exceptional service to high-profile customers. In her role as inside sales manager for Jupiter Systems, she works with the company's regional sales managers and will be involved in activities related to customer satisfaction.[22]

Sales force management links individual salespeople to general management. The sales manager performs seven basic managerial functions: (1) recruitment and selection, (2) training, (3) organization, (4) supervision, (5) motivation, (6) compensation, and (7) evaluation and control. Sales managers perform these tasks in a demanding and complex environment. They must manage an increasingly diverse sales force that includes more women and minorities. Women account for almost half of Canadian professional salespeople, and their numbers are growing at a faster rate than that for men. As the workforce composition continues to change and become more diverse, an even more diverse blend of people will be needed to fill a growing number of sales positions.[23]

RECRUITMENT AND SELECTION

Recruiting and selecting successful salespeople are among the sales manager's greatest challenges. After all, these people will collectively determine just how successful the sales manager is. New salespeople—like you—might come from colleges and universities, trade and business schools, other companies, and even the firm's current non-sales staff. A successful sales career offers satisfaction in all the following five areas that a person generally considers when deciding on a profession:

1. *Opportunity for advancement.* Salespeople work in positions of high visibility, and good salespeople can demonstrate their ability to perform in a short period of time. This places them in an excellent position for advancement as opportunities arise.

2. *Potential for high earnings.* Salespeople have the opportunity to earn among the highest salaries in many organizations.

3. *Personal satisfaction.* A salesperson derives satisfaction from achieving success in a competitive environment and from helping customers satisfy their wants and needs.

4. *Job security.* Selling provides a high degree of job security because there is always a need for good salespeople. Selling skills are also frequently transferable from one sales job to another.

During an interview, a sales manager looks for enthusiasm, organizational skills, sociability, and other traits.

5. *Independence and variety.* Salespeople often work independently, calling on customers in their territory. They have the freedom to make important decisions about meeting their customers' needs and frequently report that no two workdays are the same.

Careful selection of salespeople is important for two reasons. First, a company invests a substantial amount of time and money in the selection process. Second, hiring mistakes can damage relationships with customers and overall performance and are also costly to correct. Most larger firms use a seven-step process in selecting sales personnel: application screening, initial interview, in-depth interview, testing, reference checks, physical examination, and hiring decision. An application screening is typically followed by an initial interview. If the applicant looks promising, an in-depth interview is conducted. During the interview, a sales manager looks for the person's enthusiasm, organizational skills, ambition, persuasiveness, ability to follow instructions, and sociability.

Next, the company may administer aptitude, interest, and knowledge tests. One testing approach gaining in popularity is the assessment centre. This technique, which uses situational exercises, group discussions, and various job simulations, allows the sales manager to measure a candidate's skills, knowledge, and ability. Assessment centres enable managers to see what potential salespeople can do rather than what they say they can do. Before hiring a candidate, firms should check references and review company policies. Once a job offer has been made, firms can request a physical examination; however, they are required by law in Canada to make reasonable accommodation for people with a disability, unless it will cause undue hardship for the company.

TRAINING

To shape new sales recruits into an efficient sales organization, managers must conduct an effective training program. The principal methods used in sales training are on-the-job training, individual instruction, in-house classes, and external seminars.

Popular training techniques include instructional videos or DVDs, lectures, role-playing exercises, and interactive computer programs. Simulations can help salespeople improve their selling techniques. Many firms supplement their training by enrolling salespeople in executive development programs at local colleges and by hiring specialists to teach customized training programs. In other instances, sales reps attend courses and workshops developed by outside companies. Salespeople can earn the Certified Sales Professional (CSP) designation after successfully completing training through the Canadian Professional Sales Association. This training program focuses on consultative selling, an approach discussed earlier in this chapter, which is particularly appropriate for

SOLVING AN ETHICAL CONTROVERSY | When the Sale Doesn't Benefit the Customer

ALTHOUGH reputable sources such as *Consumer Reports* say most product failures occur late in a product's life, making extended warranties a poor value, selling such "protection" is so profitable that many companies push it anyway and provide their salespeople with incentives to do so, at prices that run to 20 percent of the item's purchase price or more. Best Buy is one retailer that aggressively pitches warranties for electronics on the grounds that products break, customers handle them clumsily, or the plans are inexpensive and save time and money. Some critics insist such plans are scams.

Is it appropriate for companies to sell extended warranties that might not be in the customer's best interest?

PRO

1. Some customers want the "peace of mind" of knowing they can repair or replace an item in a few years at no extra charge.

2. Buyers will make up their own minds about what is good value.

CON

1. Most product failures occur so early that repair is still covered under the manufacturer's own short-term warranty.
2. Some extended warranties are so overpriced that it's cheaper to buy a replacement item.

Where do you stand: pro or con?

Sources: "How to Beware of Extended Warranty Scams," eHow.com, **www.ehow.com**, accessed June 5, 2012; Damon Darlin, "Don't Worry, Be Happy: The Warranty Psychology," *The New York Times*, **www.nytimes.com**, accessed June 5, 2012; Marianne Goldstein, "Are Extended Warranties Worth the Money?" CBSNews.com, **www.cbsnews.com**, accessed June 5, 2012; Jim Henry, "Buyer Beware: Common Scams Related to Extended Warranties," *Forbes*, **www.forbes.com**, accessed April 30, 2012; Rick Aristotle Munarriz, "Best Buy's Turnaround Plan Sends Retailer in the Wrong Direction," The Motley Fool.com, **www.dailyfinance.com**, accessed March 29, 2012; Rafi Mohammed, "Consumer Reports Is Wrong about Extended Warranties," Harvard Business Review Blog Network, **http:blogs.hbr.org**, accessed March 23, 2012; Larry Downes, "The People vs. Best Buy Round Two," *Forbes*, **www.forbes.com**, accessed January 9, 2012.

business-to-business sales, but also for financial services sales, or anywhere that understanding customer needs is especially important.

Some companies incorporate training into their regular sales meetings. In such settings, colleagues share their experiences and are motivated to reassess their own skills and try new techniques. Ongoing sales training is important for both new and veteran salespeople. Best Buy recently received some negative press for training its salespeople to push extended warranties on customers, which many felt caused customer service to suffer. See the "Solving an Ethical Controversy" feature for opposing views on this strategy.

Sales managers often conduct training informally, travelling with field reps and then offering sales-related advice. Like sales meetings, classes and workshops are other ways to reinforce training. Mentoring is also a key tool in training new salespeople.

ORGANIZATION

Sales managers are responsible for the organization of the field sales force. General organizational alignments, which are usually made by top marketing management, may be based on geography, products, types of customers, or some combination of these factors. Figure 15.3 presents a streamlined organizational chart illustrating each of these alignments.

figure 15.3

Basic Approaches to Organizing the Sales Force

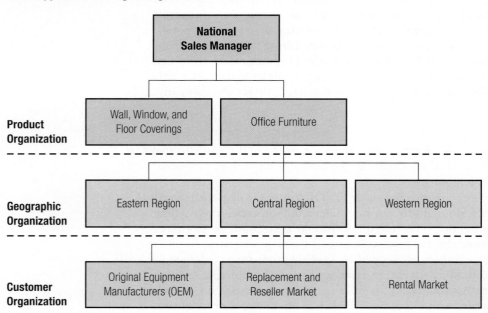

A product sales organization is likely to have a specialized sales force for each major category of the firm's products. This approach is common among industrial product companies that market large numbers of highly technical, complex products that are sold through different marketing channels.

Firms that market similar products throughout large territories often use geographic specialization. Multinational corporations may have different sales divisions in different countries. A geographic organization may also be combined with one of the other organizational methods. However, many companies are moving away from using territorial sales reps as they adopt customer-focused sales forces. For example, a single territory that contains two major customers might be redefined so the same sales rep covers both customers. Customer-oriented organizations use different sales force strategies for each major type of customer served. Some firms assign separate sales forces for their consumer and organizational customers. Others have sales forces for specific industries, such as financial services, educational, and automotive. Sales forces can also be organized by customer size, with a separate sales force assigned to large, medium, and small accounts.

Many firms using a customer-oriented structure adopt a **national accounts organization**. This format strengthens a firm's relationship with its largest customers by assigning senior sales personnel or sales teams to major accounts. Organizing by national accounts helps sales representatives develop cooperation among departments to meet special needs of the firm's most important customers. An example of national account selling is the relationship between Walmart and its major vendors. Walmart Canada is such an important account that many of its suppliers, including Procter & Gamble, have dedicated several salespeople who are responsible solely for this one account. Other examples of companies that have national accounts programs in Canada are Bell Mobility, Johnson & Johnson, Elizabeth Arden, and McCain Foods.

As companies expand their market coverage across national borders, they may use a variant of national account sales teams. These global account teams may be staffed by local sales representatives in the countries in which a company is operating. In other instances, the firm selects highly trained sales executives from its domestic operations. In either case, specialized training is critical to the success of a company's global sales force.

The individual sales manager also has the task of organizing the sales territories within his or her area of responsibility. Factors such as sales potential, strengths and weaknesses of available personnel, and workloads are considered in territory allocation decisions.

national accounts organization Promotional effort in which a dedicated sales team is assigned to a firm's major customers to provide sales and service needs.

SUPERVISION

Sales managers have differing opinions about the supervision of a sales force. Individuals and situations vary, so it is impossible to write a recipe for the exact amount of supervision needed in all cases. However, a concept known as **span of control** helps provide some general guidelines. Span of control refers to the number of sales representatives who report to first-level sales managers. The optimal span of control is affected by such factors as complexity of work activities, ability of the individual sales manager, degree of interdependence among individual salespeople, and the extent of training each salesperson receives. A 6-to-1 ratio has been suggested as the optimal span of control for first-level sales managers supervising technical or industrial salespeople. In contrast, a 10-to-1 ratio is recommended if sales representatives are calling on wholesale and retail accounts.

span of control Number of representatives who report to first-level sales managers.

MOTIVATION

What motivates salespeople to perform their best? The sales manager is responsible for finding the answer to this question. The sales process involves problem solving, which sometimes includes frustration—particularly when a sale is delayed or falls through. Information sharing, recognition, bonuses, incentives, and benefits can all be used to help defray frustration and motivate sales staff. Developing an enthusiastic sales staff who are happy at their jobs is the goal of the sales manager. Motivation is an important part of the company's success.

Creating a positive, motivating environment doesn't necessarily mean instituting complex or expensive incentive programs. Monetary reward—cash—is often considered king. But sometimes simple recognition—a thank-you, a dinner, a year-end award—can go a long way. It is important for the sales manager to figure out what types of incentives will be most effective with his or her particular group of employees. Some firms go all out, dangling luxury items such as computers, digital cameras, or trips in front of the sales force as rewards. A Caribbean cruise, a trip to Disney World, or a weekend at a luxury spa could be the carrot that works, particularly if family members are included. Some firms purchase gift cards from retailers such as Future Shop or Canadian Tire to distribute to sales staff who perform well. But not all incentive programs are effective at motivating employees. A program with targets that are set too high, that isn't publicized, or that allows only certain sales personnel to participate can backfire. So it is important for sales management to plan carefully for an incentive program to succeed.

Sales managers can also gain insight into the subject of motivation by studying the various theories of motivation developed over the years. One theory that has been applied effectively to sales force motivation is **expectancy theory**, which states that motivation depends on the expectations an individual has of his or her ability to perform the job and on how performance relates to attaining rewards that the individual values.

expectancy theory Theory that motivation depends on an individual's expectations of his or her ability to perform a job and how that performance relates to attaining a desired reward.

Sales managers can apply the expectancy theory of motivation by following a five-step process:

1. Let each salesperson know in detail what is expected with regard to selling goals, service standards, and other areas of performance. Rather than setting goals just once a year, many firms do so on a semi-annual, quarterly, or even monthly basis.

2. Make the work valuable by assessing the needs, values, and abilities of each salesperson and then assigning appropriate tasks.

3. Make the work achievable. As leaders, sales managers must inspire self-confidence in their salespeople and offer training and coaching to reassure them.

4. Provide immediate and specific feedback, guiding those who need improvement and giving positive feedback to those who do well.

5. Offer rewards that each salesperson values, whether it is an incentive as described previously, opportunity for advancement, or a bonus.

COMPENSATION

Money is an important part of any person's job, and the salesperson is no exception. So deciding how best to compensate the sales force can be a critical factor in motivation. Sales compensation can be based on a commission, a straight salary, or a combination of both. Bonuses based on end-of-year results are another popular form of compensation. The increasing popularity of team selling has also forced companies to set up reward programs to recognize performance of business units and teams. Today, about 25 percent of firms reward business-unit performance.

A **commission** is a payment tied directly to the sales or profits that a salesperson achieves. A salesperson might receive a 5 percent commission on all sales up to a specified quota and a 7 percent commission on sales beyond that point. This approach to sales compensation is increasingly popular. But while commissions reinforce selling incentives, they may cause some sales force members to overlook non-selling activities, such as completing sales reports, delivering promotion materials, and servicing existing accounts. In addition, salespeople who operate entirely on commission may become too aggressive in their approach to potential customers, a practice that could backfire.

commission Incentive compensation directly related to the sales or profits achieved by a salesperson.

A **salary** is a fixed payment made periodically to an employee. A firm that bases compensation on salaries rather than commissions might pay a salesperson a set amount weekly, bi-monthly, or monthly. A company must balance benefits and disadvantages in paying predetermined salaries to compensate managers and sales personnel. A straight salary plan gives management more control over how sales personnel allocate their efforts, but it reduces the incentive to find new markets and land new accounts.

salary Fixed compensation payment made periodically to an employee.

Many firms have found that it's best to develop compensation programs that combine features of both salary and commission plans. A new salesperson often receives a base salary while in training, even if he or she moves to full commission later on. If the salesperson does a lot of driving as part of the job, he or she may receive a vehicle. If the person works from home, there might be an allowance toward setting up an office there.

table 15.4 **Sales Compensation, Canada**

	BASE SALARY, $000s			TOTAL CASH, $000s		
	25%ile	50%ile	75%ile	25%ile	50%ile	75%ile
Inside Sales	$33.4	$37.8	$42.9			
Sales Representative	$44.6	$52.2	$61.0	$52.4	$62.7	$77.3
Sales Representative (Senior)	$59.6	$69.3	$80.7	$69.2	$80.0	$104.5
Key Accounts Representative	$65.6	$81.6	$95.3			
Sales Manager	$62.9	$74.8	$91.0	$69.4	$82.7	$121.2

NOTES

Total cash columns show base salary plus incentive compensation for obvious incentive-driven positions.

Source: Amanda Frank, Monster Contributing Writer, "Average Salaries for Jobs in Sales," **http://career-advice.monster.ca/salary -benefits/salary-information/average-salaries-for-jobs-in-sales/article.aspx**, accessed February 6, 2014. Copyright © 2014 Monster Worldwide, Inc. All Rights Reserved.

Total compensation packages vary according to industry, with the finance, insurance, and real estate industries coming out on top, followed closely by general services. Compensation also varies according to years of experience in sales. Table 15.4 provides information on base salaries and total cash for both inside and field salespeople with various levels of experience.

EVALUATION AND CONTROL

Perhaps the most difficult tasks required of sales managers are evaluation and control. Sales managers are responsible for setting standards and choosing the best methods for measuring sales performance. Sales volume, profitability, and changes in market share are the usual means of evaluating sales effectiveness. They typically involve the use of **sales quotas**—specified sales or profit targets that the firm expects salespeople to achieve. A particular sales representative might be expected to generate sales of $2.4 million in his or her territory during a given year. In many cases, the quota is tied to the compensation system. Technology has greatly improved the ability of sales managers to monitor the effectiveness of their sales staffs. Databases help sales managers to quickly divide revenues by salesperson, by account, and by geographic area.

sales quota Level of expected sales for a territory, product, customer, or salesperson against which actual results are compared.

In today's marketing environment, other measures such as customer satisfaction, profit contribution, share of product-category sales, and customer retention are also coming into play. This is the result of three factors:

1. A long-term orientation that results from emphasis on building customer relationships.

2. The fact that evaluations based on sales volume alone may lead to overselling and inventory problems that may damage customer relationships.

3. The need to encourage sales representatives to develop new accounts, provide customer service, and emphasize new products. Sales quotas tend to put focus on short-term selling goals rather than long-term relationships.

The sales manager must follow a formal system that includes a consistent series of decisions. This way, the manager can make fair and accurate evaluations. The system helps the sales manager answer three general questions:

1. *Where does each salesperson's performance rank relative to predetermined standards?* This comparison takes into consideration any uncontrollable variables on sales performance, such as a natural disaster or unforeseen change in the industry. Each adjusted rank is stated as a percentage of the standard.

2. *What are the salesperson's strong points?* The manager might list areas of the salesperson's performance in which he or she has performed above the standard. Or strong points could be placed in such categories as technical ability, processes, and end results.

3. *What are the salesperson's weak points?* No one likes to hear criticism, but when it is offered constructively, it can be motivation to improve performance. The manager and employee should establish specific objectives for improvement and set a timetable for judging the employee's improvement.

In completing the evaluation summary, the sales manager follows a set procedure so that all employees are treated equally:

- Each aspect of sales performance for which a standard exists should be measured separately. This helps prevent the so-called *halo effect,* in which the rating given on one factor influences those on other performance variables.

- Each salesperson should be judged on the basis of actual sales performance rather than potential ability. This is why rankings are important in the evaluation.

- Sales managers must judge each salesperson on the basis of sales performance for the entire period under consideration, rather than for a few particular incidents.

- The evaluation should be reviewed by a third party—such as the manager's boss or a human resources manager—for completeness and objectivity.

Once the evaluation is complete, both manager and salesperson should focus on positive action—whether it is a drive toward new goals or correcting a negative situation. An evaluation should be motivation for improved performance.

> **assessment check 6** ✓
>
> **6.1** What are the seven basic functions performed by a sales manager?
>
> **6.2** Define *span of control.*
>
> **6.3** What are the three main questions a sales manager must address as part of a salesperson's evaluation?

⑦ **Explain the role of ethical behaviour in personal selling.**

ETHICAL ISSUES IN SALES

Promotional activities can raise ethical questions, and personal selling is no exception. A difficult economy or highly competitive environment may tempt some salespeople—particularly those new to the business—to behave in ways that they might later regret. They might use the company car for personal errands or pad an expense report. They might give expensive gifts to customers. But today's experienced, highly professional salespeople know that long-term success requires a strong code of ethics. They also know that a single breach of ethics could have a devastating effect on their careers.

Some people believe that ethical problems are inevitable because of the very nature of the sales function. And in the wake of corporate scandals in which top executives have benefited at the expense of customers, employees, and shareholders, ethical managers are working harder than ever to build trust. So they reinforce ethics codes that may already be in place and strengthen ethics training. Salespeople who earn the Certified Sales Professional (CSP) designation through the Canadian Professional Sales Association (CPSA) must agree to abide by the CPSA Sales Institute Code of Ethics (Figure 15.4).

Sales managers and top executives can do a lot to foster a corporate culture that encourages honesty and ethical behaviour. Here are some characteristics of such a culture:

- *Employees understand what is expected of them.* A written code of ethics—which should be reviewed by all employees—in addition to ethics training helps educate employees in how to conduct ethical business.

- *Open communication.* Employees who feel comfortable talking with their supervisors are more apt to ask questions if they are uncertain about situations or decisions and to report any violations they come across.

- *Managers lead by example.* Workers naturally emulate the ethical behaviour of managers. A sales manager who is honest with customers, doesn't accept inappropriate gifts, and leaves the company car at home during a vacation is likely to be imitated by his or her sales staff.

figure 15.4

CPSA Sales Institute Code of Ethics

The Candian Professional Sales Association (CPSA) Sales Institute Code of Ethics is the set of principles and standards that a Certified Sales Professional (CSP) will strive to adhere to with customers, organizations, competitors, communities, and colleagues.

The CSP pledges and commits to uphold these standards in all activities:

As a Certified Sales Professional, I will:

1. Maintain honesty and integrity in all relationships with customers, prospective customers, and colleagues and continually work to earn their trust and respect.

2. Accurately represent my products or services to the best of my ability in a manner that places my customer or prospective customer and my company in a position that benefits both.

3. Respect and protect the proprietary and confidential information entrusted to me by my company and my customers and not engage in activities that may conflict with the best interest of my customers or my company.

4. Continually upgrade my knowledge of my products/services, skills, and my industry.

5. Use the time and resources available to me only for legitimate business purposes. I will only participate in activities that are ethical and legal, and when in doubt, I will seek counsel.

6. Respect my competitors and their products and services by representing them in a manner which is honest, truthful, and based on accurate information that has been substantiated.

7. Endeavour to engage in business and selling practices which contribute to a positive relationship with the community.

8. Assist and counsel my fellow sales professionals where possible in the performance of their duties.

9. Abide by and encourage others to adhere to this Code of Ethics.

As a Certified Sales Professional, I understand that the reputation and professionalism of all salespeople depends on me as well as others engaged in the sales profession, and I will adhere to these standards to strengthen the reputation and integrity for which we will strive. I understand that failure to consistently act according to this Code of Ethics may result in the loss of the privilege of using my professional sales designation.

Source: The Canadian Professional Sales Association (CPSA) Sales Institute Code of Ethics, online at: **http://www.cpsa.com/csp/cspProcess/cspCodeofEthics.aspx**

The Canadian Professional Sales Association (CPSA)

Regardless of corporate culture, every salesperson is responsible for his or her own behaviour and relationship with customers. If, as a new salesperson, you find yourself uncertain about a decision, ask yourself these questions. The answers should help you make the ethical choice.

1. Does my decision affect anyone other than myself and the bottom line?

2. Is my success based on making the sale or creating a loyal customer?

3. Are my dealings with my customers in their best interest and not exploiting their trust?

4. What price will I pay for this decision?

assessment check 7

7.1 Why is it important for salespeople to maintain ethical behaviour?

7.2 What are the characteristics of companies that foster corporate cultures that encourage ethical behaviour?

SALES PROMOTION

Sales promotion includes those marketing activities other than personal selling, advertising, and publicity designed to enhance consumer purchasing and dealer effectiveness. In Canada, companies have been giving away trinkets and premiums for more than 100 years.

Sales promotion techniques were originally intended as short-term incentives aimed at producing an immediate response—a purchase. Today, however, marketers recognize sales promotion as an integral part of the overall marketing plan, and the focus has shifted from short-term goals to long-term objectives of building brand equity and maintaining continuing purchases. A frequent-flyer program enables an airline to build a base of loyal customers. A frequent-stay program allows a hotel chain to attract regular guests.

8 **Describe the role of sales promotion in the promotional mix, and identify the different types of sales promotions.**

sales promotion Marketing activities other than personal selling, advertising, and publicity that enhance consumer purchasing and dealer effectiveness.

Both retailers and manufacturers use sales promotions to offer consumers extra incentives to buy. These promotions are likely to stress price advantages, giveaways, or special offerings. The general objectives of sales promotion are to speed up the sales process and increase sales volume. Promotions can also help build loyalty. Through a consumer promotion, a marketer encourages consumers to try the product, use more of it, and buy it again. The firm also hopes to foster sales of related items and increase impulse purchases. Holiday specials are one type of sales promotion. In 2013, Target kicked off its first Boxing Day sale in Canada with limited-quantity deals on 50-inch Toshiba televisions for $499 (regularly $899) and Dyson upright vacuums for $298 (regularly $498).[24] Online sales jumped the queue. Walmart started its online Boxing Day sale by midday Christmas Eve; Best Buy, Future Shop, and The Source were not far behind.[25] Today, consumers have many more choices among products than in the past, and for this reason many marketers create special programs to build loyalty among their customers. However, with loyalty programs no longer unique, marketing and sales professionals work to build loyalty among their customers by managing customer relationships and regularly evaluating those relationships to determine how they can enhance them.[26]

Because sales promotion is so important to a marketing effort, an entire promotion industry exists to offer expert assistance in its use and to design unique promotions, just as an entire advertising industry offers similar services for advertisers. These companies, like advertising agencies, provide other firms with assistance in promoting their goods and services.

Sales promotions often produce their best results when combined with other marketing activities. Ads create awareness, while sales promotions lead to trial or purchase. After a presentation, a salesperson may offer a potential customer a discount coupon for the good or service. Promotions encourage immediate action because they impose limited time frames. Discount coupons and rebates usually have expiration dates. In addition, sales promotions produce measurable results, making it relatively easy for marketers to evaluate their effectiveness. If more people buy shoes during a buy-one-get-one-free promotion at a shoe store, its owners know the promotion was successful.

It is important to understand what sales promotions can and cannot do. They can encourage interest in both new and mature products, help introduce new products, encourage trial and repeat purchases, increase usage rates, neutralize competition, and reinforce advertising and personal selling efforts. On the other hand, sales promotions cannot overcome poor brand images, product deficiencies, or poor training for salespeople. While sales promotions increase volume in the short term, they may not lead to sales and profit growth in the long run.

Sales promotion techniques may serve all members of a marketing channel. In addition, manufacturers may use trade promotion methods to promote their products to resellers. Sales promotion techniques include the following consumer-oriented promotions: samples, bonus packs, premiums, coupons, refunds, contests, sweepstakes, and specialty advertising. Trade-oriented promotions include trade allowances, point-of-purchase advertising, trade shows, dealer incentives, contests, and training programs.

CONSUMER-ORIENTED SALES PROMOTIONS

In the promotion industry, marketers use all types of sales promotions, including games, contests, sweepstakes, and coupons to persuade new and existing customers to try their products. Consumer-oriented

Manufacturers use sales promotions to offer consumers extra incentives to buy.

H. F. (Herb) MacKenzie

sales promotions encourage repurchases by rewarding current users, boosting sales of complementary products, and increasing impulse purchases. These promotions also attract consumer attention in the midst of advertising clutter. Figure 15.5 illustrates the objectives of popular sales promotion alternatives and identifies their strengths and weaknesses.

It's important for marketers to use sales promotions selectively because if they are overused, consumers begin to expect price discounts at all times, which ultimately diminishes brand equity. The following sections describe the various forms of consumer-oriented sales promotions.

KIND OF PROMOTION	OBJECTIVES	STRENGTHS	WEAKNESSES
Coupons	Stimulate trial or brand switching	Attract price-sensitive customers who might not otherwise buy Encourage retailer support	Not all retailers accept coupons Have often been counterfeited or redeemed by some retailers without consumer purchases
Refunds (or rebates)	Encourage customers to buy	Help halt sales declines or reduce inventories if new products are about to enter the market	May reduce perceived value of the product Easy for competition to match
Samples	Stimulate trial of new products	Low customer risk creates awareness and trial	May be very costly for the company
Bonus Packs	Encourage customers to buy and minimize brand switching	Reward loyal customers for continued purchase	Customers will not need to repurchase for a longer period
Premiums	Stimulate trial or create goodwill	Customers like free merchandise and may induce trial of complementary product	May be costly for the company
Contests	Encourage consumers to buy and channel members to increase inventories	A predetermined number of winners, hence cost is usually predictable May create excitement	Require careful thought to be creative and to avoid costly legal responsibilities
Sweepstakes	Encourage customers to buy and minimize brand switching	A predetermined number of winners, hence cost is usually predictable Consumers like them because little effort is required	Sales may decline following the promotion
Specialty Advertising	Encourage customer loyalty	Create awareness and help to reinforce previous and future advertising messages Good customer acceptance	May be very costly for company and may become less effective if competition offers a better promotional item

figure 15.5

Most Popular Sales Promotion Alternatives

Coupons and Refunds

coupon Sales promotion technique that offers a discount on the purchase price of goods or services.

Coupons, the most widely used form of sales promotion, offer discounts on the purchase price of goods and services. Consumers can redeem the coupons at retail outlets, which receive the face value of the coupon plus a handling fee from the manufacturer. The coupon industry has been somewhat "clipped" in recent years due to the growing clout of retailers and more complex accounting rules that make couponing less attractive to some marketers. In addition, consumers receive so many coupons that they cannot possibly redeem them all. The number of coupons distributed in Canada continues to climb, but the redemption rate has been decreasing. In 2012, Canadians received 6.8 billion coupons, but redeemed only 86 million of them, a redemption rate of 1.26 percent. This was down from 1.5 percent in 2010, but still well ahead of the United States where redemption rates are around 1 percent.[27]

Mail, magazines, newspapers, package inserts, and, increasingly, the Internet are the standard methods of distributing coupons. Canadians have many choices for finding rebates and coupons on the Internet, including webSaver.ca, TeamBuy.ca, RedFlagDeals.com, Coupons.ca, SaveaLoonie.ca, and more. But another distribution channel for coupons has emerged: cell phones. Thanks to advances in bar code technology, retailers can distribute coupons digitally to cell phone users, who can also redeem the coupons digitally when they shop. Social platforms such as Groupon, Living Social, and Foursquare feature daily deals that often improve when users share them. SocialTwist's platform states that it "allows users to share in order to receive a better bargain." For example, if someone shares a $1 coupon with four other people, that coupon will be worth $4.[28]

refund Cash given back to consumers who send a proof of purchase for one or more products.

Refunds, or rebates, offer cash back to consumers who send in proof of purchasing one or more products. Refunds help packaged goods companies to increase purchase rates, promote multiple purchases, and reward product users. Although many consumers find the refund forms too bothersome to complete, plenty still do.

SAMPLES, BONUS PACKS, AND PREMIUMS

sampling Free distribution of a product in an attempt to obtain future sales.

Marketers are increasingly adopting the "try it, you'll like it" approach as an effective means of getting consumers to try and then purchase their goods and services. **Sampling** refers to the free distribution of a product in an attempt to obtain future sales. Samples may be distributed door to door, by mail, via demonstrations in stores or at events, or by including them in packages with other products. Sampling produces a much higher response rate than previously believed. One study demonstrated that households that participated in sampling events created a 475 percent sales increase on the day of the event, compared to non-sampled households. Those that sampled products were also 11 percent more likely to repurchase the product in the 20 weeks following the event and were 6 percent more likely to buy another product from the same brand franchise.[29]

With sampling, marketers can target potential customers and be certain that the product reaches them. Sampling provides an especially useful way to promote new or unusual products because it gives the consumer a direct product experience.

A major disadvantage of sampling is the high cost involved. Not only must the marketer give away small quantities of a product that might otherwise have generated revenues through regular sales, but the market is also in effect closed for the time it takes consumers to use up the samples. In addition, the marketer may encounter problems in distributing the samples. Hellmann's marketers annoyed consumers instead of pleasing them when the firm distributed sample packets of Italian and French salad dressing in home-delivered newspapers. Many of the packets burst when the papers hit the driveways.

bonus pack Specially packaged item that gives the purchaser a larger quantity at the regular price.

A **bonus pack** is a specially packaged item that gives the purchaser a larger quantity at the regular price. For instance, Quaker recently offered two free extra bars in every box of its Chewy Granola Bars. **Premiums** are items given free or at reduced cost with purchases of other products. For example, 3M Canada recently offered a bonus pack of four rolls of transparent tape with the purchase of a heavy-duty tape dispenser. Premiums have proven effective in motivating consumers to try new products or different brands. A premium should have some relationship with the product or brand it accompanies, though. A home improvement centre might offer free measuring tapes to its customers, for example.

premium Item given free or at a reduced cost with purchase of other products.

Contests and Sweepstakes

Firms often sponsor contests and sweepstakes to introduce new goods and services, to attract additional customers, and to collect contact information from participants that can later be used for targeting customers. **Contests** require entrants to complete a task, such as solving a puzzle or answering questions in a trivia quiz, and they may require proof of purchase. **Sweepstakes**, on the other hand, choose winners by chance, so no product purchase is necessary. They are more popular with consumers than contests because they do not take as much effort for consumers to enter. Marketers like them, too, because they are inexpensive to run and the number of winners is predetermined. With some contests, the sponsors cannot predict the number of people who will correctly complete the puzzles or gather the right number of symbols from scratch-off cards.

Marketers are increasingly turning to the Internet for contests and sweepstakes, because of its relatively low cost and its ability to provide data immediately. Interactivity is also a key part of the online experience—as consumers become more engaged in the contest or sweepstakes event, they also build a relationship with the firm and its products. Friendly Planet Travel, which conducts group tours around the world, recently held a sweepstakes as part of its "Win the World" Facebook sweepstakes. The prize was a free, all-inclusive week-long vacation in Ireland.

contest Sales promotion technique that requires entrants to complete a task, such as solving a puzzle or answering questions on a quiz, for the chance to win a prize.

sweepstakes Sales promotion technique in which prize winners are selected by chance.

COFFEE CRISP® is a registered trademark of Société des Produits Nestlé S.A., Vevey, Switzerland

Coffee Crisp—a Canadian chocolate bar favourite—celebrated its 75th anniversary with a sweepstakes that promoted $10,000 travel experiences for winners.

Contestants entered a contact on Friendly Planet's Facebook page. If a contestant shared the page with a Facebook friend, his or her name was entered again for another chance at winning.[30] There are special laws and regulations governing contests and sweepstakes in Canada and, in particular, for online ones. A firm would be wise to consider legal advice before deciding to implement one of these promotional techniques.

Specialty Advertising

The origin of specialty advertising has been traced to the Middle Ages, when artisans gave wooden pegs bearing their names to prospects, who drove them into the walls at home to serve as convenient hangers for armour. Corporations began putting their names on a variety of products in the late 1800s, as newspapers and print shops explored new methods to earn additional revenues from their expensive printing presses. Today, just about everyone owns a cap or T-shirt with the name or logo of a company, organization, or product displayed on it.

Specialty advertising is a sales promotion technique that places the advertiser's name, address, and advertising message on useful articles that are then distributed to target customers. Wearable products are the most popular, accounting for nearly a third of specialty advertising sales. Pens, mugs, glassware, and calendars are other popular forms.

Advertising specialties help to reinforce previous or future advertising and sales messages. Consumers like these giveaways, which generate stronger responses to direct mail, resulting in three times the dollar volume of sales compared with direct mail alone. Companies use this form of promotion to highlight store openings and new products, motivate salespeople, increase visits to trade show booths, and remind customers about their products.

TRADE-ORIENTED PROMOTIONS

Sales promotion techniques can also contribute effectively to campaigns aimed at retailers and wholesalers. **Trade promotion** is sales promotion that appeals to marketing intermediaries rather than to final consumers. Marketers use trade promotions in push strategies by encouraging resellers to stock new products, continue to carry existing ones, and promote both effectively to consumers. The typical firm actually spends half its promotional budget on trade promotion—as much money as it spends on advertising and consumer-oriented sales promotions combined. Successful trade promotions offer financial incentives. They require careful timing and attention to costs and are easy to implement by retailers. These promotions should bring quick results and improve retail sales.

Trade Allowances

Among the most common trade promotion methods are **trade allowances**—special financial incentives offered to wholesalers and retailers that purchase or promote specific products. These offers take various forms. A buying allowance gives retailers a discount on goods. They include off-invoice allowances through which retailers deduct specified amounts from their invoices or receive free goods, such as one free case for every 10 ordered, when they order certain quantities. When a manufacturer offers a promotional allowance, it agrees to pay the reseller a certain amount to cover the costs of special promotional displays or extensive advertising that features the manufacturer's product. The goal is to increase sales to consumers by encouraging resellers to promote their products effectively.

Point-of-Purchase Advertising

A display or other promotion located near the site of the actual buying decision is known as **point-of-purchase (POP) advertising**. This method of sales promotion capitalizes on the fact that nearly two-thirds of shoppers make many purchase decisions within the store, so it encourages retailers to improve on-site merchandising. Product suppliers assist the retailer by creating special displays designed to stimulate sales of the item being promoted.

Free-standing POP promotions often appear at the ends of shopping aisles. On a typical trip to the supermarket, you might see a POP display for Disney videos, Coppertone sunscreen, or Duracell

specialty advertising Sales promotion technique that places the advertiser's name, address, and advertising message on useful articles that are then distributed to target consumers.

trade promotion Sales promotion that appeals to marketing intermediaries rather than to consumers.

trade allowance Financial incentive offered to wholesalers and retailers that purchase or promote specific products.

point-of-purchase (POP) advertising Display or other promotion located near the site of the actual buying decision.

batteries. Retailers such as Home Depot, Staples, and Canadian Tire all use POP advertising displays frequently. Electronic kiosks, which allow consumers to place orders for items not available in the store, have begun to transform the POP display industry, as creators of these displays look for ways to involve consumers more actively as well as entertain them.

Trade Shows

To influence resellers and other members of the distribution channel, many marketers participate in **trade shows**. These shows are often organized by industry trade associations; frequently, they are part of these associations' annual meetings or conventions. Vendors who serve the industries display and demonstrate their products for attendees. Industries that hold trade shows include manufacturers of sporting goods, medical equipment, electronics, automobiles, clothing, and home furnishings. Service industries include hair styling, health care, travel, and restaurant franchises. The Canadian Gift Association holds Canada's largest trade show—the Toronto Gift Fair—bi-annually, where 1,000 exhibitors attract more than 17,000 retail buyers from across Canada and around the world. It also owns and manages two other bi-annual trade fairs: the Alberta Gift Fair in Edmonton, Alberta, and the Quebec Gift Fair in Montreal, Quebec.[31]

> **trade show** Product exhibition organized by industry trade associations to showcase goods and services.

Because of the expense involved in trade shows, a company must assess the value of these shows on several criteria, such as direct sales, any increase in product awareness, image building, and any contribution to the firm's marketing communications efforts. Trade shows give especially effective opportunities to introduce new products and to generate sales leads as described in the "Marketing: Making Your World Better" feature. Some types of shows reach ultimate consumers as well as channel members. Home, recreation, and automobile shows, for instance, allow businesses to display and demonstrate home improvement, recreation, and other consumer products. Trade shows are particularly effective in B2B marketing, where companies spend approximately 40 percent of their total marketing budget. Research shows that more than 80 percent of trade show attendees have purchasing authority.[32]

MARKETING: MAKING YOUR WORLD BETTER   Asian ECO Fair Growing Every Year

EACH fall, a major trade show is held in Hong Kong—Eco Expo Asia—dedicated to the environmental industry. In 2013, 297 exhibitors from 19 countries participated. The four-day event featured four main exhibit categories: air quality, energy efficiency and energy, waste management and recycling, and eco-friendly products. The popularity of the trade show is growing as world interest in environmental issues continues to build. This eighth annual trade show attracted 12,952 trade visitors from 98 countries, the largest attendance yet.

Trade shows are great venues for sales and technical people to connect with important buyers and other influencers who are looking for solutions to their buying problems. Just over 60 percent of exhibitors came from Hong Kong. Other countries with more than five exhibitors were mainland China (39), Japan (21), Canada (18), Macau (8), Switzerland (7), Russia (6), and Germany (5). Ian Xiao, a senior executive at Canada's Green Power Labs, joined the fair on the recommendation of the Canadian government. He says, "We came to Eco Expo Asia to meet government officials and were very successful. The show put us in touch with all the right people. It was a very engaging and top-tier fair." Consistent with the trade fair theme, the organizers made a number of suggestions for exhibitors:

- To use natural decorative materials, and avoid excessive decorations
- To use energy-saving light bulbs or LED lights
- To use reusable panels, cabinets, signage boards, and carpets
- To travel to and from the venue by public transit or shuttle bus
- To avoid using plastic bags (or make a charity donation)
- To reduce souvenirs or choose practical ones
- To place recycling bins in booths and practise waste separation

The final day of the trade fair was open to the general public, when an additional 3,552 visitors attended. Workshops were provided on a number of eco-topics, including energy saving, food waste composting, and creating an aquaponic system. Environmentally friendly products were offered for sale at the fair's Green Mart.

Source: Hong Kong Trade Development Council website, **www.hktdc .com/fair/ecoexpoasia-en/Eco-Expo-Asia-International-Trade-Fair-on -Environmental-Protection.html**, accessed February 6, 2014.

Dealer Incentives, Contests, and Training Programs

push money Cash reward paid to retail salespeople for every unit of a product they sell.

Manufacturers run dealer incentive programs and contests to reward retailers and their salespeople who increase sales and, more generally, to promote specific products. These channel members receive incentives for performing promotion-related tasks and can win contests by reaching sales goals. Manufacturers may offer major prizes to resellers such as trips to exotic places. **Push money** (which retailers commonly refer to as *spiffs*) is another incentive that gives retail salespeople cash rewards for every unit of a product they sell. This benefit increases the likelihood that the salesperson will try to convince a customer to buy the product rather than a competing brand.

For more expensive and highly complex products, manufacturers often provide specialized training for retail salespeople. This background helps sales personnel explain features, competitive advantages, and other information to consumers. Training can be provided in several ways: a manufacturer's sales representative can conduct training sessions during regular sales calls, or the firm can distribute sales literature and DVDs.

assessment check 8

8.1 Define *sales promotion*.

8.2 Identify at least four types of consumer-oriented sales promotions.

8.3 Identify at least three types of trade-oriented sales promotions.

Strategic Implications

Today's salespeople are a new breed. Richly nourished in a tradition of sales, their roles are strengthened even further through technology. However, as many companies are discovering, nothing can replace the power of personal selling in generating sales and in building strong, loyal customer relationships.

Salespeople today are a critical link in developing relationships between the customer and the company. They communicate customer needs and wants to co-workers in various units within an organization, enabling a cooperative, company-wide effort in improving product offerings and in better satisfying individuals within the target market. For salespeople, the greatest benefit of electronic technologies is the ability to share knowledge when it is

needed with those who need to know, including customers, suppliers, and employees. Because buyers are now more sophisticated, demanding more rapid and lower-cost transactions, salespeople must be quick and creative as they find solutions to their customers' problems. Product life cycles are accelerating, and customers who demand more are apt to switch from one product to another. Recognizing the long-term impact of keeping satisfied buyers—those who make repeat and cross-purchases and provide referrals—versus dissatisfied buyers, organizations are increasingly training their sales forces to provide superior customer service and rewarding them for increasing satisfaction levels.

The traditional skills of a salesperson included persuasion, selling ability, and product knowledge. But

today's sales professional is more likely to possess communication skills; problem-solving skills; and knowledge of products, customers, industries, and applications. Earlier generations of salespeople tended to be self-driven; today's sales professional is more likely to be a team player as well as a customer advocate who serves his or her buyers by solving problems.

The modern professional salesperson is greatly assisted by the judicious use of both consumer- and trade-oriented sales promotions. Often overlooked in promotional discussions of high-profile advertising, the typical firm allocates more promotional dollars for sales promotion than for advertising. The proven effectiveness of sales promotion makes it a widely used promotional mix component for most marketers. ◆◆◆

REVIEW OF CHAPTER OBJECTIVES

① **Describe the role of today's salesperson.**

Today's salesperson seeks to form long-lasting relationships with customers by providing high levels of customer service rather than going for the quick sale. Firms have begun to integrate their computer and communications technologies into the sales function, so people involved in personal selling have an expanded role.

② **Describe the four sales channels.**

Over-the-counter selling involves providing product information and arranging for completion of the sales transaction when customers come to the seller's location. Field selling involves making personal sales calls to customers. Under certain circumstances, telemarketing is used to provide product information and answer questions from customers who call. Inside selling relies on phone, mail, and e-commerce to provide sales and product services for customers on a continuing basis.

③ **Describe the major trends in personal selling.**

Companies are turning to relationship selling, consultative selling, and team selling. Relationship selling occurs when a salesperson builds a mutually beneficial relationship with a customer on a regular basis over an extended period. Consultative selling involves meeting customer needs by listening to customers, understanding and caring about their problems, paying attention to the details, and following through after the sale. Team selling occurs when the salesperson joins with specialists from other functional areas of the firm to complete the selling process.

④ **Identify and briefly describe the three basic sales tasks.**

Order processing is the routine handling of an order. It characterizes a sales setting in which the need is made known to and is acknowledged by the customer. Creative selling is persuasion aimed at making the prospect see the value of the good or service being presented. Missionary selling is indirect selling, such as making goodwill calls and providing technical or operational assistance.

⑤ **Outline the seven steps in the sales process.**

The basic steps in the sales process are prospecting and qualifying, approach, presentation, demonstration, handling buyer concerns, closing, and follow-up.

⑥ **Identify the seven basic functions of a sales manager.**

A sales manager links the sales force to other aspects of the internal and external environments. The manager's functions are recruitment and selection, training, organization, supervision, motivation, compensation, and evaluation and control.

⑦ **Explain the role of ethical behaviour in personal selling.**

Ethical behaviour is vital to building positive, long-term relationships with customers. Although some people believe that ethical problems are inevitable, employers can do much to foster a corporate culture that encourages honesty and ethical behaviour. In addition, each salesperson is responsible for his or her own behaviour and relationship with customers.

⑧ **Describe the role of sales promotion in the promotional mix, and identify the different types of sales promotions.**

Sales promotion includes activities other than personal selling, advertising, and publicity designed to enhance consumer purchasing and dealer effectiveness. Sales promotion is an integral part of the overall marketing plan, intended to increase sales and build brand equity. Promotions often produce their best results when combined with other marketing activities. Consumer-oriented sales promotions include coupons, refunds, samples, bonus packs, premiums, contests and sweepstakes, and specialty advertising. Trade-oriented promotions include trade allowances; point-of-purchase (POP) advertising; trade shows; and dealer incentives, contests, and training programs.

assessment check answers

1.1 What is personal selling?

Personal selling is the process of a seller's person-to-person promotional presentation to a buyer.

1.2 What is the main focus of today's salespeople?

The main focus of today's salespeople is to build long-lasting relationships with customers.

2.1 What is over-the-counter selling?

Over-the-counter selling describes selling in retail and some wholesale locations. Most of these transactions take place directly with customers.

2.2 What is field selling?

Field selling involves making sales calls on prospective and existing customers at their businesses or homes.

2.3 Distinguish between outbound and inbound telemarketing.

Outbound telemarketing takes place when a salesperson phones customers; inbound telemarketing takes place when customers call the firm.

3.1 Identify the three major personal selling approaches.

The three major personal selling approaches are relationship selling, consultative selling, and team selling.

3.2 Distinguish between relationship selling and consultative selling.

Relationship selling is a technique for building a mutually beneficial partnership with a customer. Consultative selling involves meeting customer needs by listening to, understanding, and paying attention to their problems; then following up after a sale.

4.1 What are the three basic sales tasks performed by salespeople?

The three major tasks are order processing, creative selling, and missionary selling.

4.2 What are the three steps of order processing?

The three steps of order processing are identifying customer needs, pointing out the need to the customer, and completing the order.

5.1 Identify the seven steps of the sales process.

The seven steps of the sales process are prospecting and qualifying, approach, presentation, demonstration, handling buyer concerns, closing, and follow-up.

5.2 Why is follow-up important to the sales effort?

Follow-up allows the salesperson to reinforce the customer's purchase decision, strengthen the bond, and correct any problems.

6.1 What are the seven basic functions performed by a sales manager?

The seven basic functions of a sales manager are recruitment and selection, training, organization, supervision, motivation, compensation, and evaluation and control.

6.2 Define *span of control*.

Span of control refers to the number of sales representatives who report to first-level sales managers.

6.3 What are the three main questions a sales manager must address as part of a salesperson's evaluation?

The three main questions a sales manager must address are these: Where does each salesperson's performance rank relative to predetermined standards? What are the salesperson's strong points? What are the salesperson's weak points?

7.1 Why is it important for salespeople to maintain ethical behaviour?

Salespeople need to maintain ethical behaviour because it is vital to their firm's relationships with customers and because they are representing their company. A breach of ethics could also be detrimental to an individual's career.

7.2 What are the characteristics of companies that foster corporate cultures that encourage ethical behaviour?

Characteristics of corporations fostering ethical behaviour include the following: employees who understand what is expected of them, open communication, and managers who lead by example.

8.1 Define *sales promotion*.

Sales promotion includes marketing activities other than personal selling, advertising, and publicity designed to enhance consumer purchasing and dealer effectiveness.

8.2 Identify at least four types of consumer-oriented sales promotions.

Consumer-oriented sales promotions include coupons, refunds, samples, bonus packs, premiums, contests, sweepstakes, and specialty advertising.

8.3 Identify at least three types of trade-oriented sales promotions.

Trade-oriented sales promotions include trade allowances, POP advertising, trade shows, dealer incentives, contests, and training programs.

MARKETING TERMS YOU NEED TO KNOW

These terms are printed in blue in the text. They are defined in the margins of the chapter and in the Glossary that begins on p. G-1.

personal selling 436
over-the-counter selling 437
field selling 438
network marketing 439
telemarketing 439
outbound telemarketing 439
inbound telemarketing 439
inside selling 440
relationship selling 441
consultative selling 442
cross-selling 442
team selling 442
virtual sales team 443
order processing 443
creative selling 444
missionary selling 444

sales incentives 444
prospecting 445
qualifying 445
approach 446
precall planning 446
presentation 446
cold calling 447
demonstration 448
buyer concerns 449
closing 449
follow-up 450
national accounts organization 453
span of control 453
expectancy theory 454
commission 454
salary 454

sales quota 455
sales promotion 457
coupon 460
refund 460
sampling 460
bonus pack 460
premium 460
contest 461
sweepstakes 461
specialty advertising 462
trade promotion 462
trade allowance 462
point-of-purchase (POP) advertising 462
trade show 463
push money 464

PROJECTS AND TEAMWORK EXERCISES

1. Cross-selling can be an effective way for a firm to expand. On your own or with a classmate, locate an advertisement for a firm that you believe could benefit from cross-selling. List ways it could offer multiple goods or services to the same customer. Then create a new ad illustrating the multiple offerings.
2. With a partner, choose one of the following sales situations. Then take turns coming up with creative ways to close the deal—one of you plays the customer and the other plays the salesperson. Present your closing scenarios to the class.
   a. You are a new sales associate at a car dealership, and a potential customer has just test-driven one of your newest models. You have handled all the customer's concerns and settled on a price. You don't want the customer to leave without agreeing to purchase the car.
   b. You operate a lawn care business and have visited several homeowners in a new development. Three of them have already agreed to give your service a try. You are meeting with the fourth and want to close that sale, too.
3. As sales representatives for a cooperative of organic farmers, you and a classmate are invited to make a sales

presentation to a national supermarket chain. List the most important messages you wish to relate and then role-play the sales presentation.
4. On your own or with a classmate, go online and research a firm such as Cadbury, General Mills, Ford, or Burger King to find out what kinds of consumer-oriented promotions the company is conducting for its various brands or individual products. Which promotions seem the most appealing to you as a consumer? Why? Present your findings to the class.
5. With a classmate, design a specialty advertising item for one of the following companies or its products, or choose one of your own. Present your design sketches to the class.
   a. Canada's Wonderland (Toronto), La Ronde (Montreal), Calaway Park (Calgary), or Playland (Vancouver)
   b. Tim Hortons
   c. Your college or university
   d. Telus or Fido wireless
   e. The Green Beanery (www.greenbeanery.ca)
   f. Apple iPad

CRITICAL THINKING EXERCISES

1. Since the implementation of Canada's Do Not Call registry, some Canadians witnessed an increase in door-to-door selling as well as emails containing sales messages. As a marketer, do you think this type of selling is effective? Why or why not?
2. Montreal-based Van Houtte Inc. operates the largest coffee services network in North America. You will find its coffee

served in car dealerships, doctors' offices, real estate offices, and in many other types of offices across Canada. Getting equipment and supplies into these offices requires personal selling to office managers, administrative support people, doctors, and even company owners. What role does relationship selling play in this situation? What kind of training should these salespeople receive?

3. Assume that a friend asks you to solicit donations for a local charity. (You pick the charity.) Outline your approach and presentation as a salesperson would.

4. Why is the recruitment and selection stage of the hiring process one of a sales manager's greatest challenges?

5. Food manufacturers often set up tables in supermarkets and offer free samples to shoppers, along with coupons for the promoted items. Sometimes restaurants offer free coffee or drink refills. What other products might lend themselves to sampling? Make a list. Pick one of the items and come up with a sampling plan for it. Where and when would you sample? To whom would you offer samples?

ETHICS EXERCISE

You have been hired by a discount sporting-goods retailer in an over-the-counter sales position. You have completed a training course that includes learning about the products, assisting customers, and cross-selling. You have made several good friends in the training course and sometimes get together after work to go running, play golf, or have dinner. You've noticed that one of your friends has really taken the training course to heart and has adopted a very aggressive attitude toward customers in the store, pushing them to buy just about anything, whether they need it or not.

1. Do you agree with your friend's actions? Why or why not?

2. Should you discuss the situation with your friend? Should you discuss it with your supervisor? Explain your response.

CASE 15.1

Not So Skinny Bitch

In 1984, Anita Skinner founded *The Downtowner*, a St. Catharines, Ontario, newsletter dedicated to improving the city's downtown neighbourhood. The newsletter evolved to become a full-colour, glossy magazine, *Niagara Life Magazine*, which Anita sold in 2004 at the height of its success. Her plan at that time was to retire and enjoy some travel. Her husband, a financial advisor and recreational golfer, convinced her to start golfing so they could have a common activity. At first, Anita admitted, she was very self-conscious. There were too many "skinny bitches" on the course, all with comfortable, fashionable outfits. All Anita could find were poorly fitting alternatives, and nothing that could be described, even remotely, as fashionable. With a little research, Anita soon learned that there were more than half a million women golfers in Canada, and data from the United States suggested that 56 percent of women were size 14 or larger. That's when Anita decided to develop her own line of active wear for plus-size women. This was the birth of Not So Skinny Bitch, and Anita became Chief Executive Bitch (CEB) of her company. She described her target market: "A Not So Skinny Bitch woman is a successful businesswoman or mature woman, retired or approaching retirement. She wants what every woman wants—to look as good as the other ladies on the golf course, tennis court, or just walking down the street. She wants athletic fashion that makes her look and feel fabulous. She wants Not So Skinny Bitch!"

The initial products offered by Not So Skinny Bitch included the Foxy Lady shirt ($75) and the Polo with a Twist polo ($85). All products were manufactured in Canada, using the highest-quality materials. Over 600 units were sold to 33 golf clubs in Ontario during the 2013 season. Golf clubs received a 50 percent resale discount. In August 2013, the Squeeze Me skort ($110) was added to the product mix. A skort is basically a skirt with a pair of shorts underneath. They are popular among women athletes as they provide the freedom of shorts with the more attractive appearance of a skirt. Fifteen skorts were sold in the first month after its introduction. For the 2014 season, Anita added more colours and sizes and conducted a "crowd funding" campaign to launch another new product, the Squeeze Me capris ($125).

Not So Skinny Bitch had a professionally designed website: **www.notsoskinnybitch.com**. In its first month, the website received 3,000 unique visitors. A Google search for "women's large size golf clothing" or "golf wear" brought up the website second on the list; adding "Canada" to the search term brought the website to the top of the list. Visitors to the website were also encouraged to follow Not So Skinny Bitch on Facebook, where it had 81 likes at the end of the 2013 golf season, 76 followers on Twitter, and 564 connections on LinkedIn. Largely as a result of the website, the company received 25 online orders during the 2013 golf season. Visitors to the website could also find a list of retail locations where they could find the clothing, sizing instructions, and instructions concerning proper clothing care. The website also included news releases and reprints of a number of newspaper and magazine articles, including articles that appeared in *Inside Golf Magazine* and *PRO GOLF*.

For the first year of operations, Anita was the company's only salesperson. She made dozens of trips to golf clubs within a day's drive of her home and called by telephone the 300 golf clubs in her database, mostly in Ontario. In November 2013, Anita attended her first trade show, the Ontario PGA Golf Industry Expo. She failed to get a single order at the show, but she was assured that her expectations were too high because orders were seldom placed at this show. She did, however, identify a number of prospects that she was confident she could convert to customers for the 2014 golf season. She also met a manufacturers' agent while there. He suggested that a 10 percent commission was quite standard in the industry, and he would be happy to consider adding Not So Skinny Bitch to his mix of products, if Anita was interested. At the time, after considering what his commission would do to her already low gross margins, Anita didn't give his offer much thought. She continued to expand her database of prospects to include golf clubs across Canada, and by the end of December 2013, she received her first orders from golf clubs in Prince Edward Island, Manitoba, Saskatchewan, Alberta, and British Columbia. She even received a large order from one of Canada's top spas northeast of Toronto and from a golf club in Australia. She was gearing up for a blitz campaign to get orders from across Canada, and in particular from past customers and new prospects that she identified in Ontario. She had to place an order with the manufacturer by early February to ensure delivery for the start of the 2014 golf season.

As she sat at home making dozens of daily phone calls, Anita started to reconsider the option of hiring one or more manufacturers' agents. Agents would provide the needed face-to-face representation at all the golf courses, where they could also check inventory of Not So Skinny Bitch clothing, hopefully convincing pro shop managers to fill holes in their selections. Manufacturers' agents also had strong relationships with many pro shop managers and were often welcomed because they sold several noncompeting lines of products that were popular with golfers. Hiring agents would also allow her to expand quickly across Canada with little risk, and this would free her to focus on other aspects of the business. The more she thought about it, the more attractive this option appeared. But she wondered what, if any, effect this might have on her online business. She also began to have some thoughts about the brand name of her clothing. She was starting to get lots of business, but some of the club managers, although they did not openly say so, seemed uncomfortable with the Not So Skinny Bitch brand name. Regardless of whether she changed her go-to-market strategy to include one or more manufacturers' agents, if she were to make a name change, it was critical that it be done before she placed her February order.

Questions for Critical Thinking

1. What factors should Anita consider when deciding whether to add manufacturers' agents to her distribution strategy?
2. What are the pros and cons of Anita selling her clothing online, or through golf club pro shops? Should she continue to use both channels? Explain.
3. List the places where there is potential for horizontal and vertical conflict in Anita's current, and possible future, distribution channel. Explain what factors could contribute to this conflict.
4. What alternatives does Anita have regarding the brand name of her clothing? What would you do?

Sources: Company website, **www.notsoskinnybitch.com**, accessed March 10, 2014; Personal interviews and correspondence with Anita Skinner, December 2013–March 2014.

CASE 15.2

Selling Food Equipment Solutions

TFI Food Equipment Solutions (TFI) is a Canadian industrial distributor that regularly exceeds $20 million in sales revenue—sometimes exceeding this by a considerable amount when several large sales are made during a particularly good year. Sales come mainly from two major product lines—Taylor and Henny Penny. These manufacturers produce equipment used in food service operations in institutions, stores, and restaurants and account for nearly 90 percent of TFI sales. The two product lines complement each other very well. Taylor is focused on ice cream and beverage equipment. Henny Penny produces fryers, rotisseries, blast chillers/freezers, heated food display units, etc.

To service its customers, TFI employs two types of salespeople. Nine salespeople service the single-outlet market. Single-outlet customers include many smaller, independent convenience, variety, and grocery stores. Salespeople each have a protected territory that is part of the five provinces where TFI has been appointed to represent Taylor and Henny Penny— Ontario and the four Atlantic provinces (New Brunswick, Nova Scotia, Prince Edward Island, and Newfoundland and Labrador). The busiest period for sales to single-outlet customers is just prior to the summer, when demand for ice cream and beverages peaks. These salespeople get company vehicles, and their out-of-pocket expenses are reimbursed by TFI. They are not paid a salary but earn commissions of 12 to 18 percent of sales revenue, depending on what is sold and the final price that they negotiate for each sale. Salespeople are expected to sell $400,000 (usually between 35 and 50 sales) of equipment annually, although some sell considerably more.

TFI also employs three national account salespeople. Judi Saliba and Vico Singh sell to accounts such as Tim Hortons, Burger King, Esso, Harvey's, KFC, Mac's Convenience Stores, McDonald's, Milestone's Grill & Bar, Wendy's, and other large multi-outlet businesses. Bill Moyer specializes in servicing the supermarket chains: Loblaw, Sobeys, and Walmart, among others. Because the selling tasks are different—relationship management and providing service are even more important—these salespeople receive a high salary component, ranging between $50,000 and $70,000, and a smaller commission (1 to 4 percent) since the sales revenue from these accounts is so much greater. These accounts contribute approximately 43 percent of total company sales revenue, while the single-outlet customers contribute approximately 31 percent. The balance of sales revenue comes from parts and service sales.

Alex Pettes, president and co-owner of TFI, manages the selling function; that is, he fills the role as sales manager. Alex is highly motivated and his infectious enthusiasm has helped create a winning sales team at TFI. Over the last decade, Alex has developed his unique persona: Commander Alex Pettes, Sales Fighter Pilot Squadron Leader of the USS TFI. He begins each sales meeting—and the presentations he makes to salespeople and sales managers from other companies—as Commander Pettes.

Alex likes to talk about how he sees salespeople as "fighter pilots." He has developed a four-level pyramid to illustrate the similarities he sees between them. At the base, for a foundation, Alex sees good salespeople and fighter pilots as being calm and confident, yet slightly cocky. This is not arrogance, but rather the calm, controlled confidence of the well-trained and competent professional. At level two, Alex says that good salespeople and fighter pilots know their equipment, environment, competition, and mission. Neither simply fly around hoping to find opportunities; they plan for achievement. At the third level, Alex sees good salespeople and fighter pilots as "ever learning, ever improving." He recognizes the need of both to continue the learning process long after their formal education, and he likes to quote a favourite expression of McDonald's founder Ray Kroc: "Green and growing or ripe and rotting." Finally, at the top level, Alex sees both good salespeople and fighter pilots as having a whatever-it-takes winning attitude.

His personal philosophy informs how he sees and manages his salespeople. He believes that the responsibility for poor sales performance rests solely with the sales manager. He also believes that you cannot motivate other people, but that the sales manager must create an environment where salespeople can motivate themselves. Alex says, to create this environment, sales managers must provide three things: leadership, coaching, and training.

- *Leadership.* Sales managers must lead from the front, lead by example. They need to be "servant leaders," and they must remove barriers and obstacles that prevent salespeople from achieving their goals.
- *Coaching.* All the best performers—athletes, singers, actors, and even businesspeople—have a coach. It is a one-on-one, planned process of assistance, designed to help another person achieve their goals. Great sales managers are great coaches.
- *Training.* Sales managers must ensure that salespeople receive whatever product or sales training they need to succeed.

To help keep himself motivated and provide personal direction, Alex has developed his personal mission statement, which he recites three times each day:

I AM the Commander. I AM the Leader at the Front.

I AM the most positive, enthusiastic, vibrant person, who loves God and his family and continually contributes in the service to others.

I AM having everything in life I want as I help and serve enough other people get what they want.

The key to selling at TFI is to show customers how they can increase their business and make a profit; that is, TFI, and the TFI salespeople, succeed by helping their customers succeed.

Questions for Critical Thinking

1. Why does TFI employ two different types of salespeople?
2. What are the implications of having two different types of salespeople for sales management? Explain.
3. Do you agree with Alex Pettes that the responsibility for poor sales performance rests solely with the sales manager? Why or why not?

Sources: Interviews with Alex Pettes, president, TFI Food Equipment Solutions, 2007–2014; Alex Pettes, *From the Flight Deck* (Bloomington, IN: iUniverse, 2010).

chapter 16

Pricing Concepts and Strategies

CHAPTER OBJECTIVES

1. Identify the major categories of pricing objectives.

2. Explain the methods of determining prices.

3. Compare the alternative pricing strategies and explain when each strategy is most appropriate.

4. Describe how prices are quoted.

5. Identify the various pricing policy decisions that marketers must make.

6. List and explain a number of special issues in pricing.

7. Outline the legal constraints on pricing.

H. F. (Herb) MacKenzie

DOLLARAMA: FROM A HUMBLE BEGINNING TO DOMINANCE OF THE DOLLAR STORE INDUSTRY

Dollarama started with a single store in Matane, Quebec, and now spans Canada with 874 retail locations. It is approximately five times the combined size of the next four dollar store chains: Dollar Tree Canada has 185 locations, Dollar Store with More has 121 locations, Great Canadian has 93 locations, and Buck or Two has 48 locations. Sales in 2014 exceeded $2 billion. And Dollarama is planning another 400 locations for Canada in the next few years, along with further international expansion. It currently has 15 stores in El Salvador and is evaluating Colombia, Costa Rica, and Peru.

The keys to success in retailing involve achieving increased revenue or decreasing cost, or both. Dollarama has proven to be proficient at both, while maintaining its target 36 to 37 percent gross margin. It has been increasing sales through superior locations, expanded product assortments, and an increasing number of value price points. Dollarama stores are often found near Walmart locations. This generates consumer traffic but also helps attract the same customers that shop at Walmart stores. Dollarama stores have grown to an average size of nearly 10,000 square feet, providing space for merchandising products in many important consumer goods categories, including stationery and greeting cards, kitchenware, cleaning supplies, health and beauty aids, office and school supplies, toys and pet supplies, snacks and novelties, and much more. Increasing the number of price points on its products has allowed Dollarama to expand its product assortment to include an increasing number of popular consumer products, while improving product quality of many goods. Originally, there was a single price point: $1.00. In 2009, Dollarama added price points of $1.25, $1.50, and $2.00. In 2012, the range was expanded to include $2.50 and $3.00. Today, approximately 60 percent of sales come from products priced over $1.00.

Dollarama has been able to better manage its costs than many retailers. Its size and scale of operations give it bargaining power with many of its suppliers, and it sources much of its inventory directly from many low-cost foreign suppliers. Dollarama spends very little for advertising and promotion due to its strong brand name, its high-traffic locations, and its everyday fixed price points. It doesn't have sales or markdowns to advertise. The company also saves costs by accepting only cash or PIN-based debit cards, avoiding charges it would otherwise pay to credit card companies. To help manage logistics efficiently, Dollarama has been able to implement the cross-docking strategy first introduced by Walmart. With cross-docking, inventory comes to the distribution centre, is unloaded and crosses the dock floor, and is directly loaded for shipment to retail locations. As a result, inventory levels, and their costs, are minimized. All these cost savings—combined with its no-frills, self-service format—helps Dollarama keep its prices low for its many loyal customers.[1]

connecting with customers

Once favoured by a small number of low-income consumers, dollar store retailers—and Dollarama in particular—now attract shoppers from all income strata. While many competitors offer a "treasure hunt" shopping experience where product assortment changes frequently, Dollarama customers are assured of a consistent product selection—including both national-brand and private-label brand products—that meets everyday household needs. As a result, Dollarama has become the fourth most frequented destination for grocery shoppers in Canada. And Dollarama is positioned to take advantage of growth potential in the Canadian marketplace. The top five Canadian dollar store retailers have one location for every 27,000 people; the top five in the United States have a location for every 13,000 people.

Chapter Overview

One of the first questions customers ask is "How much does it cost?" Marketers understand the critical role that price plays in the customer's decision-making process. For products as varied as lipstick and business consulting services, marketers must develop strategies that price products to achieve their firms' objectives.

As a starting point for examining pricing strategies, consider the meaning of the term *price*. A price is the exchange value of a good or service—in other words, whatever that product can be exchanged for in the marketplace. Today, that usually denotes money required to purchase a product.

Prices are both difficult to set and dynamic; they shift in response to a number of variables. Higher prices may convey the image of quality or even prestige; lower prices may connote value or, sometimes, poor quality. Setting prices is neither a one-time decision nor a standard routine. Some companies change prices once a year or less frequently; others change prices monthly or more frequently.

Companies translate pricing objectives into pricing decisions, considering costs, supply and demand, competition, channel needs, and the law. This chapter introduces the concept of price and its role in the economic system and marketing strategy.

It discusses the process of determining a profitable but justifiable (or fair) price. It examines various pricing strategies and price structures, such as reductions from list prices and geographical considerations. It then looks at the primary pricing policies, including psychological pricing, price flexibility, product-line pricing, and promotional pricing, as well as price–quality relationships. Competitive and negotiated prices are discussed, as is the transfer pricing dilemma. Finally, the chapter concludes by describing important factors in pricing goods and services for online and global markets, as well as legal considerations that affect pricing decisions. ◆◆◆

price Exchange value of a good or service.

① **Identify the major categories of pricing objectives.**

PRICING OBJECTIVES AND THE MARKETING MIX

The extent to which any or all of the factors of production—natural resources, capital, human resources, and entrepreneurship—are employed depends on the prices those factors command. A firm's prices and the resulting purchases by its customers determine the company's revenue, influencing the profits it earns. Overall organizational objectives and more specific marketing objectives guide the development of pricing objectives, which in turn lead to the development and implementation of more specific pricing policies and procedures.

A firm might, for instance, set a major overall goal of becoming the dominant producer in its domestic market. It might then develop a marketing objective of achieving maximum sales penetration in each region, followed by a related pricing objective of setting prices at levels that maximize sales. These objectives might lead to the adoption of a low-price policy implemented by offering substantial price discounts to channel members.

Price affects and is affected by the other elements of the marketing mix. Product decisions, promotional plans, and distribution choices all affect the price of a good or service. For example, products distributed through complex channels involving several intermediaries must be priced high enough to cover the markups needed to compensate wholesalers and retailers for services they provide. Basic so-called *fighting brands* are intended to capture market share from higher-priced, options-laden competitors by offering relatively low prices to entice customers to give up some options in return for a cost savings.

Pricing objectives vary from firm to firm, and they can be classified into four major groups: (1) profitability objectives, (2) volume objectives, (3) meeting competition objectives, and (4) prestige objectives. Not-for-profit organizations, as well, must consider objectives of one kind or another when developing pricing strategies. Table 16.1 outlines the pricing objectives marketers rely on to meet their overall goals.

PROFITABILITY OBJECTIVES

Marketers at for-profit firms must set prices with profits in mind. Even not-for-profit organizations realize the importance of setting prices high enough to cover expenses and provide a

table 16.1 **Pricing Objectives**

OBJECTIVE	PURPOSE	EXAMPLE
Profitability objectives	Profit maximization Target return	Samsung's initially high price for the Blu-ray disc player
Volume objectives	Sales maximization Market share	Comwave's home phone plan: six months and all features free, then Canada-wide unlimited calling for one low monthly fee
Meeting competition objectives	Value pricing	Walmart's lower prices on private house brands
Prestige objectives	Lifestyle Image	High-priced luxury autos such as Lexus and stereo equipment by Bose
Not-for-profit objectives	Profit maximization Cost recovery Market incentives Market suppression	Reduced or zero tolls for high-occupancy vehicles to encourage carpooling

financial cushion to cover unforeseen needs and expenses. As the Russian proverb says, "There are two fools in every market: one asks too little; one asks too much." For consumers to pay prices that are either above or below what they consider to be the going rate, they must be convinced they are receiving fair value for their money. The "Marketing and the SME" feature describes how one consultant manages the careful balance between charging too much and charging too little.

Economic theory is based on two major assumptions. It assumes, first, that firms will behave rationally and, second, that this rational behaviour will result in an effort to maximize gains and minimize losses. Some marketers estimate profits by looking at historical sales data; others use elaborate calculations based on predicted future sales. It has been said that setting prices is an art, not a

MARKETING AND THE SME

If You Were for Sale, What Would You Charge?

WHAT are you worth? Most people don't have to seriously consider this, but if you are a consultant, and time is money, you must decide exactly how you will charge for your time.

When Laura Ricciuto was doing her MBA, she was hired by her university's MBA business consulting group and was involved in a number of marketing-related consulting projects. Pricing was not really an issue as clients paid $250 per day for consulting services, and only the time required to complete a consulting project had to be estimated. But when Laura graduated, she decided to start her own consultancy: Kaizen Marketing & Creative Design House. Under Laura's guidance, the company has evolved from projects focused on market research, business planning, and strategy development to include a number of additional marketing-related services focused more on tactical issues: brand development, graphic design, campaign advertisements, Web development, and more. When it comes to setting a price for her services, Laura says she uses one of three methods: project-based, value-based, or hourly-based pricing.

The following are some of the things that professionals such as Laura must consider when determining their worth and what they will charge:

- *Experience and expertise*: As consultants gain experience in a particular area, they become more knowledgeable and, hence, more valuable to their clients. They can charge a higher price.
- *Exclusivity*: Specialists are usually worth more than generalists. When consultants specialize in an area so that there are fewer qualified competitors, they can charge a higher price.
- *Target market*: Some customers are more price-sensitive than others. Larger corporations tend to be less price-sensitive than small business clients. Of course, a good portfolio of customers, large and small, would be a valuable asset for most consultants, and this usually requires some pricing flexibility.

Sources: Laura Ricciuto, personal correspondence, May 31, 2014; Kaizen Marketing & Creative Design House website, **http://kaizenmarketing.ca/about**, accessed June 1, 2014.

High fuel costs and increased price competition have contributed to some airlines charging additional fees for excess or overweight baggage, or for special seating requests.

science. The talent lies in a marketer's ability to strike a balance between desired profits and the customer's perception of a product's value.

Marketers should evaluate and adjust prices continually to accommodate changes in the environment. The technological environment, for example, forces Internet marketers to respond quickly to competitors' pricing strategies. Search capabilities performed by shopping bots (described later in this chapter) allow customers to compare prices locally, nationally, and globally in a matter of seconds.

Intense price competition, sometimes conducted even when it means forgoing profits altogether or reducing services, often results when rivals battle for leadership positions in new-product categories. For some years, passenger airlines cut costs in order to compete on pricing. Computer technology allowed them to automate many services and put passengers in charge of other services, such as making reservations online and checking in at electronic kiosks. As a result, passengers frequently find that amenities, such as in-flight meals, pillows and blankets, and audio headsets, all cost extra. Recently, some airlines have increased the number of seats reserved for frequent fliers—or passengers who are willing to pay extra for better seating options. For families, costs could add up to hundreds of dollars more so that parents and children can sit together.[2]

Profits are a function of revenue and expenses:

$$\text{Profits} = \text{Revenue} - \text{Expenses}$$

Revenue is determined by the product's selling price and number of units sold:

$$\text{Total Revenue} = \text{Price} \times \text{Quantity Sold}$$

Therefore, a profit-maximizing price rises to the point at which further increases will cause disproportionate decreases in the number of units sold. A 10 percent price increase that results in only an 8 percent cut in volume will add to the firm's revenue. However, a 10 percent price hike that results in an 11 percent sales decline will reduce revenue.

marginal analysis
Method of analyzing the relationship among costs, sales price, and increased sales volume.

Economists refer to this approach as **marginal analysis**. They identify **profit maximization** as the point at which the addition to total revenue is just balanced by the increase in total cost. Marketers must resolve a basic problem of how to achieve this delicate balance when they set prices. Relatively few firms actually hit this elusive target. A significantly larger number prefer to direct their effort toward more realistic goals.

profit maximization
Point at which the additional revenue gained by increasing the price of a product equals the increase in total costs.

Consequently, marketers commonly set **target-return objectives**—short-run or long-run goals usually stated as percentages of sales or investment. The practice has become particularly popular among large firms in which other pressures interfere with profit-maximization objectives. In addition to resolving pricing questions, target-return objectives offer several benefits for marketers. For example, these objectives serve as tools for evaluating performance; they also satisfy desires to generate "fair" profits as judged by management, shareholders, and the public.

target-return objectives Short-run or long-run pricing objectives of achieving a specified return on either sales or investment.

VOLUME OBJECTIVES

Some economists and business executives argue that pricing behaviour actually seeks to maximize sales within a given profit constraint. In other words, they set a minimum acceptable profit level and then seek to maximize sales (subject to this profit constraint) in the belief that the increased sales are more important in the long-run competitive picture than immediate high profits. As a result, companies should continue to expand sales as long as their total profits do not drop below the minimum return acceptable to management.

Sales maximization can also result from nonprice factors such as service and quality. A greenhouse, for example, may charge higher prices for some plants. One company president explained the importance of knowing what customers value. His company tailors its price according to the segment of the market it wants to reach. For example, in today's economy, experienced gardeners value longer life spans in the plants they buy and therefore are willing to pay more for them.[3]

Another volume-related pricing objective is the **market-share objective**—the goal of controlling a specified minimum share of the market for a firm's good or service. Procter & Gamble experienced poor sales growth in some markets when it increased prices on some products to cover its costs. Recently, the company announced it would roll back those price increases in the hope of winning back some of the market share it lost.[4]

market-share objective
Volume-related pricing objective in which the goal is to achieve control of a portion of the market for a firm's good or service.

The PIMS Studies

Market-share objectives may prove critical to the achievement of other organizational objectives. High sales, for example, often mean more profits. The **Profit Impact of Market Strategies (PIMS) project**, an extensive study conducted by the Marketing Science Institute, analyzed more than 2,000 firms and revealed that two of the most important factors influencing profitability were product quality and market share. Many companies have introduced loyalty programs to retain customers and protect their market share. However, a recent Gallup survey indicated that only a small percentage of a company's customer base actively participates in loyalty programs—and that customers who are fully involved with a loyalty program tend to spend more money. One managing consultant at Gallup says the way companies can create more value is by fully engaging customers by building an emotional connection with their brand or product.[5]

Profit Impact of Market Strategies (PIMS) project Research that discovered a strong positive relationship between a firm's market share and product quality and its return on investment.

The relationship between market share and profitability is evident in PIMS data that reveal an average 32 percent return on investment (ROI) for firms with market shares above 40 percent. In contrast, average ROI decreases to 24 percent for firms whose market shares are between 20 and 40 percent. Firms with a minor market share (less than 10 percent) generate average pre-tax investment returns of under 10 percent.[6]

The relationship also applies to a firm's individual brands. PIMS researchers compared the top four brands in each market segment they studied. Their data revealed that the leading brand typically generates after-tax ROI of 18 percent, considerably higher than the second-ranked brand. Weaker brands, on average, fail to earn adequate returns.

Marketers have developed an underlying explanation of the positive relationship between profitability and market share. Firms with large shares accumulate greater operating experience and lower overall costs relative to competitors with smaller market shares. Accordingly, effective segmentation strategies might focus on obtaining larger shares of smaller markets and on avoiding smaller shares of larger ones. A firm might achieve higher financial returns by becoming a major competitor in several smaller market segments than by remaining a relatively minor player in a larger market.

MEETING COMPETITION OBJECTIVES

A third set of pricing objectives seeks simply to meet competitors' prices. In many lines of business, firms set their own prices to match those of established industry price leaders. Price is a pivotal factor in the ongoing competition between long-distance telephone services and wireless carriers. In addition to unlimited calls within Canada for $2.99 a month and within North America for $7.99 a month, Skype, the Internet calling company owned by Microsoft, allows unlimited calls to landline phones in over 60 countries around the world for $13.99 a month. The countries include most of Europe, as well as Australia, Brazil, China, and Korea.[7]

Canadian Tire regularly offers product discounts in its retail stores across Canada.

H. F. (Herb) MacKenzie

Dollarama has recently added two new price points: $2.50 and $3.00, as it continues to use a value-pricing strategy to sell many popular items at prices often far below its competition.

Pricing objectives tied directly to meeting prices charged by major competitors de-emphasize the price element of the marketing mix and focus more strongly on nonprice variables. Pricing is a highly visible component of a firm's marketing mix and an easy and effective tool for obtaining a differential advantage over competitors. It is, however, a tool that other firms can easily duplicate through price reductions of their own. Because price changes directly affect overall profitability in an industry, many firms attempt to promote stable prices by meeting competitors' prices and competing for market share by focusing on product strategies, promotional decisions, and distribution—the nonprice elements of the marketing mix.

Value Pricing

When discounts become normal elements of a competitive marketplace, other marketing mix elements gain importance in purchase decisions. In such instances, overall product value, not just price, determines product choice. In recent years, a new strategy—**value pricing**—has emerged that emphasizes the benefits a product provides in comparison to the price and quality levels of competing offerings. This strategy typically works best for relatively low-priced goods and services. Loblaw Companies' discount banners, such as no frills, aim to be the lowest-price food stores in their markets.[8] Customers get value prices on many items throughout their stores.

Value-priced products generally cost less than premium brands, but marketers point out that value does not necessarily mean *inexpensive*. The challenge for those who compete on value is to convince customers that low-priced brands offer quality comparable to that of a higher-priced product. An increasing number of alternative products and private-label brands has resulted in a more competitive marketplace in recent years. Palazzi Bros. Carpet and Tile, with three designer showrooms in Ontario, recently celebrated its 50th anniversary.

value pricing Pricing strategy emphasizing benefits derived from a product in comparison to the price and quality levels of competing offerings.

Brothers Marco and Paul attribute their success to quality workmanship and materials. They negotiate competitive prices with their suppliers, allowing their customers to benefit from value pricing and superior products. Even customers with very limited budgets can have breathtaking floors for reasonable cost.[9]

Value pricing is perhaps best seen in the personal computer industry. In the past few years, PC prices have collapsed, but sales have still declined. The economy, increased competition from tablets, and floods in Thailand, where some components are made, were factors. Worldwide PC sales were expected to rise as economic recovery strengthened, but prices for hard drives and memory have recently increased. Apple's Macintosh computers and iPad tablets use a different type of memory, for which prices are falling, so Apple may have a competitive edge.[10]

PRESTIGE OBJECTIVES

The final category of pricing objectives, unrelated to either profitability or sales volume, is prestige objectives. Prestige pricing establishes a relatively high price to develop and maintain an image of quality and exclusiveness that appeals to status-conscious consumers. Such objectives reflect marketers' recognition of the role of price in creating an overall image of the firm and its product offerings.

Prestige objectives affect the price tags of such products as Tilley hats, Lululemon Athletica sports clothing, and Tag Heuer watches. When a perfume marketer sets a price of $400 or more

Marketoid

A 750-millilitre bottle of Penfolds Limited Edition 2004 Block 42 Kalimna Cabernet Sauvignon Ampoule recently sold at the Liquor Control Board of Ontario's Summerhill outlet in Toronto for $168,000.

per ounce, this choice reflects an emphasis on image far more than the cost of ingredients. Analyses have shown that ingredients account for less than 5 percent of a perfume's cost. Thus advertisements for Clive Christian's No. 1 that promote the fragrance as the "world's most expensive perfume" use price to promote product prestige.

In the business world, private jet ownership imparts an image of prestige, power, and high price tags—too high for most business travellers to consider. Recognizing that cost is the primary factor that makes jet ownership prohibitive, companies such as Edmonton-based Aurora Jet Partners and Calgary-based AirSprint have created an alternative: fractional ownership. Corporate boards of directors pressed to cut costs in a weak economy are much more willing to pay for a share in a jet than to purchase a whole new aircraft.[11]

PRICING OBJECTIVES OF NOT-FOR-PROFIT ORGANIZATIONS

Pricing is also a key element of the marketing mix for not-for-profit organizations. Pricing strategy can help these groups achieve a variety of organizational goals:

1. *Profit maximization.* While not-for-profit organizations by definition do not cite profitability as a primary goal, there are numerous instances in which they do try to maximize their returns on single events or a series of events. A $1,000-a-plate political fund-raiser is a classic example.

2. *Cost recovery.* Some not-for-profit organizations attempt to recover only the actual cost of operating the unit. Mass transit and toll roads and bridges are common examples. The amount of recovered costs is often dictated by tradition, competition, or public opinion.

3. *Market incentives.* Other not-for-profit groups follow a lower-than-average pricing policy or offer a free service to encourage increased usage of the good or service. OC Transpo provides public transit services in Ottawa. It has offered free bus service after 9:00 p.m. on Canada Day to encourage use during a period when there would be street closures and when downtown traffic would be congested.

4. *Market suppression.* Price can also discourage consumption. High prices help to accomplish social objectives independent of the costs of providing goods or services. Illustrations are tobacco and alcohol taxes (the so-called sin taxes), parking fines, tolls, and gasoline excise taxes.

H. F. (Herb) MacKenzie

Some prestige products stay within families for many generations. This Rolex watch is now being worn by a third-generation owner.

assessment check 1a ✓

1.1 What are target-return objectives?

1.2 What is value pricing?

1.3 How do prestige objectives affect a seller's pricing strategy?

assessment check 1b ✓

1.4 What goals does pricing strategy help a not-for-profit organization achieve?

METHODS FOR DETERMINING PRICES

② Explain the methods of determining prices.

Marketers determine prices in two basic ways—by applying the theoretical concepts of supply and demand and by completing cost-oriented analyses. During the first part of the 20th century, most discussions of price determination emphasized the classical concepts of supply and demand. During the last half of the century, however, the emphasis began to shift to a cost-oriented approach. Hindsight reveals certain flaws in both concepts.

H. F. (Herb) MacKenzie

Manufacturers have downsized such products as chocolate bars, peanut butter, paper towels, dish detergent, and orange juice to reduce costs. However, price reductions seldom follow.

customary prices
Traditional prices that customers expect to pay for certain goods and services.

demand Schedule of the amounts of a firm's product that consumers will purchase at different prices during a specified time period.

supply Schedule of the amounts of a good or service that firms will offer for sale at different prices during a specified time period.

pure competition
Market structure characterized by homogeneous products in which there are so many buyers and sellers that none has a significant influence on price.

monopolistic competition Market structure involving a heterogeneous product and product differentiation among competing suppliers, allowing the marketer some degree of control over prices.

oligopoly Market structure in which relatively few sellers compete and where high start-up costs form barriers to keep out new competitors.

Treatments of this subject often overlook another concept of price determination—one based on the impact of custom and tradition. **Customary prices** are retail prices that consumers expect as a result of tradition and social habit. Candy makers have attempted to maintain traditional price levels by greatly reducing overall product size. Similar practices have prevailed in the marketing of soft drinks as bottlers attempt to balance consumer expectations of customary prices with the realities of rising costs. Sometimes customary prices hide a real price increase, however, when the quantity of the product has been imperceptibly reduced. Kraft Foods' macaroni and cheese comes with two different noodle shapes, spiral and elbow. The spiral kind contains nearly 25 percent less pasta, but both come in the same size box and sell for the same price. The company says that the manufacturing process for spiral pasta is more complicated and that it manufactures more elbow pasta.[12]

The changing price of gasoline in Canada presents another example of supply and demand. When gas prices rise substantially, frustrated drivers begin demanding to know who, if anyone, is cashing in on the price spike. Higher gas prices have effects on other consumer costs as well. There are at least 57 different major uses of petroleum in addition to gasoline, in products as unlikely as cosmetics and chewing gum. The rising costs of raw materials and energy have caused many tire manufacturers to charge more for their tires. China mines almost 95 percent of rare earth metals, which are used in energy-efficient light bulbs and electric cars. The country has recently begun taking steps to reduce the high levels of pollution caused by the mining and processing of rare earths—steps that have driven up the price of these important metals.[13]

With fuel costs at record highs, hybrid cars are in greater demand than ever before, and some dealers have had months-long waiting lists even at premium prices. The recently unveiled Toyota Prius plug-in hybrid gives drivers the choice of running on electricity alone or hybrid without draining the battery. It can travel up to 22 kilometres in city driving, meaning that typical commuter ranges can be made without using gas.[14]

PRICE DETERMINATION IN ECONOMIC THEORY

Microeconomics suggests a way of determining prices that assumes a profit-maximization objective. This technique attempts to derive correct equilibrium prices in the marketplace by comparing supply and demand. It also requires more complete analysis than actual business firms typically conduct.

Demand refers to a schedule of the amounts of a firm's product that consumers will purchase at different prices during a specified time period. **Supply** refers to a schedule of the amounts of a good or service that will be offered for sale at different prices during a specified period. These schedules may vary for different types of market structures. Businesses operate and set prices in four types of market structures: pure competition, monopolistic competition, oligopoly, and monopoly.

Pure competition is a market structure with so many buyers and sellers that no single participant can significantly influence price. Pure competition presupposes other market conditions as well: homogeneous products and ease of entry for sellers due to low start-up costs. The agricultural sector exhibits many characteristics of a purely competitive market, making it the closest actual example. But the Canadian Organic Livestock Association (COLA) is now marketing certified organic beef across North America, attempting to differentiate a higher-quality product.

Monopolistic competition typifies most retailing and features large numbers of buyers and sellers. These diverse parties exchange heterogeneous, relatively well-differentiated products, giving marketers some control over prices.

Relatively few sellers compete in an **oligopoly**. Pricing decisions by each seller are likely to affect the market, but no single seller controls it. High start-up costs form significant barriers to entry for new competitors. Each firm's demand curve in an oligopolistic market displays a unique kink at the current market price. Because of the impact of a single competitor on total industry sales, competitors usually quickly match any attempt by one firm to generate additional sales by

table 16.2   *Distinguishing Features of the Four Market Structures*

		TYPE OF MARKETING STRUCTURE		
CHARACTERISTICS	PURE COMPETITION	MONOPOLISTIC COMPETITION	OLIGOPOLY	MONOPOLY
Number of competitors	Many	Few to many	Few	No direct competitors
Ease of entry into industry by new firms	Easy	Somewhat difficult	Difficult	Regulated by government
Similarity of goods or services offered by competing firms	Similar	Different	Can be either similar or different	No directly competing goods or services
Control over prices by individual firms	None	Some	Some	Considerable
Demand curves facing individual firms	Totally elastic	Can be either elastic or inelastic	Kinked; inelastic below kink; more elastic above	Can be either elastic or inelastic
Examples	Alberta beef farm	Best Buy stores	Air Canada	Liquor Control Board of Ontario

reducing prices. Price cutting in such industry structures is likely to reduce total industry revenues. Oligopolies operate in the petroleum refining, automobile, airline, banking, and tobacco industries.

A **monopoly** is a market structure in which only one seller of a product exists and for which there are no close substitutes. Legislation has nearly eliminated all but temporary monopolies, such as those created through patent protection. Regulated industries, such as utility companies, constitute another form of monopoly. The government allows regulated monopolies in markets in which competition would lead to an uneconomical duplication of services. In return for such a licence, government reserves the right to regulate the monopoly's rate of return.

The four types of market structures are compared in Table 16.2 on the following bases: number of competitors, ease of entry into the industry by new firms, similarity of competing products, degree of control over price by individual firms, and the elasticity or inelasticity of the demand curve facing the individual firm. Elasticity—the degree of consumer responsiveness to changes in price—is discussed in more detail in a later section.

Cost and Revenue Curves

Marketers must set a price for a product that generates sufficient revenue to cover the costs of producing and marketing it. A product's total cost is composed of total variable costs and total fixed costs. **Variable costs** change with the level of production (such as raw materials and labour costs), and **fixed costs** remain stable at any production level within a certain range (such as lease payments or insurance costs). **Average total costs** are calculated by dividing the sum of the variable and fixed costs by the number of units produced. Finally, **marginal cost** is the change in total cost that results from producing an additional unit of output.

The demand side of the pricing equation focuses on revenue curves. Average revenue is calculated by dividing total revenue by the quantity associated with these revenues. Average revenue is actually the demand curve facing the firm. Marginal revenue is the change in total revenue that results from selling an additional unit of output. Figure 16.1 shows the relationships of various cost and revenue measures; the firm maximizes its profits when marginal costs equal marginal revenues.

monopoly Market structure in which a single seller dominates trade in a good or service for which buyers can find no close substitutes.

variable costs Costs that change with the level of production (such as labour and raw materials costs).

fixed costs Costs that remain stable at any production level within a certain range (such as lease payments or insurance costs).

figure 16.1

Determining Price by Relating Marginal Revenue to Marginal Cost

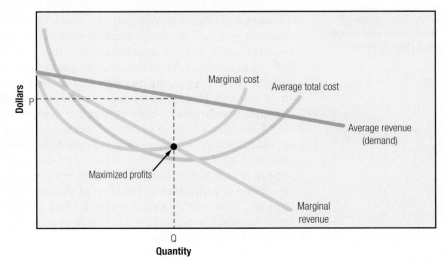

table 16.3 **Price Determination Using Marginal Analysis**

PRICE	NUMBER SOLD	TOTAL REVENUE	MARGINAL REVENUE	TOTAL COSTS	MARGINAL COSTS	PROFITS (TOTAL REVENUE MINUS TOTAL COSTS)
—	—	—	—	—	—	($50)
$34	1	$34	$34	$57	$7	(23)
32	2	64	30	62	5	2
30	3	90	26	66	4	24
28	4	112	22	69	3	43
26	5	130	18	73	4	57
24	6	144	14	78	5	66
22	7	154	10	84	6	70
20	8	160	6	91	7	69
18	9	162	2	100	9	62
16	10	160	(2)	110	11	50

average total costs
Costs calculated by dividing the sum of the variable and fixed costs by the number of units produced.

marginal cost Change in total cost that results from producing an additional unit of output.

Table 16.3 illustrates why the intersection of the marginal cost and marginal revenue curves is the logical point at which to maximize revenue for the organization. Although the firm can earn a profit at several different prices, the price at which it earns maximum profits is $22. At a price of $24, $66 in profits are earned—$4 less than the $70 profit at the $22 price. If a price of $20 is set to attract additional sales, the marginal costs of the extra sales ($7) are greater than the marginal revenues received ($6), and total profits decline.

assessment check 2a ✓

2.1 What are the two basic ways in which marketers determine prices?

2.2 What are the four types of market structures?

2.3 Identify the two types of costs that make up a product's total cost.

THE CONCEPT OF ELASTICITY IN PRICING STRATEGY

Although the intersection of the marginal cost and marginal revenue curves determines the level of output, the impact of changes in price on sales varies greatly. To understand why it fluctuates, it is necessary to understand the concept of elasticity.

elasticity Measure of responsiveness of purchasers and suppliers to a change in price.

Elasticity is the measure of the responsiveness of purchasers and suppliers to price changes. The price elasticity of demand (or elasticity of demand) is the percentage change in the quantity of a good or service demanded divided by the percentage change in its price. A 10 percent increase in the price of eggs that results in a 5 percent decrease in the quantity of eggs demanded yields a price elasticity of demand for eggs of 0.5. The price elasticity of supply of a product is the percentage change in the quantity of a good or service supplied divided by the percentage change in its price. A 10 percent increase in the price of shampoo that results in a 25 percent increase in the quantity supplied yields a price elasticity of supply for shampoo of 2.5.

Consider a case in which a 1 percent change in price causes more than a 1 percent change in the quantity supplied or demanded. Numerically, that means an elasticity measurement greater than 1.0. When the elasticity of demand or supply is greater than 1.0, that demand or supply is said to be elastic. If a 1 percent change in price results in less than a 1 percent change in quantity, a product's elasticity of demand or supply will be less than 1.0. In that case, the demand or supply is called inelastic. For example, the demand for cigarettes is relatively inelastic; research studies have shown that a 10 percent increase in cigarette prices results in only a 4 percent sales decline.

In some countries whose economies are in shambles, price levels bear little resemblance to the laws of elasticity or supply and demand. Prices in Zimbabwe are rising at unheard-of rates, the result of hyperinflation that rose to more than 7,600 percent in a *month*—estimated to be as high as 12.5 million percent a year. More recently, however, changes in the country's monetary policies, including the abandonment of its local currency, began to bring prices down and it appeared that inflation in Zimbabwe may continue to drop.[15]

Determinants of Elasticity

Why is the elasticity of supply or demand high for some products and low for others? What determines demand elasticity? One major factor influencing the elasticity of demand is the availability of substitutes or complements. If consumers can easily find close substitutes for a good or service, the product's demand tends to be elastic. A product's role as a complement to the use of another product also affects its degree of price elasticity. For example, the relatively inelastic demand for motor oil reflects its role as a complement to a more important product, gasoline. High prices of gasoline, in turn, are fuelling the search for alternative fuels.[16]

A 1 percent increase in the price of cigarettes results in a decrease of approximately 0.4 percent in demand; that is, cigarettes are price inelastic. Price elasticity will vary among different consumer segments.

As increasing numbers of buyers and sellers complete their business transactions online, the elasticity of a product's demand is drastically affected. Take major discounters and other price-competitive box stores, for example. Small businesses and individual do-it-yourselfers shop at Canadian Tire for tools, such as wheelbarrows; parents look for birthday gifts at Walmart; and homeowners go to Future Shop for new refrigerators or stoves. Today, however, the Internet lets consumers contact many more providers directly, often giving them better selections and prices for their efforts with service sites such as Shopbot.ca and PriceGrabber.ca for consumer goods and electronics; Net-à-Porter.com for high-fashion clothing; and Travelocity.ca, Hotels.com, and Expedia.ca for travel bargains. The increased options available to shoppers combine to create a market characterized by demand elasticity.

Elasticity of demand also depends on whether a product is perceived as a necessity or a luxury. The Four Seasons chain of luxury hotels and resorts enjoys such a strong reputation for service, comfort, and exclusiveness that it has become a favourite among affluent individual travellers and business professionals. In other contexts, specialty shops such as Tim Hortons are considered necessities by some consumers today.

Elasticity also depends on the portion of a person's budget that he or she spends on a good or service. For example, people no longer really need matches; they can easily find good substitutes. Nonetheless, the demand for matches remains very inelastic because people spend so little on them that they hardly notice a price change. In contrast, the demand for housing or transportation is not totally inelastic, even though they are necessities, because both consume large parts of a consumer's budget.

Elasticity of demand also responds to consumers' time perspectives. Demand often shows less elasticity in the short run than in the long run. Consider the demand for home air conditioning. In the short run, people pay rising energy prices because they find it difficult to cut back on the quantities they use. Accustomed to living with specific temperature settings and dressing in certain ways, they prefer to pay more during a few months of the year than to explore other possibilities. Over the long term, though, they may consider insulating their homes and planting shade trees to reduce cooling costs.

Elasticity and Revenue

The elasticity of demand exerts an important influence on variations in total revenue as a result of changes in the price of a good or service. Assume, for example, that the Toronto Transit Commission (TTC) officials are considering alternative methods of raising more money for their budget. One possible method for increasing revenues would be to increase fares for commuters. But should the TTC raise or lower the price of a pass? The correct answer depends on the elasticity of demand for its services. A 10 percent decrease in fares should attract more riders, but unless it stimulates

Marketoid

Cigarettes are price inelastic: in a recent 10-year period in New Brunswick, cigarette prices increased by 113 percent; consumption fell by only 11 percent.

assessment check 2b ✓

2.4 What are the determinants of elasticity?

2.5 What is the usual relationship between elasticity and revenue?

more than a 10 percent increase in riders, total revenue will fall. A 10 percent increase in fares will bring in more money per rider, but if more than 10 percent of the riders stop using TTC services, total revenue will fall. A price cut will increase revenue only for a product with elastic demand, and a price increase will raise revenue only for a product with inelastic demand. TTC officials seemed to believe that the demand for its services is inelastic; they recently raised fares as they needed more money to cover operating costs.

PRACTICAL PROBLEMS OF PRICE THEORY

Marketers may thoroughly understand price theory concepts but still encounter difficulty applying them in practice. What practical limitations interfere with setting prices? First, many firms do not attempt to maximize profits. Economic analysis is subject to the same limitations as the assumptions on which it is based—for example, the proposition that all firms attempt to maximize profits. Second, it is difficult to estimate demand curves. Modern accounting procedures provide managers with a clear understanding of cost structures, so managers can readily comprehend the supply side of the pricing equation. But they find it difficult to estimate demand at various price levels. Demand curves must be based on marketing research estimates that may be less exact than cost figures. Although the demand element can be identified, it is often difficult to measure in real-world settings.

assessment check 2c ✓

2.6 List the three reasons why it is difficult to put price theory into practice.

PRICE DETERMINATION IN PRACTICE

cost-plus pricing
Practice of adding a percentage of specified dollar amount—or markup—to the base cost of a product to cover unassigned costs and to provide a profit.

The practical limitations inherent in price theory have forced practitioners to turn to other techniques. **Cost-plus pricing,** the most popular method, uses a base-cost figure per unit and adds a markup to cover unassigned costs and to provide a profit. The only real difference among the multitude of cost-plus techniques is the relative sophistication of the costing procedures employed. For example, a local apparel shop may set prices by adding a 45 percent markup to the invoice price charged by the supplier. The markup is expected to cover all other expenses and permit the owner to earn a reasonable return on the sale of clothes. Car dealerships often rely on a markup when they set their prices; see the "Career Readiness" feature for some tips on using pricing savvy when buying a car.

CAREER READINESS   **Getting the Best Price on Your Auto Purchase**

MAKING a big purchase such as a car is good practice for other major decisions you may make in your career. Here's how to get the most for your money.

- Don't fall in love with a car until you own it. It's a mistake to buy a car you can't afford just because you decide you have to have it.
- Do your homework before you visit a dealership. Research the safety, fuel economy, and reliability of the car or cars you're considering, and test-drive well ahead of purchasing.
- Know exactly what you can afford. Find the dealer's invoice price for the car online, and be prepared to visit more than one dealer to shop for the best price.
- Make an offer close to the invoice price, and let the dealer know you plan to shop around.

- Check out financing options on your own. Even if you decide on dealer financing, you'll want to be sure it's really cheaper than the rate at a bank or credit union.
- If you have a car to trade in, find out its true value at an auto-pricing website.
- If you can, pay cash. It reduces the dealer's administrative costs and the savings should pass on to you.

Sources: Miriam Caldwell, "How to Buy Your First Car," About.com, **http://moneyfor20s.about.com**, accessed June 11, 2012; "Car Buying Advice," Consumer Reports.org, **www.consumerreports.org**, accessed June 11, 2012; "Buying Your First Car? A Guide to Successfully Closing the Deal," NYE Automotive Group, **http://nyeauto.com**, accessed June 11, 2012; Phil M. Fowler, "How to Get the Best Price on a New Car," eHow, **www.ehow.com**, accessed June 11, 2012.

In contrast to this rather simple pricing mechanism, a large manufacturer may employ a complex pricing formula requiring computer calculations. However, this method merely adds a more complicated procedure to the simpler, traditional method for calculating costs. In the end, someone still must make a decision about the markup. The apparel shop and the large manufacturer may figure costs differently, but they are remarkably similar in completing the markup side of the equation.

Cost-plus pricing often works well for a business that keeps its costs low, allowing it to set its prices lower than those of competitors and still make a profit. Walmart keeps costs low by buying most of its inventory directly from manufacturers, using a supply chain that slashes inventory costs by quickly replenishing inventory as items are sold, and relying on wholesalers and other intermediaries only in special instances like localized items. This strategy has played a major role in the discounter becoming the world's largest retailer.

Alternative Pricing Procedures

The two most common cost-oriented pricing procedures are the full-cost method and the incremental-cost method. **Full-cost pricing** uses all relevant variable costs in setting a product's price. In addition, it allocates those fixed costs that cannot be directly attributed to the production of the specific item being priced. Under the full-cost method, if job order 515 in a printing plant amounts to 0.000127 percent of the plant's total output, then 0.000127 percent of the firm's overhead expenses are charged to that job. This approach allows the marketer to recover all costs plus the amount added as a profit margin.

full-cost pricing Pricing method that uses all relevant variable costs in setting a product's price and allocates those fixed costs not directly attributed to the production of the priced item.

The full-cost approach has two basic deficiencies. First, there is no consideration of competition or demand for the item. Perhaps no one wants to pay the price the firm has calculated. Second, any method for allocating overhead (fixed expenses) is arbitrary and may be unrealistic. In manufacturing, overhead allocations often are tied to direct labour hours. In retailing, the area of each profit centre is sometimes the factor used in computations. Regardless of the technique employed, it is difficult to show a cause–effect relationship between the allocated cost and most products.

One way to overcome the arbitrary allocation of fixed expenses is with **incremental-cost pricing**, which attempts to use only those costs directly attributable to a specific output in setting prices. Consider a very small-scale manufacturer with the following income statement:

incremental-cost pricing Pricing method that attempts to use only costs directly attributable to a specific output in setting prices.

Sales (10,000 units at $10)		$100,000
Expenses:		
Variable	$50,000	
Fixed	40,000	90,000
Net Profit		$10,000

Suppose the firm is offered a contract for an additional 5,000 units. Since the peak season is over, these items can be produced at the same average variable cost. Assume that the labour force would otherwise be working on maintenance projects. How low should the firm price its product to get the contract?

Under the full-cost approach, the lowest price would be $9 per unit. This figure is obtained by dividing the $90,000 in expenses by an output of 10,000 units. The incremental approach, on the other hand, could permit any price above $5, which would significantly increase the possibility of securing the additional contract. This price would be composed of the $5 variable cost associated with each unit of production plus some additional per-unit contribution to fixed expenses and overhead. With a $5.10 proposed price ($.10 over the variable cost), for example, the income statement now looks like this:

Sales (10,000 at $10; 5,000 at $5.10)		$125,500
Expenses:		
Variable	$75,000	
Fixed	40,000	115,000
Net Profit		$10,500

Profits thus increase under the incremental approach.

assessment check 2d

2.7 What is full-cost pricing?

2.8 What is incremental-cost pricing?

Admittedly, the illustration is based on two assumptions: (1) the ability to isolate markets such that selling at the lower price will not affect the price received in other markets, and (2) the absence of legal restrictions on the firm. The example, however, does illustrate that profits can sometimes be enhanced by using the incremental approach.

Break-Even Analysis

break-even analysis
Pricing technique used to determine the number of products that must be sold at a specified price to generate enough revenue to cover total cost.

Break-even analysis is a means of determining the number of goods or services that must be sold at a given price to generate sufficient revenue to cover total costs. Figure 16.2 graphically depicts this process. The total cost curve includes both fixed and variable segments, and total fixed cost is represented by a horizontal line. Average variable cost is assumed to be constant per unit as it was in the example for incremental pricing.

The break-even point is the point at which total revenue equals total cost. In the example in Figure 16.2, a selling price of $10 and an average variable cost of $5 result in a per-unit contribution to fixed cost of $5. The break-even point in units is found by using the following formula, where the per-unit contribution equals the product's price less the variable cost per unit:

$$\text{Break-Even Point (in units)} = \frac{\text{Total Fixed Cost}}{\text{Per-Unit Contribution to Fixed Cost}}$$

$$\text{Break-Even Point (in units)} = \frac{\$40,000}{\$5} = 8,000 \text{ units}$$

The break-even point in dollars is found with the following formula:

$$\text{Break-Even Point (in dollars)} = \frac{\text{Total Fixed Cost}}{1 - \text{Variable Cost per Unit Price}}$$

$$\text{Break-Even Point (in dollars)} = \frac{\$40,000}{1 - (\$5/\$10)}$$

$$= \frac{\$40,000}{0.5} = \$80,000$$

Sometimes break-even is reached by reducing costs. After declaring bankruptcy and being bailed out by the Canadian and U.S. governments, General Motors is once again the world's biggest auto manufacturer. It regained that status by reducing costs and shutting some factories.[17]

figure 16.2

Break-Even Chart

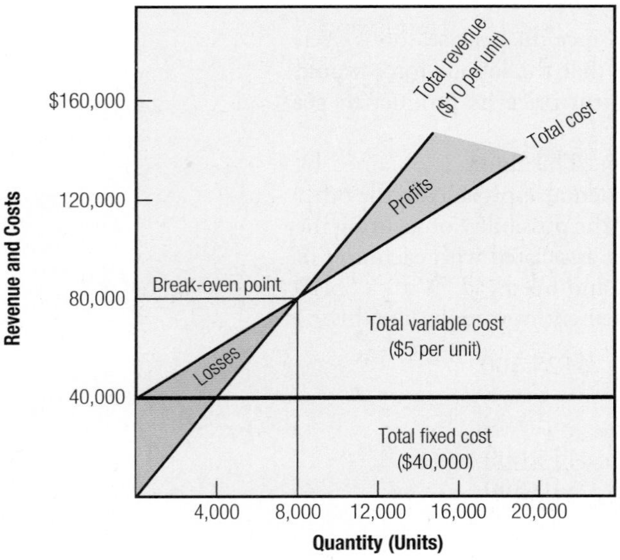

Once the break-even point has been reached, sufficient revenues will have been obtained from sales to cover all fixed costs. Any additional sales will generate per-unit profits equal to the difference between the product's selling price and the variable cost of each unit. As Figure 16.2 reveals, sales of 8,001 units (1 unit above the break-even point) will produce net profits of $5 ($10 sales price less per-unit variable cost of $5). Once all fixed costs have been covered, the per-unit contribution will become the per-unit profit.

Target Returns

Although break-even analysis indicates the sales level at which the firm will incur neither profits nor losses, most firms' managers include a targeted profit in their analyses. In some instances, management sets a desired dollar return when considering a proposed new product or other marketing action. A retailer may set a desired profit of $250,000 in considering whether to expand to a second location. In other instances, the target return may be expressed in percentages, such as a 15 percent return on sales. These target returns can be calculated as follows:

$$\text{Break-Even Point (including specific dollar target return)} = \frac{\text{Total Fixed Cost} + \text{Profit Objective}}{\text{Per-Unit Contribution}}$$

$$\text{Break-Even Point (in units)} = \frac{\$40,000 + \$15,000}{\$5} = 11,000 \text{ units}$$

If the target return is expressed as a percentage of sales, it can be included in the break-even formula as a variable cost. Suppose the marketer in the preceding example seeks a 10 percent return on sales. The desired return is $1 for each product sold (the $10 per-unit selling price multiplied by the 10 percent return on sales). In this case, the basic break-even formula will remain unchanged, although the variable cost per unit will be increased to reflect the target return, and the per-unit contribution to fixed cost will be reduced to $4. As a result, the break-even point will increase from 8,000 to 10,000 units:

$$\text{Break-Even Point} = \frac{\$40,000}{\$4} = 10,000 \text{ units}$$

assessment check 2e ✓

2.9 Give the formula for finding the break-even point, in units and in dollars.

2.10 What adjustments to the basic break-even calculation must be made to include target returns?

2.11 What are the advantages of break-even analysis?

2.12 What are the disadvantages of break-even analysis?

Evaluation of Break-Even Analysis

Break-even analysis is an effective tool for marketers in assessing the sales required for covering costs and achieving specified profit levels. It is easily understood by both marketing and nonmarketing executives and may help them decide whether required sales levels for a certain price are in fact realistic goals. However, it has its shortcomings.

First, the model assumes that costs can be divided into fixed and variable categories. Some costs, such as salaries and advertising outlays, may be either fixed or variable depending on the particular situation. In addition, the model assumes that per-unit variable costs do not change at different levels of operation. However, these may vary because of quantity discounts, more efficient utilization of the workforce, or other economies resulting from increased levels of production and sales. Finally, the basic break-even model does not consider demand. It is a cost-based model and does not directly address the crucial question of whether consumers will purchase the product at the specified price and in the quantities required for breaking even or generating profits.

Marketoid

Delays to the introduction of Bombardier's CSeries commercial jets, announced in 2014, will cost the company hundreds of millions of dollars, raising its break-even point to 800 planes.

Yield Management

When most of a firm's costs are fixed over a wide range of outputs, the primary determinant of profitability will be the amount of revenue generated by sales. **Yield management** strategies allow marketers to vary prices based on such factors as demand, even though the cost of providing those goods or services remains the same. OpenTable, a real-time online reservation network, matches empty tables at restaurants with diners and provides reservation and guest-management software to its restaurant clients. The company has more than 25,000 restaurants on its customer list and has reserved tables for more than 325 million diners in Canada, the United States, Mexico, Germany, Japan, and the United Kingdom.[18]

Similar yield management strategies typify the marketing of such goods and services as the following:

yield management
Pricing strategy that allows marketers to vary prices based on such factors as demand, even though the cost of providing those goods or services remains the same; designed to maximize revenues in situations such as airfares, lodging, auto rentals, and theatre tickets, where costs are fixed.

- *Sports teams*—the Ottawa Senators and Vancouver Canucks charge more for single-game tickets for games featuring high-profile opponents

- *Lodging*—lower prices off season and higher prices during peak season periods; low-priced weekend rates for most hotels, motels, and bed-and-breakfasts across Canada

- *Auto rental*—lower prices on weekends when business demand is low and higher prices during the week when business demand is higher

assessment check 2f ✓

2.13 Explain the goal of yield management.

- *Airfares*—lower prices on nonrefundable tickets with travel restrictions such as advance-purchase and Saturday-night-stay requirements and penalties for flight changes and higher prices on refundable tickets that can be changed without penalty

③ Compare the alternative pricing strategies and explain when each strategy is most appropriate.

PRICING STRATEGIES

The specific strategies that firms use to price goods and services grow out of the marketing strategies they formulate to accomplish overall organizational objectives. One firm's marketers may price their products to attract customers across a wide range; another group of marketers may set prices to appeal to a small segment of a larger market; still another group may simply try to match competitors' price tags. In general, firms can choose from three pricing strategies: skimming, penetration, and competitive pricing. The following sections look at these choices in more detail.

SKIMMING PRICING STRATEGY

skimming pricing strategy Pricing strategy involving the use of an initial high price relative to competitive offerings. Price is dropped in incremental steps as supply begins to exceed demand, or when competition catches up.

Derived from the expression "skimming the cream," **skimming pricing strategies** are also known as *market-plus pricing*. They involve the intentional setting of a relatively high price compared with the prices of competing products. Although some firms continue to utilize a skimming strategy throughout most stages of the product life cycle, it is more commonly used as a market entry price for distinctive goods or services with little or no initial competition. As supply begins to exceed demand, or when competition catches up, the initial high price is incrementally dropped.

Such was the case with high-definition televisions (HDTVs), whose average price was approximately $20,000, including installation, when they were introduced. The resulting sticker shock kept them out of the range of most household budgets. But nearly a decade later, price cuts have brought flat screen models into the reach of mainstream consumers. At Costco.ca, shoppers can pick up a Haier 22-inch flat panel LED model for $139.99. On the higher end, they can purchase a Sharp 80-inch Smart LED flat-panel model for $3,999.99.[19]

A company may practise a skimming strategy in setting a market-entry price when it introduces a distinctive good or service with little or no competition. Or it may use this strategy to market higher-end goods. Amazon's Kindle e-reader was first launched in 2007 and was priced at approximately $400. Today, Canadian consumers can buy a Kindle e-reader for $89, and the Paperwhite model for $139.[20] As new competitors entered the market, Amazon was forced to develop new models at much lower prices.

Sony has generally used a price skimming strategy for many of its innovative, quality products. The e-reader shown here cost $499 when it was introduced.

H. F. (Herb) MacKenzie

In some cases, a firm may maintain a skimming strategy throughout most stages of a product's life cycle. The jewellery category is a good example. Although discounters such as Costco and Walmart offer heavier gold pieces for a few hundred dollars, firms such as Tiffany and Cartier are able to command prices 10 times that amount just for the brand name. Exclusivity justifies the pricing—and the price, once set, rarely falls.

Sometimes maintaining a high price through the product's life cycle works, but sometimes it does not. High prices can drive away otherwise loyal customers. Hockey fans may shift from attending NHL games to junior league hockey games because of ticket, parking, and food prices. Amusement park visitors may shy away from high admission prices and head to the beach instead. If an industry or firm has been known to cut prices at certain points in the past, consumers—and retailers—will expect it. If the price cut doesn't come, consumers must decide whether to pay the higher tab or try a competitor's products.

Significant price changes in the retail gasoline and airline industries occur in the form of a **step out**, in which one firm raises prices and then waits to see if others follow suit. If competitors fail to respond by increasing their prices, the company making the step out usually reduces prices to the original level. Although companies are prohibited by law from collectively setting prices, they can follow each other's example.

Despite the risk of backlash, a skimming strategy does offer benefits. It allows a manufacturer to quickly recover its research and development (R&D) costs. Pharmaceutical companies, which fiercely protect their patents on new drugs, justify high prices because of astronomical R&D costs—an average of 16 cents of every sales dollar, compared with 8 cents for computer makers and 4 cents in the aerospace industry. To protect their brand names from competition from lower-cost generics, drug makers frequently make small changes to their products—such as combining the original product with a complementary prescription drug that treats different aspects of the ailment.

figure 16.3

Price Reductions to Increase Market Share

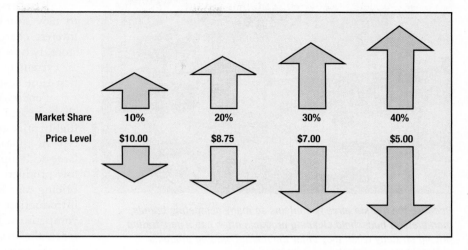

| Market Share | 10% | 20% | 30% | 40% |
| Price Level | $10.00 | $8.75 | $7.00 | $5.00 |

A skimming strategy also permits marketers to control demand in the introductory stages of a product's life cycle and then adjust productive capacity to match changing demand. A low initial price for a new product could lead to fulfillment problems and loss of shopper goodwill if demand outstrips the firm's production capacity. The result is likely to be consumer and retailer complaints and possibly permanent damage to the product's image. Excess demand occasionally leads to quality issues, as the firm strives to satisfy consumer desires for the product with inadequate production facilities.

During the late growth and early maturity stages of its life cycle, a product's price typically falls for two reasons: (1) the pressure of competition and (2) the desire to expand its market. Figure 16.3 shows that 10 percent of the market may buy Product X at $10.00, and another 20 percent could be added to its customer base at a price of $8.75. Successive price declines may expand the firm's market size and meet challenges posed by new competitors.

A skimming strategy has one inherent chief disadvantage: it attracts competition. Potential competitors see innovative firms reaping large financial returns and decide to enter the market. This new supply may force the price of the original product even lower than its eventual level under a sequential skimming procedure. However, if patent protection or some other unique proprietary ability allows a firm to exclude competitors from its market, it may extend a skimming strategy.

PENETRATION PRICING STRATEGY

A **penetration pricing strategy** sets a low price as a major marketing weapon. Marketers often price products noticeably lower than competing offerings when they enter new industries characterized by dozens of competing brands. Once the product achieves some market recognition through consumer trial purchases stimulated by its low price, marketers may increase the price to the level of competing products. Marketers of consumer products such as detergents often use this strategy. A penetration pricing strategy may also extend over several stages of the product life cycle as the firm seeks to maintain a reputation as a low-price competitor.

A penetration pricing strategy is sometimes called *market-minus pricing* when it implements the premise that a lower-than-market price will attract buyers and move a brand from an unknown newcomer to at least the brand-recognition stage or even to the brand-preference stage. Since many firms begin penetration pricing with the intention of increasing prices in the future, success depends on generating many trial purchases. Penetration pricing is common among credit card firms, which typically offer low or zero interest rates for a specified introductory period, then raise the rates. If competitors view the new product as a threat, marketers attempting to use a

step out Pricing practice in which one firm raises prices and then waits to see if others follow suit.

penetration pricing strategy Pricing strategy involving the use of a relatively low entry price compared with competitive offerings, based on the theory that this initial low price will help secure market acceptance.

Because the market already contains so many competing brands, marketers of household cleaning products often use a penetration pricing strategy when they enter the market, pricing products noticeably lower than the competition.

penetration strategy often discover that rivals will simply match their prices.

Retailers may use penetration pricing to lure shoppers to new stores. Strategies might take such forms as zero interest charges for credit purchases at a new furniture store, two-for-one offers for dinner at a new restaurant, or an extremely low price on a single product purchase for first-time customers to get them to come in and shop.

Penetration pricing works best for goods or services characterized by highly elastic demand. Large numbers of highly price-sensitive consumers pay close attention to this type of appeal. The strategy also suits situations in which large-scale operations and long production runs result in low production and marketing costs. Finally, penetration pricing may be appropriate in market situations in which introduction of a new product will likely attract strong competitors. Such a strategy may allow a new product to reach the mass market quickly and capture a large share prior to entry by competitors.

Some auto manufacturers have been using penetration pricing for some new models to attract customers who might not otherwise consider purchasing a vehicle during a given year or who might be looking at a more expensive competitor. India's Tata Motors launched the world's cheapest car: the Nano, which carries a price tag of $2,600 (U.S.) in India. Tata hopes to eventually sell a less stripped-down version of the Nano in North America and Western Europe but has not set a date—or a price. Currently, the lowest-priced car in Canada is the Nissan Micra, with a sticker price starting at $9,998.[21]

Everyday Low Pricing

Closely related to penetration pricing is **everyday low pricing (EDLP)**, a strategy devoted to continuous low prices as opposed to relying on short-term, price-cutting tactics such as cents-off coupons, rebates, and special sales. EDLP can take two forms. In the first, retailers such as Walmart and Canadian Tire compete by consistently offering consumers low prices on a broad range of items. Through its EDLP policy, Lowe's Canada offers not only to match any price the consumer sees elsewhere but also to take off an additional 10 percent. Walmart states that it achieves EDLP by negotiating better prices from suppliers and by cutting its own costs. In addition, Walmart holds suppliers to a strict four-day delivery window. Goods that arrive at the regional distribution centre before or after the window are assessed a 3 percent penalty.[22]

The second form of the EDLP pricing strategy involves its use by the manufacturer in dealing with channel members. Manufacturers may seek to set stable wholesale prices that undercut offers that competitors make to retailers, offers that typically rise and fall with the latest trade promotion deals. Many marketers reduce the list prices on a number of products while simultaneously reducing promotion allowances to retailers. While reductions in allowances mean that retailers may not fund such in-store promotions as shelf merchandising and end-aisle displays, the manufacturers hope that stable low prices will stimulate sales instead.

Some retailers oppose EDLP strategies. Many grocery stores, for instance, operate on "high-low" strategies that set profitable

Everyday low pricing was introduced to Canada by Walmart, but it is now a common strategy practised by many Canadian retailers.

regular prices to offset losses of frequent specials and promotions. Other retailers believe that EDLP will ultimately benefit both sellers and buyers. Supporters of EDLP in the grocery industry point out that it already succeeds at two of the biggest competitors, Walmart and warehouse clubs such as Costco.

One popular pricing myth is that a low price is a sure sell. Low prices are an easy means of distinguishing the offerings of one marketer from other sellers, but such moves are easy to counter by competitors. Unless overall demand is price elastic, overall price cuts will mean less revenue for all firms in the industry. In addition, low prices may generate an image of questionable quality.

COMPETITIVE PRICING STRATEGY

Although many organizations rely heavily on price as a competitive weapon, even more implement **competitive pricing strategies**. These organizations try to reduce the emphasis on price competition by matching other firms' prices and concentrating their own marketing efforts on the product, distribution, and promotion elements of the marketing mix. As pointed out earlier, while price offers a dramatic means of achieving competitive advantage, it is also the easiest marketing variable for competitors to match. In fact, in industries with relatively homogeneous products, competitors must match each other's price reductions to maintain market share and remain competitive.

Retailers such as Home Depot and Future Shop both use price-matching strategies, assuring consumers they will meet—and beat—competitors' prices. Grocery chains such as Loblaw, Sobeys, and Overwaitea Foods often compete with seasonal items: watermelon, soft drinks, and hot dogs in the summer; apples, hot chocolate, and turkeys in the winter. As soon as one store lowers the price of an item such as turkey, the rest follow suit.

Another form of competitive pricing is setting an **opening price point** within a category. Retailers often achieve this by pricing a quality private-label product below the competition. Many grocery chains have begun actively advertising their private-label goods, most of which are priced below those of their manufacturers' brands. In a tough economy, more consumers are giving private-label products a try, and many say the quality is comparable to that of national brands.[23]

Prices can really drop when companies continually match each other's prices, as has been evident periodically in the airline and computer industries. But competitive pricing can be tricky; a price reduction affects not only the first company but also the entire industry as other firms match the price reduction. Unless the lower prices can attract new customers and expand the overall market enough to offset the loss of per-unit revenue, the price cut will leave all competitors with less revenue. Research shows that nearly two-thirds of all firms set prices using competitive pricing as their primary pricing strategy.

Once competitors are routinely matching each other on price, marketers must turn away from price as a marketing strategy, emphasizing other variables to develop areas of distinctive competence and attract customers. That might mean offering personalized services such as gift wrapping or a sales associate who knows the type of clothing or books you like.

everyday low pricing (EDLP) Pricing strategy of continuously offering low prices rather than relying on such short-term price cuts as cents-off coupons, rebates, and special sales.

competitive pricing strategy Pricing strategy designed to de-emphasize price as a competitive variable by pricing a good or service at the general level of comparable offerings.

opening price point Setting an opening price below that of the competition, usually on a high-quality private-label item.

> **assessment check 3** ✓
>
> 3.1 What are the three major pricing strategies?
>
> 3.2 What is EDLP?

PRICE QUOTATIONS

④ **Describe how prices are quoted.**

The choice of the best method for quoting prices depends on many industry conditions, including competitive trends, cost structures, and traditional practices, along with the policies of individual firms. This section examines the reasoning and methodology behind price quotation practices.

Most price structures are built around **list prices**—the rates normally quoted to potential buyers. Marketers usually determine list prices by one or a combination of the methods discussed earlier in this chapter. The sticker price on a new automobile is a good example:

list price Established price normally quoted to potential buyers.

figure 16.4

Gasoline Taxes across Canada

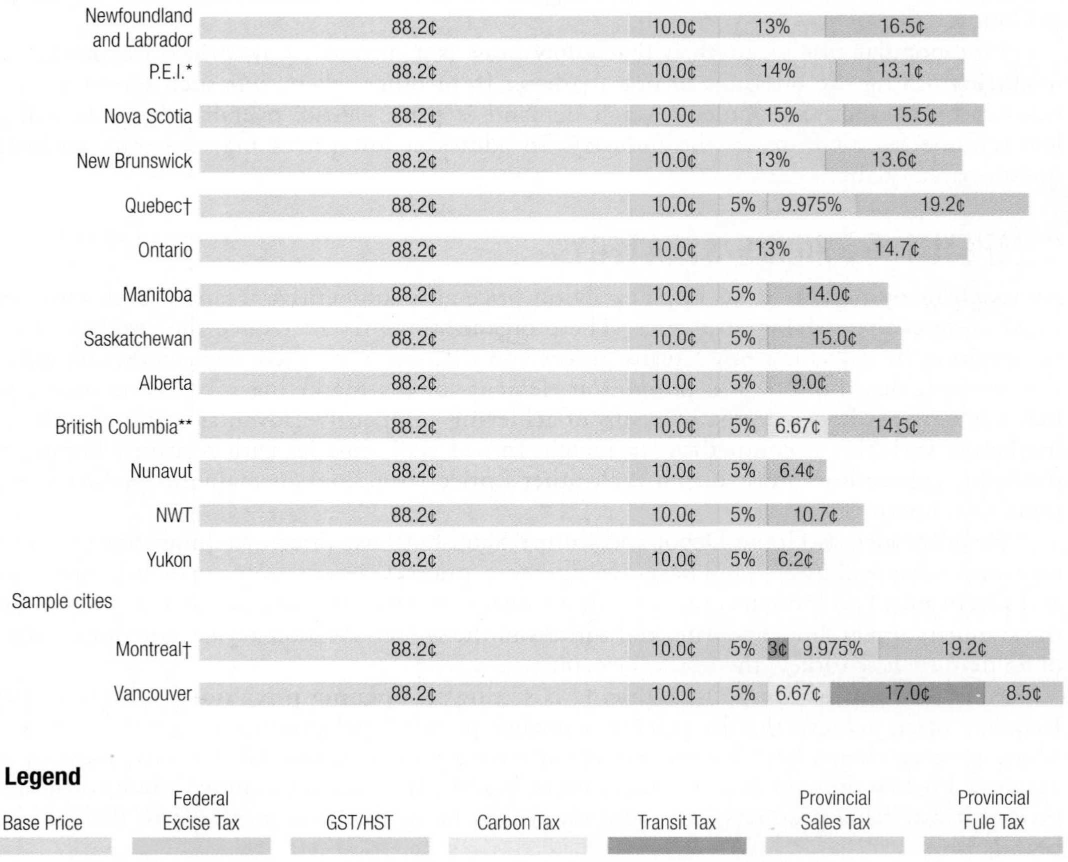

Region	Base Price	Federal Excise Tax	GST/HST	Carbon Tax	Transit Tax	Provincial Sales Tax	Provincial Fuel Tax
Newfoundland and Labrador	88.2¢	10.0¢	13%				16.5¢
P.E.I.*	88.2¢	10.0¢	14%				13.1¢
Nova Scotia	88.2¢	10.0¢	15%				15.5¢
New Brunswick	88.2¢	10.0¢	13%				13.6¢
Quebec†	88.2¢	10.0¢	5%			9.975%	19.2¢
Ontario	88.2¢	10.0¢	13%				14.7¢
Manitoba	88.2¢	10.0¢	5%				14.0¢
Saskatchewan	88.2¢	10.0¢	5%				15.0¢
Alberta	88.2¢	10.0¢	5%				9.0¢
British Columbia**	88.2¢	10.0¢	5%	6.67¢			14.5¢
Nunavut	88.2¢	10.0¢	5%				6.4¢
NWT	88.2¢	10.0¢	5%				10.7¢
Yukon	88.2¢	10.0¢	5%				6.2¢
Sample cities							
Montreal†	88.2¢	10.0¢	5%		3¢	9.975%	19.2¢
Vancouver	88.2¢	10.0¢	5%	6.67¢	17.0¢		8.5¢

Legend

Base Price	Federal Excise Tax	GST/HST	Carbon Tax	Transit Tax	Provincial Sales Tax	Provincial Fule Tax

*Prince Edward Island harmonized PST and GST on April 1, 2013
**British Columbia cancelled the HST and reverted back to the 5% GST on April 1, 2013
†Quebec harmonized QST and GST, effective January 1, 2013

Taxes play an important role in the price consumers pay for gasoline, and these vary considerably across Canada.

Source: **http://retail.petro-canada.ca/en/fuelsavings/2139.aspx.** Reproduced by permission from Petro-Canada

it shows the list price for the basic model and then adds the prices of options. The sticker price for a new Kia Forte sedan is $15,995. But you can add such features as keyless entry, front tweeter speakers, heated front seats, and more—all at additional cost. Most car manufacturers bundle features into packages for one price. So if you order trim level EX on the Forte, you automatically get those features, among other add-ons.[24] The price of oil is equally important to consumers—particularly those who drive cars—because it directly affects the list price of gasoline. Disruptions such as refinery shutdowns, hurricanes, and wars affect the price of oil and ultimately the price that drivers pay at the pump. Prices may also fluctuate seasonally, as demand for gasoline rises and falls. Demand for gasoline is much higher in Canada during the summer when tourists visit and when Canadians travel longer distances for their vacations. Figure 16.4 illustrates how taxes affect the final price that consumers pay for gasoline across Canada.

market price Price a consumer or marketing intermediary actually pays for a product after subtracting any discounts, allowances, or rebates from the list price.

REDUCTIONS FROM LIST PRICE

The amount that a consumer pays for a product—its **market price**—may or may not equal the list price. Discounts and allowances sometimes reduce list prices. A list price often defines a starting point from which discounts set a lower market price. Marketers offer discounts in several classifications: cash, trade, and quantity discounts.

Cash Discounts

Consumers, industrial purchasers, or channel members sometimes receive reductions in price in exchange for prompt payment of bills; these price cuts are known as **cash discounts**. Discount terms usually specify exact time periods, such as 2/10, net 30. This notation means that the customer must pay within 30 days, but payment within 10 days entitles the customer to subtract 2 percent from the amount due. Consumers may receive a cash discount for immediate payment—say, paying with cash instead of a credit card at the gas pump or paying the full cash amount upfront for elective dental services such as braces for teeth. Cash discounts represent a traditional pricing practice in many industries. They fulfill legal requirements provided that all customers can take the same reductions on the same terms.

In recent years, sellers have increasingly attempted to improve their own liquidity positions, reduce their bad-debt losses, and cut collection expenses by moving to a form of *negative cash discount*. Confronted with purchasers who may defer paying their bills as long as possible, a new notice has begun to appear on customer statements:

Due on Receipt. A FINANCE CHARGE of 1.5% per month (18% A.P.R.) is computed on and added to the unpaid balance as of the statement date.

Past-due accounts may be turned over to collection agencies.

cash discount Price reduction offered to a consumer, business user, or marketing intermediary in return for prompt payment of a bill.

Trade Discounts

Payments to channel members for performing marketing functions are known as **trade discounts**, or functional discounts. Services performed by various channel members and the related costs were discussed in Chapters 12 and 13. A manufacturer's list price must incorporate the costs incurred by channel members in performing required marketing functions and expected profit margins for each member.

Trade discounts initially reflected the operating expenses of each category, but they have become more or less customary practices in some industries. In the United States, the Robinson-Patman Act allows trade discounts as long as all buyers in the same category, such as all wholesalers or all retailers, receive the same discount privileges. In Canada, the Competition Act does not recognize trade discounts. Wholesalers and retailers are considered competitors, and they therefore must be treated equally with respect to pricing and related promotional allowances.

Figure 16.5 shows how a chain of trade discounts works. In the first instance, the trade discount is "40 percent, 10 percent off list price" for wholesalers. In other words, the 40 percent discount on the $40 product is the trade discount the retailer receives to cover operating expenses and earn a profit. The wholesaler receives 10 percent of the $24 price to retailers to cover expenses and earn a profit. The manufacturer receives $21.60 from the wholesaler for each order.

In the second example, the manufacturer and retailer decide to bypass the wholesaler. The producer offers a trade discount of 45 percent to the retailer. In this instance, the retailer receives $18 for each product sold at its list price, and the manufacturer receives the remaining $22. Either the retailer or the manufacturer must assume responsibility for the services previously performed by the wholesaler, or they can share these duties between them.

trade discount Payment to a channel member or buyer for performing marketing functions; also known as a *functional discount*.

quantity discount Price reduction granted for a large-volume purchase.

cumulative quantity discount Price discount determined by amounts of purchases over stated time periods.

figure 16.5

Chain of Trade Discounts

"40 PERCENT, 10 PERCENT OFF" TRADE DISCOUNT			
List Price −	Retail Trade Discount −	Wholesale Trade Discount =	Manufacturer Proceeds
$40 −	$16 ($40 x 40%) −	$2.40 ($24 x 10%) =	$21.60 ($40 − $16 − $2.40)

"45 PERCENT" TRADE DISCOUNT		
List Price −	Retail Trade Discount =	Manufacturer Proceeds
$40 −	$18 ($40 x 45%) =	$22 ($40 − $18)

Quantity Discounts

Price reductions granted for large-volume purchases are known as **quantity discounts**. Sellers justify these discounts on the grounds that large orders reduce selling expenses and may shift some costs for storage, transportation, and financing to buyers. The law allows quantity discounts provided they are applied on the same basis to all customers.

Quantity discounts may specify either cumulative or noncumulative terms. **Cumulative quantity discounts** reduce prices in amounts determined by purchases over stated time periods. Annual purchases of at least $25,000 might entitle a buyer to a 3 percent rebate, and purchases exceeding $50,000 would increase the refund to 5 percent. These reductions are really patronage discounts because they tend to bind customers to a single supply source.

noncumulative quantity discount Price reduction granted on a one-time-only basis.

Noncumulative quantity discounts provide one-time reductions in the list price. For example, a firm might offer the following discount schedule for a product priced at $100 per unit:

1 unit	List: $100
2–5 units	List less 10 percent
6–10 units	List less 20 percent
Over 10 units	List less 25 percent

allowance Specified deduction from list price, including a trade-in or promotional allowance.

trade-in Credit allowance given for a used item when a customer purchases a new item.

promotional allowance Promotional incentive in which the manufacturer agrees to pay the reseller a certain amount to cover the costs of special promotional displays or extensive advertising.

minimum advertised pricing (MAP) Fees paid to retailers who agree not to advertise products below set prices.

rebate Refund of a portion of the purchase price, usually granted by the product's manufacturer.

Many businesses have come to expect quantity discounts from suppliers. Online photo supply retailer Shutterfly offers volume discounts for photo books and discounts of up to 50 percent on prepaid orders.[25] Marketers typically favour combinations of cash, trade, and quantity discounts.

Allowances

Allowances resemble discounts by specifying deductions from list price. The major categories of allowances are trade-ins and promotional allowances. **Trade-ins** are often used in sales of durable goods such as automobiles. The new product's basic list price remains unchanged, but the seller accepts less money from the customer along with a used product—usually the same kind of product as the buyer purchases.

Promotional allowances reduce prices as part of attempts to integrate promotional strategies within distribution channels. Manufacturers often return part of the prices that buyers pay in the form of advertising and sales-support allowances for channel members. Automobile manufacturers frequently offer allowances to retail dealers to induce them to lower prices and stimulate sales. In an effort to alert consumers to the difference between a car's sticker price and the price the dealer actually pays to the manufacturer, *Consumer Reports* recently began selling car and truck buyers a breakdown on dealers' wholesale costs. The information reveals undisclosed dealer profits such as manufacturers' incentives, rebates from dealer-invoice price, and "holdbacks"—amounts refunded to the dealer after sales are completed.[26] Dealers dislike the move to reveal their markups, arguing that no other retail sector is forced to give consumers details of their promotional allowances.

Minimum advertised pricing (MAP) occurs when a manufacturer pays a retailer not to advertise a product below a certain price. However, some electronics manufacturers have announced that they are imposing unilateral pricing policies (UPPs) that set the same prices for some types of TVs no matter where they are sold. Some manufacturers plan to monitor retailers' compliance. Some manufacturers have warned retailers that, if they sell an item in the UPP program for less than the minimum advertised price, the manufacturer will remove their authorization and stop supplying products.[27]

Rebates

In still another way to reduce the price paid by customers, marketers may offer a **rebate**—a refund of a portion of the purchase price. Rebates appear everywhere—on cosmetics packages, appliances, over-the-counter medications, and in automobile promotions—by manufacturers eager to get consumers to try their products or to move products during periods of slow sales. The contact-lens manufacturer ACUVUE offers rebates to current and new customers who buy boxes of the company's disposable contact lenses.

H. F. (Herb) MacKenzie

Freight, PDI, and levies on a Honda Accord manufactured in Ontario and delivered to a customer in Ontario were $1,829 (April 2014)—to a customer in British Columbia: $1,820. Ontario customers subsidize the freight for customers in other provinces.

Rebates can have their problems. Many consumers complain of the amount of paperwork they have to fill out to get a rebate, particularly on larger items such as computers and kitchen appliances. Some say they fill out the paperwork only to be denied the claim on a technicality. Others report never receiving the rebate—or even a response—at all. The Better Business Bureau notes that the number of complaints filed relating to rebates has grown significantly in the past few years. Yet companies argue that many consumers never even apply for their legitimate rebates.[28]

GEOGRAPHIC CONSIDERATIONS

In industries dominated by catalogue and online marketers, geographic considerations weigh heavily on the firm's ability to deliver orders in a cost-effective manner at the right time and place. In other instances, geographic factors affect the marketer's ability to receive additional inventory quickly in response to demand fluctuations. And although geographic considerations strongly influence prices when costs include shipping heavy, bulky, low-unit-value products, they can also affect lightweight, lower-cost products.

Buyers and sellers can handle transportation expenses in several ways: (1) the buyer pays all transportation charges, (2) the seller pays all transportation charges, or (3) the buyer and the seller share the charges. This decision has major effects on a firm's efforts to expand its geographic coverage to distant markets. How can marketers compete with local suppliers in distant markets who are able to avoid the considerable shipping costs that their firms must pay? Sellers can implement several alternatives for handling transportation costs in their pricing policies.

FOB Pricing

FOB (free on board) origin (or **shipping point**) prices include no shipping charges. Shipments are sent freight collect, and the buyer must pay all freight charges to transport the product from the manufacturer's loading dock. The seller is responsible to load the merchandise aboard the carrier selected by the buyer. Legal title and responsibility pass to the buyer after the seller's employees load the purchase and get a receipt from the representative of the common carrier. Firms such as Walmart often handle freight charges over the entire supply chain. Because Walmart sources so many products from China, "FOB China" is now becoming common.

Many marketing intermediaries sell only on FOB plant terms to downstream channel members. These distributors believe that their customers have more clout than they do in negotiating with carriers. They prefer to assign transportation costs to the channel members in the best positions to secure the most cost-effective shipping terms.

Sellers may also quote prices **FOB destination**, sometimes referred to as *uniform delivered pricing*. In such instances, the seller pays the freight and also retains legal responsibility and title to the goods until they are received by the buyer. That means that lost and damaged shipments remain the responsibility of the seller. The price quote includes a transportation charge averaged over all of the firm's customers, meaning that distant customers actually pay a smaller share of shipping costs while nearby customers pay what is known as *phantom freight* (the amount by which the average transportation charge exceeds the actual cost of shipping). Both amazon.ca and chapters.indigo.ca use uniform-delivered pricing for orders over $25. Finally, some sellers quote **FOB origin—freight allowed and prepaid**. The freight allowed and prepaid means the customer does not pay the freight; however, the FOB origin means the customer assumes legal responsibility and title once the shipment leaves the seller's premises. This alternative is popular among firms with high fixed costs, because it helps them expand their markets by quoting the same prices to customers regardless of where the customers are located.

Zone Pricing

Zone pricing modifies a uniform-delivered pricing system by dividing the overall market into different zones and establishing a single price within each zone. This pricing structure incorporates average transportation costs for shipments within each zone as part of the delivered price of goods sold there; by narrowing distances, it greatly reduces but does not completely eliminate phantom freight. The primary advantage of zone pricing comes from easy administration methods that help a seller to compete in distant markets. Canada Post's parcel rates depend on zone pricing.

FOB (free on board) origin (or **shipping point**) Price quotation that does not include shipping charges. Legal responsibility and title pass to the buyer once the shipment leaves the seller's premises.

FOB destination Price quotation that includes freight—paid by the seller—and where the seller retains legal responsibility and title to the goods until they reach the buyer.

FOB origin—freight allowed and prepaid A hybrid price quotation system where the seller pays the freight, but the customer assumes legal responsibility and title once the shipment leaves the seller's premises.

zone pricing Pricing system for handling transportation costs under which the market is divided into geographic regions and a different price is set in each region.

basing-point pricing System used in some industries during the early 20th century in which the buyer paid the factory price plus freight charges from the basing-point city nearest the buyer.

Zone pricing helps explain why gasoline can cost more in one suburb than it costs in a neighbourhood just four or five kilometres down the road. One way in which gasoline marketers boost profits is by mapping out areas based on formulas that factor in location, affluence, or simply what the local market will bear. Dealers are then charged different wholesale prices, which are reflected in the prices paid at the pump by customers. Some dealers argue that zone pricing should be prohibited. When drivers shop around for cheaper gas in other zones, stations in high-price zones are unable to compete.

Basing-Point Pricing

In **basing-point pricing**, the price of a product includes the list price at the factory plus freight charges from the basing-point city nearest the buyer. The basing point specifies a location from which freight charges are calculated—not necessarily the point from which the goods are actually shipped. In either case, the actual shipping point does not affect the price quotation. For example, a seller might quote a customer a price of $1,000 per ton for a shipment of steel from Hamilton, Ontario, but designate the basing point as Montreal. The customer pays for the steel plus a charge equal to the freight that would have resulted had the shipment been made from Montreal. Such a system seeks to equalize competition—usually for heavy commodity-type items—between distant marketers since all competitors use Montreal as the basing point.

assessment check 4

4.1 What are the three major types of discounts?

4.2 Identify the three alternatives for handling transportation costs in pricing policies.

⑤ **Identify the various pricing policy decisions that marketers must make.**

pricing policy General guideline that reflects marketing objectives and influences specific pricing decisions.

PRICING POLICIES

Pricing policies contribute important information to buyers as they assess the firm's total image. A coherent policy provides an overall framework and consistency that guide day-to-day pricing decisions. Formally, a **pricing policy** is a general guideline that reflects marketing objectives and influences specific pricing decisions.

Decisions concerning price structure generally tend to focus on technical, detailed questions, but decisions concerning pricing policies cover broader issues. Price-structure decisions take the firm's pricing policy as a given, from which they specify applicable discounts. Pricing policies have important strategic effects, particularly in guiding competitive efforts. They form the basis for more practical price-structure decisions.

Firms implement variations of four basic types of pricing policies: psychological pricing, price flexibility, product-line pricing, and promotional pricing. Specific policies deal effectively with various competitive situations; the final choice depends on the environment within which marketers must make their pricing decisions. Regardless of the strategy selected, however, marketers sometimes must raise prices. Although it is never easy to deliver this decision to customers, if it is accomplished with honesty and tact, customers are likely to remain loyal.

psychological pricing Pricing policy based on the belief that certain prices or price ranges make a good or service more appealing than others to buyers.

PSYCHOLOGICAL PRICING

Psychological pricing applies the belief that certain prices or price ranges make products more appealing than others to buyers. No research offers a consistent foundation for such thinking, however, and studies often report mixed findings. Nevertheless, marketers practise several forms of psychological pricing. Prestige pricing, discussed in this chapter, sets a relatively high price to convey an image of quality and exclusiveness. Two more psychological pricing techniques are odd pricing and unit pricing.

odd pricing Pricing policy based on the belief that a price ending with an odd number just under a round number is more appealing, for instance, $9.97 rather than $10.

In **odd pricing**, marketers set prices at odd numbers just under round numbers. Many people assume that a price of $4.95 appeals more strongly to consumers than $5, supposedly because buyers interpret it as $4 plus change. Odd pricing originated as a way to force clerks to make change, thus serving as a cash-control device, and it remains a common feature of contemporary price quotations. Some producers and retailers practise odd pricing but avoid prices ending in 5, 9, or 0. These marketers believe that customers view price tags of $5.95, $5.99, or $6.00 as regular retail prices, but they think of an amount like $5.97 as a discount price. Walmart avoids using 9s at the end of its prices, and even uses numbers such as 3 or 7.

Unit pricing states prices in terms of some recognized unit of measurement (such as grams and litres) or a standard numerical count. Unit pricing began to be widely used during the late 1960s to make price comparisons more convenient following complaints by consumer advocates about the difficulty of comparing the true prices of products packaged in different sizes. These advocates thought that posting prices in terms of standard units would help shoppers make better informed purchases. However, unit pricing has not improved consumers' shopping habits as much as supporters originally envisioned. Instead, research shows that unit pricing most often affects purchases only by relatively well-educated consumers with high earnings.

unit pricing Pricing policy in which prices are stated in terms of a recognized unit of measurement or a standard numerical count.

PRICE FLEXIBILITY

Marketing executives must also set company policies that determine whether their firm will permit **price flexibility**—that is, the decision of whether to set one price that applies to every buyer or to permit variable prices for different customers. Generally, one-price policies suit mass-selling marketing programs, whereas variable pricing is more likely to be applied in marketing programs based on individual bargaining. In a large department store, customers do not expect to haggle over prices with retail salespeople. Instead, they expect to pay the amounts shown on the price tags. Usually, customers pay less only when the retailer replaces regular prices with sale prices or offers discounts on damaged merchandise. Variable pricing usually applies to larger purchases such as automobiles, real estate, and hotel room rates. While variable pricing adds some flexibility to selling situations, it may also lead to retaliatory pricing by competitors, and it may stir complaints among customers who find that they paid higher prices than necessary.

price flexibility Pricing policy permitting variable prices for goods and services.

In recent years, Internet service providers such as Bell Canada and Rogers Communications have set usage caps on customer accounts. Both offer a number of Internet plans with prices based on the usage allowance and the connection speed that customers choose to meet their needs.

PRODUCT-LINE PRICING

Since most firms market several product lines, an effective pricing strategy must consider the relationships among all these items instead of viewing each in isolation. **Product-line pricing** is the practice of setting a limited number of prices for a selection of merchandise. For example, a clothier might offer three lines of men's suits—one priced at $400, a second at $600, and the most expensive at $1,200. These price points help the retailer to define important product characteristics that differentiate the three product lines and assist the customer in deciding on whether to trade up or trade down.

product-line pricing Practice of setting a limited number of prices for a selection of merchandise and marketing different product lines at each of these price levels.

Retailers practise extensive product-line pricing. In earlier days, five-and-dime variety stores exemplified this technique. It remains popular, however, because it offers advantages to both retailers and customers. Shoppers can choose desired price ranges and then concentrate on other product variables such as colours, styles, and materials. Retailers can purchase and offer specific lines in limited price categories instead of more general assortments with dozens of different prices.

Sunglasses have become a hot fashion item in recent years, and prices for designer glasses have jumped from an average of approximately $250 per pair to as much as $900 for Thornhill Aviators at Fifth Avenue department store Bergdorf Goodman. While sales of other luxury goods have softened, sunglass sales are getting long looks from retailers. Younger consumers—teens and young women—seem to be snapping up designer shades most often. Bulgari, Dolce & Gabbana, Prada, Stella McCartney, and Versace all offer high-end glasses carried by luxury retailers.

Marketoid

The most expensive sunglasses in the world—from Swiss luxury house Chopard—are priced at $408,496 and are made of 51 fully cut River diamonds weighing four carats, plus 60 grams of 24-carat gold.

A potential problem with product-line pricing is that once marketers decide on a limited number of prices to use as their price lines, they may have difficulty making price changes on individual items. Rising costs, therefore, force sellers to either change the entire price-line structure, which results in confusion, or cut costs through production adjustments. The second option opens the firm to customer complaints that its merchandise is not what it used to be.

PROMOTIONAL PRICING

In **promotional pricing**, a lower than normal price is used as a temporary ingredient in a firm's marketing strategy. Some promotional pricing arrangements form part of recurrent marketing

promotional pricing Pricing policy in which a lower than normal price is used as a temporary ingredient in a firm's marketing strategy.

Many retailers are known for regularly using promotional pricing to attract consumers to their stores.

H. F. (Herb) MacKenzie

initiatives, such as a shoe store's annual "buy one pair, get the second pair for one cent" sale. Another firm may introduce a promotional model or brand with a special price to begin competing in a new market.

Managing promotional pricing efforts requires marketing skill. Customers may get hooked on sales and other promotional pricing events. If they know their favourite department store has a one-day sale every month, they are likely to wait to make their purchases on that day. Car shoppers have been offered so many price incentives that it is becoming harder and harder for manufacturers and dealers to take them away—or to come up with new ones.

In an effort to preserve customer traffic despite a tough economy, fast food restaurants are trying a variety of promotions designed to attract business. However, where franchisees operate the fast food restaurants, they often bear the brunt of those value-priced promotions, as discussed in the "Solving an Ethical Controversy" feature.

loss leader Product offered to consumers at less than cost to attract them to stores in the hope that they will buy other merchandise at regular prices.

Loss Leaders and Leader Pricing

Retailers rely most heavily on promotional pricing. In one type of technique, stores offer **loss leaders**—goods priced below cost to attract customers who, the retailer hopes, will also buy other, regularly priced merchandise. Loss leaders can form part of an effective marketing program.

SOLVING AN ETHICAL CONTROVERSY

Pricing Strategy: The New Battleground for Franchisors and Franchisees

THE rising cost of food and a struggling economy have combined to create the perfect storm in the fast-food industry, causing many companies, including McDonald's, Wendy's, Burger King, KFC, and Taco Bell, to tinker with their pricing strategy. By introducing new menu items and pricing promotions geared to draw consumers back into their restaurants, companies are raising the ire of their franchisees, who find their already slim profit margins shaved to the bone.

Should fast-food companies unilaterally set pricing policies?

PRO

1. Pricing policy cannot be left to the discretion of individual franchisees: uniformity from store to store is an important facet of the company's brand.
2. Fast-food restaurants have to be creative in trying new things to stay competitive. What's more, in devising promotions, marketers must consider every possibility as they attempt to pull customers away from their competition. For example, promoting its dollar drink days during the summer months—as McDonald's has done again in 2014—creates an opportunity to woo customers away from minimarts

and convenience stores; introducing specialty coffees puts them head to head with coffee houses.

CON

1. Franchise operators are at the mercy of the parent company because they have little say over corporate decisions like pricing policy, yet must still pay a percentage of their sales to the parent. Some promotions have actually caused franchisees to lose money because the items cost more to prepare and serve than is reflected in the selling price.
2. Because franchises represent the lifeblood of companies such as McDonald's and Burger King, it is important for the parent company to maintain a good relationship with its franchisees. If franchisees perceive they have little power in influencing their store's future, they may decide their investment was a poor one—and the company would be in trouble.

Where do you stand: pro or con?

Sources: Company website, **www.mcdonalds.ca**, accessed May 25, 2014; Lisa Baertlein, "Burger King Pulling Slice from Double Cheeseburger," Reuters, February 17, 2010, **www.reuters.com**, accessed May 25, 2014.

Paper towels at your grocery store are often a loss leader, as is fruit in season. Around Thanksgiving, many grocers offer turkey as a loss leader in the hope that customers will buy the trimmings there as well.[29]

Retailers frequently use a variant of loss-leader pricing called **leader pricing**. To earn some return on promotional sales, they offer so-called leader merchandise at prices slightly above cost. Among the most frequent practitioners of this combination pricing/promotion strategy are mass merchandisers and supermarkets such as Walmart and Sobeys. Retailers sometimes treat private label products (such as George, Equate, and Great Value products at Walmart or Our Compliments products at Sobeys) as leader merchandise because the store brands cost, on average, about 27 percent less than those of comparable national brands. While store brand items generate lower per-unit revenues than national brands would produce, higher sales volume will probably offset some of the difference, as will related sales of high-margin products such as toiletries and cosmetics.

Digital cameras are a good example. Although a digital point-and-shoot camera once ranged from $400 to $600, today, for the same money, shoppers can get a more technologically advanced digital SLR camera. Meanwhile, prices on the point-and-shoot models have dropped. Many of the cameras in Canon's PowerShot series—formerly priced in the hundreds of dollars—are now available for less than $200.[30]

But marketers should anticipate two potential pitfalls when making a promotional pricing decision:

1. Some buyers are not attracted by promotional pricing.

2. By maintaining an artificially low price for a period of time, marketers may lead customers to expect it as a customary feature of the product. That is the situation currently faced by North American car manufacturers; sales of their models lag when they do not offer price incentives.

leader pricing Variant of loss-leader pricing in which marketers offer prices slightly above cost to avoid violating minimum-markup regulations and earn a minimal return on promotional sales.

---

assessment check 5a

5.1 Define *pricing policy*.

5.2 Describe the two types of psychological pricing other than prestige pricing.

5.3 What is promotional pricing?

PRICE–QUALITY RELATIONSHIPS

One of the most thoroughly researched aspects of pricing is its relationship to consumer perceptions of product quality. In the absence of other cues, price serves as an important indicator of a product's quality to prospective purchasers. Many buyers interpret high prices as signals of high-quality products. Prestige is also often associated with high prices. However, a new type of prestige surrounds eco-friendly products. Many consumers are willing to pay more for green goods and services—those made with environmentally friendly materials and processes. These purchases make consumers feel good about themselves and convey status among others.

---

assessment check 5b

5.4 Describe the price–quality connection.

5.5 What are price limits?

Despite the appeal of prestige, nearly every consumer loves a good deal. Marketers work hard to convince consumers they are offering high-quality products at the lowest possible price. Motels were once considered both cheap and seedy. The Motel 6 chain, for example, was so named because when it opened in the United States in 1962, a room cost just $6 per night. Today, Motel 6 advertises "the lowest rates of any national chain," and, in 2014, Canadian travellers could stay in many locations for as little as $70, while still enjoying many of the same amenities offered by more expensive alternatives.[31]

Probably the best statement of the price–quality connection is the idea of price limits. Consumers define certain limits within which their product–quality perceptions vary directly with price. A potential buyer regards a price below the lower limit as too cheap, and a price above the higher limit seems too expensive. This perception holds true for both national brands and private-label products.

More consumers are concerned with sustainability, and many are willing to pay a premium for eco-friendly products.

⑥ **List and explain a number of special issues in pricing.**

SOME SPECIAL TOPICS IN PRICING

A discussion of pricing concepts and strategies would not be complete without considering some of the special topics in pricing that are important to some marketing managers, in particular marketing environments. These include competitive bidding and negotiated prices, pricing in global markets, the dilemma of transfer pricing, online pricing considerations, and bundle pricing.

COMPETITIVE BIDDING AND NEGOTIATED PRICES

competitive bidding
Inviting potential suppliers to quote prices on proposed purchases or contracts.

Many government and organizational procurement departments do not pay set prices for their purchases, particularly for large purchases. Instead, they determine the lowest prices available for items that meet specifications through **competitive bidding**. This process consists of inviting potential suppliers to quote prices on proposed purchases or contracts. Detailed specifications describe the good or service that the government agency or business organization wishes to acquire. One of the most important procurement tasks is to develop accurate descriptions of products that the organization seeks to buy. This process generally requires the assistance of the firm's technical personnel, such as engineers, designers, and chemists.

In competing for students, colleges and universities across Canada differentiate themselves on many dimensions, including price. In order to keep operating costs down, institutions routinely invite competitive bids in many areas of operation, including building maintenance and janitorial services, landscaping, and food service. With costs soaring for everything related to academic life, schools look for ways to economize without diminishing their appeal in the eyes of prospective students and their parents.

In some cases, business and government purchasers negotiate contracts with favoured suppliers instead of inviting competitive bids from all interested parties. The terms of such a contract emerge through offers and counteroffers between the buyer and the seller. When only one supplier offers a desired product, or when projects require extensive research and development, buyers and sellers often set purchase terms through negotiated contracts. In addition, some government and business customers allow their buyers to skip the formal bid process and negotiate purchases under certain dollar limits—say $500 or $1,000. This policy seeks to eliminate economic waste that would result from obtaining and processing bids for relatively minor purchases.

PRICING IN GLOBAL MARKETS

It is equally important for a firm engaging in global marketing to use a pricing strategy that reflects its overall marketing strategy. Prices must support the company's broader goals, including product development, advertising and sales, customer support, competitive plans, and financial objectives.

In general, a company can implement one of three export pricing strategies: a standard worldwide price, dual pricing, or market-differentiated pricing. Exporters often set standard worldwide prices, regardless of their target markets. This strategy can succeed if foreign marketing costs remain low enough that they do not affect overall costs or if their prices reflect average unit costs. A company that implements a standard pricing program must monitor the international marketplace carefully, however, to make sure that domestic competitors do not undercut its prices.

The dual pricing strategy distinguishes prices for domestic and export sales. Some exporters practise cost-plus pricing to establish dual prices that fully allocate their true domestic and foreign costs to product sales in those markets. These prices ensure that an exporter makes a profit on any product it sells, but final prices may exceed those of competitors. Other companies opt for flexible cost-plus pricing schemes that allow marketers to grant discounts or change prices according to shifts in the competitive environment or fluctuations in the international exchange rate.

assessment check 6a ✓

6.1 What is competitive bidding?

6.2 Why is price stability difficult to achieve in global marketing?

6.3 What are the three traditional global pricing strategies?

6.4 Which is the most flexible global pricing strategy?

The third strategy, market-differentiated pricing, makes even more flexible arrangements to set prices according to local marketplace conditions. The dynamic global marketplace often requires frequent price changes by exporters who choose this approach. Effective market-differentiated pricing depends on access to quick, accurate market information.

THE TRANSFER PRICING DILEMMA

A pricing problem peculiar to large-scale enterprises is the determination of an internal **transfer price**—the price for moving goods between **profit centres**, which are any part of the organization to which revenue and controllable costs can be assigned, such as a department. As companies expand, they tend to decentralize management and set up profit centres as a control device in the newly decentralized operation.

In a large company, profit centres might secure many needed resources from sellers within their own organization. The pricing problem thus poses several questions: What rate should profit centre A (maintenance department) charge profit centre B (production department) for the cleaning compound used on B's floors? Should the price be the same as it would be if A did the work for an outside party? Should B receive a discount? The answers to these questions depend on the philosophy of the firm involved.

Transfer pricing can be complicated, especially for multinational organizations. The government closely monitors transfer pricing practices because these exchanges offer easy ways for companies to avoid paying taxes on profits. Figure 16.6 shows how this type of pricing manipulation might work. Suppose a South Korean manufacturer of DVD players sells its machines to its Canadian subsidiary for distribution to dealers. Although each unit costs $25 to build, the manufacturer charges its subsidiary $75. In turn, the distributor sells the DVD players to retailers for $125 each. This arrangement gives the South Korean manufacturer a $50 profit on each machine, on which it pays taxes only in South Korea. Meanwhile, the Canadian subsidiary writes off $50 for advertising and shipping costs, leaving it with no profits—and no tax liability.

> **transfer price** Cost assessed when a product is moved from one profit centre in a firm to another.
>
> **profit centre** Any part of an organization to which revenue and controllable costs can be assigned.

---

assessment check 6b

6.5 Define *transfer price*.

6.6 What is a profit centre?

ONLINE PRICING CONSIDERATIONS

Throughout this text, we have seen the impact of the Internet on every component of the marketing mix. A recent online phenomenon is Kijiji, an online network of urban communities where buyers and sellers can sell, buy, or exchange goods as described in the "Marketing: Making Your World Better" feature. Sellers' expectations are frequently low: they expect to receive little for what they sell. Buyer expectations are high: they expect to pay little for what they buy. Sometimes

figure 16.6

Transfer Pricing to Escape Taxation

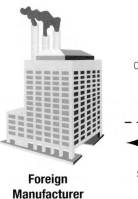

| **Foreign Manufacturer** | | **Foreign-Owned Distributor** | | **Retailer** |

Cost of unit $25

Sale price $75

Profit $50

Cost of unit $75
Advertising/shipping $50

Sale price $125

Profit $0

MARKETING: MAKING YOUR WORLD BETTER
Kijiji: Whatever You Want—To Buy or To Sell

HAVE you ever considered Kijiji—to buy or to sell? Millions of Canadians do, from teenagers looking for the latest fashions, to seniors who are downsizing and need to get rid of excess furniture. Ads can be placed on Kijiji for free, except for ads trying to sell dogs. The company recently instituted a $4.99 fee for such ads and requires that they be paid for by credit card or PayPal so that there is accountability and traceability. Animal welfare agencies and registered shelters still advertise for free, and part of the fees that Kijiji otherwise collects goes to animal welfare groups. Kijiji hopes this will eliminate the worst of the unscrupulous pet brokers.

One of the most popular categories on Kijiji is cars and vehicles. About 40 percent of shoppers for used vehicles search online—about 4 million Canadians view the 350,000 listings on Kijiji. A new listing for a pre-owned vehicle is placed on Kijiji Canada every seven seconds; the average listing takes 27 days to sell. But Kijiji can also help find very unusual items: one of the most unusual ads on Kijiji—and a successful one—was for a new calf, wanted for a mother cow that had just given birth to a pair of identical twins that were stillborn.

Kijiji can also help find very high-demand items that are otherwise unavailable without considerable delay: when Nike launched the Air Jordan 11 Retro Low Concord sneakers on May 3, 2014, approximately 350,000 pairs were sold that day across the United States. Retail stores in Canada sold out in mere minutes. But entrepreneurial "sneaker scalpers" were ready. Twenty-five pairs were posted for sale on Kijiji within a half-hour, at prices as high as double the $180 retail price. Unfortunate shoppers who did not want to wait any longer than necessary for new inventory to arrive had an option, provided they were willing to pay.

Finally, in very time-sensitive situations where there are few other alternatives, Kijiji can be the solution. When four-year-old Jaslynn Long died in May 2014, her dream to be an ice princess—like Elsa, whom she saw in Disney's movie *Frozen*—ended. Her distraught parents, hoping to still make her dream come true, wanted their daughter to be buried in the sparkling blue dress seen in the movie. A replica of the dress was almost impossible to get due to high demand. The Disney store held draws and allowed only winners to purchase one. With time at a premium, the parents explained their predicament to eight sellers they found on Kijiji. Darren Ezer of Toronto was offering a dress for $150. Ezer said, "I was kind of shocked, and very sad.... I've got three daughters of my own, so it touched me right off the bat." When he met the family, he donated the dress to them.

Users of Kijiji never know what they will find. Some are lucky enough to find special people such as Darren Ezer. Unfortunately, unaware consumers can find people whose sole purpose in life is to see how much they can get while contributing as little as possible in exchange. Shoppers should be aware of the warnings offered by Kijiji because the company wants to make your Kijiji experience a positive one.

Sources: Brian Turner, "We Really Have Issues with Our Wheels; Most Would Rather Drive Something Else," *Edmonton Journal*, May 30, 2014, p. F3; Sam Laidman, "Hampstead Cow 'Moo'ves on after Losing Babies," *Telegraph-Journal* (Saint John, N.B.), May 27, 2014, p. C6; Laurent Bastien Corbeil, "Family Finds Dress Fit for Their Princess: After Tragic Death, Girl To Be Buried in Her Fairy-Tale Gown," *Toronto Star*, May 26, 2014, p. GT1; Rory Barrs, "Sneaker No Mics; The Regulated Supply of and Intense Demand for Air Nike 11 Retro Low Concord," *National Post*, May 24, 2014, p. WP6; CBC News, "Kijiji Fee Aimed at Weeding Out Unscrupulous Pet Brokers," **www.cbc.ca**, March 13, 2014.

Marketoid

Among the recent items on the Government of Canada's online auction site: a commercial potato peeler formerly used at Kingston Penitentiary, and a 2009 Ford Crown Victoria police interceptor. Car description: broken windshield, assorted scrapes and scratches, rear doors inoperable from the inside, engine starts with a boost, opening bid is $900.

buyers and sellers negotiate price before a sale or purchase is made. Many people see the Internet as one big auction site. Whether it's toys, art, or automobiles, there seems to be an online auction site to serve every person's needs—buyer and seller alike. Auctions are the purest form of negotiated pricing.

Ticket sales are an online auction favourite. Consumers can bid on tickets for all sorts of events: Broadway shows, professional sports, and rock concerts. Razor Gator and Ticket Liquidator are two such online ticket sellers. Razor Gator specializes in finding tickets to sold-out events and providing a "VIP experience." Ticket Liquidator offers low prices on tickets for thousands of events daily.[32]

Online auctions also take place at sites such as eBid.ca and uBid.com, where consumers can snap up items as varied as diamond-and-gold cuff links and an entire—deserted—Italian village. Recently, eBay reported that more than half of its transactions concern fixed-price products, and income from its Marketplace website has been overtaken by PayPal, which eBay owns and has 110 million active accounts around the world. Home Depot recently began accepting PayPal; the pilot project spread to 2,000 stores in only two months. Fifteen new retail partners have joined this service, which translates to almost 17,000 stores. A PayPal customer swipes the PayPal card or keys in his or her mobile phone number and PIN.[33]

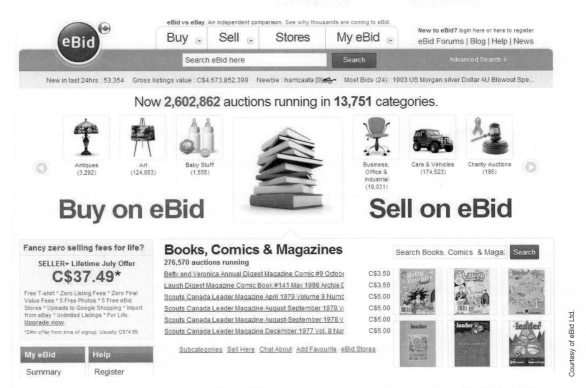

Auctions are considered the purest form of negotiating prices and can occur in many places, including online. eBid is one of the most popular online auction sites.

Another characteristic of online pricing is the use of search programs called **bots** or **shopbots**—derived from the word *robots*—that act as comparison shopping agents. Bots, such as shopbot.ca, search the Web for a specific product and print a list of sites that offer the best prices. In online selling, bots force marketers to keep prices low. However, marketing researchers report that almost four of every five online shoppers will check out several sites before buying, and price is not the only variable they consider when making a purchase decision. Service quality and support information are powerful motivators in the decision process. Also, although price is an important factor with products such as books and DVDs, it is not as important with complex or highly differentiated products, such as real estate or investment banking. Brand image and customer service may outweigh price in these purchase decisions.

To deal with the influences of the Internet on pricing policies and practices, marketers are applying old strategies in new ways and companies are updating operations to compete with new electronic technologies. Some firms offer online specials that do not appear in their stores or mail-order catalogues. These may take such forms as limited-time discounts, free shipping offers, or coupons that are good only online.

THE CANNIBALIZATION DILEMMA

By pricing the same products differently online, companies run the risk of **cannibalization**. The new twist to an old tactic is that companies are self-inflicting price cuts by creating competition among their own products. During the first decade of e-business, marketers debated whether it was worth taking the risk of alienating customers and channel members by offering lower prices for their products online—which then was an unproven retail outlet. But today, marketers are more savvy about integrating marketing channels, including online sites and affiliated stores—different stores owned by the same company. The trend is moving toward standardizing pricing across channels. As consumers become *multi-channel shoppers,* shopping their preferred retailers both online and off, they expect retailers to recognize them as regular shoppers, regardless of the channel they

bot (shopbot) Software program that allows online shoppers to compare the price of a particular product offered by several online retailers.

cannibalization Loss of sales of an existing product due to competition from a new product in the same line.

choose. Research shows that multi-channel shoppers are more profitable than those who stick to one channel.[34]

BUNDLE PRICING

bundle pricing Offering two or more complementary products and selling them for a single price.

As marketers have watched e-commerce weaken their control over prices, they have modified their use of the price variable in the marketing mix. Whenever possible, they have moved to an approach called **bundle pricing**, in which customers acquire a host of goods and services in addition to the tangible products they purchase.

Nowhere is bundle pricing more prevalent than in the telecommunications industry. Consumers are bombarded daily by advertisements for all kinds of Internet, cell phone, and cable or satellite TV packages. Telus, Rogers Communications, and Bell Canada all compete with discounted bundles of services. For example, prices on bundles from Rogers vary depending on the number of services a customer chooses, including wireless, TV, Internet, home phone, and home monitoring.

But sometimes consumers resist the practice of bundling, claiming they are forced to pay for services they don't want in order to receive the ones they do. This is particularly the case with cable television. Cable companies insist they have spent billions of dollars to expand their networks and technology and would be left with unused capacity if they sold only a few channels at a time. Consumer advocates argue that customers are not only forced to pay for unwanted services but also wind up paying inflated prices. The solution for many consumers is increasingly to simply discontinue their subscription service and stream exactly what they want to see, and only what they want to see, online.

assessment check 6c

6.7 Describe the benefits of an auction—to the buyer and to the seller.

6.8 What is cannibalization?

6.9 What is bundle pricing?

(7) **Outline the legal constraints on pricing.**

PRICING AND THE LAW

Pricing decisions are influenced by a variety of legal constraints imposed by federal, provincial, and municipal governments. Included in the price of products are not only the cost of the raw materials, processing and packaging, and profit for the business but also the various taxes that governments require providers to charge. For instance, excise taxes are levied on a variety of products—including cigarettes, alcoholic beverages, and motor fuels. Sales taxes are charged on purchases of most products and services in Canada.

In the global marketplace, prices are directly affected by special types of taxes called *tariffs*. These taxes—levied on the sale of imported goods and services—often make it possible for firms to protect their local markets and still set prices on domestically produced goods well above world market levels. Canada, the United States, and Mexico almost eliminated tariffs on goods traded between them due to the North America Free Trade Agreement (NAFTA). In 2013, Canada and the European Union—representing 28 countries—signed a tentative free trade agreement that, if ratified, would see 98 percent of tariffs both ways immediately eliminated. Ratification could take place as early as 2015.[35] After nearly ten years of negotiations, Canada and South Korea concluded a free trade agreement in 2014—Canada's first such agreement with an Asian country.[36]

Another form of pricing—often illegal—is *ticket scalping*. Scalpers camp out in ticket lines for high-demand sporting and concert events (or hire someone else to stand in line) to purchase tickets they expect to resell at a higher price. Although some cities have enacted laws prohibiting the practice, it continues to occur in many locations.

Canada's free-trade agreement with South Korea—the first with an Asian country—will eliminate the 6.1 percent tariff on Kia and Hyundai car imports into Canada.

H. F. (Herb) MacKenzie

But the ticket reselling market is both highly fragmented and susceptible to fraud and distorted pricing. In response, buyers and sellers are finding that the Internet is helping to create a market where both buyers and sellers can compare prices and seat locations. Web firms such as StubHub .com and TicketsNow.com, the latter owned by Ticketmaster, act as ticket clearinghouses for this secondary market and have signed deals with several professional sports teams that allow season ticket holders to sell unwanted tickets and for buyers to purchase them with a guarantee.

Pricing is also regulated by the general constraints of the Competition Act legislation, as outlined in Chapter 3. The following sections review some of the most important pricing laws for contemporary marketers.

COMPETITION ACT

Canada has a long history of competition legislation that goes back to the 1889 act for the prevention and suppression of combines formed in restraint of trade. The Combines Investigation Act was passed in 1923, and the current **Competition Act** has been in effect since 1986. The purpose of the competition act is to

- promote the efficiency and adaptability of the Canadian economy

- expand opportunities for Canadian participation in world markets while at the same time recognizing the role of foreign competition in Canada

- ensure that small and medium-sized enterprises have an equitable opportunity to participate in the Canadian economy

- provide consumers with competitive prices and product choices.[37]

The Competition Act tries to balance the interests of businesses and consumers; it tries to foster a fair competitive environment to protect businesses from each other and to protect consumers from unfair business practices. It focuses on a number of pricing-related practices, including *price discrimination*, *price fixing (a form of collusion)*, *bid rigging*, *predatory pricing*, *false or misleading ordinary selling price representations*, and many others.

Price discrimination, which occurs when some customers pay more than others for the same product, dates back to the very beginnings of trade and commerce. Today, however, technology has added to the frequency and complexity of price discrimination, as well as the strategies marketers adopt to get around it. For example, marketers may encourage repeat business by inviting purchasers to become preferred customers, entitling them to average discounts of 10 percent. As long as companies can demonstrate that their price discounts and promotional allowances do not restrict competition, they avoid penalties under the Competition Act. Direct mail marketers frequently send out catalogues of identical goods but with different prices in different editions of the catalogues. Postal code areas that traditionally consist of high spenders get the catalogues with the higher prices, while postal code areas where price-sensitive customers live get the catalogues with the lower prices. Victoria's Secret, Staples, and Simon & Schuster are among the hundreds of companies that employ legal price discrimination strategies.

Firms accused of price discrimination often argue that they set price differentials to meet competitors' prices and that cost differences justify variations in prices. When a firm asserts that it maintains price differentials as good-faith methods of competing with rivals, a logical question arises: What constitutes good-faith pricing behaviour? The answer depends on the particular situation.

A defence based on cost differentials works only if the price differences do not exceed the cost differences resulting from selling to various classes of buyers. Marketers must then be prepared to justify the cost differences. Many authorities consider this provision one of the most confusing areas in the Competition Act. Courts handle most charges brought under the act as individual cases. Therefore, domestic marketers must continually evaluate their pricing actions to avoid potential violations. Price discrimination becomes a more important issue when one company charges different prices to two or more companies that are in competition with each other. This clearly interferes with competition in the marketplace. There have been only three convictions for discriminatory pricing under the Competition Act, all since 1984, with fines ranging from $15,000 to $50,000.[38]

Price fixing is a form of collusion in which sellers get together and collude to set prices higher than they would otherwise be in a free market. Regulators in Canada, the United States, Europe,

Competition Act The most comprehensive legislation in Canada, designed to help both consumers and businesses by promoting a healthy competitive environment.

price discrimination Occurs when some customers pay more than others for the same product.

price fixing A form of collusion in which sellers get together and collude to set prices higher than they would otherwise be in a free market.

Marketoid

Canadians purchase approximately $1.4 billion of chocolate annually, including 90 million Easter bunnies. Celebrate Chocolate Éclair Day (June 22), Chocolate Pudding Day (June 26), and Chocolate Day (July 7).

A number of health clubs in Canada have been charged with violations under the Competition Act.

and Japan have imposed multimillion-dollar fines for automotive parts manufacturers for price fixing related to radiators, seatbelts, and other auto parts. Recently, the Competition Bureau of Canada announced that it had uncovered evidence of price fixing among Canada's largest chocolate candy makers and sellers and that it would be prosecuting the companies and several of their executives. A settlement was recently reached that saw them pay more than $23 million in fines. If found guilty of price fixing, businesses and individuals face fines up to $25 million and prison terms as long as 14 years.[39] **Bid rigging** is another form of collusion, similar to price fixing. It occurs when sellers get together and collude to set prices with respect to one or more requests for competitive proposals. The intent is that one of the sellers will provide the lowest price but, unknown to the customer, one that is higher than it would be in a free market.

bid rigging Occurs when sellers get together and collude to set prices with respect to one or more requests for competitive proposals.

Predatory pricing occurs when companies set prices below their cost for a sufficiently long period of time to discourage or eliminate competition and then raise their prices or otherwise interfere with competition. Speculation of predatory pricing recently arose when the big three telcos—Bell Canada, Rogers, and Telus—reduced wireless rates in areas of Canada serviced by much smaller regional carriers: Eastlink in the Maritimes, Videotron in Quebec, MTS in Manitoba, and SaskTel in Saskatchewan. Ron Styles, president of SaskTel, suggests if this is not predatory pricing, then the big three are charging consumers in the rest of Canada needlessly high rates.[40]

predatory pricing Occurs when companies set prices below their cost for a sufficiently long period of time to discourage or eliminate competition and then raise their prices or otherwise interfere with competition.

False or misleading price representation is one form of misleading advertising. Misleading price advertising has been common in Canada. Several Canadian retailers and health and fitness clubs have paid fines for misleading advertising. Recently, Rogers Communications was assessed a $500,000 fine as the result of poorly substantiated claims it was making regarding its Chatr discount brand.[41] Advertising Standards Canada recently reported that complaints about misleading advertising now exceed complaints about offensive advertising. In one recent year, it upheld six complaints concerning retailers who failed to honour their price-match guarantees and three complaints concerning inaccurate ads for daily deals.[42]

false or misleading price representation One form of misleading advertising.

assessment check 7 ✓

7.1 What does the Competition Act try to accomplish?

7.2 What is price discrimination? Is it always considered anticompetitive? Explain.

7.3 What is the difference between price fixing and bid rigging?

Strategic Implications

This chapter has focused on traditional pricing concepts and methods, and on setting prices as an important part of a firm's marketing program designed to help it achieve its overall business objectives. Technology has forever changed the marketplace, which affects the pricing function. A growing number of products are not made until they are ordered, and increasingly, their prices are no longer fixed; instead, prices can shift up and down in response to changing market conditions.

Customers can now compare prices quickly, heightening competitive intensity. Online price comparison engines, known as *shopping bots*, promise to help customers find the lowest price for any good or service. The Web allows for prices to be negotiated on the spot, and anything can be auctioned. Reverse auctions—gaining in popularity in both consumer and business markets—allow customers to submit the highest price they are willing to pay for an increasing number of products.

The Web connects buyers and sellers from around the globe. A customer in Halifax, Nova Scotia, might want to purchase a wool sweater from Norway. Global transportation systems have lowered delivery costs and increased delivery speeds as volumes have grown, facilitating the likelihood of such purchases. Firms today must be concerned with price competition across borders, and not simply across town.

To succeed in today's more competitive pricing environment, marketers must continue to offer value—fair prices for quality goods and services—and superior customer service. These are the critical success factors in marketing today. ◆◆◆

REVIEW OF CHAPTER OBJECTIVES

① Identify the major categories of pricing objectives.

Pricing objectives should be the natural consequence of overall organizational goals and more specific marketing goals. They can be classified into four major groups: (1) profitability objectives, including profit maximization and target returns; (2) volume objectives, including sales maximization and market share; (3) meeting competition objectives; and (4) prestige objectives.

② Explain the methods of determining prices.

Marketers determine prices in two basic ways: by applying the theoretical concepts of supply and demand and by completing cost-oriented analyses. The assumption that firms attempt to maximize profit, the difficulty of estimating demand curves, and inadequate training of managers to use economic theory all present problems with the first approach. Cost-plus pricing is the most commonly used method of setting prices today. There are two primary cost-oriented pricing procedures: full-cost pricing and incremental-cost pricing. Break-even analysis, another cost-based model, can be helpful but also has some limitations. The basic limitation of all cost-oriented pricing approaches is that they do not adequately account for product demand. When most of a firm's costs are fixed over a wide range of outputs, yield management pricing strategies can help maximize revenues and, hence, maximize profit.

③ Compare the alternative pricing strategies and explain when each strategy is most appropriate.

The alternative pricing strategies are skimming pricing strategy, penetration pricing strategy, and competitive pricing strategy. Skimming pricing is commonly used as a market-entry price for distinctive products with little or no initial competition. Penetration pricing is used when there is a wide array of competing brands. Everyday low pricing (EDLP), a variant of penetration pricing, is used by discounters that attempt to hold the line on prices without having to rely heavily on short-term coupons, rebates, and other price concessions. Competitive pricing is employed when marketers wish to concentrate their competitive efforts on marketing variables other than price.

④ Describe how prices are quoted.

Methods for quoting prices depend on such factors as cost structures, traditional practices in the particular industry, and policies of individual firms. Price quotes can involve list prices, market prices, cash discounts, trade discounts, quantity discounts, and allowances such as trade-ins, promotional allowances, and rebates. Shipping costs often figure heavily into the pricing of goods. A number of alternatives for dealing with these costs exist: FOB origin (or shipping point) pricing, in which the shipping costs are paid by the buyer; FOB destination, in which the shipping costs are paid by the seller; FOB origin—freight allowed and prepaid, in which the freight is still paid by the seller but legal responsibility and title pass to the buyer when the goods leave the seller's premises; and zone pricing, in which a set price exists within each region.

⑤ Identify the various pricing policy decisions that marketers must make.

A pricing policy is a general guideline based on pricing objectives and is intended for use in specific pricing decisions. Pricing policies include psychological pricing, unit pricing, price flexibility, product-line pricing, and promotional pricing. An important pricing consideration for marketing managers is the price–quality relationship. In the absence of other cues, price is an important influence on how the consumer perceives the product's quality.

⑥ List and explain a number of special issues in pricing.

A number of special issues in pricing were discussed. Competitive bidding and negotiated prices are pricing techniques used primarily in the B2B sector and in government and organizational markets. For global marketers, in addition to the traditional four pricing objectives, a fifth objective is often price stability. Global marketers can choose from three export pricing strategies: a standard worldwide price, dual pricing, or market-differentiated pricing. A phenomenon in large corporations—and particularly in global marketing companies—is transfer pricing, in which a company sets prices for transferring goods or services from one company profit centre to another. To deal with the influences of the Internet on pricing policies and practices, marketers are updating operations to compete with new electronic technologies. For customers, bots, also known as shopbots, act as comparison-shopping agents. Cannibalization secures additional sales through lower prices that take sales away from the marketer's other products. It can be an important problem for companies that price their products differently online than through other channels. Bundle pricing is offering two or more complementary products and selling them for a single price.

⑦ Outline the legal constraints on pricing.

A variety of laws affect pricing decisions. The Competition Act is the major legislation in Canada that governs pricing and other competitive business practices. Among the pricing-related issues covered by this legislation are price discrimination, price fixing, bid rigging, predatory pricing, and false or misleading ordinary selling price representations. The Competition Act tries to balance the interests of businesses and consumers; it tries to foster a fair competitive environment to protect businesses from each other and to protect consumers from unfair business practices.

assessment check answers ✓

1.1 What are target-return objectives?
Target-return objectives are short-run or long-run goals that are usually stated as percentages of sales or investment.

1.2 What is value pricing?
Value pricing emphasizes the benefits a product provides in comparison to the price and quality levels of competing offerings.

1.3 How do prestige objectives affect a seller's pricing strategy?
Prestige pricing establishes a relatively high price to develop and maintain an image of quality that appeals to status-conscious customers. The seller uses price to create an overall image of the firm.

1.4 What goals does pricing strategy help a not-for-profit organization achieve?
Pricing strategy helps not-for-profit organizations achieve a variety of goals: profit maximization, cost recovery, market incentives, and market suppression.

2.1 What are the two basic ways in which marketers determine prices?
Marketers determine prices by applying the theoretical concepts of supply and demand and by completing cost-oriented analysis.

2.2 What are the four types of market structures?
The four types of market structures are pure competition, monopolistic competition, oligopoly, and monopoly.

2.3 Identify the two types of costs that make up a product's total cost.
A product's total cost is composed of total variable costs and total fixed costs.

2.4 What are the determinants of elasticity?
The degree of consumer responsiveness to price changes—elasticity—is affected by such factors as (1) availability of substitute or complementary goods, (2) the classification of a good or service as a luxury or a necessity, (3) the portion of a person's budget spent on an item, and (4) the time perspective.

2.5 What is the usual relationship between elasticity and revenue?

A price cut increases revenue only for a product with elastic demand, and a price increase raises revenue only for a product with inelastic demand.

2.6 List the three reasons why it is difficult to put price theory into practice.

A basic assumption of price theory is that all firms attempt to maximize profits. This does not always happen in practice. A second reason is that demand curves can be extremely difficult to estimate. Finally, managers can be inadequately trained, causing poor communication between economists and managers, which makes it difficult to apply price theory in the real world.

2.7 What is full-cost pricing?

Full-cost pricing uses all relevant variable costs in setting a product's price.

2.8 What is incremental-cost pricing?

Incremental-cost pricing attempts to use only costs directly attributable to a specific output in setting prices to overcome the arbitrary allocation of fixed expenses.

2.9 Give the formula for finding the break-even point, in units and in dollars.

Break-even point (in units) = Total fixed cost/Per-unit contribution to fixed cost. Break-even point (in dollars) = Total fixed cost/ (1 – Variable cost per unit price).

2.10 What adjustments to the basic break-even calculation must be made to include target returns?

Break-even point (including specific dollar target return) = (Total fixed cost + Profit objective)/Per-unit contribution.

2.11 What are the advantages of break-even analysis?

Break-even analysis is easily understood by managers and may help them decide whether required sales levels for a certain price are realistic goals.

2.12 What are the disadvantages of break-even analysis?

First, the model assumes that cost can be divided into fixed and variable categories and ignores the problems of arbitrarily making some allocations. Second, it assumes that per-unit variable costs do not change at different levels of operation, ignoring the possibility of quantity discounts, more efficient use of the workforce, and other possible economies. Third, the basic break-even model does not consider demand.

2.13 Explain the goal of yield management.

Yield management pricing strategies are designed to maximize revenues in situations in which costs are fixed, such as airfares, auto rentals, and theatre tickets.

3.1 What are the three major pricing strategies?

The three major pricing strategies are skimming, penetration, and competitive.

3.2 What is EDLP?

EDLP stands for everyday low pricing. It is a variation of penetration pricing often used by discounters.

4.1 What are the three major types of discounts?

The three major types of discounts are cash discounts, trade discounts, and quantity discounts.

4.2 Identify the three alternatives for handling transportation costs in pricing policies.

The three alternatives for handling transportation costs are FOB pricing, zone pricing, and basing-point pricing.

5.1 Define *pricing policy*.

A pricing policy is a general guideline that reflects marketing objectives and influences specific pricing decisions.

5.2 Describe the two types of psychological pricing other than prestige pricing.

The two additional types of psychological pricing are odd pricing, in which marketers set prices at odd numbers just under round numbers, and unit pricing, which states prices in terms of a recognized unit of measurement.

5.3 What is promotional pricing?

Promotional pricing is a lower-than-normal price for a set period of time.

5.4 Describe the price–quality connection.

Price serves as an important indicator of a product's quality. However, many marketers now work hard to convince consumers that they are offering high-quality products at the lowest possible price.

5.5 What are price limits?

Price limits indicate certain boundaries within which consumers' product-quality perceptions vary directly with price. A price set lower than expected seems too cheap, and one set above the expected limit is seen as too expensive.

6.1 What is competitive bidding?

Competitive bidding consists of inviting potential suppliers to quote prices on proposed purchases or contracts.

6.2 Why is price stability difficult to achieve in global marketing?

Price stability is difficult to achieve because wars, terrorism, economic trends, changing governments, and shifting trade policies can alter prices.

6.3 What are the three traditional global pricing strategies?

The three global pricing strategies are standard worldwide pricing, dual pricing, and market-differentiated pricing.

6.4 Which is the most flexible global pricing strategy?

The most flexible global pricing strategy is market-differentiated pricing, which allows firms to set prices according to actual conditions.

6.5 Define *transfer price*.

A transfer price is the price for moving goods between profit centres.

6.6 What is a profit centre?

A profit centre is any part of the organization to which revenue and controllable costs can be assigned.

6.7 Describe the benefits of an auction—to the buyer and to the seller.

An auction can provide buyers with opportunities to buy goods and services at very low prices. It can also offer the seller an opportunity to sell to a wider audience (online) perhaps at a higher price than otherwise would be possible, if the item is particularly popular.

6.8 What is cannibalization?
Cannibalization involves cutting prices in one selling channel, which creates direct competition with a firm's own products.

6.9 What is bundle pricing?
Bundle pricing involves combining a number of goods or services together and offering them at a set price.

7.1 What does the Competition Act try to accomplish?
The Competition Act tries to foster a fair competitive environment to protect businesses from each other and to protect consumers from unfair business practices.

7.2 What is price discrimination? Is it always considered anticompetitive? Explain.
Price discrimination occurs when some customers pay more than others for the same product. It is acceptable when discounts are given to meet competition, or can be justified due to cost savings resulting from selling to some customers.

7.3 What is the difference between price fixing and bid rigging?
Both are forms of price collusion and are illegal; however, price fixing occurs when sellers decide to establish prices higher than would exist in a free market whereas bid rigging occurs when the prices relate to one or more competitive bids.

MARKETING TERMS YOU NEED TO KNOW

These terms are printed in blue in the text. They are defined in the margins of the chapter and in the Glossary that begins on p. G-1.

PROJECTS AND TEAMWORK EXERCISES

1. In small teams, categorize each of the following as a specific type of pricing objective. Suggest a company or product likely to use each pricing objective. Compare your findings.
   a. 5 percent increase in profits over the previous year
   b. prices no more than 6 percent higher than prices quoted by independent dealers
   c. 5 percent increase in market share
   d. 25 percent return on investment (before taxes)
   e. setting the highest prices in the product category to maintain favourable brand image

2. How are the following prices determined, and what do they have in common?
   a. admission to a local museum
   b. college or university tuition

c.   provincial sales tax
d.   printing of business cards
e.   lawn mowers

3. WebSmart Development of Winnipeg, Manitoba, is considering the introduction of a new product proposed by its research and development staff. The firm's marketing director estimates the product can be marketed at a price of $70. Total fixed cost is $278,000, and average variable cost is calculated at $48.
    a.   What is the break-even point in units for the proposed product? In sales dollars?
    b.   The firm's CEO has suggested a target return of $214,000 for the proposed product. How many units must be sold to break even and achieve this target return?

4. With a classmate, create two advertisements for the same product. One advertisement should feature a high price, and the other advertisement should feature a low price. Present your advertisements to the students in your class. Record students' perceptions of the price–quality relationship.

5. On your own or with a classmate, visit a local supermarket to find examples of promotional pricing and loss leaders. Note instances of both. Does the promotional pricing make you more apt to purchase a product? Does knowing the store uses loss-leader pricing of bananas or apples make you more inclined to buy them? Present your findings and opinions to the class.

CRITICAL THINKING EXERCISES

1. Music artists earn only about 9 percent in royalties per CD, using a royalty base of retail price less 25 percent for packaging costs. The rest goes to the producer and to cover recording costs, promotion, copies given away to radio stations and reviewers, and other costs such as videos. What do you think happens to the artist's royalties when a CD is marked down to sell faster? Consider two cases: (a) the marked-down CD sells more copies, and (b) it sells the same number of copies as before.

2. Some finance experts advise consumers not to worry about rising gasoline prices, the cost of which can easily be covered by forgoing one takeout meal a month, but to worry about how high energy prices will affect the rest of the economy. For example, each dollar-a-barrel price increase is equivalent to several millions of dollars a day "tax" on the economy. Explain what this means.

3. When Chinese automakers recently began exporting cars, rather than focusing on developed nations in the West, they turned to emerging markets in countries like Algeria, Russia, Chile, and South Africa. In these markets, even used vehicles from multinational manufacturers are relatively scarce—and relatively expensive. The Chinese automakers, whose priority is keeping costs down rather than design or even safety, applied a penetration-pricing strategy. A woman in Santiago, Chile, who bought a new Chery S21 explained, "The price factor is fairly decisive. I paid $5,500 new and full. Toyota with similar features costs around $12,000." Why do you think Chinese automakers chose that pricing strategy? Do you think it was successful? As Chinese regulators pressure these manufacturers to make their cars safer, do you think they will be able to keep their prices low compared with those of the international automakers? Why or why not?[43]

4. As a consumer, would you rather shop at a store that features a sale once a month or a store that practises everyday low pricing (EDLP)? Why?

5. Go online to a shopping site you use regularly and note the prices for different types of products. Does the firm use psychological pricing? Product line pricing? Note any pricing strategies you can identify. Do any of these strategies make you prefer the site over a competitor's site?

ETHICS EXERCISE

You work for a major restaurant in your town. The manager is facing cost pressures from rising food prices and says she needs to raise revenues. She decides to reduce the size of the meal portions and use cheaper cuts of meat and fish in some entrées while holding the menu prices constant. She tells you and other staff members not to mention the changes to customers and to deflect any questions or complaints you hear. The descriptions in the menu will not be changed, she says, "because the printing costs would be too high."

1. You know the restaurant advertises the quality of its ingredients in the local media. But the menu changes are not advertised, and it bothers you. What course of action would you take?

2. A customer mentions the beef in a dish he ordered is "tough and dry" and the order seems smaller than before. What would you do?

CASE 16.1

The Cost of Golf: Money versus Time

While we often hear that hockey is Canada's game, there are more adults who play golf in Canada than who play hockey, and twice the percentage in Canada than in the United States. In fact, one in five Canadians plays golf, according to Scott Simmons, CEO of Golf Canada. Golf, he adds, creates 350,000 jobs across Canada, contributes more than $13 billion annually to Canadian GDP, and generates more than $400 million in charitable donations through golf tournaments.

Despite its popularity, most people—even most golfers—will not recognize the name Stanley Thompson (1893–1953). But he was and, arguably, remains one of the world's most influential golf course architects. He worked on well over 100 golf courses from Nova Scotia to British Columbia, and in Brazil, Colombia, Jamaica, and the United States. In 1998, the Stanley Thompson Foundation was formed to build his legacy, catalogue and verify his courses, and provide scholarship opportunities in his name. The Thompson Graduate Studies Scholarship at the University of Guelph was recently introduced and is awarded to graduate students who pursue graduate studies in golf course design. In 2005 Stanley Thompson was designated as a Person of National Significance by the Historic Sites and Monuments Board of Canada.

For anyone interested in experiencing a Stanley Thompson course as he originally designed and built it, Allandale Golf Club just north of Toronto is intact, just as he originally designed and built it. All his other Ontario golf courses have been altered over the years. The original Allandale course was constructed in 1932 as a six-hole course at Mardon Lodge, the country estate of General Donald McDonald Hogarth. Three additional holes were added in 1937 and, today, the course remains a nine-hole course. The following is the 2014 green fees schedule.

	9-Holes	18-Holes	After 4:00 P.M.
Adults			
Mon.–Fri.	$23.00	$35.00	$22.50
Weekends and Holidays	$25.00	$40.00	$23.00

Juniors & Seniors			
Mon.–Fri.	$22.50	$31.00	$22.50
Weekends and Holidays	$25.00	$40.00	$23.00

Golfers who insist on playing 18 holes simply need to make two rounds of the course. But, today, more golfers are seeking to play a 9-hole par 36 course or an 18-hole "executive" course that is shorter—often par 60 to par 63 versus the more standard par 72. Golfers are increasingly moving away from the 18 holes of par-72 golf. In fact, historically, golf courses varied from as few as 7 to as many as 25 holes. What is driving today's preference for shorter golf games? Many golfers, particularly ones who are otherwise busy, find it much easier to spare 90 to 120 minutes for a round of golf rather than losing an entire morning or afternoon to the sport. They are willing to pay a higher price per hole but a lower overall price, while also saving the time needed to play longer games.

Questions for Critical Thinking

1. Carefully review the 2014 green fees schedule for Allandale Golf Club and explain what you believe to be the rationale for this schedule.
2. What recommendations would you suggest to improve the 2014 fees schedule? Explain the rationale for any recommendations you make.
3. Explain, from a golfer's perspective, why nine-hole golf courses are increasing in popularity. Do you see this trend increasing in the future? Explain.

Sources: The Stanley Thompson Foundation, **www.stanleythompsonsociety.com**; Ian Andrew's "Caddy Shack": A Blog about Golf Course Architecture, "Stepping Back in Time at Allandale," May 31, 2006; Allandale Golf Course website, **www.allandalegolfcourse.com**; Scott Anderson, "Golf a Big Hit in Canada: Golf Canada CEO," **www.bnn.ca**, April 12, 2013, all accessed May 28, 2014; "The Easy Sell: Nine Holes," **www.canadianbusiness.com**, July 19, 2013.

CASE 16.2

When Price Deals Fail, Consumers React

In May 2014, Lonovo offered special prices on six laptop models, including the Y410P, priced at $279 instead of its regular price of $1,329. Customers were instructed to use "DOORCRASHER" as the rebate code when they placed their orders. Unfortunately, the deal was not really a deal: Lonovo erred. However, Lenovo had already processed many orders, even charging customers' credit cards, before the error was noted and the company processed reimbursements to customers' credit cards. As a "gesture of goodwill," Lenovo offered customers a $100 gift card they could use for future computer purchases. One customer, however, complained that 12 hours after he was informed his order was cancelled, the incorrect prices were still available online. Customers were not only angry about Lenovo's response, some were unhappy that they gave Lenovo credit card and personal information when placing an order that was not honoured. More than 5,500 people signed an online petition asking Lenovo to honour its advertised price, and many complained to Canada's Competition Bureau and to the Consumers' Association of Canada. On social media, many consumers called for a boycott of Lenovo Canada. While the bureau confirmed it had received complaints, it would not confirm if it was taking action. Phil Norris, a spokesperson for the Competition Bureau, stated, "The best advice that we can give to the general public is to report these matters to the bureau, as it assists us in gathering evidence and possibly conducting an investigation." Under the Competition Act, companies that fail to prohibit "the sale or rent of a product at a price higher than its advertised price" can be fined as much as $10 million. However, the act will not be enforced if the advertised price was in error and the price was immediately corrected. A Queen's University marketing professor, Ken Wong, stated that regardless of whether it was an error, customers don't forgive such mistakes, particularly since this was not the first pricing error made by Lenovo.

The Lenovo situation is not unique. Many companies have made pricing errors in recent years. Some have honoured their mistakes; some have not. Few have generated the consumer backlash that Lenovo's mistake has caused. But, consumers are increasingly likely to complain about price issues whenever companies entice them with special prices, and then, for whatever reason, they cannot take advantage of the deals offered. What follows is an actual letter recently sent to a national grocery chain by an unhappy customer (name of both the company and the customer have been disguised).

May 27, 2014

54 Hidden Street,

Struan, ON

L5E 9X9

National Pride Stores

60 Unknown Street,

Somewhere, ON

L5A 7Z7

Mr. _____, President

Dear Mr. _____:

I am writing to complain regarding an experience I had at one of your Ontario locations this morning. I made a special trip to your store to purchase, in particular, the pork chops advertised in your weekly flyer for May 23–29. The price advertised was $2.99 per pound, or $6.59 per kg.

Unfortunately, there were no pork chops. I asked if there would be more available shortly and was told that there would be after Friday (the day after the sale was to end). I was offered a 30-day rain check, a reasonable solution. At the checkout, the cashier asked what quantity I wished and I requested 16 pork chops, but I was told there would be a limit of four. When I asked if there was a quantity limit on the in-store purchases, she advised no, but there was a rain check policy that limited quantities to four. In the meantime, another cashier came over and phoned the meat department and, while she was asking whether she could increase the limit on the rain check, a third woman approached and shook her head no. Then, the woman on the telephone confirmed that four would be the limit. I complained that this did not make good business sense; I left my other groceries on the counter and exited your store.

My first concern is that this contravenes the Competition Act, particularly with respect to misleading advertising. Your weekly flyer did not specify "limited quantities," and it did not specify that should an item be out of stock, your rain check policy would limit customers to four units. My second concern is that the advertised special was for family packs of pork chops, but the rain check would be for only four pork chops, not four family packs of pork chops as the item was advertised.

Had I really wanted this item, I would have asked my three passengers with me to come into the store and we could each ask for rain checks. That would simply have created more work for your employee, and would have aggravated three additional people.

Sincerely,

Corrine Langley

Questions for Critical Thinking

1. Will the Competition Bureau be likely to take action against either Lenovo Canada or the national grocery chain situation described in this case? Why or why not?

2. Some consumers complained to the Competition Bureau about Lenovo Canada, but it is unclear whether Corrine Langley complained to the Competition Bureau. What factors would lead consumers to complain to the Competition Bureau, and what factors would stop them from registering a complaint?

Sources: Nicole Bogart, "Scope of Lenovo Online Price Error Widens as Customers Wait for Refunds," **http://globalnews.ca**, April 28, 2014; Pete Evans, "Lenovo Offers $100 for Laptop Pricing Glitch," **www.cbc.ca**, May 27, 2014; David Paddon, "Lenovo Makes $100 'Goodwill' Offer after Cancelling Orders Due to Pricing Error," **www.ctvnews.ca**, May 27, 2014.

Creating an Effective Marketing Plan

Overview

"What are our mission and goals?"

"Who are our customers?"

"What types of products do we offer?"

"How can we provide superior customer service?"

These are some of the questions addressed by a **marketing plan**—a detailed description of the resources and actions needed to achieve stated marketing objectives. Chapter 2 discussed **strategic planning**—the process of anticipating events and market conditions and deciding how a firm can best achieve its organizational objectives. Marketing planning encompasses all the activities devoted to achieving marketing objectives, establishing a basis for designing a marketing strategy. This appendix deals in depth with the formal marketing plan, which is part of an organization's overall business plan. At the end of this appendix, you'll see what an actual marketing plan looks like. Each plan component for a hypothetical firm called Wild Canada Clothing is presented. ◆◆◆

COMPONENTS OF A BUSINESS PLAN

A company's **business plan** is one of its most important documents. The business plan puts in writing all the company's objectives, how they will be achieved, how the business will obtain financing, and how much money the company expects to earn over a specified time period. Although business plans vary in length and format, most contain at least some form of the following components:

- An *executive summary* briefly answers the who, what, when, where, how, and why questions for the plan. Although the summary appears early in the plan, it is typically written last, after the firm's executives have worked out the details of all the other sections.

- A *competitive analysis* section focuses on the environment in which the marketing plan is to be implemented. Although this section is more closely associated with the comprehensive business plan, factors specifically influencing marketing are likely to be included here.

- The *mission statement* summarizes the organization's purpose, vision, and overall goals. This statement provides the foundation upon which further planning is based.

- The overall business plan includes a series of *component* plans that present goals and strategies for each functional area of the enterprise. They typically include the following:

    The *marketing plan*, which describes strategies for informing potential customers about the goods and services offered by the firm as well as strategies for developing long-term relationships. At the end of this appendix, a sample marketing plan for Wild Canada Clothing is presented.

    The *financing plan*, which presents a realistic approach for securing needed funds and managing debt and cash flows.

    The *production plan*, which describes how the organization will develop its products in the most efficient, cost-effective manner possible.

marketing plan
Detailed description of the resources and actions needed to achieve stated marketing objectives.

strategic planning
Process of determining an organization's primary objectives and adopting courses of action that will achieve these objectives.

business plan Formal document that outlines a company's objectives, how they will be met, how the business will achieve financing, and how much money the firm expects to earn.

The *facilities plan*, which describes the physical environment and equipment required to implement the production plan.

The *human resources plan*, which estimates the firm's employment needs and the skills necessary to achieve organizational goals, including a comparison of current employees with the needs of the firm, and which establishes processes for securing adequately trained personnel if a gap exists between current employee skills and future needs.

This basic format encompasses the planning process used by nearly every successful organization. Whether a company operates in the manufacturing, wholesaling, retailing, or service sector (or a combination), the components described here are likely to appear in its overall business plan. Regardless of the size or longevity of a company, a business plan is an essential tool for a firm's owners because it helps them focus on the key elements of their business. Even small firms that are just starting out need a business plan to obtain financing. Figure 1 shows the outline of a business plan for Wild Canada Clothing.

figure 1

Outline of a Business Plan

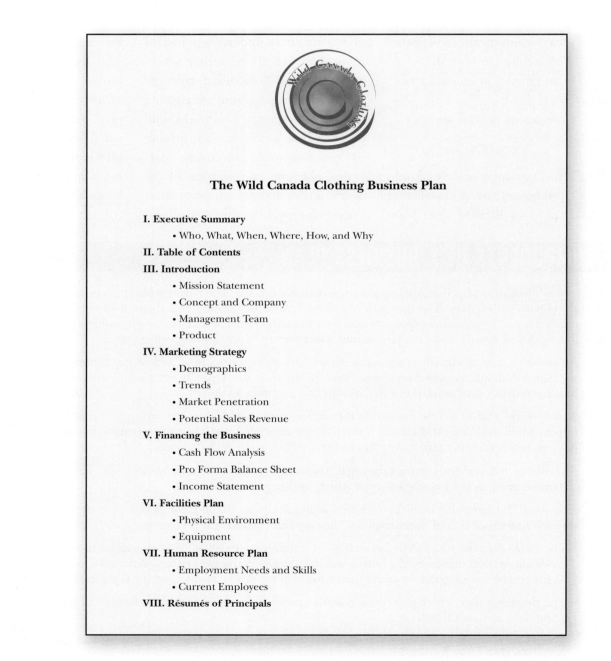

The Wild Canada Clothing Business Plan

I. Executive Summary
  • Who, What, When, Where, How, and Why

II. Table of Contents

III. Introduction
  • Mission Statement
  • Concept and Company
  • Management Team
  • Product

IV. Marketing Strategy
  • Demographics
  • Trends
  • Market Penetration
  • Potential Sales Revenue

V. Financing the Business
  • Cash Flow Analysis
  • Pro Forma Balance Sheet
  • Income Statement

VI. Facilities Plan
  • Physical Environment
  • Equipment

VII. Human Resource Plan
  • Employment Needs and Skills
  • Current Employees

VIII. Résumés of Principals

CREATING A MARKETING PLAN

Keep in mind that a marketing plan should be created in conjunction with the other elements of a firm's business plan. In addition, a marketing plan often draws from the business plan, restating the executive summary, competitive analysis, and mission statement to give its readers an overall view of the firm. The marketing plan is needed for a variety of reasons:

- To obtain financing because banks and most private investors require a detailed business plan—including a marketing plan component—before they will even consider a loan application or a venture capital investment.

- To provide direction for the firm's overall business and marketing strategies.

- To support the development of long-term and short-term organizational objectives.

- To guide employees in achieving these objectives.

- To serve as a standard against which the firm's progress can be measured and evaluated.

In addition, the marketing plan is where a firm puts into writing its commitment to its customers and to building long-lasting relationships. After creating and implementing the plan, marketers must reevaluate it periodically to gauge its success in moving the organization toward its goals. If changes are needed, they should be made as soon as possible.

FORMULATING AN OVERALL MARKETING STRATEGY

Before creating a marketing plan, a firm's marketers formulate an overall marketing strategy. A firm may use a number of tools in marketing planning, including business portfolio analysis and the BCG matrix. Its executives may conduct a SWOT analysis, take advantage of a strategic window, study Porter's Five Forces model as it relates to their business, or consider adopting a first mover or second mover strategy, all of which are described in Chapter 2.

In addition to the planning strategies discussed in Chapter 2, marketers are likely to use **spreadsheet analysis**, which lays out a grid of columns and rows that organize numerical information in a standardized, easily understood format. Spreadsheet analysis helps planners answer various "what if" questions related to the firm's financing and operations. The most popular spreadsheet software is Microsoft Excel. A spreadsheet analysis helps planners anticipate marketing performance given specified sets of circumstances. For example, a spreadsheet might project the outcomes of different pricing decisions for a new product, as shown in Figure 2.

spreadsheet analysis Grid that organizes information in a standardized, easily understood format.

Once general planning strategies are determined, marketers begin to flesh out the details of the marketing strategy. The elements of a marketing strategy include identifying the target market, studying the marketing environment, and creating a marketing mix. When marketers have identified the target market, they can develop the optimal marketing mix to reach their potential customers:

- *Product strategy*. Which goods and services should the company offer to meet its customers' needs?

- *Distribution strategy*. Through which channel(s) and physical facilities will the firm distribute its products?

- *Promotional strategy*. What mix of advertising, sales promotion, and personal selling activities will the firm use to reach its customers initially and then develop long-term relationships?

- *Pricing strategy*. At what level should the company set its prices?

THE EXECUTIVE SUMMARY, COMPETITIVE ANALYSIS, AND MISSION STATEMENT

Because these three elements of the business plan often reappear in the marketing plan, it is useful to describe them here. Recall that the executive summary answers the who, what, when, where,

figure 2

**How Spreadsheet
Analysis Works**

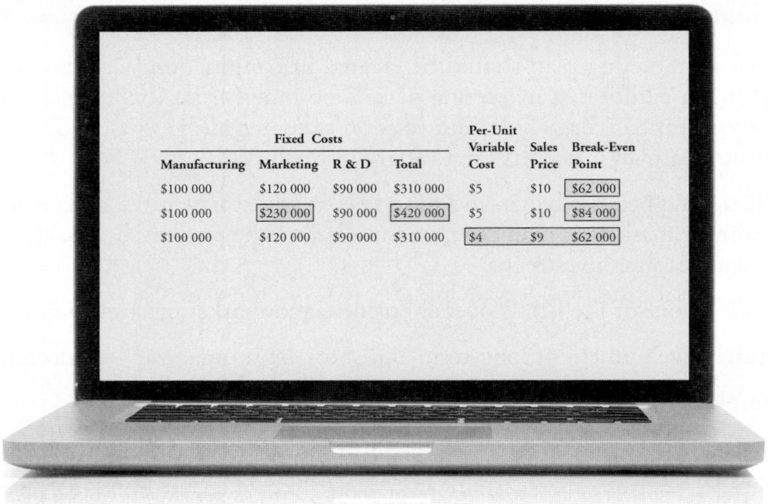

	Fixed Costs			Per-Unit Variable Cost	Sales Price	Break-Even Point
Manufacturing	Marketing	R & D	Total			
$100 000	$120 000	$90 000	$310 000	$5	$10	$62 000
$100 000	$230 000	$90 000	$420 000	$5	$10	$84 000
$100 000	$120 000	$90 000	$310 000	$4	$9	$62 000

how, and why questions for the business. In the early days of Google, the executive summary of the company's business plan included references to its strategic planning process for its search services, which involved "developing the perfect search engine … [one that] understands exactly what you mean and gives you back exactly what you want."[1] The summary also answered questions such as who is involved (key people and organizations), what length of time the plan represents, and how the goals will be met.

The competitive analysis focuses on the environment in which the marketing plan is to be implemented. TerraCycle manufactures a wide variety of products, all made from recycled materials. Believing the green movement will eventually hold sway in consumer products, TerraCycle's business goal is to become the leading eco-friendly organic brand in each of the product categories in which it competes. It doesn't attempt to overpower the category leader; instead, it aims to beat other eco-friendly competitors. For example, TerraCycle wants its window cleaner to outsell green competitors, but it is less concerned about beating Windex, the category leader. Today, many of TerraCycle's eco-friendly products are available at major retailers such as Target and Walmart.[2] The mission statement puts into words an organization's overall purpose and reason for being. According to Nintendo's corporate mission, the company is "strongly committed to producing and marketing the best products and support services available." Not only does Nintendo strive to manufacture the highest-quality video products, but it also attempts "to treat every customer with attention, consideration and respect." Nintendo is similarly committed to its employees and believes in treating them "with the same consideration and respect that we, as a company, show our customers."[3]

DESCRIPTION OF THE COMPANY

Near the beginning of the marketing plan—typically following the executive summary and before the mission statement—a description of the company is presented. The company description may include a brief history or background of the firm, the types of products it offers or plans to introduce, recent successes or achievements—in short, it consists of a few paragraphs containing the kind of information often found on the home page of a company's website.

STATEMENT OF GOALS AND CORE COMPETENCIES

The plan then includes a statement of the firm's goals and its core competencies—those things it does extremely well or better than anyone else. The goals should be specific and measurable and may be divided into financial and nonfinancial aims. A financial goal might be to add 75 new franchises in the next 12 months or to reach $10 million in revenues. A nonfinancial goal might be to enter the European market or to add a new product line every other year. Travel Alberta has a stated financial objective of achieving $10.3 billion in tourism revenue by 2020. Nonfinancial objectives are no less important.[4] A nonfinancial objective, for example, might be to achieve 80 percent satisfaction among industry users who seek information and marketing knowledge from the Travel Alberta website or to annually attract 1 million U.S. tourists to Alberta by 2020.

Core competencies are what make a firm stand out from everyone else in the market-place. Costco's core competency is offering a wide variety of consumer goods at low prices, including some luxury-brand items such as Lalique crystal vases, Mont Blanc pens, and Royal Doulton figurines. Costco leadership regards its workforce as a significant differentiator in the company's success and, for that reason, pays above-market wages. The average Costco hourly wage is considerably above the minimum wage and the hourly wage at its biggest competitor, Walmart.[5]

Small businesses often begin with a single core competency and build their business and reputation on it. It is important for a new firm to identify its core competency in the marketing plan so that investors or banks understand why they should lend the firm money to get started or to grow to the next stage. As a college student, David Kim found he enjoyed tutoring children. When he discovered a real demand for skilled tutoring, he decided to launch a tutoring business, which he named C2 Education. Because C2's core competency is helping students to excel, employees are hired and trained according to rigorous standards. Today, C2 Education serves students from elementary through high school, operating in 110 locations in Canada and the United States.[6]

OUTLINE OF THE MARKETING ENVIRONMENT (SITUATION ANALYSIS)

Every successful marketing plan takes into consideration the marketing environment—the competitive, economic, political-legal, technological, and social-cultural factors that affect the way a firm formulates and implements its marketing strategy. Marketing plans may address these issues in different ways, but the goal is to present information that describes the company's position or situation within the marketing environment. J. Crew, for instance, has a well-known brand name and a CEO with an impressive track record: Mickey Drexler, who previously headed the Gap. The retail environment for stores like J. Crew is highly competitive. Merchandise that doesn't appeal to enough customers ends up on a clearance rack and hurts the bottom line. According to Drexler, the key to J. Crew's success is that it sells merchandise that "cannot be sold anywhere else." Drexler pushes his buyers to "outproduct" their competitors.[7] A marketing plan for J. Crew would include an evaluation of competing stores such as the Gap and Urban Outfitters, any technological advances that would affect such factors as merchandise distribution or inventory, social-cultural issues such as fashion preferences and spending habits of customers, and economic issues affecting a pricing strategy.

One such method for outlining the marketing environment in the marketing plan is to include a SWOT analysis, described in Chapter 2. A SWOT analysis identifies the firm's strengths, weaknesses, opportunities, and threats within the marketing environment. A SWOT analysis for J. Crew might include strengths such as its corporate leadership, brand name, and upscale target market. Weaknesses might include the risks inherent in the business of correctly spotting fashion trends. A major opportunity lies in the fact that J. Crew can expand almost anywhere. For example, after J. Crew acquired Madewell, a retailer that sells hip, casual clothes to an upscale audience, it expanded the chain to 39 cities and launched an e-commerce site. Threats for J. Crew could include competition from other trendy stores, sudden changes in customer preferences, and financial crises that affect spending.[8] A SWOT analysis can be presented in chart format so it is easy to read as part of the marketing plan. The sample marketing plan in this appendix includes a SWOT analysis for Wild Canada Clothing.

THE TARGET MARKET AND MARKETING MIX

The marketing plan identifies the target market for the firm's products. Weight Watchers has long regarded women as its primary target market and, in fact, females currently make up 90 percent of its clientele. However, as the company saw increasing interest from men, marketers for Weight Watchers began to tap into that segment, launching a men-only website and a $10-million advertising campaign directed solely at men.[9] In another example of targeting, the Cute Overload website (**www.cuteoverload.com**) contains photos and videos of animals that visitors can share and about which they can post comments. But the site also offers a page-a-day desk calendar of the same name featuring images of puppies, kittens, birds, and chipmunks with humorous captions. Cute Overload targets women ages 18 to 34 who need a laugh and a brief escape from the real world. The calendars are also offered for sale on Amazon.ca, and the retailer's inventory sold out in one day, which astonished the developer.[10]

The marketing plan also discusses the marketing mix the firm has selected for its products. Hollywood studios are known for implementing lavish strategies for promoting their films. Not only did Columbia Pictures and Nickelodeon Movies use traditional means to launch their movie *Rango*, but they also partnered with other organizations to promote the movie. Social gaming company Zynga integrated *Rango* references and the movie trailer into its popular *FrontierVille* game on Facebook. *FrontierVille* players could embark on three different quests to find the elusive Rango somewhere on the frontier, enlist their Facebook friends to help by "sending" them water buckets, and, conceivably, win a Rango statue. With an estimated 15 million-plus Facebook users playing *FrontierVille* daily, *Rango* received great exposure.[11]

BUDGET, SCHEDULE, AND MONITORING

Every marketing plan requires a budget, a time schedule for implementation, and a system for monitoring the plan's success or failure. At age 21, entrepreneur Joe Cirulli made a to-do list of ten life goals, which included "Own a health club" and "Make it respected in the community." By age 33, Cirulli had achieved all 10 of his life goals, including the opening of his health and fitness centre. As Cirulli's business grew, however, he discovered a larger mission: to make his community the healthiest one in the country. Today, his community is the first and only city to win the Gold Well City award from the Wellness Councils of America, and Cirulli's fitness centre is widely regarded as one of the best in the industry. Whether or not he realized it at the time, Cirulli's life and business plan at age 21 had the makings of a marketing plan, with goals and budgets, setting a timeline, and measuring progress—a formula for business success.[12]

Most long-range marketing plans encompass a two- to five-year period, although companies that do business in industries such as auto manufacturing, pharmaceuticals, or lumber may extend their marketing plans further into the future because it typically takes longer to develop these products. However, marketers in most industries will have difficulty making estimates and predictions beyond five years because of the many uncertainties in the marketplace. Firms also may opt to develop short-term plans to cover marketing activities for a single year.

The marketing plan, whether it is long term or short term, predicts how long it will take to achieve the goals set out by the plan. A goal may be opening a certain number of new stores, market share growth, or achieving an expansion of the product line. Finally, the marketing program is monitored and evaluated for its performance. Monthly, quarterly, and annual sales targets are usually tracked; the efficiency with which certain tasks are completed is determined; customer satisfaction is measured; and so forth. All these factors contribute to the overall review of the program.

At some point, a firm may opt to implement an *exit strategy*, a plan for the firm leaving the market. A common way for a large company to do this is to sell off a business unit. A number of these strategies have been implemented recently. Dover Corporation is a diversified global manufacturer of equipment and components for the communication, energy, and printing industries. In keeping with the company's long-term growth strategy, it recently sold a business unit, Heil Trailer International, a manufacturer of specialty transportation trailers and equipment. With the transaction, Dover exited the transportation trailer business. The move is expected to help improve Dover's financial performance.[13]

Another example of an exit strategy involves pharmaceutical giant Pfizer. Founded in 1849, over time, the company expanded its operations beyond its core business—the development and manufacture of prescription medications—to include nutrition and animal health. To return the focus to its core business of developing new drugs, Pfizer recently sold its infant nutrition business to Nestlé.[14]

SAMPLE MARKETING PLAN

The following pages contain an annotated sample marketing plan for Wild Canada Clothing. At some point in your career, you will likely be involved in writing—or at least contributing to—a marketing plan. And you'll certainly read many marketing plans throughout your business career. Keep in mind that the plan for Wild Canada is a single example; no one format is used by all companies. Also, the Wild Canada plan has been somewhat condensed to make it easier to annotate and illustrate the most vital features. The important point to remember is that the marketing plan is a document designed to present concise, cohesive information about a company's marketing objectives to managers, lending institutions, and others who are involved in creating and carrying out the firm's overall business strategy.

Five-Year Marketing Plan
Wild Canada Clothing, Inc.

TABLE OF CONTENTS

Executive Summary

This five-year marketing plan for Wild Canada Clothing has been created by its two founders to secure additional funding for growth and to inform employees of the company's current status and direction. Although Wild Canada was launched only three years ago, the firm has experienced greater-than-anticipated demand for its products, and research has shown that the target market of sports-minded consumers and sports retailers would like to buy more casual clothing than Wild Canada currently offers. The company is also interested in extending its product line as well as adding new product lines. In addition, Wild Canada plans to explore opportunities for online sales. The marketing environment has been very receptive to the firm's high-quality goods—casual clothing in trendy colours with logos and slogans that reflect the interests of outdoor enthusiasts around the country. Over the next five years, Wild Canada can increase its distribution, offer new products, and win new customers.

> The executive summary outlines the who, what, where, when, how, and why of the marketing plan. Wild Canada is only three years old and is successful enough that it now needs a formal marketing plan to obtain additional financing from a bank or private investors for expansion and the launch of new products.

GO Play Outside

Company Description

The company description summarizes the history of Wild Canada—how it was founded and by whom, what its products are, and why they are unique. It begins to "sell" the reader on the growth possibilities for Wild Canada.

Wild Canada Clothing was founded three years ago by entrepreneurs Lucy Neuman and Nick Russell. Neuman has an undergraduate degree in marketing and worked for several years in the retail clothing industry. Russell operated an adventure business called Go West!, which arranges group trips to locations in Manitoba, Saskatchewan, Alberta, and British Columbia, before selling the enterprise to a partner. Neuman and Russell, who have been friends since college, decided to develop and market a line of clothing with a unique—yet universal—appeal to outdoor enthusiasts.

Wild Canada Clothing reflects Neuman's and Russell's passion for the outdoors. The company's original cotton T-shirts, baseball caps, and fleece jackets and vests bear logos of different sports—such as kayaking, mountain climbing, bicycling, skating, surfing, and horseback riding. But every item shows off the company's slogan "Go Play Outside." Wild Canada sells clothing for both men and women, in the hottest colours with the coolest names—such as sunrise pink, sunset red, twilight purple, desert rose, cactus green, ocean blue, mountaintop white, and river rock grey.

Wild Canada attire is currently carried by small retail stores that specialize in outdoor clothing and gear. Most of these stores are concentrated in British Columbia, Alberta, Ontario, and Quebec. The high quality, trendy colours, and unique message of the clothing have gained Wild Canada a following among consumers between the ages of 25 and 45. Sales have tripled in the last year alone, and Wild Canada is currently working to expand its manufacturing capabilities.

Wild Canada is also committed to giving back to the community by contributing to local conservation programs. Ultimately, the company would like to develop and fund its own environmental programs. This plan will outline how Wild Canada intends to introduce new products, expand its distribution, enter new markets, and give back to the community.

Wild Canada's Mission and Goals

It is important to state a firm's mission and goals, including financial and nonfinancial goals. Wild Canada's goals include growth and profits for the company as well as the ability to contribute to society through conservation programs.

Wild Canada's mission is to be the leading producer and marketer of personalized, casual clothing for consumers who love the outdoors. Wild Canada wants to inspire people to get outdoors more often and enjoy family and friends while doing so. In addition, Wild Canada strives to design programs for preserving the natural environment.

During the next five years, Wild Canada seeks to achieve the following financial and nonfinancial goals:

- Financial goals

  1. Obtain financing to expand manufacturing capabilities, increase distribution, and introduce two new product lines.

  2. Increase revenues by at least 50 percent each year.

  3. Donate at least $25,000 a year to conservation organizations.

- Nonfinancial goals

  1. Introduce two new product lines—customized logo clothing and lightweight luggage.

  2. Enter new geographic markets, including the Atlantic provinces.

  3. Develop a successful Internet site, while maintaining strong relationships with retailers.

  4. Develop its own conservation program aimed at helping communities raise money to purchase open space.

Core Competencies

Wild Canada seeks to use its core competencies to achieve a sustainable competitive advantage, in which competitors cannot provide the same value to consumers that Wild Canada does. Already, Wild Canada has developed core competencies in (1) offering a high-quality, branded product whose image is recognizable among consumers; (2) creating a sense of community among consumers who purchase the products; and (3) developing a reputation among retailers as a reliable manufacturer and delivering the requested number of products on schedule. The firm intends to build on these competencies through marketing efforts that increase the number of products offered as well as distribution outlets.

By forming strong relationships with consumers, retailers, and suppliers of fabric and other goods and services, Wild Canada believes it can create a sustainable competitive advantage over its rivals. No other clothing company can say to its customers with as much conviction "Go Play Outside"!

> This section reminds employees as well as those outside the company (such as potential lenders) exactly what Wild Canada does so well and how it plans to achieve a sustainable competitive advantage over rivals. Note that here and throughout the plan, Wild Canada focuses on relationships.

Situation Analysis

The marketing environment for Wild Canada represents overwhelming opportunities. It also contains some challenges that the firm believes it can meet successfully. Figure A illustrates a SWOT analysis of the company conducted by marketers to highlight Wild Canada's strengths, weaknesses, opportunities, and threats.

The SWOT analysis presents a thumbnail sketch of the company's position in the marketplace. In just three years, Wild Canada has built some impressive strengths while looking forward to new opportunities. Its dedicated founders, the growing number of brand-loyal customers, and sound financial management place the company in a good position to grow. However, as Wild Canada considers expansion of its product line and entrance into new markets, the firm will have to guard against marketing myopia (the failure to recognize the scope of its business) and quality slippages. As the company finalizes plans for new products and expanded Internet sales, its management will also have to guard against competitors who attempt to duplicate the products. However, building strong relationships with consumers, retailers, and suppliers should help thwart competitors.

> The situation analysis provides an outline of the marketing environment. A SWOT analysis helps marketers and others identify clearly a firm's strengths, weaknesses, opportunities, and threats. Again, relationships are a focus. Wild Canada has also conducted research on the outdoor clothing market, competitors, and consumers to determine how best to attract and keep customers.

Competitors in the Outdoor Clothing Market

The outdoor retail sales industry sells more than $500 million worth of goods annually, ranging from clothing to equipment. The outdoor apparel market has many entries. L.L. Bean, Timberland, Bass Pro Shops, Patagonia, Tilley Endurables, and Mountain Equipment Co-op are among the most recognizable companies that offer these products. Smaller competitors such as Title IX, which offers athletic clothing for women, and Ragged Mountain, which sells fleece clothing for skiers and hikers, also grab some of the market. The outlook for the industry in general—and Wild Canada in particular—is positive for several reasons. First, consumers are participating in and investing in recreational activities that are near their homes. Second, consumers are looking for ways to enjoy their leisure time with friends and family without overspending. Third, consumers are gaining more confidence in the economy and are willing and able to spend more.

While all the companies listed earlier can be considered competitors, most of them sell performance apparel in high-tech manufactured fabrics. With the exception of the fleece vests and jackets, Wild Canada's clothing is made of strictly the highest-quality cotton, so it may be worn both on the hiking trail and around town. Finally, Wild Canada products are offered at moderate prices, making

figure A

SWOT Analysis for Wild Canada Clothing, Inc.

GO Play Outside

Strengths

Wild Canada's dedicated founders understand the target market and product.

Wild Canada has achieved distribution in several markets with quick acceptance.

The firm has very little debt, with great potential for growth.

Wild Canada works with a single manufacturer, ensuring maximum quality control.

Weaknesses

Wild Canada's founders may lose sight of the potential scope of their business.

A limited number of consumers around the country are aware of the Wild Canada brand.

The firm has limited cash flow.

Wild Canada relies on a single manufacturer, which limits production capacity if the firm wants to expand.

VULNERABILITIES

CONSTRAINTS

Opportunities

Wild Canada's loyal consumers are likely to buy new products.

Gaps exist in the market that can be filled with new products, such as customized clothing items and luggage.

Wild Canada has a chance to expand across Canada into new markets.

The firm can reach more consumers via its website.

Threats

Consumers may tire of the concept; the firm needs to keep it fresh.

Large competitors such as Mountain Equipment Co-op, Timberland, and Tilley Endurables may soak up consumer dollars or launch a similar product line.

Clothing sales nationwide have generally been flat the past few years.

Relationships with retailers might deteriorate if they believe they face internal competition in the form of Internet sales.

Leverage

Problems

it affordable to buy them in quantity. For instance, a Wild Canada T-shirt sells for $15.99, compared with a competing high-performance T-shirt that sells for $29.99. Consumers can easily replace a set of shirts from one season to the next, picking up the newest colours, without having to think about the purchase.

A survey conducted by Wild Canada revealed that 67 percent of responding consumers prefer to replace their casual and active wear more often than other clothing, so they are attracted by the moderate pricing of Wild Canada products. In addition, as the trend toward health-conscious activities and concerns about the natural environment continues, consumers increasingly relate to the Wild Canada philosophy as well as the firm's contributions to socially responsible programs.

GO Play Outside

The Target Market

The target market for Wild Canada products is active consumers between the ages of 25 and 45—people who like to hike, rock climb, bicycle, surf, figure skate, in-line skate, ride horses, snowboard or ski, kayak, and other such activities. In short, they like to "Go Play Outside." They might not be experts at the sports they engage in, but they enjoy themselves outdoors.

These active consumers represent a demographic group of well-educated and successful individuals; they are single or married and raising families. Household incomes generally range between $60,000 and $120,000 annually. Despite their comfortable incomes, these consumers are price conscious and consistently seek value in their purchases. Regardless of their age (whether they fall at the upper or lower end of the target range), they lead active lifestyles. They are somewhat status oriented but not overly so. They like to be associated with high-quality products but are not willing to pay a premium price for a certain brand. Current Wild Canada customers tend to live in British Columbia, Alberta, Ontario, and Quebec. However, one future goal is to target consumers in the Atlantic Provinces, Manitoba, and Saskatchewan.

Wild Canada has identified its customers as active people between the ages of 25 and 45. However, that doesn't mean someone who is older or prefers to read about the outdoors isn't a potential customer as well. By pinpointing where existing customers live, Wild Canada can make plans for growth into new outlets.

The Marketing Mix

The following discussion outlines some of the details of the proposed marketing mix for Wild Canada products.

PRODUCT STRATEGY. Wild Canada currently offers a line of high-quality outdoor apparel items including cotton T-shirts, baseball caps, and fleece vests and jackets. All bear the company logo and slogan "Go Play Outside." The firm has researched the most popular colours for its items and given them names that consumers enjoy—sunset red, sunrise pink, cactus green, desert rose, and river rock grey, among others. Over the next five years, Wild Canada plans to expand the product line to include customized clothing items. Customers may select a logo that represents their sport—say, rock climbing. Then they can add a slogan to match the logo, such as "Get Over It." A baseball cap with a bicyclist logo might bear the slogan "Take a Spin." At the beginning, there would be 10 new logos and five new slogans; more would be added later. Eventually, some slogans and logos would be retired, and new ones introduced. This strategy will keep the concept fresh and prevent it from becoming diluted with too many variations.

The second way in which Wild Canada plans to expand its product line is to offer items of lightweight luggage—two sizes of duffel bags, two sizes of tote bags, and a daypack. These items would also come in trendy and basic colours, with a choice of logos and slogans. In addition, every product would bear the Wild Canada logo.

The strongest part of the marketing mix for Wild Canada involves sales promotions, public relations, and nontraditional marketing strategies such as attending outdoor events and organizing activities like day hikes and bike rides.

DISTRIBUTION STRATEGY. Currently, Wild Canada is marketed through regional and local specialty shops scattered throughout British Columbia, Alberta, Ontario, and Quebec. So far, Wild Canada has not been distributed through national sporting goods and apparel chains. Climate and season tend to dictate the sales at specialty shops, which sell more T-shirts and baseball caps during warm weather and more fleece vests and jackets during colder months. Wild Canada obtains much of its information about overall industry trends in different geographic areas and at different types of retail outlets from its trade organization, the Canadian Outdoor Industry Association.

Over the next three years, Wild Canada seeks to expand distribution to retail specialty shops throughout the nation, focusing next on the Atlantic provinces. The firm has not yet determined whether it would be beneficial to sell through a major national chain such as Bass Pro Shops, Mountain Equipment Co-op, or Sports Experts as these outlets could be considered competitors.

In addition, Wild Canada plans to expand online sales by offering the customized product line via Internet only, thus distinguishing between Internet offerings and specialty shop offerings.

Eventually, the company may be able to place Internet kiosks at some of the more profitable store outlets so consumers could order customized products from the stores. Regardless of its expansion plans, Wild Canada fully intends to monitor and maintain strong relationships with distribution channel members.

PROMOTIONAL STRATEGY. Wild Canada communicates with consumers and retailers about its products in a variety of ways. Information about Wild Canada—the company as well as its products—is available via the Internet, direct mailings, and in person. The firm's promotional efforts also seek to differentiate its products from those of its competitors.

The company relies on personal contact with retailers to establish the products in their stores. This contact, whether in person or by phone, helps convey the Wild Canada message, demonstrate the products' unique qualities, and build relationships. Wild Canada sales representatives visit each store two or three times a year and offer in-store training on the features of the products for new retailers or for those who want a refresher. As distribution expands, Wild Canada will adjust to meet greater demand by increasing sales staff to make sure its stores are visited more frequently.

Sales promotions and public relations currently make up the bulk of Wild Canada's promotional strategy. Wild Canada staff works with retailers to offer short-term sales promotions tied to events and contests. In addition, Nick Russell is currently working with several trip outfitters to offer Wild Canada items on a promotional basis. Because Wild Canada also engages in cause marketing through its contribution to environmental programs, good public relations have followed.

Nontraditional marketing methods that require little cash and a lot of creativity also lend themselves perfectly to Wild Canada. Because Wild Canada is a small, flexible organization, the firm can easily implement ideas such as distributing free water, stickers, and discount coupons at outdoor sporting events. During the next year, the company plans to engage in the following marketing efforts:

- Create a Wild Canada Tour, in which several employees take turns driving around the country to campgrounds to distribute promotional items such as Wild Canada stickers and discount coupons.

- Attend canoe and kayak races, bicycling events, and rock climbing competitions with the Wild Canada truck to distribute free water, stickers, and discount coupons for Wild Canada shirts or hats.

- Organize Wild Canada hikes departing from participating retailers.

- Hold a Wild Canada design contest, selecting a winning slogan and logo to be added to the customized line.

PRICING STRATEGY. As discussed earlier in this plan, Wild Canada products are priced with the competition in mind. The firm is not concerned with setting high prices to signal luxury or prestige, nor is it attempting to achieve the goals of offsetting low prices by selling high quantities of products. Instead, value pricing is practised so that customers feel comfortable purchasing new clothing to replace the old, even if it is just because they like the new colours. The pricing strategy also makes Wild Canada products good gifts—for birthdays, graduations, or "just because." The customized clothing will sell for $2 to $4 more than the regular Wild Canada logo clothing. The luggage will be priced competitively, offering good value against its competition.

Budget, Schedule, and Monitoring

Though its history is short, Wild Canada has enjoyed a steady increase in sales since its introduction three years ago. Figure B shows these three years, plus projected sales for the next three years, including the introduction of the two new product lines. Additional financial data are included in the overall business plan for the company.

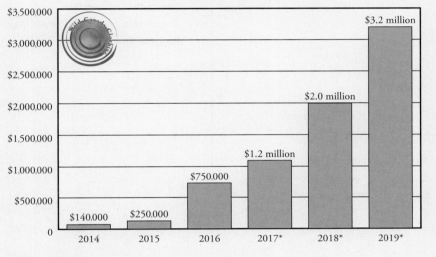

*Projected sales

figure B

Annual Sales for Wild Canada Clothing: 2014–2019

The timeline for expansion of outlets and introduction of the two new product lines is shown in Figure C. The implementation of each of these tasks will be monitored closely and evaluated for its performance.

> An actual plan will include more specific financial details, which will be folded into the overall business plan. For more information, see the "Financial Analysis in Marketing" appendix on page A-29 of this book. In addition, Wild Canada states that, at this stage, it does not have plans to make a public stock offering or exit the market by merging with another firm.

figure C

Timeline for First Three Years of Marketing Plan

YEAR 1

New outlets added: 20
Customized items: 5 slogans/10 logos
Luggage items: 0

YEAR 2

New outlets added: 50
Customized items: 10 slogans/10 logos
Luggage items: 2 (duffels and totes)

YEAR 3

New outlets added: 100
Customized items: 5 slogans/5 logos
Luggage items: 1 (backpack)

Wild Canada anticipates continuing operations into the foreseeable future, with no plans to exit this market. Instead, as discussed throughout this plan, the firm plans to increase its presence in the market. At present, there are no plans to merge with another company or to make a public stock offering.

Relationship Marketing and Customer Relationship Management (CRM)

Marketing revolves around relationships with customers and with all the business processes involved in identifying and satisfying them. The shift from transaction-based marketing, which focuses on short-term, one-time exchanges, to customer-focused relationship marketing is one of the most important trends in marketing today. Companies know that they cannot prosper simply by identifying and attracting new customers; to succeed, they must build loyal, mutually beneficial relationships with both new and existing customers, suppliers, distributors, and employees. This strategy benefits the bottom line because retaining customers costs much less than acquiring new ones. Building and managing long-term relationships between buyers and sellers are the hallmarks of relationship marketing. Relationship marketing is the development, growth, and maintenance of cost-effective, high-value relationships with individual customers, suppliers, distributors, retailers, and other partners for mutual benefit over time.

Relationship marketing is based on promises: the promise of low prices, the promise of high quality, the promise of prompt delivery, the promise of superior service. A network of promises—within the organization, between the organization and its supply chain, and between buyer and seller—determines whether a relationship will grow. A firm is responsible for keeping or exceeding the agreements it makes, with the ultimate goal of achieving customer satisfaction.

THE SHIFT FROM TRANSACTION-BASED MARKETING TO RELATIONSHIP MARKETING

Since the Industrial Revolution, most manufacturers have run production-oriented operations. They have focused on making products and then promoting them to customers in the hope of selling enough to cover costs and earn profits. The emphasis has been on individual sales or transactions. In transaction-based marketing, buyer and seller exchanges are characterized by limited communications and little or no ongoing relationships. The primary goal is to entice a buyer to make a purchase through such inducements as low price, convenience, or packaging. The goal is simple and short term: sell.

Today, many organizations have embraced an alternative approach. Relationship marketing views customers as equal partners in buyer–seller transactions. By motivating customers to enter a long-term relationship in which they repeat purchases or buy many brands from the firm, marketers obtain a clearer understanding of customer needs over time. This process leads to improved products or customer service, which pays off through increased sales and lower marketing costs. In addition, marketers have discovered that it is less expensive to retain satisfied customers than it is to attract new ones or to repair damaged relationships.

The move from transactions to relationships is reflected in the changing nature of the interactions between customers and sellers. In transaction-based marketing, exchanges with customers are generally sporadic and in some instances disrupted by conflict. As interactions become relationship oriented, however, conflict changes to cooperation, and infrequent contacts between buyers and sellers become ongoing exchanges.

figure 1

Forms of Buyer–Seller Interactions on a Continuum from Conflict to Integration

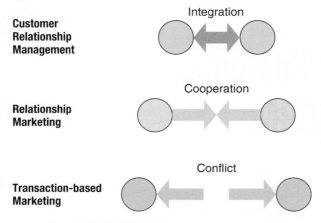

Customer Relationship Management — Integration

Relationship Marketing — Cooperation

Transaction-based Marketing — Conflict

Source: From BOONE/KURTZ. *Contemporary Marketing*, 13E. © 2008 South-Western, a part of Cengage Learning, Inc. Reproduced by permission. **www.cengage.com/permissions**

As Figure 1 illustrates, relationship marketing emphasizes cooperation rather than conflict between all the parties involved. This ongoing collaborative exchange creates value for both parties and builds customer loyalty. Customer relationship management goes a step further and integrates the customer's needs into all aspects of the firm's operations and its relationships with suppliers, distributors, and strategic partners. It combines people, processes, and technology with the long-term goal of maximizing customer value through mutually satisfying interactions and transactions.

Twenty-first-century marketers now understand they must do more than simply create products and then sell them. With so many goods and services to choose from, customers look for added value from their marketing relationships.

In general, the differences between the narrow focus of transaction marketing and the much broader view of relationship marketing can be summarized as follows:

Relationship marketing

- focuses on the long term rather than the short term,

- emphasizes retaining customers over making a sale,

- ranks customer service as a high priority,

- encourages frequent customer contact,

- fosters customer commitment with the firm,

- bases customer interactions on cooperation and trust, and

- commits all employees to provide high-quality products.

As a result, the buyer–seller bonds developed in a relationship marketing partnership last longer and cover a much wider scope than those developed in transaction marketing.

ELEMENTS OF RELATIONSHIP MARKETING

To build long-term customer relationships, marketers need to place customers at the centre of their efforts. When a company integrates customer service and quality with marketing, the result is a relationship marketing orientation.

But how do firms achieve these long-term relationships? They build them with four basic elements.

1. They gather information about their customers. Database technology, discussed later, helps a company identify current and potential customers with selected demographic, purchase, and lifestyle characteristics.

2. They analyze the data collected and use it to modify their marketing mix to deliver differentiated messages and customized marketing programs to individual consumers.

3. Through relationship marketing, they monitor their interactions with customers. They can assess the customer's level of satisfaction or dissatisfaction with their service. Marketers can also calculate the cost of attracting one new customer and figure out how much profit that customer will generate during the relationship. Information is fed back, and they are then able to seek ways to add value to the buyer–seller transaction so that the relationship will continue.

4. With customer relationship management (CRM) software, they use intimate knowledge of customers and customer preferences to orient every part of the organization, including both its internal and external partners, toward building a unique company differentiation based on strong, unbreakable bonds with customers. Sophisticated technology and the Internet help make that happen.

INTERNAL MARKETING

The concepts of customer satisfaction and relationship marketing are usually discussed in terms of **external customers**—people or organizations that buy or use a firm's goods or services. But marketing in organizations concerned with customer satisfaction and long-term relationships must also address **internal customers**—employees or departments within the organization whose success depends on the work of other employees or departments. A person processing an order for a new piece of equipment is the internal customer of the salesperson who completed the sale, just as the person who bought the product is the salesperson's external customer. Although the order processor might never directly encounter an external customer, his or her performance can have a direct impact on the overall value the firm is able to deliver.

Internal marketing involves managerial actions that enable all members of an organization to understand, accept, and fulfill their respective roles in implementing a marketing strategy. Good internal customer satisfaction helps organizations attract, select, and retain outstanding employees who appreciate and value their role in the delivery of superior service to external customers.

Employee knowledge and involvement are important goals of internal marketing. Companies that excel at satisfying customers typically place a priority on keeping employees informed about corporate goals, strategies, and customer needs. Employees must also have the necessary tools to address customer requests and problems in a timely manner. Company-wide computer networks aid the flow of communications between departments and functions. Several companies also include key suppliers in their networks to speed and ease communication of all aspects of business from product design to inventory control.

Employee satisfaction is another critical objective of internal marketing. Employees seldom, if ever, satisfy customers when they themselves are unhappy. Dissatisfied employees are likely to spread negative word-of-mouth messages to relatives, friends, and acquaintances, and these reports can affect purchasing behaviour. Satisfied employees buy their employer's products, tell friends and families how good the customer service is, and ultimately send a powerful message to customers. One recommended strategy for offering consistently good service is to attract good employees, hire good employees, and retain good employees.

external customer
People or organizations that buy or use another firm's goods or services.

internal customer
Employees or departments within an organization that depend on the work of another employee or department to perform tasks.

internal marketing
Managerial actions that help all members of the organization understand and fulfill their respective roles in implementing a marketing strategy.

employee satisfaction
Employee's level of satisfaction for his or her company and the extent to which that loyalty or lack of loyalty is communicated to external customers.

Companies like Boston Pizza often have special programs for their employees.

Courtesy of Boston Pizza International Inc.

THE RELATIONSHIP MARKETING CONTINUUM

Like all other interpersonal relationships, buyer–seller relationships function at a variety of levels. As an individual or firm progresses from the lowest level to the highest level on the continuum of relationship marketing, the strength of commitment between the parties grows. The likelihood of a continuing, long-term relationship grows as well. Whenever possible, marketers want to move their customers along this continuum, converting them from Level 1 purchasers, who focus mainly on price, to Level 3 customers, who receive specialized services and value-added benefits that may not be available from another firm.

FIRST LEVEL: FOCUS ON PRICE

Interactions at the first level of relationship marketing are the most superficial and the least likely to lead to a long-term relationship. In the most prevalent examples of this first level, relationship marketing efforts rely on pricing and other financial incentives to motivate customers to enter into buying relationships with a seller. Although price-related programs can be attractive to users, they may not create long-term buyer relationships. Because the programs are not customized to the needs of individual buyers, they are easily duplicated by competitors. The lesson is that it takes more than a low price or other financial incentives to create a long-term relationship between buyer and seller.

SECOND LEVEL: SOCIAL INTERACTIONS

As buyers and sellers reach the second level of relationship marketing, their interactions develop on a social level, one that features deeper and less superficial links than the financially motivated first level. Sellers have begun to learn that social relationships with buyers can be very effective marketing tools. Customer service and communication are key factors at this stage.

Social interaction can take many forms. The owner of a local shoe store or dry cleaner might chat with customers about local events.

THIRD LEVEL: INTERDEPENDENT PARTNERSHIP

At the third level of relationship marketing, relationships are transformed into structural changes that ensure buyer and seller are true business partners. As buyer and seller work more closely

The upscale hotel chain Four Seasons pampers its customers but also relates its high service standards directly to maintaining satisfied employees.

© iStockphoto.com/EdStock

together, they develop a dependence on one another that continues to grow over time. Companies that maintain member programs are examples of third-level relationship marketing.

ENHANCING CUSTOMER SATISFACTION

Marketers monitor customer satisfaction through various methods of marketing research. As part of an ongoing relationship with customers, marketers must continually measure and improve how well they meet customer needs. As Figure 2 shows, three major steps are involved in this process: understanding customer needs, obtaining customer feedback, and instituting an ongoing program to ensure customer satisfaction.

UNDERSTANDING CUSTOMER NEEDS

Knowledge of what customers need, want, and expect is a central concern of companies focused on building long-term relationships. This information is also a vital first step in setting up a system to measure **customer satisfaction**. Marketers must carefully monitor the characteristics of their product that really matter to customers. They also must remain constantly alert to new elements that might affect satisfaction.

Satisfaction can be measured in terms of the gaps between what customers expect and what they perceive they have received. Such gaps can produce favourable or unfavourable impressions. Goods or services may be better or worse than expected. If they are better, marketers can use the opportunity to create loyal customers. If goods or services are worse than expected, a company may start to lose customers.

To avoid unfavourable service gaps, marketers need to keep in touch with the needs of current and potential customers. They must look beyond traditional performance measures and explore the factors that determine purchasing behaviour to formulate customer-based missions, goals, and performance standards.

customer satisfaction
Extent to which customers are satisfied with their purchases.

OBTAINING CUSTOMER FEEDBACK AND ENSURING SATISFACTION

The second step in measuring customer satisfaction is to compile feedback from customers regarding current performance. Increasingly, marketers try to improve customers' access to their companies by including toll-free phone numbers or website addresses in their advertising. Most firms rely on reactive methods of collecting feedback. Rather than solicit complaints, they might, for example, monitor blogs or other online discussion groups to track customers' comments and attitudes about the value received. Some companies hire mystery shoppers, who visit or call businesses posing as customers, to evaluate the service they receive. Their unbiased appraisals are usually conducted semi-annually or quarterly to monitor employees, diagnose problem areas in customer service, and measure the impact of employee training. Other companies are using websites to obtain customers' feedback, allowing them to accurately identify and respond to customers' needs.

Unhappy customers typically talk about their experience more than happy customers do. The cost of dissatisfaction can be high so it makes sense to try to resolve problems quickly. In addition to training employees to resolve complaints, firms can benefit from providing several different ways for customers to make their dissatisfaction known, including prepaid mail

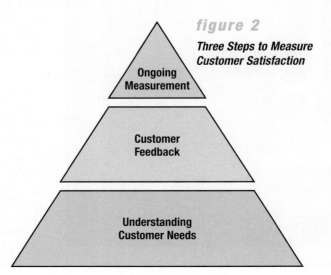

figure 2

Three Steps to Measure Customer Satisfaction

Ongoing Measurement

Customer Feedback

Understanding Customer Needs

questionnaires, telephone help lines, comment cards, and face-to-face exit surveys as people leave the premises. Any method that makes it easier for customers to complain actually benefits a firm. Customer complaints offer firms the opportunity to overcome problems and prove their commitment to service. People often have greater loyalty to a company after a conflict has been resolved than if they had never complained at all.

Many organizations also use proactive methods to assess customer satisfaction, including visiting, calling, or mailing out surveys to clients to find out their level of satisfaction. Companies are also paying more and more attention to the millions of bloggers on the Internet.

BUILDING BUYER–SELLER RELATIONSHIPS

frequency marketing
Frequent buyer or user marketing programs that reward customers with cash, rebates, merchandise, or other premiums.

Marketers of consumer goods and services have discovered that they must do more than simply create products and then sell them. With a dizzying array of products to choose from, many customers are seeking ways to simplify both their business and personal lives, and relationships provide a way to do this.

One reason consumers form continuing relationships is their desire to reduce choices. Through relationships, they can simplify information gathering and the entire buying process as well as decrease the risk of dissatisfaction. They find comfort in brands that have become familiar through their ongoing relationships with companies. Such relationships may lead to more efficient decision making by customers and higher levels of customer satisfaction. A key benefit to consumers in long-term buyer–seller relationships is the perceived positive value they receive. Relationships add value because of increased opportunities for frequent customers to save money through discounts, rebates, and similar offers; via special recognition from the relationship programs; and through convenience in shopping.

Marketers should also understand why consumers end relationships. Computerized technologies and the Internet have made consumers better informed than ever before by giving them unprecedented abilities to compare prices, merchandise, and customer service. If they perceive that a competitor's product or customer service is better, customers may switch loyalties. Many consumers dislike feeling that they are locked into a relationship with one company, and that is reason enough for them to try a competing item next time they buy. Some customers simply become bored with their current providers and decide to sample the competition.

HOW MARKETERS KEEP CUSTOMERS

One of the major forces driving the push from transaction-based marketing to relationship marketing is the realization that retaining customers is an important component of maintaining a successful business.

Also, customers usually enable a firm to generate more profits with each additional year of the relationship. Some companies use **frequency marketing**. These programs reward top customers with cash, rebates, merchandise, or other premiums. Buyers who purchase an item more often earn higher

porter
flying refined

Swap three below zero for three below par at Myrtle Beach.

Spring may not have sprung here in Toronto, but in Myrtle Beach, it's tee-off time. Fly direct, non-stop from downtown Toronto to the golf courses of Myrtle Beach. And enjoy all the Porter perks - from the lounge at Toronto City Airport to the free onboard drinks and snacks. Fore!

HALIFAX • MONCTON • MONT TREMBLANT • MONTRÉAL • OTTAWA • QUÉBEC CITY
SAULT STE. MARIE • ST. JOHN'S • SUDBURY • THUNDER BAY • TIMMINS • TORONTO • WINDSOR
BOSTON • VERMONT • CHICAGO • MYRTLE BEACH • NEW YORK • WASHINGTON DC

flyporter.com

Courtesy of Porter Airlines Inc.

Porter Airlines: Adding value by providing extra services to their customers.

rewards. Frequency marketing focuses on a company's best customers with the goal of increasing their motivation to buy even more of the same or other products from the seller. Many different types of companies use frequency programs—such as fast-food restaurants, retail stores, telecommunications companies, and travel firms. Popular programs are airline frequent-flyer programs and retail programs.

In addition to frequency programs, companies use **affinity marketing** to retain customers. Each of us holds certain things dear. Some feel strongly about their college or university, while for others it's a sports team or not-for-profit organization. These examples, along with an almost unending variety of others, are subjects of affinity programs. An affinity program is a marketing effort sponsored by an organization that solicits involvement by individuals who share common interests and activities. With affinity programs, organizations create extra value for members and encourage stronger relationships. Affinity credit cards are a popular form of this marketing technique. The sponsor's name appears prominently in promotional materials, on the card itself, and on monthly statements.

affinity marketing
Marketing effort sponsored by an organization that solicits responses from individuals who share common interests and activities.

DATABASE MARKETING

The use of information technology to analyze data about customers and their transactions is referred to as **database marketing**. The results form the basis of new advertising or promotions targeted to carefully identified groups of customers. Database marketing is a particularly effective tool for building relationships because it allows sellers to sort through huge quantities of data from many sources on the buying habits or preferences of thousands or even millions of customers. Companies can then track buying patterns, develop customer relationship profiles, customize their offerings and sales promotions, and even personalize customer service to suit the needs of targeted groups of customers. Properly used, databases can help companies in several ways, including these:

database marketing
Use of software to analyze marketing information, identifying and targeting messages toward specific groups of potential customers.

- identifying their most profitable customers

- calculating the lifetime value of each customer's business

- creating a meaningful dialogue that builds relationships and encourages genuine brand loyalty

- improving customer retention and referral rates

- reducing marketing and promotion costs

- boosting sales volume per customer or targeted customer group; and

- expanding loyalty programs[1]

Where do organizations find all the data that fill these vast marketing databases? Everywhere! Credit card applications, software registration, and product warranties all provide vital statistics of individual customers. Point-of-sale register scanners, customer opinion surveys, and sweepstakes entry forms may offer not just details of name and address, but also information on preferred brands and shopping habits. Websites offer free access in return for personal data, allowing companies to amass increasingly rich marketing information.

Newer technologies such as radio frequency identification (RFID) allow retailers to identify shipping pallets and cargo containers, but most observers anticipate that in the near future RFID will be cost effective enough to permit tagging of individual store items, allowing retailers to gather information about the purchaser as well as managing inventory and deterring theft, but raising privacy concerns.

Interactive television delivers even more valuable data—information on real consumer behaviour and attitudes toward brands. Linked to digital television, sophisticated set-top boxes already collect vast amounts of data on television viewer behaviour, organized in incredible detail. As the technology makes its way into more homes, marketers receive first-hand knowledge of the kind of programming and products their targeted customers want. In addition, rather than using television to advertise to the masses, they can talk directly to the viewers most interested in their products. At a click of a button, viewers can skip ads, but they also can click to a full-length infomercial on any brand that captures their interest.

New technologies like widgets—small software applications, such as games, easily passed from friend to friend on sites like Facebook—are becoming popular marketing tools. Cell phone advertising is increasing, and with it the prospect that it can become highly targeted because telecom companies already have access to users' personal and credit card information, and even their current locations.

Discount offers can be sent to users passing a particular store, for instance. Marketers can even build their own social networking sites rather than relying on Facebook.

As database marketing becomes more complex, a variety of software tools and services enable marketers to target consumers more and more narrowly while enriching their communications to selected groups. After all, a huge collection of data isn't valuable unless it can be turned into information that is useful to a firm's marketers. Application service providers (ASPs) assist marketers by providing software when it is needed to capture, manipulate, and analyze masses of consumer data. One type of software collects data on product specifications and details, which marketers can use to isolate products that best meet a customer's needs. This feature would be particularly important in selling expensive business products that require high involvement in making a purchase decision.

CUSTOMERS AS ADVOCATES

grassroots marketing
Efforts that connect directly with existing and potential customers through non-mainstream channels.

Recent relationship marketing efforts focus on turning customers from passive partners into active proponents of a product. Grassroots marketing involves connecting directly with existing and potential customers through non-mainstream channels. The grassroots approach relies on marketing strategies that are unconventional, nontraditional, and extremely flexible. Grassroots marketing is sometimes characterized by a relatively small budget and lots of legwork, but its hallmark is the ability to develop long-lasting, individual relationships with loyal customers. Viral and buzz marketing are examples of grassroots marketing.

CUSTOMER RELATIONSHIP MANAGEMENT

Emerging from—and closely linked to—relationship marketing, customer relationship management (CRM) is the combination of strategies and technologies that empowers relationship programs, reorienting the entire organization to a concentrated focus on satisfying customers. Made possible by technological advances, it leverages technology as a means to manage customer relationships and to integrate all stakeholders into a company's product design and development, manufacturing, marketing, sales, and customer service processes.

CRM represents a shift in thinking for everyone involved with a firm—from the CEO down and encompassing all other key stakeholders, including suppliers, dealers, and other partners. All recognize that solid customer relations are fostered by similarly strong relationships with other major stakeholders. Since CRM goes well beyond traditional sales, marketing, or customer service functions, it requires a top-down commitment and must permeate every aspect of a firm's business. Technology makes that possible by allowing firms—regardless of size and no matter how far-flung their operations—to manage activities across functions, from location to location, and among their internal and external partners.

BENEFITS OF CRM

CRM software systems are capable of making sense of the vast amounts of customer data that technology allows firms to collect. B2B firms benefit just as much as retailers. Another key benefit of customer relationship management systems is that they simplify complex business processes while keeping the best interests of customers at heart.

Selecting the right CRM software system is critical to the success of a firm's entire CRM program. CRM can be used at two different levels—on-demand accessed via the Internet as a Web-based service; and on premises, installed on a company's computer system on-site. A firm may choose to buy a system from a company or rent hosted CRM applications through websites. Purchasing a customized system can cost millions of dollars and take months to implement, while hosted solutions—rented through a website—are cheaper and quicker to get up and running. But purchasing a system allows a firm to expand and customize, whereas hosted systems are more limited. Experienced marketers also warn that it is easy to get mired in a system that is complicated for staff to use.

Software solutions are just one component of a successful CRM initiative. The most effective companies approach customer relationship management as a complete business strategy, in which

Maximizer Software: simplifying CRM systems.

people, processes, and technology are organized around delivering superior value to customers. Successful CRM systems share the following qualities:

- They create partnerships with customers in ways that align with the company's mission and goals.

- They reduce costs by empowering customers to find the information they need to manage their own orders.

- They improve customer service by centralizing data and help sales representatives guide customers to information.

- They reduce response time and thus increase customer satisfaction.

- They improve customer retention and loyalty, leading to more repeat business and new business from word of mouth.

- They can provide a complete picture of customers.

- Their results are measurable.[2]

Once the groundwork has been laid, technology solutions drive firms toward a clearer understanding of each customer and his or her needs.

PROBLEMS WITH CRM

CRM is not a magic wand. The strategy needs to be thought out in advance, and everyone in the firm must be committed to it and understand how to use it. If no one can put the system to work, it is an expensive mistake.

Experts explain that failures with CRM often result from failure to organize—or reorganize—the company's people and business processes to take advantage of the benefits the CRM system offers. For instance, it might be important to empower salespeople to negotiate price with their customers to close more sales with CRM, but if a company does not adapt its centralized pricing system, its CRM efforts will be hampered. Second, if sales and service employees do not have input in the CRM process during its design phase, they might be less willing to use its tools—no matter how much training is offered. "It is important to clearly communicate the benefits of the CRM, train employees how to use it, and have an onsite, dedicated 'go-to' person they can call on for help," says one marketing manager who managed four CRM implementations.[3] A third factor is that some CRM "failures" are actually at least partially successful, but companies or their executives have set their expectations too high. Having a realistic idea what CRM can accomplish is as important to success as properly implementing the program. Finally, truly understanding customers, their needs, and the ways they differ from customers of the past is a critical element in any successful CRM project.

RETRIEVING LOST CUSTOMERS

Customers defect from an organization's goods and services for a variety of reasons. They might be bored, they might move away from the region, they might not need the product anymore, or they might have tried—and preferred—competing products. An increasingly important part of an effective CRM strategy is **customer winback**, the process of rejuvenating lost relationships with customers.

customer winback
Process of rejuvenating lost relationships with customers.

In many cases, a relationship gone sour can be sweetened again with the right approach. A good rule for service providers is to anticipate where problems will arise and figure out in advance how to prevent them in the first place. The second part of this strategy is to accept that mistakes will occur in even the best system and to have a high-quality recovery effort in place that employees are empowered to enact. Sometimes, however, the missteps are so great that it is almost impossible for a company to repair the damage until enough time has passed for attention to simply turn elsewhere.

BUYER–SELLER RELATIONSHIPS IN BUSINESS-TO-BUSINESS MARKETS

Customer relationship management and relationship marketing are not limited to consumer goods and services. Building strong buyer–seller relationships is a critical component of business-to-business marketing as well.

Business-to-business marketing involves an organization's purchase of goods and services to support company operations or the production of other products. Buyer–seller relationships between companies involve working together to provide advantages that benefit both parties. These advantages might include lower prices for supplies, quicker delivery of inventory, improved quality and reliability, customized product features, and more favourable financing terms.

partnership Affiliation of two or more companies that help each other achieve common goals.

A **partnership** is an affiliation of two or more companies that help each other achieve common goals. Partnerships cover a wide spectrum of relationships from informal cooperative purchasing arrangements to formal production and marketing agreements. In business-to-business markets, partnerships form the basis of relationship marketing.

A variety of common goals motivates firms to form partnerships. Companies may want to protect or improve their positions in existing markets, gain access to new domestic or international markets, or quickly enter new markets. Expansion of a product line—to fill in gaps, broaden the product line, or differentiate the product—is another key reason for joining forces. Other motives include sharing resources, reducing costs, warding off threats of future competition, raising or creating barriers to entry, and learning new skills.

CHOOSING BUSINESS PARTNERS

How does an organization decide which companies to select as partners? The first priority is to locate firms that can add value to the relationship—whether through financial resources, contacts, extra manufacturing capacity, technical know-how, or distribution capabilities. The greater the value added, the greater the desirability of the partnership. In many cases, the attributes of each partner complement those of the other; each firm brings something to the relationship that the other party needs but cannot provide on its own. Other partnerships join firms with similar skills and resources to reduce costs. Organizations must share similar values and goals for a partnership to succeed in the long run.

TYPES OF PARTNERSHIPS

Companies form four key types of partnerships in business-to-business markets: buyer, seller, internal, and lateral partnerships. This section briefly examines each category.

In a buyer partnership, a firm purchases goods and services from one or more providers. When a company assumes the buyer position in a relationship, it has a unique set of needs and requirements that vendors must meet to make the relationship successful. While buyers want sellers to provide fair prices, quick delivery, and high quality levels, a lasting relationship often requires more effort. To induce a buyer to form a long-term partnership, a supplier must also be responsive to the purchaser's unique needs.

Seller partnerships set up long-term exchanges of goods and services in return for cash or other consideration. Sellers, too, have specific needs as partners in ongoing relationships. Most prefer to develop long-term relationships with their partners. Sellers want prompt payment.

The importance of internal partnerships is widely recognized in business today. The classic definition of the word *customer* as the buyer of a good or service is now more carefully defined in terms of external customers. However, customers within an organization also have their own needs. Internal partnerships are the foundation of an organization and its ability to meet its commitments to external entities. If the purchasing department selects a parts vendor that fails to ship on the dates required by manufacturing, production will halt, and products will not be delivered to customers as promised. As a result, external customers will likely seek other more reliable suppliers. Without building and maintaining internal partnerships, an organization will have difficulty meeting the needs of its external partnerships.

Lateral partnerships include strategic alliances with other companies or with not-for-profit organizations and research alliances between for-profit firms and colleges and universities. The relationship focuses on external entities—such as customers of the partner firm—and involves no direct buyer–seller interactions. Strategic alliances are discussed in a later section.

CO-BRANDING AND CO-MARKETING

Two other types of business marketing relationships are co-branding and co-marketing. Co-branding joins together two strong brand names, perhaps owned by two different companies, to sell a product. In a co-marketing effort, two or more organizations join to sell their products in an allied marketing campaign.

IMPROVING BUYER–SELLER RELATIONSHIPS IN BUSINESS-TO-BUSINESS MARKETS

Organizations that know how to find and nurture partner relationships, whether through informal deals or contracted partnerships, can enhance revenues and increase profits. Partnering often leads to lower prices, better products, and improved distribution, resulting in higher levels of customer satisfaction. Partners who know each other's needs and expectations are more likely to satisfy them and forge stronger long-term bonds. Often, partnerships can be cemented through personal relationships, no matter where firms are located.

In the past, business relationships were conducted primarily in person, over the phone, or by mail. Today, businesses are using the latest electronic, computer, and communications technology to link up. Email, the Internet, and other telecommunications services allow businesses to communicate anytime and anyplace.

NATIONAL ACCOUNT SELLING

Some relationships are more important than others due to the large investments at stake. Large manufacturers such as Procter & Gamble and Clorox pay special attention to the needs of major retailers such as Walmart. Manufacturers use a technique called national account selling to serve their largest, most profitable customers. The large collection of supplier offices in northwest Arkansas—near Walmart's home office—suggests how national account selling might be implemented. These offices are usually called teams or support teams.

The advantages of national account selling are many. By assembling a team of individuals to serve just one account, the seller demonstrates the depth of its commitment to the customer. The buyer–seller relationship is strengthened as both collaborate to find mutually beneficial solutions. Finally, cooperative buyer–seller efforts can bring about dramatic improvements in both efficiency and effectiveness for both partners. These improvements find their way to the bottom line in the form of decreased costs and increased profits.

BUSINESS-TO-BUSINESS DATABASES

As noted earlier, databases are indispensable tools in relationship marketing. They are also essential in building business-to-business relationships. Using information generated from sales reports, scanners, and many other sources, sellers can create databases that help guide their own efforts and those of buyers who resell products to final users.

ELECTRONIC DATA INTERCHANGE AND WEB SERVICES

electronic data interchange (EDI) Computer-to-computer exchanges of invoices, orders, and other business documents.

Technology has transformed the ways in which companies control their inventories and replenish stock. Gone are the days when a retailer would notice stocks were running low, call the vendor, check prices, and reorder. Today's **electronic data interchanges (EDIs)** automate the entire process. EDI involves computer-to-computer exchanges of invoices, orders, and other business documents. It allows firms to reduce costs and improve efficiency and competitiveness. Many retailers require vendors to use EDI as a core quick-response merchandising tool. Quick-response merchandising is a just-in-time strategy that reduces the time merchandise is held in inventory, resulting in substantial cost savings. An added advantage of EDI is that it opens new channels for gathering marketing information that is helpful in developing long-term business-to-business relationships.

Web services provide a way for companies to communicate even if they are not running the same or compatible software, hardware, databases, or network platforms. Companies in a customer–supplier relationship, or a partnership such as airlines and car rental firms, may have difficulty getting their computer systems to work together or exchange data easily. Web services are platform-independent information exchange systems that use the Internet to allow interaction between the firms. They are usually simple, self-contained applications that can handle functions from the simple to the complex.

Effective supply chain management can provide an important competitive advantage for a business marketer.

VENDOR-MANAGED INVENTORY

The proliferation of electronic communication technologies and the constant pressure on suppliers to improve response time have led to another way for buyers and sellers to do business. Vendor-managed inventory (VMI) has replaced buyer-managed inventory in many instances. It is an inventory management system in which the seller—based on an existing agreement with the buyer—determines how much of a product a buyer needs and automatically ships new supplies to that buyer.

Some firms have modified VMI to an approach called collaborative planning, forecasting, and replenishment (CPFaR). This approach is a planning and forecasting technique involving collaborative efforts by both purchasers and vendors.

MANAGING THE SUPPLY CHAIN

Good relationships between businesses require careful management of the supply chain, sometimes called the *value chain*, which is the entire sequence of suppliers that contribute to the creation and delivery of a product. This process affects both upstream relationships between the company and its suppliers and downstream relationships with the product's end users.

Effective supply chain management can provide an important competitive advantage for a business marketer that results in

- increased innovation,
- decreased costs,
- improved conflict resolution within the chain, and
- improved communication and involvement among members of the chain.

ColorBlind Images/Blend Images/Jupiter Images

By coordinating operations with the other companies in the chain, boosting quality, and improving its operating systems, a firm can improve speed and efficiency. Because companies spend considerable resources on goods and services from outside suppliers, cooperative relationships can pay off in many ways.

BUSINESS-TO-BUSINESS ALLIANCES

Strategic alliances are the ultimate expression of relationship marketing. A strategic alliance is a partnership formed to create a competitive advantage. These more formal long-term partnership arrangements improve each partner's supply chain relationships and enhance flexibility in operating in today's complex and rapidly changing marketplace. The size and location of strategic partners are not important. Strategic alliances include businesses of all sizes, of all kinds, and in many locations; it is what each partner can offer the other that is important.

Companies can structure strategic alliances in two ways. Alliance partners can establish a new business unit in which each takes an ownership position. In such a joint venture, one partner might own 40 percent, while the other owns 60 percent. Alternatively, the partners may decide to form a less formal cooperative relationship that does not involve ownership—for example, a joint new-product design team. The cooperative alliance can operate more flexibly and can change more easily as market forces or other conditions dictate. In either arrangement, the partners agree in advance on the skills and resources that each will bring into the alliance to achieve their mutual objectives and gain a competitive advantage. Resources typically include patents, product lines, brand equity, product and market knowledge, company and brand image, and reputation for product quality, innovation, or customer service. Relationships with customers and suppliers are also desirable resources, as are a convenient manufacturing facility, economies of scale and scope, information technology, and a large sales force. Alliance partners can contribute marketing skills such as innovation and product development, manufacturing skills including low-cost or flexible manufacturing, and planning and research and development expertise.

Companies form many types of strategic alliances. Some create horizontal alliances between firms at the same level in the supply chain; others define vertical links between firms at adjacent stages. The firms may serve the same or different industries. Alliances can involve cooperation among rivals who are market leaders or between a market leader and a follower.

EVALUATING CUSTOMER RELATIONSHIP PROGRAMS

One of the most important measures of relationship marketing programs, whether in consumer or business-to-business markets, is the lifetime value of a customer. This concept can be defined as the revenues and intangible benefits such as referrals and customer feedback that a customer brings to the seller over an average lifetime of the relationship, less the amount the company must spend to acquire, market to, and service the customer. Long-term customers are usually more valuable assets than new ones because they buy more, cost less to serve, refer other customers, and provide valuable feedback. The "average lifetime" of a customer relationship depends on industry and product characteristics. Customer lifetime for a consumer product such as microwave pizza may be very short, while that for an automobile or computer will last longer.

For a simple example of a lifetime value calculation, assume that a Chinese takeout restaurant determines that its average customer buys dinner twice a month at an average cost of $25 per order over a lifetime of five years. That business results in revenues of $600 per year and $3,000 for five years. The restaurant can calculate and subtract its average costs for food, labour, and overhead to arrive at the per-customer profit. This figure serves as a baseline against which to measure strategies to increase the restaurant's sales volume, customer retention, or customer referral rate.

Another approach is to calculate the payback from a customer relationship, or the length of time it takes to break even on customer acquisition costs. Assume that an Internet service provider spends $75 per new customer on direct mail and enrolment incentives. Based on average revenues per subscriber, the company takes about three months to recover that $75. If an average customer stays with the service 32 months and generates $800 in revenues, the rate of return is nearly 11 times the original investment. Once the customer stays past the payback period, the provider should make a profit on that business.

In addition to lifetime value analysis and payback, companies use many other techniques to evaluate relationship programs, including the following:

- Reviewing customer comments and feedback on social media sites like Facebook and Twitter

- tracking rebate requests, coupon redemption, credit card purchases, and product registrations

- monitoring complaints and returned merchandise and analyzing why customers leave

- reviewing reply cards, comment forms, and surveys

- monitoring click-through behaviour on websites to identify why customers stay and why they leave

These tools give the organization information about customer priorities so that managers can make changes to their systems, if necessary, and set appropriate, measurable goals for relationship programs.

A hotel chain may set a goal of improving the rate of repeat visits from 44 to 52 percent. A mail-order company may want to reduce time from 48 to 24 hours to process and mail orders. If a customer survey reveals late flight arrivals as the number one complaint of an airline's passengers, the airline might set an objective of increasing the number of on-time arrivals from 87 to 93 percent.

Companies large and small can implement technology to help measure the value of customers and the return on investment from expenditures on developing customer relationships. They can choose from among a growing number of software products, many of which are tailored to specific industries or flexible enough to suit companies of varying sizes.

Financial Analysis in Marketing

A number of basic concepts from accounting and finance offer invaluable tools to marketers. Understanding the contributions made by these analytic tools can improve the quality of marketing decisions. In addition, marketers are frequently called on to explain and defend their decisions in financial terms. These accounting and financial tools can be used to supply quantitative data to justify decisions made by marketing managers. In this appendix, we describe the major accounting and finance concepts that have marketing implications and explain how they assist in making informed marketing decisions.

FINANCIAL STATEMENTS

All companies prepare a set of financial statements on a regular basis. Two of the most important financial statements are the income statement and balance sheet. The analogy of a motion picture is often used to describe an *income statement*, since it presents a financial record of a company's revenues, expenses, and profits over a period of time, such as a month, quarter, or year. In contrast, the *balance sheet* is a snapshot of what a company owns—called *assets*—and what it owes—called *liabilities*—at a point in time, such as at the end of the month, quarter, or year. The difference between assets and liabilities is referred to as *owner's, partners', or shareholders' equity*—the amount of funds the firm's owners have invested in its formation and continued operations. Of the two financial statements, the income statement contains more marketing-related information.

A sample income statement for Composite Technology is shown in Figure 1. Composite Technology is a B2B producer and marketer. The firm designs and manufactures a variety of composite components for manufacturers of consumer, industrial, and government products. Total sales revenues for 2015 amounted to $675 million. Total expenses, including taxes, for the year were $583.1 million. The year 2015 proved to be profitable for Composite Technology—the firm reported a profit, referred to as net income, of $91.9 million. While total revenue is a fairly straightforward number, several of the expenses shown on the income statement require additional explanation.

For any company that makes its own products (a manufacturer) or simply markets one or more items produced by others (an importer, retailer, or wholesaler), the largest single expense is usually a category called *cost of goods sold*. This reflects the cost, to the firm, of the goods that it markets to its customers. In the case of Composite Technology, the cost of goods sold represents the cost of components and raw materials as well as the cost of designing and manufacturing the composite panels the firm produces and markets to its business customers.

The income statement illustrates how cost of goods sold is calculated. The calculation begins with the value of the firm's inventory at the beginning of 2015. Inventory is the value of raw materials, partially completed products, and finished products held by the firm at the end of a specified time period, say, the end of the year. The cost of materials purchased by Composite Technology buyers during the year and the direct cost of manufacturing the finished products are then added to the beginning inventory figure. The result is cost of goods the firm has available for sale during the year. Once the firm's accountants subtract the value of inventory held by the firm at the end of 2015, they know the cost of goods sold. By simply subtracting cost of goods sold from total sales revenues generated during the year, they determine that Composite achieved gross profits of $270 million in 2015.

figure 1

2015 Income Statement for Composite Technology, Inc.

Composite Technology, Inc.
500 Ridley Road
Somewhere, MB

CT

INCOME STATEMENT
For the Year Ended December 31, 2015
(in $ millions)

Sales	675.0
Cost of Goods Sold	405.0
Gross Income	270.0
Selling, Administrative, and General Expenses	82.1
Research and Development Expenses	25.4
Operating Income	162.5
Depreciation	18.6
Net Interest Expense	2.5
Before Tax Income	141.4
Provision for Income Taxes	49.5
Net Income	91.9

Cost of Goods Sold Calculation	($ millions)
Beginning Inventory	158.0
plus: Raw Materials Purchased	200.7
plus: Direct Manufacturing Expenses	226.3
Total Cost of Goods	585.0
minus: Ending Inventory	(180.0)
Cost of Goods Sold	405.0

Operating expenses are another significant cost for most firms. This broad category includes such marketing outlays as sales compensation and expenses, advertising and other promotions, and other expenses incurred in implementing marketing plans. Accountants typically combine these financial outlays into a single category with the label *Selling, Administrative, and General Expenses.* Other expense items included in the operating expenses section of the income statement are administrative salaries, utilities, and insurance.

Another significant expense for Composite Technology is research and development (R&D). This includes the cost of developing new products and modifying existing ones. Firms such as pharmaceutical, biotechnology, and computer companies spend significant amounts of money each year on R&D. Subtracting selling, administrative, and general expenses and R&D expenses from the gross profit equals the firm's operating income. For 2015, Composite had operating income of $162.5 million.

Depreciation represents the systematic reduction over time in the value of certain company assets, such as production machinery, office furniture, or laptops provided for the firm's sales representatives. Depreciation is an unusual expense in that it does not involve an actual cash expenditure. However, it does reflect the reality that equipment owned by the company is physically wearing out over time from use and/or from technological obsolescence. Also, charging a portion of the total cost of these long-lived items to each of the years in which they are used results in a more accurate determination of the total costs involved in the firm's operation each year.

Net interest expense is the difference between what a firm paid in interest on various loans and what it collected in interest on any investments made during the time period involved. Subtracting depreciation and net interest expense from the firm's operating profit reveals the firm's *before-tax income.* Composite had depreciation of $18.6 million and a net interest expense of $2.5 million for the year, so its 2015 taxable income was $141.4 million.

Profit-seeking firms pay taxes calculated as a percentage of their taxable income. Composite paid $49.5 million in taxes in 2015. Subtracting taxes from taxable income gives us the firm's *net income* of $91.9 million.

PERFORMANCE RATIOS

Managers often compute a variety of financial ratios to assess the performance of their firm. These ratios are calculated using data found on both the income statement and the balance sheet. Ratios are then compared with industry standards and with data from previous years. Several ratios are of particular interest to marketers.

A number of commonly used financial ratios focus on *profitability measures.* They are used to assess the firm's ability to generate revenues in excess of expenses and earn an adequate rate of return. Profitability measures include gross profit margin, net profit margin, and return on assets.

Gross Profit Margin

The gross profit margin equals the firm's gross profit divided by its sales revenues. In 2015, Composite had a gross profit margin of

$$\frac{\text{Gross Profit}}{\text{Sales}} = \frac{\$270 \text{ million}}{\$675 \text{ million}} = 40\%$$

The gross profit margin is the percentage of each sales dollar that can be used to pay other expenses and meet the firm's profit objectives. Ideally, businesses would like to see gross profit margins that are equal to or higher than those of other firms in their industry. A declining gross profit margin may indicate that the firm is under some competitive price pressures or that its prices have not been adjusted to account for increases in raw materials or other product costs.

Net Profit Margin

The net profit margin equals net income divided by sales. For 2015, Composite had a net profit margin of

$$\frac{\text{Net Income}}{\text{Sales}} = \frac{\$91.9 \text{ million}}{\$675 \text{ million}} = 13.6\%$$

The net profit margin is the percentage of each sales dollar that the firm earns in profit or retains after all expenses have been paid. Companies—and their shareholders—generally want to see rising, or at least stable, net profit margins.

Return on Assets (ROA)

A third profitability ratio, return on assets, measures the firm's efficiency in generating sales and profits from the total amount invested in the company. For 2015, Composite's ROA is calculated as follows:

$$\frac{\text{Net Income}}{\text{Sales}} = \frac{\text{Sales}}{\text{Average Assets}} \times \frac{\text{Net Income}}{\text{Sales}}$$

$$\frac{\$675 \text{ million}}{\$595 \text{ million}} \times \frac{91.9 \text{ million}}{\$675 \text{ million}} = 1.13 \times 13.6\% = 15.4\%$$

The ROA ratio actually consists of two components. The first component, called *asset turnover,* is the amount of sales generated for each dollar invested. The second component is *net profit margin.* Data for total assets are found on the firm's balance sheet.

Assume that Composite began 2015 with $560 million in assets and ended the year with $630 million in assets. Its average assets for the year would be $595 million. As was the case for the other profitability ratios, Composite's ROA should be compared with that of other firms in the industry and with its own previous performance to be meaningful.

Inventory Turnover

Inventory turnover is typically categorized as an *activity ratio* because it evaluates the effectiveness of the firm's resource use. Specifically, it measures the number of times a firm "turns" its inventory each year. The ratio can help answer the question of whether the firm has the appropriate level of inventory. Inventory turnover equals sales divided by average inventory. From the income statement, we see that Composite Technology began 2015 with $158 million in inventory and ended the year with $180 million in inventory. Therefore, the firm's average inventory was $169 million. The firm's inventory turnover ratio equals

$$\frac{\text{Sales}}{\text{Average Inventory}} = \frac{\$675 \text{ million}}{\$169 \text{ million}} = 3.99$$

For 2015, Composite Technology turned its inventory almost four times a year. While a faster inventory turn is usually a sign of greater efficiency, to be really meaningful the inventory turnover ratio must be compared with historical data and appropriate peer firm averages. Different organizations can have different inventory turnover ratios depending on the types of products they sell. For instance, a supermarket such as Safeway might turn its inventory every two weeks for an annual rate of 26 times per year. In contrast, a large furniture retailer is likely to average only about two turns per year. Again, the determination of a "good" or "inadequate" inventory turnover rate depends on typical rates in the industry and the firm's performance in previous years.

Accounts Receivable Turnover

Another activity ratio that may be of interest to marketers is accounts receivable turnover. This ratio measures the number of times per year a company "turns" its receivables. Dividing accounts receivable turnover into 365 gives us the average age of the company's receivables.

Companies make sales on either a cash or credit basis. Credit sales allow the buyer to obtain a product now and pay for it at a specified later date. In essence, the seller is providing credit to the buyer. Credit sales are common in B2B transactions. It should be noted that sales to buyers using credit cards such as MasterCard and VISA are included as cash sales since the issuer of the credit card, rather than the seller, is providing credit to the buyer. Consequently, most B2C sales are cash sales.

Receivables are uncollected credit sales. Measuring accounts receivable turnover and the average age of receivables is important for firms where credit sales make up a high proportion of total sales. Accounts receivable turnover is defined as

$$\text{Accounts Receivable Turnover} = \frac{\text{Credit Sales}}{\text{Average Accounts Receivable}}$$

Assume that all of Composite Technology's sales are credit sales. Also assume that the firm began 2015 with $50 million in receivables and ended the year with $60 million in receivables (both numbers can be found on the balance sheet). Therefore, it had an average of $55 million in receivables. The firm's receivables turnover and average age equal

$$\frac{\$675 \text{ million}}{\$55 \text{ million}} = 12.3 \text{ times}$$

$$\frac{365}{12.3} = 29.7 \text{ days}$$

Composite turned its receivables slightly more than 12 times per year. The average age of its receivables was slightly less than 30 days. Since Composite expects its customers to pay outstanding invoices within 30 days, these numbers appear appropriate. As with other ratios, however, receivables turnover and average age of receivables should also be compared with peer firms and historical data.

MARKUPS AND MARKDOWNS

In previous chapters, we discussed the importance of pricing decisions for firms. This section expands on our earlier discussion by introducing two important pricing concepts: markups and markdowns. They can help to establish selling prices and evaluate various pricing strategies and are closely tied to a firm's income statement.

Markups

The amount that a marketer adds to a product's cost to set the final selling price is the markup. The amount of the markup typically results from two marketing decisions:

1. The services performed by the marketer. Other things being equal, retailers who offer more services charge larger markups to cover their costs.

2. The inventory turnover rate. Other things being equal, retailers with a higher turnover rate can cover their costs and earn a profit while charging a smaller markup.

A marketer's markup exerts an important influence on its image among present and potential customers. In addition, it affects the retailer's ability to attract shoppers. An excessive markup may drive away customers; an inadequate markup may fail to generate sufficient revenues needed by the retailer to cover costs and earn a profit.

Markups are typically stated as percentages of either the selling prices or the costs of the products. The formulas for calculating markups are as follows:

$$\text{Markup Percentage on Selling Price} = \frac{\text{Amount Added to Cost (Markup)}}{\text{Selling Price}}$$

$$\text{Markup Percentage on Cost} = \frac{\text{Amount Added to Cost (Markup)}}{\text{Cost}}$$

Consider a product with an invoice of 60 cents and a selling price of $1. The total markup (selling price less cost) is 40 cents. The two markup percentages are calculated as follows:

$$\text{Markup Percentage on Selling Price} = \frac{\$0.40}{\$1.00} = 40\%$$

$$\text{Markup Percentage on Cost} = \frac{\$0.40}{\$0.60} = 66.7\%$$

To determine the selling price knowing only the cost and markup percentage on selling price, a marketer applies the following formula:

$$\text{Price} = \frac{\text{Cost in Dollars}}{(100\% - \text{Markup Percentage on Selling Price})}$$

In the previous example, to determine the correct selling price of $1, the marketer would make the following calculation:

$$\text{Price} = \frac{\$0.60}{(100\% - 40\%)} = \$1.00$$

Similarly, you can convert the markup percentage for a specific item based on the selling price to one based on cost and the reverse using these formulas:

$$\text{Markup Percentage on Selling Price} = \frac{\text{Markup Percentage on Cost}}{(100\% + \text{Markup Percentage on Cost})}$$

$$\text{Markup Percentage on Cost} = \frac{\text{Markup Percentage on Selling Price}}{(100\% - \text{Markup Percentage on Selling Price})}$$

Again, data from the previous example give the following conversions:

$$\text{Markup Percentage on Selling Price} = \frac{66.7\%}{(100\% + 66.7\%)} = 40\%$$

$$\text{Markup Percentage on Cost} = \frac{40\%}{(100\% - 40\%)} = 66.7\%$$

Marketers determine markups based partly on their judgments of the amounts that consumers will pay for a given product. When buyers refuse to pay a product's stated price, however, or when improvements in other products or fashion changes reduce the appeal of the current merchandise, a producer or retailer must take a markdown.

Markdowns

A markdown is a price reduction a firm makes on an item. Reasons for markdowns include sales promotions featuring price reductions or a decision that the initial price was too high. Unlike markups, markdowns cannot be determined from the income statement since the price reduction takes place before the sale occurs. The markdown percentage equals dollar markdowns divided by sales. For example, a retailer decides to reduce the price of an item by $10, from $50 to $40, and sells 1,000 units. The markdown percentage equals

$$\frac{(1,000 \times \$10)}{(1,000 \times \$40)} = \frac{\$10,000}{\$40,000} = 25\%$$

BREAK-EVEN ANALYSIS

For a discussion of break-even analysis, see Chapter 16. A sample question is included in the Project and Teamwork Exercises at the end of the chapter.

ASSIGNMENTS

1. Assume that a product has an invoice price of $45 and a selling price of $60. Calculate the markup as a percentage of both the selling price and the cost.

2. A product has an invoice price of $92.50. The seller wants to include a markup on the selling price of 25 percent. Calculate the selling price.

3. Assume a retailer decides to reduce the price of an item by $5, from $15 to $10, and sells 5,000 units. Calculate the markdown percentage.

4. Obtain a recent income statement and balance sheet for a business of your choosing whose stock is publicly traded. An easy way to find these is to visit the company's website and click on a link for "Investor Relations." Then look for the company's annual report. Use the relevant data on the income statement to calculate each of the following ratios:
   a. gross profit margin
   b. net profit margin
   c. inventory turnover
   d. return on assets
   e. price markup

5. This appendix has described how the industry in which a firm operates affects its financial ratios. Solve this critical-thinking exercise by matching the following set of financial ratios to

FINANCIAL RATIO	FIRM A	FIRM B	FIRM C	FIRM D
Net profit margin	28.4%	3.5%	13.9%	6.5%
Return on assets	20.6%	8.6%	14.6%	10.0%
Inventory turnover	2.1	7.6	3.4	4.9

each of the following firms: 3M, Gap, Pfizer, and Walmart. Consider the industry in which each company operates and the way it is likely to affect profits, return on assets, and inventory turnover rates. For example, which of the four would you expect to have the lowest profit margin and which should have the highest profit margin?

CHAPTER 1

1. John Bassett, "Motor Racing's Best of the Best 2013: From IndyCar to F1, NASCAR to Moto GP, Racing Had Its Moments," *Toronto Star,* January 4, 2014, p. W12; Billy Fellin, "NASCAR Embraces Social Media," *Hispanic Business,* April 27, 2012, **www.hispanicbusiness.com**; Cary Estes, "To Tweet or Not to Tweet at Races: Gentlemen, Start Your Arguments," *SI.com,* March 8, 2012, **sportsillustrated.cnn.com**; Richard Sandomir, "Stopped on the Track, Racing Ahead on Twitter," *The New York Times,* February 28, 2012, **www.nytimes.com**; Kevin Mullett, "Capitalizing on a Social Media Storm a la NASCAR Driver Brad Keselowski," *Cirrus Abs,* February 28, 2012, **www.cirrusabs.com**; Sam Laird, "Can Social Media Turbocharge NASCAR on TV?" *Mashable.com,* February 24, 2012, **http://mashable.com**; Jason Del Rey, "Nascar Targets New Audiences, Revs Up Social–Media Strategy," *Ad Age,* January 2, 2012, **http://adage.com**.

2. Douglas Macmillan and Brad Stone, "Facebook Delves Deeper into Search," *Bloomberg Businessweek,* March 29, 2012, **www.businessweek.com**.

3. Company website, **www.golfwithoutlimits.com**, accessed January 16, 2014.

4. Company website, **www.yoyonation.com**, accessed April 6, 2012.

5. Joseph P. Guiltinan and Gordon W. Paul, *Marketing Management,* 6th ed. (New York: McGraw-Hill), 1996, pp. 3–4.

6. American Marketing Association, "Resource Library," **www.marketingpower.com**, accessed January 17, 2014.

7. Company website, "Checked Baggage," **www.aircanada.com**, accessed January 17, 2014.

8. "Automobile Industry Introduction," Plunkett Research, Ltd., **www.plunkettresearch.com**, accessed April 7, 2012.

9. Asia Pacific Foundation of Canada, "Canada's Merchandise Trade with China," available **www.asiapacific.ca/statistics/trade/bilateral-trade-asia-product/canadas-merchandise-trade-china**, accessed January 17, 2014.

10. "2011 U.S. Manufacturing-Outsourcing Index," *Alixpartners.com,* **www.alixpartners.com**, accessed April 7, 2012.

11. Jason Fekete, "Nexen Takeover Bid Gets OK; China Completes Deal for Canadian Oilsands Firm," *Ottawa Citizen,* December 8, 2012, p. A1.

12. "New iPad Tops Three Million," press release, March 19, 2012, **www.apple.com**.

13. Vittorio Hernandez, "Boeing Dreamliner Takes off after Three Years of Delay," *iHaveNet.com,* **www.ihavenet.com**, accessed April 7, 2012.

14. Milt Freudenheim, "As Smartphones Become Health Aids, Ads May Follow," *The New York Times,* April 1, 2012, **www.nytimes.com**.

15. Katie Fehrenbacher, "SunPower Scores Deal for Apple's Huge Solar Farm," *Gigaom.com,* March 8, 2012, **http://gigaom.com**; Kit Eaton, "Apple's Solar Power Patent: Sun Powered Mac, iPods, iPhones in the Future," *Fast Company,* **www.fastcompany.com**, accessed March 8, 2012.

16. Company website, "Charities & Nonprofit Organizations," **www.imaginecanada.ca**, January 1, 2014; Imagine Canada, "Sector Impact," available **http://sectorsource.ca/research-and-impact/sector-impact**, accessed January 1, 2014.

17. Company website, **www.walmartcanada.ca**, accessed January 1, 2014.

18. Food Banks Canada 2012 Annual Report, **www.foodbankscanada.ca**, January 18, 2014.

19. Heart & Stroke Foundation website, "Our Impact," **www.heartandstroke.com**, January 18, 2014.

20. CNW Group, "Alberta Flood Aid Raises Nearly 2.2 Million Dollars through Benefit Concert," October 17, 2013, available **www.newswire.ca**, accessed January 18, 2014.

21. Organization website, **www.piryx.com**, accessed April 9, 2012; organization website, **www.yourcause.com**, accessed April 9, 2012.

22. Organization website, "Playoff-Bound Argos to Host Blue Bombers in CFL Pink Game," **www.argonauts.ca**, October 22, 2013, accessed January 18, 2014.

23. Sarah Hampson, "Hot Family Values," *The Globe and Mail,* December 14, 2013, p. L14.

24. Nick Friedell, "Derrick Rose, Adidas Sticking Together," ESPN, February 26, 2012, **http://espn.go.com**; Albert Lin, "Derrick Rose Signs Second Largest Sneaker Endorsement Ever," *Nice Kicks,* February 26, 2012, **www.nicekicks.com**.

25. Joel Rubinoff, "Shaken, Jerked and Twerked in 2013," *Toronto Star,* December 27, 2013, p. E7.

26. "Twitter Follower Flock to Perry: Year in Review," *The Province* (Vancouver), December 24, 2013, p. B2; Erin Bury, "Want to Take Your Business to the Next Level? Clinch a Celebrity Endorsement," **www.business.financialpost.com**, May 20, 2013, accessed January 16, 2014.

27. CBC News, "Canadian Tourism Declines Despite World Travel Boom," **www.cbc.ca**, November 14, 2013.

28. Ibid.

29. Ibid.; Steven Threndyle, "Why Tourists Don't Like Canada," **www.canadianbusiness.com**, October 28, 2013, accessed January 17, 2014; Adrian Brijbassi, "How Canada Can Attract Chinese Tourists," *Vacay.ca,* **http://vacay.ca**, April 11, 2013, accessed January 18, 2014.

30. Canadian Tire Jumpstart 2012 Annual Report, "Giving Kids a Sporting Chance," **http://jumpstart.canadiantire.ca**, accessed January 18, 2014.

31. "Super Bowl TV Audience Reaches Record 111.3 Million," Reuters, February 6, 2012, **www.reuters.com**; "Super Bowl Ads Cost an Average of $3.5M," *ESPN.com,* February 5, 2012, **http://espn.go.com**.

32. Official website for Sochi 2014 Winter Olympics, **http://tenders.sochi2014.com/en/**, accessed January 18, 2014.

33. University of Toronto website, "The University of Toronto Launches Boundless, Its $2-Billion Fundraising Campaign," available **www.news.utoronto.ca/**, November 20, 2011, accessed January 18, 2014.

34. Emil Protalinksi, "Facebook Passes 1.19 Billion Users, 874 Million Mobile Users, and 728 Million Daily Users," **http://thenextweb.com**, October 30, 2013, accessed January 16, 2014.

35. Emil Protalinski, "Twitter Sees 218M Monthly Active Users, 163.5M Monthly Mobile Users, and 500M Tweets Per Day," **http://thenextweb.com**, October 3, 2013, accessed January 16, 2014.

36. Cooper Smith, "Facebook Is a Daily Habit in the US, While Twitter Users Log on Less Often," **www.businessinsider.com**, December 31, 2013, accessed January 16, 2014.

37. Marissa McNaughton, "77% of Fortune Global 100 Companies Use Twitter," *Real-time Report,* **http://therealtimereport.com**, accessed April 11, 2012.

38. Mario Toneguzzi, "Alberta Entrepreneurs on Social Media," *Calgary Herald,* October 26, 2013, p. C3.

39. Gillian Shaw, "Survey Says," *Vancouver Sun,* November 20, 2013, p. C1.

40. Ibid.

41. Organization website, "Canadian Students Global Leaders in Movember Fundraising," press release, December 12, 2013, **http://ca.movember.com**; Misty Harris, "Don't Count on 'Staches for Donations; Movember Face Fur Ineffective as Pledge: Study," *Edmonton Journal,* November 13, 2013, p. D5.

42. CNW, "Sears Canada Enters into Strategic Alliance with Buffalo International to Build Nevada Apparel," **www.newswire.ca**, January 17, 2013, accessed January 1, 2014.

43. Organization website, **www.secondharvest.ca**, accessed January 18, 2014; Sobeys website, "Serving Our Communities," **www.sobeyscorporate.com**, January 18, 2014.

44. "An Interview with Linda Fisher," *Globe-Net,* February 13, 2012, **www.globe-net.com**.

45. Ibid.

46. Company website, "Sustainability on a Smarter Planet," **www.ibm.com**, accessed April 11, 2012.

47. Organization website, **www.ecofriendlysites.org**, accessed April 11, 2012.

48. Company website, "Recycling," **www.nokia.com**, accessed April 11, 2012.

49. Patrick Langston, "Lean, Green Award-Winning Machines; The Numbers May Still Be Small, But Eco-Friendly Building Is Thriving in the City," *Ottawa Citizen,* October 27, 2012, p. I1.

CHAPTER 1 MARKETOID NOTES

1. Golf Canada website, **www.golfcanada.ca**, accessed March 31, 2014.

2. Canadian Tire website, **www.corp.canadiantire.ca**, accessed March 31, 2014.

3. Mondelez International website, **www.mondelezinternational.com**, accessed March 31, 2014.

4. Hill Strategies Research, "Volunteers and Donors in Arts and Culture Organizations in Canada in 2010," available **http://canadacouncil.ca/~/media/files/research%20-%20en/arts%20funding/volunteers%20in%20arts%20and%20culture%20organizations%20in%20canada/volunteers_donors2010.pdf**, accessed March 31, 2014.

5. **www.facebook.com/sochi2014**, tracked before and after the games by H.F. (Herb) MacKenzie.

6. "Canada's Greenest Employers for 2013," **theglobeandmail.com**, April 19, 2013, accessed March 31, 2014.

CHAPTER 2

1. Jeff Bliss, "Google Wins U.S. Antitrust Approval to Buy Motorola Mobility," *Bloomberg Businessweek,* February 15, 2012, **www.businessweek.com**; Trefis Team, "Google Wins E.U., U.S. Approval to Scoop Up Motorola, Patents," *Forbes,* February 15, 2012, **www.forbes.com**; Diane Bartz and Foo Yun Chee, "Google Gets U.S., EU Nod to Buy Motorola Mobility," Reuters, February 14, 2012, **www.reuters.com**; Matt Richtel and Jenna Wortham, "Motorola's Identity Crisis," *The New York Times,* August 21, 2011, **www.nytimes.com**; Roger Cheng, "Google to Buy Motorola Mobility for $12.5B," *CNet.com,* August 15, 2011, **http://news.cnet.com**; Jay Yarrow, "Google: We Bought Motorola to 'Protect' the Android Ecosystem," *Business Insider,* August 15, 2011, **http://articles.businessinsider.com**.

2. Company website, "Our 500th Astronaut," March 22, 2012, **www.virgin.com/richard -branson/blog**; Christine Kearney, "Ashton Kutcher to Fly on Branson's First Spacecraft," Reuters, March 20, 2012, **www.reuters.com**.

3. Gordon Sinclair, Jr., "Local Biz Helps Clothe Our Athletes," *Winnipeg Free Press*, November 21, 2013, p. B1.

4. Company website, **www.pg.com**, accessed April 13, 2012.

5. Tristan Hopper, "Police Hockey Team Subdues Enraged Flyer; Flight from Poland; Drunk Passenger Attacks Crew; Storms Cockpit," *National Post*, November 27, 2013, p. A2.

6. "Companies Aim to Improve Social Media Marketing, Survey Finds," *National Post*, October 29, 2012, p. FP6.

7. Caroline Van Hasselt and Leslie Scism, "Sun Life Revamps Its U.S. Strategy," *The Wall Street Journal*, December 13, 2011, **http://online.wsj.com**.

8. Zachary Rodgers, "Microsoft Retires AdECN, Migrates to AppNexus RTB Engine," *ClickZ .com*, March 30, 2011, **www.clickz.com**.

9. Mark Brandau, "McDonald's McCafe: An Evolution," *Nation's Restaurant News*, August 16, 2011, **http://nrn.com**.

10. "Embraer Could Fly Past Bombardier," *Calgary Herald*, August 27, 2013, p. D3.

11. Dr Pepper Snapple Group 2012 Annual Report, available **www.drpeppersnapplegroup .com/**, accessed January 18, 2014; Nanette Byrnes, "Why Dr. Pepper Is in the Pink of Health," **www.businessweek.com**, accessed March 20, 2012.

12. Byrnes, "Why Dr. Pepper Is in the Pink of Health."

13. Derek F. Abell, "Strategic Windows," *Journal of Marketing*, 42, no. 3 (July 1978), pp. 21–26.

14. Cameron French, "Canadian Banks Eye Cuban Presence as Tensions Ease," *Calgary Herald*, December 20, 2011, p. D3.

15. Company website, **www.platoscloset.com**, accessed January 2, 2014.

16. Jeff Beer, "Oreo's Chinese Twist," *Canadian Business*, December 10, 2012, pp. 66–67.

17. "Connecting and Engaging with Digital Indian Consumers," *Nielsen Wire*, November 15, 2011, **http://blog.nielsen.com**.

18. Venessa Wong, "Lay's New Chocolate-Covered Potato Chips: For Women, of Course," *BusinessWeek*, November 4, 2013, **www.businessweek.com**, accessed January 18, 2014.

19. Michael Oliveira, "Soaring WestJet Viral Video Branding Win: Experts," *Telegraph-Journal* (Saint John), December 13, 2013, p. A6.

20. Brad Thomas, "Dollar Stores Take on Wal-Mart, and Are Starting to Win," *Forbes*, April 16, 2012, **www.forbes.com**; "Majority of High-Income Shoppers Visiting Dollar Stores," October 18, 2013, **www.marketingcharts.com**.

21. Norihiko Shirouzu, "Ford Revs up in China, Roars Past Toyota and Honda," **www.reuters .com**, accessed January 6, 2014.

22. Company website, **www.canadiantire.ca/en/mobile.html**, accessed January 2, 2014; Heather Loney, "Canadian App Rates 'Dirty' Ingredients in Cosmetics and Personal Care Products," October 25, 2013, **http://globalnews.ca**, accessed January 2, 2014.

23. Alice Hines, "eBay's 'Buy It New' Rebranding Angers Devoted Used Goods Sellers," *Daily Finance*, November 2, 2011, **www.dailyfinance.com**.

24. "1960s IBM Standard Issue Clock," *Hypebeast*, **http://hypebeast.com**, accessed April 16, 2012.

25. comScore, Inc. "comScore Reports November 2013 U.S. Smartphone Subscriber Market Share," January 6, 2014, **www.sacbee.com**, accessed January 7, 2014.

26. Christopher Davies, "Intel Profits up But Microsoft's Windows OS Suffers," *Manufacturing Digital*, January 20, 2012, **www.manufacturingdigital.com**.

27. "Lululemon's Next Challenge Is International Growth," *Financial Post*, October 9, 2013, **http://business.financial post.com**, accessed January 16, 2014.

28. Venessa Wong, "For Burger King's Satisfries, 'Healthier' Is a Very Relative Term," *Business-Week*, September 24, 2013, **www.businessweek.com**, accessed January 16, 2014.

29. Moon Ihlwan, "Sony and Samsung's Strategic Split," *Bloomberg Businessweek*, January 18, 2010, p. 52.

CHAPTER 2 MARKETOID NOTES

1. Search performed by H.F. (Herb) MacKenzie, March 31, 2014.

2. CBC News, "Milton Siblings Have Journeys Booked Aboard Virgin Galactic Spacecraft," January 17, 2014, **www.cbc.ca**, accessed March 22, 2014.

3. Tim Hortons website, **www.timhortons.com**, accessed March 31, 2014.

4. Statistics Canada, "Immigration and Ethnocultural Diversity in Canada," available **http:// www12.statcan.gc.ca/nhs-enm/2011/as-sa/99-010-x/99-010-x2011001-eng.cfm**, accessed March 31, 2014.

5. Industry Canada, "Combating Counterfeit Products Coming into Canada: Backgrounder," available **http://www.ic.gc.ca/eic/site/064.nsf/eng/07280.html**, accessed March 31, 2014.

CHAPTER 3

1. Company press release, "Chipotle Plans to Serve More Than 15 Million Pounds of Locally Grown Produce in 2013," June 18, 2013, **http://ir.chipotle.com**; "Chipotle Mexican Grill, Inc.: Chipotle Will Plant a Free Burrito in Your Lunch Bag to Celebrate Earth Day," *4-Traders .com*, March 26, 2012, **www.4-traders.com**; Maureen Morrison, "Chipotle Bucks Fast-Food Convention While It Still Can," *Advertising Age*, March 12, 2012, **www.adage.com**; "Chipotle Ad Upstages Some Grammy Performances," *Advertising Age*, February 13, 2012, **www.adage .com**; Elizabeth Olson, "An Animated Ad with a Plot Line and a Moral," *The New York Times*, February 10, 2012, **www.nytimes.com**; company press release, "Chipotle Mexican Grill Creates 'Chipotle Cultivate Foundation,'" August 25, 2011, **http://ir.chipotle.com**.

2. Sophie Cousineau, "High Hurdles, Nervous Airlines and a Big Year for Bombardier's Biggest Bet," *The Globe and Mail*, December 28, 2013, p. B1.

3. Company news release, "Ontario Becomes First in North America to Provide Energy Credits for Drain Water Heat Recovery (DWHR) in Building Code," March 15, 2103, **www.renewability.com**, accessed January 18, 2014; Derek Markham, "Power-Pipe Heat Exchanger Could Reduce Water Heating Costs by 40%," July 5, 2012, **http://treehugger .com**, accessed January 18, 2014.

4. Organization website, "Major Victory for Small Business as EI Rates Frozen for Three Years," **www.cfib-fcei.ca**, accessed January 9, 2014; "Federal Government Makes Promises to Act on Entrepreneurs' Needs," *National Post*, October 21, 2013, p. F9.

5. Mike Florio, "American Needle's Silver Lining Could Help NFL in Antitrust Case," *ProFootballTalk*, **http://profootballtalk.nbcsports.com**, accessed April 20, 2012; Ashby Jones, "American Needle: High Court Delivers 9-0 Shutout against NFL," *The Wall Street Journal*, **http://blogs.wsj.com**, accessed April 20, 2012.

6. Franois Shalom, "2014 Puts CSeries to the Test; Bombardier Faces a Real Challenge in Getting Its New Aircraft to Customers Before the Year Is Out," *Gazette* (Montreal), January 4, 2014, p. C1.

7. Company website, **www.costco.com**, accessed April 20, 2012.

8. Organization website, "About ENERGY STAR," **www.nrcan.gc.ca**, accessed January 18, 2014.

9. Company website, "Wifi Hotspots Set to More Than Triple by 2015," **www.informa .com**, accessed January 9, 2014.

10. Company website, **www.tweglobal.com**, accessed April 20, 2012; Matthew Stevens, "Foster's Wine-Beer Demerger to Clarify Divisions' Value," *Australian*, April 30, 2011, **www .theaustralian.com.au**.

11. Bob Evans, "Top 10 Reasons for SAP Acquisition from SuccessFactors CEO Lars Dalgaard," *Forbes*, **www.forbes.com**, accessed April 20, 2012; Ray Wang, "News Analysis: SAP Buys SuccessFactors for $3.4B Signals SAP's Commitment to Cloud, HCM, and Social," *SoftwareInsider*, **http://blog.softwareinsider.org**, accessed April 20, 2012.

12. Company website, **www.stoneyfield.com**, accessed January 18, 2014.

13. Gemma Karstens-Smith, "Tech Companies Aim to Wow: Trade Show Gets Underway to the Delight of Those Eager to Launch Their Cutting-Edge Innovations," *Toronto Star*, January 8, 2014, p. B1.

14. Government of Canada, Consumer Measures Committee website, "About the CMC," **http://cmcweb.ca/eic/site/cmc-cmc.nsf/eng/h_fe00013.html**, accessed January 18, 2014.

15. National Energy Board, "Our Responsibilities," **http://www.neb-one.gc.ca/clf-nsi/ rthnb/whwrndrgvrnnc/rrspnsblt-eng.html**, accessed January 18, 204.

16. Michael Geist, "What Will Canada's Anti-Spam Law Mean for Internet Users: Geist," *Toronto Star*, **www.thestar.com**, accessed January 10, 2014.

17. Advertising Standards Canada website, **www.adstandards.com/en/**, accessed January 16, 2014.

18. World Bank website, "Household Final Consumption Expenditure, etc. (% of GDP)," available **http://data.worldbank.org/indicator/NE.CON.PETC.ZS**, accessed January 10, 2014.

19. Navigant Research website, "Electric Bicycles," **www.navigantresearch.com/research/ electric-bicycles**, accessed January 10, 2014.

20. Bank of Canada website, **www.bankofcanada.ca/**, accessed January 10, 2014.

21. Tavia Grant, "Canadian Unemployment Growth Continues—But Soft Spots Remain," *The Globe and Mail*, December 6, 2013, **www.theglobeandmail.com**, accessed January 10, 2014.

22. Bloomberg News, "Canadian Household Debt Ratio Climbs to Record in Third Quarter as Mortgage Borrowing Hits $1.13-trillion," *Financial Post*, available **http://business .financialpost.com/2013/12/13/canada-debt-mortgages-2/**, accessed January 14, 2014.

23. John Vidal, "UN Warns of Looming Worldwide Food Crisis in 2013," *The Guardian*, October 13, 2012, available **http://www.theguardian.com/global-development/2012/oct/14/ un-global-food-crisis-warning**, accessed January 10, 2014.

24. Organization website, **www.commutegreener.com**, accessed April 21, 2012; press release, "Volvo IT's Commute Greener Appointed as This Year's Sustainable Project," **www.volvoit.com**, December 9, 2011.

25. Organization website, "New Mitsubishi i-MIEV Unseats Honda Civic Natural Gas after 8 Consecutive Years at the Top," press release, February 7, 2012, **www.aceee.org**.

26. Kenneth Rapoza, "Within a Generation, China Middle Class Four Times Larger than America's," *Forbes*, **www.forbes.com**, accessed April 20, 2012.

27. "Egypt Unrest Pushes up Global Oil Prices," The Associated Press, July 2, 2013, available **www.cbc.ca/news/business/egypt-unrest-pushes-up-global-oil-prices-1.1376431**, accessed January 10, 2014.

28. "EU Austerity Drive Country by Country," BBC News, March 30, 2012, **www.bbc .co.uk**.

29. "What Is Disney Doing with RFID at Its Theme Parks?" *Theme Park Tourist*, January 25, 2012, **www.themeparktourist.com**.

30. Sophie Bushwick, "Micro-Bubbles Cut Cost of Algae-Derived Biofuel," *Scientific American*, January 27, 2012, **www.scientificamerican.com**.

31. CETAC-WEST website, **http://cetacwest.com/**, accessed January 11, 2014.

32. "Skype Grow FY Revenues 20%, Reaches 663 Mln Users," Telecompaper, March 8, 2011, **www.telecompaper.com**.

33. Cecilia Kang, "Boomers Rapid Users of Social Media via Smartphones: Nielsen," *Washington Post*, September 12, 2011, **www.washingtonpost.com**.

34. Company website, **www.rogers.com**, accessed January 18, 2014.

35. Organization website, **www.boycott-canada.co.uk**, accessed January 18, 2014; organization website, **www.harpseals.org**, accessed January 18, 2014; company news release, "Loblaw Customers Use Five Billion Fewer Plastic Shopping Bags," April 9, 2013, **www.loblaw.ca**, accessed January 18, 2014; Kitt Doucette, "The Plastic Bag Wars," *Rolling Stone*, July 25, 2011, **www.rollingstone.com**.

36. "Professor Madoff?" *Business Casual*, April 12, 2011, **http://blogs.smeal.psu.edu**.

37. Kirk Makin, "Ontario Scores Big Win Against Bi Tobacco," *The Globe and Mail*, May 31, 2013, p. A6; "All Provinces Now Have a Lawsuit in the Works," *Gazette* (Montreal), June 9, 2012, p. A6.

38. Anthony Wing Kosner, "Target Breach of 70 Million Customers' Data Used Bargain Basement Malware," *Forbes*, January 15, 2014, **www.forbes.com**, accessed January 18, 2014; Marina Strauss, "Target's Profitability in Canada Seen as Years Away," *The Globe and Mail*, January 11, 2014, p. B2.

39. Allan Woods, "Canada Viewed as Safe Haven for Cloud Computing: U.S. Stands to Lose Billions in Business as Companies Look North to Store Data," *Toronto Star*, January 9, 2014, p. A1.

40. Jessica Silver-Greenberg and Tara Siegel Bernard, "Lenders Again Dealing Credit to Risky Clients," *New York Times*, April 12, 2012, **www.nytimes.com**.

41. Marina Strauss and Bertrand Marotte, "Loblaw Outlines Bangladesh Compensation Plan," *The Globe and Mail*, October 25, 2013, p. B8; Tanya Talaga, "When Change Comes to Bangladesh: Rana Plaza Collapse Seen as 'Defining Moment' as Brands Commit to Improve Worker Safety," *Toronto Star*, October 24, 2013, p. A22.

42. Company website, "Details About the Environmental Handling Fee," **www.thesource.ca/sitelets/ehf/**, accessed January 12, 2014.

43. Company websites, **www.bestbuy.ca** and **www.futureshop.ca**, accessed January 18, 2014.

44. Organization website, **http://sustainabilityconsortium.org**, accessed April 23, 2012.

45. Diane Jermyn, "Canada's Greenest Employers for 2013," *The Globe and Mail*, **www.theglobeandmail.com**, April 22, 2013; Leon Kaye, "Motel 6: Sustainability Means We'll No Longer Leave the Light on for You," *Triple Pundit*, **www.triplepundit.com**, accessed April 20, 2012; "Marriott LEED®'s the Way to Green Hotels," press release, **http://news.marriott.com**, accessed April 20, 2012; Marina Hanes, "How Eco-Friendly Are Fairmont Hotels & Resorts?" *1-800Recycling.com*, **http://1800recycling.com**, accessed April 20, 2012; "Motel 6 Commits to Green Key Certification in 2011," press release, January 31, 2011, **www.motel6.com**.

CHAPTER 3 MARKETOID NOTES

1. "Business Groups Fret over Possible Impact of Sanctions in Ukraine Crisis," *The Globe and Mail*, March 2, 2014, **www.theglobeandmail.com**, accessed March 31, 2014.

2. Loblaw Companies website, **www.loblaw.ca**, accessed March 31, 2014; Loblaw Companies, 2012 Annual Report.

3. "Bombardier Implicated in Brazilian Price Fixing Case," *The Globe and Mail*, March 25, 2014, **www.theglobeandmail.com**, accessed March 31, 2014.

4. "Canada Jobs Grant Ads Cost $2.5M for Non-existent Program," CBC, January 13, 2014, **www.cbc.ca**, accessed March 31, 2014.

5. Jane Gerster, "Toronto Struggling with Unemployment Despite Boom in Jobs: Report," *Toronto Star*, **www.thestar.com**, March 4, 2014, accessed March 31, 2014.

6. Federal Bureau of Investigation website, "Vancouver Man Sentenced to Over 14 Years in Prison for Running International Telemarketing Scam That Caused $1.8 Million in Losses, Primarily to Elderly Victims," available **www.fbi.gov/losangeles/press-releases/2010/la112310c.htm**, accessed March 31, 2014.

7. Chad Finkelstein, "Is Your Franchise Ready for Canada's Anti-spam Law?" **www.financialpost.com**, March 25, 2014.

8. StEP Initiative website, "StEP E-waste WorldMap," available **www.step-initiative.org/index.php/WorldMap.html**, accessed March 31, 2014.

CHAPTER 4

1. Gene Marks, "Drilling Down: What Small Businesses Should Know About Pinterest," *The New York Times*, March 26, 2012, **www.nytimes.com**; Christine Lagorio, "Where Pinterest Will Go From Here," *Inc.*, March 16, 2012, **www.inc.com**; Chas Edwards, "In Age of Pinterest, Instagram, Marketers Need an Image Strategy," *Advertising Age*, March 15, 2012, **http://adage.com**; Eric Savitz, "Four Pinterest Marketing Tips," *Forbes*, March 12, 2012, **www.forbes.com**; Janet Aronica, "Pinterest Sent More Referral Traffic than Twitter in February," *Shareaholic.com*, March 7, 2012, **http://blog.shareaholic.com**; Curt Finch, "How Pinterest's Female Audience Is Changing Social Marketing," *Mashable.com*, February 28, 2012, **http://mashable.com**; Sandra M. Jones, "Crafty, Comfy Startup Generates Interest Fast," *The Chicago Tribune*, February 5, 2012, pp. B1, B3.

2. Internet World Stats, **www.internetworldstats.com**, accessed September 29, 2013.

3. Power Reviews, "New Study Reveals Impact of Social Tools, Evolving Search Patterns and Mobile Technology on Consumer Shopping Behavior," *Marketwire*, **www.marketwire.com**, accessed April 27, 2012.

4. Company website, **www.williams-sonoma.com**, accessed September 29, 2013.

5. Russ Martin, "More Data on Canada's Online Shopping Lag," *Marketing*, August 21, 2012, **www.marketingmag.ca**.

6. Company website, **www.ae.com**, accessed October 4, 2013.

7. S.J. Johnson, "Best Websites for Travel Deals and Online Travel Deal Tips," *Yahoo! Voices*, **http://voices.yahoo.com**, accessed April 28, 2012.

8. Leena Rao, "It's Official: Google Acquires Like.com," *TechCrunch*, **http://techcrunch.com**, accessed April 29, 2012; Company website, **www.google.com/prdhp?hl=en**, accessed April 29, 2012.

9. "Canada Lags in Online and Mobile Shopping," *RetailMeNot* website, **retailmenot.mediaroom.com**, accessed, October 2, 2013; "UPS Pulse of the Online Shopper: A Customer Experience Study," Canada Study, September 2013.

10. Marcia Kaplan, "Understanding the Shift to Online Shopping," *Practical eCommerce*, **www.practicalecommerce.com**, accessed April 29, 2012.

11. Scott Beale, "Email vs. Snail Mail," *Laughing Squid*, **http://laughingsquid.com**, accessed April 30, 2012; Barry Shurtz, "Email Fun Fact: How Many Emails Are Sent Every Day," *Sendmail, Inc.*, **www.sendmail.com**, accessed April 30, 2012; Lucian Parfeni, "More than 95 Percent of All Email Is Spam," *Softpedia*, **http://news.softpedia.com**, accessed April 30, 2012.

12. Parfeni, "More than 95 Percent of All Email Is Spam."

13. Justin James, "10 Things You Should Consider Before Launching a Social Media Marketing Campaign," *TechRepublic*, **www.techrepublic.com**, accessed April 30, 2012; Marni Salup, "Social Media's Modern Day Role in PR and Marketing Campaigns: Highlights and Thoughts," *Huffington Post*, **www.huffingtonpost.com**, accessed April 30, 2012.

14. Sam Thielman, "Want to Skip Those Veloster Pre-Roll Ads? What's It Worth to You?" *Adweek*, **www.adweek.com**, accessed May 1, 2012.

15. Michelle Megna, "Widgets Offer Viral Marketing and Affiliate Revenue," *ecommerce guide*, **www.ecommerce-guide.com**, accessed May 1, 2012.

16. Sarah Kessler, "Facebook Timeline Changed the Way We See Brand Pages: Here's How," *Mashable Business*, **http://mashable.com**, accessed May 1, 2012.

17. David Gitonga, "How to Keep Your Website Up to Date on a Small Budget," *TechRepublic*, **www.techrepublic.com**, accessed May 1, 2012.

18. Chelsi Nakano, "Webtrends Analytics 10: Analytics for Mobile, Social and Web," *CMS Wire*, **www.cmswire.com**, accessed May 2, 2012.

19. Webtrends website, **webtrends.com**, accessed Oct 27, 2013.

20. *Merriam-Webster Online Dictionary*, **www.merriam-webster.com**, accessed August 18, 2013.

21. "10 Successful Social Media Campaign Tips," *Nimble*, April 9, 2012, **www.nimble.com**.

22. Rebecca Harris, "Turkish Airlines reaches out to Canadian travel bloggers," *Marketing*, August 22, 2013, **www.marketingmag.ca**.

23. "Pepsi Pulls Back Curtain on Twitter Music Push, Launches Campaign with Free Song, Video," *Washington Post*, May 30, 2012, **www.washingtonpost.com**.

24. Alissa Skelton, "Social Demographics: Who's Using Today's Biggest Networks," *Mashable.com*, March 9, 2012, **www.mashable.com**.

25. Dale Buss, "Ford Fiesta Sales Slump Despite 'Groundbreaking' Social Media Marketing Campaign," *Forbes*, May 2, 2012, **www.forbes.com**.

26. Frank Barry, "Content Marketing: 5 Non-Profit Success Stores to Learn From," *Mashable.com*, March 2, 2012, **http://mashable.com**; Big Brothers Big Sisters website, **www.bigbrothersbigsisters.ca**, accessed August 24, 2013.

27. Cara Pring, "100 Social Media Statistics for 2012," *The Social Skinny*, January 11, 2012, **http://thesocialskinny.com**.

28. Courtney Rubin, "Shoppers Combine Search, Social Media to Fuel Decisions," *Inc.*, **www.inc.com**, accessed May 11, 2012.

29. Kristin Laird, "Feature: Reventing Retail," *Marketing*, March 28, 2013, **www.marketingmag.ca**; Chris Powell, "Study Compares Canadian and U.S. 'Showroom-ers'," *Marketing*, March 13, 2013, **www.marketingmag.ca**.

30. Ron Jones, "6 Steps in Developing a Social Media Strategy," January 9, 2012, **www.clickz.com**.

31. "World's Most Powerful People," *Forbes.com*, **www.forbes.com**, accessed August 26, 2013.

32. "Alberta Floods Shape YouTube's Latest Canada Ad Leaderbord," *Marketing*, August 15, 2013, **www.marketingmag.ca**.

33. Ford Canada website, **www.ford.ca**, accessed August 28, 2013; Ford Canada YouTube page, **www.youtube.com/FordCanada**, accessed August 28, 2013.

34. "How to Target Your Audience and Engage Online," *socialmediatoday*, February 14, 2012, **http://socialmediatoday.com**.

35. Kristin Laird, "McDonald's Goes to the Movies with Social Media Fans," *Marketing*, August 26, 2013, **www.marketingmag.ca**.

36. "Top Influencers @ SXSWi 2012," *SocMetrics*, **http://sxsw.socmetrics.com**, accessed May 15, 2012.

37. Jeff Fraser, "LG's Finger-Focused Contest Promotes Lastest G2 Phone," *Marketing*, August 26, 2013, **www.marketingmag.ca**; LG Canada website, **www.lg.com/ca_en**, accessed August 31, 2013.

38. Julie Blakley, "5 Best Social Media Campaigns with User-Generated Content," *Postano*, May 10, 2012, **www.postano.com**.

39. Frank Barry, "Content Marketing: 5 Non-Profit Success Stories to Learn From," *Mashable*, March 2, 2012, **http://mashable.com**.

40. "What Is Content Marketing?" *Content Marketing Institution*, **www.junta42.com**, accessed May 18, 2012.

41. Tia Fisher, "What We Can Learn from the Crisis: Volkswagen vs. Greenpeace," *Social Media Today*, April 6, 2012, **http://socialmediatoday.com**.

42. Hootsuite website, "Social Media Dashboard," **http://hootsuite.com**, accessed May 18, 2012.

43. Jim Belosic, "6 Ways to Use Facebooks Apps for Business," *Social Media Examiner*, July 11, 2013, **www.socialmediaexaminer.com**.

44. Jason Miller, "5 Simple Metrics to Track Your Social Media Efforts," *Social Media Examiner*, May 28, 2012, **www.socialmediaexaminer.com**; Ron Jones, "6 Steps in Developing a Social Media Strategy," *Clickz*, January 9, 2012, **www.clickz.com**.

45. Sharlyn Lauby, "Ethics and Social Media: Where Should You Draw The Line?" *Mashable*, March 17, 2012, **http://mashable.com**.

46. Carol Rozwell, "Why Social Media Policies Should Focus on the Dos Rather than the Don'ts," *Forbes*, February 27, 2012, **www.forbes.com**.

47. Erica Ogg, "Sony Sued for PlayStation Network Data Breach," *CNET News*, **http://news.cnet.com**, accessed May 15, 2012.

48. Jeremiah Owyang, "What Are the Many Types of Social Media Services, Job, or Roles?" *Focus*, **www.focus.com**, accessed May 23, 2012

49. Phil Mershon, "5 Social Media Marketing Trends: New Research," *Social Media Examiner*, February 29, 2012, **www.socialmediaexaminer.com**.

50. Michael A. Stelzner, "2012 Social Media Marketing Industry Report," *Social Media Examiner*, April 2012, **www.socialmediaexaminer.com**.

CHAPTER 4 MARKETOID NOTES

All Marketoids: "Digital Technology and Internet Use, 2012," Statistics Canada, *The Daily*, Wednesday, June 12, 2013, Component of Statistics Canada catalogue no. 11-001-X.

CHAPTER 5

1. Jonathan Paul, "Back of the Mobile Pack," *Marketing*, **marketingmag.ca**, May 14, 2013; "Canadians Expect Discounts When Shopping Online: Survey," *Marketing*, **www.marketingmag.ca**, November 7, 2013; Alicia Androich, "M:Ad Women Event Analyzes the 'Digital Diva,'" *Marketing*, November 15, 2013; "Nearly 75 Percent of Consumers Use a Smartphone While Shopping, According to NPD," NPD Group, **www.npd.com**, accessed January 1, 2014; "Individual Internet Use and e-commerce, 2012," Statistics Canada, component of Statistics Canada catalogue no. 11-001-X, October 28, 2013.

2. Kristin Laird, "Video: Making Sense of 'Linsanity' and Understanding Chinese Moms," *Marketing*, **www.marketingmag.ca**, March 21, 2012.

3. "Canadian Social Values—Dominant Themes in Canadian Culture," Canadian Marketing Association, **http://canadianmarketingblog.com**, accessed March 25, 2011.

4. Michael Adams website, **www.michaeladams.ca**, accessed January 2, 2014.

5. Bethany Overland, "Starbucks Hopes New App Appeals to Smartphone Users," *TechFlash*, **www.techflash.com**, accessed April 25, 2012.

6. Company website, **www.dominosbiz.com**, accessed April 25, 2012; Annie Gasparro, "Domino's Has International Growth Spurt," *MarketWatch*, **www.marketwatch.com**, accessed April 25, 2012.

7. "Study, Projections of the Diversity of the Canadian Population," Statistics Canada website, **www.statcan.gc.ca**, March 9, 2010; "2011 National Household Survey: Immigration, Place of Birth, Citizenship, Ethnic Origin, Visible Minorities, Language and Religion," Statistics Canada, Component of Statistics Canada catalogue No. 11-001-X, May 8, 2013.

8. "Study, Projections of the Diversity of the Canadian Population," Statistics Canada website, **www.statcan.gc.ca**, March 9, 2010.

9. Government of Quebec website, **www.gouv.qc.ca**, accessed January 3, 2014.

10. Government of Quebec website, **www.gouv.qc.ca**, accessed January 4, 2014; Statistics Canada, "Population and Demography," **www.statcan.gc.ca**, accessed January 4, 2014; *Quebec Handy Numbers*, 2013 edition, Institut De La Statistique Du Québec, page 11.

11. Matt Semansky, "Plus ca change," *Marketing*, **www.marketingmag.ca**, October 27, 2008; Headspace Marketing website, **www.headspacemarketing.com**, accessed March 31, 2011; Susan Krashinsky, "Target Take Note: Quebec Market Tricky for Outsiders," *The Globe and Mail*, March 4, 2013.

12. Eric Blais, "The 36 Keys of the Quebecois Revisited," *Marketing*, November 15, 2004, pp. 11–12; Yves Leveille, "What Quebec Wants Now," *Marketing*, June 20, 2005, p. 46; Danny Kucharsky, "Redecorating Quebec's Creative Bedrooms," *Marketing*, February 11, 2002, p. 8.

13. "Indepth: China: Chinese Immigration," **www.cbc.ca**, accessed July 12, 2005; Statistics Canada, "Study: Projections of the Diversity of the Canadian Population: 2006 to 2031," **www.statcan.gc.ca**, March 9, 2010.

14. Kristin Laird, "Adams Presents the Stats Behind Canada's Multicultural Makeup," *Marketing*, **www.marketingmag.ca**, March 23, 2011; Don Miller, "Chinese Challenge," *Marketing*, March 13, 2006, p. 24; Rebecca Harris, "Embrace and Prosper," *Marketing*, January 23, 2006, p. 11; Jaime Christian, "Diversity Marketing as Strategy: Jaime Christian On Targeting Chinese Consumers in Canada," **www.starbusinessclub.ca**, February 8, 2013.

15. Council of Agencies Serving South Asians, "Constructing a Community in Diversity: The South Asian Experience," **www.cassa.on.ca**, accessed July 12, 2005.

16. Kristin Laird, "Multicultural Marketing Panel Opens Window on South Asian Pop Culture," *Marketing*, **www.marketingmag.ca**, March 24, 2011; Chris Daniels, "In-House Champions," *Marketing*, **www.marketingmag.ca**, April 30, 2010.

17. "Projections of the Diversity of the Canadian Population: 2006 to 2031," Statistics Canada, Catalogue no. 91-551-X, March 2010.

18. Ann Zimmerman, "Frontier of Frugality," *The Wall Street Journal*, **http://finance.yahoo.com**, accessed April 27, 2012.

19. Roots company website, **http://Canada.roots.com**, accessed January 5, 2014; Gap company website, **www.gapcanada.ca**, accessed January 4, 2014.

20. Pew Internet, "Teens, Kindness and Cruelty on Social Network Sites," **http://pewinternet.org**, accessed April 27, 2012; "Teens Slowly Increase Online Shopping," *eMarketer*, **www.emarketer.com**, accessed April 27, 2012.

21. Adrianne Pasquarelli, "Private Labels Are Back in Fashion," *Crain's New York Business*, **www.crainsnewyork.com**, accessed April 27, 2012; Marina Strauss, "Meet the Man Trying to Shake Up Luxury Retail in Canada," *The Globe and Mail*, **www.theglobeandmail.com**, November 27, 2013.

22. Advertisements from *The New York Times*, April 15 and 22, 2012.

23. Company website, **www.oprah.com**, accessed April 27, 2012.

24. "Fifty Years of Families in Canada: 1961 to 2011," Statistics Canada, Catalogue no. 98-312-X2011003, December 18, 2013.

25. "New Insights on Male Shoppers," *Progressive Grocer*, **www.progressivegrocer.com**, accessed April 27, 2012.

26. Jeff Fraser, "Student Shoppers Losing Interest in Brands, SPC Says," *Marketing*, **www.marketingmag.ca**, September 12, 2013.

27. "Poll Says Teens Sharing More, Moving to Twitter," *Marketing*, **www.marketingmag.ca**, May 21, 2013.

28. North Carolina Sweet Potatoes website, **www.ncsweetpotatoes.com**, accessed April 30, 2012.

29. Company website, **http://edhardyshop.com**, accessed April 30, 2012.

30. "Rational and Irrational Buying Choices—The Paradox of Choice," *Imagemakers.com*, **http://blog.imagemakers-inc.com**, accessed April 30, 2012.

31. These categories were originally suggested in John A. Howard, *Marketing Management: Analysis and Planning* (Homewood, Ill.: Richard D. Irwin, 1963); Henry Assael, "Consumer Behavior and Marketing Action," Kent Publishing Company, 1987, p. 87.

32. Nin-Hai Tseng, "Why Dollar Stores Are Thriving, Even Post-Recession," *Fortune*, April 2, 2012, **http://finance.fortune.cnn.com**.

33. Fran Jeffries, "Are You Willing to Pay for Online News?" *Atlanta Journal-Constitution*, April 4, 2012, **http://blogs.ajc.com**.

CHAPTER 5 MARKETOID NOTES

All Marketoids: "Individual Internet Use and e-commerce, 2012," Statistics Canada, components of Catalogue no. 11-001-X; *The Daily*, October 28, 2013, **www.statcan.gc.ca**.

CHAPTER 6

1. "GE: Reinventing Mobility," Apple website, **www.apple.com**, accessed April 16, 2012; Marc Brownstein, "It's Time to Bring B2B Marketers into the Social-Media World," *Advertising Age*, March 7, 2012, **www.adage.com**; Jennifer Barron and Jesse Purewal, "B2B Marketers: Creating a Great Customer Experience," *Media Post.com*, March 7, 2012, **www.mediapost.com**; "Relevance Over Reach, Says GE Digital Chief," *Wordpress.com*, February 27, 2012, **http://brandleadership.wordpress.com**; Kate Maddox, "GE's Boff Named 'BtoB's' Top Digital Marketer of the Year," *BtoBonline.com*, **www.btobonline.com**, accessed February 27, 2012; Sean Callahan, "Boff Details GE's Embrace of Social Media," *BtoBonline.com*, **www.btobonline.com**, accessed February 27, 2012; Brett Johnson, "GE and Caterpillar: B2B Mobile Is Serious Business," *Landslide.com*, **www.landslide.com**, accessed February 27, 2012; "Apple Recognizes GE as Mobile App Leader," company website, **http://careers.geblogs.com**, accessed February 27, 2012.

2. Hollie Shaw, "Online Retail Sales to Hit $34-billion in Canada by 2018," **www.financialpost.com**, July 23, 2013; "Online Sales by Businesses Rise to $136B in Canada." **www.cbcnews.ca**, June 11, 2014.

3. Bell Canada website, **http://www.bell.ca/enterprise/?ETCID=enterprise_federal_tile**, accessed February 10, 2014.

4. Company website, **www.jan-pro.com**, accessed May 7, 2014.

5. Company website, **www.acco.com**, accessed May 7, 2014.

6. Government of Canada, "View, Buy, Bid," available **www.gcsurplus.ca/mn-eng.cfm**, accessed May 7, 2014; PRWeb, "Official Auction Government High End Assets Sale—April 22, 2012," *SFGate*, **www.sfgate.com**, accessed May 3, 2012.

7. U.S. Census Bureau, "E-Stats."

8. Nick Stamoulis, "How HubSpot Does B2B Internet Marketing Right," *Business 2 Community*, **www.business2community.com**, accessed May 3, 2012.

9. Company website, **www.theseam.com**, accessed May 7, 2014.

10. Jakob Nielsen, "10 Best Intranets of 2012," *Jakob Nielsen's Alertbox,* **www.useit.com**, accessed April 27, 2012; Kelly Kass, "Staples Intranet Is a Two-Time Winner—Here's Why," *Ragan.com,* **www.ragan.com**, accessed April 27, 2012.

11. "SAP Customer Success Story: Royal Dutch/Shell Group," **www.sap.com**, accessed April 28, 2012.

12. "Kirtsy.com and Microsoft Office Live Team to Present Free 'Hands On Small Business' Sessions across the Country," **www.marketwire.com**, October 2009.

13. Company website, **www.tetratech.com**, accessed May 7, 2014.

14. "North American Industry Classification System (NAICS)," *Encyclopedia of Business and Finance,* **www.enotes.com**, accessed May 4, 2012.

15. Company website, "Miguel Cabrera Captures Triple Crown!!!" October 4, 2012, available **http://sambat.com/news/**, accessed February 11, 2014.

16. David Friend, "BlackBerry CEO Brings on Another Former Sybase Colleague to Help Revamp Company," The Canadian Press (Toronto), January 13, 2014.

17. Company website, **www.cdw.com**, accessed May 7, 2014.

18. Company website, **www.walmartcanada.ca/Pages/Community/190/190/190**, accessed February 11, 2014.

19. William J. Holstein, "How Coca-Cola Manages 90 Emerging Markets," *strategy+business,* **www.strategy-business.com**, accessed May 5, 2012.

20. Nora Bieberstein, "2011's Top Outsourcing Countries," *Miracle Technologies,* **www.miraclegroup.com**, accessed May 9, 2012.

21. "Brand Name Companies Go Bankrupt," **http://money.cnn.com**, September 25, 2009.

22. Joel Schectman, "IT Investments Pay off at Victoria's Secret, Bath & Body Works," *CIO Journal,* **http://blogs.wsj.com**, accessed May 7, 2012.

23. "Xerox at a Glance," company website, **www.xerox.com**, accessed May 7, 2012.

24. "Outsourcing and Offshoring Overview," *Plunkett Research Ltd.,* **www.plunkettresearch.com**, accessed May 8, 2012.

25. Nick Bunkley, "Toyota and Honda Bounce Back," *The New York Times,* **www.nytimes.com**, accessed May 8, 2012.

26. "The Keurig Story," company website, **www.keurig.com**, accessed May 8, 2012.

27. Laura Carroll, "Big Names in Coffee Business Convene at Trade Show," *Las Vegas Business Press,* **www.lvbusinesspress.com**, accessed May 9, 2012; Christopher MacManus, "Drinking in the Vue, Keurig's K-Cup Successor," *CNET News,* **http://news.cnet.com**, accessed May 9, 2012.

28. Business Wire, "UPS Deploys Next High-Tech Mobile Computer to Drivers," *The New York Times,* **http://markets.on.nytimes.com**, accessed May 9, 2012; Larry Dignan, "UPS Upgrades Driver Handhelds; Utilizes Gobi," *ZDNet,* **www.zdnet.com**, accessed May 9, 2012.

29. Public Works and Government Services Canada website, "Section I: Organization Overview," available **www.tpsgc-pwgsc.gc.ca/rapports-reports/rpp/2013-2014/rpp-01-eng.html**, May 7, 2014.

30. Niagara Public Purchasing Committee website, **www.nppc.ca**, accessed May 7, 2014.

CHAPTER 6 MARKETOID NOTES

1. Government of Canada, "About GCSurplus," **www.gcsurplus.ca/mn-eng.cfm**, accessed May 4, 2014.

2. Statistics Canada, "2012 NAICS Canada Structure," **www.statcan.gc.ca/subjects-sujets/standard-norme/naics-scian/2012/introduction-eng.htm**, accessed May 4, 2014.

3. Jason Chow, "China Is Now World's Biggest Consumer of Red Wine," **http://blogs.wsj.com/scene/2014/01/29/china-is-now-worlds-biggest-consumer-of-red-wine/**, accessed May 4, 2014.

4. "Just-In-Time (JIT) Manufacturing," **www.siliconfareast.com/jit.htm**, accessed May 4, 2014; "Guru Taiichi Ohno," *The Economist,* July 3, 2009, available **www.economist.com/node/13941150**, accessed May 4, 2014.

5. Supply Chain Management Association, "About SCMA," **www.scmanational.ca**, accessed May 4, 2014.

6. Public Works and Government Services Canada, "Our History," available **www.tpsgc-pwgsc.gc.ca/apropos-about/histoire-history-eng.html**, accessed May 4, 2014.

CHAPTER 7

1. Tom Krisher, "Hyundai Sales Growth Lags US Market, CEO Says Factories Can't Build Cars Fast Enough," *Canadian Business,* July 12,2013, **www.canadianbusiness.com**; "John Krafcik, CEO of Hyundai Motor America, To Step Down at Year-End: Zuchowski Tapped as CEO," *Canadian Business,* December 27, 2013, **www.canadianbusiness.com**; Youkyung Lee, "Hyundai Unveils New Genesis to Lure BMW, Mercedes-Benz Buyers, Burnish Brand Image," *Canadian Business,* November 26, 2013, **www.canadianbusiness.com**; company website, **www.hyundaicanada.com**, accessed January 23, 2014; "Awards and Reviews: Elantra," company website, **www.hyundaiusa.com**, accessed April 20, 2012; Nikhi Gulati, "Hyundai Planning Diesel Engine Factory in India," *The Wall Street Journal,* April 16, 2012, **http://blogs.wsj.com**; Alex Taylor III, "The Race to Become the World's Uber-Automaker," *CNN Money.com,* April 13, 2012, **http://money.cnn.com**; "Hyundai's U.S. Sales Could Top 700,000 in 2012, Krafcik Says," *Automotive News,* April 12, 2012, **www.autonews.com**; Andrew Ganz, "Hyundai Hoping to Apply U.S. Success Story to Europe," *Left Lane News.com,* January 26,2012, **www.leftlanenews.com**; Stephen Williams, "Hyundai—Yes, Hyundai—Aims to Be New Badge of Luxury," *Advertising Age,* January 9, 2012, **http://adage.com**; Julie Halpert, "Hyundai Marketing Boss: We're Not Just a 'Left-Brain Choice,'" *Advertising Age,* October 20, 2011, **http://adage.com**.

2. Statistics Canada, "Imports, Exports and Trade Balance of Goods on a Balance-of-Payments Basis, By Country or Country Grouping," **www.statcan.gc.ca**, accessed January 27, 2014.

3. United Nations Conference on Trade and Development, World Investment Report 2009, **www.unctad.org**, p. xxi.

4. Statistics Canada, "Canadian International Merchandise Trade" catalogue no. 65-001-X, **www.statcan.gc.ca**, November 2013, accessed January 27, 2014.

5. Statistics Canada, "Imports, Exports and Trade Balance of Goods on a Balance-of-Payments Basis, By Country or Country Grouping," *Canada Year Book 2012,* Statistics Canada, Catalogue no. 11-402-X, pp. 290–93.

6. Company website, **www.walmartstores.com**, accessed May 4, 2012; "Infographic of the Day: Walmart Dwarfs Entire Industries and Nations," *Fast Company,* December 2, 2011, **www.fastcodesign.com**.

7. Chris Powell, "Expansion on the Horizon with HootSuite's $165 Million in New Funding," *Marketing,* **www.marketingmag.ca**, August 12, 2013.

8. Statistics Canada, "Employment by Industry: Gross Domestic Product, Expenditure-based," **www.statcan.ca**, accessed January 30, 2014.

9. Christine Roy, "The Service Industries and Trade in Services," Statistics Canada, #63F0002XIB, 2001.

10. "2013 Gateway to Growth: Canadian Tourism Industry Annual Report," Tourism Industry Association Canada website, **http://tiac.travel/publications.htm**, accessed January 30, 2014.

11. Company website, **www.yum.com**, accessed May 4, 2012.

12. Company website, **www.subway.com**, accessed January 30, 2014; "How Subway Went Global," *QSR,* **www.qsrmagazine.com**, accessed May 5, 2012 .

13. *The World Factbook,* Central Intelligence Agency website, **www.cia.gov**, accessed January 31, 2014.

14. Ibid.

15. Kounteya Sinha, "Population Growth Rate Dips to 17%," *Times of India,* May 5, 2012, **http://articles.timesofindia.indiatimes.com**; Susan Yoshihara, "New UN Population Projections Have India Outpacing China," *LifeNews.com,* September 2, 2011, **www.lifenews.com**.

16. Mary Amiti and Mark Choi, "Consumer Goods from China Are Getting More Expensive," Liberty Street Economics, **http://libertystreeteconomics.newyorkfed.org**, accessed May 5, 2012.

17. "IBM Continues to Expand in India with Another New Office," *WRAL Techwire,* March 26, 2012, **http://wraltechwire.com**.

18. "Internet Usage Statistics," *Internet World Stats,* **www.internetworldstats.com**, accessed January 31, 2014.

19. Charlie Dunmore, "Danes Fail to Win EU Majority for GM Crop Ban Rules," Reuters, March 9, 2012, **www.reuters.com**.

20. Charles Duhigg and Steven Greenhouse, "Foxconn Audit Finds 'Serious' Violations of China Labor Laws," *Boston Globe,* March 30, 2012, **www.bostonglobe.com**.

21. "About ISO," International Organization for Standardization website, **www.iso.org**, accessed January 31, 2014.

22. Canadian Trade Commissioner Service website, **www.tradecommissioner.gc.ca**, accessed January 31, 2014; Canadian Business Network website, **www.canadabusiness.ca**, accessed January 31, 2014; Foreign Affairs, Trade and Development Canada website, **www.international.gc.ca**, accessed January 31, 2014; Agriculture and Agri-Food Canada website, **www.agr.gc.ca**, accessed January 31, 2014.

23. "Top 20 Countries with the Highest Number of Internet Users," *Internet World Stats,* **www.internetworldstats.com**, accessed May 6, 2012; "'Anonymous' Hackers Take on the Great Firewall," *China Digital Times,* April 7, 2012, **http://chinadigitaltimes.com**.

24. Free Trade of the Americas, **www.ftaa-alca.org**, accessed February 3, 2014.

25. Canada's Economic Action Plan, **www.actionplan.gc.ca**, accessed February 5, 2014; Canada Gazette, **www.gazette.gc.ca**, accessed February 5, 2014.

26. "Ending the Banana Wars: Who Wins and Who Loses?" *European Parliament News,* **www.europarl.europa.eu**, accessed May 5, 2012.

27. "China Unicom Offers Free iPhone 4S for $45 Monthly Contract," *Bloomberg News,* January 6, 2012, **www.bloomberg.com**.

28. "Andrew Hupert's 'Guanxi for the Busy American,'" *ChinaBizGov,* March 20, 2012, **http://chinabizgov.blogspot.com**.

29. "Anti-dumping and Countervailing," Canada Border Services Agency website, **www.cbsa-asfc.gc.ca**, accessed February 7, 2014.

30. Kevin G. Hall, "Chicken Feet at the Heart of U.S.-China Dispute," *Times-Tribune* (Scranton, Pa.), **http://thetimes-tribune.com**, accessed May 5, 2012.

31. World Trade Organization, "Ministerial Conference Approves Russia's WTO Membership," press release, **www.wto.org**, accessed May 5, 2012.

32. World Trade Organization website, **www.wto.org**, accessed May 7, 2012.

33. "NAFTA Trade Volume Increases," *Global Trade News,* **www.integrationpoint.com**, accessed May 7, 2012

34. Free Trade Area of the Americas website, **www.ftaa-alca.org**, accessed February 7, 2014.

35. European Union website, **http://europa.eu**, accessed February 7, 2014.

36. Ibid.

37. Allan Brettman, "Chicago Bulls' Derrick Rose Signs Adidas Deal Reportedly Worth $260 Million," *Oregonian*, February 26, 2012, **http://impact.oregonlive.com**; Alex Miller, "Rich Pickings as Ennis Strikes Gold with Endorsement Deals," *Daily Mail*, December 5, 2011, **www.dailymail.com**.

38. John Dudovskiy, "Self Reference Criterion: Introduction and Illustrations," Research-Methodology website, October 15, 2012, **http://research-methodology.net**.

39. Company website, **www.ikea.com**, accessed February 9, 2014.

40. "EA Sports UEFA Euro 2012 Digital Expansion Pack to FIFA Soccer 12 Available Today for Download," press release, April 24, 2012, **http://news.ea.com**.

41. Foreign Affairs, Trade and Development Canada website, **www.international.gc.ca**, accessed February 9, 2014.

42. Chuck Chiang, "Chuck Chiang: Canada Must Try Harder to Attract Chinese Investment," *Vancouver Sun*, November 11, 2013, **www.vancouversun.com**; Foreign Affairs, Trade and Development Canada website, **www.international.gc.ca**, accessed February 9, 2014.

43. Company website, **www.walmartstores.com**, accessed February 9, 2014; "Media Statement from Bharti and Walmart," October 9, 2013, Bharti company website, **www.bharti.com**, accessed August 19, 2014.

44. Corporate website, **www.abb.com**, accessed May 8, 2012; Stephanie Overby, "IT Outsourcing in Latin America: 9 Things Your Vendor Won't Tell You," *CIO*, April 6, 2011, **www.cio.com**.

45. Ildiko Szalai, "Kellogg's First Global Scale Acquisition Targets Pringles," *Euromonitor International*, February 22, 2012, **http://blog.euromonitor.com**.

46. Domino's Singapore website, **www.dominos.com.sg**, accessed May 8, 2012.

47. Mark J. Miller, "Levi's Takes Go Forth Campaign Global," *Brand Channel*, **www.brandchannel.com**, accessed May 8, 2012.

48. Tamson W. Burgess, "The Making of Mr. Claus," *Wicked Local Wareham*, **www.wickedlocal.com**, accessed May 8, 2012.

49. Evra Taylor, "FIAT Rolls on Montreal Grand Prix with Publicis Campaign," *Marketing*, June 6, 2012, **www.marktingmag.ca**; Rachel Smith, "Will the Fiat 500 Abarth Boost Fiat Sales?" *U.S. News & World Report*, March 29, 2012, **http://usnews.rankingsandreviews.com**.

50. Derek Burney and Fen Hampson, "Government Uncertainty on Foreign Investment Hampers Canada's Plan to Develop Resources," *iPolitics*, December 1, 2013, **www.ipolitics.ca**.

CHAPTER 7 MARKETOID NOTES

All Marketoids: "January 1 Marks 20th Anniversary of North American Free Trade Agreement," Foreign Affairs, Trade and Development Canada website, **www.international.gc.ca**, accessed January 29, 2014.

CHAPTER 8

1. Charles Duhigg, "How Companies Learn Your Secrets," *The New York Times Magazine*, February 16, 2012, **www.nytimes.com**; Jessica Wohl, "Target to Host Boutiques, and Apple, in Stores," *Reuters.com*, January 12, 2012, **www.reuters.com**; Stephanie Clifford, "In a Test, Target Plans to Add an Apple 'Store' Inside 25 Stores," *The New York Times*, January 12, 2012, **www.nytimes.com**; Jeff Fraser, "Adding Some Humanity to Big Data," *Marketing*, August 20, 2012, **www.marketingmag.ca**; David Thomas, "Q&A: Fifteen Years of Big Data Perspective," *Marketing*, August 19, 2013, **www.marketingmag.ca**; Emma Hall, "Hegarty Has No Time for Big Data," *Marketing*, March 21, 2013, **www.marketingmag.ca**; company website, **www.target.ca**, accessed January 11, 2014.

2. J.D. Power and Associates website, **www.canada.jdpower.com**, accessed January 12, 2014.

3. Environics Research Group, **www.environics.ca**, accessed January 12, 2014.

4. Company website, **www.bazaarvoice.com**, accessed January 12, 2014.

5. qbord company website, **www.qbord.com**, accessed January 14, 2014.

6. Elliot Zwiebach, "Target Executives Happy with PFresh Performance," *Supermarket News*, May 1, 2012, **http://supermarketnews.com**; company website, **www.target.ca**, accessed January 12, 2014.

7. Jim Utsler, "Carry-on Data," *IBM Systems*, February 2012, **www.ibmsystemsmag.com**.

8. Leonor Vivanco, "Mac Snack Wrap, Other Items Dreamed up in McDonald's Test Kitchen," *Chicago Tribune.com*, February 21, 2010, **www.chicagotribune.com**.

9. Company website, **www.ipsos-na.com**, accessed January 12, 2014.

10. Statistics Canada, **www.statcan.gc.ca**, accessed January 13, 2014.

11. Industry Canada, **www.ic.gc.ca**, accessed January 13, 2014.

12. Claire Swedberg, "American Apparel Adopting RFID at Every Store," *RFID Journal*, February 8, 2012, **www.rfidjournal.com**.

13. Company website, Datamonitor Group, **www.datamonitor.com**, accessed May 14, 2012.

14. Company website, **www.google.com**, accessed May 15, 2012; "360i POV Nielsen Facebook Ad Effectiveness Study," *eBook Browse*, February 23, 2012, **http://ebookbrowse.com**.

15. Company website, **www.youtube.com**, accessed May 15, 2012.

16. David McMillin, "4 Tips to Lowering Survey Abandonment," **http://survey.cvent.com**, March 1, 2010.

17. Matt Ryan, "How Gamers Make Real Money from Video Games," *Lockergnome*, April 20, 2012, **www.lockergnome.com**.

18. Company website, **http://tru-insights.com**, accessed May 15, 2012.

19. Company website, "Can P&G Win with $2-a-Day Consumers?" press release, **http://news.pg.com**, accessed May 16, 2012.

20. Marc Brenner, "Ethnography App Debuts on iTunes Store," *Research*, **www.research-live.com**, accessed May 16, 2012.

21. Canadian Radio-television and Telecommunications Commission website, **www.crtc.gc.ca**, accessed January 13, 2014.

22. Joanna L. Krotz, "Dos and Don'ts for Using Marketing Focus Groups," *Microsoft Business*, **www.microsoft.com**, accessed May 16, 2012.

23. Company website, "Key Facts," **http://newsroom.fb.com**, accessed May 16, 2012; "Social Networks Account for 20% of Time Spent Online," *The Wall Street Journal*, **http://blogs.wsj.com**, accessed May 16, 2012; David Murphy, "Singapore Delivers Highest Average Facebook Session Time. US: Fifth," *PC Magazine*, **www.pcmag.com**, accessed May 16, 2012.

24. Erica Swallow, "Measuring Social Media ROI: 3 Things to Consider," *Mashable.com*, **http://mashable.com**, accessed May 16, 2012.

25. Jim Edwards, "P&G to Lay off 1,600 after Discovering It's Free to Advertise on Facebook," *Business Insider*, January 30, 2012, **http://articles.businessinsider.com**.

26. Industry Canada, **www.ic.gc.ca**, accessed January 13, 2014.

27. Jeff Fraser, "Adding Some Humanity to Big Data," *Marketing*, August 20, 2013, **www.marketingmag.ca**; Alicia Androich, "Data Science: Making Something Out of Everything," *Marketing*, August 19, 2013, **www.marketingmag.ca**.

CHAPTER 8 MARKETOID NOTES

All Marketoids: "Survey of Household Spending, 2011," Statistics Canada, catalogue no. 11-001-X, January 30, 2013, **www.statscan.gc.ca**.

CHAPTER 9

1. Chris Powell, "Four Canadian Brands Go 24/7 with Rogers on Winter Classic," *Marketing*, October 30, 2013, **www.marketingmag.ca**; Dairy Farmers of Canada website, **www.dairyfarmers.ca**, accessed February 18, 2014; Rebecca Harris, "Dairy Farmers Go Flat out for New Campaign," *Marketing*, March 5, 2013, **www.marketingmag.ca**; Kristin Laird, "Dairy Farmers Take on Gatorade," *Marketing*, October 16, 2008, **www.marketingmag.ca**; Rebecca Harris, "Milk Finds Some Brotherly Love in Quebec," *Marketing*, January 20, 2014, **www.marketingmag.ca**; Jeff Fraser, "Dairy Farmers Across Canada Band Together for Milk Every Moment," *Marketing*, June 19, 2013, **www.marketingmag.ca**; Alberta Farmer Express website, **www.albertafarmexpress.ca**, accessed February 16, 2014.

2. U.S. Census Bureau, "U.S. & World Population Clock," **www.census.gov**, accessed February 18, 2014; Statistics Canada, **www.statcan.gc.ca**, accessed February 18, 2014.

3. Statistics Canada, "Projections of the Diversity of the Canadian Population; 2006–2031," **www.statcan.gc.ca**, Catalogue no. 91-551-X, March 3, 2010.

4. "Marketing to Women Quick Facts," She economy website, **she-conomy.com**, accessed February 19, 2014.

5. "Car Ads Alienate Women," B&T website, February 20, 2014, **www.bandt.com.au**; Susan Dobscha, "Column: Why Do Marketers Keep Getting Women So Wrong?," *Marketing*, December 17, 2014, **www.marketingmag.ca**.

6. "Milestone Marketing to Boomer Women," Trendsight website, **www.trendsight.com**, accessed February 20, 2014; National Association of Baby Boomer Women website, **http://nabbw.com**, accessed February 20, 2014.

7. Rich Rovito, "Harley-Davidson Launches Women Riders Month," *Milwaukee Business Journal*, **www.bizjournals.com**, accessed May 10, 2012.

8. Statistics Canada, "Population of Census Metropolitan Areas," **www.statcan.gc.ca**, accessed February 20, 2014.

9. Statistics Canada, "Population by Sex and Age Group, by Province and Territory," **www.statcan.gc.ca**, accessed February 20, 2014; Charlottetown website, **www.discovercharlottetown.com**, accessed February 20, 2014.

10. "Country Comparison: Population," *CIA World FactBook*, **www.cia.gov**, accessed February 10, 2014.

11. "World: Largest Cities and Towns and Statistics of Their Population" and "World: Metropolitan Areas," *World Gazetteer*, **http://world-gazetteer.com**, accessed May 11, 2012.

12. "Census 2011: Canada's 10 Fastest Growing Cities," HuffPost Business website, **www.huffingtonpost.ca/business/**, February 8, 2012.

13. "Census Metropolitan Area (CMA) and Census Agglomeration (CA)," Statistics Canada, **www.statcan.gc.ca**, accessed February 21, 2014.

14. Jonathan Paul, "Back of the Mobile Pack," *Marketing*, May 14, 2013, **www.marketingmag.ca**.

15. Shine website, **www.shine.yahoo.com**, accessed February 21, 2014.

16. Amanda Gardner, "Doctors Urge Ban on Junk Food Ads During Kids' Shows," *US News and World Report,* **http://health.usnews.com**, accessed May 15, 2012.

17. Companies Committed to Kids website, **http://cck-eee.ca**, accessed February 21, 2014.

18. Bea Fields, "Marketing to Gen Y: What You Can't Afford Not to Know," *Startup Nation,* **www.startupnation.com**, accessed May 15, 2012.

19. Company website, **www.ivivva.com**, accessed February 21, 2014.

20. Martin Zwilling, "Gen-X Sets High Standards for Gen-Y Entrepreneurs," *Examiner.com,* **www.examiner.com**, accessed May 15, 2012; eMarketer, "Gen X Watches More TV, Online Video Than Other Demo's," *BizReport,* **www.bizreport.com**, accessed May 15, 2012.

21. Jack Johnson website, **http://jackjohnsonmusic.com**, accessed February 21, 2014.

22. Michael Adams, *Sex in the Snow: Canadian Social Values at the End of the Millennium* (Toronto: Viking, 1997), p. 80.

23. "The 5 Indulgences of Boomers," Boomer Match to Business website, **www.bm2b.ca**, accessed February 21, 2014.

24. Bill Ness, "Boomers: 26 Percent of the Population, 40 Percent of the Economy," *55Places .com,* **www.55places.com**, accessed May 16, 2012; Zak Stambor, "As Social Commerce Spreads, Half of American Adults Say They Use Social Networks," *Internet Retailer,* **www .internetretailer.com**, accessed May 16, 2012.

25. Theresa Campbell, "No Trikes Allowed on Main Street," *Daily Commercial,* **www .dailycommercial.com**, accessed May 16, 2012; Ken Freund, "Champion Trikes," *RoadRUNNER Motorcycle Touring & Travel,* **www.roadrunner.travel**, accessed May 16, 2012.

26. Statistics Canada, **www.statcan.gc.ca**, accessed February 22, 2014.

27. Company website, "Baby Boomers & Seniors: The Most Valuable Generations in the History of Marketing," **www.comingofage.com**, accessed February 22, 2014.

28. Organization website, "Why Road Scholar?" **www.roadscholar.org,** accessed February 22, 2014.

29. Bea Fields, "Marketing to Gen Y: What You Can't Afford Not to Know," *Startup Nation,* **www.startupnation.com**, accessed May 15, 2012.

30. "Projections of the Diversity of the Canadian Population: 2006 to 2032," Statistics Canada, Catalogue no. 91-551-X, March 3, 2010.

31. "Projections of the Diversity of the Canadian Population: 2006 to 2032."

32. "The 1940's Landmark Canadian Advertisements," *Marketing,* September 28, 1998.

33. Eric Blais, "The 36 Keys of the Quebecois Revisited," *Marketing,* November 15, 2004, pp. 11–12.

34. Caroline Fortin, "Boston Pizza Takes Quebec Rival Into the Boards," *Marketing,* January 18, 2013, **www.marketingmag.ca**.

35. Patrick Fong, "Defining the Chinese Market," *Marketing,* June 3, 2002, p. 15; Michael McCullough, "Fireworks Had Died on the Morning of July 1," *Marketing,* September 8, 1997, p. 23.

36. Jaime Christian, "Diversity Marketing as Strategy: Jaime Christian on Targeting Chinese Consumers in Canada," February 8, 2013, **www.starbusinessclub.ca**; Chris Daniels, "How Do Canada's Major Multicultural Markets Spend?" *Marketing,* October 24, 2011, **www.marketingmag.ca**; Jeromy Lloyd, David Brown, and Tom Gierasimczuk, "The Incredible Rise of the Ethnic Consumer," *Marketing,* March 28, 2011, pp. 28–33.

37. Lloyd, Brown, and Gierasimczuk, "The Incredible Rise of the Ethnic Consumer."

38. Jeromy Lloyd, "Bet on Black," *Marketing,* March 28, 2011, pp. 34–38.

39. "Family Life—Age of Mother at Childbirth," Employment and Social Development Canada, **www.hrsdc.gc.ca**, accessed February 22, 2014; "Births and Total Fertility Rate, by Province and Territory," Statistics Canada, **www.statcan.gc.ca**, accessed February 22, 2014.

40. Madhavi Acharya-Tom Yew, "More Canadians Expect to Work Full-time in Retirement," *Toronto Star,* February 14, 2014, **www.thestar.com**.

41. Garry Marr, "Moving Back Home and Still Not Saving," *Financial Post,* October 6, 2012, **www.financial post.com**.

42. Cangrands website, **www.cangrands.com**, accessed February 23, 2014.

43. Statistic Canada, "Household Size, by Province and Territory (2011 Census)," **www .statcan.gc.ca**, February 26, 2014; "Household Size, by Province and Territory (2006 Census)," **www.statcan.gc.ca**, accessed December 19, 2007.

44. "Portrait of Families and Living Arrangements in Canada," Statistics Canada, January 14, 2014, **www.statcan.gc.ca**.

45. "Portrait of Families and Living Arrangements in Canada."

46. Aylin Kumcu and Phil Kaufman, "Food Spending Adjustments During Recessionary Times," *Amber Waves,* **www.ers.usda.gov,** accessed May 18, 2012.

47. U.S. Department of Agriculture, Food CPI and Expenditures: Table 7, **www.ers.usda .gov**, accessed May 18, 2012.

48. Company website, "Japan—VALS™," **www.strategicbusinessinsights.com**, accessed March 23, 2010.

49. Adams, *Sex in the Snow.*

50. Helen Leggatt, "Experian Segments Mobile Users by Behavior/Attitudes," *BizReport,* March 18, 2010, **www.bizreport.com**.

51. Kristin Laird, "Tim Hortons Dumps Ice Cream, Launches Loyalty Program," *Marketing,* February 20, 2014, **www.marketingmag.ca**; Kristin Laird, "McDonald's Launches McCafe Loyalty Program," *Marketing,* November 15, 2013, **www.marketingmag.ca**.

52. M.G. Siegler, "Apple Quantifies Their iPad 'Record Weekend': 3 Million Sold in 3 Days," *TechCrunch,* **http://techcrunch.com**, accessed May 22, 2012.

53. Competition Bureau, **www.competitionbureau.gc.ca**, accessed February 26, 2014.

54. Dan Ovsey, "Road to Redemption: How McDonald's Once Down-and-Out Brand Recaptured Hearts and Minds," *Financial Post,* January 21, 2014, **www.financialpost.com**.

55. Sierra Club website, **www.sierraclub.ca**, accessed February 27, 2014.

56. Eve Lazarus, "Prairie Milk Helps Kids Hit Their Stride," *Marketing,* January 10, 2012, **www .marketingmag.ca**; Milk Every Moment website, **http://milkeverymoment.ca**, accessed February 27, 2014.

57. Judy Keen, "Encyclopaedia Britannica Turns a Page, Ends Print Edition," *USA Today,* **www .usatoday.com**, accessed May 22, 2012.

CHAPTER 9 MARKETOID NOTES

All Marketoids: "Milk Product Consumption Per Capita," Dairy Nutrition website, **www .dairynutrition.ca**, accessed February 18, 2014.

CHAPTER 10

1. "Apple Retail Stores Serve 1 Million Customers Daily, 407 Locations Worldwide," Slash Gear website, June 10, 2013, **www.slashgear.com**; "The World's 50 Most Innovative Companies: 1. Apple," *Fast Company,* **www.fastcompany.com**, accessed May 8, 2012; Larry Dignan, "Five Not-So-Obvious Reasons Why Apple Won't Be Sony Redux," *ZDnet .com,* April 26, 2012, **www.zdnet.com**; "Apple Retail Success," *MarketingApple.com,* April 12, 2012, **www.marketingapple.com**; Carmine Gallo, "Enrich Lives: Reinvent Your Business the Apple Store Way," *Forbes,* April 2, 2012, **www.forbes.com**; John Ashcroft, "What Can We Learn About Apple Corporate Strategy from the iPad 3," *JohnAshcroft .co.uk,* March 31, 2012, **www.johnashcroft.co.uk**; Jodi Grainick, "Half of U.S. Homes Own Apple Products," *USA Today,* March 28, 2012, **www.usatoday.com**.

2. "Top 1000: Exclusive Rankings of Canada's Most Profitable Companies," *The Globe and Mail,* **www.theglobeandmail.com**, accessed March 1, 2014.

3. "Business, Consumer and Property Services," Statistics Canada, **www.statcan.gc.ca**, accessed March 1, 2014.

4. "Canada's Service Trade with the World: 2011," Parliament of Canada website, **www.parl .gc.ca**, accessed March 2, 2014.

5. Dave Coles, "Comment: Sending Jobs Offshore Hurts Canadian Workers," *Times Colonist* website, April 11, 2013, **www.timescolonist.com**.

6. Stefany Moore, "Another E-Retailer Brings Its Call Center Back to the United States," *Internet Retailer,* January 12, 2012, **www.internetretailer.com**.

7. Canada Flowers website, **www.canadaflowers.ca**, accessed March 2, 2014.

8. Concept introduced by Christopher H. Lovelock, "Classifying Services to Gain Strategic Marketing Insights," *Journal of Marketing,* Summer 1983, p. 10.

9. "Least Expensive Cars of 2012," *Cars.com,* **http://cars.about.com**, accessed May 21, 2012; "Lamborghini, Most Expensive Cars in the World," *TopCarRating.com,* **www .topcarrating.com**, accessed May 21, 2012; "The Most Expensive Cars 2012," *Forbes,* **www.forbes.com**, accessed May 21, 2012.

10. "Boeing Signs Record $22.4 Billion Order with Lion Air," *Reuters,* February 14, 2012, **www.reuters.com.**

11. Company website, **www.bose.ca**, accessed March 2, 2014.

12. Company website, **www.cargill.ca**, accessed March 2, 2014.

13. Company website, **www.staples.ca**, accessed March 2, 2014.

14. Company website, **www.cisco.com**, accessed March 3, 2014.

15. Company website, **www.regus.ca**, accessed March 3, 2014.

16. Excellence Canada website, **www.excellence.ca**, accessed March 3, 2014.

17. Organization website, "ISO 9001:2008," **www.iso.org**, accessed March 3, 2014; organization website, **www.nist.gov**, accessed March 4, 2014.

18. "New Research Shows Consumer Expectations at 20-Year High," Colloquy company website, February 4, 2014, **www.colloquy.com**.

19. Company website, **www.roots.com**, accessed March 6, 2014.

20. Company website, **www.tilley.com**, accessed March 6, 2014.

21. Calgary Stampede Park website, **www.calgarystampede.com**, accessed March 6, 2014.

22. Company website, **www.lifescan.com**, accessed March 6, 2014; company website, **www .depuy.com**, accessed March 6, 2014.

23. "Geox Fiscal Year 2011 Results," presentation, March 8, 2012, **http://geoxusa.info**; Walking On A Cloud company website, **www.walkingonacloud.ca**, accessed March 6, 2014.

24. Company website, **www.fglsports.com**, accessed March 6, 2014.

25. "The Home Depot and Martha Stewart Living Omnimedia Extend and Expand Agreement for Popular Martha Stewart Living Product Line," *The Wall Street Journal,* February 29, 2012, **http://online.wsj.com**; company website, **www.homedepot.ca**, accessed March 6, 2014.

26. Ben Sisario, "Full Album Sales Showed a Little Growth in 2011," *The New York Times,* January 4, 2012, **www.nytimes.com**.

27. "GPS Guide," *Consumer Reports,* April 2012, **www.consumerreports.org**.

28. Company website, **www.bestbuy.com**, accessed March 6, 2014.

29. "Hockey Canada and Nike Unveil Team Canada Jersey for 2014," Hockey Canada website, October 8, 2013, **www.hockeycanada.ca**.

30. Eric Felten, "It's Alive! Vinyl Makes a Comeback," *The Wall Street Journal*, January 27, 2012, **http://online.wsj.com**.

31. Dana Mattioli, "J. Crew Suits Up for Overseas," *The Wall Street Journal*, March 22, 2012, **http://online.wsj.com**.

32. Company website, **www.armandhammerbakingsoda.ca**, accessed March 6, 2014.

33. "More Cereal, Less Packaging," press release, February 22, 2012, **www.generalmills.com**.

34. Company website, **www.timhortons.com**, accessed March 8, 2014.

35. Ed Watkins, "Holiday Inn Relaunch Drives Revenues, Satisfaction," *Lodging Hospitality*, **http://lhonline.com**, accessed May 22, 2012 .

36. Aaron Smith, "Spirit Air to Charge up to $100 for Carry-on Bags," *CNN Money*, May 3, 2012, **http://money.cnn.com**.

CHAPTER 10 MARKETOID NOTES

All Marketoids: "Business, Consumer and Property Services," Statistics Canada, **www.statcan.gc.ca**, accessed March 1, 2014.

CHAPTER 11

1. "Under Armour Q4 2013 Earnings Call Transcript," company website, January 30, 2014, **www.underarmour.com**; MapMyFitness company website, **www.mapmyfitness.com**, accessed March 13, 2014; Jeromy Lloyd, "Watch This: Downhill and Into the Boards (Under Armour)," *Marketing*, January 29, 2014, **www.marketingmag.ca**; Trey Palmisano, "From Rags to Microfiber: Inside the Rapid Rise of Under Armour," *Sports Illustrated*, **www.si.com**, accessed May 14, 2012; Lorraine Mirabella, "Under Armour Poised for Greater Growth with New Products," *Baltimore Sun*, May 1, 2012, **www.baltimoresun.com**; Fred Dreier, "Under Armour Flexing Its Muscles Overseas," *Forbes*, April 4, 2012, **www.forbes.com**; Candus Thompson, "Under Armour Bets on Bobsled to Fuel Global Growth," *Baltimore Sun*, March 25, 2012, **www.baltimoresun.com**; Mark J. Miller, "Under Armour: Wicky Business," *Brand Channel.com*, **www.brandchannel.com**, accessed March 25, 2012; "Under Armour's Kevin Plank: Creating the 'Biggest, Baddest Brand on the Planet,'" *Knowledge @ Wharton*, **http://knowledge.wharton.upenn.edu**, accessed March 25, 2012.

2. "Private Label Trends: Packaged Food in Canada," Agriculture and Agri-Food Canada, Market Indicator Report, June 2013.

3. Company website, **www.staples.ca**, accessed March 14, 2014.

4. Company website, **www.canadiantire.ca**, accessed March 14, 2014.

5. Interbrand, "Best Global Brands of 2013," Interbrand website, **www.interbrand.com**, accessed March 14, 2014.

6. "Brand Asset Valuator," Young & Rubicam website, **http://young-rubicam.de**, accessed March 14, 2014.

7. Company website, **http://bavconsulting.com**, accessed August 25, 2014.

8. Category Management Association website, "What Is Category Management?" **www.cpgcatnet.org**, accessed March 15, 2014.

9. Ibid.

10. Company website, **www.igd.com**, accessed March 14, 2014.

11. Company website, **www.hersheys.com**, accessed March 14, 2014.

12. Company website, **www.amronexperimental.com**, accessed May 29, 2012; Audrey Quinn, "Dissolving Fruit Stickers," *SmartPlanet*, **www.smartplanet.com**, accessed May 29, 2012.

13. "A Guide to Trade-Marks," Industry Canada website, **www.cipo.ic.gc.ca/**, accessed March 14, 2014.

14. Mariam Noronha, "Why You Should Not Be Afraid to Use Humor in Branding—3 Reasons Small Business Owners Can Use," *Noobpreneur.com*, **www.noobpreneur.com**, accessed May 29, 2012; company website, **www.harley-davidson.com**, accessed May 29, 2012.

15. "A Guide to Trade-Marks."

16. Heidi Parsons, "Prepared and Packed," *Brand Packaging*, **www.brandpackaging.com**, accessed June 1, 2012.

17. Jim Butschli, "Kimberly-Clark Uses Packaging to Reduce Product Waste," *Packaging World*, **www.packworld.com**, accessed June 1, 2012.

18. Competition Bureau, Canada, website, **www.competitionbureau.gc.ca**, accessed March 15, 2014; Health Canada website, **www.hc-sc.gc.ca**, accessed March 15, 2014.

19. Company website, **http://wiifit.com**, accessed March 15, 2014.

20. Company website, **www.barbiemydreams.com**, accessed March 16, 2014; Michelle DiPardo, "Barbie My Dreams Mimics Mommy's Social Media," *Marketing*, February 12, 2014, **www.marketingmag.ca**.

21. "Licensing Royalty Rates," *InventionStatistics.com*, **www.inventionstatistics.com**, accessed March 16, 2014.

22. Lizzy Guterma, "The Good, the Bad & the Bizarre of Brand Extensions," *Brand Salsa*, **www.brandsalsa.com**, accessed June 1, 2012.

23. "Extension Failures: Harley Davidson Perfume," *Marketing Guides*, **http://marketingnow.biz**, accessed June 2, 2012.

24. Company website, **www.hyundaicanada.com**, accessed March 16, 2014; Jonathan Yarkony, "Interview: John Krsteski, Hyundai Genesis Chief Designer," Autos.ca website, February 27, 2014, **www.autos.ca**.

25. Sarah Barmak, "How Major Brands Wished Chinese Canadians Happy New Year," *Marketing*, February 19, 2014, **www.marketingmag.ca**.

26. Company website, **www.panasonic.com**, accessed March 18, 20014; Joshua Condon, "Major 3D TV Manufacturers Look to Adopt Technology Standard," *Inc.*, **www.technology.inc.com**, accessed June 3, 2012.

27. Company website, **www.calvinkleinfragrances.com**, accessed March 18, 2014.

28. Andrew Goodman, "PepsiCo, Re-Energized," *Forbes*, June 14, 2013, **www.forbes.com**; Mike Esterl and John Revill, "PepsiCo, Nestle to Invest in Mexico," *The Wall Street Journal*, January 24, 2014, **http://online.wsj.com**.

29. Rebecca Harris, "Colgate Palmolive Takes Deodorant Marketing to New Heights," *Marketing*, March 18, 2014, **www.marketingmag.ca**.

30. Company website, **www.bose.com**, accessed March 20, 2014.

31. Company website, **www.loreal.com**, accessed March 20, 2014.

32. Company website, **www.scottsmiraclegro.com**, accessed March 20, 2014.

33. Robert G. Cooper, "Winning at New Products: Creating Value through Innovation" (Philadelphia, PA: Basic Books, 2011).

34. "Participating in the Standards System—What Are Standards?" Industry Canada website, **www.ic.gc.ca**, accessed March 22, 2014.

CHAPTER 11 MARKETOID NOTES

All Marketoids: "Education in Canada: Attainment, Field of Study and Location of Study," Statistics Canada, Catalogue no. 99-012-X2011001, January 14, 2014.

CHAPTER 12

1. Spencer Ante, "Amazon Adds That Robotic Touch," *The Wall Street Journal*, March 20, 2012, **http://online.wsj.com**; "Amazon Acquires Robot-Coordinated Order Fulfillment Company Kiva Systems for $775 Million in Cash," *TechCrunch.com*, March 19, 2012, **http://techcrunch.com**; "Robots to the Rescue," *Alumni Bulletin*, Harvard Business School, March 2012, **www.alumni.hbs.edu**; Jennifer Alsever, "Robot Workers Take over Warehouses," *CNN Money*, **http://money.cnn.com**, accessed March 19, 2012; A. Selway Ryan, "Robots in Disguise," *Supply Chain Digital*, February 14, 2012, **www.supplychaindigital.com**.

2. James Newton, "Ubisoft Announces Avengers Game for Wii U," *Nintendo Life*, **http://wii.nintendolife.com**, accessed June 4, 2012; James Newton, "NBA 2K13 Confirmed for Wii U Launch Period," *Nintendo Life*, **http://wii.nintendolife.com**, accessed June 4, 2012; company website, **http://e3.nintendo.com**, accessed June 4, 2012.

3. Paula Bernstein, "The Right Fit: Social, Mobile, Display, Search, Video... How Marketers Are Choosing Their Digital Options," *Adweek*, **www.adweek**, accessed June 4, 2012.

4. Eric Markowitz, "Independent Coffee Shops Caught in Price Squeeze," *Inc.*, **www.inc.com**, accessed June 4, 2012; Susan J. Aluise, "Warning: Coffee Prices Are Headed Up," *InvestorPlace*, **www.investorplace.com**, accessed June 4, 2012.

5. Company website, **http://home.stelladot.com**, accessed May 7, 2014; Vikram Alexei Kansara, "Jessica Herrin of Stella & Dot on Remaking Direct Sales for the Digital Age," **www.businessoffashion.com**, October 2013, accessed May 7, 2014.

6. Don Reisinger, "Netflix Arrives on Nintendo 3DS," *CNET News*, **http://news.cnet.com**, accessed June 5, 2012.

7. "AAA/CAA Great Battery Roundup" Fast Facts," available **http://newsroom.aaa.com/wpcontent/uploads/2013/07/GBR_fast_facts_2013.pdf**, accessed March 1, 2014.

8. "Reuse-a-Shoe," May 29, 2013, available **http://www.nike.com/us/en_us/c/better-world/stories/2013/05/reuse-a-shoe**, accessed May 7, 2014.

9. Entrepreneur.com, "9 Things You Never Thought You Would Buy From a Vending Machine," available **www.entrepreneur.com/slideshow/227452**, accessed March 1, 2014.

10. Erin Bury, "Small Businesses Set Sights on Shelf Space in Target Canada's Stores," **http://business.financialpost.com**, April 21, 2013.

11. Mark Brohan, "A Conflicted Group: Top 500 Manufacturers Need to Address Channel Conflict and Speed Up Online Productivity," *Internet Retailer*, June 2012, **www.internetretailer.com**.

12. "The Changing World of Industrial Distribution," *B2B International*, **www.b2binternational.com**, accessed June 5, 2012.

13. Mario Toneguzzi, "Walmart to Build Second Distribution Centre North of Calgary as Part of $500-Million Expansion," **www.calgaryherald.com**, February 4, 2014.

14. Tom Cheredar, "Comcast Launches 'Netflix-like' Streampix to Complement Expensive Cable Packages," *VentureBeat*, **http://venturebeat.com**, accessed June 6, 2012; "Daily Report: Netflix Transitions to TV Shows," *The New York Times*, **http://bits.blogs.nytimes.com**, accessed June 6, 2012; Quentin Hardy, "The Explosion of Mobile Video," *The New York Times*, **http://bits.blogs.nytimes.com**, accessed June 6, 2012.

15. Katia Hetter, "Travel Agents Know Something You Don't," *CNN.com*, **www.cnn.com**, accessed June 6, 2012; PR Web, "Travel Agencies in the US Industry Market Research Report Now Available from IBISWorld," *Seattle pi*, **www.seattlepi.com**, accessed June 6, 2012; Daniel Bortz, "Why It Pays to Book with a Travel Agent," *US News and World Report*, **http://money.usnews.com**, accessed June 6, 2012.

16. Reuters, "Apple Eyes New Stores in Two Chinese Cities as iPad Suit Continues," *Republic* (Columbus, Indiana), June 6, 2012, **www.therepublic.com**; Michael Kan, "Half of iPads Sold in China from Gray Market," *Computerworld*, **www.computerworld.com**, accessed June 6, 2012; Kevin Voigt, "iPad Hits Hong Kong—Before Global Release," *CNN.com*,

http://articles.cnn.com, accessed June 6, 2012; Owen Fletcher, "Amazon Kindle Hits China's Grey Market," *Macworld UK,* **www.macworld.co.uk**, accessed June 6, 2012.

17. Company website, **www.3net.com**, accessed June 6, 2012; "3net: A 3E Channel by Discovery, Sony, IMAX," *Adweek,* **www.adweek.com**, accessed June 6, 2012.

18. Company website, "Company Fact Sheet," **http://canada.roots.com**, accessed May 7, 2014.

19. Company website, "Company Overview," **www.truevaluecompany.com**, accessed March 1, 2104.

20. "Selling U.S. Products and Services in Canada," available **http://export.gov/canada/doingbusinessincanada/sellingusproductsandservices/index.asp**, accessed March 1, 2014.

21. Company website, "About Pier 1 Imports," **www.pier1.com**, accessed June 6, 2012.

22. Company website, **www.jda.com**, accessed May 7, 2014.

23. Claire Swedberg, "Treehouse Labs Unveils iPhone RFID System for Locating People and Things," *RFID Journal,* **www.rfidjournal.com**, accessed May 7, 2014.

24. Mark Smith, "SAP Spends Big on Success Factors for Cloud Computing and Talent Management," *SmartData Collective,* **http://smartdatacollective.com**, accessed May 7, 2014; Aaron Racardela, "Oracle Buys Taleo for $1.9 Billion," *Bloomberg,* **www.bloomberg.com**, accessed May 7, 2014; Tien Tzuo, "The End of ERP," *Forbes,* **www.forbes.com**, accessed May 7, 2014.

25. U.S. Customs and Border Protection, "C-TPAT Program Benefits: Reference Guide," available **http://www.cbp.gov/linkhandler/cgov/trade/cargo_security/ctpat/ctpat_program_information/ctpat_prog_benefits_guide.ctt/ctpat_prog_benefits_guide.pdf**, accessed March 1, 2014.

26. Armstrong & Armstrong Inc. website, "3PL Customers Report Identifies Service Trends, 3PL Market Segment Sizes and Growth Rates," available **www.3plogistics.com/PR_3PL_Customers-2013.htm**, accessed March 1, 2014.

27. Company website, **www.canadaflowers.ca**, accessed May 7, 2014.

28. Transport Canada, "Transportation in Canada 2012," p. 2, available **https://www.tc.gc.ca/media/documents/policy/Transportation_in_Canada_2012_eng_ACCESS.pdf**, accessed May 7, 2014.

29. Ibid., p. 18.

30. Transport Canada, "Rail Transportation," available **www.tc.gc.ca/eng/policy/anre-menu-3020.htm**, accessed May 7, 2014.

31. FedEx Small Business Center, "Holtkamp Greenhouses," **www.fedex.com**, accessed May 7, 2014.

32. "Union Pacific Unveils New Aerodynamic Technology for Double-Stack Intermodal Trains," PR Newswire.com, September 3, 2013, **www.prnewswire.com/news-releases/union-pacific-unveils-new-aerodynamic-technology-for-double-stack-intermodal-trains-222163401.html**, accessed March 2, 2014.

33. Transport Canada, "Transportation in Canada 2012," p. 18.

34. Walmart Canada, "Walmart Supercube Project Gets Green Light,"press release, December 5, 2013, **www.walmart.ca**.

35. Company website, **www.cslships.com**, accessed May 7, 2014.

36. Port Metro Vancouver Statistics Overview: 2013, available **www.portmetrovancouver.com/docs/default-source/about-facts-stats/2013-statistic-overview-(new).pdf?sfvrsn=0**, accessed March 2, 2014.

37. Transport Canada, "Transportation in Canada 2012," p. 10.

38. Company website, **www.dhl.com**, accessed May 7, 2014.

39. Company website, **www.transcanada.com**, "Facts and Figures," accessed May 7, 2014.

40. Company website, **www.enbridge.com**, "Our Pipelines," accessed May 7, 2014.

41. Company website, **www.ups-scs.com**, accessed May 7, 2014.

42. Company website, **www.purolator.com**, "Facts," accessed May 7, 2014.

43. Company website, **www.coldstorage.com**, "About Conestoga," accessed May 7, 2014.

44. Marc Wulfraat, "Cornwall—a Growing Epicentre for Canadian Distribution," **www.canadiangrocer.com**, December 31, 2013.

45. Company website, **www.pwc.ca/en/about/locations**, accessed March 2, 2014.

46. Company website, **www.datalliance.com**, accessed May 7, 2014; "Datalliance Expands Staff to Support Growth in VMI for Direct Store Replenishment," press release, **www.marketwatch.com**, accessed June 9, 2012.

47. "Bags Shipped Trouble-Free without Stretch Wrap," *Powder Bulk Solids,* **www.powderbulksolids.com**, accessed June 9, 2012.

48. Inbound Logistics, "Preventing Cargo Theft," *Transport Security,* **www.transportsecurity.com**, accessed June 9, 2012.

CHAPTER 12 MARKETOID NOTES

1. Jessica Leeder, "Second Coming of the Avon Lady," *Report on Business,* May 2014, pp. 52–55.

2. Statistics Canada, "Recycling in Canada," available **www.statcan.gc.ca/pub/16-002-x/2007001/article/10174-eng.htm**, accessed May 3, 2014.

3. Transport Canada, "Rail Transportation," available **www.tc.gc.ca/eng/policy/anre-menu-3020.htm**, accessed May 3, 2014.

4. Transport Canada, "Transportation in Canada 2012," available **www.tc.gc.ca/media/documents/policy/Transportation_in_Canada_2012_eng_ACCESS.pdf**, accessed May 3, 2014.

5. The World Bank, "Container Port Traffic (TEU: 20 foot equivalent units)," available **http://data.worldbank.org/indicator/IS.SHP.GOOD.TU**, accessed May 3, 2014.

CHAPTER 13

1. Hollie Shaw, "New-Look Loblaw Pushes Healthy Lifestyle; CEO Wants Fresh Foods to Outsell Dry Goods," *National Post,* May 2, 2014, p. FP3; Derwin Gowan, "Corporate Acquisition Forcing Change at St. Stephen Pharmacy," *Telegraph-Journal* (Saint John), April 9, 2014, p. C7; Marina Strauss, "Competition Bureau Sets Stiff Limits in Loblaw's Deal for Shoppers," *The Globe and Mail,* March 22, 2014, p. B1; Romina Maurino, "Galen Weston Named Business Newsmaker of the Year," *Telegraph-Journal* (Saint John), December 31, 2013, p. B3; Kate Wilkinson, "Loblaw's 'Brilliant Tactical Move' Captures Shoppers Drug Mart," **www.canadianbusiness.com**, July 15, 2013.

2. Ibid.

3. Chris Nichols, "Burger Giants Roll Out Remodels, But Are You Noticing?" *The Exchange,* August 29, 2103, available **http://finance.yahoo.com/blogs/the-exchange/burger-giants-roll-remodels-noticing-150243628.html**, accessed May 7, 2014.

4. Richard Gilbert, "Target Opening Nine More Stores in Canada," *journalofcommerce.com,* February 5, 2014, available **www.journalofcommerce.com/article/id58874/--target-opening-nine-more-stores-in-canada**, accessed May 7, 2014.

5. "Women's Roles in Home Improvement," *ABC News,* **http://abcnews.go.com**, accessed June 14, 2012.

6. "Business Idea Center: Specialty Foods," *Entrepreneur,* **www.entrepreneur.com**, accessed June 14, 2012.

7. Company website, **www.callwave.com**, accessed June 14, 2012.

8. Company website, **www.goodlifefitness.com/about/**, accessed March 3, 2014.

9. Company website, **www.lapalmera.com**, accessed June 15, 2012.

10. Company website, **www.shopparkroyal.com**, "About Park Royal," accessed March 3, 2014; Elaine Misonzhnik, "Lifestyle Centers Launch a Comeback," *Retail Traffic,* **http://retailtrafficmag.com**, accessed June 15, 2012.

11. Company website, **www.wem.ca**, "About WEM," accessed March 3, 2014.

12. Andrew Adam Newman, "A Web Series for G.E. Tests a Refrigerator and Freshness," *The New York Times,* **www.nytimes.com**, accessed June 15, 2012.

13. Mark Walsh, "Flurry to Debut Mobile Ad Analytics Tool," *Online Media Daily,* **www.mediapost.com**, accessed June 15, 2012.

14. "Clicks and Mortar: Why In-Store Experience Matters (Now More than Ever)," *Merchandising Matters,* **http://merchandisingmatters.com**, accessed June 15, 2012.

15. PR Newswire, "IMAN Cosmetics Launches Digital Beauty Advisor," press release, **www.prnewswire.com**, accessed June 15, 2012.

16. Nichols, "Burger Giants Roll Out Remodels, But Are You Noticing?"

17. Industry Canada, "Canada's Changing Retail Market," available **www.ic.gc.ca/eic/site/oca-bc.nsf/eng/ca02855.html**, accessed May 7, 2014.

18. Company website, **www.couche-tard.com**, accessed March 3, 2014.

19. Company website, **www.denmanbikeshop.com**, accessed March 3, 2014.

20. Company website, **http://sale.vente-privee.com**, accessed May 7, 2014.

21. Company website, **www.meijer.com**, accessed May 7, 2014.

22. Mark Hachman, "Walmart, Vudu to Rip Your DVDs to the Cloud," *PCMag.com,* **www.pcmag.com**, accessed June 16, 2012.

23. Company website, **www.dominioncitrus.com**, accessed May 7, 2014.

24. Company website, **www.wfsltd.com**, accessed May 7, 2014.

25. "Merchandising Services Companies," *Product Profitability,* **www.productprofitability.com**, accessed June 16, 2012.

26. Company website, **www.jwsales.com**, accessed May 7, 2014.

27. Company website, **www.cabelas.ca**, "The Cabela's Story," accessed May 7, 2014.

28. Lesley Kennedy, "Collette Liantonio, Queen of Infomercials," *MORE* Magazine, **www.more.com**, accessed June 17, 2012.

29. "Vending Machine Operators," *Hoover's,* **www.hoovers.com**, accessed June 17, 2012.

30. Robert Ianiro, "No Vending Machines for Pot," *National Post,* October 22, 2013, p. A13; Tom Blackwell, "Canada Getting Pot Vending Machines; Would Dispense Marijuana to Licensed Producers," *National Post,* October 17, 2013, p. A1.

31. Bruce Horovitz, "Vending World Tries New Tech to Court Gen Y," *USA Today,* **www.usatoday.com**, accessed June 17, 2012.

CHAPTER 13 MARKETOID NOTES

1. Pete Evans, "Target Canada Loses $941M in 2013, Weighing on U.S. Profit," **www.cbc.ca**, February 26, 2014.

2. Dollarama website, **www.dollarama.com**, accessed May 5, 2014; Ross Marowits, "Dollarama CEO and Founder's Compensation Surged 125% in 2013," **www.theglobeandmail.com**, April 28, 2014.

3. UFA website, **www.ufa.com**, "FAQ," accessed May 5, 2014.

4. Vanessa Wong, "The World's First Kit Kat Store, and Other Brand-Building Retail Endeavors," **www.businessweek.com**, January 17, 2014.

5. Acklands-Grainger website, **www.acklandsgrainger.com**, "About Us," accessed May 5, 2014.

CHAPTER 14

1. Russ Martin, "Social Costs," *Marketing,* April 2014, pp. 40–44; Steve Olenski, "What Is Programmatic Advertising and Is It the Future?," *Forbes,* March 20, 2013; Jeff Fraser, "Get With the Mobile Program," *Marketing,* March 2014, pp. 46–49; Jeff Fraser, "It's 2 A.M.

Do You Know Where Your Ads Are?" *Marketing*, November 11, 2013, pp. 16–23; "2013 Canadian Digital Consumer Insights," *Marketing*, October 2013; Chris Powell, "Programmatic, Economic Stability Driving Global Ad Spending: ZenithOptmedia," *Marketing*, April 9, 2014, **www.marketingmag.ca**; John Ebbert, "Define It—What Is Programmatic Buying?" Adexchanger website, November 19, 2012, **www.adexchanger.com**; John Ebbert, "Define It—What Is Real-Time Bidding?" adexchanger website, November 27, 2012, **www.adexchanger.com**.

2. Ben Meyers, "Digital Marketing Spend to Eclipse TV in 2014 Says eMarketer," DX3 digest website, January 7, 2014, **http://digest.dx3canada.com**.

3. Chris Powell, "CBC Boosts Olympic Offering Through BDU, Online Licensing Deals," *Marketing*, February 6, 2014, **www.marketingmag.ca**.

4. "AARP Financial Inc. Survey Finds: When It Comes to Financial Jargon, Americans Are Befuddled," *PR Newswire*, **www.prnewswire.com**, accessed June 19, 2012.

5. Alicia Androich, "Brands Get Planned and Unplanned Oscars Exposure," *Marketing*, March 3, 2014, **www.marketingmag.ca**.

6. Mira Shenker, "Chris Hadfield Wins CPRS President's Award," *Marketing*, March 10, 2014, **www.marketingmag.ca**.

7. "Executive Summary: Advertising Expenditure Forecast June 2013," ZenthOptmedia: The ROI Agency, June 2013.

8. Ibid.

9. "The Leading Global Advertiser in 2012 by Estimated Expenditure," Adbrands website, **www.adbrands.net**, accessed March 31, 2014.

10. Jack Neff, "Does P&G Really Drop 35% of Its Marketing Dollars on Digital?," *Adage*, August 20, 2013, **http://adage.com**.

11. Michelle DiPardo, "Danone Shakes It with Shakira for Activia," *Marketing*, March 12, 2014, **www.marketingmag.ca**.

12. David Brown, "Watch This: Pick Them Back Up (P&G)," *Marketing*, January 7, 2014, **www.marketingmag.ca**.

13. Kurt Badenhausen, "LeBron James' Endorsements Breakdown: By The Numbers," *Forbes*, January 22, 2014, **www.forbes.com**.

14. Kurt Badenhausen, "Sidney Crosby Tops List of NHL's Highest-Paid Players On and Off the Ice," *Forbes*, November 25, 2013, **www.forbes.com**.

15. Samantha Ettus, "Jennifer Lopez and Angelina Jolie: When Paired with Brands, Can You Spot the Fake?" *Forbes*, accessed June 18, 2012.

16. Company website, **www.geico.com**, accessed April 1, 2014.

17. Canadian Media Directors' Council Media Digest 2012/2013, page 8.

18. Jennifer Hough, "Wonder Finds Its Next Greatest Thing for Sandwich-y Campaign," *Marketing*, March 26, 2014, **www.marketingmag.ca**.

19. Rebecca Harris, "Allstate Canada Steps up PR Efforts to Counter Distracted Driving," *Marketing*, October 22, 2013, **www.marketingmag.ca**.

20. Michelle DiPardo, "Louisville Slugger Gets Competitive with Online Batting Contest," *Marketing*, March 26, 2014, **www.marketingmag.ca**.

21. Jim Edwards, "Facebook Shares Surge on First Ever $1 Billion Mobile Ad Revenue Quarter," Business Insider website, January 29, 2014, **www.businessinsider.com**.

22. "Executive Summary: Advertising Expenditure Forecast June 2013," ZenthOptmedia: The ROI Agency, June 2013.

23. Brian Stelter, "A DVR Ad Eraser Causes Tremors at TV Upfronts," *The New York Times*, May 16, 2012, **www.nytimes.com**.

24. "Net Advertising Revenue," Television Bureau of Canada website, **www.tvb.ca**, accessed April 2, 2014.

25. Canadian Web Radio website, **www.canadianwebradio.com**, accessed April 2, 2014.

26. "Net Advertising Revenue," Television Bureau of Canada website.

27. Steve Ladurantaye, "Canadians Increasingly Going Online for Written News," *The Globe and Mail*, March 27, 2013, **www.theglobeandmail.com**.

28. "Net Advertising Revenue," Television Bureau of Canada website.

29. "Net Advertising Revenue," Television Bureau of Canada website; Magazines Canada website, **www.magazinescanada.ca**, accessed April 2, 2014.

30. "Net Advertising Revenue," Television Bureau of Canada website.

31. Ibid..

32. Ibid.

33. Seth Rosenblatt, "Google Demolishes Financial Expectations to Close 2013," cnet website, January 30, 2014, **www.cnet.com**.

34. "2012 Actual + 2013 Estimated Canadian Internet Advertising Revenue Survey Detailed Report," Interactive Advertising Bureau, September 18, 2013.

35. Dusan Belic, "Total Immersion's D'Fusion Studio 3.2 Allows Developers to Create a 'New Breed' of AR Apps and Games," *IntoMobile*, **www.intomobile.com**, accessed June 19, 2012.

36. Company website, **www.carwraps.ca**, accessed April 3, 2014.

37. Suzanne Kane, "2012 Honda Civic: Recall Alert," *Washington Post*, June 13, 2012, **www.washingtonpost.com**.

38. Advertising Standards Canada website, **www.adstandards.com**, accessed April 5, 2014.

39. "M&M's Super Bowl Ad, Teaser Puts Yellow in Peril," *Marketing*, January 23, 2014, **www.marketingmag.ca**.

CHAPTER 14 MARKETOID NOTES

All Marketoids: Television Bureau of Canada website, **www.tvb.ca**, accessed April 2, 2014.

CHAPTER 15

1. Drew Fitzgerald and Kristin Jones, "Update: Salesforce to Buy Buddy Media for $689M, Revises View," *The Wall Street Journal*, June 4, 2012, **http://online.wsj.com**; Larry Dignan, "Salesforce Doubles Down on Social with Buddy Media, Following CMO Spending," *ZDnet.com*, June 4, 2012, **www.zdnet.com**; Tim Peterson, "Salesforce Buys Buddy Media for $689 Million," *Adweek*, June 4, 2012, **www.adweek.com**; "With Buddy Media Deal, Salesforce Targets CMOs," *Advertising Age*, June 4, 2012, **http://adage.com**; Peter Kafka, "Sales Set to Snap up Facebook Friend Buddy Media for More Than $800 Million," *All Things Digital*, May 29, 2012, **http://allthingsd.com**; Ian Schafer, "Will Salesforce's Acquisition of Buddy Media Make Social CRM Real?" *Advertising Age*, May 30, 2012, **http://adage.com**; Lisa Arthur, "Five Years from Now, CMOs Will Spend More on IT Than CIOs Do," *Forbes*, February 8, 2012, **www.forbes.com**; David A. Kaplan, "Salesforce's Happy Workforce," *Fortune*, January 19, 2012, **http://tech.fortune.cnn.com**.

2. Gerald L. Manning, Michael Ahearne, Barry L. Reece, and H.F. (Herb) MacKenzie, *Selling Today: Creating Customer Value*, 7th Canadian edition (Toronto, ON: Pearson Canada, in press, 2014).

3. Best Buy website, "Investor Relations," available **http://investors.bestbuy.com/phoenix.zhtml?c=83192&p=IROL-IRhome**, accessed May 3, 2014.

4. Hayley Tsukayama, "Panasonic Expands 'Toughbook' Line to Tablets," *Washington Post*, **www.washingtonpost.com**, accessed June 23, 2012.

5. Company website, **www.dsa.ca**, accessed February 1, 2014.

6. Canadian Radio-television and Telecommunications Commission, "National Do Not Call List (DNCL) Status Report," available **www.crtc.gc.ca/eng/dncl/status-etape.htm**, accessed May 7, 2014.

7. Canadian Radio-television and Telecommunications Commission, "About Registering and Who Can Still Call You," available **www.crtc.gc.ca/eng/info_sht/t1031.htm**, accessed May 7, 2014.

8. Canadian Radio-television and Telecommunications Commission, "Telecom Decision CRTC 2012-196," available **www.crtc.gc.ca/eng/archive/2012/2012-196.htm**, accessed May 7, 2014.

9. Canadian Radio-television and Telecommunications Commission, "Telecom Decision CRTC 2012-98," available **www.crtc.gc.ca/eng/archive/2012/2012-98.htm**, accessed May 7, 2014.

10. Quentin Casey, "New Brunswick, Unknown Land of Opportunity," *Telegraph-Journal* (Saint John), December 3, 2013, p. B1.

11. Company website, **www.nba.com**, accessed June 24, 2012.

12. Company website, **www.discountcar.com**, accessed February 3, 2014.

13. "Finding the Right Fit; Inspiration Furniture's Knowledgeable Staff Take Furniture Selection and Service to the Next Level," *Vancouver Sun*, January 29, 2014, p. E8.

14. Michelle Juergen, "A Hot Business Idea—Between the Sheets," *Entrepreneur*, **www.entrepreneur.com**, accessed May 7, 2014.

15. Company website, **www.westjet.com/guest/en/about**, accessed February 3, 2014.

16. Rockfish Interactive, "BUNN Ecommerce," **http://rockfishinteractive.com**, accessed June 24, 2012.

17. Jonathan D. Rockoff, "Drug Reps Soften Their Sales Pitches," *The Wall Street Journal*, **http://online.wsj.com**, accessed June 25, 2012.

18. Ibid.

19. Kelly Liyakasa, "Brainshark Releases SlideShark Team Edition," *DestinationCRM.com*, **www.destinationcrm.com**, accessed May 7, 2014.

20. Diana Ransom, "An Old-Fashioned Approach to Finding Customers," *Entrepreneur*, **www.entrepreneur.com**, accessed May 7, 2014.

21. Company website, **www.blackanddecker.com**, accessed May 7, 2014.

22. BusinessWire, "Jupiter Systems Hires New Head of Engineering, Expands Sales and Field Support," *MarketWatch*, **www.marketwatch.com**, accessed June 25, 2012.

23. U.S. Department of Labor, Women's Bureau, "20 Leading Occupations of Employed Women: 2010 Annual Average," **www.dol.gov**, accessed June 25, 2012; U.S. Bureau of Labor Statistics, "Overview of the 2010–20 Projections," *Occupational Outlook Handbook, 2012–2013*, **www.bls.gov**, accessed June 25, 2012.

24. Hollie Shaw, "Boxing Day Still Draws a Crowd; Canadians," *The Province* (Vancouver), December 27, 2013, p. A34.

25. Derrick Penner, "Annual Retail Blowout Begins Earlier and Earlier; Many Stores Not Even Waiting until after Christmas to Start Post-Holiday Sales," *Vancouver Sun*, December 26, 2013, p. A11.

26. "CRM Best Practices," *CRM Trends*, **www.crmtrends.com**, accessed June 25, 2012.

27. "Coupon Redemption in Canada; Some Interesting Data," available **www.canadiandealsassociation.com/coupon-redemption-in-canada-some-interesting-data**, accessed May 7, 2014.

28. Jeff Hudson, "What's Next for Digital Coupons?" *Mashable*, **http://mashable.com**, accessed June 26, 2012.

29. "Study: In-Store Sampling Inspires Repeat Purchases," **www.salesandmarketingmanagement .com**, accessed July 14, 2011.

30. "Get 'A Taste of Ireland' with Friendly Planet's Facebook Sweepstakes Giveaway," *EON: Enhanced Online News,* **http://eon.businesswire.com**, accessed June 26, 2012.

31. Company website, **www.cangift.org**, "Gift Fair Facts," accessed May 7, 2014.

32. Mike Thimmesch, "16 Powerful Stats on the Value of Trade Shows," **www.tsnn.com**, accessed May 7, 14.

CHAPTER 15 MARKETOID NOTES

1. "2014 World's Longest Yardsale Set for August 7th–10th," *www.127sale.com,* available **www.127sale.com/media.htm**, accessed May 3, 2014.

2. CPSA website, **www.cpsa.com**, accessed May 3, 2014.

3. "CRTC Fines Weed Man for Do-Not-Call Breaches," January 10, 2014, **www .theglobeandmail.com**.

4. CBC Television, *The National* (Wendy Mesley, host), "Ford Mustang 00001 Bought in St. John's 50 Years Ago," April 17, 2014.

5. Wallace Kenyon, "Canadian Tire Cash Buys Dream Wheels: It Took 15 Years and $1053 in Colourful Bills to Meet Teenage Goal," *Toronto Star,* July 16, 2011, p. 10.

6. Promotional Product Professionals of Canada Website, "Who is PPPC," **www.promocan .com**, accessed May 3, 2014.

CHAPTER 16

1. Dollarama Annual Information Form 2014, **www.dollarama.com**, "Our History," accessed May 25, 2014; Ross Marowitz, "Intense Competition Will Force Dollarama to Raise Prices Slowly Due to Loonie," The Canadian Press (Toronto), April 9, 2014; Rebecca Harris, "Canada's Hottest Retailer Is Loonie," *Canadian Grocer,* April 2014, pp. 39–41; Francine Kopun, "Dollarama Hopes to Get More Bang for Its Buck: Canadian Retailer Announces Plan to Expand by 400 Stores," *Toronto Star,* March 27, 2014, p. B1.

2. Tim Hume, "Fliers Stung by Charges for Window and Aisle Seats," *CNN Travel,* June 7, 2012, **www.cnn.com**.

3. Richard Jones, "Plant Sales: Quality over Quantity," *Greenhouse Grower,* **www .greenhousegrower.com**, accessed June 1, 2014.

4. Trefis Team, "P&G Cuts Prices to Save Market Share amid Weaker Outlook," *Trefis,* **www.trefis.com**, accessed June 1, 2014.

5. Bryant Orr, "Making Loyalty Programs Work," *Gallup Business Journal,* **http:// businessjournal.gallup.com**, accessed June 1, 2014.

6. Robert D. Buzzell, Bradley T. Gale, and Ralph G. M. Sultan, "Market Share—A Key to Profitability," *Harvard Business Review,* **http://hbr.org**, accessed June 1, 2014.

7. Company website, **www.skype.com**, accessed May 24, 2014.

8. Loblaw Companies Annual Report 2013, p. 10.

9. Company website, **http://palazzibros.com**, accessed June 1, 2014; Karen Paton-Evans, "Palazzi Brothers' Golden Anniversary; Palazzi Celebrating the First 50 Years," *Windsor Star,* September 16, 2010, p. C6.

10. Agam Shah, "Hard Drive Supply Issues Weigh on Dell's Q4 Earnings," *PCWorld,* **www .pcworld.com**, accessed June 29, 2012; Brian Caulfield, "Advantage Apple: Hard Drive Shortage and Rising Memory Prices Hit PC Costs," *Forbes,* **www.forbes.com**, accessed June 29, 2012.

11. Company websites, **www.aurorajet.ca** and **www.airsprint.com**, accessed June 1, 2014; Thomas Black and Noah Buhayar, "Buffett Pounces in Private-Jet Slump with $9.6 Billion," *Bloomberg Businessweek,* June 12, 2012, **www.businessweek.com**.

12. Amy Leap, "Less for Your Money," *Mail Tribune,* **www.mailtribune.com**, accessed June 1, 2014.

13. "Raw Material Costs Rise, So Do Bridgestone Prices," *Modern Tire Dealer,* **www .moderntiredealer.com**, accessed June 1, 2014; Keith Bradsher, "China Consolidates Grip on Rare Earth," *The New York Times,* **www.nytimes.com**, accessed June 1, 2014.

14. Aaron Cole, "2012 Prius Plug-in: The 'Current' Generation of Hybrid," *Aurora Sentinel,* **www.aurorasentinel.com**, accessed June 1, 2014.

15. Anders Kelto, "After a Free Fall, Zimbabwe Finds a Bit of Stability," WBUR and NPR, **www.wbur.org**, accessed June 1, 2014; Tawanda Musarurwa, "Zimbabwe: Inflation Declines Marginally," *Zimbabwe Herald,* **http://allafrica.com**, accessed June 30, 2012.

16. David Baugher, "Lack of Infrastructure, Slow Consumer Acceptance Complicate Quest for Alternative Fuels," *St. Louis Beacon,* **www.stlbeacon.org**, accessed June 1, 2014.

17. Tim Higgins and Chris Reiter, "GM Says Opel Turnaround Plan May Take a 'Couple' of Months," *Bloomberg Businessweek,* **www.businessweek.com**, accessed June 30, 2012.

18. "About OpenTable," company website, **www.opentable.com**, accessed June 1, 2014.

19. Company website, **www.costco.ca**, accessed May 20, 2014.

20. Kyle Wagner, "The History of Amazon's Kindle So Far," *Gizmodo,* **http://gizmodo.com**, accessed July 3, 2012; company website, **www.amazon.ca**, accessed June 1, 2014.

21. "CEO Defends Tata Nano, World's Cheapest Car," *USA Today,* **http://content.usatoday .com**, accessed July 3, 2012; company website, **www.nissan.ca**, accessed June 1, 2014.

22. Trefis Team, "Lowe's Still Worth $34 Though Trails Home Depot's Recovery," *Forbes,* **www.forbes.com**, accessed June 1, 2014; H. Butler, "Macquarie Forecasts 'Benign' Peak Season," *JOC Sailings,* **www.jocsailings.com**, accessed July 3, 2012.

23. Matthew Boyle, "Why Grocers Are Boosting Private Labels," *Bloomberg Businessweek,* **www.businessweek.com**, accessed June 1, 2014.

24. Kia Canada website, **www.kia.ca**, accessed August 19, 2014.

25. Company website, **www.shutterfly.com**, accessed June 1, 2014.

26. Organization website, **www.consumerreports.org**, accessed July 7, 2012.

27. Carl Laron, "New TV Pricing Policies a Tough Sell for Customers," *Consumer Search,* **www.consumersearch.com**, accessed July 8, 2012.

28. Jill Cataldo, "Super-Couponing Tips: When Rebates Go Awry," *LehighValleyLive.com,* June 1, 2014, **www.lehighvalleylive.com**; "Advice on Rebates and Refunds," *Better Business Bureau,* **http://memphis.bbb.org**, accessed June 1, 2014.

29. Betty Beard, "Prepare to Pay More for Your Holiday Feast," *USA Today,* **www .usatoday.com**, accessed July 8, 2012.

30. Company website, **www.bestbuy.ca**, accessed June 1, 2014.

31. Company website, **www.motel6.com**, accessed June 1, 2014.

32. Company website, **www.razorgator.com**, accessed June 1, 2014; company website, **www.ticketliquidator.com**, accessed June 1, 2014.

33. Company website, **www.ubid.com**, accessed June 1, 2014; Marilyn Alva, "EBay Goes Brick-and-Mortar, Tags Future to Mobile Too," *Investor's Business Daily,* **http:// news.investors.com**, accessed June 1, 2014.

34. PR Newswire, "Walmart Announces 'Pay with Cash' for Online Purchases," *MarketWatch,* **www.marketwatch.com**, accessed July 8, 2012; company website, **www .containerstore.com**, accessed June 1, 2014; company website, **www.lowes.com**, accessed June 1, 2014.

35. Laura Payton, "CETA: Canada-EU Free Trade Deal Lauded by Harper, Barroso," **www.cbc.ca**, October 18, 2013, accessed May 26, 2014.

36. Youkyung Lee, "S. Korea, Canada Reach Free Trade Deal Meant to Help Korean Automakers, Canadian Ranchers," *The Gazette* (Montreal), March 11, 2014, **www .montrealgazette.com**, accessed May 26, 2014.

37. Competition Bureau, "About Us," **www.competitionbureau.gc.ca**, accessed June 1, 2014.

38. *Competition Law* (North York, ON: CCH Canadian Limited, 1995), p. 4202.

39. Monique Keirnan, "Chocolate Has Its Day—Many of Them, in Fact," *Times-Colonist* (Victoria, B.C.), April 19, 2014, p. A12.

40. Will Chabun, "SaskTel Fears Competition from Big 3," *Leader Post* (Regina, SK), April 12, 2014, p. B1.

41. "Court Orders Rogers to Pay $500,000 in Ad Case," *National Post,* February 25, 2014, p. FP6.

42. Hollie Shaw, "Consumers Most Irked at False Claims, Watchdog Says; Inaccurate Retail Info Beats Out Concerns about Racy Content," *National Post,* March 27, 2013, p. FP2.

43. Keith Bradsher, "Chinese Cars Make Valuable Gains in Emerging Markets," *The New York Times,* **www.nytimes.com**, accessed June 1, 2014.

CHAPTER 16 MARKETOID NOTES

1. Megan O'Toole, "LCBO Reportedly Sells $168,000 Bottle of Wine, the Most Expensive Ever Purchased in Ontario," **www.nationalpost.com**, accessed October 18, 2013.

2. John Philippe, "Getting 'Mileage' Out of Tax Hikes," *Telegraph-Journal* (Saint John, N.B.), April 6, 2011, p. A7.

3. Conan Tobias, "Winners & Losers: Netflix Is Up, Bombardier Is Down, Rob Ford Is Rob Ford," **www.canadianbusiness.com**, March 3, 2014.

4. Ealuxe Luxury & Fine Living website, "Most Expensive Sunglasses in the World," available **www.ealuxe.com/most-expensive-sunglasses-world/**, accessed May 20, 2014.

5. Laura Peyton, "Government Surplus Auction Site Sells Cars, Jewelry, Office Furniture," **www.cbc.ca**, May 29, 2014.

6. Monique Keiran, "Chocolate Has Its Day—Many of Them, in Fact," *Times-Colonist* (Victoria, B.C.), April 19, 2014, p. A12.

APPENDIX A NOTES

1. Company website, **www.google.com**, accessed June 7, 2012.

2. Company website, **www.terracycle.net**, accessed June 7, 2012; Jack Neff, "Terracycle: Building a Small Empire on a Foundation of Compost," *Advertising Age,* **http:// adage.com**, accessed June 7, 2012.

3. Company website, **www.nintendo.com**, accessed June 7, 2012.

4. Travel Alberta, "2013–2016 Business Strategy." Available **http://industry .travelalberta.com**, accessed January 7, 2014.

5. U.S. Department of Labor, "Minimum Wage Laws in the States," **www.dol.gov**, accessed June 26, 2012; Lora Keleher, "Average Salaries at Costco," Money and Business, **www.moneyandbusiness.com**, accessed June 7, 2012; Lydia Dishman, "Target vs. Walmart: Which One Is a Better Place to Work?" PayScale.com, **http://blogs .payscale.com**, accessed June 7, 2012.

6. Company website, **http://c2educate.com**, accessed June 7, 2012.

7. David Hinckley, "J. Crew CEO Knows How to Tailor a Comeback," *New York Daily News,* May 24, 2012, **http://articles.nydailynews.com**.

8. "J. Crew Group, Inc. Announces First Quarter Fiscal 2012 Results," press release, **www.prnewswire.com**, accessed June 7, 2012; Jim Tierney, "Shareholders Approve J. Crew Deal," *Multichannel Merchant*, **http://multichannelmerchant.com**, accessed June 7, 2012.

9. Company website, **http://cuteoverload.com**, accessed June 8, 2012.

10. E.J. Schultz, "Weight Watchers Picks a New Target: Men," *Crain's New York Business*, **www.crainsnewyork.com**, accessed June 7, 2012.

11. Georg Szalai, "Zynga Partners with Paramount/Nickelodeon Movies on 'Rango' Promotion," *Hollywood Reporter*, **www.hollywoodreporter.com**, accessed June 7, 2012.

12. Company website, **www.ghfc.com**, accessed June 8, 2012.

13. Company website, "Dover Completes Sale of Heil Trailer International," press release, **http://phx.corporate-ir.net**, accessed June 7, 2012.

14. David Benoit, "Pfizer Sells Infant Nutrition Business for $11.9 Billion—Analysts React," *The Wall Street Journal*, April 23, 2012, **http://blogs.wsj.com**.

APPENDIX B NOTES

1. Arthur Middleton Hughes, "The 24 Essential Database Marketing Techniques," *Database Marketing Institute*, **www.dbmarketing.com**, accessed May 25, 2012.

2. "Benefits of a CRM System," *Customer Service Point*, **www.customerservicepoint.com**, accessed May 26, 2012; "Benefits of CRM," *Systems2Business*, **www.systems2business.com**, accessed May 26, 2012; Gene Gander, "10 Ways an Integrated CRM Tool Can Improve the Forwarding Process," *The Journal of Commerce*, **www.joc.com**, accessed May 26, 2012.

3. "How to Avoid CRM Implementation Failures," *Market for Cause*, **http://marketforcause.com**, accessed May 26, 2012.

glossary

A

accessory equipment Capital items like desktop computers and printers that typically cost less and last for shorter periods of time than installations. p. 284

administered marketing system VMS that achieves channel coordination when a dominant channel member exercises its power. p. 345

adoption process Stages that consumers go through in learning about a new product, trying it, and deciding whether to purchase it again. p. 318

advertising Paid, nonpersonal communication through various media about a business, not-for-profit organization, product, or idea by a sponsor identified in a message that is intended to inform, persuade, or remind members of a particular audience. p. 402

advertising campaign Series of different but related ads that use a single theme and appear in different media within a specified time period. p. 411

affinity marketing Marketing effort sponsored by an organization that solicits responses from individuals who share common interests and activities. p. A-21

AIDA concept Steps through which an individual reaches a purchase decision: attention, interest, desire, and action. p. 400

AIO statements Items on lifestyle surveys that describe various activities, interests, and opinions of respondents. p. 261

allowance Specified deduction from list price, including a trade-in or promotional allowance. p. 494

app Short for application, a free or purchased software download that links users to a wide range of goods and services, media and text content, social media platforms, search engines, and the like. p. 108

approach Salesperson's initial contact with a prospective customer. p. 446

atmospherics Combination of physical characteristics and amenities that contribute to a store's image. p. 373

attitudes A person's enduring favourable or unfavourable evaluations, emotions, or action tendencies toward some object or idea. p. 140

average total costs Costs calculated by dividing the sum of the variable and fixed costs by the number of units produced. p. 482

B

baby boomers People born between the years of 1947 and 1965. p. 253

backward integration Process through which a firm attempts to gain greater control over inputs in its production process, such as raw materials. p. 345

banner ad Strip message placed in high-visibility areas of frequently visited websites. p. 103

basing-point pricing System used in some industries during the early 20th century in which the buyer paid the factory price plus freight charges from the basing-point city nearest the buyer. p. 496

benchmarking Method of measuring quality by comparing performance against industry leaders. p. 289

bid rigging Occurs when sellers get together and collude to set prices with respect to one or more requests for competitive proposals. p. 506

blog Short for Web log—an online journal for an individual or organization. p. 101

bonus pack Specially packaged item that gives the purchaser a larger quantity at the regular price. p. 460

bot (shopbot) Software program that allows online shoppers to compare the price of a particular product offered by several online retailers. pp. 99, 503

bottom line Reference to overall company profitability. p. 14

brand Name, term, sign, symbol, design, or some combination that identifies the products of one firm while differentiating them from the competition's. p. 306

brand equity Added value that a respected, well-known brand name gives to a product in the marketplace. p. 310

brand extension Strategy of attaching a popular brand name to a new product in an unrelated product category. p. 315

brand insistence Consumer refusal of alternatives and extensive search for desired merchandise. p. 307

brand licensing Firm's authorization of other companies to use its brand names. p. 316

brand manager Marketer within an organization who is responsible for a single brand. p. 311

brand mark Symbol or pictorial design that distinguishes a product. p. 312

brand name Part of a brand consisting of words, numbers, or letters that can be spoken and that identifies and distinguishes a firm's offerings from those of its competitors. p. 312

brand preference Consumer reliance on previous experiences with a product to choose that product again. p. 307

brand recognition Consumer awareness and identification of a brand. p. 307

break-even analysis Pricing technique used to determine the number of products that must be sold at a specified price to generate enough revenue to cover total cost. p. 486

broker Agent wholesaling intermediary who does not take title to or possession of goods in the course of its primary function, which is to bring together buyers and sellers. p. 385

B2C products *See* consumer products.

bundle pricing Offering two or more complementary products and selling them for a single price. p. 504

business cycle Pattern of stages in the level of economic activity: prosperity, recession, depression, and recovery. p. 71

business plan Formal document that outlines a company's objectives, how they will be met, how the business will achieve financing, and how much money the firm expects to earn. p. A-1

business products Goods and services purchased for use either directly or indirectly in the production of other goods and services for resale. p. 246

business services Intangible products that firms buy to facilitate their production and operating processes. p. 287

business-to-business (B2B) e-marketing Use of the Internet for business transactions between organizations. p. 159

business-to-business (B2B) marketing Organizational sales and purchases of goods and services to support production of other products, for daily company operations, or for resale. p. 156

business-to-business (B2B) product Product that contributes directly or indirectly to the output of other products for resale; also called industrial or organizational product. p. 279

business-to-consumer (B2C) digital marketing Selling directly to consumers over the Internet. p. 97

buyer Person who has the formal authority to select a supplier and to implement the procedures for securing a good or service. p. 177

buyer concerns Expressions of sales resistance by the prospect. p. 449

buyer's market Market in which there are more goods and services than people willing to buy them. p. 10

buying centre Participants in an organizational buying decision. p. 176

C

cannibalization Loss of sales of an existing product due to competition from a new product in the same line. pp. 317, 503

captive brand National brand that is sold exclusively by a retail chain. p. 309

cash discount Price reduction offered to a consumer, business user, or marketing intermediary in return for prompt payment of a bill. p. 493

category advisor (category captain) Trade industry vendor who develops a comprehensive procurement plan for a retail buyer. p. 172

category killer Store offering huge selections and low prices in single product lines. p. 377

category management Product management system in which a category manager—with profit and loss responsibility—oversees a product line. p. 311

cause marketing Identification and marketing of a social issue, cause, or idea to selected target markets. p. 17

census agglomeration (CA) Geographic area with a population over 10,000. p. 250

census metropolitan area (CMA) Geographic area surrounding an urban core with a population of at least 100,000. p. 249

channel captain Dominant and controlling member of a marketing channel. p. 343

click-through rate Percentage of people presented with a banner ad who click on it. p. 106

closed sales territory Exclusive geographic selling region of a distributor. p. 342

closing Stage of the personal selling process in which the salesperson asks the customer to make a purchase decision. p. 449

cognitive dissonance Imbalance among knowledge, beliefs, and attitudes that occurs after an action or decision is taken, such as a purchase. p. 147

cohort effect Tendency of members of a generation to be influenced and bound together by events occurring during their key formative years—roughly 17 to 22 years of age. p. 254

cold calling Contacting a prospect without a prior appointment. p. 447

commercial market Individuals and firms that acquire products to support, directly or indirectly, production of other goods and services. p. 158

commission Incentive compensation directly related to the sales or profits achieved by a salesperson. p. 454

commission merchant Agent wholesaling intermediary who takes possession of goods shipped to a central market for sale, acts as the producer's agent, and collects an agreed-upon fee at the time of the sale. p. 385

common carriers Businesses that provide transportation services as for-hire carriers to the general public. p. 351

common market Extension of a customs union by seeking to reconcile all government regulations affecting trade. p. 200

comparative advertising Advertising strategy that emphasizes messages with direct or indirect promotional comparisons between competing brands. p. 407

Competition Act The most comprehensive legislation in Canada, designed to help both consumers and businesses by promoting a healthy competitive environment. pp. 67, 505

competitive bidding Inviting potential suppliers to quote prices on proposed purchases or contracts. p. 500

competitive environment Interactive process that occurs in the marketplace among marketers of directly competitive products, marketers of products that can be substituted for one another, and marketers competing for the consumer's purchasing power. p. 63

competitive pricing strategy Pricing strategy designed to de-emphasize price as a competitive variable by pricing a good or service at the general level of comparable offerings. p. 491

competitive strategy Methods through which a firm deals with its competitive environment. p. 65

component parts and materials Finished business products of one producer that become part of the final products of another producer. p. 285

concentrated marketing Focusing marketing efforts on satisfying a single market segment; also called niche marketing. p. 266

concept testing Method for subjecting a product idea to additional study before actual development by involving consumers through focus groups, surveys, in-store polling, and the like. p. 323

consultative selling Meeting customer needs by listening to customers, understanding their problems, paying attention to details, and following through after the sale. p. 442

consumer behaviour Process through which buyers make purchase decisions. p. 128

consumer innovators People who purchase new products almost as soon as the products reach the market. p. 318

consumer orientation Business philosophy incorporating the marketing concept that emphasizes first determining unmet consumer needs and then designing a system for satisfying them. p. 10

consumer products Products bought by ultimate consumers for personal use. p. 246

consumer rights In their most basic form, these rights are a person's right to choose goods and services freely, to be informed about these products and services, to be heard, and to be safe. p. 78

consumerism Social force within the environment designed to aid and protect the consumer by exerting legal, moral, and economic pressures on business and government. p. 77

containerization Process of combining several unitized loads into a single, well-protected load for shipment. p. 357

content marketing Creating and distributing relevant and targeted material to attract and engage an audience, with the goal of driving them to a desired action. p. 114

contest Sales promotion technique that requires entrants to complete a task, such as solving a puzzle or answering questions on a quiz, for the chance to win a prize. p. 461

contract carriers For-hire transporters that do not offer their services to the general public. p. 351

contractual marketing system VMS that coordinates channel activities through formal agreements among participants. p. 345

controlled experiment Scientific investigation in which a researcher manipulates a test group (or groups) and compares the results with those of a control group that did not receive the experimental controls or manipulations. p. 231

convenience products Goods and services that consumers want to purchase frequently, immediately, and with minimal effort. p. 279

convenience retailer Store that appeals to customers with accessible location, long hours, rapid checkout, and adequate parking. p. 375

conversion rate Percentage of visitors to a website who make a purchase. p. 106

cooperative advertising Strategy in which a retailer shares advertising costs with a manufacturer or wholesaler. p. 408

core region Region from which most major brands get 40 to 80 percent of their sales. p. 250

corporate marketing system VMS in which a single owner operates the entire marketing channel. p. 345

cost-plus pricing Practice of adding a percentage of specified dollar amount—or markup—to the base cost of a product to cover unassigned costs and to provide a profit. p. 484

countertrade Form of exporting whereby goods and services are bartered rather than sold for cash. p. 209

coupon Sales promotion technique that offers a discount on the purchase price of goods or services. p. 460

creative selling Personal selling that involves situations in which a considerable degree of analytical decision making on the buyer's part results in the need for skillful proposals of solutions for the customer's needs. p. 444

cross-promotion Promotional technique in which marketing partners share the cost of a promotional campaign that meets their mutual needs. p. 420

cross-selling Selling several, often unrelated, goods and services to the same customer based on knowledge of that customer's needs. p. 442

culture Values, beliefs, preferences, and tastes handed down from one generation to the next. p. 128

cumulative quantity discount Price discount determined by amounts of purchases over stated time periods. p. 493

customary prices Traditional prices that customers expect to pay for certain goods and services. p. 480

customer relationship management (CRM) Combination of strategies and tools that drives relationship programs, reorienting the entire organization to a concentrated focus on satisfying customers. p. 164

customer satisfaction Extent to which customers are satisfied with their purchases. p. A-19

customer winback Process of rejuvenating lost relationships with customers. p. A-24

customer-based segmentation Dividing a business-to-business market into homogeneous groups based on buyers' product specifications. p. 162

customs union Establishment of a free trade area plus a uniform tariff for trade with nonmember unions. p. 200

D

data mining Process of searching through customer databases to detect patterns that guide marketing decision making. p. 233

database marketing Use of software to analyze marketing information, identifying and targeting messages toward specific groups of potential customers. p. A-21

decider Person who chooses a good or service, although another person may have the formal authority to complete the sale. p. 177

decline stage Final stage of the product life cycle, in which a decline in total industry sales occurs. p. 295

Delphi technique Qualitative sales forecasting method that gathers and redistributes several rounds of anonymous forecasts until the participants reach a consensus. p. 235

demand Schedule of the amounts of a firm's product that consumers will purchase at different prices during a specified time period. p. 480

demarketing Process of reducing consumer demand for a good or service to a level that the firm can supply. p. 74

demographic segmentation Division of an overall market into homogeneous groups based on variables such as gender, age, income, occupation, education, sexual orientation, household size, and stage in the family life cycle; also called socioeconomic segmentation. p. 250

demonstration Stage in the personal selling process in which the customer has the opportunity to try out or otherwise see how a good or service works before purchase. p. 448

department store Large store that handles a variety of merchandise, including clothing, household goods, appliances, and furniture. p. 378

derived demand Demand for a resource that results from demand for the goods and services that are produced by that resource. p. 167

differentiated marketing Strategy that focuses on producing several products and pricing, promoting, and distributing them with different marketing mixes designed to satisfy smaller segments. p. 266

diffusion process Process by which new goods or services are accepted in the marketplace. p. 318

digital marketing Strategic process of creating, distributing, promoting, and pricing goods and services to a target market over the Internet or through digital tools. p. 96

direct channel Marketing channel that moves goods directly from a producer to the business purchaser or ultimate user. p. 335

direct marketing Direct communications, other than personal sales contacts, between buyer and seller, designed to generate sales, information requests, or store or website visits. p. 386

direct selling Strategy designed to establish direct sales contact between producer and final user. p. 335

discount house Store that charges low prices but may not offer services such as credit. p. 378

discretionary income Money available to spend after buying necessities such as food, clothing, and housing. p. 73

distribution Movement of goods and services from producers to customers. p. 332

distribution strategy Planning that ensures that consumers find their products in the proper quantities at the right times and places. p. 46

downstream management Controlling part of the supply chain that involves finished product storage, outbound logistics, marketing and sales, and customer service. p. 346

drop shipper Limited-function merchant wholesaler that accepts orders from customers and forwards these orders to producers, which then ship directly to the customers who placed the orders. p. 384

dual distribution Network that moves products to a firm's target market through more than one marketing channel. p. 337

E

e-business Conducting online transactions with customers by collecting and analyzing business information, carrying out the exchanges, and maintaining online relationships with customers. p. 96

economic environment Factors that influence consumer buying power and marketing strategies, including stage of the business cycle, inflation, unemployment, income, and resource availability. p. 96

80/20 principle Generally accepted rule that 80 percent of a product's revenues come from 20 percent of its total customers. p. 263

elasticity Measure of responsiveness of purchasers and suppliers to a change in price. p. 482

electronic data interchange (EDI) Computer-to-computer exchanges of invoices, orders, and other business documents. p. A-26

electronic shopping cart File that holds items the online shopper has chosen to buy. p. 98

electronic storefronts Company websites that sell products to customers. p. 98

emergency goods and services Products bought in response to unexpected and urgent needs. p. 280

employee satisfaction Employee's level of satisfaction for his or her company and the extent to which that loyalty or lack of loyalty is communicated to external customers. p. A-17

end-use application segmentation Segmenting a business-to-business market based on how industrial purchasers will use the product. p. 164

engagement Amount of time users spend on sites. p. 106

enterprise resource planning (ERP) system Software system that consolidates data from among a firm's various business units. p. 348

environmental management Attainment of organizational objectives by predicting and influencing the competitive, political-legal, economic, technological, and social-cultural environments. p. 63

environmental scanning Process of collecting information about the external marketing environment to identify and interpret potential trends. p. 63

e-procurement Use of the Internet by organizations to solicit bids and purchase goods and services from suppliers. p. 161

ethics Moral standards of behaviour expected by a society. p. 23

European Union (EU) Customs union that is moving in the direction of an economic and monetary union by adopting a common currency, removing trade restrictions, and permitting free flow of goods and workers throughout the member nations. p. 201

evaluative criteria Features that a consumer considers in choosing among alternatives. p. 146

event marketing Marketing of sporting, cultural, and charitable activities to selected target markets. p. 17

everyday low pricing (EDLP) Pricing strategy of continuously offering low prices rather than relying on such short-term price cuts as cents-off coupons, rebates, and special sales. p. 490

evoked set Number of alternatives that a consumer actually considers in making a purchase decision. p. 146

exchange functions Buying and selling. p. 22

exchange process Activity in which two or more parties give something of value to each other to satisfy perceived needs. p. 8

exchange rate Price of one nation's currency in terms of another country's currency. p. 194

exclusive distribution Distribution of a product through a single wholesaler or retailer in a specific geographic region. p. 341

expectancy theory Theory that motivation depends on an individual's expectations of his or her ability to perform a job and how that performance relates to attaining a desired reward. p. 454

exploratory research Process of discussing a marketing problem with informed sources both within and outside the firm and examining information from secondary sources. p. 221

exponential smoothing Quantitative forecasting technique that assigns weights to historical sales data, giving the greatest weight to the most recent data. p. 237

exporting Marketing domestically produced goods and services in foreign countries. p. 190

extended problem solving Situation that involves lengthy external searches and long deliberation; results when brands are difficult to categorize or evaluate. p. 148

external customer People or organizations that buy or use another firm's goods or services. p. A-17

F

false or misleading price representation One form of misleading advertising. p. 506

family brand Single brand name that identifies several related products. p. 309

family life cycle Process of family formation and dissolution. p. 256

field selling Sales presentations made at prospective customers' locations on a face-to-face basis. p. 438

first mover strategy Theory advocating that the company that is first to offer a product in a marketplace will be the long-term market winner. p. 41

fixed costs Costs that remain stable at any production level within a certain range (such as lease payments or insurance costs). p. 481

FOB (free on board) origin (or **shipping point**) Price quotation that does not include shipping charges. Legal responsibility and title pass to the buyer once the shipment leaves the seller's premises. p. 495

FOB destination Price quotation that includes freight—paid by the seller—and where the seller retains legal responsibility and title to the goods until they reach the buyer. p. 495

FOB origin—freight allowed and prepaid A hybrid price quotation system where the seller pays the freight, but the customer assumes legal responsibility and title once the shipment leaves the seller's premises. p. 495

focus group Simultaneous personal interview of a small group of individuals, which relies on group discussion about a certain topic. p. 228

follow-up Post-sale activities that often determine whether an individual who has made a recent purchase will become a repeat customer. p. 450

foreign licensing Agreement that grants foreign marketers the right to distribute a firm's merchandise or to use its trademark, patent, or process in a specified geographic area. p. 205

forward integration Process through which a firm attempts to control downstream distribution. p. 345

franchise Contractual arrangement in which a wholesaler or retailer agrees to meet the operating requirements of a manufacturer or other franchiser. pp. 205, 346

free trade area Region in which participating nations agree to the free trade of goods among themselves, abolishing tariffs and trade restrictions. p. 200

Free Trade Area of the Americas (FTAA) Proposed free trade area stretching the length of the entire Western hemisphere and designed to extend free trade benefits to additional nations in North, Central, and South America. p. 201

frequency marketing Frequent buyer or user marketing programs that reward customers with cash, rebates, merchandise, or other premiums. p. A-20

full-cost pricing Pricing method that uses all relevant variable costs in setting a product's price and allocates those fixed costs not directly attributed to the production of the priced item. p. 485

full-service research supplier Marketing research organization that contracts with clients to conduct complete marketing research projects. p. 220

G

gatekeeper Person who controls the information that all buying centre members will review. p. 177

General Agreement on Tariffs and Trade (GATT) International trade accord that has helped reduce world tariffs. p. 201

general merchandise retailer Store that carries a wide variety of product lines, stocking all of them in some depth. p. 377

Generation X The group born between 1966 and 1981—who are in their 30s to early 40s. p. 252

generic products Products characterized by plain labels, no advertising, and the absence of brand names. p. 307

geographic segmentation Division of an overall market into homogeneous groups based on their locations. p. 248

global marketing strategy Standardized marketing mix with minimal modifications that a firm uses in all of its domestic and foreign markets. p. 207

global sourcing Purchasing goods and services from suppliers worldwide. p. 167

good Tangible products that customers can see, hear, smell, taste, or touch. p. 276

goods–services continuum Spectrum along which goods and services fall according to their attributes, from pure good to pure service. p. 276

grassroots marketing Efforts that connect directly with existing and potential customers through non-mainstream channels. p. A-22

green marketing Production, promotion, and reclamation of environmentally sensitive products. p. 87

grey goods Goods produced for sale in one market and then diverted to another market. p. 344

gross domestic product (GDP) Sum of all goods and services produced by a nation in a year. p. 70

growth stage Second stage of the product life cycle, which begins when a firm starts to realize substantial profits from its investment in the product. p. 294

guerrilla marketing Unconventional, innovative, and low-cost marketing techniques designed to get consumers' attention in unusual ways. p. 404

H

high-involvement purchase decision Buying decisions that evokes high levels of potential social or economic consequences. p. 145

hypermarket Giant one-stop shopping facility offering wide selections of grocery items and general merchandise at discount prices, typically filling up 200,000 or more square feet of selling space. p. 379

hypothesis Tentative explanation for some specific event. p. 222

I

importing Purchasing foreign goods and services. p. 190

impulse goods and services Products purchased on the spur of the moment. p. 279

inbound telemarketing Sales method in which prospects call a seller to obtain information, make reservations, and purchase goods and services. p. 439

incremental-cost pricing Pricing method that attempts to use only costs directly attributable to a specific output in setting prices. p. 485

individual brand Single brand that uniquely identifies a product itself. p. 309

inelastic demand Demand that, throughout an industry, will not change significantly due to a price change. p. 168

inflation Rising prices caused by some combination of excess consumer demand and increases in the costs of one or more factors of production. p. 72

influencers Individuals with the capability of affecting the opinions or actions of others. p. 112; Typically, technical staff such as engineers who affect the buying decision by supplying information to guide evaluation of alternatives or by setting buying specifications. p. 177

informative advertising Promotion that seeks to develop initial demand for a good, service, organization, person, place, idea, or cause. p. 407

inside selling Selling by phone, mail, and electronic commerce. p. 440

installations Business products like factories, assembly lines, and huge machinery that are major capital investments. p. 284

institutional advertising Promotion of a concept, idea, philosophy, or goodwill of an industry, company, organization, person, geographic location, or government agency. p. 406

integrated marketing communications (IMC) Coordination of all promotional activities to produce a unified, customer-focused promotional message. p. 396

intensive distribution Distribution of a product through all available channels. p. 341

interactive advertising Two-way promotional messages transmitted through communication channels that induce message recipients to participate actively in the promotional effort. p. 409

interactive marketing Buyer–seller communications in which the customer controls the amount and type of information received from a marketer through such channels as the Internet and virtual reality kiosks. p. 98

intermodal operations Combination of transport modes such as rail and highway carriers (piggyback), air and highway carriers (birdyback), and water and highway carriers (fishyback) to improve customer service and achieve cost advantages. p. 351

internal customer Employees or departments within an organization that depend on the work of another employee or department to perform tasks. p. A-17

internal marketing Managerial actions that help all members of the organization understand and fulfill their respective roles in implementing a marketing strategy. p. A-17

interpretative research Observational research method developed by social anthropologists in which customers are observed in their natural setting and their behaviour is interpreted based on an understanding of social and cultural characteristics; also known as *ethnography*, or going native. p. 227

introductory stage First stage of the product life cycle, in which a firm works to stimulate demand for the new market entry. p. 294

ISO (International Organization for Standardization) certification Internationally recognized standards that ensure a company's goods and services meet established quality levels and that ensure its operations minimize harm to the environment. p. 197

ISO 9001:2008 Standards that define international, generic criteria for quality management and quality assurance. p. 289

J

joint demand Demand for a product that depends on the demand for another product used in combination with it. p. 168

jury of executive opinion Qualitative sales forecasting method that assesses the sales expectations of various executives. p. 235

just-in-time (JIT)/JIT II Inventory practices that seek to boost efficiency by cutting inventories to absolute minimum levels. With JIT II, suppliers' representatives work at the customer's facility. p. 168

L

label Branding component that carries an item's brand name or symbol, the name and address of the manufacturer or distributor, information about the product, and recommended uses. p. 315

leader pricing Variant of loss-leader pricing in which marketers offer prices slightly above cost to avoid violating minimum-markup regulations and earn a minimal return on promotional sales. p. 499

learning Knowledge or skill that is acquired as a result of experience, which changes consumer behaviour. p. 143

limited problem solving Situation in which the consumer invests some small amount of time and energy in searching for and evaluating alternatives. p. 148

limited-line store Retailer that offers a large assortment within a single product line or within a few related product lines. p. 377

limited-service research supplier Marketing research firm that specializes in a limited number of research activities, such as conducting field interviews or performing data processing. p. 220

line extension Development of individual offerings that appeal to different market segments while remaining closely related to the existing product line. p. 293

list price Established price normally quoted to potential buyers. p. 491

logistics Process of coordinating the flow of information, goods, and services among members of the distribution channel. p. 332

loss leader Product offered to consumers at less than cost to attract them to stores in the hope that they will buy other merchandise at regular prices. p. 498

low-involvement purchase decision Routine purchase that poses little risk to the consumer, either socially or economically. p. 145

M

mail-order wholesaler Limited-function merchant wholesaler that distributes catalogues instead of sending sales personnel to contact customers. p. 384

mall intercepts Interviews conducted inside retail shopping centres. p. 228

manufacturer's brand Brand name owned by a manufacturer or other producer. p. 308

manufacturers' representative Agent wholesaling intermediary that represents manufacturers of related but noncompeting products and receives a commission on each sale. pp. 337, 385

marginal analysis Method of analyzing the relationship among costs, sales price, and increased sales volume. p. 476

marginal cost Change in total cost that results from producing an additional unit of output. p. 482

markdown Amount by which a retailer reduces the original selling price of a product. p. 371

market Group of people with sufficient purchasing power, authority, and willingness to buy. p. 246

market development strategy Strategy that concentrates on finding new markets for existing products. p. 317

market penetration strategy Strategy that seeks to increase sales of existing products in existing markets. p. 316

market price Price a consumer or marketing intermediary actually pays for a product after subtracting any discounts, allowances, or rebates from the list price. p. 492

market segmentation Division of the total market into smaller, relatively homogeneous groups. p. 247

marketing Organizational function and a set of processes for creating, communicating, and delivering value to customers and for managing customer relationships in ways that benefit the organization and its stakeholders. p. 6

marketing communications Messages that deal with buyer–seller relationships. p. 396

marketing concept Company-wide consumer orientation with the objective of achieving long-run success. p. 10

marketing decision support system (MDSS) Marketing information system component that links a decision maker with relevant databases and analysis tools. p. 233

marketing (distribution) channel System of marketing institutions that enhances the physical flow of goods and services, along with ownership title, from producer to consumer or business user. p. 332

marketing ethics Marketers' standards of conduct and moral values. p. 79

marketing information system (MIS) Planned, computer-based system designed to provide managers with a continuous flow of information relevant to their specific decisions and areas of responsibility. p. 233

marketing intermediary (middleman) Wholesaler or retailer that operates between producers and consumers or business users. p. 333

marketing mix Blending of the four strategy elements—product, distribution, promotion, and pricing—to fit the needs and preferences of a specific target market. p. 45

marketing myopia Management's failure to recognize the scope of its business. p. 12

marketing plan Detailed description of the resources and actions needed to achieve stated marketing objectives. p. A-1

marketing planning Implementing planning activities devoted to achieving marketing objectives. p. 35

marketing public relations (MPR) Narrowly focused public relations activities that directly support marketing goals. p. 419

marketing research Process of collecting and using information for marketing decision making. p. 218

marketing strategy Overall company-wide program for selecting a particular target market and then satisfying consumers in that market through the marketing mix. p. 39

market-share objective Volume-related pricing objective in which the goal is to achieve control of a portion of the market for a firm's good or service. p. 477

markup Amount that a retailer adds to the cost of a product to determine its selling price. p. 370

mass merchandiser Store that stocks a wider line of goods than a department store, usually without the same depth of assortment within each line. p. 378

materials handling system Set of activities that move production inputs and other goods within plants, warehouses, and transportation terminals. p. 356

maturity stage Third stage of the product life cycle, in which industry sales level out. p. 295

media research Advertising research that assesses how well a particular medium delivers an advertiser's message, where and when to place the advertisement, and the size of the audience. p. 424

media scheduling Setting the timing and sequence for a series of advertisements. p. 417

merchandisers Trade sector buyers who secure needed products at the best possible prices. p. 172

merchant wholesaler Independently owned wholesaling intermediary that takes title to the goods it handles; also known as an industrial distributor in the business goods market. p. 383

message Communication of information, advice, or a request by the sender to the receiver. p. 399

message research Advertising research that tests consumer reactions to an advertisement's creative message. p. 424

microcultures Smaller groups within a society that have their own distinct characteristics and modes of behaviour. p. 130

micromarketing Targeting potential customers at very narrow, basic levels, such as by postal code, specific occupation, or lifestyle—possibly even individuals themselves. p. 267

middleman *See* marketing intermediary.

minimum advertised pricing (MAP) Fees paid to retailers who agree not to advertise products below set prices. p. 494

mission Essential purpose that differentiates one company from others. p. 38

missionary selling Indirect type of selling in which specialized salespeople promote the firm's goodwill among indirect customers, often by assisting customers in product use. p. 444

mobile marketing Marketing messages transmitted via wireless technology. p. 19

modified rebuy Situation in which a purchaser is willing to reevaluate available options for repurchasing a good or service. p. 175

monopolistic competition Market structure involving a heterogeneous product and product differentiation among competing suppliers, allowing the marketer some degree of control over prices. p. 480

monopoly Market structure in which a single seller dominates trade in a good or service for which buyers can find no close substitutes. pp. 63, 481

motive Inner state that directs a person toward the goal of satisfying a need. p. 138

MRO items Business supplies made up of maintenance items, repair items, and operating supplies. p. 286

multi-domestic marketing strategy Application of market segmentation to foreign markets by tailoring the firm's marketing mix to match specific target markets in each nation. p. 207

multinational corporation Firm with significant operations and marketing activities outside its home country. p. 206

multiple sourcing Purchasing from several vendors. p. 171

N

national accounts organization Promotional effort in which a dedicated sales team is assigned to a firm's major customers to provide sales and service needs. p. 453

nearshoring Moving jobs to vendors in countries close to the business' home country. p. 169

need Imbalance between a consumer's actual and desired states. p. 138

network marketing Personal selling that relies on lists of family members and friends of the salesperson, who organizes a gathering of potential customers for a demonstration of products. p. 439

new-task buy First-time or unique purchase situation that requires considerable effort by decision makers. p. 175

noncumulative quantity discount Price reduction granted on a one-time-only basis. p. 494

nonmarketing public relations Organizational messages about general management issues. p. 418

nonpersonal selling Promotion that includes advertising, product placement, sales promotion, direct marketing, guerrilla marketing, and public relations—all conducted without being face to face with the buyer. p. 402

nonprobability sample Sample that involves personal judgment somewhere in the selection process. p. 226

North American Free Trade Agreement (NAFTA) Accord removing trade barriers among Canada, Mexico, and the United States. p. 201

North American Industry Classification System (NAICS) Classification used by NAFTA countries to categorize the business marketplace into detailed market segments. p. 164

O

odd pricing Pricing policy based on the belief that a price ending with an odd number just under a round number is more appealing, for instance, $9.97 rather than $10. p. 496

offshoring Movement of high-wage jobs from Canada to lower-cost overseas locations. p. 169

oligopoly Market structure in which relatively few sellers compete and where high start-up costs form barriers to keep out new competitors. p. 480

opening price point Setting an opening price below that of the competition, usually on a high-quality private label item. p. 491

opinion leaders Trendsetters who purchase new products before others in a group and then influence others in their purchases. p. 136

order processing Selling, mostly at the wholesale and retail levels, that involves identifying customer needs, pointing them out to customers, and completing orders. p. 443

organization marketing Marketing by mutual-benefit organizations, service organizations, and government organizations intended to influence others to accept their goals, receive their services, or contribute to them in some way. p. 18

organizational product *See* business-to-business (B2B) product.

outbound telemarketing Sales method in which sales personnel place phone calls to prospects and try to conclude the sale over the phone. p. 439

outsourcing Using outside vendors to produce goods and services formerly produced in-house. p. 169

over-the-counter selling Personal selling conducted in retail and some wholesale locations in which customers come to the seller's place of business. p. 437

P

partnership Affiliation of two or more companies that help each other achieve common goals. p. A-24

penetration pricing strategy Pricing strategy involving the use of a relatively low entry price compared with competitive offerings, based on the theory that this initial low price will help secure market acceptance. p. 489

perception Meaning that a person attributes to incoming stimuli gathered through the five senses. p. 140

perceptual screens Mental filter or block through which all inputs must pass to be noticed. p. 140

person marketing Marketing efforts designed to cultivate the attention, interest, and preference of a target market toward a person (typically a political candidate or celebrity). p. 15

personal selling Interpersonal influence process involving a seller's promotional presentation conducted on a person-to-person basis with the buyer. pp. 402, 436

persuasive advertising Promotion that attempts to increase demand for an existing good, service, organization, person, place, idea, or cause. p. 407

physical distribution Broad range of activities aimed at efficient movement of finished goods from the end of the production line to the consumer. p. 333

place marketing Marketing efforts to attract people and organizations to a particular geographic area. p. 16

planned shopping centre Group of retail stores planned, coordinated, and marketed as a unit. p. 371

planning Process of anticipating future events and conditions and of determining the best way to achieve organizational goals. p. 34

podcast Online audio or video file that can be downloaded to other digital devices. p. 102

point-of-purchase (POP) advertising Display or other promotion located near the site of the actual buying decision. p. 462

political risk assessment (PRA) Units within a firm that evaluate the political risks of the marketplaces in which they operate as well as proposed new marketplaces. p. 196

political-legal environment Component of the marketing environment consisting of laws and interpretations of laws that require firms to operate under competitive conditions and to protect consumer rights. p. 67

population Total group that researchers want to study. p. 225

pop-up ad Separate window that pops up with an advertising message. p. 103

Porter's Five Forces Model developed by strategy expert Michael Porter, which identifies five competitive forces that influence planning strategies: the threat of new entrants, the threat of substitute products, rivalry among competitors, the bargaining power of buyers, and the bargaining power of suppliers. p. 39

positioning Placing a product at a certain point or location within a market in the minds of prospective buyers. p. 267

positioning map A tool that helps marketers place products in a market by graphically illustrating consumers' perceptions of competing products within an industry. p. 268

post-testing Research that assesses advertising effectiveness after it has appeared in a print or broadcast medium. p. 425

precall planning Use of information collected during the prospecting and qualifying stages of the sales process and during previous contacts with the prospect to tailor the approach and presentation to match the customer's needs. p. 446

predatory pricing Occurs when companies set prices below their cost for a sufficiently long period of time to discourage or eliminate competition and then raise their prices or otherwise interfere with competition. p. 506

premium Item given free or at a reduced cost with purchase of other products. p. 460

preroll video ad Brief marketing message that appears before expected video content. p. 103

presentation Personal selling function of describing a product's major features and relating them to a customer's problems or needs. p. 446

pretesting Research that evaluates an ad during its development stage. p. 425

price Exchange value of a good or service. p. 474

price discrimination Occurs when some customers pay more than others for the same product. p. 505

price fixing A form of collusion in which sellers get together and collude to set prices higher than they would otherwise be in a free market. p. 505

price flexibility Pricing policy permitting variable prices for goods and services. p. 497

pricing policy General guideline that reflects marketing objectives and influences specific pricing decisions. p. 496

pricing strategy Methods of setting profitable and justifiable prices. p. 47

primary data Information collected for a specific investigation. p. 222

private brand Brand offered by a wholesaler or retailer. p. 308

private carriers Transporters that provide service solely for internally generated freight. p. 351

probability sample Sample that gives every member of the population a chance of being selected. p. 225

product Bundle of physical, service, and symbolic attributes designed to satisfy a customer's wants and needs. p. 276

product advertising Nonpersonal selling of a particular good or service. p. 406

product development Introduction of new products into identifiable or established markets. p. 317

product diversification strategy Developing entirely new products for new markets. p. 317

product liability Responsibility of manufacturers and marketers for injuries and damages caused by their products. p. 324

product life cycle Progression of a product through introduction, growth, maturity, and decline stages. p. 293

product line Series of related products offered by one company. p. 291

product manager Marketer within an organization who is responsible for an individual product or product line; also called a *brand manager*. p. 320

product mix Assortment of product lines and individual product offerings that a company sells. p. 291

product placement Form of promotion in which a marketer pays a motion picture or television program owner a fee to display a product prominently in the film or show. p. 403

product positioning Consumers' perceptions of a product's attributes, uses, quality, and advantages and disadvantages relative to competing brands. p. 317

product strategy Decisions about what goods or services a firm will offer its customers; also includes decisions about customer service, packaging, brand names, and the like. p. 46

production orientation Business philosophy stressing efficiency in producing a quality product, with the attitude toward marketing that "a good product will sell itself." p. 8

product-line pricing Practice of setting a limited number of prices for a selection of merchandise and marketing different product lines at each of these price levels. p. 497

product-related segmentation Division of a population into homogeneous groups based on their relationships to the product. p. 263

profit centre Any part of an organization to which revenue and controllable costs can be assigned. p. 501

Profit Impact of Market Strategies (PIMS) project Research that discovered a strong positive relationship between a firm's market share and product quality and its return on investment. p. 477

profit maximization Point at which the additional revenue gained by increasing the price of a product equals the increase in total costs. p. 476

promotion Communications link between buyers and sellers. Function of informing, persuading, and influencing a consumer's purchase decision. p. 396

promotion strategy Communications links between buyers and sellers. Function of informing, persuading, and influencing a buyer's purchase decision. p. 46

promotional allowance Promotional incentive in which the manufacturer agrees to pay the reseller a certain amount to cover the costs of special promotional displays or extensive advertising. p. 494

promotional mix Subset of the marketing mix in which marketers attempt to achieve the optimal blending of the elements of personal and nonpersonal selling to achieve promotional objectives. p. 402

promotional pricing Pricing policy in which a lower than normal price is used as a temporary ingredient in a firm's marketing strategy. p. 497

prospecting Personal selling function of identifying potential customers. p. 445

psychographic segmentation Division of a population into groups that have similar attitudes, values, and lifestyles. p. 260

psychological pricing Pricing policy based on the belief that certain prices or price ranges make a good or service more appealing than others to buyers. p. 496

public relations Firm's communications and relationships with its various publics. p. 403

pure competition Market structure characterized by homogeneous products in which there are so many buyers and sellers that none has a significant influence on price. p. 480

push money Cash reward paid to retail salespeople for every unit of a product they sell. p. 464

Q

qualifying Determining a prospect's needs, income, and purchase authority as a potential customer. p. 445

qualitative forecasting Use of subjective techniques to forecast sales, such as the jury of executive opinion, Delphi technique, sales force composite, and surveys of buyer intentions. p. 234

quantitative forecasting Use of statistical forecasting techniques such as trend analysis and exponential smoothing. p. 234

quantity discount Price reduction granted for a large-volume purchase. p. 493

QR code Short for "quick response," a two-dimensional bar code that can be read by some mobile phones with cameras. p. 109

R

rack jobber Full-function merchant wholesaler that markets specialized lines of merchandise to retail stores. p. 383

radio frequency identification (RFID) Technology that uses a tiny chip with identification information that can be read from a distance by a scanner using radio waves. p. 347

raw materials Natural resources such as farm products, coal, copper, or lumber, which become part of a final product. p. 285

rebate Refund of a portion of the purchase price, usually granted by the product's manufacturer. p. 494

reciprocity Buying from suppliers who are also customers. p. 176

reference groups People or institutions whose opinions are valued and to whom a person looks for guidance in his or her own behaviour, values, and conduct, such as family, friends, or celebrities. p. 134

refund Cash given back to consumers who send a proof of purchase for one or more products. p. 460

relationship marketing Development and maintenance of long-term, cost-effective relationships with individual customers, suppliers, employees, and other partners for mutual benefit. p. 11

relationship selling Regular contacts between sales representatives and customers over an extended period to establish a sustained seller–buyer relationship. p. 441

remanufacturing Efforts to restore older products to like-new condition. p. 180

reminder advertising Advertising that reinforces a previous promotional activity by keeping the name of a good, service, organization, person, place, idea, or cause before the public. p. 407

repositioning Changing the position of a product within the minds of prospective buyers relative to the positions of competing products. p. 268

resellers Marketing intermediaries that operate in the trade sector. p. 159

retail advertising Advertising by stores that sell goods or services directly to the consuming public. p. 408

retail convergence A situation in which similar merchandise is available from many retail outlets, resulting in the blurring of distinctions between type of retailer and merchandise offered. p. 379

retail cooperative Group of retailers that establish a shared wholesaling operation to help them compete with chains. p. 346

retailing Activities involved in selling merchandise to ultimate consumers. p. 366

return on investment (ROI) The rate of revenues received for every dollar spent on an expense. p. 116

reverse channel Channel designed to return goods to their producer. p. 337

routinized response behaviour Rapid consumer problem solving in which no new information is considered; the consumer has already set evaluative criteria and identified available options. p. 148

S

salary Fixed compensation payment made periodically to an employee. p. 454

sales analysis In-depth evaluation of a firm's sales. p. 222

sales force composite Qualitative sales forecasting method based on the combined sales estimates of the firm's salespeople. p. 236

sales forecast An estimate of a firm's sales for a specified future period. p. 234

sales incentives Programs that reward salespeople for superior performance. p. 444

sales orientation Belief that consumers will resist purchasing nonessential goods and services, with the attitude toward marketing that only creative advertising and personal selling can overcome consumers' resistance and persuade them to buy. p. 9

sales promotion Marketing activities other than personal selling, advertising, guerrilla marketing, and public relations that stimulate consumer purchasing and dealer effectiveness. pp. 403, 457

sales quota Level of expected sales for a territory, product, customer, or salesperson against which actual results are compared. p. 455

sampling Process of selecting survey respondents or research participants. Free distribution of a product in an attempt to obtain future sales. pp. 225, 460

scrambled merchandising Retailing practice of combining dissimilar product lines to boost sales volume. p. 379

search marketing Paying search engines, such as Google, a fee to make sure the company's listing appears toward the top of the search results. p. 103

second mover strategy Theory that advocates observing closely the innovations of first movers and then introducing new products that improve on the original offering to gain advantage in the marketplace. p. 42

secondary data Previously published information. p. 222

selective distribution Distribution of a product through a limited number of channels. p. 341

self-concept A person's multifaceted picture of himself or herself. p. 144

self-reference criteria The unconscious reference to one's own cultural values, experiences, and knowledge as a basis for decisions. p. 203

seller's market Market in which there are more buyers for fewer goods and services. p. 10

selling agent Agent wholesaling intermediary for the entire marketing program of a firm's product line. p. 385

sender Source of the message communicated to the receiver. p. 399

service Intangible task that satisfies the needs of consumer and business users. p. 276

service encounter Point at which the customer and service provider interact. p. 290

service quality Expected and perceived quality of a service offering. p. 290

shaping Process of applying a series of rewards and reinforcements to permit more complex behaviour to evolve over time. p. 143

shopping products Products that consumers purchase after comparing competing offerings. p. 281

skimming pricing strategy Pricing strategy involving the use of an initial high price relative to competitive offerings. Price is dropped in incremental steps as supply begins to exceed demand, or when competition catches up. p. 488

social-cultural environment Component of the marketing environment consisting of the relationship among the marketer and society and its culture. p. 77

social marketing The use of online social media as a communications channel for marketing messages. p. 20

social media Different forms of electronic communication through which users can create online communities to exchange information, ideas, messages, and other content, such as videos or music. p. 107

social media analytics Tools that help marketers trace, measure, and interpret data related to social media marketing initiatives. p. 115

social media marketing (SMM) The use of social media portals to create a positive influence on consumers or business customers toward an organization's brand, products, public image, or website. p. 110

social media marketing plan A formal document that identifies and describes goals and strategies, targeted audience, budget, and implementation methods, as well as tactics for monitoring, measuring, and managing the SMM effort. p. 111

social media monitoring The process of tracking, measuring, and evaluating a firm's social media marketing initiatives. p. 115

social media platform A type of software or technology that allows users to build, integrate, or facilitate a community, interaction among users, and user-generated content. p. 107

social media tool Software (such as an app or blog) that enables users to communicate with each other online. p. 107

social responsibility Marketing philosophies, policies, procedures, and actions that have the enhancement of society's welfare as a primary objective. pp. 23, 85

sole sourcing Purchasing a firm's entire stock of an item from just one vendor. p. 168

spam Popular name for junk email. p. 100

span of control Number of representatives who report to first-level sales managers. p. 453

specialty advertising Sales promotion technique that places the advertiser's name, address, and advertising message on useful articles that are then distributed to target consumers. p. 462

specialty products Products that offer unique characteristics that cause buyers to prize those particular brands. p. 281

specialty retailer Store that combines carefully defined product lines, services, and reputation to persuade shoppers to spend considerable shopping effort there. p. 376

split runs Methods of testing alternative ads by dividing a cable TV audience or a publication's subscribers in two, using two different ads, and then evaluating the relative effectiveness of each. p. 425

sponsorship Relationship in which an organization provides funds or in-kind resources to an event or activity in exchange for a direct association with that event or activity. p. 404

spreadsheet analysis Grid that organizes information in a standardized, easily understood format. p. A-3

staples Convenience goods and services that consumers constantly replenish to maintain a ready inventory. p. 280

step out Pricing practice in which one firm raises prices and then waits to see if others follow suit. p. 489

stockkeeping unit (SKU) Offering within a product line such as a specific size of liquid detergent. p. 369

straight rebuy Recurring purchase decision in which a customer repurchases a good or service that has performed satisfactorily in the past. p. 175

strategic alliances Partnerships in which two or more companies combine resources and capital to create competitive advantages in a new market. pp. 21, 63

strategic business units (SBUs) Key business units within diversified firms. p. 50

strategic planning Process of determining an organization's primary objectives and adopting courses of action that will achieve these objectives. pp. 36, A-1

strategic window Limited periods during which the key requirements of a market and the particular competencies of a firm best fit together. p. 44

subcontracting Contractual agreements that assign the production of goods or services to local or smaller firms. p. 205

suboptimization Condition that results when individual operations achieve their objectives but interfere with progress toward broader organizational goals. p. 350

supercentre Large store, usually smaller than a hypermarket, that combines groceries with discount store merchandise. p. 379

supplies Regular expenses that a firm incurs in its daily operations. p. 286

supply Schedule of the amounts of a good or service that firms will offer for sale at different prices during a specified time period. p. 480

supply chain Complete sequence of suppliers and activities that contribute to the creation and delivery of merchandise. p. 346

supply-chain management Control of the activities of purchasing, processing, and delivery through which raw materials are transformed into products and made available to final consumers. p. 333

survey of buyer intentions Qualitative sales forecasting method that samples opinions among groups of present and potential customers concerning their purchase intentions. p. 236

sustainable products Products that can be produced, used, and disposed of with minimal impact on the environment. p. 23

sweepstakes Sales promotion technique in which prize winners are selected by chance. p. 461

SWOT analysis Analysis that helps planners compare internal organizational strengths and weaknesses with external opportunities and threats. p. 42

syndicated service Organization that provides standardized data to all customers. p. 220

systems integration Centralization of the procurement function within an internal division or as a service of an external supplier. p. 172

T

tactical planning Planning that guides the implementation of activities specified in the strategic plan. p. 36

target market Group of people to whom a firm decides to direct its marketing efforts and ultimately its goods and services. p. 45; Specific group of people a firm believes is most likely to buy its goods and services. p. 246

target-return objectives Short-run or long-run pricing objectives of achieving a specified return on either sales or investment. p. 476

tariff Tax levied against imported goods. p. 198

team selling Selling situation in which several sales associates or other members of the organization are recruited to assist the lead sales representative in reaching all those who influence the purchase decision. p. 442

technological environment Applications to marketing of knowledge based on discoveries in science, inventions, and innovations. p. 75

telemarketing Promotional presentation involving the use of the telephone on an outbound basis by salespeople or on an inbound basis by customers who initiate calls to obtain information and place orders. p. 439

test-marketing Marketing research technique that involves introducing a new product in a specific area and then measuring its degree of success. p. 231

third-party (contract) logistics firm Company that specializes in handling logistics activities for other firms. p. 349

time-based competition Strategy of developing and distributing goods and services more quickly than competitors. p. 66

total quality management (TQM) Continuous effort to improve products and work processes with the goal of achieving customer satisfaction and world-class performance. p. 288

trade allowance Financial incentive offered to wholesalers and retailers that purchase or promote specific products. p. 462

trade discount Payment to a channel member or buyer for performing marketing functions; also known as a *functional discount*. p. 493

trade dress Visual components that contribute to the overall look of a brand. p. 313

trade industries Retailers or wholesalers that purchase products for resale to others. p. 159

trade promotion Sales promotion that appeals to marketing intermediaries rather than to consumers. pp. 403, 462

trade show Product exhibition organized by industry trade associations to showcase goods and services. p. 463

trade-in Credit allowance given for a used item when a customer purchases a new item. p. 494

trademark Brand for which the owner claims exclusive legal protection. p. 312

transaction-based marketing Buyer and seller exchanges characterized by limited communications and little or no ongoing relationships between the parties. p. 19

transfer price Cost assessed when a product is moved from one profit centre in a firm to another. p. 501

trend analysis Quantitative sales forecasting method that estimates future sales through statistical analyses of historical sales patterns. p. 236

truck wholesaler (truck jobber) Limited-function merchant wholesaler that markets perishable food items. p. 384

tying agreement An arrangement that requires a marketing intermediary to carry items other than those they want to sell. p. 342

U

undifferentiated marketing Strategy that focuses on producing a single product and marketing it to all customers; also called *mass marketing*. p. 266

unemployment Proportion of people in the economy who do not have jobs but are actively seeking work. p. 72

unit pricing Pricing policy in which prices are stated in terms of a recognized unit of measurement or a standard numerical count. p. 497

Universal Product Code (UPC) Numerical bar code system used to record product and price information. p. 315

unsought products Products marketed to consumers who may not yet recognize a need for them. p. 279

upstream management Controlling part of the supply chain that involves raw materials, inbound logistics, and warehouse and storage facilities. p. 346

user Individual or group that actually uses a business good or service. p. 177

utility Want-satisfying power of a good or service. p. 5

V

VALS™ Segmentation system that divides consumers into eight psychographic categories: innovators, thinkers, achievers, experiencers, believers, strivers, makers, and survivors. p. 261

value analysis Systematic study of the components of a purchase to determine the most cost-effective approach. p. 176

value pricing Pricing strategy emphasizing benefits derived from a product in comparison to the price and quality levels of competing offerings. p. 478

variable costs Costs that change with the level of production (such as labour and raw materials costs). p. 481

vendor analysis Assessment of supplier performance in areas such as price, back orders, timely delivery, and attention to special requests. p. 176

vendor-managed inventory (VMI) Inventory management system in which the seller—based on an existing agreement with a buyer—determines how much of a product is needed. p. 356

venture team Associates from different areas of an organization who work together in developing new products. p. 320

vertical marketing system (VMS) Planned channel system designed to improve distribution efficiency and cost effectiveness by integrating various functions throughout the distribution chain. p. 344

Video-Game Generation A group called by several names: Generation Y, the Millennial Generation, Generation Next, the 9/11 generation, and the Echo Boomers (an echo of baby boomers), whose preferences were shaped at the same time as video games. p. 254

virtual sales team Network of strategic partners, suppliers, and others who recommend a firm's goods or services. p. 443

VoIP—Voice over Internet Protocol A phone connection through a personal computer with any type of broadband Internet connection. p. 76

W

Web-to-store shoppers Consumers who use the Internet as a tool when shopping at brick-and-mortar retailers. p. 106

wheel of retailing Hypothesis that each new type of retailer gains a competitive foothold by offering lower prices than current outlets charge; the result of reducing or eliminating services. p. 366

wholesaler Channel intermediary that takes title to the goods it handles and then distributes these goods to retailers, other distributors, or B2B customers. pp. 334, 380

wholesaling intermediary Comprehensive term that describes wholesalers as well as agents and brokers. p. 380

widgets Tiny applications that Internet users can copy and add to their own pages to play music, video, or slide shows. p. 103

wiki Web page that anyone can edit. p. 102

World Trade Organization (WTO) Organization that replaces GATT, overseeing GATT agreements, making binding decisions in mediating disputes, and reducing trade barriers. p. 201

Y

yield management Pricing strategy that allows marketers to vary prices based on such factors as demand, even though the cost of providing those goods or services remains the same; designed to maximize revenues in situations such as airfares, lodging, auto rentals, and theatre tickets, where costs are fixed. p. 487

Z

zone pricing Pricing system for handling transportation costs under which the market is divided into geographic regions and a different price is set in each region. p. 495

name index

subject index